SOMATOFORM DISORDERS

Somatization Disorder
Conversion Disorder
Hypochondriasis
Body Dysmorphic Disorder
Pain Disorder

FACTITIOUS DISORDERS

Factitious Disorder

DISSOCIATIVE DISORDERS

Dissociative Amnesia
Dissociative Fugue
Dissociative Identity Disorder (Multiple Personality Disorder)
Depersonalization Disorder

SEXUAL AND GENDER IDENTITY DISORDERS

Sexual Dysfunctions
Sexual Desire Disorders: Hypoactive Sexual Desire Disorder;
Sexual Aversion Disorder / Sexual Arousal Disorders: Female
Sexual Arousal Disorder; Male Erectile Disorder / Orgasmic
Disorders: Female Orgasmic Disorder; Male Orgasmic Disorder;
Premature Ejaculation / Sexual Pain Disorders: Dyspareunia;
Vaginismus / Sexual Dysfunction Due to a General Medical
Condition / Substance-induced Sexual Dysfunction
Paraphilias
Exhibitionism / Fetishism / Frotteurism / Pedophilia / Sexual
Masochism / Sexual Sadism / Voyeurism / Transvestic Fetishism
Gender Identity Disorders
Gender Identity Disorder: in Children; in Adolescents or Adults

EATING DISORDERS

Anorexia Nervosa
Bulimia Nervosa

SLEEP DISORDERS

Primary Sleep Disorders
Dyssomnias: Primary Insomnia; Primary Hypersomnia;
Narcolepsy; Breathing-related Sleep Disorder; Circadian
Rhythm Sleep Disorder (Sleep-Wake Schedule Disorder) /
Parasomnias; Nightmare Disorder (Dream Anxiety Disorder);
Sleep Terror Disorder; Sleepwalking Disorder / Sleep Disorders
Related to Another Mental Disorder
Sleep Disorder Due to a General Medical Condition
Substance-induced Sleep Disorder

IMPULSE CONTROL DISORDERS NOT ELSEWHERE CLASSIFIED

Intermittent Explosive Disorder
Kleptomania
Pyromania
Pathological Gambling
Trichotillomania

ADJUSTMENT DISORDERS

Adjustment Disorder
With Anxiety / with Depressed Mood / with Disturbance of
Conduct / with Mixed Disturbance of Emotions and Conduct /
with Mixed Anxiety and Depressed Mood

Axis II

MENTAL RETARDATION

Mild Mental Retardation / Moderate Mental Retardation / Severe
Mental Retardation / Profound Mental Retardation

PERSONALITY DISORDERS

Paranoid Personality Disorder
Schizoid Personality Disorder
Schizotypal Personality Disorder
Antisocial Personality Disorder
Borderline Personality Disorder
Histrionic Personality Disorder
Narcissistic Personality Disorder
Avoidant Personality Disorder
Dependent Personality Disorder
Obsessive-Compulsive Personality Disorder

OTHER CONDITIONS THAT MAY BE A FOCUS OF CLINICAL ATTENTION

Psychological Factors Affecting Medical Condition/Medication-Induced Movement Disorders/Relational Problems
Relational Problem Related to a Mental Disorder or General
Medical Condition / Parent-Child Relational Problem / Partner
Relational Problem / Sibling Relational Problem
Problems Related to Abuse or Neglect
Physical Abuse of Child / Sexual Abuse of Child / Neglect of
Child / Physical Abuse of Adult / Sexual Abuse of Adult
Additional Conditions That May Be a Focus of Clinical Attention
Bereavement / Borderline Intellectual Functioning / Academic
Problem / Occupational Problem / Child or Adolescent
Antisocial Behavior / Adult Antisocial Behavior / Malingering /
Phase of Life Problem / Noncompliance with Treatment /
Identity Problem / Religious or Spiritual Problem / Acculturation
Problem / Age-related Cognitive Decline

WILEY PLUS

www.wileyplus.com

Wiley is committed to making your entire *WileyPLUS* experience productive & enjoyable by providing the help, resources, and personal support you & your students need, when you need it. It's all here: www.wileyplus.com –

TECHNICAL SUPPORT:

- ➕ A fully searchable knowledge base of FAQs and help documentation, available 24/7
- ➕ Live chat with a trained member of our support staff during business hours
- ➕ A form to fill out and submit online to ask any question and get a quick response
- ➕ **Instructor-only** phone line during business hours: 1.877.586.0192

FACULTY-LED TRAINING THROUGH THE WILEY FACULTY NETWORK:
Register online: www.wherefacultyconnect.com
Connect with your colleagues in a complimentary virtual seminar, with a personal mentor in your field, or at a live workshop to share best practices for teaching with technology.

1ST DAY OF CLASS...AND BEYOND!
Resources You & Your Students Need to Get Started & Use *WileyPLUS* from the first day forward.

- ➕ 2-Minute Tutorials on how to set up & maintain your *WileyPLUS* course
- ➕ User guides, links to technical support & training options
- ➕ **WileyPLUS for Dummies**: Instructors' quick reference guide to using *WileyPLUS*
- ➕ Student tutorials & instruction on how to register, buy, and use *WileyPLUS*

YOUR *WileyPLUS* ACCOUNT MANAGER:
Your personal *WileyPLUS* connection for any assistance you need!

SET UP YOUR *WileyPLUS* COURSE IN MINUTES!
Selected *WileyPLUS* courses with QuickStart contain pre-loaded assignments & presentations created by subject matter experts who are also experienced *WileyPLUS* users.

Interested? See and try WileyPLUS *in action!*
Details and Demo: www.wileyplus.com

Abnormal Psychology
Eleventh Edition

Ann M. Kring
University of California, Berkeley

Sheri L. Johnson
University of Miami

Gerald C. Davison
University of Southern California

John M. Neale
State University of New York at Stony Brook

WILEY

John Wiley & Sons, Inc.

Vice President & Executive Publisher	Jay O'Callaghan
Executive Editor	Christopher T. Johnson
Assistant Editor	Eileen McKeever
Marketing Manager	Danielle Torio
Editorial Assistant	Aaron Talwar
Production Manager	Dorothy Sinclair
Production Editor	Sandra Dumas
Photo Department Manager	Hilary Newman
Senior Photo Editor	Elle Wagner
Design Director	Jeof Vita
Designer	Lee Goldstein
Senior Media Editor	Lynn Pearlman
Production Management Services	Suzanne Ingrao

This book was set in 10/12 Berkeley Book by Prepare and printed an bound by R. R. Donnelley/Jefferson City. The cover was printed by R. R. Donnelley/Jefferson City.

This book is printed on acid-free paper. ∞

To order books or for customer service, please call 1-800-CALL-WILEY (225-5945).

ISBN-13-978-0470-38008-6

Printed in the United States of America

10 9 8 7 6 5 4 3 2

To
_____

Angela Hawk

Margaret Hunt

Kathleen C. Chambers, Eve H. Davison, and Asher Davison

Gail and Sean Neale

About the Authors

ANN M. KRING is Professor of Psychology at the University of California at Berkeley, where she is also the Director of the Clinical Science Program and Psychology Clinic. She received a B.S. from Ball State University and her M.A. and Ph.D. from the State University of New York at Stony Brook. Her internship in clinical psychology was completed at Bellevue Hospital and Kirby Forensic Psychiatric Center, in New York. Before moving to Berkeley, she was on the psychology faculty at Vanderbilt University (1991–1998). At both Vanderbilt and UC Berkeley, she has taught a course in abnormal psychology every year. She received a Distinguished Teaching Award from UC Berkeley in 2008. She is on the editorial board of *Emotion, Applied and Preventive Psychology, and Psychological Science in the Public Interest*, was formerly an Associate Editor for *Cognition and Emotion* and is currently Associate Editor for *Journal of Abnormal Psychology*. She is currently a member of the Executive Board for the Society for Research in Psychopathology and the International Society for Research on Emotion.

In 1997 she was awarded a Young Investigator award from the National Alliance for Research on Schizophrenia and Depression, and in 2006 she was awarded the Joseph Zubin Memorial Fund Award in recognition of her research in schizophrenia. In 2005, she was named a fellow of the Association for Psycological Science. Her research has been supported by grants from the Scottish Rite Schizophrenia Research program, the National Alliance for Research on Schizophrenia and Depression, and the National Institute of Mental Health. She is a co-editor (with Denise Sloan) of the forthcoming book *Emotion Regulation and Psychopathology*, and is an author on more than 60 articles and chapters. Her current research focus is on emotion and psychopathology, with a specific interest in the emotional features of schizophrenia, assessing negative symptoms in schizophrenia, and the linkage between cognition and emotion in schizophrenia. Additional foci of Kring's research include the origins and consequences of individual differences in emotional expressivity, how gender and social context shape the experience and expression of emotion, and how anticipatory processes influence emotion.

SHERI L. JOHNSON received her B.A. from Salem College in 1982 and her Ph.D. from the University of Pittsburgh in 1992. She completed an internship and postdoctoral fellowship at Brown University, and she was a clinical assistant professor at Brown from 1993 to 1995. From 1995 through 2008, she taught in the Department of Psychology at the University of Miami. In 2008, she became a professor at the University of California at Berkeley. She regularly teaches courses on abnormal psychology at undergraduate and graduate levels. In 2001, 2005, and 2007, she received the Award for Excellence in Graduate Teaching from the Department of Psychology at the University of Miami.

In 1993, Johnson received the Young Investigator Award from the National Alliance for Research in Schizophrenia and Depression. Dr. Johnson's previous books include *Psychological Treatments of Bipolar Disorder* (available in paperback), *Stress, Coping and Depression, and Emotion and Psychopathology*. She has published more than 100 articles and chapters. She is an associate editor for *Applied and Preventive Psychology* and *Cognition and Emotion*, and she serves on the editorial board for *Psychological Bulletin, Psychology* and *Psychotherapy, and International Journal of Cognitive Therapy*. She is a member of the Executive Board for the Society for Research in Psychopathology, and she is a fellow in the Academy of Behavioral Medicine Research. Her work has been supported by grants from the National Alliance of Research on Schizophrenia and Depression, the National Science Foundation, the National Institute of Mental Health, and the National Cancer Institute. Her research is focused on understanding the psychological and environmental factors that shape the course of mania and major depression.

GERALD C. DAVISON is Dean of the USC Davis School of Gerontology and Executive Director of the Andrus Gerontology Center at the University of Southern California. He is holder of the William and Sylvia Kugel Dean's Chair and is Professor of Gerontology and Psychology. Previously he was Professor and Chair of the Department of Psychology at USC and served also as Director of Clinical Training. Prior to moving to USC, he was on the psychology faculty at the State University of New York at Stony Brook. He is a Fellow of the American Psychological Association, a Charter Fellow of the Association for Psychological Science, and a member of the Gerontological Society of America. During 2006 he served as President of the Society of Clinical Psychology (Division 12 of the American Psychological Association) and as Chair of the Council of Graduate Departments of Psychology. He earned his B.A. in social relations from Harvard and his Ph.D. in psychology from Stanford.

Among his honors and awards are an outstanding achievement award from APA's Board of Social and Ethical Responsibility, the USC Associates Award for Excellence in Teaching, and the Outstanding Educator Award and the Lifetime Achievement Award of the Association for Behavioral and Cognitive Therapies.

Among his more than 150 publications, his book *Clinical Behavior Therapy*, co-authored in 1976 with Marvin Goldfried and reissued in expanded form in 1994, is one of two publications that have been recognized as Citation Classics by the Social Sciences Citation Index; it appears in German and Spanish translation. Other books are *Case Studies in Abnormal Psychology*, Seventh Edition (2007) with Tom Oltmanns and John Neale and *Exploring Abnormal Psychology* (1996) with John Neale and David Haaga. Davison is also on the editorial board of several professional journals.

His publications emphasize experimental and philosophical analyses of psychopathology, assessment, and therapeutic change. His current research focuses on the relationships between cognition and a variety of behavioral and emotional problems via his articulated thoughts in simulated situations think-aloud paradigm.

JOHN M. NEALE is Professor Emeritus of Psychology at the State University of New York at Stony Brook, where he regularly taught the undergraduate course in abnormal psychology. He received his B.A. from the University of Toronto and his M.A. and Ph.D. from Vanderbilt University. His internship in clinical psychology was as a Fellow in Medical Psychology at the Langley Porter Neuropsychiatric Institute. In 1975 he was a Visiting Fellow at the Institute of Psychiatry, London, England. In 1974 he won the American Psychological Association's Early Career Award for his research on cognitive processes in schizophrenia. In 1991 he won a Distinguished Scientist Award from the American Psychological Association's Society for a Science of Clinical Psychology. He has been on the editorial boards of several journals and has been Associate Editor of the *Journal of Abnormal Psychology*. Besides his numerous articles in professional journals, he has published books on the effects of televised violence on children, research methodology, schizophrenia, case studies in abnormal psychology, and psychological influences on health. Schizophrenia was a major focus of his research, and he also conducted research on the influence of stress on health.

Preface

It has been more than 30 years since the first edition of this book was published. Emerging from conversations about teaching abnormal psychology between Davison and Neale, then young faculty at Stony Brook, came the first edition of a textbook that was different from the texts available at the time in its balance and blending of research and clinical application; in its use of paradigms as an organizing principle; and in its effort to involve the reader in the problem solving engaged in by clinicians and scientists. These qualities have continued to be the cornerstones of subsequent editions of the book, and we have been both surprised and delighted at the favorable reception the book has received and, perhaps more importantly, the impact it has had on the lives of so many students of psychopathology throughout the years.

With the eleventh edition of the book, we continue to emphasize the recent and comprehensive research coverage that has been the hallmark of the book, and we continue to expand the pedagogical features that we added in the tenth edition. We have added additional clinical cases, figures, tables, and clarifying writing to make this material accessible to a broad audience. We continue to emphasize an integrated approach, showing how psychopathology is best understood by considering multiple perspectives and how these varying perspectives can provide us with the clearest accounting of the causes of these disorders as well as the best possible treatments.

The beautiful cover image is a satellite photograph of the Lena River Delta as it empties into the Laptev Sea. Beyond the sheer beauty of this image, it illustrates a number of key principles about our book. The image shows how different parts (tributaries of the river) flow into the whole (sea), which is what the study of psychopathology is all about: different paradigms (genetic, neuroscience, psychodynamic, cognitive behavioral) coming together to explain the whole (mental illness). This is also how science works. Layer and layer of discovery build pathways that flow into our current understanding of mental illness. Our book is first and foremost grounded in the latest science of mental illeness. However, just as rivers continually change and shift over time, so does the field of psychopathology. As new discoveries and new treatments are developed, our understanding shifts toward a better conceptualization of mental illness. Finally, although the image is of a river delta, it also resembles a colorful image of the human brain that can be obtained from the latest imaging technologies. As our understanding of the human brain has grown in recent years, so has our understanding of the causes and maintaining factors and treatments for mental illness.

Goals of the Book

With each new edition, we update, make changes, and streamline features to enhance both the scholarly and pedagogical characteristics of the book. We also devote considerable effort to couching complex concepts in prose that is sharp, clear, and vivid. In the past 30 years, the domains of psychopathology and intervention have become increasingly multifaceted and technical. Therefore, a good abnormal psychology textbook must engage the careful and focused attention of students so that they can acquire a deep and critical understanding of the issues and the material. Some of the most exciting breakthroughs in psychopathology research and treatment that we present in the book have come in areas that are complex, such as molecular genetics, neuroscience, and cognitive science. Rather than oversimplify these complex issues, we have instead added a number of pedagogical features to enhance understanding of this vital material.

We endeavor to present up-to-date theories and research in psychopathology and intervention, and also to convey some of the intellectual excitement that is associated with the search for answers to some of the most puzzling questions facing humankind. A reviewer of an earlier edition once said that our book reads like a detective story, for we do more than just state the problem and then its solution. Rather, we try to involve the student in the search for clues, the follow-up of hunches, and the evaluation of evidence that are part and parcel of the science and art of the field. We try to encourage students to participate with us in a process of discovery as we sift through the evidence on the origins of psychopathology and the effectiveness of specific interventions.

In this edition, we continue to emphasize ways in which we can take away the stigma that is unfortunately still associated with mental illness. Psychopathology is something that affects all of us in one way or another. As many as half of us may experience a psychological disorder at some time or another, and most of us know someone who has had a mental disorder. Despite the ubiquity of psychopathology, the stigma associated with it can keep some from seeking treatment, keep our legislatures from providing adequate funding for treatment and research, and keep some terms as accepted popular vernacular (*crazy, nuts, schizo*). Thus, another of our goals for the book is to combat this stigma and present a positive and hopeful view on the causes and treatments of mental illness.

Paradigms as an Organizing Principle

A recurrent theme in the book is the importance of major points of view, perspectives, or, to use Kuhn's (1962/1970) phrase, paradigms. Our experience in teaching undergraduates has made us very much aware of the importance of making explicit the unspoken assumptions underlying any quest for knowledge. In our handling of the paradigms, we have tried to make their premises clear. Long after specific facts are forgotten, we hope students will retain a grasp of the basic problems in the field of psychopathology and understand that the answers one arrives at are, in an important but often subtle way, constrained by the questions one poses and the methods employed to ask those questions.

Throughout the book we discuss four major paradigms: genetic, neuroscience, psychodynamic, and cognitive behavioral. We also emphasize the importance of factors that are important to all paradigms, including emotion, gender, culture, ethnicity, and socioeconomic status. A related issue is the use of more than one paradigm in studying abnormal psychology. Rather than force an entire field into, for example, a cognitive behavioral paradigm, we argue from the available information that different problems in psychopathology are amenable to analyses within different frameworks. For instance, genetic factors are important in bipolar disorder and attention-deficit/hyperactivity disorder, but genes do their work via the environment. In disorders such as depression, cognitive behavioral factors are essential, but neurotransmitters also exert an influence. For still other disorders, for example, dissociative disorders, psychodynamic theories can enhance our understanding, but cognitive factors involving consciousness are also important to consider. Furthermore, the importance of a diathesis–stress approach has become increasingly evident. Emerging data indicate that many, perhaps most, disorders arise from subtle interactions between genetic or psychological predispositions and stressful life events.

Organization of the Eleventh Edition

In Chapters 1 through 4, we place the field in historical context, present the concept of paradigms in science, describe the major paradigms in psychopathology, review the text revision of the fourth edition of the *Diagnostic and Statistical Manual of Mental Disorders* (DSM-IV-TR), discuss critically its validity and reliability, provide an overview of major approaches and techniques in clinical assessment, and then describe the major research methods of the field. These chapters are the foundation upon which the later chapters can be interpreted and understood. As in the 10th edition, specific disorders and their treatment are discussed in Chapters 5 through 14. We continue to provide up-to-date coverage of late-life and psychological disorders in Chapter 15. In Chapter 16 we discuss process and outcome research on treatment and controversial issues surrounding the therapy enterprise. In Chapter 17 we have updated and strengthened our chapter on legal and ethical issues.

Throughout the book we have included considerable material on culture and ethnicity in the study of psychopathology and intervention. In Chapter 2, we present a separate section that emphasizes the importance of culture and ethnicity in all paradigms. We point to the important role of culture and ethnicity in the other chapters as well. For example, in the Diagnosis and Assessment chapter (3), we have extended our earlier discussions of cultural bias in assessment and ways to guard against this selectivity in perception. We have expanded and updated information on ethnicity with respect to how stress impacts health in Chapter 7, we have provided new findings about symptom patterns across culture in Chapter 8, and we have updated coverage of culture and ethnicity in eating disorders (Chapter 9) and substance-related disorders (Chapter 10).

We continue to emphasize and expand our discussion of genetics and psychopathology throughout the book. We repeatedly emphasize that psychopathology is best understood by considering how genes do their work via the environment. Thus, rather than asking whether genes or the environment are more important in a particular disorder, we emphasize that both of these factors are important. Exciting new discoveries have made it clear that nature and nurture work together, not in opposition to one another. Without the genes, a behavior might not be possible. But without the environment, genes could not express themselves and thus contribute to the behavior. Genes are remarkably flexible at responding to different types of environments. In turn, human beings are quite flexible at adapting to different environments.

New to This Edition

The eleventh edition has many new exciting additions and changes. First, we have built upon the innovations from the tenth edition. The chapters covering the disorders all have a consistent organization, presenting sections on clinical descriptions, etiology, and treatments of the various disorders. We have further streamlined the writing across all the chapters to increase the clarity of presentation and to highlight the key issues in the field.

Second, we have continued to add additional pedagogy based on feedback from students and professors. We have added a number of new clinical case boxes and Focus on Discovery Boxes to the book in order to illustrate what the different disorders look like in the context of real people's lives. Additional Quick Summaries have been added to the chapter in order to summarize some of the more complex material. In addition, we have modified and added new Check Your Knowledge Questions in each chapter so that students may do a quick check to see if they are understanding and integrating the material. There are many new photos to provide students with additional real-world examples and applications of psychopathology. In addition, we have added several new and colorful illustrations and tables to provide additional visual clarification and explanation for more complex material. The end-of-chapter summaries continue to be consistent across the chapters, using a bulleted format and summarizing the descriptions, causes, and treatments of the disorders covered.

One of the strengths of the book has always been its current and forward-looking coverage of research in the descriptions, causes, and treatments of psychopathology, and this tradition is strongly maintained in this edition with the addition of over 1000 new references.

New and Expanded Coverage

We are excited about the new features of this edition. Some of the major new material in this eleventh edition includes:

Chapter 1: Introduction and Historical Overview

Expanded section on stigma and mental illness
New Focus on Discovery box on fighting stigma
New historical material added
Updated and revised section on the mental health professions

Chapter 2: Current Paradigms in Psychopathology

Paradigms reorganized to include: genetic, neuroscience, psychodynamic, and cognitive behavioral
Revised and updated coverage of the psychodynamic paradigm
Updated coverage on cognitive science contributions
Expanded coverage of factors that cut across paradigms: emotion, gender, and sociocultural factors
New table on racial and ethnic differences in psychopathology
New Check Your Knowledge box

Chapter 3: Diagnosis and Assessment

Updated material on intelligence testing, projective testing, and self-monitoring
Additional historical material added to Focus on Discovery 3.1
New table illustrating the costs of mental illness
New table on the prevalence of mental illnesses around the world
Updated and expanded coverage of cultural factors in diagnosis and assessment
Updated and expanded section previewing the DSM-V
New genetic and comorbidity data demonstrating the robust overlap in adulthood externalizing and internalizing disorders

Chapter 4: Research Methods in the Study of Psychopathology

Expanded material on meta-analysis, including an example of a cross-national examination of the prevalence of disorders
Updated example of single-case experimental design
Material on epidemiological and behavior genetics research integrated as examples of the use of correlational methods

Chapter 5: Anxiety Disorders

Substantially reorganized so that clinical descriptions for all disorders covered first, followed by etiology and treatment
Several new clinical cases
New sections on gender and cultural issues in anxiety disorders
Updated research on neurobiology, personality, life events, and cognition

Broader coverage of the common factors involved in treatment, including recent developments in the understanding of exposure treatment

Chapter 6: Dissociative Disorders and Somatoform Disorders

Restructured chapter to cover dissociative disorders before somatoform disorders
Updated research on controversy about DID and repressed memories
More discussion of dissociation and memory
More clinical description of depersonalization
Issues being considered for DSM-V in the diagnosis of somatoform disorders

Chapter 7: Stress and Health

Overall chapter streamlined substantially, making it more accessible to students
Section on theories of the stress-illness link revised and reorganized
Updated research on gender, ethnicity, and health
Updated research on asthma
Updated research on HIV prevention programs

Chapter 8: Mood Disorders

New data on the 10-year outcomes of dysthymic disorder
Expanded discussion on gender differences in depression
New Focus on Discovery box on seasonal affective disorder
New data on medical and occupational consequences of bipolar disorder
New data on the genetics of bipolar disorder, including a meta-analysis showing the troubling inconsistency in findings
Findings of several large-scale trials on the medication and psychological treatment of mood disorders
New data on the predictors and treatment of suicidality

Chapter 9: Eating Disorders

New research findings on descriptions and treatments for binge eating disorder
Substantially reorganized so that etiology sections are consistent with other chapters
Updated material on obesity
Updated material on ethnicity, gender, and eating disorders
New table with body mass index calculations
New research on longitudinal course of eating disorder risk factors and symptoms

Chapter 10: Substance-Related Disorders

Entire chapter substantially streamlined to make the material more accessible and easier to integrate
Section on etiology reorganized and updated
Updated statistics on prevalence rates for all disorders, including gender and ethnicity

New and updated tables
Updated research on contingency management treatment
Updated research on medication treatment
New research on nicotine dependence

Chapter 11: Schizophrenia

Entire chapter streamlined
New examples of clinical features
Updated information on genetics
New information on prenatal infections as a risk factor for schizophrenia
New information on glutamate in schizophrenia
New information on high-risk studies
New information on medication treatment and cognitive behavior therapy
Two new Focus on Discovery boxes

Chapter 12: Personality Disorders

New data on the interrater reliability and stability of measures for personality disorder, as well as the long-term validity of these diagnoses
New findings on the heritability and neurobiology of personality disorders
Treatment outcome research for new approaches to borderline personality disorder
New table demonstrating the differences in the prevalence of personality disorders in community vs. treatment settings

Chapter 13: Sexual and Gender Identity Disorders

New data on relationship satisfaction after sex-reassignment surgery
New community data on the high prevalence of voyeuristic and exhibitionistic behavior
New table describing rates of sexual problems from a representative community study of 2,0000 adults
New clinical case illustrating on fetishism
Data on predictors of recidivism among sexual offenders

Chapter 14: Disorders of Childhood

Updated information on neurobiological, environmental, and genetic factors in ADHD
Updated section on medication treatment for ADHD
Updated section on Head Start
New table describing learning disorders, streamlining this section
Updated Focus on Discovery box on controversies in developmental psychopathology, including suicide and antidepressant treatment
Updated and expanded information on etiology and treatment of mood and anxiety disorders in children
Updated and expanded sections on etiology and treatment for autism

Chapter 15: Late-Life and Psychological Disorders

New Focus on Discovery box on cardiovascular disease and depression
Less focus (removed Focus on Discovery box) on nursing homes, given that other forms of care have become more common
New diagnostic criteria for dementia with Lewy bodies
Updated evidence about treatments for dementia, including a review of the role of exercise
Many updated references throughout

Chapter 16: Psychological Treatment

Entire chapter restructured and streamlined, with distinct sections on types of therapy and therapy research
More specific descriptive information on the different therapies
Examples of therapy techniques and a new case study for emotion-focused therapy
New section on treatments that are harmful
Streamlined the chapter to focus on newer findings and approaches
Updated research on the mechanisms of change involved in cognitive therapy

Chapter 17: Legal and Ethical Issues

Greater streamlining of court case descriptions
Revised material on *Tarasoff*
Updated material on insanity pleas in the states
Updated material on Yates, Atkins, and Hinckley cases
Two new clinical case boxes
Updated material numbers of people in psychiatric hospitals

Special Features for the Student Reader

Several features of this book are designed to make it easier for students to master and enjoy the material.

Clinical Case Boxes We have expanded and added a number of new clinical cases throughout the book to provide a clinical context for the theories and research that occupy most of our attention in the chapters and to help make vivid the real-life implications of the empirical work of psychopathologists and clinicians.

Focus on Discovery Boxes There are many in-depth discussions of selected topics encased in Focus on Discovery boxes throughout the book. This feature allows us to involve the reader in specialized topics in a way that does not detract from the flow of the regular text. Sometimes a Focus on Discovery box expands on a point in the text; sometimes it deals with an entirely separate but relevant issue, often a controversial one. We have added a number of new boxes in this edition, replacing a number of the older boxes. Additional boxes feature real-life examples of individuals living with different disorders.

Quick Summaries We have added short summaries throughout the chapters to allow students to pause and assimilate the material. These should help students to keep track of the multifaceted and complex issues that surround the study of psychopathology.

End-of-Chapter Summaries Summaries at the end of each chapter have been rewritten in bulleted form. In Chapters 5–14, we organize these by clinical descriptions, etiology, and treatment—the major sections of every chapter covering the disorders. We believe this format will make it easier for readers to review and remember the material. In fact, we even suggest that the student read it before beginning the chapter itself in order to get a good sense of what lies ahead. Then re-reading the summary after completing the chapter itself will enhance the student's understanding and provide an immediate sense of what has been learned in just one reading of the chapter.

Check Your Knowledge Questions Throughout each chapter, we provide between three and six boxes that ask questions about the material covered in the chapter. These questions are intended to help students assess their understanding and retention of the material, as well as provide them with samples of the types of questions that often are found in course exams. The answers to the questions in these boxes are at the end of each chapter, just before the list of key terms. We believe that these will be useful aids for students as they make their way through the chapters.

Glossary When an important term is introduced, it is boldfaced and defined or discussed immediately. Most such terms appear again later in the book, in which case they will not be highlighted in this way. All of these terms are listed again at the end of each chapter, and definitions appear at the end of the book in a glossary.

DSM-IV-TR Table The endpapers of the book contain a summary of the current psychiatric nomenclature found in the text revision of the fourth edition of the *Diagnostic and Statistical Manual of Mental Disorders*, known as DSM-IV-TR. This provides a handy guide to where particular disorders appear in the "official" taxonomy or classification. We make considerable use of DSM-IV-TR, though in a selective and sometimes critical vein. Sometimes we find it more effective to discuss theory and research on a particular problem in a way that is different from DSM's conceptualization.

Supplements

Several supplements have been prepared, free to adopters of the text, to enhance and facilitate teaching from this textbook. These supplements include the following:

Produced by documentary film-maker Nathan Friedkin, these video modules present an encompassing view of eleven psychological disorders. Each module features interviews with those living with the disorder, as well as their friends and family, and experts in the field. These videos are presented in the WileyPlus course that accompanies *Abnormal Psychology, 11th Edition*. To review one of these modules, please visit: www.wiley.com/college/sc/kring or contact your local Wiley representative for more details.

Instructor's Resource Manual, written by Dave Smith of University of Notre Dame, includes chapter summaries, lecture launchers, perspectives on the causes and treatment of each disorder, key points students should know, key terms, discussion stimulators, and guides to instructional films and websites.

Instructor's PowerPoint slides, written by Sandra Kerr of Westchester University, provide lecture-ready slides that include the figures and tables from the text so that the instructor can create a custom classroom presentation.

Test Bank, written by Daniel Fulford of the University of Miami, contains nearly 2,000 multiple-choice questions. It is available in printed form as well as on CD. An easy-to-use computerized test bank, containing the same questions as the printed version, is accessible from the web. Instructors can customize exams by adding new questions or editing existing ones.

Study Guide, written by Douglas Hindman of Eastern Kentucky University, includes a summary of each chapter, a list of key concepts, important study questions, and practice tests written in collaboration with the test bank author to ensure consistency and to encourage active reading and learning. Students find it to be a very helpful study guide.

Book Website (http://www.wiley.com/college/kring) includes an online Instructor Resource section and an online Student Resource section, as well as active learning links to several interesting sites related to the field of abnormal psychology. Online Student Quizzes for which students can receive immediate feedback are also on the site.

Acknowledgments

It is a real pleasure to recognize the following reviewers of previous editions, for it was with their assistance that the eleventh edition had the strong base on which to build:

Ted Beauchaine, *University of Washington;* Allison Harvey, *University of California, Berkeley;* Jutta Joormann, *University of Miami;* Janice Kiecolt-Glaser, *Ohio State University;* Richard McNally, *Harvard University;* Jack Nitzcke, *University of Wisconsin;* David Arnold, *University of Massachusetts;* Jack J. Blanchard, *University of Maryland;* John Burns, *Chicago Medical School;* Laura Heatherington, *Williams College;* John Kassel, *University of Illinois at Chicago;* Joni Mihura, *University of Toledo;* Judith Moskowitz, *University of California, San Francisco;* Brady Phelps, *South Dakota State University;* Kathleen M. Pike, *Columbia University;* Judy Rauenzahn, *Kutztown University;* Melanie Domenech Rodriguez, *Utah State University;* Randall Salekin, *University of Alabama;* Carol Terry, *University of Oklahoma;* Mary Pat Kelly, *University of California, Irvine;* Judith LeMaster, *Scripps College;* David Greenway, *University of Southwestern Louisiana;* Drew Gouvier, *Louisiana State University-Baton Rouge;* Michael R. Hufford, *University of Montana;* C. Chrisman Wilson, *Tulane University;* Kathy Hoff, *Utah State University;* Jose M. Lafosse, *University of Colorado, Denver;* Kent Hutchinson, *University of Colorado;* Tibor Palfai, *Boston University;* Daniel L. Segal, *University of Colorado, Colorado Springs;* Ann Rosen Spector, *Rutgers*

University; William T. McReynolds, *University of Tampa*; Kristine Lynn Brady, *California School of Professional Psychology, San Diego*; Debra Hollister, *Valencia Community College*; Gay Melville, *Trident Technical College*; Joseph Lowman, *University of North Carolina at Chapel Hill*; Mitchell Earleywine, *University of Southern California*; Thomas Bradbury, *University of California, Los Angeles*; Frances K. Grossman, *Boston University*; Brad Schmidt, *Ohio State University*; Cooper Holmes, *Emporia State University*; Christopher Layne, *University of Toledo*; Robert D. Coursey, *University of Maryland*; Larry Jamner, *University of California, Irvine*; Kelly Champion, *Gustavus Adolphus College*; D. Growe, *Oakland Community College*; Robert Higgins, *Oakland University*; Mike Connor, *California State University, Long Beach*; James Linder, *California State University, Long Beach*; Paul Rokke, *North Dakota State University*; William G. Iacono, *University of Minnesota*; J. Tate, *Middle Tennessee State University*; Joanne Lindoerfer, *University of Texas*; John Hall, *LaSalle University*; Benjamin Blanding, *Rowan University*; John Suler, *Rider University*; Christine Gayda, *Stockton College*; Herbert Rappaport, *Temple University*; Davis Burdick, *Stockton College*; Michael Zinser, *University of Colorado, Denver*; Scott Hamilton, *Colorado State University*; Charles Gelso, *University of Maryland*; Donald Strassberg-Carson, *University of Utah*; James Alexander-Carson, *University of Utah*; Melissa Alderfer, *University of Utah*; Jennifer Skeem, *University of Utah*; Gretchen Gimpel, *Utah State University*; L. Dennis Madrid, *University of Southern Colorado*; James Cameron, *University of Southern Colorado*; Bob Coursey, *University of Southern Colorado*; Gordon D. Atlas, *Alfred University*; Frederic Desmond, *University of Florida*; Dominic Parrott, *Georgia State University*; Loretta Bradley, *Texas Tech University*; Nelly SantaMaria Stadler, *University of Pittsburg*; Jeffrey Kern, *University of Nevada at Las Vegas*; Matthew Tull, *University of Maryland*; Craig Neumann, *University of North Texas*; Renee Engeln-Maddox, *Northwestern University*; Clifton Watkins, *University North Texas*.

And we are tremendously appreciative of the wisdom and guidance that Charles Carver provided throughout the process. We would also like to thank Rachael Goldberg, Nancy Quartin, and Nicole Marquinez.

We have also benefited from the skills and dedication of the folks from Wiley. For this edition, we have many people to thank. Specifically, we thank Executive Editor, Chris Johnson; Executive Marketing Manager, Danielle Torio; Production Manager, Sandra Dumas; Photo Editor, Ellinor Wagner; Illustration Editor, Anna Melhorn; and the Outside Production Service, Suzanne Ingrao of Ingrao Associates. We also are grateful for the generous help and timely support from Eileen McKeever, the Assistant Editor for Psychology, and Aaron Talwar, Editorial Assistant.

From time to time, students and faculty colleagues have written us their comments on the book; these communications are always welcome. Readers can e-mail us: akring@berkeley.edu, Sljohnson@berkeley.edu.

Finally and most importantly, our heartfelt thanks go to the most important people in our lives for their continued support and encouragement along the way. A great big thanks to: Angela Hawk (AMK), Margaret Hunt (SLJ), Kathleen Chambers, Eve and Asher Davison (GCD), and Gail and Sean Neale (JMN), to whom this book is dedicated with love and gratitude.

DECEMBER 2008

Ann M. Kring, *Berkeley, CA*

Sheri L. Johnson, *Berkeley, CA*

Gerald C. Davison, *Los Angeles, CA*

John M. Neale, *Hilton Head, SC*

Brief Contents

Contents

1 Introduction and Historical Overview

LEARNING GOALS

1. Be able to explain the meaning of stigma as it applies to people with mental disorders.
2. Be able to describe and compare different definitions of mental disorder.
3. Be able to explain how the causes and treatments of mental disorders have changed over the course of history.
4. Be able to describe the historical forces that have helped to shape our current view of mental disorders, including biological, psychoanalytic, and behavioral views.
5. Be able to describe the different mental health professions, including the training involved and the expertise developed.

Clinical Case: Jack

Jack dreaded family gatherings. His parents' house would be filled with his brothers and their families, and all the little kids would run around making a lot of noise. His parents would urge him to "be social" and spend time with the family, even though Jack preferred to be alone. He knew that the kids called him "crazy Uncle Jack." In fact, he had even heard his younger brother Kevin call him "crazy Jack" when he stopped by to see their mother the other day. Jack's mother admonished him, reminding Kevin that Jack had been doing very well on his new medication. "Schizophrenia is an illness," his mother had said.

Jack had not been hospitalized with an acute episode of his schizophrenia for over 2 years. Even though Jack still heard voices, he learned not to talk about them in front of his mother because she would then start hassling him about taking his medication or ask him all sorts of questions about whether he needed to go back to the hospital. He hoped he would soon be able to move out of his parents' house and into his own apartment. The landlord at the last apartment he had tried to rent rejected his application once he learned that Jack had schizophrenia. His mother and father needed to cosign the lease, and they had inadvertently said that Jack was doing very well with his illness. The landlord asked about the illness, and once his parents mentioned schizophrenia, the landlord became visibly uncomfortable. The landlord called later that night and said the apartment had already been rented. When Jack's father pressed him, the landlord admitted he "didn't want any trouble" and that he was worried that people like Jack were violent.

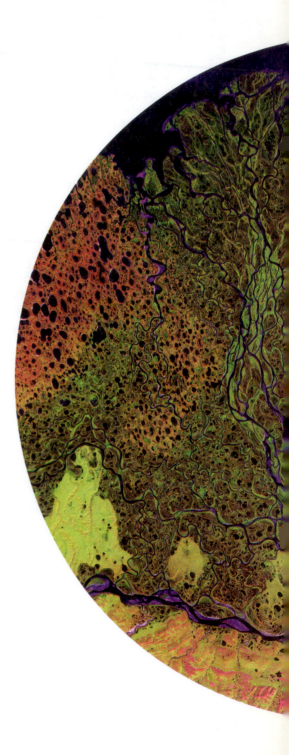

Clinical Case: Felicia

Felicia didn't like to think back to her early school years. Elementary school was not a very fun time. She couldn't sit still or follow directions very well. She often blurted out answers when it wasn't her turn to talk, and she never seemed to be able to finish her class papers without many mistakes. If that wasn't bad enough, the other girls often laughed at her and called her names. She still remembers the time she tried to join in with a group of girls during recess. They kept running away, whispering to each other, and giggling. When Felicia asked what was so funny, one of the girls laughed and said, "You are hyper, girl! You fidget so much in class, you must have ants in your pants!"

When Felicia started fourth grade, her parents took her to a psychologist. She took a number of tests and answered all sorts of questions. At the end of these testing sessions, the psychologist diagnosed Felicia with attention-deficit/hyperactivity disorder (ADHD). Felicia began seeing a different psychologist, and her pediatrician prescribed the medication Ritalin. She enjoyed seeing the psychologist because she helped her learn how to deal with the other kids' teasing and how to do a better job of paying attention. The medication helped, too—she was able to concentrate better and didn't seem to blurt out things as much anymore.

Now in high school, Felicia is much happier. She has a good group of close friends, and her grades are better than they have ever been. Though it is still hard to focus sometimes, she has learned a number of ways to deal with her distractibility. She is looking forward to college, hoping she can get into the top state school. Her guidance counselor has encouraged her, thinking her grades and extracurricular activities will make for a strong application.

WE ALL TRY TO understand other people. Determining why another person does or feels something is not easy to do. In fact, we do not always understand our own feelings and behavior. Figuring out why people behave in normal, expected ways is difficult enough; understanding seemingly abnormal behavior, such as the behavior of Jack, Felicia, and José (see p. 6), can be even more difficult.

In this book, we will consider the description, causes, and treatments of a number of different mental disorders. We will also demonstrate the numerous challenges professionals in this field face. As you approach the study of **psychopathology**, the field concerned with the nature, development, and treatment of mental disorders, keep in mind that the field is continually developing and adding new findings. As we proceed, you will see that the field's interest and importance is ever growing.

One challenge we face is to remain objective. Our subject matter, human behavior, is personal and powerfully affecting, making objectivity difficult. The pervasiveness and potentially disturbing effects of psychopathology intrude on our own lives. Who has not experienced irrational thoughts, fantasies, and feelings? Most of us have known someone, a friend or a relative, whose behavior was upsetting and impossible to fathom, and we realize how frustrating and frightening it can be to try to understand and help a person suffering psychological difficulties. You can see that this personal impact of our subject matter requires us to make a conscious, determined effort to remain objective.

The other side of this coin is that our closeness to the subject matter adds to its intrinsic fascination; undergraduate courses in abnormal psychology are among the most popular in the entire college curriculum, not just in psychology departments. Our feeling of familiarity with the subject matter draws us to the study of psychopathology, but it also has a distinct disadvantage: we bring to the study our preconceived notions of what the subject matter is. Each of us has developed certain ways of thinking and talking about mental disorders, certain words and concepts that somehow seem to fit. As you read this book and try to understand the psychological disorders it discusses, we may be asking you to adopt different ways of thinking and talking from those to which you are accustomed.

Perhaps most challenging of all, we must not only recognize our own preconceived notions of mental disorders, but we must also confront and work to change the stigma we often associate with these conditions. **Stigma** refers to the destructive beliefs and attitudes held by a society that are ascribed to groups considered different in some manner, such as people with mental illness. More specifically, stigma has four characteristics (see Figure 1.1):

1. A label is applied to a group of people that distinguishes them from others (e.g., "crazy").

2. The label is linked to deviant or undesirable attributes by society (e.g., crazy people are dangerous).

3. People with the label are seen as essentially different from those without the label, contributing to an "us" versus "them" mentality (e.g., we are not like those crazy people).

4. People with the label are discriminated against unfairly (e.g., a clinic for crazy people can't be built in our neighborhood).

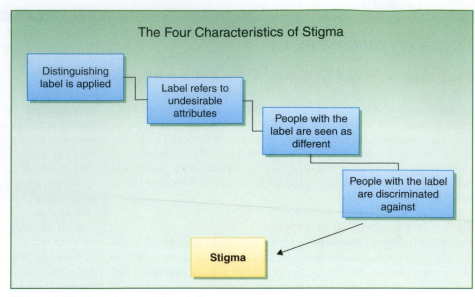

Figure 1.1 The four characteristics of stigma.

The case of Jack illustrates how stigma can lead to discrimination. Jack was denied an apartment due to his schizophrenia. The landlord believed Jack's schizophrenia meant he would be violent. This belief is based more in fiction than reality, however. A person with mental illness is not necessarily any more likely to be violent than a person without mental illness (Steadman et al., 1998; Swanson et al., 1990).

As we will see below, the treatment of individuals with mental illness throughout recorded history has not generally been good, and this has contributed to their stigmatization, to the extent that they have often been brutalized and shunned by society. Torturous treatments have been described to the public as miracle cures, and even today, terms such as *crazy*, *insane*, *retard*, and *schizo* are tossed about without thought of the people who actually suffer from mental illnesses and for whom these insults and the intensely distressing feelings and behaviors they refer to are a reality of daily life. The cases of Jack and Felicia illustrate how hurtful using such careless and mean-spirited names can be. In the 1970s, attempts were made to correct deplorably overcrowded conditions in mental hospitals by releasing many patients. But this was done without having appropriate aftercare programs in place; as a result, over a third of the homeless population in the United States would qualify for diagnosis of a mental illness of some sort (see Chapter 17).

Sadly, mental illness remains one of the most stigmatized of conditions in the twenty-first century, despite advances in the public's knowledge regarding the origins of mental disorders (Hinshaw, 2007). In 1999, David Satcher, then Surgeon General of the United States, wrote that stigma is the "most formidable obstacle to future progress in the arena of mental illness and mental health" in his groundbreaking report on mental illness (U.S. Department of Health and Human Services, 1999).

Throughout this book, we hope to fight this stigma by showing you the latest evidence about the nature, causes, and treatments for these disorders, dispelling myths and other misconceptions as we go. But you will have to help in this fight, for the mere acquisition of knowledge does not ensure the end of stigma (Penn, Chamberlin, & Mueser, 2003). As part of this effort, we will try to put a human face on mental disorders, by including descriptions of actual people with these disorders in the chapters that follow. Additional ways to fight stigma are presented in Focus on Discovery 1.1. There is much work to be done!

In this chapter, we first discuss what we mean by the term *mental disorder*. Then we look briefly at how our views of mental disorders have evolved through history to the more scientific perspectives of today. We will conclude with a discussion of the current mental health professions.

FOCUS ON DISCOVERY 1.1

Fighting against Stigma: A Strategic Approach

In 2007, psychologist Stephen Hinshaw published a book entitled *The Mark of Shame: The Stigma of Mental Illness and an Agenda for Change*. In this important book, Hinshaw outlines several steps that can be taken to end stigma surrounding mental illness. Here we briefly discuss some of the key suggestions for fighting stigma across many arenas, including law and policy, community, mental health professions, and individual/family behaviors and attitudes.

Policy and Legislative Strategies

Parity in Insurance Coverage In 1996, the Federal Mental Health Parity Act required that insurance coverage for mental illness be at the same level as for other illnesses. However, substance abuse was not included, small companies (under 50 employees) were not required to offer parity, companies could set limits on coverage, and the law allowed for companies to opt out if their costs increased over 1 percent. In February 2007, the U.S. Senate passed a new mental health parity bill to expand on the 1996 law. In March 2008, the U.S. House of Representatives passed an even broader parity bill, the Paul Wellstone Mental Health and Addiction Equity Act, which comes closer to offering true parity. House and Senate committees produced a bill that was signed into law on October 3, 2008.

Discriminatory Laws Some states have rules banning people with mental illness from voting, marrying, serving on juries, or holding public office. In a recent analysis of bills submitted for consideration in state legislatures in 2002, there were about an equal number of bills to take away liberties as there were to grant liberties to people with mental illness. Similarly, there were roughly equal numbers of new bills that would effectively increase discrimination against people with mental illness as there were bills that would diminish discrimination (Corrigan et al., 2005). Speaking to state legislators about the importance of nondiscriminatory laws is something we can all do to help fight stigma in this arena.

Employment Unemployment rates among people with mental illness are extremely high, despite the Americans with Disabilities Act (ADA) provisions that make it illegal to keep someone with mental illness from obtaining or keeping a job. The cruel irony here is that only a small number of ADA claims deal with job discrimination for people with mental illness (likely because people with mental illness are afraid to come forward due to the stigma surrounding their illness), yet these claims are among the easiest, at least in terms of cost, to fix (e.g., contrast the cost of allowing time off for therapy to the cost of redesigning and building a wheelchair-accessible area). Further training in job-relevant skills, such as provision of extra educational benefits to those whose education might have been curtailed by mental illness will help with employment opportunities. Similarly, training in social skills relevant to the workplace and other structured programs to enhance workplace success would be an important goal.

Decriminalization People with mental illness, particularly substance abuse, often end up in jail rather than a hospital. Large urban jails, such as Los Angeles County jail, Riker's Island in New York, and Cook County jail in Chicago, now house more people with mental illness than any hospital, public or private, in the United States. Many substance-related problems are first detected within the criminal justice system, and people may need more intensive treatment to address underlying substance abuse problems. Minimal or no treatment is provided in jail, and this is thus not an optimal place for people with mental illness. Many states have adopted assisted outpatient treatment (AOT) laws that provide court-mandated outpatient treatment rather than jail time for people with mental illness.

Community Strategies

Housing Options Rates of homelessness in people with mental illness are all too high, and more programs to provide community residences and group homes are needed. However, many neighborhoods are reluctant to embrace

Defining Mental Disorder

A difficult but fundamental task facing those in the field of psychopathology is to define **mental disorder**. The best current definition of mental disorder is one that contains several characteristics. The definition of mental disorder presented in the current American diagnostic manual, the *Diagnostic and Statistical Manual of Mental Disorders*, Fourth Edition, Text Revision (DSM-IV-TR), includes a number of characteristics essential to the concept of mental disorder. In DSM-IV-TR, mental disorder is defined as:

> *A clinically significant behavioral or psychological syndrome or pattern that occurs in an individual and that is associated with present distress (e.g., a painful symptom) or disability (i.e., impairment in one or more important areas of functioning) or with a significantly increased risk of suffering, death, pain, disability, or an important loss of freedom. In addition, this syndrome or pattern must not be merely an expectable and culturally sanctioned response to a particular event, for example, the death of a loved one. Whatever its original cause, it must currently be considered a manifestation of a behavioral, psychological, or biological dysfunction in the individual (American Psychiatric Association, 2000, p. xxxi)*

the idea of people with mental illness living too close. Lobbying legislatures and community leaders about the importance of adequate housing is a critically important step toward providing housing and reducing stigma.

Personal Contact Including greater housing opportunities for people with mental illness will likely mean that people with mental illness will shop and dine in local establishments alongside people without mental illness. Research suggests that this type of contact—where status is relatively equal—can reduce stigma. Informal settings, such as local parks and churches, can also help bridge the personal contact gap between people with and without mental illness.

Education Educating people about mental illness (one of the goals of this book!) is an important step toward reducing stigma. Education alone won't completely eradicate stigma, however. By learning about mental illness, people may be less hesitant to interact with people who have different disorders. Many of you know already know someone with a mental disorder. Sadly, though, stigma often prevents people from disclosing their history with mental illness. Education may help lessen the hesitancy of people to talk about their illnesses.

Mental Health and Health Profession Strategies

Mental Health Evaluations Many children see their pediatricians for well-baby or well-child exams. The goal of these is to prevent illness before it occurs. Hinshaw (2007) makes a strong case for the inclusion of similar preventive efforts for mental illness among children and adolescents by, for example, including rating scale assessments from parents and teachers in order to help identify problems before they become more serious.

Education and Training Mental health professionals should receive training in stigma issues. This type of training will undoubtedly help professionals recognize the pernicious signs of stigma, even within the very profession that is charged with helping people with mental illness. In addition, mental health professionals need to keep current in their knowledge of the descriptions, causes, and empirically supported treatments for mental illness. This will certainly lead to better interactions with patients and

may also help to educate the public about the important work that is done by mental health professionals.

Individual and Family Strategies

Education for Individuals and Families It can be frightening and disorienting for families who learn that a loved one has been diagnosed with an illness, and this may be particularly true for mental illness. Receiving current information about the causes and treatments of mental illness is crucial because it will help to alleviate blame and stereotypes families may hold about mental illness. Educating people with mental illness is also extremely important. Sometimes termed psychoeducation, this type of information is built into many types of treatments, whether they are pharmacological or psychosocial. In order for people to understand why they should adhere to certain treatment regiments, it is important for them to know the nature of their illness and the treatment alternatives available.

Support and Advocacy Groups Participating in support or advocacy groups can be a helpful adjunct to treatment for people with mental illness and their families. Recent websites, such as the Freedom Center (*http://www.freedom-center.org*) or Mind Freedom International (*http://www.mindfreedom.org*) are designed to provide a forum for people with mental illness to find support. Some such groups also encourage people not to hide their mental illness, but rather to consider it a point of pride—"Mad Pride" events are scheduled all over the world. Many people with mental illness have created their own blogs to discuss their illness and help to demystify and therefore destigmatize it. For example, Liz Spikol, a reporter for the *Philadelphia Weekly*, keeps a blog called "The Trouble with Spikol (*http://trouble.philadelphiaweekly.com*) where she writes about her own bipolar disorder and other mental health issues. These sites and events are developed and run by people with mental illness, and the sites contains useful links, blogs, and other helpful resources. In-person support groups are also helpful, and many communities have groups supported by the National Alliance on Mental Illness (*www.nami.org*). Finding peers in the context of support groups can be beneficial, especially for emotional support and empowerment.

In the following sections, we consider in more detail some of the key characteristics that are highlighted by the DSM-IV-TR definition, including disability, distress, violation of social norms, and dysfunction. We will see that no single characteristic can fully define the concept, although each has merit and each captures some part of what might be a full definition. Consequently, mental disorder is usually determined based on the presence of several characteristics at one time, as the DSM-IV-TR definition exemplifies. Figure 1.2 shows the different characteristics of the definition of mental disorder.

Personal Distress

One characteristic used to define mental disorder is personal distress—that is, a person's behavior may be classified as disordered if it causes him or her great distress. Felicia felt distress about her difficulty with paying attention and the social

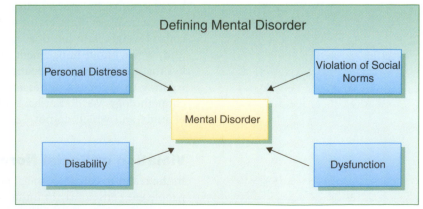

Figure 1.2 Key characteristics in the definition of mental disorder.

Clinical Case: José

José didn't know what to think about his nightmares. Ever since he returned from the war, he couldn't get the bloody images out of his head. He woke up nearly every night with nightmares about the carnage he witnessed as a soldier stationed in Falluja. Even during the day, he would have flashbacks to the moment his Humvee was nearly sliced in half by a rocket-propelled grenade. Watching his friend die sitting next to him was the worst part; even the occasional pain from shrapnel still embedded in his shoulder was not as bad as the recurring dreams and flashbacks. He seemed to be sweating all the time now, and whenever he heard a loud noise, he jumped out of his chair. Just the other day, his grandmother stepped on a balloon left over from his "welcome home" party. To José,

it sounded like a gunshot, and he immediately dropped to the ground.

His grandmother was worried about him. She thought he must have *ataque de nervios*, just like her father had back home in Puerto Rico. She said her father was afraid all the time and felt like he was going crazy. She kept going to Mass and praying for José, which he appreciated. The army doctor said he had posttraumatic stress disorder (PTSD). José was supposed to go to the Veterans Administration (VA) hospital for an evaluation, but he didn't really think there was anything wrong with him. Yet his buddy Jorge had been to a group session at the VA, and he said it made him feel better. Maybe he would check it out. He wanted these images to get out of his head.

Personal distress can be part of the definition of mental disorder. (AFP/Corbis Images.)

consequences of this difficulty—that is, being called names by other schoolgirls. Personal distress also characterizes many of the forms of mental disorder considered in this book—people experiencing anxiety disorders and depression suffer greatly. But not all mental disorders cause distress. For example, an individual with antisocial personality disorder may treat others coldheartedly and violate the law without experiencing any guilt, remorse, anxiety, or other type of distress. And not all behavior that causes distress is disordered—for example, the distress of hunger due to religious fasting or the pain of childbirth.

Disability

Disability—that is, impairment in some important area of life (e.g., work or personal relationships)—can also be used to characterize mental disorder. For example, substance-related disorders are defined in part by the social or occupational disability (e.g., serious arguments with one's spouse or poor work performance) created by substance abuse. Being rejected by peers, as Felicia was, is also an example of this characteristic. Phobias can produce both distress and disability—for example, if a severe fear of flying prevents someone living in California from taking a job in New York. Like distress, however, disability alone cannot be used to define mental disorder, because some, but not all, disorders involve disability. For example, the disorder bulimia nervosa involves binge eating and compensatory purging (e.g., vomiting) in an attempt to control weight gain but does not necessarily involve disability. Many people with bulimia lead lives without impairment, while bingeing and purging in private. Other characteristics that might, in some circumstances, be considered disabilities—such as being blind and wanting to become a professional race car driver—do not fall within the domain of psychopathology. We do not have a rule that tells us which disabilities belong in our domain of study and which do not.

Violation of Social Norms

In the realm of behavior, social norms are widely held standards (beliefs and attitudes) that people use consciously or intuitively to make judgments about where behaviors are situated on such scales as good–bad, right–wrong, justified–unjustified, and acceptable–unacceptable. Behavior that violates social norms might be classified as disorderd. For example, the repetitive rituals performed by people with obsessive-compulsive disorder (see Chapter 5) and the conversations with imaginary voices that some people with schizophrenia engage in (see Chapter 11) are behaviors that violate social norms. José's dropping to the floor at the sound of a popping balloon does not fit within most social norms. Yet this way of defining mental disorder is both too broad and too narrow. For example, it is too broad in that criminals violate social norms but are not usually studied within the domain of psychopathology; it is too narrow in that highly anxious people typically do not violate social norms.

Also, of course, social norms vary a great deal across cultures and ethnic groups, so behavior that clearly violates a social norm in one group may not do so at all in another. For example, in some cultures but not in others it violates a social norm to directly disagree with someone. In Puerto Rico, José's behavior would not likely have been interpreted in the same way as it would be in the United States. Throughout this book, we will address this important issue of cultural and ethnic diversity as it applies to the descriptions, causes, and treatments of mental disorders.

Dysfunction

In an influential and widely discussed paper, Wakefield (1992) proposed that mental disorders could be defined as **harmful dysfunction**. This definition has two parts: a value judgment ("harmful") and an objective, scientific component—the "dysfunction." A judgment that a behavior is harmful requires some standard, and this standard is likely to depend on social norms and values, the characteristic just described. Dysfunctions are said to occur when an internal mechanism is unable to perform its natural function—that is, the function that it evolved to perform. By grounding this part of the definition of mental disorder in evolutionary theory, Wakefield hoped to give the definition scientific objectivity.

Numerous critics have argued that the dysfunction component of Wakefield's definition is not so easily and objectively identifiable in relation to mental disorders (e.g., Houts, 2001; Lilienfeld & Marino, 1999). One difficulty is that the internal mechanisms involved in mental disorders are largely unknown; thus, we cannot say exactly what may not be functioning properly. Wakefield (1999) has tried to meet this objection by, in part, referring to plausible dysfunctions rather than proven ones. In the case of Jack, for example, hallucinations (hearing voices) could be construed as a failure of the mind to "turn off" unwanted sounds. Nevertheless, we have a situation in which we judge a behavior or set of behaviors to be harmful and then decide that the behavior represents a mental disorder because we believe it is caused by a dysfunction of some unknown internal mechanism. Clearly, like the other definitions of mental disorder, Wakefield's concept of harmful dysfunction has its limitations.

The broader concept of dysfunction as indicated in the DSM-IV-TR definition of mental disorder refers to behavioral, psychological, or biological dysfunctions that are supported by our current body of evidence. This broadening does not entirely avoid the problems that Wakefield's definition suffers from, but it is an attempt that formally recognizes the limits of our current understanding.

Indeed, it is crucial to keep in mind that our book presents human problems that are currently considered mental disorders. Over time, because the field is continually evolving, the disorders discussed in books like this will undoubtedly change, and so will the definition of mental disorder. It is also quite possible that we will never be able to arrive at a definition that captures mental disorder in its entirety and for all time. Nevertheless, at the current time, the characteristics that are included in the DSM-IV-TR definition constitute a useful partial definition, but keep in mind that they are not equally or invariably applicable to every diagnosis.

Quick Summary

The focus of this book will be on the description, causes, and treatments of a number of different mental disorders. It is important to note at the outset that the personal impact of our subject matter requires us to make a conscious, determined effort to remain objective. Stigma remains a central problem in the field of psychopathology. Stigma has four components that involve the labels for mental illness and their uses. Even the use of everyday language terms such as *crazy* or *schizo* can contribute to the stigmatization of people with mental illness.

Defining mental disorder remains difficult. A number of different definitions have been offered, but none can entirely account for the full range of disorders. Whether or not a behavior causes personal distress can be a characteristic of mental disorder. But not all behav-

ior that we consider to be part of mental disorders causes distress. Behaviors that cause a disability or are unexpected can be considered part of a mental disorder. But again, some behaviors do not cause disability, nor are they unexpected. Behavior that violates social norms can also be considered part of a mental disorder. However, not all such behavior is considered part of a mental disorder, and some behaviors that are characteristic of mental disorders do not necessarily violate social norms. Harmful dysfunction involves both a value component and a scientific component. Like the other definitions, however, it cannot fully account for what we study in psychopathology. Taken together, each definition of mental disorder has something helpful to offer in the study of psychopathology.

Check Your Knowledge 1.1 (Answers are at the end of the chapter.)

1. Characteristics of stigma include all of the following *except:*
   a. a label reflecting desirable characteristics
   b. discrimination against those with the label
   c. focus on differences between those with and without the label
   d. labeling a group of people who are different
2. Which of the following definitions of mental disorder is currently thought best?
   a. personal distress
   b. harmful dysfunction
   c. norm violation

   d. none of the above
3. The DSM-IV-TR definition of mental disorder is perhaps the best current definition because:
   a. It includes information about both violation of social norms and dysfunction.
   b. It includes many components, none of which can alone account for mental disorder.
   c. It is part of the current diagnostic system.
   d. It recognizes the limits of our current understanding.

History of Psychopathology

Many textbooks begin with a chapter on the history of the field. Why? It is important to consider how concepts and approaches have changed (or not) over time, because we can learn not to make the same mistakes made in the past and because we can see that our current concepts and approaches are likely to change in the future. As we consider the history of psychopathology, we will see that many new approaches to the treatment of mental illness throughout time appear to go well at first and are heralded with much excitement and fanfare. But these treatments eventually fall into disrepute. These are lessons that should not be forgotten as we consider more contemporary approaches to treatment and their attendant excitement and fanfare.

The search for causes of mental disorders has gone on for a considerable period of time. At different periods in history, explanations for mental disorders have been supernatural, biological, and psychological. As we quickly travel through these different periods, ask yourself what level of explanation was operating at different times.

Early Demonology

Before the age of scientific inquiry, all good and bad manifestations of power beyond human control—eclipses, earthquakes, storms, fire, diseases, the changing seasons—were regarded as supernatural. Behavior seemingly outside individual control was also ascribed to supernatural causes. Many early philosophers, theologians, and physicians who studied the troubled mind believed that disturbed behavior reflected the displeasure of the gods or possession by demons.

The doctrine that an evil being or spirit can dwell within a person and control his or her mind and body is called **demonology**. Examples of demonological thinking are found in the records of the early Chinese, Egyptians, Babylonians, and Greeks. Among the Hebrews, odd behavior was attributed to possession of the person by bad spirits, after God in his wrath had withdrawn protection. The New Testament includes the story of Christ curing a man with an unclean spirit by casting out the devils from within him and hurling them onto a herd of swine (Mark 5:8–13).

The belief that odd behavior was caused by possession led to treating it by **exorcism**, the ritualistic casting out of evil spirits. Exorcism typically took the form of elaborate rites of prayer, noise-making, forcing the afflicted to drink terrible-tasting brews, and on occasion more extreme measures, such as flogging and starvation, to render the body uninhabitable to devils.

Christ driving the evil spirits out of a possessed man. (Archivo Iconografico, S.A./Corbis Images.)

Early Biological Explanations

In the fifth century B.C., Hippocrates (460?–377? B.C.), often called the father of modern medicine, separated medicine from religion, magic, and superstition. He rejected the prevailing Greek belief that the gods sent mental disturbances as punishment and insisted instead that such illnesses had natural causes and hence should be treated like other, more common maladies, such as colds and constipation. Hippocrates regarded the brain as the organ of consciousness, intellectual life, and emotion; thus, he thought that disordered thinking and behavior were indications of some kind of brain pathology. Hippocrates is often considered one of the earliest proponents of the notion that something wrong with the brain disturbs thought and action.

Hippocrates classified mental disorders into three categories: mania, melancholia, and phrenitis, or brain fever. Further, Hippocrates believed that normal brain functioning, and therefore mental health, depended on a delicate balance among four humors, or fluids of the body, namely, blood, black bile, yellow bile, and phlegm. An imbalance produced disorders. If a person was sluggish and dull, for example, the body supposedly contained a preponderance of phlegm. A preponderance of black bile was the explanation for melancholia; too much yellow bile explained irritability and anxiousness; and too much blood, changeable temperament.

Through his teachings, the phenomena associated with mental disorders became more clearly the province of physicians than of priests. The treatments Hippocrates suggested were quite different from exorcism. For melancholia, for example, he prescribed tranquility, sobriety, care in choosing food and drink, and abstinence from sexual activity. Because Hippocrates believed in natural rather than supernatural causes, he depended on his own keen observations and made valuable contributions as a clinician. He also left behind remarkably detailed records clearly describing many of the symptoms now recognized in seizure disorders, alcohol dependence, stroke, and paranoia.

Hippocrates' ideas, of course, did not withstand later scientific scrutiny. However, his basic premise—that human behavior is markedly affected by bodily structures or substances and that odd behavior is produced by some kind of physical imbalance or even damage—did foreshadow aspects of contemporary thought. In the next seven centuries, Hippocrates' naturalistic approach to disease and disorder was generally accepted by other Greeks as well as by the Romans, who adopted the medicine of the Greeks after their empire became the major power in the ancient European world.

HIPOCRATI COO

The Greek physician Hippocrates held a biological view of mental illness, considering mental disorders to be diseases of the brain. (Archivo Iconografico, S.A./Corbis Images.)

The Dark Ages and Demonology

Historians have often pointed to the death of Galen (A.D. 130–200), the second-century Greek who is regarded as the last great physician of the classical era, as the beginning of the so-called Dark Ages in western European medicine and in the treatment and investigation of mental disorders. Over several centuries of decay, Greek and Roman civilization ceased to be. The churches gained in influence, and the papacy was declared independent of the state. Christian monasteries, through their missionary and educational work, replaced physicians as healers and as authorities on mental disorder.[1]

The monks in the monasteries cared for and nursed the sick, and a few of the monasteries were repositories for the classic Greek medical manuscripts, even though the monks may not have made use of the knowledge within these works. Monks cared for people with mental disorders by praying over them and touching them with relics; they also concocted fantastic potions for them to drink in the waning phase of the moon. Many people with mental illness roamed the countryside, destitute and progressively becoming worse. During this period, there was a return to a belief in supernatural causes of mental disorders.

The Persecution of Witches Beginning in the thirteenth century, in response to widespread social unrest and recurrent famines and plagues, people in Europe turned to demonology to explain these disasters. Witchcraft, now viewed as instigated by Satan, was seen as a heresy and a denial of God. Then, as today, when faced with inexplicable and frightening occurrences, people tended to seize on whatever explanation seemed most plausible. The times conspired to heap enormous blame on those regarded as witches, who were persecuted with great zeal.

In 1484, Pope Innocent VIII exhorted the clergy of Europe to leave no stone unturned in the search for witches. He sent two Dominican monks to northern Germany as inquisitors. Two years later they issued a comprehensive and explicit manual, *Malleus Maleficarum* ("the witches' hammer"), to guide the witch hunts. This legal and theological document came

In the dunking test, if the woman did not drown, she was considered to be in league with the devil (and punished accordingly); this is the ultimate no-win situation. (Corbis-Bettmann.)

to be regarded by Catholics and Protestants alike as a textbook on witchcraft. Those accused of witchcraft should be tortured if they did not confess; those convicted and penitent were to be imprisoned for life; and those convicted and unrepentant were to be handed over to the law for execution. The manual specified that a person's sudden loss of reason was a symptom of demonic possession and that burning was the usual method of driving out the supposed demon. Records of the period are not considered reliable, but it is thought that over the next several centuries hundreds of thousands of people, particularly women and children, were accused, tortured, and put to death.

Investigators initially believed that many of the people accused of being witches during the later Middle Ages were mentally ill (Zilboorg & Henry, 1941). The basis for this belief was the confessions of the accused that investigators interpreted as delusional beliefs or hallucinations.

More detailed research into this historical period, however, indicates that many of the accused were not mentally ill. Careful analyses of the witch hunts reveal that more healthy than ill people were tried. Confessions were typically obtained during brutal torture, having been suggested to the accused witches both by their accusers and by the prevailing beliefs of the times. Indeed, in England, where torture was not allowed, the confessions did not usually contain descriptions resembling delusions or hallucinations (Schoeneman, 1977).

Lunacy Trials Evaluations of other sources of information also indicate that mental illness was not primarily ascribed to witchcraft. From the thirteenth century on, as the cities of Europe grew larger, hospitals began to come under secular jurisdiction. Municipal authorities, gaining in power, tended to supplement or take over some of the activities of the church, one of these being the care of people who were mentally ill. The foundation deed for the Holy Trinity Hospital in Salisbury, England, dating from the mid-fourteenth century, specified the purposes of the hospital, among them that the "mad are kept safe until they are restored of reason." English laws

---

[1]The teachings of Galen continued to be influential in the Islamic world. For example, the Persian physician al-Razi (865–925) established a facility for the treatment of people with mental illness in Baghdad and was an early practitioner of psychotherapy.

during this period allowed people with mental illness to be hospitalized. Notably, the people who were hospitalized were not described as being possessed (Alldderidge, 1979).

Beginning in the thirteenth century, lunacy trials to determine a person's mental health were held in England. The trials were conducted under the Crown's right to protect the people with mental illness, and a judgment of insanity allowed the Crown to become guardian of the lunatic's estate (Neugebauer, 1979). The defendant's orientation, memory, intellect, daily life, and habits were at issue in the trial. Usually, strange behavior was attributed to physical illness or injury or to some emotional shock. In all the cases that Neugebauer examined, only one referred to demonic possession. Interestingly, the term *lunacy* comes from a theory espoused by the Swiss physician Paracelsus (1493–1541), who attributed odd behavior to a misalignment of the moon and stars (the Latin word for "moon" is *luna*). This lunar explanation, even if unsubstantiated, was a welcome alternative to explanations involving demons or witches. Even today, many people believe that a full moon is linked to odd behavior; however, there is no scientific evidence to support this belief.

Development of Asylums

Until the fifteenth century, there were very few hospitals for people with mental illness in Europe. However, there were many hospitals for people with leprosy—for example, in the twelfth century, England and Scotland had 220 leprosy hospitals serving a total population of a million and a half. Leprosy gradually disappeared from Europe, probably because with the end of the wars came a break with the eastern sources of the infection. With hospitals now underused, attention seems to have turned to people with mental illness. Leprosariums were converted to **asylums**, refuges for the confinement and care of people with mental illness.

Bethlehem and Other Early Asylums   The Priory of St. Mary of Bethlehem was founded in 1243. Records indicate that in 1403 it housed six men with mental illness. In 1547, Henry VIII handed it over to the city of London, thereafter to be a hospital devoted solely to the confinement of people with mental illness. The conditions in Bethlehem were deplorable. Over the years the word *bedlam*, the popular name for this hospital, came to mean a place or scene of wild uproar and confusion. Bethlehem eventually became one of London's great tourist attractions, by the eighteenth century rivaling both Westminster Abbey and the Tower of London. Even as late as the nineteenth century, viewing the patients was considered entertainment, and people bought tickets to see them. Similarly, in the Lunatics Tower, which was constructed in Vienna in 1784, patients were confined in the spaces between inner square rooms and the outer walls, where they could be viewed by passersby.

Obviously, confining people with mental illness in hospitals and placing their care in the domain of medicine did not necessarily lead to more humane and effective treatment. Medical treatments were often crude and painful. Benjamin Rush (1745–1813), for example, began practicing medicine in Philadelphia in 1769 and is considered the father of American psychiatry. Yet he believed that mental disorder was caused by an excess of blood in the brain, for which his favored treatment was to draw great quantities of blood from disordered individuals (Farina, 1976). Rush also believed that many people with mental illness could be cured by being frightened. Thus, one of his recommended procedures was for the physician to convince the patient that death was near!

In this eighteenth-century painting by Hogarth, two upper-class women find amusement in touring St. Mary's of Bethlehem (Bedlam). (Corbis-Bettmann.)

The freeing of the patients at La Bicetre (supposedly by Pinel, as pictured here) is often considered to mark the beginning of more humanitarian treatment of people with mental illness. (Stock Montage, Inc.)

Pinel's Reforms   Philippe Pinel (1745–1826) has often been considered a primary figure in the movement for humanitarian treatment of people with mental illness in asylums. In 1793, while the French Revolution raged, he was put in charge of a large asylum in Paris known as La Bicêtre. A historian described the conditions at this particular hospital:

[The patients were] shackled to the walls of their cells, by iron collars which held them flat against the wall and permitted little movement. They could not lie down at night, as a rule. Oftentimes there was a hoop of iron around the waist of the patient and in addition chains on both the hands and the feet. These chains [were] sufficiently long so that the patient could feed himself out of a bowl, the food usually being a mushy gruel—bread soaked in a weak soup. Since little was known about dietetics, [no attention] was paid to the type of diet given the patients. They were presumed to be animals and not to care whether the food was good or bad. (Selling, 1940, p. 54)

Many texts assert that Pinel removed the chains of the people imprisoned in La Bicêtre, an event that was memorialized in well-known paintings. Pinel is said to have begun to treat the patients as sick human beings rather than as beasts. Light and airy rooms replaced dungeons. Many who had been completely unmanageable became calm. Patients formerly considered dangerous now strolled through the hospital and grounds without creating disturbances or harming anyone. Some patients who had been incarcerated for years were apparently restored to health and eventually discharged from the hospital.

Historical research, however, indicates that it was not Pinel who released the patients from their chains. Rather, it was a former patient, Jean-Baptiste Pussin, who had become an orderly at the hospital. In fact, Pinel was not even present when the patients were released (Weiner, 1994). Several years later, though, Pinel did praise Pussin's efforts and began to follow the same practices.

Consistent with the egalitarianism of the new French Republic, Pinel came to believe that patients in his care were first and foremost human beings, and thus, these people should be approached with compassion and understanding and treated with dignity as. He surmised that if their reason had left them because of severe personal and social problems, it might be restored to them through comforting counsel and purposeful activity.

Pinel did much good for people with mental illness, but he was no paragon of enlightenment and egalitarianism. He reserved the more humanitarian treatment for the upper classes; patients of the lower classes were still subjected to terror and coercion as a means of control, with straitjackets replacing chains.

Moral Treatment   For a time, mental hospitals established in Europe and the United States were relatively small, privately supported, and operated along the lines of the humanitarian changes at La Bicêtre. In the United States, the Friends' Asylum, founded in 1817 in Pennsylvania, and the Hartford Retreat, established in 1824 in Connecticut, were established to provide humane treatment. In accordance with this approach, which became known as **moral treatment**, patients had close contact with attendants, who talked and read to them and encouraged them to engage in purposeful activity; residents led lives as close to normal as possible and in general took responsibility for themselves within the constraints of their disorders. Further, there were to be no more than 250 patients in a given hospital (Whitaker, 2002).

Moral treatment was largely abandoned in the latter part of the nineteenth century. Ironically, the efforts of Dorothea Dix (1802–1887), a crusader for improved conditions for people with mental illness who fought to have hospitals created for their care, helped effect this change. Dix, a Boston schoolteacher, taught a Sunday school class at the local prison and

In the nineteenth century, Dorothea Dix played a major role in establishing more mental hospitals in the United States. (Corbis Images.)

was shocked at the deplorable conditions in which the inmates lived. Her interest spread to the conditions at mental hospitals and to people with mental illness who had nowhere to go for treatment. She campaigned vigorously to improve the lives of people with mental illness and personally helped see that 32 state hospitals were built. These large, public hospitals took in many of the patients whom the private hospitals could not accommodate. Unfortunately, the small staffs of these new hospitals were unable to provide the individual attention that was a hallmark of moral treatment (Bockhoven, 1963). Moreover, the hospitals came to be administered by physicians, most of whom were interested in the biological aspects of illness and in the physical, rather than the psychological well-being of patients with mental illness. The money that had once paid the salaries of personal attendants now paid for equipment and laboratories. (See Focus on Discovery 1.2 for an examination of whether the conditions in today's mental hospitals have improved.)

FOCUS ON DISCOVERY 1.2

The Mental Hospital Today

In the late 1960s and early 1970s, concerns about the restrictive nature of confinement in a mental hospital led to the so-called deinstitutionalization of a large number of people with mental illness. Budget cuts beginning in the 1980s and continuing today have caused this trend to continue. But the problems of the chronically ill patient, who needs treatment in a hospital setting, have yet to be handled adequately (as we will discuss in more detail in Chapter 17). Treatment in public mental hospitals today is primarily custodial in nature. Patients live in a protected environment, but they may receive little treatment beyond medication; their existence is monotonous and sedentary for the most part.

Today, public mental hospitals in the United States are usually funded either by the federal government or by the state where they are located. Many Veterans Administration hospitals and general medical hospitals also contain units for people with mental illness. Since 1970, the number of public mental hospitals has decreased substantially. In 1969, there were 310 state or county hospitals; by 1998, there were just 229 (Geller, 2006).

With the decreasing numbers of state and county hospitals, private mental hospitals began to expand in numbers in the 1970s. In 1969, there were 150 private hospitals, but in 1998, there were 348 (Geller, 2006). This trend toward increasing private hospitals nonetheless peaked in 1992. Since then, private hospitals have also declined in number. The physical facilities and professional care in private hospitals tend to be superior to those of public hospitals for one reason: the private hospitals have more money. The costs to patients in these private institutions can exceed $1,000 per day, and reimbursement from private insurance, Medicaid, and Medicare continues to decline.

A somewhat specialized mental hospital, sometimes called a forensic hospital, is reserved for people who have been arrested and judged unable to stand trial and for those who have been acquitted of a crime by reason of insanity (see Chapter 17). Although these patients have not been sent to prison, security staff and tight security regiment their lives. Treatment of some kind is supposed to take place during their stay.

Many hospitals require patients to attend group therapy—here, a general term indicating only that at least two patients are supposed to relate to each other and to a group leader in a room for a specific period of time. Some patients in public hospitals have a few sessions alone with a professional therapist; many more patients in private hospitals receive individual therapy. For the most part, however, traditional hospital treatment over the past 50 years has been oriented toward dispensing drugs rather than offering psychotherapy. The institutional setting itself is used as a way to provide supportive care, to try to ensure that patients take their medication, and to protect and look after patients whose conditions make it difficult for them to care for themselves or that render them a threat to others.

Most dormitory rooms at state mental hospitals are bleak and unstimulating. (Eric Roth/Index Stock.)

Quick Summary

Early concepts of mental illness included demonology (possession by demons) but also biological approaches as evidenced by the ideas of Hippocrates. During the Dark Ages, some people with mental illness were cared for in monasteries, but many simply roamed the countryside. Some were persecuted as witches, but this was relatively rare (later analyses indicated that many of the people accused of being witches were not mentally ill). Treatments for people with mental illness have changed over time, though not always for the better. Exorcisms did not do much good. Treatments in asylums could also be cruel and unhelpful, but pioneering work by Pinel, Dix, and others made asylums more humane places for treatment. Unfortunately, their good ideas did not last, as the mental hospitals became overcrowded and understaffed.

Check Your Knowledge 1.2

True or false?
1. Benjamin Rush is credited with beginning moral treatment in the United States.
2. The most recent historical research has found that nearly all of the people persecuted as witches were mentally ill.

3. Hippocrates was one of the first to propose that mental illness had a biological cause.
4. The term *lunatic* is derived from the ideas of Paracelsus.

The Evolution of Contemporary Thought

Table 1.1 Causes of Maladies Observed among Patients in Bethlehem in the Year 1810	
Cause	**Number of Patients**
Childbed*	79
Contusions/fractures of skull	12
Drink/intoxication	58
Family/hereditary	115
Fevers	110
Fright	31
Grief	206
Jealousy	9
Love	90
Obstruction	10
Pride	8
Religion/Methodism	90
Smallpox	7
Study	15
Venereal	14
Ulcers/scabs dried up	5

Sources: Adapted from Appignannesi (2008); Hunter & Macalpine (1963).
*Childbed refers to childbirth—perhaps akin to what we now call postpartum depression.

As horrific as the conditions in Bethlehem hospital were, the physicians at the time were nonetheless interested in what caused the maladies of their patients. Table 1.1 lists the hypothesized causes of the illnesses exhibited by patients in 1810 that were recorded by a physician working at Bethlehem at the time named William Black (Appignannesi, 2008). It is interesting to observe that about half of the presumed causes were biological (e.g., fever, hereditary, venereal) and half were psychological (e.g., grief, love, jealousy). Only around 10 percent of the causes were spiritual.

Contemporary developments in biological and psychological approaches to the causes and treatments of mental disorders were heavily influenced by theorists and scientists working in the late nineteenth and early twentieth centuries. We will discuss, compare, and evaluate these approaches more fully in Chapter 2. In this section, we review the historical antecedents of these more contemporary approaches.

Recall that in the West, the death of Galen and the decline of Greco-Roman civilization temporarily ended inquiries into the nature of both physical and mental illness. Not until the late Middle Ages did any new facts begin to emerge, thanks to an emerging empirical approach to medical science, which emphasized gathering knowledge by direct observation.

Biological Approaches

Discovering Biological Origins in General Paresis and Syphilis The anatomy and workings of the nervous system were partially understood by the mid-1800s, but not enough was known to let investigators conclude whether the structural brain abnormalities presumed to cause various mental disorders were present or not. Perhaps the most striking medical success was the elucidation of the nature and origin of syphilis, a venereal disease that had been recognized for several centuries.

The story of this discovery provides a good illustration of how an empirical approach, the basis for contemporary science, works. Since the late 1700s it had been known that a number of people with mental illness manifested a syndrome characterized by a steady deterioration of both mental and physical abilities, including symptoms such as delusions of grandeur and progressive paralysis; the presumed disease associated with this syndrome was given the name **general paresis**. Soon after these symptoms were recognized, investigators realized that these people never recovered. By the mid-1800s, it had been established that some patients with general paresis also had syphilis, but a connection between the two conditions was not yet made.

In the 1860s and 1870s, Louis Pasteur established the germ theory of disease, which set forth the view that disease is caused by infection of the body by minute organisms. This theory laid the groundwork for demonstrating the relation between syphilis and general paresis. Finally, in 1905, the specific microorganism that causes syphilis was discovered. For the first time, a causal link had been established between infection, destruction of certain areas of the brain, and a form of psychopathology (general paresis). If one type of psychopathology had a biological cause, so could others. Biological approaches gained credibility, and the searches for more biological causes were off and running.

Galen was a Greek physician who followed Hippocrates's ideas and is regarded as the last great physician of the classical era. (Corbis Images.)

Genetics   Francis Galton (1822–1911) is often considered the originator of genetic research with twins, based on his study of twins in the late 1800s in England, where he attributed many behavioral characteristics to heredity. In the early twentieth century, investigators became intrigued by the idea that mental illness may run in families, and beginning at that time, a number of studies documented the heritability of mental illnesses such as schizophrenia, bipolar disorder, and depression. These studies would set the stage for later theories about the causes of mental illness.

Unfortunately, many of the early efforts in the United States to determine whether mental illness could be inherited were associated with the eugenics movement, whose advocates sought to eliminate undesirable characteristics from the population by restricting the ability of certain people to have children (e.g., by enforced sterilization). Among such "undesirable characteristics" was mental illness, and in a sad page from U.S. history, state laws were written in the late 1800s and early 1900s to prohibit marriage and force sterilization for people with mental illness in order to prevent them from "passing on" their illness. Such laws were upheld by the United States Supreme Court in 1927 (Chase, 1980), and it wasn't until the middle of the twentieth century that these abhorrent practices were halted. Nevertheless, much damage had been done: by 1945, over 45,000 people with mental illness in the United States had been forcibly sterilized (Whitaker, 2002).

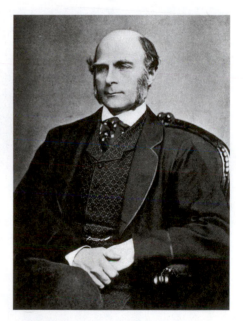

Francis Galton is considered the originator of genetics research. (Public Domain image from Wikipedia)

Biological Treatments   The general warehousing of patients in mental hospitals earlier in the twentieth century, coupled with the shortage of professional staff, created a climate that allowed, perhaps even subtly encouraged, experimentation with radical interventions. In the early 1930s, the practice of inducing a coma with large dosages of insulin was introduced by Sakel (1938), who claimed that up to three-quarters of the people with schizophrenia whom he treated showed significant improvement. Later findings by others were less encouraging, and insulin-coma therapy—which presented serious risks to health, including irreversible coma and death—was gradually abandoned.

In the early twentieth century, **electroconvulsive therapy (ECT)** was originated by two Italian physicians, Ugo Cerletti and Lucino Bini. Cerletti was interested in epilepsy and was seeking a way to induce seizures experimentally. Shortly thereafter he found that by applying electric shocks to the sides of the human head, he could produce full epileptic seizures. Then, in Rome in 1938, he used the technique on a patient with schizophrenia.

In the decades that followed, ECT was administered to people with schizophrenia and severe depression, usually in hospital settings. As we will discuss in Chapter 8, it is still used today for people with severe depression. Fortunately, important refinements in the ECT procedures have made it less problematic, and it remains an effective treatment.

In 1935, Egas Moniz, a Portuguese psychiatrist, introduced the *prefrontal lobotomy*, a surgical procedure that destroys the tracts connecting the frontal lobes to other areas of the brain. His initial reports claimed high rates of success (Moniz, 1936), and for 20 years thereafter thousands of people with mental illness underwent variations of this psychosurgery. The procedure was used especially for those whose behavior was violent. Many people did indeed quiet down and could even be discharged from hospitals, largely because the brain

Scene from *One Flew over the Cuckoo's Nest*. The character portrayed by Jack Nicholson was lobotomized in the film. (Photofest.)

Mesmer's procedure for manipulating magnetism was generally considered a form of hypnosis. (Jean-Loup Charnet/Photo Researchers.)

In this famous painting, the French psychiatrist Jean Charcot lectures on hysteria (note the woman suffering hysterical symptoms). Charcot was an important figure in reviving interest in psychological approaches. (Corbis-Bettmann.)

was damaged. During the 1950s, this intervention fell into disrepute for several reasons. After surgery, many people became dull and listless and suffered serious losses in their cognitive capacities—for example, becoming unable to carry on a coherent conversation with another person—which is not surprising given the destruction of parts of their brains that support thought and language.

Psychological Approaches

The search for biological causes dominated the field of psychopathology until well into the twentieth century, no doubt partly because of the exciting discoveries made about general paresis and genetics. But beginning in the late eighteenth century, various psychological points of view emerged that attributed mental disorders to psychological malfunctions. These theories were fashionable first in France and Austria, and later in the United States, leading to the development of psychotherapeutic interventions based on the tenets of the individual theories.

Mesmer and Charcot During the eighteenth century in western Europe, many people were observed to be subject to *hysteria*, which referred to physical incapacities, such as blindness or paralysis, for which no physical cause could be found. Franz Anton Mesmer (1734–1815), an Austrian physician practicing in Vienna and Paris in the late eighteenth century, believed that hysteria was caused by a particular distribution of a universal magnetic fluid in the body. Moreover, he felt that one person could influence the fluid of another to bring about a change in the other's behavior.

Mesmer conducted meetings cloaked in mystery and mysticism, at which afflicted patients sat around a covered wooden tub, with iron rods protruding through the cover from bottles underneath that contained various chemicals. Mesmer would enter the room, take various rods from the tub, and touch afflicted parts of his patients' bodies. The rods were believed to transmit animal magnetism and adjust the distribution of the universal magnetic fluid, thereby removing the hysterical disorder. Later, Mesmer perfected his routines by simply looking at patients rather than using rods. Whatever we may think of this questionable explanation and strange procedure, Mesmer apparently helped many people overcome their hysterical problems.

Although Mesmer regarded hysteria as having strictly biological causes, we discuss his work here because he is generally considered one of the earlier practitioners of modern-day hypnosis (the word *mesmerism* is a synonym for *hypnotism*; the phenomenon itself was known to the ancients of many cultures, as part of the sorcery and magic of conjurers, fakirs, and faith healers).

Mesmer came to be regarded as a quack by his contemporaries, which is ironic, since Mesmer had earlier contributed to the discrediting of an exorcist, Father Johann Gassner, who was performing similar rituals (Harrington, 2008). Nevertheless, hypnosis gradually became respectable. The great Parisian neurologist Jean Martin Charcot (1825–1893) also studied hysterical states. Charcot initially espoused a biological point of view. One day, however, some of his enterprising students hypnotized a healthy woman and, by suggestion, induced her to display certain hysterical symptoms. Charcot was deceived into believing that she was an actual patient with hysteria. When the students showed him how readily they could remove the symptoms by waking the woman, Charcot changed his mind about hysteria and became interested in psychological interpretations of these very puzzling phenomena.

Given Charcot's prominence in Parisian society, his support of hypnosis as a worthy treatment for hysteria helped to legitimize this form of treatment among medical professionals of the time (Harrington, 2008).

Breuer and the Cathartic Method

In the nineteenth century, a Viennese physician, Josef Breuer (1842–1925), treated a young woman, whose identity was disguised under the pseudonym Anna O., with a number of hysterical symptoms, including partial paralysis, impairment of sight and hearing, and, often, difficulty speaking. She also sometimes went into a dreamlike state, or "absence," during which she mumbled to herself, seemingly preoccupied with troubling thoughts. During one treatment session, Breuer hypnotized her and repeated some of her mumbled words back to her. Hypnosis led to her talking more freely and, ultimately, with considerable emotion about upsetting events from her past. Frequently, on awakening from a hypnotic session she felt much better. Breuer found that the relief of a particular symptom seemed to last longer if, under hypnosis, she was able to recall the event associated with the first appearance of that symptom and if she was able to express the emotion she had felt at the time. Reliving an earlier emotional trauma and releasing emotional tension by expressing previously forgotten thoughts about the event were called catharsis, and Breuer's method became known as the **cathartic method**. In 1895, Breuer and a younger colleague, Sigmund Freud (1856–1939), jointly published *Studies in Hysteria*, partly based on the case of Anna O.

Josef Breuer, an Austrian physician and physiologist, collaborated with Freud in the early development of psychoanalysis. (Corbis-Bettmann.)

The case of Anna O. became one of the best-known clinical cases in the psychoanalytic literature. Ironically, later investigation revealed that Breuer and Freud reported the case incorrectly. Historical study by Henri Ellenberger (1972) indicates that the young woman was helped only temporarily by Breuer's talking cure. This is supported by Carl Jung, a renowned colleague of Freud's, who is quoted as saying that during a conference in 1925, Freud told him that Anna O. had never been cured. Hospital records discovered by Ellenberger confirmed that Anna O. continued to rely on morphine to ease the "hysterical" problems that Breuer is reputed to have removed by catharsis.

Freud and Psychoanalysis

The apparently powerful role played by factors of which patients seemed unaware led Freud to postulate that much of human behavior is determined by forces that are inaccessible to awareness. The central assumption of Freud's theorizing, often referred to as **psychoanalytic theory**, is that psychopathology results from unconscious conflicts in the individual. In the next sections, we take a look at Freud's theory. See Focus on Discovery 1.3 for a look at Freud's theory of personality development.

Structure of the Mind   Freud divided the mind, or the **psyche**, into three principal parts: id, ego, and superego. According to Freud, the **id** is present at birth and is the repository of all of the energy needed to run the psyche, including the basic urges for food, water, elimination, warmth, affection, and sex. Trained as a neurologist, Freud saw the source of the id's energy as biological, and he called this energy **libido**. The individual cannot consciously perceive this energy—it is **unconscious**, below the level of awareness.

The id seeks immediate gratification of its urges, operating on what Freud called the **pleasure principle**. When the id is not satisfied, tension is produced, and the id impels a person to eliminate this tension as quickly as possible. For example, a baby feels hunger and is impelled to move about, sucking, in an attempt to reduce the tension arising from the unsatisfied drive. A person may also attempt to obtain gratification by generating images—in essence, fantasies—of what is desired. For instance, the hungry baby imagines sucking at the mother's breast and thereby obtains some substitute, short-term satisfaction. Of course, fantasizing cannot really satisfy such urges. This is where the ego comes in.

According to Freud, the **ego** begins to develop from the id during the second 6 months of life. Unlike the contents of the id, those of the ego are primarily conscious. The id may resort to fantasy when seeking satisfaction, but the task

Sigmund Freud developed psychoanalytic theory, both as a theory of the structure and functions of the mind (including explanations of the causes of mental disorders) and as a new method of therapy. (Corbis-Images.)

of the ego is to deal with reality. The ego thus operates on what Freud termed the **reality principle** as it mediates between the demands of reality and the id's demands for immediate gratification.

The **superego**—the third part of the psyche in Freud's theory—can be roughly conceived of as a person's conscience. Freud believed that the superego develops throughout childhood, arising from the ego much as the ego arises from the id. As children discover that many of their impulses—for example, biting and bed-wetting—are not acceptable to their parents, they begin to incorporate parental values as their own in order to receive the pleasure of parental approval and avoid the pain of disapproval.

Defense Mechanisms   According to Freud, and as elaborated by his daughter Anna (A. Freud, 1946/1966), herself an influential psychoanalyst, discomforts experienced by the ego as it attempts to resolve conflicts and satisfy the demands of the id and superego can be reduced in several ways. A **defense mechanism** is a strategy used by the ego to protect itself from anxiety. Perhaps the most important defense mechanism is **repression**, the process of pushing impulses and thoughts unacceptable to the ego into the unconscious. Of course, for the strategy to work—that is, for a person to remain unaware of the existence of these unacceptable things—repression must itself take place unconsciously, out of a person's awareness (see Focus on Discovery 6.1 for a current debates about repression). Examples of other defense mechanisms are presented in Table 1.2.

Psychoanalytic Therapy   Psychotherapy based on Freud's theory is called **psychoanalysis** or psychoanalytic therapy. It is still practiced today, although not as commonly as it once was. In Chapter 2, we will present more recent therapies derived from classical psychoanalysis. Here, we present some of the basic concepts of psychoanalysis as it was originally conceived (see Table 1.3 for a summary of psychoanalysis techniques).

Psychoanalysis attempts to help people face childhood conflicts, gain insight into them, and resolve them in the light of adult reality. Early repressions may prevent the ego from developing in an adult fashion; facing and resolving the repressed conflicts is supposed to undo such repression and enable adult development to continue.

Freud developed a number of techniques in his efforts to help people resolve repressed conflicts. With **free association**, a patient reclines on a couch, facing away from the analyst, and is encouraged to give free rein to his or her thoughts, verbalizing whatever comes to mind,

Table 1.2 Selected Defense Mechanisms

Defense Mechanism	Definition	Example
Repression	Keeping unacceptable impulses one has or wishes from conscious awareness	A professor starting a lecture she dreaded giving says, "In conclusion."
Denial	Not accepting a painful reality into conscious awareness	A victim of childhood abuse does not acknowledge it as an adult.
Projection	Attributing to someone else one's own unacceptable thoughts or feelings	A man who hates members of a racial group believes that it is they who dislike him.
Displacement	Redirecting emotional responses from their real target to someone else	A child gets mad at her brother but instead acts angrily toward her friend.
Reaction formation	Converting an unacceptable feeling into its opposite	A person with sexual feelings toward children leads a campaign against child sexual abuse.
Regression	Retreating to the behavioral patterns of an earlier stage of development	An adolescent dealing with unacceptable feelings of social inadequacy might attempt to mask those feelings by seeking oral gratification.
Rationalization	Offering acceptable reasons for an unacceptable action or attitude	A parent berates a child out of impatience, then indicates that she did so to "build character."
Sublimation	Converting unacceptable aggressive or sexual impulses into socially valued behaviors	Someone who has aggressive feelings toward his father becomes a surgeon.

Table 1.3 Major Techniques of Psychoanalysis

Technique	Description
Free association	The patient tries to say whatever comes to mind without censoring anything.
Interpretation	The analyst points out to the patient the meaning of certain of the patient's behaviors.
Analysis of transference	The patient responds to the analyst in ways that the patient has previously responded to other important figures in his or her life, and the analyst helps the patient understand and interpret these responses.

FOCUS ON DISCOVERY 1.3

Stages of Psychosexual Development

Freud conceived of the personality as developing through a series of four distinct psychosexual stages. He used the term *psychosexual* because, at each stage, a different part of the body is the most sensitive to sexual excitation and, therefore, the most capable of satisfying the id.

According to Freud, too much or too little gratification during one of the psychosexual stages may lead to regression to this stage during stress. (Jennie Woodcock; Reflections Photolibrary/Corbis Images.)

In Freud's theory, the first stage of psychosexual development is the oral stage, during which pleasure is obtained from feeding. (Banana Stock/Superstock.)

The **oral stage** is the first stage. From birth to about 18 months, the demands of an infant's id are satisfied primarily by feeding and the sucking and biting associated with it. The body parts through which the infant receives gratification at this stage are the lips, mouth, gums, and tongue. During the **anal stage**, from about 18 months to 3 years of age, a child mainly receives pleasure via the anus, by passing and retaining feces. The **phallic stage** extends from age 3 to age 5 or 6; during this stage, maximum gratification of the id is obtained through genital stimulation. Between the ages of 6 and 12, the child is in a **latency period**; during these years the id impulses do not play a major role in motivating behavior. The final and adult stage is the **genital stage**, during which heterosexual interests predominate.

During each stage, the developing person must resolve the conflicts between what the id wants and what the environment will provide. How this is accomplished is believed, in Freud's view, to determine basic personality traits that last throughout the person's life. A person who experiences either excessive or deficient amounts of gratification at a particular stage develops a **fixation** and is likely to regress to that stage when stressed.

without censoring anything. As the patient gradually masters this skill, defenses built up over many years are eventually bypassed. The patient's verbalizations more and more directly relate to the repressed material, and the patient learns to use those relationships to develop insight into the material.

Another key component of psychoanalytic therapy is the analysis of **transference**. Transference refers to the patient's responses to his or her analyst that seem to reflect attitudes and ways of behaving toward important people in the patient's past, rather than reflecting actual aspects of the analyst–patient relationship. For example, a patient might feel that the analyst is generally bored by what he or she is saying and as a result might struggle to be entertaining, and this pattern of response might reflect the patient's childhood relationship with a parent rather than what's actually going on between the patient and the analyst. Through careful observation and analysis of these transferred attitudes, Freud believed the analyst could gain insight into the childhood origins of the patient's repressed conflicts. In the example above, the analyst might find that the patient was made to feel boring and unimportant as a child and could only gain parental attention through humor.

As previously repressed material begins to appear in therapy, the technique of **interpretation** comes into play—the analyst points out to the patient the meanings of certain of the patient's behaviors. Defense mechanisms are a principal focus of interpretation. For instance, a man who appears to have trouble with intimacy may look out the window and change the subject whenever anything touches on closeness during the course of a session. The analyst will attempt at some point to interpret the patient's behavior, pointing out its defensive nature in the hope of stimulating the patient to acknowledge that he is in fact avoiding the topic.

Neo-Freudian Psychodynamic Perspectives

Several of Freud's contemporaries met with him periodically to discuss psychoanalytic theory and therapy. As often happens when a brilliant leader attracts brilliant followers and colleagues, disagreements arose about many general issues, such as the relative importance of id versus ego, of biological versus socio-cultural forces on psychological development, of unconscious versus conscious processes, and of childhood versus adult experiences; whether sexual urges drive behaviors that are not obviously sexual; and the role of reflexlike id impulses versus that of purposive behavior governed primarily by conscious ego deliberations. We discuss two influential historical figures here: Carl Jung and Alfred Adler, as well as the later development of the school of thought called ego analysis.

Jung and Analytical Psychology   Carl Gustav Jung (1875–1961), a Swiss psychiatrist originally considered Freud's heir apparent, broke with Freud in 1914 on many issues, after a 7-year period of intense correspondence about their disagreements. Jung proposed ideas radically different from Freud's, ultimately establishing **analytical psychology**.

Jung hypothesized that in addition to the personal unconscious postulated by Freud, there is a **collective unconscious**, the part of the unconscious that is common to all human beings and that consists primarily of what Jung called *archetypes*, or basic categories that all human beings use in conceptualizing about the world. In addition, Jung asserted that each of us has masculine and feminine traits that are blended and that people's spiritual and religious urges are as basic as their id urges. Jung also catalogued various personality characteristics; perhaps most important among them are extraversion (an orientation toward the external world) versus introversion (an orientation toward the inner, subjective world). This personality dimension continues to be regarded as very important, and we will encounter it again in our discussion of personality disorders in Chapter 12.

Adler and Individual Psychology   Alfred Adler (1870–1937), also an early adherent of Freud's theories, came to be even less dependent on Freud's views than was Jung, and Freud remained quite bitter toward Adler after their relationship ended. Adler's theory, which came to be known as **individual psychology**, regarded people as inextricably tied to their society because he

Carl Jung was the founder of analytical psychology. (Topham/The Image Works.)

Alfred Adler was the founder of individual psychology. (Corbis-Bettmann.)

believed that fulfillment was found in doing things for the social good. Like Jung, he stressed the importance of working toward goals (Adler, 1930).

A central element in Adler's work was his focus on helping individual patients change their illogical and mistaken ideas and expectations; Adler believed that feeling and behaving better depend on thinking more rationally, an approach that anticipated contemporary developments in cognitive behavior therapy (discussed in Chapter 2).

Ego Analysis   After Freud's death, a group of practitioners generally referred to as ego analysts introduced some important modifications to psychoanalytic theory. The major figures in this loosely formed movement included Karen Horney (1942), Anna Freud (1946/1966), Erik Erikson (1950), David Rapaport (1951), and Heinz Hartmann (1958).

Those who subscribed to ego analysis placed greater emphasis on a person's ability to control the environment and to select the time and the means for satisfying basic drives. Their fundamental contention was that the individual is as much ego as id. That is, they contended that ego functions, which are assumed to be present at birth and then develop through experience, have energies and gratifications of their own, usually separate from the gratification of id impulses. In addition, they focused more on the individual's current living conditions than did Freud, although they sometimes advocated delving deeply into the historical causes of an individual's behavior. Also, whereas Freud viewed the relationship of the individual to society as a struggle to overcome social inhibitions and achieve unfettered gratification of id urges, the ego analysts held that an individual's social interactions can provide their own special kind of gratification.

Quick Summary

The nineteenth and twentieth centuries saw a return to biological explanations for mental illness. Developments outside the field of psychopathology, such as the germ theory of disease and the discovery of the cause of syphilis, illustrated how the brain and behavior were linked. Early investigations into the genetics of mental illness led to a tragic emphasis on eugenics and the enforced sterilization of many thousands of people with mental illness. Such biological approaches to treatment as induced insulin coma, electroconvulsive therapy, and lobotomy eventually gave way to drug treatments. Psychological approaches to psychopathology evolved from Mesmer's manipulation of "magnetism" to treat hysteria (late eighteenth century) through Breuer's conceptualization of the cathartic method in his treatment of Anna O. (late nineteenth century) and culminated in Freud's psychoanalytic theories and treatment techniques (early twentieth century). Jung and Adler took Freud's basic ideas in a variety of different directions. Those who developed ego analysis maintained that the ego has energies of its own that are just as important as id energies and that it is important to focus on a person's current living situation as well as his or her social interactions.

Check Your Knowledge 1.3

Fill in the blanks.

1. _____ was a French neurologist who was influenced by the work of _____.

2. _____ developed the cathartic method, which _____ later built on in the development of psychoanalysis.

3. The _____ is driven by the pleasure principle, but the _____ is driven by the reality principle.

4. In psychoanalysis, _____ refers to interpreting the relationship between therapist and client as indicative of the client's relationship to others.

5. _____ developed the concept of the collective unconscious; _____ developed the technique of free association; _____ is associated with individual psychology.

6. Ego analysis emphasized the importance of the _____ more than the _____.

John B. Watson, an American psychologist, was the major figure in establishing behaviorism. (Underwood & Underwood/Corbis Images.)

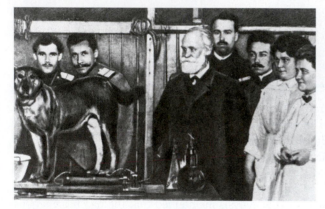

Ivan P. Pavlov, a Russian physiologist and Nobel laureate, made important contributions to the research and theory of classical conditioning. (Culver Pictures, Inc.)

The Rise of Behaviorism   After some years, many in the field began to lose faith in Freud's approach. This dissatisfaction was brought to a head by John B. Watson (1878–1958), who in 1913 revolutionized psychology with his views.

Watson looked to the experimental procedures of the psychologists who were investigating learning in animals, and because of his efforts, the dominant focus of psychology switched from thinking to learning. **Behaviorism** focuses on observable behavior rather than on consciousness or mental functioning. We will look at three types of learning that influenced the behaviorist approach in the early and middle parts of the twentieth century and that continue to be influential today: classical conditioning, operant conditioning, and modeling.

Classical Conditioning   Around the turn of the twentieth century, the Russian physiologist and Nobel laureate Ivan Pavlov (1849–1936) discovered **classical conditioning**, quite by accident. As part of his study of the digestive system, Pavlov gave a dog meat powder to make it salivate. Before long, Pavlov's laboratory assistants became aware that the dog began salivating when it saw the person who fed it. As the experiment continued, the dog began to salivate even earlier, when it heard the footsteps of its feeder. Pavlov was intrigued by these findings and decided to study the dog's reactions systematically. In the first of many experiments, a bell was rung behind the dog and then the meat powder was placed in its mouth. After this procedure had been repeated a number of times, the dog began salivating as soon as it heard the bell and before it received the meat powder.

In this experiment, because the meat powder automatically elicits salivation with no prior learning, the powder is termed an **unconditioned stimulus (UCS)** and the response of salivation an **unconditioned response (UCR)**. When the offering of meat powder is preceded several times by a neutral stimulus, the ringing of a bell, the sound of the bell alone (the **conditioned stimulus, or CS**) is able to elicit the salivary response (the **conditioned response, or CR**) (see Figure 1.3). As the number of paired presentations of the bell and the meat powder increases, the number of salivations elicited by the bell alone increases. What happens to an established CR if the CS is no longer followed by the UCS—for example, if repeated soundings of the bell are not followed by meat powder? The answer is that fewer and fewer CRs (salivations) are elicited, and the CR gradually disappears. This is termed **extinction**.

Classical conditioning can even instill pathological fear. A famous but ethically questionable experiment conducted by John Watson and Rosalie Rayner (1920) involved introducing a white rat to an 11-month-old boy, Little Albert. The boy showed no fear of the animal and appeared to want to play with it. But whenever the boy reached for the rat, the experimenter

Figure 1.3 The process of classical conditioning. (a) Before learning, the meat powder (UCS) elicits salivation (UCR), but the bell (CS) does not. (b) A training or learning trial consists of presentations of the CS, followed closely by the UCS. (c) Classical conditioning has been accomplished when the previously neutral bell elicits salivation (CR).

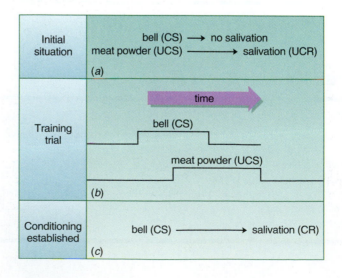

made a loud noise (the UCS) by striking a steel bar behind Albert's head. This caused Little Albert great fright (the UCR). After five such experiences, Albert became very frightened (the CR) by the sight of the white rat, even when the steel bar was not struck. The fear initially associated with the loud noise had come to be elicited by the previously neutral stimulus, the white rat (now the CS). This study suggests a possible relationship between classical conditioning and the development of certain emotional disorders, in this instance a phobia. It is important to note that this type of study could never be done today because it breaches ethical standards.

B. F. Skinner originated the study of operant conditioning and the extension of this approach to education, psychotherapy, and society as a whole. (Kathy Bendo for John Wiley & Sons.)

Operant Conditioning   In the 1890s, Edward Thorndike (1874–1949) began work that led to the discovery of another type of learning. Rather than investigate the association between stimuli, as Pavlov did, Thorndike studied the effects of consequences on behavior. Thorndike formulated what was to become an extremely important principle, the **law of effect**: behavior that is followed by consequences satisfying to the organism will be repeated, and behavior that is followed by noxious or unpleasant consequences will be discouraged.

B. F. Skinner (1904–1990) introduced the concept of **operant conditioning**, so called because it applies to behavior that operates on the environment. Renaming Thorndike's "law of effect" the "principle of reinforcement," Skinner distinguished two types of reinforcement. **Positive reinforcement** refers to the strengthening of a tendency to respond by virtue of the presentation of a pleasant event, called a positive reinforcer. For example, a water-deprived pigeon will tend to repeat behaviors (operants) that are followed by the availability of water. **Negative reinforcement** also strengthens a response, but it does so via the removal of an aversive event, such as the cessation of electric shock. Extrapolating his extensive work with pigeons to complex human behavior (his book *Walden Two* is one of the better-known utopian novels, describing an ideal society governed by his principles of reinforcement), Skinner argued that freedom of choice is a myth and that all behavior is determined by the reinforcers provided by the environment.

In a prototypical operant conditioning experiment, a hungry rat might be placed in a box, known as a Skinner box, which has a lever located at one end. The rat will explore its new environment and by chance come close to the lever. The experimenter may then drop a food pellet into the receptacle located near the lever. After a few such rewards, the animal will come to spend more and more time in the area around the lever. But now the experimenter may drop a pellet into the receptacle only when the rat happens to touch the lever. After capitalizing on a few chance touches, the rat begins to touch the lever frequently. With lever touching well established, the experimenter can make the criterion for reward more stringent—the animal must now actually press the lever. Thus the desired operant behavior, lever pressing, is gradually achieved by **shaping**, that is, by rewarding a series of responses, called successive approximations, that more and more closely resemble the desired response. The number of lever presses increases as soon as they become the criterion for the release of pellets and decreases, or extinguishes, when the pellet is no longer dropped into the receptacle after a lever press.

Operant conditioning principles may contribute to the persistence of aggressive behavior, a key feature of conduct disorder (see Chapter 14). Aggression is often rewarded, as when one child hits another to secure the possession of a toy (getting the toy is the reinforcer). Parents may also unwittingly reinforce aggression by giving in when their child becomes angry or threatens violence to achieve some goal, such as staying up late to watch TV.

Modeling   Learning often goes on even in the absence of reinforcers. We all learn by watching and imitating others, a process called **modeling**. In the 1960s, experimental work demonstrated that witnessing someone perform certain activities can increase or decrease diverse kinds of behavior, such as sharing, aggression, and fear. For example, Bandura and Menlove (1968) used

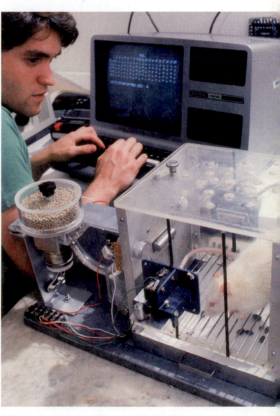

Skinner boxes are often used in studies of operant conditioning to demonstrate how behavior can be shaped by reinforcing it. (Index Stock.)

Aggressive responses in children are often rewarded, which makes them more likely to occur in the future. In this photo, the more aggressive child gets to keep the toy. (Ken Cavanagh/ Photo Researchers.)

a modeling treatment to reduce fear of dogs in children. After witnessing a fearless model engage in various activities with a dog, initially fearful children showed an increase in their willingness to approach and handle a dog. Children of parents with phobias or substance abuse problems may acquire similar behavior patterns, in part through observation.

Behavior Therapy   **Behavior therapy** emerged in the 1950s. In its initial form, this therapy applied procedures based on classical and operant conditioning to alter clinical problems. Sometimes the term *behavior modification* is used as well, and therapists who employ operant conditioning as a means of treatment often prefer that term. Behavior therapy was an attempt to change behavior, thoughts, and feelings by applying in a clinical context the methods used and the discoveries made by experimental psychologists.

One technique, **aversive conditioning**, played an important historical role in the development of behavior therapy. In aversive conditioning, a stimulus attractive to a person is paired with an unpleasant event, such as a drug that produces nausea or a painful electric shock applied to the hand, in the hope of endowing it with negative properties. For example, a person who wishes to stop drinking might be asked to smell alcohol while he or she is being made nauseous by a drug. Aversive techniques have been employed to reduce smoking, drug use, and socially inappropriate attractions such as the sexual arousal that children produce in people with pedophilia.

Aversion therapy has been controversial for ethical reasons because it involves inflicting pain and discomfort on people. Currently, it is rarely used as the only treatment for a particular problem. For example, in treating a person dependent on alcohol, the aversion treatment may help to temporarily reduce the problem behavior while the person is taught new ways of coping with stress.

One important behavior therapy technique that is still used to treat phobias and anxiety today is called **systematic desensitization**. This technique was developed by Joseph Wolpe in 1958, and it includes two components: (1) deep muscle relaxation and (2) gradual exposure to a list of feared situations, starting with those that arouse minimal anxiety and progressing to those that are the most frightening. Wolpe hypothesized that a state or response opposite to anxiety is substituted for anxiety as the person is exposed gradually to stronger and stronger doses of what he or she fears. We will cover this technique in more detail in Chapter 2, as it remains an important part of current forms of cognitive behavior therapy.

Modeling was also included in behavior therapy starting in the 1960s. For example, people reduced their fear of snakes by viewing both live and filmed encounters in which other people gradually approached and successfully handled snakes (Bandura, Blanchard, & Ritter, 1969). Fears of surgery and dental work have also been treated in a similar manner (Melamed & Siegel, 1975).

Quick Summary

Behaviorism began its ascendancy in the 1920s and continues to be an important part of various psychotherapies. John Watson built on the work of Ivan Pavlov in showing how some behaviors can be conditioned. B. F. Skinner, building on the work of Edward Thorndike, emphasized the contingencies associated with behavior, showing how positive and negative reinforcement could shape behavior. Research on modeling helped to explain how people can learn even when no obvious reinforcers are present. Early behavior therapy techniques included systematic desensitization, aversion therapy, and modeling.

Check Your Knowledge 1.4

True or false?

1. Positive reinforcement refers to increasing a desired behavior, while negative reinforcement refers to eliminating an undesirable behavior.
2. Among the different techniques in behavior therapy, aversion therapy has been criticized on ethical grounds.
3. A cat comes running at the sound of a treat jar rattling, and his human friend then gives him a treat. The conditioned stimulus in this example is the sound of the jar rattling.

The Mental Health Professions

As views of mental disorders have evolved, so, too, have the professions associated with the field. Professionals authorized to provide psychological services include clinical psychologists, psychiatrists, psychiatric nurses, counseling psychologists, social workers, and marriage and family therapists. The need for such professions has never been greater. For example, a recent study found that the cost of mental disorders in the United States is nearly $200 billion a year in lost earnings (Kessler et al., 2008). People with serious mental illness are often not able to work due to their illness, and as a result their yearly earnings are substantially less than those of people without mental illness (by as much as $16,000 a year!). In this section, we discuss the different types of mental health professionals that seek to treat people with mental disorders, the different types of training they receive, and a few related issues.

Clinical psychologists (such as the authors of this textbook) must have a Ph.D. or Psy.D. degree, which entails 4 to 8 years of graduate study. Training for the Ph.D. in clinical psychology is similar to that in other psychological specialties, such as developmental or cognitive neuroscience. It requires a heavy emphasis on research, statistics, neuroscience, and the empirically based study of human and animal behavior. As in other fields of psychology, the Ph.D. is basically a research degree, and candidates are required to write a dissertation on a specialized topic. But candidates in clinical psychology learn skills in two additional areas, which distinguish them from other Ph.D. candidates in psychology. First, they learn techniques of assessment and diagnosis of psychopathology; that is, they learn the skills necessary to determine whether a person's symptoms or problems indicate a particular disorder. Second, they learn how to practice **psychotherapy**, a primarily verbal means of helping people change their thoughts, feelings, and behavior to reduce distress and to achieve greater life satisfaction. Students take courses in which they master specific techniques and treat patients under close professional supervision; then, during an intensive internship, they assume increasing responsibility for the care of patients.

Another degree option for clinical psychologists is the Psy.D. (doctor of psychology), for which the curriculum is similar to that required of Ph.D. students, but with less emphasis on research and more on clinical training. The thinking behind this approach is that clinical psychology has advanced to a level of knowledge and certainty that justifies intensive training in specific techniques of assessment and therapeutic intervention rather than combining practice with research. On the other hand, conducting assessment or therapy without a sufficient empirical basis is professionally dubious. As of 2002, there were nearly 90,000 clinical psychologists in the United States (Duffy et al., 2004). By 2003, estimates suggested that there were more clinical psychologists than needed to adequately deliver services, and this was negatively impacting clinical psychologists' salaries (Robiner, 2006).

Psychiatrists hold an M.D. degree and have had postgraduate training, called a residency, in which they have received supervision in the practice of diagnosis and pharmacotherapy (administering medications). By virtue of the medical degree, and in contrast with psychologists, psychiatrists can function as physicians—giving physical examinations, diagnosing medical problems, and the like. Most often, however, the only aspect of medical practice in which psychiatrists engage is prescribing **psychoactive medications**, chemical compounds that can influence how people feel and think. Psychiatrists may receive some training in psychotherapy as well, though this is not a strong focus of training. In contrast to clinical psychologists, there is a shortage of psychiatrists, largely due to budget cuts in residency training programs. In 2000, there were over 40,000 psychiatrists in the United States. (Robiner, 2006).

Over the past 15 years, there has been a lively and sometimes acrimonious debate about whether to allow clinical psychologists with suitable training to prescribe psychoactive medications. Such a move is opposed not only by psychiatrists, whose turf would be invaded, but also by many psychologists, who view it as an ill-advised dilution of the basic behavioral science focus of psychology. Also at issue is the question of whether a non-M.D. can learn enough about neurobiology and neurochemistry to monitor the effects of drugs and protect patients from adverse side effects and drug interactions. Currently two states (New Mexico and Louisiana) allow psychologists to prescribe medication following the receipt of additional training; several other states are considering similar legislation.

A psychiatric nurse typically receives bachelor's or master's level training. Nurses can also receive more specialized training as a nurse practitioner that will allow them to prescribe psychoactive medications. There are currently over 18,000 psychiatric nurses in the United States, but the trend appears to be more toward emphasizing training as a nurse practitioner in order to secure prescription privileges (Robiner, 2006).

Other graduate programs are more focused on clinical practice than are the traditional Ph.D. programs. One of these is counseling psychology. **Counseling psychologists** originally dealt mostly with vocational issues; their focus today may be quite similar to that in clinical psychology, though still with less of an emphasis on mental disorders and more of an emphasis on prevention, education, and general life problems. Counseling psychologists work in a variety of settings, including schools, mental health agencies, industry, and community health centers. In 2002, there were 85,000 counseling psychologists working in mental health (Robiner, 2006).

Social workers have an M.S.W. (master of social work) degree. Training programs are shorter than Ph.D. programs, typically requiring 2 years of graduate study. The focus of training is on psychotherapy. Those in social work graduate programs do not receive training in psychological assessment. In 2002, there were close to 100,000 social workers in the United States who provided direct mental health services that were also part of the National Association of Social Workers (Duffy et al., 2004).

Marriage and family therapists (MFTs) treat families or couples, focusing on the ways in which these relationships impact a variety of mental health issues. Specialized programs in marriage and family therapy can be at the master's or doctoral levels. Some M.S.W. programs offer specialized training and certification in marriage and family therapy. In 2002, there were just over 47,000 marriage and family therapists in the United States, the majority having master's level training.

Summary

- The study of psychopathology is a search for the reasons why people behave, think, and feel in unexpected, sometimes odd, and possibly self-defeating ways. Unfortunately, people who have a mental illness are often stigmatized. Reducing the stigma associated with mental illness remains a great challenge for the field.
- In evaluating whether a behavior is part of a mental disorder, psychologists consider several different characteristics, including personal distress, disability, violation of social norms, and dysfunction. Each characteristic tells us something about what can be considered mental disorder, but no one by itself provides a fully satisfactory definition. The DSM-IV-TR definition includes all of these characteristics.

- Since the beginning of scientific inquiry into mental disorders, supernatural, biological, and psychological points of view have vied for attention. More supernatural viewpoints included early demonology, which posited that people with mental illness are possessed by demons or evil spirits, leading to treatments such as exorcism. Early biological viewpoints originated in the writings of Hippocrates. After the fall of Greco-Roman civilization, the biological perspective became less prominent in western Europe, and demonological thinking gained ascendancy, as evidenced by the persecution of so-called witches. Beginning in the fifteenth century, people with mental illness were often confined in asylums, such as Bethlehem; treatment in asylums was generally poor or nonexistent until various humanitarian reforms were instituted. In the twentieth century, genetics and mental illness became an important area of inquiry, though the findings from genetic studies were used to the detriment of people with mental illness during the eugenics movement.

- Psychological viewpoints emerged in the nineteenth century from the work of Charcot and the writings of Breuer and Freud. Freud's theory emphasized stages of psychosexual development and the importance of unconscious processes, such as repression and defense mechanisms that are traceable to early-childhood conflicts. Therapeutic interventions based on psychoanalytic theory make use of techniques such as free association and the analysis of transference in attempting to overcome repressions so that patients can confront and understand their conflicts and find healthier ways of dealing with them. Later theorists such as Jung and Adler made various modifications in Freud's basic ideas and emphasized different factors in their perspectives on therapy. A later school of thought, ego analysis, emphasized the ego more than the id, current living conditions, and gratification from social interactions.

- Behaviorism suggested that behavior develops through classical conditioning, operant conditioning, or modeling. B. F. Skinner introduced the ideas of positive and negative reinforcement and showed that operant conditioning can shape behavior. Behavior therapists try to apply these ideas to change undesired behavior, thoughts, and feelings.

- There are a number of different mental health professions, including clinical psychologist, psychiatrist, counseling psychologist, psychiatric nurse, social worker, and marriage and family therapist. Each involves different training programs of different lengths and with different emphaseis on research, psychological assessment, psychotherapy, and psychopharmacology.

Answers to Check Your Knowledge Questions

1.1   1. a; 2. d; 3. b
1.2   1. F; 2. F; 3. T; 4. T

1.3   1. Charcot, Mesmer; 2. Breuer, Freud; 3. id, ego; 4. transference; 5. Jung, Freud, Adler; 6. ego, id.
1.4   1. F; 2. T; 3. T

Key Terms

anal stage	ego	libido	psychoanalysis
analytical psychology	ego analysis	marriage and family therapist	psychoanalytic theory
asylums	electroconvulsive therapy (ECT)	mental disorder	psychopathology
aversive conditioning	exorcism	modeling	psychotherapy
behaviorism	extinction	moral treatment	reality principle
behavior therapy	fixation	negative reinforcement	represssion
cathartic method	free association	operant conditioning	shaping
classical conditioning	general paresis	oral stage	social worker
clinical psychologist	genital stage	phallic stage	stigma
collective unconscious	harmful dysfunction	pleasure principle	superego
conditioned response (CR)	id	positive reinforcement	systematic desensitization
conditioned stimulus (CS)	individual psychology	psyche	transference
counseling psychologist	interpretation	psychiatric nurse	unconditioned response (UCR)
defense mechanism	latency period	psychiatrist	unconditioned stimulus (UCS)
demonology	law of effect	psychoactive medications	unconscious

2

Current Paradigms in Psychopathology

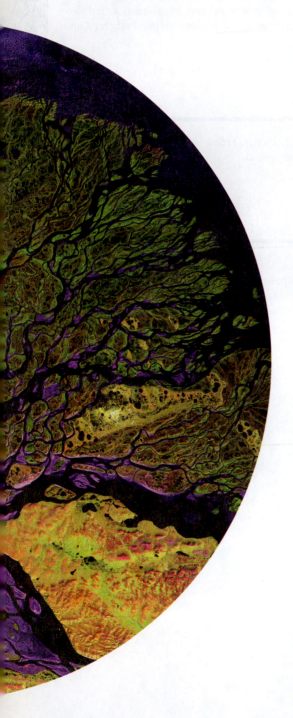

LEARNING GOALS

1. Be able to describe the essentials of the genetic, neuroscience, psychodynamic, and cognitive behavioral paradigms.
2. Be able to describe the concept of emotion and how it may be relevant to psychopathology.
3. Be able to explain how culture, ethnicity, and social factors figure into the study and treatment of psychopathology.
4. Be able to recognize the limits of adopting any one paradigm and the importance of integration across multiple levels of analysis, as in the diathesis-stress integrative paradigm.

AS WE NOTED IN Chapter 1, we face an enormous challenge to remain objective when trying to understand and study psychopathology scientifically. Science is a human enterprise that is bound by scientists' human limitations; it is also bound by the current state of scientific knowledge. We cannot ask questions or investigate phenomena that go beyond what human beings can understand, and it is very difficult even to go beyond what we currently understand. Our view is that every effort should be made to study psychopathology according to scientific principles. But science is not a completely objective and certain enterprise. Rather, as suggested by philosopher of science Thomas Kuhn (1962/1970), subjective factors as well as our human limitations enter into the conduct of scientific inquiry.

Central to scientific activity, in Kuhn's view, is the notion of a **paradigm**, a conceptual framework or approach within which a scientist works—that is, a set of basic assumptions, a general perspective, that defines how to conceptualize and study a subject, how to gather and interpret relevant data, even how to think about a particular subject.[1] A paradigm has profound implications for how scientists operate at any given time. Paradigms specify what problems scientists will investigate and how they will go about the investigation.

In this chapter we consider current paradigms of psychopathology and treatment. We present four paradigms that guide the study and treatment of psychopathology: genetic, neuroscience, psychodynamic, and cognitive behavioral. We also consider the important role of emotion and sociocultural factors in psychopathology. These factors cut across all the paradigms and are significant in terms of the description, causes, and treatments of all the disorders we will discuss in this book.

---

[1] William O'Donohue (1993) has criticized Kuhn's use of the concept of paradigm, noting that he was inconsistent in its definition. The complexities of this argument are beyond the scope of this book. Suffice to say that we find it useful to organize our thinking about mental disorders around the paradigm concept. We use the term to refer to the general perspectives that constrain the way scientists collect and interpret information in their efforts to understand the world.

Current thinking about psychopathology is multifaceted. The work of clinicians and researchers is informed by an awareness of the strengths and limitations of all the paradigms. For this reason, current views of psychopathology and its treatment typically integrate several paradigms. At the end of this chapter we describe another paradigm—diathesis–stress—that provides the basis for an integrative approach.

For researchers and clinicians, the choice of a paradigm has important consequences for the way in which they define, investigate, and treat psychopathology. Our discussion of paradigms will lay the groundwork for the topics covered in the rest of the book. We note at the outset that no one paradigm offers the "complete" conceptualization of psychopathology. Rather, for most disorders, each paradigm offers some important information with respect to etiology and treatment, but only part of the picture.

The Genetic Paradigm

. . . the more we lift the lid on the genome, the more vulnerable to experience genes appear to be.
(Ridley, 2003, p. 4).

In 2003, we celebrated the fiftieth anniversary of the discovery of human DNA's double-helix structure. That has been coupled with the virtual explosion of information regarding human genetics in just the past 8 or 9 years. The **genetic paradigm** has guided a number of discoveries regarding human behavior since the early part of the twentieth century. However, the changes that have occurred recently have transformed the way we think about genes and behavior. We no longer have to wonder, "Is nature or nurture responsible for human behavior?" We now know (1) almost all behavior is heritable to some degree (i.e., involves genes), and (2) despite this, genes do not operate in isolation from the environment. Instead, throughout the life span, the environment shapes how our genes are expressed, and our genes also shape our environments (Plomin et al., 2003; Rutter & Silberg, 2002; Turkheimer, 2000).

The more contemporary way to think about genes and the environment is cast as "nature via nurture" (Ridley, 2003). In other words, researchers are learning how environmental influences, such as stress, relationships, and culture (the nurture part), shape which of our genes are turned on or off and how our genes (the nature part) influence our bodies and brain. We know that without genes, a behavior might not be possible. But without the environment, genes could not express themselves and thus contribute to the behavior.

When the ovum, the female reproductive cell, is joined by the male's sperm, a zygote, or fertilized egg, is produced. It has 46 chromosomes, the number characteristic of a human being. Each chromosome is made up of many **genes**, the carriers of the genetic information (DNA) passed from parents to child.

In the year 2001, two different groups of researchers announced that the human genome consisted of around 30,000 genes. At first, this news was surprising, since researchers had been thinking the human genome consisted of closer to 100,000 genes. After all, the mere fruit fly has around 14,000 genes—researchers had thought that surely human beings were several times more complex than that! As it turns out, however, one of the exciting things about this discovery was the revelation from dozens of other genetic labs that the number of genes was not all that important. Instead, it is the sequencing, or ordering, of these genes as well as the expression of these genes that make us unique. Genes are essentially responsible for making proteins that in turn make the body and brain work. Some of these proteins switch, or turn, on and off other genes, a process called **gene expression**. Learning about the flexibility of genes and how they switch on or off has closed the door on beliefs about the inevitability of the effects of genes, good or bad. As we will illustrate throughout this book, the data do not often support the supposition that if you have the genes for *x*, you will necessarily get *x*. With respect to most mental illnesses, there will likely not be just one gene that contributes vulnerability. Instead, psychopathology will be **polygenic**, meaning several genes, perhaps operating at different times during the course of development, will be the essence of genetic vulnerability.

Shared environment refers to things families have in common, like marital quality. (Blend Images/SuperStock,Inc.)

An important term that will be used throughout the book is **heritability**. Heritability refers to the extent to which variability in a particular behavior (or disorder) in a population can be accounted for by genetic factors. This term can be easily misused or misunderstood. There are two important points about heritability to keep in mind.

1. Heritability estimates range from 0.0 to 1.0: the higher the number, the greater the heritability.

2. Heritability is relevant only for a large population of people, not a particular individual. Thus, it is incorrect to talk about any one person's heritability for a particular behavior or disorder. Knowing that the heritability of attention-deficit/hyperactivity disorder (ADHD) is around 0.70 does not mean that 70 percent of Jane's ADHD is because of her genes and 30 percent is due to other factors. It means that in a population (e.g., a large sample in a study), the variation in ADHD is understood as being attributed to 70 percent genes and 30 percent environment.

Other terms that are important in genetic research involve environmental factors. **Shared environment** factors include those things that members of a family have in common, such as family income level, child-rearing practices, and parents' marital status and quality. **Nonshared environment** factors are those things believed to be distinct among members of family, such as relationships with friends or specific events unique to a person (e.g., being in a car accident or on the swim team), and these are believed to be important in understanding why two siblings from the same family can be so different. Consider an example. Jason is a 34-year-old man who is dependent on alcohol and struggling to keep his job. His sister Joan is a 32-year-old executive in a computer company in San Jose and has no alcohol or drug problems. Jason did not have many friends as a child; Joan was one of the most popular girls in high school. Jason and Joan shared several influences, including their family atmosphere growing up. They also had nonshared experiences, such as differences in peer relationships. Behavior genetics research suggests that the nonshared experiences have much more to do with the development of mental illness than the shared experiences.

We now turn to review two broad approaches in the genetic paradigm, including behavior genetics and molecular genetics. We then discuss the exciting evidence on the ways in which genes and environments interact. This sets the stage for our discussion of an integrative paradigm later in this chapter.

Behavior Genetics

Behavior genetics is the study of the degree to which genes and environmental factors influence behavior. To be clear, behavior genetics is not the study of *how* genes or the environment determine behavior. Many behavior genetics studies estimate the heritability of a mental illness, without providing any information about how the genes might work. The total genetic makeup of an individual, consisting of inherited genes, is referred to as the **genotype** (physical sequence of DNA); the genotype cannot be observed outwardly. In contrast, the totality of observable, behavioral characteristics, such as level of anxiety, is referred to as the **phenotype**.

We defined gene expression earlier: the genotype should not be viewed as a static entity. Genes switch off and on at specific times, for example, to control various aspects of development. Indeed, genetic programs are quite flexible—they respond in remarkable ways to things that happen to us.

The phenotype changes over time and is the product of an interaction between the genotype and the environment. For example, a person may be born with the capacity for high intellectual achievement, but whether he or she develops this genetically given potential depends on

Nonshared environment refers to factors that are distinct among family members, such as having different groups of friends. (Pixland/SuperStock, Inc.)

environmental factors such as upbringing and education. Hence intelligence is an index of the phenotype.

A study by Turkheimer and colleagues shows how genes and environment may interact to influence IQ (Turkheimer et al., 2003). A number of studies have demonstrated high heritability for IQ (e.g., Plomin, 1999). What Turkheimer and colleagues found, though, was that heritability depended on environment. The study included 319 twin pairs of 7-year-olds (114 identical, 205 fraternal). Many of the children were living in families either below the poverty line or with a low family income. Among the families of lower socioeconomic status (SES), 60 percent of the variability in children's IQ was attributable to the environment. Among the higher-SES families, the opposite was found. That is, variability in IQ was more attributable to genes than environment. Thus, being in an impoverished environment may have deleterious effects on IQ, whereas being in a more affluent environment may not help out all that much. It is important to point out that these interesting findings deal with IQ scores, a measure of what psychologists consider to be intelligence, not achievement (we discuss this more in Chapters 3 and 14). Such interactions between genes and environments are the "new look" to behavior genetics research (Moffitt, 2005), and we discuss additional studies illustrating how genes and environments work together below. In Chapter 4, we will discuss the major research designs used in behavior genetics research—including family, twin, and adoption studies—to estimate the heritability of different disorders.

Molecular Genetics

Molecular genetics studies seek to find out what exactly is heritable by identifying particular genes and their functions. Recall that a human being has 46 chromosomes and that each chromosome is made up of thousands of genes that contain DNA. Different forms of the same gene are called **alleles**. The alleles of a gene are found at the same location, or locus, of a chromosome pair. A genetic **polymorphism** refers to a difference in DNA sequence on a gene that has occurred in a population.

The DNA in genes is transcribed to RNA. In some cases, the RNA is then translated into amino acids, which then form proteins, and proteins make cells (see Figure 2.1). Gene expression involves particular types of DNA called *promoters*. These promoters are recognized by particular proteins called *transcription factors*. Promoters and transcription factors are the focus of much new research in molecular genetics and psychopathology. All of this is a remarkably complex system, and variations along the way, such as different combinations or sequences of events, lead to different outcomes.

Researchers studying animals can actually manipulate specific genes and then observe the effects on behavior. Specific genes can be taken out of mice DNA—these studies are called "knockout studies." For example, the gene that is responsible for a specific receptor

Behavior genetics studies the degree to which characteristics, such as physical resemblance or psychopathology, are shared by family members because of shared genes. (Tony Freeman/ PhotoEdit.)

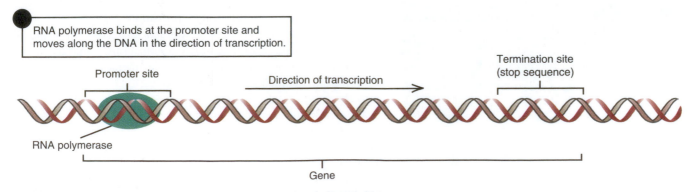

RNA polymerase binds at the promoter site and moves along the DNA in the direction of transcription.

Promoter site

Direction of transcription

Termination site (stop sequence)

RNA polymerase

Gene

Figure 2.1 This figure shows the process by which DNA is transcribed to RNA. In some cases, the RNA is then translated into amino acids, which then form proteins, and proteins make cells.

for the neurotransmitter serotonin called 5-HT$_{1A}$ has been knocked out in mice before their birth. As adults, they show what could be described as an anxious phenotype. Interestingly, one study that employed a novel technique to only temporarily knock out this gene found that the restoration of it early in development prevented the development of anxious behavior in the adult mice (Gross et al., 2002). This is a major area of molecular genetic work. Linking the findings from these animal studies to humans remains a challenge for the field, however.

Gene–Environment Interactions

As we noted earlier, we know now that genes and environments work together. Life experience shapes how our genes are expressed, and our genes guide us in behaviors that lead to the selection of different experiences. A **gene–environment interaction** means that a given person's sensitivity to an environmental event is influenced by genes.

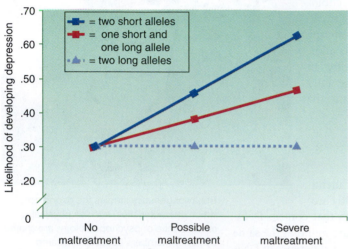

Figure 2.2 A gene–environment interaction is illustrated here. Having both the short allele of the 5-HTT gene and childhood maltreatment were associated with the greatest probability of developing depression as an adult. Adapted from Caspi et al. (2003).

Take a simple (and made-up) example. If a person has gene XYZ, he or she might respond to a snakebite by developing a fear of snakes. A person without the XYZ gene would not develop a fear of snakes after being bitten. This simple relationship involves both genes (the XYZ gene) and an environmental event (snakebite).

A different (and true) example of a gene–environment interaction involves depression. In one longitudinal study, a large sample of children in New Zealand was followed across time from the age of five until their mid-twenties (Caspi et al., 2003). Across this time, the researchers assessed a number of variables, including early childhood maltreatment (abuse) and depression as an adult. They also measured a particular gene called the **serotonin transporter gene** (5-HTT). This gene has a polymorphism such that some people have two short alleles (short-short), some have two long alleles (long-long), and some have one short and one long allele (short-long). They found that those individuals who had either the short-short allele or the short-long allele combinations of the 5-HTT gene *and* were maltreated as children were more likely to have major depressive disorder as adults than either those people who had the same gene combination but no childhood maltreatment or those people who were maltreated as children but had the long-long allele combination of the gene (see Figure 2.2). Thus, having the gene was not enough to predict an episode of depression, nor was the presence of childhood maltreatment. Rather, it was the specific combination of the gene configuration and environmental events that predicted depression. They found the same gene–environment interaction for having at least one short allele of the gene and reports of stressful life events. That is, those people who reported more severe stressful life events and had at least one short allele of the 5-HTT gene were at greater risk of developing depression.

Other exciting developments in this area have emerged in animal research. In these studies, different environments are manipulated and then changes in behavior and gene expression are measured. The study of how the environment can alter gene expression or function is called *epigenetics*.

In a series of fascinating studies with rats, Darlene Francis has shown that parenting behaviors can be passed on to offspring in a nongenetic way. Good parenting among rats consists of a lot of licking and grooming (LG) and what is called arched-back nursing (ABN). Mothers differ in the extent to which they do these LG-ABN behaviors, but mothers who do it more tend to have pups that grow up to be less reactive to stress. Francis and colleagues (1999) found that

Baby rats who are raised by a mother who does a lot of licking are more likely to do this when they grow up to be mothers, even if they were raised by an adoptive mother. (Courtesy Darlene Francis.)

pups born to mothers who were low in this LG-ABN behavior but raised by mothers high in LG-ABN (called a cross-fostering adoptee method, discussed in more detail in Chapter 4) grew up to be low in stress reactivity and as mothers themselves exhibited the high LG-ABN style. And, when they had their own pups, these "grandpups" were also low in stress reactivity and became high LG-ABN mothers. Thus, this parenting style was transmitted across two generations after an adoption. Does this suggest that genes are not important? The adoptive parent's behavior was what was transmitted across generations, not the biological parent's behavior, which would suggest that this is an environmental effect.

However, a later study showed that this transmission of good mothering was due in part to the fact that it triggered an increase in the expression of a certain gene among the adopted offspring (Weaver et al., 2004). Using cross-fostering again, pups with a low LG-ABN biological mother who were raised by a high LG-ABN mother had increases in expression of a certain gene (glucocorticoid receptor) in the same way that pups with a biological high LG-ABN mother do (but pups with a biological low LG-ABN mother do not). The environment (mothering) was responsible for turning on (or turning up) the expression of a particular gene. Once it was on, the mothering style seemed to continue across generations.

We will continue to see these types of studies in animals and humans. Understanding how environments influence the expression of genes will be important for understanding the causes of psychopathology.

Reciprocal Gene–Environment Interactions

Another important way in which genes are important in psychopathology is in how they may promote certain types of environments. This is called a **reciprocal gene–environment interaction** (Plomin et al., 2003; Rutter & Silberg, 2002). The basic idea is that genes may predispose us to seek out certain environments that then increase our risk for developing a particular disorder. For example, studies suggest that a genetic risk for alcohol dependence may predispose persons to life events that put them in high risk situations for alcohol abuse, such as being in trouble with the law (Kendler & Karkowski-Shuman, 1997). Another study found that genetic vulnerability to depression may promote certain life events, such as breaking up with a boyfriend or difficulties with parents, that can trigger depression among adolescent girls (Silberg et al., 1999). More broadly, one type of stressful life events, called dependent life events, appears to be influenced by genes more than by random bad luck. That is, people seem to select environments that increase the likelihood of certain kinds of stressful life events, at least in part, based on their genes (Kendler & Baker, 2007). Researchers now try to distinguish between these dependent life events and those that are outside of an individual's control, a topic we return to in Chapter 3 when we discuss life event assessment.

Evaluating the Genetic Paradigm

Our discussion of each paradigm will conclude with an evaluation section. Genetics is an important part of the study of psychopathology, and there are many ways in which genes might be involved in psychopathology. The models that will help us understand how genes are implicated in psychopathology are the ones that take the contemporary view that genes do their work *via* the environment. Perhaps the biggest challenge facing scientists working within the genetic paradigm is to specify exactly how genes and environments reciprocally influence one another. This is more easily done in tightly controlled laboratory studies with animals. Making the leap to understanding how genes interact with complex human environments throughout the course of development is of course a greater challenge. Nevertheless, this is an exciting time for genetics research, and important discoveries about genes, environments, and psychopathology are being made at a rapid rate. In addition, some of the most exciting breakthroughs in genetics have involved a combination of methods from genetics and neuroscience. For example, findings from neuroscience have illuminated the ways in which genes and environments exert their influence via the brain (Caspi & Moffitt, 2006). Although we present the genetic and neuroscience paradigms separately, they go hand in hand when it comes to understanding the possible causes of psychopathology.

Quick Summary

The genetic paradigm focuses on questions such as whether certain disorders are heritable and, if so, what is actually inherited. Heritability is a population statistic, not a metric of the likelihood a particular person will inherit a disorder. Environmental effects can be classified as shared and nonshared. Molecular genetics studies isolate particular genes and gene polymorphisms that may be involved in psychopathology. Research has emphasized the importance of gene–environment interactions. Genes do their work via the environment in most cases. Recent examples of genetic influence being manifested only under certain environmental conditions (e.g., poverty and IQ; early maltreatment and depression) make clear that we must not look just for the genes associated with mental illness, but also for the conditions under which these genes may be expressed.

Check Your Knowledge 2.1 (Answers are at the end of the chapter.)

Answer the questions.

1. The process by which genes are turned on or off is referred to as:
   a. heritability
   b. gene expression
   c. polygenic
   d. gene switching

2. Sam and Sally are twins raised by their biological parents. Sam excelled in music and was in the high school band; Sally was the star basketball player on the team. They both received top-notch grades, and they both had part-time jobs at the bagel store. An example of a shared environment variable would be _____; an example of a nonshared environment variable would be _____.
   a. school activities; their parent's relationship
   b. band for Sam; basketball for Sally
   c. their parent's relationship; work
   d. their parent's relationship; school activities

3. _____ refers to different forms of the same gene; _____ refers to different genes contributing to a disorder.
   a. Allele; polygenic
   b. Polygenic; allele
   c. Allele; polymorphism
   d. Polymorphism; allele

4. In the Caspi and colleagues (2003) gene–environment interaction study of depression, those who were at highest risk for developing depression were
   a. those who were maltreated as children and had a biological parent with depression
   b. those who were maltreated as children and had at least one long allele of the 5-HTT gene
   c. those who were maltreated as children and had at least one short allele of the 5-HTT gene
   d. those who were not maltreated as children but had at least one short allele of the 5-HTT gene

The Neuroscience Paradigm

The **neuroscience paradigm** holds that mental disorders are linked to aberrant processes in the brain. Considerable literature deals with the brain and psychopathology. For example, some depressions are associated with neurotransmitter problems within the brain; anxiety disorders may be related to a defect within the autonomic nervous system that causes a person to be too easily aroused; dementia can be traced to impairments in structures of the brain. In this section, we look at four components of this paradigm in which the data are particularly interesting: neurons and neurotransmitters, brain structure and function, the neuroendocrine system, and the autonomic nervous system. We then consider some of the key treatments that follow from the paradigm.

Neurons and Neurotransmitters

The cells in the nervous system are called neurons, and the nervous system is comprised of billions of neurons. Although neurons differ in some respects, each **neuron** has four major parts: (1) the cell body; (2) several dendrites, the short and thick extensions; (3) one or more axons of varying lengths, but usually only one long and thin axon that extends a considerable distance from the cell body; and (4) terminal buttons on the many end branches of the axon (Figure 2.3). When a neuron is appropriately stimulated at its cell body or through its dendrites, a **nerve impulse** travels down the axon to the terminal endings. Between the terminal endings of the sending axon and the cell membrane of the receiving neuron there is a small gap, called the **synapse** (Figure 2.4).

For neurons to send a signal to the next neuron so that communication can occur, the nerve impulse must have a way of bridging the synaptic space. The terminal buttons of each axon contain synaptic vesicles, small structures that are filled with **neurotransmitters.** Neurotransmitters are chemicals that allow neurons to send a signal across the synapse to another neuron. As the neurotransmitter flows into the synapse, some of the molecules reach the receiving, or postsynaptic, neuron. The cell membrane of the postsynaptic neuron contains receptors. Receptors are configured so that only specific neurotransmitters can fit into them. When a neurotransmitter fits into a receptor site, a message can be sent to the postsynaptic cell. What actually happens to the postsynaptic neuron depends on integrating thousands of similar messages. Sometimes these messages are excitatory, leading to the creation of a nerve impulse in the postsynaptic cell; at other times the messages are inhibitory, making the postsynaptic cell less likely to create a nerve impulse.

Once a presynaptic neuron (the sending neuron) has released its neurotransmitter, the last step is for the synapse to return to its normal state. Not all of the released neurotransmitter has found its way to postsynaptic receptors. Some of what remains in the synapse is broken down by enzymes, and some is taken back into the presynaptic cell through a process called **reuptake**.

Several key neurotransmitters have been implicated in psychopathology, including **dopamine, serotonin, norepinephrine,** and **gamma-aminobutyric acid (GABA)**. Serotonin and dopamine may be involved in depression, mania, and schizophrenia. Norepinephrine is a neurotransmitter that communicates with the sympathetic nervous system, where it is involved in producing states of high arousal and thus may be involved in the anxiety disorders and other stress-related conditions (see Focus on Discovery 2.1 for more on the sympathetic nervous system). GABA inhibits nerve impulses throughout most areas of the brain and may be involved in the anxiety disorders.

Early theories linking neurotransmitters to psychopathology sometimes proposed that a given disorder was caused by either too much or too little of a particular transmitter (e.g., mania is associated with too much norepinephrine, anxiety disorders with too little GABA). Later research has uncovered the details behind these overly simple ideas. Neurotransmitters are synthesized in the neuron through a series of metabolic steps, beginning with an amino acid. Each reaction along the way to producing an actual neurotransmitter is catalyzed by an enzyme. Too much or too little of a particular neurotransmitter could result from an error in these metabolic steps.

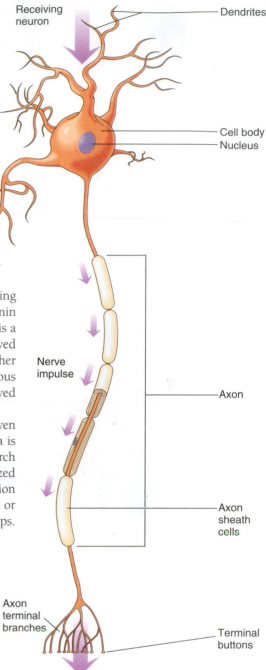

Figure 2.3 The neuron, the basic unit of the nervous system.

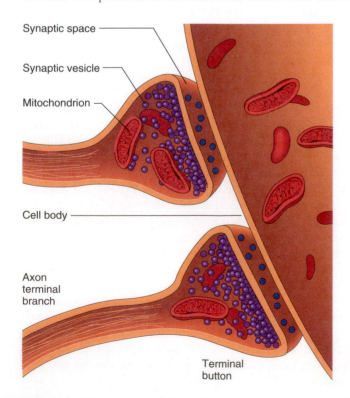

Figure 2.4 A synapse, showing the terminal buttons of two axon branches in close contact with a very small portion of the cell body of another neuron.

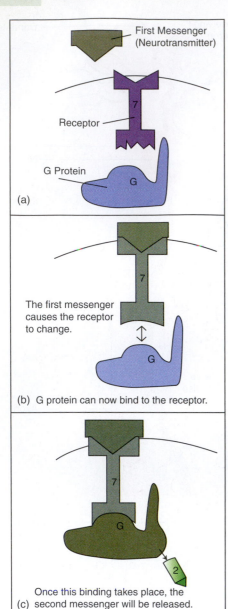

Figure 2.5 The process by which a second messenger is released.

Similar disturbances in the amounts of specific transmitters could result from alterations in the usual processes by which transmitters are deactivated after being released into the synapse. For example, a failure to pump leftover neurotransmitter back into the presynaptic cell (reuptake) would leave excess transmitter in the synapse. Then, if a new nerve impulse causes more neurotransmitter to be released into the synapse, the postsynaptic neuron would, in a sense, get a double dose of neurotransmitter, making it more likely for a new nerve impulse to be created.

Other research has focused on the possibility that the neurotransmitter receptors are at fault in some disorders. If the receptors on the postsynaptic neuron were too numerous or too easily excited, the result would be akin to having too much transmitter released. There would simply be more sites available with which the neurotransmitter could interact, increasing the chances that the postsynaptic neuron would be stimulated. The delusions and hallucinations of schizophrenia, for example, may result from an overabundance of dopamine receptors.

Many mechanisms control the sensitivity of postsynaptic neurons. For example, if a receptor has been activated extensively over time, the cell may retune the sensitivity of the receptors so that it becomes more difficult to create a nerve impulse. When a cell has been firing more frequently, this receptor releases **second messengers** (see Figure 2.5). Once second messengers are released, they play a role in adjusting the sensitivity of postsynaptic receptors to dopamine, norepinephrine, or serotonin (Duman, Heninger, & Nestler, 1997; Shelton, 2000; Shelton, Mainer, & Sulser, 1996). One can think of second messengers as helping a neuron adjust receptor sensitivity when it has been overly active. Current research on depression suggests that antidepressant medications may be effective in part due to their ability to impact second messengers (see p. 226 in Chapter 8).

One method that investigators use to study how neurotransmitters are working in the brain is to have people take a drug that stimulates a particular neurotransmitter's receptors. This kind of drug is referred to as an **agonist**. A serotonin agonist, for example, is a drug that stimulates serotonin receptors to produce the same effects as serotonin does naturally. By contrast, an **antagonist** is a drug that works on a neurotransmitter's receptors to dampen the activity of that neurotransmitter. For example, many drugs used to treat schizophrenia are dopamine antagonists that work by blocking dopamine receptors (see p. 332 in Chapter 11).

Structure and Function of the Human Brain

The brain is located within the protective coating of the skull and is enveloped with three protective layers of membranes referred to as meninges. Viewed from the top, the brain is divided by a midline fissure into two mirror-image cerebral hemispheres; together they constitute most of the cerebrum. The major connection between the two hemispheres is a band of nerve fibers, called the **corpus callosum**, that allows the two hemispheres to communicate. Figure 2.6 shows the surface of one of the cerebral hemispheres. The cortex is comprised of the neurons that form the thin outer covering of the brain, the so-called **gray matter** of the brain. The cortex consists of six layers of tightly packed neurons, estimated to number 10 to 15 billion. The cortex is vastly convoluted; the ridges are called gyri, and the depressions between them sulci, or fissures. If unfolded, the cortex would be about the size of a formal dinner napkin. The sulci are used to define different regions of the brain, much like guide points on a map. Deep fissures divide the cerebral hemispheres into four distinct areas called lobes. The **frontal lobe** lies in front of the central sulcus; the **parietal lobe** is behind it and above the lateral sulcus; the **temporal lobe** is located below the lateral sulcus; and the **occipital lobe** lies behind the parietal and temporal lobes (see Figure 2.6). Different functions tend to be associated with particular brain areas: vision with the occipital lobe; discrimination of sounds with the temporal lobe; reasoning, problem solving, working memory, and other executive processes plus the regulation of fine voluntary movement with the frontal lobe. One important area of the cortex is called the **prefrontal cortex**. This region, in the very front of the cortex, helps to regulate the amygdala (discussed below) and is important in many different disorders.

If the brain is sliced in half, separating the two cerebral hemispheres, additional important structures can be seen. The gray matter of the cerebral cortex does not extend throughout the interior of the brain (see Figure 2.7). Much of the interior is **white matter**, made up of large tracts of myelinated (sheathed) fibers that connect cell bodies in the cortex with those in the spinal cord and in other centers lower in the brain. In certain areas, called *nuclei*, sets of nerves converge and messages are integrated from different centers.

One important set of areas, collectively referred to as the *basal ganglia*, is located deep within each hemisphere. The basal ganglia help regulate starting and stopping both motor and cognitive activity. Also deep within the brain are cavities called **ventricles**. These ventricles are filled with cerebrospinal fluid. Cerebrospinal fluid circulates through the brain through these ventricles, which are connected with the spinal cord.

The **thalamus** is a relay station for all sensory pathways except the olfactory. The nuclei making up the thalamus receive nearly all impulses arriving from the different sensory areas of the body before passing them on to the cortex, where they are interpreted as conscious sensations. The **brain stem**, comprised the *pons* and the *medulla oblongata,* functions primarily as a neural relay station. The pons contains tracts that connect the cerebellum with the spinal cord and with motor areas of the cerebrum. The medulla oblongata serves as the main line of traffic for tracts ascending from the spinal cord and descending from the higher centers of the brain. The **cerebellum** receives sensory nerves from the vestibular apparatus of the ear and from muscles, tendons, and joints. The information received and integrated relates to balance and posture and equilibrium and to the smooth coordination of the body when in motion.

A set of deeper, mostly subcortical, structures are often implicated in different forms of psychopathology. There is a long history of referring to different groupings of these structures as the *limbic system*, a term that most contemporary neuroscientists consider outdated. These structures, shown in Figure 2.8, support the visceral and physical expressions of emotion—quickened heartbeat and respiration, trembling, sweating, and alterations in facial expressions—and the expression of appetitive and other primary drives, namely, hunger, thirst, mating, defense, attack, and flight. Important structures are the **anterior cingulate**, which is an area just above the corpus callosum; the **septal area**, which is anterior to the thalamus; the **hippocampus**, which stretches from the septal area into the temporal lobe; the **hypothalamus**, which regulates metabolism, temperature, perspiration, blood pressure, sleeping, and appetite; and the **amygdala**, which is embedded in the tip of the temporal lobe. The amygdala is also an important area for attention to emotionally salient stimuli and memory for emotionally relevant memories. This is one of the key brain structures for psychopathology researchers, given the ubiquity of emotion problems in the psychological disorders. For example, people with depression show more activity in the amygdala when watching pictures of emotional faces than do people without depression (Sheline et al., 2001).

The development of the human brain is a complex process that begins early in the first trimester of pregnancy and continues into early adulthood. It has been estimated that about a third of our genes are expressed in the brain,

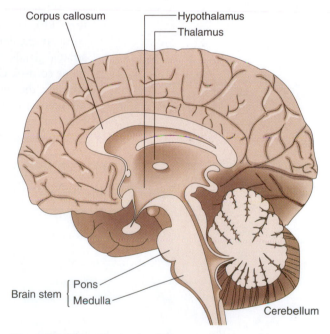

Figure 2.6 Surface of the left cerebral hemisphere, showing the four lobes and the central and lateral sulci.

Figure 2.7 Slice of brain showing some of the internal structures.

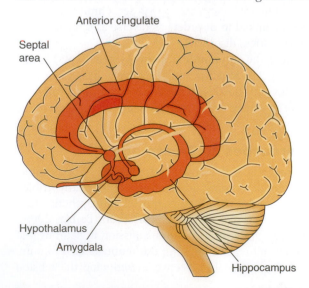

Figure 2.8 Subcortical structures of the brain.

and many of these genes are responsible for laying out the structure of the brain. The development of the cells and migration of these cells to the appropriate layers of cortex are an intricate dance. Unfortunately, missteps can happen, and current thinking about a number of disorders, such as schizophrenia, places the beginnings of the problem in these early developmental stages. Brain development continues throughout childhood, adolescence, and even into adulthood. What is happening during this time is cell development and a honing of the connections between cells and brain areas. The gray matter of the brain continues to develop, filling with cells, until early adolescence. Then, somewhat surprisingly, a number of synaptic connections begin to be eliminated—a process called **pruning**. Throughout early adulthood, the connections in the brain may become fewer, but they also become faster. The areas that develop the quickest are areas linked to sensory processes, like the cerebellum and occipital lobe. The area that develops last is the frontal lobe.

We will discuss a number of these brain areas throughout the book. For example, patients with schizophrenia, have been found to have enlarged ventricles of the brain (Chapter 11); the size of the hippocampus is reduced among some patients with posttraumatic stress disorder, depression, and schizophrenia, perhaps due to overactivity of their stress response systems (Chapters 5, 8, and 11); brain size among some children with autism expands at a much greater rate than it should in typical development (Chapter 14).

The Neuroendocrine System

The neuroendocrine system has been implicated in psychopathology as well, and we will consider this evidence throughout this book. One of the systems we will return to again and again is the **HPA axis** (shown in Figure 2.9). The HPA axis is central to the body's response to stress, and stress figures prominently in many of the disorders we discuss in this book.

When people are faced with threat, the hypothalamus releases corticotropin-releasing factor (CRF), which then communicates with the *pituitary gland*. The pituitary then releases adreno-corticotropic hormone, which travels via the blood to the adrenal glands. The outer layers of the adrenal glands are referred to as the *adrenal cortex*, and this area promotes the release of the hormone cortisol. **Cortisol** is often referred to as the stress hormone. This is not a fast-moving system, like the autonomic nervous system to be reviewed shortly. Rather, it takes about 20 to 40 minutes for cortisol release to peak. After the stress or threat has remitted, it can take up to an hour for cortisol to return to baseline (i.e., before the stress) levels (Dickerson & Kemeny, 2004).

Studies of stress and the HPA axis are uniquely integrative. That is, they begin with a psychological concept, stress, and examine how stress is manifested in the body, the HPA axis. For example, in a series of animal studies, researchers have shown that rats and primates that are exposed to early trauma, such as being separated from their mothers, show elevated activity in the HPA axis when they are exposed to stressors later in life (Gutman & Nemeroff, 2003). Like our discussion of gene–environment interactions above, it is hard to consider biology and environment separately—biology may create increased reactivity to the environment, and early experiences may influence biology. As we will see, chronic stress and its effects on the HPA axis are linked to disorders as diverse as schizophrenia, depression, and posttraumatic stress disorder.

Another important system, the **autonomic nervous system (ANS)**, is discussed in Focus on Discovery 2.1. Much of our behavior is dependent on a nervous system that operates very quickly, generally without our awareness, and that has traditionally been viewed as beyond voluntary control; hence the term *autonomic*.

Neuroscience Approaches to Treatment

The use of psychoactive drugs has been increasing dramatically. For example, between 1988 and 2000 antidepressant use among adults nearly tripled (National Center for Health Statistics, 2004). Spending on antipsychotic drugs increased from $1.3 billion in 1997 to $5.6 billion in 2006 (Barber, 2008). Antidepressants, such as Prozac, increase neural transmission in neurons that use serotonin as a neurotransmitter by inhibiting the reuptake of serotonin. Benzodiazepines, such as Xanax, can be effective in reducing the tension

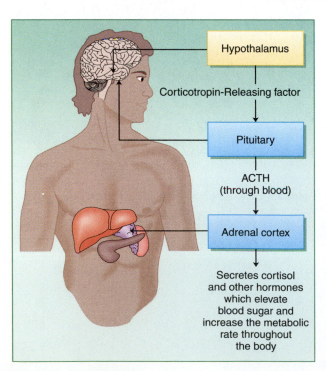

Figure 2.9 The HPA axis.

FOCUS ON DISCOVERY 2.1

The Autonomic Nervous System

The autonomic nervous system (ANS) innervates the endocrine glands, the heart, and the smooth muscles that are found in the walls of the blood vessels, stomach, intestines, kidneys, and other organs. This nervous system is itself divided into two parts, the **sympathetic nervous system** and the **parasympathetic nervous system** (Figure 2.10). A simple way to think about these two components of the ANS is that the sympathetic nervous system prepares the body for "fight or flight" and the parasympathetic nervous system helps "calm down" the body. Things are not actually that simple, though. The sympathetic portion of the ANS, when energized, accelerates the heartbeat, dilates the pupils, inhibits intestinal activity, increases electrodermal activity (i.e., sweat on the skin), and initiates other smooth muscle and glandular responses that prepare the organism for sudden activity and stress. Division of activities is not quite so clear-cut, however, for it is the parasympathetic system that increases blood flow to the genitals during sexual excitement.

The autonomic nervous system figures prominently in many of the anxiety disorders, such as panic disorder and posttraumatic stress disorder. For example, people with panic disorder tend to misinterpret normal changes in their nervous system, such as shortness of breath after running up a flight of stairs. Instead of attributing this to being out of shape, people with panic disorder may think they are about to have another panic attack. In essence, they come to fear the sensations of their own autonomic nervous system.

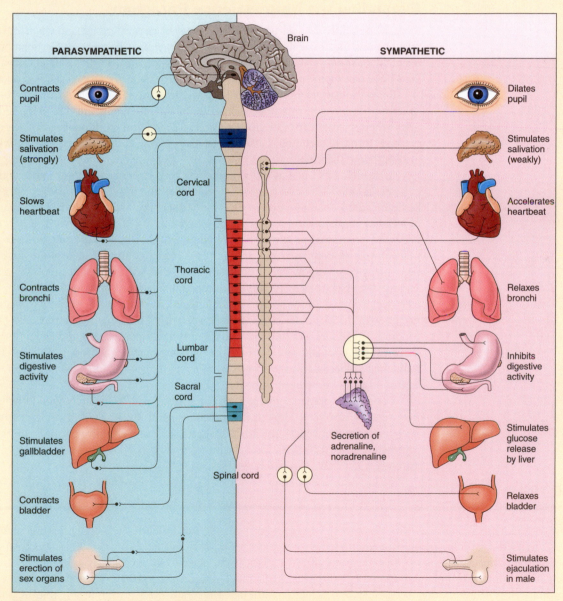

Figure 2.10 The autonomic nervous system.

associated with some anxiety disorders, perhaps by stimulating GABA neurons to inhibit other neural systems that create the physical symptoms of anxiety. Antipsychotic drugs, such as Olanzapine, used in the treatment of schizophrenia, reduce the activity of neurons that use dopamine as a neurotransmitter by blocking their receptors and also impact serotonin. Stimulants, such as Adderal, are often used to treat children with attention-deficit/hyperactivity disorder; they operate on several neurotransmitters that help children pay attention.

Although you might assume that we have learned which neurotransmitters are involved in a disorder and then used that to define pharmacological treatments, this is often not the case. Rather, the reverse has often happened, a drug is found that influences symptoms, and then researchers are inspired to study the neurotransmitters influenced by that drug.

It should be noted that a person could hold a neuroscience view about the nature of a disorder and yet recommend psychological intervention. Contemporary scientists and clinicians also appreciate that nonbiological interventions can influence brain functioning. For example, psychotherapy that teaches a person how to stop performing compulsive rituals, which is an effective and widely used behavioral treatment for obsessive-compulsive disorder, has measurable effects on brain activity (Baxter et al., 2000).

Evaluating the Neuroscience Paradigm

Over the past three decades neuroscientists have made great progress in elucidating brain–behavior relationships. Neuroscience research on both causes and treatment of psychopathology is proceeding at a rapid rate, as we will see when we discuss specific disorders in later chapters. Although we view these developments in a positive light, we also want to caution against reductionism.

Reductionism refers to the view that whatever is being studied can and should be reduced to its most basic elements or constituents. In the case of mental disorders, reductionism happens when scientists try to reduce complex mental and emotional responses to biology. In its extreme form, reductionism asserts that psychology and psychopathology will ultimately be nothing more than biology.

Basic elements, such as individual nerve cells, are organized into more complex structures or systems, such as neural networks or circuits. The properties of these neural circuits cannot be deduced from the properties of the individual nerve cells. The whole is greater than the sum of its parts. A good example is provided by computers. Students writing papers for their courses use word-processing programs like Word or Google Docs. These software programs consist of many levels of code that communicate with the computer. The word-processing program necessarily involves low-level communication with the computer, involving a series of 0's and 1's and even electronics. Yet we don't conceptualize the program in terms of binary digits or electrical impulses. If the spell-checker stopped working, our first place to begin repairs would not be with the computer chips. Instead, we would want the programmer to fix the bug in the program. To be sure, the program could not run without the computer, but the program is more than just the impulses sent by the chips. In the same way, although a complex behavior like a hallucination necessarily involves the brain and nerve impulses, it is not likely that we can fully capture this by knowing specific nerve impulses.

Certain phenomena emerge only at certain levels of analysis and will be missed by investigators who focus only at the molecular level. In the field of psychopathology, problems such as delusional beliefs, dysfunctional attitudes, and catastrophizing cognitions may well be impossible to explain neurobiologically, even with a detailed understanding of the behavior of individual neurons (Turkheimer, 1998).

Quick Summary

The neuroscience paradigm is concerned with the ways in which the brain contributes to psychopathology. Neurotransmitters such as serotonin, norepinephrine, dopamine, and GABA have been implicated in a number of disorders. A number of different brain areas are also a focus of research. The autonomic nervous system, which includes the sympathetic and parasympathetic nervous systems, is also implicated in the manifestations of some disorders. The HPA axis is responsible for the body's response to stress and thus is relevant for several stress-related disorders. Biological treatments, primarily medications, are effective treatments for different disorders, but these treatments are not necessarily treating the cause of the problems. Although the brain plays an important role in our understanding of the causes of psychopathology, we must be careful to avoid reductionism.

Check Your Knowledge 2.2

Fill in the blanks.

1. The so-called limbic system of the brain includes the following brain areas: _____, _____, _____, _____, and _____.
2. The _____ matter of the brain consists of the tracts of myelinated fibers that connect cells; the _____ matter of the brain refers to the brain's cells or neurons.

3. Neurotransmitters that are studied in psychopathology include: _____, which can produce states of high arousal, and _____, which inhibits nerve impulses.
4. The HPA axis consists of the _____, _____, and _____.

The Psychodynamic Paradigm

The central assumption of the psychoanalytic theory that Sigmund Freud developed (see Chapter 1) was that psychopathology resulted from unconscious conflicts in the individual. More specifically, Freud believed that the various forms of psychopathology resulted from the presence of strong drives or id instincts, which set the stage for the development of unconscious conflicts linked to a particular psychosexual stage. The interplay of these forces is referred to as the psychodynamics of the personality. Theorists who follow Freud's ideas (many different versions of Freudian theory have evolved over time) are therefore referred to as psychodynamic theorists. The **psychodynamic paradigm** includes psychoanalysis and its later variants.

Although the psychodynamic paradigm provides a theory about the causes of psychopathology, little research has been conducted to support the theory. Freud believed that the information obtained from therapy sessions was enough to validate his theory and demonstrate the effectiveness of the therapy. Beyond this, Freud and many of his followers were not as concerned with conducting research on the theory as they were with treating patients. Thus, many of the contributions of this paradigm are in treatment, not in understanding the causes of psychopathology.

Although traditional psychoanalysis is still practiced today, it is less common than other forms of psychotherapy. As discussed in Chapter 1, many of Freud's followers altered psychoanalysis and developed variants on this treatment, and these variants are collectively referred to as psychodynamic therapies. Even though Freud and his followers did not conduct much research, researchers in other fields, such as cognitive neuroscience and social psychology, have conducted studies to examine some of the concepts originating in psychodynamic theories. Cognitive psychologists, for example, have studied how unconscious biases can influence the way people attend to and interpret information. In the next sections we review two contemporary views of concepts that evolved from the work of psychodynamic theorists: the unconscious and interpersonal relationships. In addition, we examine two contemporary psychodynamic therapies.

The Role of the Unconscious

The behavior of human beings, as conceptualized by Freud, is a complex interplay of the three parts of the psyche (id, ego, superego), all vying for the achievement of sometimes irreconcilable goals. Much of this activity was presumed to be unconscious, or outside the awareness of the individual. Later followers of Freud continued to emphasize the role of the unconscious in human behavior and psychopathology, but the way in which the unconscious has been discussed and even empirically studied has changed throughout the years (see also Focus on Discovery 6.3).

Followers of Freud, including more contemporary ego analysts (see Chapter 1 for the historical underpinnings of this approach) have refined the theorizing about the unconscious so that it is more amenable to empirical scrutiny. For example, the concept of *pathogenic beliefs* refers to beliefs that are maladaptive and contribute to psychopathology (Weiss & Sampson, 1986). Pathogenic beliefs are believed to be nearly entirely outside of an individual's awareness (i.e., they are unconscious) and responsible for other maladaptive thoughts and emotions. For example, survivor guilt is hypothesized to flow from the (unconscious) pathogenic belief that achieving one's own success will cause others to suffer (O'Connor et al., 2000), and survivor guilt has been linked with depression (O'Connor et al., 2002).

The unconscious has been a "hot topic" of study among cognitive psychologists for over 30 years, and cognitive neuroscientists have more recently explored how the brain supports behavior that is outside conscious awareness. For example, the concept of *implicit memory* refers to the idea that a person can, without being aware of it, be influenced by prior learning. For example, a person may be shown a list of words so quickly that he or she cannot identify the words. Later, the person will be able to recall those words even though the words were not consciously perceived during the rapid, initial presentation. Thus, a memory is formed implicitly (i.e., without conscious awareness). Implicit memory paradigms have been adopted by psychopathology researchers who have found, for example, that people with social anxiety and depression have trouble with these tasks (Amir, Foa, & Coles, 1998; Watkins, 2002).

Contemporary studies of the unconscious, such as studies of implicit memory, are a long way from Freud's original theorizing about the unconscious. Even contemporary psychodynamic theorists posit different explanations for why material may be kept out of conscious awareness than do cognitive neuroscientists. For a psychodynamic theorist, the unconscious may be a "safe place" to keep unwanted thoughts or feelings in check. By contrast, for cognitive neuroscientists, the unconscious reflects the incredible efficiency and automaticity of the brain. That is, there are simply too many things going on around us all the time for us to be aware of everything. Thus, our brains have developed the capacity to register information for later use even if we are not aware of it. Despite these differences in conceptualizations of the unconscious, it is fair to say that Freud and his followers have certainly contributed to the contemporary study of the unconscious.

The Importance of Interpersonal Relationships

Recall from Chapter 1 that one of the central features of psychoanalysis is transference, which refers to a patient's responses to his or her analyst that seem to reflect attitudes and ways of behaving toward important people in the patient's past, rather than reflecting actual aspects of the analyst–patient relationship. Contemporary psychodynamic theorists have built on the concept of transference to emphasize the importance of a person's interpersonal relationships for psychological well-being. One example is **object relations theory**, which stresses the importance of long-standing patterns in close relationships, particularly within the family, that are shaped by the ways in which people think and feel. The "object" refers to another person in most versions of this theory. This theory goes beyond transference to emphasize that the way in which a person comes to understand, whether consciously or unconsciously, how the self is situated in relation to other people. For example, a woman may come to understand herself as a worthless person based on her cold and critical relationship with her mother.

Another influential theory, **attachment theory,** grew out of object relations theory. John Bowlby (1907–1990) first proposed this theory in 1969, and Mary Ainsworth (1913–1999) and colleagues (1978) developed a method to measure attachment styles in infants. The essence of the theory is that the type or style of an infant's attachment to his or her caregivers can set the stage for psychological health or problems later in life. For example, infants who are securely attached to their caregivers are more likely to grow up to be psychologically healthy adults, whereas infants who are anxiously attached to their caregivers are more likely to experience psychological difficulties. Attachment theory has been extended to adults (Main, Kaplan, & Cassidy, 1985; Pietromonaco & Barrett, 1997) and couples (e.g. Fraley & Shaver, 2000), and therapies based on attachment theory have been developed for children and adults, though these have not yet been empirically scutinized.

Social psychologists have integrated these theories into the concept of the *relational self,* which refers to the self in relation to others (Anderson & Chen, 2002; Chen, Boucher, & Parker Tapias, 2006). The concept of the relational self has garnered a tremendous amount of empirical support. For example, people will describe themselves differently depending on what other close relationships they have been asked to think about (Chen et al., 2006). Other studies show that describing a stranger in terms that are similar to a close significant other will trigger positive feel-

Children who are securely attached to parents are more likely to be psychologically healthy adults. (Blend Images/SuperStock,Inc.)

ings and facial expressions, presumably linked to the view of the self in relation to the close other person (Anderson et al., 1996). Thus, if you are given a description of a stranger you must interact with that resembles a close friend from high school, you will be more likely to smile, perhaps as a result of thinking about yourself and your interactions with your high school friend. The idea of the relational self has not yet been fully extended to the study of psychopathology, but given its theoretical basis and empirical support, it is ripe for translation to the study of interpersonal difficulties across many different psychological disorders.

In summary, contemporary psychodynamic theorizing has become more amenable to empirical research, though most research on these concepts has been done by researchers working outside the paradigm. Nevertheless, concepts such as the unconscious and interpersonal relationships have influenced the development of psychodynamic therapies, two of which we briefly review here.

Contemporary Psychodynamic Psychotherapies

Brief Psychodynamic Therapy   Although many laypeople assume that patients usually spend many months, even years, in psychodynamic **psychotherapy,** most courses of therapy last fewer than 10 sessions (Garfield, 1978). Among the many reasons for the short duration of therapy is that people today are less likely to consider the ambitious examination of the past as the best way to deal with today's realities—the essence of classical psychoanalytic therapy. Indeed, most patients expect therapy to be fairly short term and targeted to specific problems in their everyday lives. These expectations contributed to the design of briefer forms of dynamic therapy.

These factors, combined with the greater acceptability of psychotherapy in the population at large, set the stage for the development of **brief therapy**. Time-limited psychodynamic therapies share several common elements (Koss & Shiang, 1994). First, the therapist takes a more active role than a traditional psychoanalyst. Second, it is made clear right away that therapy will be limited and that improvement is expected within a small number of sessions, from 6 to 25. Third, interpretations are directed more toward present life circumstances and patient behavior than toward the historical significance of feelings. Finally, the development of transference is not encouraged, but some positive transference to the therapist is fostered to encourage the patient to follow the therapist's suggestions and advice.

Unresolved grief is one of the issues discussed in interpersonal therapy. (PhotoDisc/SuperStock, Inc.)

Interpersonal Therapy   Although also a brief therapy, we discuss **interpersonal therapy (IPT)** separately because it has been shown to be an effective treatment for depression (a topic we turn to in more detail in Chapter 8). IPT has also been used to treat eating disorders, anxiety disorders, and personality disorders.

IPT emphasizes the importance of current relationships in a person's life and how problems in these relationships can contribute to psychological symptoms. The therapist encourages the patient to identify feelings about his or her relationships and to express these feelings, and helps the patient generate solutions to interpersonal problems. In IPT, four interpersonal issues are assessed to examine whether one or more might be impacting symptoms:

- *Unresolved grief*—for example, experiencing delayed or incomplete grieving following a loss
- *Role transitions*—for example, transitioning from child to parent or from worker to retired person
- *Role disputes*—for example, resolving different relationship expectations between romantic partners
- *Interpersonal or social deficits*—for example, not being able to begin a conversation with an unfamiliar person or finding it difficult to negotiate with a boss at work

Discussions in therapy also focus on longstanding patterns in relationships that may contribute to negative feelings that the patient can now identify. Some of these patterns may emerge in the relationship between therapist and patient (i.e., transference), and this becomes a topic of discussion in the therapy. In sum, the therapist helps the patient understand that psychopathology occurs in a social or relationship context, and that getting a better handle on relationship patterns is needed to reduce symptoms of psychopathology.

Evaluating the Psychodynamic Paradigm

Many of the criticisms leveled at the psychodynamic paradigm are criticisms of Freud's original ideas and methods. For example, Freud conducted no formal research on the causes and treatments of mental illness. This remains one of the main criticisms today: because they are based on anecdotal evidence gathered during therapy sessions, some contemporary psychodynamic theories are not grounded in objectivity and therefore are not scientific. However, other contemporary psychodynamic theories, such as object relations theory, have built a limited base of research in support of the theory. Offshoots of object relations theory, such as attachment theory and the relational self, have accumulated a good bit of empirical support, both in children and adults. Moreover, some therapies, such as IPT, have also garnered empirical support.

Though perhaps not as influential as it once was, the psychodynamic paradigm continues to have an impact on the field of psychopathology (Westen, 1998). This influence is most evident in the following three commonly held assumptions:

1. *Childhood experiences help shape adult personality.* Contemporary clinicians and researchers still view childhood experiences and other environmental events as crucial. They seldom focus on the psychosexual stages about which Freud wrote, but some emphasize problematic parent–child relationships in general and how they can influence later adult relationships in negative ways.

2. *There are unconscious influences on behavior.* As discussed earlier, the unconscious is a focus of contemporary research in cognitive neuroscience and psychopathology (see also Focus on Discovery 6.3). This research shows that people can be unaware of the causes of their behavior. However, most current researchers and clinicians do not think of the unconscious as a repository of id instincts.

3. *The causes and purposes of human behavior are not always obvious.* Freud and his followers sensitized generations of clinicians and researchers to the nonobviousness of the causes and purposes of human behavior. Contemporary psychodynamic theorists continue to caution us against taking everything at face value. A person expressing disdain for another, for example, may actually like the other person very much yet be fearful of admitting positive feelings. This tendency to look under the surface, to find hidden meanings in behavior, is perhaps the best known legacy of Freud.

The Cognitive Behavioral Paradigm

The **cognitive behavioral paradigm** traces its roots to learning principles and to cognitive science. As we willl see, the basic principles from classical and operant conditioning as well as cognitive science have shaped the development of many cognitive behavioral therapies.

Influences from Behavior Therapy

One of the key influences from behaviorism is the notion that problem behavior is likely to continue if it is reinforced. Generally, problem behavior is thought to be reinforced by four possible consequences: getting attention, escaping from tasks, generating sensory feedback (such as results from the hand flapping often seen in children with autistic disorder), and gaining access to desirable things or situations (Carr et al., 1994). Once the source of reinforcement has been identified, treatment is then tailored to alter the consequences of the problem behavior. For example, if it was established that the problem behavior was reinforced by getting attention, the treatment might be to ignore the behavior. Alternatively, the problem behavior could be followed by **time-out**—the person is sent for a period of time to a location where positive reinforcers are not available. Today, time-out is a commonly used parenting technique for children who exhibit a problematic behavior of some sort.

Another technique used to increase the frequency of desirable behavior is making positive reinforcers contingent on behavior. For example, a socially withdrawn child could be reinforced for playing with others. Similarly, positive reinforcement has been used to help children with autistic disorder develop language, to remediate learning disabilities, and to help children with mental retardation develop necessary living skills.

The **token economy** is a procedure in which tokens (such as stickers) are given for desired behavior; the tokens can later be exchanged for desirable items and activities (Staats & Staats, 1963). This procedure is still used today, particularly with children. For example, each time a child completes her homework or remains seated during class, she receives a sticker; the stickers can then be traded in for items or activities, such as a DVD, computer time, or time outside.

We introduced the technique called systematic desensitization in Chapter 1. Recall that this involves two components: (1) deep muscle relaxation and (2) gradual exposure to a list of feared situations, starting with those that arouse minimal anxiety and progressing to those that are the most frightening. The still-influential contribution from this behavioral approach is the **exposure** component of this treatment. The basic idea was that the anxiety will extinguish if the person can face the object or situation for long enough with no actual harm occurring. Sometimes this exposure can be conducted **in vivo**—that is, in real-life situations. For example, if someone has a fear of flying, you might have him or her take an actual flight. At times, exposure cannot be conducted in real life, so *imaginal exposure* will be used to address fears, such as rape, trauma, or contamination. In other situations, both types of exposure are used.

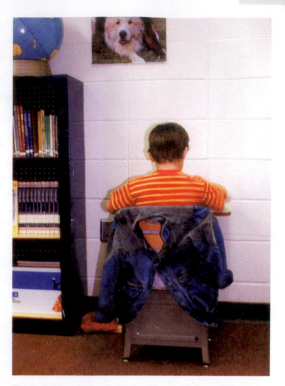

Time-out is a behavioral therapy technique based on operant conditioning; the consequence for misbehavior is removal to an environment with no positive reinforcers. (Jeff Greenberg/PhotoEdit.)

To illustrate exposure and systematic desensitization, consider a person who suffers from a fear of spiders. The person is taught to relax deeply. Next, the person develops a list of situations with spiders that vary in how frightening or anxiety producing they are. Examples of hierarchy items for someone who has a specific phobia of spiders might include the following:

- You hear the word *spider*.
- You look at an illustration of a spider in a children's book.
- You look at a photo of a spider.
- You look at a nature program on DVD about spiders.
- You look at a spider in a glass case at the zoo.
- You look at a live spider from several feet away.
- You look at a live spider up close.

Step-by-step, while relaxed, the person imagines the graded series of situations with spiders. The relaxation tends to inhibit any anxiety that might otherwise be elicited by the imagined scenes of spiders. The fearful person becomes able to tolerate increasingly more difficult imagined situations as he or she climbs the hierarchy over a number of therapy sessions.

Exposure continues to be a centrally important component of many forms of cognitive behavior therapy today. In the years since exposure treatments such as systematic desensitization were first developed, much has been learned about them. For instance, exposure to the real thing (in vivo exposure), when practical, is more effective than imagining situations. Also, even though relaxation training helps people experience less arousal when they first face the feared stimulus, there is no evidence that such training is required for good outcomes; as a result, it has been possible to develop briefer psychological treatments that do not include relaxation training.

As influential as these behavior therapy techniques were (and still are), behaviorism and behavior therapy were often criticized for minimizing the importance of two important factors: thinking and feeling. In other words, the way we think and feel about things undoubtedly influences our behavior. Yet behaviorists did not often take this into account when conceptualizing or treating psychological problems. These limitations of behavioral points of views, plus the explosion of research in the 1960s and 1970s in cognitive science, led some behavioral researchers and clinicians to include cognitive variables in their conceptualizations of psychopathology and therapy.

Cognitive Science

Cognition is a term that groups together the mental processes of perceiving, recognizing, conceiving, judging, and reasoning. Cognitive science focuses on how people (and animals) structure their experiences, how they make sense of them, and how they relate their current experiences to past ones that have been stored in memory.

At any given moment, we are bombarded by far more stimuli than we can possibly respond to. How do we filter this overwhelming input, put it into words or images, form hypotheses, and arrive at a perception of what is out there?

Cognitive scientists regard people as active interpreters of a situation, with people's past knowledge imposing a perceptual funnel on the experience. A person fits new information into an organized network of already-accumulated knowledge, often referred to as a **schema**, or cognitive set (Neisser, 1976). New information may fit the schema; if not, the person reorganizes the schema to fit the information or construes the information in such a way as to fit the schema. The following situation illustrates how a schema may alter the way in which information is processed and remembered.

> *The man stood before the mirror and combed his hair. He checked his face carefully for any places he might have missed shaving and then put on the conservative tie he had decided to wear. At breakfast, he studied the newspaper carefully and, over coffee, discussed the possibility of buying a new washing machine with his wife. Then he made several phone calls. As he was leaving the house he thought about the fact that his children would probably want to go to that private camp again this summer. When the car didn't start, he got out, slammed the door and walked down to the bus stop in a very angry mood. Now he would be late. (Bransford & Johnson, 1973, p. 415)*

Now read the excerpt again, but add the word *unemployed* before the word *man*. Now read it a third time, substituting *neurosurgeon* for *man*. Notice how differently you understand the passage. Ask yourself what parts of the newspaper these men read. If you were asked on a questionnaire to recall this information and you no longer had access to the excerpt, you might answer "the want ads" for the unemployed man and "the financial pages" for the investment banker. Since the passage does not specify which part of the paper was read, these answers are wrong, but in each instance the error would have been a meaningful, predictable one.

Other important contributions from cognitive science include the study of attention. As we shall see, people with disorders as diverse as anxiety disorders, mood disorders, and schizophrenia have problems in attention. For example, individuals with anxiety disorders tend to focus their attention on threatening or anxiety-producing events or situations in the environment. People with schizophrenia have a hard time concentrating their attention for a period of time.

One of the ways in which researchers have studied attention is with the Stroop task. In this task, the participant sees a set of color names printed in inks of *different* colors and must name the ink color of each word as rapidly as possible (see Figure 2.11). To do this, participants have to resist the natural impulse to say the printed word. For example, a participant might see the word *blue* written in the green ink. The participant is instructed to name the ink color (green) as fast as possible without making mistakes (saying the word *blue*). It is difficult to say *green* and "inhibit" the more natural tendency to say *blue*. Interference, measured as a lengthening of response time, occurs because the words are more "attention grabbing" than the ink color.

The Stroop task has been modified to focus on emotion rather than colors. In this emotion Stroop task, participants are still instructed to name the color of the ink rather than saying the word. However, the list of words now contains emotion words instead of color words. So, for example, words such as *threat, danger, happy,* or *anxious* are written in different ink colors. In such an emotion Stroop task, individuals with anxiety disorders find that some of the emotion words are so attention grabbing that the impulse to say the word is especially strong. As in the original Stroop task, the more attention grabbing the word

Black	Pink
Red	White
Blue	Red
Green	Black
Yellow	Purple
Blue	Green
Red	Blue
White	Yellow

Figure 2.11 In the Stroop task, participants must name the color of the ink instead of reading the words.

is, the more interference and the slower the response. Research has shown that people with anxiety disorders show more interference for threatening words (i.e., they say these words more slowly) than nonthreatening words, and this is used as evidence of an attention bias toward threatening information (see Chapter 5).

Of course, the concepts of schema and attention are related to each other. If a person has a particular set or schema about the world (e.g., the world is dangerous), that person may be more likely to pay attention to threatening or dangerous things in the environment. Furthermore, this person may be more likely to interpret ambiguous things in the environment as threatening. For example, seeing a stranger standing on a front porch may be interpreted as a sign of danger to someone with such a "danger" schema. For someone without such a schema, this person may be viewed simply as the person who lives in that house.

Cognitive explanations are now central in the search for the causes of psychopathology and for new methods of intervention. A widely held view of depression, for example, places the blame on a particular cognitive set, namely, the individual's overriding sense of hopelessness (see p. 234). Many people who are depressed believe that they have no important effect on their surroundings regardless of what they do. Their destiny seems to them to be out of their hands, and they expect their future to be negative. If depression does develop from a sense of hopelessness, this fact could have implications for how clinicians treat the disorder. Cognitive theorizing will be included in discussions of most of the disorders presented in subsequent chapters.

Cognitive Behavior Therapy

Cognitive behavior therapy (CBT) incorporates theory and research on cognitive processes. Cognitive behavior therapists pay attention to private events—thoughts, perceptions, judgments, self-statements, and even tacit (unconscious) assumptions—and have studied and manipulated these processes in their attempts to understand and modify overt and covert disturbed behavior. **Cognitive restructuring** is a general term for changing a pattern of thought that is presumed to be causing a disturbed emotion or behavior. This restructuring is implemented in several ways by cognitive behavior therapists.

Aaron Beck developed a cognitive theory of depression and a cognitive behavioral therapy for people with depression. (Courtesy Dr. Aaron T. Beck.)

Beck's Cognitive Therapy   Psychiatrist Aaron Beck, one of the leading cognitive behavior therapists, developed a cognitive therapy for depression based on the idea that depressed mood is caused by distortions in the way people perceive life experiences (Beck, 1976; Salkovskis, 1996). For example, a person with depression may focus exclusively on negative happenings and ignore positive ones. Imagine that a woman's romantic partner both praises and criticizes her. If the woman attends to the praise and remembers it the next day, she is likely to feel happy. But if she focuses on the criticism and continues to dwell on it the next day, she is likely to feel unhappy. Beck proposed that the attention, interpretation, and recall of negative and positive information were biased in depression. These effects on attention and memory are called information-processing biases. Beck's therapy, which has now been adapted for other disorders in addition to depression, addresses these biases by trying to persuade patients to change their opinions of themselves and the way in which they interpret life events. When a depressed person expresses feelings that nothing ever goes right, for example, the therapist offers counterexamples, pointing out how the client has overlooked favorable happenings. The general goal of Beck's therapy is to provide people with experiences, both inside and outside the consulting room, that will alter their negative schemas, enabling them to have hope rather than despair.

Albert Ellis, a cognitive behavior therapist and founder of rational-emotive behavior therapy, focused on the role of irrational beliefs as causes of psychopathology. (Courtesy Michael A. Fenichel, Ph.D.)

Ellis's Rational-Emotive Behavior Therapy   Albert Ellis (1913–2007) developed a different type of cognitive behavior therapy. His principal thesis was that sustained emotional reactions are caused by internal sentences that people repeat to themselves; these self-statements reflect sometimes unspoken assumptions—irrational beliefs—about what is necessary to lead a meaningful life. In Ellis's **rational-emotive behavior therapy (REBT)** (Ellis, 1993, 1995), the aim is to eliminate self-defeating beliefs. A person with depression, for example, may say several times a day, "What a worthless jerk I am." Ellis proposed that people interpret what is happening around them, that sometimes these interpretations can cause emotional turmoil, and that a therapist's attention should be focused on these beliefs rather than on historical causes or, indeed, on overt behavior.

Ellis used to list a number of irrational beliefs that people can harbor. He later (1991; Kendall et al., 1995) shifted from a cataloguing of specific beliefs to the more general concept of "demandingness," that is, the musts or shoulds that people impose on themselves and on others. Thus, instead of wanting something to be a certain way, feeling disappointed, and then perhaps engaging in some behavior that might bring about the desired outcome, the person demands that it be so. Ellis hypothesized that it is this unrealistic, unproductive demand that creates the kind of emotional distress and behavioral dysfunction that bring people to therapists.

Evaluating the Cognitive Behavioral Paradigm

Cognitive behavioral explanations of psychopathology tend to focus more on current determinants of a disorder and less on historical, childhood antecedents. Some cognitive explanations of psychopathology do not appear to explain much. That a person with depression has a negative schema tells us that the person thinks gloomy thoughts. But such a pattern of thinking is actually part of the diagnosis of depression. What is distinctive in the cognitive behavioral paradigm is that the thoughts are given causal status; that is, the thoughts are regarded as causing the other features of the disorder, such as sadness. Left unanswered is the question of where the negative schema came from in the first place. Much of the current research is focused on understanding what types of mechanisms sustain the biased thoughts shown in different psychopathologies.

Table 2.1 compares the basic assumptions of the psychodynamic and cognitive behavioral paradigms.

Table 2.1 Comparison of Psychodynamic and Cognitive Behavioral Paradigms

Psychodynamic	Cognitive Behavioral
We don't always say what we mean.	We usually say what we mean, or at least we are able to quite readily.
We don't always know what we mean.	We usually know what we mean.
We can have strongly inconsistent feelings about things, desires, and fears.	We do have strongly inconsistent, conflicting feelings, but such conflicts are not emphasized.
What lies on the surface is not (always) the most important aspect of ourselves; in fact, it seldom is.	What lies on the surface is usually the most important aspect of ourselves. Yet looking for controlling variables can take cognitive-behaviorists into the realm of causes.
Our earliest life experiences are pivotal, especially with our parents and parent figures.	Current factors in one's life are at least as important as past experiences.
We can come to fear our own desires and experience conflict about expressing them.	Fear of our own desires is emphasized less.
We often desire or fear what is unconventional, bizarre, taboo.	People's wishes and fears are much more prosaic. There is little presumption of taboo concerns.
"The truth shall set you free." Insight into one's actual motivations has, in itself, curative properties.	Insight can be helpful, but it is to be found more in current thoughts than the past. It facilitates control over our fears and desires.

Quick Summary

The psychodynamic paradigm derives from the work of Freud and his followers. Contemporary psychodynamic theories include ego analysis, which introduced the concept of pathogenic beliefs; object relations, which stresses the importance of relationships; and its offshoot, attachment theory, which emphasizes the role of attachment styles in infancy through adulthood. The theories of Freud and other psychodynamic theorists do not lend themselves to systematic study, which has limited their acceptance by some in the field. However, more contemporary psychodynamic researchers along with researchers in other fields, such as cognitive neuroscience and social psychology, have generated a body of empirical research on concepts such as the unconscious and interpersonal relationships. For example, research on implicit memory and the relational self has promoted acceptance of the ideas of unconscious influences on behavior and the role of the self in relation to others. Brief psychodynamic therapy and interpersonal therapy are two contemporary psychotherapies that are based in psychodynamic theory. Although Freud's early work is often criticized, this paradigm has been influential in the study of psychopathology in that it has made clear the importance of early experiences, the notion that we can do things without conscious awareness, and the point that the causes of behavior are not always obvious.

The cognitive behavioral paradigm reflects influences from behavior therapy and cognitive science. Treatment techniques designed to alter the consequences or reinforcers of a behavior, such as in time-out or a token economy, are still used today. Exposure is a key component to cognitive behavioral treatments of anxiety. Cognitive science focuses on concepts such as schemas (a network of accumulated knowledge or set), attention, and memory, and these concepts are part of cognitive behavioral theories and treatments of psychopathology. Cognitive behavior therapy uses behavior therapy techniques and cognitive restructuring. Aaron Beck and Albert Ellis are two influential cognitive behavior therapists. The boundary between what is behavioral and what is cognitive is not always so clear in the cognitive behavioral paradigm.

Check Your Knowledge 2.3

True or false?

1. One of the current contributions of the psychodynamic paradigm is the recognition that the unconscious is not important.
2. The relational self is a concept from social psychology that incorporates ideas from object relations and attachment theories.
3. Interpersonal therapy may focus on four types of interpersonal problems including unresolved grief, role transitions, role disputes, and social deficits.
4. Beck's theory suggests that emotions are caused by irrational thoughts, whereas Ellis's theory suggests that people have distortions in the way they perceive life's experiences.
5. In the Stroop task, interference is measured by how long it takes to name the color of the ink in a list of words.

Factors That Cut across the Paradigms

Two important sets of factors that we will consider throughout this book are emotion and sociocultural factors. Some type of disturbance in emotion can be found in nearly all mental disorders. In addition, we will see that gender, culture, ethnicity, and social relationships bear importantly on the descriptions, causes, and treatments of the different disorders. In the next sections, we introduce these concepts and give some examples of why they are so important in psychopathology, regardless of what paradigm has been adopted.

Emotion and Psychopathology

Emotions influence how we respond to problems and challenges in our environment; they help us organize our thoughts and actions, both explicitly and implicitly, and they guide our behavior. Perhaps because our emotions exert such widespread influence, we spend a good deal of time trying to regulate how we feel and how we present our emotions to others. Given their

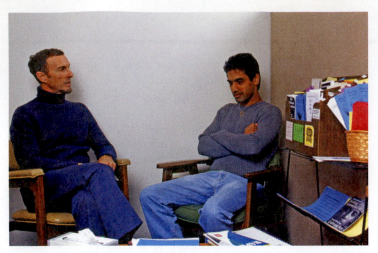

Emotion consists of many components, including expression (shown here), experience, and physiology. (Rachel Epstein/PhotoEdit.)

centrality, it is not surprising that emotion disturbances figure prominently in many different forms of psychopathology. By one analysis, as many as 85 percent of psychological disorders include disturbances in emotional processing of some kind (Thoits, 1985).

What is emotion? The answer to that question could fill an entire textbook on its own. Emotions are believed to be fairly short-lived states, lasting for a few seconds, minutes, or at most hours. Sometimes the word *affect* is used to describe short-lasting emotional feelings. Moods, on the other hand, are emotional experiences that endure for a longer period of time.

Most contemporary emotion theorists and researchers suggest that emotions are comprised of a number of components—including (but not limited to) expressive, experiential, and physiological components—that are typically coordinated within the individual. The expressive, or behavioral, component of emotion typically refers to facial expressions of emotion. For example, anger expression is an important variable in studies of heart disease. Many patients with schizophrenia display very few facial expressions. The experience, or subjective feeling, component of emotion refers to how someone reports he or she feels at any given moment or in response to some event. For example, learning that you received an A on your midterm might elicit feelings of happiness, pride, and relief. Learning you received a C might elicit feelings of anger, concern, or embarrassment. The physiological component of emotion involves changes in the body, such as those due to the autonomic nervous system activity that accompanies emotion. For example, if a car almost runs you down as you are crossing the street, you may show a frightened look on your face, feel fear, and experience an increase in your heart rate, breathing rate, and skin conductance.

When we consider emotional disturbances in psychopathology, it will be important to consider which of the emotion components are affected. In some disorders, all emotion components may be disrupted, whereas in others, just one might be problematic. For example, people with schizophrenia do not readily express their emotions outwardly, but they report feeling emotions very strongly. People with panic disorder experience excessive fear and anxiety when no actual danger is present. People with depression may experience prolonged sadness and other negative feelings. A person with antisocial personality disorder does not feel empathy. We will try to be clear in the book as to what component of emotion is being considered.

Another important consideration in the study of emotion and psychopathology is the concept of *ideal affect*, which simply refers to the kinds of emotional states that a person ideally wants to feel. At first glance, you might presume that happiness is the ideal affect for everyone. After all, who doesn't want to feel happy? However, recent research shows that ideal affects vary depending on cultural factors (Tsai, 2007). Thus, people from Western cultures, such as the United States, do indeed value happiness as their ideal state. However, people from East Asian cultures, like China, value less arousing positive emotions, such as calmness, more than happiness (Tsai, Knutson, & Fung, 2006). Tsai and colleagues have also shown a linkage between people's ideal affect and drug usage; if the ideal affect is a state of low arousal, like calmness, a person is less likely, for example, to use cocaine (Tsai, Knutson, & Rothman, 2007). Cross-nationally, more people in the United States seek treatment for cocaine and amphetamines, drugs that are stimulating and associated with feelings of excitement and happiness; more people in China seek treatment for heroin, a drug that has calming effects (Tsai, 2007; for more on the effects of these drugs see Chapter 10).

The study of emotion figures prominently in the work of neuroscientists who are examining the ways in which the brain contributes to the different emotion components. Geneticists have also begun to examine how tendencies to experience a lot of positive or negative emotion may run in families. Emotions such as anger figured prominently in Freud's views; more contemporary psychodynamic treatments also focus on changing emotion. Even cognitive behavioral therapies consider how emotion influences thinking and behavior. As noted above, emotion is the starting point for Ellis's theory. Emotion thus cuts across the paradigms and can be studied from multiple perspectives, depending on the paradigm that is adopted.

Sociocultural Factors and Psychopathology

A good deal of research has focused on the ways in which sociocultural factors, such as culture, ethnicity, gender, and social relationships, can contribute to different psychological disorders. Researchers who study such sociocultural factors and psychopathology all share the premise that environmental factors can trigger, exacerbate, or maintain the symptoms that make up the different disorders. But the range of variables considered, and the ways of studying those variables, cover a lot of ground.

An increasing number of such studies look at the role of culture and ethnicity by conducting multinational and multicultural studies. In addition, these studies have shown that some disorders affect men and women differently. For example, depression is nearly twice as common among women as among men. On the other hand, antisocial personality disorder and alcohol dependence are more common among men than women. Childhood disorders, such as attention-deficit/hyperactivity disorder, affect boys more than girls, but some researchers question whether this reflects a true difference between boys and girls or a bias in the diagnostic criteria. Other studies show that poverty is a major influence on psychological disorders. For example, poverty is related to antisocial personality disorder, anxiety disorders, and depression.

Beyond the role of culture, ethnicity, and poverty, thousands of articles have been published on how the quality of relationships influences different disorders. Family and marital relationships, social support, and even the amount of casual social contact all play a role in influencing the course of disorders. Within relationships, researchers have looked for ways to capture the relative closeness and support offered, but also the degree of hostility. In addition, current research is looking beyond whether men and women differ in the prevalence rates of certain disorders to asking questions about risk factors that may differentially impact men and women in the development of certain disorders. For example, father-to-son genetic transmission appears to be an important risk factor in the development of alcohol dependence for men, whereas sociocultural standards of thinness may be a risk factor in the development of eating disorders for women.

One tradition involves examining problem-solving interactions of family members to try to capture key dimensions in relationships. In a typical family interaction task, researchers might ask family members to discuss a topic that has been a source of concern, like whether the family is spending enough time together. An interviewer talks with each family member independently to capture the basics of his or her position. Then, in a family meeting, the interviewer briefly summarizes each person's perspective and asks the family to discuss the topic for 10 to 15 minutes and try to come to some resolution. Researchers then might code various dimensions from watching videotapes, like how family members share power, express positive sentiments, or deal with negative emotions.

Other researchers are interested in understanding the role of trauma, serious life events, and stress in psychopathology. We will describe some of the ways people measure life events in the next chapter. But the influence of stress within the context of social relationships plays a role in just about all the disorders we will consider.

Cultural and ethnic factors in psychopathology must be examined more closely. Some questions, such as whether or not the disorders we diagnose and treat in the United States are observed in other parts of the world, have been fairly well studied. This research has demonstrated that a number of disorders are indeed observed in diverse parts of the world. Indeed, no country or culture is without psychopathology of some sort. For example, Murphy (1976) examined whether schizophrenia symptoms could be observed in cultures as diverse as Eskimo and Yoruba. She found that both cultures have a concept of being "crazy" that is quite similar to the Western definition of schizophrenia. The Eskimo's *nuthkavihak* includes talking to oneself, refusing to talk, delusional beliefs, and bizarre behavior.

Culture and ethnicity play an important role in the descriptions, causes, and treatments of mental disorders. (Betsie Van der Meer/Stone/Getty Images.)

The Yoruba's *were* encompasses similar symptoms. Notably, both cultures also have shamans but draw a clear distinction between their behavior and that of mentally ill people. In Chapter 5, we discuss a number of anxiety conditions across the world that look very similar to the symptoms of panic disorder.

Although some disorders appear to occur in different cultures, other disorders appear to be specific to particular cultures. In Chapter 9, we will consider the evidence that eating disorders are specific to Western culture. The Japanese term *hikikomori* refers to a condition where a person completely withdraws from his social world (although women are affected, it is observed predominantly among men). People with hikikomori may completely shut themselves into their room or houses—in some cases, for many years—refusing to interact with other people and leaving only occasionally to buy food. As we discuss in the next chapter, the current diagnostic system includes cultural factors in the discussion of every category of disorder, and this may be an important step toward increasing research in this area.

Even though there are some cross-cultural similarities in the presence of mental illnesses across cultures, there are also a number of profound cultural influences on the symptoms expressed in different disorders, the availability of treatment, and the willingness to seek treatment. We will consider these issues throughout this book.

We must also consider the role of ethnicity in psychopathology. Some disorders, such as schizophrenia, are diagnosed more often among African Americans than Caucasians. Does this mean schizophrenia occurs more often in this group, or does it mean that some type of ethnic bias might be operating in diagnostic assessments? Drug use and abuse and their effects vary by ethnicity. Whites are more likely to use or abuse many drugs, such as nicotine, hallucinogens, methamphetamine, prescription painkillers, and, depending on the age group, alcohol. Yet African American smokers are more likely to die from lung cancer. Eating disturbances and body dissatisfaction are greater among white women than black women, particularly in college, but differences in actual eating disorders, particularly bulimia, do not appear to be as great. The reasons for these differences are not yet well understood and are the focus of current research. Table 2.2 shows recent data on ethnic and racial differences in the lifetime prevalence of DSM-IV-TR disorders.

Sociocultural factors have become more prominent in recent years in genetics and neuroscience. For example, *social neuroscience* seeks to understand what happens in the brain during complex social situations. Gene–environment interaction studies are uncovering the ways in which the social environment in combination with certain genes can increase the risk for disorders, as illustrated by the Caspi and colleagues (2003) study discussed earlier. Psychodynamic and cognitive behavior traditions have tended to focus more on the individual rather than how the individual interacts with the social world. However, this, too, is changing. New efforts are under way, for example, to develop cognitive behavior therapy for people from different cultures and ethnicities.

Table 2.2 Lifetime Prevalence Rates of DSM-IV-TR Disorders among Different Ethnic Groups

Disorder	White	Hispanic	Black
ADHD	4.6	4.6	3.4
Alcohol abuse or dependence	13.4	15.0*	9.5
Bipolar disorder	3.2	4.3	4.9*
Depression	17.9*	13.5	10.8
Drug abuse or dependence	7.9	9.1	6.3
Generalized anxiety disorder	8.6*	4.8	5.1
Panic disorder	4.9	5.4	3.1
PTSD	6.8	5.9	7.1

Table values are percentages. * indicates group with significantly highest prevalence rate.

Source: Adapted from Breslau et al. (2006). Sample came from the National Comorbidity Survey-Replication study, a study including a representative sample of people age 18 or older in the United States.

Quick Summary

Emotion disturbances figure prominently in psychopathology, but the ways in which emotions can be disrupted varies quite a bit. Emotions guide our behavior and help us to respond to problems or challenges in our environment. It is important to distinguish between components of emotion, including expression, experience, and physiology. In addition, mood can be distinguished from emotion. The concept of ideal affect points to important cultural differences in emotion that may be important for psychopathology. Psychological disorders have different types of emotion disturbances, and thus it is important to consider which of the emotion components are affected. In some disorders, all emotion components may be disrupted, whereas in others, just one might be problematic. Emotion is an important focus in the paradigms.

Sociocultural factors, such as culture, ethnicity, gender, social support, and relationships, are important factors in the study of psychopathology. Some disorders appear to be universal across cultures, like schizophrenia or anxiety, yet their manifestations may differ somewhat and the ways in which society regards them may also differ. Other disorders, like eating disorders or hikikomori, may be specific to particular cultures. Some disorders are more frequently diagnosed in some ethnic groups compared to others. It is not clear whether this reflects a true difference in the presence of disorder or perhaps a bias on the part of diagnosticians. Social relationships can be important buffers against stress and have benefits for physical and mental health. Current research is also examining whether risk factors associated with various disorders differ for men and women. Sociocultural factors have recently become the focus of people working in the other paradigms, and this trend will continue.

Diathesis–Stress: An Integrative Paradigm

Psychopathology is much too diverse to be explained or treated adequately by any one of the current paradigms. Most of the disorders we will discuss in this book likely develop through an interaction of neurobiological defects and environmental factors, a view that we turn to next.

The **diathesis–stress** paradigm is an integrative paradigm that links genetic, neurobiological, psychological, and environmental factors. It is not limited to one particular school of thought, such as cognitive behavioral, genetic, or psychodynamic. The diathesis–stress concept was introduced in the 1970s as a way to account for the multiple causes of schizophrenia (Zubin & Spring, 1977). Its appeal continues today for many disorders, however, because, like the gene–environment interaction models reviewed above, it is a model that focuses on the interaction between a predisposition toward disease—the **diathesis**—and environmental, or life, disturbances—the stress. Diathesis refers most precisely to a constitutional predisposition toward illness, but the term may be extended to any characteristic or set of characteristics of a person that increases his or her chance of developing a disorder.

In the realm of neurobiology, for example, a number of disorders considered in later chapters appear to have a genetically transmitted diathesis. Although the precise nature of these genetic diatheses is currently unknown (e.g., we don't know exactly what is inherited that makes one person more likely than another to develop bipolar disorder), it is clear that a genetic predisposition is an important component of many disorders. Other neurobiological diatheses include oxygen deprivation at birth, poor nutrition, and a maternal viral infection or smoking during pregnancy. Each of these conditions may lead to changes in the brain that predispose the individual toward psychopathology.

In the psychological realm, a diathesis for depression may be the cognitive set already mentioned, the chronic feeling of hopelessness sometimes found in people with depression. Other psychological diatheses include the ability to be easily hypnotized, which may be a diathesis for dissociative identity disorder (formerly called multiple personality disorder), and an intense fear of becoming fat, which predisposes an individual toward eating disorders.

These diatheses can arise for a variety of reasons. Some, such as hypnotizability, are personality characteristics that are probably in part genetically influenced. Others, such as a sense of hopelessness, may result from childhood experiences with harshly critical parents. Sexual or physical abuse during childhood produces psychological changes as well as changes in the brain that seem to predispose people to develop a number of different disorders.

Stressors that may activate a diathesis range from minor, such as having car trouble, to major, such as the aftermath of a hurricane. (Left: Creatas/SuperStock, Inc.; Right: AFP/Getty Images.)

Sociocultural influences also play an important role; for instance, cultural standards of what is beautiful may lead to an intense fear of being fat and thus predispose some people to eating disorders. The diathesis–stress paradigm is integrative because it draws on all these diverse sources of information about the causes of diatheses. In later chapters we will see that concepts from the major paradigms we have already discussed are differentially applicable to different disorders. For example, a genetic diathesis plays a major role in attention-deficit/hyperactivity disorder. Cognitive diatheses, in contrast, are more influential in the anxiety disorders and depression. A diathesis–stress paradigm allows us to draw on concepts from many sources and to make more or less use of them depending on the disorder being considered.

Possessing the diathesis for a disorder increases a person's risk of developing it but does not by any means guarantee that a disorder will develop. The stress part of diathesis–stress is meant to account for how a diathesis may be translated into an actual disorder. In this context stress generally refers to some noxious or unpleasant environmental stimulus that triggers psychopathology. Psychological stressors include major traumatic events (e.g., becoming unemployed, divorce, death of a spouse) as well as more mundane happenings, which many of us experience (e.g., being stuck in traffic). By including these environmental events, the diathesis–stress model goes beyond the major paradigms we have already discussed.

The key point of the diathesis–stress model is that both diathesis and stress are necessary in the development of disorders. Some people, for example, have inherited a predisposition that places them at high risk for mania (see Chapter 8); given a certain amount of stress, they stand a good chance of developing mania. Other people, those at low genetic risk, are not likely to develop mania, regardless of how difficult their lives are.

Another major feature of the diathesis–stress paradigm is that psychopathology is unlikely to result from the impact of any single factor. Like our discussion of the reciprocal relationships between genes and the environment above, a genetically transmitted diathesis may be necessary for some disorders, but it is embedded in a network of other factors that also contribute to the disorder. These factors could include genetically transmitted diatheses for other personality characteristics; childhood experiences that shape personality, the development of behavioral competencies, and coping strategies; stressors encountered in adulthood; cultural influences; and numerous other factors.

Finally, we should note that within this framework, the data gathered by researchers holding different paradigms are not incompatible with one another. For example, stress may be needed to activate a predisposition toward a problem in neurotransmitter systems. Some of the differences between the paradigms also appear to be more linguistic than substantive. A cognitive behavioral theorist may propose that maladaptive cognitions cause depression, whereas a neurobiological theorist may speak of the underactivity of a certain neural pathway. The two positions are not contradictory but merely reflect different levels of description, just as we could describe a table as pieces of wood in a particular configuration or as a collection of atoms.

Check Your Knowledge 2.4

True or false?

1. Emotion consists of at least three components: expression, experience, and physiology.
2. Sociocultural factors such as gender, culture, ethnicity, and social relationships are less important to consider from the neuroscience paradigm.
3. Examining problem-solving interactions of family members is useful for understanding key dimensions in relationships.
4. In the diathesis–stress model, the diathesis must be biological (e.g., genetic).
5. The diathesis–stress model emphasizes the importance of integrating across paradigms to understand the causes of mental illness.

Multiple Perspectives on a Clinical Problem

To provide a concrete example of how it is possible to conceptualize a clinical case using multiple paradigms, we present a case and discuss how information provided is open to a number of interpretations, depending on the paradigm adopted.

Depending on the paradigm you adopt, your conceptualization of this case may differ. If you hold a genetic point of view, you are attentive to the family history, noting that Arthur's father had similar difficulties with alcohol. You are probably aware of the research (to be reviewed in Chapter 10) that suggests a genetic factor in substance-related disorders such as alcohol dependence. You do not discount environmental contributions to Arthur's problems, but you hypothesize that some inherited defect predisposes him to react poorly to stress, which may in turn increase the likelihood that he will turn to alcohol to cope. After all, not everyone who experiences a difficult childhood and adolescence develops a drinking problem.

Clinical Case: Arthur

Arthur's childhood had not been a particularly happy one. His mother died suddenly when he was only 6, and for the next 10 years he lived either with his father or with a maternal aunt. His father drank heavily, seldom managing to get through any day without some alcohol. His father's income was so irregular that he could seldom pay bills on time or afford to live in any but the most run-down neighborhoods. At times Arthur's father was totally incapable of caring for himself, let alone his son. Arthur would then spend weeks, sometimes months, with his aunt in a nearby suburb.

Despite these early life circumstances, Arthur completed high school and entered college. He qualified for student loans and other financial aid, but he also needed to wait tables and tend bar to make ends meet. During these college years, he felt an acute self-consciousness with people he felt had authority over him—his boss, his professors, and even some of his classmates, with whom he compared himself unfavorably.

Like many people in college, Arthur attended his fair share of parties. He pledged a fraternity at the end of his freshman year, and this was the source of most of his socializing. It was also the source of a lot of alcohol. He drank heavily at the weekend parties. By his senior year, however, he was drinking daily, often as a way to deal with the stress of being in school and working at the same time.

Two years after college, Arthur married his college girlfriend. Arthur could never quite believe that his wife, as intelligent as she was beautiful, really cared for him. As the years wore on, his doubts about himself and about her feelings toward him would continue to grow. He felt she was far brighter than he, and he worried that she would make more money than he would.

After college, Arthur began a job at a publishing company, serving as an assistant editor. This job proved to be even more stressful than college. The deadlines and demands of the senior editors were difficult. He constantly questioned whether he had what it took to be an editor. Like his father, he often drank to deal with this stress.

Several years later, when it seemed that life should be getting easier, he found himself in even greater turmoil. Now 32 years old, with a fairly secure job that paid reasonably well, he and his wife were arguing more often. She continually complained about his drinking; he denied that there was a problem. After all, he was only drinking four beers a night. His wife wanted to start a family, but he was not sure if he wanted to have this additional stress in his life. His brooding over his marriage led him to drink even more heavily until finally, one day, he realized he was drinking too much and needed to seek help.

A psychodynamic point of view casts Arthur in yet another light. Believing that events in early childhood are of great importance in later patterns of adjustment, you may hypothesize that Arthur is still grieving for his mother and has blamed his father for her early death. Such strong anger at the father has been repressed, and this plus the death of his mother is negatively impacting his adult relationships with others. For treatment, you may choose interpersonal therapy to work on Arthur's relationships and to deal openly and consciously with his buried anger toward his father.

Now suppose that you are committed to a cognitive behavioral perspective, which encourages you to analyze human behavior in terms of reinforcement patterns as well as cognitive variables. You may focus on Arthur's self-consciousness at college, which seems related to the fact that compared with his fellow students, he grew up with few advantages. Economic insecurity and hardship may have made him unduly sensitive to criticism and rejection. Alcohol has been his escape from such tensions. But heavy drinking, coupled with persistent doubt about his own worth as a human being, has worsened an already deteriorating marital relationship, further undermining his confidence. As a cognitive behavior therapist, you may employ systematic desensitization, in which you teach Arthur to relax deeply as he imagines a hierarchy of situations in which he is being evaluated by others. Or you may decide on cognitive behavior therapy to convince Arthur that he need not obtain universal approval for every undertaking.

If you adopt a diathesis–stress perspective, you might follow more than one of these strategies. You would acknowledge the likely genetic contribution to Arthur's alcohol dependence, but you would also identify key triggers (e.g., job stress) that might lead to greater bouts of drinking. You would likely employ many of the therapeutic techniques noted above.

Summary

- A paradigm is a conceptual framework or general perspective. Because the paradigm within which scientists and clinicians work helps to shape what they investigate and find, understanding paradigms helps us to appreciate subjective influences that may affect their work.

- Several major paradigms are current in the study of psychopathology and therapy. The choice of a paradigm has important consequences for the way in which psychopathology is defined, investigated, and treated.

- The genetic paradigm holds that psychopathology is caused, or at least influenced, by heritable factors. Recent genetic findings show how genes and the environment interact, and it is this type of interaction that will figure most prominently in psychopathology.

- The neuroscience paradigm emphasizes the role of the brain, neurotransmitters, and other systems, such as the HPA axis. Biological treatments, including medications, attempt to rectify the specific problems in the brain.

- The psychodynamic paradigm derives from the work of Freud. More contemporary research in this paradigm includes research on the unconscious and interpersonal relationships. The psychodynamic paradigm continues to influence the field by highlighting the importance of childhood experiences, the unconscious, and the fact that the causes of behavior are not always obvious.

- The cognitive behavioral paradigm emphasizes schemas, attention, and irrational interpretations and their influence on behavior as major factors in

psychopathology. Cognitive behavior therapists such as Beck and Ellis focus on altering patients' negative schemas and interpretations.

- Emotion plays a prominent role in many disorders. It is important to distinguish among components of emotion that may be disrupted, including expression, experience, and physiology. Emotion disturbances are the focus of study across the paradigms.

- Sociocultural factors, including culture, ethnicity, gender, poverty, social support, and relationships, are also important in conceptions of psychopathology. The prevalence and meaning of disorders may vary by culture and ethnicity; men and women may have different risk factors for different disorders; and social relationships can be an important buffer against stress. Sociocultural factors are included in the work of geneticists, neuroscientists, psychodynamic theorists, and cognitive behaviorists.

- Because each paradigm seems to have something to offer to our understanding of mental disorders, it is important to develop more integrative paradigms. The diathesis–stress paradigm, which integrates several points of view, assumes that people are predisposed to react adversely to environmental stressors. The diathesis may be genetic, neurobiological, or psychological and may be caused by early-childhood experiences, genetically influenced personality traits, or sociocultural influences, among other things.

Answers to Check Your Knowledge Questions

2.1 1. b; 2. d; 3. a; 4. c
2.2 1. hypothalamus, anterior cingulate, septal area, hippocampus, amygdala; 2. white, gray; 3. norepinephrine, GABA; 4. hypothalamus, pituitary gland, adrenal cortex

2.3 1. F; 2. T; 3. T; 4. F; 5. T
2.4 1. T; 2. F; 3. T; 4. F; 5. T

Key Terms

agonist
allele
amygdala
antagonist
anterior cingulate
attachment theory
autonomic nervous system (ANS)
behavior genetics
brain stem
brief therapy
cerebellum
cognition
cognitive behavior therapy
   (CBT)
cognitive behavioral paradigm
cognitive restructuring
corpus callosum
cortisol
diathesis
diathesis–stress

dopamine
emotion
exposure
frontal lobe
gamma-aminobutyric acid
   (GABA)
gene
gene expression
gene–environment interaction
genetic paradigm
genotype
gray matter
heritability
hippocampus
HPA axis
hypothalamus
in vivo
interpersonal therapy
   (IPT)
molecular genetics

nerve impulse
neuron
neuroscience paradigm
neurotransmitters
nonshared environment
norepinephrine
object-relations theory
occipital lobe
paradigm
parasympathetic nervous
   system
parietal lobe
phenotype
polygenic
polymorphism
prefrontal cortex
pruning
psychodynamic paradigm
rational-emotive behavior
   therapy (REBT)

reciprocal gene–environment
   interaction
reuptake
schema
second messengers
septal area
serotonin
serotonin transporter gene
shared environment
sympathetic nervous system
synapse
temporal lobe
thalamus
time-out
token economy
ventricles
white matter

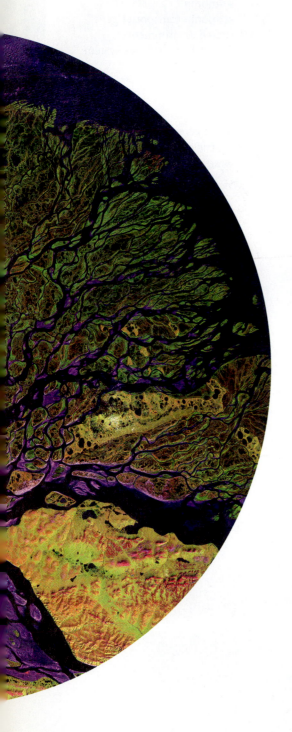

3

Diagnosis and Assessment

LEARNING GOALS

1. Be able to describe the purposes of diagnosis and assessment.
2. Be able to distinguish the different types of reliability and validity.
3. Be able to identify the basic features, strengths, and weaknesses of the DSM-IV-TR.
4. Be able to describe the goals, strengths, and weaknesses of psychological and neuro-biological approaches to assessment.
5. Be able to discuss the ways in which culture and ethnicity impact diagnosis and assessment.

Clinical Case: Aaron

Hearing the sirens in the distance, Aaron realized that someone must have called the police. He didn't mean to get upset with the people sitting next to him at the bar, but he just knew that they were talking about him and plotting to have his special status with the CIA revoked. He could not let this happen again. The last time people conspired against him, he wound up in the hospital. He did not want to go to the hospital again and endure all of the evaluations. Different doctors would ask him all sorts of questions about his work with the CIA, which he simply was not at liberty to discuss. They asked other odd questions, such as whether he heard voices or believed others were putting thoughts into his head. He was never sure how they knew that he had those experiences, but he suspected that there were electronic bugging devices in his room at his parents' house, perhaps in the electrical outlets.

Just yesterday, Aaron began to suspect that someone was watching and listening to him through the electrical outlets. He decided that the safest thing to do was to stop speaking to his parents. Besides, they were constantly hounding him to take his medication. But when he took this medication, his vision got blurry and he had trouble sitting still. He reasoned that his parents must somehow be part of the group of people trying to remove him from the CIA. If he took this medication, he would lose his special powers that allowed him to spot terrorists in any setting, and the CIA would stop leaving messages for him in phone booths or in the commercials on Channel 2. Just the other day, he found a tattered paperback book in a phone booth, which he interpreted to mean that a new assignment was imminent. The voices in his head were giving him new clues about terrorist activity. They were currently telling him that he should be wary of people wearing the color purple, as this was a sign of a terrorist. If his parents were trying to sabotage his career with the CIA, he needed to keep out of the house at all costs. That was what had led him to the bar in the first place. If only the people next to him wouldn't have laughed and looked toward the door. He knew this meant that they were about to expose him as a CIA operative. If he hadn't yelled at them to stop, his cover would have been blown.

DIAGNOSIS AND ASSESSMENT ARE the critically important "first steps" in the study and treatment of psychopathology. In the case of Aaron, a clinician may begin treatment by determining whether Aaron meets the diagnostic criteria for a mood disorder, schizophrenia, or perhaps a substance-related disorder. Having a correct **diagnosis** will allow the clinician to describe base rates, causes, and treatment for Aaron and his family, all of which are important aspects of good clinical care. More broadly, diagnosis enables clinicians and scientists to communicate accurately with one another about cases or research. Without agreed-on definitions and categories, our field would face a situation like the Tower of Babel (Hyman, 2002), in which different scientists and clinicians would be unable to understand each other.

Diagnosis is also important for research on causes and treatments. Sometimes researchers discover unique causes and treatments associated with a certain set of symptoms. For example, autism was only recognized in the *Diagnostic and Statistical Manual* in 1980. Since that time, research on the causes and treatments of autism has grown exponentially. Diagnosis also can be the first major step in good clinical care. Imagine if your doctor told you, "There is no diagnosis for what you have." Rather than this alarming scenario, hearing a diagnosis can provide relief in several different ways. Often, a diagnosis can help a person begin to understand why certain symptoms are occurring. Understanding the causes of symptoms can be a relief. Many disorders are extremely common, such as depression, anxiety, and substance abuse—knowing that his or her diagnosis is common can also help a person feel less unusual.

To help make the correct diagnosis, clinicians and researchers use a variety of assessment procedures, beginning with a clinical interview followed by other psychological and neurobiological assessment methods. Broadly speaking, all clinical assessment procedures are more or less formal ways of finding out what is wrong with a person, what may have caused problems, and what can be done to improve the person's condition. Assessment procedures can help in making a diagnosis, and they can also provide information beyond a diagnosis. Indeed, a diagnosis is only a starting point. In the case of Aaron, for example, many other questions remain to be answered. Why does Aaron behave as he does? Why does he believe he is working for the CIA? What can be done to resolve his conflicts with his parents? Has he performed up to his intellectual potential in school and in his career? What obstacles might interfere with treatment? These are also the types of questions that mental health professionals address in their assessments.

In this chapter, we will describe the official diagnostic system used by many mental health professionals, as well as the strengths and weaknesses of this system. We will then turn to a discussion of the most widely used assessment techniques, including interviews, psychological assessment, and neurobiological assessment. We then conclude the chapter with an examination of a sometimes neglected aspect of assessment, the role of cultural bias. Before considering diagnosis and assessment in detail, however, we begin with a discussion of two concepts that play a key role in diagnosis and assessment: reliability and validity.

Cornerstones of Diagnosis and Assessment

The concepts of reliability and validity are the cornerstones of any diagnostic or assessment procedure. Without them, the usefulness of our methods is seriously limited. That said, these two concepts are quite complex. There are several kinds of each, and an entire subfield of psychology—psychometrics—exists primarily for their study. Here, we provide a general overview.

Reliability

Reliability refers to consistency of measurement. An example of a reliable measure would be a wooden ruler, which produces the same value every time it is used to measure an object. In contrast, an unreliable measure would be a flexible, elastic-like ruler whose length changes every time it is used. Several types of reliability exist, and here we will discuss the types that are most central to assessment and diagnosis.

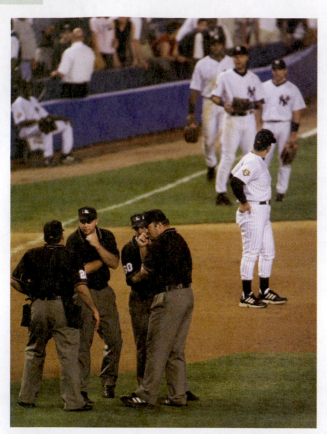

Reliability is an essential property of all assessment procedures. One means of determining reliability is to determine if different judges agree, as happens when two umpires witness the same event in a baseball game. (Reuters/NewMedia Inc./Corbis Images.)

Interrater reliability refers to the degree to which two independent observers agree on what they have observed. To take an example from baseball, two umpires may or may not agree as to whether the ball is fair or foul.

Test–retest reliability measures the extent to which people being observed twice or taking the same test twice, perhaps several weeks or months apart, receive similar scores. This kind of reliability makes sense only when we can assume that people being observed will not change appreciably between test sessions on the underlying variable being measured; a prime example of a situation in which this type of reliability is typically high is in evaluating intelligence tests. On the other hand, we cannot expect people to be in the same mood at a baseline and a follow-up assessment 4 weeks later.

Sometimes psychologists use two forms of a test rather than giving the same test twice, perhaps when there is concern that test takers will remember their answers from the first round of taking the test and aim merely to be consistent. This approach enables the tester to determine **alternate-form reliability**, the extent to which scores on the two forms of the test are consistent.

Finally, **internal consistency reliability** assesses whether the items on a test are related to one another. For example, one would expect the items on an anxiety questionnaire to be interrelated, or to correlate with one another, if they truly tap anxiety. A person who reports a dry mouth in a threatening situation would be expected to report increases in muscle tension as well, since both are common characteristics of anxiety.

Validity

Validity is a complex concept, generally related to whether a measure measures what it is supposed to measure. For example, if a questionnaire is supposed to measure a person's hostility, does it do so? Before we describe types of validity, it is important to note that validity is related to reliability—unreliable measures will not have good validity. Because an unreliable measure does not yield consistent results (recall our example of a ruler whose length is constantly changing), an unreliable measure will not relate very strongly to other measures. For example, an unreliable measure of coping is not likely to relate well to how a person adjusts to stressful life experiences. Reliability, however, does not guarantee validity. Height can be measured very reliably, but height would not be a valid measure of anxiety.

Content validity refers to whether a measure adequately samples the domain of interest. For example, later in this chapter we will describe an interview that is often used to make an Axis I diagnosis. It has excellent content validity because it contains questions about all the symptoms that are involved in Axis I diagnoses. As another example, consider a measure of life stress that we will examine in more detail below. It consists of a list of 43 life experiences. Respondents indicate which of these experiences—for example, losing one's job—they have had in some time period, for example, the past year. Content validity is less certain here because many people may have life experiences that do not appear on the questionnaire. If you read the experiences in Table 3.7, you will likely think of stressors that are not on the list (e.g., the serious illness of someone close to you).

Criterion validity is evaluated by determining whether a measure is associated in an expected way with some other measure (the criterion). If both variables are measured at the same point in time, the resulting validity is referred to as **concurrent validity**. For example, we will describe a measure below of the overly negative thoughts that are believed to play an important role in depression. Criterion validity for this measure of negative thoughts could be established by showing that people with depression score higher on the test than do people without depression. Alternatively, criterion validity can be assessed by evaluating the ability of the measure to predict some other variable that is measured at some point in the future, often referred to as **predictive validity**. For example, IQ tests were originally developed to predict future school performance. Similarly, a measure of negative thinking could be used to predict the development of depression in the future. In summary, concurrent and predictive validity are both types of criterion validity.

Construct validity is a more complex concept. It is relevant when we want to interpret a test as a measure of some characteristic or construct that is not observed simply or overtly (Cronbach & Meehl, 1955). A construct is an inferred attribute, such as anxiousness or distorted cognition. Consider an anxiety-proneness questionnaire as an example. If the questionnaire has construct validity, people who obtain different scores on our test really will differ in anxiety proneness. Just because the items seem to be about the tendency to become anxious ("I find that I become anxious in many situations"), it is not certain that the test is a valid measure of the construct of anxiety proneness.

Construct validity is evaluated by looking at a wide variety of data from multiple sources (compare this to criterion validity, where a test is typically evaluated against just one other piece of data). For example, people diagnosed as having an anxiety disorder and people without such a diagnosis could be compared on their scores on our self-report measure of anxiety proneness. The self-report measure would achieve some construct validity if the people with anxiety disorders scored higher than the people without anxiety disorders. Greater construct validity would be achieved by showing that the self-report measure was related to other measures thought to reflect anxiety, such as observations of fidgeting and trembling, and physiological indicators, such as increased heart rate and rapid breathing. When the self-report measure is associated with these multiple measures (diagnosis, observational indicators, physiological measures), its construct validity is increased.

More broadly, construct validity is related to theory. For example, we might hypothesize that being prone to anxiety is in part caused by a family history of anxiety. We could then obtain further evidence for the construct validity of our questionnaire by showing that it relates to a family history of anxiety. At the same time, we would also have gathered support for our theory of anxiety proneness. Thus, construct validation is an important part of the process of theory testing.

Construct validity is also centrally important to diagnostic categories. Below, we consider in more detail the issue of construct validity and the DSM-IV-TR.

Classification and Diagnosis

Clinical Case: Roxanne

Roxanne is a middle-aged woman who was brought to the local psychiatric emergency room by the police. They had found her running through a crowded street, laughing loudly and running into people. Her clothes were dirty and torn. When they questioned her, she was speaking very rapidly, and she was hard to follow. At the ER, she wrestled free of the police and began running down the hallway. She knocked over two staff members during her flight, while bellowing at the top of her lungs, "I am the resurrection! Come follow me!" Police brought her back to the exam room, and the staff began to form hypotheses. Clearly, she was full of energy. Had she been through some trauma? She believed she had special religious powers—could this be a delusion? Unfortunately, the staff were unable to gain much information from an interview due to her rapid and pressured speech. Rather, Roxanne sat restlessly, occasionally laughing and shouting; treatment could not proceed without understanding the reason for her unusual behavior. When efforts to calm Roxanne failed, police helped the staff to contact family members, who were relieved to hear that Roxanne was safe. She had disappeared from home the day before. Family members described a long history of bipolar disorder (formerly known as manic depression), and they reported having been concerned for the past couple weeks because Roxanne had stopped taking medications for her bipolar disorder and for her high blood pressure. Treatment was able to proceed based on the idea that Roxanne was experiencing a new manic episode of her long-standing bipolar disorder.

In this section, we focus on the official diagnostic system used by mental health professionals, the *Diagnostic and Statistical Manual of Mental Disorders*, now in its fourth edition, commonly referred to as **DSM-IV-TR**. After reviewing the major components of DSM-IV-TR, we will describe the strengths of the DSM-IV-TR, and then review some criticisms of this system as well as of diagnosis in general.

The Diagnostic System of the American Psychiatric Association (DSM-IV-TR)

In 1952, the American Psychiatric Association published its *Diagnostic and Statistical Manual* (DSM). The publication of the DSM was informed by earlier systems of classification (for a review, see Focus on Discovery 3.1), and it has been revised five times since 1952. DSM-IV was published in 1994, and in June 2000, a "text revision," DSM-IV-TR, followed. Almost no changes were made to the diagnostic categories and criteria in the 2000 revision. Rather, DSM-IV-TR provided a summary of new research findings on prevalence rates, course, and etiology (causes). The DSM-IV-TR includes several key features: the use of separate dimensions, or axes, to rate people; discrete diagnostic categories; and more focus on cultural issues.

Five Axes of Classification   As shown in Table 3.1, DSM-IV-TR includes five axes. This **multiaxial classification system**, by requiring judgments on each of the five axes, forces the diagnostician to consider a broad range of information.

Axis I includes all diagnostic categories except the personality disorders and mental retardation, which make up Axis II. Thus Axes I and II cover the classification of mental disorders. A complete listing of the DSM-IV-TR categories of Axes I and II appears inside the front cover of this book. (We will describe many of these disorders throughout the rest of this book.) Most people consult a mental health professional for an Axis I condition, such as depression or an anxiety disorder. But beyond Axis I conditions, clients might have a long-standing Axis II condition, such as dependent personality disorder. Axes I and II are separated to encourage clinicians to be attentive to the possibility of an Axis II disorder. The presence of an Axis II disorder along with an Axis I disorder generally means that a person's problems will be more difficult to treat.

Axes III, IV, and V are designed to capture the broader life context of the person. On Axis III, the clinician indicates any general medical conditions. For many diagnoses, the DSM includes a provision for indicating that the disorder is due to a medical condition or substance abuse. For example, depression resulting from an endocrine gland dysfunction would be diagnosed on Axis I but listed as caused by a medical problem. Therefore, clinicians must be sensitive to possible medical causes of symptoms. On Axis IV, the clinician codes psychosocial problems that may contribute to the disorder, including occupational problems, economic problems, or interpersonal difficulties. Finally, on Axis V, the clinician indicates the person's current level of adaptive functioning, using the Global Assessment of Functioning (GAF) scale (see Table 3.1) to consider social relationships, occupational functioning, and use of leisure time.

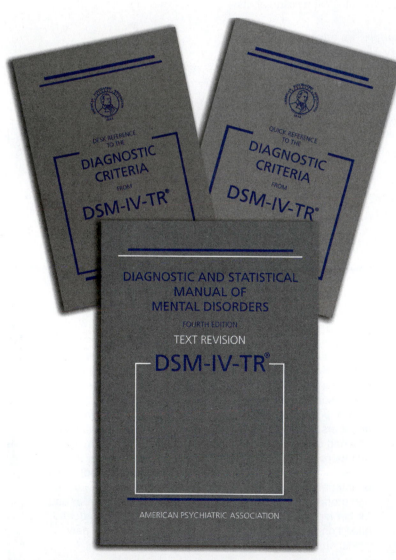

DSM-IV-TR is the official diagnostic system of the American Psychiatric Association. (Courtesy American Psychiatric Association.)

Table 3.1 DSM-IV-TR Multiaxial Classification System

Axis I

Disorders Usually First Diagnosed in Infancy, Childhood, or Adolescence

Delirium, Dementia, Amnesic and Other Cognitive Disorders

Substance-Related Disorders

Schizophrenia and Other Psychotic Disorders

Mood Disorders

Anxiety Disorders

Somatoform Disorders

Factitious Disorders

Dissociative Disorders

Sexual and Gender Identity Disorders

Eating Disorders

Sleep Disorders

Impulse Control Disorders Not Elsewhere Classified

Adjustment Disorders

Axis II

Mental Retardation

Personality Disorders

Axis III

General Medical Conditions

Axis IV Psychosocial and Environmental Problems

Check:

_____ Problems with primary support group.

Specify:

_____ Problems related to the social environment.

Specify:

_____ Educational problem.

Specify:

_____ Occupational problem.

Specify:

_____ Housing problem.

Specify:

_____ Economic problem.

Specify:

_____ Problems with access to health care services.

Specify:

_____ Problems related to interaction with the legal system/crime.

Specify:

_____ Other psychosocial and environmental problems.

Specify:

Axis V Global Assessment of Functioning Scale (GAF Scale)

Consider psychological, social, and occupational functioning on a hypothetical continuum of mental health/illness. Do not include impairment in functioning due to physical (or environmental) limitations.

Code

100 Superior functioning in a wide range of activities, life's problems never seem to get out of hand, is sought out by others because of many positive qualities. No symptoms.

90 Absent or minimal symptoms (e.g., mild anxiety before an exam), good functioning in all areas, interested and involved in a wide range of activities, socially effective, generally satisfied with life, no more than everyday problems or concerns (e.g., an occasional argument with family members).

80 If symptoms are present, they are transient and expectable reactions to psychosocial stressors (e.g., difficulty concentrating after family argument); no more than slight impairment in social, occupational, or school functioning (e.g., temporarily falling behind in schoolwork).

70 Some mild symptoms (e.g., depressed mood and mild insomnia) OR some difficulty in social, occupational, or school functioning (e.g., occasional truancy, or theft within the household), but generally functioning pretty well, has some meaningful interpersonal relationships.

60 Moderate symptoms (e.g., flat affect and circumstantial speech, occasional panic attacks) OR moderate difficulty in social, occupational, or school functioning (e.g., no friends, unable to keep a job).

50 Serious symptoms (e.g., suicidal ideation, severe obsessional rituals, frequent shoplifting) OR any serious impairment in social, occupational, or school functioning (e.g., no friends, unable to keep a job).

40 Some impairment in reality testing or communication (e.g., speech is at times illogical, obscure, or irrelevant) OR major impairment in several areas, such as work or school, family relations, judgment, thinking, or mood (e.g., depressed man avoids friends, neglects family, and is unable to work; child frequently beats up younger children, is defiant at home, and is failing at school).

30 Behavior is considerably influenced by delusions or hallucinations OR serious impairment in communication or judgment (e.g., sometimes incoherent, acts grossly inappropriately, suicidal preoccupation) OR inability to function in almost all areas (e.g., stays in bed all day; no job, home, or friends).

20 Some danger of hurting self or others (e.g., suicide attempts without clear expectation of death, frequently violent, manic excitement) OR occasionally fails to maintain minimal personal hygiene (e.g., smears feces) OR gross impairment in communication (e.g., largely incoherent or mute).

10 Persistent danger of severely hurting self or others (e.g., recurrent violence) OR persistent inability to maintain minimal personal hygiene OR serious suicidal act with clear expectation of death.

0 Inadequate information.

Note: Reprinted with permission from the Diagnostic and Statistical Manual of Mental Disorders, Text Revision, Copyright 2000, American Psychiatric Association.

FOCUS ON DISCOVERY 3.1

A Brief History of Classification and Diagnosis

By the end of the nineteenth century, as people recognized that different illnesses required different treatments, medical diagnostic procedures were improved. During the same period, other sciences, such as botany and chemistry, advanced after classification systems were developed. Impressed by these successes, investigators of mental disorders sought to develop classification schemes. Unfortunately, progress in classifying mental disorders was not gained easily.

Early Efforts at Classification of Mental Illness

Emil Kraepelin (1856–1926) authored an influential early classification system in his textbook of psychiatry first published in 1883. His classification system attempted to definitively establish the biological nature of mental illnesses. Kraepelin noted that certain symptoms clustered together as a *syndrome*. He labeled a set of syndromes and hypothesized that each had its own biological cause, course, and outcome. Even though effective treatments had not been identified, at least the course of the disease could be predicted.

Kraepelin proposed two major groups of severe mental illnesses: dementia praecox (an early term for schizophrenia) and manic-depressive psychosis (an early term for bipolar disorder). He postulated a chemical imbalance as the cause of dementia praecox and an irregularity in metabolism as the explanation of manic-depressive psychosis. Though his theories about causes were not quite correct, Kraepelin's classification scheme nonetheless influenced the current diagnostic categories.

Development of the WHO and DSM Systems

In 1939 the World Health Organization (WHO) added mental disorders to the International List of Causes of Death (ICD). In 1948 the list was expanded to become the International Statistical Classification of Diseases, Injuries, and Causes of Death, a comprehensive listing of all diseases, including a classification of abnormal behavior. Unfortunately, the mental disorders section was not widely accepted. Even though American psychiatrists had played a prominent role in the WHO effort, the American Psychiatric Association published its own Diagnostic and Statistical Manual (DSM) in 1952.

In 1969 the WHO published a new classification system, which was more widely accepted. In the United Kingdom, a glossary of definitions was produced to accompany the WHO system (General Register Office, 1968). A second version of the American Psychiatric Association's DSM, DSM-II (1968), was similar to the WHO system. But true consensus still eluded the field. Even though DSM-II and the British Glossary of Mental Disorders specified some symptoms of diagnoses, the two systems defined different symptoms for a given disorder! Thus diagnostic practices still varied widely.

In 1980 the American Psychiatric Association published an extensively revised diagnostic manual, DSM-III, and a somewhat revised version, DSM-III-R, followed in 1987. In 1988 the American Psychiatric Association began work on DSM-IV, which was published in 1994. Thirteen working groups, which included many psychologists, were established to critique DSM-III-R, review literature, analyze previously collected data, and collect new data. The committee adopted an important new approach—the reasons for changes in diagnoses would be explicitly stated and supported by data. In previous versions of the DSM, the reasons for diagnostic changes had not always been explicit.

Improvements in the DSM Beginning with the third edition of DSM and continuing today, an effort was made to create more reliable and valid diagnostic categories. Major improvements include the following:

1. Specific diagnostic criteria—the symptoms for a given diagnosis—are spelled out precisely, and clinical symptoms are defined in a glossary. Table 3.2 compares the descriptions of a manic episode given in DSM-II with the diagnostic criteria given in DSM-IV-TR. Notice how DSM-IV-TR is much more detailed and concrete.

2. The characteristics of each diagnosis in Axes I and II are described much more extensively than they were in DSM-II. For each disorder there is a description of essential features, then of associated features, such as laboratory findings (e.g., enlarged ventricles in schizophrenia) and results from physical exams (e.g., electrolyte imbalances in people who have eating disorders). Next, a summary of the research literature provides information about age of onset, course, prevalence and sex ratio, familial pattern, and differential diagnosis (i.e., how to distinguish similar diagnoses from each other).

3. With each revision of the DSM, the number of diagnostic categories has increased (see Table 3.3). For example, autism was added in DSM-III. Below, we discuss some of the implications of so many diagnostic categories. Although the number of diagnostic categories has increased dramatically over the years, some categories have been dropped because they have no research to support their validity (e.g., homosexuality).

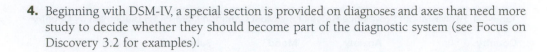

4. Beginning with DSM-IV, a special section is provided on diagnoses and axes that need more study to decide whether they should become part of the diagnostic system (see Focus on Discovery 3.2 for examples).

Table 3.2 Description of Mania in DSM-II versus DSM-IV-TR

DSM-II (1968, p. 36)

Manic-depressive illness, manic type. This disorder consists exclusively of manic episodes. These episodes are characterized by excessive elation, irritability, talkativeness, flight of ideas, and accelerated speech and motor activity. Brief periods of depression sometimes occur, but they are never true depressive episodes.

DSM-IV-TR (2000, p. 362)

Diagnostic Criteria for a Manic Episode

A. A distinct period of abnormally and persistently elevated, expansive, or irritable mood, lasting at least 1 week (or any duration if hospitalization is necessary).

B. During the period of mood disturbance, three (or more) of the following symptoms have persisted (four if the mood is only irritable) and have been present to a significant degree:

   1. inflated self-esteem or grandiosity
   2. decreased need for sleep (e.g., feels rested after only 3 hours of sleep)
   3. more talkative than usual or pressure to keep talking
   4. flight of ideas or subjective experience that thoughts are racing
   5. distractibility (i.e., attention too easily drawn to unimportant or irrelevant external stimuli)
   6. increase in goal-directed activity (either socially, at work or school, or sexually) or psychomotor agitation
   7. excessive involvement in pleasurable activities that have a high potential for painful consequences (e.g., engaging in unrestrained buying sprees, sexual indiscretions, or foolish business investments)

C. The symptoms do not meet criteria for a Mixed Episode.

D. The mood disturbance is sufficiently severe to cause marked impairment in occupational functioning or in usual social activities or relationships with others, or to necessitate hospitalization to prevent harm to self or others, or there are psychotic features.

E. The symptoms are not due to the direct physiological effects of a substance (e.g., a drug of abuse, a medication, or other treatment) or a general medical condition (e.g., hyperthyroidism).

Note: DSM-IV-TR material reprinted with permission from the DSM-IV-TR, copyright 2000, American Psychiatric Association.

Ethnic and Cultural Considerations in DSM-IV-TR   Mental illness is universal. There is not a single culture in which people are free of mental illness. But there are many different cultural influences on the risk factors for mental illness (e.g., social cohesion, poverty, access to drugs of abuse, and stress), the types of symptoms experienced, the willingness to seek help, and the treatments available. Sometimes these differences across cultures are profound. For example, although mental health care is widely available in the United States, it is estimated that there is only one psychiatrist for every 2 million people living in sub-Saharan Africa (World Health Organization, 2001).

Cultural differences do not always play out in the way one might expect. For example, even with the access to medical care in the United States, a major study found that outcomes for schizophrenia were more favorable in Nigeria, India, and Colombia than in more industrialized countries, including the United States (Sartorius et al., 1986). People who immigrate from Mexico to the United States are about half as likely to meet criteria for mental illness than native born citizens in the United States initially, but over time, they and their children begin to show an increase in certain disorders, such as substance abuse, such that their risk for disorder begins to approximate that of people born in the United States (Allegria et al., 2008). As shown in Table 3.4, rates of mental illnesses tend to be higher in the United States than in many other countries. If we hope to understand how culture defines risk, symptom

Table 3.3 Number of Diagnostic Categories per Edition of DSM

Edition of DSM	Number of Categories
DSM I	106
DSM-II	182
DSM-III	265
DSM-III-R	292
DSM-IV-TR	297

Source: Pincus et al. (1992).

Table 3.4 Twelve-Month Prevalence Rates of the Most Common DSM-IV-TR Diagnoses by Country

Country	Anxiety Disorders	Mood Disorders	Substance Disorders	Any Psychological Disorder
Americas				
Colombia	10.0	6.8	2.8	17.8
Mexico	6.8	4.8	2.5	12.2
United States	18.2	9.6	3.8	26.4
Europe				
Belgium	6.9	6.2	1.2	12.0
France	12.0	8.5	0.7	18.4
Germany	6.2	3.6	1.1	9.1
Italy	5.8	3.8	0.1	8.2
Netherlands	8.8	6.9	3.0	14.9
Spain	5.9	4.9	0.3	9.2
Middle East and Africa				
Lebanon	11.2	6.6	1.3	16.9
Nigeria	3.3	0.8	0.8	4.7
Asia				
Japan	5.3	3.1	1.7	8.8
Beijing	3.2	2.5	2.6	9.1

Source: The WHO World Mental Health Survey Consortium (2004).

Note: In the European countries, bipolar disorders and non-alcohol-related substance-use disorders were not assessed. Obsessive-compulsive disorder was not assessed in Asian countries.
Anxiety disorders include agoraphobia, generalized anxiety disorder, obsessive-compulsive disorder, panic disorder, posttraumatic stress disorder, social phobia, and specific phobia. Mood disorders include bipolar I and II disorders, dysthymia, and major depressive disorder. Substance disorders include alcohol or drug abuse or dependence. Diagnoses were assessed with the Composite International Diagnostic Interview. Tabled values are percentages.

The core symptoms of depression appear to be similar cross-culturally. (Richard Nowitz/Photo Researchers.)

expression, and outcomes, we need a diagnostic system that can be applied reliably and validly in different countries and cultures.

Previous editions of the DSM were criticized for their lack of attention to cultural and ethnic variations in psychopathology. DSM-IV-TR enhances cultural sensitivity in three ways: (1) by providing a general framework for evaluating the role of culture and ethnicity, (2) by describing cultural factors and ethnicity for each disorder, and (3) by listing culture-bound syndromes in an appendix.

In the general framework, clinicians are cautioned not to diagnose symptoms unless they are atypical and problematic within a person's culture. People vary in the degree to which they identify with their cultural or ethnic group. Some value assimilation into the majority culture, whereas others wish to maintain close ties to their cultural background. In general, clinicians are advised to be constantly mindful of how culture and ethnicity influence diagnosis and treatment. We will return to this topic when we cover assessment tools.

Much more attention is paid now to how culture can shape the symptoms of a given disorder. For example, the symptoms of both schizophrenia (e.g., delusions and hallucinations) and depression (e.g., depressed mood and loss of interest or pleasure in activities) are similar cross-culturally (Draguns, 1989). But as we will discuss in Chapter 5, it is more likely in Japan than in the United States for anxiety to be focused around fears of offending others (Kirmayer, 2001).

In evaluating symptoms, clinicians also need to be aware that cultures may shape the language used to describe distress in many cultures, for example, it is common to describe grief or anxiety in physical terms—"I am sick in my heart" or "My heart is heavy"—rather than in psychological terms.

FOCUS ON DISCOVERY 3.2

Possible Categories in Need of Further Study

One of DSM-IV-TR's appendixes is entitled "Criteria Sets and Axes Provided for Further Study." It contains several proposals for new categories that the DSM-IV task force considers promising but not sufficiently supported by data to merit inclusion in DSM-IV. By describing these potential categories, the DSM task force hopes to encourage professionals to consider whether a future DSM should contain any of these syndromes or axes officially.

Possible New Syndromes

Here is a sampling of the more than two dozen categories described as meriting further study.

Binge eating disorder. Symptoms include recurrent binges (eating an excessive amount of food within less than two hours), lack of control over the bingeing episode, and distress about bingeing, as well as other characteristics, such eating alone. It is distinguished from anorexia nervosa by the absence of weight loss and from bulimia nervosa by the absence of compensatory behaviors (purging, fasting, or excessive exercise). Most often, people with binge eating disorder are obese, and one issue is how to distinguish this category from obesity. We discuss this in more detail in Chapter 9.

Premenstrual dysphoric disorder. This proposed syndrome is marked by depression, anxiety, anger, mood swings, and decreased interest in usually pleasurable activities. The symptoms occur a week or so before menstruation for most months in a given year and are severe enough to interfere with social or occupational functioning. This category is to be distinguished from premenstrual syndrome, which is experienced by many more women and is not usually debilitating. Arguments abound for and against this possible category. On the plus side, inclusion might alert people to the hormonal bases of monthly mood changes linked to the menstrual cycle and thereby foster more tolerance and less blame. On the minus side, listing such mood changes in a manual of mental disorders would seem to convey the message that women who experience these psychological changes are mentally disordered.

Passive-aggressive personality disorder (negativistic personality disorder). This personality disorder was present in DSM-III and DSM-III-R but was moved to the appendix in DSM-IV. Symptoms include resenting, resisting, and opposing demands and expectations by means of passive activities, such as lateness, procrastination, forgetfulness, and intentional inefficiency. The implication is that the person expresses anger or resentment by not doing certain things rather than by more direct expression, such as assertiveness or aggressiveness. Such people often feel mistreated, cheated, or underappreciated.

Depressive personality disorder. In lay terms, symptoms of this personality disorder include gloominess, lack of cheer, and a tendency to worry a lot. This traitlike, long-term disorder may be a precursor to a full-blown major depressive disorder. One concern is that it is very difficult to distinguish between depressive personality disorder and other depressive disorders.

The DSM includes 25 culture-bound syndromes in the appendix. Culture-bound syndromes are diagnoses that are likely to be seen within specific regions. It is important to note that these culture-bound syndromes are not just found in cultures outside the United States. For example, some argued for listing bulimia nervosa as a Western culture-bound syndrome, a topic we return to in more detail in Chapter 9. The following are some examples of syndromes listed in the DSM appendix.

- *amok.* A dissociative episode in which there is a period of brooding followed by a violent and sometimes homicidal outburst. The episode tends to be triggered by an insult and is found primarily among men. Persecutory delusions are often present as well. The term is Malaysian and is defined by the dictionary as a murderous frenzy. You may have heard the phrase "run amok."

- *ghost sickness.* An extreme preoccupation with death and those who have died found among certain Native American tribes.

- *dhat.* A term used in India to refer to severe anxiety about the discharge of semen.

- *koro.* Reported in South and East Asia, an episode of intense anxiety about the possibility that the penis or nipples will recede into the body, possibly leading to death.

- *shenjing shuairuo* (neurasthenia). A common diagnosis in China, this syndrome is characterized by fatigue, dizziness, headaches, pain, poor concentration, sleep problems, and memory loss.

- *taijin kyofusho.* The fear that one could offend others through inappropriate eye contact, blushing, a perceived body deformation, or one's own foul body odor. This disorder is most

Clinical Case: Lola: An Example of a Multiaxial Diagnosis

Lola is a 17-year-old high school junior. She moved to the United States from Mexico with her parents and brother when she was 14 years old. A few months after they arrived, Lola's father returned to Mexico to attend the funeral of his brother. He was denied reentry to the United States due to a problem with his visa, and he has been unable to reunite with the family for nearly 3 years. Lola's mother has found it difficult to make ends meet on her salary as a bookkeeper, and the family was forced to move to a rougher neighborhood a year ago. Lola's English was fairly good when she came to the United States, and she has picked up many of the nuances of the language since arriving in the country. For the past 2 years, she has been dating a boy in her school. They have been fairly constant companions, and she describes him as the one person she would turn to if she was feeling upset. If her mother had any concern about Lola, it was that she seemed to rely on her boyfriend too much—she asked for his advice with small and large decisions, and she seemed wary of social interactions when he wasn't present. Lola's mother stated, "It is as though she is afraid to think for herself." Lola's mother noted that she had always been a bit shy and had tended to count on her brother a lot for decisions and social support when she was younger.

With little warning, her boyfriend announced that he wanted to break up with her. Lola was extremely distressed by this change and reported that almost immediately she was unable to sleep or eat. She lost weight rapidly and found herself unable to concentrate on her schoolwork. Friends complained that she no longer wanted to talk during lunch or by phone. After 2 weeks of steadily feeling worse, Lola left a suicide note and disappeared. Police found her the next day in an abandoned home, holding a bottle of medicines. She reported that she had been sitting there all night, considering ending her life. Lola's mother reported that she had never seen her this distressed but that a few other family members had what she called bouts of sadness. Still, these family members in Mexico had not made suicide attempts nor had they received any formal treatment. Instead, the family learned to give these family members support and time to heal on their own. After the police found Lola, she was hospitalized for intensive treatment.

Multiaxial Diagnosis of Lola

Axis I   Major Depressive Disorder

Axis II   Dependent Personality Disorder

Axis III None

Axis IV   Problems with primary support group (father not with family); problems related to social environment (acculturation stress; relationship with boyfriend)

Axis V   GAF: 25

---

common in Japan, but cases have been reported in the United States. Japanese cultural norms appear to proscribe more careful attention to social appropriateness and hierarchy, perhaps intensifying the risk of these symptoms (Fabrega, 2002).

- *Hikikomori* (withdrawal). This refers to a syndrome observed in Japan, Taiwan, and South Korea in which an individual, most often an adolescent boy or young adult man, shuts himself into a room (e.g., bedroom) for a period of 6 months or more and does not socialize with anyone outside the room.

Some have argued that we should try to identify broad syndromes that can be identified across cultures and, in this light, have argued against the inclusion of culture-bound syndromes (Lopez-Ibor, 2003). In support of this position, they point toward a number of culture-bound syndromes that are not so different from the main DSM-IV-TR diagnoses. For example, Kleinman (1986) interviewed 100 Chinese people who had been diagnosed with *shenjing shuairuo* and found that 87 percent of them met criteria for major depressive disorder. Many of those responded to antidepressant medications. Suzuki and colleagues (2003) have pointed out that the symptoms of *taijin kyofusho* overlap with those of social phobia (excessive fear of social interaction and evaluation) and body dysmorphic disorders (the mistaken belief that one is deformed or ugly), which are more commonly diagnosed in the United States. Other syndromes may reflect the common concerns of anxiety and distress, with the content

A therapist must be mindful of the role of cultural differences in the ways in which patients describe their problems. (Rhoda Sidney/PhotoEdit.)

Returning to Clinical Case: Roxanne: A Second Example of a Multiaxial Diagnosis

Previously, we described the case of Roxanne, who was brought to the psychiatric emergency room by the police. A multiaxial diagnosis for Roxanne might look as follows.

Axis I	Bipolar I Disorder, Manic
Axis II	None
Axis III	High blood pressure
Axis IV	Problems with housing (homeless)
Axis V	GAF: 20

shaped by life circumstances and values (Lopez-Ibor, 2003). Hence, some researchers believe it is important to look for commonalities across cultures. In contrast, others believe that culture-bound syndromes are central, as since local and personal meanings are a key issue in understanding mental illness (Gaw, 2001). Researchers already are considering various approaches to culture and diagnosis for DSM-V (Kupfer, First, & Regier, 2002).

Quick Summary

Because diagnosis provides the first step in thinking about the causes of symptoms, it is the first step in planning treatment. Because psychopathology is diagnosed on the basis of symptoms, clinical interviews are used to make diagnoses.

With all assessments, the reliability (the consistency of measurement) and validity (whether an assessment measures what it is designed to measure) should be evaluated. Reliability can be estimated by examining how well raters agree, how consistent test scores are over time, how alternate forms of a test compare, or how well items correlate with each other. There are many different forms of validity, including content, criterion, and construct validity.

Diagnostic systems for mental illness have changed a great deal in the past 100 years. Currently, the system in use in the United States is the DSM-IV-TR, a multiaxial classification system that includes approximately 300 different diagnostic categories. One of the most heartening features of the DSM is the explicit rules for diagnosis. This clarity has improved reliability and provides a systematic foundation to study whether each diagnosis is valid. In several different ways, the system guides clinicians to be more sensitive to the role of culture and ethnicity in evaluating mental health.

Check Your Knowledge 3.1 (Answers are at the end of the chapter.)

Answer the questions.

1. Match each axis with its function.
   _____ Axis I
   _____ Axis II
   _____ Axis III
   _____ Axis IV
   _____ Axis V
   a. most major mental disorders, with the exception of personality disorders and mental retardation
   b. functioning
   c. problems with the social environment
   d. personality disorders and mental retardation
   e. medical conditions

2. Which type of reliability or validity is tested with the following procedures?
   _____ A group of high school students is given the same IQ test 2 years in a row.

   _____ A group of high school students is given an IQ test, and their scores are correlated with a different IQ test they took the year before.

   _____ A measure of the tendency to blame oneself is developed, and researchers then test whether it predicts depression, whether it is related to childhood abuse, and whether it is related to less assertiveness in the workplace.

   _____ Patients are interviewed by two different doctors. Researchers examine whether the doctors agree about the diagnosis.
   a. interrater reliability
   b. test–retest reliability
   c. criterion validity
   d. construct validity

Specific Criticisms of the DSM

Some specific questions and concerns have been raised about the current version of the DSM. We review some of these concerns in the following sections.

Too Many Diagnoses? DSM-IV-TR contains almost 300 different diagnoses. Some have critiqued the burgeoning number of diagnostic categories (see Table 3.3). The DSM-IV-TR even includes an all-encompassing category for "Other conditions that may be a focus of clinical attention." This category comprises conditions that are not regarded as mental disorders per se but still may be a focus of professional attention or treatment, including academic problems, relational problems, bereavement, religious doubt, and noncompliance with treatment. This category seems to exist, perhaps, so that anyone entering the mental health system can be categorized. The DSM-IV includes a category for acute stress disorder, to capture symptoms in the first month after a severe trauma. Should these relatively common reactions to trauma be pathologized by diagnosing them as a mental disorder (Harvey & Bryant, 2002)? By expanding its coverage, the authors of the DSM seem to have made too many problems into psychiatric disorders, without good justification for doing so.

Others argue that the system includes too many minute distinctions based on small differences in symptoms. One side effect of the huge number of diagnostic categories is a phenomenon called **comorbidity**, which refers to the presence of a second diagnosis. When diagnosticians use DSM-IV-TR, comorbidity is the norm rather than the exception. Among people who meet criteria for at least one psychiatric diagnosis, 45 percent will meet criteria for at least one more psychiatric diagnosis (Kessler et al., 2005). Some argue that this overlap is a sign that we are dividing syndromes too finely. Others praise the careful specificity.

Among people who think there are too many diagnostic categories, several researchers have considered ways to collapse into broader categories. To begin, some disorders seem to co-occur more frequently than do others. For example, a person with antisocial personality disorder is highly likely to meet diagnostic criteria for substance abuse or dependence. In the DSM-IV-TR, these are diagnosed as separate disorders. Some have argued that childhood conduct disorder, adult antisocial personality disorder, alcohol dependence, and other forms of drug dependence co-occur so often that they should be considered different manifestations of one underlying disease process or vulnerability (Krueger et al., 2005). These different types of problems could be jointly considered "externalizing disorders." Others have found that a person with a diagnosis of major depressive disorder is highly likely to meet the diagnostic criteria for an anxiety disorder. Some have recommended grouping depressive and anxious disorders together (Watson, 2005).

A more subtle issue about the large number of diagnoses is that many risk factors seem to trigger more than one disorder. For example, early trauma, dysregulation of stress hormones, tendencies to attend to and remember negative information about the self, and neuroticism all seem to increase risk for a broad range of anxiety disorders as well as mood disorders (Harvey et al., 2004). Genes that increase the risk for anxiety disorders also seem to increase the risk for depression (Kendler et al., 2003). Some genes increase risk for the externalizing disorders as a whole (Kendler, Prescott, et al., 2003). Similarly, selective serotonin reuptake inhibitors (SSRIs), such as Prozac, often seem to relieve symptoms of anxiety as well as depression (Van Ameringen et al., 2001). Does this mean that we should lump anxiety and depressive disorders into one category? Beliefs about this differ. Some think we should lump, others think we should keep these finer distinctions.

Categorical Diagnoses versus Continuum In the DSM, Axes I and II rely on **categorical** (yes–no) **classification**. Does the patient have schizophrenia or not? This type of classification does not consider continuity between normal and abnormal behavior. For example, in Table 3.2 we see that the diagnosis of mania requires the presence of three symptoms from a list of seven, or four if the person's mood is irritable. But why require three symptoms rather than two or five? A categorical system forces clinicians to define one threshold as "diagnosable." There is often little research support for the threshold defined. Indeed, as many as 20–50 percent of people seeking treatment fall into the "not otherwise specified" category (Helmuth, 2003); that is, many people have mild symptoms that appear to fall just below the threshold for a diagnosis. Many people who have subthreshold symptoms of a diagnosis still seek and receive extensive health care treatment (Johnson, Weissman, & Klerman, 1992). Categorical diagnoses foster a false impression of discontinuity (Widiger & Samuel, 2005).

Consider an illustration of a problem with categorical systems. A central feature of narcissistic personality disorder is grandiosity. As Drew Westen quipped, "Anyone who has been on a bad blind date knows that narcissism and grandiosity are fairly common" (Helmuth, 2003, p. 809). If you were considering a blind date, you might rather know how much grandiosity was present, rather than whether grandiosity was present at all. Because anxiety, depression, and many personality disorder symptoms are common, it may be more helpful to know their severity rather than if they are present.

In contrast to categorical classification, **dimensional** systems describe the *degree* of an entity that is present (e.g., a 1-to-10 scale of anxiety, where 1 represents minimal and 10 extreme). Diagnosis involves a profile on several dimensions. (See Figure 3.1 for an illustration of the difference between dimensional and categorical approaches.) A **dimensional diagnostic system** can subsume a categorical system by specifying a threshold. This capability is a potential advantage of the dimensional approach.

One reason categorical systems are popular is that they define a threshold for treatment. Consider high blood pressure (hypertension), a topic discussed at length in Chapter 7. Blood pressure measurements form a continuum, which clearly fits a dimensional approach; yet by defining a threshold for high blood pressure, doctors can feel more certain about when to offer treatment. Similarly, a threshold for clinical depression may help demarcate a point where treatment is recommended. Although the cutoffs are likely to be somewhat arbitrary, they can provide helpful guidance.

In sum, the categorical versus dimensional issue is not resolved. In any categorical approach, there will be questions about thresholds for diagnosis.

Reliability of the DSM   Suppose you were concerned about your mental health, and you went to see two psychologists. Consider the distress you would feel if the two psychologists disagreed—one told you that you had schizophrenia, and the other told you that you had bipolar disorder. Diagnostic systems must have high interrater reliability to be useful. Before DSM-III, reliability for DSM diagnoses was poor, mainly because the criteria for making a diagnosis were not clear (see Figure 3.2 for an illustration of interrater reliability).

The increased explicitness of the DSM criteria has improved reliability. Nonetheless, because clinicians might not rely on the criteria precisely, the reliability of the DSM in everyday usage may be a bit lower than that seen in research studies. Even when following criteria, there is some room for disagreement in DSM-IV-TR. Consider again the criteria for mania in Table 3.2. What does it mean to say that mood is abnormally elevated? Or when is "involvement in pleasurable activities that have a high potential for painful consequences" excessive? Such judgments set the stage for the insertion of cultural biases as well as the clinician's own personal ideas of what the average person should be doing. Because different clinicians may adopt different definitions for symptoms like "elevated mood," achieving high reliability is likely to be a challenge.

How Valid Are Diagnostic Categories?   Construct validity is considered the most important type of validity for diagnosis. The diagnoses of DSM are referred to as constructs because they are inferred, not proven, entities. Every diagnosis is based on a pattern of symptoms. With the exception of IQ tests for mental retardation or polysomnography for sleep disorders, we have no

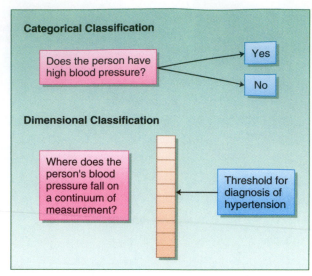

Figure 3.1 Categorical versus dimensional systems of diagnosis.

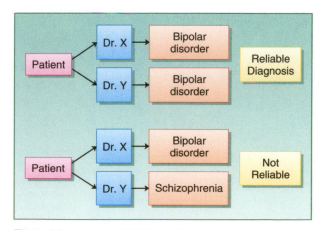

Figure 3.2 Interrater reliability. In this example, the diagnosis of the first patient is reliable—both clinicians diagnose bipolar disorder—whereas the diagnosis of the second is not reliable.

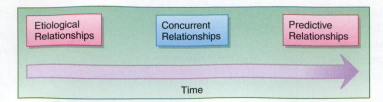

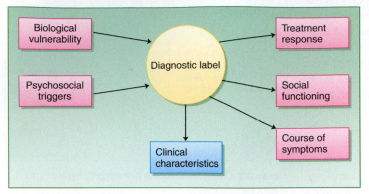

(a)

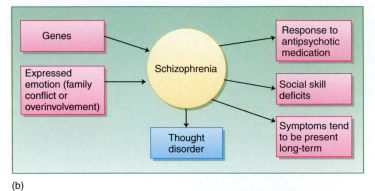

(b)

Figure 3.3 Construct validity. An example of the types of information a diagnosis might help predict.

laboratory tests, neurobiological markers, or genetic indicators to use in making diagnoses. A diagnosis of schizophrenia, then, does not have the same status as a diagnosis of diabetes, where we have laboratory tests.

One way of thinking about diagnosis is to ask whether the system helps organize different observations (see Figure 3.3 for one example of how a diagnosis might help organize different observations). Diagnoses have construct validity if they help make accurate predictions. What types of predictions should a good diagnostic category facilitate? One would hope that a diagnosis would inform us about related clinical characteristics, such as poor social skills in people with schizophrenia.

The DSM specifies that symptoms alone are not enough to qualify for a diagnosis. Rather, a person must experience either impairment or distress to meet criteria for a diagnosis. There are many different possible signs of impairment, including difficulty with employment, academic accomplishments, or relationships. As shown in Table 3.5, most major psychiatric disorders are associated with a substantial increase in the risk of marital distress as well as missed days at work.

Beyond capturing the most common difficulties for a person with a diagnosis, one would hope that a diagnosis would inform us about what to expect next—the likely course of the disorder and response to different treatments. Perhaps most importantly, one would hope that the diagnosis relates to possible causes of the disorder, for example, a genetic predisposition or a biochemical imbalance. A diagnosis with strong construct validity should help predict a broad range of characteristics (see Figure 3.3).

The central question, then, is whether diagnoses made with the DSM criteria reveal anything useful about patients. We have organized this book around the major DSM diagnostic categories because we believe that they do indeed possess some construct validity. Certain categories have less validity than others, however, and we will discuss some gaps in the validity of specific diagnostic categories

Table 3.5 Rates of Marital Distress and Missed Work Days among People with Mental Illness in the Past Year

Disorder	Odds of Marital Distress for a Given Diagnosis Compared to No Mental Illness	Odds of Missed Work Days for a Given Diagnosis Compared to No Mental Illness
Panic disorder	1.28	3.32
Specific phobia	1.34	2.82
Social phobia	1.93	2.74
Generalized anxiety disorder	2.54	1.15
Posttraumatic stress disorder	2.30	2.05
Major depressive disorder	1.68	2.14
Bipolar I or II disorder	3.60	Not assessed
Alcohol use disorder	2.78	2.54

Source: Information on marital distress drawn from M. A. Whisman (2007). Information on work-loss days drawn from The ESEMeD/MHEDEA 2000 investigators (2004).

Note: Age, gender, education, and race/ethnicity are controlled for in marital distress analyses, and age and gender are controlled for in work-loss analyses. Diagnoses were based on the Composite International Diagnostic Interview. Marital distress was measured using a 14-item version of the Dyadic Adjustment Scale. Missed work days were measured during the month before the interview.

FOCUS ON DISCOVERY 3.3

Possible Changes for DSM-V

DSM-V is not likely to appear before 2012. But researchers are well at work on the possible changes. Some of the proposals are described below (Helmuth, 2003; Kupfer et al., 2002).

Personal health index. DSM-V may include a place to list the strengths of a patient.

Reorganizing categories based on overlap. Currently, some diagnoses overlap so much that people have wondered whether they should be separated. For example, depression and anxiety often strike the same people, share many risk factors, and respond similarly to antidepressant medication (Watson, 2005). Do they still belong in separate categories? In addition, overlap is a particular issue for personality disorders and disorders usually first diagnosed in infancy, childhood, or adolescence.

Dimensional approach to diagnoses. As described in the text, some have argued against a categorical approach to diagnosis. The next round of DSM may include specific dimensions for clinicians to evaluate. This approach is receiving considerable attention as a way to think about personality disorders.

Organizing diagnoses by causes. Currently, DSM-IV-TR defines diagnoses entirely on the basis of symptoms. Some have argued that advances in neuroscience and behavioral approaches to psychology could help us rethink this approach. For example, schizophrenia and schizotypal personality disorder share a great deal of genetic overlap. Could these ties be reflected in the diagnostic system? Others have proposed organizing diagnoses based on parallels in neurotransmitter activity, temperament, emotion dysregulation, or social triggers. Most, however, agree that we still need much more knowledge to be able to develop this type of system.

Defining disability. DSM-IV-TR requires the presence of disability for a diagnosis to be made. Some have argued that we should be considering symptoms and disability separately so that we can begin to understand what types of variables predict disability in the face of symptoms.

It isn't clear whether any of these changes will be adopted; substantial debate and research are likely to occur between then and now. Ongoing updates will be posted at http://dsm5.org/index.cfm. Some have argued that changes in the next round should be minor and that science supports most of the current diagnoses.

---

in later chapters. As research findings accumulate on whether each category has construct validity, this is likely to shape the next edition of the DSM (see Focus on Discovery 3.3 for a discussion of likely changes in DSM-V).

General Criticisms of Diagnosing Mental Illness

Although we described many advantages of diagnosis in the beginning of this chapter, it is also clear that diagnoses can have negative effects on a person. Consider how your life might be changed by receiving the diagnosis of schizophrenia. You might become worried that someone will recognize your disorder. Or you might fear the onset of another episode. You might worry about your ability to deal with new challenges. The fact that you are a "former mental patient" could have a stigmatizing effect. Friends and loved ones might treat you differently, and employment might be hard to find.

There is little doubt that diagnosis can have negative consequences. Research shows that many people view people with mental illness negatively, and patients and their families often encounter stigma against mental illness (Wahl, 1999). As we discussed in Chapter 1, stigma concerning mental disorders remains a huge problem.

Another concern about diagnosis is that it can result in a loss of information about that person, because once classified by a diagnostic category, we may lose sight of the uniqueness of that person. Because of this concern, the American Psychological Association recommends that people avoid using words like *schizophrenic* or *depressive* to describe people. Consider that we do not call people with medical illnesses by their disease (e.g., you aren't likely to hear someone with cancer described as the *canceric*). Rather, psychologists are encouraged to use phrases such as *a person with schizophrenia*.

Even with more careful language, some maintain that diagnosis shapes us to focus on illnesses and, in doing so, to ignore important differences among people. Unfortunately, this criticism ignores a fundamental truth: it is human nature to categorize whenever we think about anything. Some would argue, then, that if we use categories anyway, it is best to systematically develop the categories. If one accepts this perspective, then the question is how well the current system does in grouping similar illnesses.

Quick Summary

Despite the major improvements in the DSM, a number of problems remain. Some argue that there are too many diagnoses, and others challenge the use of a categorical rather than a dimensional approach to diagnoses. Reliability is substantially higher than it was for DSM-II, but there is still some disagreement across clinicians regarding some symptoms and diagnoses. Finally, the field as a whole faces a huge challenge; researchers are focused on validating this diagnostic system by trying to identify the causal patterns, symptom patterns, and treatment that can be predicted by a given diagnosis. In sum,

although the DSM is continually improving, it is far from perfect. We can expect more changes and refinements over the next several years. Regardless of the diagnostic system used, there are certain problems inherent in diagnosing people with mental illness; it is important to be aware of the potential stigma associated with diagnoses and the tendency to ignore a person's strengths when focusing on diagnoses. APA recommends using phrases such *as person with schizophrenia* rather than *schizophrenic* as one way to be conscious that a person is much more than his or her diagnosis.

Check Your Knowledge 3.2

Answer the questions.

1. Some researchers have argued that DSM-V should "lump" diagnoses so that we have fewer categories. List three reasons why some think DSM-V should lump diagnoses.

2. Most of the axes in DSM-IV-TR are categorical, but one is dimensional. Which one is dimensional?

3. What are three broad types of characteristics that a valid diagnosis should help predict?

Psychological Assessment

To make a diagnosis, mental health professionals can use a variety of assessment measures and tools. Beyond helping to make a diagnosis, psychological assessment techniques are used in other important ways. For example, assessment methods are often used to identify appropriate therapeutic interventions. And repeated assessments are very useful in monitoring the effects of treatment over time. In addition, assessments are fundamental to conducting research on the causes of disorder.

We will see that beyond the basic interview, many of the assessment techniques stem from the paradigms presented in Chapter 2. We discuss here clinical interviews; measures for assessing stress; personality tests, including objective and projective tests; intelligence tests; and behavioral and cognitive assessment techniques. Although we present these methods individually, a complete psychological assessment of a person will often entail combining several assessment techniques. The data from the various techniques complement each other and provide a more complete picture of the person. In short, there is no one best assessment measure. Rather, using multiple techniques and multiple sources of information will provide the best assessment.

Clinical Interviews

Most of us have probably been interviewed at one time or another, although the conversation may have been so informal that we did not regard it as an interview. For mental health professionals, there are both formal, structured clinical interviews as well as informal and less structured clinical interviews that are used in psychopathological assessment.

Characteristics of Clinical Interviews
One way in which a **clinical interview** is perhaps different from a casual conversation is the attention the interviewer pays to how the respondent answers questions—or does not answer them. For example, if a client is recounting marital

conflicts, the clinician will generally be attentive to any emotion accompanying the comments. If the person does not seem upset about a difficult situation, the answers probably will be understood differently from how they would be interpreted if the person was crying or agitated while relating the story.

The interviewer's choice of paradigm influences the type of information sought, how it is obtained, and how it is interpreted. A psychodynamically trained clinician is likely to remain skeptical of verbal reports because the psychodynamic paradigm holds that the most significant aspects of a disturbed person's developmental history may be repressed into the unconscious. By the same token, the cognitive behavioral clinician is likely to focus on current environmental conditions that can be related to changes in the person's behavior—for example, the circumstances in which the person becomes anxious as well as the thoughts the person articulates about the anxiety. Thus, the informal clinical interview does not follow one prescribed course but varies with the paradigm adopted by the interviewer.

Great skill is necessary to carry out good clinical interviews. Clinicians, regardless of the paradigm adopted, recognize the importance of establishing rapport with the client. The interviewer must obtain the trust of the person; it is naive to assume that a client will easily reveal information to another, even to an authority figure with the title "Doctor." Even a client who sincerely, perhaps desperately, wants to recount intensely personal problems to a professional may not be able to do so without help.

Although it is illegal to discriminate based on mental illness, many employers do so. Stigma must be considered when giving a person a diagnosis of a mental disorder. (Ryan McVay/PhotoDisc, Inc./Getty Images.)

Most clinicians empathize with their clients in an effort to draw them out and to encourage them to elaborate on their concerns. An accurate summary statement of what the client has been saying can help sustain the momentum of talk about painful and possibly embarrassing events and feelings, and an accepting attitude toward personal disclosures dispels the fear that revealing "secrets of the heart" (London, 1964) to another human being will have disastrous consequences.

Interviews vary in the degree to which they are structured. In practice, most clinicians probably operate from only the vaguest outlines. Exactly how information is collected is left largely up to the particular interviewer and depends, too, on the responsiveness and responses of the interviewee. Through years of training and clinical experience, each clinician develops ways of asking questions with which he or she is comfortable and that seem to draw out the information that will be of maximum benefit to the client. Thus, to the extent that an interview is unstructured, the interviewer must rely on intuition and general experience. As a consequence, reliability for unstructured clinical interviews is probably lower than for structured interviews; that is, two interviewers may reach different conclusions about the same patient.

Structured Interviews At times, mental health professionals need to collect standardized information, particularly for making diagnostic judgments based on the DSM. To meet that need, investigators have developed structured interviews, such as the Structured Clinical Interview (SCID) for Axis I of DSM-IV (Spitzer, Gibbon, & Williams, 1996), that assists researchers and clinicians in making diagnostic decisions. A **structured interview** is one in which the questions are set out in a prescribed fashion for the interviewer.

The SCID is a branching interview, that is, the client's response to one question determines the next question that is asked. It also contains detailed instructions to the interviewer concerning when and how to probe in detail and when to go on to questions about another diagnosis. Most symptoms are rated on a three-point scale of severity, with instructions in the interview schedule for directly translating the symptom ratings into diagnoses. The initial questions

Structured interviews are widely used to make reliable diagnoses. (© BSIP/Phototake.)

pertaining to obsessive-compulsive disorder (discussed in Chapter 5) are presented in Figure 3.4. The interviewer begins by asking about obsessions. If the responses elicit a rating of 1 (absent), the interviewer turns to questions about compulsions. If the patient's responses again elicit a rating of 1, the interviewer is instructed to go to the questions for posttraumatic stress disorder. On the other hand, if positive responses (2 or 3) are elicited about obsessive-compulsive disorder, the interviewer continues with further questions about that problem.

Results of several studies demonstrate that the SCID achieves good interrater reliability for most diagnostic categories. As shown in Table 3.6, interrater reliability is a bit low for some of the anxiety disorders. Other structured interviews with good reliability have been developed for diagnosing personality disorders and for more specific disorders, such as the anxiety disorders, and for diagnosing disorders of childhood (DiNardo et al., 1993; Shaffer et al., 2000). With adequate training, interrater reliability for structured interviews is generally good (Blanchard & Brown, 1998).

In practice, most clinicians review the DSM symptoms in an informal manner without using a structured interview. Note, however, that clinicians using unstructured diagnostic interviews tend to miss comorbid diagnoses that often accompany a primary diagnosis (Zimmerman & Mattia, 1999).

Assessment of Stress

Given the centrality of stress to nearly all the disorders we consider in this book, measuring stress is clearly important in the total assessment picture. Broadly, **stress** can be conceptualized as the subjective experience of distress in response to perceived environmental problems. Life stressors can be defined as the environmental problems that trigger the subjective sense of stress. Various scales and methods have been developed to measure life stress. Here we examine three: the Social Readjustment Rating Scale, the Assessment of Daily Experience, and the Life Events and Difficulties Schedule.

The Social Readjustment Rating Scale

In the 1960s two researchers, Holmes and Rahe (1967), asked a large group of men in the military to describe life events they had encountered. Then they gave that list of life events to a large group of people and asked them to rate each item according to its intensity and the amount of time they thought they would need to adjust to it. Marriage was arbitrarily assigned a stress value of 500; all other items were then evaluated using this reference point. For example, an event twice as stressful as marriage would be assigned a value of 1,000, and an event one-fifth as stressful as marriage would be assigned a value of 100. The average ratings assigned to the events by the respondents in Holmes and Rahe's study are shown in Table 3.7. From this study Holmes and Rahe created the Social Readjustment Rating Scale (SRRS). A respondent checks off the life events experienced during the time period in question. Ratings are then totaled for all the events actually experienced to produce a Life Change Unit (LCU) score, a weighted sum of events.

The SRRS has been criticized because it contains items that are both the triggers and the outcomes of psychological symptoms. For example, the item "change in sleeping habits" could be the result of depression or anxiety. Moreover, the SRRS was developed over 40 years ago based on the experiences of one group of men, rendering some of the original ratings of stressful life events potentially out of sync with the times. Two studies gave the 43 original events on the SRRS to community residents and found that a number of the ratings changed compared to the original ratings from the 1960s, with some items being rated as less stressful (e.g., changing jobs) and others being rated as more stressful (e.g., change in financial status) (Miller & Rahe, 1997; Scully, Tosi, & Banning, 2000). The SRRS also has been criticized because some items (e.g., vacation or change in eating habits) could reflect positive rather than negative life changes. Another criticism of the SRRS is that it relies on a retrospective method, asking participants to recall the stressful life events that they experienced over a long time period. Retrospective reports are subject to considerable distortion and forgetting.

Table 3.6 Interrater Reliability of Selected DSM Diagnoses

Diagnosis	Kappa
Axis I disorders	
Major depressive disorder	.80
Dysthymic disorder	.76
Bipolar disorder	.84
Schizophrenia	.79
Alcohol dependence/abuse	1.00
Other substance dependence/abuse	1.00
Panic disorder	.65
Social phobia	.63
Obsessive-compulsive disorder	.57
Generalized anxiety disorder	.63
Posttraumatic stress disorder	.88
Any eating disorder	.77
Axis II disorders	
Avoidant	.97
Dependent	.86
Obsessive-compulsive	.83
Depressive	.65
Paranoid	.93
Schizotypal	.91
Schizoid	.91
Histrionic	.92
Narcissistic	.98
Borderline	.91
Antisocial	.95

Sources: Estimates for bipolar disorder are based on a study using DSM-III-R criteria (Williams et al., 1992), which are largely comparable to DSM-IV-TR. Estimates for schizophrenia are drawn from Flaum et al. (1998). Other Axis I estimates are drawn from Zanarini et al. (2000), and Axis II estimates are based on Maffei et al. (1997).

Note: The numbers here are a statistic called kappa, which measures the proportion of agreement over and above what would be expected by chance. Generally, kappas over 0.70 are considered good.

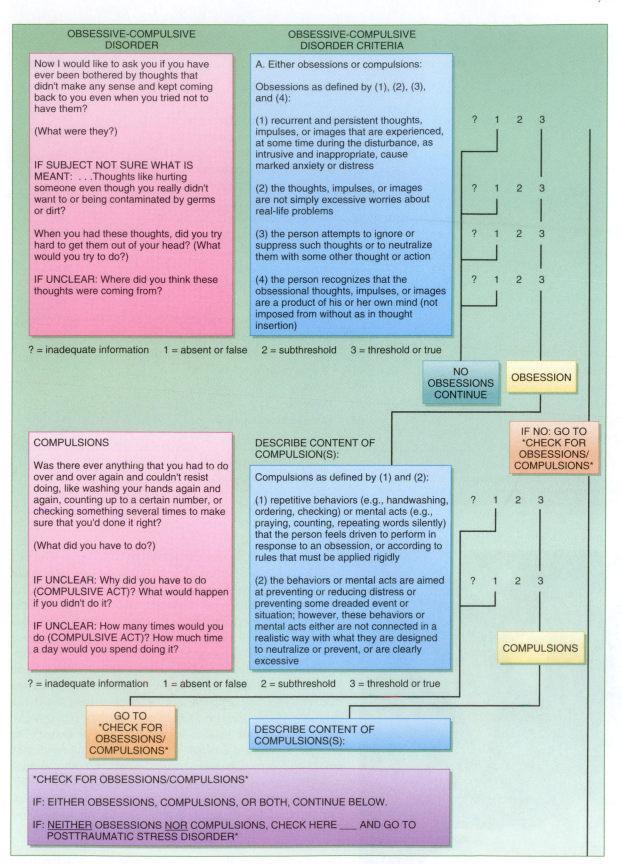

OBSESSIVE-COMPULSIVE DISORDER

Now I would like to ask you if you have ever been bothered by thoughts that didn't make any sense and kept coming back to you even when you tried not to have them?

(What were they?)

IF SUBJECT NOT SURE WHAT IS MEANT: . . .Thoughts like hurting someone even though you really didn't want to or being contaminated by germs or dirt?

When you had these thoughts, did you try hard to get them out of your head? (What would you try to do?)

IF UNCLEAR: Where did you think these thoughts were coming from?

OBSESSIVE-COMPULSIVE DISORDER CRITERIA

A. Either obsessions or compulsions:

Obsessions as defined by (1), (2), (3), and (4):

(1) recurrent and persistent thoughts, impulses, or images that are experienced, at some time during the disturbance, as intrusive and inappropriate, cause marked anxiety or distress   ? 1 2 3

(2) the thoughts, impulses, or images are not simply excessive worries about real-life problems   ? 1 2 3

(3) the person attempts to ignore or suppress such thoughts or to neutralize them with some other thought or action   ? 1 2 3

(4) the person recognizes that the obsessional thoughts, impulses, or images are a product of his or her own mind (not imposed from without as in thought insertion)   ? 1 2 3

? = inadequate information   1 = absent or false   2 = subthreshold   3 = threshold or true

NO OBSESSIONS CONTINUE

OBSESSION

IF NO: GO TO *CHECK FOR OBSESSIONS/ COMPULSIONS*

COMPULSIONS

Was there ever anything that you had to do over and over again and couldn't resist doing, like washing your hands again and again, counting up to a certain number, or checking something several times to make sure that you'd done it right?

(What did you have to do?)

IF UNCLEAR: Why did you have to do (COMPULSIVE ACT)? What would happen if you didn't do it?

IF UNCLEAR: How many times would you do (COMPULSIVE ACT)? How much time a day would you spend doing it?

DESCRIBE CONTENT OF COMPULSION(S):

Compulsions as defined by (1) and (2):

(1) repetitive behaviors (e.g., handwashing, ordering, checking) or mental acts (e.g., praying, counting, repeating words silently) that the person feels driven to perform in response to an obsession, or according to rules that must be applied rigidly   ? 1 2 3

(2) the behaviors or mental acts are aimed at preventing or reducing distress or preventing some dreaded event or situation; however, these behaviors or mental acts either are not connected in a realistic way with what they are designed to neutralize or prevent, or are clearly excessive   ? 1 2 3

? = inadequate information   1 = absent or false   2 = subthreshold   3 = threshold or true

COMPULSIONS

GO TO *CHECK FOR OBSESSIONS/ COMPULSIONS*

DESCRIBE CONTENT OF COMPULSIONS(S):

CHECK FOR OBSESSIONS/COMPULSIONS

IF: EITHER OBSESSIONS, COMPULSIONS, OR BOTH, CONTINUE BELOW.

IF: NEITHER OBSESSIONS NOR COMPULSIONS, CHECK HERE ___ AND GO TO POSTTRAUMATIC STRESS DISORDER*

Figure 3.4 Sample item from the SCID. Reprinted by permission of New York State Psychiatric Institute Biometrics Research Division. Copyright © 1996 by the Board of Trustees of the Leland Stanford Junior University.

Table 3.7 Social Readjustment Rating Scale (SRRS)

Rank	Life Event	Mean Value	Rank	Life Event	Mean Value
1	Death of spouse	100	23	Child leaving home	29
2	Divorce	73	24	Trouble with in-laws	29
3	Marital separation	65	25	Outstanding personal achievement	28
4	Jail term	63	26	Spouse begins or stops work	26
5	Death of close family member	63	27	Begin or end school	26
6	Personal injury or illness	53	28	Change in living conditions	25
7	Marriage	50[a]	29	Revision of personal habits	24
8	Fired from work	47	30	Trouble with boss	23
9	Marital reconciliation	45	31	Change in work hours or conditions	20
10	Retirement	45	32	Change in residence	20
11	Change in health of family member	44	33	Change in schools	20
12	Pregnancy	40	34	Change in recreation	19
13	Sex difficulties	39	35	Change in church activities	19
14	New family member	39	36	Change in social activities	18
15	Business readjustment	39	37	Mortgage or loan less than $10,000[b]	17
16	Change in financial state	38	38	Change in sleeping habits	16
17	Death of close friend	37	39	Change in number of family get-togethers	15
18	Change to different line of work	36	40	Change in eating habits	15
19	Change in number of arguments with spouse	35	41	Vacation	13
20	Mortgage over $10,000[b]	31	42	Christmas	12
21	Foreclosure of mortgage or loan	30	43	Minor violations of the law	11
22	Change in responsibilities at work	29			

Source: Holmes and Rahe (1967).

[a]Marriage was arbitrarily assigned a stress value of 500; no event was found to be any more than twice as stressful. Here the values are reduced proportionally and range up to 100.
[b]In the mid-1960s, a mortgage like this was considered very large.
Reprinted from Holmes, T.H., and Rahe, R.H. (1967). The social readjustment rating scale. *Journal of Psychosomatic Research,* 213–218, with permission from Elsevier.

The LEDS focuses on major stressors, such as deaths, job losses, and romantic breakups. (Bob Falcetti Reportage/Getty Images News and Sport Services.)

Assessment of Daily Experience Problems with the SRRS led Stone and Neale (1982) to develop a new assessment of stress called the Assessment of Daily Experience (ADE). Because retrospective recall of moods, thoughts, or experiences over time may be inaccurate, the ADE allows persons to record and rate their daily experiences so that researchers can trace whether day-to-day stressors predict changes in symptoms. Consider, for example, how difficult it would be for you to recall accurately the exact thoughts you had a week earlier when you received a speeding ticket. Memory researchers have shown not only that simple forgetting leads to inaccurate retrospective recall but also that recalled information can be biased. For example, a report of a person's mood is overly influenced by moods the person has experienced most recently or most strongly (e.g., Fredrickson & Kahneman, 1993). In the ADE, stressors are rated every day to avoid retrospective-recall bias. Part of the ADE is shown in Figure 3.5. We will discuss how this measure relates to health in Chapter 7.

The Bedford College Life Events and Difficulties Schedule Another assessment technique that is widely used to study life stressors is the Bedford College Life Events and Difficulties Schedule (LEDS; Brown & Harris, 1978). The LEDS includes an interview that covers over 200 different kinds of stressors. Because the interview is only semistructured, the interviewer can tailor questions to cover stressors that might only occur to a small number of people. The interviewer and the interviewee work collaboratively to produce a calendar of each of the major events within a given time period (see Figure 3.6 for an example). After the interview, raters evaluate the severity and several other dimensions of each stressor. The LEDS was designed to address a number of problems in life stress assessment, including the need to evaluate the importance of any given life event in the context of a person's life circumstances. For example, pregnancy might have quite a different meaning for an unmarried 14-year-old girl compared to a 38-year-old woman who has been trying to conceive for a long time. A second goal of the LEDS is to exclude life events that might just be consequences of symptoms. For example, if a person misses work because he or she is too depressed to get out of bed, any consequent job problems should really be seen as the symptoms of disorder rather than a triggering life event. Finally, the LEDS includes a set of strategies to carefully date when a life stressor happened. Using this more careful assessment method, researchers have found that life stressors are robust predictors of episodes of anxiety, depression, schizophrenia, and even the common cold (Brown & Harris, 1989b; Cohen et al., 1998).

Personality Tests

Psychological tests further structure the process of assessment. The two most common types of psychological tests are personality tests and intelligence tests. Here, we will examine the two types of personality tests: self-report personality inventories and projective personality tests.

Self-Report Personality Inventories   In a **personality inventory**, the person is asked to complete a self-report questionnaire indicating whether statements assessing habitual tendencies apply to him or her. When these tests are developed, they are typically administered to many people to analyze how certain kinds of people tend to respond. Statistical norms for the test can thereby be established. This process is called **standardization**. The responses of a particular person can then be compared with the statistical norms.

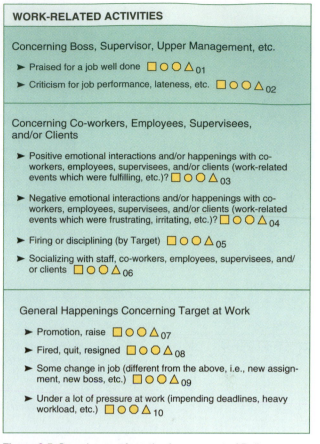

Figure 3.5 Sample page from the Assessment of Daily Experience scale (Stone & Neale, 1982). Respondents indicate whether an event occurred by circling the arrows to the left of the list of events. If an event has occurred, it is then rated on the dimensions of desirability, change, meaningfulness, and control using the enclosed spaces to the right.

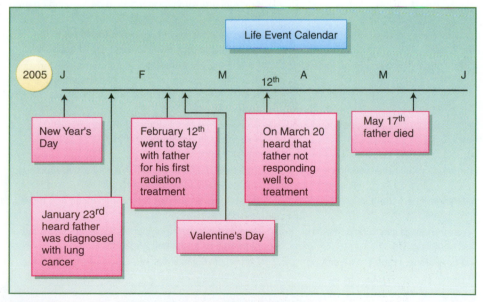

Figure 3.6 Example of a life events timeline. The LEDS interview is designed to capture the major stressors a person has encountered in the past year.

Perhaps the best known of these tests is the **Minnesota Multiphasic Personality Inventory (MMPI)**, developed in the early 1940s by Hathaway and McKinley (1943) and revised in 1989 (Butcher et al., 1989). The MMPI is called multiphasic because it was designed to detect a number of psychological problems. Over the years the MMPI has been widely used to screen large groups of people for whom clinical interviews are not feasible.

In developing the test, the investigators used several steps. First, many clinicians provided statements that they considered indicative of various mental problems. Second, patients diagnosed with particular disorders and people with no diagnoses were asked to rate whether hundreds of statements described them. Items were selected for the final version of the test if patients in one clinical group responded to them more often in a certain way than did those in other groups.

With additional refinements, sets of these items were established as scales for determining whether a respondent should be diagnosed in a particular way. If a person answered many of the items in a scale in the same way as had a certain diagnostic group, his or her behavior was expected to resemble that of the particular diagnostic group. The 10 scales are described in Table 3.8.

Table 3.8 Typical Clinical Interpretations of Items Similar to Those on the MMPI-2

Scale	Sample Item	Interpretation
? (cannot say)	This is merely the number of items left unanswered or marked both true and false.	A high score indicates evasiveness, reading difficulties, or other problems that could invalidate results of the test. A very high score could also suggest severe depression or obsessional tendencies.
L (Lie)	I approve of every person I meet. (True)	Person is trying to look good, to present self as someone with an ideal personality.
F (Infrequency) clinician.	Everything tastes sweet. (True)	Person is trying to look abnormal, perhaps to ensure getting special attention from the clinician.
K (Correction)	Things couldn't be going any better for me. (True)	Person is guarded, defensive in taking the test, wishes to avoid appearing incompetent or poorly adjusted.
1. Hs (Hypochondriasis)	I am seldom aware of tingling feelings in my body. (False)	Person is overly sensitive to and concerned about bodily sensations as signs of possible physical illness.
2. D (Depression)	Life usually feels worthwhile to me. (False)	Person is discouraged, pessimistic, sad, self-deprecating, feeling inadequate.
3. Hy (Hysteria)	My muscles often twitch for no apparent reason. (True)	Person has somatic complaints unlikely to be due to physical problems; also tends to be demanding and histrionic.
4. Pd (Psychopathy)	I don't care about what people think of me. (True)	Person expresses little concern for social mores, is irresponsible, has only superficial relationships.
5. Mf (Masculinity–Femininity)	I like taking care of plants and flowers. (True, female)	Person shows nontraditional gender characteristics (e.g., men with high scores tend to be artistic and sensitive; women with high scores tend to be rebellious and assertive).
6. Pa (Paranoia)	If they were not afraid of being caught, most people would lie and cheat. (True)	Person tends to misinterpret the motives of others, is suspicious and jealous, vengeful and brooding.
7. Pt (Psychasthenia)	I am not as competent as most other people I know. (True)	Person is overanxious, full of self-doubts, moralistic, and generally obsessive-compulsive.
8. Sc (Schizophrenia)	I sometimes smell things others don't sense. (True)	Person has bizarre sensory experiences and beliefs, is socially reclusive.
9. Ma (Hypomania)	Sometimes I have a strong impulse to do something that others will find appalling. (True)	Person has overly ambitious aspirations and can be hyperactive, impatient, and irritable.
10. Si (Social Introversion).	Rather than spend time alone, I prefer to be around other people. (False)	Person is very modest and shy, preferring solitary activities.

Sources: Hathaway & McKinley (1943); revised by Butcher et al. (1989).

Note: The first four scales assess the validity of the test; the numbered scales are the clinical or content scales.

The revised MMPI-2 (Butcher et al., 1989) was designed to improve validity and acceptability. The original sample assessed 65 years ago was composed mainly of white people from Minnesota and lacked representation of ethnic minorities. The new version was standardized using a sample that was much larger and more representative of 1980 U.S. census figures. Several items containing allusions to sexual adjustment, bowel and bladder functions, and excessive religiosity were removed because they were judged in some testing contexts to be needlessly intrusive and objectionable. Sexist wording was eliminated, along with outmoded idioms. New scales deal with substance abuse, emotions, and marital problems.

Aside from these differences, the MMPI-2 is otherwise quite similar to the original, having the same format, yielding the same scale scores and profiles (Ben-Porath & Butcher, 1989; Graham, 1988) and in general providing continuity with the vast literature already existing on the original MMPI (Graham, 1990). An extensive research literature shows that the MMPI-2 is reliable and has adequate criterion validity when it is related to diagnoses made by clinicians and to ratings made by spouses (Ganellan, 1996; Vacha-Hasse et al., 2001).

Like many other personality inventories, the MMPI-2 can now be administered and scored by computer. Many available computer programs even provide narratives about the respondent. Of course, the validity of the printouts is only as good as the program, which in turn is only as good as the competency and experience of the psychologist who wrote it. Figure 3.7 shows a hypothetical profile. Such profiles can be used in conjunction with a therapist's evaluation to help diagnose a client, assess personality functioning and coping style, and identify likely obstacles to treatment.

You may wonder whether it would be easy to fake answers that suggest no psychopathology. For example, a superficial knowledge of contemporary psychopathology research could alert

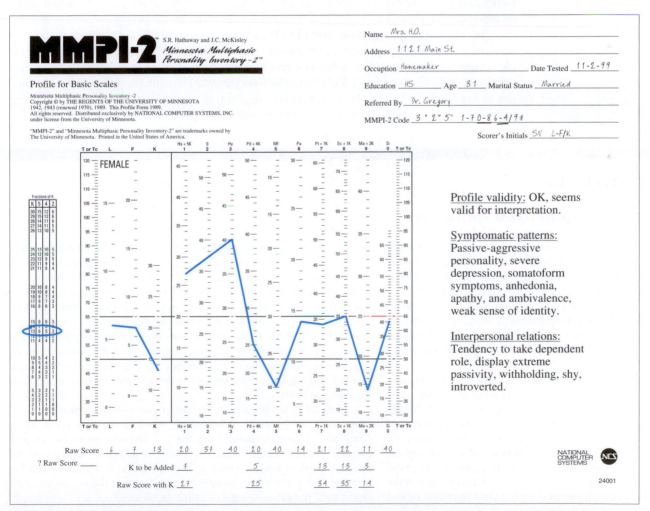

Figure 3.7 Hypothetical MMPI-2 profile.

someone that to be regarded as psychologically healthy, he or she must not admit to worrying a great deal about receiving messages from television.

As shown in Table 3.8, the MMPI-2 includes several "validity scales" designed to detect deliberately faked responses. In one of these, the lie scale, a series of statements sets a trap for the person who is trying to look too good. An item on the lie scale might be, "I read the newspaper editorials every day." The assumption is that few people would be able to endorse such a statement honestly. Persons who endorse a large number of the statements in the lie scale might be attempting to present themselves in a good light. High scores on the F scale also discriminate between people trying to fake psychopathology and real patients (Bagby et al., 2002). If a person obtains high scores on the lie or F scale, his or her profile might be viewed with skepticism. People who are aware of these validity scales, however, can effectively fake a normal profile (Baer & Sekirnjak, 1997; Walters & Clopton, 2000). In most testing circumstances, however, people do not want to falsify their responses, because they want to be helped. Focus on Discovery 3.4 discusses other issues surrounding the validity of self-report questionnaires.

Projective Personality Tests   A **projective test** is a psychological assessment tool in which a set of standard stimuli—inkblots or drawings—ambiguous enough to allow variation in responses is presented to the person. The assumption is that because the stimulus materials are unstructured and ambiguous, the person's responses will be determined primarily by unconscious processes and will reveal his or her true attitudes, motivations, and modes of behavior. This notion is referred to as the **projective hypothesis**.

If a patient reports seeing eyes in an ambiguous inkblot, for example, the projective hypothesis might be that the patient tends toward paranoia. The use of projective tests assumes that the respondent would be either unable or unwilling to express his or her true feelings if asked directly. As you might have guessed, projective techniques are derived from the psychodynamic paradigm.

The **Thematic Apperception Test (TAT)** is a projective test. In this test a person is shown a series of black-and-white pictures one by one and asked to tell a story related to each. For example, a patient seeing a picture of a boy observing a youth baseball game from behind a fence may tell a story that contains angry references to the boy's parents. The clinician may, through the projective hypothesis, infer that the patient harbors resentment toward his or her parents. There are few reliable scoring methods for this test, and the norms are based on a small and limited sample

FOCUS ON DISCOVERY 3.4

Underreporting of Stigmatized Behaviors

A survey of self-reported drug use, sexual behavior, and violence highlights the importance of the setting in establishing the validity of what people will tell about their actions and attitudes (Turner et al., 1998). Findings from self-report questionnaires were compared with results from a novel self-report method—boys and young men (ages 15 to 19) listened by themselves through headphones to questions probing risky, often stigmatized behavioral practices and then indicated whether they had engaged in those behaviors by pressing keys on a computer keyboard labeled Yes and No.

Compared to a matched control group who responded to the same items on a paper-and-pencil questionnaire, many more of the computer respondents admitted to having engaged in a range of high-risk behaviors. For example, they were almost 14 times more likely to report having sex with an intravenous drug user (2.8 percent versus 0.2 percent), more than twice as likely to report having been paid for sex (3.8 percent versus 1.6 percent), and almost twice as likely to report having used cocaine (6.0 percent versus 3.3 percent). (One can safely assume that the differences would have been even greater if the boys had been interviewed

by an adult researcher facing them across a table, another method that has been used to collect such survey data.) No differences showed up on questions directed at nonstigmatized or legal behaviors such as having sex with a female in the preceding year (47.8 percent for computer users versus 49.6 percent for paper-and-pencil questionnaires) or drinking alcohol in the past year (69.2 percent versus 65.9 percent).

If these findings show nothing else, they strongly suggest that the frequencies of problematic behavior as determined by questionnaire or interview studies may be underestimates and that social problems such as needle sharing and unsafe sex may be considerably more common than most people believe.

In an effort to obtain more accurate reports about stigmatized, sensitive, risky, or even illegal behaviors, investigators may apply for a Certificate of Confidentiality from the U.S. Department of Health and Human Services. These certificates provides additional protection for research participants by ensuring that sensitive information can be revealed during the research study without fear that the researchers will report their responses to legal or other authorities.

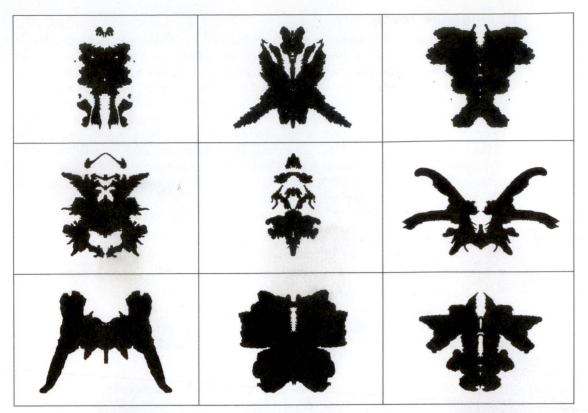

Figure 3.8 In the Rorschach test the client is shown a series of inkblots and is asked what the blots look like.

(i.e., few norms for people of different ethnic or cultural backgrounds). The construct validity of the TAT is also limited (Lilienfeld, Wood, & Garb, 2000). The **Rorschach Inkblot Test** is perhaps the best-known projective technique. In the Rorschach test, a person is shown 10 inkblots (for similar inkblots, see Figure 3.8), one at a time, and asked to tell what the blots look like. Half the inkblots are in black, white, and shades of gray; two also have red splotches; and three are in pastel colors.

Exner (1978) designed the most commonly used system for scoring the Rorschach test. The Exner scoring system concentrates on the perceptual and cognitive patterns in a person's responses. The person's responses are viewed as a sample of how he or she perceptually and cognitively organizes real-life situations (Exner, 1986). For example, Erdberg and Exner (1984) concluded from the research literature that respondents who express a great deal of human movement in their Rorschach responses (e.g., "The man is running to catch a plane") tend to use inner resources when coping with their needs, whereas those whose Rorschach responses involve color ("The red spot is a kidney") are more likely to seek interaction with the environment. Rorschach suggested this approach to scoring in his original manual, *Psychodiagnostics: A Diagnostic Test Based on Perception* (1921), but he died only 8 months after publishing his 10 inkblots, and his immediate followers devised other methods of interpreting the test.

The Exner scoring system has norms, although the sample on which they are based was rather small and did not represent different ethnicities and cultures well. Though many clinical practitioners still rely on the projective hypothesis in analyzing Rorschach responses, Exner's work has attracted a good deal of attention from academic researchers. Regarding its reliability and validity, this work has enthusiastic supporters as well as equally harsh critics (e.g., Hunsley & Bailey, 1999; Lilienfeld et al., 2000; Meyer & Archer, 2001). Perhaps trying to make a blanket statement about the validity of the Rorschach (or the MMPI-2) is not the right approach. The test appears to have more validity in assessing some issues than others. For example, limited evidence suggests that the Rorschach may have validity in identifying schizophrenia, borderline personality disorder, and dependent personality traits, but it remains unclear whether it does so better than other assessment techniques (Lilienfeld et al., 2000). In other words, it is unclear whether the Rorschach provides information that could not be obtained more simply—for example, through an interview.

During a ride in the country with his two children, Hermann Rorschach (1884–1922), Swiss psychiatrist, noticed that what they saw in the clouds reflected their personalities. From this observation came the famous inkblot test. (Courtesy National Library of Medicine.)

John Exner developed the most widely used scoring system for the Rorschach test. (Courtesy Dr. John E. Exner.)

Intelligence Tests

Alfred Binet, a French psychologist, originally constructed tests to help the Parisian school board predict which children were in need of special schooling. Intelligence testing has since developed into one of the largest psychological industries. An **intelligence test**, often referred to as an IQ test, is a way of assessing a person's current mental ability. IQ tests are based on the assumption that a detailed sample of a person's current intellectual functioning can predict how well he or she will perform in school, and most are individually administered. The most commonly administered tests include the Wechsler Adult Intelligence Scale, 4th edition (WAIS-IV, 2008); the Wechsler Intelligence Scale for Children, 4th edition (WISC-IV, 2003); the Wechsler Preschool and Primary Scale of Intelligence, 3rd edition (WPPSI-III, 2002); and the Stanford–Binet, 5th edition (SB:V,2003); IQ tests are regularly updated, and like personality inventories, they are standardized.

Beyond predicting school performance, intelligence tests are also used in other ways:

- In conjunction with achievement tests, to diagnose learning disabilities and to identify areas of strengths and weaknesses for academic planning
- To help determine whether a person has mental retardation
- To identify intellectually gifted children so that appropriate instruction can be provided them in school
- As part of neuropsychological evaluations, for example, periodically testing a person believed to be suffering from dementia so that deterioration of mental ability can be followed over time

IQ tests tap several functions believed to constitute intelligence, including language skills, abstract thinking, nonverbal reasoning, visual-spatial skills, attention and concentration, and speed of processing. Scores on most IQ tests are standardized so that 100 is the mean and 15 or 16 is the standard deviation (a measure of how scores are dispersed above and below the average). Approximately 65 percent of the population receives scores between 85 and 115. Approximately 2.5 percent of the population falls below 70 or above 130 (i.e., 2 standard deviations below or above the mean score of 100). In Chapter 14 we discuss people whose IQ falls at the low end of the distribution.

IQ tests are highly reliable (e.g., Canivez & Watkins, 1998) and have good criterion validity. For example, they distinguish between people who are intellectually gifted and those with mental retardation and between people with different occupations or educational attainment (Reynolds et al., 1997). They also predict educational attainment and occupational success (Hanson, Hunsley, & Parker, 1988), at least among Caucasians (see below for a discussion of cultural bias in assessment). Though the correlations between IQ scores and school performance are statistically significant, IQ tests explain only a small part of school performance; much more is unexplained by IQ test scores than is explained.

Regarding construct validity, it is important to keep in mind that IQ tests measure only what psychologists consider intelligence. Factors other than what we think of as intelligence play an important role in how people will do in school, such as family and circumstances, motivation to do well, expectations, performance anxiety, and difficulty of the curriculum. Another factor relevant to IQ test performance is called stereotype threat. It suggests that the social stigma of poor intellectual performance borne by some groups (e.g., African Americans do poorly on IQ tests; women perform more poorly than men on mathematics tests) actually interferes with their performance on these tests. In one study demonstrating this phenomenon, groups of men and women were given a difficult mathematics test. In one condition the participants were told that men scored higher than women on the test they were going to take (stereotype threat condition), while in the other condition they were told there were no gender differences in performance on the test. Only when the test was described as yielding gender differences did the women perform more poorly than men (Spencer, Steele, & Quinn, 1999).

Unfortunately, awareness of these stereotypes develops early. For example, a study revealed that children develop awareness of stereotypes regarding ethnicity and ability between the ages of 6 and 10, with 93 percent of children being aware of such stereotypes by age 10 (McKown & Weinstein, 2003). This awareness seems to influence stereotype threat (and performance). In the McKown and

The French psychologist Alfred Binet developed the first IQ test to predict how well children would do in school. (Courtesy Psychology Archive, University of Akron.)

Weinstein (2003) study, children also were asked to complete a puzzle task. Half of the children received instructions that the task reflected their ability (stereotype threat condition), and half the children received instructions that the test did not reflect their ability. Looking only at African American children who were aware of the stereotype about ethnicity and ability yielded evidence of stereotype threat. Specifically, among African American children, those who received the ability instructions performed more poorly on the puzzle task than the children who did not, suggesting that the instructions activated the stereotype and thus influenced their performance.

Behavioral and Cognitive Assessment

Thus far, we have discussed assessment methods that measure underlying personality structures and intellectual ability. Behavioral and cognitively oriented clinicians assess other characteristics, including the following:

- Aspects of the environment that might contribute to symptoms (e.g., an office location next to a noisy hallway might contribute to concentration problems)
- Characteristics of the person (e.g., a client's fatigue may be caused in part by a cognitive tendency toward self-deprecation manifested in such statements as "I never do anything right, so what's the point in trying?")
- The frequency and form of problematic behaviors (e.g., procrastination taking the form of missing important deadlines)
- Consequences of problem behaviors (e.g., when a client avoids a feared situation, his or her partner offers sympathy and excuses, thereby unwittingly keeping the client from facing up to his or her fears)

The hope is that understanding these aspects of cognition and behavior will guide the clinician toward more effective intervention targets.

The information necessary for a behavioral or cognitive assessment is gathered by several methods, including direct observation of behavior in real life as well as in laboratory or office settings, interviews and self-report measures, and various other methods of cognitive assessment (Bellack & Hersen, 1998). We turn to these now.

IQ tests have many subtests, including this test which assesses spatial ability. (Bob Daemmrich/The Image Works.)

Direct Observation of Behavior   It is not surprising that cognitive behavior therapists have paid considerable attention to careful observation of behavior in a variety of settings, but it should not be assumed that they simply go out and observe. Like other scientists, they try to fit events into a framework consistent with their points of view. In formal behavioral observation, the observer divides the sequence of behavior into various parts that make sense within a learning framework, including such things as the antecedents and consequences of particular behaviors. Behavioral observation is also often linked to intervention (O'Brien & Haynes, 1995). The cognitive behavioral clinician's way of conceptualizing a situation typically implies a way to try to change it.

It is difficult to observe most behavior as it actually takes place, and little control can be exercised over where and when it may occur. For this reason, many therapists contrive artificial situations in their consulting rooms or in a laboratory so they can observe how a client or a family acts under certain conditions. For example, Barkley (1981) had a mother and her child spend time together in a laboratory living room, complete with sofas and a television set. The mother was given a list of tasks for the child to complete, such as picking up toys or doing arithmetic problems. Observers behind a one-way mirror watched the proceedings and reliably coded the child's reactions to the mother's efforts to control as well as the mother's reactions to the child's compliant or noncompliant responses. These **behavioral assessment** procedures yielded data that could be used to measure the effects of treatment.

Self-Observation   Cognitive behavior therapists and researchers have also asked people to observe and track their own behavior and responses. This approach is called **self-monitoring**. Self-monitoring is used to collect a wide variety of data of interest to both clinicians and researchers, including moods, stressful experiences, coping behaviors, and thoughts (Hurlburt, 1979; Stone et al., 1998).

Behavioral assessment often involves direct observation of behavior, as in this case, where the observer is behind a one-way mirror. (Jeff Greenberg/PhotoEdit.)

Another method of self-observation is called **ecological momentary assessment**, or **EMA**. EMA involves the collection of data in real time as opposed to the more usual methods of having people reflect back over some time period and report on recently experienced thoughts, moods, or stressors. The methods for implementing EMA range from having people complete diaries at specified times during the day (perhaps signaled by a wristwatch that beeps at those times) to supplying them with PDAs (personal digital assistant) that not only signal when reports are to be made but also allow them to enter their responses directly into the device (Stone & Shiffman, 1994).

Given the problems in retrospective recall, some theories in the field of psychopathology can best be tested using EMA. For example, current theories of both anxiety disorders and depression propose that emotional reactions to a stressor are determined by thoughts that the stressor elicits. It is unlikely, however, that these thoughts can be recalled accurately in retrospect.

EMA may also be useful in clinical settings, revealing information that traditional assessment procedures might miss. For example, Hurlburt (1997) describes a case of a man with severe attacks of anxiety. In clinical interviews, the patient reported that his life was going very well, that he loved his wife and children, and that his work was both financially and personally rewarding. No cause of the anxiety attacks could be discerned. The man was asked to record his thoughts as he went about his daily routine. Surprisingly, about a third of his thoughts were concerned with annoyance with his children (e.g., "He left the fence gate open again and the dog got out").

> Once the high frequency of annoyance thoughts was pointed out to him, he. . . accepted that he was in fact often annoyed with his children. However, he believed that anger at his children was sinful and felt unfit as a father for having such thoughts and feelings. . . . [He] entered into brief therapy that focused on the normality of being annoyed by one's children and on the important distinction between being annoyed and acting out aggressively. Almost immediately, his anxiety attacks disappeared. (Hurlburt, 1997, p. 944)

Although some research indicates that self-monitoring or EMA can provide accurate measurement of such behavior, considerable research indicates that behavior may be altered by the very fact that it is being self-monitored—that is, the self-consciousness required for self-monitoring affects the behavior (Haynes & Horn, 1982). The phenomenon wherein behavior changes because it is being observed is called **reactivity**. In general, desirable behavior, such as engaging in social conversation, often increases in frequency when self-monitored (Nelson, Lipinski, & Black, 1976), whereas behavior the person wishes to reduce, such as cigarette smoking, diminishes (McFall & Hammen, 1971). Therapeutic interventions can take advantage of the reactivity that is a natural by-product of self-monitoring. Smoking, anxiety, depression, and health problems all have undergone beneficial changes in self-monitoring studies (Febbraro & Clum, 1998). Beyond reactivity, self-monitoring via PDAs has also been included effectively in cognitive behavior therapy for different anxiety disorders (Przeworski & Newman, 2006).

Cognitive-Style Questionnaires Cognitive questionnaires tend to be used to help plan targets for treatment as well as to determine whether clinical interventions are helping to change overly negative thought patterns. In format, some of these questionnaires are similar to the personality tests we have already described.

Self-monitoring generally leads to increases in desirable behaviors and decreases in undesirable ones. (Courtesy Invivo data, Inc.)

One self-report questionnaire that was developed based on Beck's theory (see Chapters 2 and 8) is the Dysfunctional Attitude Scale (DAS). The DAS contains items such as "People will probably think less of me if I make a mistake" (Weissman & Beck, 1978). Supporting construct validity, researchers have shown that they can differentiate between depressed and nondepressed people on the basis of their scores on this scale and that scores decrease (i.e., improve) after interventions that relieve depression. Furthermore, the DAS relates to other aspects of cognition in ways consistent with Beck's theory (Glass & Arnkoff, 1997).

Capturing Thoughts in a Specific Situation As mentioned, people's responses to inventories and to questions asked by interviewers about their thoughts in past situations may well be different from what they would report were they able to do so in the immediate circumstance. The Articulated Thoughts in Simulated Situations (ATSS) method of Davison and his associates (Davison, Navarre, & Vogel, 1995; Davison, Robins, & Johnson, 1983) is one way to assess immediate thoughts in specific situations. In this procedure, a person pretends that he or she is in a situation, such as listening to a teaching assistant criticize a term paper. The scenes are presented on audiotape, with a pause every 10 or 15 seconds. During the ensuing 30 seconds of silence, the participant talks aloud about whatever is going through his or her mind in reaction to the words just heard. One taped scene in which the participant overhears two pretend acquaintances criticizing him or her includes the following segments.

First acquaintance: He certainly did make a fool of himself over what he said about religion. I just find that kind of opinion very closed-minded and unaware. You have to be blind to the facts of the universe to believe that. [Thirty-second pause for subject's response.]

Second acquaintance: What really bugs me is the way he expresses himself. He never seems to stop and think, but just blurts out the first thing that comes into his head. [Thirty-second pause.]

Participants readily become involved in the pretend situations, regarding them as credible and realistic. Using this method, research has shown that people with social anxiety articulate thoughts of greater unfounded negativity (e.g., "Oh God, I wish I were dead; I'm so embarrassed") than do people without social anxiety (e.g., Davison & Zighelboim, 1987). In a study that directly compared ATSS data with overt behavior (Davison, Haaga, et al., 1991), the more anxiously participants behaved on a timed behavioral checklist measure of public-speaking anxiety, the less capable they felt they were while articulating thoughts in a stressful, simulated speech-giving situation. Thus, this method can draw out people's thinking about both inherently bothersome and "objectively" innocuous situations.

Cognitive assessment focuses on the person's perception of a situation, realizing that the same event can be perceived differently. For example, moving could be regarded as a very negative event or a very positive one, resulting in very different levels of stress. (Renata Hiller.)

Table 3.9 Psychological Assessment Methods

Interviews	Clinical interviews	The clinician learns about the patient's problems through conversation. The paradigm of the interviewer shapes the content of the interview.
	Structured interviews	Questions to be asked are spelled out in detail in a booklet. The Structured Clinical Interview for DSM-IV Axis I Disorders is a structured interview that is commonly used to make a diagnosis.
Stress measures		Self-report scales or interviews that assess stressful events and responses to these events.
Psychological tests	Personality tests	Self-report questionnaires, used to assess either a broad range of characteristics, as in the MMPI-2, or a single characteristic, such as dysfunctional attitudes.
	Projective tests	Ambiguous stimuli, such as inkblots (Rorschach test), are presented and responses are thought to be determined by unconscious processes.
	Intelligence tests	Assessments of current mental functioning. Used to predict school performance and identify cognitive strengths and weaknesses.
Direct observation		Used by behavioral clinicians to identify problem behaviors as well as antecedents and consequences. Also used to assess cognition, as in the Articulated Thoughts in Simulated Situations technique.
Self-observation		People monitor and keep records of their own behavior, as in ecological momentary assessment.

Quick Summary

The psychological assessments we have described are summarized in Table 3.9. A comprehensive psychological assessment draws on many different methods and tests. Interviews can be structured, with the questions predetermined and followed in a certain order, or unstructured to follow more closely what the client tells the interviewer. Structured interviews are more reliable. Rapport is important to establish regardless of the type of interview.

Stress can be assessed via a checklist of life events as in the SRRS, by assessing daily reports of thoughts and feelings such as with the Assessment of Daily Experience (ADE), or by a semistructured interview that captures the importance of any given life event in the context of a person's life circumstances, as in the LEDS.

The MMPI-2 is a standardized and objective personality inventory. The test has good reliability and validity and is widely used. Projective personality tests, like the Rorschach or TAT, are not as widely used today, likely due to their poor validity. Reliability can be achieved using scoring systems such as Exner's. Intelligence tests have been used for a number of years and are quite reliable. Like any test, there are limits to what an IQ test can tell a clinician or researcher.

Direct observation of behavior can be very useful in assessment, though it can take more time than a self-report inventory. Other behavioral and cognitive assessment methods include ecological momentary assessment (EMA) and the Articulated Thoughts in Simulated Situations (ATSS).

Check Your Knowledge 3.3

True or false?
1. If conducted properly, a psychological assessment typically includes just one measure most appropriate to the client.
2. Unstructured interviews may have poor reliability, but they can still be quite valuable in a psychological assessment.
3. The MMPI-2 contains scales to detect whether someone is faking their answers.

4. The projective hypothesis is based on the idea that a person does not really know what is bothering him or her; thus, a subtler means of assessment is needed.
5. Intelligence tests are highly reliable.
6. EMA is a method to assess unwanted impulses.

Neurobiological Assessment

Recall from Chapters 1 and 2 that throughout history people interested in psychopathology have assumed, quite reasonably, that some symptoms are likely to be due to or at least reflected in malfunctions of the brain or other parts of the nervous system. We turn now to contemporary work in neurobiological assessment. We'll look at four areas in particular: brain imaging, neurotransmitter assessment, neuropsychological assessment, and psychophysiological assessment (see Table 3.10 for a summary of these methods).

Table 3.10 Neurobiological Assessment Methods	
Brain imaging	CT and MRI scans reveal the structure of the brain. PET reveals brain function and, to a lesser extent, brain structure. fMRI is used to assess both brain structure and brain function.
Neurotransmitter assessment	Includes postmortem analysis of neurotransmitters and receptors, assays of metabolites of neurotransmitters, and PET scans of receptors.
Neuropsychological assessment	Behavioral tests such as the Halstead–Reitan and Luria–Nebraska assess abilities such as motor speed, memory, and spatial ability. Deficits on particular tests help point to an area of brain dysfunction.
Psychophysiological assessment	Includes measures of electrical activity in the autonomic nervous system, such as skin conductance, or in the central nervous system, such as EEG.

Brain Imaging: "Seeing" the Brain

Because many behavioral problems can be brought on by brain dysfunction, neurological tests—such as checking the reflexes, examining the retina for any indication of blood vessel damage, and evaluating motor coordination and perception—have been used for many years to identify brain dysfunction. Today, devices have become available that allow clinicians and researchers a much more direct look at both the structure and functioning of the brain.

Computerized axial tomography, the **CT** or **CAT scan**, helps to assess structural brain abnormalities (and is able to image other parts of the body for medical purposes). A moving beam of X-rays passes into a horizontal cross section of the person's brain, scanning it through 360 degrees; the moving X-ray detector on the other side measures the amount of radioactivity that penetrates, thus detecting subtle differences in tissue density. A computer uses the information to construct a two-dimensional, detailed image of the cross section, giving it optimal contrasts. Then the machine scans another cross section of the brain. The resulting images can show the enlargement of ventricles (which signals degeneration of tissue) and the locations of tumors and blood clots.

Newer devices for seeing the living brain include **magnetic resonance imaging**, also known as **MRI**, which is superior to the CT scan because it produces pictures of higher quality and does not rely on even the small amount of radiation required by a CT scan. In MRI the person is placed inside a large, circular magnet, which causes the hydrogen atoms in the body to move. When the magnetic force is turned off, the atoms return to their original positions and thereby produce an electromagnetic signal. These signals are then read by the computer and translated into pictures of brain tissue. This technique provides an enormous advance. For example, it has allowed physicians to locate delicate brain tumors that would have been considered inoperable without such sophisticated methods of viewing brain structures.

An even greater advance has been a technique called **functional MRI (fMRI)** which allows researchers to measure both brain structure and brain function. This technique takes MRI pictures so quickly that metabolic changes can be measured, providing a picture of the brain at work rather than of its structure alone. fMRI measures blood flow in the brain, and this is called the **BOLD** signal, which stands for blood oxygenation level dependent. As neurons fire, blood flow increases to that area. Therefore, blood flow in a particular region of the brain is a reasonable proxy for neural activity in that brain region.

Positron emission tomography, the **PET scan**, a more expensive and invasive procedure, also allows measurement of both brain structure and brain function, although the measurement of brain structure is not as precise as with MRI or fMRI. A substance used by the brain is labeled with a short-lived radioactive isotope and injected into the bloodstream. The radioactive molecules of the substance emit a particle called a positron, which quickly collides with an electron. A pair of high-energy light particles shoot out from the skull in opposite directions and are detected by the scanner. The computer analyzes millions of such recordings and converts them into a picture of the functioning brain. The images are in color; fuzzy spots of lighter and warmer colors are areas in which metabolic rates for the substance are higher. Because this is more invasive than fMRI, it is now used less often as a measure of brain function.

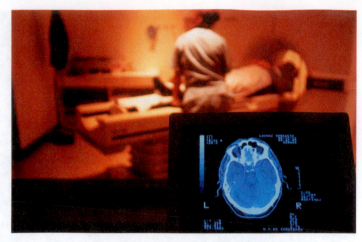

An fMRI scanner is a long tube-like structure. (age fotostock/SuperStock, Inc.)

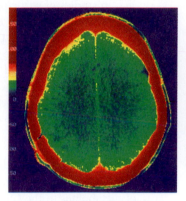 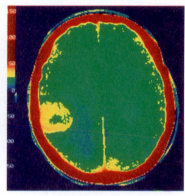

These two CT scans show a horizontal "slice" through the brain. The one on the left is normal; the one on the right has a tumor on the left side. (Dan McCoy/Rainbow.)

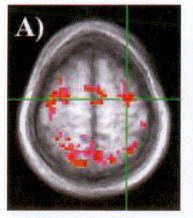 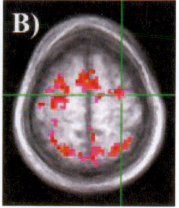

Functional magnetic resonance images (fMRI). With this method, researchers can measure how brain activity changes while a person is doing different tasks, such as viewing an emotional film, completing a memory test, looking at a visual puzzle, or hearing and learning a list of words. [From J. E. McDowell et al., *Biological Psychiatry*, 51, 216–223 (2002).]

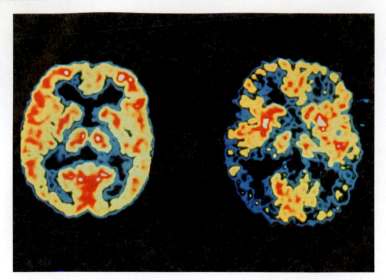

The PET scan on the left shows a normal brain; the one on the right shows the brain of a patient with Alzheimer's disease. (Dr. Robert Friedland/Photo Researchers.)

Visual images of the working brain can indicate sites of seizures, brain tumors, strokes, and trauma from head injuries, as well as the distribution of psychoactive drugs in the brain. fMRI, and to a lesser extent PET, is being used to study possible abnormal brain processes that are linked to various disorders, such as the failure of the frontal cortex of patients with schizophrenia to become activated while they attempt to perform a cognitive task.

Neurotransmitter Assessment

It might seem that assessing the amount of a particular neurotransmitter or the quantity of its receptors in the brain would be straightforward. But as we began to discuss in Chapter 2, it is not. Most of the research on neurotransmitters and psychopathology has relied on indirect assessments.

In postmortem studies, the brains of deceased patients are removed and the amount of specific neurotransmitters in particular brain areas can then be directly measured. Different brain areas can be infused with substances that bind to receptors, and the amount of binding can then be quantified; more binding indicates more receptors. In Chapter 11 we will discuss how this method has been used to study the dopamine theory of schizophrenia.

In studies of participants who are alive, one common method of neurotransmitter assessment involves analyzing the metabolites of neurotransmitters that have been broken down by enzymes. A **metabolite**, typically an acid, is produced when a neurotransmitter is deactivated. These by-products of the breakdown of neurotransmitters, such as norepinephrine, dopamine, and serotonin, are found in urine, blood serum, and cerebrospinal fluid (CSF; the fluid in the spinal column and in the brain's ventricles). For example, a major metabolite of dopamine is homovanillic acid; of serotonin, 5-hydroxyindoleacetic acid. A high level of a particular metabolite presumably indicates a high level of a neurotransmitter, and a low level indicates a low level of the transmitter.

But there is a problem with measuring metabolites from blood or urine: such measures are not direct reflections of levels of neurotransmitters in the brain; metabolites measured in this way could reflect neurotransmitters anywhere in the body. A more specific measure can be taken of metabolites in the CSF fluid drawn from a person's spinal cord. Even with CSF fluid, however, metabolites reflect activity throughout the brain and spinal cord, rather than regions that are directly involved in psychopathology. We will see in Chapter 8 that some people with depression have low CSF levels of the main metabolite of serotonin—a fact that has played an important role in the serotonin theory of depression.

Another problem with metabolite studies is that they are correlational. In Chapter 4, we discuss the limits of correlational research, including the fact that causation cannot be determined from a correlational study. That is, when researchers find that neurotransmitter levels are low among people with a particular disorder, such as depression, this could be because neurotransmitter levels cause depression, because depression causes neurotransmitter changes, or because a third variable causes shifts in both neurotransmitters and depression. For example, dopamine, norepinephrine, and serotonin levels change in response to stress. To test whether neurotransmitter levels could cause symptoms, experimental evidence is needed.

To provide more experimental data on whether these neurotransmitter systems actually help cause psychopathology, one strategy is to administer drugs that increase or decrease levels of neurotransmitters. For example, a drug that raises the level of serotonin should alleviate depression; one reducing it should trigger depressive symptoms. This strategy also has its problems, though. One might wonder about whether it is ethical to do these studies if the goal of an experiment is to produce symptoms. On this front, it is reassuring that most studies find very temporary effects of these medications; neurotransmitter systems quickly return to normal levels, allowing for recovery from these brief mood periods. Another issue is that drugs that change levels of one neurotransmitter often tend to influence other neurotransmitter systems. We will see examples of these types of studies throughout this book.

Clinicians and researchers in many disciplines are currently using brain imaging and neurotransmitter assessment techniques both to discover previously undetectable brain problems and to conduct inquiries into the neurobiological contributions to thought, emotion, and behavior. It is a very lively and exciting area of research and application. Indeed, one might reasonably assume that researchers and clinicians, with the help of such procedures and technological devices as fMRI, could observe the brain and its functions more or less directly and thus assess all brain abnormalities. Results to date, however, are not strong enough for these methods to be used in diagnosing psychopathology. Moreover, many brain abnormalities involve alterations in structure so subtle or slight in extent that they have thus far eluded direct examination. Furthermore, the problems in some disorders are so widespread that finding the contributing brain dysfunction is a daunting task. Take, for example, schizophrenia, which affects thinking, feeling, and behavior. Where in the brain might there be dysfunction? Looking for areas that influence thinking, feeling, and behavior requires looking at just about the entire brain.

Neuropsychological Assessment

It is important at this point to note a distinction between neurologists and neuropsychologists, even though both specialists are concerned with the study of the central nervous system. A **neurologist** is a physician who specializes in diseases that affect the nervous system, such as muscular dystrophy, cerebral palsy, or Alzheimer's disease. A **neuropsychologist** is a psychologist who studies how dysfunctions of the brain affect the way we think, feel, and behave. Both kinds of specialists contribute much to each other as they work in different ways, often collaboratively, to learn how the nervous system functions and how to ameliorate problems caused by disease or injury to the brain.

Neuropsychological tests are often used in conjunction with the brain imaging techniques just described to both detect brain dysfunction and to help pinpoint specific areas of the brain involved. Neuropsychological tests are based on the idea that different psychological functions (e.g., motor speed, memory, language) rely on different areas of the brain. Thus, for example, neuropsychological testing might help identify the extent of brain damage suffered during a stroke, and it can provide clues about where in the brain the damage may exist. The concept of using a battery of tests, each tapping a different function, is critical, for only by studying a person's pattern of performance can a clinician or researcher adequately determine whether the brain is damaged and where the damage is located. There are numerous neuropsychological tests used in psychopathology assessment. Here, we highlight two widely used batteries of tests.

One neuropsychological test is Reitan's modification of a battery or group of tests previously developed by Halstead, called the Halstead–Reitan neuropsychological test battery. The following are three of the Halstead-Reitan tests.

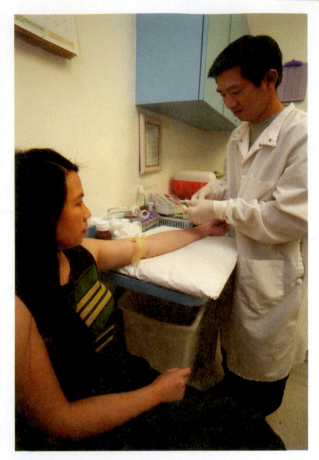
Measures of neurotransmitter metabolites in blood or urine levels do not provide a very accurate index of neurotransmitter levels in the brain. (Spencer Grant/Photo Researchers, Inc.)

1. **Tactile Performance Test—Time.** While blindfolded, the patient tries to fit variously shaped blocks into spaces of a form board, first using the preferred hand, then the other, and finally both.

2. **Tactile Performance Test—Memory.** After completing the timed test, the participant is asked to draw the form board from memory, showing the blocks in their proper location. Both this and the timed test are sensitive to damage in the right parietal lobe.

3. **Speech Sounds Perception Test.** Participants listen to a series of nonsense words, each comprising two consonants with a long-*e* sound in the middle. They then select the "word" they heard from a set of alternatives. This test measures left-hemisphere function, especially temporal and parietal areas.

Neuropsychological tests assess various performance deficits in the hope of detecting a specific area of brain malfunction. Shown here is the Tactile Performance Test. (Richard Nowitz/Photo Researchers.)

Extensive research has demonstrated that the battery is valid for detecting behavior changes linked to brain dysfunction resulting from a variety of conditions, such as tumors, stroke, and head injury (Horton, 2008).

The Luria–Nebraska battery (Golden, Hammeke, & Purisch, 1978), based on the work of the Russian psychologist Aleksandr Luria (1902–1977), is also widely used (Moses & Purisch, 1997). The battery includes 269 items divided into 11 sections designed to determine basic and complex motor skills, rhythm and pitch abilities, tactile and kinesthetic skills, verbal and spatial skills, receptive speech ability, expressive speech ability, writing, reading, arithmetic skills, memory, and intellectual processes. The pattern of scores on these sections, as well as on the 32 items found to be the most discriminating and indicative of overall impairment, helps reveal potential damage to the frontal, temporal, sensorimotor, or parietal-occipital area of the right or left hemisphere.

The Luria–Nebraska battery can be administered in $2\frac{1}{2}$ hours and can be scored in a highly reliable manner (e.g., Kashden & Franzen, 1996). It also has an alternate form. Criterion validity has been established by findings that test scores can correctly distinguish 86 percent of neurological patients and controls (Moses et al., 1992). A particular advantage of the Luria–Nebraska tests is that one can control for educational level so that a less educated person will not receive a lower score solely because of limited educational experience (Brickman et al., 1984). Finally, a version for children ages 8 to 12 (Golden, 1981a, 1981b) has been found useful in helping to pinpoint brain damage and in evaluating the educational strengths and weaknesses of children (Sweet et al., 1986).

Psychophysiological Assessment

The discipline of **psychophysiology** is concerned with the bodily changes that are associated with psychological events. Experimenters have used measures such as heart rate, tension in the muscles, blood flow in various parts of the body, and brain waves to study physiological changes when people are afraid, depressed, asleep, imagining, solving problems, and so on. Like the brain-imaging methods we have already discussed, the assessments we describe here are not sensitive enough to be used for diagnosis. They can, however, provide important information about a person's reactivity and can also be used to compare individuals. For example, in using exposure to treat a patient with an anxiety disorder, it would be useful to know the extent to which the patient shows physiological arousal when exposed to the stimuli that create anxiety. Patients who show more physiological arousal may be experiencing more fear, which predicts more benefit from the therapy (Foa et al., 1995).

The activities of the autonomic nervous system (also discussed in Chapter 2) are often assessed by electrical and chemical measurements to understand aspects of emotion. One important measure is heart rate. Each heartbeat generates electrical changes, which can be recorded by electrodes placed on the chest that convey signals to an electrocardiograph or a polygraph. The signal is graphically depicted in an **electrocardiogram (EKG)**, which may be seen as waves on a computer screen or a roll of graph paper.

A second measure of autonomic nervous system activity is **electrodermal responding**, or skin conductance. Anxiety, fear, anger, and other emotions increase activity in the sympathetic nervous system, which then boosts sweat-gland activity. Increased sweat-gland activity increases the electrical conductance of the skin. Conductance is typically measured by determining the current that flows through the skin as a small voltage is passed between two electrodes on the hand. When the sweat glands are activated, this current shows a pronounced increase. Since the sweat glands are activated by the sympathetic nervous system, increased sweat-gland activity indicates sympathetic autonomic excitation and is often taken as a measure of emotional arousal. These measures are widely used in research in psychopathology.

Advances in technology allow researchers to track changes in physiological processes, such as blood pressure in vivo, as people go about their normal business. Participants wear a portable device that automatically records blood pressure many times during the day. Combining these measures with self-reports recorded by the participants in specially designed diaries, researchers have been able to study how people's changing moods affect blood pressure—of interest to understanding hypertension (Kamarck et al., 1998; see Chapter 7).

Brain activity can be measured by an **electroencephalogram (EEG)**. Electrodes placed on the scalp record electrical activity in the underlying brain area. Abnormal patterns of electrical activity can indicate seizure activity in the brain or help in locating brain lesions or tumors. EEG indices are also used to measure attention and alertness.

As with the brain-imaging techniques reviewed earlier, a more complete picture of a human being is obtained when physiological functioning is assessed while the person is engaging in some form of behavior or cognitive activity. If experimenters are interested in psychophysiological responding in patients with obsessive-compulsive disorder, for example, they would likely study the patients while presenting stimuli, such as dirt, that would elicit the problematic behaviors.

A Cautionary Note about Neurobiological Assessment

A cautionary note regarding neurobiological assessment methods is in order here. Inasmuch as psychophysiology and brain imaging employ highly sophisticated electronic machinery, and many psychologists aspire to be as scientific as possible, researchers and clinicians sometimes believe uncritically in these apparently objective assessment devices without appreciating their real limitations and complications. Many of the measurements do not differentiate clearly among emotional states. Skin conductance, for example, increases not only with anxiety but also with other emotions—among them, happiness. In addition, being in a scanner is often a threatening experience. Thus, the investigator interested in measuring brain changes associated with emotion using fMRI must also take the scanning environment into account. It is also important to keep in mind that brain-imaging techniques do not allow us to manipulate brain activity and then measure a change in behavior (Feldman Barrett, 2003). In a typical study, we show people a list of emotionally evocative words and then measure blood flow in the brain. Does a person who fails to show the same level of activation in emotion regions during this task have a brain-based emotion deficit? Not necessarily. The person might not have paid attention, might not have understood the words, or might be focused on the loud clanging noises that the fMRI machine is making. It is important to be extremely careful in considering alternative explanations for the effects found in these studies.

Neither is there a one-to-one relationship between a score on a given neuropsychological test or a finding on an fMRI scan on the one hand and psychological dysfunction on the other. The reasons for these sometimes loose relationships have to do with such factors as how the person has, over time, reacted to and coped with the losses brought about by the brain dysfunction. And the success of coping, in turn, has to do with the social environment in which the person has lived, for example, how understanding parents and associates have been or how well the school system has provided for the special educational needs of the person. Furthermore, the brain has changed in response to these psychological and socioenvironmental factors over time. Therefore, in addition to the imperfect nature of the neurobiological assessment instruments themselves and our incomplete understanding of how the brain actually functions, clinicians and researchers must consider these environmental factors that operate over time to contribute to the clinical picture. In other words, a complete assessment must include multiple methods (clinical interviews, psychological and neurobiological methods).

A final caution is reflected in the simple yet often unappreciated fact that in attempting to understand the neurocognitive consequences of any brain dysfunction, one must understand the preexisting abilities that the patient had prior to diagnosis with a mental disorder. This straightforward truth brings to mind the story of the man who, recovering from an accident that has broken all the fingers in both hands, earnestly asks the surgeon whether he will be able to play the piano when his wounds heal. "Yes, I'm sure you will," says the doctor reassuringly. "That's wonderful," exclaims the man, "I've always wanted to be able to play the piano."

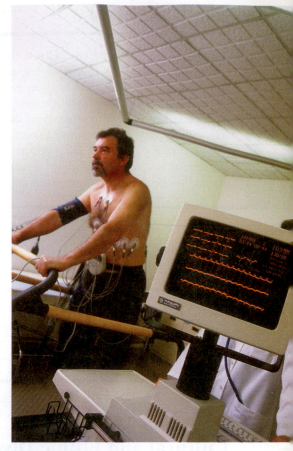

In psychophysiological assessment, physical changes in the body are measured. The electrocardiograph is one such assessment. (© BSIP/Phototake.)

Quick Summary

Advances in technology have allowed clinicians and researchers to "see" the living brain. Different imaging techniques, such as CT, MRI, and fMRI, have the potential to show areas of the brain that might not be working optimally. Direct assessment of neurotransmitters is not done often. Rather, examinations of the metabolites of neurotransmitters provide a rough way to estimate how neurotransmitters are functioning. Another approach is to administer drugs that increase or decrease the levels of a neurotransmitter. Postmortem exams also allow for measurements of neurotransmitters, particularly

receptors. Neuropsychological tests are tests that have been developed to show how changes in behavior may reflect damage or disturbance in particular areas of the brain. Psychophysiological assessment methods can show how behaviors and cognitions are linked to changes in nervous system activity, such as heart rate, skin conductance, or brain activity. These methods have as many or more limitations as other assessment measures, and the key concepts of reliability and validity are just as relevant with neurobiological assessment as with other forms of assessment

Check Your Knowledge 3.4

True or false?
1. MRI is a technique that shows both the structure and function of the brain.
2. Neurotransmitter assessment is most often done using indirect methods.

3. A neuropsychologist is a psychologist who studies how dysfunctions of the brain affect the way we think, feel, and behave.
4. Brain activity can be measured with the psychophysiological method called EKG.

Cultural and Ethnic Diversity and Assessment

Studies of the influences of culture and ethnicity on psychopathology and its assessment have proliferated in recent years. As you read about some of this research, it is critical to keep in mind that there are typically more differences within cultural and ethnic groups than there are between them. Remembering this important point can help avoid the dangers of stereotyping members of a culture.

We should also note that the reliability and validity of various forms of psychological assessment have been questioned on the grounds that their content and scoring procedures reflect the culture of white European Americans and so may not accurately assess people from other cultures. In this section we discuss problems of cultural bias and what can be done about them.

Cultural Bias in Assessment

The issue of cultural bias in assessment refers to the notion that a measure developed for one culture or ethnic group may not be equally reliable and valid with a different cultural or ethnic group. Some tests that were developed in the United States have been translated into different languages and used in different cultures successfully. For example, a Spanish-language version of the WAIS has been available for over 40 years (Wechsler, 1968) and can be useful in assessing the intellectual functioning of people from Hispanic or Latino cultures (Gomez, Piedmont, & Fleming, 1992). Additionally, the MMPI-2 has been translated into more than two dozen languages (Tsai et al., 2001).

Simply translating words into a different language, however, does not ensure that the meaning of those words will be the same across different cultures. Several steps in the translation process, including working with multiple translators, back-translating, and testing with multiple native speakers can help to ensure that the test is similar in different languages. This approach has been successful in achieving equivalence across different cultures and ethnic groups for some instruments, such as the MMPI-2 (Arbisi, Ben-Porath, & McNulty, 2002). Even with the MMPI-2, however, there are cultural differences that are not likely attributable to differences in psychopathology. For example, among Asian Americans who are not heavily assimilated into American culture, scores on most MMPI-2 scales are higher than those of Caucasians (Tsai & Pike, 2000). This is unlikely to reflect truly higher emotional disturbance among Asians. For children, the latest version of the WISC has not only been translated into Spanish (WISC-IV Spanish); it also has a complete set of norms for Spanish-speaking children in the United States, and the items have been designed explicitly to minimize cultural bias.

Despite these efforts, the field has a ways to go in reducing cultural and ethnic bias in clinical assessment. These cultural assumptions or biases may cause clinicians to over- or underestimate psychological problems in members of other cultures (Lopez, 1989, 1996). African American children are overrepresented in special education classes, which may be a result of subtle biases in the tests used to determine such placement (Artiles & Trent, 1994). At least since the 1970s, studies have found that African Americans are more likely to receive a diagnosis of schizophrenia than are Caucasian Americans, but it is

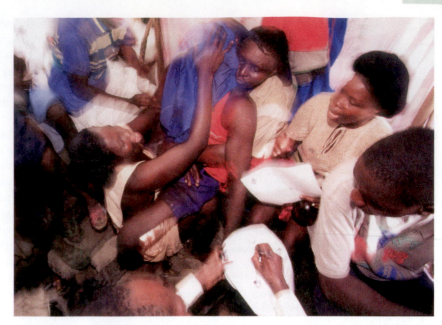

Assessment must take the person's cultural background into account. Believing in possession by spirits is common in some cultures and thus should not always be taken to mean that the believer is psychotic. (Tony Savino/The Image Works.)

still unclear whether this reflects an actual difference or a form of ethnic bias on the part of clinicians (Arnold et al., 2004; Trierweiler et al., 2000). Yet take the example of an Asian American man who is very emotionally withdrawn. Should the clinician consider that lower emotional expressiveness in men is viewed more positively in Asian cultures than in Euro American culture? A clinician who quickly attributes the behavior to a cultural difference may overlook an emotional problem that he or she would be likely to diagnose if the patient were a white male.

How do such biases come about? Cultural factors may affect assessment in various ways. Language differences, differing religious and spiritual beliefs, the alienation or timidity of members of ethnic groups when being assessed by clinicians of the Euro American culture—all these factors can play a role. For example, clinicians who encounter clients claiming to be surrounded by spirits might view this belief as a sign of schizophrenia. Yet in Puerto Rican cultures, such a belief is common; therefore, believing that one is surrounded by spirits should probably not be taken as a sign of schizophrenia in a Puerto Rican person (Rogler & Hollingshead, 1985).

Cultural and ethnic differences in psychopathology must be examined more closely. Unfortunately, the cultural and ethnic biases that can creep into clinical assessment do not necessarily yield to efforts to compensate for them. There is no simple answer. DSM-IV-TR's inclusion of cultural factors in the discussion of every category of disorder may well sensitize clinicians to the issue, a necessary first step. When practitioners were surveyed, they overwhelmingly reported taking culture into account in their clinical work (Lopez, 1994), so it appears that the problem, if not the solution, is clearly in focus.

Strategies for Avoiding Cultural Bias in Assessment

Clinicians can—and do—use various methods to minimize the negative effects of cultural biases when assessing patients. Perhaps the place to begin is with graduate training programs. Lopez (2002) has noted three important issues that should be taught to graduate students in clinical psychology programs. First, students must learn about basic issues in assessment, such as reliability and validity. Second, students must become informed about the specific ways in which culture or ethnicity may impact assessment rather than relying on more global stereotypes about a particular cultural or ethnic group. Third, students must consider that culture or ethnicity may not impact assessment in every individual case.

Assessment procedures can also be modified to ensure that the person truly understands the requirements of the task. For example, suppose that a Native American child performed

Cultural differences can lead to different results on an aptitude or IQ test. For example, Native American children may lack interest in the individualistic, competitive nature of IQ tests because of the cooperative, group-oriented values instilled by their culture. (Lawrence Migdale/Photo Researchers.)

poorly on a test measuring psychomotor speed. The examiner's hunch is that the child did not understand the importance of working quickly and was overly concerned with accuracy instead. The test could be administered again after a more thorough explanation of the importance of working quickly without worrying about mistakes. If the child's performance improves, the examiner has gained an important understanding of the child's test-taking strategy and avoids diagnosing psychomotor speed deficits.

Finally, when the examiner and client have different ethnic backgrounds, the examiner may need to make an extra effort to establish a rapport that will result in the person's best performance. For example, when testing a shy Hispanic preschooler, one of the authors was unable to obtain a verbal response to test questions. However, the boy was overheard talking in an animated and articulate manner to his mother in the waiting room, leading to a judgment that the test results did not represent a valid assessment of the child's language skills. When testing was repeated in the child's home with his mother present, advanced verbal abilities were observed.

As Lopez (1994) points out, however, "the distance between cultural responsiveness and cultural stereotyping can be short" (p. 123). To minimize such problems, clinicians are encouraged to be particularly tentative about drawing conclusions with patients from different cultural and ethnic backgrounds. Rather, they are advised to make hypotheses about the influence of culture on a particular client, entertain alternative hypotheses, and then test those hypotheses.

In a case from our files, a young man was suspected of having schizophrenia. One prominent symptom he reported was hearing voices. However, he claimed that he heard voices only while meditating and that within his (Buddhist) culture this experience was normative. To test this hypothesis, the examiner (with the permission of the client) contacted the family's religious leader. The Buddhist priest indicated that the symptom reported by this young man was very unusual, and it turned out that the religious community to which he belonged was quite concerned about his increasingly bizarre behavior. Thus, the hypothesis that his symptom should be attributed to cultural factors was refuted, and an error of failing to detect psychopathology was avoided.

Summary

In gathering diagnosis and assessment information, clinicians and researchers must be concerned with both reliability and validity. Reliability refers to whether measurements are consistent and replicable; validity, to whether assessments are tapping into what they are meant to measure. Assessment procedures vary greatly in their reliability and validity. Certain diagnostic categories are more reliable than others.

Diagnosis

- Diagnosis is the process of assessing whether a person meets criteria for a mental disorder. Having an agreed-on diagnostic system allows clinicians to communicate effectively with each other and facilitates the search for causes and treatments. Clinically, diagnosis provides the foundation for treatment planning.
- *The Diagnostic and Statistical Manual of Mental Disorders* (DSM), published by the American Psychiatric Association, is an official diagnostic system widely used by mental health professionals. A revision of the fourth edition of the manual, referred to as DSM-IV-TR, was published in 2000. An important feature of the current DSM is its multiaxial organization. In the multiaxial classification system of DSM, Axes I and II make up the mental disorders per se; Axis III lists any medical conditions believed to bear on the mental disorder in question; Axis IV is used to indicate the psychosocial and environmental problems that the person has been experiencing; and Axis V rates the person's current level of adaptive functioning.
- Some critics of the DSM argue against diagnosis in general. They point out that diagnostic classifications may ignore important information and may also increase stigma. Specific shortcomings of the DSM have also been identified. These include the high rates of comorbidity, overlap in the causes and treatments for different disorders, the reliance on a categorical classification system, limited reliability for some disorders, and questions about the validity of a few of the diagnostic categories. Most researchers and clinicians, though, recognize that the DSM is an enormous advance compared to historical systems.

Assessment

● Clinicians rely on several modes of psychological and neurobiological assessment in trying to find out how best to describe an individual, search for the reasons the person is troubled, arrive at an accurate diagnosis, and design effective treatments. A clinician's paradigm influences his or her choice of assessment methods. The best assessment involves multiple types of methods.

● Psychological assessments include clinical interviews, assessments of stress, psychological tests, and behavioral and cognitive assessments.

● Clinical interviews are structured or relatively unstructured conversations in which the clinician probes the patient for information about his or her problems. Assessing stress is key to the field of psychopathology. A number of useful methods for assessing stress have been developed, including the LEDS and ADE.

● Psychological tests are standardized procedures designed to assess personality or measure performance. Personality assessments range from empirically derived self-report questionnaires, such as the Minnesota Multiphasic Personality Inventory, to projective tests in which the patient interprets ambiguous stimuli, such as the Rorschach test. Intelligence tests, such as the Wechsler Adult Intelligence Scale, evaluate a person's intellectual ability and predict how well he or she will perform academically.

● Behavioral and cognitive assessment is concerned with how people act, feel, and think in particular situations. Approaches include direct observation of behavior; interviews and self-report measures that are situational in their focus; and specialized, think-aloud cognitive assessment procedures that attempt to uncover beliefs, attitudes, and thinking patterns related to specific situations.

● Neurobiological assessments include brain imaging techniques—such as fMRI—that enable us to see various structures and access functions of the living brain; neurochemical assays that allow clinicians to make inferences about levels of neurotransmitters; neuropsychological tests, such as the Halstead–Reitan, that seek to identify brain defects based on variations in responses to psychological tests; and psychophysiological measurements, such as heart rate and electrodermal responding, that are associated with certain psychological events or characteristics.

● Cultural and ethnic factors play a role in clinical assessment. Assessment techniques developed on the basis of research with Caucasian populations may be inaccurate when used with clients of differing ethnic or cultural backgrounds, for example. Clinicians can have biases when evaluating ethnic minority patients, which can lead to minimizing or exaggerating a patient's psychopathology. Clinicians use various methods to guard against the negative effects of cultural biases in assessment.

Answers to Check Your Knowledge Questions

3.1 1. a, d, e, c, b; 2. b, c, d, a

3.2 1. high comorbidity, many different diagnoses are related to the same causes, symptoms of many different diagnoses respond to the same treatments; 2. Axis V; 3. course, social functioning, treatment

3.3 1. F; 2. T; 3. T; 4. T; 5. T; 6. F

3.4 1. F; 2. T; 3. T; 4. F

Key Terms

alternate-form reliability
behavioral assessment
BOLD
categorical classification
clinical interview
comorbidity
concurrent validity
construct validity
content validity
criterion validity
CT or CAT scan
Diagnostic and Statistical Manual of Mental Disorders (DSM-IV-TR)
diagnosis

dimensional diagnostic system
ecological momentary assessment (EMA)
electrocardiogram (EKG)
electrodermal responding
electroencephalogram (EEG)
functional magnetic resonance imaging (fMRI)
intelligence test
internal consistency reliability
interrater reliability
magnetic resonance imaging (MRI)
metabolite

Minnesota Multiphasic Personality Inventory (MMPI)
multiaxial classification system
neurologist
neuropsychological tests
neuropsychologist
personality inventory
PET scan
predictive validity
projective hypothesis
projective test
psychological tests
psychophysiology
reactivity

reliability
Rorschach Inkblot Test
self-monitoring
standardization
stress
structured interview
test–retest reliability
Thematic Apperception Test (TAT)
validity

4 Research Methods in the Study of Psychopathology

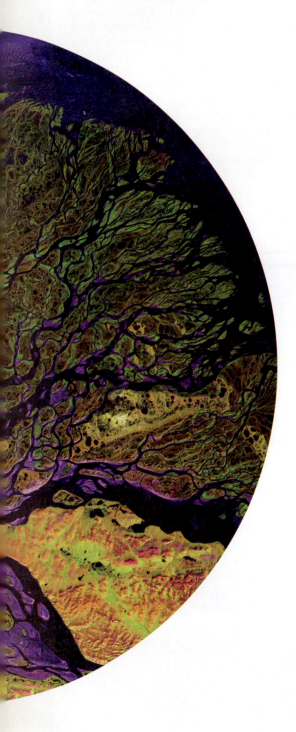

LEARNING GOALS

1. Be able to define science and the scientific method.
2. Be able to describe the advantages and disadvantages of correlational and experimental designs.
3. Be able to identify common types of correlational and experimental designs.
4. Be able to describe the basic steps in conducting a meta-analysis.

OUR ABILITY TO CONCEPTUALIZE and treat mental illness has improved vastly over the past 50 years. Nonetheless, there are still important unanswered questions about the causes and treatments of psychological disorders. Because there are unanswered questions, it is important to pursue new discoveries using scientific research methods. This chapter discusses the methods used in psychopathology research.

Science and Scientific Methods

The term science comes from the Latin *scire*, "to know." At its core, science is a way of knowing. More formally, science is the systematic pursuit of knowledge through observation. Science involves forming a theory and then systematically gathering data to test the theory.

A **theory** is a set of propositions meant to explain a class of observations. Usually, the goal of scientific theories is to understand cause–effect relationships. A theory permits the generation of more specific **hypotheses**—expectations about what should occur if a theory is true. For example, if the classical conditioning theory is valid, people with phobias should be more likely than those in the general population to have had traumatic experiences with the situations they fear, such as flying. By collecting such data, you could test your hypothesis.

People sometimes assume that a scientist formulates a theory by simply considering data that were previously collected and then deciding, in a rather straightforward fashion, that one way of thinking about the data is the most useful. Although some theory building follows this course, not all does. Theory building often involves creativity—a theory sometimes seems to leap into the scientist's head in a wonderful moment of insight. New ideas suddenly occur, and connections that were overlooked before are grasped. Formerly obscure observations might make a new kind of sense within the framework of the new theory (see Focus on Discovery 4.1).

What makes a good theory? A scientific approach requires that ideas be stated clearly and precisely. This is needed for scientific claims to be exposed to systematic tests that could negate the scientist's expectations. That is, regardless of how plausible a theory seems, it must be subject to disproof. Science proceeds by disproving theories, never by "proving

FOCUS ON DISCOVERY 4.1

Chaos Theory and Limits on Prediction

. . . the Butterfly Effect—the notion that a butterfly stirring the air today in Peking can transform storm systems next month in New York. (Gleick, 1987, p. 8)

This quotation captures the essence of chaos theory, which suggests that major events (such as a storm system) may be affected by seemingly trivial events (the air turbulence created by a flying butterfly). The chaos theory perspective argues against the ability of scientists to predict with any confidence the long-term consequences that unravel from apparently tiny changes in events (Gleick, 1987). The world is almost unfathomably complex, and we are inherently limited in what we can predict and explain. We have all experienced frustration with weather reports—it is a standing joke to blame the meteorologist for favorable forecasts that turn out to be wrong. But an appreciation of the many factors that enter into the development of a storm system justifies more tolerance of the limitations of forecasters.

In the human sciences it seems especially appropriate to view our task in terms of chaos theory (e.g., Duke, 1994). Even if we knew all the variables controlling behavior—and no one would claim that we do—our ability to predict would be limited by many unexpected and uncontrollable factors that are likely to affect a person over a period of time. People do not behave in a social vacuum. Consequently, simple cause–effect statements are exceedingly difficult to construct with confidence.

As we review the theories and evidence about the causes of and treatments for abnormal behavior, we will often encounter the complexities and shortcomings in the research literature. Our discussions of intervention in particular should be informed by the chaos perspective. Therapists have limited contact with their patients, all of whom live moment-to-moment in exquisitely complex interaction with others who themselves are affected on a moment-to-moment basis by hundreds of factors that are impossible to anticipate. We are not embracing chaos as a goal—we are not scientific nihilists; rather, we want to counsel humility, even awe, in an enterprise that tries to understand how things go awry with the human condition.

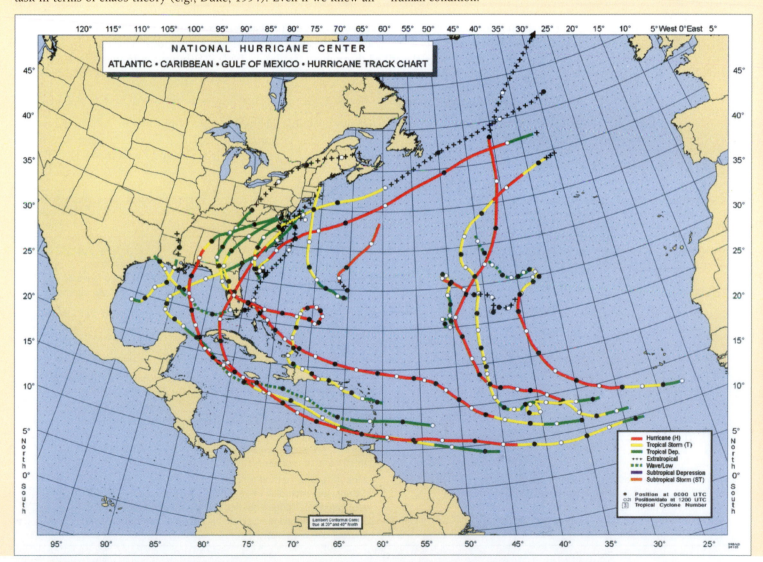

Chaos theory suggests that major weather events, such as Hurricane Katrina that hit New Orleans in 2005, can be influenced by seemingly trivial events, such as air's being disturbed by the flight of a butterfly thousands of miles away.

theories." Because of this, it is not enough to assert that traumatic experiences during childhood cause psychological maladjustment in adulthood. This is no more than a possibility. According to a scientific point of view, a hypothesis must be amenable to systematic testing that could show it to be false. That is, the focus of testing is on disproving rather than proving a theory.

In testing a theory, each scientific observation must be replicable. Each facet of a study must be carefully defined so that findings can be replicated. Much of this depends on using assessments with strong reliability and validity, as discussed in Chapter 3. Beyond choosing measures carefully, though, researchers in psychopathology choose among a set of different types of research designs.

In this chapter, we discuss some of the most common types of research designs. It is worth noting at the outset that many aspects of research involve ethical issues. For example, researchers must consider whether participants are fully informed, whether any coercion is involved in a study, and the long-term implications of findings. Ethical issues in the conduct of research are covered in Chapter 17.

Approaches to Research on Psychopathology

In this section we describe the most common research methods in the study of abnormal behavior: the case study, correlational methods, and experimental methods. These methods will be seen in the studies described throughout this book. Table 4.1 shows a summary of the strengths and weaknesses of each.

The Case Study

The **case study**, perhaps the most familiar method of observing human behavior, involves recording detailed information about one person at a time. The clinical cases described in the last chapter are examples of case studies. A comprehensive case study would cover family his-

Table 4.1 Research Methods in Psychopathology

Method	Description	Evaluation
Case study	Collection of detailed biographical information	Excellent source of hypotheses Can provide information about novel cases or procedures Can disconfirm a relationship that was believed to be universal Cannot provide causal evidence, because cannot rule out alternative hypotheses May be biased by observer's theoretical viewpoint
Correlation	Study of the relationship between two or more variables; measured as they exist in nature	Widely used because we cannot manipulate many risk variables (such as personality, trauma, or genes) or diagnosis in psychopathology research Epidemiologists often use the correlational method to study the incidence, prevalence, and risk factors of disorders in a representative sample Behavioral genetic studies often use the correlational method to study the heritability of different mental disorders Cannot determine causality because of the directionality and third-variable problems
Experiment	Includes a manipulated independent variable, a dependent variable, preferably at least one control group, and random assignment	Most powerful method for determining causal relationships Often used in studies of treatment effectiveness Also used in analogue studies of the risk factors for mental illness Single case experimental designs are also common but can have limited external validity

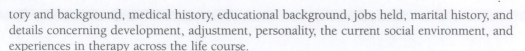

tory and background, medical history, educational background, jobs held, marital history, and details concerning development, adjustment, personality, the current social environment, and experiences in therapy across the life course.

Case studies lack the control and objectivity of other research methods. That is, the validity of the information gathered in a case study is sometimes questionable. The objectivity of case studies is limited because the clinician's paradigm will shape the kinds of information reported in a case study. To take one example, case studies by psychodynamic clinicians typically contain more information about the client's early childhood and parental conflicts than do reports by behavioral clinicians.

Despite their relative lack of control, case studies still play an important role in the study of abnormal behavior. Specifically, the case study can be used:

1. To provide a rich description of a clinical phenomenon
2. To disprove an allegedly universal hypothesis
3. To generate hypotheses that can be tested through controlled research

We discuss each of these uses next.

The Case Study as a Rich Description   Because it focuses on a single person, the case study can include much more detail than other research methods typically do. This is particularly helpful when a report covers a rare clinical phenomenon. Another typical use is to provide a detailed description of how a new intervention works. See Focus on Discovery 4.2 for an example of the level of detail that can be gathered within a case study.

The Case Study Can Disprove but Not Prove a Hypothesis   Case histories can provide examples that contradict an assumed universal relationship. Consider, for example, the proposition that depressive episodes are always preceded by life stress. Finding even a single case of non-stress-related depression would negate the theory.

Even though case studies can disprove a hypothesis, case studies do not provide good evidence in support of a particular theory, because they do not provide a way to rule out alternative hypotheses. To illustrate this problem, consider the sleep/wake intervention described in Focus on Discovery 4.2. Although it would be tempting to conclude that the therapy is effective, such a conclusion cannot be drawn legitimately because other factors could have produced the change. A stressful situation in the client's life may have resolved, or the client may have adopted better coping skills during the time period of the intervention. Thus, several plausible rival hypotheses could account for the clinical improvement. The data yielded by the case study do not allow us to determine the true cause of the change.

Generating Hypotheses   Although the case study may not provide valid support for hypotheses, it does help generate hypotheses. As they hear the life histories of many different clients, clinicians may notice patterns and then formulate important hypotheses that they could not have formed otherwise. For example, in his clinical work, Kanner (1943) noticed that some disturbed children showed a similar constellation of symptoms, including failure to develop language and extreme isolation from other people. He therefore proposed a new diagnosis—infantile autism—that was subsequently confirmed by larger-scale research and adopted into the DSM (see p. 450).

The Correlational Method

A great deal of psychopathology research relies on the **correlational method**. Correlational studies address questions of the form "Do variable X and variable Y vary together (co-relate)?" In correlational research, variables are measured as they exist in nature. This is distinct from experimental research (discussed on pp. 110–115), in which the researcher manipulates variables.

To illustrate the difference, consider that the role of stress in hypertension (high blood pressure) can be assessed with either a correlational or an experimental design. In a correlational study, we might measure stress levels by interviewing people about their recent stressful experiences. Stress would then be correlated with blood pressure measurements collected from these same people. In

FOCUS ON DISCOVERY 4.2

An Example of the Advantages and Disadvantages of Case Studies

Bipolar disorder, defined by episodes of mania, is one of the most severe of psychological illnesses. Manic episodes are defined by extreme happiness or anger, along with increased confidence, energy, talkativeness, goal-directed behavior, and decreased need for sleep. Of particular concern, when people are manic, they may not be aware of potential dangers, and so they are likely to engage in reckless behaviors, such as driving too fast, spending too much money, or being more sexual. Beyond the manic episodes, depressive episodes are also common for people with this disorder. The manic and the depressive symptoms both take a toll on jobs, relationships, and self-esteem.

Although bipolar disorder is believed to be inherited, sleep loss can trigger episodic symptoms of bipolar disorder (Colombo et al., 1999). Wehr and his colleagues (1998) noted that electric lights might disrupt our natural sleep schedules and that this might be of particular concern for people with this disorder. Given this, they theorized that a more natural light–dark cycle that mirrored the natural rhythm of the sun might help protect sleep and thereby reduce symptoms in bipolar disorder. To test the influence of natural light–dark cycles on the course of bipolar disorder, Wehr's group tried a unique treatment idea: they asked a person with bipolar disorder to extend his hours of bedrest.

At the time the case study began, the patient was a 51-year-old married man who had worked as a chief engineer in a technology firm. He had always had a great deal of energy and drive. He reported that his mother had a history of depression. The patient developed depression in 1990 and was treated with two antidepressants. As is relatively common for people diagnosed with bipolar disorder (Ghaemi & Goodwin, 2003), the antidepressants triggered mild manic symptoms. In his case, though, the symptoms of depression and mania continued for more than 2 years, despite the addition of mood-stabilizing medications such as lithium and divalproex. Antidepressants were discontinued, but then he became depressed. When a new antidepressant was started, he developed manic symptoms again. Over a period of several years, he frequently shifted between depression and mania. During his manic periods, he was overly active, slept only 3–4 hours, and woke

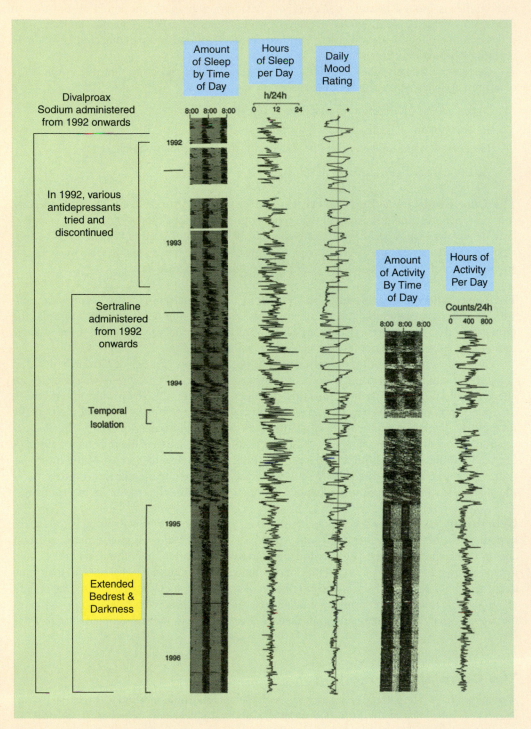

Figure 4.1 Relationship of extended bedrest with sleep, mood, and activity patterns in patient treated with extended bed rest. Adapted from Wehr et al. (1998).

up before dawn. When he was depressed, he would spend long hours of the day inactive, then sleep for 10 or 12 hours, waking up late in the morning or even during the afternoon.

After several years of monitoring his symptoms and trying different medications, Wehr and his colleagues began the novel sleep/wake intervention in May 1995. For the first 3 months, he slept in a bedroom on a research ward where lights could be carefully controlled. The room was sealed to protect against accidental light exposure. During the dark period, he was asked not to take part in any activities and even to avoid using the radio, TV or telephone. During the first part of the intervention, he was asked to spend 14 hours resting in the dark. Over the next 18 months, the dark period was gradually reduced to 10 hours. Medications were kept stable throughout the sleep/wake intervention phase.

As shown in Figure 4.1, the number of hours per night that the client slept varied a good deal up until 1995, when the intervention began. At that point, the number of hours of sleep per night became much more routine. Also at that time, the amount of daily activity began to vary much less; the patient no longer displayed days of extreme inactivity or days of extreme hyperactivity. Most importantly, almost all of his mood ratings after the sleep/wake intervention began were in a neutral range, neither depressed nor manic. Hence the increase in the rest period appeared to be an effective way to bolster the effects of medication.

Although the findings were encouraging, this case study leaves many questions unanswered. These include whether the critical ingredient in the intervention is time spent sleeping, time spent resting, or just a focus on calmer routines. It is also possible that something other than sleep/wake cycles changed for this patient during the period of the intervention, such that the symptom reductions were unrelated to sleep/wake. Perhaps most importantly, case studies can never reveal whether a treatment will work well for other patients.

Fortunately, several researchers have extended these findings. In other case studies (Wirz-Justice et al., 1999) and uncontrolled studies (Barbini et al., 2005), researchers have achieved good results with encouraging people with bipolar disorder to extend their time spent in bed. Other researchers have tried to help people with bipolar disorder to create more stable patterns of daily activities, along with improving sleep routines (Frank et al., 2005; Shen et al., 2008; Totterdell & Kellett, 2008). Hence this early case report helped to generate interest in whether treatments focused on sleep could enhance the effects of medication in bipolar disorder. Although controlled trials have generated mixed results (Frank et al., 2005; Shen et al., 2008), researchers continue to refine this approach.

In short, case studies provide a way to demonstrate new and interesting treatments. Case studies, though, cannot address whether treatment is the sole cause of the change, nor can they address whether findings can be applied to other people.

an experimental study, in contrast, the experimenter might create stress in the laboratory; for example, some participants might be asked to give a speech to an audience about the aspect of their personal appearance they find least appealing (see Figure 4.2). The key difference between these methods is whether or not a variable is manipulated. Psychopathologists will rely on correlational methods when there are ethical reasons not to manipulate a variable; for example, no researcher would try to manipulate genes, trauma, severe stressors, or neurobiological deficits.

Numerous examples of **correlation** can be drawn from mental health research. For example, depression tends to correlate with anxiety; people who feel depressed tend to report feeling anxious. It is worth highlighting that comparisons of people with and without a diagnosis can be correlational as well. See Table 4.2 for a description of how such data might be coded. For example, two diagnostic groups may be compared to see how much stress was experienced before the onset of their disorders. In other words, questions are asked about relationships between a given diagnosis and some other variable; for

Although the information yielded by a case study does not fare well as a source of evidence, it is an important source of hypotheses. (Greg Smith/Cortis Images.)

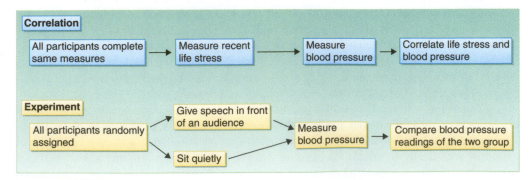

Figure 4.2 Correlational versus experimental studies.

Table 4.2 Data for a Correlational Study with Diagnosis

Participant	Diagnosis	Stress Score
1	1	65
2	1	72
3	0	40
4	1	86
5	0	72
6	0	21
7	1	65
8	0	40
9	1	37
10	0	28

Note: Diagnosis—having an anxiety disorder or not, with having an anxiety disorder designated as 1 and not as 0—is correlated with an assessment of recent life stress on a 0–100 scale. Higher scores indicate greater recent stress. To make the point clearly, we present a smaller sample of cases than would be used in an actual research study. Notice that diagnosis is associated with recent life stress. Patients with an anxiety disorder tend to have higher stress scores than people without an anxiety disorder. In this example, the correlation between stress and anxiety scores = + .60.

Table 4.3 Data for Determining a Correlation

	Height	Weight in Pounds
John	5'10''	170
Asher	5'10''	140
Eve	5'4''	112
Gail	5'3''	105
Jerry	5'10''	177
Gayla	5'2''	100
Steve	5'8''	145
Margy	5'5''	128
Gert	5'6''	143
Sean	5'10''	140
Kathleen	5'4''	116

Note: For these figures r = + .88.

example, "Is schizophrenia related to social class?" or "Are anxiety disorders related to neurotransmitter function?"

In the next sections, we discuss how to measure the relationship (correlation) between two variables, how to test whether the relationship is statistically and clinically significant, and some issues in determining whether variables are causally related. Then we discuss two specific domains of research that tend to use correlational designs: epidemiology as well as behavior and molecular genetics.

Measuring Correlation   The first step in determining a correlation is to obtain pairs of observations of the two variables in question. One example would be the height and weight of each participant. Another example would be the intelligence of mothers and daughters. Once such pairs of measurements are obtained, the strength of the relationship between the paired observations can be computed to determine the **correlation coefficient**, denoted by the symbol r. This statistic may take any value between -1.00 and +1.00, and it measures both the magnitude and the direction of a relationship. The higher the absolute value of r, the stronger the relationship between the two variables. That is, an r of either +1.00 or −1.00 indicates the strongest possible, or perfect, relationship, whereas an r of .00 indicates that the variables are unrelated. If the sign of r is positive, the two variables are said to be positively related; in other words, as the values for variable X increase, those for variable Y also tend to increase. Table 4.3 shows data for a correlation of +.88 between height and weight, indicating a very strong positive relationship; as height increases, so does weight. Conversely, when the sign of r is negative, variables are said to be negatively related; as scores on one variable increase, those for the other tend to decrease. For example, the number of hours spent watching television is negatively correlated with grade point average.

One way to think about the strength of a correlation is to plot the two variables. In Figure 4.3, each point represents the scores for a given person on variable X and variable Y. In a perfect correlation, all the points fall on a straight line; if we know the value of only one of the variables for a person, we can know the value of the other variable. Similarly, when the correlation is relatively large, there is only a small degree of scatter about the line of perfect correlation. The values tend to scatter increasingly far from the line as the correlations become lower. When the correlation reaches .00, knowledge of a person's score on one variable tells us nothing about his or her score on the other.

Statistical and Clinical Significance   Thus far we have established that the magnitude of a correlation coefficient tells us the strength of a relationship between two variables. But scientists use **statistical significance** for a more rigorous test of the importance of a relationship. (Significance is considered with many different statistics, but here we focus on correlation coefficients.) A statistically significant correlation is unlikely to have occurred by chance. A nonsignificant correlation may have occurred by chance, so it does not provide evidence for an important relationship. When a correlation is not statistically significant, it is highly likely that no significant relationship will be observed if the study is repeated.

A statistical finding is usually considered significant if the probability that it is a chance finding is 5 or less in 100. This level of significance is called the alpha level, commonly written as $p < .05$ (the p stands for probability). In general, as the absolute size of the correlation coefficient increases, the result is more likely to be statistically significant. For example, a correlation of .80 is more likely than a correlation of .40 to be significant.

Statistical significance is influenced not only by the size of the relationship between variables but also by the number of participants in a study. The more people studied, the smaller the correlation needs to be to reach statistical significance. For example, a correlation of r = .30 is statistically significant when the number of observations is large—say, 300—but is not significant if only 20 observations were made. Thus, if the alcohol consumption of 30 men was studied and the correlation between depression and drinking was found to be .32, the correlation would not be statistically significant. The same correlation, however, would be significant if 300 men were studied.

Beyond statistical significance, it is important to consider clinical significance. **Clinical significance** is defined by whether a relationship between variables is large enough to matter. In a survey as large as the United States Census, almost every correlation you could conceive of would be statistically significant. Because of this issue, researchers also attend to whether a correlation is large enough to be of clinical significance. For example, one might want to see

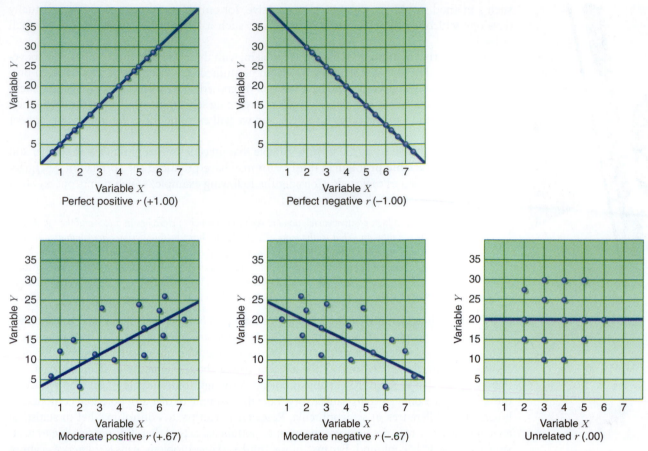

Figure 4.3 Scatter diagrams showing various degrees of correlation.

that a risk factor has a moderately strong relationship with the severity of symptoms. Clinical significance is also considered with statistics other than correlations. For a treatment effect to be considered clinically significant, a researcher might want to see that symptoms in the active treatment condition were decreased by 50 percent or that patients appeared comparable to those without disorder at the end of treatment. In other words, researchers should evaluate not only whether an effect is statistically significant but also whether the effect is large enough to be meaningful in predicting or treating a clinical disorder (Jacobson et al., 1999).

Problems of Causality   Even though it is commonly used, the correlational method has a critical drawback: it does not allow determination of cause–effect relationships. A large correlation between two variables tells us only that they are related to each other, but we do not know if either variable is the cause of the other. For example, a correlation has been found between the diagnosis of schizophrenia and social class; lower-class people are diagnosed with schizophrenia more often than middle-and upper-class people are. One possible explanation is that the stresses of living in the lowest social class cause an increase in the prevalence of schizophrenia. But a second hypothesis has been supported. It may be that the disorganized behavior patterns of persons with schizophrenia cause them to perform poorly in their occupational endeavors and thus to become impoverished.

The **directionality problem** is present in most correlational research designs—hence the often-cited dictum "Correlation does not imply causation." One way of overcoming the directionality problem is based on the idea that causes must precede effects. In a **longitudinal design,** the researcher tests whether causes are present before a disorder has developed. This is in contrast to a **cross-sectional design**, in which the causes and effects are measured at the same point in time. A classic longitudinal design to study the development of schizophrenia, for example, would involve selecting a large sample of babies, measuring risk variables repeatedly throughout development, and following the sample for 45 years to determine who develops schizophrenia. But

In some epidemiological research, interviewers go door-to-door to conduct interviews. (Creatas/SuperStock, Inc.)

such a method would be prohibitively expensive, for only about 1 person in 100 eventually develops schizophrenia. The yield of data from such a longitudinal study would be small indeed.

The **high-risk method** overcomes this problem; with this approach, only people with above-average risk of developing schizophrenia would be studied. For example, several research programs involve studying people who have a parent diagnosed with schizophrenia (having a parent with schizophrenia increases a person's risk for developing schizophrenia). The high-risk method is also used to study several other disorders, and we will examine these findings in subsequent chapters.

Even if a high-risk study identifies a variable that precedes schizophrenia, a researcher still faces the **third-variable problem**: a third factor may have produced the correlation. Such factors are often labeled as *confounds*. Consider the following example, which points out an obvious third variable.

> One regularly finds a high positive correlation between the number of churches in a city and the number of crimes committed in that city. That is, the more churches a city has, the more crimes are committed in it. Does this mean that religion fosters crime, or does it mean that crime fosters religion? It means neither. The relationship is due to a particular third variable—population. The higher the population of a particular community, the greater . . . the number of churches and . . . the frequency of criminal activity. (Neale & Liebert, 1986, p. 109)

Psychopathology research offers numerous examples of third variables. Biochemical differences between people with and without schizophrenia are often reported. These differences could reflect the influence of medications used for schizophrenia or even dietary differences between groups; the differences do not reveal anything about the nature of schizophrenia. Are there ways to resolve the third-variable problem? Although some strategies can help reduce it, the solutions are only partially satisfactory. Take the example of diet as a potential confound in biochemical differences in schizophrenia. Researchers can try to control for diet in statistical analyses, but they may not measure the most important aspects of diet. It is not feasible to measure every possible confound. Because of the third-variable problem, causal inferences cannot be made from correlational data.

One Example of Correlational Research: Epidemiological Research

Epidemiology is the study of the distribution of disorders in a population. That is, data are gathered about the rates of a disorder and its possible correlates in a large sample. Epidemiological research focuses on three features of a disorder:

1. **Prevalence**. The proportion of people with the disorder either currently or during their lifetime
2. **Incidence**. The proportion of people who develop *new* cases of the disorder in some period, usually a year
3. **Risk factor**. Variables that are related to the likelihood of developing the disorder

Epidemiological studies of risk factors are usually correlational studies because they examine how variables relate to each other without including a manipulation of the independent variable.

Epidemiological studies are designed to be *representative* of the population being studied—researchers test a group of people who match the population on key characteristics, like gender, economic status, and ethnicity. Unfortunately, much of mental health research does not follow these principles but rather draws on samples that are not representative. For example, many studies use undergraduate samples. Undergraduates, though, are likely to be wealthier and more educated than the general population. If we only studied undergraduates with anxiety disorders, we could end up concluding that people with anxiety disorders are above average in intelligence. Other studies use samples drawn from treatment centers. But people who seek treatment may be those with the more severe forms of disorders. For example, estimates of suicide rates for a given disorder are much higher when measured in hospitalized samples as compared to rates in representative community samples. These types of bias can skew our perceptions of factors related to mental disorders. Epidemiological studies, then, are needed to carefully identify risk variables and outcomes for disorders.

The National Comorbidity Survey–Replication is an example of one large-scale national survey that used structured interviews to collect information on the prevalence of several diagnoses (Kessler, Berglund et al., 2005). Table 4.4 shows some data from this study. The table presents lifetime prevalence rates—the proportion of people who experienced a disorder during their lifetime. From the table, we can see that major depression, alcoholism, and anxiety disorders are very common—so common, in fact, that as many as half (46.4 percent) of the people in the United States describe meeting criteria for a mental disorder at some point during their lives. Knowing that mental disorders will strike one out of every two people should help reduce stigma. People who experience the disorders may take comfort in knowing that so many other people struggle with similar issues.

Knowledge about risk factors may give clues to the causes of disorders. For example, depression is about twice as common in women as in men. Thus, gender is a risk factor for depression. In Chapter 8, we will review theories about this gender difference. The results of epidemiological research may inform us about risk factors (like gender and social class) that can be more thoroughly investigated using other research methods.

Another Example of Correlational Research: Behavior and Molecular Genetics

Research on behavior genetics has relied on three basic methods to uncover whether a genetic predisposition for psychopathology is inherited—comparison of members of a family, comparison of pairs of twins, and the investigation of adoptees. In each case, researchers are interested in whether relatives demonstrate similarity (correlations) in their patterns of disorder.

The **family method** can be used to study a genetic predisposition among members of a family because the average number of genes shared by two blood relatives is known. Children receive a random sample of half their genes from one parent and half from the other, so on average siblings and parents and children share 50 percent of their genes. People who share 50 percent of their genes with a given person are called first-degree relatives of that person. Relatives not as closely related share fewer genes. For example, nephews and nieces share 25 percent of the genetic makeup of an uncle and are called second-degree relatives. If a predisposition for a mental disorder can be inherited, a study of the family should reveal a relationship between the proportion of shared genes and the *concordance* of the disorder in relatives (that is, whether the relatives are matched on presence or absence of a disorder).

The starting point in such investigations is the collection of a sample of persons with the diagnosis in question. These people are referred to as **index cases** or **probands**. Then relatives are studied to determine the frequency with which the same diagnosis might be applied to them. If a genetic predisposition to the disorder being studied is present, first-degree relatives of the index cases should have the disorder at a rate higher than that found in the general population. This is the case with schizophrenia: about 10 percent of the first-degree relatives of index cases with schizophrenia can be diagnosed as having this disorder, compared with about 1 percent of the general population.

Epidemiological research has shown that mood disorders, anxiety disorders, and substance abuse are extremely common. (Stone/Getty Images.)

Table 4.4 Lifetime Prevalence Rates of Selected Diagnoses

Disorder	Male	Female	Total
Major depressive disorder	13.2	20.2	16.6
Bipolar I or II disorder	na	na	3.9
Dysthymia	1.8	3.1	2.5
Panic disorder	3.1	6.2	4.7
Agoraphobia without panic	1.1	1.6	1.4
Social phobia	11.1	13.0	12.1
Specific phobia	8.9	15.8	12.5
Generalized anxiety disorder	na	na	5.7
Alcohol abuse	19.6	7.5	13.2
Drug abuse	11.6	4.8	7.9

Source: From data collected in the National Comorbidity Survey–Replication (Kessler, Berglund et al., 2005).

Although the methodology of family studies is clear, the data they yield are not always easy to interpret. For example, children of parents with agoraphobia—people suffering from a fear of being in places where it would be hard to escape if they were to become highly anxious— are themselves more likely than average to have agoraphobia. Does this mean that a predisposition for this anxiety disorder is genetically transmitted? Not necessarily. The greater number of family members with agoraphobia could reflect the child-rearing practices and modeling of the phobic parents. In other words, family studies show that agoraphobia runs in families but not necessarily that a genetic predisposition is involved.

In the **twin method** both **monozygotic (MZ) twins** and **dizygotic (DZ) twins** are compared. MZ, or identical, twins develop from a single fertilized egg and are genetically the same. DZ, or fraternal, pairs develop from separate eggs and are on average only 50 percent alike genetically, no more alike than are any two siblings. MZ twins are always the same sex, but DZ twins can be either the same sex or opposite in sex. Twin studies begin with diagnosed cases and then search for the presence of the disorder in the other twin. When the twins are similar diagnostically, they are said to be concordant. To the extent that a predisposition for a mental disorder can be inherited, **concordance** for the disorder should be greater in genetically identical MZ pairs than in DZ pairs. When the MZ concordance rate is higher than the DZ rate, the characteristic being studied is said to be heritable. We will see in later chapters that the concordance for many forms of psychopathology is higher in MZ twins than in DZ twins.

The ability to offer a genetic interpretation of data from twin studies hinges on what is called the "equal environment assumption." The equal environment assumption is that the environmental factors that are partial causes of concordance are equally influential for both MZ pairs and DZ pairs. This does not mean that the environments of MZ and DZ twins are equal in all respects; the assumption of equality applies only to factors that are plausible environmental causes of psychopathology. For example, the equal environment assumption would assert that MZ pairs and DZ pairs are equally matched on numbers of stressful life experiences. In general, the equal environment assumption seems to be reasonable, although it is clearly in need of further study (Kendler, 1993).

The **adoptees method** studies children who were adopted and reared completely apart from their biological parents. Though infrequent, findings from this method are more clear-cut because the child is not raised by the parent with a disorder. If a high frequency of agoraphobia was found in children reared apart from their parents who also had agoraphobia, we would have convincing support for the theory that the disorder is heritable. Another adoptee method is called **cross-fostering**. In this method, children are adopted and reared completely apart from their biological parents. In this case, however, the adoptive parent has a particular disorder, not the biological parent. The adoptee method is also used to examine gene–environment interactions. For example, one study found that adoptees who had a biological parent with antisocial personality disorder (APD) and were raised in an unhealthy adoptive family (e.g., parental conflict, abuse, alcohol/drugs in the adoptive family) were more likely to develop APD than two other groups of adoptees: (1) adoptees who had a biological parent with APD but were raised in a healthy family and (2) adoptees who had no biological parent with APD but were raised in an unhealthy adoptive family (Cadoret et al., 1995). Thus, genes (APD in a biological parent) and environment (unhealthy adoptive family) worked together to increase the risk for developing antisocial personality disorder.

Two methods used in molecular genetics research (see Chapter 2) include linkage analysis and association studies. The **linkage analysis** method studies families in which a disorder is heavily concentrated and collects diagnostic information and blood samples from affected people and their relatives. Linkage analysis relies on the study of **genetic markers.** Genetic markers are diseases or characteristics for which we know the chromosomal location of the genes involved. If the occurrence of a form of psychopathology among relatives co-occurs with the genetic marker, it is concluded that one of the genes predisposing to the psychopathology is on the same chromosome and in a similar location on that chromosome (i.e., it is linked) as the gene controlling the other characteristic. We will see several examples of linkage analysis in subsequent chapters, especially when we study schizophrenia (Chapter 11), though "breakthrough" findings have often failed to be replicated. The greatest success of the method thus far has been in identifying specific genes on several chromosomes that are extremely important in Alzheimer's disease, drawing on a correlation between Alzheimer's disease and Down syndrome (Chapter 15). Linkage analysis will be most successful with disorders for which a single gene is involved, like Huntington's Chorea (Plomin & McGuffin, 2003). As we noted earlier, the disorders we cover in this book undoubtedly involve many, many genes.

Association studies are another method of molecular genetics. In these studies, researchers examine the relationship between a specific allele and a trait or behavior in the population. Because the researchers are measuring a specific allele rather than the general chromosome location (as in linkage studies), association studies are more precise. Association studies have become much more common as technologies have become more affordable for measuring alleles. In Chapter 15, we will describe a particular allele called APOE-4 that is related to later-onset Alzheimer's disease. Not all people with Alzheimer's have this, and not all people who have APOE-4 develop Alzheimer's. Still, there is a strong association between this allele and Alzheimer's disease (Williams, 2003).

Quick Summary

Science is the systematic pursuit of knowledge through observation. The first step of science is to define a theory and related hypotheses. A good theory is precise and could be disproven.

The case study is an excellent way of examining the behavior of a single person in rich detail and of generating hypotheses that can be evaluated by controlled research. Sometimes, the evidence provided goes against a universal law or illustrates a rare disorder or technique. But findings from a case study may or may not be valid—they may be biased by the observer's theories, and the patterns observed in one case may not apply to others. Furthermore, the case study cannot provide satisfactory evidence concerning cause–effect relationships because alternative hypotheses are not examined.

Correlational studies allow a researcher to gather data about variables and to see if these variables covary. No variables are manipulated; rather, the researcher assesses whether a naturally occurring relationship is large enough to appear statistically significant and clinically meaningful. Psychopathologists are forced to make heavy use of the correlational method because there are many key variables, including diagnosis, genes, trauma, and neurobiological deficits, that they do not have the freedom to manipulate. But correlational findings are clouded by third-variable and directionality problems.

Studies of epidemiology and behavior genetics often use correlational designs. Researchers use epidemiological studies to assess how common disorders are (incidence and prevalence) and what risk factors are associated with them. Behavior genetics research uses the family method, looking to see how the presence of a disorder varies by the amount of genes shared by family members; the twin method, comparing monozygotic and dizygotic twins to see whether twins with more shared genes are at greater risk for developing a disorder; and the adoptees method to help separate gene and environmental effects. Molecular genetics research includes linkage analysis and association studies.

Check Your Knowledge 4.2

Answer the questions.

1. Which of the following are good uses of case studies (circle all that apply):
   a. to illustrate a rare disorder or treatment
   b. to show that a theory does not fit for everyone
   c. to prove a model
   d. to show cause and effect
2. Correlational studies involve:
   a. manipulating the independent variable
   b. manipulating the dependent variable
   c. manipulating the independent and dependent variable
   d. none of the above
3. The most central problem that is unique to correlational studies, regardless of how carefully a researcher designs a study, is:
   a. Findings are qualitative rather than statistical.
   b. It is impossible to know which variable changes first.
   c. Third variables may explain a correlation.
   d. Findings may not generalize.
4. Incidence refers to:
   a. the number of people who will develop a disorder during their lifetime
   b. the number of people who report a disorder at the time of an interview
   c. the number of people who develop a disorder during a given time period
   d. none of the above
5. In behavior genetics studies, researchers can rule out the influence of parenting variables most carefully if they conduct studies using the:
   a. correlational method
   b. family method
   c. twin method
   d. adoptee method

The Experiment

The **experiment** is the most powerful tool for determining causal relationships. It involves the **random assignment** of participants to conditions, the manipulation of an **independent variable**, and the measurement of a **dependent variable**. In the field of psychopathology, the experiment is most often used to evaluate the effects of therapies.

As an introduction to the basics of experimental research, consider a study of how emotional expression relates to health (Pennebaker, Kiecolt-Glaser, & Glaser, 1988). In this experiment, 50 undergraduates came to a laboratory for four consecutive days. On each of the four days, half the students wrote a short essay about a past traumatic event. They were instructed as follows:

During each of the four writing days, I want you to write about the most traumatic and upsetting experiences of your entire life. You can write on different topics each day or on the same topic for all four days. The important thing is that you write about your deepest thoughts and feelings. Ideally, whatever you write about should deal with an event or experience that you have not talked with others about in detail.

The remaining students also came to the laboratory each day but wrote essays describing topics like their daily activities, a recent social event, the shoes they were wearing, and their plans for the rest of the day.

Information about how often the participants used the university health center was available for the 15-week period before the study began and for the six weeks after it had begun. Figure 4.4 shows these data. Members of the two groups had visited the health center about equally before the experiment. After writing the essays, however, the number of visits declined for students who wrote about their emotions and increased for the remaining students. (This increase may have been due to seasonal variation in rates of visits to the health center. The second measure of number of visits was taken in February, just before midterm exams.) From these data the investigators concluded that expressing emotions has a beneficial effect on health.

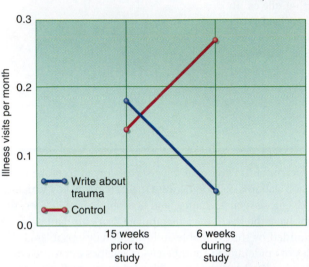

Figure 4.4 Health-center illness visits for the periods before and during the experiment. Visits for students who wrote about past traumas decreased while visits for those who wrote about mundane events actually rose. After Pennebaker et al. (1988).

Basic Features of Experimental Design   The emotional expression study illustrates many of the basic features of an experiment.

1. The investigator manipulates an independent variable. In this study, the independent variable was the writing topic.
2. Participants are assigned to the two conditions (emotions versus mundane happenings) by random assignment.
3. The researcher measures a dependent variable that is expected to vary with conditions of the independent variable. The dependent variable in this study was the number of visits to the health center.
4. Differences between conditions on the dependent variable are called the **experimental effect**.

To illustrate, consider a hypothetical study of the effectiveness of cognitive therapy in reducing depression among 20 depressed patients. (In actual research, 20 patients would be regarded as a very small sample; we present a small number of cases so the example is easier to follow.) The independent variable is treatment condition (cognitive therapy versus no treatment); 10 patients are randomly assigned to receive cognitive therapy and 10 are randomly assigned to a no-treatment control group. The dependent variable is the score on a standardized measure of the severity of depression, assessed after 12 weeks of treatment or no treatment; higher scores reflect more severe depression. Table 4.5 presents data for the hypothetical patients in each group. Note that the average scores of the two groups differ considerably (8.3 for the cognitive therapy group and 21.7 for the no-treatment group). This difference between groups, called the experimental effect, is an index of whether the independent variable influences the dependent variable. To evaluate the importance of an experimental effect, as with correlations, researchers determine statistical significance.

Internal Validity   **Internal validity** refers to the extent to which the experimental effect can be attributed to the independent variable. For example, for a treatment study to have inter-

Table 4.5 Results of a Hypothetical Study Comparing Cognitive Therapy to No Treatment for Depression

Cognitive Treatment Participants	Depression Score at End of Study	No Treatment Participants	Depression Score at End of Study
Participant 1	8	Participant 11	22
Participant 2	6	Participant 12	14
Participant 3	12	Participant 13	26
Participant 4	4	Participant 14	28
Participant 5	3	Participant 15	19
Participant 6	6	Participant 16	27
Participant 7	18	Participant 17	6
Participant 8	14	Participant 18	32
Participant 9	7	Participant 19	21
Participant 10	5	Participant 20	23
Group average	**8.3**		**21.7**

Note: Low scores indicate less depression after treatment.

nal validity, the researchers must include at least one **control group** that does not receive the experimental treatment. That is, a control group is needed to claim that the effects of an experiment are due to the independent variable. In the Pennebaker study, the control group wrote about mundane happenings. In the cognitive therapy example, the control group received no treatment. The data from a control group provide a standard against which the effects of an independent variable can be assessed.

To illustrate the importance of a control group with another example, consider a study of the effectiveness of a particular therapy in reducing anxiety. Let us assume that persons with anxiety disorders receive therapy to remedy their condition. With no control group against which to compare the improvement, we cannot argue that changes are due to the treatment or that this study is an experiment. The improvement in anxiety from the beginning of the treatment to the end could have been due to factors other than the treatment, such as the resolution of stressors, the passage of time, or support from friends. Without a control group, any changes during treatment are difficult to interpret.

In the example just outlined, including a control group would improve internal validity. For example, a control group might consist of persons with equally severe anxiety who do not receive the treatment. The effects of the independent variable could be assessed by comparing changes in anxiety of the treatment and control groups. If the treatment group experiences more relief from anxiety than does the control group, we can be relatively confident that this difference is attributable to the treatment. See Focus on Discovery 4.3 for a discussion of some special considerations when a control group includes a **placebo**.

The inclusion of a control group does not always ensure internal validity, however. Consider another therapy study involving two psychiatric inpatient units. An investigator may decide to select one inpatient unit to receive an experimental treatment and the other unit as a control. In this study, the researcher cannot claim that group differences are the result of treatment because a competing hypothesis cannot be disproven: patients in the two units might have differed because staff on the two units might offer care that differs in many ways. Without true random assignment, potential confounds make results hard to interpret. This study design is poor because the researchers did not use random assignment. To randomly assign participants in a two-group experiment, for example, the researchers could toss a coin for each participant. If the coin turned up heads, the participant would be assigned to one group; if tails, to the other group. Random assignment helps ensure that groups are similar on variables other than the independent variable.

External Validity   **External validity** is defined as the extent to which results can be generalized beyond the study. If investigators find that a particular treatment helps a particular group of patients, they will want to conclude that this treatment will be effective for other

FOCUS ON DISCOVERY 4.3

The Placebo Effect

Research on the effects of treatment—psychological or biological—should consider the **placebo effect**. This term refers to an improvement in physical or psychological condition that is due to a patient's expectations of help rather than to any active ingredient in a treatment. The classic example of a placebo effect occurs when a doctor prescribes a sugar pill but describes the pill as a proven treatment, and the patient reports symptom relief. J. D. Frank (1978) related placebo effects to faith healing in nonscientific societies. For centuries, people have made pilgrimages to sanctified places and ingested sometimes foul-smelling concoctions in the belief that these efforts would improve their health. Sometimes they did.

In psychotherapy research, patients in placebo groups receive support and encouragement but do not receive the active ingredient in the kind of therapy under study. For example, in a cognitive therapy study, the person in the placebo control condition would not get help with changing self-critical thoughts.

The effects of placebos are significant and sometimes even long lasting. For example, a meta-analysis of 75 research studies revealed that 29.7 percent of patients with depression improved after they received a placebo (Walsh et al., 2002). Among depressed patients who respond to antidepressant medication, many may actually be showing a placebo response (Kirsch, 2000). To know whether a treatment is effective because of the active chemical ingredients or a placebo response, medication trials often include a placebo control group.

In most medication studies with a placebo control group, a **double-blind procedure** is used. That is, researchers and patients are not told whether the patient receives active medication or placebo, so as to reduce bias in evaluating outcomes. A double-blind procedure can be hard to implement. Researchers and patients may figure out who is getting the active treatment because medications are much more likely to produce side effects than placebos are (Salamone, 2000).

The use of placebo control has become hotly contested. First, it raises ethical issues because effective treatment is being withheld from some patients. Second, for ethical reasons, potential participants must be informed about the details of the study in which they are being asked to participate (see p. 542), including if they have a chance of being assigned to a placebo condition. What does this knowledge do to the possibility of experiencing a placebo effect? Can the findings be generalized if people who feel an intense need for an active treatment won't sign up for a study?

Problems such as these have led the World Medical Association (2000, as cited in Forster, Emanuel, & Grady, 2001) to suggest that placebo and no-treatment control groups should only be used if the experimenter can justify the need for such groups scientifically and if the study does not include people who might be irreversibly harmed by the lack of treatment (e.g., people who are acutely suicidal). Instead of a placebo control, they recommend comparing an experimental treatment to the standard treatment. Of course, this approach can only be used if there is a standard treatment. In sum, there is considerable pressure against the use of placebo trials.

Others have argued that placebo control groups are vital for testing how treatments work (Charney et al., 2002). For example, consider studies of St.-John's-wort, an herbal remedy that many people believed could be helpful for depression. In one study, St.-John's-wort performed comparably to a standard antidepressant in producing relief from depressive symptoms (Hypericum Depression Trial Study Group, 2002). If no placebo control group were included, the conclusion of the study would have seemed supportive of St.-John's-wort. But the researchers also included a placebo control group, and they showed that neither St.-John's-wort nor the standard antidepressant treatment fared better than placebo. These results, then, suggest that St.-John's-wort is not an effective treatment. The inclusion of the placebo control group changes the conclusions of the study rather dramatically!

The debate continues over whether or not to use placebo control groups. The answers are not easy, and they are likely to vary for different disorders, different patients, and different researchers.

The effects of pilgrimages to shrines, such as Fatima, may be placebo effects. (Hans Georg Roth/Corbis Images.)

similar patients, at other times, and in other places. For example, Pennebaker and his colleagues would hope that their findings would generalize to other instances of emotional expression (e.g., confiding to a close friend), to other situations, and to people other than the study participants.

Determining the external validity of the results of an experiment is extremely difficult. For example, participants in studies often behave in certain ways because they are being observed, and thus results that are produced in the laboratory may not automatically be produced in the natural environment. External validity may also be threatened by including only a select group of persons in a study, such as college students (Coyne, 1994) or Caucasian middle-class Americans (Hall, 2001). Many treatment studies have recruited participants who suffer only from the illness being considered and excluded people who have additional mental illnesses. Because many people suffer from more than one mental illness, participants in these treatment studies may not mirror patients in the real world. Researchers must be alert to the extent to which they can claim findings are likely to generalize to people and instances not studied. Often, they must perform similar studies in new settings to test the generalizability of a finding.

Analogue Experiments   The experimental method is the most telling way to determine cause–effect relationships. Even though experiments are typically used to test treatments, there are many situations in which the experimental method cannot be used to understand the causes of abnormal behavior. Why?

Suppose that a researcher has hypothesized that a child's emotionally charged, overly dependent relationship with his or her mother causes generalized anxiety disorder. An experimental test of this hypothesis would require assigning infants randomly to either of two groups of mothers. The mothers in one group would undergo an extensive training program to ensure that they would be able to create a highly emotional atmosphere and foster overdependence in children. The mothers in the second group would be trained not to create such a relationship with their children. The researcher would then wait until the participants in each group reached adulthood and determine how many of them had developed generalized anxiety disorder. Clearly, this is unethical. (Ethical issues are considered in detail in Chapter 17.)

Studies of college students with mild symptoms may not provide a good analogue for major mental illness. (B. Daemmrich/The Image Works.)

In an effort to take advantage of the power of the experimental method, researchers sometimes use an **analogue experiment**. Investigators attempt to bring a related phenomenon—that is, an analogue—into the laboratory for more intensive study. Because a true experiment is conducted, results with good internal validity can be obtained. The problem of external validity arises, however, because the researchers are no longer studying the actual phenomenon of interest.

In one type of analogue study, temporary symptoms are produced through experimental manipulations. For example, lactate infusion can elicit a panic attack, hypnotic suggestion can produce blindness similar to that seen in conversion disorder, and threats to self-esteem can produce anxiety or sadness. If mild symptoms can be experimentally induced by such manipulations, this may provide clues into the causes of more severe symptoms.

In another type of analogue study, participants are selected because they are considered similar to people with certain diagnoses. Thousands of studies, for example, have been conducted with college students who received high scores on questionnaire measures of anxiety or depression.

A third type of analogue study involves using animals as a way to understand human behavior. For example, researchers found that dogs who were exposed to electrical shocks that they could not control developed many of the symptoms of depression, including seeming despair and passivity (Seligman, Maier, & Geer, 1968). Similarly, researchers interested in studying anxiety disorder in humans sometimes study how animals become conditioned to fear previously unthreatening stimuli (Grillon, 2002). Such animal models have helped us understand more about the neurotransmitter systems involved in depression and anxiety disorders in humans.

The key to interpreting such studies lies in the validity of the analogue. Is a stressor encountered in the laboratory fundamentally similar to the death of a parent or other serious stressors? Are distressed college students similar to people with clinically diagnosable depression? Are lethargy and decreased eating in mice akin to depressive symptoms in humans? Some would argue against such approaches overall, even when researchers are careful to discuss the limits of generalizability. For example, Coyne (1994) has argued that clinical depression is caused by different processes than those that cause common distress. He would argue that analogue studies with undergraduates have poor external validity.

Harlow's famous analogue research examined the effects of early separation from the mother on infant monkeys. Even a cloth surrogate mother is better than isolation for preventing subsequent emotional distress and depression. (Martin Rogers/Woodfin Camp & Associates.)

We believe that analogue studies can be very helpful but that findings from these types of studies must be considered conjointly with studies that do not rely on analogues. Science often depends on comparing the results of experimental analogue studies to those of longitudinal correlational studies. For example, analogue studies have shown that people with depression respond more negatively to laboratory stressors (an analogue of life stress), and correlational studies have shown that major life events predict the onset of clinical depression. Because the findings from correlational and analogue studies complement each other, this provides strong support for life event models of depression. Analogue studies can provide the precision of an experiment (high internal validity), whereas correlational studies provide the ability to study very important influences that cannot be manipulated, like the influence of death and trauma (high external validity).

Single-Subject Experiments   We have been discussing experimental research with groups of participants, but experiments do not always have to be conducted on groups. In **single-subject experimental design**, the experimenter studies how one person responds to manipulations of the independent variable. Unlike the traditional case studies described above, single-subject experimental designs can have high internal validity.

Chorpita, Vitali, and Barlow (1997) provide an example of how single case studies can provide well-controlled data. They describe their treatment of a 13-year-old girl with a phobia (intense fear) of choking, such that she was no longer able to eat solid foods. At times, her fear was so intense that she would experience fast heart rate, chest pain, dizziness, and other symptoms. She reported that the most frightening foods were hard foods, such as raw vegetables.

A behavioral treatment was designed based on exposure, a common strategy for treating anxiety. During the first 2 weeks, baseline ratings were taken of the amount of different foods eaten, along with her level of discomfort in eating those foods. Discomfort ratings were made on a "subjective units of distress scale" (SUDS) ranging from 0 to 9. Figure 4.5 shows her SUDS ratings and eating behavior over time for each food group. During the third week, she was asked to begin eating foods she described as less threatening—crackers and cookies—in three 4-minute blocks each day. The authors hoped that exposure to feared foods would reduce her anxiety.

Despite this intervention, though, the patient's SUDS ratings and food consumption did not improve. When the therapist talked with the client and her parents, he discovered that the patient was eating only the absolute minimum of foods, such that she was not getting enough exposure to the feared stimulus. To increase her exposure to foods, reinforcement was added to the program—her parents were instructed to give her ice cream at the end of any day in which the patient had consumed at least three servings of the target food. Within a week, she reported being able to consume crackers and cereals without distress. Gradually, she was asked to begin eating more frightening foods. One week, she was asked to begin consuming soft vegetables, pasta, and cheese, followed the next week by meat, and the next week by raw vegetables, salad, and hard fruit. As shown by the graphs, with the introduction of exposure to each new food group, the client experienced a reduction in SUDS ratings within the next week; effects do not look like they were due to just simply time or maturation, as anxiety was only reduced after the client began exposure for the new food group. The repeated decrements in anxiety are hard to explain using any variable other than treatment. Gains were maintained through a 19-month follow-up.

In one form of single-case design, referred to as a **reversal design** or **ABAB design**, the participant's behavior must be carefully measured in a specific sequence:

1. An initial time period, the baseline (A)
2. A period when a treatment is introduced (B)
3. A reinstatement of the conditions of the baseline period (A)
4. A reintroduction of the treatment (B)

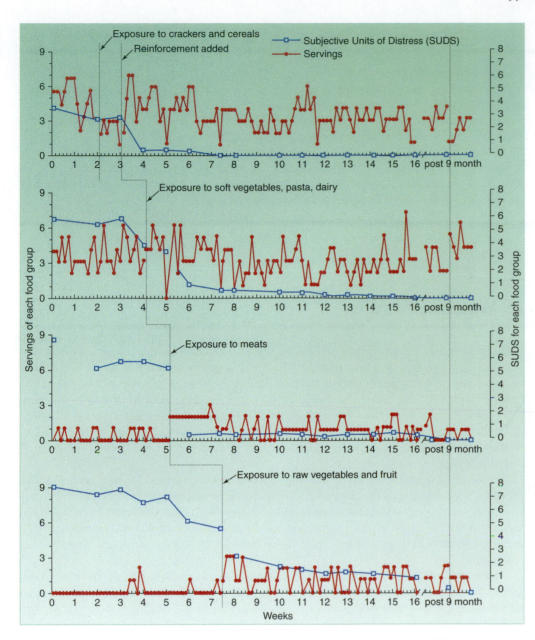

Figure 4.5 Effects of exposure treatment and reinforcement for food phobia in a single-subject design. Note the rapid shifts in SUDS ratings as exposure for each new food group is introduced. Reprinted from, Chorpita et al., Behavioral treatment of choking phobia in adolescent: An experimental analysis, *Journal of Behavior Therapy and Experimental Psychiatry*, 28, 307–315, copyright 1997, with permission from Elsevier.

If behavior in the experimental period is different from that in the baseline period, reverses when the treatment is removed, and re-reverses when the treatment is again introduced, there is little doubt that the manipulation, rather than chance or uncontrolled factors, has produced the change. Hence, even though there is no control group, there are time periods that serve as control comparisons for the treatment (Hersen & Barlow, 1976).

The reversal technique cannot always be employed, however, because the initial state of a participant may not be recoverable. Remember that most treatments aim to produce enduring change, so just removing an intervention may not return a person to the pretreatment state. This reversal technique, then, is most applicable when researchers believe that the effects of their manipulation are temporary.

Perhaps the biggest drawback of single-case designs is the potential lack of external validity. The fact that a treatment works for a single person does not necessarily imply that it will be effective for others. Findings may relate to a unique aspect of the one person whose behavior has been explored. Often researchers will present data from a small series of cases. Even then, it is important to consider whether results can be generalized to other people. Results of single-case experimental studies may help investigators to decide whether research with larger groups is warranted.

Quick Summary

The experimental method entails the manipulation of independent variables and the measurement of their effects on dependent variables. Generally, participants are randomly assigned to one of at least two groups: an experimental group, which experiences the active condition of the independent variable, and a control group, which does not. The researcher tests to see if the independent variable had an effect by looking for differences between the experimental and control groups on the dependent variable. Treatment studies are a common form of experimental research.

Placebo control groups are often used in treatment research. Considerable controversy surrounds the use of placebo and no-treatment control groups.

Internal validity refers to whether an effect can be confidently attributed to the independent variable. External validity refers to whether experimental effects can be generalized to situations and people outside of this specific study. Experimental designs can provide internal validity but external validity is sometimes of concern. Correlational studies can provide solid external validity but poorer internal validity.

Integrating the Findings of Multiple Studies

Understanding the pros and cons of different research designs should suggest a natural conclusion—there is no perfect research study. Rather, a body of research studies is often needed to test a theory. When an important research finding emerges, a key goal is to replicate the finding by conducting the study again and seeing if the same pattern of results emerges. Over time, dozens of studies may emerge on important topics. Sometimes the results of different studies will be similar, but more often, differences will emerge across studies. Researchers must synthesize the information across studies to arrive at a general understanding of findings.

How does a researcher go about drawing conclusions from a series of investigations? A simple way of drawing general conclusions is to read individual studies, mull them over, and decide what they mean overall. The disadvantage with this approach is that the researcher's biases and subjective impressions can play a significant role in determining what conclusion is drawn. It is fairly common for two scientists to read the same set of studies and reach very different conclusions.

Meta-analysis was developed as a partial solution to this problem (Smith, Glass, & Miller, 1980). The first step in a meta-analysis is a thorough literature search, so that all relevant studies are identified. Because these studies have typically used different statistical tests, meta-analysis then puts all the results into a common scale, using a statistic called the *effect size*. For example, in treatment studies, the effect size offers a way of standardizing the differences in improvement between a therapy group and a control group so that the results of many different studies can be averaged. Figure 4.6 summarizes the steps in a meta-analysis.

In their often-cited report, Smith and colleagues (1980) meta-analyzed 475 psychotherapy outcome studies involving more than 25,000 patients and 1,700 effect sizes; they came to conclusions that have attracted considerable attention and some controversy. Most importantly, they concluded that psychotherapies produce more improvement than does no treatment. Specifically, treated patients were found to be better off than almost 80 percent of untreated patients. Subsequent meta-analyses have confirmed that therapy appears effective (Lambert & Ogles, 2004).

Meta-analysis has been criticized by a number of researchers. The central problem is that researchers sometimes include studies that are of poor quality in a meta-analysis. Smith and colleagues gave equal weight to all studies, so that a poorly controlled outcome study (such as one that did not evaluate what the therapists actually did in each session) received as much weight as a well-controlled one (such as a study in which therapists used a manual that specified what they did with each research participant). When Smith and colleagues attempted to address this problem by comparing effect sizes of good versus poor studies and found no differences,

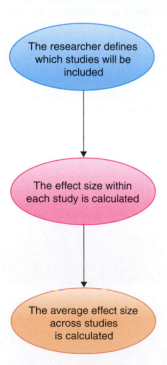

Figure 4.6 Steps in conducting a meta-analysis.

Table 4.6 An Example of a Meta-Analysis: One-Year Prevalence Rates for Mental Illness across 21 European Studies

DSM-IV Diagnosis	Number of Studies	Combined N	12-Month Prevalence (%) across the Combined Sample	Range of Prevalence Estimates within Different Studies
Alcohol dependence	12	60,891	3.3	0.1–6.6
Illicit substance dependence	6	28,429	1.1	0.1–2.2
Psychotic disorders	6	27,291	.9	0.2–2.6
Major depressive disorder	17	152,044	6.4	3.1–10.1
Bipolar I disorder	6	21,848	.8	0.2–1.1
Anxiety disorders	12	53,597	1.6	0.7–3.1
Somatoform disorders	7	18,894	6.4	1.1–11
Eating disorders	5	19,761	4.8	0.2–0.7

Source: Adapted from Wittchen & Jacobi (2005).

Note: In this meta-analysis, researchers combined the findings of 27 major epidemiological studies on the 12-month prevalence of psychiatric disorders in European countries. Across these studies, more than 155,000 participants were interviewed. Researchers were able not only to determine the percentage of participants who met criteria for diagnoses but also to illustrate that there is a broad range of prevalence estimates across different studies.

they were further criticized for the criteria they employed in separating the good from the not so good (Rachman & Wilson, 1980)! O'Leary and Wilson (1987) concluded that the ultimate problem is that someone has to make a judgment of good versus poor quality in research and that others can find fault with that judgment. A good meta-analysis, though, will be clear about the criteria for including or excluding studies.

Table 4.6 provides another example of a meta-analysis. In this meta-analysis, researchers integrated the findings of 21 epidemiological studies conducted in Europe on the 12-month prevalence of mental disorders (Wittchen & Jacobi, 2005). Across these studies, more than 155,000 participants were interviewed. Prevalence estimates from the different studies were fairly varied. Tallying the findings across studies should give a stronger estimate of how common the disorders are.

Check Your Knowledge 4.3

Choose the best answer for each question.
1. In an experimental design, the researcher manipulates:
   a. the independent variable
   b. the dependent variable
2. Dr. Jones is interested in whether a new treatment for autism will be helpful. She recruits 30 participants, and she randomly assigns 15 to receive drug X and 15 to receive a placebo. After 3 weeks of treatment, she measures social engagement. In this study, the independent variable is:
   a. medication condition
   b. drug X
   c. social engagement
   d. autism
3. The dependent variable is:
   a. treatment
   b. drug X
   c. social engagement
   d. autism
4. Single-case experimental designs may lack:
   a. internal validity
   b. external validity
5. Correlational studies may lack:
   a. internal validity
   b. external validity
6. The step in meta-analysis that has received extensive criticism is:
   a. defining which studies should be included
   b. calculating the effect size of each study
   c. calculating the average effect size across studies
   d. none of the above

Summary

Science and Scientific Methods

- Science involves forming a theory and then systematically gathering data to test the theory. It is important for researchers to replicate findings from a given study, which requires being precise about the methods used.

Approaches to Research on Psychopathology

- Common methods for studying abnormal behavior include case studies, correlational studies, and experimental studies. Each method has strengths and weaknesses.
- Case studies provide detailed descriptions of rare phenomena or novel procedures. Case studies also can disconfirm that a relationship is universal and can generate hypotheses that can be tested through controlled research. Case studies, however, may not always be valid, and they are of limited value in providing evidence to support a theory.
- Correlational methods are the most common way to study the causes of abnormal behavior, because we cannot manipulate most of the key risk variables in psychopathology, nor can we manipulate diagnosis.
- Conclusions drawn from cross-sectional correlational studies cannot be interpreted in cause–effect terms because of the directionality. Longitudinal studies help address which variable came first but can still suffer from the third-variable problems.
- One form of correlational study, epidemiological research, involves gathering information about the prevalence and incidence of disorders in populations and about risk factors that relate to higher probability of developing a disorder. Epidemiological studies avoid the sampling biases seen in studies of people drawn from undergraduate psychology classes or from treatment clinics.
- Studies of behavior genetics often rely on correlational techniques as well. The most common behavior genetics methods include the family method, the twin method, and the adoptees method. Molecular genetics studies use linkage analysis and association studies.
- In the experimental method, the researcher randomly assigns people to an experimental group or a control group. Effects of the independent variable, or experimental condition, on a dependent variable are then tested. Treatment studies are a common example of experimental research. Some controversy has arisen about the use of placebos. Many different forms of analogue studies are conducted in psychopathology research. Single-case experimental designs can provide well-controlled data.
- Generally, experimental methods help enhance internal validity, but correlational methods sometimes offer greater external validity.

Integrating the Findings of Multiple Studies

- Meta-analysis is an important tool for reaching conclusions from a group of research studies. It entails putting the statistical comparisons from single studies into a common format—the effect size—so the results of many studies can be averaged.

Answers to Check Your Knowledge Questions

4.1 1. F; 2. F; 3. F
4.2 1. a and b; 2. d; 3. c; 4. c; 5. d

4.3 1. a; 2. a; 3. c; 4. b; 5. a; 6. a

Key Terms

adoptees method	dependent variable	hypothesis	prevalence
analogue experiment	directionality problem	incidence	random assignment
case study	dizygotic (DZ) twins	independent variable	reversal (ABAB) designs
clinical significance	double-blind procedure	index cases (probands)	risk factors
concordance	epidemiology	internal validity	single-subject experimental
control group	experiment	linkage analysis	design
correlation	experimental effect	longitudinal design	statistical significance
correlation coefficient	external validity	meta-analysis	theory
correlational method	family method	monozygotic (MZ) twins	third-variable problem
cross-fostering	genetic markers	placebo	twin method
cross-sectional design	high-risk method	placebo effect	

5 Anxiety Disorders

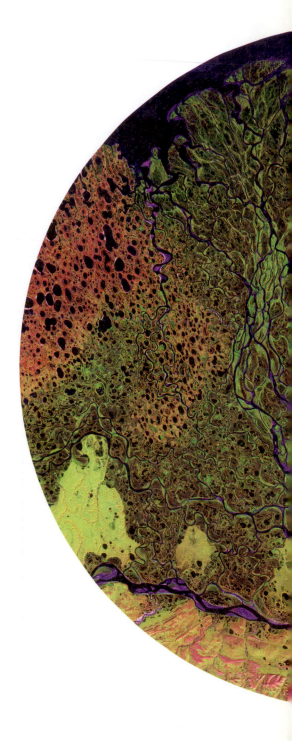

Clinical Case: Jenny

Jenny was a 23-year-old student completing her first year of medical school. The year had been a hard one, not only because of the long hours and academic challenges of medical school, but also because her mother had developed cancer. One day, while attending rounds, Jenny found herself feeling lightheaded and dizzy. During rounds, the attending physician would ask students to diagnose and explain a given case, and on that day Jenny became extremely worried about whether she would be able to answer these questions when her turn came. As she thought about this, her heart began to pound and her palms began to sweat. Overwhelmed by a deep sense of fear that something was horribly wrong, she abruptly fled the room without explaining her departure. Later in the day, she thought about how to explain leaving rounds but could not figure out how to describe the situation to the attending physician. That night, she could not sleep, wondering what had happened and worrying about whether it would happen again. She worried about how this would affect her ability not only to take part in rounds but also to perform well in other roles, such as leading a small research group and meeting with other medical staff and clients. One week later, while driving to school, she experienced a sudden attack of similar symptoms, which forced her to pull off to the side of the road. She took the day off from school. Over the next several weeks, she began to avoid public situations as much as possible because she feared being humiliated by the return of these symptoms. She avoided study groups and going out with friends, and she turned down opportunities for training that involved public interviews of patients. Although she had enjoyed being part of a choir for several years, she resigned from the choir. Despite her withdrawal, she experienced three more attacks, each in unexpected situations. She began to think that maybe medical school was a poor choice for her because she had such deep fears about experiencing another attack during rounds. After she read about panic disorder in one of her textbooks, she decided to visit a psychologist. The psychologist confirmed that she was experiencing an anxiety disorder called panic disorder, and they started cognitive behavioral treatment.

VERY FEW OF US go through even a week of our lives without experiencing anxiety or fear. In this chapter, we focus on a group of disorders called *anxiety disorders*. Both anxiety and fear play a significant role in these disorders, and so it is important to understand some of the similarities and differences between these two emotions.

Anxiety is defined as apprehension over an anticipated problem. In contrast, **fear** is defined as a reaction to immediate danger. Psychologists focus on the "immediate" aspect of fear versus the "anticipated" aspect of anxiety—fear tends to be about a threat that's happening now, whereas anxiety tends to be about a future threat. Thus, a person facing a bear experiences fear, whereas a college student concerned about the possibility of unemployment after graduation experiences anxiety.

Both anxiety and fear can involve arousal, or sympathetic nervous system activity. Anxiety often involves moderate arousal, and fear involves higher arousal. At the low end, a person experiencing anxiety may feel no more than restless energy and physiological tension; at the high end, a person experiencing fear may sweat profusely, breathe rapidly, and feel an overpowering urge to run.

Anxiety and fear are not necessarily "bad"—in fact, both are adaptive. Fear is fundamental for "flight-or-fight" reactions—that is, fear triggers rapid changes in the sympathetic nervous system that prepare the body for escape or fighting. In the right circumstance, fear saves lives. (Imagine a person who faces a bear and experiences no impulse to flee, no surge in energy, and no marshaling of that energy to run quickly!) In some anxiety disorders, though, the fear system seems to misfire—a person experiences fear at a time when there is no danger in the environment (see the discussion of panic attacks later in this chapter).

Anxiety is adaptive in helping us notice and plan for future threats—that is, to increase our preparedness, to help people avoid potentially dangerous situations, and to think through potential problems before they happen. In laboratory studies first conducted 100 years ago and since verified many times over, a small degree of anxiety has been found to improve performance on laboratory tasks (Yerkes & Dodson, 1908). Ask anyone with extreme test anxiety, though, and they will tell you that too much anxiety interferes with performance. Anxiety, then, provides a classic example of a U-shaped curve with performance—an absence of anxiety is a problem, a little anxiety is adaptive, a lot of anxiety is detrimental.

In this chapter, we examine the **anxiety disorders** included in DSM-IV-TR: specific phobias, social phobia, panic disorder (along with agoraphobia), generalized anxiety disorder, obsessive-compulsive disorder, and posttraumatic disorder (along with acute stress disorder). Anxiety disorders as a group are the most common type of psychiatric diagnosis. For example, in one study of over 8,000 adults in the United States, approximately 28 percent of people reported having experienced symptoms at some point during their life that met the DSM-IV-TR criteria for diagnosis of an anxiety disorder (Kessler, Berlund et al., 2005). Phobias are particularly common. As a group, anxiety disorders are very costly to society and to people with the disorders. These disorders are associated with twice the average rate of medical costs (Simon et al., 1995), higher risk of cardiovascular disease (Smoller et al., 2007), twice the risk of suicidal ideation and attempts compared to people without a psychiatric diagnosis (Sareen et al., 2005), difficulties in employment (APA, 2004), and serious interpersonal concerns (Zatzick et al., 1997). All of the anxiety disorders are associated with substantial decrements in the quality of life (Olatunji, Cisler, & Tolin, 2007).

We begin by defining the symptoms of the anxiety disorders. Then we turn to the common themes in the etiology for these disorders as a group. We will then describe specific etiological factors that shape the onset of specific anxiety disorders. Like most disorders, many different paradigms have helped shed light on the anxiety disorders. Hence, throughout our discussions of etiology we look at issues from various perspectives, with particular focus on genetic, neurobiological, personality, cognitive, and behavioral research. Finally, we consider the treatment of the anxiety disorders. We describe commonalities in the psychological treatment of the various anxiety disorders, and then we describe how these general treatment principles are modified to address specific anxiety disorders. Finally, we discuss biological treatments of the anxiety disorders.

Clinical Descriptions of the Anxiety Disorders

The anxiety disorders all share excessively high or frequent anxiety. Panic disorder and phobias are distinguished by high fear as well as anxiety (Cox, Clara, & Enns, 2002). Each disorder, though, is defined by a different set of symptoms related to anxiety or fear (see Table 5.1 for a brief summary). In each disorder, criteria specify that these anxieties or fears must interfere with functioning or cause marked distress in order to be diagnosed.

Table 5.1 Summary of Major Anxiety Disorders

Disorder	Description
Specific phobia	Fear of objects or situations that is out of proportion to any real danger
Social phobia	Fear of unfamiliar people or social scrutiny
Panic disorder	Anxiety about recurrent panic attacks; sometimes accompanied by agoraphobia, a fear of being in places where panic attacks could occur
Generalized anxiety disorder	Uncontrollable worry for at least 6 months
Obsessive-compulsive disorder	Obsessions, which are uncontrollable thoughts, impulses or images; or compulsions, which are repetitive behaviors or mental acts
Posttraumatic stress disorder	Aftermath of a traumatic experience in which the person reexperiences the traumatic event, avoids stimuli associated with the event, and experiences increased arousal
Acute stress disorder	Symptoms are similar to those of posttraumatic stress disorder but occur for less than 4 weeks after the traumatic event

Phobias

DSM-IV-TR defines a **phobia** as a disruptive fear of a particular object or situation that is out of proportion to any danger posed. The person recognizes that the fear is excessive but still goes to great lengths to avoid the feared object or situation. The symptoms are so intense that they cause distress or interfere with the person's social or occupational activities. Here, we discuss two types of phobias: specific phobias and social phobia. (We will discuss agoraphobia below, in the context of panic disorder.)

Specific Phobias   A **specific phobia** is an unwarranted fear caused by the presence of a specific object or situation. Some examples of specific phobias are fear of flying, fear of snakes, and fear of heights. The names for these fears consist of a Greek word for the feared object or situation followed by the suffix *-phobia* (derived from the name of the Greek god Phobos, who frightened his enemies). Two of the more familiar phobias are claustrophobia (fear of closed spaces) and acrophobia (fear of heights). Table 5.2 describes potential names of some highly unlikely phobias. Despite this array of possible phobias, in reality, specific phobias tend to cluster around a small number of feared objects and situations. DSM-IV-TR categorizes specific phobias according

---

● DSM-IV-TR Criteria for Specific Phobia

- Persistent and excessive fear triggered by specific objects or situations
- Exposure to the trigger almost always leads to intense anxiety
- The person recognizes the fear is unrealistic
- The object or situation is avoided or else endured with intense anxiety

---

Table 5.2 Words Used to Describe Highly Unlikely Phobias

Fear	Phobia
Anything new	Neophobia
Asymmetrical things	Asymmetriphobia
Books	Bibliophobia
Children	Pedophobia
Dancing	Chorophobia
Englishness	Anglophobia
Garlic	Alliumphobia
Peanut butter sticking to the roof of the mouth	Arachibutyrophobia
Technology	Technophobia
Mice	Musophobia
Pseudoscientific terms	Hellenophobia

Source: Drawn from www.phobialist.com.

Clinical Case: Jan

Jan was a 42-year-old woman who was offered a high-paying job in Florida. She was considering turning the position down because it would force her to live in an area known for having snakes. Before making this decision, she decided to see a therapist. She described avoiding nature programs that might show snakes, refusing to read nature books to her children because they might contain pictures of snakes, and avoiding outdoor activities because of her fear of snakes. Although she had been able to cope without too many negative consequences so far, the idea of living in an area with snakes had greatly increased her apprehension. Aside from her phobia, Jan reported that she had always been a bit of a nervous person, like her mother.

Table 5.3 Types of Specific Phobias

Type of Phobia	Source of Fear	Associated Characteristics
Animal	Animals (e.g., snakes, insects)	Generally begins during childhood
Natural environment	Aspects of the natural environment (e.g., storms, heights, water)	Generally begins during childhood
Blood, injection, injury	Blood, injury, injections, or other invasive medical procedures	Clearly runs in families
Situational	Specific situations (e.g., public transportation, tunnels, bridges, elevators, flying, driving, closed spaces)	Tends to begin either in childhood or in mid-twenties.
Other	Fear of choking, fear of contracting an illness, etc.; children's fears of loud sounds, clowns, etc.	

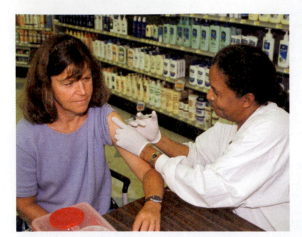

One form of specific phobia is an intense fear of blood, injection, or injuries. (David Young-Wolf/PhotoEdit.)

to these sources of fear (see Table 5.3). A person with one type of specific phobia is very likely to have another type of specific phobia as well—that is, there is high **comorbidity** of specific phobias (Kendler et al., 2001). The clinical case of Jan provides a glimpse of how specific phobias can interfere with important life goals.

Social Phobia   **Social phobia** is a persistent, unrealistically intense fear of social situations that might involve being scrutinized by, or even just exposed to, unfamiliar people. The term *social anxiety disorder* has been proposed as a more appropriate label for this disorder because the problems caused by it tend to be much more pervasive and to interfere much more with normal activities than the problems caused by other phobias (Liebowitz et al., 2000). People with social phobia, like Maureen described in the clinical case, usually try to avoid situations in which they might be evaluated, show signs of anxiety, or behave in embarrassing ways. Although this may sound like shyness, people with social phobia avoid more social situations, feel more discomfort socially, and experience these symptoms for longer periods of their life than people who are shy (Turner, Beidel, & Townsley, 1990). They often fear that they will blush or sweat excessively. Speaking or performing in public, eating in public, using public restrooms, or engaging in virtually any activity in the presence of others can cause extreme anxiety. People with social phobia often work in occupations far below their talents because of their extreme social fears. Better to resign oneself to a less rewarding job with limited social demand than deal with social situations every day.

Among people with social phobia, at least a third also meet the DSM-IV-TR criteria for diagnosis of avoidant personality disorder (see p. 372; Chavira, Stein, & Malcarne, 2002). The symptoms of the two conditions overlap a great deal, and there is overlap in the genetic vulnerability for

DSM-IV-TR Criteria for Social Phobia

- Marked, persistent fear triggered by exposure to unfamiliar people or social scrutiny
- Exposure to the trigger leads to intense anxiety about being humiliated or embarrassed
- The person recognizes the fear is unrealistic
- Trigger situations are avoided or else endured with intense anxiety

Aerophobia, or phobia of heights is common. Other specific phobias include fears of animals, injections, and enclosed spaces. (Bill Aron/PhotoEdit.)

Clinical Case: Maureen

Maureen, a 30-year-old accountant, sought psychotherapy after reading a newspaper notice advertising group therapy for people with difficulties in social situations. Maureen appeared nervous during the interview and described deep distress over the amount of anxiety she experienced in conversations with others. She described the problem as becoming worse over the years, to the point where she no longer interacted socially with anyone other than her husband. She would not even go to the supermarket for fear of having to interact with others. Maureen explained that she was afraid of interacting with others because she would feel extreme shame if others thought that she was stupid or could not express herself well. This fear made Maureen so nervous that she would often stammer or forget what she was going to say while talking to others, thus adding to her apprehension that others would see her as stupid and creating a vicious cycle of ever-increasing fear.

the two conditions (Reichborn-Kjennerud, Czajkowski, Torgersen, et al., 2007). Avoidant personality disorder, though, is considered a more severe disorder with an earlier onset and more pervasive symptoms. See Figure 5.1 for one way of thinking about shyness, social phobia, and avoidant personality disorder. Social phobia generally begins during adolescence, when social interactions become more important, but social phobia is sometimes found in children as well. Without treatment, social phobia tends to be chronic.

Social phobia is diagnosed as either generalized or specific, depending on the range of situations that the person fears and avoids. For example, a person who is anxious about writing in public, but is not anxious about other social situations, would be diagnosed with specific social phobia. In contrast, a person who fears most social situations would be diagnosed with generalized social phobia. The generalized type is associated with an earlier age of onset, more comorbidity with other disorders such as depression and alcohol abuse, and more negative effects on the person's social and occupational activities (Wittchen, Stein, & Kessler, 1999).

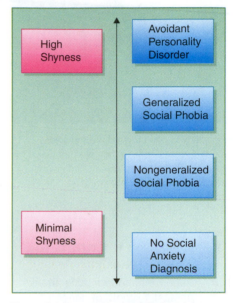

Figure 5.1 A spectrum model of social phobia and avoidant personality disorder. Adapted from Chavira et al. (2002).

Panic Disorder and Agoraphobia

Panic disorder is characterized by frequent panic attacks that are unrelated to specific situations and by worry about having more panic attacks (see the case of Jenny, described at the beginning of this chapter). A **panic attack** is a sudden attack of intense apprehension, terror, and feelings of impending doom, accompanied by at least four other symptoms. Physical symptoms can include labored breathing, heart palpitations, nausea, upset stomach, chest pain, feelings of choking and smothering, dizziness, lightheadedness, sweating, chills, hot flashes, and trembling. Other symptoms that may occur during a panic attack include **depersonalization** (a feeling of being outside one's body); **derealization** (a feeling of the world's not being real); and fears of losing control, of going crazy, or even of dying. Not surprisingly, people often report that they have an intense urge to flee whatever situation they are in when a panic attack occurs. The symptoms tend to come on very rapidly and reach a peak of intensity within 10 minutes.

We can think about a panic attack as a misfire of the fear system—physiologically, the person experiences sympathetic nervous system arousal appropriate to an immediate threat to life. Because the symptoms are inexplicable, the person tries to make sense of the experience. A person who begins to think that he or she is dying, losing control, or going crazy, is likely to feel even more fear. Among people with panic disorder, 90 percent report just these types of beliefs when panic attacks occur.

When panic attacks occur unexpectedly, they are called *uncued* attacks. When panic attacks are clearly triggered by specific situations, such as seeing a snake, they are referred to as *cued* panic attacks. People who only have cued attacks most likely suffer from a phobia. According to DSM-IV-TR criteria, for a diagnosis of

Social phobia typically begins in adolescence and interferes with developing friendships with peers. (Spencer Grant/PhotoEdit.)

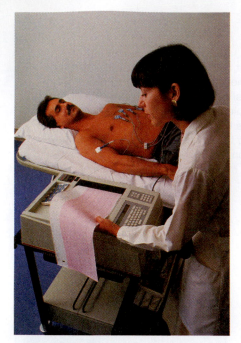

People with panic disorder often seek cardiac tests because they are frightened by changes in their heart rate.
(David Joel/Stone/Getty Images.)

panic disorder, a person must experience recurrent uncued panic attacks. They also must worry about the attacks or change their behavior because of the attacks for at least 1 month—hence, the response to panic attacks is as important as the attacks themselves in making this diagnosis.

In DSM-IV-TR, there are two types of panic disorder: with agoraphobia and without agoraphobia. **Agoraphobia** (from the Greek *agora*, meaning "marketplace") is defined by anxiety about situations in which it would be embarrassing or difficult to escape if panic symptoms occurred. Often, the person fears public places where it would be embarrassing to experience a panic attack. Commonly feared situations include driving, bridges, crowds, and crowded places such as grocery stores, malls, and churches. Many people with agoraphobia are unable to leave their house, and even those who can leave their home do so only with great distress. Agoraphobia can also be diagnosed in the absence of panic disorder. In such a case, the person's fears still focus on developing panic-like symptoms (e.g., dizziness) in a place from which it would be hard to escape.

Panic disorder typically begins in adolescence, and over time it can take a heavy toll; for example, as many as one-quarter of people with panic disorder report being unemployed for more than 5 years (Leon, Portera, & Weissman, 1995). Among people with panic disorder, those with agoraphobia tend to have much more chronic symptoms. In a 22-month follow-up study, only 18 percent of those diagnosed with panic disorder with agoraphobia recovered from these symptoms, compared to 43 percent of those without agoraphobia (Keller et al., 1994).

Remember that the criteria for panic disorder specify that panic attacks must be recurrent. But it is fairly common for people to experience a single panic attack—more than a quarter of people in the United States report that they have experienced at least one panic attack during their lifetime (Kessler et al., 2006), and 3–5 percent report a panic attack in the past year (Norton, Cox, & Malan, 1992). As Table 5.4 shows, though, many fewer people develop full-blown panic disorder.

● **DSM-IV-TR Criteria for Panic Disorder**

● Recurrent uncued panic attacks
● At least 1 month of concern about the possibility of more attacks, worry about the consequences of an attack, or behavioral changes because of the attacks

Table 5.4 Percent of People in the General Population Who Meet Diagnostic Criteria for Anxiety Disorders in the Past Year and in Their Lifetime

Anxiety Disorder	12-Month Prevalence			Lifetime prevalence
	Male	**Female**	**Total**	**Total**
Panic disorder	1.7	3.0	2.3	6.0
Any phobia	7.5	17.7	12.6	n/a
Social phobia				12.10
Specific phobia				12.15
Generalized anxiety disorder	1.0	2.1	1.5	5.7
Obsessive-compulsive disorder	0.6	0.9	0.7	1.6

Sources: Past year estimates from Jacobi (2004). Lifetime estimates from Kessler, Berglund, et al. (2005).

Generalized Anxiety Disorder

One of the central features of **generalized anxiety disorder (GAD)** is worry. Like Joe described in the clinical case on the next page, people with GAD are persistently worried, often about minor things. The term *worry* refers to the cognitive tendency to chew on a problem and to be unable to let go of it (Mennin, Heimberg, & Turk, 2004). Often, worry continues because a person cannot settle on a solution to the problem.

Most of us worry from time to time but the worries of people with GAD are excessive, uncontrollable, and long lasting. Other symptoms of GAD include difficulty concentrating, tiring easily, restlessness, irritability, and muscle tension. A person must have symptoms for at least 6 months to qualify for a diagnosis of GAD. Also, GAD is not diagnosed if a person only worries about concerns driven by another Axis I disorder; for example, a person with claustrophobia who only worried about being in closed spaces would not meet the criteria for GAD. The worries of people with GAD are similar in focus to those of most people: they worry about rela-

Clinical Case: Joe

Joe, a 24-year-old mechanic, had been referred for psychotherapy by his physician, whom he had consulted because of difficulty falling asleep. He was quite visibly distressed during the entire initial interview, gulping before he spoke and continually fidgeting in his chair. He repeatedly requested water to slake a seemingly unquenchable thirst. Although he described his physical concerns first, a picture of pervasive anxiety soon emerged. He reported that he nearly always felt tense. He seemed to worry about everything. He was apprehensive of disasters that could befall him as he interacted with other people and worked,

and he described worrying much of the time about his ability to form a relationship, his finances, and other issues. He reported a long history of difficulties relating to others, which had led to his being fired from several jobs. As he put it, "I really like people and try to get along with them, but it seems like I fly off the handle too easily. Little things upset me too much. I just can't cope unless everything is going exactly right." Joe reported that he had always felt more nervous than other people but that his anxiety had become much worse after a romantic breakup one year ago.

tionships, health, finances, and daily hassles (Roemer, Molina, & Borkovec, 1997)—but they worry more about these issues, and these persistent worries interfere with daily life.

GAD typically begins in adolescence, though many people who have generalized anxiety disorder report having had a tendency to worry all their lives (Barlow et al., 1986). GAD is often chronic; in one study, about half of people with GAD reported ongoing symptoms five years after an initial interview (Yonkers et al., 2000).

Obsessive-Compulsive Disorder

Obsessive-compulsive disorder (OCD) is characterized by persistent and uncontrollable thoughts or urges (obsessions) and by the need to repeat certain acts again and again (compulsions). Of course, most of us have unwanted thoughts from time to time, like an advertising jingle that gets stuck in our mind. And most of us also have urges now and then to behave in ways that would be embarrassing or dangerous. But few of us have thoughts or urges that are persistent and intrusive enough to qualify us for a diagnosis of OCD.

Obsessions are intrusive and recurring thoughts, images, or impulses that are persistent and uncontrollable (i.e., the person cannot stop the thoughts) and that usually appear irrational to the person experiencing them. For Bernice (described in the clinical case on the next page) and others with OCD, obsessions have such force and frequency that they interfere with normal activities. The most frequent obsessions concern fears of contamination, sexual or aggressive impulses, and body problems (Jenike, Baer, & Minichiello, 1986). People with obsessions may also be prone to extreme doubts, procrastination, and indecision.

Compulsions are repetitive, clearly excessive behaviors or mental acts that the person feels driven to perform to reduce the anxiety caused by obsessive thoughts or to prevent some calamity from occurring. Bernice's rituals while washing and eating, described in the case example below, fit this definition. Samuel Johnson, one of most famous authors of the eighteenth century, has been described as suffering from multiple compulsions. For example, he felt compelled "to touch every post in a street or step exactly in the center of every paving stone. If he perceived one of these acts to be inaccurate, his friends were obliged to wait, dumbfounded, while he went back to fix it" (Stephen, 1900, cited in Szechtman & Woody, 2004). Even though the person rationally understands that there is no need for this behavior, he or she feels as though something dire will happen if the act is not performed. The sheer frequency with which compulsions are repeated may be staggering (for example, Bernice chewed each mouthful of food 300 times). Commonly reported compulsions include the following:

- Pursuing cleanliness and orderliness, sometimes through elaborate rituals
- Performing repetitive, magically protective acts, such as counting or touching a body part

In agoraphobia, a person is afraid of being in shopping malls, crowds, and other public situations from which escape would be difficult if anxiety symptoms occurred; people with agoraphobia can become housebound. (Frank Siteman/Stone/Getty Images.)

Clinical Case: Bernice

Bernice was a 46-year-old woman. This was her fourth time seeking outpatient therapy, and she had been hospitalized twice previously. Her obsessive-compulsive disorder had begun 12 years earlier, shortly after the death of her father. Since then, it had waxed and waned but currently was as severe as ever.

Bernice was obsessed with a fear of contamination, a fear she developed after her father's death from pneumonia (which she related to germs). Although she reported that she was afraid of nearly everything because germs could be anywhere, she was particularly afraid of touching wood, "scratchy objects," mail, canned goods, silver embossing on a greeting card, eyeglass frames, shiny appliances, and silverware. She was unable to state why these particular objects were sources of possible contamination.

To try to reduce her discomfort, Bernice engaged in a variety of compulsive rituals that took up almost all her waking hours. In the morning, she spent 3 to 4 hours in the bathroom, washing and rewashing herself. Before each washing, she scraped away the outside layer of her bar of soap so that it would be free of germs. Mealtimes lasted for hours because of rituals designed to decontaminate her food, such as eating three bites of food at a time and chewing each mouthful 300 times. Her rituals had taken over her life—she did almost nothing else. Because of her fear of contamination, she would not leave the house, do housework, or even talk on the telephone.

DSM-IV-TR Criteria for Obsessive-Compulsive Disorder

- Obsessions (recurrent, intrusive, persistent thoughts, impulses or images that are more than just worries or compulsions) or
- Compulsions (repetitive behaviors or thoughts that a person feels compelled to perform to prevent distress or a dreaded event)
- The person tries to suppress, ignore, or neutralize the obsessions
- The person understands the compulsions are excessive and that they will not prevent dreaded events

- Repetitive checking to ensure that certain acts are carried out—for example, returning seven or eight times in a row to see that lights, gas jets, or faucets were turned off, windows fastened, and doors locked.

We often hear people described as compulsive gamblers, compulsive eaters, and compulsive drinkers. Even though people may report irresistible urges to gamble, eat, and drink, clinicians do not regard these behaviors as compulsions because they are often experienced as pleasurable. In one study, 78 percent of people with compulsions viewed their rituals as "rather silly or absurd" even though they were unable to stop performing them (Stern & Cobb, 1978).

The symptoms of OCD can vary a good deal across people. While one of the most common compulsions is cleaning, as many as one-third of patients diagnosed with OCD have problems with hoarding, defined as difficulty discarding items even though they would seem to have no objective value (Steketee & Frost, 2003). Extreme hoarding can render rooms of a house unusable, and it may even create fire and health hazards. Although hoarding may seem similar to a tendency to collect antiques, stamps, or other objects, hoarding is distinguished from collecting in that it creates distress and functional impairment. Among people diagnosed with OCD, hoarding symptoms are associated with an early age of onset, more indecisiveness, more anxiety and depression, and less insight into symptoms.

Obsessive-compulsive disorder tends to begin either before age 10 or else in late adolescence/early adulthood (Conceicao do Rosario-Campos et al., 2001). It has been described in children as young as age 2 (Rapoport, Swedo, & Leonard, 1992). Early onset is more common among men; later onset is more frequent among women and is often linked with cleaning compulsions (Noshirvani et al., 1991). OCD is a chronic disorder—a 40-year follow-up study of people hospitalized for OCD in the 1950s showed that only 20 percent had recovered completely (Skoog & Skoog, 1999).

Posttraumatic Stress Disorder and Acute Stress Disorder

Posttraumatic stress disorder (PTSD) entails an extreme response to a severe stressor, including increased anxiety, avoidance of stimuli associated with the trauma, and a general numbing of emotional responses. Although people have known for many years that the stresses of combat can have powerful adverse effects on soldiers, the aftermath of the Vietnam War spurred the development of this diagnosis.

Like other disorders in the DSM-IV-TR, PTSD is defined by a cluster of symptoms, but unlike other disorders, one criterion for diagnosis is exposure to a specific type of situation—a traumatic event. The person must have experienced or witnessed an event that involved actual or threatened death, serious injury, or a threat to the physical

A crowd is likely to be very distressing to people with agoraphobia because escape would be difficult if a panic attack occurred. (Cosmo Siteman/Stone/Getty Images.)

integrity of the self or others. The trauma must have created intense fear, horror, or a sense of helplessness. As noted above, war veterans have often been exposed to these sorts of severe traumas. For women, rape is the most common type of trauma preceding PTSD (Creamer, Burgess, & McFarlane, 2001), with at least one-third of women meeting criteria for PTSD after a rape (cf. Breslau et al., 1999).

The symptoms for PTSD are grouped into three major categories:

- *Reexperiencing* the traumatic event. The person often recalls the event or has nightmares about it. The person may be intensely upset by reminders of the event (e.g., helicopter sounds that remind a veteran of the battlefield; darkness that reminds a woman of a rape).

- *Avoidance* of stimuli associated with the event or a general numbing of responsiveness. Some may try to avoid all reminders of the event. For example, a Turkish earthquake survivor stopped sleeping indoors after he was buried alive at night (McNally, 2003). Other people try to avoid thinking about the trauma; some may remember only disorganized fragments of the event. *Numbing* refers to a decreased interest in others, a sense of estrangement from others, and an inability to feel positive emotions. These symptoms may seem contradictory to reexperiencing symptoms; generally, the person goes back and forth between reexperiencing and numbing.

- Symptoms of *increased arousal*. These symptoms include difficulty falling asleep or staying asleep, irritability, difficulty concentrating, hypervigilance, and an exaggerated startle response. Laboratory studies have confirmed these clinical symptoms by documenting the heightened physiological responses of people with PTSD to images of combat (Orr et al., 2003).

Once PTSD develops, symptoms are relatively chronic. In one study of people diagnosed with PTSD, about half continued to experience diagnosable symptoms when interviewed several years later (Perkonigg et al., 2005). Suicidal thoughts are common among people with PTSD, as are incidents of explosive anger and stress-related physical symptoms, such as low back pain, headaches, and gastrointestinal disorders (Hobfoll et al., 1991).

In addition to PTSD, DSM-IV-TR includes a diagnosis for **acute stress disorder (ASD)**. According to DSM-IV-TR, if symptoms occur between 2 days and 1 month after a trauma, acute stress disorder (ASD) is diagnosed. Other than duration, the symptoms of ASD are fairly similar to those of PTSD. The ASD diagnosis is not as well accepted as the PTSD diagnosis. Some have criticized the ASD diagnosis because it seems to pathologize short-term reactions to serious traumas, even though these are quite common (Harvey & Bryant, 2002). The number of people who experience symptoms of ASD varies with the type of trauma. For example, after a rape, as many as 90 percent of women report at least some (subsyndromal) symptoms (Rothbaum et al., 1992); in contrast, among people who have been exposed to a mass shooting, approximately one-third develop symptoms of ASD (Classen et al., 1998). One reason to consider this diagnosis, though, is that more than two-thirds of those diagnosed with ASD develop PTSD within 2 years (Harvey & Bryant, 2002).

> ### DSM-IV-TR Criteria for PTSD
>
> - Exposure to a traumatic event that involved threat of death or injury to self or others
> - The event caused extreme fear, helplessness, or horror
> - The event is reexperienced in dreams, memories, or intense reactivity to reminders
> - The person avoids stimuli associated with the trauma or has a numbing of responsiveness
> - Increased arousal
> - Duration of symptoms is more than 1 month

Clinical Case: John

John was a 54-year-old man who was referred for treatment by his physician at the VA hospital. John had recently separated from his wife, was currently unemployed, and reported having no close friends. He stated that he had felt haunted by images of the Vietnam War ever since he had returned from military service decades before. More recently, these symptoms had become worse when he began seeing coverage of the Iraq War on TV. He reported that he frequently experienced nightmares about a particular scene in the jungle in Vietnam, and he would wake up with his heart pounding. He tried to avoid reminders of the war, including parades, political conversations, and helicopters, but this was not feasible—he often stumbled into reminders unexpectedly. When he did, he found that he was quickly overwhelmed by emotional horror and physical shakiness. He reported feeling hopeless ever since returning from war.

He had had many separations from his wife, who would often respond with angry outbursts when she was unable to take his emotional distance. He believed that his wife loved him, but when asked if he wanted to work toward a reunion with her, he stated that he wasn't sure what he felt about her and that he had not really felt emotionally engaged with her or anyone else since the war.

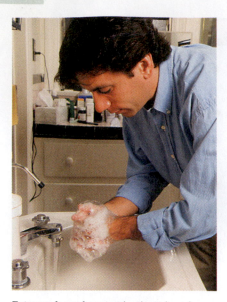

Extreme fear of contamination triggering abnormally frequent hand washing is common in obsessive-compulsive disorder. (Bill Aron/PhotoEdit.)

● DSM-IV-TR Criteria for Acute Stress Disorder
- Exposure to a traumatic event causing extreme fear, helplessness, or horror
- During or after the event, the person experiences dissociative symptoms
- The event is reexperienced intrusively in dreams, thoughts, or intense reactivity to reminders
- The person feels numb, detached, or unable to remember the event
- Increased arousal or anxiety
- Symptoms occur within the first month after the trauma

Comorbidity in Anxiety Disorders

More than half of people with one anxiety disorder meet the criteria for another anxiety disorder during their life (Brown et al., 2001). **Subthreshold symptoms** of other anxiety disorders—that is, symptoms that do not meet full diagnostic criteria—are also common. For example, more than 80 percent of people diagnosed with an anxiety disorder other than panic disorder also experience panic attacks (Barlow et al., 1985). Comorbidity within anxiety disorders arises for two primary reasons:

- The symptoms used to diagnose the various anxiety disorders overlap; for example, somatic signs of anxiety (e.g., perspiration, fast heart rate) are among the diagnostic criteria for panic disorder, phobias, and posttraumatic stress disorder.
- Some etiological factors, like certain neurobiological or personality characteristics, may increase risk for more than one anxiety disorder. (See the next section for discussion of some of these risk factors.)

Anxiety disorders are also highly comorbid with other disorders. Three-quarters of people with an anxiety disorder meet the diagnostic criteria for at least one other psychological disorder (Kessler et al., 1997). More specifically, about 60 percent of people in treatment for anxiety disorders meet the diagnostic criteria for major depression (Brown et al., 2001). Other conditions commonly comorbid with anxiety disorders include substance abuse (Jacobsen, Southwick, & Kosten, 2001) and personality disorders (Johnson, Weissman, & Klerman, 1992), especially avoidant, dependent, and histrionic personality disorders (see chapter 12). As with many disorders, comorbidity is associated with greater severity and poorer outcomes of the anxiety disorders (Newman et al., 1998). Anxiety disorders also are often comorbid with medical disorders—for example, in one study of men, those with high levels of phobic symptoms were three times more likely to develop coronary heart disease than those with low levels of phobic symptoms (Kawachi et al., 1994).

Gender and Sociocultural Factors in the Anxiety Disorders

It is well-known that gender and culture are closely tied to the risk for anxiety disorders, as are the specific types of symptoms that a person develops. As you will see, there are still some puzzles about why these differences exist.

Gender

Consistent with the numbers in Table 5.4 (see p. 124), the German Health Interview and Examination Survey indicated that women are at least twice as likely as men to be diagnosed with an anxiety disorder (de Graaf et al., 2002). The gender disparity is particularly evident for agoraphobia. Among people exposed to a trauma, women are twice as likely to develop PTSD as are men (Breslau et al., 1999). OCD is the only anxiety disorder that is equally common in women and men.

There are many different theories about why women are more likely to develop anxiety disorders than men are. Women may be more likely to report their symptoms. Psychological differences also might help explain these gender gaps. For example, men may be raised to believe more in their personal control over situations, a variable we will discuss later as protective against anxiety disorders. Social factors, like gender roles are also likely to play a role. For example, men may experience more social pressure than women to face fears—as you will see below, facing fears may be the basis for one of the most effective treatments available. Women may also face different life circumstances than do men. For example, women are much more likely than men to be sexually assaulted during childhood and adulthood (Tolin & Foa, 2006). In studies that control for sexual abuse and assault, men and women have comparable rates of PTSD (Tolin & Foa, 2006). As we will see below, having less control over one's environment may set the stage for anxiety disorders. It also appears that women show more biological stress reactivity than do men (Olff et al., 2007), perhaps as a result of these cultural and psychological influences. Although the gender gap is not fully understood, it is an important phenomenon.

Culture

People in every culture seem to experience problems with anxiety disorders. But the focus of these problem appears to vary by culture. For example, in Japan a syndrome called *taijin kyofusho* involves fear of displeasing or embarrassing others; people with this syndrome typically fear such things as making direct eye contact, blushing, having body odor, or having a bodily deformity. The symptoms of this disorder overlap with those of social phobia, but the focus on others' feelings is distinct. Perhaps this focus is related to characteristics of traditional Japanese culture that encourage extreme concern for the feelings of others and discourage the direct communication of one's own feelings (McNally, 1997).

Kayak-angst, a disorder similar to panic disorder, occurs among the Inuit people of western Greenland; seal hunters who are alone at sea may experience intense fear, disorientation, and concerns about drowning. In more religious cultures, the obsessions involved in OCD are more likely to involve religious themes (Seedat & Matsunaga, 2006). And *ataque de nervios*, originally identified in Puerto Rico, involves physical symptoms and fears of going crazy in the aftermath of severe stress and thus is similar to PTSD.

Other syndromes, such as *koro* (a sudden fear that one's genitals will recede into the body—reported in southern and eastern Asia), *shenkui* (intense anxiety and somatic symptoms attributed to the loss of semen, as through masturbation or excessive sexual activity—reported in China and similar to other syndromes reported in India and Sri Lanka), and *susto* (fright-illness, the belief that a severe fright has caused the soul to leave the body—reported in Latin America and among Latinos in the United States) also involve symptoms similar to those of the anxiety disorders defined in DSM-IV-TR. As with the Japanese syndrome taijin kyofusho, it seems that the objects of anxiety and fear in these syndromes relate to environmental challenges as well as to beliefs and attitudes that are prevalent in the cultures where the syndromes occur. In other words, culture seems to influence what people come to fear (Kirmayer, 2001). (See p. 67 for more discussion of culturally specific syndromes.)

Beyond culturally specific syndromes, the prevalence of DSM-IV-TR anxiety disorders varies across cultures. This is not surprising given that cultures differ with regard to factors such as attitudes toward mental illness, stress levels, the nature of relationships within families, and the prevalence of poverty—all of which are known to play a role in the occurrence or reporting of anxiety disorders. For example, in Taiwan and Japan, the prevalence of anxiety disorders seems to be quite low; however, this may reflect a strong stigma associated with having mental problems, which could lead to underreporting in those countries (Kawakami et al., 2004). In Cambodia and among Cambodian refugees, very elevated rates of panic disorder (often diagnosed traditionally as *kyol goeu*, or "wind overload") have been reported, perhaps because of the extreme stress experienced by Cambodians over the past several decades (Hinton et al., 2000; Hinton, Um, & Ba, 2001). Latinos living in the United States also report high rates of

Disorders similar to panic attacks occur cross-culturally. Among the Inuit, kayak-angst is defined by intense fear in lone hunters. (B & C Alexander/Photo Researchers.)

PTSD, perhaps related to the frequent exposure to political violence they experienced in their native countries (Pole, Gone, & Kaekarni, 2008). In the United States, where trauma exposure is often elevated among nonwhites, a study of over 14,000 people found higher rates of PTSD symptoms among people of color (Ritsher et al., 2002).

When researchers consider the more specific symptoms that comprise the anxiety disorders, findings are more controversial. For some time, researchers have thought that people from different cultures express symptoms of psychological distress and anxiety in different ways, but new research questions how major those cultural differences are. At one time, many researchers believed that somatic (physical) expressions of distress were more common in "collectivistic" cultures—that is, in cultures where, in some sense, the group is held to be more important than the individual (supposedly in contrast to "individualistic" Western cultures). It now seems, however, that this conclusion might reflect sampling problems—that is, researchers often studied anxiety and depression in psychological clinics in the United States but in medical clinics in other cultures. One can imagine that a person seeing a medical doctor might be likely to emphasize somatic concerns! Indeed, many people, regardless of culture, tend to describe anxiety and depression initially in terms of bodily sensations when visiting a medical clinic. When researchers interview people in similar settings and ask specifically about psychological concerns, the ratio of somatic to psychological expression of symptoms appears much more similar across cultures (Kirmayer, 2001).

Check Your Knowledge 5.1 (Answers are at the end of the chapter.)

For items 1–7, match the word to the definition.

1. fear
2. anxiety
3. worry
4. panic attack
5. obsession
6. compulsion
7. specific phobia
   a. an intense state of fear, accompanied by somatic symptoms, often in the absence of any clear danger
   b. an emotional response to immediate danger
   c. an excessive fear of a specific object or situation that causes distress or impairment
   d. a state of apprehension, often accompanied by autonomic arousal
   e. an intrusive and distressing thought that is hard to dispel and often does not make sense to the person
   f. thinking about potential problems, often without settling on a solution
   g. a behavior or thought that the person feels must be repeated again and again

8. PTSD is defined by symptoms of (circle all that apply):
   a. intense worry
   b. high arousal
   c. excessive sleeping
   d. numbing and avoidance
   e. intrusive thoughts and memories regarding the initial trauma

9. GAD is defined by:
   a. worry
   b. panic attacks
   c. fear of situations in which escape would be hard
   d. obsessions and compulsions

10. A person with one anxiety disorder has about a _____ percent chance of developing a second disorder and about a _____ percent chance of developing major depressive disorder.
    a. 35, 25
    b. 55, 35
    c. 75, 60
    d. 90, 60

11. The odds that a person will develop an anxiety disorder sometime during his or her lifetime are approximately:
    a. 1 in 10
    b. 1 in 5
    c. 1 in 4
    d. 1 in 2

Common Risk Factors across the Anxiety Disorders

In this section, we consider risk factors associated with anxiety disorders. We begin by describing a set of factors that seem to increase risk for all of the anxiety disorders. The existence of such risk factors may help explain why people with one anxiety disorder are likely to develop a second anxiety disorder—that is, some risk factors increase the odds of having more than one anxiety disorder. For example, the factors that increase risk for social phobia may also increase risk for PTSD. Psychoanalytic models dominated the field until the 1960s (see Focus on Discovery 5.1). Today, however, researchers focus more on biology, life events, personality, and cognition. Table 5.5 summarizes the factors that researchers have related to a broad range of anxiety disorders.

Genetic Factors: Are Genes a Diathesis for Anxiety Disorders?

Twin studies suggest a heritability of 20–40 percent for phobias, GAD, and PTSD and about 50 percent for panic disorder (Hettema, Neale, & Kendler, 2001; True et al., 1993). Some genes may elevate risk for several different types of anxiety disorder, while other genes may elevate risk for a specific type of anxiety disorder (Hettema et al., 2005). For example, having a family member with a phobia seems to increase the risk of developing not only a phobia but also developing other anxiety disorders (Kendler et al., 2001).

Neurobiological Factors: The Fear Circuit and the Activity of Neurotransmitters

A set of brain structures, called the **fear circuit**, tends to be activated when people are feeling anxious or fearful (Malizia, 2003). The fear circuit, shown in Figure 5.2, appears to be especially active among people with anxiety disorders. One part of the fear circuit that seems centrally involved in anxiety disorders is the amygdala. The amygdala is a small almond-shaped structure in the temporal lobe that appears to be involved in assigning emotional significance to stimuli. In animals, the amygdala has been shown to be critical for the conditioning of fear. The amygdala sends signals to a range of different brain structures involved in the fear circuit (see Figure 5.2). Studies suggest that when shown pictures of sad or angry faces, people with several different anxiety disorders respond with greater activity in the amygdala than do people without anxiety disorders (Thomas et al., 2001). Hence, elevated activity in the fear circuit, and particularly the amygdala, may help explain many different anxiety disorders. The medial prefrontal cortex appears to be important in helping to regulate amygdala activity. Researchers have found that people who meet diagnostic criteria for anxiety disorders display less activity in the medial prefrontal cortex (Shin et al., 2005). Deficits in the medial prefrontal cortex may interfere with the effective regulation of

Table 5.5 Factors That May Increase Risk for More than One Anxiety Disorder
Genetic vulnerability
Increased activity in the fear circuit of the brain
Decreased functioning of GABA and serotonin; increased norepinephrine activity
Negative life events
Behavioral inhibition
Neuroticism
Cognitive factors, including attention to cues of threat and low perception of control

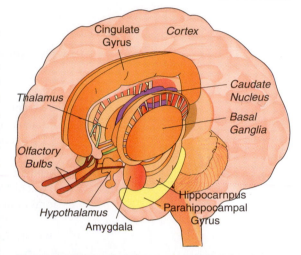

Figure 5.2 Fear and anxiety appear to be related to a set of structures in the brain called the fear circuit.

FOCUS ON DISCOVERY 5.1

Psychoanalytic Perspective: Anxiety and Defense Mechanisms

Many years ago, psychoanalytic theories of anxiety disorders dominated the field. Psychoanalysts provided a number of early case reports using the then-current diagnostic category neurosis. **Neurosis** included both anxiety and depression and was distinguished from *psychosis*, a disorder in which a person loses insight into reality.

The prevailing idea was that anxiety resulted from conflicts between the id and the ego, triggered by intense sexual or aggressive impulses from the id. Anxiety was seen as a signal to the ego that renewed efforts were needed to defend against expression of urges. The ego feared punishment if these urges were expressed and used defense mechanisms to keep the urges under control. When defense mechanisms were overworked, the result might be frequent or chronic feelings of anxiety, like the worry seen in GAD; that is, the anxiety "signal" would persist because the defense mechanisms were unable to completely repress the urges. More specific types of anxiety would be determined by the developmental stage when the conflict began, the specific defense mechanisms used by the ego, and

how well those defense mechanisms were working. For example, a fixation in the anal stage of development (a time when toilet-training is occurring and there is a focus on defecation) could promote intense conflict about whether to control impulses or not. Impulses to soil could be transformed into a desire to be compulsively neat, clean, and orderly (note the parallel with symptoms of OCD). When defense mechanisms break down, the person might experience the aggressive or sexual urge as an intrusive obsessive thought.

Attaching the anxiety to a specific object might result in a phobia. For example, Freud reported on the case of Little Hans, who was afraid of encountering horses if he went outside. Hans described "black things around horses' mouths and the things in front of their eyes." To Freud, this seemed parallel with the image of Hans's father, who had a mustache and eyeglasses. He theorized that Hans had an underlying Oedipal fear of his father. The fear was too intense for Hans to manage, so Hans had symbolically transformed it into a fear of horses.

the amygdala, contributing to a tendency toward greater emotionality. We will discuss other parts of the fear circuit, like the hippocampus, when we discuss specific anxiety disorders.

Many of the neurotransmitters involved in the fear circuit are involved in anxiety disorders. For instance, anxiety disorders seem to be related to poor functioning of the serotonin system (Chang, Cloak, & Ernst, 2003; Stein, 1998) and higher-than-normal levels of norepinephrine (Geracioti et al., 2001). GABA appears to be involved in inhibiting activity throughout the brain, and one of its effects is decreased anxiety (Sinha, Mohlman, & Gorman, 2004). Poor GABA function, then, could contribute to anxiety.

The Social Environment: Actual Threats

Negative life events, particularly those portending danger of something bad happening in the future, often precede the onset of anxiety disorders (Kendler, Prescott, et al., 2003). For example, as many as 80 percent of people with panic disorder describe a severe stressor that occurred just before the onset of the disorder (Barlow, 2004). More broadly, about 70 percent of people report a severe stressor before the onset of an anxiety disorder (Finlay-Jones, 1989).

Personality: Behavioral Inhibition and Neuroticism

Some infants show the trait of **behavioral inhibition**, a tendency to become agitated and cry when faced with novel toys, people, or other stimuli. This behavior pattern, which has been described in infants as young as 4 months old, may be inherited and may set the stage for the later development of anxiety disorders. One study followed infants from 14 months through 7.5 years; 45 percent of those who showed elevated behavioral inhibition levels at 14 months showed symptoms of anxiety at age 7.5, compared to only 15 percent of those who had shown low behavioral inhibition levels (Kagan & Snidman, 1999). Behavioral inhibition appears to be a particularly strong predictor of social phobia: thirty percent of infants showing elevated behavioral inhibition levels developed social phobia by adolescence (Biederman, 1990).

Neuroticism is a personality trait defined by the tendency to react to events with greater-than-average negative affect. How does neuroticism relate to anxiety disorders? In a sample of 7,076 adults, neuroticism predicted the onset of both anxiety disorders and depression (de Graaf et al., 2002). People with high levels of neuroticism were more than twice as likely to develop an anxiety disorder as those with low neuroticism.

Similar findings emerge when researchers use psychophysiological measures to study reactivity to even subtle negative events. In one study, researchers studied 87 firefighters just as they enlisted. They measured how much of a skin conductance response participants showed in response to a loud tone, as a measure of response to a mildly aversive stimulus. Participants who had a larger psychophysiological response to the tones were at greater risk of developing PTSD symptoms after exposure to trauma on the job (Guthrie & Bryant, 2005). In sum, whether measured using observational coding, questionnaires, or psychophysiological responses, people who tend to have stronger reactions to negative stimuli and events appear to be at greater risk for anxiety disorders.

Cognitive Factors: Perceived Control and Attending to Threat

People with anxiety disorders often report believing that bad things are likely to happen. For example, people with panic disorder might believe that they will die when their heart begins to pound, whereas people with social phobia might believe that they will suffer humiliating rejection if they blush. As pointed out by David Clark and colleagues (1999), the key issue is not why people think so negatively initially but, rather, how are these beliefs sustained? For example, by the time a person survives 100 panic attacks, you might expect the belief "this attack means I am about to die" would fade. One reason these beliefs might be sustained is that people think and act in ways that maintain these beliefs. That is, to protect against feared consequences, they engage in **safety behaviors**. For example, people who fear they will die from a fast heart rate stop all physical activity the minute they feel their heart race. They come to believe that only their safety behaviors have saved their life. Hence, safety behaviors allow a person to maintain overly negative cognitions.

Researchers have focused on several separate cognitive aspects of anxiety disorders. Here, we focus on two: a lack of control and attention to signs of threat.

Perceived Control   People who think that they lack control over their environment appear to be at greater risk for a broad range of anxiety disorders than people who do not have that belief. For example, people with anxiety disorders report experiencing little sense of control over their surroundings (Mineka & Zinbarg, 1998). Childhood experiences, such as traumatic events (Hofmann et al., 2001) and punitive, restrictive parenting (Chorpita, Brown, & Barlow, 1998), could promote a view that life is not controllable.

Animal studies have illustrated that a lack of control over the environment can promote anxiety. For example, Insel and colleagues (1988) randomly assigned monkeys to one of two conditions. One group of monkeys grew up with the ability to choose whether and when they would receive treats. A second group of monkeys had no control over whether and when they received treats—that is, a given monkey in this second group was given a treat whenever a given monkey in the first group received a treat. The two groups of monkeys received the same num-

Infants and toddlers showing behavioral inhibition—high anxiety about novel situations and people—are at greater risk of developing anxiety disorders during their lifetime. (David Young-Wolff/PhotoEdit.)

ber of treats. In the third year of life, monkeys who had grown up without control behaved in ways that looked anxious when facing new situations and interacting with other monkeys; monkeys who had grown up with control showed less anxiety. In sum, animal and human studies both point toward the importance of a perception of lack of control in the development of anxiety disorders.

As we will discuss below, many anxiety disorders develop after exposure to a traumatic incident. The amount of control that people have during that incident seems to be a major variable in whether anxiety disorders develop. For example, people who are used to dogs and feel comfortable about controlling dogs' behavior are much less likely to develop a phobia after a dog bite. Similarly, people who have been provided with coping strategies for dealing with torture (and so have a sense of control during torture sessions) are less likely to develop PTSD if imprisoned and tortured. Hence, early lifetime experiences of control, as well as experiences of control during a highly threatening circumstance, both influence whether a person develops an anxiety disorder (Mineka & Zinbarg, 2006).

Attention to Threat   People with anxiety disorders have been found to pay more attention to negative cues in their environment than do people without anxiety disorders. Many research studies have tested for negative attention patterns among people with anxiety disorders, using measures such as the emotion Stroop task (see Figure 2.11, p. 46) (Williams et al., 1997). Such studies provide evidence that anxiety disorders are associated with greater attention toward threatening stimuli (Williams et al., 1997). For example, Vietnam veterans with PTSD have been found to selectively attend to words related to war (e.g., *body bags*), whereas people with snake phobias attend to cues related to snakes (McNally et al., 1990; Öhman, Flykt, & Esteves, 2001). Researchers have also shown that this attention to threatening stimuli happens automatically and very quickly—before people are even consciously aware of the stimuli (Öhman & Soares, 1994). In a meta-analysis of 172 studies, each of the specific anxiety disorders was associated with a similar level of attention to threatening stimuli (Bar-Haim et al., 2007). In sum, anxiety disorders are associated with selective attention to signs of threat.

Is Negative Cognition a Cause or an Effect of Anxiety?   A key question is whether the negative cognitions seen among people with anxiety disorder are the cause or the effect of being anxious. There is some evidence for both sides.

First screen

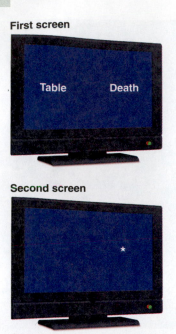

Second screen

Figure 5.3 The dot probe task is used to test biases in attention and then to train people to learn biases. In the first screen of each trial, participants see one neutral word and one negative word. In the second screen, a dot appears in the location where one of the two words was. The participant is asked to press a button as quickly as possible to indicate whether the dot appears on the left or right side of the screen. In the case shown here, a person who was looking at the word *death* will see the dot and respond more quickly than a person who was looking at the word table. To teach people a negative bias, researchers present the dot in the same location where the negative word was for hundreds of trials. For a control group, the dot randomly appears on the left or right side of the screen.

To examine the longitudinal course of beliefs about vulnerability and control, one team of researchers studied soldiers before and after they were deployed to Iraq (Engelhard et al., 2007). As one might expect, soldiers reported much more negative thinking after they had spent time in Iraq than they had reported before deployment. In this study, the negativity of cognitions before the trauma did not predict whether or not PTSD developed. These findings, then, suggest that negative cognition appears to be a consequence of anxiety. A person who has experienced threatening life experiences may learn to focus more on negatives. Other studies have found that more negative cognitive styles predict greater risk for the development of PTSD (Bryant & Guthrie, 2007). Hence, it is hard to know from these naturalistic studies whether cognition consistently predicts the onset of anxiety disorders.

Experimental research can be helpful in disentangling potential confounds that could explain the inconsistency in results of naturalistic studies. In one line of experimental research, investigators examined whether attention to anxiety-related information could actually be created, and then whether this attentional "bias" would lead to more anxiety (Mathews & MacLeod, 2002). They trained people to attend to threatening words, and then examined whether this influenced anxiety levels. To train people to attend to threat, they used hundreds of trials of a computerized task called the dot probe (see Figure 5.3). That is, researchers trained people to have a negative bias in their attention. People who are trained to attend to negative words report a more anxious mood after training, especially if they are given a challenging task like an unsolvable puzzle to perform. The control group did not show an increase in anxious mood after training. Of course, researchers could not ethically create anxiety disorders, so these studies look at milder levels of anxiety. But the results provide evidence that the way we focus our attention influences anxious mood.

Could these types of trained biases help us understand diagnosable levels of anxiety? Researchers have examined this by training people diagnosed with generalized anxiety disorder to develop a positive bias (Amir et al., 2008). Training was conducted twice a week for four weeks, and during each session, participants completed 240 trials. To train a positive bias, the dots appeared where the positive words had appeared. For a control group, there was no systematic pattern to where the dot occurred. Anxiety levels were unchanged in the control group. Participants in the positive bias training condition obtained lower anxiety scores on self-report and interview measures post-training: fifty percent of the people who received positive-bias training no longer met the diagnostic criteria for GAD. Although it is not clear how long these gains were maintained, these findings provide exciting support for the role of cognition in anxiety.

Etiology of Specific Anxiety Disorders

In the next sections, we look at the various approaches to the etiology of the specific anxiety disorders. Above, we discussed genetic, neurobiological, cognitive, and behavioral research on factors that might set the stage for development of anxiety disorders in general. Here, we turn to the question of how each of the specific anxiety disorders arise. That is, why does one person develop a specific phobia while another person develops generalized anxiety disorder? Keep in mind the common etiological factors already described and think about how these commonalities relate to and combine with the specifics described next.

Etiology of Specific Phobias

Much of the research on phobias focuses on traumatic experiences and conditioning. This model focuses on the idea that people develop phobias after exposure to an aversive stimulus. As you read this section, keep in mind that many people who are exposed to aversive stimuli don't develop phobias. The risk factors described above, such as genetic vulnerability, neuroticism and negative cognition, probably operate as diatheses—vulnerability factors that shape whether or not a phobia will develop in the context of a conditioning experience (Mineka & Sutton, 2006).

Behavioral Factors: Conditioning of Specific Phobias   Behavioral theories of specific phobias focus on conditioning, based on **Mowrer's two-factor model** (see Figure 5.4). This model suggests two steps in phobic conditioning (Mowrer, 1947):

1. Through *classical conditioning*, a person learns to fear a neutral stimulus (the CS) that is paired with an intrinsically aversive stimulus (the UCS).
2. Through *operant conditioning*, the person gains relief from this conditioned fear by avoiding the CS. The avoidant response is maintained by its reinforcing consequence of reducing fear.

Consider an example. Imagine that a man is bitten by a dog and then develops a phobia of dogs. Through classical conditioning, he has learned to associate dogs (the CS) with painful bites (the UCS). This corresponds to step 1 above. In step 2, the man reduces his fear by avoiding dogs as much as possible; the avoidant behavior is reinforced by the reduction in fear. This second step explains why the phobia isn't extinguished. With repeated exposure to dogs that don't bite, the man should lose his fear of dogs, but by avoiding dogs, the man gets little or no such exposure. We should note that Mowrer's early version of the two-factor model does not actually fit the evidence very well; several extensions of this model, which we look at next, have been developed that fit the evidence better (Mineka & Zinbarg, 1998).

One extension of the model has been to consider different ways in which classical conditioning could occur (Rachman, 1977). These include the following:

- It could occur by direct experience, like the conditioned fear of dogs in the example above.
- It could occur by seeing another person harmed or frightened by a stimulus (e.g., seeing a dog bite a man or watching a YouTube video of a vicious dog attack). This type of learning is called modeling (Fredrikson, Annas, & Wik, 1997). In one study, researchers showed participants a movie of a man who received shocks. Participants were told that they would receive shocks next. When watching the stranger receive shocks, participants demonstrated increased activity in the amygdala, just as they would if they had personally experienced the aversive stimulus (Olsson, Nearing, & Phelps, 2007).
- It could occur by verbal instruction—for example, by a parent warning a child that dogs are dangerous.

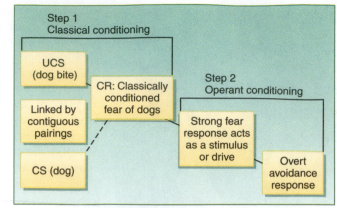

Figure 5.4 Two-factor model of conditioning.

Little Albert, shown here with Watson and Rayner, was classically conditioned to develop a fear of a white rat. (Courtesy Benjamin Harris.)

Current theory suggests that phobias *could* be conditioned by any of these types of experiences: direct trauma, modeling, or verbal instruction. But do most people with a phobia report one of these types of conditioning experiences? In one study, 1,937 people were asked whether they had had these types of conditioning experiences before the onset of their phobias (Kendler, Myers, & Prescott, 2002). Although conditioning experiences were common, about half of the people in the study could not remember any such experiences (see Table 5.6). Obviously, if

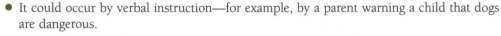

Table 5.6 Percent of People Reporting Conditioning Experiences Before the Onset of a Phobia

Type of Fear	Direct Trauma	Observed Trauma or Fear in Others	Taught Fear	No Memory of Conditioning Experience
Agoraphobia	27.0	3.4	4.6	65.1
Social	23.3	4.6	7.3	65.0
Animal	48.1	9.1	11.6	31.2
Situational	32.7	8.1	6.3	52.9
Blood/injection/injury	46.7	13.6	7.2	32.4

Source: From a survey of 1,937 people conducted by Kendler, Myers, and Prescott (2002).

Many people report that they develop a phobia after a traumatic event. Debate exists about why some people don't report that they had experienced a traumatic event before the onset of their phobia. (Bruce Herman/Stone/Getty Images.)

Susan Mineka's research showed that when monkeys observe another monkey display fear of a snake, they also acquire the fear. This indicates that modeling may play a role in the etiology of phobias. (Courtesy of Susan Mineka.)

Kim Basinger, the Oscar-winning actress, is reported to have suffered from panic disorder with agoraphobia as well as social phobia. (Matthew Simmons/Getty Images News and Sport Services.)

many phobias start without a conditioning experience, this is a big problem for the behavioral model. But proponents of the behavioral model argue that people may forget conditioning experiences (Mineka & Öhman, 2002). Because of memory gaps, simple surveys of how many people remember a conditioning experience do not provide very accurate evidence about the behavioral model.

Another extension of the model considers the types of stimuli that become feared. Mowrer's original two-factor model suggests that people could be conditioned to be afraid of all types of stimuli. But people with phobias tend to fear certain types of stimuli. Typically, people do not develop phobias of flowers, lambs, or lamp shades! But phobias of insects or other animals, natural environments, and blood are common. As many as half of women report a fear of snakes; moreover, many different types of animals also show fear in response to snakes (Öhman & Mineka, 2003). Researchers have suggested that during the evolution of our species, people learned to react strongly to stimuli that could be life-threatening, such as heights, snakes, and angry humans (Seligman, 1971). Perhaps our fear circuit has evolved to respond especially rapidly and automatically to these types of stimuli. That is, our fear circuit may have been "prepared" by evolution to learn fear of certain stimuli; hence, this type of learning is called **prepared learning**. As researchers have tested this model, some have discovered that people can be initially conditioned to fear many different types of stimuli (McNally, 1987). Fears to most types of stimuli fade quickly with ongoing exposure, though, whereas fears of naturally dangerous stimuli are sustained in most studies (Dawson, Schell, & Banis, 1986).

Prepared learning is also relevant to modeling, as indicated by a study involving four groups of rhesus monkeys (Cook & Mineka, 1989). Each group of monkeys was shown a videotape of a monkey exhibiting intense fear, but for each group, videotape editing was used to make the feared object appear to be different: a toy snake, a toy crocodile, flowers, or a toy rabbit. Only the monkeys exposed to the tapes showing a monkey who expressed fear of a toy snake or toy crocodile acquired fear of the object shown. These findings suggest that, with rhesus monkeys as with people, it is easier to condition fear of potentially life-threatening stimuli than of neutral stimuli.

Despite the volume of research on conditioning models of phobia, controversy remains. Some authors have suggested that at least some fears might be biologically preprogrammed, such that no conditioning experience is required (Menzies & Clarke, 1995). Infants tend to show fears of water, heights, and strangers even if they have no previous exposure to these stimuli. Hence, conditioning models of phobias will need to be integrated with biological models of the fear system.

Etiology of Social Phobia

In this section, we review behavioral and cognitive factors related to social phobia. The trait of behavioral inhibition, discussed above, may also be important in the development of social phobia.

Behavioral Factors: Conditioning of Social Phobia   Behavioral perspectives on the causes of social phobia are similar to those on specific phobias, insofar as they are based on a two-factor conditioning model. That is, a person could have a negative social experience (directly, through modeling, or through verbal instruction) and become classically conditioned to fear similar situations, which the person then avoids. Through operant conditioning, this avoidance behavior is maintained because it reduces the fear the person experiences. There are few opportunities for the conditioned fear to be extinguished because the person tends to avoid social situations. Even when the person interacts with others, he or she may show avoidant behavior in smaller ways that have been labeled as safety behaviors. Examples of safety behaviors in social phobia include avoiding eye contact, disengaging from conversation, and standing apart from others. Although these behaviors are used to avoid negative feedback, they create other problems. Other people tend to disapprove of these types of avoidant behaviors, which then intensifies the problem (Wells, 1998). (Think about how you might respond if you were trying to talk to someone who looks at the floor, fails to answer your questions, and leaves the room in the middle of the conversation.)

Cognitive Factors: Too Much Focus on Negative Self-Evaluations Theory focuses on several different ways in which cognitive processes might intensify social anxiety (Clark & Wells, 1995). First, people with social phobias appear to hold much higher standards for their performance and to have unrealistically negative beliefs about the consequences of their social behaviors—for example, they may believe that others will reject them if they blush or pause while speaking. Second, they attend more to how they are doing in social situations and their own internal sensations than other people do. Instead of attending to their conversation partner, they are often thinking about how others might perceive them (e.g., "He must think I'm an idiot"). They often form powerful negative visual images of how others will react to them (Hirsch & Clark, 2004). Of course, good conversation requires a focus on the other person, so too much thinking about inner feelings and evaluative cognitions can foster social awkwardness. The resultant anxiety interferes with their ability to perform well socially, creating a vicious cycle—for example, the person doesn't pay enough attention to others, who then perceive the person as not interested in them, which leads the person to perceive others as judging her or him negatively (in this case, an accurate perception).

There is plenty of evidence that people with social phobia are overly negative in evaluating their social performance, even when they are not socially awkward (Stopa & Clark, 2000). For example, in one study, researchers assessed blushing in people with and without social phobia. Participants were asked to estimate how much they would blush during different tasks, such as singing a children's song. Then they were asked to engage in these different tasks. Participants with social phobia overestimated how much they would blush (Gerlach et al., 2001). Similarly, one research team asked people with social phobia to rate videos of their performance in giving a short speech. Socially anxious people rated their speeches more negatively than objective raters did, whereas people who were not socially anxious were not harsh in rating their performance (Ashbaugh et al., 2005). Therefore, people with social phobia may be unfairly harsh in the way they evaluate their performance.

There is also evidence that social phobia is related to attention to internal cues rather than external (social) cues. For example, people with social phobia appear to spend more time than other people do monitoring for signs of their own anxiety. In one recent study, researchers gave participants a chance to watch their own heart rate displayed on a computer screen or to watch video material. People diagnosed with social phobia attended more closely to their own heart rate than did the people who were not diagnosed with social phobia (Pineles & Mineka, 2005). Hence, it seems that rather than focusing on external stimuli, people with this disorder tend to be busy monitoring their own anxiety levels.

How might all these risk variables fit together when we consider a person with social phobia, like Maureen? Maureen is likely to have inherited some tendency to be anxious when faced with new people. As she grew up, this may have interfered with her chances to acquire social skills and to gain self-confidence. Her fear of other people's opinions and her own negative thoughts about her social abilities create a vicious cycle in which her intolerable anxiety leads her to avoid social situations, and then the avoidance leads to increased anxiety.

Etiology of Panic Disorder

In this section, we look at current thinking about the etiology of panic disorder, from neurobiological, behavioral, and cognitive perspectives. As you will see, the neurobiological, behavioral, and cognitive perspectives each focus on how people respond to somatic (bodily) changes like increased heart rate.

Neurobiological Factors Remember that a panic attack seems to reflect a misfire of the fear circuit, with a concomitant surge in activity in the sympathetic nervous system. We have seen that the fear circuit appears to play an important role in many of the anxiety disorders. Now we will see that a particular part of the fear circuit seems to be especially important in panic disorder: the **locus ceruleus** (see Figure 5.5). The locus ceruleus is the major source of the neurotransmitter norepinephrine in the brain, and norepinephrine plays a major role in triggering sympathetic nervous system activity.

The notion of prepared learning suggests that we have evolved to pay special attention to signs of danger, including angry people, threatening animals, and dangerous natural environments. (Top to bottom: Digital Vision/Getty Images; Gail Shumway/Taxi/Getty Images; S. F. Vincent/Taxi/Getty Images.)

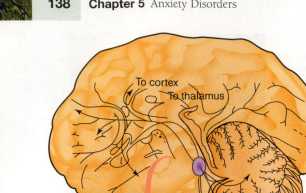

Figure 5.5 Locus ceruleus. Drawn from Martin, J. H. (1996). *Neuroanatomy Text and Atlas*, second edition. NY-McGraw-Hill Professions Division. With permission, McGraw-Hill Companies.

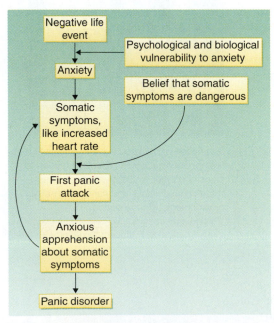

Figure 5.6 Interoceptive conditioning.

Monkeys exposed to feared stimuli, such as snakes, show high activity in the locus ceruleus. Further, when activity in the locus ceruleus is triggered using an electrical signal, monkeys behave as if they were having a panic attack (Redmond, 1977). In humans, drugs that increase activity in the locus ceruleus can trigger panic attacks, and drugs that decrease activity in the locus ceruleus, including clonidine and some antidepressants, decrease the risk of panic attacks.

Behavioral Factors: Classical Conditioning The behavioral perspective on the etiology of panic disorder focuses on classical conditioning. This model draws from an interesting pattern—panic attacks are often triggered by internal bodily sensations of arousal (Kenardy & Taylor, 1999). Theory suggests that panic attacks are classically conditioned responses to either the situations that trigger anxiety or the internal bodily sensations of arousal (Bouton, Mineka, & Barlow, 2001). Classical conditioning of panic attacks in response to bodily sensations has been called **interoceptive conditioning**: a person experiences somatic signs of anxiety, which are followed by the person's first panic attack; panic attacks then become a conditioned response to the somatic changes (see Figure 5.6).

There is some evidence that people with panic disorder might be more easily conditioned to fear aversive stimuli. In one study, researchers conditioned people to fear a neutral picture of a Rorschach card (see p. 83) by pairing the card with a shock six times (Michael et al., 2007). Regardless of whether they met diagnostic criteria for panic disorder, people learned to fear the Rorschach card, as measured using skin conductance responses to seeing the card. People who were not diagnosed with panic disorder showed a quick drop in their fear responses during the extinction phase of the study, when the card was shown without a shock being provided. People with panic disorder, though, showed very little drop in their fear response during the extinction phase of the disorder. Hence, people with panic disorder appear to sustain classically conditioned fears longer.

Cognitive Factors in Panic Disorder Cognitive perspectives focus on catastrophic misinterpretations of somatic changes (Clark, 1996). According to this model, panic attacks develop when a person interprets bodily sensations as signs of impending doom (see Figure 5.7). For example, the person may interpret the sensation of an increase in heart rate as a sign of an impending heart attack. Obviously, such thoughts will increase the person's anxiety, which produces more physical sensations, creating a vicious cycle.

Research has focused on triggering panic attacks experimentally for more than 75 years. This research provides strong support for the idea that people who experience panic attacks are overly fearful about somatic changes because they respond to many different body changes with a panic attack.

More specifically, these studies suggest that more than a dozen different types of drugs can trigger panic attacks among people with a history of panic attacks (Swain et al., 2003). People who do and do not develop panic attacks after being exposed to these agents seem to vary on only one characteristic—the extent to which they are frightened by the body changes (Margraf, Ehlers, & Roth, 1986). Furthermore, drugs that have opposite effects can even set off panic attacks! In one study, for example, 20 people with panic disorder were given either adrenaline (a drug that increases sympathetic nervous system activity) or acetylcholine (a drug that increases parasympathetic nervous system activity). The sympathetic and parasympathetic nervous systems work in opposition to each other. With either drug, about half of people had a panic attack (Lindemann & Finesinger, 1938). Even exercise alone, simple relaxation, or the physical sensations caused by an illness such as inner ear disease can induce panic attacks (Asmundson, Larsen, & Stein, 1998). In short, drugs with many different effects and even other body sensations can trigger panic attacks (Barlow, 2004).

In an important test of how cognitions influence this fear, people with a history of panic attacks were exposed to air with high levels of carbon dioxide, which has been shown to induce panic attacks for many people. Before breathing the air, some people

Table 5.7 Sample Items from the Anxiety Sensitivity Index

Unusual body sensations scare me.

When I notice that my heart is beating rapidly, I worry that I might have a heart attack.

It scares me when I feel faint.

It scares me when I feel "shaky" (trembling).

Source: Peterson & Reiss, 1987.
Note: People respond to each item on a 0 (very little) to 4 (very much) scale.

were given a full explanation regarding the physical sensations they were likely to experience, and others were given no explanation. After breathing the air, those who received a full explanation reported that they had fewer catastrophic interpretations of their bodily sensations, and they were much less likely to have a panic attack than those who did not receive an explanation (Rapee, Mattick, & Murrell, 1986). Catastrophic interpretations of bodily sensations, then, seem to be important in triggering panic attacks.

A key question, though, is whether the propensity toward catastrophic interpretations can be detected before panic disorder develops. Many researchers have used a test called the **Anxiety Sensitivity Index**, which measures the extent to which people respond fearfully to their bodily sensations (Telch, Shermis, & Lucas, 1989). (Sample items from the questionnaire used in this study are shown in Table 5.7.) In one study, college students with no history of panic attacks were divided into high and low scorers on the Anxiety Sensitivity Index (Telch & Harrington, 1992). All the participants went through two trials. In one trial they breathed regular air. In the other they breathed air with a higher-than-usual concentration of carbon dioxide. Before the trials, they were told that they would be breathing air with a high concentration of carbon dioxide. Half the participants in each trial were told that the carbon dioxide would be relaxing, and half were told that it would produce high arousal. The frequency of panic attacks in each group is shown in Table 5.8. Note that panic attacks did not occur among people breathing regular air. In the condition involving increased carbon dioxide, panic attacks were most common among people who feared their bodily sensations, particularly if they did not expect breathing carbon dioxide to be arousing. This result is exactly what the model predicts: unexplained physiological arousal in someone who is fearful of such sensations leads to panic attacks.

Another study bearing on this theory of panic disorder followed 1,296 Air Force recruits as they went through the stressful experiences of basic training (Schmidt, Lerew, & Jackson, 1999). Each participant completed the Anxiety Sensitivity Index. Consistent with the model, high scores on the Anxiety Sensitivity Index predicted the development of panic attacks during basic training.

Agoraphobia: Cognitive Factors in the Fear-of-Fear Hypothesis   As mentioned earlier, panic disorder is often accompanied by agoraphobia. The principal cognitive model for the etiology of agoraphobia is the **fear-of-fear hypothesis** (Goldstein & Chambless, 1978), which suggests that agoraphobia is driven by negative thoughts about the consequences of having a panic attack in public. There is evidence that people with agoraphobia think the consequences of a public panic attack would be horrible, and they spend more time worrying about public places where panic attacks could occur. People with panic disorder without agoraphobia do not seem to worry as much about specific places, so they spend less time avoiding specific places (Clark, 1997).

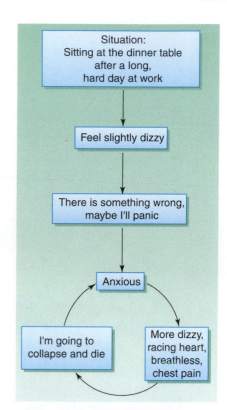

Figure 5.7 An example of catastrophic misinterpretation of bodily cues. Drawn from Clark, D. M. (1997). Panic disorder and social phobia. In D. M. Clark & C. G. Fairburn (eds.), *Science and Practice of Cognitive Behaviour Therapy* (pp. 121–153). With permission, Oxford University Press.

Table 5.8 Frequency of Panic Attacks as a Function of Breathing Regular Air versus Breathing Air with Carbon Dioxide, Fear of Bodily Sensations, and Expectations

Inhale	High Fear of Bodily Sensations		Low Fear of Bodily Sensations	
	Expect Relaxation	Expect Arousal	Expect Relaxation	Expect Arousal
Regular air	0	0	0	0
Carbon dioxide	52	17	5	5

Source: from Telch and Harrington (1992).

Etiology of Generalized Anxiety Disorder

Generalized anxiety disorder (GAD) tends to co-occur with other anxiety disorders and with depression. Because the comorbidity is so high, researchers believe that many of the factors involved in predicting anxiety disorders in general are particularly important for understanding GAD. For example, deficits in the functioning of the GABA system, which are important for many anxiety disorders, appear to be involved in GAD (Tihonen et al., 1997). Beyond these general risk factors, recent research has focused on cognitive factors.

Cognitive Factors: Why Do People Worry?

Cognitive factors may help answer why some people worry more than others. Tom Borkovec and colleagues focus on the main symptom of GAD—worry—in their cognitive model (Borkovec & Newman, 1998). Worry would seem so unpleasant that one might ask why anyone would worry a lot. Borkovec and colleagues have marshaled evidence that worry is actually reinforcing because it distracts people from more powerful negative emotions and images. The key to understanding this argument is to realize that worry does not involve powerful visual images and does not produce the physiological changes that usually accompany emotion. Indeed, worrying actually seems to decrease psychophysiological signs of arousal (Freeston, Dugas, & Ladoceur, 1996). Thus, by worrying, people with GAD may be avoiding unpleasant emotions that would be more powerful than worry. But as a consequence of this avoidance, their underlying anxiety about these images does not extinguish. What kinds of anxiety-evoking images might people with GAD be avoiding? A possible answer comes from studies showing that many people with GAD report past traumas involving death, injury, or illness (Borkovec & Newman, 1998). It may be that worry distracts people with GAD from the distress of remembering these past traumas. People diagnosed with GAD do report that it is harder to understand and label their feelings, so their difficulty in coping with negative feelings may make them more motivated to try to avoid their emotions (Mennin, et al., 2002). Some research suggests that people who have a hard time accepting ambiguity, that is, who find it intolerable to think that something bad *might* happen in the future, are more likely to worry and to develop GAD (Dugas, Marchand, & Ladouceur, 2005).

Etiology of Obsessive-Compulsive Disorder

We now turn to neurobiological, behavioral, and cognitive perspectives on the etiology of obsessive-compulsive disorder (OCD). Brain-imaging studies of OCD provide an excellent example of how neurobiology can help us understand mental illness; behavioral and cognitive models tend to provide distinct explanations for compulsions versus obsessions.

Neurobiological Factors: Hyperactive Regions of the Brain

It has been noted for decades that OCD symptoms are relatively common among people with certain neurological disorders, such as Huntington's chorea (Cummings & Cunningham, 1992). Brain-imaging studies indicate that three closely related areas of the brain are unusually active in people with OCD (see Figure 5.2, p. 131): the **orbitofrontal cortex** (an area of the frontal lobe located just above the eyes), the caudate nucleus (part of the basal ganglia), and the **anterior cingulate (cingulate gyrus)** (Micallef & Blin, 2001). When people with OCD are shown objects that tend to cause symptoms (such as a soiled glove for a person who fears contamination), activity in these three areas increases (McGuire et al., 1994). Overall, evidence is fairly strong that the symptoms of OCD are tied to overactivity in these three brain areas. One recent brain imaging study which allowed researchers to examine the biochemical function of neurons suggested that there may be some loss of neuronal function in the anterior cingulate and that the hyperactivity of neurons in this area reflects an attempt to compensate for the underlying abnormality (Yücel et al., 2007). Studies indicate that when symptoms of OCD decrease with either medication or psychological treatment, neurobiological deficits normalize (Baxter et al., 2000).

Panic attacks can be experimentally triggered by a variety of agents that change body sensations, including drugs and even exercise. (Robin Nelson/PhotoEdit.)

Behavioral Factors in Compulsions Behavioral models consider compulsions to be operantly conditioned responses. That is, compulsions are reinforced because they reduce anxiety (Meyer & Chesser, 1970). For example, compulsive hand washing would provide immediate relief from the anxiety associated with obsessions about germs. Similarly, checking the stove may provide immediate relief from the anxiety associated with the thought that the house will catch fire. Consistent with this view, after compulsive behavior, self-reported anxiety and even psychophysiological arousal drop (Carr, 1971).

Cognitive Factors in OCD: Lack of a Satiety Signal and Attempts to Suppress Thoughts At least 80 percent of people experience brief intrusive thoughts from time to time—a terrible song or image gets stuck in your head (Rachman & DeSilva, 1978). Because intrusive thoughts are so common, much of the cognitive research has focused on why such thoughts persist, rather than on why such thoughts happen in the first place. After all, we don't diagnose OCD until intrusive thoughts are so persistent that they cause real distress or impairment.

Consider for a moment how we know to stop thinking about something, to stop cleaning, or to quit studying for a test or organizing our desk. There is no absolute signal from the environment. Rather, most of us stop when we have the sense of "that is enough." Yedasentience is defined as this subjective feeling of knowing (Szechtman & Woody, 2004). Just like you have a signal that you have eaten enough food, yedasentience is an intuitive signal that you have thought enough, cleaned enough, or in other ways done what you should to prevent chaos and danger. One theory suggests that people with OCD suffer from a deficit in yedasentience. Because they fail to gain the internal sense of completion, they have a hard time stopping their thoughts and behaviors. Objectively, they seem to know that there is no need to check the stove or wash their hands again, but they suffer from an anxious internal sense that things are not complete.

A different model focuses on cognitive factors and obsessions. This model suggests that people with OCD may try harder to suppress their obsessions than other people and, in doing so, may actually make the situation worse. Several researchers have shown that people with OCD tend to believe that thinking about something can make it more likely to occur (Rachman, 1997). People with OCD are also likely to describe especially deep feelings of responsibility for what occurs (Ladoceur et al., 2000). As a consequence of these two factors, they are more likely to attempt **thought suppression** (Salkovskis, 1996).

Unfortunately, it is hard to suppress thoughts. One study looked at what happens when people are asked to suppress a thought (Wegner et al., 1987). Two groups of college students were asked either to think about a white bear or not to think about one; they were also told to ring a bell every time they thought about a white bear. The findings indicated that attempts to avoid thinking about the white bear did not work—students thought about the bear more than once a minute when trying not to do so. Beyond that, there was a rebound effect—after students tried to suppress thoughts about the bear for 5 minutes, they thought about the bear much more often during the next 5 minutes. Trying to suppress a thought may have the paradoxical effect of inducing preoccupation with it.

Most studies look at the effects of suppression over a matter of minutes, but the effects of trying to suppress a thought can continue for days. In one study, for example, people were asked to identify a recent intrusive thought and then were told to pay attention to the thought, were told to suppress the thought, or were given no instructions about the thought (Trinder & Salkoviskis, 1994). Participants recorded how often they had the intrusive thought and how uncomfortable the experience was for the next 4 days. People told to suppress the thought had more frequent intrusions of the thought and rated the intrusions as more uncomfortable over the 4-day period.

Beyond these studies of how hard it is to suppress thoughts, there is some evidence that thought suppression does actually play a role in OCD—namely, people with OCD tend to give more reasons why they should try to suppress thoughts than do people without OCD. For example, people who say they believe that bad things will happen if you think about them are more likely to try to suppress thoughts, and people who report more thought suppression also report more obsessive symptoms (Rassin et al., 2000). Research also indicates, however, that people with a wide range of anxiety disorders worry that bad things will happen if you think about them. So it is not clear if thought suppression gives us an explanation of OCD in particular or if it relates to anxiety disorders in general (Rassin et al., 2001).

Etiology of Posttraumatic Stress Disorder

As with other anxiety disorders, posttraumatic stress disorder (PTSD) tends to occur more often among people with childhood experiences of trauma, people with other anxiety or depressive disorders, people who are high in neuroticism (Breslau, Davis, & Andreski, 1995), and women (McNally, 2003). Also, as with other anxiety disorders, people with PTSD tend to show high levels of brain activity in areas of the fear circuit, such as the amygdala (Rauch et al., 2000). Keeping these things in mind, in this section we focus on factors that are uniquely associated with PTSD. Even among people who experience traumas, not everyone develops PTSD. Thus, a great deal of research has been conducted on aspects of the trauma and the person that help predict the onset of PTSD. We begin by describing aspects of the trauma and then turn to individual differences.

Nature of the Trauma: Severity and the Type of Trauma Matter   The severity of the trauma influences whether or not a person will develop PTSD. Consider the case of people who are exposed to war. About 20 percent of American fighters wounded in Vietnam developed PTSD, contrasted with 50 percent of those who were prisoners of war there (Engdahl et

Survivors of natural disasters, such as the tsunami at the end of 2004, are at risk for PTSD. (NAMAS BHOJANI/Bloomberg News/Landov LLC.)

al., 1997). During Operation Desert Storm (in the 1990–1991 conflict following the Iraqi invasion of Kuwait), among those assigned to collect, tag, and bury scattered body parts of the dead, 65 percent developed PTSD (Sutker et al., 1994). During World War II, doctors believed that 98 percent of men would develop psychiatric problems with 60 days of continuous combat (Grossman, 1995).

The occurrence of PTSD among residents of New York City after the terrorist attack on the World Trade Center on September 11, 2001 showed a similar correspondence with the severity of the trauma. Based on a telephone survey after the attack, researchers determined that 7 percent of the adults living south of 110th Street in New York City (but well north of the World Trade Center) reported symptoms that would have warranted a diagnosis of PTSD, but 20 percent of those living south of Canal Street (close to the disaster site) reported such symptoms (Galea et al., 2002). In short, among people who have been exposed to traumas, those exposed to the most severe traumas seem most likely to develop PTSD.

Beyond severity, the nature of the trauma matters. Traumas caused by humans are more likely to cause PTSD than are natural disasters (Charuvastra & Cloitre, 2008). For example, rapes, combat experience, abuse, and assault all are associated with higher risk than are naturally occurring fires and other disasters. It may be that these events are seen as more distressing because they challenge ideas about humans as benevolent.

Neurobiological Factors: Hippocampus and Hormones   The hippocampus is an area in the brain known for its role in memory, including memories related to emotions (see Figure 5.2). Brain-imaging studies show that among people with PTSD, the hippocampus has a smaller volume than among people who do not have PTSD (Bremner et al., 2003). A study of multiple pairs of identical twins, one of whom was a Vietnam veteran and the other not, is especially revealing of how hippocampal volume and PTSD are related (Gilbertson et al., 2002). As in previous studies of veterans, smaller hippocampal volume was associated with PTSD symptoms, but this study went on to find an additional important pattern. That is, there was a relationship between hippocampal volume in the nonveteran twins and the likelihood of PTSD in the veteran twins. Smaller hippocampal volume fo the nonveteran twin was related to greater likelihood that the veteran twin would develop PTSD after military service. This suggests that smaller-than-average hippocampal volume probably precedes the onset of disorder. See Focus on Discovery 5.2 for more perspectives on how these findings regarding the hippocampus can be integrated with cognitive models to understand memory complaints in PTSD.

Other neurobiological research has indicated that PTSD is associated with an increased sensitivity of receptors to the stress hormone cortisol (Golier & Yehuda, 1998; see p. 38 for a description of cortisol). This supersensitivity to cortisol could be the aftermath of the stress exposure. During initial exposure to stress, cortisol levels are high (Miller, Chen, & Zhou, 2007). Sustained high levels of cortisol change the sensitivity of the cortisol receptors, resulting in their becoming more sensitive and the body becoming more reactive to changes in cortisol. One consequence of the elevated sensitivity of cortisol receptors may be the high levels of norepinephrine (a stress-related neurotransmitter) found in PTSD (Geracioti et al., 2001).

Behavioral Factors: The Two-Factor Model
Like phobias, PTSD has been related to the two-factor model of conditioning. In this model, the initial fear in PTSD is assumed to arise from classical conditioning (Keane, Zimering, & Caddell, 1985). For example, a woman may come to fear walking in the neighborhood (the CS) where she was raped (the UCS). This classically conditioned fear is so intense that the woman avoids the neighborhood as much as possible. This avoidance behavior (the CR) is operantly conditioned; the avoidance is reinforced by the reduction of fear that comes from not being in the presence of the CS. And as we have seen before, the avoidant behavior interferes with chances for the fear to extinguish.

Psychological Factors: Cognition and Coping
From the cognitive perspective, it is important to consider how a person thinks about the event—particularly his or her sense of perceived control (Brewin & Holmes, 2003). People who cope with a trauma by trying to avoid thinking about it are more likely than others to develop PTSD (Sharkansky et al., 2000). People who had symptoms of **dissociation** (including depersonalization, derealization, amnesia, and out-of-body experiences) at the time of the trauma also are more likely to develop PTSD, as are people who try to suppress memories of the trauma (Ehlers, Mayou, & Bryant, 1998).

Rescue workers, such as this firefighter who was at the World Trade Center in the aftermath of the 9/11 terrorist attack, could be vulnerable to PTSD. (AFP/Getty Images.)

FOCUS ON DISCOVERY 5.2

Perspectives on Memory: Integrating Neurobiology and Cognition

People with PTSD seem to have frequent intrusions of memories cued by sensory stimuli. This is consistent with findings that surges of norepinephrine, which are typically present during periods of extreme stress, lead to stronger memory formation, particularly for the central aspects of a threatening experience. Now consider the fact that people with PTSD often report fragmented and disjointed memories of their trauma, making it hard for them to construct a coherent narrative about the event. How can we account for both facts at once—that memories occur too often but are also disjointed?

Brewin and Holmes (2003) theorize that people with PTSD may have deficits in their ability to access memories verbally yet retain the ability to access memories using cues such as smells, sounds, and other sensory stimuli. Bremner and colleagues highlight the possible role of hippocampal damage in this fragmentation of verbal memory (Bremner et al., 2003). The hippocampus plays a central role in our ability to locate autobiographical memories in space, time, and context, letting us give clear, organized descriptions of them. Perhaps people with decreased hippocampal volume are less able to organize their verbal memories. Other brain systems may play a more central role in **nonver-**

bal memories—that is, memories based on a link between sensory stimuli and external events. Hence, poor functioning of the hippocampus may not influence nonverbal memories. This could explain why smells, sounds, and other sensory stimuli continue to trigger memories among people with PTSD. Thus, a person may be prone to powerful memories, often triggered by sensory stimuli, but be unable to consolidate and organize those memories verbally in a way that allows for effective coping and decreased anxiety.

A meta-analysis of 27 studies found support for this theory. People diagnosed with PTSD consistently demonstrate deficits on neuropsychological tests of verbal memory even while performing adequately on tests of visual memory (Brewin et al., 2007).

This theory helps us understand how a person could simultaneously have a hard time describing the trauma and yet still be tortured by reminders of the trauma that set off reexperiencing of the original emotions. It is also hoped that this theory will help shape therapeutic techniques in the future, as effective treatment will likely require adjustments in how we ask people to remember and talk about their traumas.

Dissociation and memory suppression may play a role in maintaining the disorder, as they keep the person from confronting memories of the trauma. A compelling study of dissociation assessed rape victims within 2 weeks of the assault (Griffin, Resick, & Mechanic, 1997). The women talked about the rape and about neutral topics. While talking, the women reported when they felt stress and were measured for psychophysiological arousal. Based on their responses to questions about dissociation during the rape (e.g., "Did you feel numb?" "Did you have moments of losing track of what was going on?"), the women were divided into a high-dissociation group and a low-dissociation group. Women in the high-dissociation group were much more likely to have PTSD symptoms than women in the low-dissociation group. Furthermore, even though the women in the high-dissociation group reported emotional stress while talking about being raped, they actually showed less physiological arousal than did the women in the low-dissociation group. A range of studies now show that symptoms of dissociation shortly after being raped predict the development of PTSD (Brewin & Holmes, 2003). Moreover, people who continue to use dissociation in the years after the trauma are at risk for ongoing PTSD symptoms (Briere, Scott, & Weathers, 2005). We will discuss dissociation more in the chapter on dissociative disorders.

Other factors may help a person cope with severe traumas more adaptively. Two that seem particularly important include high intelligence (Breslau, Lucia, & Alvardo, 2006; Macklin et al., 1998) and strong social support (Brewin, Andrews, & Valentine, 2000). Having better intellectual ability to make sense of horrifying events, and more friends and family members to help with that process, seems to help people avoid symptoms after traumatic events.

Intriguingly, one line of research focuses on people who report growth in the context of a traumatic experience. For some, trauma awakens an increased appreciation of life, renews a focus on life priorities, and provides an opportunity to understand one's strengths in overcoming adversity (Bonanno, 2004; Tedeschi, Park, & Calhoun, 1998). Hence, despite the challenges of trauma, some people may learn better coping skills and develop improved resourcefulness.

Quick Summary

As a group, anxiety disorders are the most common type of mental illness. The DSM-IV-TR defines seven anxiety disorders. As Table 5.1 shows, the specific anxiety disorders are each defined by a different type of key symptom. That is, a specific phobia is defined by an intense fear of an object or situation, social phobia by an intense fear of strangers or social scrutiny, panic disorder by anxiety about recurrent panic attacks, generalized anxiety disorder by worries lasting at least 6 months, and obsessive-compulsive disorder by obsessions and/or compulsions. Posttraumatic stress disorder and acute stress disorder are both severe reactions to trauma; acute stress disorder occurs in the first four weeks after a trauma, and posttraumatic stress disorder lasts for more than four weeks after a trauma.

People with one anxiety disorder are very likely to experience a second anxiety disorder during their life. About 60 percent of people will experience an episode of major depression during their life. Women are much more likely than men to report an anxiety disorder. Culture influences the focus of fears, the ways that symptoms are expressed, and even the prevalence of different anxiety disorders.

Genes increase risk for anxiety disorders. Neurobiological research on anxiety focuses on elevated activity in the brain's fear circuit. Anxiety disorders also appear to involve poor functioning of the GABA and serotonin systems as well as high levels of norepineph-

rine. The personality traits of behavioral inhibition and neuroticism both are related to the development of anxiety disorders. From the cognitive perspective, anxiety disorders are associated with negative expectations that intensify the experience of anxiety. These expectations may be sustained because people hold long-standing beliefs that life is uncontrollable and because they tend to pay attention to negative stimuli. Severe negative life events often precede the development of an anxiety disorder.

Behavioral perspectives on specific phobias and social phobia are based on a two-factor model (classical conditioning followed by operant conditioning). Many people report that they experienced traumatic conditioning experiences before developing specific phobias, but many people don't, perhaps because the conditioning experience has been forgotten. Prepared learning refers to the fact that people are likely to sustain conditioned responses to fear stimuli that have some evolutionary significance. Cognitive factors are also considered significant in the maintenance of social phobia, and the trait of behavioral inhibition may play a role as well.

Neurobiological research demonstrates that panic attacks are related to high activity in the locus ceruleus. Behavioral models emphasize the possibility that people could become classically conditioned to experience panic attacks in response to external situations or internal somatic signs of anxiety. Conditioning to somatic signs is called interoceptive conditioning. Cognitive perspectives focus on catastrophic misinterpretations of somatic symptoms.

Generalized anxiety disorder (GAD) has been related to deficits in the GABA system. One cognitive model emphasizes that worry might actually protect people from intensely disturbing emotional images.

Obsessive-compulsive disorder (OCD) is characterized by higher activity in the orbitofrontal cortex, the caudate nucleus, and the anterior cingulate. Behavioral models of compulsions focus on the relief provided by performing these acts, which could be reinforcing. Cognitive models focus on yedasentience and thought suppression.

Posttraumatic stress disorder (PTSD) can be diagnosed only among people who have experienced a severe trauma. Even

among people who have been traumatized, though, the likelihood that a person will develop PTSD depends on the severity of the trauma. Neurobiological research has found that people with small hippocampal volume are more likely to develop PTSD. Other neurobiological research has found that PTSD is associated with elevated sensitivity to the stress hormone cortisol. After exposure to trauma, people who rely on dissociative coping strategies (i.e., who avoid thinking about the trauma) seem more likely to develop PTSD than people who rely on other strategies. The behavioral perspective focuses on the same two-factor model used to explain phobias: classical conditioning of fear, followed by operant conditioning of avoidant behavior that prevents the fear from extinguishing.

Check Your Knowledge 5.2

Fill in the blanks.

1. Research suggests that _____ percent of the variance in anxiety disorders other than panic disorder can be explained by genes.
   a. 0–20 percent
   b. 20–40 percent
   c. 40–60 percent
   d. 60–80 percent
2. _____ is a personality trait characterized by a tendency to react to events with intense negative affect.
   a. Extraversion
   b. Neurosis
   c. Neuroticism
   d. Psychosis

Answer the questions.

3. Cognitive factors found to correlate with anxiety disorders include (circle all that apply):
   a. low self-esteem
   b. attention to signs of threat
   c. hopelessness
   d. lack of perceived control
4. A key structure in the fear circuit is the:
   a. cerebellum
   b. amygdala

   c. occipital cortex
   d. inferior colliculi

Match the theory to the model of etiology:

5. Panic disorder
6. GAD
7. OCD
8. PTSD
9. Specific phobias
   a. anxiety sensitivity
   b. overly sensitive cortisol receptors and small volume of the hippocampus
   c. prepared learning
   d. increased activity in the orbitofrontal cortex, caudate nucleus, and anterior cingulate
   e. avoidance of powerful negative emotions

Fill in the blanks.

10. The first step in Mowrer's two-factor model includes _____ conditioning, and the second step involves _____ conditioning.
    a. operant, operant
    b. classical, classical
    c. classical, operant
    d. operant, classical

Treatments of the Anxiety Disorders

Only a small proportion of people with anxiety disorders seek treatment. Although public awareness campaigns and pharmaceutical company advertising have increased treatment seeking, a community survey of 5,877 individuals suggested that fewer than 20 percent of people with anxiety disorders receive minimally adequate treatment (Wang, Demler, & Kessler, 2002). One reason for the lack of treatment seeking may be the chronic nature of symptoms; a person suffering from an anxiety disorder might think "I'm just an anxious person" and not realize that treatment could help. Even when people do seek treatment, many will only visit a family doctor.

Research has found that family physicians are less effective than psychiatrists in prescribing drugs that successfully treat anxiety disorders, mostly due to doses that are too low or treatments that are discontinued too quickly (Roy-Byrne et al., 2001).

Commonalities across Psychological Treatments

Effective psychological treatments for anxiety disorders share a common focus: exposure—that is, the person must face what he or she deems too terrifying to face. Therapists from varying perspectives all agree that we must face up to the source of our fear or, as an ancient Chinese proverb puts it, "Go straight to the heart of danger, for there you will find safety." Even psychoanalysts, who believe that the unconscious sources of anxiety are buried in the past eventually encourage confronting the source of fears (Zane, 1984). Although exposure is a core aspect of many treatments, treatments differ in their strategies.

Systematic desensitization was the first widely used exposure treatment (Wolpe, 1958). In this treatment, the client is first taught relaxation skills. Then the client uses these skills to relax while undergoing exposure to a list of feared situations developed with the therapist—starting with the least feared and working up to the most feared (see p. 45 for a more detailed description). Although this technique is quite effective, researchers have now documented that exposure treatment works even if the relaxation component is not included (Marks et al., 1998).

Exposure treatment is effective for 70–90 percent of clients. A concern, though, is that fear and anxiety sometimes return. A couple of key principles appear important in protecting against relapse (Craske & Mystkowski, 2006). First, exposure should include as many features of the feared object as possible. For example, exposure for a person with a spider phobia might include a focus on the hairy legs, the beady eyes, and other features of spiders. Second, exposure should be conducted in as many different contexts as possible (Bouton & Waddell, 2007). As an example, it might be important to expose a person to a spider in an office, but also outside in nature.

The behavioral view of exposure is that it works by extinguishing the fear response. A cognitive view has also been proposed. According to this view, exposure helps people correct their mistaken beliefs that they are unable to cope with the stimulus. In this view, exposure relieves symptoms by allowing people to realize that, contrary to their beliefs, they can tolerate aversive situations without loss of control (Foa & Meadows, 1997). Cognitive approaches to treatment of anxiety disorders typically focus on challenging a person's beliefs about the likelihood of negative outcomes if he or she faces an anxiety-provoking object or situation, and by challenging the expectation that he or she will be unable to cope. Even behavioral treatments, though, are more effective if people begin to believe that they will be able to cope with the source of their anxiety.

Psychological Treatments of Specific Anxiety Disorders

Next, we look at how psychotherapy can be tailored to the specific anxiety disorders. Even though exposure treatment is used with each anxiety disorder, how can it be tailored to specific anxiety disorders?

Psychological Treatment of Phobias Many different types of exposure treatments have been developed for phobias, Over time, exposure treatments have become more and more efficient and now often include **in vivo** (real-life) exposure to feared objects. For phobias involving fear of animals, injections, or dental work, very brief treatments lasting only a couple of hours have been found to be highly effective—most people experience relief from phobic symptoms. Although systematic desensitization is effective (Barlow, Raffa, & Cohen, 2002), in vivo exposure is more effective than systematic desensitization (Choy et al., 2007). Virtual reality programs have also been developed to simulate many of the situations that are feared most in phobias, such as flying. Exposure to these simulated situations appears to be as effective as in vivo exposure (Choy et al., 2007).

Many studies indicate that the effects of exposure therapy last for at least a year (Ost, Ferebee, & Furmark, 1997). However, one study found that many people experienced at least some return of fear over a 12-year period (Lipsitz et al., 1999).

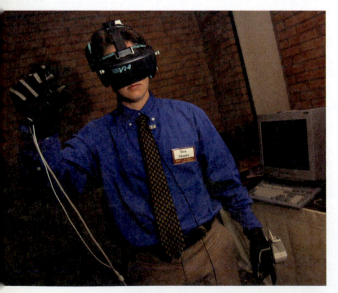

Virtual reality technology is sometimes used to facilitate exposure to feared stimuli. (Kim Kulish/Corbis Images.)

Most studies have found that cognitive therapy for specific phobias is not as effective as exposure treatment; in addition, there is not much evidence to suggest that outcomes are better when cognitive therapy is added to exposure (Antony & Barlow, 2004). One reason for this may be that cognitive therapy aims at getting the person to recognize that the phobic fear is excessive or unreasonable, but this is something that most people with specific phobias already know.

Exposure also appears to be an effective treatment for social phobia; such treatments often begin with role playing or practicing with the therapist or in small therapy groups before undergoing exposure in more public social situations (Marks, 1995). With prolonged exposure, anxiety typically extinguishes (Hope, Heimberg, & Bruch, 1995). Social skills training, in which a therapist might provide extensive modeling of behavior, can help people with social phobia who may not know what to do or say in social situations. Remember that safety behaviors, like avoiding eye contact, are believed to interfere with the extinction of social anxiety (Clark & Wells, 1995). Consistent with this idea, the effects of exposure treatment seem to be enhanced when people with social phobia are taught to stop using safety behaviors (Kim, 2005). That is, not only are people asked to engage in social activities, but while doing so, they are asked to make direct eye contact, to engage in conversation, and to be fully present. All in all, several studies attest to the effectiveness of exposure approaches (Turk, Heimberg, & Hope 2001).

Despite the relatively poor effects of cognitive therapy for specific phobias, some studies indicate that cognitive therapy added to exposure therapy is better than exposure alone in the treatment of social phobia (Turk et al., 2001). Cognitive approaches may include challenging the person's belief that others are appraising him or her negatively (e.g., a frown from a teacher is probably not directed at the person but rather a response to something else on the teacher's mind) and helping the person not to rely on approval from others for a sense of self-worth (e.g., being criticized doesn't imply worthlessness). Richard Heimberg and colleagues (1990) have developed a cognitive therapy of social phobia, and studies suggest that treatment based on this manual is more effective than supportive psychotherapy (Telch et al., 1993). David Clark (1997) has also developed a version of cognitive therapy for social phobia that expands on other treatments in a couple ways. The therapist helps people learn not to focus their attention internally. The therapist also helps them combat their very negative images of how others will react to them. This cognitive therapy has been shown to be more effective than fluoxetine (Clark et al., 2003) or than exposure treatment plus relaxation (Clark et al., 2006).

Social phobia appears to be harder to treat than specific phobias. Research suggests that treatment for social phobia is helpful, but many people experience only a partial reduction of anxiety (DeRubeis & Crits-Christoph, 1998). Nevertheless, that partial reduction is meaningful for most clients.

Social phobia is often treated in groups, which provide exposure to social threats and provide opportunities to practice new skills. (David Harry Stewart/Stone/Getty Images.)

Psychological Treatment of Panic Disorder and Agoraphobia

A psychodynamic treatment for panic disorder has been developed. The treatment involves 24 sessions focused on identifying the emotions and meanings surrounding panic attacks. Therapists help clients gain insight into areas believed to relate to the panic attacks, such as issues surrounding separation, anger, and autonomy. In one randomized controlled trial, patients who were assigned to receive psychodynamic treatment achieved more symptom relief than those who were assigned to a control condition of relaxation training (Milrod et al., 2007). In a separate trial, psychodynamic treatment for panic disorder was related to diminished rates of relapse when added as a supplement to antidepressant treatment (Wiborg & Dahl, 1996). More research is needed, though, because both of these studies were small.

Analysis of the more than 40 treatment studies indicated that cognitive behavioral treatment of panic disorder consistently yields results that are more robust than the findings obtained with medication treatment (Gould, Otto, & Pollack, 1995). Seventy to 80 percent of people with panic disorder who are treated with cognitive behavioral therapy are free of panic at the end of treatment (DeRubeis & Crits-Cristoph, 1998). Other studies have shown that therapeutic gains generally are maintained after two years and are superior in this respect to drug treatment (Clark 1994). Cognitive behavioral treatment is one of the most successful treatments available for panic disorder.

Like the behavioral treatments for phobias already discussed, cognitive behavioral treatments for panic disorder focus on exposure (White & Barlow, 2004). One well-validated cognitive behavioral treatment approach called **panic control therapy (PCT**; Craske & Barlow, 2001) is based on the tendency of people with panic disorder to overreact to bodily sensations (as discussed above).

In PCT, the therapist uses exposure techniques—that is, he or she persuades the client to deliberately elicit the sensations associated with panic. For example, a person whose panic attacks begin with hyperventilation is asked to breathe rapidly for 3 minutes, or someone whose panic attacks are associated with dizziness might be requested to spin in a chair for several minutes. When sensations such as dizziness, dry mouth, lightheadedness, increased heart rate, and other signs of panic begin, the person experiences them under safe conditions; in addition, the person practices coping tactics for dealing with somatic symptoms (e.g., breathing from the diaphragm to avoid hyperventilation). With practice and encouragement from the therapist, the person learns to stop seeing internal sensations as signals of loss of control and to see them instead as intrinsically harmless sensations that can be controlled. The person's ability to create these physical sensations and then cope with them makes them seem more predictable and less frightening (Craske, Maidenberg, & Bystritsky, 1995).

The Multisite Comparative Study for the Treatment of Panic Disorder (Barlow et al., 2000) compared the effects of PCT, the drug imipramine, PCT plus imipramine, and placebo. Initial treatment was offered once a week for three months, and if it was working, treatment was continued for another six months. Throughout treatment, both PCT and imipramine each provided better results than the placebo. Moreover, adding imipramine to PCT did not yield better results than PCT alone. Six months after treatment ended, relapse was significantly more common among people who had taken imipramine alone than among those given PCT alone. That is, medication was protective only while people continued treatment, but PCT offered protection even after treatment was finished.

A similar cognitive treatment has been developed for panic disorder (Clark, 1996). This treatment focuses on helping a person identify thoughts that may make physical sensations threatening (see Figure 5.7 for an example of one patient's thoughts). The therapist then helps a person challenge those beliefs. For example, if a person with panic disorder imagines that he or she will collapse, the therapist might help the person to examine the evidence for this belief and to develop a different image of the consequences of a panic attack. This treatment has been shown to work well in at least seven research studies, with specific evidence that this form of treatment is more helpful than relaxation or pure exposure and that few people drop out of treatment (Clark et al., 1999).

An Internet-based version of cognitive therapy for panic disorder has been developed. The program involves 10 sessions of educational material, exercises, and weekly telephone calls from the therapist. To test the program, researchers randomly assigned 30 participants to receive the program immediately, and 30 were assigned to a waiting list (Carlbring et al., 2006). Participants who received the internet therapy reported much more decrease in their panic symptoms than did those in the wait-list control groups, and the improvements were sustained through a nine-month follow-up. Three-quarters of the participants who received the Internet program no longer met diagnostic criteria for panic disorder at the end of the treatment. At the current time, Internet therapy for panic disorder has not been tested in comparison to face-to-face therapy sessions.

Within panic disorder, severe agoraphobic symptoms predict worse outcomes in therapy (Williams & Falbo, 1996). Cognitive behavioral treatments of agoraphobia also focus on exposure—specifically, on systematic exposure to feared situations. A series of studies support the efficacy of this approach (DeRubeis & Crits-Cristoph, 1998). Married people who suffer primarily from agoraphobia have benefited from family-oriented treatments in which the spouse without agoraphobia is encouraged to stop catering to the partner's avoidance of leaving the home. Exposure treatment of agoraphobia is more effective when the spouse is involved (Cerny et al., 1987).

Psychological Treatment of Generalized Anxiety Disorder   Success rates are lower for GAD treatment than they are for other anxiety disorders (Roemer, Orsillo & Barlow, 2004). A prominent behavioral approach to the treatment of GAD involves relaxation training, in which the therapist teaches the person strategies for behaving in ways that promote calmness. These strategies can involve relaxing muscle groups one-by-one or generating mental pictures of relaxing images. With practice, clients typically learn to relax rapidly. Studies suggest that relaxation training is more effective than nondirective treatment or no treatment (DeRubeis & Crits-Christoph, 1998).

Studies also suggest that cognitive behavioral treatment is effective compared to treatment with a placebo (Gould et al., 2004). Most studies of cognitive behavioral treatment are based on an approach that involves challenging the person's negative thoughts about potential threats or losses of control (Beck & Emery, 1985). Almost all studies have included several cognitive or behavioral components, such as training in detecting cues of anxiety, relaxation training, and strategies to counter negative thoughts (Roemer et al., 2004).

One study tested a version of cognitive therapy that included helping people tolerate uncertainty, as people with GAD seem to be more distressed by uncertainty than are those without GAD (Ladoceur et al., 2000). Tom Borkovec and colleagues have also designed a supplement to cognitive behavioral treatment; their supplement focuses on reducing worry with innovative strategies that include asking people to worry only during scheduled times, asking people to test whether worry "works" by keeping a diary of the outcomes of worrying, helping people focus their thoughts on the present moment instead of worrying, and helping people address core fears that they may be avoiding through worry (Borkovec, Alcaine, & Behar, 2004).

Psychological Treatment of Obsessive-Compulsive Disorder   The most widely used psychological treatment of OCD is **exposure and response prevention (ERP),** pioneered in England by Victor Meyer (1966). OCD sufferers often hold an almost magical belief that their compulsive behavior will prevent awful things from happening. With ERP, people expose themselves to situations that elicit the compulsive act and then refrain from performing the compulsive ritual—for instance, the person touches a dirty dish and then refrains from washing his or her hands. The reasoning behind this approach goes like this:

1. Not performing the ritual exposes the person to the full force of the anxiety provoked by the stimulus.
2. The exposure results in the extinction of the conditioned response (the anxiety).

The first study of ERP as a treatment for OCD involved creating a controlled environment at Middlesex Hospital in London (Meyer, 1966). These days, the therapist guides exposure to feared stimuli in the home, often with help from family members (Foa & Franklin, 2001).

Studies suggest that ERP is at least partially effective for more than half of people with OCD (Stanley & Turner, 1995), including children and adolescents (Franklin & Foa, 1998). Even though most people experience a clinically significant reduction in symptoms, some mild symptoms are likely to remain (Steketee & Frost, 1998).

In the short term, refraining from performing a ritual is extremely unpleasant for people with OCD. (To get some idea of how unpleasant, try delaying for a minute or two before scratching an itch.) Typically, ERP involves refraining from performing rituals during sessions lasting upwards of 90 minutes, with 15 to 20 sessions within a 3-week period, and with instructions to practice between sessions as well. Given the intensity of treatment, it is not surprising that about 25 percent of clients refuse ERP treatment (Foa & Franklin, 2001). Clients with OCD tend to fear changes, and these tendencies create special problems for behavior therapy and medication approaches (Jenike & Rauch, 1994).

Several studies suggest that standard behavioral treatments, including ERP, may not work well when hoarding symptoms are present (Steketee & Frost, 2003). Specialized treatments have been developed to help address hoarding. Therapists help people make decisions about their objects, provide tools to help people get their clutter organized, and schedule sessions to work on "de-cluttering." Although randomized controlled trials of these treatments have not been conducted yet, early evidence looks promising (Steketee & Frost, 2003).

Cognitive approaches to OCD focus on challenging a person's beliefs about what will happen if they do not engage in rituals (Van Oppen et al., 1995). Eventually, to help test such beliefs, these approaches will use exposure. Several studies suggest that cognitive approaches perform as well as ERP (DeRubeis & Crits-Cristoph, 1998).

Exposure treatment for OCD can include confronting one's worst fears, such as contamination by dirty objects. (Copyright John Wiley & Sons, Inc.)

Psychological Treatment of Posttraumatic Stress Disorder In PTSD, the focus of exposure treatment is on memories and reminders of the original trauma, with the person being encouraged to confront the trauma to gain mastery and extinguish the anxiety. Where possible, the person is directly exposed to reminders of the trauma—for example, by returning to the scene of the event. In other cases, imaginal exposure is used—the person deliberately remembers the event. Evidence indicates that exposure treatment that focuses on trauma-related events, either in imagination or directly, is more effective in treating PTSD than medication or supportive unstructured psychotherapy (Bradley et al., 2005). The treatment has been used successfully with a broad range of people, even performing well in a study of Sudanese refugees (Neuner et al., 2004). Despite the success of this approach, recent years have seen a great deal of controversy over another treatment of PTSD. See Focus on Discovery 5.3 for more discussion of these controversies.

Many different exposure techniques have been used. In one study, for example, Vietnam veterans with PTSD were assigned either to receive no treatment (the control group) or to take part in an **imaginal exposure** treatment that involved visualizing trauma-related scenes for extended periods of time. The exposure treatment led to significantly greater reductions in depression, anxiety, re-experiencing of the trauma, startle reactions, and irritability than did no treatment (Keane et al., 1989).

Therapists have also used virtual reality (VR) technology to treat PTSD, because this technology can provide more vivid exposure than some clients may be able to generate in their imaginations. In one study, Vietnam veterans with PTSD benefited from taking a VR helicopter trip replete with the sounds of battle (Rothbaum et al., 1999).

Exposure therapy is hard for both the patient and the therapist, however, because it requires such intense contact with traumatizing events. For example, women who have developed PTSD after rape might be asked to relive the fearsome events of the attack, imagining them in vivid detail (Rothbaum & Foa, 1993). The patient's symptoms may even increase temporarily in the initial stages of therapy, and therapists may become upset when they hear about their patient's horrifying experiences (Keane et al., 1992). Treatment is likely to be particularly hard and to require more time when the client has experienced recurrent traumas, which is often the case with child abuse.

Cognitive therapy for PTSD, which helps address a person's thoughts about their ability to cope with the initial trauma, has been shown to fare well as an intervention for PTSD in a series

FOCUS ON DISCOVERY 5.3

Eye Movement Desensitization and Reprocessing

In 1989, Francine Shapiro began to promulgate an approach to trauma treatment called eye movement desensitization and reprocessing (EMDR). In this procedure, the person imagines a situation related to the trauma, such as seeing a horrible automobile accident. Keeping the image in mind, the person visually tracks the therapist's fingers as the therapist moves them back and forth about a foot in front of the person's eyes. This process continues for a minute or so, or until the person reports that the image is becoming less painful. At this point, the therapist tells the person to say whatever negative thoughts he or she is having, while continuing to track the therapist's fingers. Finally, the therapist tells the person to think a positive thought (e.g., "I can deal with this") and to hold this thought in mind, still tracking the therapist's fingers. This treatment, then, consists of classic imaginal exposure techniques, along with the extra technique of eye movement. Studies in which EMDR was used to treat people with PTSD have reported dramatically rapid symptom relief; EMDR proponents argue that combining eye movements with thoughts about the feared event promotes rapid extinction of the conditioned fear and cor-

rection of mistaken beliefs about fear-provoking stimuli (Shapiro, 1999). The claims of dramatic efficacy have extended to disorders other than PTSD, including attention-deficit hyperactivity disorder, dissociative disorders, panic disorder, public-speaking fears, test anxiety, and specific phobias (Lohr et al., 1998).

Despite the remarkable claims about this approach, several studies have indicated that the eye movement component of treatment is not necessary. For example, one researcher developed a version of EMDR that included all its techniques except eye movement and then conducted a study in which people were randomly assigned to receive either a version without eye movement or a version with eye movement (Pitman, 1996). The two groups achieved similar symptom relief. Since the time of this study, findings from a series of studies have found that this therapy is no more effective than traditional cognitive behavioral treatment of PTSD (Seidler & Wagner, 2006). Some have argued that EMDR should not be offered as a treatment because the eye movement component is not supported either by studies or by adequate theoretical explanations (Goldstein et al., 2000).

FOCUS ON DISCOVERY 5.4

Critical Incident Stress Debriefing

Critical incident stress debriefing (CISD) involves immediate treatment of trauma victims within 72 hours of the traumatic event (Mitchell & Everly, 2000). Unlike cognitive behavioral treatment, the therapy is usually limited to one long session and is given regardless of whether the person has developed symptoms. Therapists encourage people to remember the details of the trauma and to express their feelings as fully as they can. Therapists who practice this approach often visit disaster sites immediately after events—sometimes invited by local authorities (as in the aftermath of the World Trade Center attack) and sometimes not; they offer therapy both to victims and to their families.

Like EMDR, CISD is highly controversial. A review of six studies, all of which included randomly assigning clients to receive CISD or no treatment, found that those who received CISD tended to fare worse (Litz et al., 2002). No one is certain why harmful effects occur, but remember that many people who experience a trauma do not develop PTSD. Many experts are dubious about the idea of providing therapy for people who have not developed a disorder. Some researchers raise the objection to CISD that a person's natural coping strategies may work better than those recommended by someone else (Bonanno et al., 2002).

of studies (Keane, Marshall, & Taft, 2006), even when patients are experiencing comorbid conditions (Gillespie et al., 2002). Cognitive processing therapy for victims of rape and childhood sexual abuse has received empirical support (Chard 2005; Resick et al., 2002). In this work, the victim is encouraged to dispute any tendency to attribute the blame to himself/herself. Although both cognitive therapy and exposure treatment are helpful, adding cognitive therapy to exposure treatment does not appear to offer additional benefit in reducing most symptoms (Foa et al., 2005). On the other hand, cognitive therapy is particularly helpful in reducing guilt (Resick et al., 2003).

Psychological Treatment of Acute Stress Disorder   Is it possible to prevent the development of PTSD by offering treatment to people who have developed acute stress disorder (ASD)? Short-term (five or six session) cognitive behavioral approaches that include exposure appear to do so. For example, Richard Bryant and colleagues (1999) found that early intervention decreased the risk that ASD would develop into PTSD—specifically, they found that exposure therapy reduced the risk of PTSD to 14 percent, compared to 67 percent among people who received unstructured support from therapists.

The positive effects of these early interventions appear to last for years. Researchers examined the effect of treatment on symptoms over a five-year period among adolescents who survived a devastating earthquake. Even five years after the earthquake, adolescents who had received cognitive behavioral intervention reported lower PTSD symptoms than did those who had not received treatment (Goenjian et al., 2005).

Exposure treatment appears to be more effective than cognitive restructuring in preventing the development of PTSD (Bryant et al., 2008). Unfortunately, not all approaches to prevention seem to work as well as exposure treatment (see Focus on Discovery 5.4).

Quick Summary

Psychological treatments often focus on exposure. Cognitive treatments include an exposure component but add a specific set of interventions to challenge the negative beliefs about what will happen when a person faces their fears.

For specific phobias, exposure treatments can work quite quickly. Social phobia is harder to treat, and cognitive components may be a helpful addition to exposure treatment. The most effective treatments for panic disorder include exposure to somatic sensations, along with some cognitive techniques to challenge catastrophic mis-

interpretations of those symptoms. Cognitive behavioral treatment of GAD focuses on helping a person challenge his or her thoughts about potential threats or loss of control, coupled with relaxation therapy. Exposure and ritual prevention is an effective behavioral treatment for OCD. Treatments that integrate cognitive components with this exposure-based treatment have been found to perform similarly. For PTSD, several forms of exposure treatment are helpful. Early intervention may help prevent ASD from developing into PTSD.

Barbra Streisand has used medications to relieve her anxiety about performing. (Carlo Allegri/Getty Images)

Medications That Reduce Anxiety

Drugs that reduce anxiety are referred to as sedatives, minor tranquilizers, or **anxiolytics** (the suffix *-lytic* comes from a Greek word meaning "to loosen or dissolve"). Two types of medications are most commonly used for the treatment of anxiety disorders: **benzodiazepines** (e.g., Valium and Xanax) and **antidepressants**, including **tricyclic antidepressants** and **selective serotonin reuptake inhibitors (SSRIs)**. Hundreds of studies have now confirmed that these medications provide more benefit than do placebos for anxiety disorders (Kapczinski et al., 2002; Roemer et al., 2004; Stein, Ipser, & Seedat, 2000; Stein, Ipser & Balkom, 2004).

Although medication treatments for most anxiety disorders are quite similar, there are some ways to tailor choice of medication to the different anxiety disorders. SSRIs are effective in the treatment of OCD (Soomro et al., 2008), but a particular class of antidepressants that is closely related to SSRIs, serotonin reuptake inhibitors (SRIs), are also effective in the treatment of OCD (Steketee & Barlow, 2004). The most commonly prescribed SRI for OCD is clomipramine (Anafranil; McDonough & Kennedy, 2002). In one multisite study, clomipramine led to an approximately 50 percent reduction in symptoms (Mundo, Maina, & Uslenghi, 2000). Hoarding symptoms often do not diminish with medication treatments (Steketee & Frost, 2003). For the treatment of panic disorder, SSRIs do not seem as effective as tricyclic antidepressants (Roy-Byrne & Cowley, 1998; White & Barlow, 2004). Researchers are also examining other drugs as potential anxiolytics for specific anxiety disorders, including buspirone (BuSpar) for generalized anxiety disorder (Pollack et al., 2001) and the anticonvulsant gabapentin (Neurontin) for social phobia (Ashton & Young, 2003).

When people are anxious, they can experience a surge of adrenaline, which then produces sympathetic nervous system arousal. **Beta blockers** diminish some of the effects of adrenaline on the body, such as increased heart rate. For this reason, beta blockers are among the most commonly prescribed medications for social phobia. Despite their common use, research doesn't indicate that beta blockers are effective for this use (Hofmann & Barlow, 2004).

Because several different types of medications help relieve anxiety symptoms, how does one choose between the different medications? The choice of drugs is often guided by concerns about side effects and withdrawal symptoms. All anxiolytics have side effects. Many people report being surprised by the extent of side effects and wishing they had known more about what to expect (Haslam et al., 2004). Benzodiazepines can have significant cognitive and motor side effects, such as memory lapses and difficulty driving. Also, people may experience severe withdrawal symptoms (Schweizer et al., 1990), so it can be difficult to stop using benzodiazepines—that is, they can be addictive. Antidepressants tend to have fewer side effects than benzodiazepines. Nonetheless, as many as half of people discontinue tricyclic antidepressants because of side effects like jitteriness, weight gain, elevated heart rate, and high blood pressure (cf. Taylor et al., 1990). Compared to tricyclic antidepressants, SSRIs tend to have fewer side effects, but some of their side effects may be significant, such as interference with sexual functioning (Rauch & Jenike, 1998).

This leads us to the key problem: most people relapse once they stop taking medications (Herbert, 1995). That is why medications are only effective during the time when they are taken. Because of this, and the general effectiveness of exposure treatments, psychological treatments are typically considered the preferred treatment of most anxiety disorders (Foa et al., 2005; Keane & Barlow, 2004; Kozak, Liebowitz, & Foa, 2000; McDonough & Kennedy, 2002), with the possible exception of GAD (Mitte, 2005).

Combining Medications with Psychological Treatment for Phobias

In general, adding anxiolytics to exposure treatment actually leads to worse outcomes than exposure treatment without anxiolytics, perhaps because people do not get the same chance to face their fears. D-cycloserine (DCS), though, is a different type of drug that enhances learning. Researchers have examined this drug as a way to bolster exposure treatment (Ressler et al., 2004). In one study, 28 patients with acrophobia (fear of heights) were treated using two sessions of virtual reality exposure to heights. Half of the patients were randomly assigned to receive the medicine DCS while they completed the exposure sessions; the other half received placebo. The patients who received DCS were less afraid of heights at the end of treatment and three months later than were the patients were who did not receive DCS. Similarly, DCS has been found to enhance the effects of exposure treatment for social phobia (Guastella et al., 2008; Hofmann et al., 2006). Hence, this a learning-enhancement medication appears to bolster the effects of a psychotherapy based on conditioning principles.

Check Your Knowledge 5.3

Fill in the blanks.

1. In vivo exposure is generally more effective than imaginal exposure but often cannot be conducted for _____:
   a. social phobia
   b. panic disorder
   c. most anxiety disorders
   d. PTSD
2. Cognitive therapy when added to exposure bolsters symptom relief for _____ but not _____.
   a. social phobia, specific phobia
   b. specific phobia, social phobia
   c. PTSD; any other anxiety disorders
   d. GAD; PTSD

Answer the questions.

3. Which of the following is true?
   a. Anxiolytic medications work better than CBT.
   b. Anxiety symptoms often return when a person stops taking anxiolytic medications.
   c. Antidepressants are addicting.
   d. Side effects are no longer a concern with modern anxiolytics.
4. Which of the following are the most valid treatment approaches to anxiety disorders? (Circle all that apply.)
   a. supportive listening
   b. benzodiazepines
   c. barbituates
   d. antidepressants
   e. exposure

Summary

Clinical Descriptions of the Anxiety Disorders

- As a group, anxiety disorders are the most common type of mental illness.
- DSM-IV-TR lists seven principal anxiety diagnoses: specific phobia, social phobia, panic disorder (with and without agoraphobia), generalized anxiety disorder, obsessive-compulsive disorder, posttraumatic stress disorder, and acute stress disorder. Anxiety is common to all the anxiety disorders, but phobias and panic also involve fear as a clinical feature.
- Phobias are intense, unreasonable fears that interfere with functioning. Specific phobias commonly include fears of animals; heights; enclosed spaces; and blood, injury, or injections. Social phobia is defined by intense fear of unknown people or social scrutiny.
- A patient with panic disorder has recurrent attacks of intense fear that occur out of the blue. Panic attacks alone are not sufficient for the diagnosis; a person must be worried about the potential of having another attack. Agoraphobia is defined by fear and avoidance of being in places from which escape would be hard if panic symptoms were to occur.
- In generalized anxiety disorder, the person is beset with virtually constant tension, apprehension, and worry that lasts for at least six months.
- People with obsessive-compulsive disorder have intrusive, unwanted thoughts and feel pressure to engage in rituals to avoid overwhelming anxiety.
- Posttraumatic stress disorder is only diagnosed after a traumatic event. It is marked by symptoms of reexperiencing the trauma, arousal, and avoidance or emotional numbing. Acute stress disorder is defined by similar symptoms but lasts less than one month.

Gender and Sociocultural Factors in the Anxiety Disorders

- Anxiety disorders are much more common among women than men.
- The focus of anxiety, the prevalence of anxiety disorders, and the specific symptoms expressed may be shaped by culture.

Common Risk Factors across the Anxiety Disorders

- The psychoanalytic view of anxiety disorders is that they are a defense against repressed conflicts.
- Genes increase risk for a broad range of anxiety disorders. Beyond this general risk for anxiety disorders, there may be more specific heritability for certain anxiety disorders. Beyond genetic diatheses, other factors that appear to be involved in a range of anxiety disorders include elevated activity in the fear circuit, poor regulation of several neurotransmitter systems (GABA, serotonin, and norepinephrine), negative life events, lack of perceived control, and a tendency to pay closer attention to signs of potential danger.

Etiology of Specific Anxiety Disorders

- Behavioral models of phobias typically emphasize two stages of conditioning. The first stage involves classical conditioning, in which a formerly innocuous object is paired with a feared object. This can occur through direct exposure, modeling, or cognition. The evolutionary preparedness model suggests that fears of objects with evolutionary significance may be more sustained after conditioning. The second stage involves avoidance that is reinforced because it reduces anxiety. Because not all people with negative experiences develop phobias, diatheses must be important.

- Neurobiological models of panic disorder have focused on the locus ceruleus, the brain region responsible for norepinephrine release. Behavioral theories of panic attacks have posited that the attacks are classically conditioned to internal bodily sensations. Cognitive theories suggest that such sensations are more frightening due to catastrophic misinterpretation of somatic cues.

- Cognitive behavioral theories hold that GAD results from distorted cognitive processes. One model suggests that worry actually helps people avoid more intense emotions. Neurobiological approaches focus on the neurotransmitter GABA, which may be deficient in those with the disorder.

- OCD has been robustly linked to activity in the orbitofrontal cortex, the caudate, nucleus, and the anterior cingulate. In behavioral accounts, compulsions are considered avoidance responses that are reinforced because they provide relief. Checking behaviors may be intensified by a lack of yedasentience, or failure to subjectively experience closure. Obsessions may be intensified by attempts to suppress unwanted thoughts, in part because people with OCD seem to feel that thinking about something is as bad as doing it.

- Research and theory on the causes of posttraumatic stress disorder focus on risk factors such as small hippocampal volume, the severity of the event, dissociation, and other factors that may influence the ability to cope with stress, such as social support and intelligence.

Psychological Treatment for the Anxiety Disorders

- Behavior therapists focus on exposure to what is feared. Systematic desensitization and modeling may be used as parts of exposure therapy. For some anxiety disorders, cognitive components may also be helpful in therapy.

- Exposure treatment for specific phobias tends to work quickly and well. Social phobia is harder to treat, and adding cognitive components to behavioral treatments may help.

- Relaxation and cognitive behavioral approaches may be helpful for GAD.

- ERP is a well-validated approach for the treatment of OCD that involves exposure.

- Psychological treatment of PTSD involves exposure, but often imaginal exposure is used.

Medications to Relieve Anxiety Symptoms

- Antidepressants and benzodiazepines are the most commonly used medications for anxiety disorders. There are some concerns that benzodiazapines are subject to abuse.

- Discontinuing medications usually leads to relapse. For this reason, cognitive behavior therapy is considered a more helpful approach than medication treatment for most anxiety disorders.

- Research also has begun to focus on medications like the anticonvulsant medication gabapentin (Neurontin) and Buspirone (Buspar). The SRI clomipramine appears helpful in the treatment of OCD, as do other antidepressant medications. One new approach involves providing D-cycloserine during exposure treatment for phobia.

Answers to Check Your Knowledge Questions

5.1 1. b; 2. d; 3. f; 4. a; 5. e; 6. g; 7. c; 8. b, d, e; 9. a; 10. c; 11. c

5.2 1. b; 2. c; 3. b, d; 4. b; 5. a; 6. e; 7. d; 8. b; 9. c; 10. c

5.3 1. d; 2. a; 3. b; 4. b, d, e

Key Terms

acute stress disorder (ASD)
agoraphobia
anterior cingulate
antidepressants
anxiety
anxiety disorders
anxiety sensitivity index
anxiolytics
behavioral inhibition
benzodiazepines
beta blockers
comorbidity
compulsion

depersonalization
derealization
dissociation
exposure and response
    prevention (ERP)
fear
fear circuit
fear-of-fear hypothesis
generalized anxiety disorder
    (GAD)
in vivo
imaginal exposure
interoceptive conditioning

locus ceruleus
Mowrer's two-factor model
neuroses
neuroticism
nonverbal memories
obsession
obsessive-compulsive disorder
    (OCD)
orbitofrontal cortex
panic attack
panic control therapy (PCT)
panic disorder
phobia

posttraumatic stress disorder
    (PTSD)
prepared learning
safety behaviors
selective serotonin reuptake
    inhibitors (SSRIs)
social phobia
specific phobia
subthreshold symptoms
thought suppression
tricyclic antidepressants

6 Dissociative Disorders and Somatoform Disorders

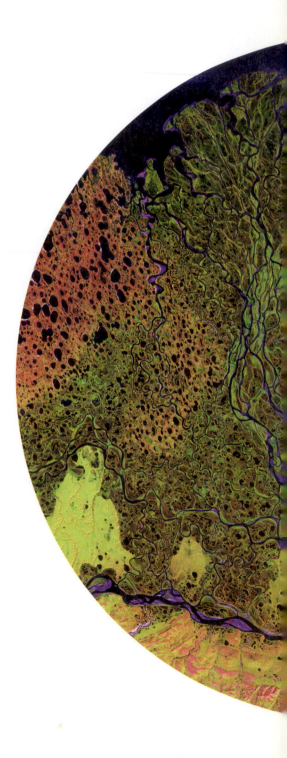

LEARNING GOALS

1. Be able to define the symptoms of the dissociative and somatoform disorders.
2. Be able to summarize current debate regarding the etiology of dissociative identity disorder.
3. Be able to explain the psychodynamic and sociocultural perspectives on conversion disorder.
4. Be able to discuss neurobiological and cognitive behavioral models of other somatoform disorders.
5. Be able to describe the available treatments for dissociative and somatoform disorders.

Clinical Case: Gina

In December 1965, Dr. Robert Jeans was consulted by a woman named Gina Rinaldi, who had been referred to him by her friends. Gina, single and 31 years old, lived with another single woman and was working successfully as a writer at a large educational publishing firm. She was considered to be efficient, businesslike, and productive, but her friends had observed that she was becoming forgetful and sometimes acted out of character. The youngest of nine siblings, Gina reported that she had been sleepwalking since her early teens; her present roommate had told her that she sometimes screamed in her sleep.

Gina described her 74-year-old mother as the most domineering woman she had ever known. She reported that as a child she had been a fearful and obedient daughter. At age 28 she had an "affair," her first, with a former Jesuit priest, although it was apparently not sexual in nature. Then she became involved with T.C., a married man who assured her he would get a divorce and marry her. She indicated that she had been faithful to him since the start of their relationship. T.C., however, fell out of her favor as he did not come through with his promised divorce and stopped seeing Gina regularly.

After several sessions with Gina, Jeans began to notice a second personality emerging. Mary Sunshine, as she came to be called by Jeans and Gina, was quite different from Gina. She seemed more childlike, more traditionally feminine, ebullient, and seductive. Gina felt that she walked like a coal miner, but Mary certainly did not. Some concrete incidents indicated Mary's existence. Sometimes while cleaning her home Gina found cups that had had hot chocolate in them—neither Gina nor her roommate liked hot chocolate. There were large withdrawals from Gina's bank account that she could not remember making. She even discovered herself ordering a sewing machine on the telephone, although she disliked sewing; some weeks later, she arrived at her therapy session wearing a new dress that Mary had sewn. At work, Gina reported, people were finding her more pleasant, and her colleagues took to consulting her on how to encourage people to work better with one another. All these phenomena were entirely alien to Gina. Jeans and Gina came to realize that sometimes Gina was transformed into Mary.

More and more often, Jeans witnessed Gina turning into Mary in the consulting room. T.C. accompanied Gina to a session during which her posture and demeanor became more relaxed, her tone of voice warmer. At another session Mary was upset and, as Jeans put it, chewed off Gina's fingernails. Then the two of them started having conversations with each other in front of Jeans.

A year after the start of therapy, an apparent synthesis of Gina and Mary began to emerge. At first it seemed that Gina had taken over entirely, but then Jeans noticed that Gina was not as serious as before, particularly about "getting the job done," that is, working extremely hard on the therapy. Jeans encouraged Gina to talk with Mary. The following is that conversation:

I was lying in bed trying to go to sleep. Someone started to cry about T.C. I was sure that it was Mary. I started to talk to her. The person told me that she didn't have a name. Later she said that Mary called her Evelyn. I was suspicious at first that it was Mary pretending to be Evelyn. I changed my mind, however, because the person I talked to had too much sense to be Mary. She said that she realized that T.C. was unreliable but she still loved him and was very lonely. She agreed that it would be best to find a reliable man. She told me that she comes out once a day for a very short time to get used to the world. She promised that she will come out to see you [Jeans] sometime when she is stronger. (Jeans, 1976, pp. 254–255)

Throughout January, Evelyn appeared more and more often, and Jeans felt that his patient was improving rapidly. Within a few months, she seemed to be Evelyn all the time; soon thereafter, this woman married a physician. Now, years later, she has had no recurrences of the other personalities. (Drawn from "The Three Faces of Evelyn," which appeared in 1976 in the *Journal of Abnormal Psychology*.)

IN THIS CHAPTER, WE discuss the dissociative disorders and the somatoform disorders. In early versions of the DSM, these disorders and the anxiety disorders were all classified together as neuroses, because anxiety was considered the predominant cause of these symptoms. Signs of anxiety, however, are not always observable in the dissociative and somatoform disorders, whereas anxiety is always clearly present in the anxiety disorders. Starting with DSM-III, in which classification is based on observable symptoms instead of presumed etiology, the diagnostic category of neurosis was abandoned, and the dissociative and somatoform disorders became diagnostic categories separate from each other and from the anxiety disorders.

We cover dissociative disorders and somatoform disorders together in this chapter because the onset of disorders of both classes is hypothesized to be related to some stressful experience, yet symptoms do not involve direct expressions of anxiety. In the dissociative disorders, the person experiences disruptions of consciousness—he or she loses track of self-awareness, memory, and identity. In the somatoform disorders, the person complains of bodily symptoms that suggest a physical defect or dysfunction—sometimes dramatic in nature—for which no physiological basis can be found.

Researchers know less about the dissociative and somatoform disorders compared to other disorders, and there is a great deal of controversy about the risk factors for these disorders, as well as the best treatments. To some, this controversy may seem daunting. We believe, however, that issues like this make a fascinating focus, as researchers strive to untangle a complex puzzle. Because so little is known about most of these disorders, though, we will focus on two of these disorders in more depth: dissociative identity disorder and conversion disorder.

Dissociative Disorders

The **dissociative disorders** defined in DSM-IV-TR include dissociative amnesia, dissociative fugue, dissociative identity disorder (formerly known as multiple personality disorder), and depersonalization disorder. The dissociative disorders are all presumed to be caused by a common mechanism, **dissociation**, which results in some aspects of cognition or experience being inaccessible consciously. Thus, dissociation involves the failure of consciousness to perform its usual role of integrating our cognitions, emotions, motivations, and other aspects of experience in our awareness. Some mild dissociative states are very common—in one example of a loss of self-awareness, a preoccupied person may miss a turn on the road home when thinking about problems. In contrast to common dissociative experiences like these, dissociative disorders are thought to result from extremely high levels of dissociation. Both psychodynamic and behavioral theorists consider pathological dissociation to be an avoidance response that protects the person from consciously experiencing stressful events. Among people undergoing very intense stressors, such as advanced military survival training, most participants report brief moments of dissociation (Morgan et al., 2001).

People with these disorders may be unable to recall important personal events, may temporarily forget their identity or assume a new identity, or may wander far from their usual surroundings. Few high-quality studies have been done of the prevalence of the dissociative disorders; perhaps the best study to date found lifetime prevalence rates of 7.0 percent, 2.4 percent, and 0.2 percent for dissociative amnesia, depersonalization disorder, and dissociative fugue, respectively (Ross, 1991). Table 6.1 summarizes the key clinical features of the dissociative disorders.

Table 6.1 Summary of Dissociative Disorders	
Disorder	**Description**
Dissociative amnesia	Memory loss, typically of a stressful experience
Dissociative fugue	Memory loss accompanied by leaving home and establishing a new identity
Depersonalization disorder	Alteration in the experience of the self
Dissociative identity disorder	At least two distinct personalities that act independently of each other

Because these disorders are rarely diagnosed, there is very little research on the etiology and treatment of dissociative amnesia, depersonalization disorder, and fugue states. For this reason, we focus on etiology and treatment only when we discuss dissociative identity disorder (DID).

Dissociation and Memory

Dissociative disorders raise fundamental questions about how memory works under stress. Some have suggested that in dissociative disorders, traumatic events are forgotten (i.e., dissociated) because they are so aversive. Cognitive scientists have questioned how this could happen, because research shows that extreme stress usually enhances rather than impairs memory (Shobe & Kihlstrom, 1997). For example, children who go through extremely painful medical procedures have accurate, detailed memories of the experience. The nature of attention and memory, however, does change during periods of intense stress. Memory for emotionally relevant stimuli is enhanced by stress, while memory for neutral stimuli is impaired (Jelicic et al., 2004). People under stress tend to focus on the central features of the threatening situation and to stop paying attention to peripheral features (McNally, 2003). For example, people might remember every detail about a gun that was trained on them yet be unable to remember the face of the person who held the gun. On recall, then, they are likely to be unable to connect all aspects of the stressful situation into a coherent whole. Given that the usual response to trauma is enhanced memory of the central features of the threat, how does the stress-related memory loss arise that we seem to see in the dissociative disorders?

One answer might be that dissociative disorders involve unusual ways of responding to stress—for example, extremely high levels of stress hormones could interfere with memory formation (Andreano & Cahill, 2006). Some theorists believe that as the intensity and frequency of dissociations increase, they can interfere with memory. That is, in the face of severe trauma, memories may be stored in such a way that they are not accessible to awareness later when the person has returned to a more normal state (Kihlstrom, Tataryn, & Hoyt, 1993). Dissociative disorders are considered an extreme outcome of this process. Debate continues about how to understand memory in the context of trauma and dissociation (see Focus on Discovery 6.1).

FOCUS ON DISCOVERY 6.1

Debates about Repression: Memories of Abuse in Childhood

A history of severe abuse in childhood is thought to be an important cause of dissociative disorders. About 13.5 percent of women and 2.5 percent of men report that they have experienced some form of childhood sexual abuse (CSA; Molnar, Buka, & Kessler, 2001) and more have experienced other forms of abuse.

Here we focus on recovered memories of childhood abuse—that is, on cases in which a person had no memory of being abused as a child but then "recovered" the memory. Few issues are more hotly debated in psychology than whether these recovered memories are real.

This is an important issue, because recovered memories of abuse have been used in hundreds of court cases (Pope, 1998). In a typical scenario, a woman recovers a memory during psychotherapy, accuses one of her parents of having abused her during childhood, and brings charges against the parent. For most crimes, plaintiffs must file suit within a certain number of years of a crime. In the 1980s, courts in more than 30 states increased the time allowed for filing suit in cases where plaintiffs claimed to have recovered memories of CSA (Brown, Scheflin, & Whitfield, 1999). By the late 1990s, however, the tide had turned, and many appellate courts refused to allow testimony based on recovered memories (Piper, Pope, & Borowiecki, 2000). More than 100 former patients have sued therapists for malpractice, claiming that the therapists implanted false memories of abuse (McNally, 2003).

Beyond the legal implications, there is a good deal of debate about whether recovered memories provide support for the idea of repression. What does the research evidence say about repression? In laboratory studies of memory, researchers have asked people to forget information, such as a list of words, and have shown that people can do so (Anderson & Green, 2001). This demonstrates that people can deliberately forget material, but other evidence does not support the idea that people with a history of trauma are any better at forgetting than are people without such a history. Indeed, people with a history of trauma are not better than aver-

age at forgetting neutral words or even cues related to their traumas (McNally, Clancy, et al., 2004). Even people with recovered memories of childhood sexual abuse do not show any superior ability to forget words related to their trauma (McNally, Ristuccia, & Perlman, 2005).

Other researchers have focused on trying to understand memory for trauma outside of the laboratory setting. In one study of whether memories of abuse can be forgotten, 94 percent of people with documented abuse still reported a memory of the abuse when they were asked about it almost 15 years later (Goodman et al., 2003). On the other hand, six percent of people reported that they had no memory of abuse.

Would a failure to remember mean that repression has occurred? Perhaps not—people might not want to think about or discuss such distressing events during an interview. People were less likely to report the memory at the 15-year follow-up if they had been under age five at the time the abuse occurred. Most people report that their earliest memories start at age three or four, so some people may have been too young to remember. Some of the traumas may have caused brain injury which could explain gaps in memory. Thus, a failure to describe a memory may not be the same thing as repression.

If repression is responsible for the failure to report events, one might expect less recall accuracy when events are more severe. In fact, the opposite is found. For example, in the 15-year follow-up study of abuse memories, people with more severe abuse memories were more likely to remember and disclose their abuse (Goodman et al., 2003). Similar findings emerged in a sample of Vietnam veterans, who were more likely to have consistent descriptions of events over time if their war-related events were more severe (Krinsley et al., 2003).

There is also plenty of evidence that memories are sometimes inaccurate. One interesting series of case reports described several people who thought that they had recovered memories of childhood abuse. Intriguingly, for two of the women who believed that they had

---

DSM-IV-TR Criteria for Dissociative Amnesia

- One or more episodes of inability to remember important personal information, usually of a traumatic experience, that is too extensive to be ordinary forgetfulness
- The amnesia occurs outside of other dissociative disorders, PTSD or acute stress disorder, or somatization disorder, and is not explained by other medical or psychological conditions

Dissociative Amnesia

As illustrated in the clinical case of the man with no name described below, the person with **dissociative amnesia** is unable to recall important personal information, usually information about some traumatic experience. The holes in memory are too extensive to be explained by ordinary forgetfulness. The information is not permanently lost, but it cannot be retrieved during the episode of amnesia, which may last for as short a period as several hours or as long as several years. The amnesia usually disappears as suddenly as it began, with complete recovery and only a small chance of recurrence.

Most often the memory loss involves information about some part of a traumatic experience, such as witnessing the sudden death of a loved one. More rarely the amnesia is for entire events during a circumscribed period of distress, is continuous from a traumatic event to the present, or is total, covering the person's entire life. During the period of amnesia the person's behavior is otherwise unremarkable, except that the memory loss may cause some disorientation. With total amnesia the person does not recognize other people, not even close relatives and friends, but retains the ability to talk, read, and reason and also retains talents and previously acquired knowledge of the world and how to function in it.

The pattern of memory deficits highlights an important distinction. Typically, dissociative disorders involve deficits in explicit memory but not implicit memory. **Explicit memory** involves the

recovered memories, their partners reported that they had spoken of the abuse in the past. Rather than recovered memories, these women seemed to have forgotten that they had experienced these memories in the past (Shobe & Schooler, 2001).

Cognitive psychologists have also shown that it is possible for people to firmly believe in an inaccurate memory. For example, in a study of people's memories of the explosion of the space shuttle *Challenger* on January 28, 1986, participants were interviewed the day after the disaster and then two years later (Neisser & Harsch, 1991). No later accounts were entirely accurate, and many were way off the mark, even though participants reported still having vivid memories of the event. This would lead us to suppose that, at least in some cases, memories are not accurate.

Where could recovered memories come from, if not from actual experiences? A leading researcher suggests a couple possibilities (Loftus, 1993):

1. **Popular writings.** *The Courage to Heal* (Bass & Davis, 1994) is an extremely popular guide for victims of CSA. It repeatedly suggests to readers that they were probably abused and offers as signs of abuse low self-esteem, feeling different from others, substance abuse, sexual dysfunction, and depression. The problem is that symptoms such as these can result from many factors other than CSA.

2. **Therapists' suggestions.** By their own accounts (Poole et al., 1995), many therapists who genuinely believe that many adult disorders result from abuse will suggest to their clients that they were probably sexually abused as children; sometimes the therapist does this with the assistance of hypnotic age regression and guided imagery (Poole et al., 1995). Unfortunately, techniques like hypnosis may actually contribute to the development of false memories (Lynn et al., 2003). Guided imagery,

Studies of memory show that recall of even a major event such as the explosion of the space shuttle *Challenger* can be considerably distorted. (© AP/Wide World Photos.)

in which a person closes their eyes and tries to imagine an event occurring, tends to increase confidence that a false memory actually occurred. One group of researchers found that with guided imagery, at least 55 percent of college students were able to develop at least a partial memory for a childhood event that never occurred, such as getting lost or being hurt (Porter, Yuille, & Lehman, 1999). To examine the validity of memories recovered in therapy, one group of researchers studied three groups of people: persons who had continuous memories of childhood sexual abuse, those who had recovered memories without a therapist, and those who had recovered memories within the context of therapy. Striking differences emerged in the ability to corroborate memories. That is, while about half of the continuous memories or those recalled outside of therapy could be corroborated by another source, none of the 16 events recalled within a therapy could be corroborated (Geraerts et al., 2007).

Not only do memory distortions occur, but once they do, they hold emotional power. In one study, researchers interviewed people who reported having been abducted by space aliens (a presumably false memory). While participants talked about the experience, the researchers recorded heart rate, sweating, and other signs of arousal. People describing their abduction demonstrated just as much arousal as others did when they recounted experiences of war or trauma (McNally, Lasko, et al., 2004). Even false memories, then, can be associated with a lot of pain!

There is little doubt that abuse occurs. But we must be wary of uncritically accepting reports of abuse. Social scientists and the courts share a heavy responsibility in deciding whether a given recovered memory is an accurate reflection of a criminal event. Erring in either direction could result in an injustice to either the accused or the accuser.

conscious recall of experiences—for example, explicit memory would be involved in describing a bicycle that you had as a child. **Implicit memory** underlies behaviors based on experiences that are not consciously recalled—for example, implicit memory of how to ride a bike underlies the behavior of actually riding one. There are numerous examples of patients with dissociative disorders whose implicit memory remains intact (Kihlstrom, 1994). One woman, for example, became amnesic after being victimized by a practical joke. She had no explicit memory of the event, but she became terrified when passing the location of the incident (implicit memory). We will discuss some recent intriguing tests of implicit memory when we discuss the etiology of dissociative identity disorder.

In diagnosing dissociative amnesia, it is important to rule out other common causes of memory loss, such as dementia and substance abuse. Dementia can be fairly easily distinguished from dissociative amnesia. In dementia, memory fails slowly over time, is not linked to stress, and is accompanied by other cognitive deficits, such as an inability to learn new information. Memory loss after a brain injury or substance abuse can be linked to the time of the injury or substance use.

In *Spellbound*, Gregory Peck played a man with amnesia. Dissociative amnesia is typically triggered by a stressful event, as it was in the film. (Springer/Corbis-Bettmann.)

Clinical Case: A Man with No Name

A 27-year-old man was brought to a hospital emergency room by the police because he had lain down in the middle of a busy intersection. He said that he wanted to die and was very depressed. He had no memory of any events before being picked up by the police—he could not tell the hospital staff his name or anything else about himself.

Neurological tests revealed no abnormality. After the first week in the hospital, his memory returned. He had just come to town to look for work. Two men had approached him and asked if he wanted a job. All three had then left in a pickup truck. Later, after smoking some marijuana, the other men had forced him at gunpoint to have sex with them. [Adapted from Kaszniak et al. (1988).]

● DSM-IV-TR Criteria for Dissociative Fugue

- Sudden, unexpected travel away from home or work
- Inability to recall one's past
- Confusion about identity or assumption of a new identity
- Symptoms are not explained by another medical or psychological disorder

Dissociative Fugue

In **dissociative fugue** (from the Latin *fugere*, "to flee") the memory loss is more extensive than in dissociative amnesia. Like the clinical case of Burt/Gene described on the next page, the person not only becomes totally amnesic but suddenly leaves home and work and assumes a new identity. Sometimes the person takes on a new name, a new home, a new job, and even a new set of personality characteristics. The person may even succeed in establishing a fairly complex social life. More often, however, the new life does not crystallize to this extent, and the fugue is of relatively brief duration, consisting for the most part of limited but apparently purposeful travel, during which social contacts are minimal or absent. Recovery is usually complete, although it takes varying amounts of time; after recovery, the person does not recollect what took place during the fugue.

Fugues can occur after a person has experienced some severe stress, such as marital discord, personal rejection, financial or occupational difficulties, war service, or a natural disaster, but not all fugues seem to immediately follow trauma (Hacking, 1998). It should also be noted that even among people who have experienced intense trauma, such as imprisonment in a concentration camp, dissociative amnesia and fugue are rare (Merckelbach et al., 2003).

Depersonalization Disorder

In **depersonalization disorder**, the person's perception or experience of the self is disconcertingly and disruptively altered. Unlike the other dissociative disorders in DSM-IV-TR, it involves no disturbance of memory. In a depersonalization episode, which is typically triggered by stress, people rather suddenly lose their sense of self. This involves unusual sensory experiences. For example, their limbs may seem drastically changed in size or their voices may sound strange to them. They may have the impression that they are outside their bodies, viewing themselves from a distance. Sometimes they feel mechanical, as though they and others are robots, or as though the world has lost its reality.

The following quote, drawn from a 1953 medical textbook, captures some of the experience of this disorder:

To the depersonalized individual, the world appears strange, peculiar, foreign, dream-like. Objects appear at times strangely diminished in size, at times flat. Sounds appear to come from a distance. . . . The emotions likewise undergo marked alteration. Patients complain that they are capable of experiencing neither pain nor pleasure; love and hate have perished with them. They experience a fundamental change in their personality, and the climax is reached with their complaints that they have become strangers to themselves. It as though they were dead, lifeless, mere automatons . . . (Schilder, 1953, p. 304–305).

Depersonalization disorder usually begins in adolescence and has a chronic course—that is, it lasts a long time. Comorbid personality disorders are frequent, as are anxiety disorders and depression (Simeon et al., 1997). As in the case of Mrs. A., described on the next page, childhood trauma is often reported.

In the show *Samantha Who*, Christina Applegate plays a 30-year-old vice president of a real estate firm who develops full amnesia and has to rediscover her life and her relationships. In this case, Samantha's amnesia would not qualify for the DSM diagnosis of Dissociative Amnesia, because it was caused by the physical trauma of a car accident. (Richard Cartwright/Retna)

Clinical Case: Burt/Gene

A 42-year-old male was brought to the emergency room by the police after he was involved in a fight at the diner where he worked. The patient had given his name as Burt Tate but when the police arrived, he was unable to provide any identification. Several weeks before the fight, Burt had arrived in town and begun working as a short-order cook. He had no memory of where he had worked or lived before he had arrived in town.

At the emergency room, Burt could answer questions about the date and his location but could not remember anything about his previous life. He was not concerned by his memory gaps. There was no evidence that alcohol, drugs, head trauma, or any medical condition could explain the gaps in his memory. A missing person search revealed that he fit the description of a man named Gene who had disappeared a month before from a city about 200 miles away. Gene's wife was contacted, and she was able to confirm that "Burt" was her husband. Gene's wife explained that he had been experiencing considerable stress in his job as a manager at a manufacturing plant for 18 months leading up to his disappearance. Two days before his disappearance, Gene had a violent fight with his adolescent son, who called him a failure and moved out of the home. Gene claimed not to recognize his wife. [Adapted from Spitzer et al. (1994).]

Diagnostic criteria for depersonalization disorder specify that the depersonalization cannot be explained by another disorder, so it is important to rule out disorders that commonly involve the symptom of depersonalization, including schizophrenia, posttraumatic stress disorder, and borderline personality disorder (Maldonado, Butler, & Spiegel, 1998). Depersonalization also can be triggered by hyperventilation, a common symptom of panic attacks. It should be noted that some have criticized the existence of this diagnosis, pointing out that depersonalization disorder requires just one symptom for diagnosis, whereas diagnosis of most other disorders requires a cluster of symptoms (McNally, 2003).

Dissociative Identity Disorder

Consider what it would be like to have **dissociative identity disorder (DID)**, as did Gina, the woman described in the opening of this chapter. People tell you about things you have done that seem out of character, events of which you have no memory. How can you explain these happenings?

Clinical Description of DID   According to DSM-IV-TR, a diagnosis of dissociative identity disorder (DID) requires that a person have at least two separate personalities, or alters—different modes of being, thinking, feeling, and acting that exist independently of each other and that come forth at different times. Each determines the person's nature and activities when it is in command. The primary alter may be totally unaware that the other alters exist and may have no memory of what those other alters do and experience when they are in control. Sometimes there is one primary personality, and this is typically the alter that seeks treatment. Usually, there are two to four alters at the time a diagnosis is made, but over the course of treatment others may emerge. The diagnosis also requires that the existence of different alters be chronic; it cannot be a temporary change resulting from the ingestion of a drug, for example.

> **DSM-IV-TR Criteria for Depersonalization Disorder**
>
> - Persistent or recurrent experiences of detachment from one's mental processes or body, as though one is in a dream, despite intact reality testing
> - Symptoms are not explained by another dissociative disorder, by any other psychological disorder, or by a medical condition

Clinical Case: Mrs. A.

Mrs. A was a 43-year-old woman who lived with her mother and son and worked in a clerical job. She had experienced symptoms of depersonalization several times per year for as long as she could remember. "It's as if the real me is taken out and put on a shelf or stored somewhere inside of me. Whatever makes me me is not there. It is like an opaque curtain. . . like going through the motions and having to exert discipline to keep the unit together." She had found these symptoms to be extremely distressing. She had experienced panic attacks for one year when she was 35 and had also been diagnosed with self-defeating personality disorder. She described a childhood trauma history that included nightly genital fondling and frequent enemas by her mother from earliest memory to age 10. (Simeon et al., 1997, p. 1109)

Each alter may be quite complex, with its own behavior patterns, memories, and relationships. Usually the personalities of the different alters are quite different from one another, even polar opposites. They may have different handedness, wear glasses with different prescriptions, like different foods, and have allergies to different substances. The alters are all aware of lost periods of time, and the voices of the others may sometimes echo in an alter's consciousness, even though the alter does not know to whom these voices belong.

DID usually begins in childhood, but it is rarely diagnosed until adulthood. It is more severe and extensive than the other dissociative disorders, and recovery may be less complete. It is much more common in women than in men. Other diagnoses—in particular, post-traumatic stress disorder, major depressive disorder, substance abuse, phobias, borderline personality disorder, sexual dysfunction, and somatization disorder—are often present (Boon & Draijer, 1993a, 1993b; Loewenstein, 1991). DID is commonly accompanied by other symptoms such as headaches, hallucinations, suicide attempts, and self-abusive behavior, as well as by other dissociative symptoms such as amnesia and depersonalization (Scroppo et al., 1998).

Cases of dissociative identity disorder are sometimes mislabeled in the popular press as schizophrenia (see Chapter 11), which derives part of its name from the Greek root *schizo*, which means "splitting away from"—hence the confusion. A split into two or more fairly separate and coherent personalities that exist alternately in the same person is entirely different from the symptoms of schizophrenia. People with DID do not show the thought disorder and behavioral disorganization characteristic of schizophrenia.

The inclusion of DID as a diagnosis in DSM-IV-TR is a matter of some controversy. For example, in a survey of board-certified psychiatrists, two-thirds reported reservations about the presence of DID in the DSM (Pope et al., 1999). Students and the public often ask, "Does DID exist?" Clinicians can describe DID reliably; it "exists" in this sense. As we will discuss later, though, controversy swirls about the reasons these symptoms occur.

● DSM-IV-TR Criteria for Dissociative Identity Disorder

- Presence of two or more personalities (alters)
- At least two of the alters recurrently take control of behavior
- Inability of at least one of the alters to recall important personal information

---

Check Your Knowledge 6.1 (Answers are at the end of the chapter.)

Answer the questions.

1. Dissociative fugue differs from dissociative amnesia in the following ways (circle all that apply):
   a. longer periods for which there is no memory
   b. assumption of a new identity
   c. symptoms often triggered by a trauma
   d. typically triggered by drug use
2. Most typically, dissociative amnesia involves being unable to remember:
   a. the entire life
   b. childhood

   c. a trauma
   d. life up until a trauma
3. In the context of dissociative identity disorder, *alter* refers to:
   a. extreme splitting
   b. a distinct personality
   c. the host personality
   d. the bridge between different personalities

The Epidemiology of DID: Increases over Time   Although descriptions of anxiety, depression, and psychosis have abounded in literature from ancient times through today, there were no identified reports of DID or dissociative amnesia before 1800 (Pope et al., 2006). A review of the literature identified a total of 77 cases of DID, most of which were reported in the period between 1890 and 1920 (Sutcliffe & Jones, 1962). After 1920, reports of DID declined until the 1970s, when they increased markedly, not only in the United States but also in countries such as Japan (Uchinuma & Sekine, 2000). More formal data on the prevalence of DID were collected on samples of adults in Winnipeg, Canada, and in Sivas, Turkey (Akyuez et al., 1999; Ross, 1991). Prevalence was 1.3 percent in the Canadian study and 0.4 percent in the Turkish one. Although these prevalence figures may not seem high, they are; prevalence was earlier thought to be about one in a million.

What has caused the vast increases in the rates of the DID diagnosis over time? It is possible that more people began to experience symptoms of DID. But there are other possible explanations for the increase. DSM-III, which was published in 1980, provided diagnostic criteria for DID for the first time (Putnam, 1996). The 1973 publication of the popular book, *Sybil*, presented a dramatic case with 16 personalities (Schreiber, 1973). A series of other case reports were published in the 1970s as well. The case of Eve White, popularized in the book *The Three Faces of Eve* as well as a movie, provided a highly detailed report of DID. The diagnostic criteria and growing literature may have increased detection and recognition of symptoms. Some critics, though, hypothesize that this heightened interest led some therapists to suggest strongly to clients that they had DID, sometimes using hypnosis to probe for alters. It has even been claimed that in Sybil's case, the alters were created by a therapist who gave substance to Sybil's different emotional states by giving them names (Borch-Jacobsen, 1997). There has been significant controversy about *The Three Faces of Eve* as well.

Etiology of DID   Almost all patients with DID report severe childhood abuse. There is evidence that children who are abused are at risk for developing dissociative symptoms, although whether these symptoms reach diagnosable levels is less clear (Chu et al., 1999).

There are two major theories of DID: the **posttraumatic model** and the **sociocognitive model**. Despite their confusing names both theories actually suggest that severe physical or sexual abuse during childhood sets the stage for DID. Since few people who are abused develop DID, both models focus on why some people develop DID after abuse. As we will see, there is considerable debate between proponents of these two approaches regarding this issue.

The posttraumatic model proposes that some people are particularly likely to use dissociation to cope with trauma, and this is seen as a key factor in causing people to develop alters after trauma (Gleaves, 1996). There is evidence that children who dissociate are more likely to develop some psychological symptoms after trauma (Kisiel & Lyons, 2001). But because DID is so rare, no prospective studies have focused on dissociative coping styles and the development of DID.

The other theory, the sociocognitive model, considers DID to be the result of learning to enact social roles. According to this model, alters appear in response to suggestions by therapists, exposure to media reports of DID, or other cultural influences (S.O. Lilienfeld et al., 1999; Spanos, 1994). An important implication of this model, then, is that DID could be created within therapy. This does not mean, however, that DID is viewed as conscious deception; the issue is not whether DID is real, but how it develops.

A leading advocate of the idea that DID is basically a role-play suggests that people with histories of trauma may be particularly likely to have a rich fantasy life, to have had consider-

In the film version of *Sybil*, about a famous case of dissociative identity disorder, the title role was played by Sally Field. (Jerry Ohlinger's Movie Material Store.)

Clinical Case: Elizabeth, an Example of Unwarranted Diagnosis

In one book, a personal account was provided of a person who received a false diagnosis of DID. Elizabeth Carlson, a 35-year-old married woman, was referred to a psychiatrist after being hospitalized for severe depression. Elizabeth reported that soon after treatment began, her psychiatrist suggested to her that perhaps her problem was the elusive, often undiagnosed condition of multiple personality disorder [MPD, now referred to as DID]. Her psychiatrist reviewed "certain telltale signs of MPD. Did Carlson ever 'zone out' while driving and arrive at her destination without remembering how she got there? Why yes,

Carlson said. Well, that was an alter taking over the driving and then vanishing again, leaving her, the 'host' personality, to account for the blackout. Another sign of MPD [the psychiatrist] said, was 'voices in the head.' Did Carlson ever have internal arguments—for example, telling herself, 'Turn right' and then 'No, turn left'? Yes, Carlson replied, that happened sometimes. Well, that was the alters fighting with each other inside her head. Carlson was amazed and embarrassed. All these years, she had done these things, never realizing that they were symptoms of a severe mental disorder" (Acocella, 1999, p. 1).

Roseanne Barr, a famous actress, has talked about her history of dissociative identity disorder. (Frederick M.Brown/Getty ImagesNews and Sport Services.)

able practice at imagining they are other people, and to have a deep desire to please others (Spanos, 1994). S.O. Lilienfeld and colleagues (1999) note that many of the therapeutic techniques being used with DID reinforce clients for identifying different alters; this researcher argues that repeated probing and reinforcement for describing alters may promote these symptoms within vulnerable people. The clinical case of Elizabeth provides an extreme example of a therapist who unwittingly encourages her client to adopt a diagnosis of DID when it isn't justified by the symptoms. Each of the symptoms described are common experiences; indeed, none of the symptoms listed are actual diagnostic criteria for DID. According to this theory, people adopt the DID role when given suggestions by a therapist.

We will never have experimental evidence for either the posttraumatic model or the sociocognitive model, since it would be unethical to intentionally reinforce dissociative symptoms. Given this, what kinds of evidence have been raised in this debate?

DID Symptoms Can Be Role-Played It has been established that people are capable of role-playing the symptoms of DID. One relevant study was conducted in the 1980s after the trial of a serial murderer in California known as the Hillside strangler (Spanos, Weekes, & Bertrand, 1985). The accused murderer, Ken Bianchi, unsuccessfully pled not guilty by reason of insanity, claiming that the murders had been committed by an alter, Steve. (For a discussion of the insanity defense, see p. 519.) In the study, undergraduate students were told that they would play the role of an accused murderer and that despite much evidence of guilt, a plea of not guilty had been entered. They were also told that they were to participate in a simulated psychiatric interview that might involve hypnosis. Then the students were taken to another room and introduced to the "psychiatrist," actually an experimental assistant. After a number of standard questions, the students were assigned to one of three experimental conditions. In the most important of these, the Bianchi condition, students were hypnotized and instructed to let a second personality come forward, just as had happened when Bianchi had been hypnotized.

After the experimental manipulations, the possible existence of a second personality was probed directly by the "psychiatrist." In addition, students were asked questions about the facts of the murders. Finally, in a second session, those who acknowledged another personality were asked to take personality tests twice—once for each of their two personalities. Eighty-one percent of the students in the Bianchi condition adopted a new name, and many of these admitted guilt for the murders. Even the personality test results of the two personalities differed considerably.

Physical or sexual abuse in childhood is regarded as a major factor in the development of dissociative disorders. (Robert Brenner/PhotoEdit.)

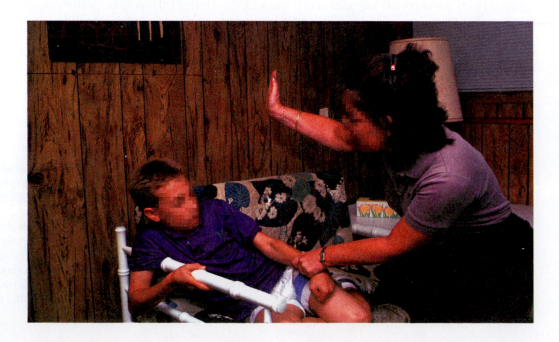

Clearly, then, when the situation demands, people can adopt a second personality. However, this demonstration illustrates only that such role-playing is possible; it in no way demonstrates that DID results from role-playing.

Patients with DID Do Not Show Deficits in Some Forms of Implicit Memory   Several studies suggest that even though different alters report being unable to share memories, they actually do share a fair amount of information, as revealed by subtle tests. For example, one group of researchers tested two different alters of people with DID on explicit and implicit tests of memory (Huntjen et al., 2003). In explicit memory tests, a person is taught a word list and then asked to recall the words at a second session. In implicit memory tests, experimenters determine if the word lists have subtler effects on performance. For example, if the first word list included the word *lullaby*, people might be quicker to identify *lullaby* as the word that fills in the puzzle l_l_a_y. Of the 31 people with DID who were tested, 21 claimed at the second testing session that they had no memory of the first session, but these 21 people performed comparably to people without DID on tests of implicit memory. That is, word lists learned during the first session affected performance during the second session, when a different alter was tested. The researchers interpreted the findings as supportive of a role-playing explanation of DID—people with DID demonstrated more accurate memories than they had acknowledged.

It should be noted, however, that even cognitive scientists disagree on whether implicit memory deficits actually exist in DID. Some authors have suggested that only certain types of implicit memory seem to transfer between alters. In two studies, memories that required complex verbal processing were less likely to be transferred between alters than were memories that were less verbal, such as those involving pictures (Eich et al., 1997; Elzinga et al., 2003). Studies like this support the idea that DID involves deficits in certain forms of implicit memory, even though some aspects of implicit memory appear to be preserved. So controversy continues.

The Detection of DID Differs by Clinician   A small number of clinicians contribute most of the diagnoses of DID within a time period. For example, a survey conducted in Switzerland found that 66 percent of the diagnoses of DID were made by fewer than 10 percent of the psychiatrists who responded (Modestin, 1992). Therapists who are most likely to diagnose DID tend to use hypnosis, to urge clients to try to unbury unremembered abuse experiences, or to name different alters. Proponents of the sociocognitive model argue that the extremes in diagnostic rates support the idea that certain clinicians are likely to elicit DID in their patients. Proponents of the posttraumatic model, however, point out that people with DID may be referred to clinicians who specialize in treating this condition (Gleaves, 1996). Once again, the data are inconclusive.

Many DID Symptoms Emerge after Treatment Starts   Studies have shown that when patients with DID enter therapy, they are usually unaware of having alters. But as treatment progresses, they tend to become aware of alters, and they report a rapid increase in the number of alters they can identify. This pattern is consistent with the idea that treatment is evoking the DID symptoms (S.O. Lilienfeld et al., 1999). Proponents of posttraumatic theory, however, explain this pattern by suggesting that most alters began their existence during childhood and that therapy just allows the person to become aware of and describe alters.

One study, however, has provided evidence regarding childhood onset in cases of DID (Lewis et al., 1997). The study, which was conducted over a period of two decades, involved detailed examination of 150 convicted murderers. Fourteen of them were found to have DID. Twelve of the 14 people had long-standing psychological symptoms that preceded their incarceration: 8 had experienced trances during childhood, and 10 had had imaginary companions (experiences that are frequently reported by people with DID). Each of these symptoms was corroborated by at least three outside sources (e.g., by interviews with family members, teachers, and parole officers). Furthermore, several of the people with DID had shown distinctly different handwriting styles (consistent with the existence of alters) well before committing their crimes (see Figure 6.1). The results of this study, then, support the idea that some symptoms begin in childhood for at least some people who are diagnosed with DID during adulthood. It is not clear, though, that the early symptoms included the presence of alters.

Ken Bianchi, a serial killer known as the Hillside strangler, unsuccessfully attempted an insanity defense. The jury decided that he was faking the symptoms of DID. (© AP/Wide World Photos.)

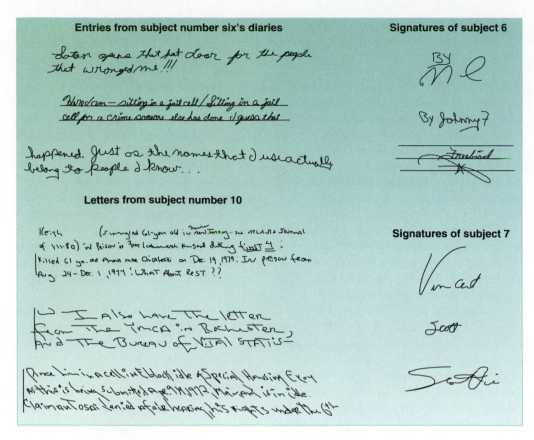

Figure 6.1 Handwriting samples from four DID cases. From Lewis et al., 1997. Reprinted with permission from the *American Journal of Psychiatry*, Copyright 1997. American Psychiatric Association.

Check Your Knowledge 6.2

True or false?

1. Prevalence of DID is currently at an all-time high.
2. Most people with DID report childhood abuse.

3. The sociocognitive model of DID emphasizes role enactment.

Treatment of DID There seems to be widespread agreement on several principles in the treatment of dissociative identity disorder, whatever the clinician's orientation (Kluft, 1994; Ross, 1989). These include an empathic and gentle stance, with the goal of helping the client function as one wholly integrated person. The goal of treatment should be to convince the person that splitting into different personalities is no longer necessary to deal with traumas. In addition, assuming that DID is a means of escaping from severe stress, treatment can help teach the person to cope better with stress. Often, people with DID are hospitalized to help them avoid self-harm and to begin the treatment in a more intensive fashion.

Psychodynamic treatment is probably used more for DID and the other dissociative disorders than for any other psychological disorders. The goal of this treatment is to overcome repressions, using basic psychodynamic techniques (MacGregor, 1996). DID, like posttraumatic stress disorder (PTSD), is widely believed to arise from traumatic events that the person is trying to block from consciousness.

Hypnosis is often used with patients diagnosed with dissociative disorders as a means of helping them gain access to repressed material (Putnam, 1993). DID patients are unusually hypnotizable (Butler et al., 1996). Typically, the person is hypnotized and encouraged to go back in his or her mind to traumatic events in childhood—a technique called *age regression*. The hope is that accessing these traumatic memories will allow the person to realize that childhood threats are no longer present and that adult life need not be governed by these ghosts from the past (Grinker & Spiegel, 1944). It has been cautioned, however, that there is little evidence that age regression relieves symptoms. Indeed, treatment involving recovered memories could result in a worsening of DID symptoms (Fetkewicz, Sharma, & Merskey, 2000; Lilienfeld, 2007; Powell & Gee, 2000).

Because of the rarity of diagnosed cases of DID, there are no controlled studies of the results of treatment. Most of the reports come from the clinical observations of one highly experienced therapist, Richard Kluft (1994). The greater the number of alters, the longer the treatment lasted (Putnam et al., 1986); in general, therapy took almost 2 years and upwards of 500 hours per patient. Years after treatment started, Kluft (1994) reported that 84 percent of an original 123 patients had achieved stable integration of alters and another 10 percent were at least functioning better. In a different follow-up study of 12 patients, six patients achieved full integration of their alters within a 10-year period (Coons & Bowman, 2001).

DID is often comorbid with anxiety and depression, which can sometimes be lessened with antidepressant medications. These medications have no effect on the DID itself, however (Simon, 1998).

Quick Summary

Dissociative disorders are defined on the basis of disruptions in consciousness or memory. Dissociative amnesia is diagnosed based on the inability to recall important personal experience, usually about a traumatic experience. Dissociative fugue is more severe than amnesia, because the person not only has an inability to recall important information but also moves and assumes a new identity. In depersonalization disorders, the person's perception of the self is altered; he or she may experience being outside the body or perceive changes in the size of body parts. The person with dissociative identity disorder has two or more distinct personalities, each with unique memories, behavior patterns, and relationships.

Little research is available concerning the causes of these disorders. Considerable debate exists about the causes of DID. The posttraumatic model suggests that DID is the result of extreme abuse, coupled with a tendency to use dissociation as a coping strategy. The sociocognitive model suggests that DID is caused by role-playing of symptoms among patients with a history of abuse and a deep need to satisfy authority figures like therapists. Debate about these two viewpoints has focused on the dramatic shifts in diagnosis over time, the differences between clinicians in recognition of the disorder, the evidence that people can role-play symptoms of DID, the indications on subtle memory tests of alters sharing information that they deny conscious awareness of, and findings that many people develop symptoms only after treatment begins.

Some mental health specialists have proposed strategies for treating DID that are reminiscent of the strategies used in treating PTSD. For example, in the safe, supportive context of therapy, patients are encouraged to think back to the traumatic events that are believed to have triggered their problems and to view those events with the expectation that they can come to terms with the horrible things that happened to them.

Somatoform Disorders

In **somatoform disorders**, psychological problems take a physical form (*soma* means "body")—that is, the person experiences bodily symptoms that have no known physical cause. These disorders are not under voluntary control, nor are they intentionally produced by the person. People with these disorders tend to seek medical treatment, sometimes at great expense. It has been estimated that somatoform disorders lead to medical expenditures of $256 billion per year in the United States (Barsky, Orav, & Bates, 2005). Patients are typically distressed and confused when doctors are unable to provide a physiological explanation for their complaints.

In this section, we begin by briefly considering the less well understood somatoform disorders—pain disorder, body dysmorphic disorder, hypochondriasis, and somatization disorder; we then take an in-depth look at one other somatoform disorder—conversion disorder.

Table 6.2 Summary of Somatoform and Related Disorders

Disorder	Description
Pain disorder	Pain that is brought on and maintained to a significant extent by psychological factors
Body dysmorphic disorder	Preoccupation with imagined or exaggerated defects in physical appearance
Hypochondriasis	Preoccupation with fears of having a serious illness
Somatization disorder	Recurrent, multiple physical complaints that have no biological basis
Conversion disorder	Sensory or motor symptoms without any physiological cause
Malingering	Physical incapacity faked to avoid responsibility
Factitious disorder	Intentionally produced symptoms

Table 6.2 summarizes the key clinical features of the somatoform disorders; the table also lists two related disorders (malingering and factitious disorder) that we discuss in Focus on Discovery 6.2.

FOCUS ON DISCOVERY 6.2

Malingering and Factitious Disorder

In DSM-IV-TR, **malingering** is classified among the "Other Conditions That May Be a Focus of Clinical Attention" (see p. 70). In malingering, a person intentionally fakes an incapacity to avoid a responsibility, such as work or military duty, or to achieve some goal, such as being awarded an insurance settlement. Thus, it is related to the somatoform disorders, in which people also show symptoms that have no physical basis.

To distinguish between malingering and conversion disorder, clinicians try to determine whether the symptoms have been consciously or unconsciously adopted; in malingering, the symptoms are under voluntary control, which is not thought to be the case in conversion disorder. Insurance companies often go to great lengths to show that a person is faking symptoms and can actually function well outside of doctors' offices. When such detective work fails, though, it is often difficult, if not impossible, to know whether behavior is consciously or unconsciously motivated. An aspect of behavior that can sometimes help distinguish the two disorders is known as **la belle indifférence**, which is defined as a relative lack of concern or a blasé attitude toward the symptoms that is out of keeping with their severity. Patients with conversion disorder sometimes demonstrate this behavior; they also appear eager to talk endlessly and dramatically about their symptoms. In contrast, malingerers are likely to be more guarded and cautious, perhaps because they consider interviews a threat to the success of the lie. But this distinction is not foolproof, for only about one-third of people with conversion disorder show la belle indifférence (Stephens & Kamp, 1962). Furthermore, a stoic attitude that resembles la belle indifférence is sometimes found among patients with actual medical diseases.

Factitious disorder, which is listed in a category of its own in DSM-IV-TR, is also related to the somatoform disorders. In factitious disorder, as in malingering, people intentionally produce physical symptoms (or sometimes psychological ones). They may make up symptoms—for example, reporting acute pain—or may inflict injuries on themselves. In contrast to malingering, however, in factitious disorder, the motivation for adopting the symptoms is much less clear. The person, for some unknown reason, wants to assume the role of a patient.

Factitious disorder may also be diagnosed in a parent who creates physical illnesses in a child; in this case it is called *factitious disorder by proxy* or *Munchausen syndrome by proxy*. In one extreme case, a 7-year-old girl was hospitalized over 150 times and experienced 40 surgeries at a cost of over $2 million. Her mother caused her illnesses by using drugs and even contaminating her feeding tube with fecal material (*Time*, 1996). The motivation in a case such as this appears to be a need to be regarded as an excellent parent who is tireless in seeing to the child's needs.

Kathleen Bush is taken into custody, charged with child abuse and fraud for deliberately causing her child's illnesses. (Sun-Sentinel.)

The grouping of somatoform disorders as a set of diagnoses has been criticized for several reasons:

- Body dysmorphic disorder, defined by worries about appearance, does not have much in common with the other somatoform disorders, which are defined by disease or pain concerns (Mayou et al., 2005).
- There is incredible diversity among people diagnosed with these conditions. For example, some people develop somatoform symptoms in the context of anxiety and depressive disorders, whereas others do not (Lieb et al., 2007).
- The common concern across somatoform disorders is that the person has a physical symptom that does not seem to be explained by a medical condition. This defining feature, though, implies that physical and psychological processes can be separated, a concept that does not translate well to many Eastern cultures, where mind–body connections are emphasized (Mayou et al., 2005). Indeed, research has shown that most physical concerns are influenced to some extent by the mind (see Chapter 7 for more detail) and that many people experience at least mild unexplained physical symptoms at some point in their lifetime (Simon et al., 1999).

Hence, it is possible that we will see major changes in the way that somatoform disorders are described and defined in DSM-V.

Pain Disorder

In **pain disorder**, psychological factors play a major role in the onset, maintenance, and severity of physical pain. The pain causes significant distress or impairment; for example, the patient may be unable to work or may become dependent on painkillers. As seen for the clinical case of Katherine, described below, the pain may begin or intensify after some conflict or stress. To an outside observer, it may seem that the person is using the pain to avoid some unpleasant activity or to get attention and sympathy, but people with pain disorder have no sense of this—they experience their pain as a completely physical symptom.

Accurate diagnosis is difficult because pain is a subjective experience—there is no way to objectively measure someone's pain. To some degree, however, people with pain disorder may describe their pain differently from people whose pain is clearly linked to a physical problem, who tend to localize pain more specifically, give more detailed descriptions of their pain sensations, and more clearly describe factors that increase or decrease their pain (Adler et al., 1997).

Understanding psychological aspects of pain is important, because millions of Americans experience chronic pain, accounting for billions of dollars of lost work time and incalculable personal and familial suffering (Turk, 2001). Traditional medical treatments seldom help with pain disorder.

Clinical Case: Katherine

Katherine, a 29-year-old married woman, was referred to a psychiatrist after extensive medical tests failed to identify a cause of her pain. Four months before the interview, she and her husband had been involved in a car accident. During the accident, Katherine was thrown forward but did not hit the window or dashboard. Her neck, arms, back, and legs began to ache 3 days later, and she had experienced pain daily since that time.

During the interview, Katherine completed all neurological tests carefully and described her pain in vivid detail. All neurological tests were within normal limits. She reported no history of psychological disorder. She and her husband had been married for 4 years, and until recently they had enjoyed a smooth marriage with the exception of complaints from her husband that he would like more frequent and "imaginative" sex. Two weeks before the accident, though, Katherine had discovered a woman's phone number in her husband's wallet. When she confronted him, he admitted that he had seen several women during the past year for "sexual release." They argued for the two weeks before the accident. After the accident, they had renewed their commitment to the marriage and had agreed to begin working on their sexual relationship. Katherine's pain, though, interfered with her ability to engage in sexual activity. Because the pain seemed to be genuine, malingering and factitious disorder were not diagnosed. But because the pain seemed to offer some protection from facing difficult marital issues, pain disorder was diagnosed. [Adapted from Spitzer et al. (1994).]

DSM-IV-TR Criteria for Body Dysmorphic Disorder

- Preoccupation with an imagined defect or markedly excessive concern over a slight defect in appearance
- Preoccupation is not explained by another psychological disorder, like anorexia nervosa

Katherine Phillips has conducted extensive research on body dysmorphic disorder. (Courtesy of Katherine Phillips, Butler Hospital, Brown University.)

Body Dysmorphic Disorder

People with **body dysmorphic disorder** are preoccupied with an imagined or exaggerated defect in their appearance. Although people with this disorder may appear attractive to others, they perceive themselves as ugly or even "monstrous" in their appearance (Phillips, 2006). Women tend to focus on their skin (like Joann in the clinical case below), hips, breasts, and legs, whereas men are more likely to focus on their height, penis size, or body hair (Perugi et al., 1997). Some patients with the disorder spend hours each day compulsively looking at themselves in mirrors to check on their defect. Others try to avoid being reminded of the defect by avoiding mirrors and camouflaging the defect—for example, by wearing very loose clothing to cover the imagined flaw (Albertini & Phillips, 1999). Some people become housebound to keep others from seeing their imagined defect. The symptoms are extremely distressing—as many as a fifth of people with this disorder report that they have thought about committing suicide (Rief et al., 2006), and as many as a quarter have plastic surgery (Phillips et al., 2001). Unfortunately, plastic surgery does little to allay their concerns (Veale, 2000), and many people report wanting to sue or hurt their physicians after the surgery because they are so disappointed.

Social and cultural factors surely play a role in how people decide whether they are attractive. Among college students, concerns about body appearance appear to be more common in America than in Europe—as many as 74 percent of American students report at least some concern about their body image, with women being more likely than men to report dissatisfaction (Bohne et al., 2002). Most of these concerns, though, are not extreme enough to be characterized as psychological disorders. The person with body dysmorphic disorder experiences agonizing distress over their perceived physical flaws.

There is some evidence that body dysmorphic disorder occurs slightly more often in women than in men, but even among women it is relatively rare, with a prevalence of less than 2 percent (Otto et al., 2001; Rief et al., 2006). Among women seeking plastic surgery, however, about 5–7 percent meet the diagnostic criteria for this disorder (Altamura et al., 2001). Body dysmorphic disorder typically begins in late adolescence. As many as 90 percent of persons diagnosed with the disorder report symptoms one year later (Phillips et al., 2006).

Nearly all people with body dysmorphic disorder meet the diagnostic criteria for another disorder. The most common comorbid disorders include major depressive disorder, social phobia, obsessive-compulsive disorder, substance abuse, and personality disorders (Gustad & Phillips, 2003). Some comorbidity may be explained by the similarity of symptoms used in making different diagnoses—body dysmorphic disorder and obsessive-compulsive disorder, for example, share symptoms of repetitive unwanted thoughts and checking behaviors.

Clinical Case: Joann

Joann was a 23-year-old woman who sought psychotherapy after losing her job as a salesclerk for a record store because she had been taking very long breaks. At the first therapy session, she seemed extremely uncomfortable; she huddled in her coat and told her story while looking at the floor. She said that she had been taking long breaks at work because she was uncomfortable when customers were in the store—she had the feeling they were staring at her. When asked why she thought that, she said that she knew they were looking at her skin, which was far too dark. She described feeling compelled to spend hours a day in her home examining her appearance in the mirror, and she described those hours as torture. She would spend all morning getting dressed and putting on makeup, but she never felt satisfied with the results. Throughout the day, she would think about how her skin, nose, and lips were "repulsively ugly." She often avoided leaving home, and when in public, she was paralyzed by extreme anxiety when others looked at her. She said that these symptoms had come and gone since adolescence but had become much worse over the last two years.

Hypochondriasis

The main feature of **hypochondriasis** is a preoccupation with fears of having a serious disease. To meet the DSM criteria for diagnosis, these fears must persist for at least 6 months despite medical reassurances that no serious disease is present. The disorder typically begins in early adulthood, and it tends to be chronic. In one study, over 60 percent of people who had been diagnosed still met the criteria four or five years later (Barsky et al., 1998). The diagnosis is rarely used, but people who do receive it are frequent—and dissatisfied—consumers of medical services, as seen in the clinical case of Louis, described below. They often view their physicians as incompetent and uncaring (Persing et al., 2000).

Hypochondriasis often co-occurs with anxiety and mood disorders, which has led some researchers to conclude that it is not a discrete disorder but a symptom of other disorders (Noyes, 1999). In addition, hypochondriasis is not easy to differentiate from somatization disorder (see below), which is also characterized by a long history of complaints of medical illnesses. The key difference is that people with hypochondriasis, like Louis in the clinical case below, are concerned that their symptoms are a sign of a very serious disease.

Somatization Disorder

In 1859 the French physician Pierre Briquet described a syndrome that was then called *Briquet's syndrome* and is now known as **somatization disorder**. As illustrated by the case history of Maria, described on the next page, this disorder is defined by multiple, recurrent somatic complaints that have no apparent physical explanation but still cause the person to seek treatment. To qualify for the diagnosis, a person must have several different kinds of physical symptoms, and the symptoms must cause impairment.

> ### ■ DSM-IV-TR Criteria for Hypochondriasis
>
> - Preoccupation with fears about having a serious disease
> - The preoccupation continues despite medical reassurance
> - Not explained by a delusional disorder or body dysmorphic disorder
> - Symptoms last at least 6 months

Clinical Case: Louis

Louis was a 66-year-old man who was referred to a psychiatrist by his cardiologist because of concerns about anxiety. Although Louis acknowledged anxiety, he reported being much more concerned about his potential for heart problems. Several years before, he had developed intermittent symptoms of heart palpitations and chest pressure. Although extensive medical tests were within the normal range, he continued to seek additional tests and to monitor the results carefully. He had gathered a thick file of articles on cardiovascular conditions, had adopted strenuous diet and exercise routines, and had stopped all activities that might be too exciting and therefore challenging to his heart, such as travel and sex. He had even retired early from running his restaurant. By the time he sought treatment, he was measuring his blood pressure four times a day using two machines to average readings, and he was keeping extensive logs of his blood pressure readings. Like many people with hypochondriasis, Louis reported years of depressive and anxiety symptoms.

Before treatment could begin, Louis had to understand that the way he was thinking about his physical symptoms was intensifying those physical symptoms as well as creating emotional distress. His therapist taught him a model of symptom amplification, in which initial physical symptoms are intensified

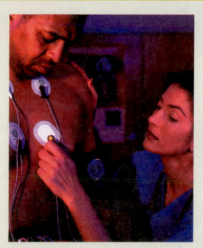

People with hypochondriasis are not easily reassured that they are healthy, even when extensive medical tests indicate no problems. (Dynamich GraphicsValue/SUPERSTOCK.)

by negative thoughts and emotions. The therapist used statements such as "A headache you believe is due to a brain tumor hurts much more than a headache you believe is due to eye strain." Once Louis understood that his thoughts and behavior might be increasing his medical concerns, treatment consisted of four goals. First, Louis was coached to identify one doctor with whom to routinely discuss health concerns and to stop seeking multiple medical opinions. Second, Louis was taught to reduce the time spent engaging in excessive illness-related behaviors, such as logging his blood pressure. His therapist showed him that these behaviors were actually increasing his anxiety rather than providing relief. Third, Louis was taught to consider the thoughts he had in response to his symptoms, which tended to be very negative and pessimistic. For example, the therapist and Louis identified ways in which he tended to catastrophize harmless physical sensations by viewing them as evidence for heart disease. Louis was taught to consider more benign reasons for his physical symptoms. Finally Louis was encouraged to build other aspects of his life in order to diminish the focus on physical symptoms. Louis began to consult for restaurants. Taken together, these interventions helped Louis reduce his anxiety, diminish his focus on and concern about his health, and begin to lead a more enjoyable life. [Adapted from Barsky (2006).]

Clinical Case: Maria

Maria, a 32-year-old woman, was referred to a psychologist by her physician. Over a period of about six months, her physician had seen Maria 23 times. Maria had dwelt on a number of rather vague complaints—general aches and pains, bouts of nausea, fatigue, irregular menstruation, and dizziness. But various tests—complete blood workups, X-rays, spinal taps, and so on—had not revealed any pathology.

On meeting her therapist, Maria immediately let him know that she was a somewhat reluctant client: "I'm here only because I trust my doctor and she urged me to come. I'm physically sick and don't see how a psychologist is going to help." But when Maria was asked to describe the history of her physical problems, she quickly warmed to the task. According to Maria, she had always been sick. As a child she had had episodes of high fever, frequent respiratory infections, convulsions, and her first two operations—an appendectomy and a tonsillectomy. As she continued her account, her descriptions of her problems became more and more colorful: "Yes, when I was in my early twenties I had some problems with vomiting.

For weeks at a time I'd vomit up everything I ate. I'd even vomit up liquids, even water. Just the sight of food would make me vomit. The smell of food cooking was absolutely unbearable. I must have been vomiting every 10 minutes."

During her twenties Maria had gone from one physician to another. She had seen several gynecologists for her menstrual irregularity and pain during intercourse, and she had undergone dilation and curettage (scraping the lining of the uterus). She had been referred to neurologists for her headaches, dizziness, and fainting spells, and they had performed EEGs, spinal taps, and even a CT scan. Other physicians had ordered X-rays to look for causes of her abdominal pain and EKGs for her chest pains. Doctors responding to her desperate pleas for a cure had performed rectal and gallbladder surgery.

When the interview shifted away from Maria's medical history, it became apparent that she was highly anxious in many situations, particularly those in which she thought she might be evaluated by other people. Indeed, some of her physical complaints could be regarded as consequences of anxiety.

People with body dysmorphic disorder may spend hours a day checking on their appearance. (Tony Latham/Stone/Getty Images.)

People with somatization disorder tend to make frequent visits to physicians, to visit several different physicians for a given symptom, and to try many different medications. Hospitalization and even surgery are common. Patients typically express their complaints in an emotional and exaggerated fashion or as part of a long and complicated medical history. Like Maria, many believe that they have been ailing all their lives.

Somatization disorder typically begins in early adulthood (Cloninger et al., 1986). It may not be as stable as the DSM-IV-TR diagnostic criteria imply, though, for in one study only one-third of patients with the disorder still met the criteria when reassessed 12 months later (Simon & Gureje, 1999). People with somatization disorder often report a host of behavioral and interpersonal problems, such as truancy, poor work history, and marital difficulties. Comorbidity is high with anxiety disorders, mood disorders, substance abuse, a number of personality disorders (Golding, Smith, & Kashner, 1991; Kirmayer, Robbins, & Paris, 1994), and conversion disorder (see below; Ford & Folks, 1985).

The lifetime prevalence of somatization disorder is estimated at less than 0.5 percent of the U.S. population, but it is commonly diagnosable among people who make very frequent medical visits. Somatization disorder is more frequent among women, especially African American and Hispanic women (Escobar et al., 1987). The specific symptoms of the disorder may vary across cultures (APA, 2000). For example, burning pains in the hands and the sensation of ants crawling under the skin are more frequent in Asia and Africa than in North America. Furthermore, the disorder is thought to be most frequent in cultures that discourage the overt display of emotion (Ford, 1995).

Interpreting these cultural differences is not straightforward (Kirmayer & Young, 1998). There is some evidence that doctors are more likely to miss a true medical problem in people from sociocultural backgrounds different from their own. Thus, some of the elevated rates of somatization disorder could reflect misdiagnosis (Schuepbach et al., 2002), but this is not likely to be the whole explanation of cultural differences. The Western perspective sometimes suggests that physical presentation of psychological problems is somehow primitive or unsophisticated. But this distinction between physical and psychological is not necessarily made in non-Western medical traditions (e.g., in Chinese medicine). Culture provides people with a concept of how distress should be communicated, and so culture may influence how and when people seek treatment for symptoms. People in Asian, Latin American, and African countries are more likely to describe their distress in physical terms (Halbreich et al., 2007) and to seek care through medical clinics, whereas more people in the United States seek help in psychiatric clinics and would probably tend to use psychological terms (Kirmayer, 2001).

Conversion Disorder

In **conversion disorder**, sensory or motor symptoms begin suddenly, such as a loss of vision or paralysis. The symptoms suggest an illness related to neurological damage, but medical tests indicate that the bodily organs and nervous system are fine. People may experience partial or complete paralysis of arms or legs; seizures and coordination disturbances; a sensation of prickling, tingling, or creeping on the skin; insensitivity to pain; or **anesthesia**—the loss of sensation. Vision may be seriously impaired; the person may become partially or completely blind or have *tunnel vision*, in which the visual field is constricted as it would be if the person were peering through a tube. *Aphonia*, loss of the voice other than whispered speech, and *anosmia*, loss of the sense of smell, can also be symptoms of conversion disorder. Some people with conversion disorder seem complacent or even serene, are not particularly eager to part with their symptoms, and do not connect their symptoms with their stressful situations.

Conversion disorder has a long history, dating back to the earliest writings on mental disorders. *Hysteria* was the term originally used to describe the disorder, which the Greek physician Hippocrates considered to be an affliction limited to women and brought on by the wandering of the uterus through the body. (The Greek word *hystera* means "womb"; the wandering uterus symbolized the longing of the woman's body for the production of a child.) The term *conversion* originated with Sigmund Freud, who thought that anxiety and psychological conflict were converted into physical symptoms (see the clinical case of Anna O. on the next page, an influential case for his theory).

Symptoms of conversion disorder usually develop in adolescence or early adulthood, typically after a major life stressor. An episode may end abruptly, but sooner or later the disorder is likely to return, either in its original form or with a different symptom. The prevalence of conversion disorder is less than 1 percent, and more women than men are given the diagnosis (Faravelli et al., 1997). Conversion disorder is often comorbid with other Axis I disorders—for example, major depressive disorder and substance abuse—and with personality disorders, notably borderline and histrionic personality disorders (Binzer & Kullgren, 1996; Rechlin, Loew, & Joraschky, 1997).

It is important to distinguish the symptoms of conversion disorder, such as a paralysis or a sensory dysfunction, from similar symptoms that have a true neurological basis. Sometimes this task seems easy, as when the paralysis does not make anatomical sense, but even then the diagnostician has to be careful. Consider, for instance, the classic example of "glove anesthesia," a rare symptom of conversion disorder in which the person experiences little or no sensation in the part of the hand and lower arm that would be covered by a glove (see Figure 6.2).

DSM-IV-TR Criteria for Somatization Disorder

- History of seeking treatment for many physical complaints beginning before the age of 30 and lasting for several years
- At least four pain symptoms, as well as at least two gastrointestinal symptoms, one sexual symptom, and one pseudoneurological symptom (e.g., unexplained paralysis)
- Symptoms are not due to a medical condition or are excessive given the person's medical condition
- Symptoms do not appear to be faked

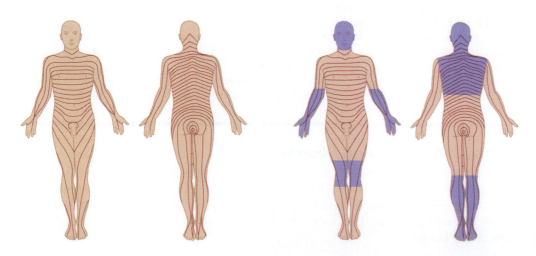

Figure 6.2 The anesthesias of conversion disorder can be distinguished from neurological dysfunctions. The patterns of neural innervation are shown on the left. Typical areas of anesthesia in conversion disorder are superimposed on the right. The anesthesias of conversion disorder do not make anatomical sense. Adapted from an original painting by Frank H. Netter, M.D. From *The CIBA Collection of Medical Illustrations*, copyright © by CIBA Pharmaceutical Company, Division of CIBA-GEIGY Corporation.

Clinical Case: Anna O.

As described in the initial case report, Anna O. was sitting at the bedside of her seriously ill father when she dropped off into a waking dream. She saw a black snake come toward her sick father to bite him. She tried to ward it away, but her arm had gone to sleep. When she looked at her hand, her fingers seemed to turn into little snakes with death's heads. The next day, when a bent branch recalled her hallucination of the snake, her right arm became rigidly extended. After that, whenever some object revived her hallucination, her arm responded in the same way—with rigid extension. Later, her symptoms extended to paralysis and anesthesia of her entire right side. [Drawn from Breuer and Freud (1895/1982)]

DSM-IV-TR Criteria for Conversion Disorder

- One or more symptoms affecting motor or sensory functioning and suggesting a neurological or medical condition
- Symptoms are related to conflict or stress
- Symptoms are not intentionally produced and cannot be explained by a medical condition
- Symptoms cause significant distress or functional impairment or warrant medical evaluation

For years this was considered a textbook illustration of anatomical nonsense because the nerves run continuously from the hand up the arm. Yet even in this case it now appears that misdiagnosis can occur if the person has carpal tunnel syndrome, a disease that can produce symptoms similar to those of glove anesthesia. Nerves in the wrist run through a tunnel formed by the wrist bones and membranes. The tunnel can become swollen and may pinch the nerves, leading to tingling, numbness, and pain in the hand. People who sit at computer keyboards for many hours a day seem to be at risk for this condition.

Since most paralyses, analgesias, and sensory failures do have neurological causes, true neurological problems sometimes may be misdiagnosed as conversion disorder. Follow-up studies conducted during the 1960s indicated that many patients diagnosed with conversion disorder were misdiagnosed. One of these studies found that nine years after diagnosis, an alarming number—60 percent—of these people had either died or developed further symptoms of neurological disease (Slater & Glithero, 1965)! Fortunately, with technological advances in diagnosing neurological problems (such as MRI), the misdiagnosis of conversion disorder among patients with a true neurological problem is much lower now (Moene et al., 2000).

Check Your Knowledge 6.3

Match the case description to the disorder, assuming that the symptoms cause significant distress or impairment.

1. Paula, a 24-year-old librarian, sought psychological help on the advice of her sister because of her deep fears about medical conditions. In daily phone calls with her sister, she had described worries that she had cancer or a brain tumor. She had seen doctors several times per month for several years, but when they reassured her that she was healthy, she became annoyed with them, criticized the insensitivity of their medical tests, and sought a new consultant.

2. Jan, a 41-year-old woman, was referred by her husband. He was worried because she spent hours and hours in the bathroom each day, crying while looking in the mirror at her hairline. She was convinced that her face and hairline were horribly asymmetrical and that others would dislike her as a result. She had visited two doctors to inquire about getting hair implants along her forehead, but both doctors felt that this was not advised, as they saw no evidence that her hairline was in any way atypical.

3. John, a 35-year-old man, was referred for psychological treatment by his surgeon. In the past five years, John had sought a stunning array of medical treatments and tests for stomach distress, itching, frequent urination, and any number of other complaints. By the time he was referred, he had received 10 MRIs and too many X-rays to count, and he had seen 15 different specialists. Each test had been negative.

4. Thomas, a 50-year-old man, was referred for psychological treatment by an ophthalmologist. He reported that 2 weeks before, he had suddenly become blind. Extensive medical tests had failed to reveal any reason for his blindness.

   a. pain disorder
   b. hypochondriasis
   c. somatization disorder
   d. conversion disorder
   e. body dysmorphic disorder
   f. cannot be determined based on this information

Etiology of Conversion Disorder

Much of the work on the etiology of somatoform disorders has been directed toward understanding conversion disorder. Although it was originally proposed that conversion disorder could be related to genetic factors, twin studies do not support this idea (Slater, 1961). In this section, we begin by discussing psychodynamic views of conversion disorder and then consider sociocultural factors.

Psychodynamic Perspective   Conversion disorder occupies a central place in psychodynamic theories because the symptoms provide a clear example of the role of the unconscious. Consider trying to diagnose a woman who says that she awakened one morning with a paralyzed left arm. Assume that a series of neurological tests reveal no neurological disorder. Perhaps she has decided to fake paralysis to achieve some end—this would be an example of malingering (see Focus on Discovery 6.2). But what if you believe her? You would almost be forced to conclude that unconscious processes were operating. On a conscious level, she is telling the truth; she believes that her arm is paralyzed. On an unconscious level, some psychological factor is at work, making her unable to move her arm despite the absence of any physical cause.

Freud and his colleague Josef Breuer (1895/1982) developed a psychoanalytic model of conversion disorder by drawing on cases like that of Anna O. They proposed that a conversion disorder results when a person experiences an emotionally overwhelming event, but the emotion is not expressed and the memory of the event is cut off from consciousness. In addition, they pointed out that the symptoms could let the person avoid an unpleasant life situation or obtain attention. This theory of conversion disorder is intriguing, but there is no empirical support for it.

A more recent psychodynamic interpretation of one form of conversion disorder, hysterical blindness, is based on a review of two case studies of hysterically blind teenage women (Sackeim, Nordlie, & Gur, 1979). In one case, a young woman who reported being blind performed more poorly on a vision test than would a person who was actually blind (i.e., she performed below chance levels). In the other case, a teenage girl reported that she could not see to read, but tests showed that she could readily identify objects of various sizes and shapes and count fingers at a distance of 15 feet.

Drawing on these cases, Sackeim and colleagues (1979) proposed a two-stage model to account for the discrepancies between the women's vision tests and their reports of blindness. The first stage focuses on the idea that people can process visual information outside of their conscious awareness. Research on patients with lesions in the visual cortex supports this idea. These patients are missing some of the key cells in the visual system of the brain and believe they are blind, but they can perform well on some specific types of visual tests (their condition is called **blindsight**). So it is possible for people to claim truthfully that they cannot see, even when tests suggest that they can. More generally, many different studies show that perceptions formed outside of consciousness can influence behavior (see Focus on Discovery 6.3). Hence, because some perceptual abilities may be unconscious (outside of awareness), hysterically blind persons are able to genuinely say that they cannot see, even when visual stimuli clearly influence their behavior. That is, one way to understand conversion disorder is that there is a disruption in the normal functions of consciousness, such that the person fails to have an explicit awareness of sensory and motor information (Kihlstrom, 1994).

The second stage of this model focuses on motivation—that is, some people, perhaps because of their personality, are motivated to appear blind. Such people would be expected to perform below chance levels on visual tests. Support for the importance of motivation comes from a study in which a man with hysterical blindness had his vision tested over a large number of sessions. The man was given different motivational instructions in different sessions, and motivation was found to influence performance (Bryant & McConkey, 1989).

The degree to which people need to be considered blind (their motivation) will shape how much they show signs of being able to see. In sum, recent psychodynamic models of conversion disorder focus on the idea that people could be unconscious of certain perceptions and be motivated to have certain symptoms. Unfortunately, despite the fact that case studies set the stage for further empirical work, this work has not yet been done.

Social and Cultural Factors

Over the past century, there has been an apparent decrease in the incidence of conversion disorder, which suggests a possible role for social and cultural factors. During the nineteenth century, Freud and his colleague Charcot seemed to have an abundance of female patients with

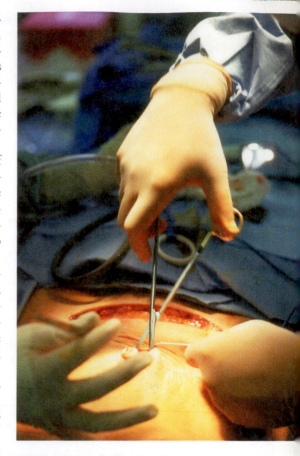

People with somatization disorder may undergo unnecessary surgeries in hopes of finding a cure for their medical symptoms. (Michelle Del Guercio/Photo Researchers, Inc.)

Some psychoanalysts believe that the high frequency of conversion disorder in nineteenth-century Europe was due to the repressive sexual attitudes of the time. (Hulton-Archive/Stone/Getty Images.)

FOCUS ON DISCOVERY 6.3

Evidence for the Unconscious

We are unaware of much that goes on in our minds as we perceive our environment—that is, much of the working of the mind proceeds outside consciousness (awareness). We can find a good deal of support for this idea in studies by cognitive psychologists. Consider these examples.

- In one study, participants were presented with different shapes for 1 millisecond (one-thousandth of a second) (Kunst-Wilson & Zajonc, 1980). Later they showed virtually no ability to recognize the shapes they had seen, but when they rated how much they liked the shapes, they preferred the ones they had been shown to other ones. It is known that familiarity affects judgments of stimuli; people tend to like familiar stimuli more than unfamiliar ones. This indicates that some aspects of the stimuli must have been absorbed, even though participants said that they did not recognize the shapes.

- Similarly, when people are presented with pictures of fearful faces for 33 milliseconds, they report no awareness of seeing the faces but show increased activity in the amygdala, a brain region involved in responding to emotionally relevant stimuli (Whalen 1998).

These experiments—and others like them—have begun to document that humans do have an unconscious. But the modern cognitive perspective understands the unconscious processes in a different way from psychoanalysis. Freud postulated that the unconscious was a repository of instinctual energy and repressed impulses. Contemporary researchers reject the notions of an energy reservoir and of repression, holding more simply that we are not aware of everything in our mind. While the original psychoanalytic view of the unconscious emphasized aggressive and sexual motivations, the newer cognitive perspective focuses on the brain as a highly efficient machine, in which some tasks are conducted automatically without entering consciousness.

A child participates in a dichotic listening experiment. Although he attends to information presented to only one ear, the information reaching the unattended ear can affect behavior. (Phanie/Photo Researchers, Inc.)

conversion disorder, but contemporary clinicians rarely see anyone with such problems. Studies show that the diagnosis of hysteria has declined in Western societies such as the United States and England (Hare, 1969) but has remained more common in countries that may place less emphasis on "psychologizing" distress, such as Libya (Pu et al., 1986), China, and India (Tseng, 2001). During World War I, a large number of men in combat developed symptoms resembling those in conversion disorder (Ziegler, Imboden, & Meyer, 1960), but by World War II, conversion disorder was less common among soldiers and occurred mainly in elite combat units (e.g., paratroopers) whose subculture prohibited psychological expressions of distress (Marlowe, 2001). Support for the role of social and cultural factors also comes from studies showing that conversion disorder is more common among people from rural areas and people of lower socioeconomic status (Binzer & Kullgren, 1996).

Several hypotheses have been proposed to explain the cultural and historical patterns in diagnostic rates. For example, psychodynamic therapists point out that in the second half of the nineteenth century, when the incidence of these problems was apparently high in France and Austria, repressive sexual attitudes may have contributed to the increased prevalence of the disorder. The decrease in the incidence of such symptoms may be attributed to the greater psychological and medical sophistication of contemporary culture, which is more tolerant of anxiety than it is of dysfunctions that do not make physiological sense. But they might instead indicate that medical diagnostic practices vary from country to country, producing the different rates. A cross-national study conducted by diagnosticians trained to follow the same procedures in each country is needed.

Etiology of Somatoform Disorders Other Than Conversion Disorder

Now that we've considered conversion disorder in depth, let's look at various perspectives on the etiology of the other somatoform disorders. We begin by briefly discussing genetic research on somatoform disorders and neurobiological risk factors for body dysmorphic disorder. Then we consider cognitive behavioral models used to explain a range of somatoform disorders, since these reflect the dominant perspective on somatoform disorders other than conversion disorder.

Genetic Research on Somatoform Disorders Torgersen (1986) reported the results of a twin study of somatoform disorders that included 10 cases of conversion disorder, 12 of somatization disorder, and 7 of pain disorder. No co-twin had the same diagnosis as his or her proband! Genetic factors, then, from the studies so far, seem to be of no importance for most somatoform disorders, with the possible exception of body dysmorphic disorder, discussed next.

Neurobiology of Body Dysmorphic Disorder Above, we described some parallels in the symptoms of body dysmorphic disorder and obsessive-compulsive disorder. These two disorders are often comorbid as well. Some researchers have suggested that body dysmorphic disorder may be a special form of obsessive-compulsive disorder. For example, the rates of obsessive-compulsive disorder are higher than average in the family members of people with body dysmorphic disorder (Gustad & Phillips, 2003), and both disorders are associated with changes in the volume of the caudate nucleus region of the brain (Rauch et al., 2003). Thus, some of the neurobiological risk factors for obsessive-compulsive disorder may be involved in the genesis of body dysmorphic disorder.

Cognitive Behavioral Models Cognitive behavioral models suggest that a number of different mechanisms contribute to somatoform disorders. Figure 6.3 illustrates one model of how these mechanisms could fit together for somatoform disorders other than body dysmorphic disorder. The process is believed to start with a physiological symptom, as a result of either a medical illness or a nonpathological change in physiological functioning (e.g., increased heart rate from effort). For body dysmorphic disorder, the process is thought to begin when a person notices a physical anomaly. Because physical symptoms are so common, these models tend to focus on cognitive and behavioral processes that amplify responses to physical symptoms.

Everybody experiences physical sensations and pays a certain amount of attention to their appearance, but people who are prone to somatoform disorders appear to have a cognitive style characterized by paying much greater attention to these things. In one study, researchers used a version of the emotion Stroop task (see p. 46) to examine attention to cues of physical health problems among patients with somatoform disorder, depression, or panic disorder (Lim & Kim, 2005). Patients with somatoform disorder attended more to words that were related to physical health, whereas other patients did not. Several researchers have replicated these findings (cf. Lecci & Cohen, 2007). Hence, people with somatoform disorder may automatically focus on cues of physical health problems.

Once people with somatoform disorder notice physical symptoms, they also seem to make more negative attributions about them. (An attribution is a person's idea about why something is happening.) The specific attributions will vary with the somatoform disorder. For example, a woman with hypochondriasis might interpret a red blotch as a sign of skin cancer (Marcus et al., 2007). Or a man with body dysmorphic disorder might focus

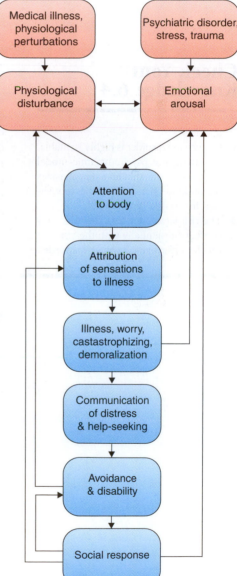

Figure 6.3 Mechanisms involved in somatoform disorders. From Looper and Kirmayer (2002).

obsessively on unnoticeable facial wrinkles, convinced that they make him unlovable. A person with somatoform disorder might overestimate the odds that a symptom is a sign of a disease (Rief et al., 2006). The exact form of the cognitive bias may vary, but most somatoform disorders seem to be characterized by worry about health and a tendency to catastrophize the symptoms (i.e., to interpret them in the worst possible way). Once these negative thoughts begin, elevated anxiety and cortisol reactivity may exacerbate somatic symptoms and distress over those symptoms (Rief & Auer, 2001).

In Chapter 5, we described a very similar cognitive process as part of panic disorder (see p. 138). That is, people with panic disorder are likely to overreact to physiological symptoms. In panic disorder, the person often believes that the symptoms are a sign of an immediate threat (e.g., a heart attack), whereas in hypochondriasis, the person believes the symptoms are a sign of an underlying long-term disease (e.g., cancer or AIDS). The types of physical cues that a person focuses on also differ for people with panic disorder compared to hypochondriasis. The person with panic disorder often focuses on symptoms that will actually become worse as they become more anxious—for example, a fast heart rate, shortness of breath, or sweaty palms. In contrast, a patient with hypochondriasis cannot, for example, increase the size of a spot on the skin by misconstruing it as cancer.

The tendency to believe that one is physically ill may have evolved from early experiences of medical symptoms or from family attitudes that became internalized. Consistent with the idea of developmental influences on cognitive biases, people with somatoform disorders report that, as children, they often missed school because of illness (Barsky et al., 1995).

Fear that a bodily sensation signifies illness (or one's physical appearance signifies ugliness) is likely to have two behavioral consequences. First, the person may assume the role of being sick and avoid work and social tasks, and this can intensify symptoms by limiting exercise and other healthy behaviors. Second, the person may seek reassurance, both from doctors and from family members, and this help-seeking behavior may be reinforced if it results in the person getting attention or sympathy. Often, people with these disorders tend to have trouble eliciting socially reinforcing interactions in other ways. For example, people with the symptoms of somatoform disorders often have trouble identifying their emotions and describing them directly (Bankier, Aigner, & Bach, 2001), so they may find attention and sympathy for health concerns particularly reinforcing. Beyond the attention, people may receive other types of behavioral reinforcers for somatoform symptoms—for example, people receive disability payments based on the amount that symptoms interfere with their daily activities.

Check Your Knowledge 6.4

True or false?
1. Conversion disorder is highly heritable.
2. The two-stage psychodynamic model of conversion disorder emphasizes unconscious perceptions and motivation for having symptoms.
3. The risk factors for pain disorder may overlap substantially with the risk factors for obsessive-compulsive disorder.

Treatment of Somatoform Disorders

One of the major obstacles to treatment is that most people with somatoform disorders do not want to consult mental health professionals. They resent referrals from their physician to "shrinks" because they interpret such a referral as a sign that the doctor thinks the illness is "all in their head." Innovative programs in which general practitioners help people think less negatively about symptoms, or insurance companies work with comprehensive teams to offer psychological and medical care, are likely to be needed.

Psychodynamic treatment has been found to be effective in alleviating the symptoms of somatoform disorders in one study (Junkert-Tress et al., 2001) and the symptoms of pain disorder in one other study (Monsen & Monsen, 2000), but there have been few other controlled studies comparing psychodynamic treatment to other treatments. In this section, therefore, we focus mainly on cognitive behavioral treatments and on the use of antidepressant medications.

Cognitive behavioral therapists have applied many different techniques in trying to help people with somatoform disorders. As illustrated with the clinical case of Louis described earlier, these include helping people (1) identify and change the emotions that trigger their somatic concerns, (2) change their cognitions regarding their somatic symptoms, and (3) change their behaviors so they stop playing the role of a sick person and gain more reinforcement for engaging in other types of social interactions (Looper & Kirmayer, 2002).

The negative emotions that accompany anxiety and depressive disorders often trigger physiological symptoms and intensify the symptoms of somatoform disorders (Simon, Goreje, & Fullerton, 2001). Indeed, as shown in Chapters 5 and 8, concern about physical health is common among people suffering from anxiety or depression. It should therefore come as no surprise that treating anxiety and depression often reduces somatoform symptoms (Phillips, Li, Zhang, 2002; Smith, 1992).

Cognitive strategies involve training people to pay less attention to their body. Alternatively, cognitive strategies might help people identify and challenge negative thoughts about their bodies.

Behavioral techniques might involve helping people resume healthy activities and decrease their reliance on playing the sick role. For example, a therapist might use operant conditioning approaches with family or friends to reduce the amount of attention they give the person who is displaying somatic symptoms, or they might help the person rebuild a lifestyle that has been damaged by too much focus on illness-related concerns.

Doctors' responses may help shape whether initial concerns about symptoms intensify or diminish. For example, in one study, patients with medically unexplained gastrointestinal symptoms were randomly assigned to receive high or low levels of warmth, attention, and reassurance from doctors. Those who received high levels of support showed more improvement in symptoms and quality of life over the next six weeks compared to those who received low levels of support (Kaptchuk et al., 2008). Hence, a new focus of research is on how to help primary care doctors best respond to somatoform disorders. With these general principles in mind, we turn to treatments that have been tested for specific somatoform disorders.

Pain Disorder   There is evidence from a number of double-blind experiments that low doses of some antidepressant drugs, most especially imipramine (Tofranil), are superior to a placebo in reducing chronic pain and distress (Fishbain et al., 2000). Interestingly, these antidepressants reduce pain even when, in the low dosages given, they don't alleviate the associated depression (Simon, 1998). Increasing attention has been given to the high rates of addiction to opioid medications among people treated for pain (Streltzer & Johansen, 2006).

Current thinking suggests that, in conducting psychotherapy, it is fruitless to make a sharp distinction between psychogenic pain and medically caused pain, such as pain resulting from injury to muscle tissue. Typically, clinicians assume that pain has physical and psychological components. Effective treatments for pain disorder tend to include the following ingredients:

- Validating that the pain is real, not just "in the patient's head"
- Rewarding the person for less focus on pain and more focus on life
- Relaxation training

In general, it is advisable to focus less on what the patient cannot do because of pain and more on teaching the patient how to deal with stress, encouraging the patient to engage in more activities, and helping the patient gain a greater sense of control. The cognitive behavioral techniques used to do this are described in greater detail in Focus on Discovery 6.4.

Body Dysmorphic Disorder   At least four trials have been conducted in which people with body dysmorphic disorder were randomly assigned to receive either a cognitive behavioral treatment or a control treatment. In each study, cognitive behavioral treatment was shown to produce a major decrease in symptoms of the disorder (Looper & Kirmayer, 2002).

Given the parallels between body dysmorphic disorder and obsessive-compulsive disorder, cognitive behavioral treatment for obsessive-compulsive disorder—exposure and response prevention (ERP, see p. 149)—has been modified to address the symptoms of body dysmorphic disorder. For example, for response prevention, people may be asked to avoid checking their appearance in mirrors and other reflective surfaces. Cognitive behavioral approaches that include response prevention have been found to reduce symptoms of body dysmorphic disorder (Veale et al., 1996).

FOCUS ON DISCOVERY 6.4

The Management of Pain

There is no one-to-one relationship between a stimulus that is capable of triggering pain, referred to as nociceptive stimulation, and the actual sensation of pain. Soldiers in combat can be wounded by a bullet and yet be so involved in their efforts to survive that they do not feel any pain until later. This well-known fact hints at ways of controlling pain: if one is distracted from a nociceptive stimulus, one may not experience as much pain as when one attends to the stimulation (Turk, 2001). It is also well-known that pain can be increased by anxiety, depression, and stress hormones (Gatchel et al., 2007).

Brain regions activated by physical pain overlap with the brain regions activated by psychological pain (such as the pain of remembering a relationship loss). That is, both types of pain increase activity in the region of the brain called the medial anterior cingulate. Researchers have begun to examine whether persons with unexplained physical pain demonstrate overreactivity in the medial anterior cingulate to physical sensations. Indeed, people with gastrointestinal pain that is unexplained by medical causes show more activity of the medial anterior cingulate in response to gastric sensations than do people with gastrointestinal pain due to medical illnesses (Mayer et al., 2005). One of the fascinating aspects of this finding is that attention and mood have strong influences on the activity of the medial anterior cingulate.

Because it is so hard to regulate pain, researchers have drawn on basic research to develop treatment programs that teach people specialized skills for managing pain and its consequences for that their lifestyle. These programs typically begin by providing information about the nature of pain, including the fact that being in a negative mood can make the pain worse (Morley, 1997). Often, treatment programs include training in the use of distraction and cognitive techniques for controlling pain, as illustrated by the following:

> The patient may be encouraged to alter the focus of their attention to the pain without switching attention directly away from the pain. In this instance, the subject may be asked to focus on the sensory qualities of the pain and transform it to a less threatening quality. For example, a young man with a severe "shooting" pain was able to reinterpret the sensory quality into an image which included him shooting a goal in a soccer match. As a result of this transformation, the impact of the pain was greatly reduced. (Morley, 1997, p. 236)

Treatment programs also tend to distinguish between pain per se—that is, the perception of nociceptive stimulation—and suffering and pain behaviors. Suffering refers to the emotional response to nociception. Pain behaviors refer to observable behaviors associated with pain or suffering; examples include moaning, clenching teeth, irritability, and avoidance of activity (Turk, Wack, & Kerns, 1985). Pain programs often focus on reducing suffering and pain behaviors. The emphasis is on restoring a lifestyle rather than allowing pain to destroy a person's lifestyle. The goal is increased activity and function, which can sometimes even reduce the actual experience of pain.

Hypochondriasis Cognitive behavioral treatment for people with hypochondriasis aims at reducing their excessive attention to bodily sensations, challenging their negative thoughts about those sensations, and discouraging them from seeking reassurance from doctors (Warwick & Salkovskis, 2001). The behavioral components of the treatment focus on keeping people from repetitively checking on their health, increasing their engagement in activities, and decreasing their focus on seeking treatment. Cognitive behavioral approaches have proven effective in reducing health concerns, symptoms of depression and anxiety, and health care utilization compared to no treatment conditions (Thomson & Page, 2007). For example, in one study, patients who received cognitive behavioral treatment reported being much less concerned about physical symptoms when they were present (Barksy & Ahern, 2004). In one study, cognitive behavioral treatment was as effective as an antidepressant in reducing the health anxiety symptoms of hypochondriasis (Greeven et al., 2007).

Somatization Disorder In a widely accepted approach to somatization disorder, the physician does not dispute the validity of the person's physical complaints but minimizes the use of diagnostic tests and medications, as well as maintaining contact with the person regardless of whether he or she is complaining of illness (Monson & Smith, 1983). A study of this approach found that it resulted in less frequent use of health care services (Rost, Kashner, & Smith, 1994).

Several studies have found that cognitive behavioral treatment can reduce somatic symptoms compared to control conditions, although effects have tended to be small (Deary et al., 2007). Available cognitive behavioral treatments have included a range of specific techniques. For Maria described on page 172, cognitive treatment could help her monitor her negative cognitions about her physical symptoms and help her evaluate the accuracy of those cognitions. She could also practice focusing less on physical symptoms. One goal of treatment is to help the person reduce the anxiety and depression that may underlie unexplained somatic symptoms. Techniques such as relaxation training and various forms of cognitive treatment have proven useful in this regard (Payne & Blanchard, 1995).

Cognitive behavioral therapists often focus on addressing the social concerns associated with somatization disorder. Maria, the woman described earlier, revealed that she was extremely anxious about her shaky marriage and about situations in which other people might judge her. Techniques such as exposure and cognitive restructuring could address her interpersonal fears, which might help lessen her somatic complaints. Assertion training and social skills training—for example, coaching Maria in effective ways to approach and talk to people, to maintain eye contact, to give compliments, to accept criticism, and to make requests—could be useful in helping her to develop healthier interpersonal interactions that do not focus on her physical illness.

Behavioral approaches could help change her reliance on playing the role of a sick person. If the people who live with Maria have adjusted to her illness by reinforcing her avoidance of normal adult responsibilities, family therapy might help. Maria and the members of her family might be able to change relationships to support her movement away from a focus on physical complaints.

Conversion Disorder   There have been no psychological treatments that have reduced symptoms of conversion disorder in controlled trials. Traditional long-term psychoanalysis, psychodynamic psychotherapy, and hypnosis, have not been demonstrated to be useful with conversion disorder (Kroenke, 2007; Simon, 1998). Case studies suggest that it is usually not a good idea to try to convince people with conversion disorder that their symptoms are related to psychological factors; rather, it is better to offer gentle support. Case studies also have suggested that reinforcing a person for being able to improve his or her functioning can be helpful.

Quick Summary

The somatoform disorders are defined by physical symptoms that are believed to be related to psychological causes. Somatoform disorders include body dysmorphic disorder, pain disorder, hypochondriasis, somatization, and conversion disorder. In pain disorder, psychological factors are believed to create or intensify pain. In body dysmorphic disorder, a person experiences distress and impairment over imagined ugliness or physical flaws. Hypochondriasis is characterized by belief in a severe disease, despite evidence to the contrary. Conversion disorder is characterized by sensory and motor dysfunctions suggesting neurological impairments that cannot be explained by medical tests. In somatization disorder, multiple physical complaints, not adequately explained by physical disorder or injury, eventuate in frequent visits to physicians, hospitalization, and even unnecessary surgery. The symptoms of somatoform disorders may arise suddenly in stressful situations.

Psychodynamic theories of conversion disorder have focused on the idea that people can be unaware of their perceptions and abilities and that some people may be motivated to have symptoms. Body dysmorphic disorder is often comorbid with obsessive-compulsive disorder, and these two disorders may be related to some of the same genetic and neurobiological risk factors. Cognitive behavioral models of somatoform disorders focus on cognitive beliefs that promote negative responses to bodily sensations and appearance. Little systematic research is available on the etiology of somatoform disorders.

One problem in treating somatoform disorders is that few people will want to see a mental health provider for their physical symptoms. Nonetheless, cognitive behavioral techniques have been found to be helpful, including strategies to help people address emotions more directly, change their cognitive responses to physical symptoms, and shift from assuming the sick role. Beyond these cognitive behavioral approaches, some other techniques have been found to be helpful for specific somatoform disorders. For pain disorder, cognitive behavioral therapy (CBT) and low levels of antidepressant medication may be helpful. For body dysmorphic disorder, CBT techniques that are highly parallel with those used to treat obsessive-compulsive disorder are helpful. For somatization disorder, physicians can reduce health care utilization by minimizing the use of diagnostic tests.

Summary

Dissociative Disorders

- Dissociative disorders are defined by disruptions of consciousness, memory, and identity.
- The dissociative disorders include dissociative amnesia, dissociative fugue, depersonalization disorder, and dissociative identity disorder.
- Most of the writing about the causes of dissociative disorders focuses on dissociative identity disorder. People with dissociative identity disorder very often report severe physical or sexual abuse during childhood. One model, the posttraumatic model, suggests that extensive reliance on dissociation to fend off overwhelming feelings from abuse puts people at risk for developing dissociative identity disorder. The sociocognitive model, though, raises the question of whether these symptoms are elicited by treatment. Proponents of the sociocognitive model point out that abuse in childhood may result in heightened suggestibility, that some therapists use strategies that suggest such symptoms to people, and that most people do not recognize the presence of any alters until after they see a therapist.
- Regardless of theoretical orientation, all clinicians focus their treatment efforts on helping a clients cope with anxiety, face fears more directly, and operate in a manner that integrates their memory and consciousness.
- Psychodynamic treatment is perhaps the most commonly used treatment for dissociative disorders, but some of the techniques involved, such as hypnosis and age regression, may make symptoms worse.

Somatoform Disorders

- In somatoform disorder, biological explanations for physical symptoms cannot be found. The major somatoform diagnoses include pain disorder, body dysmorphic disorder, hypochondriasis, conversion disorder, and somatization disorder.
- Psychodynamic theory proposes that in conversion disorder, repressed impulses are converted into physical symptoms. Sackeim has proposed a two-stage model of conversion disorder that focuses on lack of conscious awareness of perceptions as well as motivation for symptoms. Cultural factors that influence how people think about and express distress may shape the rates of disorder as well.
- Data regarding other somatoform disorder are less available. Most somatoform disorders do not appear to be inherited. There may be some neurobiological overlap between body dysmorphic disorder and obsessive-compulsive disorder. Cognitive behavioral models emphasize that some people may have a cognitive style that leads them to be overly attentive to physical concerns and to make negative attributions about these symptoms and their implications. The form of the cognitive bias may differ for the various somatoform disorders. Behavioral reinforcement may maintain help-seeking behavior.
- Antidepressants have been shown to be effective for some somatoform disorders. Cognitive behavioral treatments, which have received a great deal of support, try to address the maladaptively negative cognitions about physical symptoms, to reduce anxiety, and to reinforce behavior that is not consistent with the sick role.

Answers to Check Your Knowledge Questions

6.1 1. a, b; 2. c; 3. b
6.2 1. T; 2. T; 3. T

6.3 1. b; 2. e; 3. c; 4. d
6.4 1. F; 2. T; 3. F

Key Terms

anesthesia
blindsight
body dysmorphic disorder
conversion disorder
depersonalization disorder
dissociation

dissociative amnesia
dissociative disorders
dissociative fugue
dissociative identity disorder
   (DID)
explicit memory

factitious disorder
hypochondriasis
implicit memory
la belle indifférence
malingering
pain disorder

posttraumatic model (of DID)
sociocognitive model (of DID)
somatization disorder
somatoform disorders

7 Stress and Health

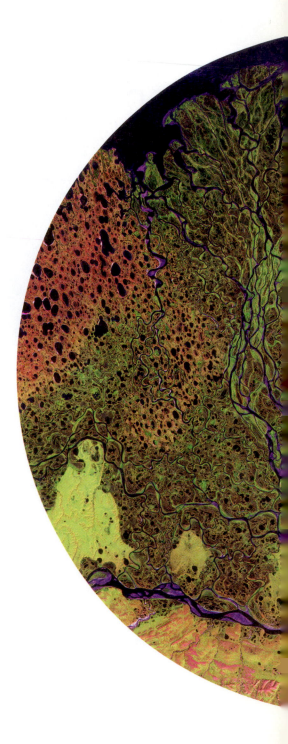

1. Be able to distinguish the definitions of *stress*, *coping*, and *social support*.
2. Be able to understand the theories of the stress–illness link as well as the concept of allostatic load and the basic components of the immune system.
3. Be able to describe how psychological factors impact cardiovascular disorders, asthma, and AIDS.
4. Be able to delineate the importance of gender, socioeconomic status, and ethnicity in health.
5. Be able to describe the major psychological treatments for psychological factors affecting medical conditions, including psychological approaches to reduce anger, anxiety, and depression as well as the concept of stress management.

Clinical Case: Mark

Mark Howard was 38. After earning an M.B.A., he had joined the marketing division of a large corporation and had worked his way up in the company. His talent and long hours of work had recently culminated in a promotion to head of his division. The promotion had left him with mixed feelings. On the one hand, it was what he had been working so hard to achieve; but on the other hand, he had never been comfortable giving orders to others and he especially dreaded the staff meetings he would have to run.

Soon after the promotion, during a routine checkup, Mark's physician discovered that Mark's blood pressure had moved into the borderline hypertension range, around 150 over 100. Before implementing any treatment, the physician asked Mark to wear an ambulatory monitor for a few days so that his blood pressure could be assessed as he went about his usual routine. The device was programmed to take blood pressure readings 20 times a day.

On the first day of monitoring, Mark had a staff meeting scheduled for 10 o'clock. While he was laying out the marketing plans for a new product, the cuff inflated to take his blood pressure. A couple of minutes later, he checked the reading. It was 195 over 140—not a borderline reading, but seriously high blood pressure. The next day he signed up for a yoga class and consulted a therapist for help with stress management. He also went to a trainer to help redesign his exercise plan and diet. He hoped that with these behavioral changes, he could continue in his managerial role and reduce the stress associated with the position.

Experiencing major life events such as starting school is associated with increased risk of illness. (Will McIntyre/Photo Researchers.)

A NUMBER OF DISORDERS characterized by genuine physical symptoms are worsened by stress. These disorders include those that we focus on in this chapter—cardiovascular disorders (including essential hypertension and coronary heart disease), asthma, and AIDS—as well as other, perhaps less serious but extremely common conditions such as headache and gastritis.

DSM-IV-TR approaches this topic under the rubric **psychological factors affecting medical conditions**, in the broad section "Other Conditions That May Be a Focus of Clinical Attention." The psychological factors that may be involved include Axis I and II disorders; personality traits, such as neuroticism; coping styles, expression and experience of emotions such as anger; and behavioral issues, such as failing to exercise regularly.

The many demonstrations of the pervasive role of psychological factors in health form the basis for the fields of **behavioral medicine** and **health psychology**. Since the 1970s these fields have dealt with the role of psychological factors in all facets of health and illness. Beyond examining the role of stress in the exacerbation or maintenance of illness, researchers in these fields study psychological treatments (e.g., stress management) and the health care system itself (e.g., how better to deliver services to underserved populations) (Appel et al., 1997; Stone, 1982).

Prevention is also a major focus of health psychology. As the twentieth century progressed and infectious diseases were brought under better control, people were dying more often from such illnesses as coronary heart disease (CHD). The causes of CHD involve behavior—people's lifestyles—such as smoking, eating too much, and excessive alcohol use. Thus, it is believed that changing unhealthy lifestyles can prevent many cases of CHD. Health psychologists are at the forefront of these preventative efforts, some of which we describe later in this chapter.

Health psychology and behavioral medicine are not restricted to a set of techniques or to particular principles of changing behavior. Clinicians in the field employ a wide variety of techniques—from contingency management, to stress reduction, to cognitive behavioral approaches—all of which share the goal of altering unhealthy living habits, distressed psychological states, and aberrant physiological processes in order to bring about health benefits.

We begin our discussion by reviewing general findings on the relationship among stress, health, and illness. Then we turn to an in-depth examination of three disorders—cardiovascular disorders, asthma, and AIDS. Next we look at the relationships between health and gender, socioeconomic status, and ethnicity. Finally, we consider various approaches to the treatment of psychological factors affecting medical conditions.

What Is Stress?

To understand the role of stress, we must first be able to define and measure it. Neither task is simple, as we discussed in Chapter 3. Stress has been defined in many ways. Perhaps one of the more influential antecedents to our current conceptualizations of stress was the work by the physician Hans Selye. He introduced the term *general adaptation syndrome* (GAS) to describe the biological response to sustained and high levels of stress. In Selye's model there are three phases of the response (see Figure 7.1):

1. During the first phase, the alarm reaction, the autonomic nervous system is activated by the stress.

2. During the second phase, resistance, the organism tries to adapt to the stress through available coping mechanisms.

3. If the stressor persists or the organism is unable to adapt effectively, the third phase, exhaustion, follows, and the organism dies or suffers irreversible damage (Selye, 1950).

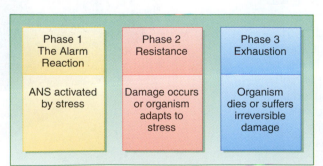

Phase 1 The Alarm Reaction	Phase 2 Resistance	Phase 3 Exhaustion
ANS activated by stress	Damage occurs or organism adapts to stress	Organism dies or suffers irreversible damage

Figure 7.1 Selye's general adaptation syndrome.

In Selye's syndrome, the emphasis was on the body's response, not the environmental events that trigger that response. Psychological researchers later broadened Selye's concept to account for the diverse stress responses that people exhibited, including emotional upset, deterioration of performance, or physiological changes such as increases in the levels of certain hormones. The problem with these response-focused definitions of stress is that the criteria are not clear-cut. Physiological changes in the body can occur in response to a number of things that we would not consider stressful (e.g., anticipating a pleasurable event).

Other researchers defined stress as a stimulus, often referred to as a stressor, rather than a response, and identified stress with a long list of environmental conditions, such as electric shock, boredom, catastrophic life events, daily hassles, and sleep deprivation. Stimuli that are considered stressors can be major (the death of a loved one), minor (daily hassles, such as being stuck in traffic), acute (failing an exam), or chronic (a persistently unpleasant work environment). For the most part, they are experiences that people regard as unpleasant, but they can also be pleasant events.

Like response-based definitions of stress, stimulus-based definitions present problems. It is important to acknowledge, that people vary widely in how they respond to life's challenges. A given event does not elicit the same amount of stress in everyone. For example, a family that has lost its home in a flood but has money enough to rebuild and strong social support from a network of friends nearby will experience less stress from this event than will a family that has neither adequate money to rebuild nor a network of friends to provide social support.

As a way of addressing the limitations associated with defining stress as either a response or a stimulus, researchers have emphasized that how we perceive or *appraise* the environment determines whether a stressor is present. Stress is perhaps most completely conceptualized as the subjective experience of distress in response to perceived environmental problems. A final exam that is merely challenging to some students may be highly stressful to others who do not feel prepared to take it (whether their concerns are realistic or not).

Studies Using the Assessment of Daily Experience (ADE)

As discussed in Chapter 3, one of the currently effective methods for measuring stress and its relationship to health is the Assessment of Daily Experience (ADE). Recall that the ADE does not rely on retrospective reports as much as other measures of stress do. Studies using the ADE ask people for responses at the end of the day for several days.

Researchers used the ADE to study the relationship between events in daily life and the onset of respiratory infection (Stone, Reed, & Neale, 1987). After reviewing the data, the researchers identified 30 people who had experienced episodes of respiratory infection during the assessment period. Next, they examined the daily frequency of undesirable and desirable events during a period of 1 to 10 days before the start of an episode. For each person, they also selected a set of control days without an episode, matching that set to the days examined before the start of an episode, to control for the higher ratio of desirable versus undesirable events typically reported on weekends. Results of this analysis are shown in Figure 7.2 and Figure 7.3. As expected, prior to the onset of illness, there were significant decreases in the number of desirable events and significant increases in the number of undesirable events.

These results, which have been replicated (Evans & Edgerton, 1990), were the first to show a relationship between life events and health with both factors measured daily over a period of several days. By carefully controlling for relevant factors, this study lets us come much closer to asserting with confidence that negative life events can make people more vulnerable to episodes of infectious illness.

Daily hassles can be upsetting and increase risk for illness. (Herve Donnezan Photo Researchers.)

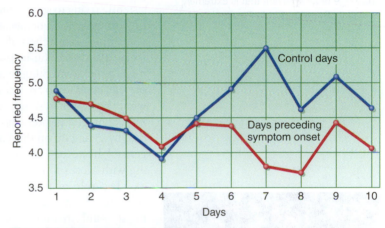

Figure 7.2 Mean number of desirable events in the 10 days preceding an episode of respiratory infection. After Stone et al. (1987).

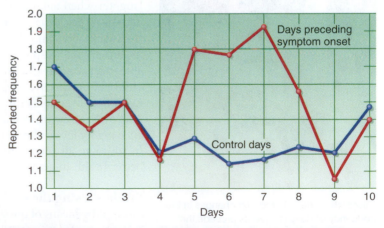

Figure 7.3 Mean number of undesirable events in the 10 days preceding an episode of respiratory infection. After Stone et al. (1987).

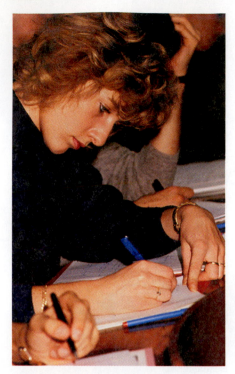

An exam may be appraised as an interesting challenge or as an event that is extremely stressful. (Borrfdon/Photo Researchers.)

Several experimental studies have confirmed the relationship between stress and respiratory infection. In these studies, volunteers took nasal drops containing a mild cold virus and also completed a battery of measures of recent stress. The advantage of this method was that exposure to the virus was under experimental control. Researchers found that stress was clearly linked to developing a cold (Cohen, Tyrell, & Smith, 1991; Stone et al., 1992) and that the stressors most often implicated were interpersonal problems and work difficulties (Cohen et al., 1998).

Coping and Health

Relevant to individual differences in perceptions of potentially stressful situations is the concept of **coping**, or how people try to deal with problems, including the problem of handling the typically negative emotions stress produces. Even among those who perceive a situation as stressful, the effects of the stress may vary depending on how the person copes with it. Researchers have identified two broad dimensions of coping (Lazarus & Folkman, 1984):

- *Problem-focused coping* involves taking direct action to solve the problem or seeking information that will be relevant to the solution. An example would be developing a study schedule covering an entire semester in order to reduce end-of-semester pressure.

- *Emotion-focused coping* involves efforts to reduce the negative emotional reactions to stress—for example, by distracting oneself from the problem, relaxing, or seeking comfort from others.

Problem-focused and emotion-focused coping are more effective depending upon the situation. For example, distraction may be an effective way of dealing with the emotional upset produced by impending surgery, for example, but it would be a poor way to handle the upset produced by the discovery of a lump on the breast (Lazarus & Folkman, 1984). Similarly, persistently trying to solve a problem that is unsolvable leads to increases in frustration, rather than providing any psychological benefit (Terry & Hynes, 1998).

Coping researchers also refer to *avoidance coping,* which involves aspects of both problem-focused and emotion-focused coping (Carver & Scheier, 1999). The essence of avoidance coping is either attempting to avoid admitting that there is a problem to deal with (e.g., by denial) or neglecting to do anything about the problem (e.g., by giving up or just wishing the problem would go away). In some cases, avoidance coping (e.g., giving up) may be a practical approach—for example, a person who has repeatedly been denied admission to graduate school may do best by giving up on this endeavor and instead focusing on pursuing a different career path. In general, however, evidence indicates that avoidance coping is the least effective method of dealing with most problems (Roesch & Weiner, 2001).

The role of positive emotions in coping is an area of current interest to researchers (Folkman & Moskowitz, 2000). Positive emotions may co-occur with negative emotions during stressful situations, and they can provide some benefit. For example, positive emotions can "undo" some of the ill effects of negative emotions, particularly the physiological effects (Fredrickson & Levenson, 1998). In one study, people who expressed genuine smiling and laughter when talking about their relationship with a spouse who had died 6 months earlier had fewer grief-related symptoms and better relationships with others 2 years after the loss (Keltner & Bonanno, 1997). Another study found that people who were able to find positive meaning, such as spiritual growth or an appreciation of life, following a traumatic event were able to respond to a laboratory stressor in a more adaptive fashion (Epel, McEwen, & Ickovics, 1998). A prospective study found that men with AIDS who reported experiencing more positive affect lived longer than men with AIDS who experienced less positive affect (Moskowitz, 2003). A review of several studies reported that older people in the community who experience higher levels of positive affect were more likely to live longer (Pressman & Cohen, 2005). In addition, all people, regardless of age, who reported experiencing more positive affect had better health in general.

Studies Using the COPE Scale   The relationship between health and coping is most often assessed by means of questionnaires that ask respondents to indicate how much they used various ways of coping to handle a recent stressor. One such measure, the COPE (Coping Orientations to Problems Experienced) scale, is presented in Table 7.1.

Researchers have found that changes in the frequency of daily life events precede the onset of episodes of respiratory infection. (Michael P. Gadomski/Photo Researchers.)

As with the relationship between stress and health, the best way to examine links between coping and health is by means of longitudinal study. Breast cancer, which strikes about one woman in nine and is the second most deadly cancer among women (behind lung cancer), has been investigated in this way. Breast cancer is a major stressor on many levels: it is life-threatening; surgical interventions are often disfiguring and thus have serious implications for psychological well-being; and both radiation therapy and chemotherapy often have very unpleasant side effects.

In one study, the coping methods of women who had just been diagnosed with breast cancer were assessed several times during the year following the diagnosis (Carver et al., 1993). Women who accepted their diagnosis and retained a sense of humor had lower levels of distress. Avoidant coping methods, such as denial and behavioral disengagement (see Table 7.1), were associated with higher levels of distress, and this negative relationship between denial and adjustment to breast cancer has been replicated (Heim, Valach, & Schaffner, 1997). Another longitudinal study of several types of cancer found that avoidant coping ("I try not to think about it") predicted greater progression of the disease at a 1-year follow-up (Epping-Jordan, Compas, & Howell, 1994). These results show that how a person reacts to a stressor is as crucial as the stressor itself in predicting its physical and emotional effects. In the case of cancer, reducing stress by ignoring the problem is not a good idea.

Social Support and Health

Another factor that can significantly reduce the negative effects of stress is social support. **Structural social support** refers to a person's basic network of social relationships, which includes factors such as marital status and number of friends. **Functional social support** refers more to the quality of a person's relationships—for example, whether a woman believes she can call on friends in a time of need (Cohen & Wills, 1985).

Structural support is a well-established predictor of mortality (i.e., death). People with few friends or relatives tend to have a higher mortality rate than those with a higher level of structural support (Kaplan et al., 1994). Similarly, unmarried people have a higher mortality rate than married people, and this is particularly true for men (N. J. Johnson et al., 2000). In one study, people with more diverse social networks were found to be less likely to develop a cold following exposure to a virus (S. Cohen et al., 1997). Higher levels of functional support have been found to be related to lower rates of atherosclerosis (clogging of the arteries) (Seeman & Syme, 1987), to an increased ability among women to adjust to chronic rheumatoid arthritis (Goodenow, Reisine, & Grady, 1990), and to less distress among women following surgery for breast cancer (Alferi et al., 2001).

How does social support exert its beneficial effects? One possibility is that people with higher levels of social support are more likely to have healthy lifestyles—for example, eating right, not smoking, and not drinking too much alcohol. Another possibility is that social support (or the lack of it) could have a direct effect on physiological processes (Uchino, Cacioppo, & Kiecolt-Glaser, 1996). For example, low levels of social support are related to an increase in negative emotions (Kessler & McLeod, 1985), which may affect some hormone levels and the immune system (S. Cohen et al., 1997; Kiecolt-Glaser et al., 1984). In fact, both psychological and physiological mechanisms are at work, and theories that take both into account are able to account for the link between social support and health most completely.

Social support has also been studied in the laboratory, where cause and effect can be more readily established than is possible in the naturalistic studies already described. In one such study, college-age women were required to complete a challenging task while experiencing high or low stress with or without social support (Kamarck, Annunziato, & Amateau, 1995). Stress was created by having the experimenter behave coldly and impersonally as she told the women to improve their performance on the task. Social support was created by having a close friend "silently cheer on" each woman while sitting close to her and placing a hand on her wrist. The researchers measured each woman's blood pressure while she performed the task. As Figure 7.4 shows, high stress

Table 7.1 Scales and Sample Items from the COPE
Active Coping
I've been concentrating my efforts on doing something about the situation I'm in.
Suppression of Competing Activities
I've been putting aside other activities in order to concentrate on this.
Planning
I've been trying to come up with a strategy about what to do.
Restraint
I've been making sure not to make matters worse by acting too soon.
Use of Social Support
I've been getting sympathy and understanding from someone.
Positive Reframing
I've been looking for something good in what is happening.
Religion
I've been putting my trust in God.
Acceptance
I've been accepting the reality of the fact that it happened.
Denial
I've been refusing to believe that it has happened.
Behavioral Disengagement
I've been giving up the attempt to cope.
Use of Humor
I've been making jokes about it.
Self-Distraction
I've been going to movies, watching TV, or reading, to think about it less.

Source: From Carver et al., 1993.

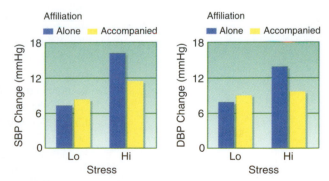

Figure 7.4 Stress led to increased blood pressure, but less so for people who experienced the stressor with a friend. DBP, diastolic blood pressure; SBP, systolic blood pressure. From Kamarck et al. (1995).

Seeking comfort or social support from others can be beneficial for health. (Bruce Ayers/Stone/Getty Images.)

led to higher blood pressure, but this effect was much greater in women who experienced the stress alone, without social support. This shows that social support can have a causal effect on a physiological process.

Research on the relationship between marriage and health has suggested that social support can affect health by impacting the married couple's relationship and each partner's emotions, cognitions, and physiology. For example, a review of laboratory studies of marital conflict discussions concluded that these interactions, which are full of negative emotions and cognitions, have a negative impact on cardiovascular reactivity, the immune system, and the endocrine system (Robles & Kiecolt-Glaser, 2004). These short-term psychological and physiological effects of marital conflict have prospectively predicted cardiovascular and blood pressure dysregulation (Baker et al., 2000) and divorce (Kiecolt-Glaser et al., 2003).

Check Your Knowledge 7.1 (Answers are at the end of the chapter.)

Answer the questions.

1. Which of the following describes the phases of Selye's general adaptation syndrome?
   a. alarm, resistance, exhaustion
   b. alarm, adapt, change
   c. stress, react, move on
   d. stress, resist, adapt
2. Problem-focused coping differs from emotion-focused in that:
   a. Problem-focused coping emphasizes reducing emotions that problems cause; emotion-focused coping emphasizes acting on emotions, particularly negative emotions.
   b. Problem-focused coping emphasizes taking action to solve a problem; emotion-focused coping emphasizes reducing negative feelings.
   c. Both are forms of structural social support.
   d. None of the above are correct.
3. Which of the following statements is incorrect regarding the relationship between social support and health?
   a. People with social support may perform more healthy behaviors.
   b. Social support may buffer against negative emotions, which can influence the immune system.
   c. Marital conflict can negatively impact health.
   d. All of the above are correct.

Understanding the Stress–Illness Link

Theories of the stress–illness link are developed to understand how psychological factors such as negative emotions impact health and disease. Theories in this domain are invariably diathesis–stress in nature—that is, theories that focus on individual vulnerabilities to stress. It is clear that not all people respond to stress in the same way, and some people are much more vulnerable. Some people are vulnerable to certain disorders and not to others. Researchers are focused on understanding psychological and neurobiological diatheses, or vulnerabilities to stress.

Before discussing these vulnerabilities, it is important to consider some indirect influences of stress on health. For example, stress may lead to health changes that are not directly due to biological or psychological factors but to changes in health-related behaviors. High stress may result in increased smoking, disrupted sleep, increased alcohol consumption, and altered diet (the opposite of what we saw with social support). These behavioral changes may then increase the risk of illness. For example, low socioeconomic status (often thought of as a stressor) has been shown to be related to greater mortality from several diseases, and this relationship is accounted for by a higher incidence among poor people of such behaviors as smoking and excessive use of alcohol (Lynch et al., 1996). In addition, high stress may result in changes in cardiovascular reactivity to stress or in changes in the immune system, such as an increase in cytokine production. These physiological changes may then increase the risk of illness. Thus, the stress–illness association is real but is likely to be mediated through changes in health behaviors or in physiology rather than to be a direct effect of stress.

Neurobiological Perspectives

Biological responses are a healthy and regular part of responding to stress. It is only when biological responses to stress are continuously activated or when other neurobiological processes do not bring the body's systems back to their pre-stress levels within a reasonable amount of time that physiological damage can occur. The major biological responses to stress involve activation of the sympathetic nervous system and the HPA axis (see Figure 2.9, on p. 38).

Theories about the ways in which stress impacts health take specific factors into consideration, such as different kinds of stressors and differences among peoples' responses to stress, appraisals of stressful situations, and perceptions of control (Kemeny, 2003). We will discuss two neurobiological systems that have been the focus of much research—stress hormones (the endocrine system) and the immune system. Before we begin, however, we should note that these systems do not respond to stress in isolation—indeed, we now know that the autonomic nervous system, the endocrine system, and the immune system all impact one another.

Allostatic Load: Prolonged Exposure to Stress Hormones   The body pays a price if it must constantly adapt to stress, and this price can be expressed in terms of what is referred to as **allostatic load**. For example, if the body is exposed to high levels of stress hormones such as cortisol and becomes susceptible to disease because of altered immune system functioning, we can view this as an effect of a high allostatic load. Furthermore, high levels of cortisol can have direct effects on the brain—for example, by damaging cells in the hippocampus, which regulates the secretion of cortisol. The result may be that, over time, the allostatic load makes the person even more susceptible to the effects of stress.

People can manifest allostatic load in different ways (McEwen & Seeman, 1999). Some people may have high levels of stress hormones simply because they experience frequent stress, whereas high levels in other people may be due to some difficulty in adapting to stress. For example, some people may have a genetically slow-to-adapt biological stress reaction. Other people may have learned behaviors that interfere with adaptation (such as poor eating habits, too little exercise, smoking, and excessive alcohol consumption). Still others may have trouble "shutting down" the biological stress response (e.g., they may exhibit an unusually high level of cortisol secretion even after the stress has abated). And some may have a weakened biological stress response, reflected by low levels of cortisol release in response to stress, which in turn causes other parts of the immune system to overrespond.

A real-world example of the way in which stress can interfere with our biological systems involves public speaking. Most people react to the stress of public speaking with an increase in cortisol secretion. After repeated exposure to such a stress (i.e., many public speaking experiences), most people adapt to the stress, and the amount of cortisol secreted declines. However, about 10 percent of people show no adaptation and even increase their secretion of cortisol (Kirschbaum, Prussner, & Stone, 1995), and these are the people at risk for health problems. A study measuring the presumed effects of allostatic load on the body (e.g., elevated blood pressure, cholesterol levels, and cortisol secretion) found that higher allostatic load effects predicted greater risk for cardiovascular disease $2\frac{1}{2}$ years later (Seeman et al., 1997).

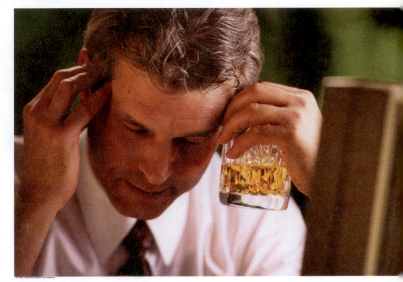

Stress may indirectly increase the risk of illness by causing people to engage in behaviors such as increased consumption of alcohol. (MTPA Stock/Masterfile.)

Stress and the Immune System   Stressors have multiple effects on the body—on the autonomic nervous system, on hormone levels, and on brain activity. One major area of current interest is the immune system, which is an important consideration in infectious diseases, cancer, and allergies as well as in autoimmune diseases, such as rheumatoid arthritis, in which the immune system attacks the body. The field that studies how psychological factors impact the immune system is called **psychoneuroimmunology**. Reviews of nearly 300 studies confirmed that a wide range of stressors produce problematic changes in the immune system, including medical school examinations, depression and bereavement, marital discord and divorce, job loss, caring for a relative with Alzheimer's disease, and the Three Mile Island nuclear disaster, among others (Kiecolt-Glaser et al., 2002; Segerstrom & Miller, 2004).

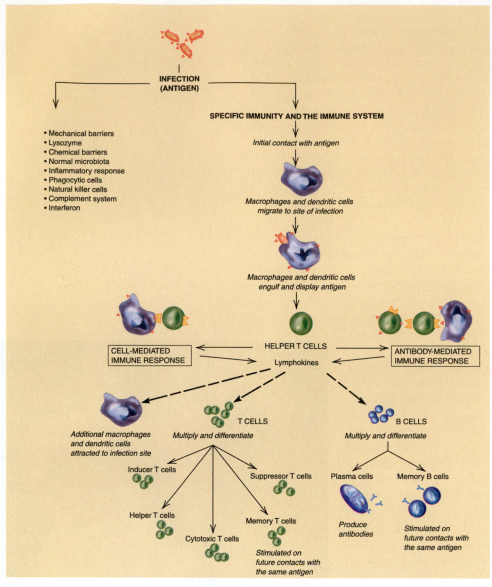

INFECTION (ANTIGEN)

- Mechanical barriers
- Lysozyme
- Chemical barriers
- Normal microbiota
- Inflammatory response
- Phagocytic cells
- Natural killer cells
- Complement system
- Interferon

SPECIFIC IMMUNITY AND THE IMMUNE SYSTEM

Initial contact with antigen

Macrophages and dendritic cells migrate to site of infection

Macrophages and dendritic cells engulf and display antigen

| CELL-MEDIATED IMMUNE RESPONSE | HELPER T CELLS | ANTIBODY-MEDIATED IMMUNE RESPONSE |

Lymphokines

Additional macrophages and dendritic cells attracted to infection site

T CELLS — *Multiply and differentiate*

Inducer T cells
Helper T cells
Cytotoxic T cells
Suppressor T cells
Memory T cells — *Stimulated on future contacts with the same antigen*

B CELLS — *Multiply and differentiate*

Plasma cells — *Produce antibodies*
Memory B cells — *Stimulated on future contacts with the same antigen*

Figure 7.5 Components of the immune system.

The immune system involves a broad array of cells and proteins that respond when the body is infected or invaded. A useful way of thinking about the immune system is to consider two broad types of immunity, natural and specific (Segerstrom & Miller, 2004).

Natural immunity is the body's first and quickest line of defense against infectious microorganisms or other invaders. A number of different cells, such as macrophages and natural killer cells, are unleashed on the invaders and begin to destroy them. Inflammation or swelling is a sign of these natural immunity cells at work. Activation of macrophages in turn stimulates the release of substances called **cytokines**, which help initiate such bodily responses to infection as fatigue, fever, and activation of the HPA axis. Although unpleasant, fever is actually a sign that the body is responding as it should to an infection.

Specific immunity involves cells that respond more slowly to infection, such as lymphocytes, which are involved in responding to specific pathogens or invading agents. Lymphocytes include T-helper cells and B cells. T-helper cells promote the release of cytokines; B cells release antibodies that deal with specific pathogens.

Figure 7.5 shows the components of the immune system. In the following sections, we illustrate the role of stress and immune system changes in infectious diseases.

The effects of stress on the immune system are direct, and they can happen very early in life. In fact, a series of studies with animals has convincingly demonstrated that prenatal stress experienced by a mother can produce long-lasting changes in behavior and the immune system in her offspring (Coe & Lubach, 2005). For example, compared to infants of mothers who experienced no stress during pregnancy, the infants of rhesus monkey mothers who were exposed to chronic stress during pregnancy (exposure to loud and unpredictable noises 5 days a week for one-quarter of their pregnancy) were observed to have emotion regulation difficulties as babies and adolescents that negatively impacted their place in the social group (Coe et al., 1999; Roughten et al., 1998). In addition, these babies exhibited immune system disturbances that continued into adolescence, including a deficiency of pro-inflammatory cytokines, such as interleukin-6 (Coe et al., 2002). **Interleukin-6 (IL-6)** promotes inflammation in response to infection and is importantly linked to human diseases.

In the past 15 years, much progress has been made toward answering a key question: whether such immune system changes are great enough to actually increase the risk of disease, leading to outcomes such as early death from cancer or the onset of arthritis. For example, we now know that stress-induced changes to the immune system can hasten the progression of AIDS (see the more detailed discussion later in this chapter). Recent studies that examine the body's response to different types of vaccines (e.g., flu and herpes vaccines) show that people exposed to stress are slower to develop antibodies in response to vaccines than those not exposed to stress. This slower response could increase the chance of illness. In addition, exposure to stress also slows the process of wound healing, which relies on the immune system (Kiecolt-Glaser et al., 2002). Across a number of studies, age appears to be a factor—that is, older adults are more likely than younger adults to show a harmful immune response to stress.

Other evidence indicates that stress can trigger the release of cytokines such as interleukin-1 and interleukin-6, as if the body were fighting off an infection (Maier & Watkins, 1998). Why is this important for health? Inflammation and higher levels of IL-6 have been linked to a number of diseases in older adults, such as coronary heart disease, arthritis, multiple myeloma, non-Hodgkin's lymphoma, osteoporosis, and type 2 diabetes. Thus, if stress increases the release of IL-6, the impact on health is likely to be negative. Based on the studies with animals reviewed above, the effects of stress on the immune system can even occur prenatally. It remains to be seen if these same effects are observed in humans. Nevertheless, the effects of stress on the immune system can be substantial.

Psychodynamic Perspectives

Psychodynamic theories propose that specific conflicts and their associated negative emotional states give rise to health problems. Of the psychodynamic theorists who studied the stress-illness link, Franz Alexander (1950) had the greatest impact. In his view, repressed emotional impulses created a chronic negative emotional state that impacted health, thus setting the stage for problems like ulcers, asthma, or essential hypertension. Alexander formulated this theory of unexpressed anger, or **anger-in theory**, on the basis of his observations of patients undergoing psychoanalysis. Although this theory has not received much empirical support, the role of anger expression as a psychological factor in essential hypertension and coronary heart disease continues to be investigated, as discussed in the sections below on those disorders.

Cognitive and Personality Perspectives

We experience stress in relation to a wide variety of conditions and situations. Physical threats obviously create stress, but so do negative emotions such as resentment, regret, and worry, which often do not easily pass and which cannot be fought against or escaped from as readily as can physical threats. Negative emotions stimulate sympathetic nervous system activity and may keep the body's stress systems aroused and the body in a continual state of emergency, sometimes for far longer than it can bear, as suggested by the notion of allostatic load.

In our general discussion of stress, we saw that the appraisal of a potential stressor is central to how it affects the person. People who continually appraise life events and experiences as exceeding their resources may be chronically stressed and at risk for the stress to adversely affect their health. We have also seen that how people cope with stress can be relevant. In addition, personality traits are implicated in several disorders, most notably cardiovascular disease. People who chronically experience high levels of negative emotions are at increased risk for the development of heart problems.

Personality traits have also been linked to immune system functioning. For example, the predisposition to experience negative emotions has been linked to slowed antibody production following a flu vaccine (Rosenkranz et al., 2003). In a study of first-year law school students, optimism predicted better mood and a stronger immune system (Segerstrom et al., 1998). This link between optimism and immune functioning was mediated in part by students' cognitive appraisals of stress—that is, optimistic students appraised law school as less aversive than did nonoptimistic students, which presumably made school less stressful and led to better immune system functioning.

Quick Summary

DSM-IV-TR covers stress and health under "Psychological Factors Affecting Medical Conditions," which can be applied to just about any illness. The fields of health psychology and behavioral medicine are dedicated to the study of how psychological factors and associated stress impact health.

Stress can be viewed as a response to a stimulus or as the stimulus itself, but neither view is without problems. Different people experience different degrees of stress in relation to the same stimuli. These differences relate to ways in which people perceive or appraise events and to people's coping styles, some of which are beneficial for health whereas others are not. Longitudinal studies using the ADE have shown a link between stress and respiratory infections, and longitudinal studies using the COPE scale have shown a link between coping styles and breast cancer. People with structural social support have better health.

Theories about the ways in which stress impacts health are diathesis–stress theories that involve both psychological and neurobiological factors. One neurobiological factor is the allostatic load that results when stress results in high levels of stress hormones. Some people may have high levels of stress hormones because they experience frequent stress, whereas high levels in other people may be due to some difficulty in adapting to stress. Another neurobiological factor is the effect of stress on the immune system. The field that studies how psychological factors impact the immune system is called psychoneuroimmunology. A wide range of stressors produce problematic changes in the immune system, and this can impact disease, for example, in hastening the progression of AIDS. Cytokines help initiate such bodily responses to infection as fatigue, fever, and activation of the HPA axis. Inflammation and higher levels of the cytokine IL-6 have been linked to a number of diseases in older adults. Psychological variables can include unexpressed anger and high levels of negative emotions, both of which can increase stress, and optimism, which then can reduce stress.

Check Your Knowledge 7.2

True or false?
1. Allostatic load refers to the body's need to adapt to stress.
2. The body's first line of defense against infection involves lymphocytes.
3. Cytokines are linked to the relationship between stress and illness.
4. Anger-in refers to expressing the experience of anger.

Cardiovascular Disorders

Cardiovascular disorders (collectively referred to as "cardiovascular disease") are diseases involving the heart and blood-circulation system. Cardiovascular disease accounts for almost half of the deaths in the United States each year, is one of the leading killers of men and women from all ethnicities, and affects nearly 65 million Americans. In 2004, the estimated costs associated with cardiovascular disease, including health care and reductions in productivity, amounted to $368.4 billion (American Heart Association, 2004).

In this section we focus on two forms of cardiovascular disease that appear to be adversely affected by stress—essential hypertension and coronary heart disease. Of all the cardiovascular disorders, coronary heart disease causes the greatest number of deaths. Experts generally agree that many of the deaths resulting from cardiovascular disorders could be prevented or delayed by dealing with behavioral risk factors. One of the American Heart Association's web slogans is "Your lifestyle is your best defense against a heart attack" (www.americanheart.org).

Essential Hypertension

Hypertension, commonly called high blood pressure, increases the risk of atherosclerosis (clogging of the arteries), heart attacks, and strokes; it can also cause death through kidney failure. Hypertension without an evident biological cause is called **essential hypertension** (or sometimes *primary hypertension*), and no more than 10 percent of all cases of hypertension in the United States have an evident biological cause—thus, essential hypertension accounts for about 90 percent of all cases. According to recent estimates, varying degrees of hypertension are found in about 20 percent of the adult population of the United States; it is twice as frequent in African Americans as in whites. As many as 10 percent of American college students have hypertension, and most of them are unaware of their illness. Around the world, hypertension affects between 25 and 33 percent of the adult population (Kearney et al., 2004). People who do not have their blood pressure checked may go for years without knowing that they are hypertensive, which is why this disease is known as the silent killer.

Clinical Description   Blood pressure is measured by two numbers, one for systolic pressure (arterial pressure when the ventricles contract and the heart is pumping) and the other for diastolic pressure (arterial pressure when the ventricles relax and the heart is resting). Normal blood pressure in a young adult is about 120 (systolic) over about 80 (diastolic). High blood pressure is defined as 140 or higher (systolic) over 90 or higher (diastolic).

Etiology   Essential hypertension is viewed as a heterogeneous condition—that is, a condition brought on by some combination of the many possible disturbances in bodily systems responsible for regulating blood pressure. Risk factors for hypertension include genes, which play a substantial role in blood pressure; obesity; excessive intake of alcohol; and excessive salt consumption. In addition, blood pressure may be elevated by increased cardiac output (the amount of blood leaving the left ventricle of the heart), by increased resistance to the passage of blood through the arteries (vasoconstriction), or by both. The physiological mechanisms that regulate blood pressure interact in an extremely complex manner—activation of the sympathetic nervous system is a key factor, but hormones, salt metabolism, and central nervous system mechanisms are all involved—and many of these physiological mechanisms can be affected by psychological stress.

The Role of Stress   Various stressful real-world conditions have been examined to determine their role in the etiology of essential hypertension. Stressful interviews, natural disasters such as earthquakes, and job stress have all been found to produce short-term elevations in blood pressure (Niedhammer et al., 1998).

It is also relatively easy to produce increased blood pressure in the laboratory. The induction of various emotional states, such as anger, fear, and sadness, increases blood pressure (Caccioppo et al., 1998). Similarly, challenging tasks such as mental arithmetic, mirror drawing, putting a hand in ice water (known as the cold pressor test), and giving a speech in front of an audience all lead to increased blood pressure (Manuck, Kaplan, & Clarkson, 1983; Tuomisto, 1997).

Although the results from laboratory studies are interesting, ultimately we must understand blood pressure increases in people's natural environments. Therefore, researchers have also undertaken studies of ambulatory blood pressure, wherein participants wear a blood pressure cuff that takes readings as they go about their daily lives. Many of these studies have asked participants about their emotional state at the time a blood pressure reading is taken. The general finding has been that both positive and negative emotional states are associated with higher blood pressure (Jacob et al., 1999; Kamarck et al., 1998). Because there is evidence that anger is the negative emotion most strongly linked to elevated blood pressure (Faber & Burns, 1996; Schwartz, Warren, & Pickering, 1994), we discuss anger more later.

Other ambulatory monitoring studies have examined environmental conditions associated with blood pressure. For example, a series of studies examined the effects of stress on blood pressure among paramedics (Shapiro, Jamner, & Goldstein, 1993). In one of these analyses, ambulance calls were divided into high- and low-stress types. As expected, the high-stress calls were associated with higher blood pressure. Even more interesting were the results when the paramedics were divided into groups on the basis of personality test measures of anger and defensiveness. The groups did not differ in blood pressure during the low-stress calls. However, during the high-stress calls, paramedics high in anger and defensiveness had higher blood pressure. In another study, participants rated job strain each time blood pressure readings were taken (Kamarck et al., 1998). Blood pressure was lower at times when participants felt in control of their work environment—for example, when they felt they could exercise choice over what they were working on. Still another ambulatory blood pressure study found that, for women, the combination of job strain and family responsibilities was associated with increases in systolic and diastolic blood pressure (Brisson et al., 1999).

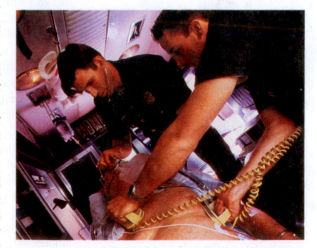

In a study of paramedics, high-stress ambulance calls, as when the victim had to be revived, led to greater blood pressure increases than low-stress calls. (Bruce Ayres/Stone/Getty Images.)

Among men, the expression of anger has been linked to cardiovascular disease. (Stone/Getty Images.)

In the ambulatory monitoring studies just described, the overall amount of blood pressure increase associated with emotional states or environmental conditions was rather small. But some people experience large increases, suggesting that only people who have some predisposition, or diathesis, will experience large blood pressure increases that over time may lead to sustained hypertension. Next, we discuss three possible diatheses, including anger, the Type A behavior pattern, and cardiovascular reactivity.

Anger   Anger per se is not bad for our cardiovascular health; rather, it is excessive or inappropriate anger that is linked to poor health (Mayne, 2001). What is less clear is the relative importance of different aspects of anger: becoming angry easily, becoming angry and not expressing it, or having a cynical or suspicious attitude toward others. Research has not totally resolved this issue, but the evidence suggests that being easily angered may be the most important factor (e.g., Räikkönen et al., 1999).

Complicating the picture further, anger may function differently in men and women, depending on the situation. With respect to cardiovascular health, expressing anger has been related to increased blood pressure reactivity in men, whereas suppressing anger has been linked to increased blood pressure reactivity in women (Faber & Burns, 1996; Shapiro, Goldstein, & Jamner, 1995). Sex differences have also been found in the relationship between becoming angry easily and ambulatory blood pressure. Among men, but not among women, this trait is related to higher blood pressure (Guyll & Contrada, 1998). We return to this issue in our discussion of myocardial infarction.

Type A Behavior Pattern   In 1958, two cardiologists, Meyer Friedman and Ray Rosenman, identified a behavior pattern called **Type A behavior pattern** (Friedman, 1969; Rosenman et al., 1975). A structured interview identifies three components of the Type A behavior pattern. *Achievement striving/competitiveness* characterizes someone with an intense and competitive drive for achievement and advancement. *Time urgency/impatience* characterizes someone with an exaggerated sense of urgency—of time passing and of the need to hurry. *Hostility* captures someone who exhibits considerable aggressiveness and hostility toward others. The Type A behavior pattern has been most often studied as a risk factor for coronary heart disease, but it has also been examined as a predisposing factor for hypertension.

A large, prospective, and longitudinal study called the Coronary Artery Risk Development in Young Adults Study (CARDIA) examined whether the three components of Type A could predict the development of hypertension among black and white men and women. The study began in 1985 with over 5,000 participants between the ages of 18 and 30. Fifteen years later, a team of investigators examined Type A and hypertension among 3,308 of these original participants (Yan et al., 2003). They found that the time urgency/impatience and hostility components from the Type A structured interview predicted a twofold increase in risk of developing hypertension. The findings for time urgency/impatience were stronger for men than women; the findings for hostility were just about equally strong for both men and women. Achievement striving/competitiveness was a predictor of later hypertension for white men only. These findings provide strong support for the role of psychological factors like these in hypertension.

One characteristic of the Type A behavior pattern is feeling under time pressure and consequently trying to do several things at once. (GoodShoot/SUPERSTOCK.)

Cardiovascular Reactivity   In the past 15 years or so there has been a great deal of interest in cardiovascular reactivity as a risk factor for hypertension (and coronary heart disease as well). *Cardiovascular reactivity* refers to the extent to which blood pressure and heart rate increase in response to stress. Typically, researchers assess cardiovascular reactivity to a laboratory stressor (or, even better, a battery of stressors) among people who are not currently hypertensive and then assess the participants again some years later to determine whether the reactivity measure (usually, the amount by which the stressor causes change from a baseline condition) predicts blood pressure.

In one study, cardiovascular reactivity was measured while participants performed a laboratory reaction-time task in which they were threatened with shock if their responses were slow (Light et al., 1992). A follow-up 10 to 15 years later found that heart-rate reactivity was the strongest predictor of high blood pressure. Of importance, these reactivity measures predicted subsequent blood pressure over and above the contribution of standard clinical predictors such as family history of hypertension. Other research has shown that cardiovascular reactivity is related to other known risk factors for hypertension, such as socioeconomic status and race (Gump, Matthews, & Räikkönen, 1999; Jackson et al., 1999).

These findings concern levels of blood pressure but not the actual disease of hypertension. A different study entailed a 4-year follow-up of 508 Finnish men whose blood pressure reactivity had been assessed as they anticipated a bicycle exercise test (Everson et al., 1996). Men whose systolic blood pressure increased by 30 points or more were almost four times more likely to have developed hypertension 4 years later. One limitation of this study is that reactivity was assessed in an unusual situation. Thus, we can't be sure that the results would generalize to the more usual tests that have been used to assess reactivity.

Further support for the importance of cardiovascular reactivity comes from high-risk research comparing people with and without a family history of hypertension (Adler & Ditto, 1998; Lovallo & Al'Absi, 1998). People with such a history show greater blood pressure reactivity to various stressors. Coupled with research showing the heritability of hypertension, these findings suggest that blood pressure reactivity is a good candidate for a genetically transmitted diathesis. But what exactly is inherited?

Research has focused on genes linked to the neurotransmitter serotonin. This evidence suggests that people with one or two long alleles in the promoter region of the serotonin transporter gene (see Chapter 2) show greater cardiovascular reactivity in response to tasks involving mental arithmetic (R. B. Williams et al., 2001) and are at greater risk for myocardial infarction (Fumeron et al., 2002). Needed next are studies that examine how stress interacts with the presence of a long allele on this gene. This type of work has been done for depression: recall from our discussions in Chapter 2 that having one or two *short* alleles in this gene was associated with an increased risk of depression, but only among those people who had experienced early life stress.

Coronary Heart Disease

Coronary heart disease (CHD) takes two principal forms, angina pectoris and myocardial infarction, or heart attack.

Clinical Description   The symptoms of **angina pectoris** are periodic chest pains, usually located behind the sternum and frequently radiating into the back and sometimes the left shoulder and arm. The major cause of these severe attacks of pain is an insufficient supply of oxygen to the heart, called *ischemia*, which in turn is due to coronary atherosclerosis, a narrowing or plugging of the coronary arteries by deposits of cholesterol, a fatty material, or to constriction of these blood vessels. Some episodes of ischemia do not cause pain, so these are called episodes of silent ischemia. Both angina and episodes of silent ischemia are precipitated by physical exertion or emotional stress and are commonly relieved by rest or medication. Angina and silent ischemia rarely result in serious physical damage to the heart, because blood flow to the heart is reduced but not cut off. If, however, the narrowing of one or more coronary arteries progresses to the point of producing a total blockage, a myocardial infarction, or heart attack, is likely to occur.

Myocardial infarction, perhaps better known as heart attack, is a much more serious disorder; it is the leading cause of death in the United States today. Like angina pectoris, it is caused by an insufficient supply of oxygen to the heart. But unlike angina, a heart attack usually results in permanent damage to the heart.

Etiology   Several factors increase the risk of CHD; the risk generally increases with the number and severity of these factors. Table 7.2 lists these risk factors.

A combination of particular risk factors has been named the **metabolic syndrome**. It is defined by the presence of a number of related metabolic factors, including abdominal obesity, insulin resistance, high blood pressure, low HDL cholesterol (the "good" cholesterol), and heightened inflammation as indexed by the presence of a protein called CRP (Grundy et al., 2004). Adults with the metabolic syndrome are more likely to die from CHD than those without it (Malik et al., 2004). People who have what is referred to as "high-normal" blood pressure (i.e. systolic pressure of 130–139 and diastolic pressure of 80–85) are also at elevated risk of CHD (Vasan et al. 2001).

Table 7.2 Risk Factors for Cardiovascular Disease

Age (older people are at greater risk)

Cigarette smoking

Trans fats

Diabetes

Elevated blood pressure

Elevated serum cholesterol

Excessive use of alcohol

Increase in the size of the left ventricle of the heart

Long-standing pattern of physical inactivity

Obesity

Sex (men are at greater risk)

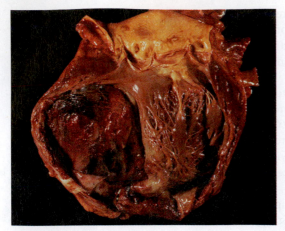

Myocardial infarction can do serious damage to the heart. (CNRI/ Photo Researchers, Inc.)

In the next three sections, we examine research on psychological risk factors for CHD. As with research on the links between stress and health, psychological and biological risk factors are intertwined, and a complete explanation of the etiology of CHD must include both. Results from the INTERHEART study of over 15,000 people who had had a heart attack and nearly 15,000 people who had not (the control group), which spanned 52 countries, found that psychosocial risk factors, such as stress, accounted for a third of the risk of a later heart attack (Rosengren et al., 2004; Yusuf et al., 2004).

Stress and Myocardial Infarction   In the short term, physical exertion can trigger a myocardial infarction, as can episodes of anger (Mittleman et al., 1997). Acute stress is another short-term factor—the frequency of myocardial infarction, for example, increased among residents of Tel Aviv on the day of an Iraqi missile attack (NHLBI, 1998). Death from myocardial infarction did not increase following the September 11, 2001, terrorist attacks in the United States (Chi et al., 2003); however, there were almost twice as many heart arrhythmias among people who had a cardiac defibrillator implanted (Steinberg et al., 2004). Over the longer term, more chronic stressors, such as marital conflict and financial worries, are also relevant.

One of the most studied chronic stressors is job strain (Karasek, 1979), an employment situation involving too much work, too little time, a lack of control over decision making, and a lack of opportunity to make full use of skills on the job. Several studies have found that a high level of job strain is associated with increased risk for myocardial infarction. In one study, over 10,000 British workers were assessed for the degree of control they could exercise over their jobs. They were then followed for about 5 years to determine the incidence of CHD. As in earlier studies, more CHD was found at follow-up among workers in lower-status jobs (e.g., clerical work). This result, in turn, was related to these workers' reports of having little control on the job (Marmot et al., 1997). In a large-scale study conducted in Finland, a high level of job demands was related to the progression of atherosclerosis (Lynch, Kaplan, et al., 1997) and to cardiovascular disease mortality and morbidity (Lynch, Krause, et al., 1997).

Other Psychological Risk Factors   Contemporary evidence linking CHD to psychological risk factors stems from the early investigations of the Type A behavior pattern. Initial support for the idea that the Type A pattern predicts CHD came from the classic Western Collaborative Group Study (WCGS) (Rosenman et al., 1975). In this double-blind, prospective investigation, 3,154 men aged 39 to 59 were followed over a period of $8^1/_2$ years. People who had been identified as Type A by interview were more than twice as likely to develop CHD as were Type B men (Type B behavior pattern is characterized by a less driven and less hostile way of life). Traditional risk factors, such as high levels of cholesterol, were also found to be related to CHD, but even when these factors were controlled for, Type A individuals were still twice as likely to develop CHD.

Hostility is linked to coronary-artery blockage. (Somos Images LLC/Alamy)

More recent research, however, has not supported the predictive power of Type A behavior (e.g., Eaker, Pinsky, & Castelli, 1992; Orth-Gomer & Unden, 1990). There are several reasons for these conflicting results. One is that later investigators used different methods of assessing Type A (e.g., questionnaires) that may not have been adequate. Second, it became apparent that not all aspects of the Type A behavior pattern were truly related to CHD. For example, in further analyses of the WCGS data, anger and hostility emerged as the major predictors of CHD (Hecker et al., 1988). A longitudinal study also found that difficulty controlling one's anger is related to higher rates of CHD (Kawachi et al., 1996). Anger and hostility are also related to several other variables that play a role in CHD. For example, high levels of anger and hostility are related to greater blood pressure reactivity to stress, higher levels of cholesterol, abnormal deposits of calcium on the walls of coronary arteries, cigarette smoking and alcohol use, the metabolic syndrome among adolescents, and greater activation of platelets, which play a major role in the formation of blockages in the coronary arteries (Fredrickson et al., 2000; Iribarren et al., 2000; Räikkönen, Matthews, & Salomen, 2003; Weidner et al., 1989).

Anger and hostility may be differentially related to CHD risk for men and women. For example, researchers found that indirect expressions of anger were associated with CHD risk for women, whereas overt expressions of anger were related to CHD risk for men (Siegman et al., 2000). These findings are similar to those discussed earlier showing that expression of anger was related to increased blood pressure reactivity in men, but the suppression of anger was related to increased blood pressure reactivity in women (Faber & Burns, 1996; Shapiro et al., 1995).

Other findings suggest that cynicism (an approach to life that involves hostility) is an important component of the Type A behavior pattern (Almada, 1991). For example, the amount of coronary artery blockage was especially high in Type A participants who had earlier given responses to MMPI items reflecting a cynical or hostile attitude (e.g., agreeing with the statement "Most people will use somewhat unfair means to gain profit or advantage, rather than lose it"). A study of medical students who had been healthy when they took the MMPI 25 years earlier found a higher rate of CHD and death in those whose answers had indicated cynicism toward others (Barefoot, Dahlstrom, & Williams, 1983). More recently, cynicism was found to predict atherosclerosis, myocardial infarctions, and death from CHD in the large Finnish study mentioned earlier (Everson et al., 1997; Kamarck et al., 1997). Cynicism also prospectively predicted a broad array of cardiovascular disorders (angina, stroke, heart attack) among older adults, and the link between cynicism and disease was accounted for in part by the presence of the metabolic syndrome among participants (Nelson, Palmer, & Pederson, 2004).

What is not yet clear is the best way to think about these results concerning anger, hostility, and cynicism. Are they the same or different? Is one more important than another in predicting cardiovascular disease? The answers to these questions remain unanswered at this point.

Research has also examined the relationship between other negative emotions—particularly anxiety and depression—and CHD. For example, anxiety has been shown to be related to the onset of CHD (Kawachi et al., 1994; Kubzansky & Kawachi, 2000) and to prospectively predict cardiac events among men with coronary artery disease (Frasure-Smith & Lesperance, 2008). Similarly, research has found that depression is related to the development of CHD (reviewed by Suls & Bunde, 2005). Two separate meta-analyses have found that depression increases the risk for CHD (Barth, Schumacher, & Hermann-Lingen, 2004; Nicholson, Kuper, & Hemingway, 2006). In addition, cardiac patients who also have a mood disorder are over five times more likely than others to die within 6 months of a heart attack (Glassman & Shapiro, 1998).

It is almost certain that these factors interact with biological factors to produce their effects on CHD. Anxiety, for example, is associated with activation of the sympathetic nervous system, which can lead to both hypertension and atherosclerosis. Research has also shown that depression is linked to a greater tendency for platelets to aggregate and thus produce obstructions in the arteries. Furthermore, depression is often associated with increases in steroidal hormones, which increase blood pressure and damage cells in arteries (Musselman, Evans, & Nemeroff, 1998).

Check Your Knowledge 7.3

Fill in the blanks.
1. _____ hypertension has no known biological cause.
2. Type A behavior pattern is linked to the disorders _____ and _____.
3. Cardiovascular reactivity is linked to changes in _____ in laboratory studies, but its link to _____ is less well established.

Asthma

Asthma, a disorder of the respiratory system (see Figure 7.6), afflicts over 22 million people in the United States (NHLBI, 2003). In 2000, the economic costs of asthma in the United States, including both medical expenditures and lost productivity, amounted to $14.5 billion (NHLBI, 2001). The prevalence of asthma increased 74 percent from 1984 to 1994, but it seems to have remained stable since 1997, perhaps due to the fact that the survey is now more reliable (NHLBI, 2003). The prevalence of asthma among children has risen 60 percent since 1980 (Eder, Ege, & von Mutius, 2006). Of the over 22 million Americans with asthma, nearly one-third are children. In California, children with asthma missed an average of one week of school in 2005 (UCLA Center for Health Policy Research, 2008). During childhood, asthma is more common among boys than among girls. But by age 18 it becomes more prevalent in women and remains so until after age 45, when men again predominate (NHLBI, 2004). Asthma is more common among smokers, people who are obese, and people of lower socioeconomic status (Gwynn, 2004).

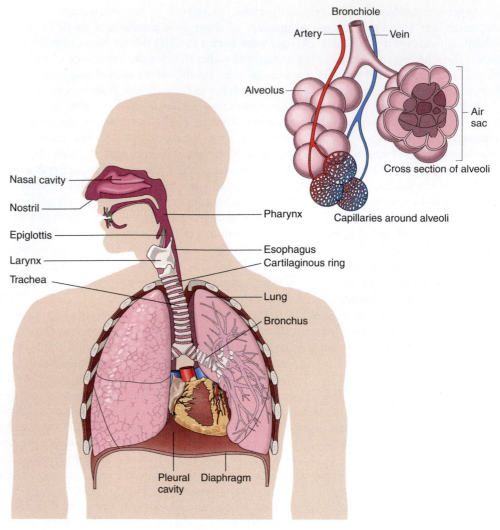

Figure 7.6 Major structures of the respiratory system—trachea, lungs, bronchi, bronchioles, and alveoli—and the ancillary organs. In asthma, the air passages, especially the bronchioles, become constricted and fluid and mucus build up in the lungs.

Clinical Description

In an asthma attack, the air passages in the lungs become narrowed, causing extremely labored and wheezy breathing. In addition, activity of the immune system during asthma attacks leads to inflammation of lung tissue, resulting in an increase in mucus secretion and edema (accumulation of fluid in the tissues) (Moran, 1991).

Clinical Case: Tom

During his childhood, Tom had frequent asthma attacks. His asthma was triggered principally by pollen, and each year he went through a particularly bad period that included several trips to the emergency room of a local hospital. He also seemed to get more than his share of colds, which frequently developed into bronchitis. As he reached his teenage years, the attacks of asthma mysteriously vanished, and he was symptom-free for the next 20 years. But at age 34 the attacks returned with a vengeance following a bout of pneumonia. In contrast to his childhood attacks, emotional stress now appeared to be the major precipitant. This hypothesis was confirmed when his physician asked Tom to keep a diary for 2 weeks in which he recorded how he had been feeling and what had been going on before each attack. He had four attacks over the period, three preceded by unpleasant interactions with his boss at work and one by an argument with his wife over an impending visit by her parents.

Asthma attacks occur intermittently, sometimes almost daily and sometimes separated by weeks or months, and vary in severity. The frequency of attacks may increase seasonally, when certain pollens are present. The airways are not continuously blocked; rather, the respiratory system returns to normal or near normal either spontaneously or after treatment, and this differentiates asthma from chronic respiratory problems such as emphysema (Creer, 1982). Symptoms may last an hour or may continue for several hours or sometimes even for days.

For people with exercise-induced asthma, the attacks follow strenuous exercise. Although some athletes are debilitated by the attacks, others are able to perform at the highest level despite their asthma—for example, Jackie Joyner-Kersee, a six-time Olympic medalist in track and field.

Most often, asthma attacks begin suddenly. A severe attack is a frightening experience and may cause a panic attack (Carr, 1998, 1999), which exacerbates the asthma. People with asthma have immense difficulty getting air into and out of the lungs and feel as though they are suffocating; the gasping, wheezing, and coughing can compound the fear. After an attack, a person may become exhausted by the exertion and fall asleep as soon as breathing is more normal.

Etiology

Asthma attacks seem to be brought on by a very wide variety of factors, including allergens, environmental toxins such as secondhand smoke, viral infections, cold, and exercise. Air pollution is known to be a contributing factor—for example, emergency room visits for asthma declined considerably in urban Atlanta during the 1996 Olympic games when automobile traffic was severely restricted (Friedman et al., 2001). As you will see from the discussions below, stress or negative emotions can exacerbate the impact of environmental toxins on asthma.

Olympic medalist Jackie Joyner-Kersee suffers from exercise-induced asthma. (© AP/Wide World Photos.)

Biological Factors   Diatheses leading to asthma might include the effects of respiratory infections, as seems to have been the case with Tom. Allergies, too, can predispose people to this disorder. When asthma is caused primarily by allergens, the cells in the respiratory tract are especially sensitive to one or more substances (allergens), such as pollen, molds, fur, air pollution, smoke, and dust mites, which bring on an attack. People whose asthma is primarily allergic may have an inherited hypersensitivity of the respiratory mucosa, which then overresponds to one or more of such usually harmless substances. Asthma runs in families, which is consistent with genetic transmission of a diathesis (Eder et al., 2006). Studies are narrowing in on how genes may interact with environmental factors to produce asthma (e.g., Cookson & Moffatt, 1997, 2000).

Stressful Life Events and Negative Emotions   The importance of psychological factors in asthma attacks is a topic of debate. Psychological factors that may interfere with the functioning of the respiratory system and thus bring on an asthma attack include stressful life events, anxiety, anger, depression, and frustration. Even when asthma is originally induced by an infection or allergy, psychological stress can precipitate an attack. Because of the link between the autonomic nervous system (ANS) and the constriction and dilation of the airways, and the connection between the ANS and emotions, research has focused on heightened experience and expression of negative emotions. Asthma patients report that many attacks are precipitated by emotions such as anxiety (Rumbak et al., 1993). In both laboratory and real-life settings, people with asthma show greater constriction of the bronchial tubes in response to stressors (Affleck et al., 2000; Miller & Wood, 1994).

Negative emotions have also been found to be directly related to reports of asthma symptoms and to peak expiratory flow, which is an assessment of airway obstruction obtained by taking a deep breath and then exhaling as hard as possible into a device that measures the force of the air expelled. One study assessed people with asthma over a period of several days (Smyth et al., 1999). Five times each day the participants were signaled to measure their peak expiratory flow and to record in a diary any asthma symptoms they were experiencing, their level of stress, and the mood they were in. Reports of higher levels of stress and negative emotions were

Asthma attacks are often treated by using a nebulizer to spray a fine mist of a bronchodilator into the bronchial tubes. (Hattye Young/Photo Researchers.)

related to lower peak flow and more reports of asthma symptoms. A prospective study asked children ages 6 to 13 and their parents to keep daily records of asthma symptom reports and peak expiratory flow for 18 months (Sandberg et al., 2004). The parents and children were also interviewed about stressful life events during the period of the study. The investigators found that the children were nearly five times as likely to have an asthma attack if they experienced a stressful life event 1 or 2 days before the attack. In addition, the children who experienced stressful life events were more likely to have another attack 5 to 7 weeks later.

In interpreting these results it is probably reasonable to assume that some of this heightened negative emotional experience is a reaction to having a chronic disease. But some research also shows that negative emotions precede asthma attacks, indicating that negative emotion may play a role in precipitating attacks (Hyland, 1990). In contrast, a prospective study found that pleasant emotions predicted better lung functioning among people with asthma (Apter et al., 1997).

Role of the Family   Sources of psychological stress associated with asthma include parent–child interactions and other family-related factors. One investigation looked at 150 pregnant women who had asthma (Klinnert, Mrazek, & Mrazek, 1994). The investigators intended to study the mothers' children, who were at genetic risk, and to assess parental characteristics as well. Both parents were interviewed 3 weeks after the child's birth to determine their attitudes and sensitivity toward the infant, their strategy for sharing parenting duties, and the presence of any stress. The amount of stress experienced by the mother in the past year was also assessed. The children were closely monitored over the next 3 years, and the frequency of asthma was then related to parenting problems in the family. Results showed a high rate of asthma among children whose mothers had high levels of stress and whose families were rated as having parenting problems (see Figure 7.7).

Not all research, however, has found that parent–child relationships figure in asthma. One study used cross-sectional and prospective analyses to study the link between family factors and (re)hospitalization for asthma (Chen et al., 2003). The cross-sectional analyses revealed that a higher level of family conflict and strain was associated with an increased number of hospitalizations for asthma among children in the family. Although this factor did not prospectively predict rehospitalization among the children, parental reports of less mastery and less emotional concern over their child's illness were predictive of later rehospitalization. These cross-sectional findings, however, do not tell us about the direction of the effects—that is, family stress could be greater due to having a serious illness in the family, or the severity of the asthma could be greater due to family stress. Nevertheless, the longitudinal, prospective findings suggest that higher levels of family stress do not cause an exacerbation in asthma, at least not with respect to rehospitalization, whereas lower levels of parental mastery and emotional concern seem to predict a later exacerbation.

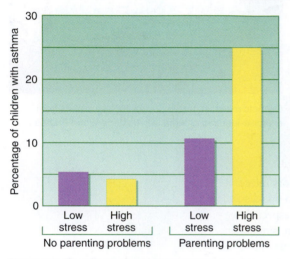

Figure 7.7 The effects of parenting problems and mothers' prior stress on the frequency of asthma in their children. Children whose mothers had been under a high level of stress and who were raised in families with parenting problems had high rates of asthma. From Klinnert et al. (1994).

AIDS

AIDS (acquired immunodeficiency syndrome) is a significant public health concern worldwide. We discuss this invariably fatal illness here because it can be prevented by psychological means.

In the United States, AIDS was originally proclaimed a disease of gay men, but it never was exclusively a "gay disease." In Africa and parts of Latin America, AIDS is found primarily among heterosexuals, and throughout the world HIV-positive women [i.e., women who are infected with HIV (human immunodeficiency virus), which causes AIDS] give birth to HIV-positive babies. The following statistics give some sense of the scope of AIDS (CDC, 2004, 2008; Epstein, 2007; UNAIDS, 2007 at http://www.unaids.org/en):

- Since the start of the epidemic, more than 25 million people worldwide have died of AIDS.
- As of 2007, over 33 million people worldwide are now HIV-positive. Of these, nearly 23 million live in sub-Saharan Africa. In 2007, an estimated 1.6 million people died from AIDS in sub-Saharan Africa; an estimated 21,000 people died from AIDS in North America.
- In 2005, 40 percent of pregnant women in Botswana and Swaziland were HIV-positive.

- There were nearly 5 million new cases worldwide in 2003. This was the largest number of new cases in any single year since the epidemic began. The number of new cases appears to have leveled off since then.
- Worldwide, women now account for nearly 50 percent of people infected with HIV.
- In the United States, African American and Hispanic women are 17 times more likely than white women to become infected.
- In 2006, 49 percent of the new HIV diagnoses in the United States were found in African Americans.
- In 2003, AIDS was the fifth leading cause of death among adults ages 35 to 44, a remarkable statistic given that it wasn't even included as a cause of death just over 25 years ago.

Clinical Description

The medical complexities of AIDS are beyond the scope of this book, but it is important to understand a few fundamentals. AIDS is a disease in which the body's immune system is severely compromised by HIV, putting the person at high risk for fatal diseases such as Kaposi's sarcoma, rare forms of lymph cancer, and a wide range of dangerous fungal, viral, and bacterial infections. The term *opportunistic* is often used to describe these illnesses, which are seldom found in people with healthy immune systems, because we can say that these diseases take advantage of the opportunity afforded by a weakened immune system (Kalichman, 1996). Strictly speaking, people do not die of AIDS but of the diseases to which AIDS makes them vulnerable.

Spread of the Disease

HIV is most often transmitted from one person to another through unsafe sexual practices, regardless of sexual orientation. HIV is present in blood, semen, and vaginal secretions and can be transmitted only when infected fluids get into the bloodstream. It cannot be transmitted through casual social contact. Among intravenous drug users, sharing unsterilized needles can introduce HIV-carrying blood into the bloodstream of another. Infants born to HIV-positive mothers are at risk, for the virus can cross the placental barrier and infect the developing fetus.

Risk is elevated in people who abuse drugs, including drugs that are not injected, perhaps because the effects of drugs can compromise a person's ability or willingness to consider the consequences of behavior. Another possible mechanism is a risk-taking disposition, for which frequent drug use is a marker; that is, engaging in unprotected sex may be another sign of a tendency to take risks (Chesney, Barrett, & Stall, 1998). Whatever the reasons, ample evidence shows that unsafe sex is associated with the frequent use of many kinds of drugs, including alcohol and methamphetamine (Colfax et al., 2004; Halkitis, Parsons, & Stirratt, 2001).

AIDS Prevention Efforts

Despite promising advances in drug treatment (e.g., AZT, saquinavir), there is widespread agreement that by far the best strategy is prevention through behavioral changes. For example, scientists generally agree that needle-exchange programs or the free distribution of needles to intravenous drug users reduces needle sharing and thereby the spread of infectious diseases (Gibson, 2001; Yoast et al., 2001). The primary focus in preventing sexually transmitted AIDS is on changing sexual practices. Early efforts in this regard were successful. For example, in the 1980s, when prevention efforts focused on encouraging the use of condoms during every sexual contact, new cases of HIV dropped in many large cities, from an annual infection rate among gay men of around 10 percent or more to 1 or 2 percent. But more recent data have indicated that younger gay men are engaging in more unprotected sexual behaviors than are older gay men (CDC, 2001; 2008). In 2006, the most common type of transmission of HIV in the United States was male-to-male sexual contact, with over 50 percent of new HIV infections being transmitted in this way (CDC, 2008).

Why might this be happening? Perhaps young gay men do not see as many of their age cohort infected as do older gay men, and so they don't consider AIDS as much of a threat for

Encouraging information about HIV testing is a key component to AIDS prevention efforts. This advertisement emphasizes the importance of HIV testing in the country of Namibia. (Sean sprague/Alamy)

themselves as it is for others. After the Food and Drug Administration (FDA) permitted direct marketing of AIDS medicines to consumers in 1997, ads from drug companies began to appear that portrayed HIV-positive men as healthy, active, robust, and happy and as engaging in all sorts of activities and sports; such ads may have given the impression that these drugs can cure AIDS.

Even if such ads accurately portrayed some small percentage of HIV-positive men, their relevance for women seems doubtful. Moreover, many HIV-positive men are not as healthy and active as the ads suggested. More importantly, these drugs can neither cure AIDS nor reduce its transmission. The FDA has since ordered that such ads be discontinued.

Other prevention efforts focus on encouraging monogamous relationships. One can eliminate the possibility of exposure by being in a monogamous relationship with a partner who tests negative for HIV. However, monogamous relationships are rare among young people and are not invariably found among married people or those in other committed relationships. Moreover, monogamous relationships are not the social norms in some eastern and southern African countries, such as Uganda. Instead, "concurrent long-term partnerships" are more common (Epstein, 2007). These relationships are faithful relationships, in that partners know about other partners and relationships outside these partnerships are not typically formed. Programs aimed at reducing the number of sexual partners has been shown to be effective in Uganda and Thailand (Shelton et al. 2004). Nonetheless, promoting faithful, monogamous relationships in this region of the world as a prevention strategy runs counter to the social and cultural norms of the region, making such programs more difficult to implement.

Although advocating monogamous relationships remains a prevalent approach in the public health arena, at least in Western countries, prevention is best directed at encouraging sexually active people to use condoms, which are about 90 percent effective in preventing HIV infection. Avoiding sex after using alcohol or drugs is also prudent because, as noted, use of these substances increases the tendency to engage in risky sex (e.g., Colfax et al., 2004).

Abstinence-only programs in schools do not appear to be effective HIV prevention programs among adolescents in the United States. A review of 13 different programs involving nearly 16,000 students found no evidence that abstinence-only programs decreased risky sexual behaviors, pregnancy, or the risk of developing HIV (Underhill, Montgomery, & Operario, 2007).

How can changes be brought about, especially in generations of sexually active people? Social psychological and cognitive behavior theory and research suggest strategies that can form the basis of effective preventive interventions (Chernoff, 1998; Kalichman, 1995; Kelly, 1995):

- Provide accurate information about HIV transmission. Such information is readily available online from the Centers for Disease Control and from local AIDS organizations.
- Explain clearly what the person's risks are (e.g., people with many sexual partners are at higher risk, regardless of sexual orientation; sharing needles with other intravenous drug users is very risky).
- Identify cues to high-risk situations (e.g., drinking alcohol in a sexually provocative situation is associated with higher-risk sexual behavior).
- Provide instruction in condom use (and, as appropriate, needle cleaning and exchanging).
- Provide social skills training that includes sexual assertiveness skills (e.g., resisting pressure to have sex or insisting that safer sex be practiced) and other communication skills that can help preserve relationships while reducing the risk of infection with HIV.
- Work at the community level to generate large-scale social support for making safer sex the expected thing, creating a "we're all in this together" atmosphere.

An early review (Chernoff, 1998) revealed that interventions implementing these principles often, but not always, leads to increases in sexual assertiveness, reductions in unprotected anal intercourse, and increased use of condoms in gay and bisexual men, low-income minority women, female prostitutes, and substance abusers. These programs also show some promise among high school and college-age students in the United States, but not with middle or junior high students.

A more recent meta-analysis (Albarracon et al., 2005) of over 300 prevention programs found that prevention programs were more likely to be effective if they included (1) educational information, (2) the positives associated with condom use (e.g., better relationship quality and health), (3) active (e.g., role-playing) rather than passive (e.g., lecture) interventions, and (4) behavioral skills training (e.g. how to use a condom, how to say no). Prevention programs that tried to induce fear into participants were least effective, particularly for people over the age of 21. School-based programs that included condom use skills and support for condom use by family and friends were also effective. A different meta-analysis concluded that prevention programs that included experts as group leaders (rather than peers) were more effective for some groups—gay men, partners of IV drug users, and commercial sex workers—but that laypeople were more effective than experts for other groups—IV drug users and heterosexuals with multiple sex partners (Durantini et al., 2006). Prevention programs for women were more effective when run by women; younger people responded better when group leaders were also young people; and people of color responded better when group leaders were also people of color. These findings suggest that a "one-size-fits-all" approach to HIV prevention will not work well.

AIDS prevention efforts are more successful if they include educational information and role playing. (Keith Dannemiller/©Corbis)

To illustrate the promise of HIV prevention programs, we describe two examples in some detail. One noteworthy study involved over 3,700 heterosexual men and women at the highest risk for HIV infection in 37 sexually transmitted disease (STD) clinics across the United States (NIMH Multisite HIV Prevention Trial Group, 1998). In this study, three-quarters of the participants were African American and the rest were Latino; most were unemployed and single. All met one or more of the following high-risk criteria: having sex with multiple partners, being infected with an STD, having sex with someone known to have multiple partners, having sex with an intravenous drug user, and having sex with someone known to be HIV-positive. A 4-week behavioral intervention applying several of the principles mentioned here, compared with a one-session information-only control group, led to significantly more reduction in unprotected sex, with some indications also of fewer cases of STDs over a 12-month period following the intervention. In addition, the estimated cost per person in the 4-week behavioral intervention was less than $300, which is equivalent to the cost of about 1 week of treatment with the AIDS medications.

An additional large study, the EXPLORE study, conducted across six U.S. cities, included nearly 4,300 men who have sex with men. The men were randomly assigned to either a prevention intervention group or a standard group. Men in the standard group received counseling two times a year on the risks associated with unprotected sex, as recommended by the Centers for Disease Control. Men in the prevention intervention group received 10 individual counseling sessions that focused on individual and social factors that contribute to risky sexual behaviors, such as alcohol and drugs, mood states, communication issues, and pleasure associated with risky sexual behavior. Counselors followed a treatment manual for each of the 10 sessions. At both 12 and 18 months after the interventions, men in the prevention intervention group tended to be less likely than men in the standard group to have been infected with HIV; however, the difference between the two groups in HIV infection rates was not statistically significant. Does this mean the intervention was not successful? Not necessarily. The men in the prevention intervention group engaged in fewer risky sexual behaviors, such as unprotected anal receptive sex and unprotected sex with an HIV-positive partner (EXPLORE Study Team, 2004).

Unfortunately, prevention efforts aimed at women have been less successful. A meta-analysis of all such studies found that despite an abundance of findings on social and contextual risk factors associated with women and HIV, there are few prevention intervention studies designed to address them. The studies that have been done to date do not yield very promising results (Logan, Cole, & Leukefeld, 2002). This is clearly an area in need of research, as women account for about half of the HIV infections worldwide, and the rates of HIV infection among women of color in the United States are much higher than among men or white women.

Quick Summary

The reasons people have hypertension are not well understood, but psychological factors such as Type A behavior pattern and anger as well as behavioral factors such as diet and exercise play a key role. Laboratory and naturalistic studies have shown that stress, anger, Type A, and cardiovascular reactivity all contribute to short-term increases in blood pressure. There is less research showing how these factors are linked to hypertension.

Type A behavior pattern has predicted CHD in some studies but not others. Researchers have looked at more specific components of Type A, and evidence suggests that anger, hostility, and cynicism may be important predictors of CHD. Anxiety and depression are also related to CHD. Cardiovascular reactivity and heart-rate variability are possible biological risk factors for CHD.

Asthma involves severe constriction of the airways; the air passages in the lungs become narrowed, causing extremely labored and wheezy breathing. There are many causes of asthma, several of which involve allergens or air pollutants. Psychological factors, such as stressful life events, negative emotions, and family conflict, may trigger attacks.

AIDS remains an epidemic worldwide, with over half of the 33 million people with HIV living in sub-Saharan Africa. Prevention has been a key focus of psychological researchers since the disease can be prevented with changes in behavior. Much work has been done to change risky sexual behaviors among gay and straight men as well as straight women. These programs have been effective in the short term, but longer-term follow-ups have not yet been conducted. Additional work is needed to develop effective prevention programs for adolescents.

Clinical Case: Juana

Juana was a 58-year-old veterinarian. She was slightly overweight but exercised regularly, did not smoke, and had only an occasional glass of wine with dinner. She had been happily married for 22 years, and her children were both in college. She enjoyed her job quite a bit, despite the long hours and the after-hours calls she often received from worried pet owners.

For several weeks, Juana had been experiencing fatigue and had found herself taking short naps during the day. She had had increasingly frequent bouts of indigestion, and occasionally she had become dizzy or lightheaded. She wondered if these were the beginning signs of menopause. She consulted with her doctor, who examined her and concluded that the symptoms would probably resolve on their own. If they didn't go away in a few weeks, the doctor said,

Juana should contact him again. About a week later, Juana began to experience shortness of breath. Then, on a long hike with her husband, she had a fainting spell. Thinking it was the heat, she dismissed it. The next night, she awoke from sleep feeling nauseous and sweaty. She was sure this was a symptom of menopause until she felt a shooting pain in her arm. She awakened her husband, and he took her to the hospital. An electrocardiogram revealed that Juana had had a small heart attack. The next day, Juana had an angiogram that showed three completely occluded coronary arteries. She needed bypass surgery. Beyond her concerns about her health, Juana was quite surprised by this turn of events—didn't heart attacks and heart disease affect men more than women, and shouldn't her doctor have diagnosed her condition?

Gender and Health

At every age from birth to 85 and older, more men die than women. Men are more than twice as likely to die in automobile accidents and of homicides, cirrhosis, heart disease, lung cancer and other lung diseases, and suicide. Women, however, have higher rates of morbidity (i.e., poor heath). That is, general poor health is more frequent among women, and women have a higher incidence of several specific diseases. For example, women have higher rates of diabetes, anemia, gastrointestinal problems, and rheumatoid arthritis; and they report more visits to physicians, use more prescription drugs, and account for two-thirds of all surgical procedures performed in the United States.

What are some of the possible reasons for the differences in mortality and morbidity rates in men and women? It might be that women have some biological mechanism that protects them from certain life-threatening diseases. For example, epidemiological and observational studies suggested that estrogen might offer protection from cardiovascular disease. Based on this evidence, many women began hormone replacement therapy (HRT) following menopause (when estrogen naturally declines) in an attempt to reduce the risk of cardiovascular disease. However, the first randomized clinical trial of HRT for postmenopausal women, called the Heart and Estrogen/Progestin Replacement Study, failed to find a reduced risk with respect to one type of cardiovascular disease—coronary heart disease (CHD) (Hulley et al., 1998).

A later randomized trial, called the Women's Health Initiative (WHI), began in 1993 with a sample of over 150,000 women. It was a large, prospective study designed to examine the effects of HRT as possible protective factors against osteoporosis, CHD, and cancer. One group of women was randomly assigned to receive estrogen plus progesterone therapy (combined therapy), another group was randomly assigned to receive estrogen only, and a third group was randomly assigned to receive a placebo. The researchers originally planned to follow women prospectively for 9 years. However, the study was stopped for women in the combined therapy group after 5 years because the data suggested that the combined treatment was *increasing* the risk of CHD, stroke, and breast cancer (Writing Group for the Women's Health Initiative Investigators, 2002). A follow-up assessment of these women was conducted 2 to 3 years after the study was stopped (Heiss et al., 2008). Women who had received the combined therapy were no longer at greater risk for developing CHD and stroke, but they still had a greater risk of developing breast cancer than those who had received placebo.

Research shows that women live longer than men but women have more health problems than men. (Thomas Langreder VISUM/The Image Works.)

The estrogen-only portion of the study was similarly discontinued after 7 years because there was no evidence for a decreased risk of CHD or breast cancer, though there was a protective effect for hip fractures, which are related to osteoporosis (WHI, 2004). Other findings from this large study suggested that neither form of hormone replacement therapy reduced the risk of dementia and that the combined therapy actually seemed to increase the risk (Shumaker et al., 2003, 2004). These findings may not be the last word on HRT. The WHI study was limited in that most of the women were postmenopausal, leaving open the possibility that HRT during the period of transition to menopause could afford some health benefits.

Early evidence suggested that women are less likely than men to exhibit the Type A behavior pattern and are also less hostile than men (Waldron, 1976; Weidner & Collins, 1993). Newer evidence, however, indicates that anger is not necessarily more commonly experienced and expressed by men (Kring, 2000; Lavoie et al., 2001). Moreover, increased hostility and both the suppression and expression of anger are associated with risk factors for CHD among women (Matthews et al., 1998; Rutledge et al., 2001). In addition, anxiety and depression are more common among women than men (see Chapters 5 and 8) and are also linked to cardiovascular disease (e.g., Suls & Bunde, 2005).

Another question concerns why the gap between mortality rates in men and women is decreasing. In the early twentieth century, most deaths were due to infectious diseases, but now most deaths result from diseases that are affected by lifestyle. One possibility, then, is that lifestyle differences between men and women account for the sex difference in mortality and that these lifestyle differences are decreasing. Although men still smoke more than women and consume more alcohol, women are catching up in their use of alcohol and cigarettes. Not surprisingly then, these behavior changes in women are paralleled by increases in lung cancer and by the failure of the mortality rate for cardiovascular disease to decrease among women (lung cancer has been the leading cause of cancer death among women since 1987). In 2004, a report issued by the National Women's Law Center and the Oregon Health and Sciences University, called "Making the Grade: A National and State-by-State Report Card," showed that 39 states received a failing grade in their efforts to curb smoking among women. Only one state, Utah, received a semisatisfactory grade (Waxman et al., 2004).

Other explanations focus on the identification and treatment of disease in women. For example, even though cardiovascular disease is the number one killer of women and more women than men have died from heart disease since 1984, there is still a widespread belief that men should be more concerned with heart disease than women, as Juana believed. Furthermore, a common diagnostic procedure for heart disease risk, the so-called stress test, which involves measuring heart rate while on a treadmill, is not a good predictor of heart problems among women (Mora et al., 2003), particularly women who do not have chest pains (L.J. Shaw et al., 2006).

In addition, a low dose of aspirin does not appear to prevent myocardial infarction in women as it does in men (though it does appear to prevent stroke in women, which is not true for men) (Ridker et al., 2005). Other research shows that women are less likely to be referred to a cardiovascular rehabilitation program following a heart attack, perhaps contributing to their persistent rates of mortality (Abbey & Stewart, 2000).

There are several possible explanations for the difference in morbidity of men and women. First, because women live longer than men, they may be more likely to experience certain diseases that are associated with aging. Second, women may be more attentive to their health than are men and thus may be more likely to visit physicians and be diagnosed. Third, women are exposed to more stress than men and they rate stress as having a greater impact on them, particularly stress related to major life events (Davis, Matthews, & Twamley, 1999). Fourth, physicians tend to treat women's health concerns and complaints less seriously than men's concerns, as Juana's physician appeared to do (Weisman & Teitelbaum, 1985). Finally, evidence indicates that women's morbidity differs depending on socioeconomic and demographic variables, such as income, education, and ethnicity. For example, having more education and a higher income are associated with fewer risk factors for cardiovascular disease, including obesity, smoking, hypertension, and reduced amounts of exercise. In the United States, women tend to have lower income than men. Also, 16.5 million women in the United States do not have health insurance. However, even after controlling for differences in income level and education, Mexican American and African American women still had a greater likelihood of having more risk factors for CHD than men (Winkleby et al., 1999). Furthermore, death from cardiovascular disease is more common among African American women than European American women (Casper et al., 2000).

Socioeconomic Status, Ethnicity, and Health

Low socioeconomic status (SES) is associated with higher rates of health problems and mortality from all causes. A number of explanations have been proposed for the correlation between SES and poor health and mortality, but many of these are still in need of empirical support. Recent research attempts to trace the connections between health and SES, encompassing economic, societal, relationship, individual, and biological factors. For example, one pathway to poor health has to do with environmental factors that reinforce poor health behaviors. Poorer neighborhoods often have high numbers of liquor stores, grocery stores offering fewer healthy food choices, and fewer opportunities for exercise at health clubs or parks. Given these environmental constraints, it is perhaps not surprising to learn that lower SES people are more likely than higher SES people to engage in behaviors that increase the risk of disease, such as smoking, eating fewer fruits and vegetables, and drinking more alcohol (Lantz et al., 1998).

Other pathways include limited access to health services and greater exposure to stressors. Recall our earlier discussion of allostatic load, the bodily effects of repeated and chronic stress. In a longitudinal study, researchers found that people who were the most economically disadvantaged had the highest allostatic load (Singer & Ryff, 1999). These investigators also found that, regardless of SES, people who reported having poor relationships with parents or negative relationships with spouses had a higher allostatic load than people with positive parental and spousal relationships. Not surprisingly, the combination of lower SES and negative relationships had the greatest effect on allostatic load. These findings indicate that lower SES is a likely source of chronic stress that impacts the body. They also illustrate the complicated relationship of individual, social, and economic factors with health.

Certainly discrimination and prejudice are sources of chronic stress, and these abhorrent social conditions continue to affect people of color as well as people of lower SES and, in turn, impact health (Mayes, Cochran, & Barnes, 2007). Since people of color are found in high numbers among lower SES groups, ethnicity has also been a feature of research into the relationship of SES to health. Consider, for example, that the mortality rate for African Americans is nearly two times as high as it is for whites in the United States (Williams, 1999). Why might this be? The reasons are complex and not completely understood. Some research suggests that certain risk factors for disease are more common in people of color. For example, risk factors for cardiovascular disease (such as smoking, obesity, hypertension, and reduced exercise) are higher among women from ethnic minorities than among white women. This finding holds even when members of the two groups are comparable in SES (Winkleby et al., 1998). The increased prevalence of some of these risk factors shows up in studies of children as young as 6 to 9 years of age. For example, African American and Mexican American girls in this age range have higher body mass indexes and higher fat intake than do non-Hispanic white girls (Winkleby et al., 1999). Other studies have found that increased stress associated with discrimination is linked to cardiovascular reactivity among African American women (Guyll, Matthews, & Bromberger, 2001). Consideration of SES at multiple levels, including the individual, family, and neighborhood, is also important (Mayes et al., 2007). For example, lower family SES and neighborhood SES were found to be associated with greater cardiovascular reactivity for African American children and adolescents, but only lower family SES was associated with greater cardiovascular reactivity among white children and adolescents (Gump et al., 1999). In sum, both SES and ethnicity are important factors in health.

Ethnicity is also an important factor in how people cope with cancer, and it is associated with detection of illness, adherence to treatment regimens, survival, and quality of life (these relationships were examined in a review by Meyerowitz et al., 1998). Among the many ethnicity-related findings based on data from the National Cancer Institute are the following:

- African Americans have the highest rates of cancer overall, as a result of very high rates of lung and prostate cancer among men.

- Although African American women have lower breast cancer rates than do white women, their mortality rates 5 years after diagnosis are the same because their survival rates are lower.

- Latino men and women have low rates of cancer in general, but Latina women have high rates of cervical cancer.

- Asian Americans have low rates for all cancers except stomach cancer. These and other findings are illustrative of ethnic differences in the incidence and outcomes of cancer. What might account for these differences? The answers appear to lie less with ethnic and biological factors than with social and psychological factors such as access to and willingness to seek out medical care (e.g., Bach et al., 1999).

As one might expect, the ability to afford health care is not uniform across ethnic and socioeconomic lines. The years of research on SES and health have clearly demonstrated that there is a linear relationship between morbidity/mortality and SES: the higher the SES, the better the health. But the reasons this is so are less clear. Taken together, the explanations posited above can account for part of the relationship between SES and health, but not all. Investigators are now proposing models that cut across these different explanations in an effort to do a better job of accounting for the SES–health link.

Poverty is stressful and is associated with poor health. (Jeff Greenberg/PhotoEdit.)

Quick Summary

Women live longer than men, yet women have poorer health than men. Researchers wondered if sex hormones might protect women from death, but controlled studies of estrogen replacement failed to show that it decreased risk for CHD. Men may be more likely than women to exhibit the Type A behavior pattern, but there are few gender differences in anger, and women are more likely to experience anxiety and depression. Even though CHD is the number one killer of women, some diagnostic procedures (e.g., stress test) and preventative measures (e.g., aspirin therapy) are not as effective for women as they are for men. Women may have poorer health than men because they live longer. Lower socioeconomic status (SES) is associated with poorer health, and women are more likely than men to have lower SES.

The reasons lower SES is linked to poorer health are many and include environmental factors such as limited resources in poorer neighborhoods, greater stress associated with lower SES, less social support, discrimination, and less access to health care. Ethnicity impacts some diseases, such as cancer, but the reasons for this are not well understood. Some differences attributed to ethnicity may have more to do with SES.

Check Your Knowledge 7.4

True or false?

1. Negative emotions don't exacerbate asthma attacks.
2. HIV prevention efforts that emphasize monogamous relationships have been highly successful in Africa.
3. HIV prevention programs have shown promise in the short term, except among young adolescents.
4. Among the reasons women may have poorer health than men is that their concerns are not taken as seriously by doctors.
5. Higher SES is associated with greater allostatic load.

Treatment of Psychological Factors Affecting Medical Conditions

Whether high blood pressure is biologically caused or, as in essential hypertension, linked to psychological stress, a number of medications can reduce it. Asthma attacks can also be alleviated by medications, taken either by inhalation or injection, which dilate the bronchial tubes. The help drugs provide in ameliorating damage and discomfort in particular bodily systems cannot be underestimated. They are frequently lifesaving. Mental health and medical professionals recognize, however, that most drug interventions do not address the fact that the person is reacting to psychological stress. Therapists of all persuasions agree that reducing anxiety, depression, and anger is important for health.

Treating Hypertension and Reducing the Risk of Coronary Heart Disease

Before the advent of effective drugs for treating hypertension in the late 1950s, physicians generally advised patients basically to "take it easy," lose weight, and restrict salt intake—all reasonably helpful measures. It is noteworthy that simple verbal reassurance was also considered important and was even demonstrated to be helpful in an early study (Reiser et al., 1950) in which non-psychiatrically-trained internists (physicians specializing in internal medicine, which includes the diagnosis and treatment of hypertension) provided what we today call nonspecific supportive psychotherapy. Clinically significant reductions in blood pressure were observed after 2 years of regular, albeit infrequent, contact.

The advent of effective drugs to lower blood pressure shifted the direction of treatment strongly toward their use from the 1960s onward. But over time the undesirable side effects of these medications—drowsiness, lightheadedness, and, in men, erectile difficulties—as well as the growth of behavioral approaches to treatment led many investigators to explore nonpharmacological treatments for borderline essential hypertension. Successful nonpharmacological efforts have been directed at losing weight, restricting salt intake, giving up cigarettes, exercising regularly, and reducing alcohol consumption. Still, those with more severe hypertension usually have to take drugs to control its deleterious long-term effects.

Two out of three Americans over the age of 60 have high blood pressure, and more than half of them take costly and sometimes risky hypertensive medication (risky because all drugs pose particularly serious risks to older people). As just mentioned, the importance of losing weight and reducing salt intake has been recognized for many years as useful in keeping blood pressure under control, but until recently there was little optimism that diet and weight loss could play a positive role among older adults, who often have had undesirable dietary habits for a lifetime.

A report from TONE, the controlled Trial of Nonpharmacologic Interventions in the Elderly (Whelton et al., 1998), indicated for the first time that significant benefits can be achieved by people between the ages of 60 and 80 who are obese and who are taking blood pressure medication. Specifically, half the overweight people in the study who reduced their salt intake by 25 percent and lost as little as 8 pounds over the course of 3 months were able to come off their antihypertensive medications and maintain normal blood pressure. The ability to maintain normal blood pressure was achieved by 31 percent of the patients who reduced their salt intake,

36 percent of those who lost weight, and more than half of those who reduced both their salt intake and their weight. Furthermore, these results—the dietary and weight changes as well as the maintenance of normal blood pressure without medication—lasted for more than 3 years.

Research has shown that increasing exercise—for example, walking up stairs rather than using an elevator, and walking short distances rather than driving—yields as much cardiovascular benefit as a structured program of aerobic exercise (Whelton et al., 2002). Other research indicates that people with essential hypertension, as well as those whose blood pressure is within the normal range, should adopt regular exercise habits, such as walking briskly almost every day for about half an hour or engaging in other aerobic exercise that raises the heart and respiration rates (Whelton et al., 2002). Most people can engage in such activity without even checking with their physician if the activity is not so strenuous that it prevents them from carrying on a conversation at the same time. In fact, the research suggests that people with high blood pressure and no other health complications should try exercise for about a year before turning to drugs to lower their blood pressure. For those already taking antihypertension drugs, a regular and not necessarily strenuous exercise regimen can sometimes reduce or even eliminate their dependence on medication. Decreases of 10 points in both systolic and diastolic blood pressure—a significant reduction—can be achieved by most people after just a few weeks. All these beneficial results may be mediated by the favorable effects that exercise has on stress, weight, and blood cholesterol. And if the sense of well-being that accompanies regular exercise and weight loss generalizes to the adoption of other health-enhancing habits, such as stopping smoking and avoiding drinking to excess, the positive effects on blood pressure will be stronger and more enduring.

Exercise, such as walking briskly, can help to reduce blood pressure. (Ariel Skelley/Corbis Images.)

Exercising regularly can also reduce mortality from cardiovascular disease (Blumenthal et al., 2002; Wannamethee, Shaper, & Walker, 1998). One study compared a stress-management intervention with an exercise intervention for men who had a history of CHD (Blumenthal et al., 2002). Patients were randomly assigned to either a weekly stress-management group, an aerobic exercise group, or a no-treatment group. The interventions lasted for 4 months. Five years after the intervention, the men who had received stress-management training or exercise were significantly less likely to have had another cardiac problem than the men who did not receive treatment.

Evidence suggesting the importance of cognitive change, as well as the role of anger, has been reported. Borderline hypertensive patients who achieved significant reductions in angry thoughts showed decreases in blood pressure—as their articulated thoughts became less angry, their blood pressure became lower (Davison, Haaga, et al., 1991). This finding is consistent with the research discussed earlier linking anger with hypertension.

Reducing Anger and Hostility, Depression, and Social Isolation

Reducing anger and hostility has been a focus of behavioral medicine interventions for many years, especially in hypertension and coronary heart disease. These studies generally involved men who had suffered a heart attack, and the focus was on reducing the likelihood that they would have a second one.

Early programs focused on reducing Type A behavior (Friedman et al., 1982). As evidence now shows that the hostility component of Type A behavior is most predictive (Williams, 2001), researchers have targeted hostility more specifically. In one study, men who had experienced myocardial infarction were randomly assigned to a hostility reduction treatment or an information-only treatment. Men who received the hostility treatment reported less hostility, were rated as less hostile, and evidenced a decrease in diastolic blood pressure (Gidron, Davidson, & Bata, 1999).

The focus on anger and hostility has been widened to include depression and social isolation, also discovered to be risk factors in cardiovascular disorders as well as in other illnesses. The Enhancing Recovery in Coronary Heart Disease (ENRICHD) project targeted depression and social isolation among people recovering from myocardial infarction. Although the treatment was successful in reducing depression and social isolation, those in the treatment group did not have better heart health at the end of the study compared to the control group (Writing Committee for the ENRICHD Investigators, 2003). See Focus on Discovery 7.1 for a discussion of coping with cancer.

FOCUS ON DISCOVERY 7.1

Coping with Cancer

An optimistic, upbeat attitude can be important in combating illness, including illnesses as serious as cancer (Carver et al., 1993) and HIV-positive status (Taylor et al., 1992). The mechanism by which an optimistic attitude helps people with life-threatening illnesses may be its link to adaptive coping. Optimistic people may be more likely to engage in risk-reducing behaviors such as avoiding risky sex or engaging in prescribed regular exercise following coronary bypass surgery (Scheier & Carver, 1987).

Psychological Interventions to Help People Cope

Problem-solving therapy (PST) has shown its value in helping cancer patients cope with the myriad life challenges facing them, from daily hassles to dealing with isolation and depression (Nezu et al., 1997). An important component of PST is that it gives patients an enhanced sense of control, which seems to be particularly important for people with a life-threatening illness who are experiencing the side effects of treatment. PST has also been shown to be helpful for caregivers, who have to cope with the patient's many cancer-related problems, including fears about death, severe fatigue, and medication side effects such as hair loss (Bucher et al., 1999).

The stressfulness of a cancer diagnosis and its treatment makes stress-management approaches relevant, like those described earlier. Clear information about the treatment procedures themselves, including what the patient is likely to experience during and following treatment, as well as training in relaxation and hypnosis, can be helpful in reducing anxiety both prior to and following various cancer treatments. It is especially important that patients understand that fatigue is a natural accompaniment of many treatments for cancer, especially radiation and chemotherapy. A common side effect is conditioned food aversions that result from associating certain foods with nausea from chemotherapy or radiation (Chambers & Bernstein, 1995).

Interventions to Encourage Prevention

Psychological interventions also focus on preventing cancer by encouraging healthy behaviors and discouraging unhealthy ones. For example, logical programs to help people stop smoking are discussed in Chapter 10. Other interventions are aimed at getting women to perform breast self-examination (BSE). The main hurdle in accomplishing this is that BSE significantly raises the probability of an aversive consequence, that is, finding a lump. Logically, it is better to take this risk than not, but the fact is that the fear of learning something unpleasant is a major deterrent to doing the exam (Mahoney, 1977). For the same reason, many high-risk women (those with first-degree relatives who had breast cancer) do not have regular mammograms (Vogel et al., 1990).

In an effort to develop ways to help women perform BSE regularly, researchers compared two pamphlets on BSE (Meyerowitz & Chaiken, 1987). One contained persuasive arguments for performing BSE while emphasizing the negative consequences of not performing BSE; the other emphasized the positive consequences of performing BSE. Both pamphlets also contained factual information about breast cancer and instructions about how to do BSE. In the following examples from these pamphlets, words in parentheses were included in the positive condition, those in brackets in the negative.

By [not] doing BSE now, you (can) [will not] learn what your normal healthy breasts feel like so that you will be (better) [ill] prepared to notice any small, abnormal changes that might occur as you get older.

Research shows that women who (do) [do not do] BSE have (an increased) [a decreased] chance of finding a tumor in the early, more treatable stage of the disease. (Meyerowitz & Chaiken, 1987, p. 504)

Stress Management

Stress management is a set of techniques for helping people who are seldom labeled as patients (e.g., hospital personnel, factory workers, and students) to cope with the challenges that life poses for all of us. Stress management has also been used successfully for several specific diseases, including tension headaches, cancer, hypertension, AIDS, coronary heart disease, and chronic pain (e.g., Antoni et al., 2000). For CHD, stress management is most effective when the intervention focuses on behavioral targets, such as quitting smoking, exercising regularly, and reducing blood pressure (Dusseldorp et al., 1999).

Stress management encompasses a variety of techniques, and more than one is typically used in any given instance (Davison & Thompson, 1988; Lehrer & Woolfolk, 1993; Steptoe, 1997). Techniques include the following:

- *Relaxation training.* The most common form of relaxation training is progressive muscle relaxation, which involves systematically tensing and then relaxing each major muscle group

A community psychology approach to stress management focuses on the environment rather than on the person. To reduce stress, an office can be redesigned with partitions to provide some privacy for employees. (Dick Luria/Photo Researchers, Inc.)

The groups given the different pamphlets did not differ in their attitudes toward BSE immediately after reading the pamphlets. However, four months later, women who had received the negatively framed information were more likely to have engaged in BSE. This effect may have occurred because those who do not engage in regular BSE take an ignorance-is-bliss attitude, but by making the possible negative consequences of not doing BSE more salient, the pamphlet made doing the exam more acceptable. This finding is particularly important because most information intended to help women do BSE stress the positive rather than the negative.

Other researchers extended this work by asking whether messages of the kind that were found effective in encouraging BSE—sometimes referred to as "loss-frame" communications—might under certain circumstances be less effective than messages that emphasize the benefits of a certain behavior (referred to as "gain-frame" messages). The results from two experiments suggest that loss-frame communications are superior when people are being encouraged to detect signs of illness, while gain-frame communications are better when people are being encouraged to prevent illness (Rothman & Salovey, 1997).

What is the difference? BSE and mammography are designed to detect signs of illness. The person lacks information about whether she has an illness and has to decide whether to engage in

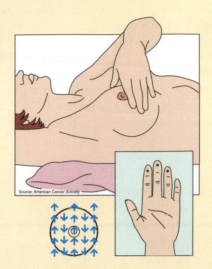

Encouraging women to perform breast self-examination (BSE) can lead to earlier detection of cancer and better treatment outcomes. Shown here is an advertisement from the American Cancer Society demonstrating how to perform BSE.

behavior that could provide information on her status, in this case, whether she might have breast cancer. In contrast, a person going to the beach has a choice about putting on sunscreen with a protection factor of 15 or greater, the strength recommended to reduce the chances of getting skin cancer in the future. Such behavior is preventive in nature, that is, it is designed to have a direct effect on reducing the chances of getting skin cancer.

In a study that replicated the findings of Meyerowitz and Chaiken, women told of the risks arising from not taking a mammography exam—the loss-frame approach—were more likely to have a mammogram than were women told of the benefits of doing so (Banks et al., 1995). In a later study, sunbathers at a beach who were told of the benefits of using sunscreen—a gain-frame communication—were more likely to use sunscreen after reading a communication that emphasized the benefits of such preventive health behavior than were those who read something that focused on the risks of not using sunscreen (Detweiler et al., 1999).

The implications of these studies are important. If one wants to foster healthful detection-related behaviors, one should emphasize the risks associated with not taking a certain action that could detect a problem. But if one wants to foster healthful preventive behaviors, it is best to emphasize the benefits that arise from doing something that can forestall a problem.

in the body. Teaching people to relax deeply and to apply these skills to real-life stressors can be helpful in lowering their stress levels. There is also evidence that the immune function can be improved by relaxation training (Jasnoski & Kugler, 1987; Kiecolt-Glaser et al., 1985), although enduring benefits are doubtful unless relaxation is practiced regularly over a long period of time (Davison & Thompson, 1988; Goldfried & Davison, 1994).

- *Cognitive restructuring.* Cognitive restructuring includes approaches to alter people's belief systems and reduce the negativity of their interpretations of experience. Providing information to reduce uncertainty and enhance the person's sense of control has also been helpful in reducing stress.

- *Behavioral skills training.* Because it is natural to feel overwhelmed if one lacks the skills to execute a challenging task, stress management often includes instruction and practice in skills such as time management and effective prioritizing. Also included under this rubric is training in assertion skills—expressing likes and dislikes without encroaching on the rights of others.

- *Environmental-change approaches.* Whereas the other individual strategies aim at helping the person deal with a particular environment, environmental-change approaches take the position that sometimes the environment is the problem and that efforts are best directed at altering it. One kind of environmental approach draws on research on the positive role of social support on health. If social support helps keep people healthy or helps them cope with illnesses, then it is reasonable to assume that enhancing such support can only be beneficial. Another kind of environmental change involves the workplace. Altering management practices or providing greater privacy and fewer interruptions can reduce stress in the world where people work and live for a significant portion of their waking hours (Murphy et al., 1995).

Cognitive Behavioral Interventions

Cognitive behavioral interventions have shown some success. For asthma sufferers, behavioral treatments that emphasize breathing training are associated with taking fewer medications, but they do not really improve lung functioning significantly (Ritz & Roth, 2003). For men and women with AIDS, group-based cognitive behavioral treatments have been effective in reducing distress, increasing coping and perceived social support, and reducing depression (Lechner et al., 2003; Lutgendorf et al., 1997). Bereavement group therapy for HIV-positive gay men who had lost a partner or close friend to AIDS was beneficial in decreasing distress and viral load, a biological predictor of the progression to AIDS (Goodkin et al., 2001).

Check Your Knowledge 7.5

True or False?
1. Behavioral interventions aimed at reducing salt intake and increasing exercise are effective in reducing CHD risk.
2. Stress management involves arousal reduction, cognitive restructuring, behavioral skills training, and environmental change.
3. Cognitive behavioral approaches have been shown to be effective with AIDS and, to a lesser extent, asthma.

Summary

- Psychological factors affecting a medical condition refers to diseases produced or influenced in part by psychological factors, including stress, social support, and negative emotions.
- In attempting to understand the complex stress–illness relationship, researchers have focused on precisely defining what stress is, on assessing differences in how people cope with perceived stress, and on how social support impacts the stress–illness relationship.
- Theories of the stress–illness relationship are diathesis–stress in nature but differ in whether the diathesis is described in psychological or neurobiological terms. Theories emphasizing a neurobiological diathesis emphasize the effects of allostatic load or changes in the immune system that are caused by stress. Theories emphasizing a psychological diathesis focus on such factors as emotional states, personality traits, cognitive appraisals, and specific styles of coping with stress. The most successful accounts of etiology are those that integrate psychological and neurobiological factors.

- Cardiovascular disorders, which involve the heart and circulatory system, include essential hypertension and coronary heart disease (CHD). While both conditions are complex and multifaceted, their etiologies appear to include a tendency to respond to stress with increases in blood pressure or heart rate. Anger, hostility, cynicism, anxiety, and depression are linked to these conditions.
- People with asthma tend to have respiratory systems that overrespond to allergens or that have been weakened by prior infection. Psychological factors such as anxiety, anger, depression, stressful life events, and family conflict may trigger an asthma attack.
- Acquired immunodeficiency syndrome (AIDS) has psychological elements in that it can be preventable by psychological means. The primary focus of prevention is to change people's behavior—specifically, to encourage safer sex and to discourage the sharing of needles in intravenous substance abuse.

- Treatment for CHD, hypertension, asthma, and AIDS usually includes medication. The general aim of psychotherapies for these disorders is to reduce stress, anxiety, depression, or anger.
- Researchers in the field of behavioral medicine try to find psychological interventions that can improve patients' physiological state by changing unhealthy behaviors and reducing stress. They have developed ways of helping people relax, smoke less, eat fewer unhealthy foods, and engage in behaviors that can prevent or alleviate illnesses, such as encouraging breast self-examination and adhering to medical treatment recommendations.
- Stress management interventions help teach people techniques to cope with stress and thereby ameliorate the toll that stress can take on the body.

Answers to Check Your Knowledge Questions

7.1 1. a; 2. b; 3. d

7.2 1. T; 2. F; 3. T; 4. F

7.3 1. Essential or primary; 2. essential hypertension, CHD; 3. blood pressure, hypertension

7.4 1. F; 2. F; 3. T; 4. T; 5. F

7.5 1. T; 2. T; 3. T

Key Terms

AIDS (acquired immuno deficiency syndrome)
allostatic load
anger-in theory
angina pectoris
asthma

behavioral medicine
cardiovascular disorders
coping
coronary heart disease (CHD)
cytokines
essential hypertension

functional social support
health psychology
interleukin-6 (IL-6)
metabolic syndrome
myocardial infarction

psychological factors affecting medical condition
psychoneuroimmunology
stress management
structural social support
Type A behavior pattern

8 Mood Disorders

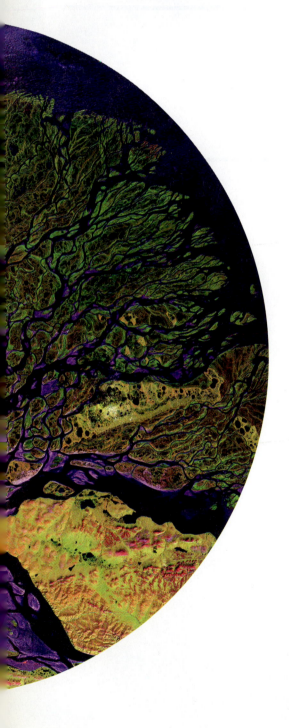

LEARNING GOALS

1. Be able to describe the symptoms of depression and mania, the diagnostic criteria for depressive disorders and bipolar disorders, and the epidemiology of these disorders.
2. Be able to discuss the genetic, neurobiological, social, and psychological factors that contribute to the mood disorders.
3. Be able to identify the medication and psychological treatments of depressive and manic symptoms as well as the current views of electroconvulsive therapy.
4. Be able to explain the epidemiology of suicide as well as the neurobiological, social, and psychological risk factors associated with suicide and the methods for preventing suicide.

Clinical Case: Mary

Mary M., a 38-year-old mother of four children, had been deeply depressed for about 2 months when she first went to see a psychologist. Three years earlier, she had returned to work when health care bills made it hard for her family to get by on her husband's income as a high school teacher. About 7 months before her visit to the psychologist, she was laid off from her job as an administrative assistant, which was a serious blow to the family's finances. She felt guilty about the loss of her job and became preoccupied with signs of her overall incompetence. Each night, she struggled for more than an hour to fall asleep, only to wake up frequently throughout the night. She had little appetite and as a result had lost 10 pounds. She also had little energy for and no interest in activities that she had enjoyed in the past. Household chores became impossible for her to do, and her husband began to complain. Their marriage had already been strained for two years, and her negativity and lack of energy contributed to further arguments. Finally, realizing that something serious had happened to his wife, Mr. M. cajoled her into making an appointment with a psychologist. (You will read about the outcome of Mary's treatment later in this chapter.)

MOOD DISORDERS INVOLVE DISABLING disturbances in emotion—from the extreme sadness and disengagement of depression to the extreme elation and irritability of mania. In this chapter, we begin by discussing the clinical description and the epidemiology of the different mood disorders. Next, we consider various perspectives on the etiology of these disorders, and then we consider approaches to treating them. We conclude with an examination of suicide, an action far too often associated with mood disorders.

Clinical Descriptions and Epidemiology of Mood Disorders

DSM-IV-TR recognizes two broad types of **mood disorders**: those that involve only depressive symptoms and those that involve manic symptoms (bipolar disorders). We begin by considering the signs of depression, the formal criteria for diagnosis of the depressive disorders (including major depressive disorder and dysthymic disorder), and the epidemiology and consequences of depressive disorders. Then we turn to bipolar disorders. There, we describe the signs of mania, followed by the formal criteria for diagnosing bipolar I disorder, bipolar II disorder, and cyclothymic disorder, and then the epidemiology and consequences of bipolar disorders. Table 8.1 presents a summary of the symptoms of each of these disorders. After covering the basic diagnostic categories, we describe DSM-IV-TR subtypes that are used to further define depressive disorders and bipolar disorders.

Depressive Disorders

The cardinal symptoms of depression include profound sadness and/or an inability to experience pleasure. Most of us experience sadness during our lives, and most of us say that we are "depressed" at one time or another. But most of these experiences do not have the intensity and duration to be diagnosable. The author William Styron (1992) wrote about his depression, "Like anyone else I have always had times when I felt deeply depressed, but this was something altogether new in my experience—a despairing, unchanging paralysis of the spirit beyond anything I had ever known or imagined could exist."

When people develop a depressive disorder, their heads may reverberate with self-recriminations. Like Mary, described in the clinical case, they may become focused on their flaws and deficits. Paying attention can be so exhausting that they have difficulty absorbing what they read and hear. They often view things in a very negative light, and they tend to lose hope.

Physical symptoms of depression are also common, including fatigue and low energy as well as physical aches and pains. These symptoms can be profound enough to convince afflicted persons that they must be suffering from some serious medical condition, even though the symptoms have no apparent physical cause (Simon et al., 1999). Although people with depression typically feel exhausted, they may find it hard to fall asleep and may wake up frequently. Other people sleep throughout the day. They may find that food

Some people with depression have trouble falling asleep and staying asleep. Others find themselves sleeping for more than 10 hours but still feeling exhausted. (Shannon Fagan/Stone/Getty Images.)

Table 8.1 A Summary of Mood Disorder Diagnoses			
Depressive Disorders	**Diagnostic Criteria**	**Bipolar Disorders**	**Diagnostic Criteria**
Major depressive disorder	Sad mood or loss of pleasure for 2 weeks, along with at least four other symptoms	Bipolar I disorder	At least one lifetime manic or mixed episode
		Bipolar II disorder	At least one lifetime episode of hypomania and episodes of major depression
Dysthymic disorder	Mood is down and other symptoms are present at least 50 percent of the time for at least 2 years	Cyclothymic disorder	Recurrent mood changes from high to low, without manic episodes for at least 2 years

tastes bland or that their appetite is gone, or they may experience an increase in appetite. Sexual interest disappears. Some may find their limbs feel heavy. Thoughts and movements may slow for some (*psychomotor retardation*), but others cannot sit still—they pace, fidget, and wring their hands (*psychomotor agitation*). Beyond these cognitive and physical symptoms, initiative may disappear. Social withdrawal is common; many prefer to sit alone and be silent. Some people with depression neglect their appearance. When people become utterly dejected and hopeless, thoughts about suicide are common.

Major Depressive Disorder   The DSM-IV-TR diagnosis of **major depressive disorder (MDD)** requires depressive symptoms to be present for at least 2 weeks. These symptoms must include either depressed mood or loss of interest and pleasure. As shown in the DSM-IV-TR criteria, at least four additional symptoms must be present, such as changes in sleep, appetite, concentration or decision-making, feelings of worthlessness, suicidality, or psychomotor agitation or retardation.

MDD is called an **episodic disorder**, because symptoms tend to be present for a period of time and then clear. Even though episodes tend to dissipate over time, an untreated episode may stretch on for 5 months or even longer. For a small percentage of people, the depression becomes chronic—the person does not completely snap back to the prior level of functioning. Even among those who improve enough that they no longer meet the criteria for diagnosis of MDD, some people experience subclinical depression for years (Judd et al., 1998).

Major depressive episodes tend to recur—once a given episode clears, a person is likely to experience another episode. About two-thirds of people with an episode of major depression will experience at least one more episode during their lifetime (Solomon et al., 2000). The average number of episodes is about four (Judd, 1997). With every new episode that a person experiences, his or her risk for experiencing another episode goes up by 16 percent (Solomon et al., 2000).

There is controversy about whether a person with five symptoms lasting two weeks (i.e., someone who meets the criteria for diagnosis with MDD) is distinctly different from someone who has only three symptoms for 10 days (i.e., someone who meets the criteria for so-called *subclinical depression*). A study of twins found that subclinical depression predicted the occurrence of future episodes of MDD and even the diagnosis of MDD in a co-twin. That is, when one twin had subclinical depression, both twins were likely to have future episodes of major depression (Kendler & Gardner, 1998). Another study found that subclinical depression resulted in as much trouble functioning in everyday activities as did a diagnosis of MDD (Gotlib, Lewinsohn, & Seeley, 1995).

Dysthymic Disorder   People with **dysthymic disorder** (also called *dysthymia*) are chronically depressed—more than half of the time for at least two years, they feel blue or derive little pleasure from usual activities and pastimes. In addition, they have at least two of the other symptoms of depression. DSM-IV-TR distinguishes dysthymia from MDD by the initial duration, type, and number of symptoms. Compare the diagnostic criteria for MDD and dysthymic disorder—note that one of the diagnostic criteria for dysthymia is that the person does not have enough symptoms to warrant a diagnosis of MDD. Over time, though, symptoms of dysthymic disorder tend to worsen if people do not receive treatment; in a 10-year follow-up study, 95 percent of patients with dysthymic disorder developed MDD (Klein, Shankman, & Rose, 2006). The key difference between dysthymic disorder and MDD is chronicity.

Kirsten Dunst has described her problems with major depressive disorder (MDD). One out of every five women will experience an episode of depression during her lifetime. (Allstar Picture Library/Alamy.)

Epidemiology and Consequences of Depressive Disorders   MDD is one of the most prevalent psychiatric disorders. One large-scale epidemiological study in the United States estimated that 16.2 percent of people meet the criteria for diagnosis of MDD at some point in their lives (Kessler Berglund, et al., 2005). Dysthymia is rarer than MDD: about 2.5 percent of people meet criteria for dysthymia during their lives (Kessler et al., 2005).

MDD is approximately two times more common among women than among men (see Focus on Discovery 8.1 for a discussion of possible reasons for this gender difference in rates of MDD). Socioeconomic status also matters—that is, MDD is three times as common among people who are impoverished compared to those who are not (Kessler et al., 2005).

The prevalence of depression varies considerably across cultures. In a major cross-cultural study using the same diagnostic criteria and structured interview in each country, prevalence of MDD varied from a low of 1.5 percent in Taiwan to a high of 19 percent in Beirut, Lebanon (Weissman et al., 1996). Similar findings have emerged in a study of depression rates among 26,000 people receiving care through primary care doctors in 14 countries (Simon et al., 2002). Another study yielded the intriguing result that people who have moved to the United States from Mexico have lower rates of MDD and other psychiatric disorders than do people of Mexican descent who were born in the United States (Vega et al., 1998). Why? People have speculated that traditional Mexican

FOCUS ON DISCOVERY 8.1

Gender Differences in Depression

Major depression occurs about twice as often in women as in men. Similar gender ratios in the prevalence of depression have been documented in many countries around the world, including the United States, France, Lebanon, and New Zealand (Weissman & Olfson, 1995). Intriguingly, the ratio does not hold in some cultural groups. For example, this gender difference does not hold between Jewish adults, because depression is more common among Jewish men than among other men (Levav et al., 1997). But for most ethnic and cultural groups, a clear gender difference in MDD begins to emerge during early adolescence and is documented consistently by late adolescence. Some of you might wonder if these findings just reflect a tendency for men to be less likely to describe symptoms. So far, evidence does not support that idea (Kessler, 2003). Although a fair amount of research has focused on hormonal factors that could explain the vulnerability of women, findings have been mixed for this idea, too (Brems, 1995). Several social and psychological factors may help explain this gender difference (Nolen-Hoeksema, 2001):

- Twice as many girls as boys are exposed to childhood sexual abuse.
- During adulthood, women are more likely than men to be exposed to chronic stressors such as poverty and caretaker responsibilities.
- Acceptance of established social roles among girls may intensify self-critical attitudes about appearance. Adolescent girls worry more than adolescent boys about their body image, a factor that does appear tied to depression (Hankin & Abramson, 2001).

The gender difference in depression does not emerge until adolescence. At that time, young women encounter many stressors and more pressure concerning social roles and body image, and they tend to ruminate about the resulting negative feelings. (Jeff Greenberg/Photo Researchers.)

- Social roles may interfere with pursuit of some potentially rewarding activities that are not considered "feminine."
- Exposure to childhood and chronic stressors, as well as the effects of female hormones, could change the reactivity of the HPA axis, a biological system guiding reactions to stress.
- A focus on gaining approval and closeness within interpersonal relationships, which is more commonly endorsed by women, may intensify reactions to interpersonal stressors (Hankin, Mermelstein, & Roesch, 2007).
- Social roles promote emotion-focused coping among women, which may then extend the duration of sad moods after major stressors. More specifically, women tend to spend more time ruminating about sad moods or wondering about the reasons why unhappy events have occurred. Men tend to spend more time using distracting or action-focused coping, such as playing a sport or engaging in other activities that shake off the sad mood. A fair amount of research suggests that rumination will intensify and prolong sad moods (Nolen-Hoeksema, Morrow, & Fredrickson, 1993).

In all likelihood, gender differences in depression are related to multiple factors. In considering these issues, bear in mind that men are more likely to demonstrate other types of disorders, such as alcohol and substance abuse as well as and antisocial personality disorder (Kessler et al., 1994). Hence, understanding gender differences in psychopathology is likely to require attending to many different risk factors and syndromes.

FOCUS ON DISCOVERY 8.2

Seasonal Affective Disorder: The Winter Blues

Criteria for the seasonal subtype of MDD specify that a person experiences depression during two consecutive winters and that the symptoms clear during the summer. These winter depressions appear to be much more common in northern climates than southern climates; while less than 2 percent of people living in sunny Florida report these patterns, about 10 percent of people living in New Hampshire report **seasonal affective disorder** (Rosen et al., 1990).

For mammals living in the wild, a slower metabolism in the winter could have been a lifesaver during periods of scarce food. For some unlucky humans, though, this same mechanism might contribute to seasonal affective disorder. It is believed that seasonal affective disorder is related to changes in the levels of melatonin in the brain. Melatonin is exquisitely sensitive to light and dark cycles and is only released during dark periods. People with seasonal affective disorder show greater changes in melatonin in the winter than do people without seasonal affective disorder (Wehr et al., 2001).

This woman is having light therapy, which is an effective treatment for patients with seasonal depression. (David White /Alamy.)

Fortunately, several treatment options are available for seasonal affective disorder. Like other subtypes of depression, seasonal affective disorder responds to antidepressant medications and cognitive behavioral therapy (Rohan et al., 2007). Winter blues, though, are as likely to remit with 30 minutes of bright light each morning as with fluoxetine (Prozac) (Lam et al., 2006). At least eight high-quality studies have examined bright light as a treatment for seasonal affective disorder (Golden et al., 2005), and it is established as a first-line recommendation in the American Psychiatric Association treatment guidelines for depression.

In one surprising finding, researchers were trying to find a good control condition to compare to bright light. To have a similar apparatus, they used negative air ionizers. Researchers were surprised when the control condition actually worked! That is, patients who received 30-minute intense doses of negative air ions each morning also demonstrated significant improvements in mood (Terman, Terman, & Ross, 1998). Researchers are continuing to examine the use of negative air ionizers (Terman & Terman, 2006).

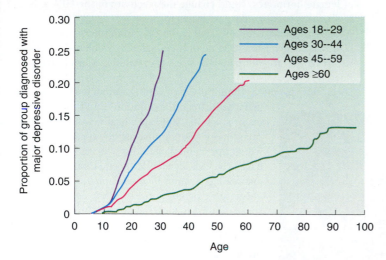

Figure 8.1 With each generation, the median age of onset for major depression gets younger. Adapted from Kessler et al. (2003). *JAMA, 289,* 3095–3105.

values may help protect against depression or that the resiliency of people who are able to immigrate could be protective. Symptoms of depression also show some cross-cultural variation, probably resulting from differences in cultural standards of acceptable expressions of emotional distress. For example, people in South Korea are less likely to describe a sad mood or suicidal thoughts than are people in the United States (Chang et al., 2008). Complaints of nerves and headaches are common in Latino culture, and reports of weakness, fatigue, and poor concentration are common in some Asian cultures. On the other hand, these symptom differences do not appear to be major enough to explain the differing rates of depression across countries (Simon et al., 2002).

It is tempting to assume that differences in prevalence rates by country indicate a strong role for culture. It turns out that differences between countries in rates of depression may be fairly complex to understand. As noted in Focus on Discovery 8.2, one factor may be distance from the equator. Rates of winter depression, or seasonal affective disorder, are higher farther from the equator, where days are shorter. There is also a robust correlation of per capita fish consumption with depression; countries with more fish consumption, such as Japan and Iceland, have much lower rates of MDD and bipolar disorder (Hibbeln et al., 2006). Undoubtedly, cultural and economic factors, such as wealth disparity and family cohesion, play an important role in rates of depression as well.

In most countries, the prevalence of MDD increased steadily during the mid to late twentieth century (Klerman, 1988); at the same time, the age of onset decreased. Figure 8.1 shows that the age of onset has become lower for each recent generation of people in the United States: among people in their sixties, less than 5 percent reported that they had experienced an episode of MDD by age 20, whereas among people ages 18–29, almost 10 percent reported that they had experienced an episode of MDD by age 20. The median age of onset is now the late teens to early twenties. One possible explanation for the increasing depression rates lies in the social changes that have occurred over the past 100 years. Support structures—such as a tightly knit extended families and marital stability, which were a more central part of society in the past— are often absent for people today. Yet there are no clear data about why depression seems to strike earlier and earlier. Beyond the prevalence rates, the symptoms of depression vary some- what across the life span. Depression in children often results in somatic complaints, such as headaches or stomachaches (see p. 433). In older adults, depression is often characterized by distractibility and complaints of memory loss (see p. 478).

Both MDD and dysthymia are often associated, or comorbid, with other psychological prob- lems. The most common comorbid conditions include anxiety disorders, substance-related dis- orders, sexual dysfunctions, and personality disorders. As many as two-thirds of people who meet the criteria for diagnosis of MDD during their lifetime also will meet the criteria for diag- nosis of an anxiety disorder at some point (Mineka, Watson, & Clark, 1998).

Depression has many serious consequences. As we will discuss later, suicide is a real risk. MDD is also one of the world's leading causes of disability (Murray & Lopez, 1996); it is estimated that MDD is associated with $31 billion per year in lost productivity in the United States (Stewart et al., 2003). MDD is also related to a high risk of other health prob- lems, particularly cardiovascular disease (Osby et al., 2001).

Although the diagnostic criteria for dysthymia require fewer symptoms than for MDD, do not make the mistake of thinking that dysthymia is a less severe disorder than MDD. Unlike MDD, dysthymia is chronic. One study found that the average duration of dysthymic symp- toms was more than five years (Klein et al., 2006). The chronicity of these symptoms takes a toll. Indeed, a study following patients for five years found that people with dysthymia were more likely to require hospitalization, to attempt suicide, and to be impaired in their functioning than were people with MDD (Klein et al., 2000).

Margaret Trudeau, the former first lady of Canada, has become an advocate for better mental health services since her own diagnosis with bipolar disorder. (Neil Burstyn/NewsCom.)

Bipolar Disorders

DSM-IV-TR recognizes three forms of bipolar disorders: bipolar I disorder, bipolar II dis- order, and cyclothymic disorder. Manic symptoms are the defining feature of each of these disorders. The bipolar disorders are differentiated by how severe and long-lasting the manic symptoms are.

These disorders are labeled "bipolar" because most people who experience mania will also experience depression during their lifetime (mania and depression are considered opposite poles). An episode of depression is not required for a diagnosis of bipolar I, but it is required for a diagnosis of bipolar II disorder. Most people seeking treatment for bipo- lar I disorder are likely to have experienced depressive episodes (Johnson & Kizer, 2002).

Mania is a state of intense elation or irritability accompanied by other symptoms shown in the diagnostic criteria. During a manic episode, people may become louder and make an incessant stream of remarks, sometimes full of puns, jokes, rhymes, and interjections about nearby stimuli that have attracted their attention (like Wayne in the clinical case). These remarks may be difficult to interrupt and may shift rapidly from topic to topic, reflecting an underlying **flight of ideas**. During mania, people may become sociable to the point of intrusiveness. They can also become excessively self-confident. Unfortunately, they can be oblivious to the potentially disastrous consequences of their behavior, which can include imprudent sexual activities, overspending, and reckless driving. They may stop sleeping but stay incredibly energetic. Attempts by others to curb such excesses can quickly bring anger and even rage. Mania usually comes on suddenly over a period of a day or two.

Most manic episodes are "purely" manic, but sometimes, people experience **mixed episodes**, characterized by severe symptoms of both mania and depression within the same week. DSM-IV-TR also includes criteria for **hypomania** (see diagnostic criteria for mania and hypomania). *Hypo-* comes from the Greek for "under"; hypomania is "under"—less extreme than—mania. Although mania involves significant impairment, hypomania does not. Rather, hypomania involves a change in functioning that does not cause serious problems.

DSM-IV-TR Criteria for Manic and Hypomanic Episodes

Distinctly elevated or irritable mood.
At least three of the following (four if mood is irritable):

- Increase in goal-directed activity or physical restlessness
- Unusual talkativeness; rapid speech
- Flight of ideas or subjective impression that thoughts are racing
- Decreased need for sleep
- Inflated self-esteem; belief that one has special talents, powers, or abilities
- Distractibility; attention easily diverted
- Excessive involvement in pleasurable activities that are likely to have undesirable consequences, such as reckless spending, sexual behavior, or driving.

For a manic episode:

- Symptoms last for 1 week or require hospitalization
- Symptoms cause significant distress or functional impairment.

For a hypomanic episode:

- Symptoms last at least 4 days
- Clear changes in functioning that are observable to others, but impairment is not marked.

Clinical Case: Wayne

Wayne, a 32-year-old insurance appraiser, had been married for 8 years. He and his wife and their two children lived comfortably and happily in a middle-class neighborhood. He had not experienced any clear symptoms until age 32. One morning, Wayne told his wife that he was bursting with energy and ideas, that his job was unfulfilling, and that he was just wasting his talent. That night he slept little, spending most of the time at his desk, writing furiously. The next morning he left for work at the usual time but returned home at 11:00 A.M., his car overflowing with aquariums and other equipment for tropical fish. He had quit his job, then withdrawn all the money from the family's savings account and spent it on tropical fish equipment. Wayne reported that the previous night he had worked out a way to modify existing equipment so that fish "won't die anymore. We'll be millionaires." After unloading the paraphernalia, Wayne set off to canvass the neighborhood for possible buyers, going door-to-door and talking to anyone who would listen.

Wayne reported that no one in his family had been treated for bipolar disorder. But his mother had gone through periods when she would stop sleeping and become extremely adventurous. For the most part, the family had regarded these episodes as unproblematic, but during one period, she had set off across the country without the children and had returned only after spending a major amount of money.

The following bit of conversation indicates Wayne's incorrigible optimism and provocativeness:

Therapist: Well, you seem pretty happy today.
Wayne: Happy! Happy! You certainly are a master of understatement, you rogue! [Shouting, literally jumping out of his seat.] Why, I'm ecstatic! I'm leaving for the West Coast today, on my daughter's bicycle. Only 3,100 miles. That's nothing, you know. I could probably walk, but I want to get there by next week. And along the way I plan to contact a lot of people about investing in my fish equipment. I'll get to know more people that way—you know, Doc, "know" in the biblical sense [leering at the therapist seductively]. Oh, God, how good it feels.

Bipolar I Disorder In DSM-IV-TR, the criteria for diagnosis of **bipolar I disorder** (formerly known as manic-depressive disorder) include a single episode of mania or a single mixed episode during the course of a person's life. Note, then, that a person who is diagnosed with bipolar I disorder may or may not be experiencing current symptoms of mania. In fact, even if they experienced only one week of manic symptoms years ago, they are still diagnosed with bipolar I disorder. Even more than MDD, bipolar disorders tend to recur. Over 50 percent of people with bipolar I disorder have four or more episodes (Goodwin & Jamison, 1990).

Bipolar II Disorder DSM-IV-TR also includes a milder form of bipolar disorder, called **bipolar II disorder**. To be diagnosed with bipolar II disorder, a person must have experienced at least one major depressive episode and at least one episode of *hypomania*.

Cyclothymic Disorder (also called *cyclothymia*) is a second chronic mood disorder (the other is dysthymic disorder). As with diagnosis of dysthymic disorder, DSM-IV-TR requires that symptoms be present for at least two years (see diagnostic criteria). In cyclothymic disorder, the person has frequent but mild symptoms of depression, alternating with mild symptoms of mania. Although the symptoms do not reach the severity of full-blown manic or depressive episodes, people with the disorder and those close to them typically notice the ups and downs. During lows, a person may be sad, feel inadequate, withdraw from people, and sleep for 10 hours a night. During highs, a person may be boisterous, overly confident, socially uninhibited and gregarious, and need little sleep.

Epidemiology and Consequences of Bipolar Disorders Bipolar I disorder is much rarer than MDD—about 1 percent of people will meet the criteria for bipolar I disorder (Weissman et al., 1996). It is hard to know with certainty, but researchers estimate that about 2 percent of people experience bipolar II disorder (Merikangas et al., 2007) and perhaps another 4 percent experience cyclothymic disorder (Regeer et al., 2004). The average age of onset of bipolar disorders is in the early twenties, but these conditions are being seen with increasing frequency among children and adolescents (Kessler et al., 2005). Bipolar disorders occur equally often in men and women, but women experience more episodes of depression than do men (Leibenluft, 1996). Most people with bipolar disorder also meet diagnostic criteria for anxiety disorders (Merikangas et al., 2007).

DSM-IV-TR Criteria for Cyclothymic Disorder

For at least 2 years:
- Numerous periods with hypomanic symptoms that do not meet criteria for a manic episode
- Numerous periods with depressive symptoms that do not meet criteria for a major depressive episode.

The symptoms do not clear for more than 2 months at a time.
Symptoms cause significant distress or functional impairment.

Bipolar I disorder is among the most severe forms of mental illnesses. One-third of people remain unemployed a full year after hospitalization for mania (Harrow et al., 1990). In one study, researchers interviewed patients every month for 15 years. People with bipolar I disorder reported that symptoms led to an inability to work about 30 percent of the time (Judd et al., 2008). Suicide rates are high for both bipolar I and bipolar II disorders (Angst et al., 2002). People with bipolar disorders are at high risk for a range of other medical conditions, including cardiovascular disease, diabetes mellitus, obesity, and thyroid disease (Kupfer, 2005). Not only are medical problems present, they are often quite severe. People who have been hospitalized for bipolar I disorder are twice as likely to die from medical illnesses in a given year as are people without mood disorders (Osby et al., 2001). The sad consequences of bipolar disorders are not offset by evidence that hypomania is associated with creativity and achievement (see Focus on Discovery 8.3).

People with cyclothymia are at elevated risk for developing episodes of mania and major depression. Even if full-blown manic episodes do not emerge, the chronicity of cyclothymic symptoms takes a toll.

FOCUS ON DISCOVERY 8.3

Creativity and Mood Disorders

Noted psychologist Kay Redfield Jamison has written extensively about creativity and mood disorders. (Courtesy of Kay Redfield Jamison.)

In her book *Touched with Fire: Manic-Depressive Illness and the Artistic Temperament* (1992), Kay Jamison, an expert on bipolar disorders and herself a longtime sufferer from bipolar I disorder, assembled much evidence linking mood disorders, especially bipolar disorder, to artistic creativity. Of course, most people with mood disorders are not particularly creative, and most creative people do not have mood disorders—but the list of visual artists, composers, and writers who seem to have experienced mood disorders is impressive, including Michelangelo, van Gogh, Tchaikovsky, Schumann, Gauguin, Tennyson, Shelley, and Whitman, among others.

Many people assume that the manic state itself fosters creativity through elated mood, increased energy, rapid thoughts, and a heightened ability to make connections

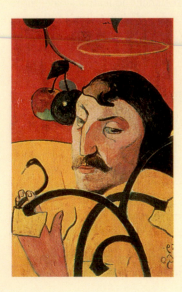

Self-portrait by Paul Gauguin. He is one of the many artists and writers who apparently suffered from a mood disorder. (Paul Gauguin/SUPERSTOCK.)

among seemingly unrelated events. Extreme mania, however, lowers creative output, and even if people produce more work during a manic period, the quality of that work might suffer, as seems to have been the case for the composer Robert Schumann (Weisberg, 1994). Moreover, studies have shown that people who have experienced episodes of mania tend to be less creative than those who have had the milder episodes of hypomania, and both groups tend to produce less creative output than do non-ill family members (Richards et al., 1988). These findings are important, because many people with bipolar disorder worry that taking medications may limit their creativity. Rather, reducing manic symptoms should help, rather than hurt, creativity.

Mood disorders are common among artists and writers. Tchaikovsky was affected, and so is Axl Rose. (Left: Photo Researchers; right: Timothy A. Clary/AFP/Getty Images News and Sport Services.)

Check Your Knowledge 8.1 (Answers are at the end of the chapter.)

Fill in the blanks.

1. Major depressive disorder is diagnosed based on at least _____ symptoms lasting at least _____ weeks.

2. Approximately _____ percent of people will experience depression during their lifetime.

3. Depressive symptoms must last for at least _____ years to qualify for a DSM-IV-TR diagnosis of dysthymia.

4. Approximately _____ out of every 100 people will experience a manic episode during their lifetime.

5. Bipolar I disorder is diagnosed on the basis of _____ or _____ episodes, and bipolar II disorder is diagnosed on the basis of _____ episodes.

Subtypes of Depressive Disorders and Bipolar Disorders

The mood disorders are highly heterogeneous—that is, people who have been diagnosed with the same disorder may show very different symptoms. DSM-IV-TR deals with this by providing criteria for dividing MDD and bipolar disorders into a number of subtypes, based on either specific symptoms or the pattern of symptoms over time.

DSM-IV-TR states that MDD, bipolar I disorder, and bipolar II disorder qualify as **seasonal** if episodes happen regularly at a particular time of the year (see Focus on Discovery 8.2 for a discussion of seasonal affective disorder). Bipolar I disorder and bipolar II disorder qualify as **rapid cycling** if the person has experienced at least four episodes within the past year (see Figure 8.2). Other subtypes are applied to a given episode of MDD or mania. These include subtypes to label the presence of **psychotic features** (delusions or hallucinations), **catatonic features** (extreme physical immobility or excessive peculiar physical movement), or a **postpartum onset** (onset within 4 weeks postpartum).

Although psychotic, catatonic, and postpartum subtypes can be applied to both depressed and manic episodes, the term **melancholic** is used only for episodes of depression. As described in DSM-IV-TR, a person suffering from depression with melancholic features finds no pleasure in any activity, does not feel better even temporarily when good things happen, and also experiences at least three other symptoms of depression, such as a distinct quality of mood, depressive symptoms that are worse in the morning than at other times of day, waking at least 2 hours too early, loss of appetite, psychomotor retardation or agitation, or guilt. Studies of the distinction between depressions with or without melancholic features have not always supported the validity of this subtype. One study, for example, suggested that MDD with melancholic features may just be a more severe type of depression—that is, people with melancholic features have more comorbidity (e.g., with anxiety disorders), more frequent episodes of depression, and more impairment in everyday activities (Kendler, 1997).

Mike Wallace, an internationally recognized reporter, has talked openly about his struggles with major depressive disorder. (AP/Wide World Photos.)

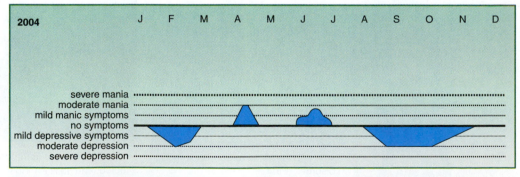

Figure 8.2 The rapid cycling subtype of bipolar disorder is defined by at least four mood episodes per year, as shown in this case.

Quick Summary

DSM-IV-TR contains two broad types of mood disorders: depressive disorders and bipolar disorders. Depressive disorders include major depressive disorder and dysthymic disorder, and bipolar disorders include bipolar I disorder, bipolar II disorder, and cyclothymic disorder. Major depression is characterized by severe episodes lasting at least 2 weeks, whereas dysthymia is characterized by milder symptoms that last at least 2 years. Bipolar I disorder is diagnosed on the basis of a single lifetime manic or mixed episode, and bipolar II disorder is diagnosed on the basis of hypomania and major depression. Cyclothymia is defined by frequent shifts between mild depressive and manic symptoms that last at least 2 years. Subtypes of mood disorders are used to differentiate different patterns of symptoms. These subtypes include distinctions based on a seasonal pattern, rapid cycling, psychotic features, catatonic features, postpartum onset, and, for depression, melancholia. MDD is one of the most common psychological disorders, whereas bipolar I disorder affects approximately 1 percent of the population. Most people with MDD will experience another episode. Bipolar disorder is even more recurrent—about 50 percent of people with bipolar I disorder experience four or more episodes.

Etiology of Mood Disorders

When we think of the profound extremes embodied in the mood disorders, it is natural to ask why these happen. How can we explain Mary sinking into the depths of depression? What factors combined to drive Wayne into his frenzied state of unrealistic ambitions? Studies of etiology focus on why these disorders unfold. No single cause can explain mood disorders. A number of different factors combine to explain their onset.

While the diagnostic criteria specify several different depressive disorders and bipolar disorders, the research on etiology and treatment has tended to focus on major depressive disorder and bipolar I disorder. For simplicity, we refer to these conditions as depression and bipolar disorder through the remainder of this chapter.

We begin by discussing neurobiological factors involved in depression and bipolar disorder. We then discuss psychosocial predictors of depression, then turn to psychosocial models of bipolar disorder.

Neurobiological Factors in Mood Disorders

As Table 8.2 shows, there are many different approaches to understanding the neurobiological factors involved in mood disorders. Here, we will discuss genetic, neurotransmitter, brain imaging, and neuroendocrine research.

Genetic Factors   A meta-analysis found that, on average, the more careful studies of MZ (identical) and DZ (fraternal) twins yield heritability estimates of 37 percent for MDD (Sullivan, Neale, & Kendler, 2000). That is, about 37 percent of the variance in depression is explained

Table 8.2 Summary of Neurobiological Hypotheses about Major Depression and Bipolar Disorder

	Genetic Contribution	Neurotransmitter Dysfunction	Cortisol	Brain Imaging
Major depressive disorder	Modest	Serotonin receptor dysfunction Possible change in the dopamine receptors within the reward system	High	Changes in the dorsolateral prefrontal cortex, amygdala, hippocampus, and dorsal anterior cingulate
Bipolar disorder	High	Serotonin receptor dysfunction Possible involvement of dopamine receptors in the reward system Possible deficits in cell membranes and neuronal functioning	High	Changes in the dorsolateral prefrontal cortex, amygdala, hippocampus, and dorsal anterior cingulate Increased activity in the basal ganglia during mania

by genes. Heritability estimates are higher when researchers study more severe samples (e.g., when the people in the study are recruited in inpatient hospitals rather than outpatient clinics). Beyond the twin studies, several small-scale adoption studies also support the modest heritability of MDD (Wender et al., 1986). Genes appear to be more important among women than among men, in that heritability estimates are higher for women than for men (Kendler, Gatz et al., 2006a).

Bipolar disorder is among the most heritable of disorders. Much of the evidence for this comes from studies of twins. The most careful twin studies involve community studies where a representative sample is interviewed (rather than focusing only on people who seek treatment, who may have more severe cases of the disorder than those who are not treated). A Finnish community-based twin sample that used structured interviews to verify diagnoses obtained a heritability estimate of 93 percent (Kieseppa et al., 2004). Adoption studies also confirm the importance of heritability in bipolar disorder (e.g., Wender et al., 1986). Bipolar II disorder is also highly heritable (Edvardsen et al., 2008). Genetic models, however, do not explain the timing of manic symptoms. Other factors must be considered as the immediate triggers of symptoms.

There is a huge amount of interest in finding the specific genes involved in mood disorders through molecular genetics research (see Chapter 4 for a review of these methods). You should be aware of the large number of nonreplications within this field. For example, in a meta-analysis of bipolar disorder and MDD, Kato (2007) identified 166 genetic loci (i.e., locations on specific chromosomes) that had been linked with bipolar disorder and with MDD in initial studies. Of those 166 loci, only 6 have been studied multiple times and replicated in more than 75 percent of relevant studies.

These inconsistencies are even more troubling because positive results are much more likely to be published than null findings. Segurado and colleagues (2003) took an extra step to avoid these publication biases. Whereas previous analyses had compiled only published data, they gathered 18 original data sets, each with more than 20 probands affected by bipolar disorder, to be able to analyze even the negative, unpublished findings for genetic regions associated with bipolar disorder. Their meta-analysis provided the strongest support for three out of 120 regions implicated in bipolar disorder: 9p22.3-21.1, 10g11.21-22.1, and 14q24.1-32.12. Even these 4 regions have not been replicated in more than 10 of the 18 studies. Positive findings should be taken with a grain of salt, as disconfirmation appears to be the rule rather than the exception.

Despite the complexities of this area, there are some consistent patterns emerging across studies. We will discuss findings below that suggest that a polymorphism of the serotonin transporter gene may influence vulnerability to depression when life stress occurs. In addition, there is evidence that a gene that influences dopamine function, the DRD4.2, is related to MDD. A meta-analysis of 917 patients and 1,164 controls revealed that MDD was more common among people with a polymorphism in the DRD4.2 gene (Lopez Leon et al., 2005). These findings help provide an understanding of how the neurotransmitter deficits associated with mood disorders might develop.

Because the mood disorders are characterized by so many different symptoms, most researchers think that these disorders will eventually be related to a set of genes rather than to any single gene. Even if we can identify the genes involved in mood disorders, many questions still remain about how they will work. It is unlikely that genes will simply control whether or not a person develops depression. Rather, as we will discuss later, genes may guide the way people regulate emotions or respond to life stressors (Kendler, Gatz, Gardner, & Pedersen, 2006a). As such, they may set the stage for mood disorders to occur when other conditions are present.

Neurotransmitters Three neurotransmitters have been studied the most in terms of their possible role in mood disorders: **norepinephrine**, **dopamine**, and **serotonin**. Each of these neurotransmitters is present in many different areas of the brain. Figure 8.3 illustrates how widespread serotonin and dopamine pathways are in the brain.

Original models suggested that depression would be tied to low levels of norepinephrine and dopamine, and mania would be tied to high levels of norepinephrine and dopamine. Mania and depression were also both posited to be tied

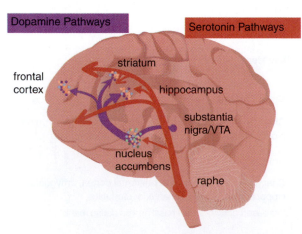

Figure 8.3 Serotonin and dopamine pathways are widespread in the brain.

to low levels of serotonin, a neurotransmitter that is believed to help regulate norepinephrine and dopamine (Thase, Jindal, & Howland, 2002). Researchers initially believed that mood disorders would be explained by absolute levels of neurotransmitters in the synaptic cleft that were either too high or too low. Emerging evidence, however, did not support the idea that levels of neurotransmitters were important in the mood disorders.

Studies of antidepressants were one source of contradictory evidence. On the one hand, these studies do suggest that depression is related in some way to these neurotransmitters. For example, effective antidepressants promote an immediate increase in levels of serotonin, norepinephrine, and/or dopamine. See Figure 8.4 for an overview of these immediate effects. But when researchers studied the time course of how antidepressants change neurotransmitter levels, they began to realize that depression could not be explained just by the absolute level of the neurotransmitters. Antidepressants take 7 to 14 days to relieve depression; by that time, the neurotransmitter levels have already returned to their previous state. It would seem, then, that a simple change in norepinephrine, dopamine, or serotonin levels is not a good explanation for why the drugs alleviate depression.

Other evidence also indicates that absolute levels of neurotransmitters did not tell the whole story. For decades, researchers studied the metabolites of neurotransmitters as an index of how much of a neurotransmitter was being released into the synaptic cleft. Recall that after a neurotransmitter is released into the synaptic cleft, enzymes begin to break down the neurotransmitter that is not reabsorbed by the cell. Metabolite studies, then, assess how much neurotransmitter has been broken down and carried into the cerebrospinal fluid, the blood, or the urine. Findings from metabolite studies were not consistent, suggesting that many people with depression did not have disturbances in the absolute levels of neurotransmitters; similarly, many people with mania did not have disturbances in the absolute levels of neurotransmitters (Placidi et al., 2001; Ressler & Nemeroff, 1999).

Given this inconsistent evidence, researchers began to focus on the idea that mood disorders might be related to the sensitivity of postsynaptic receptors that respond to the presence of neurotransmitter in the synaptic cleft. How can researchers test models of high or low receptor sensitivity? If receptors are more or less sensitive, one might expect people to react differently to drugs that influence the level of a given neurotransmitter. For example, receptors that are overly sensitive may respond to even the smallest amount of a neurotransmitter in the synaptic cleft. Researchers have focused more on dopamine and serotonin in these studies than on norepinephrine. People with depression respond differently from other people to drugs that increase dopamine levels, and it is thought that the functioning of the dopamine might be lowered in depression (Naranjo, Tremblay, & Busto, 2001). Among people with bipolar disorder, several different drugs that increase dopamine levels have been found to trigger manic symptoms, suggesting that dopamine receptors may be overly sensitive in bipolar disorder (Anand et al., 2000; Strakowski et al., 1997). Some theories suggest that we will need to look at dopamine receptors within specific regions of the brain, a topic we will return to when we discuss brain imaging studies below.

In addition to links between dopamine and mania, studies focused on depression and receptor sensitivity to serotonin. Researchers have conducted a set of studies that involve experimentally lowering serotonin levels. By raising or lowering serotonin levels, researchers can check how sensitive receptors are to fluctuations. A person who has insensitive receptors is expected to experience depressive symptoms as levels drop. To lower serotonin levels, researchers deplete levels of **tryptophan**, the major precursor of serotonin. Tryptophan can be depleted with a drink that contains high levels of 15 amino acids but no tryptophan. Within hours, serotonin levels are lowered, an effect that lasts for several hours. As a control condition, people can be given a similar-tasting drink that has no effect on tryptophan. Studies show that depleting tryptophan (and so lowering serotonin levels) causes temporary depressive symptoms among people with a history of depression or a family history of depression (Benkelfat et al., 1994; Neumeister et al., 2002). Current thinking is that people who are vulnerable to depression may have less sensitive serotonin receptors, so that they respond more dramatically to lower levels of serotonin.

Researchers have also examined the effects of tryptophan depletion in bipolar disorder. These studies have focused on family members of people with bipolar disorder. By studying relatives who

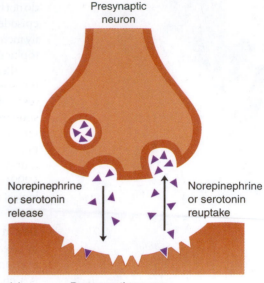

Presynaptic neuron

Norepinephrine or serotonin release

Norepinephrine or serotonin reuptake

(a)   Postsynaptic neuron

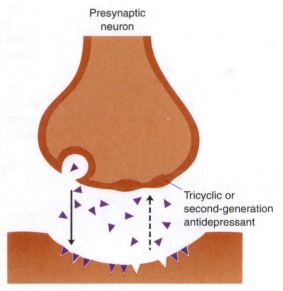

Presynaptic neuron

Tricyclic or second-generation antidepressant

(b)   Postsynaptic neuron

Figure 8.4 (a) When a neuron releases norepinephrine or serotonin into a synapse, a pumplike reuptake mechanism immediately begins to recapture some of the neurotransmitter molecules before they are received by the postsynaptic (receptor) neuron. (b) Tricyclic drugs block this reuptake process, enabling more norepinephrine or serotonin to reach and stimulate the postsynaptic (receptor) neuron. Selective serotonin reuptake inhibitors act more selectively on serotonin. Adapted from Snyder (1986), p. 106.

do not have the disorder, researchers can be certain that any effects are not scars from having had manic episodes or from taking medications for the disorder. Like people diagnosed with MDD and their family members, relatives of those with bipolar disorder demonstrate elevated mood reactions after tryptophan depletion compared to matched controls (Sobczak, Honig, Nicolson, Riedel et al., 2002).

Researchers are also beginning to study how medications influence receptor sensitivity. These types of studies are being conducted for both mania and depression. For example, one line of research is examining whether antidepressants alter chemical messengers called **second messengers** (see Figure 2.5), which then adjust postsynaptic receptor sensitivity. Another area of current research focuses on **G-proteins** (guanine nucleotide-binding proteins), which play an important role in modulating activity in the postsynaptic cell. High levels of G-proteins have been found in patients with mania and low levels in patients with depression (Avissar et al., 1997, 1999). Some have argued that the therapeutic effects of lithium, the most effective pharmacological treatment for mania, may result from its ability to regulate G-proteins (Manji et al., 1995).

Brain Imaging Studies   Two different types of brain imaging studies are commonly used in research on mood disorders. *Structural studies* focus on whether there are fewer cells or connections within a given region of the brain. *Functional activation studies* focus on whether there is a change in the activity of a brain region. Structural studies can indicate whether a person has lost connections between brain cells; functional studies are used to gain information on how people use the cells they have.

Brain imaging studies suggest that episodes of MDD are associated with changes in many of the brain systems that are activated when a person without symptoms of depression experiences strong emotions (Davidson, Pizzagalli, & Nitschke, 2002). As one might expect, many different brain structures become involved when a person experiences emotion: the person needs to attend to and interpret the stimuli that are causing the emotion and then must make plans to deal with those stimuli (Phillips et al., 2003). Because these brain systems are so complex, researchers are still working to understand how depression relates to brain activity. We will provide a brief overview of current theory (see Davidson et al., 2002 for more detail).

Table 8.3 shows the four primary brain structures involved in depression: the **amygdala**, the **hippocampus**, the **prefrontal cortex**, and the **subgenual anterior cingulate** (Figure 8.5). The amygdala helps a person to assess how emotionally important a stimulus is. For example, animals with damage to the amygdala fail to react with fear to threatening stimuli and also fail to respond positively to food. In humans, the amygdala has been shown to respond when people are shown pictures of threatening stimuli. The other structures help a person retrieve previous memories of this type of stimulus (hippocampus) and then focus on the situation and execute appropriate plans (the prefrontal cortex and the subgenual anterior cingulate). Taken together, then, these brain structures function to assess how emotionally important a stimulus is, to focus effectively, and to make plans based on emotionally relevant cues.

Functional activation studies show elevated activity of the amygdala among people with MDD. For example, when shown sad or angry faces, people with current MDD have a more intense and sustained reaction in the amygdala than do people with no MDD (Sheline et al., 2001). Similarly, when shown negative words, people with current MDD have a more sustained reaction in the amygdala than do people with no MDD (Siegle et al., 2002). This pattern of amygdala overreactivity to emotional stimuli does not look like a medication effect or even a consequence of being in a depressed state, because it can be shown even when people are not taking medications (Siegle et al., 2007) and among relatives of people with depression who have no personal history of MDD (van der Veen et al., 2007). These findings suggest that amygdala hyperreactivity to emotional stimuli in depression

Table 8.3 Brain Structures Involved in Major Depression

Brain Structure	Functional Activation Studies
Prefrontal cortex (dorsolateral portion)	Diminished
Anterior cingulate (subgenual portion)	Diminished
Hippocampus	Diminished
Amygdala	Elevated

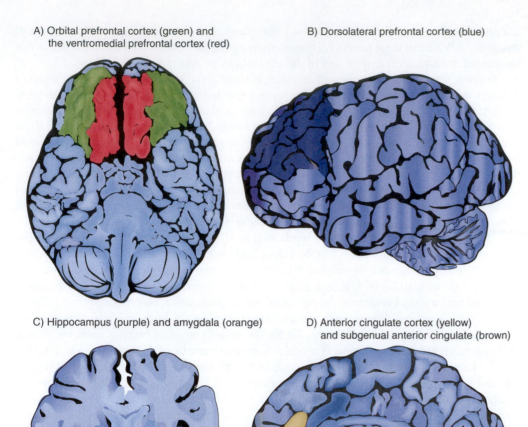

A) Orbital prefrontal cortex (green) and
the ventromedial prefrontal cortex (red)

B) Dorsolateral prefrontal cortex (blue)

C) Hippocampus (purple) and amygdala (orange)

D) Anterior cingulate cortex (yellow)
and subgenual anterior cingulate (brown)

Figure 8.5 Key brain structures involved in major depressive disorder. (Reprinted with permission from the *Annual Review of Psychology*, Vol. 53, © 2002 by Annual Reviews, www.annualreviews.org.)

might be part of the vulnerability to depression rather than just part of the aftermath of being depressed. Functional studies show that MDD is also associated with diminished activation of the subgenual anterior cingulate, the prefrontal cortex, and the hippocampus during exposure to emotional stimuli (Davidson et al., 2002; Schaefer et al., 2006).

Structural studies show many parallels with the findings of the functional studies. That is, structural studies of people with depression also find diminished volume of the subgenual anterior cingulate (Drevets et al., 1997), the prefrontal cortex, and, for people who have had depression for many years, the hippocampus (Sheline, 2000).

How might these findings fit together? One theory is that the overactivity in the amygdala during depression causes oversensitivity to emotionally relevant stimuli. At the same time, systems involved in weighing rewards and costs, making decisions, and systematically pursuing goals in the face of emotions appear less active (the subgenual anterior cingulate, the hippocampus, and the prefrontal cortex). In response to emotionally relevant stimuli, then, a person with depression may react with increased emotion but decreased ability to plan (Davidson et al., 2002).

Given this pattern of findings related to greater emotional reactivity, one might expect that people who are vulnerable to depression would show a robust shift in brain activity in the context of a sad mood. One study found just that (Liotti et al., 2002). That is, people with current major depression, with a history of major depression, and with no current or previous depression were asked to think about sad events in their lives and to try to place themselves in a sad mood. All three groups reported a similar level of sadness after this induction. Before and after the sad mood induction, PET scans were taken to measure brain activity. Among people with either current or previous major depression, activity of the orbitofrontal cortex decreased after the sadness induction compared to baseline; activity of the orbitofrontal cortex did not change among people with no current or previous depression. Stated differently, as people with current depression become sad, they display less activity in brain regions that are involved with planning and executing goals. The findings of this study indicate that these patterns of brain activity can be seen even after the depressive episode has cleared; such patterns may be part of the vulnerability to depression.

Beyond brain systems involved in emotion, another set of studies have examined whether depression is related to the sensitivity of the reward system in the brain. Remember that depressive symptoms include decreased pleasure, motivation, and energy, and manic symptoms include increased pleasure, motivation, and energy. Some researchers think that symptoms like these could be explained by changes in the sensitivity of the **reward system** in the brain (Depue & Iacono, 1989). That is, changes in this brain structure could help explain why people seem less motivated to pursue rewards during depression and overly focused on possible rewards during mania. Although findings are not entirely consistent, many researchers are studying one part of the reward system, the basal ganglia, to see if dopamine receptors in this area are less sensitive during depression (Meyer et al., 2001; Neumeister et al., 2001; Tremblay et al. 2005).

Many of the same brain structures implicated in MDD also appear to be involved in bipolar disorder. In functional studies, bipolar I disorder is associated with elevated responsiveness in the amygdala, along with diminished activity of the hippocampus and prefrontal cortex (cf. Green, Cahill, & Malhi, 2007; Kruger et al., 2003). In structural studies, bipolar disorder is associated with a loss of volume in the prefrontal cortex (Rajkowska, Halaris, & Selemon, 2001).

There is a great deal of controversy about whether the volume of other brain regions is increased or decreased in bipolar disorder (Sheline, 2003). The mixed pattern of findings might be because medications for bipolar disorder can change the volume of these brain regions (Harrison, 2002).

To date, brain imaging research tells us little about what differentiates people with bipolar disorder from those with MDD. Many of the neuroimaing findings for bipolar disorder are very similar to those seen among patients with MDD. One clue might emerge from studying what happens in the brain during manic periods. Many of the brain patterns that are shown during mania are very similar to those shown during depression. On the other hand, one difference emerges. During mania, it appears that a brain region that is very involved in reactions to reward, the basal ganglia, is overly active (Blumberg et al., 1999; Caligiuri et al., 2003). These findings, though, are quite tentative, and more research is needed.

Another set of promising findings suggest that MDD and bipolar disorder might be differentiated by changes in the way that neurons throughout the brain function. People with bipolar disorder often have deficits in the membranes of their neurons (Looney & el-Mallakh, 1997). These deficits seem to operate across the brain, and they influence how readily neurons can be activated. These cellular membrane deficits are not seen in people with MDD (Thiruvengadam & Chandrasekaran, 2007). Similar research is focused on a protein involved in the functioning of many aspects of the neuron, protein kinase C. Protein kinase C has a major role in how receptors function and how messages are sent between neurons. Protein kinase C activity appears to be abnormally high among people with mania (Yildiz et al., 2008). Although these findings for neuronal function are less well established than are other brain findings, they suggest intriguing differences between bipolar disorder and MDD.

The Neuroendocrine System: Cortisol Dysregulation and Depression

The **HPA axis** (hypothalamic–pituitary–adrenocortical axis; see Figure 2.9 on p. 38), the biological system that manages reactivity to stress, may be overly active during episodes of MDD. As described above, there is evidence that the amygdala is overly reactive among people with MDD. The HPA axis receives input from structures related to the amygdala and so thus may also be overly active in people with MDD. The HPA axis triggers the release of **cortisol**, the main stress hormone. Cortisol is secreted at times of stress and triggers changes that help the body prepare for threats.

Various findings link depression to high cortisol levels. For example, people with **Cushing's syndrome**, which causes oversecretion of cortisol, frequently experience depressive symptoms. A second line of research with animals has shown that when chemicals that trigger cortisol release are injected into the brain, many of the classic symptoms of depression are produced, including decreased interest in sex, decreased appetite, and sleep disturbances (Gutman & Nemeroff, 2003). In animals and humans, then, too much cortisol seems to produce depressive symptoms.

Even among people who are depressed but do not have Cushing's syndrome, cortisol levels are often poorly regulated—that is, the system does not seem to respond well to signals to decrease cortisol levels (Garbutt et al., 1994). The dexamethasone suppression test (dex/CRH) is used to measure cortisol regulation. Among people who do not have a mood disorder, dexamethasone suppresses cortisol secretion over the course of the night. In contrast, for some people with mood disorders, dexamethasone does not suppress cortisol secretion, particularly among people whose disorder has psychotic features (Nelson & Davis, 1997). This lack of cortisol suppression is seen as a sign of poor regulation of the HPA axis during episodes of MDD. Challenging the HPA system even further by administering both dexamethasone and corticotropin-releasing hormone (which increases cortisol levels) results in deficits in the regulation of cortisol in 80 percent of people with depression (Heuser, Yassouridis, & Holsboer, 1994). These abnormal responses to dexamethasone, though, normalize when the depressive episode ends for most people. People who continue to show elevated cortisol responses to the dex/CRH test are more likely to relapse within the next year (e.g., Aubry et al., 2007).

Although cortisol helps mobilize beneficial short-term stress responses, prolonged high levels of cortisol can cause harm to body systems. For example, long-term excesses of cortisol have been linked to damage to the hippocampus—studies have found smaller-than-normal hippocampi among people who have experienced depression for years (e.g., Dunman et al., 1997).

Like people with MDD, people with bipolar disorder fail to demonstrate the typical suppression of cortisol after the dex/CRH test. This suggests that bipolar disorder is also characterized by a poorly regulated cortisol system (Watson et al., 2006). Like those with MDD, people with bipolar disorder who continue to show abnormal responses to cortisol challenge tests after their episode clears are at high risk for more episodes in the future (Vieta et al., 1999).

In sum, both bipolar disorder and MDD are characterized by problems in the regulation of cortisol levels. Dysregulation in cortisol levels also predicts a worse course of illness for bipolar disorder and MDD.

Quick Summary

Bipolar disorder is highly heritable, and major depression is modestly heritable. Neurotransmitter models focus on serotonin, dopamine, and norepinephrine. Researchers have begun to focus on receptor sensitivity rather than levels of neurotransmitters. Consistent with this idea, studies that involve experimentally manipulating levels of neurotransmitters provide support for the role of poor serotonin sensitivity in depression and in bipolar disorder. It appears that people with depression may be less sensitive to dopamine and those with mania may be more sensitive to dopamine.

Neuroimaging studies suggest that depression is associated with changes in regions of the brain that are involved in emotion. These changes seem consistent with a greater emotional reactivity (heightened activity of the amygdala) but less planful thinking in the face of emotion (diminished activity of the prefrontal cortex, hippocampus, and subgenual anterior cingulate).

The neurobiological dysfunctions associated with depression are also observed in bipolar disorder. Both disorders are characterized by changes in the amygdala, prefrontal cortex, hippocampus, and anterior cingulate; by low functioning of the serotonin system; and by high cortisol levels. Compared to major depressive disorder, bipolar disorder appears to be uniquely related to increased activity in a region of the brain called the basal ganglia and to changes in the membranes of neurons.

Major depressive disorder and bipolar disorder are both related to poor regulation of cortisol.

Check Your Knowledge 8.2

Answer the questions.

1. Estimates of heritability are approximately _____ percent for MDD and _____ percent for bipolar I disorder.
   a. 60, 93
   b. 20, 100
   c. 37, 93
   d. 10, 59
2. Which of the following neurotransmitters is **not** believed to be involved in depression and mania:
   a. acetylcholine
   b. serotonin
   c. dopamine
   d. norepinephrine
3. Recent models suggest that depression is
   a. related to absolute levels of neurotransmitters
   b. related to changes in receptor sensitivity for neurotransmitters
   c. unrelated to neurotransmitter systems
4. In depression, dysregulation of the HPA axis is shown by:
   a. hypersensitivity of the pituitary gland
   b. failure to suppress cortisol by dexamethasone
   c. too little cortisol
   d. elevated parasympathetic nervous system activity
5. One brain region that appears to be overly active among people with mood disorders is the:
   a. hippocampus
   b. prefrontal cortex
   c. cerebellum
   d. amygdala

Social Factors in Depression: Life Events and Interpersonal Difficulties

Data indicate that neurobiological factors influence whether or not a person develops a mood disorder. Does this mean that social and psychological theories are useless? Not in the least. For example, neurobiological theories are consistent with vulnerability to stressors among people with mood disorders. Neurobiological factors, then, may be *diatheses* (p. 53) that increase risk for mood disorders in the context of other triggers or stressors.

The role of stressful life events in triggering episodes of depression is well established (Kendler, Karkowski, & Prescott, 1999). A great deal of research has focused on cause–effect relationships: do life events cause depression, or does depression cause life events? Prospective studies have been particularly important, because they have shown that life events typically happen before the depressive episode begins. Even with a prospective study, though, it remains possible that some life events are caused by early symptoms of depression that have not yet developed into a full-blown disorder. Remember the case of Mary, who developed symptoms after she was laid off from her job. Maybe Mary lost her job because she was sleeping too much and then arriving at work late; trouble sleeping can be a sign of depression.

Even when researchers exclude stressful life events that were caused by mild depressive symptoms, there is much evidence that stress can cause major depressive disorder. In careful prospective studies, 42 to 67 percent of people report that they experienced a very serious life event (that was not caused by symptoms) in the year before their depression began. Common events include losing a job, a key friendship, or a romantic relationship. These findings have been replicated in at least 12 studies, conducted in six different countries (Brown & Harris, 1989b). Certain types of life events, such as loss and humiliation, appear particularly likely to trigger depressive episodes (Kendler, Hettema, et al., 2003). Above and beyond the people who report stressful life events that happened suddenly, many people with depression report that they had been experiencing long-term chronic stressors before the depression, such as poverty (Brown & Harris, 1989b). Life events appear to be particularly important in the first episode of depression but less likely to be involved in later episodes (Monroe & Harkness, 2005).

Although many depressions follow a stressful life event, most people do not become depressed after such an event. Why do some people, but not others, become depressed after stressful life events? The obvious answer is that some people must be more vulnerable to stress than others. In the previous section, we described neurobiological systems involved in depression; many of these systems could be involved in reactivity to stress. Psychological and cognitive vulnerabilities also appear important. The most common models, then, are diathesis–stress models—that is, models that consider both preexisting vulnerabilities (diatheses) and stressors. Diatheses could be biological, social, or psychological.

One diathesis may be a lack of social support. People who are depressed tend to have sparse social networks and to regard those networks as providing little support (Keltner & Kring, 1998). Low social support may lessen a person's ability to handle stressful life events and make the person vulnerable to depression. One study showed that women experiencing a severely stressful life event without support from a confidant had a 40 percent risk of developing depression, whereas those with a confidant's support had only a four percent risk (Brown & Andrews, 1986). Social support, then, seems to minimize the effects of major stressors.

There is also some evidence that interpersonal problems within the family are particularly likely to trigger depression. A long line of research has focused on **expressed emotion (EE)**, defined as a family member's critical or hostile comments toward or emotional overinvolvement with the person with depression. High EE strongly predicts relapse in depression. Indeed, one review of six studies found that 69.5 percent of patients in families with high EE relapsed within 1 year, compared to 30.5 percent of patient in families with low EE (Butzlaff & Hooley, 1998). In a community study, marital discord also predicted the onset of depression (Whisman & Bruce, 1999).

Clearly, interpersonal problems can trigger the onset of depressive symptoms, but it is also important to consider the flip side of the coin. Once depressive symptoms emerge, they can create interpersonal problems—that is, depressive symptoms seem to elicit negative reactions from others (Coyne, 1976). For example, roommates of college students with depression rated social contacts with them as less enjoyable, and they reported feeling aggressive and rejecting toward them (Joiner, Alfano, & Metalsky, 1992).

What is it about the person who is depressed that elicits these negative reactions? Researchers have studied this aspect of depression by coding how people with depression interact with their spouses and with strangers, and then doing studies in which people mimic key depressive behaviors. The following signs of depression seem to elicit negative reactions in others: slow speech, silences, negative self-disclosures, negative affect, poor eye contact, and fewer positive facial expressions (Gotlib & Robinson, 1982; Gottman & Krokoff, 1989). People who are depressed also tend to make hostile comments more frequently to their spouses than do people without depression (Biglan, Hops, & Sherman, 1988).

Other research has explored the interpersonal effects of constant reassurance seeking (Joiner, 1995). More than most, people who are depressed seek reassurance that others truly care about them. But even when others express support, they are only temporarily satisfied. Their negative self-concept causes them to doubt the positive feedback, and their constant efforts to obtain reassurance come to irritate others. Ultimately, people experiencing depression actually elicit negative feedback (e.g., by asking questions like "How do you *truly* feel about me?" after the other person has already given support); eventually, other people's responses typically confirm the person's negative self-concept. Ultimately, the person's excessive reassurance seeking can lead to rejection (Joiner & Metalsky, 1995).

Many of the negative social behaviors, such as excessive reassurance seeking, could be the result of depression. If some of these same social problems are present before symptoms appear, can the problems increase the risk for depression? Research suggests that the answer is yes. Among a group of undergraduates who were not initially depressed, those who were high in reassurance seeking were more likely to develop depressive symptoms over a 10-week period (Joiner & Metalsky, 2001). Similarly, research using high-risk samples, identified before the onset of depression, suggests that interpersonal problems may precede depression. For example, the behavior of elementary school children of parents with depression was rated negatively by both peers and teachers (Weintraub, Prinz, & Neale, 1978); low social competence predicted the onset of depression among elementary school children (Cole et al., 1990); and poor interpersonal problem-solving skills predicted increases in depression among adolescents (Davila et al., 1995). It seems clear that interpersonal problems are one risk factor for depression.

Psychological Factors in Depression

Many different psychological factors may play a role in depressive disorders. In this section, we discuss Freud's psychoanalytic views, which emphasize the unconscious conflicts associated with grief and loss; personality factors, such as neuroticism and positive and negative affectivity; and cognitive factors, such as thoughts about the self and life events. These theories describe different diatheses to answer the question, "what are the characteristics of people who respond to negative life events with a depressive episode."

Freud's Theory In his celebrated paper "Mourning and Melancholia," Freud (1917/1950) drew from clinical observations to develop a model of depression. He theorized that the potential for depression is created early in childhood, during the oral period. If the child's needs are insufficiently or overly gratified, the person becomes fixated in the oral stage (see p. 19). This arrest in development may cause the person to become excessively dependent on other people for the maintenance of self-esteem.

Why do people with this childhood history come to suffer from depression? Freud hypothesized that after the loss of a loved one—whether by death, separation, or withdrawal of affection—the mourner identifies with the lost one—perhaps in a fruitless attempt to undo the loss. Freud asserted that the mourner unconsciously resents being deserted and feels anger toward the loved one for the loss. In addition, the mourner feels guilt for real or imagined sins against the lost person. According to the theory, the mourner's anger toward the lost one becomes directed inward, developing into ongoing self-blame and depression. In this view, depression can be described as anger turned against oneself. Overly dependent persons are believed to be particularly susceptible to this process, and, as noted above, people fixated in the oral stage are overly dependent on others.

Not much research has been carried out to test this theory, but the little information available does not strongly support it. Contrary to the idea that depression is a result of anger turned inward, people with depression express much more anger than do people without depression (Biglan et al., 1988). Despite this, some of Freud's ideas continue to influence more recent models of depression. For example, Freud maintained that depression could be triggered by the loss of a loved one. As we have seen, a large body of evidence indicates that episodes of MDD are precipitated by stressful life events, which often involve losses. Researchers have consistently shown that people who are high in dependency are prone to depressive symptoms after a rejection (Nietzel & Harris, 1990), a finding that also is congruent with Freud's theory. Although some of Freud's ideas still influence theories of depression, researchers have gone far beyond the clinical observations that were the foundation of his ideas.

Affect and Neuroticism   Current personality research has focused on the propensity to experience negative and positive affect as a risk factor for mood disorders. To understand the personality research, though, it is helpful to understand a bit about how depression and anxiety disorders relate to negative and positive affect.

As we have noted, major depression and anxiety disorders frequently co-occur. How can we differentiate anxiety and depression? One model conceptualizes depression and anxiety along three broad dimensions (see Table 8.4): **negative affect** (distress and worry), **positive affect** (happiness and contentment), and **somatic arousal** (sweaty palms, fast heart rate, etc.). Anxiety and depression are both expected to involve negative affect. Anxiety, but not depression, is expected to involve somatic arousal (Clark, Watson, & Mineka, 1994). And depression, but not anxiety, is expected to involve low levels of positive affect. People who show high negative affect, low positive affect, and high somatic arousal may be at risk for comorbid anxiety and depressive disorders.

According to this model, depressive disorders should be differentiated from anxiety disorders by the lack of positive affect. Many of the symptoms of depression seem closely related to lack of positive affect—a loss of interest in pleasurable activities and even symptoms like lack of appetite and lack of interest in sex. Other than the clinical symptoms, what is the evidence? Studies of responses to positive pictures and films suggest that people with MDD show fewer positive facial expressions, report less pleasant emotion, show less motivation, and demonstrate less psychophysiological activity in response to positive stimuli than do people without depression (Berenbaum & Oltmanns, 1992; Henriques & Davidson, 2000, Shestyuk et al., 2005; Sloan, Strauss, & Wisner, 2001). Research, then, does support the idea that episodes of MDD are characterized by high negative affect and low positive affect.

Can high negative affect and low positive affect be used to predict depression? Studies of personality help address this question. Several longitudinal studies suggest that **neuroticism**, a personality trait that involves the tendency to react to events with greater than average negative affect, predicts the onset of depression (Jorm et al., 2000). (As you would expect, neuroticism is associated with anxiety, too—see p. 132). A major study of twins suggests that neuroticism explains at least part of the genetic vulnerability to depression (Fanous, Prescott, & Kendler, 2004). In fact, neuroticism is the personality trait most strongly associated with depression. Thus, there is good evidence that people who tend to experience negative affect are at elevated risk for developing depression.

The evidence for positive affect as a predictor is not as clear. For example, **extraversion** is a personality trait associated with frequent experiences of positive affect. Some, but not all, studies suggest that low extraversion predicts the onset of depression (Klein et al., 2002). How would this fit with the idea that once a person is depressed, he or she experiences less positive affect? Some people might be fairly happy until the depressive symptoms kick in, at which point their level of happiness might decrease. In this way, depression may suppress positive affect.

In sum, neuroticism predicts both anxiety and depression. But low extraversion doesn't always precede depression. Once people are depressed, though, they seem to experience less positive affect than do people with no disorder.

Table 8.4 Affective Dimensions in Depressive Disorders and Anxiety Disorders

	Negative Affect	Positive Affect	Somatic Arousal
Depressive disorders	High	Low	Moderate
Anxiety disorders	High	Moderate	High
Comorbid anxiety disorders and depressive disorders	High	Low	High

Cognitive Theories   In some theories, negative thoughts and beliefs are seen as major causes of depression. One can easily think of people who interpret life events differently; some people seem to see the downside of events much more easily than others do. Because cognitive theories are the most common focus of research on depression, we discuss two of them: Beck's theory and hopelessness theory.

Beck's Theory   The most important cognitive theory of depression is that of Aaron Beck (1967). His thesis is that people develop depression because their thinking is negative (see Figure 8.6). That is, Beck proposed that depression is associated with the **negative triad**: negative views of the self, the world, and the future. The "world" part of the depressive triad refers to the person's own corner of the world—the situations he or she faces. For example, the person might think "I cannot possibly cope with all these demands and responsibilities" as opposed to worrying about problems in the broader world outside of their life.

According to this model, in childhood, people with depression acquired negative **schemata** through experiences such as loss of a parent, the social rejection of peers, or the depressive attitude of a parent. Schemata are different from conscious thoughts—they are an underlying set of beliefs that operate outside of a person's awareness to shape the way a person makes sense of his or her experiences. The negative schema is activated whenever the person encounters situations similar to those that originally caused the schema to form.

Once activated, negative schemata are believed to cause **cognitive biases**, or tendencies to process information in certain negative ways (Kendall & Ingram, 1989). That is, Beck suggested that people with depression might be overly attentive to negative feedback about themselves and more likely to remember such negative information than other people are. Likewise, they might fail to notice or to remember positive feedback about themselves. People with an underlying ineptness schema might readily notice signs that they are inept and remember feedback that they are inept. Signs that they are competent, though, are not noted or remembered. Overall, people who are depressed make certain cognitive errors to arrive at biased conclusions. Their conclusions are consistent with the underlying schema, which then maintains the schema (a vicious cycle).

How has Beck's theory been tested? One widely used instrument in studies of Beck's theory is a self-report scale called the Dysfunctional Attitudes Scale (DAS), which includes items concerning whether people would consider themselves worthwhile or lovable. Hundreds of studies have shown that people do demonstrate negative thinking on scales like the DAS during depression (Haaga, Dyck, & Ernst, 1991). In studies of how people process information, depression is associated with a tendency to pay more attention to negative stimuli than to positive stimuli (Gotlib & Krasnoperova, 1998). Once people with depression notice negative information, they tend to dwell on or ruminate about that negative information (Nolen-Hoeksema, Morrow, & Fredrickson, 1993). Not surprisingly, then, they tend to remember negative information more than positive information (Matt, Vazquez, & Campbell, 1992).

Despite the clear evidence that thinking is negative during a depressive episode, the greatest challenge for cognitive theories of depression is to resolve questions of cause and effect. That is, can certain cognitive styles cause depression, or do depressive symptoms cause those cognitive styles? Some studies suggest that people with negative cognitive styles are at elevated risk for developing depression. For example, in a study of 1,507 adolescents, very high scores on the DAS in combination with negative life events predicted the onset of MDD (Lewinsohn, Joiner, & Rohde, 2001). Other researchers found that high scores on the DAS predicted relapse for several years after treatment for depression (Segal et al., 2006). On the other hand, in a study of 770 women followed for 3 years, the DAS did not predict first episodes of depression, nor did the DAS scores predict recurrent episodes of depression once history of depression was controlled (Otto et al., 2007). Hence, findings are not consistent regarding the DAS.

Other studies have examined related cognitive variables as a way to predict depression. For example, cognitive biases in the way people

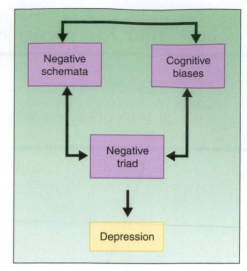

Figure 8.6 The interrelationships among different kinds of cognitions in Beck's theory of depression.

Being rejected by peers may lead to the development of the negative schema that, according to Beck's theory, plays a key role in depression. (Richard Hutchings/ Photo Researchers.)

Check Your Knowledge 8.3

True or False?

1. As many as 42 to 67 percent of people experience a stressful life event before an episode of major depression.
2. Most people who experience a stressful life event develop MDD.
3. Depressive episodes are differentiated from anxiety by low levels of positive affect.
4. Extraversion is more predictive of depression than neuroticism is.

process positive and negative information were found to predict depression over a 12- to 18-month period in a large sample of undergraduate students (Rude et al., 2003). Other studies of cognition have focused on hopelessness theory, described next.

Hopelessness Theory   In this section we discuss the evolution of an influential cognitive theory of depression—the hopelessness theory. The initial version of this theory was called learned helplessness; it was then modified to incorporate attributions and then modified again to emphasize hopelessness (see Figure 8.7).

Martin Seligman (1974) formulated **learned helplessness theory** to explain the behavior of dogs given electric shocks. He compared two groups of dogs that both received repeated shocks: one group could escape from the shocks, and the other could not. The dogs that received inescapable shocks seemed to give up. Later, when the experimental conditions were changed and the shocks could be avoided, these dogs were less likely to learn an avoidance response than dogs that had been able to escape from shocks. Rather, after a shock, most of them would lay down in a corner and whimper. Seligman proposed that animals acquire a sense of helplessness when confronted with uncontrollable aversive situations. This sense of helplessness then impairs their performance even when aversive situations are controllable. Animals exposed to uncontrollable shocks also developed symptoms that look like depressive symptoms, such as decreased appetite. On the basis of neurobiological and behavioral studies on the effects of uncontrollable stress, Seligman concluded that learned helplessness in animals could provide a model for human depression.

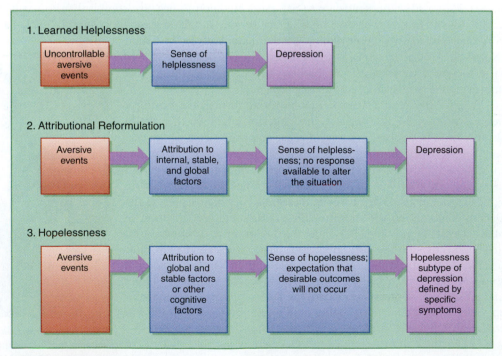

Figure 8.7 The three helplessness/ hopelessness theories of depression.

As researchers began to apply this research to humans, they found that aversive experiences triggered helplessness in some people but not others. With a moment's reflection, you can probably think of people who went through terrible stressors and still did not become depressed. Others seem to react with depression after even minor stressors. To deal with this problem, researchers revised the learned helplessness model to incorporate cognition (Abramson, Seligman, & Teasdale, 1978). The revised theory focused on three key dimensions of **attributions**—the explanations a person forms about why a stressor has occurred (Weiner et al., 1971):

1. Internal (personal) versus external (environmental) causes
2. Stable (permanent) versus unstable (temporary) causes
3. Global (relevant to many life domains) versus specific (limited to one area) causes

Table 8.5 illustrates these dimensions by considering how different people might explain their low score on the Graduate Record Examination (GRE). This revised model suggests that people whose **attributional style** leads them to believe that negative life events are due to internal, stable, and global causes are likely to become depressed.

Attributional style predicts increases in depressive symptoms (Peterson, Maier, & Seligman, 1993), but it is unclear whether attributional style predicts full diagnoses of MDD. For instance, attributional style has predicted the onset of MDD among children (Nolen-Hoeksema, Girgus, & Seligman, 1986), but some studies have found that attributional style did not predict the onset of diagnosable MDD in adolescents (Lewinsohn, Joiner, & Rohde, 2001) or adults (Barnett & Gotlib, 1988).

The current version of the theory, **hopelessness theory** (Abramson, Metalsky, & Alloy, 1989), suggests that cognitive processes explain only one type of depression (hopelessness depression). Symptoms of hopelessness depression include decreased motivation, sadness, suicidality, decreased energy, psychomotor retardation, sleep disturbances, poor concentration, and negative cognitions. In this view, the most important trigger of this type of depression is hopelessness, which is defined as an expectation that (1) desirable outcomes will not occur and that (2) the person has no responses available to change this situation. As in the revised model incorporating attributions, hopelessness can be triggered by stable and global attributions about the causes of stressors. But the model also suggests that there are other ways in which a person can become hopeless, including through low self-esteem or through the sometimes accurate recognition that life events will have severe negative consequences.

Gerald Metalsky and colleagues conducted the first test of hopelessness theory. Early in the semester, college students completed the Attributional Style Questionnaire (ASQ), as well as questionnaires to assess their grade aspirations, their depressive symptoms, hopelessness, and self-esteem. These measures were used to predict the persistence of depressive symptoms after a test among the students whose grades were below their expectations. Those who attributed poor grades to global and stable factors experienced more hopelessness, but this pattern was found only among students whose self-esteem was low. Hopelessness predicted depressive symptoms. Clearly, these results support the hopelessness theory. Also, a similar study conducted with children in the sixth and seventh grades yielded almost identical results (Robinson, Garber, & Hillsman, 1995).

One study has assessed several different aspects of cognitive theories of depression. In the Temple-Wisconsin Cognitive Vulnerability to Depression study, both the DAS and the ASQ were used to predict the development of first episodes of MDD, recurrent episodes of MDD, and also the hopelessness subtype of MDD. In this study, high- and low-risk groups were defined based on scores on the DAS and the ASQ and then followed for $2\frac{1}{2}$ years. The 173 students in the

Table 8.5 An Example of Attributions: Why I Failed My GRE Math Exam

| | Internal (Personal) | | External (Environmental) | |
	Stable	Unstable	Stable	Unstable
Global	I lack intelligence.	I am exhausted.	These tests are all unfair.	It's an unlucky day, Friday the 13th.
Specific	I lack mathematical ability.	I am fed up with math.	The math tests are unfair.	My math test was numbered "13."

upper 25 percent of the distributions for both measures were classified as high risk; the 176 students in the bottom 25 percent of the distributions were classified as low risk. Findings from this study provided support for cognitive theories: students in the high-risk group were more likely to develop first episodes of MDD as well as recurrent MDD than were students in the low-risk group (Alloy et al., 2006). Unfortunately, though, because both the DAS, a measure used to test Beck's theory, and the ASQ, the measure used in tests of the hopelessness theory, were used to define the high-risk group, we do not know whether this finding supports the hopelessness theory, Beck's theory, or both. Findings did provide support for one part of the hopelessness model, in that the cognitive measures predicted the specific symptoms defined as hopelessness depression (Alloy et al., 2000).

Fitting Together the Etiological Factors in Depressive Disorders

Research integrating the neurobiological and psychosocial etiology of depressive disorders is increasingly common. One example of this integration is the growing attention to the serotonin transporter gene. In rhesus monkeys, the presence of a polymorphism (at least one short allele) in this gene is associated with poor serotonergic function. A study found that people with this polymorphism were at greater risk for depression after a stressful life event than those without the polymorphism (Caspi et al., 2003). That is, having at least one short allele was associated with elevated reactivity to stress (see Figure 8.8). Thus, some people seem to inherit a propensity for a weaker serotonin system, which is then expressed as a greater likelihood to experience depression after a major stressor. This finding has been replicated in other large-scale studies (Kendler et al., 2005). This type of neurobiological vulnerability could set the stage for depressive disorder after major negative life events. Intriguingly, a polymorphism in the serotonin transporter gene has also been related to elevated activity of the amygdala (Hariri et al., 2005). This type of work, drawing together genetic and neurobiological risk factors with social and psychological variables, is increasingly common. By considering the set of variables together, researchers can begin to develop more precise models of who is likely to become depressed under what circumstances.

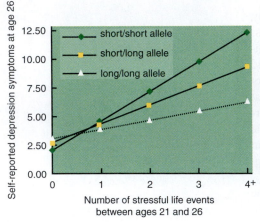

Figure 8.8 Life events interact with the serotonin transporter gene to predict symptoms of depression. Adapted from Caspi et al. (2003). *Science, 301,* 387. Reprinted with permission from AAAS.

Social and Psychological Factors in Bipolar Disorder

Most people who experience a manic episode during their life will also experience a major depressive episode—but not everyone will. Given this, researchers often study the triggers of manic and depressive episodes separately within bipolar disorder.

Depression in Bipolar Disorder   The triggers of depressive episodes in bipolar disorder appear similar to the triggers of major depressive episodes (Johnson & Kizer, 2002). As in MDD, negative life events appear important in precipitating depressive episodes in bipolar disorder. Similarly, neuroticism, negative cognitions (Reilly-Harrington et al., 1999), expressed emotion (Yan et al., 2004), and lack of social support predict depressive symptoms in bipolar disorder.

Mania   One psychological model hypothesizes that mania reflects a disturbance in the reward system of the brain (Depue, Collins, & Luciano, 1996). Researchers have demonstrated that people with bipolar disorder describe themselves as highly responsive to rewards on a self-report measure (Meyer et al., 2001). In addition, a particular kind of life event predicts increases in manic symptoms in people with bipolar I disorder over a 2-year period (Johnson et al., 2000, 2008)—specifically, life events that involved attaining goals, such as gaining acceptance to graduate school or getting married.

How could successes like these promote increases in symptoms? In studies that have provided (false) success feedback, people with a history of mild hypomanic symptoms seem to develop more confidence after an initial success compared to those with no history of hypomanic symptoms (Stern & Berrenberg, 1979). Thus, researchers have proposed that life events involving success may trigger cognitive changes in confidence, which then spiral into excessive goal pursuit (Johnson, 2005). This excessive goal pursuit may help trigger manic symptoms among people with bipolar disorder.

Quick Summary

Research strongly supports the role of life events as a trigger for MDD. Because many people do not become depressed after a life event, researchers have studied diatheses that could explain vulnerability to life events. Interpersonal research highlights the role of low social support, high expressed emotion, high need for reassurance, and poor social skills as risk factors for depression. Once a person becomes depressed, increases in negativity and reassurance-seeking may lead to more negativity and rejection from other people, potentially prolonging the episodes.

Beyond social factors, researchers have focused on psychological factors. Freud's theory—that depression is due to anger turned inward—has not obtained much support. But other psychological risk factors can help explain why some people become depressed. Evidence suggests that neuroticism, which involves high negative affect, predicts the onset of depression. Cognitive factors include a negative schema; negative beliefs about the self, world, and future; biases to attend to and recall negative rather than positive information; stable, global, and internal attributions for stressors; and hopelessness.

Less psychological research is available on bipolar disorder. Nonetheless, many of the variables that predict MDD also appear to predict depressive symptoms within bipolar disorder. For mania, one model suggests that mania may arise after life events involving goal attainment and excess involvement in pursuing goals.

Treatment of Mood Disorders

Most episodes of depression end after a few months, but the time may seem immeasurably longer to people with depression and to those close to them. With mania, even a few days of acute symptoms can create troubles for relationships and jobs. Moreover, suicide is a risk for people with mood disorders. Thus, it is important to treat mood disorders. Indeed, recent research suggests that it pays to treat depression. In one study, researchers ran a program at 16 major U.S. companies to identify depression, provide referrals for people with depression, and even offer therapy by phone (Wang, Simon, et al., 2007). Although the program cost several hundred dollars per worker, it saved about $1,800 per employee in lost time at work, employee turnover, and other costs.

A major public health goal is to increase the number of people who receive adequate treatment. Certainly, many people try to obtain treatment; more than 180,000,000 prescriptions per year are filled for antidepressants in the United States (IMS Health, 2006; see Figure 8.9). Despite this, surveys suggest that three-quarters of people do not receive effective treatments for MDD (Young et al., 2001). The first treatment with either psychotherapy or antidepressant medications is likely to help about 50–70 percent of people with MDD. Why do up to half of people not get relief? Many people stop treatment early. For example, among patients who are prescribed an antidepressant, 40 percent stop taking the medication within the first month (Olfson et al., 2006). Others are not provided with enough medication or therapy.

In this section, we cover psychological treatments of depressive disorders and bipolar disorder. Then we turn to biological treatments of depressive disorders and bipolar disorder.

Psychological Treatment of Depression

Several different forms of psychological treatment have been shown to help relieve depression. As with studies of etiology, most of the research has focused on MDD. We note when treatments have been shown to be effective in the treatment of dysthymia.

Here, we review treatments that have been shown to perform well in comparison with placebo. For this reason, we do not discuss psychoanalytic therapy—a report from the American Psychiatric Association (1993) concluded that there is no reliable evidence indicating that long-term psychoanalysis is effective in treating depression.

Interpersonal Psychotherapy A treatment known as **interpersonal psychotherapy (IPT)** has fared well in clinical trials. As we described in Chapter 2, IPT builds on the idea that depression is closely tied to interpersonal problems (Klerman et al., 1984). The core of the therapy is to examine major interpersonal problems, such as role transitions, interpersonal conflicts,

Figure 8.9 More than 180,000,000 prescriptions per year are filled for antidepressants in the United States. The percentage of people who filled a prescription for an antidepressant more than doubled between 1996 and 2003. [Drawn from Meyerhoefer & Zuvekas (2008).]

bereavement, and interpersonal isolation. Typically, the therapist and the patient focus on one or two such issues, with the goal of helping the person identify his or her feelings about these issues, make important decisions, and make changes to resolve problems related to these issues. Like cognitive behavioral treatments, IPT is typically brief (e.g., 16 sessions). Techniques include discussing interpersonal problems, exploring negative feelings and encouraging their expression, improving both verbal and nonverbal communications, problem solving, and suggesting new and more satisfying modes of behavior.

Several studies have found that IPT is effective in relieving MDD (Elkin et al., 1989) and that it appears to prevent relapse when treatment is continued after recovery (Frank et al., 1990). In addition, studies indicate that IPT can be effective in treating MDD among adolescents (Mufson et al., 1999) and postpartum women (Zlotnick et al., 2001). In a study among villagers in Uganda, group sessions of IPT provided relief from depressive symptoms (Bolton et al., 2003). IPT has also been found to be effective in the treatment of dysthymia (Markowitz, 1994). In recent studies of elderly patients, though, IPT did not perform better than a placebo and appeared less helpful than an antidepressant medication (Dombrovsky et al., 2007; Lesperance et al., 2007). In most studies, though, IPT appears helpful.

Cognitive Therapy   In keeping with their theory that depression is caused by negative schemata and cognitive biases, Beck and associates devised a **cognitive therapy** aimed at altering maladaptive thought patterns. The therapist tries to help the person with depression to change his or her opinions about the self. When a person states that he or she is worthless because "nothing goes right, and everything I try to do ends in a disaster," the therapist helps the person look for evidence that contradicts this overgeneralization, such as abilities that the person is overlooking or discounting. The therapist also teaches the person to monitor private monologues and to identify thought patterns that contribute to depression. The therapist then teaches the person to challenge negative beliefs and to learn strategies that promote making realistic and positive assumptions. Beck's emphasis is on cognitive restructuring (i.e., persuading the person to think less negatively).

Clinical Case: An Example of Challenging a Negative Thought in Cognitive Therapy

The following dialogue is an example of one way that a therapist might begin to challenge a person's negative thoughts in cognitive therapy, although it would take several sessions to help a client learn the cognitive model and to identify overly negative thoughts. It should be noted that the therapist and client are likely to challenge thoughts in several different ways over the course of treatment. Another example of thought restructuring with this client is described in Chapter 16.

Therapist: *You said that you are a "loser" because you and Roger got divorced. Now we already defined what it is to be a loser—not to achieve anything.*
Patient: *Right. That sounds really extreme.*
Therapist: *OK. Let's look at the evidence for and against the thought that you have achieved something. Draw a line down the center of the page. On the top I'd like you to write, "I have achieved some things."*
Patient: *[draws line and writes statement]*
Therapist: *What is the evidence that you have achieved some things?*
Patient: *I graduated from college, I raised my son, I worked at the office, I have some friends, and I exercise. I am reliable. I care about my friends.*

Therapist: *OK. Let's write all of that down. Now in the right column let's write down evidence against the thought that you have achieved some things.*
Patient: *Well, maybe it's irrational, but I would have to write down that I got divorced.*
Therapist: *OK. Now in looking at the evidence for and against your thought that you have achieved some things, how do you weigh it out? 50–50? Differently than 50–50?*
Patient: *I'd have to say it's 95% in favor of the positive thought.*
Therapist: *So, how much do you believe now that you have achieved some things?*
Patient: *100%.*
Therapist: *And how much do you believe that you are a failure because you got divorced?*
Patient: *Maybe I'm not a failure, but the marriage failed. I'd give myself about 10%.*
(quoted in Leahy, 2003).

Note: As is typical, this dialogue challenges some, but not all, negative thoughts. Future sessions are likely to examine other negative thoughts.

Beck also includes a behavioral technique in his therapy called **behavioral activation (BA)**, in which people are given activity assignments to provide them with successful experiences and to allow them to think well of themselves. For example, the therapist encourages patients to do things that increase the opportunity to have positive experiences, such as going for a walk and talking with friends.

Considerable research has been conducted on Beck's therapy, beginning with a widely cited study indicating that cognitive therapy was more successful than the tricyclic antidepressant imipramine (Tofranil) in alleviating depression (Rush et al., 1977). Many other studies have confirmed the efficacy of cognitive therapy for relieving symptoms of MDD and preventing subsequent bouts of depression (Hollon, Thase, & Markowitz, 2002). With modifications, early results show that cognitive therapy (CT) is promising in the treatment of dysthymia (Hollon et al., 2002). The strategies that clients learn in CT help diminish the risk of relapse even after therapy ends, an important issue in MDD (Vittengl et al., 2007). CT is particularly helpful in preventing relapse for those who need this protection the most—people with at least five episodes of previous depression gain protection from relapse through CT (Bockting et al., 2005).

An adaptation of cognitive therapy called **mindfulness-based cognitive therapy (MBCT)** focuses on relapse prevention after successful treatment for recurrent episodes of major depression (Segal, Williams, & Teasdale, 2001). MBCT is based on the assumption that a person becomes vulnerable to relapse because of repeated associations between sad mood and patterns of self-devaluative, hopeless thinking during major depressive episodes. As a result, when people who have recovered from depression become sad, they begin to think as negatively as they had when they were severely depressed. These reactivated patterns of thinking in turn intensify the sadness (Teasdale, 1988). Thus, in people with a history of major depression, sadness is more likely to escalate, which may contribute to the onset of new episodes of depression.

The goal of MBCT is to teach people to recognize when they start to become depressed and to try adopting what can be called a "decentered" perspective, viewing their thoughts merely as "mental events" rather than as core aspects of the self or as accurate reflections of reality. For example, the person might say to himself or herself such statements as "thoughts are not facts" and "I am not my thoughts" (Teasdale et al., 2000, p. 616). In other words, using a wide array of strategies, including meditation, the person is taught over time to develop a detached relationship to depression-related thoughts and feelings. This perspective, it is believed, can prevent the escalation of negative thinking patterns that may cause depression.

In one multisite study (Teasdale et al., 2000) people who formerly had depression were randomly assigned to MBCT or to "treatment as usual" (e.g., patients were instructed to seek help from other sources, as they normally would). Results of this study showed that MBCT was more effective than "treatment as usual" in reducing the risk of relapse among people with three or more previous major depressive episodes. MBCT does not appear to protect against relapse among people with only one or two previous major depressive episodes (Ma & Teasdale, 2004). This treatment, then, shows promise for patients with highly recurrent major depression.

Behavioral Activation (BA) Therapy   Some studies have focused on a treatment that uses just the behavioral activation (BA) component of Beck's therapy (Jacobson & Gortner, 2000). Inactivity, withdrawal, and inertia are common symptoms of depression. From a behavioral activation perspective, however, the *function* of these behaviors is crucial. Proponents of BA contend that these behaviors will diminish the already low levels of positive reinforcement associated with depression. Consequently, BA seeks to increase participation in positively reinforcing activities so as to disrupt the spiral of depression, withdrawal, and avoidance (Martell, Addis, & Jacobson, 2001).

BA has received a great deal of attention after positive findings in a study of which ingredients in Beck's therapy are most effective (Gortner et al., 1998). These findings suggested that the BA component of Beck's therapy performed as well as the full package in relieving MDD and preventing relapse over a 2-year follow-up period. A replication study provided support for the efficacy of BA in a study of 214 patients with MDD (Dimidjian et al., 2006). These findings challenge the notion that people must directly modify their negative thinking to alleviate depression and suggest instead that engaging in rewarding activities may be enough. Group versions of behavioral therapy also appear to be effective (Oei & Dingle, 2008).

Behavioral Couples Therapy   As described above, depression is often tied to relationship problems, including marital and family distress. Drawing on these findings, researchers have studied behavioral couples therapy as a treatment for depression. In this approach, researchers work with both members of a couple to improve communication and relationship satisfaction. Findings indicate that when a person with depression is also experiencing marital distress, **behavioral couples therapy** is as effective in relieving depression as individual cognitive therapy (Jacobson et al., 1991) or antidepressant medication (Barbato & D'Avanzo, 2008). As you might expect, marital therapy has the advantage that it relieves relationship distress more than individual therapy does.

Psychological Treatment of Bipolar Disorder

Medication is a necessary part of treatment for bipolar disorder, but psychological treatments can supplement medications. Psychological treatments show promise in dealing with many of the social and cognitive problems associated with bipolar disorder (Johnson & Leahy, 2004).

Educating people about their illness is a common component to treating many disorders, including bipolar disorder and schizophrenia. **Psychoeducational approaches** typically help people learn about the symptoms of the disorder, the expected time course of symptoms, the biological and psychological triggers for symptoms, and treatment strategies. Studies confirm that careful education about bipolar disorder can help people adhere to treatment with medications such as lithium (Colom et al., 2003). This is an important goal, because as many as half of people being treated for bipolar disorder do not take medication consistently (Regier et al., 1993). A friend of one of the authors put it like this: "Lithium cuts out the highs as well as the lows. I don't miss the lows, but I gotta admit that there were some aspects of the highs that I do miss. It took me a while to accept that I had to give up those highs. Wanting to keep my job and my marriage helped!" A drug alone does not address this kind of concern. Beyond helping people be more consistent about their medications, psychoeducational programs have been shown to help people avoid hospitalization (Morris et al., 2007).

Studies have begun to suggest that psychotherapies can also help reduce relapse in bipolar disorder. For example, cognitive therapy like that offered for MDD appears effective as a supplement to medications (Lam et al., 2000).

Expressed emotion (see p. 230) predicts faster relapse in bipolar I disorder (Miklowitz et al., 1996). This points to the need for family interventions. **Family-focused treatment (FFT)** aims to educate the family about the illness, enhance family communication, and develop problem-solving skills (Miklowitz & Goldstein, 1997). FFT leads to lower rates of relapse when added to medication treatment (Miklowitz et al., 2003). Not surprisingly, however, cognitive treatment and FFT seem to relieve symptoms of depression more than those of mania.

In a major study of therapy for bipolar disorder, researchers studied people who had bipolar disorder and who were depressed at the time they sought treatment (Miklowitz et al., 2007). To make sure that findings would generalize to different types of treatment centers, patients were recruited from 14 widely different treatment clinics across the United States. All of the patients in the trial received intensive medication treatment, because researchers were interested in whether adding psychotherapy to medication treatment for bipolar disorder is helpful. Patients were randomly assigned to receive either psychotherapy or collaborative care. The 130 patients assigned to collaborative care were offered three supportive sessions with a treatment provider. The 163 patients in the psychotherapy condition were further assigned to receive either cognitive therapy, FFT, or IPT (interpersonal psychotherapy). Psychotherapy was offered for up to 9 months. About 30 percent of the patients in the study discontinued treatment, and these rates did not differ by treatment condition. Each type of psychotherapy helped relieve depression more than the collaborative care condition did. There was no evidence that cognitive therapy, FFT, or IPT differed in their effects on depression. These findings suggest that it is important for people with bipolar disorder to receive psychotherapy when they are experiencing depression and that several types of therapy can be helpful.

Biological Treatment of Mood Disorders

A variety of biological therapies are used to treat depression and mania. The two major biological treatments are electroconvulsive therapy and drugs.

Electroconvulsive Therapy for Depression   Perhaps the most dramatic and controversial treatment for MDD is **electroconvulsive therapy (ECT)** (see p. 15). For the most part now, ECT is only used to treat MDD that has not responded to medication. ECT entails deliberately inducting a momentary seizure and unconsciousness by passing a 70–130 volt current through the patient's brain. Formerly, electrodes were placed on each side of the forehead, a method known as *bilateral ECT*. Today, *unilateral ECT,* in which the current passes through only the nondominant (typically the right) cerebral hemisphere, is more common. In the past, the patient was usually awake until the current triggered the seizure, and the electric shock often created frightening contortions of the body, sometimes even causing bone fractures. Now the patient is given a muscle relaxant before the current is applied. The convulsive spasms of muscles are barely perceptible, and the patient awakens a few minutes later remembering nothing about the treatment. Typically, patients receive between 6 and 12 treatments, spaced several days apart.

Even with these improvements in procedures, inducing a seizure is drastic treatment. Why should anyone agree to undergo such radical therapy? The answer is simple. ECT is the most reliable treatment available for depression with psychotic features (Sackheim et al., 2001), even though we don't know why it works. Most professionals acknowledge that people undergoing ECT face some risks of short-term confusion and memory loss. It is fairly common for patients to have no memory of the period during which they received ECT and, sometimes, for the weeks surrounding the procedure. Unilateral ECT, produces fewer cognitive side effects than bilateral ECT does (Sackeim et al., 2001). Nonetheless, even unilateral ECT is associated with deficits in cognitive functioning 6 months after treatment (Sackeim et al., 2007). In any case, clinicians typically resort to ECT only if less drastic treatments have failed. Given that suicide is a real possibility among people who are depressed, many experts regard the use of ECT after other treatments have failed as a responsible approach.

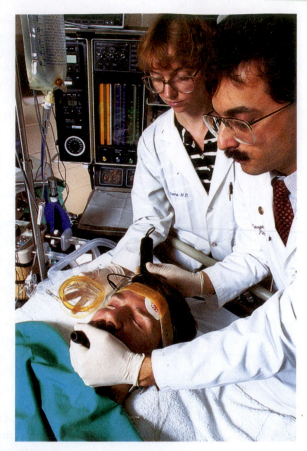

Electroconvulsive therapy is an effective treatment for depression that has not responded to medication. Using unilateral shock and muscle relaxants has reduced its undesirable side effects. (Will & Deni McIntyre/Photo Researchers.)

Medications for Depressive Disorders   Drugs are the most commonly used and best-researched treatments—biological or otherwise—for depressive disorders (and, as we will see, for bipolar disorders as well). As shown in Table 8.6, there are three major categories of antidepressant drugs: **monoamine oxidase (MAO) inhibitors**, **tricyclic antidepressants**, and **selective serotonin reuptake inhibitors (SSRIs)**. The clinical effectiveness of all three classes of drugs

Table 8.6 Medications for Treating Mood Disorders

Category	Generic Name	Trade Name	Side Effects
MAO inhibitor antidepressants	tranylcypromine	Parnate	Possibly fatal hypertension, dry mouth, dizziness, nausea, headaches
Tricyclic antidepressants	imipramine amitriptyline	Tofranil Elavil	Heart attack, stroke, hypotension, blurred vision, anxiety, tiredness, dry mouth, constipation, gastric disorders, erectile dysfunction, weight gain
Selective serotonin reuptake inhibitor (SSRI) antidepressants	fluoxetine sertraline	Prozac Zoloft	Nervousness, fatigue, gastrointestinal complaints, dizziness, headaches, insomnia, suicidality
Mood stabilizers	lithium	Lithium	Tremors, gastric distress, lack of coordination, dizziness, cardiac arrhythmia, blurred vision, fatigue, death (in rare cases)
Anticonvulsants	divalproex sodium	Depakote	Pancreatitis
Antipsychotics	olanzapine	Zyprexa	Hyperglycemia, diabetes, tardive dyskinesia, and, in elderly patients, cardiovascular problems, neuroleptic malignant syndrome

is about the same (Depression Guidelines Panel, 1993). A number of double-blind studies have shown these medications to be effective in treating depressive disorders, with 50–70 percent of people who complete treatment showing major improvement (Depression Guidelines Panel, 1993; Nemeroff & Schatzberg, 1998). These medications have been found to be effective in treating dysthymia as well as major depression (Hollon, Thase, & Markowitz, 2002).

One report, however, suggests that these published studies may overestimate how many people respond well to antidepressant medications. When pharmaceutical companies conduct studies to apply for either initial approval to market a medication or to support a change in the use of a medication, the data must be filed with the Food and Drug Administration (FDA). One research team recently examined what happened to the data from antidepressant studies conducted between 1987 and 2004 (Turner et al., 2008). The FDA rated 38 studies as having positive findings (e.g., supported the use of the antidepressant) and 36 as having neutral or negative findings. Of the studies that the FDA deemed to have positive findings, 37 out of 38 studies were eventually published. Of the 36 studies that the FDA deemed to have either neutral or negative findings, only 14 were published; in 11 of these 14 published studies, the published version of the findings seemed positive even though the FDA had rated findings as neutral or negative. Overall, then, published findings may be biased to be positive. These types of findings are difficult to interpret. Journals are less likely to publish an article with negative results, because they are interested in conveying news to practitioners about strategies that work. But it is also the case that some negative results emerge because a study is flawed, and so some studies may not have merited publication. One way to get around this issue is to create public databases that allow practitioners, scientists, and the public to have more access to the raw facts. Another strategy is to conduct very large-scale trials to help understand who does and does not respond to antidepressants and what to do when a person does not gain relief.

In an attempt to study antidepressant medication in the real world using a large sample, the STAR-D trial examined antidepressant response among 3,671 patients across 41 sites, including 18 primary care facilities (Rush et al., 2006). Many of the studies of treatment have screened for patients with "pure" depression (i.e., no other comorbid disorders) and offered treatment in specialized university clinics. In sharp contrast to the types of clean, non-comorbid depression histories reported in most medication trials, 75 percent of the patients enrolled in STAR-D suffered from chronic or recurrent depression, 61.5 percent had comorbid psychiatric conditions, and 83 percent had already received some (unsuccessful) treatment for the current episode. Rather than assessing whether antidepressant medication or psychotherapy was more helpful than a placebo treatment, the goal of the study was to consider the types of practical questions that physicians face in daily practice. For example, if initial treatment does not work, will switching to a second antidepressant work or should two antidepressants be given at the same time? What is the best treatment option if this second stage of treatment fails?

Patients were all started on citalopram (Celexa), an SSRI. If they did not respond to citalopram, they were offered (1) a choice of a different medication to replace the citalopram, (2) a chance to add a second medication to the citalopram, or (3) cognitive therapy if they were willing to pay part of the cost. Findings were generally sobering. Only about one-third of patients achieved full symptom relief when treated with citalopram (Trivedi et al., 2006). Among those who did not respond, very few wanted to pay for cognitive therapy. Among patients who did not respond to citalopram and were switched to a second round of medication treatment, about 30.6 percent achieved remission, regardless of which type of medication treatment they received. Among patients who did not respond well to either the first or second round of treatment, few responded to a third antidepressant (13.7 percent), and even fewer responded to a fourth antidepressant (13 percent). Even among those who achieved remission at one of these steps, relapse rates were high, so that even with this complex array of treatments offered, only 43 percent of people achieved sustained recovery (Nelson, 2006). Findings from this study highlight a number of important gaps in our science. First, there is a need for more careful testing of treatments in the real world, as findings may differ from findings obtained in specialty clinics. Second, there is a need for new treatments for those who do not respond well to currently available treatments.

One major problem with drug treatments is that many people stop taking their medications, often because they find the side effects unpleasant (see Table 8.6) (Thase & Rush, 1997). The MAO inhibitors are the least used antidepressants because of their potentially life-threatening side effects. The SSRIs have become the most commonly prescribed antidepressants because they tend to produce fewer side effects than the other classes of antidepressants (Enserink, 1999). In March 2004, however, the Food and Drug Administration asked manufacturers to include packaging information warning people that there have been case reports of suicidality associated with SSRIs, particularly during the early phases of treatment or after increases in dosage. There is specific concern about the potential for suicidality in children, adolescents, and young adults, and researchers continue to look at this important issue, as findings have been controversial (see Chapter 14). Such effects seem very rare, but the FDA approach is designed to protect against risk, even if that risk is faced by only a small number of people.

Although the various antidepressants hasten recovery from an episode of depression, relapse is common after the drugs are withdrawn (Reimherr et al., 2001). This is not to dismiss the advantages of temporary relief, given the potential for social problems, suicide, and hospitalization as depression continues. Results from one meta-analysis of 31 different drug trials suggest that continuing antidepressants after remission lowers the risk of recurrence from approximately 40 percent to about 20 percent (Geddes et al., 2003). Treatment guidelines recommend continuing antidepressant medications for at least 6 months after a depressive episode ends—and longer if a person has experienced several episodes. To prevent recurrence, medication doses should be as high as those offered during acute treatment.

Research Comparing Treatments for Major Depressive Disorder   Combining psychotherapy and antidepressant medications bolsters the odds of recovery by more than 10–20 percent above either psychotherapy or medications alone for most people with depression, but each treatment offers unique advantages (Hollon, Thase, & Markowitz, 2002). Antidepressants work more quickly than psychotherapy, thus providing immediate relief. Psychotherapy may take longer but may help people learn skills that they can use after treatment is finished to protect against recurrent depressive episodes. Most patients are interested in knowing whether medications or therapy will be more effective in relieving symptoms. In most studies, cognitive therapy has performed as well as medication in relieving acute symptoms of depression. In one major exception, findings of the NIMH Collaborative Study on the Treatment of Depression indicated that cognitive therapy did not provide as much symptom relief as did medication for severe depression (Elkin et al., 1996; Shea et al., 1992). Some researchers questioned whether the quality of the cognitive therapy offered in the study was up to par. In a meta-analysis of other studies comparing cognitive therapy and antidepressant medications, cognitive therapy was equally effective to antidepressant medication for the treatment of people with severe depression (DeRubeis et al.,1999).

In response to the unanswered questions, researchers designed a clinical trial to compare CT versus antidepressants in the treatment of severe depression (Hollon & DeRubeis, 2003).

Clinical Case: Treatment Decisions for Mary

Mary, the woman described in the beginning of this chapter, reported increasing problems because of her depression. Given this, her therapist referred her to a psychiatrist, who prescribed Prozac (fluoxetine). Both the psychologist and the psychiatrist agreed that medication might help by quickly relieving her symptoms. But after 2 weeks, Mary decided she did not want to continue taking Prozac because she found the side effects uncomfortable and did not like the idea of taking medication over the long term. She had not gotten much relief, but she also explained that she had missed many doses because of her concerns.

With so many different types of treatment available, determining the best therapy for each client can be a challenge. Mary had experienced a major life event and transition, suggesting that interpersonal psychotherapy might fit. But she was blaming herself for her job loss and other issues, suggesting that cognitive therapy (CT) might help. Marital

conflicts suggest behavioral couples therapy could be appropriate. How does a therapist choose which approach to use? Sometimes this decision reflects personal preferences and training of the therapist. Ideally, it incorporates the treatment preferences of the client as well. Her therapist began CT, in the belief that Mary's tendency to blame herself excessively when things went wrong was a key force in her depression. CT helped her learn to identify and challenge irrationally negative cognitions about herself. Therapy began by helping her identify times in day-to-day life when her sad moods could be explained by overly negative conclusions about small events. For example, when her children would misbehave, Mary would quickly assume this was evidence that she was a bad mother. Over time, Mary began to examine and challenge long-held beliefs about her lack of competence. By the end of 16 weeks of treatment, she had obtained relief from her symptoms of depression.

Researchers randomly assigned 240 patients with severe depression to receive antidepressant medication, CT, or a placebo for 4 months. Those who recovered were followed for another 12 months. The researchers found that CT was at least as effective as antidepressant medication for severe depression. They also found that experienced therapists were more effective than therapists without CT experience. Although both CT and medication helped people recover from depression more than a placebo did, CT had an advantage over the long term in that it helped protect against relapse once treatment was finished (Hollon et al., 2005). The researchers also noted that CT was less expensive than treatment with medication.

In a more recent study to compare different forms of treatment, 241 patients with MDD were randomly assigned to receive behavioral activation (BA) therapy, CT, antidepressant medication, or a placebo. Behavioral activation therapy and antidepressant medication both performed better than CT for those patients with severe depression (Dimidjian et al., 2006). In sum, comparisons of CT with antidepressant treatment have not provided consistent answers. This remains a hot topic of research.

Medications for Bipolar Disorder

Medications that reduce manic symptoms are called *mood-stabilizing medications*. **Lithium**, a naturally occurring chemical element, was the first mood stabilizer identified. Up to 80 percent of people with bipolar I disorder experience at least mild benefit from taking this drug (Prien & Potter, 1993). Even though symptoms may become milder with medications, most patients continue to experience at least mild manic and depressive symptoms. The median time to relapse on lithium is approximately 1 year (Keller et al., 1992). Lithium is more effective in preventing manic episodes than depressive episodes, but it does help somewhat with depression.

Because of possibly serious side effects, lithium has to be prescribed and used very carefully. When serum levels of lithium get too high, lithium toxicity can result, so patients taking lithium must have regular blood tests. Signs of lithium toxicity range from mild symptoms like tremor, nausea, blurred vision, vertigo, and confusion, to very severe symptoms, including cardiac dysrhythmias, seizures, coma, and even death. It is recommended that lithium be used continually for the person's entire life (Bowden et al., 2000), but many patients discontinue treatment (Maj et al., 1998).

Two classes of medications other than lithium have been approved by the FDA for the treatment of acute mania: anticonvulsant (antiseizure) medications such as divalproex sodium (Depakote) and antipsychotic medications such as Olanzapine (Zyprexa). Lithium is still recommended as the first choice, but these other treatments are recommended for people who are unable to tolerate lithium's side effects. Like lithium, these medications help reduce mania and, to some extent, depression. Unfortunately, even these medications have serious side effects. Anticonvulsants have been found to be related to a twofold increase in suicidal ideation compared to rates on placebo (FDA, 2008). Beyond anticonvulsant and antipsychotic medications, several other medications show promising early results (Stahl, 2006).

Typically, lithium is used in combination with other medications. Because lithium takes effect gradually, therapy typically begins with both lithium and an antipsychotic medication, such as olanzapine, which has an immediate calming effect (Scherk, Pajonk, Leucht, 2007).

Many people continue to experience depression even when taking a mood-stabilizing medication like lithium. For these people, an antidepressant medication is often added to the regimen (Sachs & Thase, 2000). But new findings call this practice into question. Initially, concerns were raised because if administered without a mood stabilizer, an antidepressant can actually trigger manic symptoms for 25–30 percent of people with bipolar I disorder (Ghaemi, Boiman, & Goodwin, 2000; Leverich et al., 2006). Beyond these concerns about harmful effects, recent findings cast doubt on whether antidepressants actually help reduce depression among persons who are already taking a mood stabilizer (the first type of treatment provided in bipolar disorder). In one trial, patients with bipolar disorder who were already taking a mood stabilizer were randomly assigned to receive an antidepressant or placebo for 26 weeks. Findings indicated that antidepressants were not effective in combating bipolar depression when added to a mood stabilizer (Sachs et al., 2007).

A major focus of current research is on identifying the best treatments for depression in bipolar disorder. Some of these studies indicate that the anticonvulsant medication lamotrigine (Lamictal) might be effective (Calabrese et al., 1999, 2003).

Depression and Primary Care

About half of all antidepressant prescriptions are written by primary care physicians. Research has shown that primary care doctors, perhaps because of time pressure, often fail to diagnose episodes of depression, and even when they offer treatment, these treatments tend to be too short, medication doses tend to be too small, and opportunities for psychotherapy tend to be limited. In health maintenance organization (HMO) settings, too, time pressures may interfere with optimal care. One group of researchers studied antidepressant treatment at an HMO and found that only about half of the patients received an adequate regimen of drug therapy (Simon et al., 2001).

Researchers are studying how to improve the quality of care offered by primary care physicians or within HMOs. Simply telling doctors to diagnose and treat depression does not work very well; studies of written treatment guidelines and workshops for doctors do not show much effect on treatment practices (Gilbody et al., 2003). More intensive programs, however, do seem to help. For example, promising results have been obtained with telephone follow-ups, increased nursing care, or specific guidelines that help physicians identify patients who should receive more intensive care (Gilbody et al., 2003). Similar programs, involving more nursing support and more patient psychoeducation, have been shown to be helpful in bipolar disorder (Simon et al., 2006).

A Final Note on the Treatment of Depression

Some of the most exciting research today is focused on how treatments work. Researchers have shown that successful treatments, whether with psychotherapy, medications, or ECT, change activity in the brain regions related to depression (Brody et al., 2001; Goldapple et al., 2004; Nobler et al., 2001). Intriguingly, antidepressant medications and ECT both stimulate growth of neurons in the hippocampus in rats (Duman, Malberg, & Nakagawa, 2001), and the effects of antidepressants, at least in animals, appear to depend on whether these neurons grow (Santarelli et al., 2003). Understanding more about how psychological and medication treatments change underlying neurobiological processes may help us refine treatments for the future.

Quick Summary

Many different treatments are available for depression. Cognitive therapy, interpersonal psychotherapy, behavioral activation treatment, and behavioral couples therapy have received support. The three forms of antidepressants have been found to be similarly effective; SSRIs have become more popular because they have fewer side effects than MAO inhibitors and tricyclic antidepressants. Two studies found that cognitive therapy was not as powerful as antidepressant medication in relieving MDD, but most research has found strong support for CT in the treatment of even severe MDD.

Medication treatment is the first line of defense against bipolar disorder. The best-researched mood stabilizer is lithium, but anticonvulsants and antipsychotic medications are also used. Recent findings cast doubt on whether antidepressant medication is helpful in bipolar disorder. Some psychological treatments may help when offered as supplements to medications for the treatment of bipolar disorder. These include psychoeducational approaches, cognitive therapy, and family therapy. These treatments appear particularly helpful in improving adherence to medication and relieving depressive symptoms within bipolar disorder.

Check Your Knowledge 8.4

Circle all answers that apply.

1. Which of the following psychotherapies have obtained support in the treatment of MDD?
   a. interpersonal psychotherapy
   b. behavioral activation
   c. psychoanalytic therapy
   d. cognitive therapy
2. The most effective treatment for MDD with psychotic features is
   a. Prozac
   b. any antidepressant medication
   c. ECT
   d. psychotherapy
3. Selective serotonin reuptake inhibitors (SSRIs) are more popular than other antidepressants because
   a. they are more effective
   b. they have fewer side effects
   c. they are cheaper

Suicide

Clinical Case: Steven

"Shannon Neal can instantly tell you the best night of her life: Tuesday, Dec. 23, 2003, the Hinsdale Academy debutante ball. Her father, Steven Neal, a 54-year-old political columnist for The Chicago Sun-Times, was in his tux, white gloves and tie. 'My dad walked me down and took a little bow,' she said, and then the two of them goofed it up on the dance floor as they laughed and laughed. A few weeks later, Mr. Neal parked his car in his garage, turned on the motor and waited until carbon monoxide filled the enclosed space and took his breath, and his life, away."

Thinking back, his wife reported that he had been under stress as he finished a book and had been hospitalized for heart problems. "Still, those who knew him were blindsided. 'If I had just 30 seconds with him now,' Ms. Neal said of her father, 'I would want all these answers.'"
(Quoted from Cohen, 2008)

No other kind of death leaves friends and relatives with such long-lasting feelings of distress, shame, guilt, and puzzlement as does suicide (Gallo & Pfeffer, 2003). Survivors have an especially high mortality rate in the year after the suicide of a loved one.

We will focus on quantitative research on suicide, but those who study suicide learn from many different sources. Many philosophers have written searchingly on the topic, including Descartes, Voltaire, Kant, Heidegger, and Camus. In addition, novelists such as Herman Melville and Leo Tolstoy have provided insights on suicide, as have writers who have killed themselves, such as Virginia Woolf (see p. 247 for her note) and Sylvia Plath.

It is important to begin by differentiating suicidal ideation, suicide attempts, and suicide. Suicidal ideation refers to thoughts of killing oneself and is much more common than attempted successful suicide. Suicide attempts involve behaviors that are intended to cause death but do not result in death. **Suicides** involve behaviors that are intended to cause death and actually do so.

Writers who killed themselves, such as Sylvia Plath, have provided insights into the causes of suicide. (Corbis-Bettmann.)

Epidemiology of Suicide and Suicide Attempts

Suicide rates may be grossly underestimated because some deaths are ambiguous—for example, seemingly accidental death may involve suicidal intentions. Nonetheless, it has been estimated that, on average, every 20 minutes someone in the United States dies from suicide (Arias et al., 2003).

Studies on the epidemiology of suicidality suggest the following:

- The overall suicide rate in the United States is about 1 per 10,000 in a given year (Centers for Disease Control and Prevention, 2006). In the United States, it is estimated that approximately 1 in 20 suicide attempts results in death (Moscicki, 1995).

  - About 10–20 percent of people report suicidal ideation at least once in their lives, and 3–5 percent have made at least one suicide attempt (Weissman et al., 1999).

  - Men are four times more likely than women to kill themselves (Arias et al., 2003).

  - Three times as many women as men make suicide attempts that do not result in death.

  - Guns are by far the most common means of suicide in the United States (Arias et al., 2003), accounting for about 60 percent of all suicides. Men usually choose to shoot or hang themselves; women are more likely to use pills, a less lethal method, which may account for their lower rate of completed suicide.

  - The suicide rate increases in old age. The highest rates of suicide in the United States are for white males over age 50.

  - The rates of suicide for adolescents and children in the United States are increasing dramatically but are still far below the rates of adults (see Figure 8.10). Some estimates suggest that at least 40 percent of

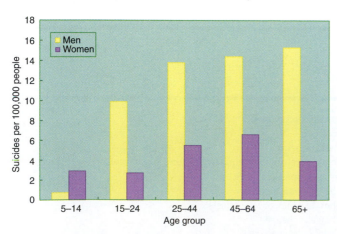

Figure 8.10 Annual deaths due to suicides per 100,000 people. From Arias et al. (2003).

children and adolescents experience suicidal ideation at least once. Because young people are less likely to die from other causes, suicide ranks as the third leading cause of death among those aged 10 to 24.

- Being divorced or widowed elevates suicide risk four- or fivefold.

Models of Suicide

Suicide is such a complex and multifaceted act that no single model can hope to explain it. Myths about suicide abound, highlighting the need for careful research (see Table 8.7). The study of suicide involves many different ethical questions and forces people to consider their own views on life and death. As an example of how complex these questions can be, Focus on Discovery 8.4 discusses physician-assisted suicide.

Psychological Disorders   Suicide does not usually happen out of the blue. Rather, suicide is discussed in this chapter because many persons with mood disorders have suicidal thoughts and some engage in suicidal behaviors. More than half of those who try to kill themselves are depressed at the time of the act (Centers for Disease Control and Prevention, 2006) and as many as 15 percent of people who have been hospitalized with depression ultimately die from suicide (Angst et al., 2002). Other mental illnesses also are important in understanding suicide: as many as 90 percent of people who attempt suicide are suffering from a mental illness. Among people hospitalized for schizophrenia, bipolar I disorder, or bipolar II disorder, 10–12 percent die from suicide eventually (Angst et al., 2002; Roy, 1982). Even less severe mental disorders, such as panic disorder, eating disorders, and, among men, alcohol dependence are associated with suicide (Linehan, 1997; Schmidt, Woolaway-Bickel, & Bates, 2000).

With most disorders, suicides are most likely when a person is experiencing comorbid depression (Angst et al., 2002; Linehan, 1997; Schmidt et al., 2000). A significant number of people who are not depressed, however, make suicidal attempts or kill themselves—most notably, people who have been diagnosed with borderline personality disorder (Linehan, 1997; see p. 362). Although understanding suicide within the context of mental disorders is extremely important, most people with mental illnesses do not die from suicide.

Neurobiological Models   Twin studies suggest that heritability is about 48 percent for suicide attempts (Joiner, Brown, & Wingate, 2005). Adoption studies also support the heritability of suicidality.

Research has established that, just as low levels of serotonin appear related to depression, there is a connection between serotonin and suicide. Low levels of serotonin's major metabolite, 5-HIAA, have been found among people who committed suicide (van Praag, Plutchik, & Apter, 1990). Particularly low 5-HIAA levels have been found in cases of violent and impulsive suicide (Roy, 1994; Winchel, Stanley, & Stanley, 1990). Several studies suggest that serotonin may play a role in the predisposition to suicide (Mann et al., 2000).

On March 28, 1941, at the age of 59, Virginia Woolf drowned herself in the river near her Sussex home. Two suicide notes were found in the house, similar in content; one may have been written 10 days earlier, and it is possible that she may have made an unsuccessful attempt then, for she returned from a walk soaking wet, saying that she had fallen. The first was addressed to her sister Vanessa and the second to her husband, Leonard. To him, she wrote:

Dearest, I feel certain I am going mad again. I feel we can't go through another of those terrible times. And I shan't recover this time. I begin to hear voices, and I can't concentrate. So I am doing what seems the best thing to do. You have given me the greatest possible happiness. You have been in every way all that anyone could be. I don't think two people could have been happier till this terrible disease came. I can't fight it any longer. I know that I am spoiling your life, that without me you could work. And you will I know. You see I can't even write this properly. I can't read. What I want to say is I owe all the happiness of my life to you. You have been entirely patient with me and incredibly good. I want to say that—everybody knows it. If anybody could have saved me it would have been you. Everything has gone from me but the certainty of your goodness. I can't go on spoiling your life any longer. I don't think two people could have been happier than we have been. V.

Quoted from pp. 400–401, Briggs, J. (2005). Virginia Woolf: An Inner Life. Orlando, Fl: Harcourt, Inc.

English novelist and critic Virginia Woolf (1882–1941). (Photo by George C. Beresford/Getty Images.)

Table 8.7 Myths about Suicide

Common Myth	Contrary Evidence
People who discuss suicide will not actually commit suicide.	Up to three-quarters of those who take their own lives communicate their intention beforehand.
Suicide is committed without warning.	People usually give many warnings, such as saying that the world would be better off without them or making unexpected and inexplicable gifts of highly valued possessions.
Suicidal people want to die.	Most people are thankful after suicide is prevented.
People who attempt suicide by low-lethal means are not serious about killing themselves.	Many people are not well informed about pill dosages or human anatomy. Because of this, people who really want to die sometimes make nonlethal attempts.

Sources: Drawn from Fremouw, De Perzel, & Ellis (1990); Shneidman (1973).

FOCUS ON DISCOVERY 8.4

Physician-Assisted Suicide

Decisions not to resuscitate terminally ill patients are made every day in hospitals. About 15 percent of physicians in the United States report that they have written at least one prescription to hasten death (Meier et al., 1998). Are these examples of physician-assisted suicide? Physician-assisted suicide is a highly charged issue that came to the fore in the early 1990s when a Michigan physician, Jack Kevorkian, helped a 54-year-old Oregon woman in the early stages of Alzheimer's disease commit suicide. Kevorkian designed a machine to inject a drug that induced unconsciousness and a lethal dose of potassium chloride (Egan, 1990), and then he helped the woman press a button on the machine. Kevorkian assisted more than a hundred terminally ill people in taking their lives. At the same time, he steadfastly provoked a searching discussion about the ethical issues involved in considering whether a physician may take the life of a dying patient. Kevorkian was brought to trial several times on charges both of murder and of professional misconduct but was not convicted until 1999, when he was found guilty of murder and sentenced to prison.

Passionate arguments pro and con continue. Among powerful groups opposing assisted suicide are the American Medical Association and the Catholic Church. In contrast, others, such as the American Civil Liberties Union, believe that terminally ill

Jack Kevorkian, a Michigan physician, assisted many patients in taking their own lives. The controversy stimulated by his actions focused attention on the moral and ethical issues surrounding physician-assisted suicide. (Blake Discher/Corbis Sygma.)

people should have the right to end their suffering and that the state should not intrude in such decisions.

Oregon became the first state to have a law—the Death with Dignity Act, originally approved by voters in 1994 and reaffirmed by an even greater margin in 1997—that made physician-assisted suicide legal. This law permits a patient diagnosed by two physicians as having less than 6 months to live to seek a doctor's prescription for a lethal dose of barbiturates. But the law also requires that the prescribing physician determine that the patient is not suffering from mental illness and that there be a waiting period of 15 days before the prescription can be filled. Since the law went into effect, there has been no increase in suicide rates in Oregon.

In 2001, then Attorney General John Ashcroft attempted to overturn Oregon's Death with Dignity Act, declaring that assisted suicide is not an appropriate practice for physicians. The state of Oregon responded by filing suit (*State of Oregon* v. *Attorney General John Ashcroft*), and in April 2002, a federal judge ruled that a federal agency cannot usurp powers relegated to the states without specific authority from Congress, thus leaving the Oregon law in place. The Death with Dignity Act was upheld by the Supreme Court in 2006.

Beyond the serotonin system, other research has found that among patients with MDD, those who had an abnormal dexamethasone suppression test response had a 14-fold increase in the risk of suicide over the next 14 years (Coryell & Schlesser, 2001). This is consistent with the idea that the HPA axis is overly reactive to stress among people at risk for suicide.

Sociocultural Models   Some of the strongest evidence for the role of the social environment in suicide comes from the major effects of media reports of suicide. In one example of these effects, suicides rose 12 percent in the month after Marilyn Monroe's death (Phillips, 1985). A review of 293 studies found that media coverage of a celebrity suicide is much more likely to spark an increase in suicidality than coverage of a noncelebrity suicide (Stack, 2000). Media reports of natural deaths of famous people are not followed by increases in suicide, suggesting that it is not grief per se that is the influential factor (Phillips, 1974). These statistics suggest that sociocultural factors matter.

Based on patterns of suicide across different countries, Emile Durkheim (1897/1951) developed a sociological theory of suicide. He focused on three different types of suicide: egoistic, altruistic, and anomic.

Egoistic suicide is committed by people who have few ties to family, society, or community. Social isolation is profoundly important in understanding suicide, whether measured using social support measures or even simpler measures like whether a person is a parent or is married (Joiner, Brown, & Wingate, 2005). Consistent with the importance of social connectedness, recent widows often report suicidal ideation (Stroebe, Stroebe, & Abakoumkin, 2005).

Altruistic suicide is committed because the person believes it will be for the good of society. Examples of this type of suicide can be observed in many Eastern cultures; including the self-immolations of Buddhist monks and nuns to protest the Vietnam War and hara-kiri among the Japanese.

Anomic suicide is triggered by a sudden change in a person's relation to society. That is, societies experiencing serious economic and cultural changes can promote anomie and even suicidality. For example, as rural China has gone through massive changes in the past decade, suicide has become one of the leading causes of death (Phillips et al., 2002).

Without a doubt, when trying to understand suicide, social factors matter. But as with all sociological theories, Durkheim's hypotheses do not account for how different people react to the same societal conditions. For example, most people who are lonely do not kill themselves. Durkheim, aware of this problem, suggested that psychological factors would interact with the social causes of suicide.

Psychological Models Suicide has been viewed as retaliation, intended to induce guilt in others; as an effort to force love from others; as an effort to make amends for wrongs; as an effort to rid oneself of unacceptable feelings; as an expression of a desire to rejoin a dead loved one; and as an expression of a desire to escape from emotional pain or an emotional vacuum. Undoubtedly, the psychological variables involved in suicide vary across people, but many researchers have attempted to identify risk factors.

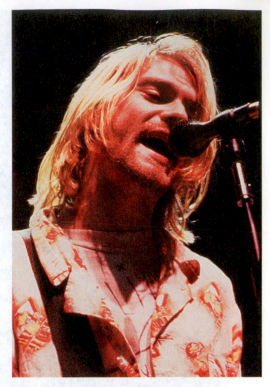

The suicide of Nirvana's lead singer, Kurt Cobain, triggered an increase in suicide among teenagers. (Kevin Estrada/Retna.)

Several researchers relate suicide to difficulties in problem solving (Linehan & Shearin, 1988). Problem-solving deficits do predict suicide attempts prospectively (Dieserud et al., 2003). Problem-solving deficits also relate to the seriousness of previous suicide attempts, even after controlling for depression severity, age, and intellectual functioning (Keilp et al., 2001).

One might expect that a person who has trouble resolving problems would be more vulnerable to hopelessness. Hopelessness, which can be defined as the expectation that life will be no better in the future than it is now, is strongly tied to suicidality. High levels of hopelessness are associated with a fourfold elevation in the risk of suicide (Brown et al., 2000), and hopelessness is important even after controlling for depression levels (Beck, Kovacs, & Weissman, 1975).

While many people become hopeless and begin to think about death as a way to ease pain, few actually hurt themselves. Among people who are experiencing suicidal thoughts, hundreds of studies document that people who are more impulsive are more likely to attempt suicide or to die from suicide (Brezo, Paris, & Turecki, 2006). While other difficulties might get a person thinking about suicide, impulsivity seems to shape whether people take the step of killing themselves rather than waiting for a better problem resolution.

Beyond these negative characteristics (e.g., poor problem solving, hopelessness, impulsivity), positive qualities may motivate a person to live and help a clinician build a case for choosing life (Malone et al., 2000). One line of research builds on Marsha Linehan's Reasons for Living (RFL) Inventory (Linehan et al., 1983). Items on this inventory tap into what is important to the person, such as responsibility to family and concerns about children. People with more reasons to live tend to be less suicidal than those with few reasons to live (Ivanoff et al., 1994).

Another factor that has been studied is life satisfaction. One prospective study in Finland found that people who expressed relatively high life satisfaction on a simple four-item questionnaire at the beginning of the study were significantly less likely to have attempted or committed suicide up to 20 years later. For example, men with the highest levels of life dissatisfaction were 25 times more likely to commit suicide than men with the lowest levels (Koivuma-Honkanen et al., 2001).

Preventing Suicide

Many people worry that talking about suicide will make it more likely to happen. Rather, clinicians have learned that it is helpful to talk about suicide openly and matter-of-factly. Giving a person permission to talk about suicide may relieve a sense of isolation.

After a broken engagement at age 31, Abraham Lincoln developed symptoms of depression that were so severe that his friends feared that he would hurt himself, and they removed any sharp objects from his room. "I am now the most miserable man living," he confessed. "Whether I shall ever be better I cannot tell; I awfully forebode I shall not. To remain as I am is impossible; I must die or be better." (Cited in Goodwin, 2003.) (Granger Collection.)

Sadly, some colleges seem to be creating policies that keep students from talking about suicidal ideas. About 10 percent of college students report that they thought about suicide in the past year. Even though suicide rates remain relatively low (about 7.5 per 100,000 students), colleges have increasingly encouraged students who endorse suicidality to withdraw (Appelbaum, 2006). More progressive schools have implemented outreach programs to allow students a chance to discuss these thoughts, offering web-based counseling that allows a student to remain anonymous.

Most people are ambivalent about their suicidal intentions, and they will communicate their intentions in some way. "The prototypical suicidal state is one in which a person cuts his or her throat, cries for help at the same time, and is genuine in both of these acts. . . . Individuals would be happy not to do it, if they didn't have to" (Shneidman, 1987, p. 170). Among those who attempt suicide but do not die, 80 percent report within the next two days that they are either glad to be alive or ambivalent about whether they want to die (Henriques et al., 2005). This ambivalence gives the clinician an important foothold.

Treating the Associated Mental Disorder One way to look at the prevention of suicide is to bear in mind that most people who kill themselves are suffering from a mental disorder. Thus, when Beck's cognitive approach successfully lessens a patient's depression, that patient's suicidal risk is also reduced. Marsha Linehan's dialectical behavior therapy with borderline patients provides another example of a treatment that is designed for a specific disorder but also provides protection from suicide (p. 377).

Studies have found that medications for mood disorders reduce the risk of suicidality three- to fourfold (Angst et al., 2002). Specifically, lithium appears effective in suicide prevention for people with bipolar disorder (Cipriani et al., 2005). Among people who have been diagnosed with depressive disorders, ECT reduces suicidality (Kellner et al., 2005), as do antidepressants among elderly people diagnosed with depression (Bruce et al., 2004). Risperidone (Clozapine), an antipsychotic medication, also appears to reduce the risk of suicide attempts among people with schizophrenia (Meltzer, 2003). Findings like these highlight the importance of helping people with mental illnesses to obtain appropriate care. Most studies of treatment though, exclude people who are highly suicidal, a fact that sadly limits our knowledge (Linehan, 1997).

Treating Suicidality Directly Cognitive behavioral approaches appear to be the most promising therapies for reducing suicidality (van der Sande, et al., 1997). Despite some findings that are not supportive (Tyrer et al., 2003), these programs have been found to reduce the risk of a future attempt among suicide attempters by 50 percent compared to treatment as usually offered in the community (Brown et al., 2005). They have also been found to reduce suicidal ideation (Joiner, Voelz, & Rudd, 2001).

Cognitive behavioral treatments include a set of strategies to prevent suicide (Brown, Henriques, Ratto, & Beck, 2002). Therapists help the clients understand the emotions and thoughts that they held just before a suicide attempt. The therapist works with the client to challenge the negative thoughts and to provide new ways to tolerate emotional distress. They also help the client problem solve about the life situations they are facing. The goal is to improve problem solving and social support and thereby to reduce the feelings of hopelessness that often precede these episodes.

Professional organizations such as the American Psychiatric Association, the National Association of Social Workers, and the American Psychological Association charge their members with protecting people from suicide even if doing so requires breaking the confidentiality of the therapist–patient relationship. Therapists are expected to take reasonable precautions when they learn a patient is suicidal (Roy, 1995). One approach to keeping such patients alive is to hospitalize them as a short-term means of keeping them safe until they can begin to consider ways of improving their life.

Some have argued against involuntary hospitalizations and other efforts to keep people from killing themselves. Boldly and controversially, Thomas Szasz (1999) argues that it is impractical and immoral to prevent suicide. It is impractical because people who are determined to die will be able to do so (even hospitalized patients manage to take their own lives). In his view, it is immoral because people should be free to make choices. In our view, his principal omissions are that treatment and hospitalization often do deter people from suicide, and most people who are prevented from killing themselves are grateful afterward for another chance at life. There are no easy answers here, but it is important to raise the questions.

Suicide Prevention Centers   There are more than 200 **suicide prevention centers** in the United States, plus others abroad (Lester, 1995). These centers typically aim to provide 24-hour phone hotline support to people in suicidal crises. It is exceedingly difficult to do controlled research on suicide prevention, and outcome studies have yielded inconsistent results. A meta-analysis of five studies on the effectiveness of suicide prevention centers failed to demonstrate that suicide rates decline after the implementation of services (Dew et al., 1987). A similarly negative finding was reported from Canada (Leenaars & Lester, 1995). Other research, however, has found that suicide rates declined in the years after suicide prevention centers were started in several cities (Lester, 1991). Thus, we are left with conflicting evidence. Human lives are precious, though, and since many people who contact prevention centers weather a suicidal crisis successfully, these efforts will continue.

Community mental health centers often provide a 24-hour-a-day hotline for people who are considering suicide. (Mark Antman/The Image Works.)

Check Your Knowledge 8.5

True or false?
1. Men have higher rates of suicide than women.
2. Men have higher rates of suicide attempts than women.
3. Adolescents have higher rates of suicide than older adults do.
4. Dopamine dysfunction is implicated in suicidality.
5. Most people with MDD will make a suicide attempt.

Summary

Clinical Descriptions and Epidemiology

- There are two broad types of mood disorders: depressive disorders and bipolar disorders.
- Depressive disorders include major depression and dysthymia, and bipolar disorders include bipolar I disorder, bipolar II disorder, and cyclothymia.
- Bipolar I disorder is defined by mania or mixed episodes. Bipolar II disorder is defined by hypomania and episodes of depression. Major depressive disorder, bipolar I disorder, and bipolar II disorder are episodic. Recurrence is very common in these disorders.
- Dysthymia and cyclothymia are characterized by low levels of symptoms that last for at least 2 years.
- Major depression is one of the most common psychiatric disorders, affecting as many as 16.2 percent of people during their lifetime. Rates of

depression are twice as high in women as in men. Bipolar I disorder is much rarer, affecting about 1 percent of people.

Etiology

- Genetic studies provide evidence that bipolar disorder is strongly heritable and that depression is somewhat heritable.
- Neurobiological research has focused on the sensitivity of receptors rather than on the amount of various transmitters, with the strongest evidence for changes in serotonin receptors in depression and potential changes in the dopamine receptors within the reward system as related to mania and depression.
- Bipolar and unipolar disorders seem tied to elevated activity of the amygdala and diminished activity in regions of the prefrontal cortex, the hippocampus, and the anterior cingulate.

● Overactivity of the hypothalamic–pituitary–adrenal axis is also found among depressive patients, manifested by high levels of cortisol and poor suppression of cortisol by dexamethasone.

● Socioenvironmental models focus on the role of negative life events, lack of social support, and family criticism as triggers for episodes but also consider ways in which a person with depression may elicit negative responses from others. People with less social skill and those who tend to seek more excessive reassurance are at elevated risk for the development of depression.

● Psychological theories of depression include psychoanalytic, emotion and personality, and cognitive models. Psychoanalytic formulations focus on anger turned inward, but this idea has not been supported. Neuroticism and excess negative emotionality appear to predict the onset of depression. Beck's cognitive theory ascribes causal significance to negative schemata and cognitive biases. According to hopelessness theory, low self-esteem or beliefs that an event will have long-term meaningful consequences can instill a sense of hopelessness, which is expressed in a specific set of depressive symptoms called hopelessness depression.

● Psychological theories of depression in bipolar disorder are similar to those proposed for unipolar depression. Some researchers have proposed that manic symptoms arise because of dysregulation in the reward system in the brain. Mania can be triggered by life events involving success.

Treatment

● Several psychological therapies are effective for depression, including interpersonal therapy, cognitive therapy, behavioral activation therapy, and behavioral couples therapy.

● The major approaches that have been found to help as adjuncts to medication for bipolar disorder include psychoeducation, family therapy, and cognitive therapy.

● Electroconvulsive shock and several antidepressant drugs (tricyclics, selective serotonin reuptake inhibitors, and MAO inhibitors) have proved their worth in lifting depression. Lithium is the best-researched treatment for prevention of mania, but antipsychotic and anticonvulsant medications also help decrease manic symptoms. Antidepressant treatments have become controversial in the treatment of bipolar disorder.

Suicide

● Men, elderly people, and people who are divorced or widowed are at elevated risk for suicide. Most people who commit suicide meet diagnostic criteria for psychiatric disorders, with more than half experiencing depression. Suicide is at least partially heritable, and neurobiological models focus on serotonin and overactivity in the HPA. Social changes are common precedents to anomic suicide. Vulnerability may be tied to poor problem solving, hopelessness, impulsivity, lack of reasons to live, and low life satisfaction.

● Several approaches have been taken to prevention. For people with a mental illness, psychological treatments and medications to quell symptoms help reduce suicidality. Many people believe it is important to address suicidality more directly, though. Problem-solving therapy has shown promise in reducing suicidal behavior, but not all results have been positive. Suicide hotlines are found in most cities, but it has been hard to conduct research demonstrating that these work.

Answers to Check Your Knowledge Questions

8.1 1. five (including mood), two; 2. 16–17; 3. two; 4. one; 5. manic, mixed, hypomanic

8.2 1. c; 2. a; 3. b; 4. b; 5. d

8.3 1. T; 2. F; 3. T; 4. F

8.4 1. a, b, d; 2. c; 3. b

8.5 1. T; 2. F; 3. F; 4. F; 5. F

Key Terms

altruistic suicide
amygdala
anomic suicide
anterior cingulate
attribution
attributional style
behavioral activation (BA) therapy
behavioral couples therapy
bipolar I disorder
bipolar II disorder
catatonic features
cognitive biases
cognitive therapy
cortisol
Cushing's syndrome
cyclothymic disorder

dopamine
dysthymic disorder
egoistic suicide
electroconvulsive therapy (ECT)
episodic disorder
expressed emotion (EE)
extraversion
family-focused treatment (FFT)
flight of ideas
G-proteins
hippocampus
hopelessness theory
HPA axis
hypomania
interpersonal psychotherapy (IPT)
learned helplessness theory

lithium
major depressive disorder (MDD)
mania
melancholic
mindfulness-based cognitive therapy (MBCT)
mixed episodes
monoamine oxidase inhibitors (MAO)
mood disorders
negative affect
negative triad
neuroticism
norepinephrine
positive affect
postpartum onset

prefrontal cortex
psychoeducational approaches
psychotic features
rapid cycling
reward system
schema
seasonal affective disorder
second messengers
selective serotonin reuptake inhibitors (SSRIs)
serotonin
somatic arousal
suicide
suicide prevention centers
tricyclic antidepressants
tryptophan

9 Eating Disorders

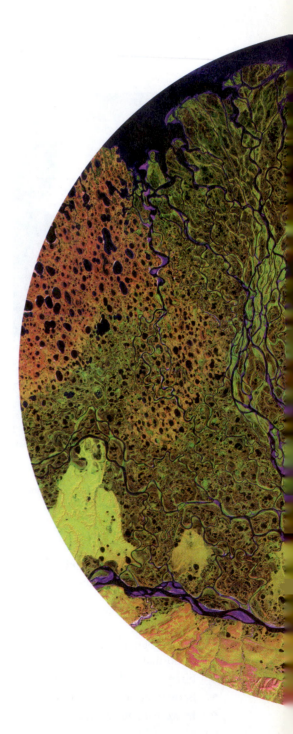

LEARNING GOALS

1. Be able to distinguish the symptoms associated with anorexia, bulimia, and binge eating disorder and be able to distinguish among the different eating disorders.
2. Be able to describe the neurobiological, sociocultural, and psychological factors implicated in the etiology of eating disorders.
3. Be able to discuss the issues surrounding the growing epidemic of obesity in the United States.
4. Be able to describe the treatments for eating disorders and the evidence supporting their effectiveness.

Clinical Case: Lynne

Lynne, a 24-year-old Caucasian woman, was admitted to the psychiatric ward of a general hospital for treatment of anorexia nervosa. Although she didn't really think anything was wrong with her, her parents had consulted with a psychiatrist, and the three of them had confronted her with a choice of admitting herself or being committed involuntarily.

At the time Lynne was 5 feet, 5 inches and weighed only 78 pounds. She hadn't menstruated for 3 years, and she had a variety of medical problems— hypotension, irregularities in her heartbeat, and abnormally low levels of potassium and calcium.

Lynne had experienced several episodes of dramatic weight loss, beginning at age 18 when she first left home for college. But none of the prior episodes had been this severe, and she had not sought treatment before. She had an intense fear of becoming fat, and although she had never really been overweight, she felt that her buttocks and abdomen were far too large. (This belief persisted even when she weighed 78 pounds.) During the periods of weight loss, she severely restricted food intake and used laxatives heavily. She had occasionally had episodes of binge eating, typically followed by self-induced vomiting so that she would not gain any weight.

MANY CULTURES ARE PREOCCUPIED with food. In the United States today, gourmet restaurants abound, and numerous magazines and television shows are devoted to food preparation. At the same time, many people are overweight. Dieting to lose weight is common, and the desire of many people, especially women, to be thinner has created a multibillion-dollar-a-year business. Given this intense interest in food and eating, it is not surprising that this aspect of human behavior is subject to disorder.

Although clinical descriptions of eating disorders can be traced back many years, particularly for anorexia nervosa, these disorders appeared in the DSM for the first time in 1980 as one subcategory of disorders beginning in childhood or adolescence. With the publication of DSM-IV, the eating disorders became a distinct category, reflecting the increased attention they have received from clinicians and researchers over the past three decades.

Clinical Descriptions of Eating Disorders

We begin by describing anorexia nervosa and bulimia nervosa. The diagnoses of these two disorders share several clinical features. We then discuss binge eating disorder, which is not yet in the current diagnostic system but has generated a good deal of attention, in part due to its association with obesity.

Anorexia Nervosa

Lynne, the woman just described, had **anorexia nervosa**. The term *anorexia* refers to loss of appetite, and *nervosa* indicates that the loss is due to emotional reasons. The term is something of a misnomer because most people with anorexia nervosa actually do not lose their appetite or interest in food. On the contrary, while starving themselves, most people with the disorder become preoccupied with food; they may read cookbooks constantly and prepare gourmet meals for their families.

Lynne met all four features required for the diagnosis:

1. *Refusal to maintain normal body weight.* This is usually taken to mean that the person weighs less than 85 percent of what is considered normal for that person's age and height. Weight loss is typically achieved through dieting, although purging (self-induced vomiting, heavy use of laxatives or diuretics) and excessive exercise can also be part of the picture.

2. *Intense fear of gaining weight and being fat.* This fear is not reduced by weight loss. There is no such thing as "too thin."

3. *Distorted body image or sense of their body shape.* Even when emaciated, those with anorexia nervosa maintain that they are overweight or that certain parts of their bodies, particularly the abdomen, buttocks, and thighs, are too fat. To check on their body size, they typically weigh themselves frequently, measure the size of different parts of the body, and gaze critically at their reflections in mirrors. Their self-esteem is closely linked to maintaining thinness.

4. *Amenorrhea (loss of menstrual period).* In females, this is caused by extreme emaciation. Of the four diagnostic criteria, amenorrhea seems least important; few differences have been found between women who meet all four criteria and those who meet the other three but not amenorrhea (Garfinkel et al., 1996).

The distorted body image that accompanies anorexia nervosa has been assessed in several ways, most frequently by a questionnaire such as the Eating Disorders Inventory (Garner, Olmsted, & Polivy, 1983). Some of the items on this questionnaire are presented in Table 9.1. In another type of assessment, people with anorexia nervosa are shown line drawings of women with varying body weights and asked to pick the one closest to their own and the one that represents their ideal shape (see Figure 9.1). People with anorexia overestimate their own body size and choose a thin figure as their ideal. Despite this distortion in body size, people with anorexia nervosa are fairly accurate when reporting their actual weight (McCabe et al., 2001), perhaps because they weigh themselves frequently.

A recent study found a slightly different pattern for men with eating disorders. Men with eating disorders didn't differ from men without eating disorders when pointing to their ideal male body type. However, the men with eating disorders overestimated their own body size considerably, thus demonstrating a distortion in their own body images (Mangweth et al., 2004).

DSM-IV-TR distinguishes two types of anorexia nervosa. In the *restricting type*, weight loss is achieved by severely limiting food intake; in the *binge-eating/purging type*, as illustrated in

Despite being thin, women with anorexia believe that parts of their bodies are too fat and spend a lot of time critically examining themselves in front of mirrors. (Susan Rosenberg/Photo Researchers.)

DSM-IV-TR Criteria for Anorexia Nervosa

- Refusal to maintain normal body weight
- Body weight less than 85 percent of normal
- Intense fear of weight gain
- Body image disturbance
- In women, amenorrhea

Table 9.1 Subscales and Illustrative Items from the Eating Disorders Inventory

Drive for thinness	I think about dieting.
	I feel extremely guilty after overeating.
	I am preoccupied with the desire to be thinner.
Bulimia	I stuff myself with food.
	I have gone on eating binges where I have felt that I could not stop.
	I have the thought of trying to vomit in order to lose weight.
Body dissatisfaction	I think that my thighs are too large.
	I think that my buttocks are too large.
	I think that my hips are too big.
Ineffectiveness	I feel inadequate.
	I have a low opinion of myself.
	I feel empty inside (emotionally).
Perfectionism	Only outstanding performance is good enough in my family.
	As a child, I tried hard to avoid disappointing my parents and teachers.
	I hate being less than best at things.
Interpersonal distrust	I have trouble expressing my emotions to others.
	I need to keep people at a certain distance (feel uncomfortable if someone tries to get too close).
Interoceptive awareness	I get confused about what emotion I am feeling.
	I don't know what's going on inside me.
	I get confused as to whether or not I am hungry.
Maturity fears	I wish that I could return to the security of childhood.
	I feel that people are happiest when they are children.
	The demands of adulthood are too great.

Source: From Garner et al. (1983).

Note: Responses use a six-point scale ranging from "always" to "never."

Lynne's case, the person has also regularly engaged in binge eating and purging. Initial research indicated a number of differences between these two subtypes, thus supporting the validity of this distinction. For example, studies have shown that people with the binge-eating/purging subtype exhibit more personality disorders, impulsive behavior, stealing, alcohol and drug abuse, social withdrawal, and suicide attempts than do people with the restricting type of anorexia (e.g., Herzog et al., 2000; Pryor, Wiederman, & McGilley, 1996). Longitudinal research, however, suggests the distinction between subtypes may not be all that useful (Eddy et al., 2002). Nearly two-thirds of women who initially met criteria for the restricting subtype had switched over to the binge-eating/purging type 8 years later. Furthermore, this study found few differences in substance abuse or personality disturbances between the two subtypes. A summary of the diagnostic criteria for anorexia nervosa appears in the margin.

Anorexia nervosa typically begins in the early to middle teenage years, often after an episode of dieting and the occurrence of a life stress. Lifetime prevalence of anorexia is less than 1 percent, and it is at least 10 times more frequent in women

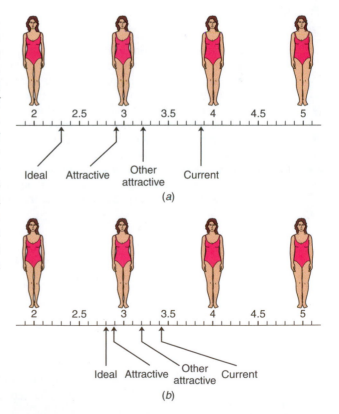

Figure 9.1 In this assessment of body image, respondents indicate their current shape, their ideal shape, and the shape they think is most attractive to the opposite sex. The figure actually rated as most attractive by members of the opposite sex is shown in both panels. Ratings of women who scored high on a measure of distorted attitudes toward eating are shown in (a); ratings of women who scored low are shown in (b). The high scorers overestimated their current size and ideally would be very thin. From Zellner, Harner, & Adler (1989).

Anorexia nervosa can be a life-threatening condition. It is especially prevalent among young women who are under intense pressure to keep their weight low. Brazilian model Ana Carolina Reston died from the condition in 2006 at age 21. (Reuters/Landov)

than in men (Hoek & van Hoeken, 2003). When anorexia nervosa does occur in men, symptomatology and other characteristics, such as reports of family conflict, are generally similar to those reported by women with the disorder (Olivardia et al., 1995). As we discuss more fully later, the gender difference in the prevalence of anorexia most likely reflects the greater cultural emphasis on women's beauty, which has promoted a thin shape as the ideal over the past several decades.

Women with anorexia nervosa are frequently diagnosed with depression, obsessive-compulsive disorder, phobias, panic disorder, alcoholism, and various personality disorders (Godart et al., 2000; Ivarsson et al., 2000). Men with anorexia nervosa are also likely to have a diagnosis of a mood disorder, schizophrenia, or substance dependence (Striegel-Moore et al., 1999b). Suicide rates are quite high for people with anorexia, with as many as 5 percent completing suicide and 20 percent attempting suicide (Franko & Keel, 2006).

Physical Consequences of Anorexia Nervosa   Self-starvation and use of laxatives produce numerous undesirable biological consequences in people with anorexia nervosa. Blood pressure often falls, heart rate slows, kidney and gastrointestinal problems develop, bone mass declines, the skin dries out, nails become brittle, hormone levels change, and mild anemia may occur. Some people lose hair from the scalp, and they may develop lanugo—a fine, soft hair—on their bodies. As in Lynne's case, levels of electrolytes, such as potassium and sodium, are altered. These ionized salts, present in various bodily fluids, are essential to neural transmission, and lowered levels can lead to tiredness, weakness, cardiac arrythmias, and even sudden death.

Prognosis   About 70 percent of people with anorexia eventually recover. However, recovery often takes 6 or 7 years, and relapses are common before a stable pattern of eating and weight maintenance is achieved (Strober, Freeman, & Morrell, 1997). As we discuss later, changing peoples' distorted views of themselves is very difficult, particularly in cultures that value thinness.

Anorexia nervosa is a life-threatening illness; death rates are 10 times higher among people with the disorder than among the general population and twice as high as among people with other psychological disorders. Death most often results from physical complications of the illness—for example, congestive heart failure—and from suicide (Herzog et al., 2000; Sullivan, 1995).

Clinical Case: Jill

Jill was the second child born to her parents. Both she and her brother became intensely involved in athletics at an early age, Jill in gymnastics and her brother in Little League baseball. At age 4 Jill was enrolled in gymnastics school, where she excelled. By the time she was 9, her mother had decided that Jill had outgrown the coaching abilities of the local instructors and began driving her to a nationally recognized coach several times a week. Over the next few years, Jill's trophy case swelled and her aspirations for a place on the Olympic team grew. As she reached puberty, though, her thin frame began to fill out, raising concerns about the effects of

weight gain on her performance as a gymnast. She began to restrict her intake of food but found that after several days of semistarvation she would lose control and go on an eating binge. This pattern of dieting and bingeing lasted for several months, and Jill's fear of becoming fat seemed to increase during that time. At age 13, she hit on the solution of self-induced vomiting. She quickly fell into a pattern of episodes of bingeing and vomiting three or four times per week. Although she maintained this pattern in secret for a while, eventually her parents caught on and initiated treatment for her.

Bulimia Nervosa

Jill's behavior illustrates the features of **bulimia nervosa**. *Bulimia* is from a Greek word meaning "ox hunger." This disorder involves episodes of rapid consumption of a large amount of food, followed by compensatory behavior, such as vomiting, fasting, or excessive exercise, to prevent weight gain. The DSM defines a *binge* as eating an excessive amount of food within less than 2 hours. Bulimia nervosa is not diagnosed if the bingeing and purging occur only in the context of anorexia nervosa and its extreme weight loss; the diagnosis in such a case is anorexia nervosa, binge-eating/purging type. The key difference between anorexia and bulimia is weight loss: people with anorexia nervosa lose a tremendous amount of weight, whereas people with bulimia nervosa do not.

In bulimia, binges typically occur in secret; they may be triggered by stress and the negative emotions they arouse, and continue until the person is uncomfortably full (Grilo, Shiffman, & Carter-Campbell, 1994). In the case of Jill, she was likely to binge after periods of stress associated with being an elite athlete. Foods that can be rapidly consumed, especially sweets such as ice cream and cake, are usually part of a binge. One study found that women with bulimia nervosa were more likely to binge while alone and during the morning or afternoon. In addition, avoiding a craved food on one day was associated with a binge episode the next morning (Waters, Hill, & Waller, 2001). Other studies show that a binge is likely to occur after a negative social interaction, or at least the perception of a negative social exchange (Steiger et al., 1999).

Research suggests that people with bulimia nervosa sometimes ingest enormous quantities of food during binges, often more than what a person eats in an entire day; however, binges are not always as large as the DSM implies, and there is wide variation in the caloric content consumed by people with bulimia nervosa during binges (e.g., Rossiter & Agras, 1990). People report that they lose control during a binge, even to the point of experiencing something akin to a dissociative state, perhaps losing awareness of their behavior or feeling that it is not really they who are bingeing. They are usually ashamed of their binges and try to conceal them.

After the binge is over, feelings of discomfort, disgust, and fear of weight gain lead to the second step of bulimia nervosa—purging to attempt to undo the caloric effects of the binge. People with bulimia most often stick fingers down their throats to cause gagging, but after a time many can induce vomiting at will without gagging themselves. Laxative and diuretic abuse (which do little to reduce body weight) as well as fasting and excessive exercise are also used to prevent weight gain.

Although many people binge occasionally and some people also experiment with purging, the DSM diagnosis of bulimia nervosa requires that the episodes of bingeing and purging occur at least twice a week for 3 months. Is twice a week a well-established cutoff point? Probably not. Few differences are found between people who binge twice a week and those who do so less frequently, suggesting that we are dealing with a continuum of severity rather than a sharp distinction (Garfinkel, Kennedy, & Kaplan, 1995).

Like those with anorexia nervosa, people with bulimia nervosa are afraid of gaining weight, and their self-esteem depends heavily on maintaining normal weight. Whereas people without eating disorders typically underreport their weight and say they are taller than they actually are, people with bulimia nervosa are more accurate in their reports (Doll & Fairburn, 1998; McCabe et al., 2001). Yet people with bulimia nervosa are also likely to be highly dissatisfied with their bodies.

Two subtypes of bulimia nervosa are distinguished: a *purging type* and a *nonpurging type* in which the compensatory behaviors are fasting or excessive exercise. And, as with anorexia, evidence for the validity of this distinction is mixed. In some studies, people diagnosed with nonpurging bulimia were heavier, binged less frequently, and showed less psychopathology than did people with purging-type bulimia (e.g., Mitchell, 1992). But in other research, few differences emerged between the two types (e.g., Tobin, Griffing, & Griffing, 1997). Given the limited validity of these two subtypes, researchers have investigated other possible subtypes. Three different studies have now validated two different subtypes: a *dietary subtype*, which is characterized by dietary restraint, and a *dietary-depressive subtype*, which is characterized by both dietary restraint and persistent negative affect (Stice & Fairburn, 2003). Dietary restraint refers to rigid and strict patterns of eating that are very restrictive with respect to what, when, and how much to eat. People with the dietary-depressive subtype are more likely to have comorbid mood and anxiety disorders, personality disorders, more severe bulimia, social impairment, more persistent binge eating, and a poor response to cognitive behavioral treatment (Stice & Agras, 1999; Stice & Fairburn, 2003). These two subtypes appear to have greater validity than the purging/nonpurging types, and perhaps they will be included in the next version of DSM.

Bulimia nervosa typically begins in late adolescence or early adulthood. About 90 percent of cases are women, and prevalence among women is thought to be about 1 to 2 percent of the population (Hoek & van Hoeken, 2003). Many people with bulimia nervosa were somewhat overweight before the onset of the disorder, and the binge eating often started during an episode of dieting.

Bulimia nervosa is comorbid with numerous other diagnoses, notably depression, personality disorders, anxiety disorders, substance abuse, and conduct disorder (Godart et al., 2000;

● DSM-IV-TR Criteria for Bulimia Nervosa

- Recurrent episodes of binge eating
- Recurrent compensatory behaviors to prevent weight gain, for example, vomiting
- Body shape and weight are extremely important for self-evaluation

Stice, Burton, & Shaw, 2004). Men with bulimia are also likely to be diagnosed with a mood disorder or substance dependence (Striegel-Moore et al., 1999). Suicide rates are much higher among people with bulimia nervosa than in the general population (Favaro & Santonastaso, 1997) but substantially lower than among people with anorexia (Franko & Keel, 2006).

A prospective study examined the relationship between bulimia and depression symptoms among adolescent girls (Stice et al., 2004). This study found that bulimia symptoms predicted the onset of depression symptoms. However, the converse was also true: depression symptoms predicted the onset of bulimia symptoms. Thus, it appears each disorder increases the risk for the other.

Physical Consequences of Bulimia Nervosa Like anorexia, bulimia is associated with several physical side effects. Although less common than in anorexia, menstrual irregularities, including amenorrhea, can occur, even though people with bulimia typically have a normal body mass index (BMI) (Gendall et al., 2000). The BMI is calculated by dividing weight in kilograms by height in meters squared and is considered a more valid estimate of body fat than many others. For women, a normal BMI is between 20 and 25. To calculate your own BMI, see Table 9.2. Bulimia nervosa, like anorexia, is a serious disorder with many unfortunate medical consequences (Garner, 1997). For example, frequent purging can cause potassium depletion. Heavy use of laxatives induces diarrhea, which can also lead to changes in electrolytes and cause irregularities in the heartbeat. Recurrent vomiting has been linked to menstrual problems and may lead to tearing of tissue in the stomach and throat and to loss of dental enamel as stomach acids eat away at the teeth, which become ragged. The salivary glands may become swollen. Death from bulimia nervosa appears to be much less common than in anorexia nervosa (Herzog et al., 2000; Keel & Mitchell, 1997).

Prognosis Long-term follow-ups of people with bulimia nervosa reveal that about 70 percent recover, although about 10 percent remain fully symptomatic (Keel et al., 1999; Reas et al., 2000). Intervening soon after a diagnosis is made (i.e., within the first few years) is linked with an even better prognosis (Reas et al., 2000). People with bulimia nervosa who binge and vomit more, and have comorbid substance abuse or a history of depression, have a poorer prognosis than people without these factors (Wilson et al., 1999).

Table 9.2 Computing Your Body Mass Index (BMI)

WEIGHT lbs	100	105	110	115	120	125	130	135	140	145	150	155	160	165	170	175	180	185	190	195	200	205	210	215
kgs	45.5	47.7	50.0	52.3	54.5	56.8	59.1	61.4	63.6	65.9	68.2	70.5	72.7	75.0	77.3	79.5	81.8	84.1	86.4	88.6	90.9	93.2	95.5	97.7
HEIGHT in/cm □ Underweight ■ Healthy □ Overweight □ Obese ■ Extremely obese																								
5'0" - 152.4	19	20	21	22	23	24	25	26	27	28	29	30	31	32	33	34	35	36	37	38	39	40	41	42
5'1" - 154.9	18	19	20	21	22	23	24	25	26	27	28	29	30	31	32	33	34	35	36	36	37	38	39	40
5'2" - 157.4	18	19	20	21	22	22	23	24	25	26	27	28	29	30	31	32	33	33	34	35	36	37	38	39
5'3" - 160.0	17	18	19	20	21	22	23	24	24	25	26	27	28	29	30	31	32	32	33	34	35	36	37	38
5'4" - 162.5	17	18	18	19	20	21	22	23	24	24	25	26	27	28	29	30	31	31	32	33	34	35	36	37
5'5" - 165.1	16	17	18	19	20	20	21	22	23	24	25	25	26	27	28	29	30	30	31	32	33	34	35	35
5'6" - 167.6	16	17	17	18	19	20	21	21	22	23	24	25	25	26	27	28	29	29	30	31	32	33	34	34
5'7" - 170.1	15	16	17	18	18	19	20	21	22	22	23	24	25	25	26	27	28	29	29	30	31	32	33	33
5'8" - 172.7	15	16	16	17	18	19	19	20	21	22	22	23	24	25	25	26	27	28	28	29	30	31	32	32
5'9" - 175.2	14	15	16	17	17	18	19	20	20	21	22	22	23	24	25	25	26	27	28	28	29	30	31	31
5'10" - 177.8	14	15	15	16	17	18	18	19	20	20	21	22	23	23	24	25	25	26	27	28	28	29	30	30
5'11" - 180.3	14	14	15	16	16	17	18	18	19	20	21	21	22	23	23	24	25	25	26	27	28	28	29	30
6'0" - 182.8	13	14	14	15	16	17	17	18	19	19	20	21	21	22	23	23	24	25	25	26	27	27	28	29
6'1" - 185.4	13	13	14	15	15	16	17	17	18	19	19	20	21	21	22	23	23	24	25	25	26	27	27	28
6'2" - 187.9	12	13	14	14	15	16	16	17	18	18	19	19	20	21	21	22	23	23	24	25	25	26	27	27
6'3" - 190.5	12	13	13	14	15	15	16	16	17	18	18	19	20	20	21	21	22	23	23	24	25	25	26	26
6'4" - 193.0	12	12	13	14	14	15	15	16	17	17	18	18	19	20	20	21	22	22	23	23	24	25	25	26

Binge Eating Disorder

DSM-IV-TR includes **binge eating disorder** as a diagnosis in need of further study rather than as a formal diagnosis. This disorder includes recurrent binges (two times per week for at least 6 months), lack of control during the bingeing episode, and distress about bingeing, as well as other characteristics, such as rapid eating and eating alone. It is distinguished from anorexia nervosa by the absence of weight loss and from bulimia nervosa by the absence of compensatory behaviors (purging, fasting, or excessive exercise). Most often, people with binge eating disorder are **obese**. A person with a BMI of greater than 30 is considered obese. With the current explosion in the prevalence of obesity in the United States, it is perhaps not surprising that research on binge eating disorder continues to increase (Yanovski, 2003). It is important to point out, however, that not all obese people meet criteria for binge eating disorder. Indeed, only those who have binge episodes and report feeling a loss of control over their eating will qualify, which amounts to anywhere from 2 to 25 percent of obese people (Yanovski, 2003). For further discussion of obesity, see Focus on Discovery 9.1.

Though it did not meet the threshold for inclusion in the current DSM (Fairburn, Walsh, & Hay, 1993), binge eating disorder has several features that support its validity, and the bulk of evidence supports its inclusion in DSM-V (Striegel-Moore & Franco, 2008). It can be reliably defined and measured (Striegel-Moore & Franco, 2003). It is associated with obesity and a history of dieting (Kinzl et al., 1999; Pike et al., 2001). It is linked to impaired work and social functioning, depression, low self-esteem, substance abuse, and dissatisfaction with body shape (Spitzer et al., 1993; Striegel-Moore et al., 1998, 2001). Risk factors for developing binge eating disorder include childhood obesity, critical comments regarding being overweight, low self-concept, depression, and childhood physical or sexual abuse (Fairburn et al., 1998). A recent behavior genetics study (Hudson et al., 2006) found that relatives of obese people with binge eating disorder were more likely to have binge eating disorder themselves (20 percent) than were relatives of obese people without binge eating disorder (9 percent).

Binge eating disorder appears to be more prevalent than either anorexia nervosa or bulimia nervosa (Hudson et al., 2007). In the National Comorbidity Survey–Replication study, the prevalence was 3.5 percent for women and 2 percent for men. Research suggests that binge eating disorder is more common in women than men, although the gender difference is not as great as it is in anorexia or bulimia. Though only a few epidemiological studies have been done, binge eating disorder appears to be equally prevalent among Euro-, African-, Asian-, and Hispanic-Americans (Striegel-Moore & Franco, 2008).

Some researchers do not view binge eating disorder as a discrete diagnostic category but rather as a less severe version of bulimia nervosa, at least the nonpurging form of bulimia (Hay & Fairburn, 1998; Joiner, Vohs, & Heatherton, 2000; Striegal-Moore et al., 2001). On the other hand, more recent research suggests that these two conditions do differ. For example, bulimia nervosa affects women far more frequently than men, a gender difference that is not observed in binge eating disorder.

Quick Summary

Anorexia nervosa has four characteristics: refusal to maintain a normal body weight, an intense fear of gaining weight and being fat, a distorted body image, and amenorrhea. Anorexia usually begins in the early teen years and is more common in women than men. Bodily changes that can occur after severe weight loss can be serious and life threatening. About 70 percent of women with anorexia eventually recover, but it can take many years.

Bulimia nervosa involves both bingeing and purging. Bingeing often involves sweet foods and is more likely to occur when someone is alone, after a negative social encounter, and in the morning or afternoon. One striking difference between anorexia and bulimia is weight loss: people with anorexia nervosa lose a tremendous amount of weight whereas people with bulimia nervosa do not. Bulimia typically begins in late adolescence and is more common in women than men. Depression often co-occurs with bulimia, and each condition appears to be a risk factor for the other. Dangerous changes to the body can also occur as a result of bulimia, such as menstrual problems, tearing in the stomach and throat, and swelling of the salivary glands.

Binge eating disorder is characterized by several binges, and most (but not all) people are obese (defined as having a BMI greater than 30). Not all obese people meet criteria for binge eating disorder—only those who have binge episodes and report feeling a loss of control over their eating qualify. Binge eating disorder is more common than anorexia and bulimia and is more common in women than men, though the gender difference is not as great as it is in anorexia and bulimia.

FOCUS ON DISCOVERY 9.1

Obesity: A Twenty-First Century Epidemic?

Obesity is not an eating disorder, though it is an increasing public health problem, with estimated health care costs of nearly $117 billion in the year 2000 alone (U.S. Department of Health Human Services, 2001b). For example, obesity is linked to diabetes, hypertension, cardiovascular disease, and several forms of cancer. Studies have found that blood pressure is rising among children, and this may be in part due to the increase in the number of children who are overweight or obese (Muntner et al., 2004). Indeed, 90 percent of children who are overweight or obese have at least one additional heart disease risk factor such as high blood pressure or high cholesterol (*Time*, June 23, 2008).

Compared to the early 1990's, obesity among adults has increased 30 percent. Among children, it has increased 100 percent. In 2004, nearly 19 percent of children in the United States were obese and one-third of children were overweight. There is a glimmer of good news, however. Rates of obesity among adult women in the U.S. have remained steady since 1999. The news for men is less optimistic, though a recent report from the Centers for Disease Control and Prevention suggests that the rates among men may be leveling off as well (Ogden et al., 2007). Among children, the rates may have stopped increasing in 2006, though it is still too early to tell if this trend will remain (Ogden, Carroll, & Flegal, 2008). Even with prevalence rates appearing to plateau, large numbers of people in the United States are nevertheless obese or overweight. In 2006, more than a third of adult men and women in the United States were obese (Ogden et al., 2007). Obesity is also increasing in other parts of the world, from the Australian Aborigines to children in Egypt, from Siberia to Peru (Friedrich, 2002). Why are so many people overweight?

Obesity has become quite prevalent across the world in recent years. (Bourreau/Photo Researchers, Inc.)

A number of factors play a role, including the environment we live in. In *Food Fight: The Inside Story of the Food Industry, America's Obesity Crisis, and What We Can Do About It*, Yale University psychologist Kelly Brownell calls our environment "toxic" with respect to the food and exercise options available to most people in the United States (Brownell & Horgen, 2003). The availability and amount of fast food have exponentially increased in the past decades. At the same time, many people, including children, have become more sedentary, spending more time working or playing at the computer and watching TV than ever before. Furthermore, physical education programs for children in schools have been declining (Critser, 2003). People eat in restaurants more than ever before, and portion sizes of foods, both in restaurants and in the grocery stores, are larger than ever. In fact, most people do not know the portion size of most foods recommended by the U.S. Department of Agriculture. A 20-ounce bottle of soda is not one serving, but two and one-half. The recommended serving of cheese is $1\frac{1}{2}$ ounces, about the size of a 9-volt battery. The ever-increasing portion sizes as well

as the greater availability of unhealthy foods impact the amount we eat. In addition, the availability of healthy foods varies depending on economics. Research has shown that poorer neighborhoods have fewer grocery stores, more fast-food restaurants, and fewer healthy food selections in the stores (Moreland et al., 2002).

We are all subject to the continuing impact of advertisements, especially those promoting alluring high-calorie products such as snack foods, desserts, and meals at fast-food restaurants. For example, the advertising budget for Coke and Pepsi combined was $3 billion in 2001 (Brownell & Horgen, 2003). Compare this to the $2 million advertising campaign by the National Cancer Institute to promote eating more fruits and vegetables (Nestle, 2002). Children are particularly susceptible to advertising. A task force of the American Psychological Association concluded in 2004 that television advertisements of unhealthy foods (e.g., sugary cereals, soda) contribute to unhealthy eating habits of children under 8 years of age, largely because these children lack the requisite cognitive skills to discern truth from advertising (Kunkel et al., 2004).

Along with the environment, heredity plays a role in obesity. In behavior genetics terms, between 25 and 40 percent of the variance in obesity can be accounted for by genetic factors (Brownell & Horgen, 2003). Adoption studies have found that children's weight is more strongly related to the weight of their biological parents than to the weight of their adoptive parents (Price et al., 1987). Similarly, 40 percent of the children of an obese parent will be obese, compared with 7 percent of the children of normal-weight parents. Heredity could produce its effects by regulating metabolic rate, impacting the hypothalamus, or influencing the production of enzymes that make it easier to store fat and gain weight. Recent molecular genetics studies have identified a number of possible genes that might contribute to obesity. A variation (polymorphism) of the Insig2 gene has sparked interest among researchers. This gene is associated with regulating fatty acids and cholesterol and is found among 10 percent of people who are obese (Herbert et al., 2006). Though genetic factors tell an important part of the story, they do not tell the entire story. Clearly, the environment plays a critical role.

Stress and its associated negative moods can induce eating in some people (Arnow, Kenardy, & Agras, 1992; Heatherton & Baumeister, 1991), and research in rats shows that foods rich in fat and sugar may actually reduce stress in the short term, giving new meaning to the term *comfort food* (Dallman et al., 2003).

The stigma associated with being overweight remains a problem. Some people think that obesity is simply a matter of personal responsibility; they believe that if people would just eat less and exercise more, obesity would not be a problem. Given the multitude of factors contributing to obesity just noted, such a simple solution is not reasonable. Yet some members of the U.S. Congress ascribe to such beliefs. In 2004, the U.S. House of Representatives passed what became known as the "cheeseburger bill," which prevents people from suing fast-food companies for contributing to their obesity. Despite the evidence that environmental factors, including the availability and relatively unhealthy nature of a lot of fast food, some members of the House said that obesity was a matter of personal responsibility, not the responsibility of the fast-food industry. Of course, personal respon-

sibility is important. People can and should make better choices about what and how much they eat. Nevertheless, other environmental factors can sometimes work against such choices. Other governmental agencies seem to agree that there is more to obesity than simply personal responsibility. Also in 2004, the Department of Health and Human Services announced that Medicare, the national health insurance program for the elderly or disabled, would cover treatment for obesity by removing language that had previously said obesity was not a disease (USDHHSB, 2004).

Check Your Knowledge 9.1 (Answers are at the end of the chapter.)

Answer the questions.
1. All of the following are symptoms of anorexia *except*:
    a. fear of fat and gaining weight
    b. unwillingness to maintain normal weight
    c. perfectionism
    d. distorted body image
2. Which statement is true regarding binge eating disorder?
    a. It is more common in men than women.

b. It is a third type of eating disorder in DSM-IV-TR.
c. It is synonymous with obesity.
d. It includes binges but not purges.
3. Which of the following are characteristics of both anorexia and bulimia?
    a. They involve a good deal of weight loss.
    b. They are more common in women than men.
    c. They have physical side effects (e.g., menstrual irregularities).
    d. All of the above but *a* are correct.

Etiology of Eating Disorders

As with other disorders, a single factor is unlikely to cause an eating disorder. Several areas of current research—genetics, neurobiology, sociocultural pressures to be thin, personality, the role of the family, and the role of environmental stress—suggest that eating disorders result when several influences converge in a person's life.

Genetic Factors

Both anorexia nervosa and bulimia nervosa run in families. First-degree relatives of young women with anorexia nervosa are over 10 times more likely than average to have the disorder themselves (e.g., Strober et al., 2000). Similar results are found for bulimia nervosa, where first-degree relatives of women with bulimia nervosa are about four times more likely than average to have the disorder (e.g., Kassett et al., 1989; Strober et al., 2000). Furthermore, first-degree relatives of women with eating disorders appear to be at higher risk for anorexia or bulimia (Lilenfeld et al., 1998; Strober et al., 1990, 2000). Although eating disorders are quite rare among men, one study found that first-degree relatives of men with anorexia nervosa were at greater risk for having anorexia nervosa (though not bulimia) than relatives of men without anorexia (Strober et al., 2001). Finally, relatives of people with eating disorders are more likely than average to have symptoms of eating disorders that do not meet the complete criteria for a diagnosis (Lilenfeld et al., 1998; Strober et al., 2000).

Twin studies of eating disorders also suggest a genetic influence. Most studies of both anorexia and bulimia report higher MZ than DZ concordance rates (Bulik, Wade, & Kendler, 2000) and that genes account for a substantial portion of the variance among twins with eating disorders (Wade et al., 2000). On the other hand, research has shown that nonshared environmental factors (see p. 30), like different interactions with parents or different peer groups, also contribute to the development of eating disorders (Klump, McGue, & Iacono, 2002). Research also suggests that key features of the eating disorders, such as dissatisfaction with one's body, a strong desire to be thin, binge eating, and preoccupation with weight, are heritable (Klump, McGue, & Iacono, 2000). Additional evidence suggests that common genetic factors may account for the relationship between certain personality characteristics, such as negative emotionality and constraint, and eating disorders (Klump, McGue, & Iacono, 2002). The results of these studies are consistent with the possibility that a genetic diathesis is operating, but adoption studies are also needed. Using the method of genetic linkage analysis (discussed in Chapter 4), one study reported evidence for linkage on chromosome 1 among people with anorexia (Grice et al., 2002). It will be important to replicate this finding in future studies, but all of these findings suggest that genetics do indeed play a role in eating disorders.

Neurobiological Factors

The hypothalamus is a key brain center in regulating hunger and eating. Research on animals with lesions to the lateral hypothalamus indicates that they lose weight and have no appetite (Hoebel & Teitelbaum, 1966). Thus, it is not surprising that the hypothalamus has been proposed to play a role in anorexia. The level of some hormones regulated by the hypothalamus, such as cortisol, is indeed abnormal in people with anorexia. Rather than causing the disorder, however, these hormonal abnormalities occur as a result of self-starvation, and levels return to normal after weight gain (Doerr et al., 1980; Stoving et al., 1999). Furthermore, the weight loss of animals with hypothalamic lesions does not parallel what we know about anorexia. These animals appear to have no hunger and to become indifferent to food, whereas people with anorexia continue to starve themselves despite being hungry and having an interest in food. Nor does the hypothalamic model account for body-image disturbance or fear of becoming fat. A dysfunctional hypothalamus thus does not seem highly likely as a factor in anorexia nervosa.

Endogenous opioids are substances produced by the body that reduce pain sensations, enhance mood, and suppress appetite. Opioids are released during starvation and have been hypothesized to play a role in both anorexia and bulimia. Starvation among people with anorexia may increase the levels of endogenous opioids, resulting in a positively reinforcing euphoric state (Marrazzi & Luby, 1986). Furthermore, the excessive exercise seen among some people with eating disorders would increase opioids and thus be reinforcing (Davis, 1996; Epling & Pierce, 1992).

Some research supports the theory that endogenous opioids play a role in eating disorders, at least in bulimia. For example, two studies found low levels of the endogenous opioid beta-endorphin (see Figure 9.2) in people with bulimia (Brewerton et al., 1992; Waller et al., 1986). In one of these studies, the researchers observed that the people with more severe cases of bulimia had the lowest levels of beta-endorphin (Waller et al., 1986). It is important to note, however, that these findings demonstrate that low levels of opioids are seen concurrently with bulimia, not that such levels are seen before the onset of the disorder. In other words, we don't know if the low levels of opioids are a cause of bulimia or an effect of changes in food intake.

Finally, some research has focused on neurotransmitters related to eating and satiety (feeling full). Animal research has shown that serotonin promotes satiety. Therefore, it could be that the binges of people with bulimia result from a serotonin deficit that causes them not to feel

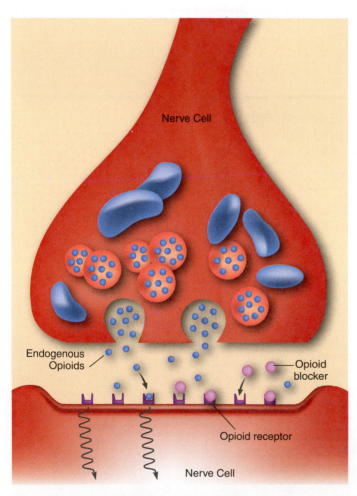

Figure 9.2 Endogenous opiod systems in the brain.

satiated as they eat. Animal research has also shown that food restriction interferes with serotonin synthesis in the brain. Thus, among people with anorexia, the severe food intake restrictions could interfere with the serotonin system.

Researchers have examined levels of serotonin metabolites among people with anorexia and bulimia. With respect to anorexia, several studies have reported low levels of serotonin metabolites among people with anorexia (e.g., Kaye et al., 1984) and bulimia (e.g., Carrasco et al., 2000; Jimerson et al., 1992; Kaye et al., 1998). Lower levels of a neurotransmitter's metabolites are one indicator that the neurotransmitter activity is underactive. In addition, people with anorexia who have not been restored to a healthy weight show a poorer response to serotonin agonists (i.e., a drug that stimulates serotonin receptors) than those people who have regained a good portion of their weight, again suggesting an underactive serotonin system (Attia et al., 1998; Ferguson et al., 1999). People with bulimia also show smaller responses to serotonin agonists (Jimerson et al., 1997; Levitan et al., 1997). The antidepressant drugs that are often effective treatments for anorexia and bulimia (discussed later) are known to increase serotonin activity, adding to the possible importance of serotonin. Serotonin, though, could be also be linked to the comorbid depression often found in anorexia and bulimia.

Researchers have recently begun to more closely examine the role of the neurotransmitter dopamine in eating behavior. Studies with animals have shown that dopamine is linked to the pleasurable aspects of food that compel an animal to go after food (e.g., Szczypka et al., 2001) and brain imaging studies in humans have shown how dopamine is linked to the motivation to obtain food. In one study with healthy people, participants were presented with smells and tastes of food while undergoing a PET scan (Volkow et al., 2002). The participants also filled out a measure of dietary restraint (see Table 9.3). People who scored higher on dietary restraint exhibited greater dopamine activity in the dorsal striatum area of the brain during the presentation of food. This finding suggests that restrained eaters may be more sensitive to cues of food, since one of the functions of dopamine is to signal the salience of particular stimuli. Whether or not these findings will be relevant to people with eating disorders remains to be seen.

Though we can expect further neurotransmitter research in the future, keep in mind that much of this work focuses on brain mechanisms relevant to hunger, eating, and satiety and does little to account for other key features of both disorders, in particular the intense fear of becoming fat. Furthermore, as suggested, the evidence so far does not show that brain changes predate the onset of eating disorders.

Table 9.3 The Restraint Scale

1.	How often are you dieting? Never; rarely; sometimes; often; always.
2.	What is the maximum amount of weight (in pounds) you have ever lost within 1 month? 0–4; 5–9; 10–14; 15–19; 20+.
3.	What is your maximum weight gain within a week? 0–1; 1.1–2; 2.1–3; 3.1–5; 5.1+.
4.	In a typical week, how much does your weight fluctuate? 0–1; 1.1–2; 2.1–3; 3.1–5; 5.1+.
5.	Would a weight fluctuation of 5 pounds affect the way you live your life? Not at all; slightly; moderately; very much.
6.	Do you eat sensibly in front of others and splurge alone? Never; rarely; often; always.
7.	Do you give too much time and thought to food? Never; rarely; often; always.
8.	Do you have feelings of guilt after overeating? Never; rarely; often; always.
9.	How conscious are you of what you are eating? Not at all; slightly; moderately; extremely.
10.	How many pounds over your desired weight were you at your maximum weight? 0–1; 1–5; 6–10; 11–20; 21+.

Source: From Polivy Herman, & Howard (1980).

Psychodynamic Views

Many psychodynamic theories of eating disorders propose that the core cause is to be found in disturbed parent–child relationships and that certain core personality traits, such as low self-esteem and perfectionism, are found among people with eating disorders. As we will see in a later section, these personality characteristics are not solely the province of psychodynamic theorists. Psychodynamic theories also propose that the symptoms of an eating disorder fulfill some need, such as increasing one's sense of personal effectiveness by being successful in maintaining a strict diet or avoiding growing up sexually by being very thin and thus not achieving the usual female shape (Goodsitt, 1997).

One view holds that anorexia nervosa is an attempt by children who have been raised to feel ineffectual to gain competence and respect and to ward off feelings of helplessness, ineffectiveness, and powerlessness (Bruch, 1980). This sense of ineffectiveness is believed to be created by a parenting style in which the parents' wishes are imposed on the child without consideration of the child's needs or wishes. For example, parents may arbitrarily decide when the child is hungry or tired, failing to perceive the child's actual state. Children reared in this way do not learn to identify their own internal states and do not become self-reliant. Facing the demands of adolescence, the child seizes on the societal emphasis on thinness and turns dieting into a means of acquiring control and identity. Moreover, negative self-perceptions about weight become the broad lens through which the child sees other aspects of the self, thus contributing to an overall poor self-evaluation.

Another psychodynamic theory, described by Goodsitt (1997), proposes that bulimia nervosa in women stems from a failure to develop an adequate sense of self because of a conflictual mother–daughter relationship. Food becomes a symbol of this failed relationship. The daughter's bingeing and purging represent the conflict between the need for the mother and the desire to reject her.

Although interesting theories, the evidence in favor of these psychodynamic views is limited. Independent of these psychodynamic theories, studies of personality characteristics of people with eating disorders and studies of the characteristics of their families have revealed interesting relationships between these variables and eating disorders. But it is difficult to reach definitive conclusions in either area of research because the disorder itself may have resulted in changes in personality or in the patient's family.

Cognitive Behavioral Views

Anorexia Nervosa Cognitive behavioral theories of anorexia nervosa emphasize fear of fatness and body-image disturbance as the motivating factors that powerfully reinforce weight loss. Many who develop anorexia symptoms report that the onset followed a period of weight loss and dieting. Behaviors that achieve or maintain thinness are negatively reinforced by the reduction of anxiety about becoming fat. Furthermore, dieting and weight loss may be positively reinforced by the sense of mastery or self-control they create (Fairburn, Shafran, & Cooper, 1999; Garner, Vitousek, & Pike, 1997). Some theories also include personality and sociocultural variables in an attempt to explain how fear of fatness and body-image disturbances develop. For example, perfectionism and a sense of personal inadequacy may lead a person to become especially concerned with his or her appearance, making dieting a potent reinforcer. Similarly, seeing portrayals in the media of thinness as an ideal, being overweight, and tending to compare oneself with especially attractive others all contribute to dissatisfaction with one's body (Stormer & Thompson, 1996).

Another important factor in producing a strong drive for thinness and a disturbed body image is criticism from peers and parents about being overweight (Paxton et al., 1999). In one study supporting this conclusion, adolescent girls aged 10 to 15 were evaluated twice, with a 3-year interval between assessments. Obesity at the first assessment was related to being teased by peers and at the second assessment was linked to dissatisfaction with their bodies. Dissatisfaction was in turn related to symptoms of eating disorder.

It is known that bingeing frequently results when diets are broken (Polivy & Herman, 1985). Thus, when a lapse occurs in the strict dieting of a person with anorexia nervosa, the lapse is likely to escalate into a binge. The purging after an episode of binge eating can

The fear of being fat, which is so important in eating disorders, is partly based on society's negative stereotypes about overweight people. (The Copyright Group/SUPERSTOCK.)

again be seen as motivated by the fear of weight gain that the binge elicited. People with anorexia who do not have episodes of bingeing and purging may have a more intense preoccupation with and fear of weight gain (Schlundt & Johnson, 1990) or may be more able to exercise self-control.

Bulimia Nervosa   People with bulimia nervosa are also thought to be overconcerned with weight gain and body appearance; indeed, they judge their self-worth mainly by their weight and shape. They also have low self-esteem, and because weight and shape are somewhat more controllable than are other features of the self, they tend to focus on weight and shape, hoping their efforts in this area will make them feel better generally. They try to follow a pattern of restric-tive eating that is very rigid, with strict rules regarding how much to eat, what kinds of food to eat, and when to eat. These strict rules inevitably are broken, and the lapse escalates into a binge. After the binge, feelings of disgust and fear of becoming fat build up, leading to compensatory actions such as vomiting (Fairburn, 1997). Although purging temporarily reduces the anxiety from having eaten too much, this cycle lowers the person's self-esteem, which triggers still more bingeing and purging, a vicious circle that maintains desired body weight but has serious med-ical consequences (see Figure 9.3 for a summary of this theory).

One group of researchers developed the Restraint Scale (see Table 9.3), a questionnaire mea-sure of concerns about dieting and overeating (Polivy et al., 1980). These researchers have con-ducted a series of laboratory studies on people with high scores on this measure. These studies are generally conducted under the guise of being taste tests. One such study was described as an assessment of the effects of temperature on taste (Polivy, Heatherton, & Herman, 1988). To achieve a "cold" condition, some participants first drank a 15-ounce chocolate milk shake (termed a *preload* by the investigators) and were then given three bowls of ice cream to taste and rate for flavor. Participants were told that once they had completed their ratings, they could eat as much of the ice cream as they wanted. The researchers then measured the amount of ice cream eaten.

In laboratory studies following this general design, people who scored high on the Restraint Scale ate more than nondieters after a fattening preload, even when the preload was perceived as fattening but was actually low in calories (e.g., Polivy, 1976) and even when the food was relatively unpalatable (Polivy, Herman, & McFarlane, 1994). Thus, people who score high on the Restraint Scale show a pattern similar to that of people with bulimia nervosa, albeit at a much less intense level.

Several additional conditions have been found to further increase the eating of restrained eaters after a preload, most notably various negative mood states, such as anxiety and depres-sion (e.g., Herman et al., 1987). The increased consumption of restrained eaters is especially pronounced when their self-image is threatened (Heatherton, Herman, & Polivy, 1991) and if they have low self-esteem (Polivy et al., 1988). Finally, when restrained eaters are given false feedback indicating that their weight is high, they respond with increases in negative emotion and increased food consumption (McFarlane, Polivy, & Herman, 1998).

The eating pattern of people with bulimia is similar to, but more extreme than, the behavior highlighted in the studies of restrained eaters. People with bulimia nervosa typically binge when they encounter stress and experience negative affect, and this has been shown in several studies. In experience sampling studies, the investigators were able to show how specific binge-and-purge events were linked to changes in emotions and stress in the course of daily life (Smyth et al, 2007).

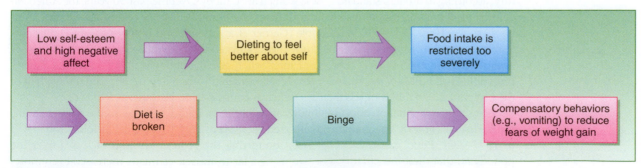

Figure 9.3 Schematic of cognitive behavioral theory of bulimia nervosa.

They found that high negative affect and stress alongside low positive affect predicted later binge-ing. The binge may therefore function as a means of regulating negative affect (Stice & Agras, 1999; Smyth et al., 2007). Evidence also supports the idea that stress and negative affect are relieved by purging. People with bulimia report increased anxiety and show heightened skin conductance when they eat a meal and are not allowed to purge (Leitenberg et al., 1984; Williamson et al., 1988). In addition, negative affect levels decline and positive affect levels increase after a purge event, sup-porting the idea that purging is reinforced by negative affect reduction (Jarrell, Johnson, & Williamson, 1986; Smyth et al., 2007). Given the similarities between people who score high on the Restraint Scale and people with bulimia nervosa, we might expect that restrained eating would play a central role in bulimia. In fact, a study of the naturalistic course of bulimia (i.e., the course of bulimia left untreated) has found that the relationship between concern over shape and weight and binge eating was partially mediated by restrained eating (Fairburn et al., 2003). In other words, concerns about body shape and weight predicted restrained eating, which in turn predicted an increase in binge eating across 5 years of follow-up assessments. Other studies have failed to find this relationship (Burne & McLean, 2002), however, and thus additional research will need to sort out the ways in which restraint is linked with the symptoms of bulimia.

Sociocultural factors appear to play a role in the faulty perceptions and eating habits of those with eating disorders. We turn to these influences next.

Quick Summary

Genetic factors appear to play a role in both anorexia and bulimia. Both disorders tend to run in families, and twin studies support the role of genetics in the actual disorders and particular characteristics of the disorders, such as body dissatisfaction, preoccupation with thinness, and binge eating. The hypothalamus does not appear to be directly involved in eating disorders, and low levels of endogenous opioids are seen concurrently with bulimia, but not before the onset of the disorder. Thus, changes in food intake could affect the opioid system instead of changes in the opioid system affecting food intake. Research findings on the role of serotonin in anorexia are mixed. Serotonin may play a role in bulimia, with studies finding a decrease in serotonin metabolites, smaller responses to serotonin agonists, and an increase in cognitions related to eating disorders, such as feeling fat, among people formerly diagnosed with bulimia who had their serotonin levels reduced. Newer research suggests dopamine may play a role in restrained eating, a characteristic that is found in people with eating disorders. The neurobiological factors do not do a particularly good job of accounting for some key features of anorexia and bulimia, in particular the intense fear of becoming fat.

Psychodynamic theories focus on disturbed parent–child rela-tionships and personality characteristics. There is not much research support for these views.

Cognitive behavioral theories focus on body dissatisfaction and preoccupation with thinness. The Restraint Scale measures concerns about dieting and overeating, and high scores are linked to binge eat-ing among people without eating disorders. The eating pattern of people with bulimia is similar to, but more extreme than, the behav-ior highlighted in the studies of restrained eaters. Studies have found that concerns about body shape and weight predicted restrained eat-ing, which in turn predicted an increase in binge eating.

Sociocultural Factors

Throughout history, the standards societies have set for the ideal body—especially the ideal female body—have varied greatly. Think of the famous nudes painted by Rubens in the seventeenth cen-tury: according to modern standards, these women are chubby. Over the past 50 years, the American cultural ideal has progressed steadily toward increasing thinness. *Playboy* centerfolds became thin-ner between 1959 and 1978, for example (Garner et al., 1980), and beauty pageant contestants also became thinner through 1988. A study that calculated the body mass index (BMI) of *Playboy* centerfolds from 1985 to 1997 (Owen & Laurel-Seller, 2000) found that all but one of the *Playboy* centerfolds had a BMI of less than 20, which is considered to be a low weight, and almost half of the centerfolds had a BMI of less than 18, which is considered to be underweight.

For men, the situation appears somewhat different. In a study parallel to the studies exam-ining *Playboy* centerfolds, researchers analyzed the BMI of *Playgirl* male centerfolds from 1973 to 1997 (Leit, Pope, & Gray, 2001). They found that the centerfolds' BMI *increased* over the period and that their muscularity, assessed using a fat-to-muscle estimate, increased even more. Thus for men, magazines focus attention on the masculine ideal of normal body weight or on increased muscle mass (Mishkind et al., 1986).

Somewhat paradoxically, as cultural standards were moving in the direction of thinness over the later part of the twentieth century, more and more people were becoming overweight. The prevalence of obesity has doubled since 1900 (see Focus on Discovery 9.1). Currently, nearly 30 percent of Americans are obese (BMI greater than 30), setting the stage for greater conflict between the cultural ideal and reality.

As society has become more health and fat conscious, dieting to lose weight has become more common; the number of dieters increased from 7 percent of men and 14 percent of women in 1950 to 29 percent of men and 44 percent of women in 1999 (Serdula et al., 1999). The focus on cutting carbohydrates, so widespread during the past few years, added yet another craze to dieting. For example, the sale of low-carb foods yielded nearly $30 billion in 2004; more than 1,500 new low-carb foods were introduced in a 2-year period; the number of low-carb diet books increased from 15 to 194 between 1999 and 2004; and 26 million people in the United States were on a diet that severely limited carbohydrate consumption in 2004 (*Time*, May 3, 2004). Like many diet fads, the low-carb craze has quieted a bit since 2004. Finally, surgeries such as liposuction (vacuuming out fat deposits just under the skin) and gastroplasty (surgically changing the stomach so it cannot digest as much food) are becoming more common despite their risk (Brownell & Horgen, 2003).

The percentages above indicate that women are more likely than men to be dieters. The onset of eating disorders is typically preceded by dieting and other concerns about weight, supporting the idea that social standards stressing the importance of thinness play a role in the development of these disorders (Killen et al., 1994; Stice, 2001).

It is likely that women who either are actually overweight or fear being fat are also dissatisfied with their bodies. Not surprisingly, studies have found people with both a high BMI and body dissatisfaction are at higher risk for developing eating disorders (Fairburn et al., 1997; Killen et al., 1996). Body dissatisfaction is also a robust predictor of the development of eating disorders among adolescent girls (Killen et al., 1996). In addition, preoccupation with being thin or feeling pressure to be thin predicts an increase in body dissatisfaction among adolescent girls, which in turn predicts more dieting and negative emotions. Preoccupation with thinness and body dissatisfaction both predict greater eating disorder pathology (Stice, 2001), and these factors were operating in the case of Jill, presented earlier. Finally, exposure to media portrayals of unrealistically thin models can influence reports of body dissatisfaction. One study reviewed results from 25 experiments that presented images of thin models to women and then asked the women to report on their body satisfaction. Perhaps not surprisingly, results from these studies showed that women reported a decline in body satisfaction after viewing these images (Groesz, Levine, & Murnen, 2002). Another study found that men's body dissatisfaction, as indexed by a greater discrepancy between the muscularity of the actual and ideal self, increased after viewing images of muscular men (Leit, Gray, & Pope, 2002).

The sociocultural ideal of thinness is a likely vehicle through which people learn to fear being or even feeling fat, and this was probably influential in the cases of both Lynne and Jill. In addition to creating an undesired physical shape, fat has negative connotations, such as being unsuccessful and having little self-control. Obese people are viewed by others as less smart and are stereotyped as lonely, shy, and greedy for the affection of others (DeJong & Kleck, 1986). Even more disturbing, health professionals who specialize in obesity have also exhibited beliefs that obese people are lazy, stupid, or worthless (Schwartz et al., 2003). Reducing the stigma associated with being overweight will be beneficial to those with eating disorders as well as obesity.

Not only does the fear of being fat contribute to eating pathology, but more recently the celebration of extreme thinness via websites, blogs, and magazines may also play a role. Websites that are "pro-ana" (short for anorexia) or "pro-mia" (short for bulimia) and other "thinsperation" websites and blogs have developed a following of women who seek support and encouragement for losing weight, often to a dangerously low level. These sites often post photos of female celebrities who are extremely thin as inspiration (hence, the term *thinsperation*). Some of these women have publicly discussed their struggles with eating disorders (e.g., the actress Christina Ricci), but others have not.

Gender Influences   We have discussed the fact that eating disorders are more common in women than in men. One primary reason for the greater prevalence of eating disorders among women is likely due to the fact that Western cultural standards about thinness have changed over the past 50 years, today reinforcing the desirability of being thin for women more than for men.

Al Roker, the weatherperson on NBC's *Today Show*, had Gastric Bypass surgery to accomplish weight loss. (Evan Agostini/Getty Images News and Sport Services.)

Celebrities such as Christina Ricci have publicly discussed their struggles with eating disorders. (Allstar Picture Library/Alamy.)

Cultural standards regarding the ideal feminine shape have changed over time. Even in the 1950s and 1960s, the feminine ideal was considerably heavier than what it became in the 1970s, 1980s, 1990s, and today. (Top: Corbis Images; center: Eve Arnold/Magnum Photos, Inc.; bottom: Maria C. Valentino/Corbis Sygma.)

Another sociocultural factor, though, has remained remarkably resilient to change—namely, the objectification of women's bodies. Women's bodies are often viewed through a sexual lens; in effect, women are defined by their bodies, whereas men are esteemed more for their accomplishments. According to objectification theory (Fredrickson & Roberts, 1997), the prevalence of objectification messages in Western culture (in television, advertisements, and so forth) has led some women to "self-objectify," which means that they see their own bodies through the eyes of others. Research has shown that self-objectification causes women to feel more shame about their bodies. The emotion of shame is most often elicited in situations where an individual's ideal falls short of a cultural ideal or standard. Thus, women are likely experiencing body shame when they see a mismatch between their ideal self and the cultural (objectified) view of a woman. Research has also shown that both self-objectification and body shame are associated with disordered eating (Fredrickson et al., 1998; McKinley & Hyde, 1996; Noll & Fredrickson, 1998). The risk for eating disorders among groups of women who might be expected to be particularly concerned with their weight—for example, models, dancers, and gymnasts, as in the case of Jill—appears to be especially high (Garner et al., 1980).

Do eating disorders and weight concerns go away as women get older? A large, 20-year prospective study of over 600 men and women recently reported important differences in dieting and other eating disorder risk factors for men and women (Keel et al., 2007). The men and women were first surveyed about dieting, BMI, weight, body image, and eating disorder symptoms when they were in college. Follow-up surveys were completed 10 and 20 years after college. Thus, the men and women were around age 40 at the 20-year follow-up assessment. The researchers found that after 20 years, women dieted less and were less concerned about their weight and body image compared to when they were in college, even though they actually weighed more. In addition, eating disorder symptoms decreased over the 20 years for women, as did the risk factors for eating disorders (body-image perception, frequency of dieting). Changes in life roles—having a life partner, having a child—were also associated with decreases in eating disorder symptoms for women. By contrast, men were more concerned about their weight and were dieting more. Like women, they weighed more in their early forties than when they were in college. Decreases in risk factors such as body image and dieting frequency were also associated with decreases in eating disorder symptoms for men.

Cross-Cultural Studies Evidence for eating disorders across cultures depends on the disorder. Anorexia has been observed across a number of cultures and countries besides the United States; for example, in Hong Kong, China, Taiwan, England, Korea, Japan, Denmark, Nigeria, South Africa, Zimbabwe, Ethiopia, Iran, Malaysia, India, Pakistan, Australia, the Netherlands, and Egypt (Keel & Klump, 2003). Furthermore, cases of anorexia have been documented in cultures with very little Western culture influence. An important caveat must be made, however. The anorexia observed in these diverse cultures does not always include the intense fear of gaining weight or being fat that is part of the DSM-IV-TR criteria. Thus, intense fear of fat likely reflects an ideal more widely espoused in more Westernized cultures. For example, Lee (1994) has described a disorder similar to anorexia nervosa that exists in several nonindustrialized Asian countries (India, Malaysia, the Philippines). This disorder involves severe emaciation, food refusal, and amenorrhea, but not a fear of becoming fat. Is this a cultural variant of anorexia or a different disorder, such as depression? This question is but one of the challenges that face cross-cultural researchers (Lee et al., 2001). Indeed, in some other cultures, higher weight among women is especially valued and considered a sign of fertility and healthiness (Nasser, 1988). The wide variation in the clinical presentation of anorexia across cultures provides a window into the importance of culture in establishing realistic versus potentially disordered views of one's body.

Another feature of eating disorders that may be heavily influenced by Western ideals of beauty and thinness is body image. In a study supporting the notion of cross-cultural differences in body-image perception, Ugandan and British college students rated the attractiveness of drawings of nudes ranging from very emaciated to very obese (Furnham & Baguma, 1994). Ugandan students rated the obese females as more attractive than did the British students.

Bulimia nervosa appears to be more common in industrialized societies, such as the United States, Canada, Japan, Australia, and Europe, than in nonindustrialized nations. In addition, as cultures undergo social changes associated with adopting the practices of more Westernized cultures, the incidence of bulimia appears to increase (Abou-Saleh, Younis, & Karim, 1998; Nasser, 1997). Indeed, a comprehensive review of research on culture and eating disorders could not find evidence of bulimia outside of a Westernized culture (Keel & Klump, 2003).

Ethnic Differences   In the United States, it was reported at one time that the incidence of anorexia was eight times greater in white women than in women of color (Dolan, 1991). More recent studies confirm somewhat greater eating disturbances and body dissatisfaction among white women than black women (Grabe & Hyde, 2006; Perez & Joiner, 2003), but differences in actual eating disorders, particularly bulimia, do not appear to be as great (Wildes, Emery, & Simons, 2001). In addition, the greatest differences between white and black women in eating disorder pathology appear to be most pronounced in college student samples; fewer differences are observed in either high school or nonclinical community samples (Wildes et al., 2001). Finally, a recent meta-analysis found more similarities than differences in body dissatisfaction between ethnic groups in the United States (Grabe & Hyde, 2006). White women and Hispanic women reported greater body dissatisfaction than African American women, but no other ethnic differences were reliably found.

Another indication of our society's preoccupation with thinness is what happened with Miss Universe of 1996, Alicia Machado. When, after winning the title, she gained a few pounds, some people became outraged and suggested she give up her crown. (AP/Wide World Photos.)

Differences have been observed in the United States in some areas, however. Studies show that white teenage girls diet more frequently than do African American teenage girls and are more likely to be dissatisfied with their bodies (Fitzgibbons et al., 1998; Striegel-Moore et al., 2000). The relationship between BMI and body dissatisfaction also differs by ethnicity. Compared with African American adolescents, white adolescents become more dissatisfied with their bodies as their BMI rises (Striegel-Moore et al., 2000). As already noted, both dieting and body dissatisfaction are related to an increased risk for developing an eating disorder. Indeed, one study found that white women with binge eating disorder were more dissatisfied with their bodies than African American women with binge eating disorder, and the white women were more likely to have a history of bulimia nervosa than the African American women (Pike et al., 2001).

Ethnic group membership is not the only critical variable in observed differences. Socioeconomic status may also be important (Caldwell, Brownell, & Wilfley, 1997; French et al., 1997). The emphasis on thinness and dieting has spread beyond white women of upper and middle socioeconomic status to women of lower socioeconomic status, as has the prevalence of eating disorder pathology (e.g., Story et al., 1995; Striegel-Moore et al., 2000). In addition, acculturation, the extent to which someone assimilates their own culture with a new culture, may be another important variable to consider. This process can at times be quite stressful. A recent study found that the relationship between body dissatisfaction and bulimia symptoms was stronger for African American and Hispanic college students who reported higher levels of acculturative stress compared to those students who reported lower levels of this type of stress (Perez et al., 2002).

Finally, very little is known about the prevalence of eating disorders among Latina or Native American women, and this remains a much-needed research focus. Data from a recent epidemiological study of Latina women age 18 or older found that binge eating disorder was more prevalent than bulimia nervosa but that the prevalence rates for both disorders were comparable to prevalence rates in Caucasian women (Alegria et al., 2007). The diagnosis of bulimia was more likely for women who had lived in the United States for several years than for women who had recently immigrated, indicating that acculturation may play a role. In contrast to other eating disorders, anorexia nervosa was very rare among Latina women (only 2 out of over 2,500 women had a lifetime history of anorexia).

Beyond the study of racial or ethnic differences in eating disorders, attention should also be paid to stereotyped beliefs about race and eating disorders.

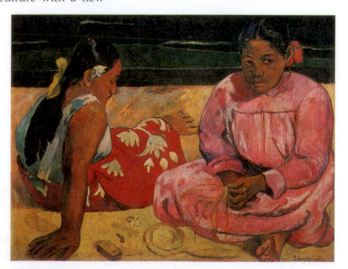

Standards of beauty vary vary cross-culturally as shown by Gaugain's painting of Tahitian women. (Musee d'Orsay, Paris/Lauris-Giraudon, Paris/SUPERSTOCK.)

One study found that college students who read a fictional case study about a woman with eating disorder symptoms were more likely to ascribe an eating disorder to the woman if her race was presented as Caucasian rather than African American or Hispanic (Gordon, Perez, & Joiner, 2002). In other words, the symptoms were only rated as clinically significant for the white case presentation, not for the African American or Hispanic ones, even though the details were identical. Although it remains to be seen if mental health professionals would also exhibit the same stereotypes when making clinical judgments, it suggests that symptoms may be more easily overlooked among non-Caucasian women.

Other Factors Contributing to the Etiology of Eating Disorders

Personality Influences   We have already seen that neurobiological changes occur as a result of an eating disorder. It is also important to keep in mind that an eating disorder itself can affect personality. A study of semistarvation in male conscientious objectors conducted in the late 1940s supports the idea that the personality of people with eating disorders, particularly those with anorexia, is affected by their weight loss (Keys et al., 1950). For a period of 6 weeks, the men were given two meals a day, totaling 1,500 calories, to simulate the meals in a concentration camp. On average, the men lost 25 percent of their body weight. They all soon became preoccupied with food; they also reported increased fatigue, poor concentration, lack of sexual interest, irritability, moodiness, and insomnia. Four became depressed, and one developed bipolar disorder. This research shows vividly how severe restriction of food intake can have powerful effects on personality and behavior, which we need to consider when evaluating the personalities of people with anorexia and bulimia.

In part as a response to the findings just mentioned, some researchers have collected retrospective reports of personality before the onset of an eating disorder. This research describes people with anorexia as having been perfectionistic, shy, and compliant before the onset of the disorder. The description of people with bulimia includes the additional characteristics of histrionic features, affective instability, and an outgoing social disposition (Vitousek & Manke, 1994). It is important to remember, however, that retrospective reports in which people with an eating disorder and their families recall what the person was like before diagnosis can be inaccurate and biased by awareness of the patient's current problem.

Prospective studies examine personality characteristics before an eating disorder is present. In one study, more than 2,000 students in a suburban Minneapolis school district completed a variety of tests for three consecutive years. Among the measures were assessments of personality characteristics as well as an index of the risk for developing an eating disorder based on the Eating Disorders Inventory. During year 1 of the study, cross-sectional predictors of disordered eating included body dissatisfaction; a measure of interoceptive awareness, which is the extent to which people can distinguish different biological states of their bodies (see Table 9.1 for items that assess interoceptive awareness); and a propensity to experience negative emotions (Leon et al., 1995). At year 3, these same variables were found to have prospectively predicted disordered eating (Leon et al., 1999). An additional study found that perfectionism prospectively predicted the onset of anorexia in young adult women (Tyrka et al., 2002).

Severe food restriction can have profound effects on behavior and personality, as illustrated by the Keyes study. (Wallace Kirkland/Time & Life Pictures/Getty Images, Inc.)

Additional research has taken a closer look at the link between perfectionism and anorexia. Perfectionism is multifaceted and may be self-oriented (setting high standards for oneself), other-oriented (setting high standards for others), or socially oriented (trying to conform to the high standards imposed by others). A recent review of many studies concludes that perfectionism, no matter how it is measured, is higher among girls with anorexia than girls without anorexia and that perfectionism remains high even after successful treatment for anorexia (Bardone-Cone et al, 2007). A multinational study found that people with anorexia scored higher on self and other-oriented types of perfectionism than people without anorexia (Halmi et al., 2000). Finally, mothers of girls with anorexia scored higher on perfectionism than mothers of girls without anorexia (Woodside et al., 2002). This intriguing finding needs to be replicated, but it suggests that what is genetically transmitted in anorexia could be a personality characteristic, such as perfectionism, that increases the vulnerability for the disorder rather than the disorder per se.

Characteristics of Families   Studies of the characteristics of families of people with eating disorders have yielded variable results. Some of the variation stems, in part, from the different methods used to collect the data and from the sources of the information. For example, self-reports of people with eating disorders consistently reveal high levels of conflict in the family (e.g., Bulik, Sullivan, et al., 2000; Hodges, Cochrane, & Brewerton, 1998). Reports of parents, however, do not necessarily indicate high levels of family problems.

Family characteristics may contribute to the risk for developing an eating disorder; however, eating disorders also likely have an impact on family functioning. One study assessed both people with eating disorders and their parents on tests designed to measure rigidity, closeness, emotional overinvolvement, critical comments, and hostility (Dare et al., 1994). The families showed considerable variation in whether parents were overinvolved with their children; the families were also quite low in conflict (low levels of criticism and hostility). A family study in which assessments were conducted before and after treatment of the patient found that ratings of family functioning improved after treatment (Woodside et al., 1995). Finally, one study examined identical twins discordant for bulimia (i.e., one twin had the disorder; the other didn't). The twin who developed bulimia reported greater family discord than the twin who did not develop the disorder. Because these studies rely on retrospective self-report, it remains unclear whether the family discord was a contributory factor or consequence of the eating disorder.

To better understand the role of family functioning, it will be necessary to study these families directly by observational measures rather than by self-reports alone. Although an adolescent's perception of his or her family's characteristics is important, we also need to know how much of reported family discord is perceived and how much is consistent with others' perceptions. In one of the few observational studies conducted thus far, parents of children with eating disorders did not appear to be very different from control parents. The two groups did not differ in the frequency of positive and negative messages given to their children, and the parents of children with eating disorders were more self-disclosing than were the controls. The parents of children with eating disorders did lack some communication skills, however, such as the ability to request clarification of vague statements (van den Broucke, Vandereycken, & Vertommen, 1995). Observational studies such as this, coupled with data on perceived family characteristics, would help determine whether actual or perceived family characteristics are related to eating disorders.

People with eating disorders consistently report that their family life was high in conflict. (Penny Tweedie/Stone/Getty Images.)

Child Abuse and Eating Disorders   Some studies have indicated that self-reports of childhood sexual abuse are higher among people with eating disorders than among people without eating disorders, especially those with bulimia nervosa (Deep et al., 1999; Webster & Palmer, 2000). Since, as discussed in Chapter 6, some research indicates that reports of abuse may be created in therapy, it is notable that high rates of sexual abuse have been found among people with eating disorders who have not been in treatment as well as those who have (Romans et al., 2001; Wonderlich et al., 1996, 2001). Still, the role of childhood sexual abuse in the etiology of eating disorders remains uncertain. Furthermore, high rates of childhood sexual abuse are found among people with different diagnoses so if it plays some role, it may not be highly specific to eating disorders (Fairburn et al., 1999; Romans et al., 2001).

Research has also found higher rates of childhood physical abuse among people with eating disorders. These data suggest that future studies should focus on a broad range of abusive experiences. Furthermore, it has been suggested that the presence or absence of abuse may be too general a variable. Abuse at a very early age, involving force and by a family member, may bear a stronger relationship to eating disorders than abuse of any other type (Everill & Waller, 1995).

Quick Summary

Sociocultural factors, including society's preoccupation with thinness, may play a role in eating disorders. This preoccupation is linked to dieting efforts, and dieting precedes the development of eating disorders among many people. In addition, the preoccupation with thinness, as well as media portrayals of thin models, predicts an increase in body dissatisfaction, which also precedes the development of eating disorders. Stigma associated with being overweight also contributes. Women are more likely to have eating disorders than men, and the ways in which women's bodies are objectified may lead some women to see their bodies as others do (self-objectify), which in turn may increase body dissatisfaction and eating pathology. Anorexia appears to occur in many cultures; bulimia appears to be more common in industrialized and Westernized societies. Eating disorders are slightly more common among white women than women of color, with the difference being most pronounced in college student samples. Eating disorders used to be more common among women of higher socioeconomic status, but this is less true today.

Research on personality characteristics finds that perfectionism may play a role. Other personality characteristics that predicted disordered eating across 3 years include body dissatisfaction, the extent to which people can distinguish different biological states of their bodies, and a propensity to experience negative emotions. Troubled family relationships are fairly common among people with eating disorders, but this could be a result of the eating disorder and not necessarily a cause of it. High rates of sexual and physical abuse are found among people with eating disorders, but these are not risk factors specific to the development of eating disorders.

Check Your Knowledge 9.2

True or false?
1. The brain structure linked to the cause of eating disorders is the hypothalamus.
2. Prospective studies of personality and eating disorders indicate that the tendency to experience negative emotions is related to disordered eating.
3. Anorexia appears to be specific to Western culture; bulimia is seen all over the world and is thus not culture specific.
4. Child abuse appears to be a specific causal factor for eating disorders.
5. Cognitive behavioral views of bulimia suggest that women judge their self-worth by their weight and shape.

Treatment of Eating Disorders

Hospitalization is frequently required to treat people with anorexia so that their ingestion of food can be gradually increased and carefully monitored. This was necessary for Lynne. Weight loss can be so severe that intravenous feeding is necessary to save the patient's life. The medical complications of anorexia, such as electrolyte imbalances, also require treatment. For both anorexia and bulimia, both medications and psychological treatments have been used.

Medications

Because bulimia nervosa is often comorbid with depression, it has been treated with various antidepressants, such as fluoxetine (Prozac). In one multicenter study, 387 women with bulimia were treated as outpatients for 8 weeks. Fluoxetine was shown to be superior to a placebo in reducing binge eating and vomiting; it also decreased depression and lessened distorted attitudes toward food and eating. Findings from most studies, including double-blind studies with placebo controls, confirm the efficacy of a variety of antidepressants in reducing purging and binge eating, even among people who had not responded to prior psychological treatment (Walsh et al., 2000; Wilson & Fairburn, 1998; Wilson & Pike, 2001).

On the negative side, many people with bulimia drop out of drug treatment (Fairburn, Agras, & Wilson, 1992). In the multicenter fluoxetine study cited, almost one-third of the women dropped out before the end of the 8-week treatment, primarily because of the side effects of the medication. In contrast, fewer than 5 percent of women dropped out of cognitive behavioral therapy (Agras et al., 1992). Moreover, most people relapse when various kinds of antidepressant medication are withdrawn (Wilson & Pike, 2001), as is the case with most psychoactive drugs. There is some evidence that this tendency to relapse is reduced if antidepressants are given in the context of cognitive behavior therapy (Agras et al., 1994).

Medications have also been used to treat anorexia nervosa. Unfortunately, they have not been very successful in improving weight or other core features of anorexia (Attia et al., 1998; Johnson, Tsoh, & Varnado, 1996). Medication treatment for binge eating disorder has not been as well studied. Limited evidence suggests that antidepressant medications are not effective in reducing binges or weight loss (Grilo, 2007). Recent trials of antiobesity drugs, such as sibutramine and atomoxetine, show some promise in binge eating disorder, but additional clinical trials are needed.

Psychological Treatment of Anorexia Nervosa

Little in the way of controlled research exists on psychological treatments for anorexia nervosa, but we will present what appear to be the most promising of the psychotherapeutic approaches to this life-threatening disorder.

Therapy for anorexia is generally believed to be a two-tiered process. The immediate goal is to help the patient gain weight in order to avoid medical complications and the possibility of death. The patient is often so weak and physiological functioning so disturbed that hospital treatment is medically imperative (in addition to being needed to ensure that the patient ingests some food). Operant conditioning behavior therapy programs (e.g. providing reinforcers for weight gain) have been somewhat successful in achieving weight gain in the short term (Hsu, 1990). However, the second goal of treatment—long-term maintenance of weight gain—remains a challenge for the field.

Beyond immediate weight gain, psychological treatment for anorexia can also involve cognitive behavior therapy (CBT). One study that combined hospital treatment with CBT found that reductions in many anorexia symptoms persisted up to 1 year after treatment (Bowers & Ansher, 2008).

Family therapy is the principal form of psychological treatment for anorexia, based on the notion that interactions among members of the patient's family can play a role in the disorder (le Grange & Lock, 2005). In one kind of family therapy, anorexia is cast as an interpersonal rather than individual issue and attempts to bring the family conflict to the fore. How is this accomplished? The therapist holds family lunch sessions, since conflicts related to anorexia are believed to be most evident at mealtime. These lunch sessions have three major goals:

Family therapy is a main form of treatment for anorexia nervosa. (Michael Newman/PhotoEdit.)

1. Changing the patient role of the person with anorexia
2. Redefining the eating problem as an interpersonal problem
3. Preventing the parents from using their child's anorexia as a means of avoiding conflict

One strategy is to instruct each parent to try individually to force the child to eat. The other parent may leave the room. The individual efforts are expected to fail. But through this failure and frustration, the mother and father may now work together to persuade the child to eat. Thus, rather than being a focus of conflict, the child's eating will produce cooperation and increase parental effectiveness in dealing with the child (Rosman, Minuchin, & Liebman, 1975).

Family therapy has not yet been sufficiently studied for its long-term effects. One study of 50 girls being treated for anorexia with family therapy suggested that as many as 86 percent of the girls were still functioning well when assessed at times ranging from 3 months to 4 years after treatment (Rosman, Minuchin, & Liebman, 1976). A newer family-based therapy (FBT) was developed in England, and preliminary evidence suggests that it is effective (Lock & le Grange, 2001; Lock et al., 2001; Loeb et al., 2007).

Actress Mary-Kate Olsen has been treated for an eating disorder. (Peter Kramer/Getty Images News and Sport Services.)

Psychological Treatment of Bulimia Nervosa

Cognitive behavior therapy (CBT) is the best-validated and most current standard for the treatment of bulimia (Fairburn, 1985; Fairburn, Marcus, & Wilson, 1993). In CBT, people with bulimia are encouraged to question society's standards for physical attractiveness. People with bulimia must also uncover and then change beliefs that encourage them to starve themselves to avoid becoming overweight. They must be helped to see that normal body weight can be maintained without severe dieting and that unrealistic restriction of food intake can often trigger a binge. They are taught that all is not lost with just one bite of high-calorie food and that snacking need not trigger a binge, which will be followed by induced vomiting or taking laxatives that will lead to still lower self-esteem and depression. Altering this all-or-nothing thinking can help people begin to eat more moderately. They are also taught assertiveness skills to help them cope with unreasonable demands placed on them by others, and they also learn more satisfying ways of relating to people.

The overall goal of treatment in bulimia nervosa is to develop normal eating patterns. People with bulimia need to learn to eat three meals a day and even some snacks between meals without sliding back into bingeing and purging. Regular meals control hunger and thereby, it is hoped, the urge to eat enormous amounts of food, the effects of which are counteracted by purging. To help people with bulimia develop less extreme beliefs about themselves, the cognitive behavior therapist gently but firmly challenges such irrational beliefs as "No one will respect me if I am a few pounds heavier than I am now" or "Eric loves me only because I weigh 112 pounds and would surely reject me if I ballooned to 120 pounds." A generalized assumption underlying these and related cognitions for women might be that a woman has value only if she is a few pounds underweight—a belief that is put forth in the media and advertisements.

One intervention that is sometimes used in the cognitive behavioral treatment approach has the patient bring small amounts of forbidden food to eat in the session. Relaxation is employed to control the urge to induce vomiting. Unrealistic demands and other cognitive distortions—such as the belief that eating a small amount of high-calorie food means that the patient is an utter failure and doomed never to improve—are continually challenged. The therapist and patient work together to determine events, thoughts, and feelings that trigger an urge to binge and then to learn more adaptive ways to cope with these situations. In the case of Jill, she and her therapist discovered that bingeing often took place after she was criticized by her coach. Therapy included the following:

- Encouraging Jill to assert herself if the criticism is unwarranted
- Desensitizing her to social evaluation and encouraging her to question society's standards for ideal weight and the pressures on women to be thin—not an easy task by any means
- Teaching her that it is not a catastrophe to make a mistake and it is not necessary to be perfect, even if the coach's criticism is valid

The outcomes of cognitive behavioral therapies are rather promising, both in the short term and over time. A meta-analysis showed that CBT yielded better results than antidepressant drug treatments (Whittal, Agras, & Gould, 1999), and therapeutic gains were maintained at 1-year follow-up (Agras et al., 2000), nearly 6 years later (Fairburn et al., 1995), and 10 years later (Keel et al., 2002). But there are limitations to these positive outcomes, as we will see.

Findings from a number of studies indicate that CBT often results in less frequent bingeing and purging, with reductions ranging from 70 to more than 90 percent. Extreme dietary restraint is also reduced significantly, and there is improvement in attitudes toward body shape and weight (Compas et al., 1998; Richards et al., 2000). However, if we focus on the people themselves rather than on numbers of binges and purges across people, we find that at least half of those treated with CBT improve very little (Wilson, 1995; Wilson & Pike, 1993). Clearly, while CBT may be the most effective treatment available for bulimia, it still has room for improvement!

To better understand how it works and how it might be improved, some investigators are conducting what are called component analyses of the CBT therapy package just described. One important aspect that has been examined is the exposure and ritual prevention (ERP) component (recall this aspect of the cognitive behavioral treatment of obsessive-compulsive disorder in Chapter 5). This ERP component involves discouraging the patient from purging after eating foods that usually elicit an urge to vomit. Indications are that this is an important component, because ERP and CBT combined appear to be more effective than CBT without ERP, at least in the short term (e.g., Fairburn et al., 1995). The ERP component may have its strongest effect early in treatment. A research review found that about 70 percent of the total improvement in frequency of bingeing and vomiting is evident by the third week of treatment (Wilson & Pike, 2001). ERP may not continue to be an advantage over the long term, however. One study examined outcome 3 years after treatment for people with bulimia who had received CBT either with or without ERP. They found similar outcomes for the two groups (Carter et al., 2003). That is, 85 percent of people with bulimia did not meet criteria for bulimia 3 years after treatment, regardless of which treatment they received.

People with bulimia who are successful in overcoming their urge to binge and purge also improve in associated problems such as depression and low self-esteem. This result is not surprising. If a person is able to achieve normal eating patterns after viewing bulimia as an uncontrollable problem, she can be expected to feel less depressed and to feel generally better about herself.

CBT alone is more effective than any available drug treatment (Compas et al., 1998; Walsh et al., 1997). But are outcomes better when antidepressant medication is added to CBT? Evidence on this front is mixed. Adding antidepressant drugs, however, may be useful in alleviating the depression that often occurs with bulimia (Keel et al., 2002; Wilson & Fairburn, 1998).

In several other studies (Fairburn et al., 1991, 1993), interpersonal therapy (IPT) fared well in comparisons with CBT, though it did not produce results as quickly. The two modes of intervention were equivalent at 1-year follow-up in effecting change across all four of the specific aspects of bulimia: binge eating, purging, dietary restraint, and maladaptive attitudes about body shape and weight (Wilson, 1995). This pattern—CBT superior to IPT immediately after treatment but IPT catching up at follow-up—was replicated in a later study (Agras et al., 2000).

Family therapy is also effective for bulimia, though it has been studied less frequently than either CBT or IPT. A recent randomized clinical trial demonstrated that family-based therapy was superior to supportive psychotherapy for adolescents with bulimia with respect to decreasing bingeing and purging up to 6 months after treatment was completed (le Grange et al., 2007).

Psychological Treatment of Binge Eating Disorder

Although not as extensively studied as with bulimia nervosa, cognitive behavior therapy has been shown to be effective for binge eating disorder in several studies (Grilo, 2007). CBT for binge eating disorder targets binges as well as restrained eating and other associated features (e.g., depression). Gains from CBT appear to last for up to 1 year after treatment. CBT also appears to be more effective than treatment with fluoxetine (Grilo, 2007). To date, one randomized controlled clinical trial has shown that interpersonal therapy (IPT) is equally effective as CBT for binge eating disorder (Wilfley et al., 2002).

Quick Summary

Antidepressant medications have shown some benefit for the treatment of bulimia, but not anorexia. However, people with bulimia are more likely to discontinue the medication than discontinue therapy. Psychological treatment of anorexia must first focus on weight gain. Family therapy is common for anorexia, but studies are needed to demonstrate whether this is effective. The most effective psychological treatment for bulimia is cognitive behavior therapy. CBT involves changing a patient's beliefs and thinking about thinness, being overweight, dieting, and restriction of food, with the overall goal being to reestablish normal eating patterns. Exposure plus ritual prevention is one CBT component that is effective early in treatment. CBT alone is more effective than medication treatment, though antidepressants can help lessen comorbid depression. CBT is also effective for binge eating disorder.

Preventive Interventions for Eating Disorders

A different approach to treating eating disorders involves prevention. Intervening with children or adolescents before the onset of eating disorders may help to prevent these disorders from ever developing. Broadly speaking, three different types of preventive interventions have been developed and implemented:

1. *Psychoeducational approaches.* The focus is on educating children and adolescents about eating disorders in order to prevent them from developing the symptoms.
2. *Deemphasizing sociocultural influences.* The focus here is on helping children and adolescents resist or reject sociocultural pressures to be thin.
3. *Risk factor approach.* The focus here is on identifying people with known risk factors for developing eating disorders (e.g., weight and body concern, dietary restraint) and intervening to alter these factors.

Stice, Shaw, and Marti (2007) conducted a meta-analysis of all such prevention studies conducted between 1980 and 2006, and they found modest support for some of these prevention approaches. The most effective prevention programs are those that are interactive rather than didactic, include adolescents age 15 or older, include girls only, and involve multiple sessions rather than just one session. Some effects appear to last as long as two years.

One recent randomized trial found that two types of preventive interventions show promise for reducing eating disorder symptoms among adolescent girls (average age of 17). One program, called the dissonance reduction intervention, focused on deemphasizing sociocultural influences; the other, called the healthy weight intervention, targeted risk factors (Stice et al., 2008). Both programs included just one 3-hour session. Specifically, girls in the dissonance reduction intervention talked, wrote, and role-played with one another to challenge the society's notions of beauty (i.e., the thin-ideal). Girls in the healthy weight intervention worked together on developing healthy weight and exercise programs for themselves. Participation in either program was associated with less negative affect, less body dissatisfaction, lower thin-ideal internalization, and lower risk of developing eating disorder symptoms 2 to 3 years after the session compared to girls who did not participate in a session. These findings point to the importance of continuing to develop and implement prevention programs.

Prevention programs that are interactive have been effective for girls with eating disorders. (Tony Freeman/PhotoEdit.)

Check Your Knowledge 9.3

Fill in the blanks.
1. Research suggests that _____ therapy is an effective treatment for bulimia, both in the short and long term.
2. For anorexia, _____ may be required to get the patient to gain weight. There are not many _____ that have been shown to be effective. The most common type of therapy used to treat anorexia is _____.
3. Research on prevention programs has shown that two programs show promise up to 3 years after the intervention: A _____ intervention and a _____ intervention.

Summary

Clinical Descriptions

- The two main eating disorders are anorexia nervosa and bulimia nervosa. Binge eating disorder is being studied for possible inclusion in the DSM-V. The symptoms of anorexia nervosa include refusal to maintain normal body weight, an intense fear of being fat, a distorted sense of body shape, and, in women, amenorrhea. Anorexia typically begins in the mid-teens, is 10 times more frequent in women than in men, and is comorbid with several other disorders, notably depression. Its course is not favorable, and it can be life threatening. The symptoms of bulimia nervosa include episodes of binge eating followed by purging, fear of being fat, and a distorted body image. Like anorexia, bulimia begins in adolescence, is much more frequent in women than in men, and is comorbid with other diagnoses, such as depression. Prognosis is somewhat more favorable than for anorexia.

Etiology

- Research in the eating disorders has examined genetics and brain mechanisms. Evidence is consistent with a possible genetic diathesis. Endogenous opioids and serotonin, both of which play a role in mediating hunger and satiety, have been examined in eating disorders. Low levels of both these brain chemicals have been found in people with eating disorders, but evidence that these cause eating disorders is limited. Dopamine is also involved with eating, but its role in eating disorders is less well studied.
- On a psychological level, several factors play important roles. Psychodynamic theories of eating disorders emphasize parent–child relationships and personality characteristics. Research on characteristics of families with an eating-disordered child have yielded different data depending on how the data were collected. Reports of people with eating disorders show high levels of conflict, but actual observations of the families do not find them especially troubled. Studies of personality have found that people with eating disorders are high in neuroticism and perfectionism and low in self-esteem. Many women with eating disorders report being abused as children, but early abuse does not appear to be a specific risk factor for eating disorders.

- Cognitive behavioral theories of eating disorders propose that fear of being fat and body-image distortion make weight loss a powerful reinforcer. Among people with bulimia nervosa, negative affect and stress precipitate binges that create anxiety, which is then relieved by purging.
- As sociocultural standards changed to favor a thinner shape as the ideal for women, the frequency of eating disorders increased. The objectification of women's bodies also exerts pressure for women to see themselves through a sociocultural lens. The prevalence of eating disorders is higher in industrialized countries, where the cultural pressure to be thin is strongest. White women tend to have greater body dissatisfaction and general eating disturbances than African American women, though the prevalence rates for actual eating disorders are not markedly different between these two ethnic groups.

Treatment

- The main neurobiological treatment of eating disorders is the use of antidepressants. Although somewhat effective, dropout rates from drug-treatment programs are high and relapse is common when people stop taking the medication. Treatment of anorexia often requires hospitalization to reduce the medical complications of the disorder. Providing reinforcers for weight gain has been somewhat successful, but no treatment has yet been shown to produce long-term maintenance of weight gain.
- Cognitive behavioral treatment for bulimia focuses on questioning society's standards for physical attractiveness, challenging beliefs that encourage severe food restriction, and developing normal eating patterns. Outcomes are promising, both in the short and long term.
- Prevention programs show promise, particularly those programs that include girls age 15 or older, involve more than one session, and are interactive rather than didactic (i.e., lecture format). Outcomes appear promising up to 3 years after the prevention programs are instituted.

Answers to Check Your Knowledge Questions

9.1 1. c; 2. d; 3. d
9.2 1. F; 2. T; 3. F; 4. F; 5. T

9.3 1. cognitive behavior therapy; 2. hospitalization, medications, family therapy; 3. dissonance reduction, healthy weight.

Key Terms

anorexia nervosa
binge eating disorder

body mass index (BMI)
bulimia nervosa

obese

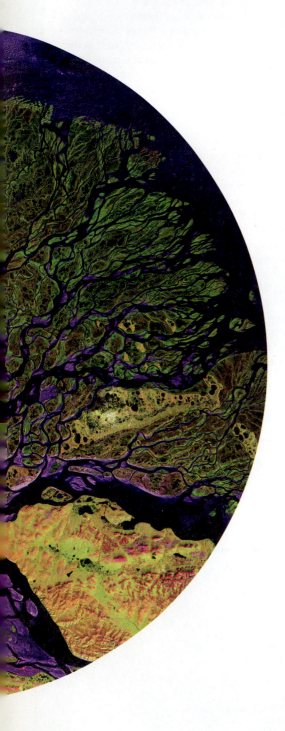

10 Substance-Related Disorders

LEARNING GOALS

1. Be able to differentiate between substance dependence and abuse.
2. Be able to describe the epidemiology and symptoms of drug and alcohol abuse and dependence.
3. Be able to understand the major etiological factors for substance-related disorders, including genetic factors, neurobiological factors, mood and expectancy effects, and sociocultural factors.
4. Be able to describe the approaches to treating substance-related disorders, including psychological treatments, medications, and drug substitution treatments.
5. Be able to delineate the major approaches to prevention of substance-related disorders.

PEOPLE HAVE USED VARIOUS substances in the hope of reducing physical pain or altering states of consciousness for centuries. Around the world, almost all people use one or more substances that affect the central nervous system, relieving physical and mental anguish or producing euphoria. Despite the often devastating consequences of taking such substances into the body, their initial effects are usually pleasing, a factor that is perhaps at the root of **substance-related disorders**.

Clinical Descriptions, Prevalence, and Effects of Substance-Related Disorders

The United States is a drug culture. Americans use drugs to wake up (coffee or tea), to stay alert throughout the day (cigarettes, soft drinks), to relax (alcohol), and to reduce pain (aspirin). The widespread availability and frequent use of various drugs sets the stage for the potential abuse of drugs, the topic of this chapter.

In 2006, over 20 million people over the age of 12 in the United States reported having used an illicit drug [Substance Abuse and Mental Health Services Administration (SAMHSA), 2007]. In addition, 125 million Americans over the age of 12 reported alcohol use of some kind, and 57 million Americans reported at least one episode of binge drinking (defined as having five or more drinks) in the last 30 days (SAMHSA, 2007). Over 15 million people abused prescription drugs such as pain medication in 2003, more than double the number that did so in 1992 (National Center on Addiction and Substance Abuse, 2005). Recent data on the frequency of use of several drugs, legal and illegal, are presented in Table 10.1. These figures do not represent the frequency of abuse or dependence but simply provide an indication of the pervasiveness of drug use in the United States.

Table 10.1 Percentage of U.S. Population Reporting Drug Use in Past Month (2006)	
Substance	**Percentage Reporting Use**
Alcohol	50.9
Cigarettes	29.6
Marijuana	6.0
Nonmedical psychotherapeutics	2.8
Cocaine	1.0
Hallucinogens	0.4
Inhalants	0.2

Source: Substance Abuse and Mental Health Services Administration (2007).

Drug use by adolescents is considerable, but the percentage of adolescents (ages 12–17) who used any illicit drug decreased between 2002 and 2006 from 11.6 to 9.8 percent (SAMHSA, 2007). In 2006, 16.6 percent of youths reported using alcohol.

The pathological use of substances falls into two categories: substance abuse and substance dependence. **Substance dependence**, also referred to as **addiction**, is characterized by DSM-IV-TR as the presence of many problems related to taking the substance. These include using more of the substance than intended, trying unsuccessfully to stop, having physical or psychological problems made worse by the drug, and experiencing problems at work or with friends.

Substance dependence typically involves either tolerance or withdrawal. **Tolerance** is indicated by either (1) larger doses of the substance being needed to produce the desired effect or (2) the effects of the drug becoming markedly less if the usual amount is taken. **Withdrawal** refers to the negative physical and psychological effects that develop when a person stops taking the substance or reduces the amount. Substance withdrawal symptoms can include muscle pains and twitching, sweats, vomiting, diarrhea, and insomnia. Some investigators argue that withdrawal should be mandatory for the diagnosis of substance dependence (Langenbucher et al., 2000). In general, being dependent on a drug is associated with more severe problems (Schuckit et al., 1998).

For the less serious diagnosis of **substance abuse,** the person must experience problems such as failure to meet obligations at work or within the family. Use of the substance may also expose the person to physical dangers, as in driving while drunk. Social relationships may be strained, and legal problems may be frequent.

In 2006, over 22 million people in the United States met the diagnostic criteria for substance abuse or dependence. This figure represents over 9 percent of the U.S. population—not a trivial number. Of this large number of people, most (nearly 15 million) met criteria for alcohol abuse or dependence. Close to 4 million met the criteria for drug abuse or dependence, and over 3 million met the criteria for both drug and alcohol problems (SAMHSA, 2007).

Drug and alcohol dependence are among the most stigmatized of disorders. Terms such as "*addict*" or "*alcoholic*" are tossed about carelessly, as if these words capture the essence of people, not the disorder that they suffer from. Historically, drug and alcohol problems have been viewed as moral lapses rather than as conditions in need of treatment. Unfortunately, such attitudes persist today. Yet there is convincing evidence that becoming dependent on drugs or alcohol is not, in fact, only a matter of personal choice. True, people make decisions about whether or not to try alcohol or drugs, but the ways in which these decisions and the substances involved interact with an individual's neurobiology, social setting, culture, and other environmental factors all conspire to create dependence. Such factors put some people at higher risk for substance dependence than others; it is a mistake to consider substance-related disorders as somehow solely the result of moral failing or personal choice. But it is also a mistake to consider those dependent on drugs or alcohol as being without recourse to change the course of their disorder. Treatment and behavioral change can work in this sphere in much the same way they can work for diseases such as diabetes, where people can change the course of their disease with insulin and diet control.

We turn now to an overview of the major substance-related disorders, those involving alcohol, nicotine, marijuana, opiates, stimulants, and hallucinogens.

DSM-IV-TR Criteria for Substance Dependence

Three or more of the following:
- Tolerance
- Withdrawal
- Substance taken for a longer time or in greater amounts than intended
- Desire or efforts to reduce or control use
- Much time spent trying to obtain the substance
- Social, recreational, or occupational activities given up or reduced
- Continued use despite knowing problems caused by substance

DSM-IV-TR Criteria for Substance Abuse

Maladaptive use of a substance shown by 1 of the following:
- Failure to meet obligations
- Repeated use in situations where it is physically dangerous
- Repeated substance-related legal problems
- Continued use despite problems caused by the substance

Clinical Case: Alice

Alice was 54 years old and living alone when her family finally persuaded her to check into an alcohol rehabilitation clinic. She had taken a bad fall while drunk, and it may have been this event that finally got her to admit that something was wrong. Her drinking had been out of control for several years. She began each day with a drink, continued through the morning, and was totally intoxicated by the afternoon. She seldom had any memory for events after noon of any day. Since early adulthood she had drunk regularly, but rarely during the day and never to the point of drunkenness. The sudden death of her husband in an automobile accident two years earlier had triggered a quick increase in her drinking, and within 6 months she had slipped into a pattern of severe alcohol dependence. She had little desire to go out of her house and had cut back on social activities with family and friends. Repeated efforts by her family to get her to curtail her intake of alcohol had only led to angry confrontations.

Alcohol Abuse and Dependence

The term "*alcoholic*" is familiar to most people, yet it does not have a precise meaning. DSM-IV-TR distinguishes between alcohol dependence and alcohol abuse. Unfortunately, some researchers have only measured abuse without distinguishing dependence. People who meet DSM-IV-TR criteria for alcohol abuse experience negative social and occupational effects from the drug. However, they do not show tolerance, withdrawal, or a compulsive pattern of abuse.

People who are dependent on alcohol generally have more severe symptoms, such as tolerance or withdrawal, than do people who only abuse alcohol without being dependent (Schuckit et al., 1998). The effects of the abrupt withdrawal of alcohol in a chronic, heavy user may be rather dramatic because the body has become accustomed to alcohol. Specifically, a person may feel anxious, depressed, weak, restless, and unable to sleep. He or she may have muscle tremors, especially of the fingers, face, eyelids, lips, and tongue, and pulse, blood pressure, and temperature may be elevated.

In relatively rare cases, a person who has been drinking heavily for a number of years may also experience **delirium tremens (DTs)** when the level of alcohol in the blood drops suddenly. The person becomes delirious as well as tremulous and has hallucinations that are primarily visual but may be tactile as well. Unpleasant and very active creatures—snakes, cockroaches, spiders, and the like—may appear to be crawling up the wall or over the person's body or to be filling the room. Feverish, disoriented, and terrified, the person may claw frantically at his or her skin to get rid of the creatures.

Although changes in the liver enzymes that metabolize alcohol can account to a small extent for tolerance, research suggests that the central nervous system is responsible as well. Some research suggests that tolerance results from changes in the number or sensitivity of GABA or glutamate receptors (Tsai et al., 1998). Withdrawal may result because some neural pathways increase their activation to compensate for alcohol's inhibitory effects in the brain.

Both alcohol abuse and dependence are often part of **polydrug abuse**, abusing more than one drug at a time. It is estimated, for example, that 80 to 85 percent of people who abuse alcohol are smokers. This very high comorbidity may occur because alcohol and nicotine are cross-tolerant; that is, nicotine can induce tolerance for the rewarding effects of alcohol and vice versa. Thus, consumption of both drugs may be increased to maintain their rewarding effects (Rose et al., 2004).

Most people who meet criteria for alcohol abuse do not go on to develop alcohol dependence. For example, one prospective study found that only 3.5 percent of

An etching showing the vivid portrayal of delirium tremens in a scene in a play. (Culver Pictures, Inc.)

persons meeting DSM-IV-TR criteria for alcohol abuse had developed alcohol dependence 5 years later, a number not significantly greater than the 2.5 percent of the population who developed alcohol dependence for the first time over the same 5-year period (Schuckit et al., 2001).

Prevalence and Cost of Alcohol Abuse and Dependence

In a recent U.S. epidemiological study based on the 2001–2002 National Epidemiologic Survey on Alcohol and Related Conditions (NESARC), lifetime prevalence rates for alcohol dependence defined by DSM-IV criteria were greater than 12 percent, and lifetime prevalence rates for alcohol abuse were over 17 percent (Hasin et al., 2007).

Alcohol use is especially frequent among college-age adults. This is true for binge drinking, defined as having five drinks in a short period of time (e.g., within an hour), and heavy-use drinking, defined as having five drinks on the same occasion five or more times in a 30-day period. Among both male and female college students, binge and heavy-use prevalence rates are 43.5 and 17.6 percent, respectively (SAMHSA, 2004). Binge drinking even occurs with high frequency among high school students. Generally speaking, the prevalence of binge drinking is highest among people aged 18 to 25, with a peak prevalence at age 22 (SAMHSA, 2007).

Binge drinking can have serious consequences. Estimates suggest that as many as 1,400 college students die from alcohol-related incidents (e.g., driving under the influence, toxicity) each year. An additional 600,000 are assaulted by other students who have been drinking, and as many as 70,000 students are sexually assaulted [National Institute on Alcohol Abuse and Alcoholism (NIAAA), 2002].

The prevalence of alcohol problems differs by ethnicity and education level as well. White adolescents and adults are more likely to abuse alcohol than African American adolescents and adults. Binge and heavy-use drinking is lowest among Asian Americans (SAMHSA, 2007). Alcohol dependence is most prevalent among Native Americans and Hispanic and least prevalent among Asian Americans and African Americans (Smith et al., 2006).

Alcohol abuse and dependence are comorbid with several personality disorders, mood disorders, schizophrenia, and anxiety disorders as well as with other drug use (Kessler et al., 1997; Morgenstern et al., 1997; Skinstad & Swain, 2001). According to the Substance Abuse and Mental Health Services Administration (2004), 21.3 percent of people suffering from alcohol or drug dependence or abuse also have at least one other mental disorder.

Expenditures on health care for people dependent on alcohol have been estimated to be over $26 billion annually (NIAAA, 2001). Alcohol-related traffic fatalities are a serious problem, and the highest-risk drivers are young men. Through vigorous law enforcement efforts and educational campaigns such as those waged by MADD (Mothers Against Drunk Driving), the situation has improved. Alcohol-related traffic fatalities declined 5 percent between 1993 and 2003, and another 2.4 percent between 2003 and 2004. Still, there were 16,694 deaths from drinking-related driving in 2004, representing nearly 4 out of every 10 traffic fatalities that year. [National Highway Transportation & Safety Administration (NHTSA), 2003, 2005]. More men than women died in alcohol-related fatalities in 2003, and the highest percentage of fatalities with blood alcohol contents of greater than .08 (the legal limit in many states) was among adults aged 21–24 (NHTSA, 2003; SAMHSA, 2004).

Polydrug abuse involves the abuse of multiple drugs. Alcohol and nicotine are a frequent combination, although most people who smoke and drink in social situations do not abuse substances. (Timothy Shonnard/Stone/Getty Images.)

Alcohol is often implicated in vehicular accidents. The driver of this New York subway train, which derailed, killing 5 and injuring over 100 people, was intoxicated. (Corbis Images.)

Blood Alcohol Concentration Calculator

# OF DRINKS CONSUMED/SEX		WEIGHT							
		100	120	140	160	180	200	220	240
1	Male	.04	.04	.03	.03	.02	.02	.02	.02
	Female	.05	.04	.04	.03	.03	.03	.02	.02
2	Male	.09	.07	.06	.05	.05	.04	.04	.04
	Female	.10	.08	.07	.06	.06	.05	.05	.04
3	Male	.13	.11	.09	.08	.07	.07	.06	.05
	Female	.15	.13	.11	.10	.08	.08	.07	.06
4	Male	.17	.15	.13	.11	.10	.09	.08	.07
	Female	.20	.17	.15	.13	.11	.10	.09	.09
5	Male	.22	.18	.16	.14	.12	.11	.10	.09
	Female	.25	.21	.18	.16	.14	.13	.12	.11
6	Male	.26	.22	.19	.16	.15	.13	.12	.11
	Female	.30	.26	.22	.19	.17	.15	.14	.13
7	Male	.30	.25	.22	.19	.17	.15	.14	.13
	Female	.36	.30	.26	.22	.20	.18	.16	.15
8	Male	.35	.29	.25	.22	.19	.17	.16	.15
	Female	.41	.33	.29	.26	.23	.20	.18	.16
9	Male	.39	.35	.28	.25	.22	.20	.18	.16
	Female	.46	38	.33	.29	.26	.23	.21	.19
10	Male	.39	.35	.28	.25	.22	.20	.18	.16
	Female	.51	.42	.36	.32	.28	.25	.23	.21
11	Male	.48	.40	.34	.30	.26	.24	.22	.20
	Female	.56	.46	.40	.35	.31	.27	.25	.23
12	Male	.53	.43	.37	.32	.29	.26	.24	.21
	Female	.61	.50	.43	.37	.33	.30	.28	.25
13	Male	.57	.47	.40	.35	.31	.29	.26	.23
	Female	.66	.55	.47	.40	.36	.32	.30	.27
14	Male	.62	.50	.43	.37	.34	.31	.28	.25
	Female	.71	.59	.51	.43	.39	.35	.32	.29
15	Male	.66	.54	.47	.40	.36	.34	.30	.27
	Female	.76	.63	.55	.46	.42	.37	.35	.32

Figure 10.1 Blood alcohol concentration calculator. Note that values are just estimates. An actual BAC will vary depending on metabolism and amount of food in the stomach.

Short-Term Effects of Alcohol How does alcohol produce its short-term effects? After being swallowed and reaching the stomach, alcohol begins to be metabolized by enzymes. Most of it goes into the small intestine, and from there is absorbed into the blood. It is then broken down, primarily in the liver, which can metabolize about 1 ounce of 100-proof (50 percent alcohol) liquor per hour. Quantities in excess of this amount remain in the bloodstream. Whereas absorption of alcohol can be very quick, removal is always slow.

Although Figure 10.1 shows mean blood alcohol levels based on a person's weight and amount of alcohol consumption, the effects of alcohol vary with its concentration in the bloodstream. Levels in the bloodstream depend on the amount ingested in a particular period of time, the presence of food in the stomach (food retains the alcohol and reduces its absorption rate), the weight and body fat of the person drinking, and the efficiency of the liver. Two ounces of alcohol will thus have a different effect on a 180-pound man who has just eaten than on a 110-pound woman with an empty stomach. However, women achieve higher blood alcohol concentrations even after adjustment for differences in body weight, perhaps due to differences in body water content between men and women.

Alcohol produces its effects through its interactions with several neural systems in the brain. It stimulates GABA receptors, which may account for its ability to reduce tension. (GABA is a major inhibitory neurotransmitter; the benzodiazepines, such as Xanax, have an effect on GABA receptors similar to that of alcohol.) Alcohol also increases levels of serotonin and dopamine, and this may be the source of its ability to produce pleasurable effects. Finally, alcohol inhibits glutamate receptors, which may cause the cognitive effects of alcohol intoxication, such as slowed thinking and memory loss.

A novel study examined the effects of alcohol on both the brain and behavior. Participants were given different doses of alcohol while in an fMRI scanner performing a simulated driving test (Calhoun, Pekar, & Pearlson, 2004). The low dose (.04 blood alcohol content) led to just a small impairment in motor functioning, but the high dose (.08 blood alcohol content) led to more significant motor impairment that interfered with driving ability. Furthermore, the effects of the alcohol in the brain were in areas associated with monitoring errors and making decisions (the anterior cingulate and orbitofrontal cortex), which suggested to the researchers that people at the legal limit of alcohol may make poor decisions about driving and not realize they are making mistakes.

Long-Term Effects of Prolonged Alcohol Abuse Almost every tissue and organ of the body is adversely affected by prolonged consumption of alcohol. For example, alcohol provides so many calories—a pint of 80-proof spirits supplies about half a day's caloric requirements—that drinkers often reduce their intake of food. But the calories provided by alcohol are empty; they do not supply the nutrients essential for health, and the result can be severe malnutrition. Alcohol also contributes directly to malnutrition by impairing the digestion of food and absorption of vitamins. In older people who have chronically abused alcohol, a deficiency of B-complex vitamins can cause amnestic syndrome, a severe loss of memory for both recent and long-past events. These memory gaps are often filled in by reporting imaginary events (confabulation).

Prolonged alcohol use plus reduction in the intake of proteins contributes to the development of cirrhosis of the liver, a disease in which some liver cells become engorged with fat and protein, impeding their function; some cells die, triggering an inflammatory process, and when scar tissue develops, blood flow is obstructed. Taken together, chronic liver disease and cirrhosis rank 12th among causes of death in the United States, with 27,257 deaths in 2002 (Kochanek et al., 2004).

Other common changes to the body due to drinking include damage to the endocrine glands and pancreas, heart failure, erectile dysfunction, hypertension, stroke, and capillary hemorrhages, which are responsible for the swelling and redness in the face, and especially the nose, of people who chronically abuse alcohol. Chronic heavy drinking is associated with damage to many areas of the brain, many of which are implicated in memory functions.

Heavy alcohol consumption by a woman during pregnancy is the leading known cause of mental retardation among children. The growth of the fetus is slowed, and cranial, facial, and limb anomalies can be produced, a condition known as **fetal alcohol syndrome (FAS)**. Even moderate drinking can produce undesirable, if less severe, effects on the fetus, leading the National Institute on Alcohol Abuse and Alcoholism to counsel total abstention during pregnancy as the safest course. Research with children who did not have FAS but whose mothers drank moderately (i.e., about one drink per day) during the first trimester revealed that these children had impairments in learning and memory (Willford et al., 2004) and exhibited growth deficits (such as smaller head size and lower height and weight) at age 14 (Day et al., 2004). Newer research is beginning to solve the puzzle of why some fetuses exposed to alcohol will not develop any problems, whereas others will have profound problems. For example, by 6 months of age, infants exposed to alcohol prenatally may exhibit problems in attention that can then contribute to the development of other cognitive problems later in childhood (Kable & Coles, 2004). The news is not all bad. Animal research has shown that some of the problems associated with prenatal alcohol exposure, such as deficits in learning and memory, can be turned around (Klintsova et al., 2002). In addition, research suggests that growth deficits associated with prenatal alcohol exposure can be mitigated if children are raised in a more stable and healthy environment, indicating that the biological effects of early alcohol exposure are sensitive to environmental conditions (Day & Richardson, 2004).

Although it is appropriate and accurate to pay attention to the negative effects of alcohol, other evidence points to the positive health benefits for some people. Light drinking, especially of red wine, has been related to lower risk for coronary heart disease and stroke (Sacco et al., 1999; Theobald et al., 2000). If alcohol does have a beneficial effect, it could be either physiological (e.g., acetate, a metabolite of alcohol, increases coronary blood flow) or psychological (a less-driven lifestyle and diminished hostility). Some hypothesize that consumption of low to moderate amounts of red wine may lower cholesterol levels. Indirect evidence for this hypothesis has recently been found in an animal study, where researchers discovered that pigment substances in red wine called polyphenols interfered with the synthesis of a peptide called endothelin-1, which is believed to contribute to atherosclerosis (Corder et al., 2001).

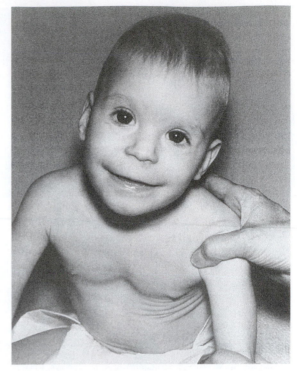

Heavy drinking during pregnancy can cause fetal alcohol syndrome. Children with this disorder can have facial abnormalities and mental retardation. (Courtesy of James W. Hanson.)

Check Your Knowledge 10.1 (Answers are at the end of the chapter.)

True or false?

1. The diagnosis of substance dependence requires both tolerance and withdrawal.
2. Research suggests that nicotine can enhance the rewarding properties of alcohol.
3. Even moderate drinking by pregnant women can cause learning and attention problems in their children.

WARNING: SMOKING CAUSES IMPOTENCE

California's Tobacco Education Media Campaign parodies tobacco ads to illustrate health risks associated with smoking and to attack pro-tobacco influences. (Courtesy of California Department of Health Services.)

Parental smoking greatly increases the chances that children will begin to smoke. (Peter Poulides/Stone/Getty Images.)

Nicotine and Cigarette Smoking

Not long after Columbus's first commerce with Native Americans, sailors and merchants began to imitate the Native Americans' smoking of rolled leaves of tobacco, with the result that they, too, began to crave it. When not smoked, tobacco was—and is—chewed or ground into small pieces and inhaled as snuff. **Nicotine** is the addicting agent of tobacco. The neural pathways that become activated stimulate the dopamine neurons in the mesolimbic area that seem to be involved in producing the reinforcing effects of most drugs (Stein et al., 1998).

Prevalence and Health Consequences of Smoking   The threat to health posed by smoking has been documented convincingly by the Surgeon General of the United States in a series of reports since 1964. It is estimated that more than 440,000 American tobacco users die prematurely each year [U.S. Department of Health and Human Sources (USDHHS) 2004)]. Cigarette smoking is responsible in some way for one of every six deaths in the United States, killing more than 1,100 people each day. It remains the single most preventable cause of premature death in the United States as well as in other parts of the world. Lung cancer kills more people than any other cancer, and cigarette smoking is probably the cause of as many as 87 percent of lung cancers.

Among the other medical problems associated with, and almost certainly caused or exacerbated by, long-term cigarette smoking are emphysema; cancers of the larynx and of the esophagus, pancreas, bladder, cervix, and stomach; complications during pregnancy; sudden infant death syndrome; periodontitis; and a number of cardiovascular disorders (USDHHS, 2004). The most probable harmful components in the smoke from burning tobacco are nicotine, carbon monoxide, and tar, which consist primarily of certain hydrocarbons, many of which are known carcinogens (Jaffe, 1985).

In 2006, nearly 73 million people in the United States used a tobacco product (cigarette, cigar, smokeless tobacco, pipe), and over 3 million youths between the ages of 12 and 17 reported using a tobacco product in the past month. Smoking is more prevalent among white and Hispanic adolescents than among African American or Asian American adolescents. In general, smoking is more prevalent among men than women. However, prevalence among girls and boys between the ages of 12 and 17 is the same (SAMSHA, 2007). The Surgeon General's report in 2004 estimated that the costs of smoking in the United States exceeded $157 billion a year, with half of that reflecting medical costs and the other half reflecting costs of lost productivity.

Research demonstrates the significance of ethnicity in nicotine addiction as well as the intricate interplay among behavioral, social, and biological factors (Leischow, Ranger-Moore, & Lawrence, 2000). It has been known for years that African American cigarette smokers are less likely to quit and are more likely, if they continue to smoke, to get lung cancer. Why? It turns out that they retain nicotine in their blood longer than do whites, that is, they metabolize it more slowly (Mustonen et al. 2005). Another reason has to do with the type of cigarette smoked. African Americans are more likely to smoke menthol cigarettes, and research shows that people who smoke menthol inhale more deeply and hold the smoke in for longer, thus providing more opportunity for deleterious effects (Celebucki et al., 2005).

Research has found that Chinese Americans metabolize less nicotine from cigarettes than either white or Latino smokers (Benowitz et al., 2002). In general, lung cancer rates are lower among Asians than whites or Latinos. The relatively lower metabolism of nicotine among Chinese Americans may help explain why lung cancer rates are lower in this group.

Health Consequences of Secondhand Smoke   As we have known for many years, the health hazards of smoking are not restricted to those who smoke. The smoke coming from the burning end of a cigarette, so-called **secondhand smoke**, or environmental tobacco smoke (ETS), contains higher concentrations of ammonia, carbon monoxide, nicotine, and tar than does the smoke actually inhaled by the smoker. Environmental tobacco smoke is blamed for close to 40,000 deaths a year in the United States. In 1993 the Environmental Protection Agency classified ETS as a hazard

Children of mothers who smoke are at increased risk for respiratory infections, bronchitis, and inner ear infections. (Jennie Woodcock, Reflections Photolibrary/Corbis Images.)

The Surgeon General's report from 2006 noted that no amount of secondhand smoke is safe. (Courtesy The U.S. Department of Health and Human Services.)

on a par with asbestos and radon. In 2006, the Surgeon General issued a report detailing the health hazards of secondhand smoke. The National Institute of Health has classified ETS as a known carcinogen, indicating that evidence has established a cause–effect relationship between ETS and cancer. Effects of ETS include the following:

- Nonsmokers can suffer lung damage, possibly permanent, from extended exposure to cigarette smoke. Those living with smokers are at greatest risk. Precancerous lung abnormalities have been observed in those living with smokers, and nonsmokers are at greater risk for developing cardiovascular disease and lung cancer. In addition, some nonsmokers have allergic reactions to the smoke from burning tobacco.
- Babies of women exposed to secondhand smoke during pregnancy are more likely to be born prematurely, to have lower birth weights, and to have birth defects.
- Children of smokers are more likely to have upper respiratory infections, asthma, bronchitis, and inner ear infections than are their peers whose parents do not smoke. Secondhand smoke can cause sudden infant death syndrome (SIDS).

The Surgeon General has stated that the best form of prevention for exposure to secondhand smoke is to promote smoke-free environments as there is really no safe level of exposure to secondhand smoke (USDHHS, 2006). In recent years, various local governments have passed ordinances regulating cigarette smoking in public places and work settings. Smoking is banned in many supermarkets, buses, hospitals, and government buildings and on all domestic U.S. airline flights. Restaurants must often post signs indicating whether they have an area for nonsmokers, and in many states, such as California, New York, Delaware, Connecticut, Massachusetts, Rhode Island, and Maine, smoking is banned altogether in restaurants. Indeed, smoking is banned in nearly all public places in these seven states, and it is likely that more states will adopt similar regulations.

Marijuana

Marijuana consists of the dried and crushed leaves and flowering tops of the hemp plant, *Cannabis sativa*. It is most often smoked, but it may be chewed, prepared as a tea, or eaten in baked goods. **Hashish**, much stronger than marijuana, is produced by removing and drying the resin exudate of the tops of cannabis plants.

Originally the hemp plant was extensively cultivated in the United States not for smoking but for its fibers, which were used in the manufacture of cloth and rope. By the nineteenth century, the medicinal properties of cannabis resin had been noted, and it was marketed by several drug companies as a treatment for rheumatism, gout, depression, cholera, and neuralgia.

Recreational use of hashish in a fashionable apartment in New York City in the nineteenth century. An 1876 issue of the *Illustrated Police News* carried this picture with the title "Secret Dissipation of New York Belles: Interior of a Hasheesh Hell on Fifth Avenue." (Culver Pictures, Inc.)

It was also smoked for pleasure, though this was little seen in the United States until 1920. At that time, the passage of the Eighteenth Amendment prohibiting the sale of alcohol prompted some people to begin smoking marijuana brought across the border from Mexico. Unfavorable reports in the press attributing crimes to marijuana use led to the enactment of a federal law against the sale of the drug in 1937. Today marijuana use is illegal in most countries.

Prevalence of Marijuana Use   Marijuana is the most frequently used illicit drug. In 2006, nearly 15 million people over the age of 12 reported using marijuana (SAMHSA, 2007). See Figure 10.2 for data on usage from 2002 to 2006. The prevalence is higher among men than women, with nearly twice as many men than women reporting use in the past month in 2006 (SAMHSA, 2007). Marijuana abuse and dependence is more common among Native Americans and European-Americans, and less common among African Americans, Hispanics, and Asian Americans (Stinson et al., 2006). Marijuana use is generally greater in the United States, Australia, and New Zealand than in the European Union, Africa, Asia, South America, and Canada (Rey, Martin, & Krabman, 2004).

Effects of Marijuana   As with most other drugs, marijuana use has its risks. Generally, the more we learn about a drug, the less benign it turns out to be, and marijuana is no exception (see Focus on Discovery 10.1).

Psychological Effects   The intoxicating effects of marijuana, like those of most drugs, depend in part on its potency and the size of the dose. Smokers of marijuana find it makes them feel relaxed and sociable. Large doses have been reported to bring rapid shifts in emotion, to dull attention, to fragment thoughts, to impair memory, and to give the sense that time is moving more slowly. Extremely heavy doses have sometimes been found to induce hallucinations and other effects similar to those of LSD, including extreme panic, sometimes arising from the belief that a frightening experience will never end. Dosage can be difficult to regulate because it may take up to half an hour after smoking marijuana for its effects to appear; many users thus get much higher than intended.

The major active chemical in marijuana is delta-9-tetrahydrocannabinol (THC). The amount of THC in marijuana is variable, but marijuana is more potent now than it was two decades ago (Zimmer & Morgan, 1995). In addition, users smoke more in a session now than in the past (e.g., a "blunt" contains more cannabis than a joint).

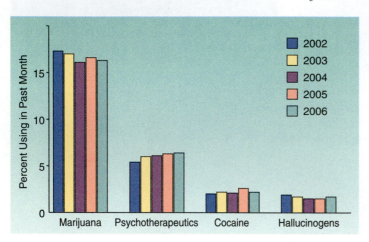

Figure 10.2 Trends in young adults' use of marijuana in the previous month.

An abundance of scientific evidence indicates that marijuana can interfere with a wide range of cognitive functions. Of special significance are findings that show loss of short-term memory. One prospective study assessed IQ scores at multiple time points among users between the ages of 17 and 23 and found a decline of about 4 points in current users (Fried et al., 2002).

Several studies have demonstrated that being high on marijuana impairs complex psychomotor skills necessary for driving. Poor performance after smoking one or two marijuana cigarettes containing 2 percent THC can persist for up to eight hours after a person believes he or she is no longer high, creating the danger that people will drive when they are not functioning adequately.

Does chronic use of marijuana affect intellectual functioning even when the person is not using the drug? Unfortunately, there are not many well-controlled studies that have been conducted to address this question. Collectively, current evidence suggests that long-term users may exhibit a slight impairment in learning and memory, but there is not strong evidence to suggest such impairments persist after discontinuation of use (Rey et al., 2004).

Physical Consequences   The short-term effects of marijuana include bloodshot and itchy eyes, dry mouth and throat, increased appetite, reduced pressure within the eye, and somewhat raised blood pressure.

We know that the long-term use of marijuana seriously impairs lung structure and function (Grinspoon & Bakalar, 1995). Even though marijuana users smoke far fewer cigarettes than do tobacco smokers, most inhale marijuana smoke more deeply and retain it in their lungs for

FOCUS ON DISCOVERY 10.1

Is Marijuana a Gateway Drug?

The so-called stepping-stone, or gateway, theory of marijuana use has been around for a long time. According to this view, marijuana is dangerous not only in itself but also because it is a first step for young people on the path to becoming addicted to other drugs, such as heroin.

Studies have established several specific dangers from using marijuana, as described in the text. But is marijuana a gateway to more serious substance abuse or dependence? First of all, there is little evidence to suggest that this theory applies to African Americans. Furthermore, about 40 percent of regular marijuana users do not go on to use such drugs as heroin and cocaine (Stephens, Roffman, & Simpson, 1993). So if by *gateway* we mean that escalation to a more serious drug is inevitable, then marijuana is not a gateway drug. However, we do know that many, but far from all,

who abuse heroin and cocaine began their drug experimentation with marijuana. And at least in the United States and New Zealand, users of marijuana are more likely than nonusers to experiment later with heroin and cocaine (Fergusson & Horwood, 2000; Kandel, 2002; Miller & Volk, 1996).

Thus, even though marijuana use often precedes other drug use, it does not appear to *cause* later drug use, as the term *gateway* implies. Rather, it may be that marijuana is the first drug to be tried because it is more socially acceptable than other drugs.

Most people who use marijuana do not go on to use heroin, but many heroin users do begin their drug use with marijuana. (Mauritius/SuperStock, Inc.)

much longer periods of time. Since marijuana has some of the same carcinogens found in tobacco, its harmful effects are greater than would be expected were only the absolute number of cigarettes or pipefuls considered. For example, one marijuana cigarette smoked in the typical way is the equivalent of five tobacco cigarettes in carbon monoxide intake, four in tar intake, and ten in terms of damage to cells lining the airways (Sussman et al., 1996).

How does marijuana affect the brain? In the early 1990s, researchers identified two cannabinoid brain receptors, called CB1 and CB2 (Matsuda et al., 1990; Munro, et al., 1993). CB1 receptors are found throughout the body and the brain, with a particularly high number in the hippocampus, an important region of the brain for learning and memory. Based on accumulating evidence, researchers have concluded that the well-documented short-term memory problems associated with marijuana use are linked to the effects of marijuana on these receptors in the hippocampus (e.g., Sullivan, 2000).

In addition, a PET study found that smoking marijuana was associated with increased blood flow to regions in the brain often associated with emotion, including the amygdala and the anterior cingulate. Decreased blood flow was observed in regions of the temporal lobe that have been associated with auditory attention, and participants in this study who were high on marijuana performed poorly on a listening task (O'Leary et al., 2000). These findings might help explain some of the psychological effects associated with marijuana use, including changes in emotion and attentional capabilities.

Is marijuana addictive? Contrary to widespread earlier belief, it may be. Controlled observations have confirmed that habitual use of marijuana does produce tolerance (Compton, Dewey, & Martin, 1990). Whether long-term users experience withdrawal when accustomed amounts of marijuana are not available is less clear, though surveys and laboratory studies conducted in the past 10 years suggest that withdrawal symptoms, such as restlessness, anxiety, tension, stomach pains, and insomnia do occur (Rey et al., 2004).

Therapeutic Effects   Ironically, therapeutic uses of marijuana came to light just as the negative effects of regular and heavy usage of the drug were being uncovered. In the 1970s several double-blind studies showed that THC and related drugs could reduce the nausea and loss of appetite that accompany chemotherapy for some people with cancer (e.g., Salan, Zinberg, & Frei, 1975). Later findings confirmed this result (Grinspoon & Bakalar, 1995). Marijuana often appears to reduce nausea when other antinausea agents fail. Marijuana is also a treatment for the discomfort of AIDS (Sussman et al., 1996).

Demonstrators in New York advocate the legalization of marijuana for medical purposes. (Spencer Platt/Liaison Agency, Inc./Getty Images.)

The potential benefits of smoking marijuana were confirmed in reports by a panel of experts to the National Institutes of Health (NIH; Ad Hoc Advisory Group of Experts, 1998) and a committee of the Institute of Medicine, a branch of the National Academy of Sciences (Institute of Medicine, 1999). These reports suggested that these benefits be taken more seriously by medical researchers and clinicians. The NIH agreed to fund research on the subject, including research on whether the benefits from taking THC in pill form are comparable to what people report from smoking marijuana. (Most people report more beneficial effects from smoking than from swallowing THC in capsule form; this may be due to other compounds than THC in marijuana leaves that are separate from THC.) The Institute of Medicine report recommended that people with "debilitating symptoms" or terminal illnesses be allowed to smoke marijuana under close medical supervision for up to 6 months; the rationale for smoking was based on the just-mentioned findings that THC swallowed by mouth does not provide the same relief. But the Institute of Medicine report also emphasized the dangers of smoking per se and urged the development of alternative delivery systems, such as inhalers.

The recommendations of medical experts represent sharp disagreement with the federal government. California passed Proposition 215 in 1996, a law that makes it legal for physicians to recommend marijuana to help people with AIDS and other seriously ill people cope with pain and relieve nausea from medications used in treating their illnesses. Federal authorities took issue with the California law, and the U.S. Supreme Court ruled in May 2001 that federal law prohibits the dispensing of marijuana for those medical purposes. Interestingly, this ruling did not expressly forbid the *use* of the drug to alleviate pain and nausea. In June 2005, the Supreme Court ruled that the federal government could prohibit the use of marijuana for medical purposes even though the voters in California had approved it. California is not the only state to approve the use of marijuana for medical purposes—11 other states have approved laws similar to California's—so this ruling will likely extend beyond California. State officials in these 12 states will not prosecute people for using medical marijuana even though federal officials may do so. It seems likely that the debate on this issue will continue for years to come.

Quick Summary

Alcohol and drug use is common in the United States. The DSM-IV-TR lists substance dependence, which typically includes either tolerance or withdrawal, and substance abuse as two major categories of substance-related disorders.

Withdrawal from alcohol can involve hallucinations and delirium tremens. People who abuse or are dependent on alcohol may use other drugs, particularly nicotine. Alcohol dependence can have quite a variable course. Alcohol use is particularly high among college students; men are more likely to drink alcohol than women, and differences in use, abuse, and dependence by ethnicity have been observed. Even light or moderate drinking during pregnancy can be associated with later problems in learning for the child.

Smoking remains prevalent, though it has been on the decline. Cigarette smoking causes a number of illnesses, including several cancers, heart disease, and other lung diseases. Although more men smoke than women, the rates are the same among adolescent boys and girls. The ill effects of tobacco are greater for African Americans. Secondhand smoke, also called environmental tobacco smoke, is also linked to a number of serious health problems.

Marijuana makes people feel relaxed and sociable, but it can also interfere with attention, memory, and thinking. In addition, it has been linked to lung-related problems. It remains among the most prevalently used drugs, particularly among younger people. Men use it more than women. Users can develop tolerance to marijuana; it is less clear whether withdrawal symptoms occur after users stop smoking it. Marijuana also has therapeutic benefits, particularly for those suffering from the side effects of chemotherapy and for people with AIDS.

Check Your Knowledge 10.2

Fill in the blanks.
1. List three types of cancer that are caused by smoking.
2. Marijuana can have _____ effects on learning and memory; it is less clear if there are _____ effects.

3. List three of the therapeutic benefits of marijuana.

Opiates

The **opiates**, which fall under the broader category of *sedatives*, include opium and its derivatives morphine, heroin, and codeine. Synthetic barbiturates and minor tranquilizers (benzodiazepines used in the treatment of anxiety), such as secobarbital (Seconal) and diazepam (Valium), are also considered sedatives.

The opiates are a group of addictive sedatives that in moderate doses relieve pain and induce sleep. Foremost among them is **opium**, originally the principal drug of illegal international traffic; it was known to the people of the Sumerian civilization, dating as far back as 7000 B.C. They gave the poppy that supplied this drug the name opium, meaning "the plant of joy."

In 1806 the alkaloid **morphine**, named after Morpheus, the Greek god of dreams, was separated from raw opium. This bitter-tasting powder proved to be a powerful sedative and pain reliever. Before its addictive properties were noted, it was commonly used in medicines. In the middle of the nineteenth century, when the hypodermic needle was introduced in the United States, morphine began to be injected directly into the veins to relieve pain.

Concerned about administering a drug that could disturb the lives of people, scientists began studying morphine. In 1874 they found that morphine could be converted into another powerful pain-relieving drug, which they named **heroin**. Used initially as a cure for morphine addiction, heroin was substituted for morphine in cough syrups and other patent medicines. So many maladies were treated with heroin that it came to be known as G.O.M., or "God's own medicine" (Brecher, 1972). However, heroin proved to be even more addictive and more potent than morphine. Today, heroin is most often injected, though it can also be smoked, snorted, or taken orally.

More recently, opiates legally prescribed as pain medications, including **hydrocodone** and **oxycodone,** have become drugs of abuse [National Drug Intelligence Center (NDIC), 2001]. Hydrocodone is most often combined with other drugs, such as acetaminophen (the active agent in Tylenol) to create prescription pain medicines such as Vicodin, Zydone, or Lortab. Oxycodone is found in medicines such as Percodan, Tylox, and OxyContin. Vicodin is one of the most commonly abused drugs containing hydrocodone, and OxyContin is one of the most commonly abused drugs containing oxycodone.

An opium poppy. Opium is harvested by slitting the seed capsule, which allows the raw opium to seep out. (Dr. Jeremy Burgess/Photo Researchers.)

Prevalence of Opiate Abuse and Dependence   There are enormous difficulties in gathering data, but the considered opinion is that there are more than a million people addicted to heroin in the United States, with an estimated 300,000 users in 2006 alone (SAMHSA, 2007).

Heroin used to be confined to poor neighborhoods and urban environments. In the early 1990s, it became popular among middle- and upper-middle-class college students and young professionals. From 1995 to 2002, rates of use among adults 18 to 25 increased from 0.8 percent to

---

Clinical Case: James

James was a 27-year-old man who had been addicted to heroin for 7 years. He first tried heroin during his time in the Marine Corps. Unable to control his habit, he was dishonorably discharged from the Marines a year later. He lived with his family for a short time, but after stealing money and valuables to support his habit, he was asked to leave the house. He then began living on the street, panhandling for money to support his habit. He also donated blood platelets when he was physically able. Over the years, James lost a tremendous amount of weight and became quite malnourished. He was over 6 feet tall, but he weighed only 150 pounds. Food wasn't a priority on most days, though he was usually able to gather a meal of scraps from the local diner. James tried to get into several rehabilitation programs, but they required that he remain free of heroin for at least a week before he could be admitted. James

was able to resist for a day or two, but then withdrawal symptoms would begin, making it too painful to continue without the drug. A friend from the streets, formerly addicted to heroin, had recently helped James get to a methadone clinic. James tried methadone for a few weeks but was unable to tolerate the long waits outside the clinic each morning and the shame of being stared at by people passing on their way to work. Still, having been free of heroin for over a week, James gained admittance to a residential treatment program. One of the physicians at the program prescribed a newly approved medication called Suboxone that eased the discomfort of heroin withdrawal while also replacing the cravings for heroin. James no longer needed to go to the methadone clinic, and he was getting job training at the treatment program. He was hopeful that he would shake his habit for good.

Heroin was synthesized from opium in 1874 and was soon being added to a variety of medicines that could be purchased without prescription. This ad shows a teething remedy containing heroin. It probably worked. (National Library of Medicine/Photo Researchers.)

1.6 percent. In Baltimore, Boston, and Newark, heroin accounted for between 62 and 82 percent of drug-related hospital admissions in 2003. Deaths attributable to heroin in Baltimore, Chicago, Detroit, and Philadelphia ranged from 275 to nearly 500 in 2003 [Community Epidemiology Work Group (CEWG), 2003].

From 1990 to 1997, reports of hydrocodone abuse increased by 173 percent in the United States, and between 2002 and 2003, use of hydrocodone among people age 12 and older increased from 4.5 million to 5.7 million. Reports of oxycodone abuse increased 43 percent in just 1 year, from 1997 to 1998 (SAMHSA, 2004). Prescriptions for OxyContin, a drug containing oxycodone, jumped 1,800 percent between 1996 and 2000 [Drug Enforcement Administration (DEA), 2001]. The rates of abuse of these drugs have remained relatively stable since 2002 (SAMHSA, 2007).

The illicit supply seems to come largely from prescriptions that are forged, stolen, or diverted to dealers on the black market. As prescribed, OxyContin comes in a pill format with polymer coating. Unfortunately, the pills can easily be dissolved into a form that can then be injected or snorted. The legitimate sales price of a 40-milligram OxyContin pill ranges from $0.50 to $1.00, but pills sell on the street for $25.00 to $40.00 each. Abuse of OxyContin appears to be more prevalent in rural areas, but it is rapidly spreading to large metropolitan areas (DEA, 2001; Meier, 2003). OxyContin's effects are quite similar to those of heroin, so health professionals are concerned that people dependent on OxyContin who can no longer afford its hefty street price will turn to heroin, which is less expensive. As shown in Figure 10.3, visits to hospital emergency rooms after overdoses of hydrocodone and oxycodone have been steadily increasing since 1994, with nearly 48,000 such visits in 2002 (Ball & Lehder Roberts, 2004).

Psychological and Physical Effects Opiates produce euphoria, drowsiness, and sometimes a lack of coordination. Heroin and OxyContin also produce a "rush," a feeling of warm, suffusing ecstasy immediately after an intravenous injection. The user sheds worries and fears and has great self-confidence for 4 to 6 hours. However, the user then experiences a severe letdown, bordering on stupor.

Opiates produce their effects by stimulating neural receptors of the body's own opioid system (the body naturally produces opioids, called endorphins and enkephalins). Heroin, for example, is converted into morphine in the brain and then binds to opioid receptors, which are located throughout the brain. Some evidence suggests that a link between these receptors and the dopamine system is responsible for opiates' pleasurable effects. However, evidence from animal studies suggests that opiates may achieve their pleasurable effects via their action in the area of the brain called the nucleus accumbens, perhaps independently from the dopamine system (Koob et al., 1999).

Opiates are clearly addicting, for users develop tolerance and show withdrawal symptoms. Withdrawal from heroin may begin within 8 hours of the last injection, at least after high tolerance has built up. During the next few hours after withdrawal begins, the person typically

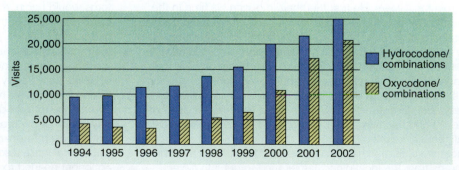

Figure 10.3 Emergency room visits after overdoses of hydrocodone and oxycodone have increased dramatically in less than 10 years. From Office of Applied Studies, SAMHSA, Drug Abuse Warning Network, 2002 (03/2003 update).

experiences muscle pain, sneezes, and sweating; becomes tearful; and yawns a great deal. The symptoms resemble those of influenza. Within 36 hours, the withdrawal symptoms become more severe. There may be uncontrollable muscle twitching, cramps, chills alternating with excessive flushing and sweating, and a rise in heart rate and blood pressure. The person is unable to sleep, vomits, and has diarrhea. These symptoms typically persist for about 72 hours and then diminish gradually over a 5 to 10-day period.

People who abuse opiates face serious problems. In a 29-year follow-up of 500 people addicted to heroin, about 28 percent had died by age 40; half of these deaths were from homicide, suicide, or accident, and one-third were from overdose (Hser, Anglin, & Powers, 1993). The social consequences of using an illegal drug are also serious. The drug and obtaining it become the center of the person's existence, governing all activities and social relationships. The high cost of drugs—users must often spend upwards of $200 per day for opiates—often drives users into acquiring money through illegal activities, such as theft, prostitution, or selling drugs.

An additional problem associated with intravenous drug use is exposure, through sharing needles, to infectious agents such as the human immunodeficiency virus (HIV), which causes AIDS. Notably, there is good consensus among scientists that the free distribution of needles and syringes reduces needle sharing and the spread of infectious agents associated with intravenous drug use (Gibson, 2001; Yoast et al., 2001). Contrary to popular political rhetoric, such programs in combination with methadone treatment (discussed later in this chapter) do not lead to an increase in either initial or continued use of drugs. In 2004, California adopted a law that allows pharmacists to sell up to 10 syringes without a prescription.

Synthetic Sedatives   **Barbiturates** were first synthesized in 1903 as aids for sleeping and relaxation. Since then, hundreds of different barbiturates have been synthesized. These drugs were initially prescribed frequently, but in the 1940s a campaign was mounted against them because they were discovered to be addictive. Physicians then began to prescribe barbiturates less frequently. From 1975 to the early 1990s, use steadily declined, but it now appears to be on the rise (Johnston, O'Malley, & Bachman, 2001). Other types of synthetic sedatives are also part of this upward trend. Benzodiazepines, such as Valium, are commonly used and abused.

Synthetic sedatives relax the muscles, reduce anxiety, and in small doses produce a mildly euphoric state. Like alcohol, they are thought to produce these psychological effects by stimulating the GABA system. With excessive doses, however, speech becomes slurred and gait unsteady. Judgment, concentration, and ability to work may be extremely impaired. The user loses emotional control and may become irritable and combative before falling into a deep sleep. Very large doses can be fatal because the diaphragm muscles relax to such an extent that a person suffocates. Many users accidentally kill themselves by drinking alcohol, which magnifies the effects of sedatives. Not surprisingly, prolonged excessive use can damage the brain.

Increased tolerance follows prolonged use of synthetic sedatives. The withdrawal reactions after abrupt termination are particularly severe and long lasting and can cause sudden death. The delirium, convulsions, and other symptoms resemble the symptoms that follow abrupt withdrawal from alcohol.

Stimulants

Stimulants act on the brain and the sympathetic nervous system to increase alertness and motor activity. Amphetamines are synthetic stimulants; cocaine is a natural stimulant extracted from the coca leaf. Focus on Discovery 10.2 discusses a less risky and more prevalent stimulant, caffeine.

Amphetamines   The first **amphetamine**, benzedrine, was synthesized in 1927, and other amphetamines were synthesized soon after. Almost as soon as benzedrine became commercially available in the early 1930s as an inhalant to relieve stuffy noses, the public discovered its stimulating effects, and physicians soon began to prescribe it and the other amphetamines to control mild depression and appetite. During World War II, soldiers on both sides were supplied with amphetamines to ward off fatigue.

Amphetamines such as benzedrine, dexedrine, and methedrine produce their effects by causing the release of norepinephrine and dopamine and blocking the reuptake of these neurotransmitters. Amphetamines are taken orally or intravenously and can be addicting. Wakefulness

FOCUS ON DISCOVERY 10.2

Our Tastiest Addiction—Caffeine

What may be the world's most popular drug is seldom viewed as a drug at all, and yet it has strong effects, produces tolerance in people, and even subjects habitual users to withdrawal (Hughes et al., 1991). Users and nonusers joke about it, and most readers of this book have probably had some this very day. We are, of course, referring to **caffeine**, a substance found in coffee, tea, cocoa, cola and other soft drinks, some cold remedies, and some diet pills.

Two cups of coffee, containing between 150 and 300 milligrams of caffeine, affect most people within half an hour. Metabolism, body temperature, and blood pressure all increase; urine production goes up, as most of us will attest; there may be hand tremors, appetite can diminish, and, most familiar of all, sleepiness is warded off. Panic disorder can be exacerbated by caffeine, not surprising in light of the heightened sympathetic nervous system arousal occasioned by the drug. Extremely large doses of caffeine can cause headache, diarrhea, nervousness, severe agitation, even convulsions and death. Death, though, is virtually impossible unless the person grossly overuses tablets containing caffeine, because

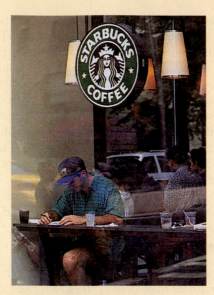

The caffeine found in coffee, tea, and soft drinks is probably the world's favorite drug. (Sepp Seitz/Woodfin Camp & Associates.)

the drug is excreted by the kidneys without any appreciable accumulation.

Although it has long been recognized that drinkers of very large amounts of regular (caffeinated) coffee daily can experience withdrawal symptoms when consumption ceases, people who drink no more than two cups of regular coffee a day can suffer from clinically significant headaches, fatigue, and anxiety if caffeine is withdrawn from their daily diet (Silverman et al., 1992), and these symptoms can interfere with social and occupational functioning. These findings are disturbing because more than three-quarters of Americans consume a little more than two cups of regular coffee a day (Roan, 1992). And although parents usually deny their children access to coffee and tea, they often do allow them to imbibe caffeine-laden soft drinks, hot chocolate, and cocoa, and to eat chocolate candy and chocolate and coffee ice cream. Thus, our addiction to caffeine can begin to develop as early as 6 months of age, the form of it changing as we move from childhood to adulthood.

is heightened, intestinal functions are inhibited, and appetite is reduced—hence their use in dieting. The heart rate quickens, and blood vessels in the skin and mucous membranes constrict. The person becomes alert, euphoric, and outgoing and is possessed with seemingly boundless energy and self-confidence. Larger doses can make a person nervous, agitated, and confused; other symptoms include palpitations, headaches, dizziness, and sleeplessness. Sometimes heavy users become extremely suspicious and hostile, to the extent that they can be dangerous to others. Large doses taken over a period of time can induce a state quite similar to paranoid schizophrenia.

Tolerance to amphetamines develops rapidly, so more and more of the drug is required to produce the stimulating effect. One study demonstrated tolerance after just 6 days of repeated use (Comer et al., 2001). As tolerance increases, some users may stop taking pills and start injecting methedrine, the strongest of the amphetamines, directly into the veins. Users may give themselves repeated injections of the drug and maintain intense and euphoric activity for a few days, without eating or sleeping, after which, exhausted and depressed, they sleep, or crash, for several days. Then the cycle starts again. After several repetitions of this pattern, the physical and social functioning of the person deteriorates considerably. Behavior becomes erratic and hostile, and users may become dangerous to themselves and others.

Clinical Case: Anton

Anton, a 37-year-old man, had just been arrested for a parole violation, stealing a package of string cheese from a convenience store. He was also found to be under the influence of methamphetamine. Two months earlier, he had been released from prison after serving time for petty theft and for purchasing methamphetamine. He was determined to remain out of prison, but his cravings for meth were so intense that he was unable to abide by the terms of his parole. He had been using meth since he was 26 years old, and he had been arrested numerous times for drug-related offenses, including prostitution (to get money to support his habit).

Methamphetamine   Abuse of an amphetamine derivative called **methamphetamine** skyrocketed in the 1990s. Some estimates indicate that as many as 4.7 million people in the United States have tried methamphetamine at some point (Anglin et al., 2000). In 2006, over 700,000 people used methamphetamine (SAMHSA, 2007).

Men tend to abuse methamphetamine more often than women in contrast with abuse of other amphetamines, where few gender differences occur. Among adolescents, however, abuse by both males and females has almost doubled since 1992 (Oetting et al., 2000). White males are most likely to abuse meth, but studies suggest that use among Hispanic Americans and Native Americans is on the rise (Oetting et al., 2000).

Like other amphetamines, methamphetamine can be taken orally or intravenously. It can also be taken intranasally (i.e., by snorting). In a clear crystal form, the drug is often referred to as "crystal meth" or "ice." Craving for methamphetamine is particularly strong, often lasting several years after use of the drug is discontinued. Craving is also a reliable predictor of later use (Hartz, Fredrick-Osborne, & Galloway, 2001).

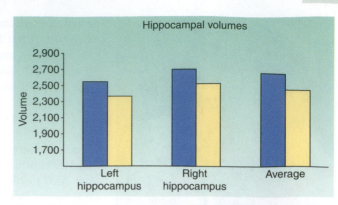

Figure 10.4   Results from an fMRI study showing that those who abused methamphetamine (yellow bars) had smaller hippocampal volume (size) than those in the control group (blue bars) who did not abuse methamphetamine. Adapted from Thompson et al. (2004).

Several studies done with animals have indicated that chronic use of methamphetamine causes damage to the brain, affecting both the dopamine system and the serotonin system (Frost & Cadet, 2000). Neuroimaging studies have found similar effects in the human brain, particularly in the dopamine system. For example, one study of chronic meth users who met DSM diagnostic criteria for dependence found a number of users with damage to the hippocampus (see Figure 10.4). The volume of the hippocampus was smaller among chronic meth users, and this correlated with poorer performance on a memory test (Thompson et al., 2004). Another study reported that people who abused methamphetamine but who were currently clean of the substance, some for as long as 11 months, had a significant reduction in a dopamine transporter gene (a transporter gene is a gene that either lets a drug enter a cell or prevents a drug from entering a cell) (Volkow et al., 2001). In fact, in 3 of the 15 people studied, the reduction in dopamine reuptake was similar to that seen in the less severe stages of Parkinson's disease. Moreover, those with a history of methamphetamine abuse performed more slowly than a comparison group on several motor tasks, a finding similar to that seen with people with Parkinson's disease.

In a different study, men who were in treatment for methamphetamine dependence participated in a laboratory task of decision making while having their brains scanned with fMRI (Paulus, Tapert, & Schuckit, 2005). The researchers found that lower activation in several brain areas (dorsolateral prefrontal cortex, insula, and areas of the temporal and parietal lobes) during the decision-making task predicted relapse in methamphetamine abuse 1 year after treatment. It seems obvious that poor decision making might put one at higher risk for relapse. What this study also showed was that the brain areas that contribute to sound decision making are disrupted in some people who are dependent on methamphetamine. What is less clear is whether the methamphetamine damaged these areas or whether these areas were damaged before methamphetamine use began.

A caveat should be noted here. One difficulty with conducting these types of studies is finding participants who use only the drug of interest (in this case, methamphetamine) so that any observed effects can be linked to that drug and not others. However, it is difficult to find meth users who have not at some point used other substances, particularly alcohol and nicotine. For example, in one of the studies described above, the meth users did not differ from the control group in alcohol consumption, but they did smoke more (Thompson et al., 2004). Nevertheless, it seems clear that the deleterious effects of methamphetamine are many and serious.

Chemicals for manufacturing methamphetamine, such as ephedrine, are readily available, though laws such as the Methamphetamine Control Act of 1996 have been passed to try to cut off the supply. When supplies of ephedrine became low, pseudoephedrine, a common substance in many over-the-counter decongestants, was substituted, but these substances are now also better regulated. Some chemicals used to make methamphetamine are highly volatile and dangerous to breathe, causing damage ranging from eye irritation and nausea to coma and death.

Cocaine   The alkaloid **cocaine** was first extracted from the leaves of the coca shrub in the mid-1800s and has been used since then as a local anesthetic. In the mid-1980s a new form of cocaine, called **crack**, appeared on the streets. Crack comes in a rock-crystal form that is then

A coca plant. The leaves contain about 1 percent cocaine. (Dr. Morley Read/Photo Researchers.)

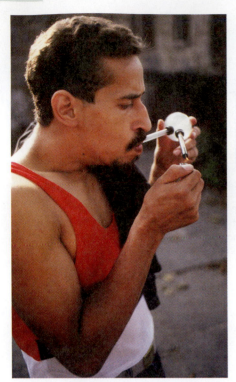

Crack use is highest in urban areas. (Wesley Bocxe/Photo Researchers, Inc.)

heated, melted, and smoked. The name *crack* comes from the crackling sound the rock makes when being heated. The presence of crack brought about an increase in the number of users of cocaine and in casualties. Because it was available in small, relatively inexpensive doses ($10 for about 100 milligrams versus $100 per gram of cocaine), younger and less affluent buyers began to experiment with the drug and to become addicted (Kozel & Adams, 1986). Crack is now most often used in poorer urban areas.

Cocaine use in general soared in the 1970s and 1980s, increasing by more than 260 percent between 1974 and 1985. Men use cocaine and crack more often than women do. Although the use of cocaine dramatically decreased in the late 1980s and early 1990s, it began to rise again in the mid-1990s, particularly among high school and college students and young adults in general. Indeed, from 2000 to 2002, there were about a million new users per year. Among users, 25 percent met DSM criteria for cocaine dependence in 2003 (SAMHSA, 2004). In 2006, 2.4 million people over the age of 12 reported using cocaine, and 700,000 reported using crack (SAMHSA, 2007). In short, cocaine and crack remain significant drugs of abuse.

Cocaine has other effects, in addition to reducing pain. It acts rapidly on the brain, blocking the reuptake of dopamine in mesolimbic areas. Cocaine yields pleasurable states because dopamine left in the synapse facilitates neural transmission. Self-reports of pleasure induced by cocaine are strongly related to the extent to which cocaine has blocked dopamine reuptake (Volkow et al., 1997). Cocaine can increase sexual desire and produce feelings of self-confidence, well-being, and indefatigability. An overdose may bring on chills, nausea, and insomnia, as well as strong paranoid feelings and terrifying hallucinations of insects crawling beneath the skin. Chronic use can lead to heightened irritability, impaired social relationships, paranoid thinking, and disturbances in eating and sleeping. Some, but not all, users develop tolerance to cocaine, requiring a large dose to achieve the same effect. Other users may become more sensitive to cocaine's effects, which are believed to be a contributing factor in deaths after a fairly small dosage. Stopping cocaine use appears to cause severe withdrawal symptoms.

Cocaine is a vasoconstrictor, causing the blood vessels to narrow. As users take larger and larger doses of the purer forms of cocaine now available, they are more often rushed to emergency rooms and may die of an overdose, often from a heart attack [National Institute on Drug Abuse (NIDA), 2004a]. Cocaine also increases a person's risk for stroke and causes cognitive impairments, such as difficulty paying attention and remembering. Because of its strong vasoconstricting properties, cocaine poses special dangers in pregnancy, for the blood supply to the developing fetus may be compromised.

Cocaine can be sniffed (snorted), smoked in pipes or cigarettes, swallowed, or even injected into the veins; some heroin users mix the two drugs. In the 1970s cocaine users in the United States began to separate, or free, a component of cocaine by heating it with ether. When purified by this chemical process, the cocaine base—or freebase—produces very powerful effects because it is absorbed so rapidly. Like most drugs, the faster it is absorbed, the quicker and more intense the high. Freebase is usually smoked in a water pipe or sprinkled on a tobacco or marijuana cigarette. It is rapidly absorbed into the lungs and carried to the brain in a few seconds, where it induces an intense 2-minute high, followed by restlessness and discomfort.

Hallucinogens, Ecstasy, and PCP

LSD and Other Hallucinogens   In 1938 the Swiss chemist Albert Hofmann manufactured a few milligrams of *d*-lysergic acid diethylamide into a drug know today as **LSD**. The term *psychedelic*, from the Greek words for "soul" and "to make manifest," was applied to emphasize the subjectively experienced expansion of consciousness reported by users of LSD and often referred to by them as a "trip." The term in current use for LSD and other drugs with similar effects is **hallucinogen**, which refers to the main effects of such drugs, hallucinations. Unlike the hallucinations in schizophrenia, however, these are usually recognized by the person as being caused by the drug.

The use of LSD and other hallucinogens peaked in the 1960s; by the 1980s, only 1 or 2 percent of people could be classified as regular users. In 2006, there were about 100,000 users (SAMHSA, 2007) down from 1 million in 2002 (SAMHSA, 2004). There is no evidence of withdrawal symptoms during abstinence, but tolerance appears to develop rapidly (McKim, 1991). Among youths between the ages of 12 and 17, African Americans are less likely to use hallucinogens than whites, Asian Americans, or Hispanics [Office of Applied Studies (OAS), 2002].

Cocaine can be smoked, swallowed, injected, or snorted as shown here. (Mark Antman/The Image Works.)

In addition to hallucinations, LSD can alter a person's sense of time (it seems to go slowly). A person using LSD may have sharp mood swings but can also experience an expanded consciousness such that he or she seems to appreciate sights and sounds like never before.

The effects of hallucinogens depend on a number of psychological variables in addition to the dose itself. A person's set—that is, attitudes, expectancies, and motivations with regard to taking drugs—is widely held to be an important determinant of his or her reactions to hallucinogens. The context in which the drug is experienced is also important.

Many users experience intense anxiety after taking LSD, in part because the perceptual experiences and hallucinations can provoke fears that they are "going crazy." For some, these anxieties unfold into full-blown panic attacks. The anxiety usually subsides as the drug is metabolized. A minority of people, however, go into a psychotic state that can require hospitalization and extended treatment.

Flashbacks (also referred to as hallucinogen persisting perception disorder, or HPPD) are visual recurrences of psychedelic experiences after the physiological effects of the drug have worn off. They occur in some people who have used LSD, most frequently in times of stress, illness, or fatigue. Flashbacks seem to have a force of their own; they may come to haunt people weeks and months after they have taken the drug and are very upsetting for those who experience them.

Other hallucinogens include mescaline and psilocybin, whose effects are thought to be due to stimulating serotonin receptors. **Mescaline**, an alkaloid and the active ingredient of peyote, was isolated in 1896 from small, disklike growths of the top of the peyote cactus. The drug has been used for centuries in the religious rites of Native American people living in the U.S. Southwest and northern Mexico. **Psilocybin** is a crystalline powder that Hofmann isolated from the mushroom *Psilocybe mexicana* in 1958.

Mescaline, obtained from the peyote cactus, is used in certain religious rites of Native American people of the American Southwest and northern Mexico. (Kal Muller/Woodfin Camp & Associates.)

Ecstasy and PCP   A newer hallucinogen-like substance, **Ecstasy**, became illegal in 1985. Ecstasy includes both MDA (methylenedioxyamphetamine) and MDMA (methylenedioxymethamphetamine). **MDMA** was first synthesized in the early 1900s, and it was used as an appetite suppressant for World War I soldiers. Chemical precursors to MDMA are found in several commonly used spices, such as nutmeg, dill, saffron, and sassafras. Not until the 1970s were the psychoactive properties of MDMA reported in the scientific literature. **MDA** was first synthesized in 1910, but it was not until the 1960s that its psychedelic properties came to the attention of the drug-using, consciousness-expanding generation of the times.

Ecstasy contains compounds from both the hallucinogen and amphetamine families, but its effects are sufficiently different from either that some have suggested putting it in its own category, called the "entactogens" (Morgan, 2000). Today it remains popular on college campuses and in clubs. Focus on Discovery 10.3 discusses the use and effects of another club drug, nitrous oxide. Across all ages, Ecstasy use seems to have peaked in 2001, with 1.8 million users. From 2002 to 2003, the number of users age 12 and over decreased from 676,000

Clinical Case: Tamara

Tamara tried Ecstasy (X) for the first time when she was a freshman in college. She went to her first rave, and a friend gave her a pill she thought was a Sweet Tart. Within a short period of time, she began to feel almost magical, as if she was seeing everything around her in a new light. She felt incredibly close to her friends and even to men and women she had just met. Hugging and close dancing were intensely pleasurable, in a completely new way. A few days after the

party, she asked her friend about the "Sweet Tart" and found out how she could obtain more. But the next time she tried X, she was unable to achieve the same pleasurable feelings. Instead, she felt more subdued, even anxious. After several more times using X, she noticed that despite her enthusiasm and even craving for the effects, she found instead that she felt a little depressed and anxious, even several days after taking the drug.

FOCUS ON DISCOVERY 10.3

Nitrous Oxide—Not a Laughing Matter

Nitrous oxide is a colorless gas that has been available since the nineteenth century. Within seconds, it induces lightheadedness and a state of euphoria in most people; for some, important insights seem to flood the mind. Many people find otherwise mundane events and thoughts irresistibly funny, hence the nickname *laughing gas*.

Many people have received nitrous oxide at a dentist's office to facilitate relaxation and otherwise make a potentially uncomfortable and intimidating dental procedure more palatable. A major advantage of nitrous oxide over other analgesics and relaxants is that a person can return to a normal waking state within minutes of breathing enriched oxygen or normal air.

Nitrous oxide fits in the broader category of inhalants and has been used recreationally since it first became available, although it has been illegal for many years in most states except as administered by appropriate health professionals. As with the other drugs examined in this chapter, illegality has not prevented unsupervised use. It is one of the most prevalently used inhalants among teens (sniffing glue, gasoline, and paint are more prevalent), with rates of use as high as 22 percent among those who use inhalants (Wu, Pilowsky,

& Schlenger, 2004). Sometimes called "hippie crack" or "whippets," nitrous oxide balloons are often combined with the use of Ecstasy and other drugs at parties with bright laser lights and loud dance music (i.e., at raves).

Nitrous oxide is no laughing matter.
(BananaStock/SUPERSTOCK.)

to 470,000. Despite this general decline, use among Hispanics does not appear to be declining (SAMHSA, 2004).

Ecstasy acts primarily by contributing to both the release and the subsequent reuptake of serotonin (Huether, Zhou, & Ruther, 1997; Liechti et al., 2000; Morgan, 2000). It was believed at one time that the use of Ecstasy was relatively harmless, but accumulating scientific evidence suggests that it may have neurotoxic effects on the serotonin system (De Souza, Battaglia, & Insel, 1990; Gerra et al., 2000). It is difficult to say if these toxic effects are directly due to drug use, since no studies in humans to date have assessed serotonin functioning both before and after Ecstasy use. Studies with animals, however, have shown that a single dose of Ecstasy causes serotonin depletion and that prolonged use can damage serotonin axons and nerve terminals (Harkin et al., 2001; Morgan, 2000).

Users report that Ecstasy enhances intimacy and insight, improves interpersonal relationships, elevates mood and self-confidence, and promotes aesthetic awareness. It can also cause muscle tension, rapid eye movements, jaw clenching, nausea, faintness, chills or sweating, anxiety, depression, depersonalization, and confusion. Some evidence suggests that the subjective and physiological effects of Ecstasy, both pleasurable and adverse, may be stronger for women than men (Liechti et al., 2000).

PCP, phencyclidine, often called *angel dust*, is another drug that is not easy to classify. Developed as a tranquilizer for horses and other large animals, it generally causes serious negative reactions, including severe paranoia and violence. Coma and death are also possible. PCP affects multiple neurotransmitters in the brain, and chronic use is associated with a variety of neuropsychological deficits. People who abuse PCP are likely to have used other drugs either before or concurrently with PCP, so it is difficult to sort out whether neuropsychological impairments are due solely to PCP, to other drugs, or to the combination. Use of PCP increased in the early to mid-1990s but was believed to be on the decline in the late 1990s. However, between 2000 and 2002, the number of arrests, emergency room visits, and treatment admissions linked to PCP increased in urban areas such as Chicago, Dallas, Los Angeles, Philadelphia, Phoenix, and Washington, D.C. (NIDA, 2004c).

Ecstasy is a popular party drug but, like many drugs, is not free of ill effects. (Lynne Sobol/Montes De Oca & Associates.)

Quick Summary

Opiates include heroin and other pain medications like hydrocodone and oxycodone. Abuse of prescription pain medications has risen dramatically, and overdoses are common. Initial effects of opiates include euphoria; later, users experience a letdown. Death by overdose from opiates is a severe problem. Other problems include exposure to HIV and other infectious agents through the use of shared needles. Synthetic sedatives are prescribed less than they used to be. They relax the muscles, reduce anxiety, and can produce a mildly euphoric state. Large doses can be fatal. Withdrawal is severe for opiates and synthetic sedatives.

Amphetamines are stimulants that produce wakefulness, alertness, and euphoria. Men and women use these equally. Tolerance develops quickly. Methamphetamine is a synthesized amphetamine, and use has increased dramatically since the 1990s. Men use it more than women and whites more than other ethnic groups. Methamphetamine can damage the brain, including the hippocampus. Cocaine and crack remain serious problems. Cocaine can increase sexual desire, feelings of well-being, and alertness, but chronic use is associated with problems in relationships, paranoia, and trouble sleeping, among other things. The faster crack or cocaine is absorbed, the more quickly and intensely the person becomes high.

LSD was a popular hallucinogen in the 1960s and 1970s, often billed as a mind-expanding drug. The mind-expanding drug of the 1990s became Ecstasy. Although these drugs do not typically elicit withdrawal symptoms, tolerance can develop. There is some indication that Ecstasy use may be on the decline, but not among all ethnic groups. PCP remains a problem in urban areas. This drug can cause severe paranoia and violence.

Check Your Knowledge 10.3

True or false?
1. Withdrawal from heroin begins slowly, days after use has been discontinued.
2. The use of OxyContin began in urban areas but quickly spread to rural areas.
3. Methamphetamine is a less potent form of amphetamine, less likely to be associated with brain impairment.
4. Ecstasy contains compounds associated with hallucinogens and amphetamines.

Etiology of Substance-Related Disorders

Becoming substance dependent is generally a developmental process. The person must first have a positive attitude toward the substance, then begin to experiment with using it, then begin using it regularly, then use it heavily, and finally abuse or become dependent on it (see Figure 10.5). The general idea is that after prolonged heavy use, some people become ensnared by the biological effects of tolerance and withdrawal.

It appears that the factors that contribute to substance dependence may depend on the point in the process that is being considered. For example, developing a positive attitude toward smoking and beginning to experiment with tobacco are strongly related to smoking by other family members (Robinson et al., 1997). In contrast, becoming a regular smoker is more strongly related to smoking by peers and being able to acquire cigarettes readily (Robinson et al., 1997; Wang et al., 1997).

More generally, adopting a developmental approach to understanding the etiology of substance-related disorders requires the study of persons across time, beginning at the earliest sign of substance use. Studies of the trajectories of substance-related problems among adolescents are becoming more frequent, and the findings suggest, not surprisingly, that different adolescents follow different trajectories (Jackson, Sher, & Wood, 2000; Wills et al., 1999). For example, one study identified two typical trajectories toward alcohol abuse in adolescence: (1) a group that began drinking early in

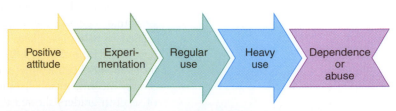

Figure 10.5 The process of becoming dependent on a drug.

adolescence and continued to increase their drinking throughout high school and (2) a group that started drinking a lesser amount in early adolescence and increased drinking at two peak points, one in middle school and another later in high school. Boys were more likely to follow the trajectory of the first group; girls were more likely to follow the trajectory of the second group, with even steeper trajectories in drinking than the boys (Li, Duncan, & Hops, 2001).

Other views incorporate what we know about the developing brain, particularly in adolescence. A review of the literature points to the fact that the area of the brain linked to judgment and decision making, novelty seeking, and impulse control—that is, the frontal cortex—is still developing at the time when adolescents are beginning to experiment with drugs and alcohol (Chambers, Taylor, & Potenza, 2003). The neural systems believed to be important for reward, including dopaminergic, serotonergic, and glutamatergic pathways, all pass through the developing frontal cortex.

Although applicable in many cases, a developmental approach does not account for all cases of substance abuse or dependence. For example, there are documented cases in which heavy use of tobacco or heroin did not result in dependence. Furthermore, we must remember that we are not talking about an inevitable progression through stages. Some people have periods of heavy use of a substance—for example, alcohol—and then return to moderate use. In the following sections, we discuss genetic, neurobiological, psychological, and sociocultural factors associated with substance-related disorders. Keep in mind that these factors are likely to be differently related to different substances. Genetic factors, for example, may play some role in alcohol dependence but be less important in hallucinogen abuse.

Genetic Factors

Much research has addressed the possibility that there is a genetic predisposition for drug and alcohol abuse and dependence. Several studies have shown that relatives and children of problem drinkers have higher-than-expected rates of alcohol abuse or dependence (e.g., Chassin et al., 1999). Furthermore, family studies show that the relatives of those who abuse substances are at increased risk for abusing many substances, not just the one that was the basis for selecting the proband (Bierut et al., 1998; Merilkangas et al., 1998). Stronger evidence for a genetic diathesis comes from twin studies, which have revealed greater concordance in identical twins than in fraternal twins for alcohol abuse by men (McGue, Pickens, & Svikis, 1992), smoking (True et al., 1999), heavy use or abuse of marijuana (Kendler & Prescott, 1998), and drug abuse in general (Tsuang et al., 1998). Behavioral genetics studies indicate that the genetic and shared environmental risk factors (see Chapter 2) for illicit drug abuse and dependence may be rather nonspecific (Karkowski, et al., 2000; Kendler, Jacobsen, et al., 2003). That is, genetic and shared environmental risk factors appear to be the same no matter what the drug (marijuana, cocaine, opiates, hallucinogens, sedatives, stimulants). This appears to be true for both men and women (Kendler, Prescott, et al., 2003).

The ability to tolerate large quantities of alcohol may be an inherited diathesis for alcohol abuse or dependence. That is, to become a dependent on alcohol, a person has to be able to drink a lot. Some ethnic groups, such as Asians, may have a low rate of alcohol abuse because of physiological intolerance, which is caused by an inherited deficiency in an enzyme involved in alcohol metabolism. About three-quarters of Asians experience unpleasant effects like flushing (blood flow to the face) from small quantities of alcohol, which may protect them from alcohol abuse or dependence. Research has also emerged on the mechanism through which genetics plays a role in smoking. Like most drugs, nicotine appears to stimulate dopamine release and inhibit its reuptake, and people who are more sensitive to these effects of nicotine are more likely to become regular smokers (Pomerleau et al., 1993). Research has examined a link between a gene that regulates the reuptake of dopamine and smoking. One form of this gene has been related to being less likely to begin smoking (Lerman et al., 1999) and being more likely to have quit (Sabo et al., 1999). Research has also found that genes contribute to the body's ability to metabolize nicotine, with some people able to do this quickly and others more slowly. Slower nicotine metabolism means that nicotine stays in the brain longer. A longitudinal study of seventh graders showed that those adolescents who had genes linked with slower nicotine metabolism were more likely to become dependent on it 5 years later (O'Loughlin et al., 2005).

Other evidence has found that people with a defect in a gene called CYP2A6, which is associated with the metabolism of nicotine, smoke fewer cigarettes and are less likely to become dependent on nicotine (Rao et al., 2000). This is an interesting example of a gene defect serving a protective function. It will be important to replicate this finding with other samples.

Neurobiological Factors

You may have noticed that in our discussions of specific drugs, the neurotransmitter dopamine has almost always been mentioned. This is not surprising given that dopamine pathways in the brain are importantly linked to pleasure and reward. Drug use typically results in rewarding or pleasurable feelings, and it is via the dopamine system that these feelings are produced. In short, people take drugs to feel good. Research with both humans and animals shows that nearly all drugs, including alcohol, stimulate the dopamine systems in the brain (see Figure 10.6), particularly the mesolimbic pathway (Camí & Farré, 2003; Koob, 2008). Researchers have wondered, then, if problems in the dopamine pathways in the brain might somehow account for why certain people become dependent on drugs. Some evidence suggests that people dependent on drugs or alcohol have a deficiency in the dopamine receptor DRD2 (Noble, 2003).

People take drugs not only to feel good. They also take them to feel less bad. This is particularly true once a person becomes dependent on a substance, such as alcohol, methamphetamine, or heroin, whose withdrawal symptoms are excruciatingly unpleasant. In other words, people take drugs to avoid the bad feelings associated with withdrawal. A substantial body of research with animals supports this motivation for drug-taking behavior (Koob & Le Moal, 2008), and this research helps to explain why relapse is so common.

Investigators have proposed a neurobiological theory, referred to as an *incentive-sensitization theory*, that considers both the craving for drugs (what they term "wanting") and the pleasure that comes with taking the drug (what they term "liking") (Robinson & Berridge, 1993, 2003). In their view, the dopamine system linked to reward, or liking, becomes supersensitive not just to the direct effects of drugs but also to the cues associated with drugs (e.g., needles, spoons, rolling paper). This sensitivity to cues induces craving, or wanting, and people go to extreme lengths to seek out and obtain drugs. Over time, the liking of drugs decreases, but the wanting remains very intense. These investigators argue that the transition from liking to powerful wanting, accomplished by the drug's effects on brain pathways involving dopamine, is what maintains the addiction.

Many researchers study the neurobiology of wanting or craving. A number of laboratory studies have shown that cues for a particular drug can elicit responses not altogether unlike

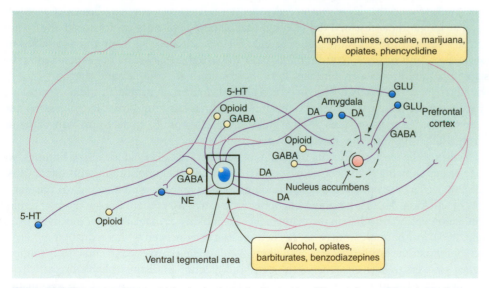

Figure 10.6 Reward pathways in the brain that are affected by different drugs. DA = dopamine; GABA = gamma-aminobutyric acid; GLU = glutamate; 5-HT = serotonin. Adapted from Camí & Farré (2003).

those associated with actual use of the drug. For example, those who were dependent on cocaine showed changes in physiological arousal, cravings, "high" feelings, and more negative emotions in response to cues of cocaine, which consisted of audio- and videotapes of people preparing to inject or snort cocaine, than did people not dependent on cocaine (e.g., Robbins et al., 2000). Brain imaging studies have shown that cues for a drug, such as a needle or a cigarette, activate the reward and pleasure areas of the brain implicated in drug use.

Of course, neurobiological, genetic, and environmental factors do not operate in isolation. The most comprehensive explanations for substance-related disorders will be those that consider how environmental factors enable genetic or neurobiological factors to have their effects. Research with animals shows this quite clearly. For example, studies of mice that were separated from their mothers at birth (a very stressful occurrence, even for mice!) responded to injections of amphetamine or cocaine later in life very differently from mice that had not been separated but had experienced stress early in life (a lot of handling by humans). The investigators showed that these two types of early stress differently impacted the way in which the dopamine system developed in these animals, which then contributed to their drug responses (Meaney, Brake, & Gratton, 2002).

Psychological Factors

In this section, we look at three types of psychological factors that may contribute to the etiology of substance-related disorders. First, we consider the effects of drugs (particularly alcohol and nicotine) on mood; we examine the situations in which a tension-reducing effect occurs and the role of cognition in this process. Second, we consider people's expectancies about the effects of substances on behavior, including beliefs about the prevalence with which a drug is used and about the health risks associated with using that drug. Third, we consider personality traits that may make it more likely for some people to use drugs heavily.

Mood Alteration   It is generally assumed that one of the main psychological motives for using drugs is to alter mood—that is, drug use is reinforced because it enhances positive moods or diminishes negative ones. For example, most people believe that an increase in tension (e.g., because of a bad day at the office) leads to increased alcohol consumption. It has also been argued that stress might causes increases in smoking, at least the initiation of smoking and relapse after quitting smoking (Kassel, Stroud, & Paronis, 2003; Shiffman & Waters, 2004).

Longitudinal studies of stress and consumption have provided some support for this idea. For example, a longitudinal study of adolescent smokers found that increases in negative affect and negative life events were associated with increases in smoking (Wills, Sandy, & Yaeger, 2002). Other studies found that life stress precedes alcohol-related relapses (e.g., Brown et al., 1990). But other longitudinal research did not find that alcohol consumption increased after reports of greater life stress (Brennan, Schutte, & Moos, 1999). Because so many third variables may relate to stress and substance consumption, most would agree that laboratory experimental studies are important in this area. Findings from those studies are complex and suggest that if tension reduction works, it only does so in certain contexts for certain people. In addition, substances can reduce more than just tension. For example, research has found that alcohol lessens negative emotions, but it also lessens positive emotions in response to anxiety-provoking situations (Curtin et al., 1998; Stritzke, Patrick, & Lang, 1995).

Studies of the tension-reducing properties of nicotine have also yielded mixed findings, with some studies showing that nicotine reduces tension and others not finding this effect (Kassel et al., 2003). The reasons for the mixed findings may have to do with a failure to consider the stages of smoking. That is, tension reduction and negative affect seem to play more of a role in the initiation of smoking than in the maintenance of smoking or in relapse after treatment (Kassel et al., 2003). Furthermore, it may not be nicotine that is associated with a reduction in negative affect, but rather the sensory aspects of smoking (i.e., inhaling). An experimental study randomly assigned smokers to have cigarettes with or without nicotine (indistinguishable by participants) after inducing a negative or positive mood (Perkins et al., 2008). The researchers also manipulated smokers' expectancies. That is, some smokers expected and received a cigarette with nicotine, others expected nicotine but didn't get it, others expected no nicotine and didn't get it, and others expected no nicotine but received it anyway. Smoking reduced negative affect after both mood inductions, but this was true for smokers regardless of what they expected and actually received to smoke (i.e., a cigarette with or without nicotine). Instead, the effects of inhaling, whether there was nicotine or not, had the greatest association with reducing negative affect.

Subsequent research to examine the reasons for these inconsistent results has focused on the situation in which alcohol or nicotine is consumed—specifically, a situation in which distraction is present. Findings indicate that alcohol may reduce tension by altering cognition and perception (Curtin et al., 1998; Steele & Josephs, 1988, 1990). Alcohol impairs cognitive processing and narrows attention to the most immediately available cues, resulting in "alcohol myopia" (Steele & Josephs, 1990). In other words, the intoxicated person has less cognitive capacity and tends to use that capacity to focus on an immediate distraction, if available, rather than on tension-producing thoughts, with a resultant decrease in anxiety. Experimental studies have also shown that cognitive distraction can also reduce aggressive behavior in people who are intoxicated (Giancola & Corman, 2007).

The benefits of distraction have also been documented for nicotine. Specifically, smokers who smoked in the presence of a distracting activity had a reduction in anxiety, whereas smokers who smoked without a distracting activity did not experience a reduction in anxiety (Kassel & Shiffman, 1997; Kassel & Unrod, 2000). However, alcohol and nicotine may increase tension when no distractions are present. For example, a person drinking alone may focus all his or her limited cognitive capacity on unpleasant thoughts, begin brooding, and become increasingly tense and anxious, a situation reflected in the expression "crying in one's beer."

In sum, the few available experimental studies suggest that there are important limits to when and how substances may reduce tension. Much more experimental research is needed (Kassel et al., 2003).

Tension reduction is only one aspect of the possible effects of drugs on mood. Some people may use drugs to reduce negative affect, whereas others may use drugs to increase positive affect when they are bored (Cooper et al., 1995). In this case, increased drug use results from a high need for stimulation combined with expectancies that drugs will promote increased positive affect. These patterns have been confirmed among people who abuse alcohol and cocaine (Cooper et al., 1995; Hussong et al., 2001).

Expectancies about Alcohol and Drug Effects   If it is true that alcohol does not reduce stress when consumed after the fact, why do so many people who drink believe that it helps them unwind? Expectation may play a role here—that is, people may drink after stress not because it actually reduces tension but because they expect it to do so. In support of this idea, studies have shown that people who expect alcohol to reduce stress and anxiety are those likely to be frequent users (Rather et al., 1992; Sher et al., 1991; Tran, Haaga, & Chambless, 1997). Furthermore, drinking amount and positive expectancies about alcohol appear to influence each other. The expectation that drinking will reduce anxiety increases drinking, which in turn makes the positive expectancies even stronger (Smith et al., 1995).

Other research has shown that expectancies about a drug's effects—for example, the beliefs that a drug will stimulate aggression and increase sexual responsiveness—predict increased drug use in general (Stacy, Newcomb, & Bentler, 1991). Similarly, people who believe (falsely) that alcohol will make them seem more socially skilled are likely to drink more heavily than those who accurately perceive that alcohol can interfere with social interactions. In now-classic experiments demonstrating the power of expectancies, participants who believe they are consuming a quantity of alcohol when they are actually consuming an alcohol-free beverage subsequently become more aggressive (Lang et al., 1975). Alcohol consumption is associated with increased aggression, but expectancies about alcohol's effects can also play a role (Bushman & Cooper, 1990; Ito, Miller, & Pollack, 1996). Thus, as we have seen in other contexts, cognitions can have a powerful effect on behavior. Research also suggests a reciprocal relationship between expectancies and alcohol use: positive expectancies predict alcohol use, and alcohol use helps to maintain and strengthen positive expectancies (e.g., Sher et al., 1996).

The extent to which a person believes a drug is harmful and the perceived prevalence of use by others are also factors related to use. In general, the greater the perceived risk of a drug, the less likely it will be used. For example, in 2003, marijuana use among adolescents who perceived great risk was 1.8 percent, whereas use among youths who perceived no, little, or moderate risk was 11.2 percent (SAMHSA, 2004). Similarly, many smokers do not believe that they are at increased risk for cancer or cardiovascular disease (Ayanian & Cleary, 1999). Furthermore, alcohol and tobacco are used more frequently among people who overestimate the frequency with which these substances are used by others (Jackson, 1997).

Personality Factors Personality factors may help to explain why certain people are more likely to abuse or become dependent on drugs and alcohol. Personality factors that appear to be important in predicting the later onset of substance-related disorders include high levels of negative affect, sometimes called *negative emotionality*; a persistent desire for arousal along with increased positive affect; and constraint, which refers to cautious behavior, harm avoidance, and conservative moral standards. One longitudinal study found that 18-year-old adolescents who were low in constraint but high in negative emotionality were more likely to develop a substance-related disorder as young adults (Krueger, 1999).

Another longitudinal, prospective study investigated whether personality factors could predict the onset of substance-related disorders in over 1,000 male and female adolescents at age 17 and then again at age 20 (Elkins et al., 2006). Low constraint and high negative emotionality predicted the onset of alcohol, nicotine, and illicit drug abuse and dependence for both men and women.

In another study, kindergarten children were rated by their teachers on several personality traits and were followed up several years later (Killen et al., 1997). Anxiety (e.g., worries about things, fear of new situations) and novelty seeking (e.g., being restless, fidgety) predicted the onset of getting drunk, using drugs, and smoking. Prospective, longitudinal studies do not support depression and anxiety as predictors of whether people initiate smoking (Kassel et al., 2003).

Sociocultural Factors

Sociocultural factors play a widely varying role in substance abuse and dependence. People's interest in and access to drugs are influenced by peers, parents, the media, and cultural norms about acceptable behavior.

At the broadest level, for example, we can look at great cross-national variation in substance consumption. Some research suggests that there are commonalities in substance use across countries. For example, a cross-national study of alcohol and drug use among high school students in 36 countries found that alcohol was the most common substance used across countries, despite great variation in the proportions of students who consumed alcohol, ranging from 32 percent in Zimbabwe to 99 percent in Wales (Smart & Ogburne, 2000). In all but two of the countries studied, marijuana was the next most commonly used drug. In those countries where marijuana was used most often (with more than 15 percent of high school students having ever used marijuana), there were also higher rates of use of amphetamines, Ecstasy, and cocaine.

Despite the commonalities across countries, other research documents striking cross-national differences in alcohol consumption. For example, the highest consumption rates have typically been found in wine-drinking societies, such as France, Spain, and Italy, where drinking alcohol regularly is widely accepted (deLint, 1978). Cultural attitudes and patterns of drinking thus influence the likelihood of drinking heavily and therefore of abusing alcohol. One finding that seems quite similar across different cultures is that men consume more alcohol than women. An analysis conducted by the International Research Group on Gender and Alcohol found that men drank more than women in Australia, Canada, the Czech Republic, Estonia, Finland, Israel, the Netherlands, Russia, Sweden, and the United States. Despite this consistency in gender differences, there was a large disparity across countries in the extent to which men drank more than women. For example, men drank

Alcohol dependence is more prevalent in countries in which alcohol use is heavy, such as major wine-producing countries. Everyone is drinking wine in this French bar. (Eric Brissaud/Liaison Agency, Inc./Getty Images.)

three times more than women in Israel but only one and a half times more than women in the Netherlands (Wilsnack et al., 2000). These findings suggest that cultural prescriptions about drinking by men and women are important to consider.

Ready availability of the substance is also a factor. For example, in wine-drinking societies, wine is present in many settings, even in university cafeterias. Also, rates of alcohol abuse are high among bartenders and liquor store owners, people for whom alcohol is readily available (Fillmore & Caetano, 1980). In 2003, drug use among youths who had been approached by drug dealers was 35 percent, compared to just under 7 percent among youths who had not been approached (SAMHSA, 2004). With regard to smoking, if cigarettes are perceived as being easy to get and affordable, the rate of smoking increases (Robinson et al., 1997). This is one of the reasons states raise taxes on alcohol and cigarettes so frequently. Of course, this tactic disproportionately affects the poor, which is not only unfair but does not necessarily target all who would benefit from substances being less available.

Family factors are important as well. For example, exposure to alcohol use by parents increases children's likelihood of drinking (Hawkins et al., 1997). Unhappy marriages predicted the onset of alcohol abuse or dependence in a study of nearly 2,000 married couples (Whisman et al., 2006). Acculturation into American society may interact with family factors for people of other cultural and ethnic backgrounds. For example, a study of middle school Hispanic students in New York found that children who spoke English with their parents were more likely to smoke marijuana than children who spoke Spanish (Epstein, Botvin, & Diaz, 2001). Psychiatric, marital, or legal problems in the family are also related to drug abuse, and a lack of emotional support from parents is linked to increased use of cigarettes, marijuana, and alcohol (Cadoret et al., 1995; Wills, DuHamel, & Vaccaro, 1995). Finally, longitudinal studies have shown that a lack of parental monitoring leads to increased association with drug-abusing peers and subsequent higher use of drugs (Chassin et al., 1996; Thomas et al., 2000).

The social setting in which a person operates can also affect substance abuse. For example, studies of smokers in daily life show that they are more likely to smoke with other smokers than with nonsmokers. In addition, smoking was more likely to occur in or outside bars restaurants, or at home, rather than in the workplace or in others' homes (Shiffman et al., 2002, 2004). Another study showed that having friends who smoke predicts smoking (Killen et al., 1997). In longitudinal studies, peer-group identification in the seventh grade predicted smoking in the eighth grade (Sussman et al., 1994) and increased drug use over a 3-year period (Chassin et al., 1996). Peer influences are also important in promoting alcohol and marijuana use (Hussong et al., 2001; Stice, Barrera, & Chassin, 1998; Wills & Cleary, 1999).

These findings support the idea that social networks influence a person's drug or alcohol behavior. However, other evidence indicates that people who are inclined to abuse substances may actually select social networks that conform to their own drinking or drug use patterns. Thus, we have two broad explanations for how the social environment is related to substance abuse: a social influence model and a social selection model. A longitudinal study of over 1,200 adults designed to test which model best accounted for drinking behavior found support for both models (Bullers, Cooper, & Russell, 2001). A person's social network predicted individual drinking, but individual drinking also predicted subsequent social network drinking. In fact, the social selection effects were stronger, indicating that people often choose social networks with drinking patterns similar to their own. No doubt the selected networks then support or reinforce their drinking.

Another variable to be considered is the media. Television commercials associate beer with athletic-looking males, bikini-clad women, and good times. Billboards equate cigarettes with excitement, relaxation, and being in style. Alcohol advertising in magazines has increased in recent years, and it seems that these ads are reaching girls more than boys. For example, between 2001 and 2002, exposure to alcohol ads for girls increased 216 percent, whereas exposure to such ads increased 46 percent for boys (Jernigan et al., 2004). A review of studies found that

Advertising is one way that expectancies develop. (Bill Aron/PhotoEdit.)

F.T.C. Charges Joe Camel Ad Illegally Takes Aim at Minors

Internal Documents of R. J. Reynolds Are Cited by Agency

By JOHN M. BRODER

Linda Rosier for The New York Times

WASHINGTON, May 28 — In another blow to an industry under siege, the Federal Trade Commission charged today that the R. J. Reynolds Tobacco Company illegally aimed its Joe Camel advertising campaign at minors.

The agency asserted in an administrative complaint that the company violated Federal fair trade practice laws by promoting a lethal and addictive product to children and adolescents who could not legally purchase or use it.

This is the first time that the commission has accused the tobacco industry of peddling its products to minors. The complaint will be supported, agency officials said, by extensive citations from internal company documents.

The Government says it believes that R. J. Reynolds papers will prove that the company deliberately designed its cartoon-based advertising campaign in the mid-1980's to increase its shrinking market share among young smokers.

The complaint amounts to a civil indictment of a company for mis... s... fficial

Advertising is an important factor in stimulating drug use. The Joe Camel campaign greatly increased Camel's share of the market among elementary and high school students. (New York Times.)

tobacco billboards were over two times more common in primarily African American neighborhoods than they were in primarily European American neighborhoods (Primack et al., 2007). It is clear that advertising for drinking targets girls and advertising for smoking targets African Americans, but does advertising change smoking or drinking patterns?

The evidence indicates that it does. An analysis of consumption in 17 countries between 1970 and 1983 supports the role of advertising in promoting alcohol use. Those countries that banned ads for alcohol had 16 percent less consumption than those that did not (Saffer, 1991). In a longitudinal study of nonsmoking adolescents, those who had a favorite cigarette ad were twice as likely subsequently to begin smoking or to be willing to do so (Pierce et al., 1998). A particularly striking example of this was the Joe Camel campaign for Camel cigarettes. Camel launched its campaign in 1988 with the Joe Camel character, which was modeled after either James Bond or the character played by Don Johnson in the television program *Miami Vice*, a popular show of the time. Before the campaign, in the period from 1976 to 1988, Camel was the preferred brand of less than 0.5 percent of seventh through twelfth graders. By 1991, Camel's share of this illegal market had increased to 33 percent (DiFranza et al., 1991)!

It seemed like the days of Joe Camel and other advertisements that appeal to young people were over. Indeed, the Liggett Group, manufacturers of cigarettes, agreed to stop using such advertising tools and to take other steps to discourage smoking among minors in 1996. These actions were part of a settlement in a class action lawsuit, which included 46 states, that charged U.S. tobacco companies with manipulating nicotine levels to keep smokers addicted. Another cigarette maker, Philip Morris, stopped advertising in magazines in 2004. Furthermore, the American Legacy Foundation was formed as part of the settlement that followed this class action lawsuit (www.americanlegacy.org). The goals of this group are to prevent smoking among young people and to make sure information about smoking and how to stop smoking is accessible to everyone. We will discuss the important efforts of this group later in the chapter when we discuss prevention.

Despite these efforts, a recent analysis of internal documents of several tobacco companies (made public thanks to the lawsuit mentioned above) by researchers at the Harvard School of Public Health revealed that tobacco companies were still targeting their advertising toward young people as recently as 2007 (Kreslake et al, 2008). Some tobacco companies, such as R.J. Reynolds, still advertise, and all magazine ads in 2005 were for menthol brands. The researchers found that tobacco companies' own research had found that cigarettes with lower levels of menthol appealed more to young people and that efforts were then made to market these milder menthol brands to young people. In 2005, nearly half of adolescent smokers chose menthol cigarettes.

Quick Summary

A number of etiological factors have been proposed to account for alcohol and drug dependence, and some have more support than others. Genetic factors play a role in alcohol dependence and perhaps also nicotine dependence. The ability to tolerate alcohol and metabolize nicotine may be what is passed on in the genes. Genes that are important for the operation of the dopamine system may be an important factor in explaining how genes influence substance dependence, although more research is needed. The most-studied neurobiological factors are brain systems associated with dopamine pathways—the major reward pathways in the brain. The incentive-sensitization theory describes brain pathways involved in liking (i.e., consuming) drugs and wanting (i.e., craving) drugs.

Psychological factors have also been evaluated, and there is support for the idea that tension reduction plays a role, but only under certain circumstances, such as when distractions are present. Expectancies about the effects of drugs, such as reducing tension, increasing aggression, and increasing sexual prowess, have been shown to predict drug and alcohol use. Expectancies about the effects of drugs are also powerful; the greater the perceived risk of a drug, the less likely it will be used. Studies of personality factors also help us understand why some people may be more prone to abuse drugs and alcohol.

Sociocultural factors play a role, including the culture, availability of a substance, family factors, social settings and networks, and advertising. There is support for both a social influence model and a social selection model.

Check Your Knowledge 10.4

Answer the questions.

1. Which of the following is not one of the sociocultural factors implicated in the etiology of substance abuse or dependence?
   a. the media
   b. gender
   c. availability of a substance
   d. social networks
2. Which of the following statements best captures the link between depression and smoking?
   a. Depression causes smoking.

   b. Smoking causes depression.
   c. It does not predict initiation.
   d. We just don't know yet.
3. Genetic research on substance dependence indicates that:
   a. Genetic factors may be the same for many drugs.
   b. Additional studies need to be done to determine heritability.
   c. The dopamine receptor DRD1 may be faulty.
   d. Twin studies show that the environment is just as important as genes.

Treatment of Substance-Related Disorders

The chronicity of addiction is really a kind of fatalism writ large. If an addict knows in his heart he is going to use again, why not today? But if a thin reed of hope appears, the possibility that it will not always be so, things change. You live another day and then get up and do it again. Hope is oxygen to someone who is suffocating on despair. (Excerpt from David Carr's book "The Night of the Gun" as adapted in an article for the New York Times Magazine, July 20, 2008.)

The challenges in treating people who are dependent on substances are great, as illustrated by the quote above. Substance dependence is chronic, and relapse occurs often. In view of these challenges, the field is constantly working to develop new and effective treatments, many of which we review in this section. The author of the quote, David Carr, was formerly addicted to cocaine, crack, and alcohol. Currently, he is a media columnist for the *New York Times*. For him, residential treatment was successful.

Many who work with those dependent on alcohol or drugs suggest that the first step to successful treatment is admitting there is a problem. To a certain extent, this makes sense. Why would someone get treatment for something that is not deemed a problem? Unfortunately, a number of treatment programs require people not only to admit a problem but also to demonstrate their commitment to treatment by stopping their use of alcohol or drugs before beginning treatment. This requirement can exclude many who desire and need treatment. For example, James (in the clinical case presented earlier) might not have been admitted to a residential program had he not been free of heroin for a week before trying to gain admission. Imagine if people with lung cancer were told they had to demonstrate their commitment to treatment by stopping smoking before the cancer could be treated. In the next sections, we review treatments for alcohol-related problems, nicotine dependence, and other drug dependence.

Treatment of Alcohol Abuse and Dependence

In 2006, 4 million people over the age of 12 received treatment for alcohol abuse or dependence (SAMHSA, 2007). Unfortunately, over 21 million people over the age of 12 were in need of treatment for alcohol or drug problems in 2006 who did not receive it. A large epidemiological study found that only 24 percent of people with alcohol dependence ever receive treatment (Hasin et al., 2007). We have far to go in developing and providing effective treatments.

Inpatient Hospital Treatment   Often, the first step in treatment for substance dependence is called **detoxification**. Withdrawal from substances including alcohol, can be difficult, both physically and psychologically. Although detoxification does not have to occur in a hospital setting, it can be less unpleasant in a supervised setting. Many people have to go through the detoxification process multiple times. Unfortunately, multiple previous detoxifications are associated with a poorer response to treatment (Malcolm et al., 2000). In recent years, the population served in detoxification centers has changed demographically: There have been large increases in admissions of women, African Americans, and Hispanics, as well as a decline in the mean age at admission and an increase in people who are unemployed (McCarty et al., 2000). Alice, the woman described in the earlier clinical case, would likely need hospital treatment, at least for detoxification.

The number of for-profit hospitals treating alcohol abuse increased dramatically until the mid-1990s, in part because such treatment was covered in large measure by both private insurance companies and the federal government (Holder et al., 1991). Because inpatient treatment is much more expensive than outpatient treatment, its cost-effectiveness has been questioned. Is it worth the expense? Apparently not, at least in many cases. The therapeutic results of hospital treatment are not superior to those of outpatient treatment (Mundle et al., 2001; Soyka et al., 2001). In addition, short stays (less than 8 days) in detoxification hospitals may be as effective as longer stays (Foster, Marshall, & Peters, 2000). Some data even suggest that home detoxification may be a viable alternative to day hospital or inpatient treatment for selected groups of people (Allan, Smith, & Melting, 2000). However, an analysis of treatment for alcohol dependence concludes that an inpatient approach is probably necessary for people with few sources of social support who are living in environments that encourage the abuse of alcohol, especially people with serious psychological problems in addition to their substance abuse (Finney & Moos, 1998). Unfortunately, changes in health insurance in the United States over the past 10 years, including affordability, availability, and coverage, have made it more difficult for those dependent on alcohol to get hospital treatment when they need it. Between 2002 and 2003, the number of people receiving inpatient treatment at a hospital went from over 800,000 to just under 600,000 (SAMHSA, 2004).

Alcoholics Anonymous The largest and most widely known self-help group in the world is Alcoholics Anonymous (AA), founded in 1935 by two recovering alcoholics. It has well over 70,000 chapters and a membership numbering more than 2 million people in the United States and in more than 100 other countries. In 2003, nearly two-thirds of people who received treatment for alcohol or drug dependence did so through a self-help program (SAMHSA, 2004).

Each AA chapter runs regular and frequent meetings at which newcomers rise to announce that they are alcoholics and older, sober members give testimonials, relating the stories of their problems with alcohol and indicating how their lives are better now. The group provides emotional support, understanding, and close counseling as well as a social network. Members are urged to call on one another around the clock when they need companionship and encouragement not to relapse. Programs modeled after AA are available for other substances, for example, Cocaine Anonymous and Marijuana Anonymous.

The AA program tries to instill in each member the belief that alcohol dependence is a disease that can never be cured and that continuing vigilance is necessary to resist taking even a single drink, lest uncontrollable drinking begin all over again. Even if the person has not consumed any alcohol for 15 years or more, the designation "alcoholic" is still necessary according to the tenets of AA, since the person is always an alcoholic, always carrying the disease, even if it is currently under control.

The spiritual aspect of AA is apparent in the 12 steps of AA shown in Table 10.2, and there is evidence that belief in this philosophy is linked with achieving abstinence (Fiorentine & Hillhouse, 2000; Tonigan, Miller, & Connors, 2000). Other self-help groups do not have the religious overtones of AA, relying instead on social support, reassurance, encouragement, and suggestions for leading a life without alcohol. One such approach, termed *Rational Recovery*, focuses on promoting renewed self-reliance rather than reliance on a higher power (Trimpey, Velton, & Dain, 1993).

Alcoholics Anonymous is the largest self-help group in the world. At their regular meetings, newcomers rise to announce their addiction and receive advice and support from others. (Hank Morgan/Photo Researchers.)

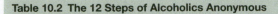

Table 10.2 The 12 Steps of Alcoholics Anonymous

1. We admitted we were powerless over alcohol—that our lives had become unmanageable.
2. Came to believe that a power greater than ourselves could restore us to sanity.
3. Made a decision to turn our will and our lives over to the care of God as we understood Him.
4. Made a searching and fearless moral inventory of ourselves.
5. Admitted to God, to ourselves, and to another human being the exact nature of our wrongs.
6. Were entirely ready to have God remove all these defects of character.
7. Humbly asked Him to remove our shortcomings.
8. Made a list of all persons we had harmed, and became willing to make amends to them all.
9. Made direct amends to such people wherever possible, except when to do so would injure them or others.
10. Continued to take personal inventory and, when we were wrong, promptly admitted it.
11. Sought through prayer and meditation to improve our conscious contact with God as we understood Him, praying only for knowledge of His will for us and the power to carry that out.
12. Having had a spiritual awakening as the result of these steps, we tried to carry this message to alcoholics and to practice these principles in all our affairs.

Source: The Twelve Steps and Twelve Traditions. Copyright © 1952 by Alcoholics Anonymous World Services, Inc. Reprinted with permission of Alcoholics Anonymous World Services, Inc.

Noncontrolled trials show that AA provides significant benefit to participants (Ouimette, Finney, & Moos, 1997; Timko et al., 2001). A large prospective study of over 2,000 men with alcohol dependence found that participation in AA predicted a better outcome 2 years later (McKeller, Stewart, & Humphreys, 2003). In addition, becoming an AA member early in treatment and staying involved for a longer period of time is associated with a better outcome 8 years after treatment began (Moos & Humphreys, 2004).

All of this sounds like good news for people participating in AA. However, a review of the eight randomized controlled clinical trials found little benefit of AA over other types of treatment, including motivational enhancement, inpatient treatment, couples therapy, or cognitive behavior therapy (Ferri, Amato, & Davoli, 2008). In addition, AA has high dropout rates, and the dropouts are not always factored into the results of studies. There have been no controlled studies testing the efficacy of Rational Recovery, though two findings from preliminary studies suggest that it may be effective (Schmidt, Carns, & Chandler, 2001).

Couples Therapy Behaviorally oriented marital or couples therapy (O'Farrell & Fals-Stewart, 2000) has been found to achieve some reductions in problem drinking, even a year after treatment has stopped, as well as some improvement in couples' distress generally (McCrady & Epstein, 1995).

Cognitive and Behavioral Treatments Contingency management therapy is a cognitive behavior treatment for alcohol abuse and dependence that involves teaching people and those close to them to reinforce behaviors inconsistent with drinking—for example, taking Antabuse (on page 309) and avoiding situations that were associated with drinking in the past. It is based on the belief that environmental contingencies can play an important role in encouraging or discouraging drinking. Vouchers are provided for not using alcohol a substance (cocaine, heroin, marijuana; verified by urine samples), and the tokens are exchangeable for things that the person would like to have more of (Dallery et al., 2001; Katz et al., 2001; Silverman et al., 1996). This therapy also includes teaching job-hunting and social skills, as well as assertiveness training for refusing drinks. For socially isolated people, assistance and encouragement are provided to establish contacts with other people who are not associated with drinking. Other effective contingency-based treatments include providing reinforcers for sobriety, such as opportunities to win prizes (Petry et al., 2000) and abstinence-contingent partial support for housing, food, recreational activities, and access to supportive therapy (Gruber, Chutuape, & Stitzer, 2000). Often referred to as the *community-reinforcement approach*, contingency management therapy has generated very promising results (Bauemetol, 1998; Sisson & Azrin, 1989; Spitzer & Petry, 2006). A review of the literature shows that it is consistently found to be one of the most effective and cost-effective treatments available (Smith, Meyers, & Miller, 2001).

Relapse prevention is another cognitive behavioral treatment that has been effective with alcohol and drug dependence and abuse. It can be a stand-alone treatment or a part of other interventions. Broadly, the goal is to help people avoid relapsing back into drinking once they have stopped. Focus on Discovery 10.4 discusses this important treatment in more detail.

Brief Motivational Interventions As we described earlier, heavy drinking is particularly common among college students. One team of investigators designed a brief intervention to try to curb such heavy drinking in college (Carey et al., 2006). The intervention contained two parts: (1) a comprehensive assessment that included the Timeline Follow Back (TLFB) interview (Sobell & Sobell, 1996), an interview that carefully assess drinking in the past 3 months, and (2) a brief motivational treatment that included individualized feedback about a person's drinking in relation to community and national averages, education about the effects of alcohol,

FOCUS ON DISCOVERY 10.4

Relapse Prevention

Relapse prevention is an important part of any treatment for drug or alcohol dependence. Mark Twain quipped that stopping smoking was easy—he'd done it hundreds of times! Marlatt and Gordon (1985) developed an approach to treatment called relapse prevention specifically to prevent relapse in substance abuse. In this approach, people dependent on alcohol are encouraged to believe that a lapse will not inevitably precipitate a total relapse and should be regarded as a learning experience rather than as a sign that the battle is lost, a marked contrast from the AA perspective (Marlatt & Gordon, 1985). This noncatastrophizing approach to relapse after therapy—falling off the wagon—is important because the overwhelming majority of people who are dependent on alcohol who become abstinent experience one or more relapses over a 4-year period (Polich, Armor, & Braiker, 1980). People dependent on alcohol examine sources of stress in their work, family, and relationships so that they can become active and responsible in anticipating and resisting situations that might lead them into excessive drinking (Marlatt, 1983; Sobell, Toneatto, & Sobell, 1990). The sources of stress that precipitate a relapse in alcohol dependence may be different for men and women. For women, marital stress is a predictor of relapse. For men, however, marriage seems to protect them from relapse (Walitzer & Dearing, 2006).

Relapse prevention treatment appears to be more effective with some substances than with others. A meta-analysis of 26 randomized controlled clinical trials found that relapse prevention was most effective for alcohol and drug dependence and least effective for nicotine dependence (Irvin et al. 1999). Most smokers relapse within a year of stopping, regardless of the means used to stop. In a pattern we have already seen, people who smoked the most—and are presumably more addicted to nicotine—relapse more often and more quickly than moderate or light smokers. Frequent slips, intense cravings and withdrawal symptoms, low tolerance for distress, younger age, nicotine dependence, low self-efficacy, stressful life events, observations of other smokers, weight concerns, and previous quitting attempts are all predictors of relapse (Brown et al., 2005; McCarthy et al., 2006; Ockene et al., 2000; Piasecki, 2006). One very detailed analysis, using ecological momentary assessment, of smokers' thoughts, feelings, and symptoms both before and after they quit smoking revealed that many smokers experience high levels of negative affect before their target quit day and that this anticipatory negative affect pre-

dicted a greater likelihood of relapse (McCarthy et al., 2006). Despite these difficulties, there is some encouraging evidence that self-help relapse prevention programs can be effective in reducing smoking relapse (Brandon, Vidrine, & Litvin, 2007). In these programs, smokers receive booklets in the mail describing the relapse prevention approach. These brochures appear to be effective up to 1 year after smoking was stopped.

What factors contribute to success? Research results (and common sense) tell us that ex-smokers who do not live with a smoker do better at follow-up than those who do live with a smoker (McIntyre-Kingsolver, Lichtenstein, & Mermelstein, 1986). So-called booster or maintenance sessions help, but in a very real sense they represent a continuation of treatment; when they stop, relapse is the rule (Brandon, Zelman, & Baker, 1987). Intensive interventions, such as a telephone counseling (Brandon et al., 2000), also help; however, they reach relatively few smokers. Brief relapse prevention interventions during medical visits are cost-effective and could potentially reach most smokers but are not consistently delivered (Ockene et al., 2000). On a positive note, there is considerably more social support for not smoking than there was just 10 years ago, at least in the United States. Perhaps as time goes on, societal sanctions against smoking will help those who have succeeded in quitting remain abstinent. (It is certainly more difficult to find a place to light up nowadays.)

One specific approach to the relapse problem is to focus on the cognitions of ex-smokers (Baer & Lichtenstein, 1988). Using the articulated thoughts paradigm (see p. 87), a study found that recent ex-smokers who tended to think of smoking without prompting relapsed more readily 3 months later (Haaga, 1989). However, if ex-smokers learned some effective ways of countering these smoking-related thoughts, such as distracting themselves, their abstinence was better months later. Using a questionnaire measure, a study found that ex-smokers' self-efficacy in facing their most difficult challenge—for example, not smoking while having coffee and dessert after a pleasant dinner—was a good predictor of abstinence a year later (Haaga, 1990). These and related studies indicate that the prediction of continued abstinence or relapse is enhanced by measuring the cognitions of ex-smokers. Such information may help therapists design programs that will improve the ability of a specific person to remain a nonsmoker (Compas et al., 1998).

and tips for reducing harm and moderating drinking. Results from the study showed that the TLFB alone decreased drinking behavior, but that the combination of the TLFB and motivational intervention was associated with a longer lasting-reduction in drinking behavior, up to 1 year after the interview and intervention.

Moderation in Drinking   At least since the advent of Alcoholics Anonymous, many have believed that people dependent on alcohol had to abstain completely if they were to be successfully treated, for they were assumed to have no control over drinking once they had taken that first drink. This continues to be the belief of Alcoholics Anonymous, but research mentioned earlier, indicating that drinkers' beliefs about themselves and alcohol may be as important as the addiction to the drug itself, has called this assumption into question. Considering the difficulty in society of avoiding alcohol altogether, it may be preferable to teach a person who does not abuse alcohol in an extreme fashion to drink with moderation. Drinkers' self-esteem will certainly benefit from being able to control a problem and from feeling in charge of their life.

The term **controlled drinking** was introduced into the domain of alcohol treatment by Mark and Linda Sobell (Sobell & Sobell, 1993). It refers to a pattern of alcohol consumption that is moderate, avoiding the extremes of total abstinence and inebriation. Findings of one well-known treatment program suggested that at least some people who abuse alcohol can learn to control their drinking and improve other aspects of their lives as well (Sobell & Sobell, 1976).

Controlled-drinking treatment programs were further developed to teach people to respond adaptively to situations in which they might otherwise drink excessively. They learn various social skills to help them resist pressures to drink; they receive assertiveness, relaxation, and stress-management training, sometimes including biofeedback and meditation; and they are encouraged to exercise and maintain a healthy diet.

The Sobells' current approach to teaching moderation to people with alcohol dependence has evolved even further. Termed *guided self-change*, this outpatient approach emphasizes personal responsibility and control. The basic assumption is that people have more potential control over their immoderate drinking than they typically believe and that heightened awareness of the costs of drinking to excess as well as of the benefits of abstaining or cutting down can be of material help. People are encouraged to view themselves as basically healthy people who have been making unwise, often self-destructive, choices about how to deal with life's inevitable stresses rather than as victims of an addiction.

In guided self-change, the therapist is empathic and supportive while making salient to the person the negative aspects of excessive drinking that the person may have been overlooking. For example, getting the person to delay 20 minutes before taking a second or third drink can help him or her reflect on the costs versus the benefits of drinking to excess. Evidence supports the effectiveness of this approach in helping people moderate their intake and otherwise improve their lives (Sobell & Sobell, 1993).

Whether abstinence or controlled drinking should be the goal of treatment remains controversial. This issue pits influential forces, such as AA, that uphold abstinence as the only proper goal for people dependent on alcohol, against more recent researchers, such as the Sobells and those adopting their general approach, who have shown that moderation can work for many people, including those with severe drinking problems. If the therapeutic means of achieving the goal of moderate drinking are available—and research strongly suggests that they are—then controlled drinking may be a more realistic goal even for a person dependent on alcohol. Controlled drinking is currently much more widely accepted in Canada and Europe than it is in the United States.

Medications   Some people who are in treatment for alcohol dependence, inpatient or outpatient, take disulfiram, or **Antabuse**, a drug that discourages drinking by causing violent vomiting if alcohol is ingested. As one can imagine, adherence to an Antabuse regimen can be a problem.

For it to be effective, a person must already be strongly committed to change. However, in a large, multicenter study, Antabuse was not shown to have any benefit, and dropout rates were as high as 80 percent (Fuller, 1988).

Mark and Linda Sobell introduced controlled drinking approaches to the treatment of alcohol abuse. (Courtesy of Mark Sobell; Courtesy of Linda Sobell.)

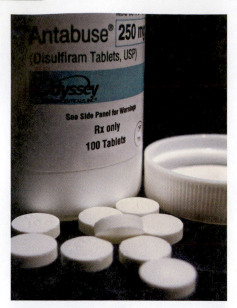

Antabuse is used to treat alcohol dependence, but it is not a very effective treatment because many people stop taking it. (Mark Alberhasky/imagema.com.)

The Food and Drug Administration has approved the opiate antagonists naltrexone and naloxone (discussed in the section on treatment for heroin dependence), which block the activity of endorphins that are stimulated by alcohol, thus reducing the craving for it. Evidence is mixed regarding whether these drugs are more effective than a placebo in reducing drinking when they are the only treatment (Krystal et al., 2001). But they do appear to add to overall treatment effectiveness when combined with cognitive behavioral therapy (Streeton & Whelan, 2001; Volpicelli et al., 1995, 1997).

Acamprosate, which has been in regular use in Europe for nearly 20 years under the brand name Campral, was approved by the FDA in 2004. Although its action is not completely understood, researchers believe that it impacts the glutamate and GABA neurotransmitter systems and thereby reduces the cravings associated with withdrawal. A review of data from all published double-blind, placebo-controlled clinical trials of acamprosate for people dependent on alcohol suggests that it is highly effective (Mason, 2001). A meta-analysis comparing the effectiveness of acamprosate and naltrexone found them equally effective (Kranzler & Van Kirk, 2001). There is, of course, the more general question of whether treating a substance abuse problem by giving another drug is necessarily a prudent strategy if one believes that some people come to rely on drugs in part because they are looking for a chemical solution to problems in their lives. Nevertheless, to the extent that medications are an effective treatment for alcohol dependence, disallowing them due to a concern over substituting one drug for another seems misguided.

Quick Summary

Inpatient hospital treatment for alcohol dependence is not as common today as it was in earlier years, primarily due to the cost. Detoxification from alcohol does often take place in hospitals, but treatment after this is more commonly done in outpatient settings.

Alcoholics Anonymous (AA) is the most common form of treatment for alcohol dependence. It is a group-based self-help treatment that instills the notion of alcohol dependence as disease. Though not widely studied, available research suggests that AA is an effective treatment.

There is some evidence that behavioral couples therapy is an effective treatment.

Contingency management therapy, which involves teaching people and those close to them to reinforce behaviors inconsistent with drinking, has shown some promise. Controlled drinking refers to a pattern of alcohol consumption that is moderate, avoiding the extremes of total abstinence and inebriation. The guided self-change treatment approach emphasizes control over moderate drinking, the costs of drinking to excess, and the benefits of abstaining.

Medications for alcohol dependence treatment include Antabuse, naltrexone and naloxone, and acamprosate. Antabuse is not an effective treatment in the long run. Noncompliance is a big problem. It is not clear that other medications are effective on their own, but they do seem to be beneficial in combination with cognitive behavior therapy. Early evidence suggests that acamprosate may be an effective medication.

Treatment of Nicotine Dependence

The numerous laws that currently prohibit smoking in restaurants, trains, airplanes, and public buildings are part of a social context that provides incentives and support to stop smoking. In addition, people are more likely to quit smoking if other people around them quit. A longitudinal study of over 12,000 people documented that if people in one's social network quit smoking (spouses, siblings, friends, co-workers), the odds that a person will quit smoking are much greater (Christakis & Fowler, 2008). For example, if a person's spouse stopped smoking, his or her chances of continued smoking decreased by nearly 70 percent. In short, peer pressure to quit smoking appears to be as effective as peer pressure to start smoking once was.

Some smokers who want to quit attend smoking clinics or consult with professionals for other specialized smoking-reduction programs. Even so, it is estimated that only about half of those who go through smoking-cessation programs succeed in abstaining by the time the program is over; only about 20 percent of those who have succeeded in the short term actually remain nonsmoking after a year. The greatest success overall is found among smokers who are better educated, older, or have acute health problems (USDHHS, 1998b).

Psychological Treatments   Probably the most widespread psychological treatment consists of a physician telling the person to stop smoking. Each year millions of smokers are given this counsel—because of hypertension, heart disease, lung disease, or diabetes, on general grounds of preserving or improving health. Indeed, by age 65, most smokers have managed to quit (USDHHS, 1998b). There is some evidence that a physician's advice can get some people to stop smoking, at least for a while, especially when the person also chews nicotine gum (Law & Tang, 1995). But much more needs to be learned about the nature of the advice, the manner in which it is given, its timing, and other factors that must surely play a role in determining whether smokers are prepared and able to alter their behavior primarily on a physician's say-so (USDHHS, 1998b).

Cognitively oriented investigators have tried to encourage more control in people who smoke; treatments aim at having people develop and use coping skills, such as relaxation and positive self-talk, when confronted with tempting situations—for example, after a meal or when sitting down to read a book. Results are not very promising, however (Smith et al., 2001).

Laws that have banned smoking in many places have probably increased the frequency of quitting. (Digital Vision/SuperStock, Inc.)

In contrast, a review indicated that scheduled smoking shows real promise (Compas et al., 1998). The strategy is to reduce nicotine intake gradually over a period of a few weeks by getting smokers to agree to increase the time between cigarettes. For example, during the first week of treatment, a one-pack-a-day smoker would be put on a schedule allowing only 10 cigarettes per day; during the second week, only 5 cigarettes a day would be allowed; and during the third week, the person would taper off to zero. The cigarettes would have to be smoked on a schedule provided by the treatment team, not when the smoker feels an intense craving. In this way, the person's smoking behavior is controlled by the passage of time rather than by urges, mood states, or situations. Smokers who are able to stay with the agreed-upon schedule showed a 44 percent abstinence rate after 1 year, a very impressive outcome (Cinciripini et al., 1994).

By age 18, about two-thirds of cigarette smokers regret having started smoking, one-half have already made an attempt to quit, and nearly 40 percent show interest in obtaining treatment for their dependence (Henningfield, Michaelides, & Sussman, 2000). A school-based program called Project EX includes training in coping skills and a psychoeducational component about the harmful effects of smoking. Two studies have found this program to be effective, both in the United States (Sussman, Dent, & Lichtman, 2001) and in China (Zheng et al., 2004), where the program was adapted to fit Chinese culture and language.

Nicotine Replacement Treatments and Medications   Reducing a smoker's craving for nicotine by providing it in a different way is the goal of nicotine replacement treatments. Attention to nicotine dependence is clearly important because the more cigarettes people smoke daily, the less successful they are at quitting. Nicotine may be supplied in gum, patches, or inhalers. The idea is to help smokers endure the nicotine withdrawal that accompanies any effort to stop smoking. Although nicotine replacement alleviates withdrawal symptoms—which justifies its use in gum and in the nicotine patches to be described next—the severity of withdrawal is only minimally related to success in stopping smoking (Ferguson, Shiffman, & Gwaltney, 2006; Hughes, et al., 1990).

Gum containing nicotine has been available in the United States since 1984 by doctor's prescription, and it is now available over the counter. The nicotine in gum is absorbed much more slowly and steadily than that in tobacco. The long-term goal is for the former smoker to be able to cut back on the use of the gum as well, eventually eliminating reliance on nicotine altogether.

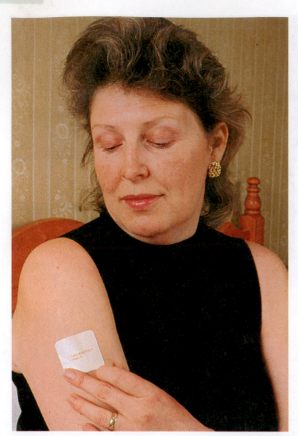

Nicotine patches are available over the counter to help relieve withdrawal symptoms. (Jim Selby/ Photo Researchers.)

This treatment involves some controversy, however. Ex-smokers can become dependent on the gum. Moreover, in doses that deliver an amount of nicotine equivalent to smoking one cigarette an hour, the gum causes cardiovascular changes, such as increased blood pressure, that can be dangerous to people with cardiovascular diseases. Nevertheless, some experts believe that even prolonged, continued use of the gum is healthier than obtaining nicotine by smoking, because at least the poisons in the smoke are avoided (de Wit & Zacny, 2000).

Nicotine patches became available in 1991 with a doctor's prescription and in 1996 over the counter. A polyethylene patch taped to the arm serves as a transdermal (through the skin) nicotine delivery system that slowly and steadily releases the drug into the bloodstream and thence to the brain. An advantage of the patch over nicotine gum is that the person need only apply one patch each day and not remove it until applying the next patch, making compliance easier. Treatment can be effective after 8 weeks of use for most smokers (Stead et al., 2008), with smaller and smaller patches used as treatment progresses. A drawback is that people who continue smoking while wearing the patch risk increasing the amount of nicotine in their body to dangerous levels.

Evidence suggests that the nicotine patch is superior to the use of a placebo patch in terms of both abstinence and subjective craving (Hughes et al., 1990). A meta-analysis of 111 trials of all types of nicotine replacement treatments (NRT: patch, gum, nasal spray, inhaler, tablets) found that NRT was more effective than placebo in smoking cessation (Stead et al., 2008). However, NRT is not a panacea. Abstinence rates are only about 50 percent at 12-month follow-ups. The manufacturers state that the patch is to be used only as part of a psychological smoking-cessation program and then for not more than 3 months at a time.

Combining the antidepressant medication buprioprion and nicotine patches yielded a 12-month abstinence rate of 35 percent in one study (Jorenby et al., 1999) but less promising results in others (Hughes, Stead, & Lancaster, 2004; Killen et al., 2006). Other promising non-nicotine pharmacotherapy for smoking cessation has included the drug clonidine and silver acetate (Benowitz & Peng, 2000). The FDA approved the prescription drug Varenicline in 2006 for treatment of nicotine dependence, and early results suggest that this medication is effective in combination with behavioral treatment and that is more effective than buprioprion (Cahill, Stead, & Lancaster, 2007; Tonstad et al., 2006).

Treatment of Illicit Drug Abuse and Dependence

Central to the treatment of people who use illegal drugs such as heroin and cocaine is detoxification—withdrawal from the drug itself. Heroin withdrawal reactions range from relatively mild bouts of anxiety, nausea, and restlessness for several days to more severe and frightening bouts of delirium and panic. The type of reaction depends primarily on the purity of the heroin that the person has been using. Withdrawal reactions from barbiturates are especially severe, even life threatening; they begin about 24 hours after the last dose and peak 2 or 3 days later. They usually abate by the end of the first week but may last for a month if large doses were taken. Withdrawal from barbiturates is best undertaken gradually, not cold turkey (a term that derives from the goosebumps that occur during withdrawal, making the person's skin resemble that of a plucked turkey), and should take place under close medical supervision.

Detoxification is the first way in which therapists try to help a person dependent on a drug, and it may be the easiest part of the rehabilitation process. Enabling the drug user to function without drugs after detoxification is extremely difficult—typically, both therapist and client experience more disappointment and sadness than success in this process. A variety of approaches to this task are available, including psychological treatments, drug substitution treatments, and medications.

Psychological Treatments   In the first direct comparison in a controlled study, the antidepressant medication desipramine and cognitive behavioral therapy (CBT) were both found to be somewhat effective in reducing cocaine use as well as in improving a person's family, social, and general psychological functioning (Carroll, Rounsaville, Gordon, et al., 1994; Carroll et al.,

1995). In this 12-week study, desipramine was better than a placebo for people with a low degree of dependence on cocaine, whereas CBT was better for people with a high degree of dependence. This finding illustrates the significance of the psychological aspects of substance abuse.

In this study, people receiving CBT learned how to avoid high-risk situations (e.g., being around people using cocaine), recognize the lure of the drug for them, and develop alternatives to using cocaine (e.g., recreational activities with nonusers). People who abused cocaine in this study also learned strategies for coping with the craving and for resisting the tendency to regard a slip as a catastrophe ("relapse prevention training," see Focus on Discovery 10.4). A more recent study testing the effectiveness of CBT for drug abuse in a community setting found that there was no difference in outcomes between CBT and standard substance-abuse counseling (Morgenstern et al., 2001). We have a ways to go in order to make our treatments more effective in community settings.

Contingency management with vouchers has shown promise for cocaine, heroin, and marijuana

Group therapy in residential settings is frequently used to treat heroin addiction. (David M. Grossman/Photo Researchers.)

dependence (Dallery et al., 2001; Katz et al., 2001; Petry et al., 2005; Silverman et al., 1996). For example, a randomized treatment trial for people with marijuana dependence compared a voucher treatment, CBT, and CBT plus vouchers (Budney et al., 2006). During the treatment, people who received the voucher treatment were more likely to remain abstinent than those in the CBT treatment or in the CBT plus vouchers treatment. After treatment was over, however, people who received CBT plus vouchers were most likely to remain abstinent. Thus, vouchers appear to work in the short term, but CBT appears to be an effective component of treatment for marijuana dependence in the long term with respect to maintaining abstinence after treatment is over.

Studies of contingency management for cocaine abuse find that it is associated not only with a greater likelihood of abstinence but also with a better quality of life (Petry, Alessi, & Hanson, 2007). In an analysis that looked at four different studies of contingency management treatment for cocaine abuse, the researchers found that people who received contingency management treatment were more likely to remain abstinent than people who received treatment as usual and that the duration of their abstinence during treatment was related to a higher quality of life after treatment. A meta-analysis of four randomized controlled clinical trials comparing contingency management, day treatment, or both treatments (combined condition) for cocaine abuse among homeless people found that the combined treatment and contingency management were both more effective than day treatment alone (Schumacher et al., 2007).

A treatment called *motivational interviewing* or *enhancement* therapy has also shown promise. This treatment involves a combination of CBT techniques and techniques associated with the humanistic therapy of Carl Rogers (see p. 491). A meta-analysis of this treatment found that it was effective for both alcohol and illegal drug dependence and abuse (Burke, Arkowitz, & Menchola, 2003). Another study found that motivational enhancement combined with CBT and contingency management was an effective treatment package for young people (ages 18–5) who were dependent on marijuana (Carroll et al. 2006).

Self-help residential homes are another psychological approach to treating heroin and other types of drug abuse and dependence. Daytop Village, Phoenix House, Odyssey House, and other drug-rehabilitation homes share the following features:

- Separation of people from previous social contacts, on the assumption that these relationships have been instrumental in maintaining the drug dependence
- A comprehensive environment in which drugs are not available and continuing support is offered to ease the transition from regular drug use to a drug-free existence

- The presence of charismatic role models, people formerly dependent on drugs who appear to be meeting life's challenges without drugs
- Direct, often intense confrontation in group therapy, in which people are goaded into accepting responsibility for their problems and for their drug habits and are urged to take charge of their lives
- A setting in which people are respected as human beings rather than stigmatized as failures or criminals

There are several obstacles to evaluating the efficacy of residential drug-treatment programs. Since entrance is voluntary, only a small minority of dependent users enter such settings. Furthermore, because the dropout rate is high, those who remain cannot be regarded as representative of the population of people addicted to illegal drugs; their motivation to stop using drugs is probably much stronger than that of people who don't volunteer for treatment or people who dropout. Any improvement participants in these programs make may reflect their uncommonly strong desire to rid themselves of the habit more than the specific qualities of the treatment program. Such self-regulating residential communities do, however, appear to help a large number of those who remain in them for a year or so (Institute of Medicine, 1990; Jaffe, 1985).

In 2000, voters in California approved Proposition 36, enacted into law in 2001 as the Substance Abuse and Crime Prevention Act (SACPA). The act allows nonviolent drug offenders to be sent to drug treatment rather than prison. Participation in this program is voluntary—someone meeting the criteria of SACPA has the choice of treatment or prison. In the first 4 years of the program, over 200,000 offenders were eligible and about 74 percent chose treatment over standard criminal justice proceedings. Researchers at UCLA studied the program for its first 4 years and released yearly reports. Findings from the first 4 years suggest that the program is working, at least with respect to treatment completion. Just over one-third completed the treatment. This may seem low, but it is actually quite favorable in comparison to completion rates of other programs, particularly those to which offenders are referred by the criminal justice system (Longshore et al., 2003, 2005). Cost savings from this program during its first 2 years were substantial. Every dollar invested in a SACPA participant would have cost as much as four times more had the participant been sent to prison (Longshore et al., 2006). The news is not all good, however. Participants who went into treatment under SACPA were more likely to be rearrested for drug offenses than people who had similar offenses before the beginning of SACPA (Longshore et al., 2005). Time will tell if the program is successful in keeping people out of the criminal justice system.

Drug Replacement Treatments and Medications

Two widely used programs for heroin dependence involve the administration of *heroin substitutes*, drugs chemically similar to heroin that can replace the body's craving for it, or *opiate antagonists*, drugs that prevent the user from experiencing the heroin high. Recall from Chapter 2 (p. 36) that an antagonist is a drug that dampens the activity of neurotransmitters, and an agonist is a drug that stimulates neurotransmitters. The first category includes **methadone**, levomethadyl acetate, and bupreophine, synthetic narcotics designed to take the place of heroin. Since these drugs are themselves addicting, successful treatment essentially converts the person's dependence on heroin into dependence on a different substance. This conversion occurs because these synthetic narcotics are **cross-dependent** with heroin; that is, by acting on the same central nervous system receptors, they become a substitute for the original dependency. Abrupt discontinuation of methadone results in its own pattern of withdrawal reactions, but because these reactions are less severe than those of heroin, methadone has potential for weaning heroin users altogether from drug dependence (Strain et al., 1999).

Treatment with a heroin substitute usually involves going to a drug-treatment clinic and swallowing the drug in the presence of a staff member, once a day for methadone and three times a week for levomethadyl acetate and bupreophine. There is some evidence that methadone maintenance can be carried out more simply and just as effectively by weekly visits to a physician (Fiellin et al., 2001). The effectiveness of methadone treatment is improved if a high (80–100 milligram) dose is used as opposed to the more typical 40–50 milligram dose (Strain et al., 1999) and

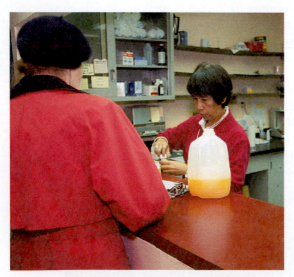

Methadone is a synthetic heroin substitute. People formerly addicted to heroin come to clinics each day and swallow their dose. (John Giordano/Corbis SABA.)

if it is combined with regular psychological counseling (Ball & Ross, 1991). Drug treatment experts generally believe that treatment with heroin substitutes is best conducted in the context of a supportive social interaction, not merely as a medical encounter (Lilly et al., 2000).

Since methadone does not provide a euphoric high, many people will return to heroin if it becomes available to them. In an effort to improve outcomes, researchers have tried adding contingency management to the usual treatment at a methadone clinic. In one randomized controlled trial (Pierce et al., 2006), people receiving methadone from a clinic could draw for prizes each time they submitted a (carefully supervised and obtained) urine sample that had no trace of illegal drugs or alcohol. Prizes ranged from praise to televisions. People who were in the contingency group were more likely to remain drug-free than those people who received only usual care from the methadone clinic. Of course, it remains to be seen whether such abstinence gains can be maintained after treatment ends and therapists are no longer providing such incentives.

Unfortunately, many people drop out of methadone programs, in part because of side effects such as insomnia, constipation, excessive sweating, and diminished sexual functioning. The stigma associated with going to methadone clinics is also linked to dropout rates, as illustrated in the clinical case of James described earlier. Age of entry into treatment may be important— the older the person, the greater the likelihood that he or she will stick with the treatment regimen (Friedmann, Lemon, & Stein, 2001).

In treatment with the opiate or heroin antagonists such as naloxone or naltrexone, people are first gradually weaned from heroin. Then they receive increasing dosages of one of these drugs, which prevents them from experiencing any high should they later take heroin. These drugs work because they have great affinity for the receptors to which opiates usually bind; their molecules occupy the receptors without stimulating them. This leaves heroin molecules with no place to go, and therefore heroin does not have its usual effect on the user. As with methadone, however, treatment with heroin antagonists involves frequent and regular visits to a clinic, which requires motivation. In addition, people do not lose the craving for heroin for some time. Both clinical effectiveness and treatment compliance can be increased by adding a contingency management component to the therapy (Carroll et al., 2001). Giving people vouchers that they can exchange for food and clothing in return for taking naltrexone and having drug-free urine samples markedly improves effectiveness.

Given the limitations of heroin substitutes such as methadone and other opiate antagonists, researchers have been searching for alternative medications. In 2003, a new prescription drug was introduced for the treatment of heroin dependence. Buprenorphine (Suboxone) is a medication that actually contains two agents: buprenorphine and naloxone. Buprenorphine is a partial opiate agonist, which means it does not have the same powerfully addicting properties as heroin, which is a full agonist. Naloxone is one of the opiate antagonists described above. This unique combination in Suboxone does not produce an intense high, is only mildly addictive, and lasts for as long as 3 days. Heroin users do not need to go to a clinic to receive this medication since it can be prescribed to individual people. Thus, this treatment avoids the stigma associated with visiting methadone clinics. Suboxone is effective at relieving withdrawal symptoms, and because it lasts longer than methadone, researchers are hopeful that relapse will be less likely. Still, some users may miss the more euphoric high associated with heroin, thus hastening a relapse.

Drug replacement does not appear to be an effective treatment for cocaine abuse and dependence. A meta-analysis of nine randomized controlled clinical trials of stimulant medication as a treatment for cocaine abuse revealed little evidence that this type of medication is effective (Castells et al., 2007). Two double-blind experiments found poor results for the antidepressant desipramine (Norpramine) (Arndt et al., 1992; Kosten et al., 1992). Researchers are also working on a possible vaccine to help stave off the cravings for cocaine. The vaccine contains tiny amounts of cocaine attached to otherwise harmless pathogens. The body's immune system responds to this invasion by developing antibodies that then squelch the cocaine. It is hoped that with repeated exposure, the antibodies will be able to keep a good deal of the cocaine from reaching the brain.

Developing effective treatments for methamphetamine dependence remains a challenge for the field. People like Anton, described in the clinical case earlier, do not have many places to turn for treatment. The largest effort to date is a randomized controlled clinical trial conducted across eight different sites referred to as the Methamphetamine Treatment Project (Rawson et al., 2004). This study compared a multifaceted treatment called Matrix with treatment as usual. The Matrix treatment consisted of 16 cognitive behavior therapy group sessions, 12 family education sessions, 4 individual therapy sessions, and 4 social support group sessions. Treatment as usual (TAU) consisted of the best available treatment currently offered at the eight outpatient clinics. This varied quite a bit across the sites, with some offering individual counseling and others offering group counseling; some offering 4 weeks of treatment, others offering 16 weeks. Results of the study are somewhat supportive of the Matrix treatment. Compared to those in TAU, those people receiving Matrix stayed in treatment longer and were less likely to use methamphetamine during treatment (confirmed with urine analysis). Unfortunately, at the end of treatment and at the 6-month follow-up, people who received Matrix were no less likely to have used methamphetamine than those in TAU. The good news is that all participants were less likely to use methamphetamine after 6 months, regardless of whether they received Matrix or TAU. Although these results are promising, additional work is clearly needed to develop effective treatments for methamphetamine abuse and dependence.

Quick Summary

Psychological treatments have not been all that effective for nicotine dependence. Scheduled smoking involves reducing nicotine intake gradually over a period of a few weeks, and it has shown some promise. Nicotine gum appears to be somewhat effective, though users can become dependent on the gum. Nicotine patches are more effective than placebo patches, but 9 months after the treatment, abstinence differences between these receiving the drug and those receiving a placebo disappear. Adding buprioprion or therapy along with nicotine patches may be effective.

Detoxification is usually the first step in treatment for drug dependence. There is some evidence that CBT is an effective treatment for cocaine dependence. Motivational interviewing has shown promise for the treatment of alcohol and other drug dependence. Residential treatment homes have not been adequately evaluated for their efficacy, though they are a common form of treatment.

The use of heroin substitutes, such as methadone, is an effective treatment for heroin dependence. Methadone can only be administered in a special clinic, and there is stigma associated with this type of treatment. A newly approved prescription drug called buprenorphine can be taken at home. Treating methamphetamine dependence remains a challenge.

Check Your Knowledge 10.5

Match the treatment approach to the type of substance(s).

Treatment	Substance
1. Suboxone	**a.** alcohol
2. AA	**b.** heroin
3. couples therapy	**c.** cocaine
4. opiate antagonist	**d.** nicotine
5. antidepressant	**e.** methamphetamine
6. patch	
7. Matrix	

Prevention of Substance-Related Disorders

Many prevention efforts have been aimed at adolescents because substance abuse in adulthood often follows experimentation in the teens and earlier. Programs, usually conducted in schools, have been directed at enhancing the young adolescent's self-esteem, teaching social skills, and encouraging the young person to say no to peer pressure. The results are mixed (Hansen, 1993; Jansen et al., 1996). Self-esteem enhancement has not demonstrated its effectiveness. In contrast, social skills training and resistance training (learning to say no) have shown some positive results, particularly with girls. A highly publicized program, Project DARE (Drug Abuse Resistance Education), which combines effective education and resistance training and is delivered by police officers in fifth- and sixth-grade classrooms, has shown disappointing results (Clayton, Catterello, & Walden, 1991; Ringwalt, Ennett, & Holt, 1991).

Half of adult smokers began their habit before the age of 15, and nearly all before the age of 19 (USDHHS, 1998b). Thus, developing ways of discouraging young people from experimenting with tobacco has become a top priority among health researchers and politicians, with encouragement from the Surgeon General and funding from the National Cancer Institute, one of the National Institutes of Health. The American Legacy Foundation is an organization developed to prevent smoking among young people, and this organization was funded in part from the settlement that followed this class action lawsuit against tobacco companies in 1999.

The measures that hold promise for persuading young people to resist smoking may also be useful in dissuading them from trying illicit drugs and alcohol. Brief family interventions show such promise. In Iowa, the Iowa Strengthening Families Program and the five-session Preparing for the Drug Free Years Program have been found to forestall the onset of nicotine and alcohol use among teens (Spoth et al., 2004). For adolescents, family treatments may also have preventative effects. Research has shown that two different brief family interventions were associated with less initiation of alcohol use among teens (Spoth, Guyll, & Day, 2002). Other evidence suggests that the longer alcohol use is delayed, the less likely alcohol dependence will develop (Grant & Dawson, 1997), suggesting that preventive interventions can play a big role in keeping the prevalence of alcohol dependence down.

These programs target families with early adolescents and include skills-based training in risk and protective factors linked to substance abuse.

Statewide comprehensive tobacco control programs, which include increasing taxes on cigarettes, restricting tobacco advertising, conducting public education campaigns, and creating smoke-free environments, appear to be an effective strategy for reducing teenage smoking (Wakefield & Chaloupka, 2000). In addition, recent years have seen scores of school-based programs aimed at preventing young people from starting to use tobacco. By and large, such programs have succeeded in delaying the onset of smoking (Sussman et al., 1995). These programs share some common components, not all of them shown to be effective (Evans, 2001; Hansen, 1992; Sussman, 1996):

- *Peer-pressure resistance training.* Students learn about the nature of peer pressure and ways to say no. Overall, programs based on peer-pressure resistance training appear to be effective in reducing the onset and level of tobacco use, as well as illegal drug use, in young people (Tobler et al., 2000).

- *Correction of beliefs and expectations.* Many young people believe that cigarette smoking is more prevalent (and by implication, more okay) than it actually is. Changing beliefs about the prevalence of smoking has been shown to be an effective strategy, perhaps because young people are so sensitive to what others their age do and believe. Establishing that it is not standard behavior to smoke cigarettes (or drink alcohol or use marijuana) appears to be significantly more effective than resistance training (Hansen & Graham, 1991).

- *Inoculation against mass media messages.* Some prevention programs try to counter the positive images of smokers that have been put forth in the media (e.g., the Joe Camel ads mentioned earlier). Sophisticated mass media campaigns, similar to the ones that have made tobacco a profitable consumer product, can be successful in discouraging smoking. For example, the *truth* campaign, instituted by the American Legacy Foundation, developed websites (www.thetruth.com and www.fairenough.com) and radio and television ads to tell youth about the health and social consequences of smoking and the ways in which the tobacco industry targets them so that they can make informed choices about whether to smoke. This campaign has been well received among young people, and one study found that awareness and agreement with the *truth* messages were associated with less smoking among teens (Niederdeppe, Farrelly, & Haviland, 2004). These findings are particularly encouraging since we know that teenagers' receptivity to tobacco marketing is strongly related to whether or not they will actually smoke (Unger et al., 2001).

- *Peer leadership.* Most smoking and other drug prevention programs involve peers of recognized status, which adds to the impact of the messages being conveyed.

Summary

Clinical Descriptions

- DSM-IV-TR distinguishes between substance dependence and substance abuse. Dependence refers to a pattern of substance use and consequent serious psychological and physical impairments, often including tolerance and withdrawal. In substance abuse, drug use leads to failure to meet obligations and to interpersonal and legal problems.

- Alcohol has a variety of short-term and long-term effects on human beings, ranging from poor judgment and impaired motor coordination to chronic health problems.

- People can become dependent on nicotine, most often via smoking cigarettes. Despite somberly phrased warnings from public health officials, it continues to be used. Medical problems associated with long-term cigarette smoking include many cancers, emphysema, and cardiovascular disease. Moreover, the health hazards of smoking are not restricted to those who smoke, for secondhand (environmental) smoke can also cause lung damage and other problems.

- When used regularly, marijuana can damage the lungs and cardiovascular system and lead to cognitive impairments. Tolerance to marijuana can develop. Ironically, just as the possible dangers of marijuana began to be uncovered, it was found to have therapeutic effects, easing the nausea of people undergoing chemotherapy and easing discomfort associated with AIDS.

- Opiates slow the activities of the body and, in moderate doses, are used to relieve pain and induce sleep. Heroin has been a focus of concern because usage is up and stronger varieties have become available. Another group is the synthetic sedatives and tranquilizers. Barbiturates are particularly lethal when taken with alcohol.

- Stimulants, which include amphetamines and cocaine, act on the brain and the sympathetic nervous system to increase alertness and motor activity. Tolerance and withdrawal are associated with all these drugs. Abuse of methamphetamine, a derivative of amphetamine, has risen dramatically since the 1990s.

- The hallucinogens—LSD, mescaline, and psilocybin—alter or expand consciousness. Use of the hallucinogen-like drug Ecstasy has dramatically risen, and it is also considered a threat to health. PCP use often leads to violence.

Etiology

- Several factors are related to the etiology of substance abuse and dependence. Neurobiological factors, most notably a genetic predisposition or diathesis and the brain's reward pathways, appear to play a role in the use of some substances. Many substances are used to alter mood (e.g., to reduce tension or increase positive affect), and people with certain personality traits, such as those high in negative affect or constraint, are especially likely to use drugs. Cognitive variables, such as the expectation that the drug will yield positive effects, are also important. Finally, sociocultural variables, such as attitudes toward the substance, peer pressure, and how the substance is portrayed by the media, are all related to how frequently a substance is used.

Treatment

- Treatments of all kinds have been used to help people refrain from the use of both legal drugs (e.g., alcohol and nicotine) and illegal drugs (e.g., heroin and cocaine). Biological treatments have attempted to release users from their dependency, often by substituting another drug. Some benefits have been observed for treatments using such drugs as clonidine, naltrexone, and methadone. Nicotine replacement via gum, patches, or inhalers has met with some success in reducing cigarette smoking. None of these approaches appears to lead to enduring change, however, unless accompanied by psychological treatments with such goals as helping people resist pressures to indulge, cope with normal life stress, control emotions without relying on chemicals, and make use of social supports, such as Alcoholics Anonymous.

- Since it is far easier never to begin using drugs than to stop using them, considerable effort has been expended to prevent substance abuse by implementing educational and social programs to equip young people to develop their lives without a reliance on drugs.

Answers to Check Your Knowledge Questions

10.1 1. F; 2. T; 3. T
10.2 1. lung, larynx, esophagus, pancreas, bladder, cervix, stomach; 2. short-term, long-term; 3. pain relief, reduction of nausea, increased appetite, relief from the discomfort from AIDS

10.3 1. F; 2. F; 3. F; 4. T
10.4 1. b; 2. c; 3. a
10.5 1. b; 2. a; 3. a; 4. b; 5. a, c, d; 6. d; 7. e

Key Terms

addiction	Ecstasy	mescaline	psilocybin
amphetamines	fetal alcohol syndrome (FAS)	methadone	secondhand smoke
Antabuse	flashback	methamphetamine	stimulants
barbiturates	hallucinogen	morphine	substance abuse
caffeine	hashish	nicotine	substance dependence
cocaine	heroin	nitrous oxide	substance-related disorders
controlled drinking	hydrocodone	opiates	tolerance
crack	LSD	opium	withdrawal
cross-dependent	marijuana	oxycodone	
delirium tremens (DTs)	MDA	PCP	
detoxification	MDMA	polydrug abuse	

11 Schizophrenia

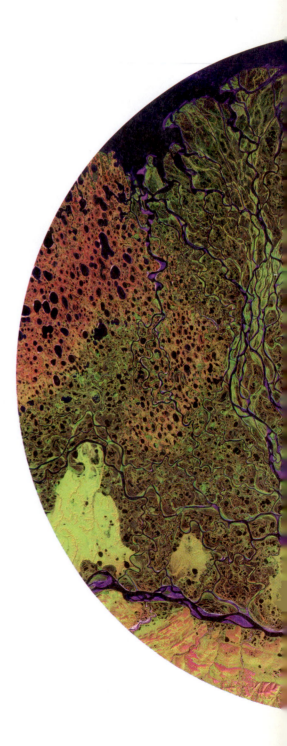

LEARNING GOALS

1. Be able to describe the clinical symptoms of schizophrenia, including positive, negative, and disorganized symptoms.
2. Be able to differentiate the genetic factors, both behavioral and molecular, in the etiology of schizophrenia.
3. Be able to discuss how the brain has been implicated in schizophrenia.
4. Be able to describe the role of stress and other psychosocial factors in the etiology and relapse of schizophrenia.
5. Be able to distinguish the medication treatments and psychological treatments for schizophrenia.

All of a sudden things weren't going so well. I began to lose control of my life and, most of all, myself. I couldn't concentrate on my schoolwork, I couldn't sleep, and when I did sleep, I had dreams about dying. I was afraid to go to class, imagined that people were talking about me, and on top of that I heard voices. I called my mother in Pittsburgh and asked for her advice. She told me to move off campus into an apartment with my sister.

After I moved in with my sister, things got worse. I was afraid to go outside and when I looked out of the window, it seemed that everyone outside was yelling, "Kill her, kill her." My sister forced me to go to school. I would go out of the house until I knew she had gone to work; then I would return home. Things continued to get worse. I imagined that I had a foul body odor and I sometimes took up to 6 showers a day. I recall going to the grocery store one day, and I imagined that the people in the store were saying, "Get saved, Jesus is the answer." Things worsened—I couldn't remember a thing. I had a notebook full of reminders telling me what to do on that particular day. I couldn't remember my schoolwork, and I would study from 6:00 P.M. until 4:00 A.M. but never had the courage to go to class on the following day. I tried to tell my sister about it, but she didn't understand. She suggested that I see a psychiatrist, but I was afraid to go out of the house to see him.

One day I decided that I couldn't take this trauma anymore, so I took an overdose of 35 Darvon pills. At the same moment, a voice inside me said, "What did you do that for? Now you won't go to heaven." At that instant, I realized that I didn't really want to die. I wanted to live, and I was afraid. I got on the phone and called the psychiatrist whom my sister had recommended.

I told him I had taken an overdose of Darvon and that I was afraid. He told me to take a taxi to the hospital. When I arrived at the hospital, I began vomiting, but I didn't pass out. Somehow, I just couldn't accept the fact that I was really going to see a psychiatrist. I thought that psychiatrists were only for crazy people, and I definitely didn't think I was crazy. As a result, I did not admit myself right away. As a matter of fact, I left the hospital and ended up meeting my sister on the way home. She told me to turn right back around because I was definitely going to be admitted. We then called my mother, and she said she would fly down the following day. (quoted in O'Neal, 1984, pp. 109–110)

THE YOUNG WOMAN DESCRIBED in this case study was diagnosed with schizophrenia. **Schizophrenia** is a disorder characterized by disturbances in thought, emotion, and behavior—disordered thinking, in which ideas are not logically related; faulty perception and attention; a lack of emotional expressiveness or, at times, inappropriate expressions; and disturbances in movement and behavior, such as a disheveled appearance. People with schizophrenia may withdraw from other people and from everyday reality, often into a life of odd beliefs (delusions) and hallucinations. Given that schizophrenia is associated with such widespread disruptions in the person's life, we should not be surprised that it has been difficult to uncover the causes of the disorder and develop methods to treat it. We still have a long way to go before we fully understand the multiple factors that trigger schizophrenia and have treatments that are both effective and free of unpleasant side effects.

The symptoms of schizophrenia can make stable employment difficult, often leading to impoverishment and homelessness. Strange behavior and social skills deficits lead to loss of friends, a solitary existence, and sometimes ridicule and persecution. Substance abuse rates are high (Fowler et al., 1998), perhaps reflecting an attempt to achieve some relief from negative emotions (Blanchard et al., 1999). Little wonder, then, that the suicide rate among people with schizophrenia is high. Indeed, people with schizophrenia are 12 times more likely to die of suicide than people in the general population (Saha, Chant, & McGrath, 2007). The symptoms of schizophrenia also have a profound effect on the lives of families and friends. Delusions and hallucinations may cause considerable distress, compounded by the fact that hopes and dreams have been shattered.

Schizophrenia is one of the most severe disorders we will describe in this book. Its lifetime prevalence is slightly less than 1 percent, and it affects men slightly more often than women (Kirkbride et al., 2006; Walker et al., 2004). Schizophrenia is diagnosed more frequently among some groups, such as African Americans, though it remains unclear whether this reflects an actual difference among groups or bias among clinicians (Kirkbride et al., 2006; [U.S. Department of Health and Human Services (USDHHS), 2001a]. Schizophrenia sometimes begins in childhood, but it usually appears in late adolescence or early adulthood, and usually somewhat earlier in men than in women. People with schizophrenia typically have a number of acute episodes of their symptoms and less severe but still debilitating symptoms between episodes. Comorbid substance abuse occurs in about 50 percent of people with schizophrenia, and so it is a major problem (Kesten & Ziedonis, 1997). Not only are people with schizophrenia more likely to die from suicide than people in the general population, they are also more likely to die from any cause (Saha et al., 2007).

In this chapter, we first describe the clinical features of schizophrenia. Then we discuss the etiology of schizophrenia and treatments for the disorder.

Clinical Descriptions of Schizophrenia

The range of symptoms in the diagnosis of schizophrenia is extensive, although people with schizophrenia typically have only some of these problems at any given time. No single essential symptom must be present for a diagnosis of schizophrenia (see DSM-IV-TR criteria box in the margin). Thus, people with schizophrenia can differ from one another quite a bit.

About 30 years ago, symptoms were divided into two categories called positive and negative (Crow, 1980; Strauss, Carpenter, & Bartko, 1974). Subsequently, the original category of positive symptoms was divided into two categories—positive (hallucinations and delusions) and disorganized (disorganized speech and behavior) (Lenzenweger, Dworkin, & Wethington, 1991). The distinction between positive, negative, and disorganized symptoms has been very useful in research on etiology and treatment of schizophrenia—even more useful than the DSM-IV-TR subtypes that we describe later. Table 11.1 shows the symptoms that comprise these categories.

In the following sections, we describe in some detail the individual symptoms that make up the positive, negative, and disorganized categories. We also describe some symptoms that do not fit neatly into these three categories.

Positive Symptoms

Positive symptoms comprise excesses and distortions, such as hallucinations and delusions. For the most part, acute episodes of schizophrenia are characterized by positive symptoms.

Delusions   No doubt all of us at one time or another have been concerned because we believed that others thought ill of us. Some of the time this belief may be justified. After all, who is universally loved? Consider, though, the anguish that you would feel if you were firmly convinced that many people did not like you—indeed, that they disliked you so much that they were plotting against you. Imagine that your persecutors have sophisticated listening devices that let them tune in on your most private conversations and gather evidence in a plot to discredit you. Those around you, including your loved ones, are unable to reassure you that people are not spying on you. Even your closest friends are gradually joining forces with your tormentor. Anxious and angry, you begin taking counteractions against the persecutors. You carefully check any new room you enter for listening devices. When you meet people for the first time, you question them at great length to determine whether they are part of the plot against you.

Such **delusions**, which are beliefs held contrary to reality and firmly held in spite of disconfirming evidence, are common positive symptoms of schizophrenia. Persecutory delusions such as those just described were found in 65 percent of a large, cross-national sample of people diagnosed with schizophrenia (Sartorius, Shapiro, & Jablonsky, 1974). Delusions may take several other forms as well, including the following:

- A person may believe that thoughts that are not his or her own have been placed in his or her mind by an external source; this is called *thought insertion*. For example, a woman may believe that the government has inserted a computer chip in her brain so that thoughts can be inserted into her head.

- A person may believe that his or her thoughts are broadcast or transmitted, so that others know what he or she is thinking; this is called *thought broadcasting*. When walking down the street, a man may look suspiciously at passersby, thinking that they are able to hear what he is thinking even though he is not saying anything out loud.

⬤ DSM-IV-TR Criteria for Schizophrenia

- Two or more of the following symptoms for a significant portion of time for at least 1 month: delusions, hallucinations, disorganized speech, disorganized or catatonic behavior, negative symptoms
- Social and occupational functioning have declined since onset
- Signs of disturbance for at least 6 months; at least 1 month duration for delusions, hallucinations, disorganized speech, disorganized or catatonic behavior; during the remaining time either negative symptoms or other symptoms in attenuated form

Table 11.1 Summary of the Major Symptom Domains in Schizophrenia

Positive Symptoms	Negative Symptoms	Disorganized Symptoms
Delusions, hallucinations	Avolition, alogia, anhedonia, flat affect, asociality	Disorganized behavior, disorganized speech

- A person may believe that his or her feelings or behaviors are controlled by an external force. For example, a person may believe that his or her behavior is being controlled by the radiofrequency (RF) waves emitted from cell phone towers.

- A person may believe that he or she is being persecuted by others. For example, a man may believe that his friends and neighbors are plotting together to get him arrested by the CIA because he can read signals from cloud formations about the government's plans.

- A person may have **grandiose delusions**, in which a person has an exaggerated sense of his or her own importance, power, knowledge, or identity. For example, a woman may believe that she can cause the wind to change direction just by moving her hands.

- A person may have **ideas of reference** in which he or she incorporates unimportant events within a delusional framework and reads personal significance into the trivial activities of others. For instance, people with this symptom might think that overheard segments of conversations are about them, that the frequent appearance of the same person on a street where they customarily walk means that they are being watched, and that what they see on television or read in magazines somehow refers to them.

Although delusions are found among more than half of people with schizophrenia, they are also found among people with other diagnoses, particularly bipolar disorder, depression with psychotic features, and delusional disorder.

Hallucinations and Other Disturbances of Perception

People with schizophrenia frequently report that the world seems somehow different or even unreal to them. A patient may mention changes in how his or her body feels, or a person may become so depersonalized that his or her body feels as though it is a machine. As in the case at the beginning of this chapter, some people report difficulties in paying attention to what is happening around them:

> *I can't concentrate on television because I can't watch the screen and listen to what is being said at the same time. I can't seem to take in two things like this at the same time especially when one of them means watching and the other means listening. On the other hand I seem to be always taking in too much at the one time, and then I can't handle it and can't make sense of it.* (quoted in McGhie & Chapman, 1961, p. 106)

The most dramatic distortions of perception are **hallucinations**, sensory experiences in the absence of any relevant stimulation from the environment. They are more often auditory than visual; 74 percent of one sample of people with schizophrenia reported having auditory hallucinations (Sartorius et al., 1974). Like delusions, hallucinations can be very frightening experiences.

Some types of hallucinations are thought to be particularly important diagnostically because they occur more often in people with schizophrenia than in people with other psychotic disorders. For example, some people with schizophrenia report hearing their own thoughts spoken by another voice. Other people may claim that they hear voices arguing, and others hear voices commenting on their behavior. Many people with schizophrenia experience their hallucinations as frightening or annoying. In one study of nearly 200 people with schizophrenia, those who had hallucinations that were longer, louder, more frequent, and experienced in the third person found them unpleasant. Hallucinations that were believed to come from a known person were experienced more positively (Copolov, Mackinnon, & Trauer, 2004).

Some theorists propose that a person who has auditory hallucinations misattributes their own voice as being someone else's voice. Behavioral studies have shown that people with hallucinations are more likely to misattribute recordings of their own speech to a different source than are people without hallucinations or healthy controls (Allen et al., 2004). Neuroimaging studies have examined what happens in the brain during auditory hallucinations. For example, studies using fMRI have found greater activity in Broca's area, the productive language area of the brain, when people with schizophrenia report hearing voices (McGuire, Shah, & Murray, 1993). Why might people make this misattribution? There may be a problem in the connections between the frontal lobe areas that enable the production of speech and the temporal lobe areas that enable the understanding of speech. Studies using both psychophysiological (Ford et al., 2002) and brain imaging methods (McGuire, Silbersweig, & Frith 1996; Shergill et al., 2000) support this idea.

Negative Symptoms

The **negative symptoms** of schizophrenia consist of behavioral deficits; they include avolition, alogia, anhedonia, flat affect, and asociality (Kirkpatrick et al., 2006), all of which we describe below. These symptoms tend to endure beyond an acute episode and have profound effects on the lives of people with schizophrenia. They are also important prognostically; the presence of many negative symptoms is a strong predictor of a poor quality of life (e.g., occupational impairment, few friends) 2 years following hospitalization (Ho et al., 1998).

When assessing negative symptoms, it is important to distinguish among those that are truly symptoms of schizophrenia and those that are due to some other factor (Carpenter, Heinrichs, & Wagman, 1988). For example, flat affect (a lack of emotional expressiveness) can be a side effect of antipsychotic medication. Observing people over extended time periods is probably the only way to address this issue.

Avolition   Apathy, or **avolition**, refers to a lack of motivation and a seeming absence of interest in or an inability to persist in what are usually routine activities, including work or school, self-care, hobbies, or social activities. For example, people with avolition may become inattentive to grooming and personal hygiene, with uncombed hair, dirty nails, unbrushed teeth, and disheveled clothes. They may have difficulty persisting at work, school, or household chores and may spend much of their time sitting around doing nothing.

Alogia   **Alogia** refers to a significant reduction in the amount of speech. Simply put, people with this symptom do not talk much. A person may answer a question with one or two words and will not be likely to elaborate on an answer with additional detail. For example, if you ask a person with alogia to describe a happy life experience, the person might respond "getting married" and then fail to elaborate even when asked for additional information.

Anhedonia   A loss of interest in or a reported lessening of the experience of pleasure is called **anhedonia**. There are two types of pleasure experiences in the anhedonia construct. The first, called **consummatory pleasure**, refers to the amount of pleasure experienced in-the-moment or in the presence of something pleasurable. For example, the amount of pleasure you experience as you are eating a good meal is consummatory pleasure. The second type of pleasure, called **anticipatory pleasure**, refers to the amount of expected or anticipated pleasure from future events or activities. For example, the amount of pleasure you expect to receive after graduating from college is anticipatory pleasure. People with schizophrenia appear to have a deficit in anticipatory pleasure but not consummatory pleasure (Gard et al., 2007; Kring, 1999). That is, when people with schizophrenia are asked about expected future situations or activities that are pleasurable for most people (e.g., good food, recreational activities, social interactions) on an anhedonia questionnaire, people with schizophrenia report that they derive less pleasure from these sorts of activities than people without schizophrenia (Gard et al., 2007; Horan, Kring, & Blanchard, 2006). However, when presented with actual pleasant activities, such as amusing films or tasty beverages, people with schizophrenia report experiencing as much pleasure as do people without schizophrenia (Gard et al., 2007). Thus, the anhedonia deficit in schizophrenia appears to be in anticipating pleasure, not experiencing pleasure in-the-moment or in the presence of pleasurable things.

Flat Affect   **Flat affect** refers to a lack of outward expression of emotion. A person with this symptom may stare vacantly, the muscles of the face motionless, the eyes lifeless. When spoken to, the person may answer in a flat and toneless voice and not look at his or her conversational partner. Flat affect was found in 66 percent of a large sample of people with schizophrenia (Sartorius et al., 1974).

The concept of flat affect refers only to the outward expression of emotion, not to the patient's inner experience, which is not impoverished at all. In one study, people with schizophrenia and a control group of people without schizophrenia watched excerpts from films while their facial reactions and skin conductance were recorded (Kring & Neale, 1996). After each film clip, participants self-reported on the emotions the films had elicited. As expected, the people with schizophrenia were much less facially expressive than were the people without

People with schizophrenia who have flat affect may not outwardly show happiness, but they will feel it as strongly as people who smile. (Top: Blend Images/SuperStock,Inc.; bottom: ThinkStock/SUPERSTOCK)

schizophrenia, but they reported experiencing the same amount of emotion and were even more physiologically aroused (as measured by skin conductance). This same pattern—diminished expression and comparable experience in people with schizophrenia compared to people without schizophrenia—has been found in over 20 different studies (Kring & Moran, 2008).

Asociality   Some people with schizophrenia have severe impairments in social relationships, referred to as **asociality**. They may have few friends, poor social skills, and very little interest in being with other people. They may not desire close relationships with family, friends, or romantic partners. Instead, they may wish to spend much of their time alone. When around others, people with this symptom may interact only superficially and briefly and appear aloof or indifferent to the social interaction.

Disorganized Symptoms

Disorganized symptoms include disorganized speech and disorganized behavior.

Disorganized Speech   Also known as *formal thought disorder*, **disorganized speech** refers to problems in organizing ideas and in speaking so that a listener can understand. The following excerpt illustrates the incoherence sometimes found in the conversation of people with schizophrenia as an interviewer tries to ask John, a person with schizophrenia, several questions.

Interviewer: Have you been nervous or tense lately?
John: No, I got a head of lettuce.
Interviewer: You got a head of lettuce? I don't understand.
John: Well, it's just a head of lettuce.
Interviewer: Tell me about lettuce. What do you mean?
John: Well . . . lettuce is a transformation of a dead cougar that suffered a relapse on the lion's toe. And he swallowed the lion and something happened. The . . . see, the . . . Gloria and Tommy, they're two heads and they're not whales. But they escaped with herds of vomit, and things like that.
Interviewer: Who are Tommy and Gloria?
John: Uh, . . . there's Joe DiMaggio, Tommy Henrich, Bill Dickey, Phil Rizzuto, John Esclavera, Del Crandell, Ted Williams, Mickey Mantle, Roy Mantle, Ray Mantle, Bob Chance . . .
Interviewer: Who are they? Who are those people?
John: Dead people . . . they want to be fucked . . . by this outlaw.
Interviewer: What does all that mean?
John: Well, you see, I have to leave the hospital. I'm supposed to have an operation on my legs, you know. And it comes to be pretty sickly that I don't want to keep my legs. That's why I wish I could have an operation.
Interviewer: You want to have your legs taken off?
John: It's possible, you know.
Interviewer: Why would you want to do that?
John: I didn't have any legs to begin with. So I would imagine that if I was a fast runner, I'd be scared to be a wife, because I had a splinter inside of my head of lettuce. (Neale & Oltmanns, 1980, pp. 103–104)

Although John may make repeated references to central ideas or themes, the images and fragments of thought are not connected; it is difficult to understand what he is trying to tell the interviewer.

Speech may also be disorganized by what are called **loose associations**, or **derailment**, in which case the person may be more successful in communicating with a listener but has difficulty sticking to one topic. Steve Lopez, a reporter for the *Los Angeles Times*, befriended a man with schizophrenia named Nathanial in the LA area who was a gifted musician (and also homeless). Lopez wrote about their friendship in the book *The Soloist* (Lopez, 2008). Nathanial often exhibited loose associations. For example, in response to a question about Beethoven, Nathanial replied:

Cleveland doesn't have the Beethoven statue. That's a military-oriented city, occupied, preoccupied, with all the military figures of American history, the great soldiers and generals, but you don't see the musicians on parade, although you do have Severance Hall, Cleveland Music School Settlement, Ohio

University Bobcats, Buckeyes of Ohio State. All the great soldiers are there from the United States Military, World War Two, Korean War, whereas in Los Angeles you have the LAPD, Los Angeles County Jail, Los Angeles Times, Mr. Steve Lopez. That's an army, right? (quoted in Lopez, 2008, pp. 23–24)

As this quote illustrates, a person with this symptom seems to drift off on a train of associations evoked by an idea from the past. People with schizophrenia have also described what it is like to experience disorganized speech.

My thoughts get all jumbled up. I start thinking or talking about something but I never get there. Instead, I wander off in the wrong direction and get caught up with all sorts of different things that may be connected with things I want to say but in a way I can't explain. People listening to me get more lost than I do. My trouble is that I've got too many thoughts. You might think about something, let's say that ashtray and just think, oh yes, that's for putting my cigarette in, but I would think of it and then I would think of a dozen different things connected with it at the same time. (quoted in McGhie & Chapman, 1961, p. 108)

It would seem logical to expect disorganized speech to be associated with problems in language production, but this does not appear to be the case. Instead, disorganized speech is associated with problems in what is called *executive functioning*—problem solving, planning, and making associations between thinking and feeling. Disorganized speech is also related to the ability to perceive semantic information (i.e., the meaning of words) (Kerns & Berenbaum, 2002, 2003)

Disorganized Behavior   **Disorganized behavior** takes many forms. People with this symptom may go into inexplicable bouts of agitation, dress in unusual clothes, act in a childlike or silly manner, hoard food, or collect garbage. They seem to lose the ability to organize their behavior and make it conform to community standards. They also have difficulty performing the tasks of everyday living.

Other Symptoms

Two other symptoms of schizophrenia do not fit neatly into the categories we have just presented: catatonia and inappropriate affect.

Catatonia   Several motor abnormalities define **catatonia**. People with this symptom may gesture repeatedly, using peculiar and sometimes complex sequences of finger, hand, and arm movements, which often seem to be purposeful. Some people manifest an unusual increase in their overall level of activity, including much excitement, wild flailing of the limbs, and great expenditure of energy similar to that seen in mania. At the other end of the spectrum is **catatonic immobility**: people adopt unusual postures and maintain them for very long periods of time. Catatonia can also involve *waxy flexibility*—another person can move the patient's limbs into positions that the patient will then maintain for long periods of time.

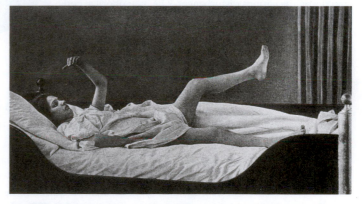

An 1894 photo showing a woman with catatonic schizophrenia. She held this unusual posture for long periods of time. (The Burns Archive.)

Catatonia is seldom seen today, perhaps because medications work effectively on these disturbed motor processes. Alternatively, Boyle (1991) has argued that the apparent high prevalence of catatonia during the early part of the twentieth century reflected misdiagnosis. Specifically, the similarities between encephalitis lethargica (sleeping sickness) and catatonic schizophrenia suggest that many cases of the former were misdiagnosed as the latter. This idea was portrayed in the film *Awakenings*, which was based on the career and writings of Oliver Sacks. See Focus on Discovery 11.1 for more on the history of schizophrenia and its symptoms.

Inappropriate Affect   Some people with schizophrenia show **inappropriate affect**—their emotional responses are out of context. Such a person may laugh on hearing that his or her mother just died or become enraged when asked a simple question about how a new jacket fits. People with this symptom are likely to shift rapidly from one emotional state to another for no discernible reason. Like catatonia, this symptom is rare, and it is relatively specific to schizophrenia.

FOCUS ON DISCOVERY 11.1

History of the Concept of Schizophrenia

Two European psychiatrists, Emil Kraepelin and Eugen Bleuler, initially formulated the concept of schizophrenia. Kraepelin first described **dementia praecox**, his term for what we now call schizophrenia, in 1898. Dementia praecox included several diagnostic subtypes—dementia paranoides, catatonia, and hebephrenia—that had been regarded as distinct entities by clinicians in the previous few decades. Although these disorders were symptomatically diverse, Kraepelin believed that they shared a common core, and the term **dementia praecox** reflected what he believed was that core—an early onset (praecox) and a progressive, inevitable intellectual deterioration (dementia). The dementia in dementia praecox is not the same as the dementias we discuss in the chapter on late life (Chapter 15), which are defined principally by severe memory impairments. Kraepelin's term referred to a general "mental enfeeblement."

Bleuler broke with Kraepelin's description on two major points: he believed that the disorder did not necessarily have an early onset, and he believed that it did not inevitably progress toward dementia. Thus the label "dementia praecox" was no longer appropriate, and in 1908 Bleuler proposed his own term, *schizophrenia*, from the Greek words *schizein* ("to split"), and *phren* ("mind"), capturing what he viewed as the essential nature of the condition.

With age of onset and deteriorating course no longer considered defining features of the disorder, Bleuler faced a conceptual problem. The symptoms of schizophrenia could vary widely among people, so he had to provide some justification for putting them into a single diagnostic category. That is, he needed to specify some common denominator, or essential property, that would link the various disturbances. The metaphorical concept that he adopted for this purpose was the "breaking of associative threads."

Emil Kraepelin (1856–1926), German psychiatrist, articulated descriptions of schizophrenia (then called dementia praecox) that have proved remarkably durable in the light of contemporary research. (Hueton Archive Getty Images.)

For Bleuler, associative threads joined not only words but also thoughts. Thus, goal-directed, efficient thinking and communication were possible only when these hypothetical structures were intact. The notion that associative threads were disrupted in people with schizophrenia could then be used to account for the range of other disturbances. Bleuler viewed attentional difficulties, for example, as resulting from a loss of purposeful direction in thought, in turn causing passive responses to objects and people in the immediate surroundings.

Kraepelin had recognized that a small percentage of people with symptoms of dementia praecox did not deteriorate, but he preferred to limit this diagnostic category to people who had a poor prognosis. Bleuler's work, in contrast, led to a broader concept of the disorder. He diagnosed some people with a good prognosis as having schizophrenia, and he also diagnosed schizophrenia in many people who would have received different diagnoses from other clinicians.

Eugen Bleuler (1857–1939), Swiss psychiatrist, contributed to our conceptions of schizophrenia and coined the term. (Corbis Bettmann.)

Schizophrenia in DSM-IV-TR

DSM-IV-TR requires that the symptoms last for at least 6 months for the diagnosis. The 6-month period must include at least 1 month of an acute episode, or active phase, defined by the presence of at least two of the following: delusions, hallucinations, disorganized speech, grossly disorganized or catatonic behavior, and negative symptoms. (Only one of these symptoms is required if the delusions are bizarre or if the hallucinations consist of voices commenting or arguing.) The remaining time required for the diagnosis can occur either before the active phase or after the active phase. This time criterion eliminates people who have a brief psychotic episode and then recover quickly.

Are the DSM-IV-TR diagnostic criteria applicable across cultures? Evidence bearing on this question was collected in a World Health Organization study of both industrialized and developing countries (Jablonsky et al., 1994). The symptomatic criteria held up well cross-culturally. However, for reasons not yet fully understood, people with schizophrenia in developing countries have a more acute onset and a more favorable course than those in industrialized societies (Susser & Wanderling, 1994).

Table 11.2 Key Features of DSM-IV-TR Subtypes of Schizophrenia

Disorganized schizophrenia The subtype called **disorganized schizophrenia** in DSM-IV-TR is manifested by speech that is disorganized and difficult for a listener to follow. The person may have flat affect or experience constant shifts of emotion, breaking into inexplicable fits of laughter and crying. The person's behavior is also generally disorganized and not goal directed.

Catatonic schizophrenia The most obvious symptoms of **catatonic schizophrenia** are the catatonic symptoms. A person may alternate between catatonic immobility and wild excitement, but one of these symptoms may predominate. Negative symptoms are also likely present.

Paranoid schizophrenia The key to the diagnosis of **paranoid schizophrenia** is the presence of prominent delusions, such as delusions of persecution, grandiose delusions, or ideas of reference. Vivid auditory hallucinations may accompany the delusions. Speech is not disorganized, and flat affect is not typically present even though a person may be somewhat stilted, formal, and intense with others.

Undifferentiated schizophrenia The subtype of **undifferentiated schizophrenia** is applied to people who meet the diagnostic criteria for schizophrenia but not for any of the three main subtypes.

Residual schizophrenia The subtype of **residual schizophrenia** is used when a person no longer meets the full criteria for schizophrenia but still shows some signs of the illness.

Table 11.2 presents the subtypes of schizophrenia in the DSM-IV-TR. Although the subtypes of schizophrenia in DSM-IV-TR form the basis of current diagnostic practices, their usefulness is often questioned. Actually, diagnosing the subtypes is extremely difficult, so diagnostic reliability is very low. Furthermore, the subtypes have little predictive validity; that is, the diagnosis of one or another type of schizophrenia provides little information helpful in either treating the disorder or predicting its course. There is also considerable overlap of symptoms among the subtypes. For example, people with all subtypes of schizophrenia may have delusions.

Other Psychotic Disorders in the DSM-IV-TR

Two brief psychotic disorders are **schizophreniform disorder** and **brief psychotic disorder**. The symptoms of schizophreniform disorder are the same as those of schizophrenia but last only from 1 to 6 months. Brief psychotic disorder lasts from 1 day to 1 month and is often brought on by extreme stress, such as bereavement. **Schizoaffective disorder** comprises a mixture of symptoms of schizophrenia and mood disorders.

A person with **delusional disorder** is troubled by persistent delusions of persecution or by delusional jealousy, the unfounded conviction that a spouse or lover is unfaithful. Other delusions seen in this disorder include delusions of being followed, delusions of erotomania (believing that one is loved by some other person, usually a complete stranger with a higher social status), and somatic delusions (believing that some internal organ is malfunctioning). Unlike the person with paranoid schizophrenia, the person with delusional disorder does not have hallucinations, and his or her delusions are less bizarre.

Quick Summary

Schizophrenia is a very heterogeneous disorder. It affects men slightly more than women and typically begins in late adolescence or early adulthood. Symptoms can be distinguished as positive, negative, and disorganized. Positive symptoms include hallucinations and delusions. Negative symptoms include avolition, alogia, flat affect, anhedonia, and asociality. Disorganized symptoms include disorganized speech and disorganized behavior. No one of these symptoms is critical for the diagnosis of schizophrenia. The DSM-IV-TR subtypes include catatonic, paranoid, disorganized, undifferentiated, and residual. Despite their presence in the DSM-IV-TR, they do not have a good deal of validity and are not that useful. Other psychotic disorders include schizophreniform disorder and brief psychotic disorder, which differ from schizophrenia in duration. Schizoaffective disorder involves symptoms of both schizophrenia and mood disorders. Delusional disorder involves delusions but no other symptoms of schizophrenia, and the delusions are less bizarre than those in schizophrenia.

Check Your Knowledge 11.1 (Answers are at the end of the chapter.)

List the symptom that each clinical vignette describes.

1. Charlie enjoyed going to movies. He particularly liked to see horror movies because they made him feel really scared. His sister was surprised to learn this, because when she went to movies with Charlie, he didn't gasp out loud or show fear on his face.
2. Marlene was convinced that Christian Bale was sending her messages. In his movie *The Dark Knight*, his battles with the Joker were a signal that he was prepared to fight for them to be together. That he signed autographs at his movie opening also told her that he was trying to get in touch with her.

3. Sophia didn't want to go out to dinner with her family. She reasoned that these dinners were always the same food and conversation, so why bother? Later in the week, her mother mentioned that Sophia was not doing much around the house. Sophia said that nothing she could think of to do would be fun.
4. Jevon was talking with his doctor about the side effects of his medication. He talked about having dry mouth and then immediately began talking about cottonmouth snakes and jungle safaris and how hiking was good for your health but that Barack Obama was in better shape than George Bush.

Etiology of Schizophrenia

What can explain the scattering and disconnection of thoughts, the lack of emotion expression, the odd delusions, and bewildering hallucinations of people with schizophrenia? Broad theoretical perspectives, such as psychoanalysis, have not had much of an impact in research on schizophrenia. Other perspectives, however, have yielded many interesting research results, as we discuss in the following sections.

Genetic Factors

A good deal of research supports the idea that schizophrenia has a genetic component, as we discuss in the sections below on behavior genetics and molecular genetics research. The evidence is somewhat more convincing from behavior genetics studies, largely because they have been well replicated. Many molecular genetics studies are still in need of replication to bolster confidence in their findings.

Behavior Genetics Research   The family, twin, and adoption methods employed in this research, as in other behavior genetics research projects, have led researchers to conclude that a predisposition to schizophrenia is inherited. It should be noted that many genetic studies of schizophrenia were conducted when the definition of schizophrenia was considerably broader than it is now. However, genetic investigators collected extensive descriptive data on their samples, allowing the results to be reanalyzed later using newer diagnostic criteria.

Family Studies   Table 11.3 presents a summary of the risk for schizophrenia in various relatives of index cases with schizophrenia. (In evaluating the figures, bear in mind that the risk for schizophrenia in the general population is a little less than 1 percent.) Quite clearly, relatives of people with schizophrenia are at increased risk, and the risk increases as the genetic relationship between proband and relative becomes closer (Kendler, Karkowski-Shuman, & Walsh, 1996).

Furthermore, people who have schizophrenia in their family histories have more negative symptoms than those whose families are free of schizophrenia (Malaspina et al., 2000), suggesting that negative symptoms may have a stronger genetic component. The relatives of people with schizophrenia are also at increased risk for other disorders (e.g., schizotypal personality disorder) that are thought to be less severe forms of schizophrenia (Kendler, Neale, & Walsh, 1995).

The results of family studies thus support the notion that a predisposition for schizophrenia can be transmitted genetically. Yet the relatives of a person with schizophrenia share not only genes but also common experiences. Recall from Chapter 2 that genes do much of their work via the environment. Therefore, the influence of the environment cannot be discounted in explaining the higher risks among relatives.

Table 11.3 Summary of Major Family and Twin Studies of the Genetics of Schizophrenia

Relation to Proband	Percentage with Schizophrenia
Spouse	1.00
Grandchildren	2.84
Nieces/nephews	2.65
Children	9.35
Siblings	7.30
DZ twins	12.08
MZ twins	44.30

Source: After Gottesman, McGuffin, & Farmer (1987).

Twin Studies   Table 11.3 also shows the risk for identical (MZ) and fraternal (DZ) twins of people with schizophrenia. The risk for MZ twins (44.3 percent), although greater than that for DZ twins (12.08 percent), is still much less than 100 percent. Similar results have been obtained in more recent studies (Cannon et al., 1998; Cardno et al., 1999). The less-than-100-percent concordance in MZ twins is important: if genetic transmission alone accounted for schizophrenia and one twin had schizophrenia, the other twin would also have schizophrenia because MZ twins are genetically identical. The importance of genetic factors is supported, however, by the fact that the risk among MZ twins increases when the twin with schizophrenia is more severely ill (Gottesman & Shields, 1972). As with the family studies, twin study research suggests that negative symptoms may have a stronger genetic component than do positive symptoms (Dworkin & Lenzenweger, 1984; Dworkin, Lenzenweger, & Moldin, 1987).

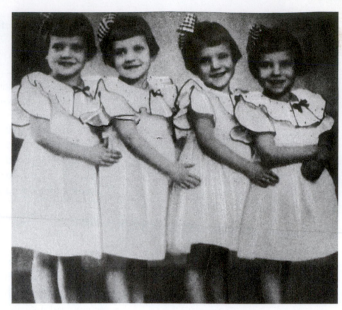

Childhood photograph of the Genain quadruplets. Each of the girls developed schizophrenia later in life. (Courtesy of Monte S. Buchsbaum, M.D., Mt. Sinai School of Medicine, New York, NY.)

As with family studies, of course, there is a critical problem in interpreting the results of twin studies. A common environment rather than common genetic factors could account for some portion of the increased risk. By common environment, we mean not only similar shared and non-shared environmental factors, such as child-rearing practices or peer relationships, but also a more similar intrauterine environment, for MZ twins are more likely than DZ twins to share a single blood supply.

A clever analysis supporting a genetic interpretation of the high risk found for identical twins was performed by Fischer (1971). She reasoned that if these rates indeed reflected a genetic effect, the twins without schizophrenia should be at high risk for the disorder. These MZ twins without schizophrenia would presumably have the genotype for schizophrenia, even though it was not expressed behaviorally, and thus might pass along an increased risk for the disorder to their children. In agreement with this line of reasoning, the rate of schizophrenia and schizophrenia-like psychoses in the children of the MZ twins without schizophrenia was 9.4 percent, while the rate among the children of the twins with schizophrenia was only slightly and non-significantly higher, 12.3 percent. Both rates are substantially higher than the 1 percent prevalence found in the general population, and this lends further support to the importance of genetic factors in schizophrenia.

Adoption Studies   The study of children whose mothers had schizophrenia but who were reared from early infancy by adoptive parents without schizophrenia has provided clearer confirmation of the role of genes in schizophrenia because such studies eliminate the possible effects of being reared in an environment where a parent has schizophrenia. In a now-classic study, Heston (1966) followed up 47 people born between 1915 and 1945 to women with schizophrenia. The infants were separated from their mothers at birth and raised by foster or adoptive parents. Fifty control participants were selected from the same adoption agency that had placed the children of the women with schizophrenia.

The follow-up assessment revealed that none of the controls was diagnosed with schizophrenia, versus 16.6 percent (five) of the offspring of women with schizophrenia. Children of women with schizophrenia were also more likely to be diagnosed with mental retardation, psychopathy, and neuroses (the older term for anxiety) (Table 11.4). This study provides strong support for the importance of genetic factors in the development of schizophrenia.

Another large study of adopted offspring of mothers with schizophrenia found similar results. In this study, the risk for developing schizophrenia among the 164 adoptees who had a biological parent with schizophrenia was 8.1 percent; the risk for the 197 control adoptees who did not have a biological parent with schizophrenia was significantly lower at 2.3 percent. The risk for other disorders, such as schizoaffective, schizophreniform, and schizotypal personality disorder, was also greater among the adoptees with a biological parent with schizophrenia than among the control adoptees (Tienari et al., 2000).

A similar study was carried out in Denmark (Kety et al., 1976, 1994), where researchers examined the records of children who had been adopted at a young age. All adoptees who had

Table 11.4 Characteristics of Participants Separated from Their Mothers in Early Infancy

Characteristic	Offspring of Mothers with Schizophrenia	Control Offspring
Number of participants	47	50
Mean age at follow-up	35.8	36.3
Overall ratings of disability (low score indicates more pathology)	65.2	80.1
Number diagnosed with schizophrenia	5	0
Number diagnosed with mental retardation	4	0
Number diagnosed with psychopathy	9	2
Number diagnosed with neurosis	13	7

Source: From Heston (1966).

later been admitted to a psychiatric facility and diagnosed with schizophrenia were selected as the index cases. From the remaining cases, the investigators chose a control group of people who had no psychiatric history and who were matched to the index group on such variables as sex and age. Both the adoptive and the biological parents and the siblings and half-siblings of the two groups were then identified, and a search was made to determine who among them had a psychiatric history. As might be expected if genetic factors figure in schizophrenia, the biological relatives of the group with schizophrenia were diagnosed with schizophrenia more often than were members of the general population; the adoptive relatives were not.

Molecular Genetics Research Knowing that schizophrenia has a genetic component is in many ways just the starting point for research. Understanding exactly what constitutes the genetic predisposition is the challenge faced by molecular genetics researchers. As with nearly all of the disorders we cover in this book, it does not appear that the predisposition for schizophrenia is transmitted by a single gene.

The results of linkage analysis studies (see p.108), in which family pedigrees are studied to try to determine on which chromosome or chromosomes the schizophrenia genes are located, have been inconsistent. Studies have reported positive findings for linkage at locations on a number of different chromosomes, including 1, 2, 5, 6, 8, 10, 11, 13, 15, 18, and 22 (Faraone, Taylor, & Tsuang, 2002: Lewis et al., 2003). Although finding so many chromosomal locations to be possibly connected with schizophrenia is consistent with the idea that multiple genes are involved, the results of these studies are simply too varied to justify any firm conclusions. A meta-analysis of 20 genome-wide studies of schizophrenia found some support for linkage on chromosome 2 (Lewis et al., 2003). However, such results have a history of not being replicated (DeLisi et al., 2002), possibly because these types of studies work better for conditions with a predisposition that is transmitted by a single gene or a small set of genes. It is also highly likely that schizophrenia is genetically heterogeneous—that is, the genetic diathesis may vary from case to case—mirroring the fact, noted earlier, that schizophrenia is certainly symptomatically heterogeneous. As with the case of any gene or genes, they do their work via the environment, so gene–environment interaction studies are likely to help more clearly pinpoint the nature of the genetic contribution to schizophrenia (Walker & Tessner, 2008).

Association studies (see p. 109) have begun to focus on specific genes associated with schizophrenia. In an association study, the goal is to establish how often a specific gene and a particular phenotype co-occur. As with the linkage studies, positive findings are often followed by failures to replicate. For example, research was initially focused on genes associated with the dopamine D2 receptor because, as we discuss below, this receptor is associated with the positive effectiveness of some medications used to treat schizophrenia. Although there are some positive findings (Glatt, Faraone, & Tsuang, 2003), a number of other studies are negative (Owen, Williams, & O'Donovan, 2004). Other studies have found associations with the serotonin receptor 5HT2 gene, though its role appears to be very small (Lohmueller et al., 2003; J. Williams et al., 1997).

Two promising candidate genes have received some recent support from association studies (Owen et al., 2004). One, a gene called DTNBP1, encodes a protein called dysbindin that is expressed throughout the brain, but it is not yet clear what the function is of either the gene or the protein. However, it appears to impact the glutamate neurotransmitter system throughout the brain (MacDonald & Chafee, 2006), and five studies have replicated an association between DTNBP1 and schizophrenia. In addition, a postmortem study has shown that compared to people without schizophrenia, those with schizophrenia appear to have less dysbindin in a number of brain areas, including the frontal cortex, temporal cortex, hippocampus, and limbic system structures (Weickert et al., 2004). Another gene, NGR1, which has been linked to the neurotransmitter glutamate's NMDA (*N*-methyl-*D*-aspartate) receptor and is helpful with the process of myelination (see p. 36), has also been found to be associated with schizophrenia. Time will tell if these results can be replicated.

Another approach to research on specific genes that may improve our understanding of schizophrenia is association studies that examine the relationship between genes and cognitive functions among people without psychopathology. For example, some research has found that a gene called COMT is associated with executive functions that rely on the **prefrontal cortex** (reviewed by Goldberg & Weinberger, 2004). A number of studies have demonstrated that people with schizophrenia have deficits in executive functions, which include planning, working memory, and problem solving, and other studies have shown problems in the prefrontal cortex. A few association studies have implicated COMT in schizophrenia (Harrison & Weinberger, 2004; Owen et al., 2004). Another gene called BDNF has been studied and linked with cognitive function in people with and without schizophrenia. This gene has a polymorphism called Val66Met, where a person can have two Val alleles (Val/Val), two Met alleles (Met/Met), or one Val and one Met allele (Val/Met). In a large study of people with and without schizophrenia, verbal memory was better for people who had two Val alleles (Val/Val) compared to people who had either one or two Met alleles (Val/Met or Met/Met) (Ho et al., 2006).

Finally, newer techniques in molecular genetics that allow for the rapid scanning of a person's entire genome, a so-called genome-wide scan, have been applied to the study of schizophrenia. This technique allows researchers to identify rare mutations in genes rather than just known gene loci from previous linkage and association studies. Mutations are changes in a gene that occur randomly and for unknown reasons. In one study, researchers identified over 50 such mutations that were three times more common among people with schizophrenia than in people without schizophrenia across two different samples of people (Walsh et al., 2008). Some of the identified gene mutations are known to be associated with other presumed risk factors in the etiology of schizophrenia, including the neurotransmitter glutamate (discussed below) and proteins that promote the proper placement of neurons in the brain during brain development. Although encouraging, these findings will need to be replicated. Furthermore, even though the identified mutations were more common in people with schizophrenia than people without schizophrenia, they were identified only in about 20 percent of the people with schizophrenia. Thus, other genetic factors await discovery in future studies.

Evaluation of the Genetic Research   Research results indicate that genetic factors play an important role in the development of schizophrenia. Of particular importance, adoption studies that do a better job of separating genetic and environmental effects provide support for the heritability of schizophrenia.

Despite this evidence, we cannot conclude that schizophrenia is a disorder completely determined by genetic transmission, for we must always keep in mind the distinction between phenotype and genotype (see p. 30). Like other mental disorders, schizophrenia is defined by behavior; it is a phenotype, and thus it reflects the influence of both genes and environment. The diathesis–stress model introduced in Chapter 2 seems appropriate for guiding theory and research into the etiology of schizophrenia. Genetic factors can only predispose people to schizophrenia. Some kind of stress is required to cause this predisposition to be expressed as an observable disorder.

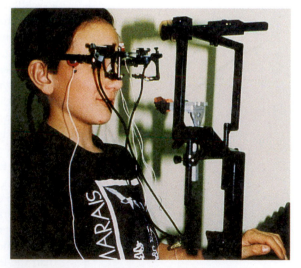

This apparatus is used to assess a person's ability to track a moving target. This ability is impaired both in people with schizophrenia and in their relatives, suggesting that eye tracking is a genetic marker for the disorder. (Courtesy of Dr. William Iacono, University of Minnesota.)

The genetic research in schizophrenia has some further limitations as well. First, as reviewed in the molecular genetics section above, it has not yet been possible to specify exactly how a predisposition for schizophrenia is transmitted. Second, the nature of the inherited diathesis remains unknown. What exactly is inherited that puts some people at risk for schizophrenia? One way of addressing this question is to study relatives of people with schizophrenia. Although not necessarily disordered, these people, who are at increased risk for schizophrenia, may reveal signs of the genetic predisposition. One area of research has been the study of how well the eyes track a moving target, such as a pendulum. People with schizophrenia do poorly on this task, as do about 50 percent of their first-degree relatives (Holzman, 1985). The importance of eye tracking is supported by data showing that it is influenced by genetic factors (Greenwood et al., 2007; Iacono et al., 1992). Deficient eye tracking may reflect a problem in several areas of the brain, including the frontal and temporal lobes as well as the cerebellum (Chen et al., 1999). We will soon see that these brain areas are thought to be very important in schizophrenia.

Despite the problems and loose ends, the results of genetics research represent an impressive body of evidence. The strong positive correlation between genetic relatedness and the prevalence of schizophrenia remains one of the strongest links in the chain of information about the causes of schizophrenia.

Neurotransmitters

Present research is examining several different neurotransmitters, such as norepinephrine, serotonin, and glutamate, to see what role they might play in the etiology of schizophrenia. The first neurotransmitter to receive substantial research attention was dopamine. We trace the history of this research here, highlighting how it has both helped and hindered efforts toward identifying causes and treatments for schizophrenia.

Dopamine Theory   The theory that schizophrenia is related to excess activity of the neurotransmitter dopamine is based principally on the knowledge that drugs effective in treating schizophrenia reduce dopamine activity. Researchers noted that antipsychotic drugs, in addition to being useful in treating some symptoms of schizophrenia, produce side effects resembling the symptoms of Parkinson's disease. Parkinson's disease is known to be caused in part by low levels of dopamine in a particular nerve tract of the brain. It was subsequently confirmed that antipsychotic drugs fit into and thereby block a particular type of postsynaptic dopamine receptors, called D2 receptors. From this knowledge about the action of the drugs that help people with schizophrenia, it was natural to conjecture that schizophrenia resulted from excess activity in dopamine nerve tracts.

Further indirect support for this **dopamine theory** of schizophrenia came from the literature on *amphetamine psychosis*. Amphetamines can produce a state that closely resembles paranoid schizophrenia, and they can exacerbate the symptoms of people with schizophrenia (Angrist, Lee, & Gershon, 1974). The amphetamines cause the release of norepinephrine and dopamine into the synaptic cleft and prevent their inactivation. We can be relatively confident that the psychosis-inducing effects of amphetamines are a result of increasing activity of dopamine rather than of norepinephrine, because antipsychotics are effective in treating amphetamine psychosis.

Based on the evidence just reviewed, researchers at first assumed that schizophrenia was caused by an excess of dopamine. But as other studies progressed, this assumption did not gain support. For example, the major metabolite of dopamine, homovanillic acid (HVA), was not found in greater amounts in people with schizophrenia (Bowers, 1974).

Such evidence, plus improved technologies for studying neurotransmitters in humans, led researchers to propose excess numbers of dopamine receptors or oversensitive dopamine receptors, rather than a high level of dopamine, as factors in schizophrenia. Research on the antipsychotics' mode of action suggests that the dopamine receptors are a more likely locus of disorder than the level of dopamine itself. Some postmortem studies of brains of people with schizophrenia, as well as PET scans of people with schizophrenia, have revealed that dopamine receptors are greater in number or are hypersensitive in some people with schizophrenia (Hietala et al., 1994; Tune et al., 1993; Wong et al., 1986). Having too many dopamine receptors would be functionally akin to having an overactive dopamine system. The reason is that when dopamine

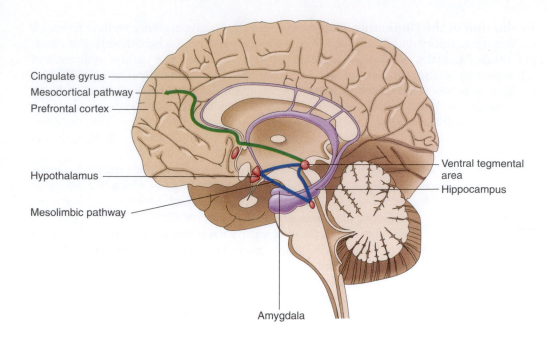

Figure 11.1 The brain and schizophrenia. The mesocortical pathway begins in the ventral tegmental area and projects to the prefrontal cortex. The mesolimbic pathway also begins in the ventral tegmental area but projects to the hypothalamus, amygdala, hippocampus, and nucleus accumbens.

(or any neurotransmitter) is released into the synapse, only some of it actually interacts with postsynaptic receptors. Having more receptors gives a greater opportunity for the dopamine that is released to stimulate a receptor, hence a greater opportunity for dopamine activity.

An excess of dopamine receptors may not be responsible for all the symptoms of schizophrenia; such an excess appears to be related mainly to positive symptoms. Amphetamines worsen positive symptoms. Antipsychotics lessen positive symptoms but have little or no effect on negative symptoms.

Subsequent developments in the dopamine theory (e.g., Davis et al., 1991) expanded its scope. The key change involved the recognition of differences among the neural pathways that use dopamine as a transmitter. The excess dopamine activity that is thought to be most relevant to schizophrenia is localized in the mesolimbic pathway (see Figure 11.1), and the therapeutic effects of antipsychotics on positive symptoms occur by blocking dopamine receptors in this neural system, thereby lowering dopamine activity.

The mesocortical pathway is another scene of dopamine activity. It begins in the same brain region as the mesolimbic pathway but projects to the prefrontal cortex. The prefrontal cortex also projects to other areas that are innervated by dopamine. The dopamine neurons in the prefrontal cortex may be underactive and thus fail to exert inhibitory control over the dopamine neurons in the limbic area, with the result that there is dopamine overactivity in the pathways. Because the prefrontal cortex is thought to be especially relevant to the negative symptoms of schizophrenia, the underactivity of the dopamine neurons in this part of the brain may also be the cause of the negative symptoms of schizophrenia (see Figure 11.2). This proposal has the advantage of accounting for the simultaneous presence of positive and negative symptoms in the same person with schizophrenia. Furthermore, because antipsychotics do not have major effects on the dopamine neurons in the prefrontal cortex, we would expect them to be relatively ineffective as treatments for negative symptoms, and they are. When we examine research on structural abnormalities in the brains of people with schizophrenia, we will see some close connections between these two domains.

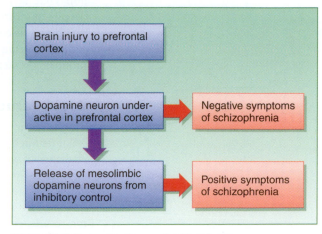

Figure 11.2 Dopamine theory of schizophrenia.

Evaluation of the Dopamine Theory Despite the positive evidence we have reviewed, the dopamine theory does not appear to be a complete theory of schizophrenia. For example, it takes several weeks for antipsychotics to begin lessening the positive symptoms of schizophrenia, although they begin blocking dopamine receptors rapidly (Davis, 1978). This disjunction between the behavioral and pharmacological effects of antipsychotics is difficult to understand within the context of the theory. One possibility is that although antipsychotics do indeed block D2 receptors, their ultimate therapeutic effect may result from the effect this blockade has on other brain areas and other neurotransmitter systems (R. M. Cohen et al., 1997).

It is also puzzling that to be therapeutically effective, antipsychotics must reduce dopamine levels or receptor activity to below normal, in some cases producing side effects like the symptoms of Parkinson's disease. According to the theory, reducing dopamine levels or receptor activity to normal should be sufficient for a therapeutic effect.

In sum, although dopamine remains the most actively researched neurotransmitter in schizophrenia, it is not likely to provide a complete explanation of the etiology of schizophrenia. Schizophrenia is a disorder with widespread symptoms covering perception, cognition, motor activity, and social behavior. It is unlikely that a single neurotransmitter could account for all of them. Thus, schizophrenia researchers have cast a broader neurotransmitter net, moving away from an almost exclusive emphasis on dopamine.

Other Neurotransmitters As we discuss later, newer drugs used in treating schizophrenia implicate other neurotransmitters, such as serotonin, in the disorder. These newer drugs partially block D2 receptors, but they also work by blocking the serotonin receptor 5HT2 (e.g., Burris et al., 2002). Dopamine neurons generally modulate the activity of other neural systems; for example, in the prefrontal cortex they regulate GABA neurons. Thus, it is not surprising that GABA transmission is disrupted in the prefrontal cortex of people with schizophrenia (Volk et al., 2000). Similarly, serotonin neurons regulate dopamine neurons in the mesolimbic pathway.

Glutamate, a neurotransmitter that is widespread in the human brain, may also play a role (Carlsson et al., 1999). Low levels of glutamate have been found in the cerebrospinal fluid of people with schizophrenia (Faustman et al., 1999), and postmortem studies have revealed low levels of the enzyme needed to produce glutamate (Tsai et al., 1995). Studies have found elevated levels of the amino acid homocysteine, a substance that is known to interact with the NMDA receptor among people with schizophrenia and in the blood of pregnant women during their third trimester whose offspring developed schizophrenia as adults (Brown et al., 2007; Regland et al., 1995). The street drug PCP (p. 296) can induce both positive and negative symptoms in people without schizophrenia, and it produces this effect by interfering with one of glutamate's receptors (O'Donnell & Grace, 1998). Furthermore, a decrease in glutamate inputs from either the prefrontal cortex or the hippocampus (both of these brain structures are implicated in schizophrenia) to the corpus striatum (a temporal lobe structure) could result in increased dopamine activity (O'Donnell & Grace, 1998). Additional evidence suggests that cognitive deficits in schizophrenia supported by the prefrontal cortex as well as symptoms of disorganization may be connected to deficits involving NMDA (MacDonald & Chafee, 2006). A new medication that targets glutamate receptors is currently being tested, and the early results are promising (Patel et al., 2007).

Brain Structure and Function

The search for a brain abnormality that causes schizophrenia began as early as the syndrome was identified, but studies did not begin to yield consistent findings until fairly recently. The challenge of such a task is indeed daunting. Schizophrenia affects everything about us that makes us human—our thinking, feeling, and behaving. It is thus unlikely that a single type of brain abnormality can account for schizophrenia's wide array of symptoms. In the last two decades, however, spurred by a number of technological advances, research has yielded some promising results. Among the most well-replicated findings of brain abnormalities in schizophrenia are enlargement of the ventricles and dysfunction in the prefrontal cortex.

Enlarged Ventricles   Postmortem studies of the brains of people with schizophrenia consistently reveal enlarged ventricles, which implies a loss of brain cells, although there are also contradictory findings. Findings from neuroimaging studies are even more impressive. Thus far, these studies have most consistently revealed that some people with schizophrenia, especially men (Nopoulos, Flaum, & Andreasen, 1997), have enlarged ventricles[1]. Further evidence concerning enlarged ventricles comes from two MRI studies of pairs of MZ twins only one of whom had schizophrenia (McNeil, Cantor-Graae, & Weinberger, 2000; Suddath et al., 1990). In both studies the ill twin had larger ventricles than the well twin, and in one of the studies most of the twins with schizophrenia could be identified by simple visual inspection of the scan. Because the twins were genetically identical in these studies, these results suggest that the origin of these brain abnormalities may not be genetic.

Large ventricles in people with schizophrenia are correlated with impaired performance on neuropsychological tests, poor adjustment prior to the onset of the disorder, and poor response to drug treatment (Andreasen et al., 1982; Weinberger et al., 1980). The extent to which the ventricles are enlarged, however, is modest, and many people with schizophrenia do not differ from people without schizophrenia in this respect. Furthermore, enlarged ventricles are not specific to schizophrenia, as they are also evident in the CT scans of people with other disorders, such as bipolar disorder with psychotic features (Rieder et al., 1983). People with these disorders can show ventricular enlargement almost as great as that seen in schizophrenia (Elkis et al., 1995)[2].

Factors Involving the Prefrontal Cortex   A variety of evidence suggests that the prefrontal cortex is of particular importance in schizophrenia.

- The prefrontal cortex is known to play a role in behaviors such as speech, decision making, and goal-directed behavior, which are disrupted in schizophrenia.
- MRI studies have shown reductions in gray matter in the prefrontal cortex (Buchanan, Vladar, et al., 1998).
- People with schizophrenia perform more poorly on neuropsychological tests designed to tap functions promoted by the prefrontal region, including working memory or the ability to hold bits of information in memory (Barch et al., 2002, 2003; Heinrichs & Zakzanis, 1998).
- In a type of functional imaging in which glucose metabolism is studied in various brain regions while people perform psychological tests, people with schizophrenia have shown low metabolic rates in the prefrontal cortex (Buchsbaum et al., 1984). Glucose metabolism in the prefrontal cortex has also been studied while people with schizophrenia are performing neuropsychological tests of prefrontal function. Because the tests place demands on the prefrontal cortex, glucose metabolism normally goes up as energy is used. People with schizophrenia, especially those with prominent negative symptoms, do poorly on the tests and also fail to show activation in the prefrontal region (Potkin et al., 2002; Weinberger, Berman, & Illowsky, 1988). Failure to show frontal activation has also been found using fMRI (Barch et al., 2001; MacDonald & Carter, 2003).
- Finally, failure to show frontal activation is related to the severity of negative symptoms (O'Donnell & Grace, 1998) and thus parallels the work on dopamine underactivity in the frontal cortex already discussed.

Despite the reduced volume of the gray matter in the prefrontal cortex (and also the temporal cortex), the number of neurons in this area does not appear to be reduced. More detailed studies indicate that what is lost may be what are called "dendritic spines" (Goldman-Rakic & Selemon, 1997; McGlashan & Hoffman, 2000). Dendritic spines are small projections on

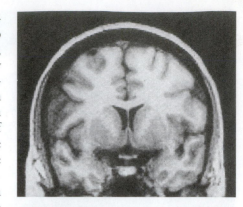

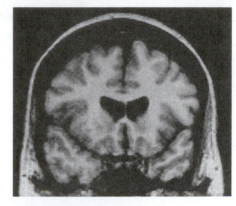

MRI of the brain of a woman with schizophrenia (bottom) and the brain of a woman without schizophrenia (top). Enlarged ventricles (the dark spaces at center of photos) are one of the best-validated biological features of schizophrenia. (Courtesy of J. Lieberman, American Journal of Psychiatry.)

---

[1]This difference between men and women with schizophrenia prompts us to mention that there are other gender differences as well. For example, men with schizophrenia have an earlier age of onset and are more likely to express negative symptoms and to have a more deteriorating course than are women with schizophrenia (Salem & Kring, 1998).

[2]Other findings also suggest that the schizophrenia and psychotic mood disorders should not perhaps be totally separate diagnostic categories. The disorders share some symptoms (notably, delusions) and some possible etiological factors (e.g., genetic factors, increased dopamine activity), and they respond similarly to medications. An important implication is that researchers would be well served to focus some of their efforts on psychotic symptoms in other disorders as well as in schizophrenia.

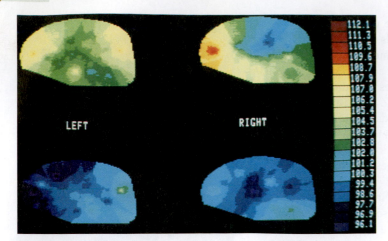

Differences in regional cerebral blood flow between people with schizophrenia (bottom) and people without schizophrenia (top) for each hemisphere. The values shown were scored as the percentage change in cerebral blood flow while performing a control task to the Wisconsin Card Sort that was expected to activate the prefrontal cortex. The participants without schizophrenia showed greater prefrontal cortical activation as indicated by the "hotter" color of this brain region. *Source:* Weinberger et al., 1988. (Courtesy of Daniel Weinberger, National Institute of Health.)

Figure 11.3 Micrograph of a neuron. The bumps on the dendrites are dendritic spines, which receive inputs from other neurons. Fewer dendritic spines may impair connections among neurons and may be a factor in schizophrenia. (BSIP/Sercomi/Photo Researchers, Inc.)

the shafts of dendrites where nerve impulses are received from other neurons (see Figure 11.3). The loss of these dendritic spines would mean that communication among neurons would be disrupted, resulting in what some have termed a "disconnection syndrome." One possible result of the failure of neural systems to communicate could be the speech and behavioral disorganization seen in schizophrenia.

Congenital and Developmental Factors   A possible cause of some of these brain abnormalities is damage during gestation or birth. Many studies have shown high rates of delivery complications in people with schizophrenia (Walker et al., 2004); such complications could have resulted in a reduced supply of oxygen to the brain, resulting in loss of cortical gray matter (Cannon et al., 2002). These obstetrical complications do not raise the rate of schizophrenia in everyone who experiences them; rather, the risk for schizophrenia is increased in those who experience complications and have a genetic diathesis (Cannon & Mednick, 1993).

Although the data are not entirely consistent (Westergaard et al., 1999), another possibility is that a virus invades the brain and damages it during fetal development (Mednick, Huttonen, & Machon, 1994; Mednick et al., 1988). During a 5-week period in 1957, Helsinki, Finland, experienced an epidemic of influenza virus. Researchers examined rates of schizophrenia among adults who had likely been exposed during their mothers' pregnancies. People who had been exposed to the virus during the second trimester of pregnancy had much higher rates than those who had been exposed in either of the other trimesters and much higher rates than in nonexposed control adults. This finding was intriguing because we know that the second trimester is a critical period for cortical development; however, only half of nearly 30 later studies were able to replicate this finding. And a more recent study found evidence that mothers' exposure to the flu during the *first* trimester of pregnancy, as directly measured by the presence of flu antibodies in the blood, was associated with a sevenfold increase in the risk for schizophrenia among their children (Brown et al., 2004). Though the increase in risk sounds large, the difference from the control group was not quite statistically different, suggesting that it will be important to replicate this finding.

Additional research suggests that other types of maternal infections during pregnancy are associated with greater risk of their children developing schizophrenia when they become adults (Brown, 2006). Specifically, one study found that maternal exposure to the parasite toxoplasma gondii was associated with a nearly 2.5 times greater risk of schizophrenia among the mothers' children when they became adults (A.S. Brown et al., 2005). This is a common parasite, and many people carry it with no ill effects.

If, as the findings we have just reviewed suggest, the development of the brains of people with schizophrenia goes awry very early, why does the disorder begin many years later, in adolescence or early adulthood? The prefrontal cortex is a brain structure that matures late, typically in adolescence or early adulthood. Thus a problem in this area, even one that begins early in the course of development, may not show itself in the person's behavior until the period of development when the prefrontal cortex begins to play a larger role in behavior (Weinberger, 1987). Notably, dopamine activity also peaks in adolescence, which may further set the stage for the onset of schizophrenia symptoms (Walker et al., 2008). Adolescence is also typically a developmental period that is fraught with stress. Recall from our discussions in Chapter 2 that stress activates the hypothalamic–pituitary–adrenal (HPA) axis (see p. 38), causing cortisol to be secreted. Research in the past 10 years has demonstrated that cortisol increases dopamine activity, particularly in the mesolimbic pathway, perhaps increasing the likelihood of the development of schizophrenia symptoms (Walker et al., 2008).

Another proposed explanation is that the development of symptoms in adolescence could reflect a loss of synapses due to excessive pruning, the elimination of synaptic connections. Pruning is a normal part of brain development that occurs at different rates in different areas of the brain. It is mostly complete in sensory areas by about 2 years of age but continues in the prefrontal cortex until mid-adolescence. If too extensive, pruning would result in the loss of necessary communication among neurons (McGlashan & Hoffman, 2000).

Current Research   Further work on the relationship of schizophrenia to brain structure and function is proceeding at a rapid rate. Recognizing that the symptoms of schizophrenia implicate many areas of the brain, researchers have moved away from trying to find a highly specific "lesion" and are beginning to examine neural systems and the ways in which different areas of the brain interact. This work is beginning to call attention to the possible roles of a wider range of brain structures, such as the thalamus and the cerebellum, in schizophrenia (Byne et al., 2002; Gilbert et al., 2001). Research also shows a reduction in cortical gray matter in both the temporal and frontal regions (Gur et al., 2000) and reduced volume in basal ganglia (e.g., the caudate nucleus), hippocampus, and limbic structures (Chua & McKenna, 1995; Gur & Pearlson, 1993; Keshavan et al., 1998; Lim et al., 1998; Nelson et al., 1998; Velakoulis et al., 1999; Walker et al., 2008). A twin study found reduced hippocampus volume among twins with schizophrenia, but not among the twins without schizophrenia (van Erp et al., 2004). A meta-analysis of MRI studies conducted with people during their first episode of schizophrenia concluded that the volume of the hippocampus was significantly reduced compared to people without schizophrenia (Steen et al., 2006).

What makes these findings about the hippocampus all the more intriguing is the fact that the HPA axis is closely connected to this area of the brain. Chronic stress is associated with reductions in hippocampal volume in other disorders, such as PTSD. Although people with schizophrenia do not necessarily experience more stress compared to people without schizophrenia, they are more reactive to stress. Other evidence indicates that the HPA axis is disrupted in schizophrenia. Taken together, stress reactivity and a disrupted HPA axis likely contribute to the reductions in hippocampal volume observed in people with schizophrenia (Walker et al., 2008). An additional interesting piece of evidence regarding the hippocampus comes from a meta-analysis of 9 studies assessing brain volume of over 400 first-degree relatives of people with schizophrenia and over 600 first-degree relatives of people without schizophrenia (Boos et al., 2007). Relatives of people with schizophrenia had smaller hippocampal volumes than relatives of people without schizophrenia. These findings suggest that reduced hippocampal volume in people with schizophrenia may reflect a combination of genetic and environmental factors.

Psychological Stress

We have discussed several possible neurobiological diatheses for schizophrenia, but more than a diathesis is required to produce schizophrenia. Psychological stress plays a role by interacting with a genetic or neurobiological vulnerability to produce this illness. Research shows that, as with many of the disorders we have discussed, increases in life stress increase the likelihood of a relapse (Ventura et al., 1989; Walker et al., 2008). People with schizophrenia do not appear to experience more stress in daily life than people without schizophrenia (Phillips et al., 2007; Walker, Mittal, & Tessner, 2008). However, people with schizophrenia appear to be very reactive to the stressors we all encounter in daily living. In one study, people with psychotic disorders (92 percent with schizophrenia), their first-degree relatives, and people without any psychiatric disorder participated in a 6-day ecological momentary assessment study in which they recorded stress and mood several times each day. Stress led to greater decreases in positive moods in both people with schizophrenia and their relatives compared with controls. Stress also led to greater increases in negative moods in the people with schizophrenia compared with both relatives and controls (Myin-Gremeys et al., 2001). Thus, people with schizophrenia were particularly vulnerable to daily stress.

Additional research on the role of life stress in the development and relapse of schizophrenia has focused on socioeconomic status and the family.

Socioeconomic Status   For many years we have known that the highest rates of schizophrenia are found in urban areas inhabited by people of the lowest socioeconomic status (SES) in several countries, including the United States, Denmark, Norway, and the United Kingdom (Hollingshead & Redlich, 1958; Kohn, 1968). The relationship between SES and schizophrenia is not such that the prevalence of schizophrenia goes up as SES goes down. Rather, there is a sharp upturn in the prevalence of schizophrenia in people of the lowest socioeconomic status.

The correlation between SES and schizophrenia is consistent but difficult to interpret in causal terms. Some people believe that stressors associated with SES may cause or contribute to the development of schizophrenia—the **sociogenic hypothesis**. Degrading treatment by others of higher status, low levels of education, and lack of rewards and opportunities may, taken together, make very low SES so stressful that people who are predisposed to develop schizophrenia readily develop the disorder. Alternatively, these stressors could have neurobiological effects; for example, children of mothers whose nutrition during pregnancy was poor are at increased risk for schizophrenia (Susser et al., 1996).

Another explanation of the correlation between schizophrenia and low SES is the **social selection theory**, which reverses the direction of causality. The theory proposes that during the course of their developing illness, people with schizophrenia may drift into poor neighborhoods because their illness impairs their earning power and they cannot afford to live elsewhere.

A study in Israel evaluated the two theories by investigating both SES and ethnic background (Dohrenwend et al., 1992). The rates of schizophrenia were examined in Israeli Jews of European ethnic background and in more recent immigrants to Israel from North Africa and the Middle East. The latter group experienced considerable racial prejudice and discrimination in Israel. The sociogenic hypothesis would predict that because they experienced high levels of stress regardless of socioeconomic status, the members of the disadvantaged ethnic group should have consistently higher rates of schizophrenia regardless of status. However, this pattern did not emerge, supporting the social selection theory.

In sum, research results are more supportive of the social selection theory than of the sociogenic hypothesis. But we should not conclude that the social environment plays no role in schizophrenia. For example, the prevalence of schizophrenia among Africans from the Caribbean who remain in their native country is much lower than among those who have emigrated to London (Hutchinson et al., 1996). This difference could well be caused by the stress associated with trying to assimilate into a new culture.

Family-Related Factors   Early theorists regarded family relationships, especially those between a mother and her son, as crucial in the development of schizophrenia. At one time the view was so prevalent that the term "*schizophrenogenic mother*" was coined for the supposedly cold and dominant, conflict-inducing parent who was said to produce schizophrenia in her offspring (Fromm-Reichmann, 1948). These mothers were characterized as rejecting, overprotective, self-sacrificing, impervious to the feelings of others, rigid and moralistic about sex, and fearful of intimacy. Controlled studies evaluating the schizophrenogenic-mother theory have not supported it. The damage done to families by this theory, however, was significant. For generations, parents blamed themselves for their child's illness, and until the 1970s, psychiatrists often joined in this blame game.

How Do Families Influence Schizophrenia?   Other studies continued to explore the possibility that the family plays some role in the etiology of schizophrenia. For the most part, the findings are only suggestive, not conclusive. For example, a few studies of families of people with schizophrenia have found that they communicate more vaguely with one another and have higher levels of conflict than families of people without schizophrenia. It is plausible, though, that the conflict and unclear communication are a response to having a young family member with schizophrenia.

Some other findings suggest that faulty communications by parents may play a role in the etiology of schizophrenia. One type of communication pattern studied is called *communication deviance (CD)*, which is characterized by hostility and poor communication. In a longitudinal study of adolescents with behavior problems, CD in the families was found to predict the later onset of schizophrenia (Norton, 1982). However, not all people who develop schizophrenia exhibit behavior problems as adolescents. Furthermore, it does not appear that CD is specifically associated with schizophrenia, since parents of people with bipolar disorder are equally likely to show CD (Miklowitz, 1985).

Further evidence favoring some role for the family comes from the Finnish adoption study described above (Tienari et al., 2000). Various aspects of family life in the adoptive families were extensively studied and then related to the adjustment of the children (Tienari et al., 1994). The families were categorized into levels of maladjustment based on material from clinical interviews and psychological tests. More serious psychopathology was found among the adoptees reared in a disturbed family environment. Furthermore, among children reared in a disturbed family environment, those having a biological parent with schizophrenia showed more psychopathology than did the control participants. Although it is tempting to conclude that both a genetic predisposition and a noxious family environment are necessary to increase risk for psychopathology, a problem in interpretation remains: the disturbed family environment could be a response to a disturbed child. Thus we cannot firmly conclude that an etiological role for the family has been established.

Families and Relapse   A series of studies initiated in London indicate that the family can have an important impact on the adjustment of patients after they leave the hospital. In one study, investigators conducted a 9-month follow-up study of a sample of people with schizophrenia who returned to live with their families after being discharged from the hospital (Brown et al., 1966). Interviews were conducted with parents or spouses before discharge and rated for the number of critical comments made about the patient and for expressions of hostility toward or emotional overinvolvement with the patient. The following is an example of a critical comment made by a father remarking on his daughter's behavior, in which he is expressing the idea that his daughter is deliberately symptomatic to avoid housework: "My view is that Maria acts this way so my wife doesn't give her any responsibilities around the house" (quoted in Weisman et al., 1998). On the basis of this variable, called **expressed emotion (EE)**, families were divided into two groups: those revealing a great deal of expressed emotion (high-EE families) and those revealing little (low-EE families). At the end of the follow-up period, only 10 percent of the patients returning to low-EE homes had relapsed, but 58 percent of the patients returning to high-EE homes had gone back to the hospital.

This research, which has since been replicated (see Butzlaff & Hooley, 1998, for a meta-analysis), indicates that the environment to which people with schizophrenia are discharged has great bearing on how soon they are rehospitalized. Researchers have also found that negative symptoms of schizophrenia are most likely to elicit critical comments, as in the example presented in the previous paragraph, and that the relatives who make the most critical comments are the most likely to view people with schizophrenia as being able to control their symptoms (Lopez et al., 1999; Weisman et al., 1998).

What is not yet clear is exactly how to interpret the effects of EE. Is EE causal, or does it reflect a reaction to the ill relative's behavior? For example, if the condition of a patient with schizophrenia begins to deteriorate, family concern and involvement may increase. Indeed, disorganized or dangerous behavior by the patient might seem to warrant limit setting and other familial efforts that could increase the level of EE. Research indicates that both interpretations of the operation of EE may be correct. Recently discharged people with schizophrenia and their high- or low-EE families were observed as they engaged in a discussion of a family problem. Two key findings emerged (Rosenfarb et al., 1994).

1. The expression of unusual thoughts by the people with schizophrenia ("If that kid bites you, you'll get rabies") elicited a greater number of critical comments by family members who had previously been characterized as high in EE than by those characterized as low in EE.

2. In high-EE families, critical comments by family members led to increased expression of unusual thoughts by the people with schizophrenia.

Thus, this study found a bidirectional relationship in high-EE families: critical comments by family members elicited more unusual thoughts by relatives with schizophrenia, and unusual thoughts expressed by the relatives with schizophrenia led to increased critical comments.

Expressed emotion, which includes hostility, critical comments, and emotional overinvolvement, has been linked with relapse in schizophrenia. (Lisette Le Bon/SUPERSTOCK.)

How does stress, such as a high level of EE, increase the symptoms of schizophrenia and precipitate relapses? One answer to this question relates the effects of stress on the HPA axis and its link to dopamine (Walker et al., 2008). Stress activates the HPA axis, causing cortisol to be secreted, which can then increase dopamine activity (Walker et al., 2008). Furthermore, heightened dopamine activity itself can increase HPA activation, which may make a person overly sensitive to stress. Thus, there is a bidirectional relationship between HPA activation and dopamine activity.

Developmental Studies

What are people who develop schizophrenia like before their symptoms begin? An early method of answering this question was to construct developmental histories by examining the childhood records of those who had later developed schizophrenia. In the 1960s, researchers found that children who later developed schizophrenia had lower IQs and were more often delinquent and withdrawn than members of various control groups, usually comprising siblings and neighborhood peers (Albee, Lane, & Reuter, 1964; Lane & Albee, 1965; Berry, 1967). Other studies found that boys who later developed schizophrenia were rated by teachers as disagreeable, whereas girls who later developed schizophrenia were rated as passive (Watt, 1974; Watt et al., 1970).

More recently, researchers have examined home movies before the onset of schizophrenia, made as part of normal family life (Walker, Davis, & Savoie, 1994; Walker et al., 1993). Compared with their siblings who did not later develop schizophrenia, the children who later developed schizophrenia as young adults showed poorer motor skills and more expressions of negative emotions.

As intriguing as these findings are, the major limitation of such developmental research is that the data were not originally collected with the intention of predicting the development of schizophrenia from childhood behavior. More specific information is required if developmental histories are to provide clear evidence regarding etiology.

The high-risk method can yield this information. The first such study of schizophrenia was begun in the 1960s (Mednick & Schulsinger, 1968). The researchers chose Denmark because Danish registries make it possible to keep track of people for long periods of time. The high-risk participants were 207 young people whose mothers had schizophrenia (The researchers decided that the mother should be the parent with the disorder because paternity is not always easy to determine.) Then, 104 low-risk participants, people whose mothers did not have schizophrenia, were matched to the high-risk subjects on variables such as sex, age, father's occupation, rural or urban residence, years of education, and institutional upbringing versus rearing by the family. In 1972 the now-grown men and women were followed up with a number of measures, including a battery of diagnostic tests. Fifteen of the high-risk participants were diagnosed with schizophrenia; none of the control participants was so diagnosed.

Additional analyses of the group of participants who were diagnosed with schizophrenia suggested that positive and negative symptoms of schizophrenia may have different etiologies (Cannon, Mednick, & Parnas, 1990). People with predominantly negative symptoms had a history of pregnancy and birth complications and a failure to show electrodermal responses to simple stimuli. By contrast, people with predominantly positive symptoms had a history of family instability, such as separation from parents and placement in foster homes or institutions for periods of time.

In the wake of this pioneering study, other high-risk investigations were undertaken, some of which have also yielded information concerning the possible causes of adult psychopathology, but not necessarily schizophrenia specifically. The New York High-Risk Study found that a composite measure of attentional dysfunction predicted behavioral disturbance at follow-up (Cornblatt & Erlenmeyer-Kimling, 1985). Furthermore, low IQ was a characteristic of the first high-risk children to be hospitalized (Erlenmeyer-Kimling & Cornblatt, 1987). In an Israeli study, poor neurobehavioral functioning (poor concentration, poor verbal ability, lack of motor control and coordination) predicted schizophrenia-like outcomes, as did earlier interpersonal problems (Marcus et al., 1987).

One of the difficulties with these types of high-risk studies has to do with the large sample sizes that are required. As shown in Table 11.3, the percentage of children with a biological parent who has schizophrenia who go on to themselves develop schizophrenia is around 10 percent. If a study begins with 200 high-risk children, only about 20 of them may go on to develop schizophrenia. In addition, is not particularly easy to locate a large sample of women or men with schizophrenia who have had their own children.

Because of these difficulties, other high-risk research designs have been used in more recent research. One such study has been ongoing in Australia for the past several years, following people between the ages of 14 and 30 who were referred to a mental health clinic in the mid-1990s (Yung et al., 1995). None of the participants had schizophrenia when they entered the study, but many later exhibited varying degrees of schizophrenia symptoms and some, but not all, had a biological relative with a psychotic disorder. These participants were deemed to be at "ultra-high risk" of developing schizophrenia or psychotic disorders. Since the study began, 41 of the original 104 participants have developed some type of psychotic disorder (Yung et al., 2004). An MRI study of 75 of the 104 participants found that those people who later developed a psychotic disorder had lower gray matter volumes than those who had not developed a psychotic disorder (Pantelis et al., 2003). Recall that reduced gray matter volume has been found in people with schizophrenia; this study suggests that this characteristic may predate the onset of schizophrenia and other psychotic disorders.

A similar study is ongoing in the United States and Canada, called the North American Prodrome Longitudinal Study (NAPLS). Prodrome refers to the period before a person meets diagnostic criteria for schizophrenia but nonetheless shows some symptoms. In this study, 82 of the 291 ultra-high risk participants had developed schizophrenia or some type of psychotic disorder (Cannon et al., 2008). The researchers identified a number of factors that predicted a greater likelihood of developing a psychotic disorder, including having a biological relative with schizophrenia, a recent decline in functioning, high levels of positive symptoms, and high levels of social impairment. It will be important in future studies to see if these factors can prospectively predict the onset of schizophrenia.

Sarnoff Mednick, a psychologist at the University of Southern California, pioneered the use of the high-risk method for studying schizophrenia. He has also contributed to the hypothesis that a maternal viral infection is implicated in this disorder. (Sarnoff Mednick.)

Quick Summary

Given its complexity, a number of causal factors are likely to contribute to schizophrenia. The genetic evidence is strong, with much of the evidence coming from family, twin, and adoption studies. Learning what is inherited remains a challenge for molecular genetics studies. Linkage studies have found linkage on several chromosomes, but these studies need to be replicated. Promising genes from association studies include DTNBP1, NGR1, and COMT, but replication is also needed here.

Neurotransmitters play a role in schizophrenia. For years, dopamine was the focus of study, but later findings led investigators to conclude that this one neurotransmitter could not fully account for schizophrenia. Other neurotransmitters are also the focus of study, such as serotonin, GABA, and glutamate. A number of different brain areas have been implicated in schizophrenia. One of the most widely replicated findings is of enlarged ventricles. Other research supports the role of the prefrontal cortex, particularly reduced activation of this area, in schizophrenia.

Research has examined the role of socioeconomic status in schizophrenia, and generally this work supports the social selection theory more than the sociogenic hypothesis. Early theories blamed families, particularly mothers, for causing schizophrenia, but research does not support this view. Communication in families is important and could perhaps constitute the stress in the diathesis–stress theory for schizophrenia. Expressed emotion has also been found to predict relapse in schizophrenia.

Early developmental studies looked back at the childhood records of adults with schizophrenia and found that some adults with schizophrenia had lower IQs and were withdrawn and delinquent as children. Other studies found that adults who later developed schizophrenia expressed a lot of negative emotion and had poor motor skills. The problem with these studies is that the studies were not designed to predict the onset of schizophrenia. High-risk designs deal with this problem, and these studies have found that children at risk for adult psychopathology have difficulties with attention and motor control, among other things.

Check Your Knowledge 11.2

Fill in the blanks.
1. _____ studies do not do such a good job of teasing out genetic and environmental effects: _____ studies do a better job.
2. _____ and _____ are two genes that have recently been associated with schizophrenia.
3. Some studies showing the _____ area of the brain to be disrupted in schizophrenia also show that people with schizophrenia do poorly on tasks that rely on this area, such as planning and problem solving.
4. _____, _____, and _____ are the three components of expressed emotion.

Treatment of Schizophrenia

Treatments for schizophrenia most often include a combination of short-term hospital stays (during the acute phases of the illness), medication, and psychosocial treatment. A problem with any kind of treatment for schizophrenia is that some people with schizophrenia lack insight into their impaired condition and refuse any treatment at all (Amador et al., 1994). Results from one study suggest that gender (female) and age (older) are predictors of better insight among people in their first episode of the illness (McEvoy et al., 2006), and this may help account for why women with schizophrenia tend to respond better to treatment (Salem & Kring, 1998). For those who lack insight and thus don't believe they have an illness, they don't see the need for professional help, particularly when it includes hospitalization or drugs. This may be especially true for those with paranoid schizophrenia, who may regard treatment as a threat from hostile outside forces. Family members therefore face a major challenge in getting their relatives into treatment, which is one reason they sometimes turn to involuntary hospitalization via civil commitment.

Before we examine the range of treatments for schizophrenia, it is important to point out that the appropriateness of a given treatment depends on the stage of illness that the patient is in. That is, when a patient is in an acutely psychotic phase of the illness, psychological interventions are not likely to be successful because the patient is too distracted, unable to concentrate on what the therapist is saying. In such a phase some sort of medication is likely necessary, and perhaps a short hospital stay. Once the person becomes less psychotic, a psychological intervention can begin to have a beneficial impact, and the dosage of the medication can be reduced as the person learns ways to reduce the stress that may have precipitated the episode (Kopelowicz, Liberman, & Zarate, 2002).

Medications

One of the most important developments in the treatment of schizophrenia was the advent in the 1950s of several medications collectively referred to as **antipsychotic drugs**, also referred to as *neuroleptics* because they produce side effects similar to the symptoms of a neurological disease. Focus on Discovery 11.2 presents a brief history of the development of these drugs.

First-Generation Antipsychotic Drugs and Their Side Effects
The discovery of the phenothiazines, including the drug Thorazine, in the 1950s led to a complete change in the treatment of schizophrenia. Just 20 years after their discovery, these drugs were the primary form of treatment for schizophrenia. Other antipsychotics that have been used for years to treat schizophrenia include the butyrophenones (e.g., haloperidol, trade name Haldol) and the thioxanthenes (e.g., thiothixene, trade name Navane). Both types seem generally as effective as the phenothiazines and work in similar ways. These classes of drugs can reduce the positive and disorganized symptoms of schizophrenia but have little or no effect on the negative symptoms, perhaps because their primary mechanism of action involves blocking dopamine D2 receptors. Recall from our discussion earlier that the dopamine theory helps account for positive symptoms, but not negative symptoms. Despite their effectiveness at reducing some of the symptoms of schizophrenia

FOCUS ON DISCOVERY 11.2

Stumbling Toward a Cure: The Development of Antipsychotic Medications

One of the more frequently prescribed antipsychotic drugs, phenothiazine, was first produced by a German chemist in the late nineteenth century. But it was not until the discovery of the antihistamines, which have a phenothiazine nucleus, in the 1940s, that phenothiazines received much attention.

Reaching beyond their use to treat the common cold and asthma, the French surgeon Henri Laborit pioneered the use of antihistamines to reduce surgical shock. He noticed that they made his patients somewhat sleepy and less fearful about the impending operation. Laborit's work encouraged pharmaceutical companies to reexamine antihistamines in light of their tranquilizing effects. Shortly thereafter the French chemist Paul Charpentier prepared a new phenothiazine derivative, which he called chlorpromazine. This drug proved very effective in calming people with schizophrenia. Phenothiazines derive their therapeutic properties by blocking dopamine receptors in the brain, thus reducing the influence of dopamine on thought, emotion, and behavior.

Chlorpromazine (trade name Thorazine) was first used therapeutically in the United States in 1954 and rapidly became the preferred treatment for schizophrenia. By 1970, more than 85 percent of all patients in state mental hospitals were receiving chlorpromazine or another phenothiazine.

and allowing many patients to be released from the hospital, these so-called first-generation antipsychotics are not a cure. They are referred to as first-generation antipsychotics because they came out of the first "wave" of significant research discoveries of effective medication treatments for schizophrenia. The second wave produced a group of drugs referred to as second-generation antipsychotics, a class of drugs we will discuss in more detail later. About 30 percent of people with schizophrenia do not respond favorably to the first-generation antipsychotics, and about half the people who take any antipsychotic drug quit after 1 year and up to three-quarters quit before 2 years because the side effects are so unpleasant (Harvard Mental Health Letter, 1995; Lieberman et al. 2005).

People who respond positively to the antipsychotics are kept on so-called maintenance doses of the drug, just enough to continue the therapeutic effect. Some people who are maintained on medication may make only marginal adjustment to the community, however. For example, they may be unable to live unsupervised or to hold down the kind of job for which they would otherwise be qualified, and their social relationships may be sparse. And again, although the first-generation antipsychotics keep positive and disorganized symptoms from returning, they tend to have little effect on negative symptoms, such as flat affect. The first-generation antipsychotics significantly reduced long-term hospitalization, but they have also initiated the revolving-door pattern of admission, discharge, and readmission seen in some people with schizophrenia.

Commonly reported side effects of the antipsychotics include sedation, dizziness, blurred vision, restlessness, and sexual dysfunction. In addition, some particularly disturbing side effects, termed *extrapyramidal side effects*, resemble the symptoms of Parkinson's disease. People taking antipsychotics may develop tremors of the fingers, a shuffling gait, and drooling. Other side effects include dystonia, a state of muscular rigidity, and dyskinesia, an abnormal motion of voluntary and involuntary muscles, producing chewing movements as well as other movements of the lips, fingers, and legs; together they cause arching of the back and a twisted posture of the neck and body. Another side effect is akasthesia, an inability to remain still; people pace constantly and fidget. These perturbing symptoms can be treated by drugs used with people who have Parkinson's disease.

In a rare muscular disturbance called *tardive dyskinesia*, the mouth muscles involuntarily make sucking, lip-smacking, and chin-wagging motions. In more severe cases, the whole body can be subject to involuntary motor movements. This syndrome is observed mainly in older people with schizophrenia who had been treated with first-generation medications before drugs were developed to prevent tardive dyskinesia from developing. It affects about 10 to 20 percent of these older people treated with first-generation antipsychotics for a long period of time and is not responsive to any known treatment (Sweet et al., 1995). Finally, a side effect called *neuroleptic malignant syndrome* occurs in about 1 percent of cases. In this condition, which can sometimes be fatal, severe muscular rigidity develops, accompanied by fever. The heart races, blood pressure increases, and the patient may lapse into a coma.

Because of these serious side effects, some clinicians believe it is unwise to prescribe high doses of first-generation antipsychotics for extended periods of time. Current clinical practice guidelines from the American Psychiatric Association call for treating people with the smallest possible doses of drugs (APA, 2004). The clinician is put in a bind by this situation: if medication is reduced, the chance of relapse increases; but if medication is continued, serious and untreatable side effects may develop.

Second-Generation Antipsychotic Drugs and Their Side Effects   In the decades following the introduction of the first-generation antipsychotic drugs, there appeared to be little interest in developing new drugs to treat schizophrenia. This situation changed about 20 years ago, with the introduction of clozapine (trade name Clozaril) in the United States. Early studies of this drug suggested it could produce therapeutic gains in people with schizophrenia who did not respond well to first-generation antipsychotics (Kane et al., 1988). Additional studies suggested that clozapine has greater therapeutic gains in reducing positive and disorganization symptoms (Rosenheck et al., 1999; Wahlbeck et al., 1999), is associated with less treatment dropout (Kane et al., 2001), reduces relapse (Conley et al., 1999), and produces fewer motor side effects than the first-generation antipsychotics. Although the precise mechanism of the therapeutic effects of clozapine is not yet completely understood, we do know that it has a major impact on serotonin receptors.

However, researchers and clinicians soon learned that clozapine has its own set of serious side effects. It can impair the functioning of the immune system in a small percentage of people (about 1 percent) by lowering the number of white blood cells, a condition called agranulocytosis, which makes people vulnerable to infection and even death. For this reason, people taking clozapine have to be carefully monitored with routine blood tests. It also can produce seizures and other side effects, such as dizziness, fatigue, drooling, and weight gain (Meltzer, Cola, & Way, 1993).

Nevertheless, the apparent success of clozapine stimulated drug companies to begin a more earnest search for other drugs that might be more effective than first-generation antipsychotics. These drugs, including clozapine, are referred to as the **second-generation antipsychotic drugs** because their mechanism of action is not like that of the typical or first-generation antipsychotic medications. Two second-generation antipsychotics developed after clozapine are olanzapine (trade name Zyprexa) and risperidone (trade name Risperdal). Early studies showed that olanzapine and risperidone produced fewer of the side effects that first-generation antipsychotics produce, suggesting people were somewhat less likely to discontinue treatment (Dolder et al., 2002), but later studies have not always replicated this (Lieberman, 2006). The second-generation antipsychotics appear to be equally as effective as first-generation antipsychotics in reducing positive and disorganized symptoms (Conley & Mahmoud, 2001), particularly for people who have not responded to at least two other medications (Lewis et al., 2006), and some studies suggest that they are superior to the first-generation antipsychotics in reducing rehospitalization rates and relapse and in reducing negative symptoms (Csernansky, Mahmoud, & Brenner, 2002; Leucht et al., 2003). A meta-analysis of 124 studies comparing first- and second-generation antipsychotic drugs found that some, but not all, second-generation drugs were modestly more effective than the first-generation drugs in reducing negative symptoms and improving cognitive deficits (Davis, Chen, & Glick, 2003).

However, the news is not all good. A comprehensive randomized controlled clinical trial compared four second-generation drugs (olanzapine, risperidone, ziprasidone, and quetiapine) and one first-generation drug (perphenazine) against one another (Lieberman et al., 2005). Close to 1,500 people from all over the United States were in the study. What set this study apart from others included in the meta-analysis mentioned above was that it was not sponsored by one of the drug companies that makes the drugs (see p. 224 in Chapter 8 for a discussion of publication bias). Among the many findings from this study, three stand out. First, the second-generation drugs were not more effective than the older, first-generation drug. Second, the second-generation drugs did not produce fewer unpleasant side effects. And third, nearly three-quarters of the people stopped taking the medications before the 18 months of the study design had ended. Similar results have been found in another large study (Jones et al., 2006). Despite the early promise of second-generation drugs, more work is needed to develop better treatments for schizophrenia.

In addition, other studies suggest that second-generation antipsychotics may have serious side effects of their own (Freedman, 2003). For example, clozapine and olanzapine have been related to the development of type 2 diabetes (Leslie & Rosenheck, 2004); however, it is not clear whether the medicine itself increases this risk, perhaps via the side effect of weight gain, or whether people taking the medications were predisposed to developing diabetes independent of their medication usage. Other evidence suggests that these drugs may increase the risk for pancreatitis (Koller et al., 2003). In 2005, the drug company that produces olanzapine, Eli Lilly, agreed to settle a series of lawsuits, paying out over $700 million to patients taking the drug. The company was sued for failing to adequately warn patients of these serious side effects. The drug's label now contains warnings about possible side effects, including weight gain, elevated blood sugar, and elevated cholesterol levels.

Another disturbing aspect of the second-generation antipsychotic medications is that they tend not to be used among people of color. Two different studies recently found that African Americans were more likely to be prescribed the first-generation antipsychotics and less likely to be prescribed the second-generation antipsychotics (Kreyenbuhl et al., 2003; Valenti, Narendran, & Pristach, 2003). This is unfortunate for a number of reasons, but particularly since there is some evidence that African Americans may experience more side effects than whites in response to the first-generation medications (Frackeiwicz et al., 1997). More broadly, these results echo the findings of the Surgeon General's supplement to his landmark report on mental health in 2001 that elucidated a number of disparities in mental health treatment among members of ethnic minority groups (USD-HHS, 2001a). Compared with other disorders reviewed in this book, there has been relatively less research on schizophrenia across different ethnic groups. This must be a focus of future research.

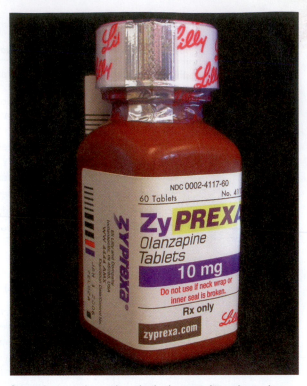

Second-generation antipsychotic drugs such as olanzapine may have fewer side effects than first-generation antipsychotic drugs, but they still have side effects. (Copyright Eli Lilly and Company. All Rights Reserved. Used with permission.)

A psychological approach to the study of the second-generation antipsychotics examines fundamental aspects of cognition, such as attention and memory, that are known to be deficient in many people with schizophrenia (Heinrichs & Zakzanis, 1998) and are associated with poor social adaptation (Green, 1996). A number of studies suggest that these medications may be more effective than the first-generation drugs at improving cognitive functioning (P. D. Harvey, et al., 2003, 2004; Keefe et al., 2007). For example, evidence suggests that risperidone improves short-term memory—involved in, for example, remembering an email address long enough to be able to type it—more than other antipsychotic drugs, apparently by reducing the activity of serotonin-sensitive receptors in the frontal cortex (Green et al., 1997). Research has also shown that improvements in memory are correlated with improvements in learning social skills in psychosocial rehabilitation programs (Green, 1996; Marder et al., 1999). More generally, the second-generation antipsychotics may thus make possible more thoroughgoing changes in schizophrenia and its behavioral consequences than do drugs that do not have these cognitive effects. However, other evidence suggests that psychological treatments (reviewed below) are also effective, perhaps more so, at alleviating cognitive deficits.

Development of New Drugs   Some people with schizophrenia do not respond to any of the available medications, suggesting the need for new medications to be developed. One exciting approach in this area was the MATRICS project. MATRICS (Measurement and Treatment Research to Improve Cognition in Schizophrenia) was a collaborative effort among psychologists, psychiatrists, pharmaceutical companies, the FDA, and the National Institute of Mental Health. One goal of this project was to develop a consensus battery of cognitive and neuropsychological tests that can be used to evaluate and compare the efficacy of medications to treat schizophrenia (Green et al., 2004). To achieve this goal, several systematic and transparent steps were followed, which included deciding on the most important cognitive domains to be studied, finding the best and most practical ways to measure these domains, and determining the extent to which improving performance in those domains is related to a better outcome in schizophrenia. Results from each step were made available to the public via a website (www.matrics.ucla.edu).

Table 11.5 Summary of Major Drugs Used in Treating Schizophrenia

Drug Category	Generic Name	Trade Name
First-Generation Drugs	Chlorpromazine	Thorazine
	Fluphenazine decanoate	Prolixin
	Haloperidol	Haldol
	Thiothixene	Navane
	Trifluoperazine	Stelazine
Second-Generation Drugs	Clozapine	Clozaril
	Aripiprazole	Ablify
	Olanzapine	Zyprexa
	Risperidone	Risperdal
	Ziprasidone	Geodon
	Quetiapine	Seroquel

Evaluation of Drug Treatments   Antipsychotic drugs are an indispensable part of treatment for schizophrenia and will undoubtedly continue to be an important component. Furthermore, the limited success of clozapine, olanzapine, and risperidone has stimulated a continued effort to find new and more effective drug therapies for schizophrenia. Many other drugs are currently being evaluated, so we may be on the verge of a new era in the treatment of schizophrenia. See Table 11.5 for a summary of major drugs used to treat schizophrenia.

Psychological Treatments

Our growing knowledge about neurobiological factors in schizophrenia and the continuing improvement in antipsychotic medications should not lead us to neglect the importance of psychosocial factors in both the etiology and treatment of schizophrenia. This is made clear in the following excerpt from a review of empirically supported psychological treatments for schizophrenia:

> For veteran practitioners who have long considered only biological treatments as effective in protecting schizophrenic individuals from stress-induced relapse and disability . . . evidence [on reducing expressed emotion in families, reviewed later] that supports the protective value of psychosocial treatments . . . may serve as an antidote to the insidious biological reductionism that often characterizes the field of schizophrenia research and treatment. . . . It is essential to view treatments of schizophrenia in their biopsychosocial matrix—leaving out any of the three components . . . will diminish the impact and efficacy of treatment. (Kopelowicz & Liberman, 1998, p. 192)

Neglecting the psychological and social aspect of schizophrenia compromises efforts to help people and their families who are struggling with this illness. Indeed, the current treatment recommendations for schizophrenia as compiled by the schizophrenia Patient Outcomes Research Team (PORT) are medications plus psychosocial interventions (Lehman et al., 2004). The PORT recommendations are based on extensive reviews of treatment research. In addition, review of 37 prospective studies of people after their first episode of schizophrenia found that the combination of medication and psychosocial treatment predicted the best outcome (Menezes, Arenovich, & Zipursky, 2006).

For example, a promising procedure for reducing rehospitalization rates involves both medication and psychosocial treatment. In one study, people with schizophrenia were randomly assigned to maintenance treatment as usual (medication and supportive group therapy) or a new treatment involving the following components (Herz et al., 2000):

1. Educating people with schizophrenia about relapse and recognizing early signs of relapse
2. Monitoring early signs of relapse by staff
3. Weekly supportive group or individual therapy
4. Family educational sessions
5. Quick intervention, involving both increased doses of medication and crisis-oriented problem-solving therapy, when early signs of relapse were detected

Importantly, staff were able to accurately recognize early signs of relapse and implement procedures to deal with them. Over 18 months, the new treatment cut relapse rates in half and reduced rehospitalization rates by about 44 percent. Other psychosocial treatments have been developed for schizophrenia, some with more success than others. We turn to these next.

Psychoanalytic Therapy   Freud did little, either in his clinical practice or through his writings, to adapt psychoanalysis to the treatment of people with schizophrenia. He believed that they were incapable of establishing the close interpersonal relationship essential for analysis. Later analysts, such as Harry Stack Sullivan and Frieda Fromm-Reichmann, promoted the use

FOCUS ON DISCOVERY 11.3

Living with Schizophrenia

A heartening example of one woman's struggles with and triumphs over schizophrenia is found in the 2007 book entitled *The Center Cannot Hold: My Journey Through Madness*. This book was written by Elyn Saks, an endowed professor of law at the University of Southern California who also happens to have schizophrenia. In the book, she describes her lifelong experience with this illness. Prior to the publication of the book, only a few of Professor Saks' close friends even knew that she had schizophrenia. Why did she keep it a secret? Certainly stigma is part of the reason. As we have discussed throughout this book, stigma toward people with mental illness is very much alive in the 21st century, and stigma can have seriously negative consequences for people with illnesses like schizophrenia.

What makes Professor Saks' life story particularly encouraging is that she has achieved exceptional professional and personal success in her life despite having such a serious mental illness. She grew up in a loving and supportive family, earned a bachelor's degree from Vanderbilt University, graduating as her class valedictorian, earned a prestigious Marshall fellowship to study philosophy at Oxford in the United Kingdom, graduated from Yale Law School as editor of the prestigious *Yale Law Review*, and is a tenured professor of law at a major university. How did she do it?

She believes that a combination of treatments, including psychoanalysis and medications, social support from family and friends, hard work, and acknowledging that she has a serious illness have all helped her cope with schizophrenia and its sometimes unpredictable and frightening symptoms. Although psychoanalysis does not have a good deal of empirical support for its efficacy with schizophrenia, it was and remains a central part of Professor Saks' treatment regimen. This illustrates nicely the fact that even though some treatments may not be effective for a group of people, they can nonetheless be effective for individuals (see Chapter 16 for more on this). One of the things that appears to have been helpful for Professor Saks, from her early days in psychoanalysis as a Marshall scholar at Oxford University until the present, has been her ability to "be psychotic" when

Elyn Saks, a law professor at USC, has schizophrenia. (Photo courtesy Will Vinet.)

she is with her psychoanalyst. So much of her energy was spent trying to hide her symptoms and keep them from interfering with her life, psychoanalysis became a safe place for her to let these symptoms more fully out into the open. The different analysts she has had over the year were also among the chief proponents of adding antipsychotic medication to her treatment, something that Professor Saks resisted for many years. Having the unwavering support of close friends and her husband has also been a tremendous help, particularly during her more symptomatic periods. Her loved ones would not turn and run the other way when she was psychotic. Instead, they would support her and help her get additional treatment if it was needed.

She still experiences symptoms, sometimes every day. Her symptoms include paranoid delusions, which she describes as very frightening (e.g., believing that her thoughts have killed people). She also experiences disorganization symptoms, which she eloquently describes in the book:

Consciousness gradually loses its coherence. One's center gives way. The center cannot hold. The "me" becomes a haze, and the solid center from which one experiences reality breaks up like a bad radio signal. There is no longer a sturdy vantage point from which to look out, take things in, assess what's happening. No core holds things together, providing the lens through which to see the world, to make judgments and comprehend risk. (Saks, 2007, p. 13).

Even though she still experiences symptoms, she has been able to come to terms with the fact that schizophrenia is a part of her life. Would she prefer not to have the illness? Sure. But she also recognizes that she has a wonderful life filled with friends, loved ones, and meaningful work. She is not defined by her illness, and she importantly notes that "the humanity we all share is more important than the mental illness we may not" (Saks, 2007, p. 336). Her life is an inspiration to all, not just those with mental illness. Her story reminds us that life is difficult, more so for some than others, but that it can be lived, and lived to the fullest.

---

of psychoanalysis for people with schizophrenia. However, research results do not support the efficacy of this treatment for schizophrenia. For some people, it may do more harm than good (Katz & Gunderson, 1990; Mueser & Berenbaum, 1990; Stanton et al., 1984). Nevertheless, anecdotal reports and case studies point to some successes with this type of treatment. See Focus on Discovery 11.3 for an example of this.

More recent types of psychosocial treatments are more active, present-focused, and reality-oriented than psychoanalytic approaches, as therapists try to help patients and their families deal more directly with the everyday problems they face in coping with this disruptive and debilitating illness. Inherent to this work is the assumption that a good deal of the stress experienced by people with schizophrenia is due to their difficulties in negotiating everyday social challenges, including the pressures that arise in their families when they return home after hospitalization. We turn now to these newer and more effective approaches.

Social Skills Training **Social skills training** is designed to teach people with schizophrenia how to successfully manage a wide variety of interpersonal situations—discussing their medications with their psychiatrist, ordering meals in a restaurant, filling out job applications, interviewing for jobs, saying no to drug dealers on the street, and reading bus schedules. Most of us take these skills for granted and give little thought to them in our daily lives, but people with schizophrenia cannot take them for granted—they need to work hard to acquire or reacquire such skills (Heinssen, Liberman, & Kopelowicz, 2000; Liberman et al., 2000). Social skills training typically involves role-playing and other group exercises to practice skills, both in a therapy group and in actual social situations.

Research has shown that people with schizophrenia can be taught new social behaviors that help them achieve fewer relapses, better social functioning, and a higher quality of life (Kopelowicz et al., 2002). Some of the studies are noteworthy in demonstrating benefits over a period of 2 years following treatment (Liberman et al., 1998; Marder et al., 1999), though not all results are positive (Pilling et al., 2002). Social skills training is usually a component of treatments for schizophrenia that go beyond the use of medications alone, including family therapies for lowering expressed emotion, which we discuss next. For example, social skills training that included family therapy was found to be more effective than treatment as usual (medication plus a 20-minute monthly meeting with a psychiatrist) in a randomized controlled trial conducted in Mexico (Valencia et al., 2007).

Family Therapies Many people with schizophrenia who are discharged from hospitals go home to their families. Earlier we discussed research showing that high levels of expressed emotion (EE) within the family, including being hostile, hypercritical, and overprotective, have been linked to relapse and rehospitalization. Based on this finding, a number of family therapies have been developed. These therapies may differ in length, setting, and specific techniques, but they have several features in common:

- *Education about schizophrenia—specifically about the genetic or neurobiological factors that predispose some people to the illness, the cognitive problems associated with schizophrenia, the symptoms of schizophrenia, and the signs of impending relapse.* High-EE families are typically not well informed about schizophrenia, and giving them some basic information helps them be less critical of the relative with schizophrenia. Knowing, for example, that neurobiology has a lot to do with having schizophrenia and that the illness involves problems in thinking clearly and rationally might help family members be more accepting and understanding of their relative's inappropriate or ineffectual actions. Therapists encourage family members to lower their expectations of their relative with schizophrenia, and they make clear to family and the person with schizophrenia alike that proper medication and therapy can reduce stress on the patient and prevent deterioration.

- *Information about antipsychotic medication.* Therapists impress on both the family and the ill relative the importance of taking antipsychotic medication, becoming better informed about the intended effects and the side effects of the medication, taking responsibility for monitoring response to medication, and seeking medical consultation rather than just discontinuing the medication if adverse side effects occur.

- *Blame avoidance and reduction.* Therapists encourage family members to blame neither themselves nor their relative for the illness and for the difficulties all are having in coping with it.

- *Communication and problem-solving skills within the family.* Therapists focus on teaching the family ways to express both positive and negative feelings in a constructive, empathic, nondemanding manner rather than in a finger-pointing, critical, or overprotective way. They focus as well on making personal conflicts less stressful by teaching family members ways to work together to solve everyday problems.

- *Social network* expansion. Therapists encourage people with schizophrenia and their families to expand their social contacts, especially their support networks.

- *Hope.* Therapists instill hope that things can improve, including the hope that the person with schizophrenia may not have to return to the hospital.

Therapists use various techniques to implement these strategies. Examples include identifying stressors that could cause relapse, training families in communication skills and problem solving, and having high-EE family members watch videotapes of interactions of low-EE families (Penn & Mueser, 1996). Compared with standard treatments (usually just medication), family therapy plus medication has typically lowered relapse over periods of 1 to 2 years. This positive finding is evident particularly in studies in which the treatment lasted for at least 9 months (Falloon et al., 1982, 1985; Hogarty et al., 1986, 1991; Kopelowicz & Liberman, 1998; McFarlane et al., 1995; Penn & Mueser, 1996).

Cognitive Behavior Therapy   At one time, researchers assumed that it was futile to try to alter the cognitive distortions, including delusions, of people with schizophrenia. Now, however, a growing body of evidence demonstrates that the maladaptive beliefs of some people with schizophrenia can in fact benefit from cognitive behavior therapy (CBT) (Garety, Fowler, & Kuipers, 2000; Wykes et al., 2008).

People with schizophrenia can be encouraged to test out their delusional beliefs in much the same way as people without schizophrenia do. Through collaborative discussions (and in the context of other modes of treatment, including antipsychotic drugs), some people with schizophrenia have been helped to attach a nonpsychotic meaning to paranoid symptoms and thereby reduce their intensity and aversive nature, similar to what is done for depression and panic disorder (Beck & Rector, 2000; Drury et al., 1996; Haddock et al., 1998). Researchers have found that CBT can also reduce negative symptoms, for example, by challenging belief structures tied to low expectations for success (avolition) and low expectations for pleasure (anticipatory pleasure deficit in anhedonia) (Beck, Rector, & Stolar, 2004; Rector, Beck, & Stolar, 2005; Wykes et al., 2008).

Family therapy can help educate people with schizophrenia and their families about schizophrenia and reduce expressed emotion. (Bruce Ayres/Stone/Getty Images.)

Findings from the first few randomized controlled trials of CBT in schizophrenia suggest that this treatment, along with medication, can help reduce hallucinations and delusions (Bustillo et al., 2001). A more recent meta-analysis of 34 studies of close to 2,000 people with schizophrenia across 8 different countries found small to moderate effect sizes for positive symptoms, negative symptoms, mood, and general life functioning (Wykes et al., 2008). CBT has been used as an adjunctive treatment for schizophrenia in Great Britain for over 10 years, and the results have been positive, even in community settings (Sensky et al., 2000; Turkington, Kingdom, & Turner, 2002; Wykes et al., 2008). One study has found that stress management training (discussed in Chapter 7) was effective in reducing stress among people with schizophrenia—a noteworthy outcome indeed, given the link between stress and relapse (Norman et al., 2002).

Therapies That Focus on Basic Cognitive Functions   In recent years researchers have been attending to fundamental aspects of cognition that are disordered in schizophrenia, in an attempt to improve these functions and thereby favorably affect behavior. The fact that positive clinical outcomes from risperidone are associated with improvements in certain kinds of memory (Green et al., 1997) lends support to the more general notion that therapies directed at basic cognitive processes—the kind that nonclinical cognitive scientists study—holds promise for improving the social and emotional lives of people with schizophrenia. This general approach concentrates on trying to normalize such functions as attention and memory, which are known to be deficient in many people with schizophrenia and are associated with poor social adaptation (Green et al., 2000).

Recently developed treatments that seek to enhance basic cognitive functions such as verbal learning ability are referred to as **cognitive enhancement therapy (CET)** or *cognitive training*. A 2-year randomized controlled clinical trial compared group-based CET with enriched supportive therapy (EST). CET consisted of nearly 80 hours of computer-based training in attention, memory, and problem solving. Groups also worked on such daily-life, social-cognitive skills as reading and understanding newspaper editorials, solving social problems, and starting and maintaining conversations. EST included supportive and educational elements. All people were also taking medications. At the 1- and 2-year follow-up assessments, CET was more effective than EST in improving cognitive abilities in problem solving, attention, social cognition, and social adjustment, while symptom reduction was the same for both treatments (Hogarty et al., 2004). People who received CET were also rated as being more ready for employment and, in fact, tended to be employed at the end of 2 years, largely driven by the fact that these people were more likely to be in volunteer positions than those in the EST group. Thus, CET is effective at reducing symptoms and improving cognitive abilities, and it appears to be linked to good functional outcomes, such as employment.

A recent review of 17 other randomized trials of cognitive training therapies shows that these interventions, for the most part, improve cognitive abilities, whether the treatments focus on specific tasks (e.g., a memory test) or on broader strategies (e.g., problem solving) or whether done via computer-based training (Twamley, Jeste, & Bellack, 2003). Only a few of these studies included measures of symptoms and functional outcomes, such as employment or general functioning, but those that did generally found that cognitive training improved symptoms and functional outcomes. As promising as these findings are, nearly all of the studies have been with white men; thus, their generalizability remains to be established. And not all studies yield positive results (Pilling et al., 2002).

Case Management After large numbers of people were discharged from hospitals (referred to as deinstitutionalization) in the 1960s, many people with schizophrenia no longer resided in hospitals and thus had to fend for themselves in securing needed services. Lacking the centralized hospital as the site where most services were delivered, the mental health system became more complex. In 1977, fearing that many people with schizophrenia were not accessing services, the National Institute of Mental Health established a program giving grants to states to help people with schizophrenia cope with the mental health system. Out of this program, a new mental health specialty, the case manager, was created.

Initially, case managers were basically brokers of services; because they were familiar with the system, they were able to get people with schizophrenia into contact with providers of whatever services they required. As the years passed, different models of case management developed. The major innovation was the recognition that case managers often needed to provide direct clinical services and that services might best be delivered by a team rather than brokered out. The Assertive Community Treatment model (Stein & Test, 1980) and the Intensive Case Management model (Surles et al., 1992) both entail a multidisciplinary team that provides services in the community, such as medication, treatment for substance abuse, help in dealing with stressors people with schizophrenia face regularly (such as managing money), psychotherapy, vocational training, and assistance in obtaining housing and employment. Case managers hold together and coordinate the range of medical and psychological services that people with schizophrenia need to keep functioning outside of institutions and with some degree of independence and peace of mind (Kopelowicz et al., 2002).

Indications are that this more intensive treatment is superior to less intensive methods in reducing time spent in the hospital, improving housing stability, and ameliorating symptoms (Mueser et al., 1998). However, more intensive case management has not shown positive effects in other domains, such as improvement in social functioning. In order for this approach to be effective, there have to be enough case managers for people with schizophrenia. Too often, the caseloads of these mental health professionals are much too high.

Residential Treatment Residential treatment homes, or "halfway houses," are sometimes good alternatives for people who do not need to be in the hospital but are not quite well enough to live on their own or even with their family. These are protected living units, typically located in large, formerly private residences. Here people discharged from the hospital live, take their meals, and gradually return to ordinary community life by holding a part-time job or going to school. As part of what is called *vocational rehabilitation*, residents learn marketable skills that can help them secure employment and thereby increase their chances of remaining in the community. Living arrangements may be relatively unstructured; some houses set up money-making enterprises that help train and support the residents.

Depending on how well funded the residential treatment facility is, the staff may include psychiatrists or clinical psychologists or both. The frontline staff members are paraprofessionals, often undergraduate psychology majors or graduate students in clinical psychology or social work, who live at the facility and act both as administrators and as friends to the residents. Group meetings, at which residents talk out their frustrations and learn to relate to others in honest and constructive ways, are often part of the routine. There are many such programs across the United States that have helped thousands of people with schizophrenia make enough of a social adaptation to be able to remain out of the hospital.

The need in the United States for effective residential treatment cannot be underestimated, especially in light of the deinstitutionalization that has seen tens of thousands of people discharged from hospitals. People with schizophrenia almost always need follow-up community-based services, and these are scarce. Indeed, today a large percentage of homeless people in the United States are mentally ill, including many people with schizophrenia. Social Security benefits are available to those with schizophrenia, but if they do not have an address, they often do not receive all the benefits to which they are entitled. Though there are good residential treatment programs available, there are not enough of them.

Integrating therapy with gainful employment is important in keeping people with schizophrenia out of hospitals (Kopelowicz & Liberman, 1998; Kopelowicz et al., 2002). For example, the U.S. government has begun to recognize the importance of employment by allowing people with schizophrenia to continue receiving Social Security benefits for up to 2 years while they are earning money from (low-paying) jobs that can increase their chances of living independently or at least outside of the hospital. This welcome change in policy (from one that terminated such benefits once the person began earning money) represents a recognition of the harmful effects of not working and not being able to live in a reasonably independent manner.

Still, obtaining employment can pose a major challenge because of bias and stigma against people with schizophrenia. Although the Americans with Disabilities Act of 1990 prohibits employers from asking applicants if they have a history of serious mental illness, people with schizophrenia still have a difficult time obtaining regular employment because their symptoms make negatively biased employers fearful of hiring them. Also a factor is how much leeway employers are willing to give people whose thinking, emotions, and behavior can be unconventional to some degree.

Despite these difficulties, the trend seems to be to do whatever is necessary to assist people in working and living in as autonomous a manner as their physical and mental condition will allow (Kopelowicz & Liberman, 1998). Additional funding will be needed to create more residential treatment facilities with the hope of reducing the number of people with schizophrenia who are without treatment.

Remaining Challenges in the Treatment of Schizophrenia

It is increasingly recognized that early intervention is important and useful in affecting the course of schizophrenia over time. That is, getting people with schizophrenia onto the right medications and providing support and information to the family and appropriate psychotherapy can reduce the severity of relapses in the future (Drury et al., 1996). It is also important to teach people with schizophrenia social skills and more reality-based thinking so that they can function outside the hospital and probably reduce the EE encountered both inside and outside the home. Families affected by schizophrenia are encouraged to join support groups and formal organizations, such as the National Alliance on Mental Illness, to reduce the isolation and stigma associated with having a family member who has schizophrenia.

Despite the promise of these interventions, there is often a gap between what treatments are available and what treatments are actually received. This issue was highlighted in a study that involved interviewing over 700 people with schizophrenia and reviewing their medical records (Lehman et al., 1998). As expected, almost 90 percent had been prescribed antipsychotic drugs, but of these people only 62 percent received a dose in the recommended range. About 15 percent got too little, and the remainder got too much. Further, although over 90 percent of people with schizophrenia were prescribed maintenance doses of drugs, only 29 percent of these received a dose in the recommended range; of the 71 percent who did not receive a recommended dose, about half were getting too much and half too little. African Americans were much more likely than whites to be prescribed maintenance doses that were too high.

Psychosocial treatments were also examined, but these were more difficult to evaluate because records of patient reports did not allow the researchers to know whether the treatment was one of those considered effective (such as family therapies or social skills training). Just in terms of whether any psychosocial treatments at all were prescribed for people with schizophrenia, the study shows that some sort of individual or group therapy was provided for over 90 percent of patients in the hospital. But for people with schizophrenia who had regular contact with their families, family treatment of some sort was prescribed for only about 40 percent. For unemployed people with schizophrenia, vocational rehabilitation (teaching job skills) was prescribed for only about 30 percent.

Conclusion? Many people with schizophrenia are not getting anything near optimal therapy. Indeed, though the kind of integrated treatment we have been describing is promising, the sad fact is that it is not widely available or accessible to most people with schizophrenia and their families. The reasons for this are unclear (Baucom et al., 1998; Dixon et al., 1997).

Preventing substance abuse among people with schizophrenia is largely an unmet challenge. The lifetime prevalence rate for substance abuse among people with schizophrenia is an astounding 50 percent (Kosten & Ziedonis, 1997); the rate is even higher among the homeless mentally ill population. Programs for treating substance abuse usually exclude people who are seriously mentally ill, and programs for treating people who are seriously mentally ill usually exclude substance abusers. In both instances the reason is that the comorbid condition is considered disruptive to the treatment (Mueser, Bellack, & Blanchard, 1992). This is a situation that simply must be turned around.

Check Your Knowledge 11.3

True or false?
1. First-generation antipsychotics include medications like Haldol or Prolixin; second-generation antipsychotics include clozapine and olanzapine.
2. Second-generation antipsychotics produce more motor side effects than first-generation antipsychotics.
3. Cognitive behavior therapy, but not cognitive enhancement therapy, is effective for schizophrenia, if given along with medications.
4. One important focus of residential treatment programs is to help people with schizophrenia become employed.

Summary

Clinical Description

- The symptoms of schizophrenia involve disturbances in several major areas, including thought, perception, and attention; motor behavior; affect; and life functioning. Symptoms are typically divided into positive, negative, and disorganized categories. Positive symptoms include excesses and distortions, such as delusions and hallucinations. Negative symptoms are behavioral deficits, which include flat affect, avolition, alogia, asociality, and anhedonia. Disorganized symptoms include disorganized speech and behavior. Other more rare symptoms include catatonia and inappropriate affect.

- The DSM-IV-TR includes several subtypes of schizophrenia, including disorganized, catatonic, and paranoid. These subtypes are based on the prominence of particular symptoms (e.g., delusions in the paranoid subtype) and reflect the variations in behavior found among people diagnosed with schizophrenia. However, the subtypes have little predictive validity.

Etiology

- The evidence for genetic transmission of schizophrenia is impressive. Family and twin studies suggest a genetic component; adoption studies show a strong relationship between having a parent with schizophrenia and the likelihood of developing the disorder, typically in early adulthood. Molecular genetics studies are still in need of replication. The most promising findings to date seem to indicate genes such as DTNBP1, NGR1, and COMT.

- The genetic predisposition to develop schizophrenia may involve neurotransmitters. It appears that increased sensitivity of dopamine receptors in the limbic area of the brain is related to the positive symptoms of schizophrenia. The negative symptoms may be due to dopamine underactivity in the prefrontal cortex. Other neurotransmitters, such as serotonin, glutamate, and GABA, may also be involved.

- The brains of some people with schizophrenia have enlarged ventricles and problems with the prefrontal cortex. Some of these structural abnormalities could result from maternal viral infection during the second trimester of pregnancy or from damage sustained during a difficult birth.

- The diagnosis of schizophrenia is most frequently applied to people of the lowest socioeconomic status, apparently because of downward social mobility created by the disorder. In addition, vague communications and conflicts are evident in the family life of people with schizophrenia, though it is less clear whether these contribute to their disorder. High levels of expressed emotion in families, as well as increases in general life stress, have been shown to be an important determinant of relapse. Developmental studies have identified problems in childhood that were there prior to the onset of schizophrenia, but these studies were not designed to predict schizophrenia, so it is difficult to interpret the findings. High-risk studies suggest that the causes of positive and negative symptoms may be different. Other studies have found cognitive problems in childhood to predict the onset of adult psychopathology, but not specifically schizophrenia.

Treatment

- Antipsychotic drugs, especially the phenothiazines, have been widely used to treat schizophrenia since the 1950s. Second-generation antipsychotic drugs, such as clozapine and risperidone, are also effective and produce fewer motoric side effects, though they have their own set of side effects. Drugs alone are not a completely effective treatment, though, as people with schizophrenia need to be (re)taught ways of dealing with the challenges of everyday life.

- The efficacy of psychoanalytic treatments has not been supported by evidence. In contrast, family therapy aimed at reducing high levels of expressed emotion has been shown to be valuable in preventing relapse. In addition, social skills training and various cognitive behavioral therapies have helped people with schizophrenia meet the inevitable stresses of family and community living. Recent efforts to change the thinking of people with schizophrenia with cognitive behavior therapy are showing promise as well.

- The most promising approaches to treatment today emphasize the importance of both pharmacological and psychosocial interventions. Unfortunately, such integrated treatments are not widely available.

Answers to Check Your Knowledge Questions

11.1 1. flat affect; 2. delusion or ideas of reference; 3. anhedonia (anticipatory); 4. disorganized thinking or derailment.

11.2 1. Family, adoption; 2. DTNBP1, NGR1; 3. prefrontal; 4. Hostility, critical comments, emotional overinvolvement.

11.3 1. T; 2. F; 3. F; 4. T

Key Terms

alogia
anhedonia
anticipatory pleasure
antipsychotic drugs
asociality
avolition
brief psychotic disorder
catatonia
catatonic immobility
catatonic schizophrenia

cognitive enhancement therapy (CET)
consummatory pleasure
delusional disorder
delusions
dementia praecox
disorganized behavior
disorganized schizophrenia
disorganized speech
disorganized symptoms
dopamine theory

expressed emotion (EE)
flat affect
grandiose delusions
hallucinations
ideas of reference
inappropriate affect
loose associations (derailment)
negative symptoms
paranoid schizophrenia
positive symptoms
prefrontal cortex

residual schizophrenia
schizoaffective disorder
schizophrenia
schizophreniform disorder
second-generation antipsychotic drugs
social selection theory
social skills training
sociogenic hypothesis
undifferentiated schizophrenia

12 Personality Disorders

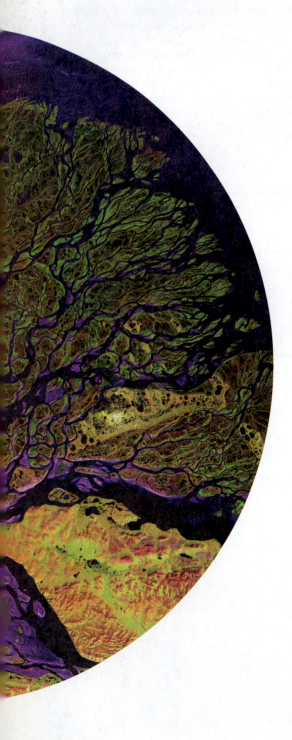

LEARNING GOALS

1. Be able to explain the issues in classifying personality disorders and to describe alternative dimensional approaches to diagnosis.
2. Be able to define the key features of each personality disorder.
3. Be able to describe the genetic, neurobiological, social, and other risk factors for personality disorders, and be able to discuss problems in the research on etiology.
4. Be able to describe the available medication and psychological treatments of personality disorders.

Clinical Case: Mary

Mary was single and 26 years old when she was first admitted to a psychiatric hospital. She had been in outpatient treatment with a psychologist for several months when her persistent thoughts of cutting, burning, and killing herself led her therapist to conclude that she needed more than outpatient treatment.

Mary's first experience with psychotherapy occurred when she was an adolescent. Her grades declined sharply in the eleventh grade, and her parents suspected she was using drugs. She began to miss curfews and, occasionally, to stay out all night. She often skipped school. Family therapy was started, and it seemed to go well at first. Mary was enthusiastic about the therapist and asked for additional, private sessions with him.

During the private sessions, Mary revealed she had used drugs extensively, including "everything I can get my hands on." She had been promiscuous and had prostituted herself several times to get drug money. Her relationships with her peers were changeable, to say the least. There was a constant parade of new friends, whom Mary at first thought to be the greatest ever but who soon disappointed her and were cast aside, often in very unpleasant ways. Except for the one person with whom she was currently enamored, Mary had no friends. She said that she stayed away from others for fear that they would harm her in some way.

After several weeks of family therapy, Mary's parents noticed that Mary was angry and abusive toward the therapist. After a few more weeks had passed, Mary refused to attend any more sessions. In a subsequent conversation with the therapist, Mary's father learned that she had behaved seductively toward the therapist during their private sessions and that her changed attitude coincided with his rejection of her advances, despite the therapist's attempt to mix firmness with warmth and empathy.

Mary managed to graduate from high school and enrolled in a local community college, but the old patterns returned. Poor grades, cutting classes, continuing drug use, and lack of interest in her studies finally led her to quit college in the middle of the first semester of her second year. After leaving school, Mary held a series of low-paying jobs. Most of them didn't last long, as her relationships with co-workers paralleled her relationships with her peers in high school. When Mary started a new job she would find someone she really liked, but something would come between them, and the relationship would end angrily. She was often suspicious of her co-workers and reported that she heard them plotting how to prevent her from getting ahead on the job. She was quick to find hidden meanings in their behavior, as when she interpreted being the last person asked to sign a birthday card to mean that she was the least liked person in the office. She indicated that she "received vibrations" from others and could tell when they really didn't like her even in the absence of any direct evidence.

Mary's frequent mood swings, with periods of depression and extreme irritability, led her to seek therapy several times. But after initial enthusiasm, her relationships with therapists always deteriorated, resulting in premature termination of therapy. By the time of her hospitalization, she had seen six therapists.

T**HE PERSONALITY DISORDERS ARE** a heterogeneous group of disorders defined by long-standing, pervasive, and inflexible patterns of behavior and inner experience that deviate from the expectations of a person's culture. These problematic patterns are manifested in at least two of the following areas: cognition, emotions, relationships, and impulse control. Like all other DSM-IV-TR disorders, personality disorders are not diagnosed unless they cause distress or functional impairment.

As we examine the personality disorders, some might seem to fit people we know, not to mention ourselves! This seems a good time to remind readers about the medical student syndrome, so called because medical students (and psychology students) have a tendency to see themselves or their families and friends in descriptions of the disorders they study. For example, suppose you hear a loud burst of laughter just as you enter a crowded room, and this makes you feel that you are the target of some joke and that people are talking about you. Such concerns would qualify as symptoms of paranoid personality disorder only if they occurred often enough and intensely enough to prevent you from developing close personal relationships. This illustrates a general point: from time to time, we all behave, think, and feel in ways that look similar to symptoms of personality disorders, but an actual personality disorder is defined by the extreme, inflexible, and maladaptive ways in which these traits are expressed. The symptoms of personality disorders are pervasive and persistent.

In this chapter we begin by looking at how personality disorders are classified in the DSM, at issues related to the DSM diagnostic system for personality disorders, and at an alternative system of classification. Next, we turn to clinical descriptions of the personality disorders and to discussions of their etiology. We conclude with discussions of the treatment of personality disorders. Throughout, the extent of our coverage depends on how much is known about the specific personality disorder under consideration; for example, there have been few studies of histrionic personality disorder, but there is a vast literature on antisocial personality disorder.

Classifying Personality Disorders

There is considerable debate about the best way to classify personality disorders. We begin by providing an overview of the DSM-IV-TR approach, then turn to an alternate dimensional approach.

The DSM Approach to Classification

In DSM-IV-TR, the 10 different personality disorders are classified in three clusters, reflecting the idea that these disorders are characterized by odd or eccentric behavior (cluster A); dramatic, emotional, or erratic behavior (cluster B); or anxious or fearful behavior (cluster C). These clusters form a useful organizational framework for our discussions in this chapter. Table 12.1 presents the personality disorders, their key features, and their grouping in clusters.

Beginning with DSM-III, personality disorders were placed on a separate axis, Axis II, to ensure that clinicians would consider whether a personality disorder is also present. Typically, clients seek help for the symptoms of an Axis I disorder (such as panic disorder), without initially emphasizing symptoms of personality disorders. It is important to note, though, that many people with an Axis I disorder will also experience an Axis II disorder. When this comorbidity occurs, the personality disorder shapes the form of the Axis I symptoms. For example, a person diagnosed with an anxiety disorder on Axis I and obsessive-compulsive personality disorder on Axis II will express anxiety in perfectionistic and controlling ways. As one researcher put it, different personality disorders "evoke contrasting ways of perceiving and coping" with Axis I disorders, which means that clinicians should consider the "context of personality" when dealing with Axis I disorders (Millon, 1996, p. vii). Comorbid personality disorders are associated with more severe symptoms, poorer social functioning, and worse treatment outcomes for Axis I disorders (Clark, 2007). As a result, personality disorders are commonly encountered in treatment settings. See Table 12.2 for the rates of personality disorders in the general community as compared to treatment settings.

Diagnostic Reliability Before DSM-III, the diagnosis of personality disorders was very unreliable—one clinician might diagnose a flamboyant patient with narcissistic personality disorder, whereas another might diagnose the patient with histrionic personality disorder. DSM-III began a trend toward improved reliability by including specific diagnostic criteria for personality disorders, as it did for other disorders (Coolidge & Segal, 1998). Structured interviews were also developed to assess personality disorders, and these, too, helped improve diagnostic reliability.

Table 12.1 Key Features of the DSM-IV-TR Personality Disorders

Cluster A (odd/eccentric)	
Paranoid	Distrust and suspiciousness of others
Schizoid	Detachment from social relationships and restricted range of emotional expression
Schizotypal	Lack of capacity for close relationships, cognitive distortions, and eccentric behavior
Cluster B (dramatic/erratic)	
Antisocial	Disregard for and violation of the rights of others
Borderline	Instability of interpersonal relationships, self-image, and affect, as well as marked impulsivity
Histrionic	Excessive emotionality and attention seeking
Narcissistic	Grandiosity, need for admiration, and lack of empathy
Cluster C (anxious/fearful)	
Avoidant	Social inhibition, feelings of inadequacy, and hypersensitivity to negative evaluation
Dependent	Excessive need to be taken care of, submissive behavior, and fears of separation
Obsessive-compulsive	Preoccupation with order, perfection, and control

Table 12.2 Rates of DSM-IV Personality Disorders in the Community and in Treatment Settings

Disorder	Prevalence in the Community (%)	Prevalence in Treatment Settings (%)	Gender Ratio
Paranoid	0.7–5.1	4.2	Males > females
Schizoid	0.9–1.7	1.4	Males > females
Schizotypal	0.6–1.10	0.6	Males > females
Antisocial	1.2–4.1	3.6	Males > females
Borderline	0.5–3.9	9.3	Females > males
Histrionic	0.2–0.9	1.0	Females > males
Narcissistic	0.0–2.2	2.3	Males > females
Avoidant	1.8–6.4	14.7	Males = females
Dependent	0.1–0.8	1.4	Females > males
Obsessive-compulsive	4.7	8.7	Males > females

Source: Prevalence estimates for community settings are drawn from Crawford et al. (2005) and Samuels et al. (2002). Prevalence estimates for treatment settings are drawn from Zimmerman, Rothschild, & Chelminski (2005).

Table 12.3 shows interrater reliabilities from a study of the DSM-IV personality disorders using a structured diagnostic interview administered by experts (Zanarini et al., 2000). Although diagnoses of most personality disorders have adequate or good reliability when structured interviews are used, schizoid personality disorder is still characterized by relatively low interrater reliability. This may be because clinicians differ in their thresholds for seeing a behavior as pathological. Of concern, most clinicians do not use structured interviews to assess personality, so in real life, the reliability of personality diagnoses is likely to be relatively low (Heumann & Moreg, 1990).

When there is disagreement about how to apply diagnostic criteria, there is a potential for the personal biases of a clinician to influence decisions. Some have noted that clinicians tend to be more likely to decide that certain behaviors are pathological for women more than they are for men. (See Focus on Discovery 12.1 for discussion of gender biases in diagnosing personality disorders.)

One issue in assessing personality disorders is whether people can accurately describe their own personalities. When clients' reports of their personality disorder symptoms are compared

Table 12.3 Interrater Reliability for the Personality Disorders

Diagnosis	Interrater Reliability
Paranoid	.86
Schizoid	.69
Schizotypal	.91
Antisocial	.97
Borderline	.90
Histrionic	.83
Narcissistic	.88
Avoidant	.79
Dependent	.87
Obsessive-compulsive	.85

Source: Zanarini et al. (2000).

FOCUS ON DISCOVERY 12.1

Gender and Personality Disorders

For many personality disorders, prevalence varies a great deal by gender (see Table 12.2). For example, women are more likely than men to be diagnosed with borderline, histrionic, and dependent personality disorders, and men are more likely than women to be diagnosed with antisocial, narcissistic, and obsessive-compulsive personality disorders. Before the publication of DSM-IV, some researchers argued that certain of the diagnostic criteria for personality disorders pathologized feminine traits (Kaplan, 1983). For example, histrionic personality disorder included criteria for emotional lability, a focus on physical appearance, and sexual seductiveness. Are these traits more reinforced, and therefore more common, among women? In response to these types of criticisms, DSM-IV refined such criteria to make them more gender-neutral. For example, the criterion for a focus on physical appearance was modified to read as "consistently uses physical appearance to draw attention to self," and the text now includes descriptions of ways in

which men might show macho behaviors that fit this criterion (Hartung & Widiger, 1998).

Despite these changes to the criteria, research has suggested that clinicians are still biased by gender stereotypes in the way they diagnose personality disorders. For example, clinicians might focus on different behaviors, depending on whether they are diagnosing a man or a woman. In a typical test of this issue, two different vignettes are written involving people with personality disorders. The versions are identical except that in one, the person in the vignette is named Joan, and in the other, the person is named John. Clinicians read the vignettes and provide the most likely diagnosis. In these types of studies, clinicians are more likely to diagnose the person as having histrionic personality disorder if the vignette is about a woman and more likely to diagnose the person as having antisocial personality disorder if the vignette is about a man (Garb, 1997). These findings highlight how important it is for clinicians to be aware of biases.

to the reports of friends and families, agreement tends to be low (Klonsky, Oltmanns, & Turkheimer, 2002). Intriguingly, it is not the case that people always downplay their difficulties; sometimes clients are more harsh than are their friends and family members, and sometimes they are less harsh in describing their personality symptoms. Nonetheless, having more than one perspective on personality disorders is important. Interviews with people who know the patient well improve the reliability of diagnosis (Bernstein et al., 1997). However, fewer than 10 percent of published studies of personality disorders gather data from people other than the person being diagnosed (Bornstein, 2003), even though the diagnostic criteria often specify that people with personality disorders tend to see themselves in distorted ways (Thomas, Turkheimer, & Oltmanns, 2003).

By definition, personality disorders are supposed to be more stable over time than episodic Axis I disorders like major depressive disorder. Therefore, studies of test–retest reliability—whether clients receive the same diagnosis at two assessments separated by some time interval—are an important test of the basic definition of the disorder. Figure 12.1 shows a summary of test–retest reliability (i.e., diagnostic stability) from one study (Shea et al., 2002). The figure indicates that diagnoses of personality disorders are much more stable than diagnoses for major depressive disorder; nevertheless, about half of the people initially diagnosed with a personality disorder did not receive the same personality disorder diagnosis when they were interviewed one and two years later. These results, then, indicate that many of the personality disorders may not be as enduring as the DSM asserts.

Even though the personality disorders do not have high diagnostic stability, there are several issues that are important to consider. First, many of the people in the study still had symptoms at the second interview, just not at the levels required for diagnosis. Second, even if people no longer meet the full criteria for personality disorder, there might be a sustained influence of personality disorders on functioning. In one study, people with and without personality disorders were reinterviewed at a 15-year follow-up; baseline diagnoses of personality disorders were a significant predictor of lower functioning 15 years later (Hong et al., 2005).

In sum, there are many issues to consider in obtaining reliable estimates of personality. Using structured interviews and multiple informants can improve reliability, but a core concern is that many diagnoses are not stable. As pointed out by Lee Anna Clark (2007), most laypeople know that understanding personality requires gathering data across multiple situations, over time, from many different perspectives. Perhaps it is not so surprising, then, that obtaining high-quality assessments of personality disorder would require careful assessments gathered from different informants at different time points.

Comorbidity   A major problem in classifying personality disorders arises from their comorbidity with Axis I disorders and with each other. The clinical case of Mary illustrates this issue: Mary met the diagnostic criteria not only for borderline personality disorder but also for paranoid personality disorder. More than 50 percent of people diagnosed with a personality disorder meet the diagnostic criteria for another personality disorder, and more than two-thirds meet lifetime criteria for an Axis I disorder (Lenzenweger et al., 2007). These facts are discouraging when we try to interpret the results of research that compares people who have a specific personality disorder with some control group. If, for example, we find that people with borderline personality disorder differ from healthy people, is our finding related to borderline personality disorder or to personality disorders in general, or perhaps even to comorbid Axis I disorders?

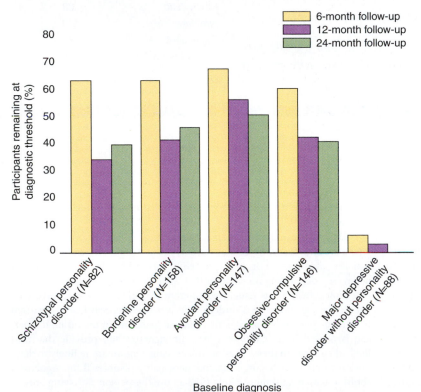

Figure 12.1 Test–retest stability for personality disorders and major depressive disorder across 6-, 12-, and 24-month follow-up interviews. Drawn from Grilo et al. (2004); Shea et al. (2002).

In sum, the categorical system of the DSM might not be ideal for classifying personality disorders, because of concerns about the lack of test–retest stability, the potential for gender bias, and the high rates of comorbidity. These types of concerns have led some authors to recommend shifting to a dimensional approach.

A Dimensional Approach to Personality: The Five-Factor Model

The personality traits used for classification form a continuum; that is, most of these traits are present in varying degrees across people (see p. 70 for a discussion of dimensional versus categorical systems). When people with a personality disorder take a personality inventory, they endorse more extreme personality traits than those seen in the general population (Clark & Livesley, 2002). Thus, personality disorders might be defined by extremes of characteristics we all possess. Given this, a dimensional approach to personality is being considered as one option for DSM-V.

There are a number of advantages of using a dimensional approach to personality. Most importantly, it handles the comorbidity problem, because comorbidity is a difficulty only in a categorical classification system like the one used in DSM-IV-TR. A dimensional system also links normal and abnormal personality, so general findings on personality traits become relevant to the study of personality disorders. Clinicians also report that they find a dimensional approach to personality to be more helpful than the current categorical system in describing clients and considering treatment options (Samuel & Widiger, 2006; Verheul, 2005).

Although there are many different models of personality, a major focus is on the **five-factor model** (McCrae & Costa, 1990), in which the five factors, or major dimensions, of personality are neuroticism, extraversion/introversion, openness to experience, agreeableness/antagonism, and conscientiousness. Table 12.4 presents questionnaire items that assess each of these dimensions; by reading the items, you can get a sense of what each dimension means. These dimensions of personality are moderately heritable (Jang et al., 2002), and the patterns of heritability for these dimensions are consistent across cultures (Yamagata et al., 2006). These personality traits prospectively predict important life outcomes, such as divorce, educational attainment, and occupational status (Roberts et al., 2007).

Several studies have shown that each of the different personality disorders can be explained using a set of these personality traits (Widiger & Costa, 1994). A meta-analysis shows that findings are fairly consistent across a range of studies that have mapped personality disorder diagnoses onto the dimensions of the five-factor model. Most personality disorders are characterized by high neuroticism and antagonism. High extraversion was tied to histrionic and narcissistic disorders (two disorders that involve dramatic behavior), whereas low extraversion was tied to disorders that involve social isolation, such as schizoid, schizotypal, and avoidant personality disorders (Saulsman & Page, 2004).

The five-factor model is not without its critics, however. In a study in which people with personality disorders completed a questionnaire to assess the five factors, the profiles of the various personality disorders turned out to be rather similar to one another (Morey et al., 2000). Some might say this is fine, and that fewer dimensions would simplify things. But proponents of the need to be more specific have responded to this difficulty by claiming that differentiating the personality disorders requires breaking down the five factors into their "facets" (Lynam

Table 12.4 Sample Items from the Revised NEO Personality Inventory Assessing the Five-Factor Model

Personality Trait	Sample Items
Neuroticism	I often feel tense or jittery.
Extraversion/introversion	I really like most people I meet.
Openness to experience	I have a very active imagination.
Agreeableness/antagonism	I tend to be cynical and skeptical of others' intentions (reverse scored).
Conscientiousness	I often come into situations without being prepared (reverse scored).

Reproduced by special permission of the Publisher, Psychological Assessment Resources, Inc., 16204 North Florida Avenue, Lutz, FL 33549, from the NEO Personality Inventory-Revised by Paul Costa and Robert McCrae, Copyright 1978, 1985, 1989, 1991, 1992 by Psychological Assessment Resources, Inc. (PAR). Further reproduction is prohibited without permission of PAR.

& Widiger, 2001). Each of the five factors has six facets, or components; for example, the extraversion factor includes the facets of warmth, gregariousness, assertiveness, activity, excitement seeking, and positive emotionality. Differentiating among the personality disorders might require a more detailed assessment that includes these specific personality facets.

Beyond the need to consider facets, it appears that some disorders, such as schizotypal personality disorder, are more distinct than being just extreme points along a dimension; statistical analyses suggest that people with these disorders tend to be qualitatively different from other people. For example, people with schizotypal personality disorder tend to experience perceptual oddities that others don't experience even in mild degrees (Haslam & Kim, 2002). The five-factor model is not a total solution to the problem of classifying personality disorders, but the important point is that a dimensional model has several distinct advantages compared to the current categorical system.

Problems with classifying personality disorders should not lead us to underestimate the importance of being able to identify them. Personality disorders are prevalent, and they cause severe impairments. We now turn to a review of the clinical description and etiology of the personality disorders in cluster A, cluster B, and cluster C.

Check Your Knowledge 12.1 (Answers are at the end of the chapter.)

True or false?

1. Most of the DSM-IV-TR personality disorders can be diagnosed with good interrater reliability.
2. Most people diagnosed with a personality disorder will still show that personality disorder one year later.

3. People who meet diagnostic criteria for a personality disorder are likely to meet diagnostic criteria for a second or third personality disorder as well.
4. Most studies of personality disorders include informants.
5. The seven-factor model is a popular approach to personality dimensions.

Odd/Eccentric Cluster

● DSM-IV-TR Criteria for Paranoid Personality Disorder

Presence of four or more of the following signs of distrust and suspiciousness, beginning in early adulthood and shown in many contexts:

- Pervasive unjustified suspiciousness of being harmed, deceived, or exploited
- Unwarranted doubts about the loyalty or trustworthiness of friends or associates
- Reluctance to confide in others because of suspiciousness
- The tendency to read hidden meanings into the innocuous actions of others
- Bears grudges for perceived wrongs
- Angry reactions to perceived attacks on character or reputation
- Unwarranted suspiciousness of the fidelity of partner

The odd/eccentric cluster of personality disorders includes paranoid personality disorder, schizoid personality disorder, and schizotypal personality disorder. The symptoms of these three disorders bear some similarity to the types of bizarre thinking and experiences seen in schizophrenia. In personality disorders, though, the bizarre thinking and experiences are less severe than they are in schizophrenia.

Paranoid Personality Disorder

People with **paranoid personality disorder** are suspicious of others. This suspicion influences relationships with family, colleagues, and casual acquaintances. They expect to be mistreated or exploited and thus are secretive and continually on the lookout for signs of trickery and abuse. They are often hostile and react angrily to perceived insults. They might read hidden threatening messages into events.

This disorder is different from paranoid schizophrenia because other symptoms of schizophrenia, such as hallucinations, are not present and there is less impairment in social and occupational functioning. Also absent is the cognitive disorganization that is characteristic of schizophrenia. It differs from delusional disorder because full-blown delusions are not present. Paranoid personality disorder co-occurs most often with schizotypal, borderline, and avoidant personality disorders.

Schizoid Personality Disorder

Like Joe (see clinical case), people with **schizoid personality disorder** do not desire or enjoy social relationships and usually have no close friends. They appear dull, bland, and aloof and have no warm, tender feelings for other people. They rarely experience strong emotions, are not interested in sex, and have few pleasurable activities. Indifferent to praise, criticism, and the sentiments of

Clinical Case: Joe

Joe was a 53-year-old unmarried Vietnam veteran who was referred for treatment by his general practitioner, who was concerned about Joe's disconnection from life. Joe reluctantly agreed to see a therapist. He had not worked in several years and survived on a small disability pension from the Veterans Administration. He said that he found it unpleasant to shop for groceries because he didn't like having other people around him. The landlady at his boarding house persisted in trying to introduce him to women, even though he had declared his lack of interest in each and every one of the 10 women she had pestered him to meet. He stated that he did not like talking,

and in treatment he was often silent for long periods. He did talk about his sense that he had little connection with life and that he experienced little emotion other than mild irritability. Indeed, he was unable to describe a single person or activity that made him happy. After six weeks of treatment, Joe announced that he didn't think that he was a person who was going to feel any better from talking about things and that he had decided to spend his remaining savings to purchase a small cabin in a remote section of Maine. He seemed content with his decision, stating that by living there, he could avoid most interactions with people. He moved the next week.

others, people with this disorder are loners who pursue solitary interests. Comorbidity is highest for schizotypal, avoidant, and paranoid personality disorders, most likely because of the similar diagnostic criteria for the four disorders (see the DSM-IV-TR diagnostic criteria).

Schizotypal Personality Disorder

People with **schizotypal personality disorder** are often socially isolated, like people with schizoid personality, but they also show other, more eccentric symptoms, which are milder versions of the symptoms that define schizophrenia. (See the DSM-IV-TR diagnostic criteria for schizotypal personality disorder.) People with this disorder might have odd beliefs or magical thinking—for instance, the belief that they can read other people's minds and see into the future. It is also common for them to have ideas of reference (the belief that events have a particular and unusual meaning for them personally) and to show suspiciousness and paranoid ideation. They might also have recurrent illusions (inaccurate sensory perceptions), such as sensing the presence of a force or a person that is not actually there. In their speech, they might use words in an unusual and unclear fashion—for example, they might say "not a very talkable person" to mean a person who is not easy to talk to. Their behavior and appearance might also be eccentric—for example, they might talk to themselves or wear dirty and disheveled clothing. Their affect appears constricted and flat. A study of the relative importance of these symptoms for diagnosis found that paranoid ideation, ideas of reference, and illusions were most telling (Widiger, Frances, & Trull, 1987).

Comorbidity with other personality disorders is particularly high, even given the generally high comorbidity among personality disorders; on average, people with schizotypal personality disorder meet the diagnostic criteria for at least two other personality disorders, the most likely being avoidant personality disorder and paranoid personality disorder, perhaps because of overlapping criteria (McGlashon et al., 2000).

Etiology of the Personality Disorders in the Odd/Eccentric Cluster

What causes the odd thinking, bizarre behavior, and interpersonal difficulties that appear in this cluster of personality disorders? Each of the cluster A personality disorders appears to be highly heritable (Kendler et al., 2007). Beyond this, researchers don't know much about the etiology of paranoid personality disorder or schizoid personality disorder—as you can imagine, people with these disorders aren't likely to be interested in completing lengthy research interviews.

The genes that increase risk for schizotypal personality disorder appear to overlap with the genes that increase risk for schizophrenia. That is, family studies have shown that the relatives of clients with schizophrenia are at increased risk for schizotypal personality disorder (Nigg & Goldsmith, 1994), as are adopted children of biological mothers with schizophrenia (Tienari et al., 2003). People with schizotypal personality disorder also have deficits in cognitive and

● DSM-IV-TR Criteria for Schizoid Personality Disorder

Presence of four or more of the following are present from early adulthood:
- Lack of desire for or enjoyment of close relationships
- Almost always prefers solitude to companionship
- Little interest in sex
- Few or no pleasurable activities
- Lack of friends
- Indifference to praise or criticism from others
- Flat affect, emotional detachment

● DSM-IV-TR Criteria for Schizotypal Personality Disorder

Presence of five or more of the following in many contexts beginning in early adulthood:
- Ideas of reference
- Peculiar beliefs or magical thinking, e.g., belief in extrasensory perception
- Unusual perceptions, e.g., distorted feelings about one's body
- Peculiar patterns of thought and speech
- Suspiciousness or paranoia
- Inappropriate or restricted affect
- Odd or eccentric behavior or appearance
- Lack of close friends
- Anxiety around other people, which does not diminish with familiarity

neuropsychological functioning that are similar to but milder than those seen in schizophrenia (Cadenhead et al., 2002; Lenzenweger, 2001). Furthermore, and again paralleling findings from schizophrenia research, people with schizotypal personality disorder have enlarged ventricles and less temporal lobe gray matter (Dickey, McCarley, & Shenton, 2002).

Quick Summary

Personality disorders are defined by long-standing and pervasive ways of being that cause distress and impairment through their influence on cognition, emotions, relationships, and impulse control. Most people with personality disorders experience comorbid Axis I conditions as well as other personality disorders. In DSM-IV-TR, personality disorders are classified in three clusters, reflecting the idea that these disorders are characterized by odd or eccentric behavior (cluster A); dramatic, emotional, or erratic behavior (cluster B); or anxious or fearful behavior (cluster C). Interrater reliability of personality disorder diagnoses, particularly when clinicians use structured interviews, is strong. But despite the idea that personality disorders are defined as long-standing, test–retest reliability is only modest. Concerns have also been raised about gender bias in diagnoses. Some have argued that we should be measuring personality

traits as dimensions rather than attempting to classify people with personality disorders. A key issue is how many personality traits should be assessed to adequately differentiate the types of problems that are encountered in clinical settings, but much of current research focuses on five personality factors.

The odd/eccentric cluster of personality disorders (cluster A) includes paranoid personality disorder, schizoid personality disorder, and schizotypal personality disorder. People with paranoid personality disorder are suspicious of others, people with schizoid personality disorder are socially aloof, and people with schizotypal personality disorder are eccentric in their thoughts and behavior. Genetic studies indicate that schizotypal personality disorder and schizophrenia are related. Cluster A personality disorders appear to be highly heritable.

Dramatic/Erratic Cluster

DSM-IV-TR Criteria for Borderline Personality Disorder

Presence of five or more of the following in many contexts beginning in early adulthood:
- Frantic efforts to avoid abandonment
- Unstable interpersonal relationships in which others are either idealized or devalued
- Unstable sense of self
- Self-damaging, impulsive behaviors in at least two areas, such as spending, sex, substance abuse, reckless driving, binge eating
- Recurrent suicidal behavior, gestures, or self-injurious behavior (e.g., cutting self)
- Chronic feelings of emptiness
- Recurrent bouts of intense or poorly controlled anger
- During stress, a tendency to experience transient paranoid thoughts and dissociative symptoms

The disorders in the dramatic/erratic cluster—borderline personality disorder, histrionic personality disorder, narcissistic personality disorder, and antisocial personality disorder—are characterized by symptoms that range from highly inconsistent behavior to inflated self-esteem, exaggerated emotional displays, and rule-breaking behavior. More is known about the etiology of personality disorders in the dramatic/erratic cluster than those in the other clusters.

Borderline Personality Disorder

Borderline personality disorder (BPD) has been a major focus of interest for several reasons. Among these reasons, BPD is very common in clinical settings, very hard to treat, and associated with suicidality.

Clinical Description The core features of **borderline personality disorder** (BPD) are impulsivity and instability in relationships and mood. For example, attitudes and feelings toward other people might change drastically and inexplicably very quickly. Emotions are intense, erratic and can shift abruptly, particularly from passionate idealization to contemptuous anger. As in the clinical case of Mary, which opened this chapter, the intense anger of people with BPD often damages relationships. People with BPD are overly sensitive to small signs of emotions in others (Lynch et al., 2006). Their unpredictable, impulsive, and potentially self-damaging behavior might include gambling, reckless spending, indiscriminate sexual activity, and substance abuse. People with BPD often have not developed a clear and coherent sense of self—they sometimes experience major swings in such basic aspects of identity as their values, loyalties, and career choices. They cannot bear to be alone, have fears of abandonment, demand attention, and experience chronic feelings of depression and emptiness. They may experience transient psychotic and dissociative symptoms when stressed.

Suicidal behavior is a particular concern in BPD. One study found that, over a 20-year period, approximately 7.5 percent of people with BPD committed suicide (Linehan & Heard, 1999). In a study of 621 people with BPD, 15.5 percent were found to have engaged in at least one suicidal behavior within the previous year (Yen et al., 2003). People with BPD are also particularly likely to engage in *self-mutilating behavior*. For example, they might slice their legs with a razor blade or burn their arms with cigarettes—behaviors that are harmful but unlikely to cause death. At least two-thirds of people with BPD will engage in self-mutilation at some point during their lives (Stone, 1993).

Over a 10- or 15-year period, as many as three-quarters of people with BPD stabilize so that they no longer meet diagnostic criteria, and their functioning approximates that of the general population (Zanarini et al., 2006). Most people no longer meet the diagnostic criteria by age 40 (Paris, 2002). Symptoms of self-harm and suicidality diminish more quickly than do other symptoms, such as tendencies toward anger and impulsivity (Zanarini et al., 2006).

People with BPD are highly likely to have a comorbid Axis I anxiety disorder (especially posttraumatic stress disorder) or mood disorder (McGlashan et al., 2000). They are also at risk for comorbid substance-related disorders and eating disorders, as well as for other personality disorders from the odd/eccentric cluster (McGlashan et al., 2000). When present, comorbid Axis I conditions predict greater likelihood that BPD symptoms will be sustained over a 6-year period (Zanarini et al., 2004).

A colorful account by Jonathan Kellerman, a clinical psychologist and successful mystery writer, gives a good sense of what people with BPD are like.

> They're the chronically depressed, the determinedly addictive, the compulsively divorced, living from one emotional disaster to the next. Bed hoppers, stomach pumpers, freeway jumpers, and sad-eyed bench-sitters with arms stitched up like footballs and psychic wounds that can never be sutured. Their egos are as fragile as spun sugar, their psyches irretrievably fragmented, like a jigsaw puzzle with crucial pieces missing. They play roles with alacrity, excel at being anyone but themselves, crave intimacy but repel it when they find it. Some of them gravitate toward stage or screen; others do their acting in more subtle ways. . . .
>
> Borderlines go from therapist to therapist, hoping to find a magic bullet for the crushing feelings of emptiness. They turn to chemical bullets, gobble tranquilizers and antidepressants, alcohol and cocaine. Embrace gurus and heaven-hucksters, any charismatic creep promising a quick fix of the pain. And they end up taking temporary vacations in psychiatric wards and prison cells, emerge looking good, raising everyone's hopes. Until the next letdown, real or imagined, the next excursion into self damage. (Kellerman, 1989, pp. 113–114)

Fortunately, research on new treatments for BPD, discussed later in the chapter, indicates a more positive outlook than Kellerman offers.

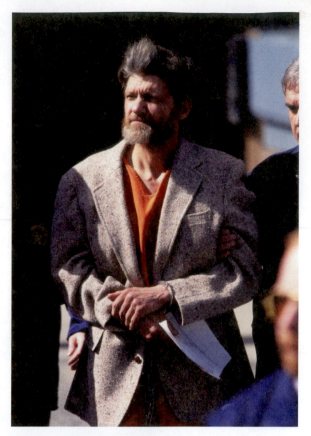

Ted Kaczynski, the "unibomber," is believed to have schizoid personality disorder; he has a long history of extreme detachment from interpersonal relationships. (Ralf-Finn Hestoft/Corbis Images.)

Etiology of Borderline Personality Disorder   There are several views concerning the causes of BPD. We discuss neurobiological factors, social factors, object relations theory, and Linehan's diathesis–stress theory.

Neurobiological Factors   Both twin studies and family studies support a strong heritability for BPD. Genes account for more than 60 percent of the variance in the development of this disorder. To understand the neurobiology of BPD, it helps to separate two types of symptoms of BPD—emotion dysregulation and impulsivity. Deficits in sensitivity to the neurotransmitter serotonin are associated with impulsivity and emotion dysregulation. People with BPD demonstrate lower serotonin function than do controls (Soloff et al., 2000).

Beyond serotonin, separable aspects of genetic and neurobiological vulnerability may contribute to the components of emotion dysregulation or impulsivity, rather than to the disorder as a whole (Siever et al., 2000). Consistent with the idea that emotional dysregulation may be one of the components of this disorder, the parents of people with BPD have elevated rates of mood disorders (Shachnow et al., 1997). Hence some of the genetic vulnerability to BPD might overlap with genetic vulnerability to mood disorders.

Otto Kernberg, one of the leading object relations theorists, has been very influential in the study of borderline personality disorder. (Courtesy Dr. Otto Kernberg.)

Some neurobiological characteristics might be closely related to emotional dysregulation. For example, people with BPD show increased activation of the amygdala (Herpetz et al., 2001; Silbersweig et al., 2007). Amygdala activation appears to be correlated with several disorders that involve intense emotions, including mood disorders and anxiety disorders, so it might be relevant for understanding the emotion dysregulation of BPD.

The prefrontal cortex is thought to help control impulsiveness, and in some studies, people with BPD perform poorly on neuropsychological tests of frontal lobe functioning (Bazanis et al., 2002; Fertuck et al., 2006; Ruchsow et al., 2006). In brain-imaging studies, people with BPD show low levels of activity and structural changes in the prefrontal cortex (van Elst et al., 2001, van Elst, 2003).

Social Factors: Childhood Abuse   People with BPD are much more likely to report a history of parental separation, verbal abuse, and emotional abuse during childhood than are people diagnosed with other Axis II disorders (Reich & Zanarini, 2001). Indeed, such abuse is believed to be more frequent among people with BPD than among people diagnosed with most other disorders (Herman, Perry, & van der Kolk, 1989), with the exception of dissociative identity disorder (see Chapter 6), which is also characterized by very high rates of childhood abuse. Given the frequency of dissociative symptoms in people with BPD, we can speculate that BPD and dissociative identity disorder might be related and that, in both, dissociation is caused by the extreme stress of child abuse. Indeed, one study found that people who dissociated after child abuse were more likely to develop symptoms of BPD (Ross et al., 1998). Two major psychological models build on these high rates of reported abuse to explain how a person might come to develop the symptoms of BPD. We review these theories in the next two sections.

Object Relations Theory   Object relations theory (see Chapter 2) focuses on the way children internalize their images of the people who are important to them, such as their parents. In other words, the central focus is how children identify with people to whom they have strong emotional attachments. These internalized images (***object relations***) become part of the person's ego and influence how the person reacts to the world. But internalized values can come into conflict with the wishes and ideals of the adult—for example, when a college-age woman has internalized the idea that all relationships will be abusive but strives to relate to a warm and supportive partner without conveying mistrust and suspicion.

Otto Kernberg is a leading object relations theorist who has written extensively about BPD. Kernberg (1985) proposed that adverse childhood experiences—for example, having parents who provide love and attention inconsistently, perhaps praising achievements but being unable to offer emotional support and warmth—cause children to internalize disturbed object representations that fail to integrate the loving and unloving aspects of the people who are close to them. As a result of these disturbed object relations, they develop insecure egos, a major feature of BPD. People with BPD cope with their fragile sense of self by seeking almost continuous reassurance.

To avoid perceived relationship threats, people with BPD often use a defense mechanism called splitting—dichotomizing objects into all good or all bad and failing to integrate positive and negative aspects of another person or the self into a whole. This tendency causes extreme difficulty in regulating emotions because people with BPD see the world, including themselves, in black-and-white terms. One week, they might see their therapist as a perfect human being, capable of saving them from pain and turmoil, but then might become scathingly angry the next week if the therapist is unavailable for some reason.

Linehan's Diathesis–Stress Theory   Marsha Linehan proposes that BPD develops when people who have difficulty controlling their emotions because of a biological diathesis (possibly genetic) are raised in a family environment that is invalidating. That is, a diathesis of emotional dysregulation interacts with experiences of invalidation to promote the development of BPD.

In an invalidating environment, the person's feelings are discounted and disrespected—that is, the person's efforts to communicate feelings are disregarded or even punished. An extreme form of invalidation is child abuse, either sexual or nonsexual, where the abusive parent claims to love the child and yet hurts the child.

The two main hypothesized factors—emotional dysregulation and invalidation—interact with each other in a dynamic fashion (see Figure 12.2). For example, the emotionally dysregulated child makes enormous demands on his or her family. The exasperated parents ignore or even punish the child's outbursts, which leads the child to suppress his or her emotions. The suppressed emotions build up to an explosion, which then gets the attention of the parents. Thus, the parents end up reinforcing the very behaviors that they find aversive. Many other patterns are possible, of course, but what they have in common is a vicious circle, a constant back-and-forth between dysregulation and invalidation.

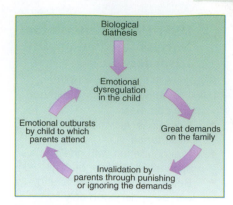

Figure 12.2 Marsha Linehan's diathesis–stress theory of borderline personality disorder.

Histrionic Personality Disorder

The key feature of **histrionic personality disorder** is overly dramatic and attention-seeking behavior. People with this disorder often use their physical appearance, such as unusual clothes, makeup, or hair color, to draw attention to themselves. Despite displaying extravagant and intense emotions, they are thought to be emotionally shallow. For example, someone with this disorder might gush about and call a person his or her best friend, only to have trouble remembering a conversation with that person the next day. They are self-centered, overly concerned with their physical attractiveness, and uncomfortable when not the center of attention. They can be inappropriately sexually provocative and seductive and are easily influenced by others. Their speech is often impressionistic and lacking in detail. For example, they might state a strong opinion yet be completely unable to support it. (*Patient:* "She was absolutely the greatest." *Interviewer:* "What did you like best about her?" *Patient:* "Gosh, I'm not sure I could describe that."). Histrionic personality disorder is highly comorbid with depression, borderline personality disorder, and medical problems (Nestadt et al., 1990).

Etiology of Histrionic Personality Disorder   Psychodyanmic theory proposes that the emotional display and seductiveness that are characteristic of this disorder are encouraged by parental seductiveness, especially a father's seductive behavior toward his daughter. The theory also proposes that people with this disorder were raised in a family environment in which parents talked about sex as something dirty yet behaved as though it was exciting and desirable. Such an upbringing might explain a preoccupation with sex, coupled with a fear of actually behaving sexually. Exaggerated displays of emotion are seen as symptoms of such underlying conflicts. Being the center of attention is seen as a way of defending against low self-esteem (Apt & Hurlbert, 1994). Unfortunately, this theory has not been tested.

Narcissistic Personality Disorder

People with **narcissistic personality disorder** have a grandiose view of their abilities and are preoccupied with fantasies of great success (as demonstrated by Bob in the clinical case below). They are more than a little self-centered—they require almost constant attention

DSM-IV-TR Criteria for Histrionic Personality Disorder

Presence of five or more of the following shown in many contexts by early adulthood:

- Strong need to be the center of attention
- Inappropriate sexually seductive behavior
- Rapidly shifting expression of emotions
- Use of physical appearance to draw attention to self
- Speech that is excessively impressionistic and lacking in detail
- Exaggerated, theatrical emotional expression
- Overly suggestible
- Misreads relationships as more intimate than they are

Clinical Case: Bob

Bob, a 50-year-old college professor, sought treatment only after urging from his wife. During the interview, Bob's wife noted concerns that he seemed so focused on himself and his own advancement that he often belittled others. Bob was dismissive of these concerns, stating that he had never been the sort of person to tolerate fools, and he could see no reason why he should begin offering such tolerance now—in rapid fire, he described his supervisor, his students, his parents, and a set of former friends as lacking the intelligence to merit his friendship. He willingly acknowledged working long hours but stated that his research had the potential to change life for people and that other activities could not be allowed to interfere with his success.

and excessive admiration. Their interpersonal relationships are disturbed by their lack of empathy, by their arrogance coupled with feelings of envy, by their habit of taking advantage of others, and by their feelings of entitlement—they expect others to do special favors for them. People with this disorder are extremely sensitive to criticism and might become enraged when others do not admire them. They tend to seek out high-status partners whom they idealize, but when, inevitably, these partners fall short of their unrealistic expectations, they become angry and rejecting (like those with borderline personality disorder). They are also likely to change partners if given an opportunity to be with a person of higher status. This disorder most often co-occurs with borderline personality disorder (Morey, 1988).

Etiology of Narcissistic Personality Disorder   In this section, we discuss the two most influential models of the etiology of this disorder: the self-psychology model and the social-cognitive model. Both theories are attempts to understand how a person develops these traits.

Self-Psychology Model   Heinz Kohut established a variant of psychoanalysis known as *self-psychology,* which he described in his two books, *The Analysis of the Self* (1971) and *The Restoration of the Self* (1977). Kohut noted that the person with narcissistic personality disorder projects remarkable self-importance, self-absorption, and fantasies of limitless success on the surface. But Kohut theorizes that these characteristics mask a very fragile self-esteem. People with narcissistic personality disorder strive to bolster their sense of self-worth through unending quests for respect from others.

Kohut described parenting styles that might contribute to the development of narcissism. When parents respond to a child with respect, warmth, and empathy, they endow the youngster with a normal sense of self-worth. Parental coldness may contribute to an insecure sense of self. Beyond this, Kohut described a pattern in which the child is valued as a means of fostering the parents' self-esteem, and the child's talents and abilities are overly emphasized. The child will experience a deep sense of shame over any of his or her shortcomings. Hence, Kohut hypothesized that two parenting dimensions would increase risk of narcissism: emotional coldness and an overemphasis on the child's achievements. Recent research indicates that people with high levels of narcissism report experiencing both of these parenting issues when they were children (Otway & Vignoles, 2006).

Narcissistic personality disorder draws its name from the Greek mythological figure Narcissus, who fell in love with his own reflection, was consumed by his own desire, and was transformed into a flower. (Museum Bojimans Van Beuningen, Rotterdam, Netherlands/Bridgeman Art Library/SuperStock, Inc.)

Social-Cognitive Model   A model of narcissistic personality disorder developed by Carolyn Morf and Frederick Rhodewalt (2001) is built around two basic ideas: first, that people with this disorder have fragile self-esteem, in part because they are trying to maintain the belief that they are special and second, that interpersonal interactions are important to them for bolstering self-esteem, rather than for gaining closeness or warmth. In other words, they are captive to the goal of maintaining a grand vision of themselves, and this goal pervades their experiences. The work of Morf and Rhodewalt is impressive in that they have designed laboratory research studies aimed at elucidating the cognitive, emotional, and interpersonal processes associated with narcissistic personality disorder.

To assess the idea that people with narcissistic personality disorder are trying to maintain grandiose beliefs about themselves, they examine biases in how people with this disorder rate themselves in various settings. For example, in laboratory studies, people with narcissistic personality disorder overestimate their attractiveness to others and their contributions to group activities. ("Others must be jealous of me, I've been responsible for the lion-share of our progress here today.") In some studies, researchers have provided people with feedback that they were successful on a task (regardless of their actual performance), then asked participants to rate the reasons why they were successful. In these types of studies, people with narcissistic personality disorder attribute successes to their abilities rather than chance or luck. So, a set of studies suggest that people with narcissistic personality disorder show cognitive biases that would help maintain grandiose beliefs about the self.

To assess whether people with narcissistic personality disorder have fragile self-esteem, Morf and Rhodewalt review studies of how much self-esteem depends on external feedback. For example, when falsely told they have done poorly on an IQ test, they show much more reactivity than others do; similarly, they show more reactivity to being told they have succeeded at something. Morf and Rhodewalt argue that this vulnerability of self-esteem to external feedback arises from the attempt to maintain an inflated self-view.

According to this theory, when people with narcissistic personality disorder interact with others, their primary goal is to bolster their own self-esteem. This goal influences how they act toward others in several ways. First, they tend to brag a lot; this often works well initially, but over time, repeated bragging comes to be perceived negatively by others (Paulhus, 1998). Second, when someone else performs better than they do on a task that is relevant to self-esteem, they will denigrate the other person, even if they have to do so to that person's face. That is, it is more important for them to be admired or to achieve competitive success than it is to have closeness with others. This framework makes it easy to understand why people with narcissistic personality disorder do things that alienate others; their sense of self depends on "winning," not in gaining or maintaining closeness (Campbell et al., 2007).

Check Your Knowledge 12.2

Answer the questions.

1. Which personality disorder is most related to schizophrenia in family history studies?
   a. schizoid
   b. schizotypal
   c. antisocial
   d. borderline

2. Which of the following factors play a central role in Linehan's model of BPD (choose all that apply)?
   a. emotional dysregulation

   b. parental invalidation
   c. conflicts between introjected values and current needs
   d. splitting as a defense mechanism

3. Which personality disorder is most common in clinical settings?
   a. schizoid
   b. schizotypal
   c. antisocial
   d. borderline

Antisocial Personality Disorder and Psychopathy

Informally, the terms *antisocial personality disorder* and *psychopathy* (sometimes referred to as *sociopathy*) often are used interchangeably. Antisocial behavior, such as breaking laws, is an important component of both, but there are important differences between the two disorders. One difference is that antisocial personality disorder is included in the DSM-IV-TR, whereas psychopathy is not. In this next section, we will review the definitions of these two highly related constructs, then discuss research on the etiology of these syndromes.

Clinical Case

A 19-year-old man with irregular breathing, a rapid pulse, and dilated pupils was brought to the hospital by a friend, who eventually admitted that they had been using a lot of cocaine before the symptoms began. The men didn't want to identify themselves, but eventually the medical team was able to get enough information to contact the patient's mother, who arrived at the hospital distraught and smelling of alcohol. When interviewed, she reported that her son had a long history of disobedience and disengagement from family activities. When she attempted to set rules, he became violently argumentative; he often stayed out all night. She said that the father was not present to help with parenting. She believed that her son was a good student and a star basketball player, but both of these beliefs turned out to be false. Later research revealed, though, that her son was deeply involved in drugs and in drag racing, and he bragged that he typically consumed a case of beer per day. He used various schemes to get money for drugs, including stealing car radios and taking money from his mother. He denied that he had any problems and ended his first interview with a therapist early. [Adapted from Spitzer et al. (1994).]

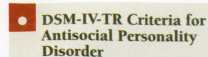

DSM-IV-TR Criteria for Antisocial Personality Disorder

- Age at least 18
- Evidence of conduct disorder before age 15
- Pervasive pattern of disregard for the rights of others since the age of 15 as shown by at least three of the following:
  1. Repeated law-breaking
  2. Deceitfulness, lying
  3. Impulsivity
  4. Irritability and aggressiveness
  5. Reckless disregard for own safety and that of others
  6. Irresponsibility as seen in unreliable employment or financial history
  7. Lack of remorse

Antisocial Personality Disorder: Clinical Description   The DSM-IV-TR diagnostic criteria for **antisocial personality disorder** (APD) include two major components: (1) a pervasive pattern of disregard for the rights of others since the age of 15, and (2) the presence of a conduct disorder (see Chapter 14) before the age of 15. Truancy, running away from home, frequent lying, theft, arson, and deliberate destruction of property are major symptoms of conduct disorder. People with APD show irresponsible behavior such as working only inconsistently, breaking laws, being irritable and physically aggressive, defaulting on debts, being reckless and impulsive, and neglecting to plan ahead. They show little regard for truth and little remorse for their misdeeds.

The disorder is more common among people of low socioeconomic status, and there is evidence that culture influences whether or not people develop this disorder—for example, rates of APD are higher in the United States than in Scotland (Cooke & Michie, 1999). Rates are also higher among younger adults than among older adults, and some people seem to mature out of the symptoms. In one study, people who had been hospitalized for APD were followed up 16 to 45 years later. About one-quarter of them no longer had APD, and another third had improved (Black, Baumgard, & Bell, 1995). About three-quarters of people with APD meet the diagnostic criteria for another disorder, with substance abuse being the most common comorbid disorder (Newman et al., 1998). Not surprisingly, then, high rates of APD are observed in drug and alcohol rehabilitation facilities (Sutker & Adams, 2001).

Psychopathy: Clinical Description   The concept of psychopathy predates the DSM-IV-TR diagnosis of antisocial personality disorder. In his classic book *The Mask of Sanity* (1941/1976), Hervey Cleckley drew on his clinical experience to formulate diagnostic criteria for psychopathy. Unlike the DSM diagnostic criteria for APD that focus on observable symptoms, Cleckley's criteria for psychopathy refer less to behavior per se and more to the person's thoughts and feelings.

In Cleckley's description, one of the key characteristics of psychopathy is poverty of emotions, both positive and negative: Psychopathic people have no sense of shame, and their seemingly positive feelings for others are merely an act. They are superficially charming and use that charm to manipulate others for personal gain. Their lack of anxiety might make it impossible for them to learn from their mistakes, and their lack of remorse leads them to behave irresponsibly and often cruelly toward others. Another key point in Cleckley's description is that the antisocial behavior of a person with psychopathy is performed impulsively, as much for thrills as for a reason such as financial gain.

The most commonly used scale to assess psychopathy is the Psychopathy Checklist–Revised (Hare, 2003). Raters using this scale conduct an extensive interview but also gather information from other sources, such as criminal records and social worker reports, to rate 20 items. Some of the items overlap with the criteria for APD, including juvenile delinquency, criminality, impulsivity, and irresponsibility. The scale also includes interpersonal items (such as superficial charm, pathological lying, and manipulativeness) and affective symptoms (such as lack of remorse, shallow affect, and lack of empathy) (Hare & Neumann, 2006).

As you can see, the criteria for APD and psychopathy differ a good deal. Note that the criteria for psychopathy do not require onset of symptoms before age 15. Some researchers criticize the APD criteria for relying on retrospective reports of people who may not describe their behavior accurately (Hare, Hart, & Harpur, 1991)

Because the criteria for psychopathy criteria cover a broader range of problems than do the criteria for APD, many of the people diagnosed with APD do not meet criteria for psychopathy. Indeed, only 20 percent of people diagnosed with APD obtain high scores on the Psychopathy Checklist (Rutherford, Cacciola, & Alterman, 1999). However, because the APD criteria emphasize observable behaviors, APD is three times as common in criminal settings as is psychopathy (Hare & Neumann, 2006). Both APD and psychopathy are observed much more frequently among men than women.

Etiology of Antisocial Personality Disorder and Psychopathy   In this section, we consider the etiology of APD and psychopathy. As we review the research in this area, keep in mind two issues that make findings a little hard to integrate. First, research has been conducted on persons diagnosed in different ways—some with APD and some with psychopathy. Second, most research on APD and psychopathy has been conducted on persons who have been convicted as criminals. Thus, the results of this research might not be applicable to psychopaths who are not criminals or who avoid arrest. Indeed, on cognitive and psychophysiological measures, psychopaths who have been convicted show more deficits than those who have not been caught (Ishikawa et al., 2001).

Genetic Factors   Adoption studies reveal a higher-than-normal prevalence of antisocial behavior in adopted children of biological parents with APD and substance abuse (Cadoret et al., 1995; Ge et al., 1996). Older studies suggested that criminality (Gottesman & Goldsmith, 1994), psychopathy (Taylor et al., 2003), and APD (Eley, Lichtenstein, & Moffitt, 2003) were moderately heritable, with heritability estimates of 40 to 50 percent. Remember, though, that poor reliability will limit validity and that test–retest and multiple informant reliability estimates for personality disorders can be low.

Three-quarters of convicted felons meet the DSM criteria for antisocial personality disorder. (Chris Steele-Perkins/Magnum Photos, Inc.)

Recent studies have addressed this by gathering repeated measures of symptoms (Burt et al., 2007), by gathering multiple indices of psychopathy (Larsson, Andershed, & Lichtenstein, 2006), or by gathering reports of antisocial symptoms from teachers, parents, and children (Baker et al., 2007). By combining multiple measures, one can obtain an index of psychopathy or antisocial behavior that is much more reliable. Each study using this type of approach has found much higher heritability estimates; in one case, it was estimated that heritability of antisocial behavior symptoms was .96 (Baker et al., 2007).

Genetic risk for APD, psychopathy, conduct disorder, and substance abuse appear to be related. A person might inherit a general vulnerability for these types of symptoms, and then environmental factors might shape which of the symptoms evolve (Kendler, Prescott, et al., 2003; Larsson et al., 2007). Some genetic risk, however, is very specific—for example, some genes might influence aggressive behavior within APD (Eley et al., 2003).

Adoption research has also shown that genetic, behavioral, and family influences are very hard to disentangle (Ge et al., 1996). That is, the genetically influenced antisocial behavior of the child can provoke harsh discipline and lack of warmth, even in adoptive parents, and these parental characteristics in turn exacerbate the child's antisocial tendencies.

Social Factors: Family Environment and Poverty   Since much psychopathic behavior violates social norms, many investigators focus on the primary agent of socialization, the family, in their search for the explanation of such behavior. High negativity, low warmth, and parental inconsistency predict antisocial behavior (Marshall & Cooke, 1999; Reiss et al., 1995). The family environment might be particularly important when a child has an inherited tendency toward antisocial behavior. For example, in the adoption study referred to above (Cadoret et al., 1995), an adverse environment in the adoptive home (such as marital problems and substance abuse) was related to the development of APD, particularly when the biological parents had APD.

Outside of twin studies, there is substantial prospective research to show that social factors, including poverty and exposure to violence, predict antisocial behavior in children (Loeber & Hay, 1997), even when children are not genetically at risk for APD (Jaffee et al., 2002). Among adolescents with conduct disorder, those who are impoverished are twice as likely to develop APD as are those from higher socioeconomic status backgrounds (Lahey et al., 2005).

Emotion and Psychopathy   There is a large body of work on the emotional components of psychopathy. In defining the psychopathic syndrome, Cleckley noted the inability of people with psychopathy to profit from experience or even from punishment; they seem to be unable to avoid the negative consequences of social misbehavior. Many are chronic lawbreakers despite their experiences with jail sentences. They seem immune to the anxiety or pangs of conscience that keep most of us from breaking the law, lying, or injuring others, and they have difficulty curbing their impulses. In the terminology of learning theory, psychopaths do not learn to avoid certain behaviors because they are unresponsive to punishments for their antisocial behavior. Presumably, they do not experience conditioned fear responses when they encounter situations in which such responses would normally serve to inhibit antisocial behavior.

A classic study tested the idea that people with psychopathy have few inhibitions about committing antisocial acts because they experience little anxiety (Lykken, 1957). It is believed that anxiety mediates the ability to learn to avoid aversive stimuli, such as shocks. Lykken assessed how well people with psychopathy learned to avoid shock. Consistent with the idea that psychopathy is associated with low anxiety levels, people with psychopathy were poorer than controls at learning to avoid shock.

Studies of the activity of the autonomic nervous system have also yielded with supported the idea that psychopaths respond to fear-eliciting stimuli with less anxiety than other people. At rest, people with psychopathy have lower-than-normal levels of skin conductance, and their skin conductance is less reactive when they are confronted with or anticipate an aversive stimulus (Lorber, 2004). In one study, skin conductance reactivity to aversive stimuli (loud tones) at age 3 was found to predict psychopathy scores at age 28 (Glenn et al., 2007). Research using other methods of assessing emotion has confirmed these results. One study measured the eyeblink component of the startle response, a good nonverbal indicator of whether a person is in a negative emotional state. When people are anxious, they demonstrate a larger startle response in response to a sudden loud noise. People with psychopathy do not show increased startle while they are viewing negative stimuli, like a picture of a gun or a horrible accident (Levenston et al., 2000), confirming the idea that they do not experience anxiety in response to aversive stimuli.

In an interesting extension of this theory, researchers used brain activity as a way to examine what happens with classical conditioning in which an unconditioned stimulus (painful pressure) was repeatedly paired with a neutral picture (the conditioned stimuli). To measure responses to the CS after these repeated pairings, the researchers measured activity of the amygdala and other brain regions involved in emotion responsivity (Birbaumer et al., 2005). After conditioning, healthy control participants showed increases in amygdala activity when viewing the neutral pictures. People with psychopathy, though, did not show this expected increase in amgydala activity. These findings suggest that the people with psychopathy are failing to show classical conditioning to aversive stimuli at a very basic level.

The research we have described so far has been based on the idea that punishment does not arouse strong emotions in people with psychopathy and thus does not inhibit antisocial behavior. But some researchers believe that empathy, not punishment, is the critical agent of socialization. Empathy means being in tune with the emotional reactions of others; thus, empathizing with someone's distress could inhibit the tendency toward callous exploitation. From this perspective, one could argue that some features of psychopathy arise from a lack of empathy.

This idea has been tested by monitoring the skin conductance of men with and without psychopathy as they viewed slides showing three different types of pictures: threatening (e.g., gun, shark), neutral (e.g., book), and others' distress (e.g., a crying person). Unlike the results of the studies described above, the two groups did not differ in their responses to threatening stimuli, but the people with psychopathy were less responsive to the slides of others' distress (Blair et al., 1997)—that is, those with psychopathy indeed appeared to show less empathy (see Figure 12.3). Similarly, when asked to identify the emotion conveyed in pictures of various strangers, men with psychopathy did very poorly in recognizing others' fear, even though they recognized other emotions well (Marsh & Blair, 2008).

Response Modulation, Impulsivity, and Psychopathy Impulsivity is defined as the tendency to pursue potential rewards without attending to potential threats. Remember that the prefrontal cortex is involved in inhibiting impulsivity. More specifically, poor functioning of the

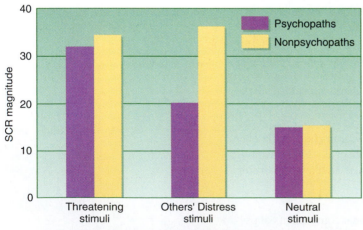

Figure 12.3 Skin-conductance response (SCR) of men with and without psychopathy to three types of stimuli. The men with psychopathy showed less responsiveness to the distress stimuli, indicating a deficit in empathy. (Blair et al.1997).

prefrontal cortex is related to the tendency to respond impulsively to immediate rewards and to the inability to learn to avoid punishment. Some researchers have suggested that deficits in the prefrontal cortex may drive psychopathy (Gorenstein & Newman, 1980). This idea is supported by studies showing that people with psychopathy have less gray matter in the prefrontal cortex than people without psychopathy (Raine & Yang, 2007).

People with psychopathy also show impulsivity when presented with a task designed to test the ability to modify responses depending on success or failure (Patterson & Newman, 1993). In one study demonstrating this phenomenon, participants viewed played a computerized card game (Newman, Patterson, & Kosson, 1987). If a face card appeared, the participant won five cents; if a nonface card appeared, the participant lost five cents. After each trial, the participant had the opportunity to continue or stop the game. The probability of losing was controlled by the experimenter and started at 10 percent. Thereafter, the probability of losing increased by 10 percent for every 10 cards played until it reached 100 percent. People with psychopathy continued to play the game much longer than did people without psychopathy. Nine of twelve people in the psychopathy group never quit, even though they had lost money on 19 of the last 20 trials. That is, they did not quit pursuing reward even though they were being punished.

The same game was played again with one variation—a 5-second waiting period was imposed after feedback, thus delaying the decision about whether to play again. This dramatically reduced the number of trials for which people with psychopathy played the game. It seems that enforcing a delay might lead people with psychopathy to reflect on negative feedback and behave less impulsively. Insensitivity to feedback of many forms (particularly without a pause for reflection) appears to be a feature of psychopathy (Newman, Schmitt, & Voss, 1997).

A card-guessing task that manipulates the odds of winning and losing was used to demonstrate psychopaths' impulsivity (Newman, Patterson, & Kosson, 1987). (Courtesy of Joseph Newman.)

Check Your Knowledge 12.3

True or false?
1. Psychopathy and borderline personality disorder are tied to impulsivity.
2. Psychopathy is tied to increased amygdala activation.
3. Psychopathy appears related to decreased emotional responsiveness.
4. Conduct disorder is not required for a DSM-IV-TR diagnosis of APD.

Quick Summary

The dramatic/erratic cluster (cluster B) includes borderline personality disorder, histrionic personality disorder, narcissistic personality disorder, and antisocial personality disorder. The key features of borderline personality disorder include intense emotionality, unstable identity, and impulsivity. Histrionic personality disorder is characterized by exaggerated emotional displays. Narcissistic personality disorder is characterized by highly inflated self-esteem but a deep need for admiration. Antisocial personality disorder is defined by violation of rules, and a disregard for others' feelings and social norms. Psychopathy is related to antisocial personality disorder but is not defined in the DSM. Psychopathy criteria focus on internal experiences as well as observable behavior.

There is evidence that BPD is inherited, and that heritability might be particularly related to the greater emotional dysregulation and impulsivity. Consistent with the symptoms of impulsivity, research indicates diminished activity in the prefrontal cortex among people with BPD. Consistent with the greater emotionality, people with BPD have also been found to demonstrate increased activity in the amygdala and decreased functioning of the serotonin system.

People with BPD report elevated rates of abuse. Both object relations theories and Linehan's model build on the high rates of abuse reported by people with BPD. Linehan's model also emphasizes the biological diathesis for emotional dysregulation. Object relations theory places an emphasis on conflicts between the internalized values drawn from major relationships and defense mechanisms such as splitting. Linehan's model focuses on emotional dysregulation coupled with parental invalidation.

Researchers know relatively little about the roots of histrionic personality disorder. This personality disorder is believed to be related to poor parenting.

According to the self-psychology theory of narcissistic personality disorder, parents who are inconsistent and focused on their own worth fail to help the child develop a stable sense of self-worth. Social-cognitive theory proposes that the behavior of the person with narcissistic personality disorder is shaped by the goal of maintaining specialness and the belief that that the purpose of interpersonal interactions is to bolster self-esteem.

When carefully measured, antisocial personality disorder and psychopathy are both highly heritable. Beyond genes, family environment and poverty seem to play a role in the development of this disorder.

People with psychopathy have little anxiety. Their callous treatment of others might also be linked to their lack of empathy.

People with psychopathy are deficient in using negative feedback when pursuing reward—that is, they behave impulsively. This lack of anxiety and empathy, as well as their impulsivity, may drive misconduct without regret.

Anxious/Fearful Cluster

The anxious/fearful cluster includes avoidant personality disorder, dependent personality disorder, and obsessive-compulsive personality disorder. People with these disorders are prone to worry and distress.

Avoidant Personality Disorder

People with **avoidant personality disorder** are so fearful of criticism, rejection, and disapproval that they will avoid jobs or relationships to protect themselves from negative feedback. In social situations they are restrained because of an extreme fear of saying something foolish, being embarrassed, blushing, or showing other signs of anxiety. They believe they are incompetent and inferior to others and are reluctant to take risks or try new activities.

About 80 percent of people with avoidant personality disorder have comorbid major depression, as Leon did in the clinical case. Other common comorbid conditions include borderline personality disorder, schizotypal personality disorder, and alcohol abuse (McGlashan et al., 2000). The very high rate of comorbidity with social phobia is probably a result of the fact that the diagnostic criteria for these two disorders are so similar; avoidant personality disorder might actually be a more chronic variant of social phobia (Alden et al., 2002). See Figure 5.1 (p. 0) for one way of thinking about these two disorders.

Both avoidant personality disorder and social phobia are related to a syndrome called taijin kyofusho that occurs in Japan (*taijin* means "interpersonal" and *kyofusho* means "fear"). Like people with avoidant personality disorder and social phobia, those with taijin kyofusho are overly sensitive in interpersonal situations and avoid interpersonal contact. But what they fear is somewhat different from the usual fears of those with the DSM diagnoses. People with taijin kyofusho tend to be anxious or ashamed about how they affect or appear to others—for example, they fear that they are ugly or have body odor (Ono et al., 1996).

Dependent Personality Disorder

The core features of **dependent personality disorder** are an overreliance on others and a lack of self-confidence. People with dependent personality disorder have an intense need to be taken care of, which often leads them to feel uncomfortable when alone. They subordinate their own

Clinical Case: Leon

Leon was a 45-year-old man who sought treatment for depression, which he claimed to have experienced almost continuously since the first grade. During the interview, Leon described feeling uncomfortable socially for as long as he could remember. By age five, he would experience intense anxiety with other children, and his mind would "go blank" if he had to speak in front of others. He grew up dreading birthday parties, teacher's classroom questions, and meeting new children. Although he was able to play with some of the children in his neighborhood, he never had a "best friend," and he never went out on a date. Although he did well academically through high school, his grades worsened during college. He took a job at the post office after graduation because it involved little social interaction. [Adapted from Spitzer et al. (1994).]

Clinical Case: Matthew

Matthew was a 34-year-old man who sought treatment after breaking up with a girlfriend. His mother, with whom he lived, had disapproved of his marriage plans because his girlfriend came from a different religious background. Matthew felt that he could not marry his girlfriend without his mother's approval because "blood is thicker than water." Although he canceled the engagement, he was angry with his mother and feared that she would never approve of anyone he wanted to marry. He said that he feared disagreeing with his mother because he did not want to have to "fend for himself." [Adapted from Spitzer et al. (2002).]

needs to ensure that they do not break up the protective relationships they have established. When a close relationship ends, they urgently seek another relationship to replace it. They see themselves as weak, and they turn to others for support and decision-making. The clinical case history of Matthew provides an example of dependent personality disorder.

The DSM diagnostic criteria for dependent personality disorder include some features that do not appear to be well supported by research. Specifically, the criteria portray people with dependent personality disorder as being very passive (e.g., having difficulty initiating projects or doing things on their own, not being able to disagree with others, allowing others to make decisions for them). Research indicates, however, that people with dependent personality disorder actually can do what is necessary to maintain a close relationship; this might involve being very deferential and passive, but it might involve taking active steps to preserve the relationship (Bornstein, 1997).

The prevalence of dependent personality disorder is higher in India and Japan than in the United States, perhaps because these societies encourage some behaviors that might be construed as dependent. Dependent personality disorder often co-occurs with borderline, schizoid, histrionic, schizotypal, and avoidant personality disorders, as well as with mood disorders, anxiety disorders, and bulimia.

Obsessive-Compulsive Personality Disorder

The person with **obsessive-compulsive personality disorder** is a perfectionist, preoccupied with details, rules, and schedules. People with this disorder often pay so much attention to detail that they fail to finish projects. They are more oriented toward work than pleasure. They have inordinate difficulty making decisions (lest they err) and allocating time (lest they focus on the wrong thing). Their interpersonal relationships are often troubled because they demand that everything be done the right way—their way. They often become known as "control freaks." Generally, they are serious, rigid, formal, and inflexible, especially regarding moral issues. They are unable to discard worn-out and useless objects, even those with no sentimental value, and they are likely to be excessively frugal to a level that causes concern for those around them.

Obsessive-compulsive personality disorder is quite different from obsessive-compulsive disorder (OCD), despite the similarity in names. The personality disorder does not include the obsessions and compulsions that define the latter. Indeed, only a minority of people with OCD meet the diagnostic criteria for obsessive-compulsive personality disorder (Baer & Jenike, 1992). The disorder most frequently comorbid with obsessive-compulsive personality disorder is avoidant personality disorder (see DSM-IV-TR criteria on the next page).

Etiology of the Personality Disorders in the Anxious/Fearful Cluster

We briefly review ideas about the etiology of avoidant personality disorders, then obsessive-compulsive personality disorder, followed by dependent personality disorder. We begin by describing the evidence for heritability and then highlight social and psychological models.

> ### DSM-IV-TR Criteria for Dependent Personality Disorder
>
> An excessive need to be taken care of, as shown by the presence of at least five of the following beginning in early adulthood and shown in many contexts:
> - Difficulty making decisions without excessive advice and reassurance from others
> - Need for others to take responsibility for most major areas of life
> - Difficulty disagreeing with others for fear of losing their support
> - Difficulty doing things on own because of lack of self-confidence
> - Doing unpleasant things as a way to obtain the approval and support of others
> - Feelings of helplessness when alone because of lack of confidence in ability to handle things without others
> - Urgently seeking new relationship when one ends
> - Preoccupation with fears of having to take care of self

DSM-IV-TR Criteria for Obsessive-Compulsive Personality Disorder

Intense need for order and control, as shown by the presence of at least four of the following beginning by early adulthood and evidenced in many contexts:

- Preoccupation with rules, details, and organization to the extent that the point of an activity is lost
- Extreme perfectionism interferes with task completion
- Excessive devotion to work to the exclusion of leisure and friendships
- Inflexibility about morals and values
- Difficulty discarding worthless items
- Reluctance to delegate unless others conform to one's standards
- Miserliness
- Rigidity and stubbornness

Very little research has been conducted to examine the heritability of cluster C personality disorders. Heritability appears to be about 27–35 percent for avoidant personality disorder (Reichborn-Kjennerud, Czajkowski, Neale et al., 2007; Torgersen et al., 2000). Although it is clear that genes influence the other personality disorders in cluster C, two available twin studies vary widely in their heritability estimates (Reichborn-Kjennerud, Czajkowski, Neale, et al., 2007; Torgersen et al., 2000).

For decades, theorists have suggested that the cluster C personality disorders relate to early childhood experiences. For example, avoidant personality disorder was thought to result when a child was taught, perhaps through modeling, to fear people and situations that others would regard as harmless.

Obsessive-compulsive personality traits were originally viewed by Freud as caused by fixation at the anal stage of psychosexual development. More contemporary psychodynamic theories emphasize a fear of loss of control, which is handled by overcompensation. For example, the man who is a compulsive workaholic might fear that his life will fall apart if he allows himself to relax and have fun.

Investigators have argued that dependent personality disorder may result from an overprotective and authoritarian parenting style that prevents the development of feelings of self-efficacy (Bornstein, 1997). Dependent personality disorder might also be related to "attachment" problems (Livesley, Schroeder, & Jackson, 1990). Developmental psychologists regard attachment as one of the major influences on personality development (see Chapter 2). In healthy development, infants become attached to an adult and use the adult as a secure base from which to explore and pursue other goals. Separation from the adult leads to anger and distress. As development proceeds, children become less dependent on the presence of the attachment figure for security. It is possible that the abnormal attachment behaviors seen in dependent personality disorder reflect something gone wrong in the usual developmental process, such as a disruption of the early parent–child relationship caused by death, neglect, rejection, or overprotectiveness. Persons with dependent personality disorder engage in a number of tactics, originally established to maintain their relationship with their parents, to keep their relationships with other people at any cost—for example, agreeing to do unpleasant tasks to keep others happy (Stone, 1993).

Check Your Knowledge 12.4

You are the director of human resources for a major corporation. You are asked to review a set of situations in which employees had interpersonal and task-focused problems that were severe and persistent enough to raise concerns in the workplace. Name the most likely personality disorder for each of the following.

1. José refuses to meet with his boss; he says that the boss is stupid and that only the top guns could understand the type of brilliant ideas he is generating. When asked to write his ideas down in a memo that could be shared, he refuses, stating that he doesn't have time for such petty exercises. When you sit down to meet with him, his first question is whether you are in a position of power to help him negotiate a higher salary.

2. Mariana refuses to meet with customers. She states that she is terrified that they will see that she does not know much. It turns out that she has called in sick the last three times her boss scheduled an appointment with her, and her colleagues barely know her name. When asked, she says that meeting with any of these people makes her feel horribly nervous about potential rejection of her ideas. She asks for a position that would involve little social contact.

3. Sheila has had three subordinate employees request transfers from her department. They each stated that she was too controlling, picked on

small mistakes, and would not listen to any new ideas for solving problems. At the interview, she brought in a typed, 15-page chart of the goals she would like to execute for the company. Despite having an inordinate number of goals, she has failed to complete a single project during her first year with the company.

4. Seth, a 52-year-old man who has worked in the mailroom for 10 years, has been the subject of complaints from many other staff members. They say that he seems cold and indifferent, even though they attempt to include him in conversations. Other mailroom staff say they can't get him to talk. When you meet with Seth, he explains that he really has no interest in having friends or joining parties; socializing is just not part of his life in general. He is completely unenthusiastic about his colleagues, but he does his work without any other problems.

5. Police contact you to let you know that they have arrested Sam, one of your employees. He was caught at a bank trying to cash a $10,000 company check on which he had forged the signature. You learn that Sam had previously defrauded three other companies. When you meet with Sam, he laughs about how easy it was to get access to the checkbook, and he does not seem the least bit sorry.

Treatment of Personality Disorders

It is important to bear in mind that many people with personality disorders enter treatment because of an Axis I disorder rather than a personality disorder. For example, a person with antisocial personality disorder might seek treatment of substance-abuse problems; a person with avoidant personality disorder might seek treatment for social phobia; and a patient with obsessive-compulsive personality disorder might seek help for depression. In this connection, it can be mentioned that people with Axis I disorders and personality disorders usually do not improve as much from various forms of psychotherapy as do people with Axis I disorders alone (Crits-Christoph & Barber, 2002). The reason seems pretty clear: people with both types of disorders are more seriously disturbed than are those with only Axis I disorders and therefore might require treatment that is both more intensive (because of the long-standing nature of personality disorders) and more extensive (i.e., focused on a broad range of psychological problems).

Medications are often used to treat personality disorders (Koenigsberg, Woo-Ming, & Siever, 2002), the choice of drug being determined by the Axis I problem that the personality disorder resembles. For example, clients with avoidant personality disorder can be prescribed antidepressants in hopes of reducing their social anxieties. Given the connections noted earlier between schizophrenia and schizotypal personality disorder, it is not surprising that antipsychotic drugs (e.g., risperidone, trade name Risperdal) have shown some effectiveness with schizotypal personality disorder (Koenigsberg et al., 2003).

People with serious symptoms of personality disorders might attend a day treatment program that offers psychotherapy, in both group and individual formats, for several hours per day. Typically, psychotherapy sessions are interspersed with social and occupational therapy. The length of such programs varies, but some last several months. Programs tend to vary in their treatment approaches, with some offering psychodynamic approaches, others offering supportive approaches, and still others offering cognitive behavioral treatments. The early findings suggest that day treatment programs lead to improvements in symptoms and social functioning (Ogrodniczuk & Piper, 2001). Beyond day treatment programs, many clients are seen in individual outpatient psychological treatment. A review of 15 studies suggested that 52 percent of clients recovered within about 15 months of treatment (Perry, Banon, & Ianni, 1999). Most of these studies of the effectiveness of either day treatment or psychotherapy, though, do not include a control group but rather compare clients to those receiving standard care. This is of concern—Remember that half of personality disorders seem to dissipate over time naturally (see Figure 12.1). Given this, psychotherapy studies comparing active treatment to a control treatment are needed.

Psychodynamic therapists aim to alter the patient's present-day views of the childhood problems assumed to underlie the personality disorder. For example, they might guide a man with obsessive-compulsive personality disorder to the realization that his childhood quest to win his parents' love by being perfect does not need be carried into adulthood—that he does not need to be perfect to win the approval of others and that it is possible to make mistakes without being abandoned by those whose love he seeks. Studies of psychodynamic treatment often include a broad range of different personality disorders. In one trial that focused on more specific personality disorders, brief psychodynamic treatment was shown to be helpful in reducing symptoms of histrionic personality disorder and of personality disorders in the anxious/fearful cluster (Winston et al., 1994).

Cognitive behavioral therapists tend to break a personality disorder down into a set of separate problems. For example, a person diagnosed as having a paranoid personality disorder or avoidant personality disorder is extremely sensitive to criticism. This sensitivity might be treated by social skills training in how to address criticism, by systematic desensitization, or by cognitive therapy (Renneberg et al., 1990). Since the argumentativeness of people with paranoid personality disorder provokes counterattacks from others, the behavior therapist might help the person learn less antagonizing ways of relating to other people. Social skills training in a support group might encourage people with avoidant personality disorder to be more assertive with other people; one controlled study confirmed that this is a promising strategy (Alden, 1989).

Table 12.5 Examples of Maladaptive Cognitions Hypothesized to Be Associated with Each Personality Disorder

Personality Disorder	Maladaptive Cognitions
Avoidant	If people *know* the real me, they will reject me.
Dependent	I need people to survive, and I need constant encouragement and reassurance.
Obsessive-compulsive	I know what's best.
	People *should* do better and try harder.
Paranoid	Don't trust anyone.
	Be on guard.
Antisocial	I am entitled to *break* rules.
	Others are exploitative.
Narcissistic	Since I am special, I *deserve* special rules.
	I am better than others.
Histrionic	People are there to serve or admire me.
Schizoid	Others are unrewarding.
	Relationships are messy and undesirable.

Source: Beck & Freeman (1990).

Children normally go through a phase in which separation from a parent is distressing. People with dependent personality disorder might be experiencing a similar phenomenon in their adult relationships. (Mary Kate Denny/PhotoEdit.)

In cognitive therapy for personality disorders, Aaron Beck and colleagues (1990) apply the same kind of analysis used in the treatment of depression (see p. 238). Each disorder is analyzed in terms of negative cognitive beliefs that could help explain the pattern of symptoms (see Table 12.5). For example, cognitive therapy for a perfectionistic person with obsessive-compulsive personality disorder entails first persuading the patient to accept the essence of the cognitive model—that feelings and behaviors are primarily a function of thoughts. Biases in thinking are then explored, such as when the patient concludes that he or she cannot do anything right because of failing in one particular endeavor. The therapist also looks for dysfunctional assumptions or schemata that might underlie the person's thoughts and feelings—for example, the belief that it is critical for every decision to be correct. Beyond challenging cognitions, Beck's approach to personality disorders incorporates a variety of other cognitive behavioral techniques.

The traits that characterize the personality disorders are probably too ingrained to change thoroughly. Instead, the therapist—regardless of theoretical orientation—might find it more realistic to change a disorder into a style or a more adaptive way of approaching life (Millon, 1996).

Treatment of Borderline Personality Disorder

Few clients pose a greater challenge to treatment than do those with borderline personality disorder, regardless of the type of treatment being used. Clients with borderline personality disorder tend to show their interpersonal problems in the therapeutic relationship as much as they do in other relationships. Because these clients find it inordinately difficult to trust others, therapists find it inordinately difficult to develop and maintain the therapeutic relationship. The patient alternately idealizes and vilifies the therapist, demanding special attention and consideration one moment—such as therapy sessions at odd hours and countless phone calls during periods of particular crisis—and refusing to keep appointments the next; they beg the therapist for understanding and support but insist that certain topics are off-limits.

Suicide is always a serious risk, but it is often difficult for the therapist to judge whether a frantic phone call at 2:00 A.M. is a call for help or a manipulative gesture designed to test how special the patient is to the therapist and to what lengths the therapist will go to meet the patient's needs at the moment. As in the case of Mary (see the clinical case at the beginning of this chapter), hospitalization is often necessary to protect against the threat of suicide. Seeing such clients is so stressful that it is common for a therapist to regularly consult with another therapist for advice and for support in dealing with their own emotions as they cope with the extraordinary challenges of helping these clients.

A number of drugs have been tried in the treatment of people with borderline personality disorder. There is some evidence that fluvoxamine decreases some of the aggressiveness and depression often found in these clients (Rinne et al., 2002) and that lithium can reduce some of their irritability, anger, and suicidality (Links et al., 1990). Similarly, antiseizure medications, which have been used to treat mood changes in bipolar disorder, appear helpful in the treatment of borderline personality disorder (Hollander et al., 2001). Newer antipsychotic medications, such as olanzapine, seem to reduce the symptoms of borderline personality disorder when offered alone (Bogenschutz & Nurnberg, 2004) or as supplements to psychotherapy (Soler et al., 2005). Because such clients often abuse drugs and engage in suicidal behavior, extreme caution must be used in drug therapy (Waldenger & Frank, 1989).

Object Relations Psychotherapy   Otto Kernberg (1985) developed a modified psychodynamic object relations treatment, sometimes called transference-focused therapy, in which the overall goal is to strengthen the patient's weak ego so that he or she stops splitting—seeing everything according to a simple good–bad dichotomy (see p. 364). The therapist points out how the patient is allowing his or her emotions and behavior to be regulated by such defenses as splitting. Kernberg's approach is more directive than that of most analysts. In addition to interpreting defensive behavior, he recommends giving clients concrete suggestions for behaving more adaptively and hospitalizing clients whose behavior becomes dangerous.

Dialectical Behavior Therapy   Marsha Linehan (1987) introduced an approach that she called **dialectical behavior therapy** (DBT), combining client-centered empathy and acceptance with cognitive behavioral problem-solving, emotion regulation techniques, and social skills training. The concept of dialectics comes from the work of German philosopher Georg Wilhelm Friedrich Hegel (1770–1831). It refers to a constant tension between any phenomenon (any idea, event, etc., called the *thesis*) and its opposite (the *antithesis*), which is resolved by the creation of a new phenomenon (the *synthesis*). In DBT, the term *dialectical* is used in two main ways:

- In one sense, it refers to the seemingly opposite strategies that the therapist must use when treating people with borderline personality disorder—accepting them as they are and yet helping them change. (For a closer look at the dialectic between acceptance and change, see Focus on Discovery 12.2.)

- In the other sense, it refers to the patient's realization that splitting the world into good and bad is not necessary; instead, one can achieve a synthesis of these apparent opposites. For example, instead of seeing a friend as either all bad (thesis) or all good (antithesis), the friend can be seen as having both kinds of qualities (synthesis).

Hence, the therapist and the client in DBT are both encouraged to adopt a dialectical view of the world.

The cognitive behavioral aspect of DBT, conducted both individually and in groups, involves four stages. In the first stage, dangerously impulsive behaviors are addressed, with the goal of promoting greater control. In the second stage, the focus is on learning to modulate the extreme emotionality. This phase might involve coaching to help a person learn to tolerate emotional distress. Stage three focuses on improving relationships and self-esteem. Stage four is designed to promote connectedness and happiness. Throughout, clients learn more effective and socially acceptable ways of handling their day-to-day problems. Basically, DBT involves cognitive behavioral therapy combined with interventions to provide validation and acceptance to the client.

FOCUS ON DISCOVERY 12.2

Acceptance in Dialectical Behavior Therapy

Marsha Linehan (1987) argues that a therapist treating clients with borderline personality disorder has to adopt a posture that might seem inconsistent to the Western mind. The therapist must work for change while at the same time accepting the real possibility that no changes are going to occur. Linehan's notions of acceptance are drawn from Zen philosophy and from Rogerian approaches to psychotherapy.

Linehan's reasoning is that people with borderline personality disorder are so sensitive to rejection and criticism that even gentle encouragement to behave or think differently can be misinterpreted as a serious rebuke, leading to extreme emotional reactions. When this happens, the therapist, who may have been revered a moment earlier, is suddenly vilified. Thus, while observing limits—"I would be very sad if you killed yourself, so I hope very much that you won't"—the therapist must convey to the patient that he or she is fully accepted. This is hard to do if the patient is threatening suicide, showing uncontrolled anger, or railing against imagined rebukes from the therapist.

Completely accepting the patient does not mean approving of everything the patient does;

Marsha Linehan created dialectical behavior therapy, which combines cognitive behavioral therapy with acceptance. (Courtesy of Marsha M. Linehan.)

rather, it means that the therapist must accept the situation for what it is. And this acceptance, argues Linehan, must be real: the therapist must truly accept clients as they are; acceptance should not be in the service of change, an indirect way of encouraging clients to behave differently. "Acceptance can transform but if you accept in order to transform, it is not acceptance. It is like loving. Love seeks no reward but when given freely comes back a hundredfold. He who loses his life finds it. He who accepts, changes" (Linehan, personal communication, November 16, 1992). Full acceptance does not, in Linehan's view, preclude change. Indeed, she proposes the opposite—that it is the refusal to accept that precludes change.

Linehan's approach also emphasizes that clients, too, must accept who they are and what they have been through. Clients are asked to accept that their childhood is now unchangeable, that their behaviors might have caused relationships to end, and that they feel emotions more intensely than others do. This approach, it is hoped, will provide a basis for understanding the self.

Schema-Schema-Focused Cognitive Therapy for BPD   Schema-focused cognitive therapy enriches traditional cognitive therapy with a broader focus on how early childhood antecedents and parenting shape current cognitive patterns. In schema-focused therapy, the therapist and the patient work to identify the maladaptive assumptions (schema) that a client holds about relationships from his or her early experiences. It is assumed that the person also has a schema for healthy relationships, and the goal of therapy is to increase the use of this healthy schema, rather than automatic behaviors reflecting the problematic relationship schema. Similar to object relations therapy, the therapist is working to change internalized representations of relationships drawn from early difficult experiences. Similar to cognitive therapy, though, the therapist might place more emphasis on how these patterns are being expressed in current life and might use more homework assignments to try to change these patterns.

Studies of the Efficacy of Psychotherapy for BPD   Linehan and colleagues (1991) were the first to publish the results of a randomized controlled study of a psychological treatment for borderline personality disorder. Clients were randomly assigned either to DBT or to treatment as usual, meaning any therapy available in the community (Seattle, Washington). After one year of treatment and again six and 12 months later, clients in the two groups were compared on a variety of measures (Linehan, Heard, & Armstrong, 1993). The findings immediately after treatment revealed that DBT was superior to treatment as usual—clients showed less intentional self-injurious behavior, including fewer suicide attempts; dropped out of treatment less; and spent fewer days in the hospital. There were, however, no differences in self-reported depression and feelings of hopelessness between the two treatment groups. At the follow-ups, the superiority of DBT was maintained. Additionally, DBT clients had better work records, reported less anger, and were judged as better adjusted than the comparison therapy clients. But most clients were still feeling quite miserable at the one-year follow-up, underscoring the extreme difficulty of treating such clients. A second randomized controlled trial found that DBT provided more relief from depressive and other symptoms than did treatment as usual (Koons et al., 2001). A similarly designed study of women with borderline personality disorder who were also drug dependent found less substance abuse after DBT than after treatment as usual (Linehan et al., 1999).

Beyond DBT, studies suggest that Kernberg's object relations psychodynamic therapy (Trull, Stepp, & Durrett, 2003) and adaptations of this approach (Bateman & Fonagy, 2004) help relieve symptoms of borderline personality disorder. It is worth noting that a long-term study suggested that, unlike object relations therapy, classical psychoanalysis was not helpful for BPD (Stone, 1987).

Most of the psychotherapy studies have compared the specific treatments for BPD to treatment as usual. How do DBT, object relations therapy, or schema-focused therapy compare to each other? One study is available comparing DBT, object relations therapy, and a control condition consisting of supportive therapy (Clarkin et al., 2007). All three approaches helped reduce depression and anxiety. Generally, DBT and object relations therapy did not achieve significant gains compared to supportive therapy on many of the outcome measures. Key group differences emerged in one important area: Clients who received either DBT or object relations therapy demonstrated reduced suicidality, whereas clients in supportive therapy did not. Object relations therapy also showed significant effects in reducing anger, assaultiveness, and irritability, whereas DBT did not. On most measures, then, object relations therapy and DBT performed similarly, although object relations therapy appeared to be slightly more helpful in reducing anger-related symptoms.

In a separate study, clients with BPD were randomly assigned to receive three years of either schema-focused therapy or object relations therapy (Giesen-Bloo et al., 2006). Clients receiving either treatment showed significant gains in their quality of life. But schema-focused therapy helped clients achieve more gains by the end of treatment than did object relations therapy in specific borderline symptoms, such as relationship problems, impulsivity, dissociative and paranoid ideas, and abandonment fears.

At this early stage, then, three treatments each show an ability to help reduce symptoms of BPD. One study suggests that object relations therapy has an advantage compared to DBT in treating anger, and another study shows that schema-focused therapy has an advantage compared to object relations therapy.

Treatment of Psychopathy

Experts of varying theoretical persuasions have asserted for years that it is pointless to try to alter the callous and remorseless nature of people with psychopathy (e.g., Cleckley, 1941/1976). These pessimistic views have been challenged in a comprehensive meta-analysis of 42 studies of the psychological treatment of psychopathy (Salekin, 2002). These studies had many methodological problems, but 17 of them, involving 88 people with psychopathy, found that psychoanalytic psychotherapy was very helpful in domains such as improving interpersonal relationships, increasing the capacity for feeling remorse and empathy, reducing the amount of lying, being released from probation, and holding down a job. Similar positive therapeutic effects were found in five studies employing cognitive behavioral techniques with 246 people with psychopathy. Therapy was more beneficial for younger clients. To be at all effective, treatment had to be quite intensive: four times a week for at least a year—a very heavy dose of psychosocial treatment whatever one's theoretical orientation.

These are remarkably positive findings given the widely held belief that psychopathy is basically untreatable. And yet, as optimistic as one researcher is about current and future treatment efforts for psychopaths, he cautions at the end of his article that ". . . research needs to make some attempt to determine whether clients are 'faking good' in treatment studies or whether the changes are genuine" (Salekin, 2002, p. 107).

Summary

- Coded on Axis II in DSM-IV-TR, personality disorders are defined as enduring patterns of behavior and inner experience that disrupt functioning. Personality disorders are grouped into three clusters in DSM-IV-TR: odd/eccentric, dramatic/erratic, and anxious/fearful.
- Personality disorders are usually comorbid with Axis I disorders such as depression and anxiety disorders, and they tend to predict poorer outcomes for these disorders.
- The high comorbidity of personality disorders with each other, and the fact that personality disorders are seen as the extremes of continuously distributed personality traits, have led to proposals to develop a dimensional rather than a categorical approach to personality diagnoses.

Odd/Eccentric Cluster

- Specific diagnoses in the odd/eccentric cluster include paranoid, schizoid, and schizotypal.
- The major symptom of paranoid personality disorder is suspiciousness and mistrust; of schizoid personality disorder, interpersonal detachment; and of schizotypal personality disorder, unusual thought and behavior.
- Genetic research supports the idea that schizotypal personality disorder is related to schizophrenia.

Dramatic/Erratic Cluster

- The dramatic/erratic cluster includes borderline, histrionic, narcissistic, and antisocial personality disorders.
- The major symptom of borderline personality disorder is unstable, highly changeable emotion and behavior; of histrionic personality disorder, exaggerated emotional displays; and of narcissistic personality disorder, highly inflated self-esteem. Antisocial personality disorder and psychopathy overlap a great deal but are not equivalent. The diagnosis of antisocial personality focuses on behavior, whereas that of psychopathy emphasizes emotional deficits.
- There is evidence that much of the vulnerability to borderline personality disorder is inherited, and there are also findings regarding deficits in frontal lobe functioning and regarding greater amygdala activation.
- Psychosocial theories of the etiology of borderline, histrionic, and narcissistic disorders focus on early parent–child relationships. It is clear that people with borderline personality disorder report extremely high rates of child abuse and parental separation compared to the general population.
- The object relations theorist Kernberg and the self-psychologist Kohut have detailed proposals concerning borderline and narcissistic personality disorders, focusing on the child developing an insecure ego because of inconsistent love and attention from the parents. Linehan's cognitive behavioral theory of borderline personality disorder proposes an interaction between emotional dysregulation and an invalidating family environment.
- When designs involving repeated measurements or multiple informants are used to bolster the reliability of pathology measures, antisocial personality disorder and psychopathy appear to be highly heritable.
- Psychopathy and antisocial behavior also appear to be related to family environment and poverty.
- Psychopathy is related to lack of response to punishment, poor empathy, and elevated impulsivity.

Anxious/Fearful Cluster

- The anxious/fearful cluster includes avoidant, dependent, and obsessive-compulsive personality disorders.
- The major symptom of avoidant personality disorder is fear of rejection or criticism; of dependent personality disorder, excessive reliance on others; and of obsessive-compulsive personality disorder, a perfectionistic, detail-oriented style.
- Avoidant personality disorder is modestly heritable, but estimates of heritability vary for dependent and obsessive-compulsive personality disorders.
- Social theories of etiology for the anxious/fearful cluster focus on parenting. Avoidant personality disorder might result from the transmission of fear from parent to child via modeling. Dependent personality might be caused by disruptions of the parent–child relationship (e.g., through separation or loss) that lead the person to fear losing other relationships in adulthood. Dependency as a personality trait is only modestly heritable.

Treatment of Personality Disorders

- Although psychodynamic, behavioral and cognitive, and pharmacological treatments are all used for personality disorders, less research has been conducted for these disorders compared to Axis I disorders.
- Several medications appear to be helpful for quelling specific symptoms.
- Early research on day treatment programs is promising.
- Some promising evidence is emerging for the utility of dialectical behavior therapy, object relations therapy, and schema-focused therapy for borderline personality disorder. Other research suggests that even psychopathy, formerly considered virtually untreatable, might respond to intensive psychological treatment.

Answers to Check Your Knowledge Questions

12.1 1. T; 2. F; 3. T; 4. F; 5. F
12.2 1. b; 2. a, b; 3. d
12.3 1. T; 2. F; 3. T; 4. F

12.4 1. narcissistic; 2. avoidant; 3. obsessive-compulsive; 4. schizoid; 5. antisocial

Key Terms

antisocial personality disorder
avoidant personality disorder
borderline personality disorder
dependent personality disorder

dialectical behavior therapy
five-factor model
histrionic personality disorder
narcissistic personality disorder

obsessive-compulsive
   personality disorder
paranoid personality disorder
personality disorders

psychopathy
schizoid personality disorder
schizotypal personality disorder

13 Sexual and Gender Identity Disorders

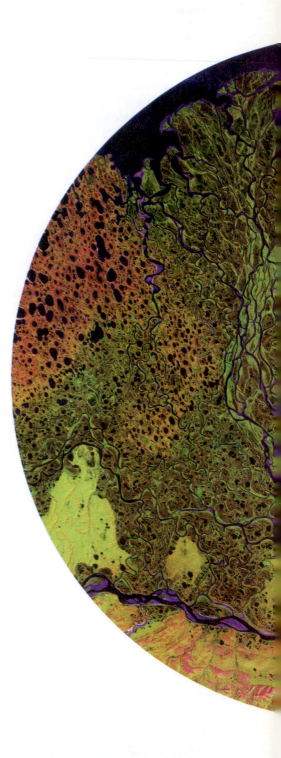

SEXUALITY IS ONE OF the most personal areas of a person's life. Each of us is a sexual being with preferences and fantasies that may surprise or even shock us from time to time. Usually these are part of normal sexual functioning. But when our fantasies or desires begin to affect us or others in unwanted or harmful ways, they begin to qualify as abnormal. In this chapter we consider the range of human sexual thoughts, feelings, and actions that are listed in DSM-IV-TR as sexual and gender identity disorders (see Table 13.1).

For perspective, we begin by briefly describing norms and healthy sexual behavior. Then we divide our study of sexual disorders and problems into three major sections: **sexual dysfunctions**, disruptions in sexual functioning found in many people who are in otherwise good psychological health; **gender identity disorder**, a diagnosis used to describe people who believe they are of the opposite sex and are troubled by this belief; and the **paraphilias**, in which people are attracted to unusual sexual activities or objects. We close this chapter with a discussion of rape. Although rape is not a diagnosis in DSM-IV-TR, we examine this issue because it is a harmful form of sexual behavior.

Sexual Norms and Behavior

Definitions of what is normal or desirable in human sexual behavior vary with time and place. Consider contemporary Western worldviews that *inhibition* of sexual expression causes problems. Contrast this with nineteenth- and early-twentieth-century views that *excess* was the culprit; in particular, excessive masturbation in childhood was widely believed to lead to sexual problems in adulthood. Von Krafft-Ebing (1902) postulated that early masturbation damaged the sexual organs and exhausted a finite reservoir of sexual energy, resulting in diminished ability to function sexually in adulthood. Even in adulthood, excessive sexual activity was thought to underlie problems such as erectile failure. The general Victorian view was that sexual appetite was dangerous and therefore had to be restrained. For example, to discourage handling of the genitals by children, metal mittens were promoted; and to distract adults from too much sex, outdoor exercise and a bland diet were recommended. In fact, Kellogg's Corn Flakes and graham crackers were developed as foods that would lessen sexual interest. They didn't.

Table 13.1 Sexual and Gender Identity Disorders

Sexual dysfunctions
  Sexual desire disorders
    Hypoactive sexual desire disorder
    Sexual aversion disorder
  Sexual arousal disorders
    Female sexual arousal disorder
    Male erectile disorder
  Orgasmic disorders
    Female orgasmic disorder
    Male orgasmic disorder
    Premature ejaculation
  Sexual pain disorders
    Dyspareunia
    Vaginismus
Gender identity disorder
Paraphilias
  Fetishism
  Transvestic fetishism
  Pedophilia
  Exhibitionism
  Voyeurism
  Frotteurism
  Sexual masochism
  Sexual sadism
  Paraphilias not otherwise specified
  (e.g., coprophilia, necrophilia)

Source: From DSM-IV-TR (APH, 2000).

Other changes over time have influenced people's attitudes and experiences of sexuality. For example, technology is changing sexual experiences, as the number of people accessing sexual content on the Internet increases dramatically. Even as the accessibility of sexual content increases so dramatically, the specter of AIDS and other sexually transmitted diseases changes the risks associated with sexual behavior. Other changes in sexual norms are occurring as well. As the population of the United States ages, a newfound emphasis on the right to a good sex life until the day of death has emerged, perhaps most visibly expressed in the barrage of television commercials for medications to improve erectile function among older men (Tiefer, 2003). Clearly, we must keep varying cultural norms in mind as we study human sexual behavior.

At the current point in time in our culture, what are the norms? Several major surveys have been conducted to assess typical levels of sexual activity. In one study that included a representative sample of almost 3,000 adults, Laumann and colleagues (1994) asked participants to describe their involvement in different sexual activities (see Table 13.2). Some of the findings were surprising. Although researchers had thought for some time that as many as 10 percent of people had engaged in sex with a same-sex partner, Laumann's study, which involved a more representative sample of participants, revealed much lower rates. In his study, approximately 5.1 percent of men and 3.3 percent of women reported that they had had sex with a same-sex partner during their adult lives. On the other hand, about 30 percent of people reported that they would find a same-sex partner to be appealing. See Focus on Discovery 13.1 for a look at the complicated path taken by health professionals in response to changing attitudes toward sexual orientation.

Gender and Sexuality

Few topics raise as much political debate or personal turmoil as gender differences in sexuality. Across a wide range of indices, men report more engagement in sexual thought and behavior than do women. Of course, these are averages, there are going to be exceptions, and most of these differences are small (Andersen, Cyranowski & Aarested, 2000). But compared to women, men report thinking about sex, masturbating, and desiring sex more often, as well as desiring more sexual partners and having more partners (Baumeister, Catanese, & Vohs, 2001).

Table 13.2 Participation in Selected Sexual Behaviors in the Past Year

Behavior	Male (%)	Female (%)
Give oral sex		
Never	30	35.2
Occasionally	49.4	53.0
Always	20.7	11.8
Receive oral sex		
Never	30.5	33.2
Occasionally	50.4	52.2
Always	19.0	14.6
Number of sex partners		
0	9.9	13.6
1	66.7	74.7
2–4	18.3	10.0
5+	5.1	1.7
Frequency of sexual intercourse		
For unmarried participants		
None	22.1	30.6
< 3x/month	38.9	36.6
At least 1x/week	38.9	32.8
For married participants		
None	1.3	2.6
< 3x/month	31.4	33.9
At least 1x/week	67.3	63.5

Source: Laumann et al. (1994).

FOCUS ON DISCOVERY 13.1

Learning from History

Until 1973, homosexuality was listed in the DSM as one of the sexual disorders. In 1973 the Nomenclature Committee of the American Psychiatric Association, under pressure from professional and activist groups, recommended the elimination of the category "homosexuality" and the substitution of "sexual orientation disturbance." This new diagnosis was to be applied to gay men and women who are "disturbed by, in conflict with, or wish to change their sexual orientation." The change was approved, but not without vehement protests from several renowned psychiatrists who remained convinced that homosexuality reflects a fixation at an early stage of psychosexual development and is therefore inherently abnormal. Today, these protests would be considered misguided, prejudiced, and antiscientific.

In the 1980 publication of the DSM-III, the Nomenclature Committee waffled by adding a new category called *ego-dystonic homosexuality*, which referred to a person who is homosexually aroused, is persistently distressed by this arousal, and wishes to become heterosexual. In doing so, the crafters of DSM-III took an inconsistent position: a gay man or lesbian is abnormal if he or she has been persuaded by a prejudiced society that his or her sexual orientation is disordered. At the same time, according to DSM-III, homosexuality was not in itself abnormal!

In the years after publication of DSM-III, mental health professionals made very little use of the diagnosis of ego-dystonic homosexuality. When the American Psychiatric Association published DSM-III-R in 1987, the category of ego-dystonic homosexuality was dropped. Instead, the catchall category of "sexual disorder not otherwise specified," which refers to "persistent and marked distress about one's sexual orientation" (p. 296), has been included in DSM-IV and DSM-IV-TR. It is noteworthy that the new category does not specify a sexual orientation but, rather, can be applied when a person is distressed over a heterosexual or homosexual orientation.

Beyond these differences in sex drive, Peplau (2003) has described several other ways in which the genders tend to differ in sexuality. Women tend to be more ashamed of any flaws in their appearance than do men, and this shame can interfere with sexual satisfaction (Sanchez & Kiefer, 2007). For women, sexuality appears more closely tied to relationship status and social norms than for men (Baumeister, 2000). For example, women tend to engage less in sexual activities like masturbation when they are not in a relationship; men don't experience the same shift when a relationship ends. Some argue that the DSM pays too little attention to the relational components of human sexuality in describing sexual dysfunction, especially for women. Some propose that there should be a more women-centered definition that includes "discontent or dissatisfaction with any emotional, physical, or relational aspect of sexual experience" (Tiefer, Hall, & Tavris, 2002, pp. 228–229). Although there are many parallels in how men and women think about sex, men are more likely to think about their sexuality in terms of power than are women (Andersen, Cyranowski, & Espindle, 1999). Men develop more sexual dysfunctions as they age, such as erectile dysfunctions; in contrast, sexually active older women do not report more sexual problems than younger women do (Laumann et al., 2005).

Debate continues about the reasons for these gender differences. Are they based on cultural prohibitions regarding women's sexuality? Are they based on biological differences? Are they tied to women's greater investment in parenting? It is hard to design research to tease apart cultural and biological influences on sexuality. Intriguingly, though, at least some research suggests that some gender differences seem to be remarkably consistent across cultures. In one study of more than 16,000 people (albeit mostly college students), men in 52 different countries reported that they wanted more partners over the course of a lifetime than did women (Schmitt et al., 2003). These findings suggest that biology may shape men's desire for many lifetime partners more than culture does. We know less about the basis for other gender differences in sexuality. There must be some reason for these differences, though. As Baumeister (2000) points out, in a perfect world, wouldn't men and women be well matched on their sexual preferences?

Norms about sexuality have fluctuated a great deal over time. In the early twentieth century, corn flakes were promoted as part of a bland diet to reduce sexual desire. (Corbis Images.)

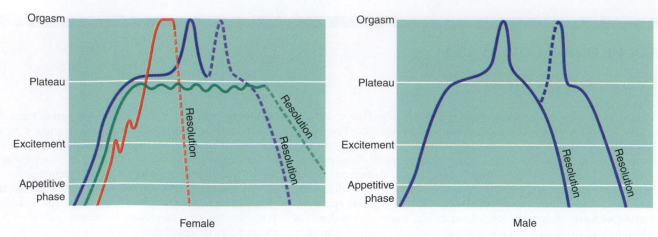

Figure 13.1 The sexual response cycle differs for women and men. Some women report no orgasms (as shown in the green line in the left-hand figure), others report one (as shown in the orange line in the left-hand figure), and some report multiple orgasms (as shown in the blue line). A single orgasm is the typical pattern for men, but a second orgasm may be possible after a refractory period.

Despite debate about gender differences in sexuality, we will see throughout this chapter that gender shapes sexual disorders in a number of ways. Women are much more likely to report symptoms of sexual dysfunction than are men, but men are much more likely to meet diagnostic criteria for paraphilias. A better understanding of gender differences in sexuality is needed to understand why there are such major gender differences in sexual diagnoses.

The Sexual Response Cycle

Many researchers have focused on understanding the **sexual response cycle**. The Kinsey group made breakthroughs in the 1940s by interviewing people about their sexuality (Kinsey, Pomeroy, & Martin, 1948). Masters and Johnson created another revolution in research on human sexuality 50 years ago when they began to gather direct observations and physiological measurements of people masturbating and having sexual intercourse. Most contemporary conceptualizations distill proposals by Masters and Johnson (1966) and Kaplan (1974). Figure 13.1 shows the four phases in the human sexual response cycle typically identified for both men and women.

1. **Desire phase**. A concept introduced by Kaplan (1974), this stage refers to sexual interest or desire, often associated with sexually arousing fantasies.
2. **Excitement phase**. During this phase, men and women experience pleasure and increased blood flow to the genitalia (see Figure 13.2 for the sexual anatomy of men and women). Women also experience increased blood flow to the breasts. In men, this flow of blood into tissues produces an erection of the penis. In women, blood flow creates enlargement of the breasts and changes in the vagina, such as increased lubrication. Interestingly, the amount of blood flow to the vagina has little correlation with women's subjective level of desire (Basson et al., 2005).
3. **Orgasm phase**. In this phase, sexual pleasure peaks in ways that have fascinated poets and the rest of us ordinary people for thousands of years. In men, ejaculation feels inevitable and indeed almost always occurs (in rare instances, men have an orgasm without ejaculating, and vice versa). In women, the outer walls of the vagina contract. In both sexes there is general muscle tension.
4. **Resolution phase**. This last stage refers to the relaxation and sense of well-being that usually follow an orgasm. In men there is an associated refractory period during which further erection and arousal are not possible. The duration of the refractory period varies across men and even in the same man across occasions. Women are often able to respond again with sexual excitement almost immediately, a capability that permits multiple orgasms.

As portrayed in the movie *Kinsey*, Alfred Kinsey shocked people when he began to interview people to understand more about norms in sexual behavior. (Courtesy Kinsey Institute for Research in Sex, Gender, and Reproduction.)

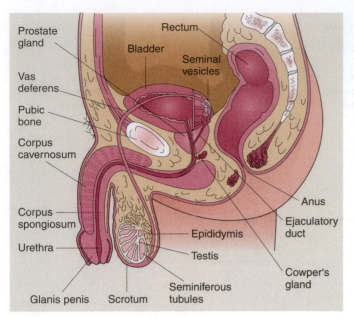
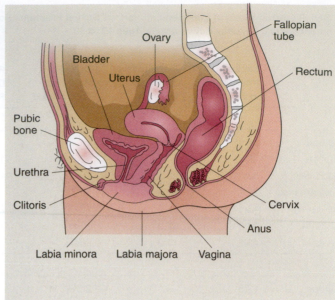

Figure 13.2 The male and female sexual anatomy.

Check Your Knowledge 13.1 (Answers are at the end of the chapter.)

Answer the questions.

1. Which of the following is **not** documented:
   a. Men report more sex drive than women do.
   b. Women's sexuality is more closely tied to relationship status than is men's sexuality.
   c. Men describe their sexuality as more related to power than women do.
   d. Men are able to have more orgasms within a given sexual experience than are women.

2. Which of the following is **not** a phase of the human sexual response cycle?
   a. desire
   b. ejaculation
   c. excitement
   d. resolution

3. Gender differences in the desired number of lifetime partners:
   a. appear similar across cultures
   b. are only observed in Western cultures

Sexual Dysfunctions

Sexuality usually occurs in the context of an intimate personal relationship. At its best, it provides a forum for closeness and connection. For better or for worse, most of us base part of our self-concept on our sexuality. Do we please the people we love, do we gratify ourselves, or, more simply, are we able to enjoy the fulfillment and relaxation that can come from a pleasurable sexual experience? When sexual problems emerge, they can wreak havoc on our self-esteem and relationships. A marriage is likely to suffer as sexual dysfunctions become so severe that the intense satisfaction and tenderness of sexual activity is lost.

We turn now to sexual problems that interfere with sexual enjoyment for many people at some time during their life. We begin by describing the different types of sexual dysfunctions described in DSM-IV-TR. Then we discuss etiologies and treatments for these problems.

Clinical Descriptions of Sexual Dysfunctions

As Table 13.1 shows, DSM-IV-TR divides **sexual dysfunctions** into four categories: sexual desire disorders, sexual arousal disorders, orgasmic disorders, and sexual pain disorders. The dysfunction should be persistent and recurrent, a clinical judgment acknowledged in the DSM to entail some subjectivity. The dysfunction also should cause marked distress or interpersonal

Table 13.3 Self-Reported Rates of Experiencing Various Sexual Problems For 2 Out of the Past 12 Months by Region among 20,000 Sexually Active Adults Ages 40 to 80

	Lacked Interest in Sex	Inability to Reach Orgasm	Orgasm Reached Too Quickly	Pain During Sex	Sex Not Pleasurable	Trouble Lubricating	Trouble Maintaining or Achieving an Erection
Women							
Northern Europe	25.6	17.7	7.7	9.0	17.1	18.4	NA
Southern Europe	29.6	24.2	11.5	11.9	22.1	16.1	NA
Non-European West	32.9	25.2	10.5	14.0	21.5	27.1	NA
Central/South America	28.1	22.4	18.3	16.6	19.5	22.5	NA
Middle East	43.4	23.0	10.0	21.0	31.0	23.0	NA
East Asia	34.8	32.3	17.6	31.6	29.7	37.9	NA
Southeast Asia	43.3	41.2	26.3	29.2	35.9	34.2	NA
Men							
Northern Europe	12.5	9.1	20.7	2.9	7.7	NA	13.3
Southern Europe	13.0	12.2	21.5	4.4	9.1	NA	12.9
Non-European West	17.6	14.5	27.4	3.6	12.1	NA	20.6
Central/South America	12.6	13.6	28.3	4.7	9.0	NA	13.7
Middle East	21.6	13.2	12.4	10.2	14.3	NA	14.1
East Asia	19.6	17.2	29.1	5.8	12.2	NA	27.1
Southeast Asia	28.0	21.1	30.5	12.0	17.4	NA	28.1

Source: After Laumann et al. (2005).

Note: Non-European West includes Australia, Canada, New Zealand, South Africa, and the United States.

The pioneering work of the sex therapists William H. Masters and Virginia Johnson helped launch a candid and scientific appraisal of human sexuality. (Ira Wyman/Corbis Sygma.)

problems. A diagnosis of sexual dysfunction is not made if the problem is believed to be due entirely to a medical illness (such as advanced diabetes, which can cause erectile problems in men) or if it is due to another Axis I disorder (such as major depression).

One might not expect people to report problems as personal as sexual dysfunction in community surveys. But many people do report these symptoms—the prevalence of occasional symptoms of sexual dysfunctions is actually quite high. Table 13.3 presents data from a survey of more than 20,000 men and women who were asked whether they had experienced various symptoms of sexual dysfunction for at least two of the past 12 months (Laumann et al., 2005). More women (43 percent) than men (31 percent) report symptoms of sexual dysfunction (Laumann, Paik, & Rosen, 1999).

Although a lot of people endorsed symptoms, clinical diagnoses are not made unless a person experiences distress or impairment from symptoms; distress or impairment were not assessed in the Laumann survey. In a study of over 1,000 women who were engaged in heterosexual relationships, Bancroft, Loftus, and Long (2003) found a very similar rate of women who reported symptoms of sexual dysfunction (44.3 percent). But when they asked women whether they were distressed by these symptoms, one-quarter of the women experiencing dysfunction reported distress (11 percent). To be sure, 11 percent is still a relatively high prevalence rate, but note that most women experiencing a symptom did not meet criteria for a clinical diagnosis. Unfortunately, we have almost no data on how many people have experienced sexual dysfunctions at a diagnosable level (APA, 2000).

Although the diagnostic system for sexual dysfunction reflects the stages in the sexual cycle (see Figure 13.3), the problems often don't break out so cleanly in real life. Many people with problems in one phase of a sexual cycle will report problems in another phase (Segraves & Segraves, 1991). Some of this may just be a vicious spiral. For example, women with low desire often have troubles with arousal and orgasms. Men who develop premature ejaculation may begin to worry about sex and then experience problems with sexual desire or sexual arousal

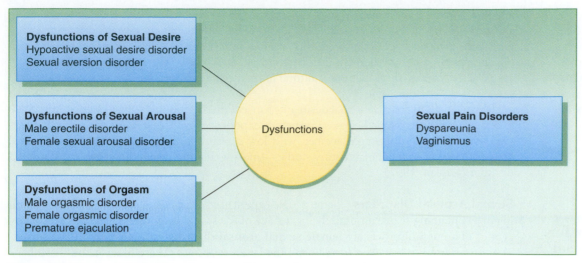

Figure 13.3 The sexual dysfunctions by phase of the sexual response cycle.

(Rowland, Cooper, & Slob, 1996). Beyond the consequences for the individual, sexual problems in one person may lead to sexual problems in the partner. Nonetheless, in the following section, we review the specific sexual dysfunction disorders defined by DSM-IV-TR.

Sexual Desire Disorders   DSM-IV-TR distinguishes two kinds of sexual desire disorders. **Hypoactive sexual desire disorder** refers to deficient or absent sexual fantasies and urges; **sexual aversion disorder** represents a more extreme disorder, in which the person actively avoids nearly all genital contact with another person. Among people seeking treatment for sexual dysfunctions, more than half complain of low desire. Diagnoses of hypoactive sexual desire increased in samples of men and women seeking treatment from the 1970s to the 1990s (Beck, 1995). As Table 13.3 shows, women are more likely than men to report at least occasional concerns about their level of sexual desire.

Of all the DSM-IV-TR diagnoses, the sexual desire disorders, often colloquially referred to as low sex drive (as illustrated in the clinical case of Robert), seem the most subjective and influenced by cultural norms. How often should a person want sex? And with what intensity? Often, partners are the ones who encourage a person to see a clinician. The hypoactive desire category appeared for the first time in DSM-III in 1980 under the title of "inhibited sexual desire"

DSM-IV-TR Criteria for Hypoactive Sexual Desire Disorder

- Persistently deficient or absent sexual fantasies and desires, as judged by the clinician
- Causes marked distress or interpersonal problems
- Not due to a medical illness, another Axis I disorder (except another sexual dysfunction), or the effects of a drug

Clinical Case: Robert

Robert was a highly intelligent 25-year-old graduate student in physics at a leading East Coast university who sought treatment for what he called "sexual diffidence." He was engaged to a young woman, and he said he loved his fiancée very much and felt compatible with her in every conceivable way except in bed. There, try as he might, and with apparent understanding from his fiancée, he found himself uninterested in responding to or initiating sexual contact. Both parties had attributed these problems to the academic pressures he had faced for the past two years, but a discussion with the therapist revealed that Robert had had little interest in sex—either with men or with women—for as far back as he could remember, even when work pressures decreased. He asserted that he found his fiancée very attractive and appealing, but as with other women he had known, his feelings were not passionate.

He had masturbated very rarely in adolescence and did not begin dating until late in college, though he had had many female acquaintances. His general approach to life, including sex, was analytical and intellectual, and he described his problems in a very dispassionate and detached way to the therapist. He freely admitted that he would not have contacted a therapist at all were it not for the quietly stated wishes of his fiancée, who worried that his lack of interest in sex would interfere with their future marital relationship.

After a few individual sessions the therapist asked the young man to invite his fiancée to a therapy session, which the client readily agreed to do. During a conjoint session the couple appeared to be very much in love and looking forward to a life together, though the woman expressed concern about her fiancé's lack of sexual interest.

DSM-IV-TR Criteria for Sexual Aversion Disorder

- Persistent avoidance of almost all sexual contact
- Causes marked distress or interpersonal problems
- Not due to another Axis I disorder (except another sexual dysfunction)

DSM-IV-TR Criteria for Female Sexual Arousal Disorder

- Persistent inability to attain or maintain sexual excitement (lubrication and swelling of the genitalia) adequate for completion of sexual activity
- Causes marked distress or interpersonal problems
- Not due to a medical illness, another Axis I disorder (except another sexual dysfunction), or the effects of a drug

DSM-IV-TR Criteria for Male Erectile Disorder

- Persistent inability to attain or maintain an erection adequate for completion of sexual activity
- Causes marked distress or interpersonal problems
- Not due to a medical illness, another Axis I disorder (except another sexual dysfunction), or the effects of a drug

and may owe its existence to the high expectations some people have about being sexual. Data attest to the significance of subjective and cultural factors in defining low sex drive; for example, hypoactive sexual desire disorder was reported more often by American men than by British (Hawton et al., 1986) or German men (Arentewicz & Schmidt, 1983) despite similar levels of sexual activity across these cultures. Cultural norms seem to influence perceptions of how much sex a person "should" want.

People with hypoactive sexual desire often meet criteria for other sexual dysfunctions, such as orgasmic disorder. Nonetheless, some people experience low sexual desire without other sexual dysfunctions. For example, women with low sexual desire show normal levels of sexual arousal to sexual stimuli in laboratory studies—most would not meet criteria for sexual arousal disorder (Kaplan, 1997).

Sexual Arousal Disorders Some people experience sexual desire but have difficulty attaining or maintaining sexual arousal, the next stage of the sexual response cycle. The two subcategories of arousal disorders are **female sexual arousal disorder** and **male erectile disorder**. The former used to be called *frigidity* and the latter, *impotence*. These older names have been dropped because of their perjorative connotations.

The diagnosis of arousal disorder is made for a woman when there is consistently inadequate vaginal lubrication for comfortable completion of intercourse and for a man when there is persistent failure to attain or maintain an erection through completion of the sexual activity. As shown in Table 13.3, occasional symptoms of erectile disorder are the most common sexual concern among men, with rates ranging from 13 to 28 percent, depending on the country (Laumann et al., 2005). Male erectile disorder increases greatly with age, with as many as 15 percent of men in their seventies reporting erectile disorder (Feldman et al., 1994) and as many as 70 percent reporting occasional erectile dysfunction (Kim & Lipshultz, 1997). The availability of new drugs for erectile dysfunction may change the rates at which we recognize these disorders. It is important to rule out biological explanations for these symptoms for both men and women. For example, laboratory tests of hormone levels are a routine part of assessment for postmenopausal women (Bartlik & Goldberg, 2000).

Orgasmic Disorders The DSM-IV-TR describes one kind of orgasmic disorder in women and two in men. **Female orgasmic disorder** refers to the persistent absence of orgasm after sexual excitement. Women have different thresholds for orgasm. Although some have orgasms quickly and without much clitoral stimulation, others seem to need intense and prolonged stimulation during sexual contact. Given this, it is not surprising that about one-third of women report that they do not consistently experience orgasms with their partners (Laumann et al., 2005). Female orgasmic disorder is not diagnosed unless the absence of orgasms is persistent and troubling. Beyond the distress some women feel about this issue, partners may come to believe they are unskilled or insensitive lovers, or that their partner no longer cares for them (both of which could be true). Worries about protecting a partner's feelings probably account for the fact that up to 60 percent of women report faking an orgasm on occasion (McConaghy, 1993).

Women's problems reaching orgasm are distinct from problems with sexual arousal. Many women achieve arousal during sexual activity but then do not reach orgasm. Indeed, laboratory

Clinical Case: Paul and Petula

Paul and Petula seek treatment at a sex therapy clinic. They are a young, middle-class couple who have been living together for 6 months and are engaged to be married. Petula reports that Paul "hasn't been able to keep his erection after he enters me" for the past two months. Paul experiences initial sexual arousal but loses his erection almost immediately after he enters Petula. Although they enjoyed sexual intercourse in the beginning of their relationship, the erectile problems started after they moved in together. During the interview, the psychiatrist learns that they have considerable conflict over time spent together and commitment, and at times Petula has been violent toward Paul. Neither person is depressed, and no medical problems appear to be involved. (Drawn from Spitzer et al., 1994.)

research has shown that arousal levels while viewing erotic stimuli do not distinguish women with orgasmic disorder from those without orgasmic disorder (Meston & Gorzalka, 1996).

DSM-IV-TR includes two orgasmic disorders of men: **male orgasmic disorder**, defined by persistent difficulty in ejaculating, and **premature ejaculation**, defined by ejaculation that occurs too quickly. Sometimes premature ejaculation occurs even before the penis enters the vagina, but more often it occurs within the first minute or two of insertion into the vagina (Strassberg et al., 1987). Although researchers do not know how many men meet formal diagnostic criteria, 10 to 20 percent of men reported that they had trouble reaching orgasm and 20 to 30 percent of men reported premature ejaculation for at least a couple months in the past year in the Laumann survey (Laumann et al., 2005). Premature ejaculation can provoke considerable anxiety.

Sexual Pain Disorders   Two pain disorders associated with sex are listed in the DSM: dyspareunia and vaginismus. **Dyspareunia** is diagnosed when there is persistent or recurrent pain during sexual intercourse. Dyspareunia can be diagnosed in men and women. Some people report that the pain starts at entry, whereas others report pain only after penetration (Meana et al., 1997). In women, the most common form of dyspareunia is vulvar vestibulitis syndrome, or pain concentrated at the entrance to the vagina. A first step in making this diagnosis is ensuring that the pain is not caused by a medical problem, such as an infection (McCormick, 1999), or, in women, to a lack of vaginal lubrication due to low desire or postmenopausal changes. Women with dyspareunia show normal sexual arousal to films of oral sex, but, not surprisingly, their arousal declines when they watch a depiction of intercourse (Wouda et al., 1998).

Vaginismus is marked by involuntary spasms of the outer third of the vagina to a degree that makes intercourse impossible. It can also occur in response to penetration by a finger or tampon as well as during gynecological examinations. Despite not being able to have intercourse, women with vaginismus have normal sexual arousal and can have orgasms from manual or oral stimulation that does not involve penetration.

Prevalence rates for occasional symptoms of dyspareunia among women have been estimated to range from 10 to 30 percent (Laumann et al., 2005), but dyspareunia in men is rare. Estimates for vaginismus range from 12 to 17 percent of women seeking sex therapy (Rosen & Leiblum, 1995), and it is a very common complaint seen by gynecologists (Leiblum, 1997).

Etiology of Sexual Dysfunctions

Because sexuality can be so difficult to study, case studies have dominated the literature on the causes of sexual dysfunctions. Psychoanalytic case studies focus on underlying repressed conflicts as an explanation for sexual dysfunctions. For example, the theme of repressed aggression competing with the gratification of sexual needs pervades psychoanalytic writings. Thus, a man who ejaculates so quickly that he frustrates his female partner could be expressing repressed hostility toward women, who remind him unconsciously of his mother. A woman with vaginismus could be expressing her hostility toward men, perhaps as a result of her husband's overbearing manner. Empirical evidence has failed to support these suppositions.

In 1970, Masters and Johnson (1970) published their widely acclaimed book *Human Sexual Inadequacy*, which included a theory of why sexual dysfunctions develop based on case studies from their practice. Masters and Johnson used a two-tier model of current and historical causes to conceptualize the etiology of human sexual inadequacy (see Figure 13.4). The current causes can be distilled down to two: fears about performance and the adoption of a spectator role. Fears about performance involve concerns with how one is "performing" during sex. **Spectator role** refers to being an observer rather than a participant in a sexual experience. Both involve a focus on sexual performance that impedes the natural sexual responses. These current reasons for sexual dysfunctions were hypothesized to have one or more historical antecedents, such as sociocultural influences, biological causes, sexual traumas, or homosexual inclinations. Masters and Johnson's work set the tone for researchers to begin systematically studying risk factors for sexual dysfunction in much the same way case studies in other areas set the stage for empirical research. It is important to note, however, that many people who have one or more of the pathogenic factors discussed by Masters and Johnson do not develop sexual dysfunctions.

DSM-IV-TR Criteria for Female Orgasmic Disorder and Male Orgasmic Disorder

- Persistent delay in or absence of orgasm after a normal period of sexual arousal
- Not explained by age, sexual experience, or adequacy of sexual stimulation
- Causes marked distress or interpersonal problems
- Not due to a medical illness, another Axis I disorder (except another sexual dysfunction), or the effects of a drug

DSM-IV-TR Criteria for Premature Ejaculation

- Persistent tendency to ejaculate after minimal stimulation and before the man wishes it
- Not explained by the man's age, novelty of the situation or the partner, or recent frequency of sexual contacts
- Causes marked distress or interpersonal problems
- Not due to the effects of a drug

DSM-IV-TR Criteria for Dyspareunia

- Recurrent genital pain associated with sexual intercourse
- Causes marked distress or interpersonal problems
- Not due to vaginismus, lack of vaginal lubrication, another Axis I disorder (except another sexual dysfunction), medical illness, or the effects of a drug

DSM-IV-TR Criteria for Vaginismus

- Recurrent spasm of the outer third of the vagina interferes with intercourse
- Causes marked distress or interpersonal problems
- Not due to another Axis I disorder or to the physiological effects of a medical illness

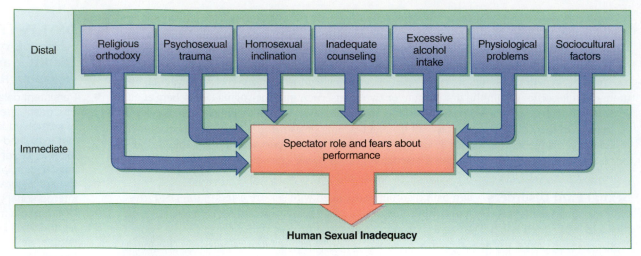

Figure 13.4 Distal and immediate causes of human sexual inadequacies, according to Masters and Johnson.

We turn now to research on the causes of sexual dysfunctions. Figure 13.5 summarizes factors related to sexual dysfunctions. One thing is clear—sexual functioning is complex and multifaceted.

Biological Factors   Biological causes of sexual dysfunctions can include diseases of the vascular (blood vessel) system such as atherosclerosis; diseases that affect the nervous system such as diabetes, multiple sclerosis, and spinal cord injury; low levels of testosterone or estrogen; heavy alcohol use before sex; chronic alcohol dependence; and heavy cigarette smoking (Bach, Wincze, & Barlow, 2001). Certain medications, such as antihypertensive drugs and especially SSRI antidepressant drugs like Prozac and Zoloft, have effects on sexual function, including delayed orgasm, decreased libido, and diminished lubrication (Segraves, 2003).

Some laboratory-based evidence exists that men with premature ejaculation are more sexually responsive to tactile stimulation than men who don't have this problem (Rowland et al., 1996). Perhaps, then, their penises are very sensitive, causing them to ejaculate more quickly.

	Successful sexual functioning	**Poor sexual functioning**
Psychological factors	Good emotional health Attraction toward partner Positive attitude toward partner Positive sex attitude	Depression or anxiety disorders Focus on performance Routine Poor self-esteem Uncomfortable environment for sex Rigid, narrow attitude toward sex Negative thoughts about sex
Physical factors	Good physical health Regular appropriate exercise Good nutrition	Smoking Heavy drinking Cardiovascular problems Diabetes Neurological diseases Low physiological arousal SSRI medications Antihypertensive medication Other drugs
Social and sexual history factors	Positive sexual experiences in past Good relationship with partner Sexual knowledge and skills	Rape or sexual abuse Relationship problems, such as anger or poor communication Long periods of abstinence History of hurried sex

Figure 13.5 Predictors of sexual functioning. Adapted from *Enhancing Sexuality: A Problem-Solving Approach* (1997), Graywind Publications.

Psychosocial Factors   Some sexual dysfunctions can be traced to rape, childhood sexual abuse, or other degrading encounters. Sexual contact with an adult during childhood is associated with high rates of arousal disorder in women and twice the rate of premature ejaculation and low sexual desire in men (Laumann et al., 1999). See Focus on Discovery 13.3, later in this chapter, for more discussion of childhood sexual abuse and its repercussions. Beyond the role of traumatic experiences, it is important to consider the benefits of previous positive experiences—many people with sexual problems lack knowledge and skill because they have not had opportunities to learn about their sexuality (LoPiccolo & Hogan, 1979).

Broader relationship problems can intrude into the sexual situation and thereby inhibit whatever arousal and pleasure might otherwise be found (Bach et al., 2001). For people who tend to be anxious about their relationships, sexual problems may exacerbate underlying worries about relationship security (Birnbaum et al., 2006). As one might expect, people who are angry with their partners are less likely to want sex. Anger seems to be more detrimental to desire among men than among women (Beck & Bozman, 1995). Even in couples who are satisfied in other realms of the relationship, poor communication can contribute to sexual dysfunction. For any number of reasons, including embarrassment, worry about the partner's feelings, or fear, one lover may not tell the other about preferences even if a partner is engaging in unstimulating or even aversive behaviors. After all, open discussions of sex by partners, among friends, in the media, and even in professional training programs are relatively recent phenomena.

Specific sexual experiences may shape premature ejaculation. Men with premature ejaculation have longer periods of abstinence from climactic sex than do men who are not premature ejaculators (Spiess, Geer, & O'Donohue, 1984). It has also been proposed that men may acquire the tendency to ejaculate quickly as a result of having hurried sex because of not being in a private place and fearing detection (Metz et al., 1997).

Several mental disorders are associated with increased risk of sexual dysfunctions. People who are depressed are more than twice as likely as nondepressed people (62 percent to 26 percent) to have a sexual dysfunction (Angst, 1998). People with a panic disorder, who are often fearful of physical sensations like rapid heart rate and sweating, are also at risk for sexual dysfunction (Sbrocco et al., 1997). Anxiety and depression are particularly comorbid with dyspareunia (Meana et al., 1998) and erectile disorder (Araujo et al., 1998).

Beyond evidence that depression and anxiety are detrimental, several studies suggest that low general physiological arousal can interfere with specific sexual arousal. Meston and Gorzalka (1995) looked at the role of arousal by assigning women to exercise or no-exercise conditions, and then asked women to watch erotic films. Consistent with the positive role of higher arousal, exercise facilitated sexual arousal. No wonder, then, that exhausted couples, turning to sex after a full day of work, parenting, socializing, and other roles, can encounter problems with sexuality. Too much stress and exhaustion clearly impede sexual functioning (Morokoff & Gilliland, 1993).

Negative cognitions, such as worries about pregnancy or AIDS, negative attitudes about sex, or concerns about the partner, interfere with sexual functioning (e.g., Reissing, Binik, & Khalife, 1999). But as Masters and Johnson first suggested, cognitions concerning sexual performance are particularly important. Consider the idea that variability in sexual performance is common; a stressful day, a distracting context, a relationship concern, or any number of other issues may diminish sexual responsiveness. The key issue may be how people think about their diminished physical response when it happens. One theory is that people who blame themselves for decreased sexual performance will be more likely to develop recurrent problems.

In a test of the role of self-blame and erectile dysfunction, Weisberg and colleagues (2001) asked 52 male participants to watch erotic videos. During the videos, their sexual arousal (penile circumference) was measured using a **penile plethysmograph** (see Figure 13.6). Regardless of their actual arousal, the men were given false feedback that the size of their erection was smaller than that typically measured among aroused men. Men were randomly assigned to receive two different explanations for this false feedback. In the first, they were told that the films did not seem to be working for most men (external explanation). In the second, they were told that the pattern of their responses on questionnaires about sexuality might help explain the low arousal (internal explanation). After receiving this feedback, the men were asked to watch one more

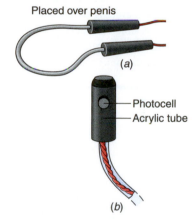

Placed over penis

(a)

Photocell
Acrylic tube

(b)

Figure 13.6 Behavioral researchers use two genital devices for measuring sexual arousal. Both are sensitive indicators of blood flow into the genitalia, a key physiological process in sexual arousal. (a) For men, the penile plethysmograph measures changes in the circumference of the penis by means of a strain gauge, consisting of a very thin rubber tube filled with mercury. As the penis enlarges with blood, the tube stretches, changing its electrical resistance. (b) For women, sexual arousal can be measured by a vaginal plethysmograph. Shaped like a tampon, this apparatus can be inserted into the vagina to measure increases in blood flow.

film. The men who were given an internal explanation reported less arousal and also showed less physiological evidence of arousal during the next film than those given an external explanation. These results, then, support the idea that people who blame themselves when their body doesn't perform will diminish their subsequent arousal. Needless to say, men in this study were carefully debriefed after the experiment!

Masters and Johnson found that many of their sexually dysfunctional patients had learned negative views of sexuality from their social and cultural surroundings. For example, some religions and cultures may discourage sexuality for the sake of pleasure, particularly outside marriage. Other cultures may disapprove of sexual initiative or behavior among women, other than for the sake of procreation. When people learn such negative views about sexuality, it can affect how they behave sexually. One female patient suffering from hypoactive sexual desire, for example, had been taught as she was growing up not to look at herself naked in the mirror and that intercourse was reserved for marriage and then only to be endured for purposes of having children.

Quick Summary

Sexuality is profoundly shaped by culture and experience, so it is important to be aware of subjective biases in thinking about diagnoses. Gender also shapes sexuality: men report more frequent sexual thoughts and behaviors than do women. For men and women, four phases of the sexual response cycle have been recognized: desire, excitement, orgasm, and resolution.

In DSM-IV-TR, the sexual dysfunction disorders are divided into the following:

- The sexual desire disorders (hypoactive sexual desire disorder and sexual aversion disorder)
- The sexual arousal disorders (female sexual arousal disorder and male erectile disorder)
- The orgasmic disorders (female orgasmic disorder, male orgasmic disorder, and premature ejaculation)
- The sexual pain disorders (dyspareunia and vaginismus).

Although there are no good estimates of how many people meet full diagnostic criteria for sexual dysfunction disorders, in one major survey, 43 percent of women and 31 percent of men reported at least some symptoms of sexual dysfunction. People who experience one sexual dysfunction disorder often experience a comorbid sexual dysfunction disorder; for example, a man who is experiencing premature ejaculation may develop hypoactive sexual desire disorder. Before diagnosing sexual dysfunction, it is important to rule out medical explanations for a symptom. The key etiological variables involved in sexual dysfunctions appear to be previous sexual abuse, relationship problems, lack of sexual knowledge, mental disorders like depression or anxiety or alcohol abuse, low arousal and exhaustion, and negative cognitions and attitudes about sexuality. For premature ejaculation, one possible cause is an overly sensitive penis.

Treatments of Sexual Dysfunctions

The pioneering work of Masters and Johnson (1970) in the treatment of sexual dysfunctions is described in Focus on Discovery 13.2. Over the past decades, therapists and researchers have elaborated on Masters and Johnson's work and created new procedures. We will describe several of the procedures that extend the Masters and Johnson work. A therapist may choose only one technique for a given case, but the multifaceted nature of sexual dysfunctions often requires the use of a combination of techniques. These approaches are generally suitable for treating sexual dysfunctions in homosexual as well as heterosexual clients.

Anxiety Reduction   Well before the publication of the Masters and Johnson therapy program, behavior therapists appreciated that their sexually dysfunctional clients needed gradual and systematic exposure to anxiety-provoking aspects of the sexual situation. Wolpe's systematic desensitization and in vivo desensitization (desensitization by real-life encounters) have been employed with some success (Wolpe, 1958), especially when combined with skills training. For example, a woman with vaginismus might first receive psychoeducation about her body, be trained in relaxation, and then practice inserting her fingers or dilators into her vagina, starting with small insertions and working up to larger ones (Leiblum, 1997). Such programs have been shown to be effective for most women with vaginismus (Jeng et al., 2006).

In vivo desensitization would appear to be the principal technique of the Masters and Johnson program, although additional components probably contribute to its overall effectiveness. Interestingly, simple psychoeducation programs about sexuality also do a great deal to reduce anxiety, and accordingly, several studies have now shown minimal or no benefit of systematic desensitization compared to psychoeducation for male erectile disorder, female arousal disorder, and female orgasmic disorder (Emmelkamp, 2004).

FOCUS ON DISCOVERY 13.2

Masters and Johnson's Therapy for Sexual Dysfunctions

In the 1970 book *Human Sexual Inadequacy,* Masters and Johnson reported on the successful results of one of the first sex therapy programs, which they had carried out with almost 800 sexually dysfunctional people. Each couple had traveled to St. Louis and spent two weeks attending intensive therapy during the day and completing sexual homework in a motel at night.

Many therapists continue to use the Masters and Johnson techniques, although success rates have tended to be lower than those originally reported (Segraves & Althof, 1998). Some believe that the lower success rates may be attributed more to the couples seeking treatment than to the therapy itself; as sex therapy has become more popular, the treatment-seeking couples have poorer marital relationships than did those who sought treatment in the early years of sex therapy.

In the Masters and Johnson work, couples were always seen by one male therapist and one female therapist. For several days, couples completed an assessment of social history, sexual history, sexual values, and medical concerns. During the assessment and first couple of days of treatment, sexual intercourse was forbidden. Sometimes the couple discussed sex for the first time at the clinic. Therapists adopted a calm and open manner to help couples feel comfortable discussing sex.

On the third day, the therapists began to offer interpretations about the sources of problems. If a person had negative attitudes toward sex, this would be addressed. But the basic emphasis was on relationship problems, not on individual difficulties of either partner. A premise of the therapy was that "there is no such thing as an uninvolved partner in any marriage in which there is some form of sexual inadequacy" (1970, p. 2). Whatever the problem, the couple was encouraged to see it as their mutual responsibility. At the same time, the clients were introduced to the idea of the spectator role. They were told, for example, that a male with erectile problems—and often his partner as well—usually worries about how well he is doing and that this pattern of observing the state of the erection, although totally understandable, blocks his natural responses and interferes with sexual enjoyment.

At the end of the third day, the couple was asked to engage in **sensate focus**. The couple was instructed to choose a time when both partners felt a sense of warmth and compatibility. During sensate focus exercises, the couple was instructed not to have intercourse. Indeed, initially they were instructed not to touch each other's genitalia. Rather they were to undress and give each other pleasure by touching each other's bodies. The co-therapists appointed one marital partner to do the first pleasuring; the partner who was "getting" was simply to be allowed to enjoy being touched. The one being touched was not required to feel a sexual response and was responsible for immediately telling the partner if something became uncomfortable. Then the roles were to be switched. The sensate-focus assignment usually promoted contact, constituting a first step toward reestablishing sexual intimacy.

Most of the time, partners began to realize that their physical encounters could be intimate and pleasurable without necessarily being a prelude to sexual intercourse. On the next evening, the partner being pleasured was instructed to give specific direction by guiding his or her partner's hand to regulate pressure and rate of stroking. Touching of genitals and breasts was now allowed, but still no intercourse. After two days of sensate focus, treatment began to be tailored to specific problems. To illustrate the process, we will outline the therapy for female orgasmic disorder.

After the sensate-focus exercises increased comfort, the woman was encouraged to focus on maximizing her own sexual stimulation without trying to have an orgasm. Her sexual excitement usually increased as a result. The therapists gave her partner explicit instructions about generally effective means of manually stroking the female genital area, although the female partner was encouraged to make decisions and express her wishes to her partner in the moment. At this stage it was emphasized that having orgasms was not the focus.

After the woman began to enjoy being pleasured by manual stimulation, she was told to place herself on top of the man, gently insert the penis, and simply attend in to her feelings. When she felt inclined, she could begin slowly to move her pelvis. She was encouraged to regard the penis as something for her to play with, something that could provide her with pleasure. The male could begin to thrust slowly. At all times, however, the woman was to decide what should happen next. When the couple was able to maintain this exploration for minutes at a time, without the man thrusting forcefully toward orgasm, a major change had usually taken place in their sexual interactions: for perhaps the first time, the woman was allowed to think sexually about her own pleasure. In their subsequent encounters, most couples began to have mutually satisfying intercourse.

A caveat about sensate focus is in order. As LoPiccolo (1992) pointed out, more and more people are aware that not getting an erection from sensate focus is at the same time expected and not expected! That is, although the instruction from the therapist is not to engage in sex, even a moderately knowledgeable man knows that at some point he is supposed to get an erection from this situation. Thus, rather than reducing performance anxiety and the spectator role, some men may experience a phenomenon called *metaperformance anxiety* during sensate focus, taking the form of self-statements such as, "Okay, I don't have any pressure to get an erection and have intercourse. Right. So now 10 minutes have passed, there's no pressure to perform, but I don't have an erection yet. When am I going to get an erection? And if I do, will I be able to maintain it long enough to insert it?" Sensate-focus treatment and other aspects of Masters and Johnson's sex therapy have elements of a paradoxical approach to treatment, which is based on the idea that telling people not to do something will reduce their anxiety about doing something.

For the treatment of premature ejaculation, anxiety-reduction techniques sometimes have a different focus. Anxiety about ejaculating too soon may be a natural result of an overemphasis on intercourse as a sole focus of sexual behavior. Sex therapists advise couples to expand their repertoire of activities to include techniques not requiring an engorged penis, such as oral or manual manipulation, so that gratification of the partner is possible after the man has climaxed. When the exclusive focus on penile insertion is removed, a couple's anxieties about sex usually diminish enough to permit greater ejaculatory control.

Directed Masturbation   Directed masturbation was devised by LoPiccolo and Lobitz (1972) to enhance women's comfort with and enjoyment of their sexuality. The first step is for the woman to carefully examine her nude body, including her genitals, and to identify various areas with the aid of diagrams. Next, she is instructed to touch her genitals and to find areas that produce pleasure. Then she increases the intensity of masturbation using erotic fantasies. If orgasm is not achieved, she is to use a vibrator in her masturbation. Finally, her partner enters the picture, first watching her masturbate, then doing for her what she has been doing for herself, and finally having intercourse in a position that allows him to stimulate the woman's genitals manually or with a vibrator. Directed masturbation appears to significantly improve the effectiveness of the treatment of orgasmic disorder (O'Donohue, Dopke, & Swingen, 1997); it is also helpful in the treatment of sexual desire disorder (Renshaw, 2001). Directed masturbation with partner involvement has been found to be effective for 90 percent of women with a lifelong inability to experience orgasm (Riley & Riley, 1978).

Procedures to Change Attitudes and Thoughts   In *sensory-awareness procedures*, clients are encouraged to tune in to the pleasant sensations that accompany even incipient sexual arousal. The sensate-focus exercises described in Focus on Discovery 13.2, for example, are a way of helping the person be more aware of and comfortable with sexual feelings. Rational-emotive behavior therapy tries to challenge self-demanding, perfectionistic thoughts that often cause problems for people with sexual dysfunctions. A therapist might try to reduce the pressure a man with erectile dysfunction feels by challenging his belief that intercourse is the only true form of sexual activity. Kaplan (1997) recommends several procedures to try to increase the attractiveness of sex. She has clients engage in erotic fantasies and gives them courtship and dating assignments, such as getting away for a weekend.

Skills and Communication Training   To improve sexual skill and communication, therapists assign written materials and show clients explicit videotapes and films demonstrating sexual techniques (McMullen & Rosen, 1979). Encouraging partners to communicate their likes and dislikes to each other has been shown to be helpful for a range of sexual dysfunctions (Rosen, Leiblum, & Spector, 1994). Taken together, skills and communication training also exposes partners to potentially anxiety-provoking material, such as expressing sexual preferences, which allows for a desensitizing effect. Telling a partner one's preferences in sex is often made more difficult by tensions that go beyond the sexual relationship, which leads us to the next strategy.

Couples Therapy   Masters and Johnson considered sexual dysfunctions as problems that could be treated directly, rather than as symptoms of other psychological or interpersonal difficulties. Many of the couples they treated had marriages that, in spite of sexual problems, were marked by caring and closeness. But as society changed and people became more comfortable seeking help, sex therapists began to see people whose relationships were seriously impaired. In current treatment settings, sexual dysfunctions are often embedded in a distressed relationship, and troubled couples usually need special training in nonsexual communication skills (Rosen, 2000). Sex therapists now often work from a systems perspective; that is, the therapist appreciates that a sexual problem is embedded in a complex network of relationship factors (Wylie, 1997). Some therapists focus on nonsexual issues, such as difficulties with in-laws or with child rearing—either in addition to or instead of a Masters and Johnson type of sex therapy. For women with sexual dysfunctions in the context of relationship distress, behavioral couples therapy has been found to improve many aspects of sexual functioning (Zimmer, 1987).

Medications and Physical Treatments Sometimes medical treatments are used to correct an underlying physical condition. The current trend toward viewing sexual dysfunctions as medical problems may divert the attention of therapists and patients from the inherently interpersonal nature of sexual problems, giving rise to a quick-fix mentality that is probably ill advised (Rosen & Leiblum, 1995). Exclusively medical approaches have been particularly criticized as inappropriate for women, given the strong links between sexuality and relationship satisfaction (Tiefer, 2001). Despite these caveats, medication treatments for sexual dysfunction have become increasingly popular. Antidepressant drugs have been found to be helpful when depression appears to contribute to diminished sex drive. Antianxiety medications also can be used as an adjunct to anxiety-reduction techniques. A complicating factor, though, is that some of these psychoactive drugs themselves interfere with sexual responsiveness. Sometimes a second medication may be used to counteract the sexual side effects of the first; for example, buproprion (Wellbutrin) has been shown to help address the libido problems caused by SSRI medications (Segraves, 2003).

"YOU WANT A RAISE, BREWSTER? HOW ABOUT A VIAGRA PILL?"

(© Harley Schwadron.)

Premature Ejaculation For the treatment of premature ejaculation, the squeeze technique is often used, in which a partner is trained to squeeze the penis in the area where the head and shaft meet to rapidly reduce arousal. This technique is practiced without insertion, and then during insertion, the penis is withdrawn and the squeeze is repeated as needed. Success rates initially tend to be high (60 to 90 percent), but there is some relapse over time (Polonsky, 2000). Antidepressant drugs have also been found to be helpful in the treatment of premature ejaculation (Bettocchi et al., 2008).

Erectile Dysfunction The most common medical interventions for erectile dysfunction include sildenafil (Viagra) and related medications [e.g., tadafil (Cialis) and vardenafil (Levitra)]. Viagra was approved by the FDA in March 1998 and in its first 3 months was prescribed over 3 million times. Viagra relaxes smooth muscles and thereby allows blood to flow into the penis during sexual stimulation, creating an erection. It is taken one hour before sex, and its effects last about four hours. Viagra does not cause an erection in the absence of sexual stimulation, so the psychological dimension of erectile dysfunction must be attended to if this drug is to be effective (Rosen, 2000). Although promising, research reports indicate that between 16 and 44 percent of men do not derive much benefit from the drug (Bach et al., 2001). Viagra also produces side effects such as headaches and indigestion. Moreover, it may be dangerous for men with cardiovascular disease, and this is a concern since many of the older men who use Viagra are at risk for hypertension and coronary artery disease. Several trials of Viagra and related medicines have been conducted with women, but so far, the results are not promising, with the exception of Viagra for postmenopausal women who retain desire but have low arousal (Berman et al., 2003).

In the movie *Something's Gotta Give,* Jack Nicholson portrays a man whose use of Viagra complicates his cardiovascular treatment. (The Kobal Collection, Ltd.)

Quick Summary

Psychological treatments for sexual dysfunction include techniques to reduce anxiety, to increase knowledge and awareness of the body, to reduce negative thoughts about sexuality, to improve couples' communication, and to reduce performance anxiety. Medical treatments are increasingly popular, despite some criticism. Medications such as Viagra and Cialis are commonly used to treat erectile dysfunction. Antidepressant drugs can be helpful in the treatment of premature ejaculation.

Gender Identity Disorder

"Are you a man or a woman?" For virtually all people, the answer to such a question is obvious. And others would agree unequivocally with the answer. The sense of self as male or female, or **gender identity**, is so deeply ingrained from earliest childhood that the vast majority of people are absolutely certain of their gender. In contrast to gender identity, **sexual orientation** is the preference for the sex of a partner. Sexual orientation and gender identity are distinct. For example, a man may be attracted to men—a matter of sexual orientation—without believing he is a woman—a matter of gender identity. Here, we discuss gender identity disorder (formerly known as transsexualism).

Clinical Description of Gender Identity Disorder

People with **gender identity disorder (GID)** feel deep within themselves, usually from early childhood, that they are of the opposite sex. They are not persuaded by the presence of normal genitals, nor by others' perceptions of their gender. A man can look at himself in a mirror, see the body of a biological man, and yet experience that body as belonging to a woman. He may want to surgically alter his body to bring it in line with his gender identity. The diagnosis of GID is only applicable when the desire to be a member of the opposite sex causes significant distress or impairment. Persons who are comfortable perceiving themselves as a member of the opposite sex should not be diagnosed. In keeping with the distinctions between gender identity and sexual orientation, it is important to note that a person with GID may be attracted to people from the same or the opposite sex (Carroll, 2000).

The prevalence rates for GID are small: one in about 12,000 for men and one in 30,000 in women (Meyer et al., 2001). The higher prevalence in men may reflect societal acceptance of women who choose to adopt a male role.

GID is one of the most debated categories in the DSM-IV-TR. Few would argue that there are people with the intense belief that they are a member of the opposite sex. But should this be labeled as a disorder? Despite its controversial status, GID is still in the DSM-IV; it remains to be seen whether future versions of the DSM will be more sensitive to the changing scientific and political opinions on this issue. Even for those who believe this should be classified as a disorder, there are controversies about the causes and treatment (Bailey, 2003). For example, some have argued that inclusion of this phenomenon as a diagnosis pathologizes a natural diversity. A lead spokesperson for this perspective is Joan Roughgarden (2004), a Stanford professor of biology. Roughgarden points to the tremendous diversity of gender roles in the animal kingdom. She describes countless examples of species in which biologically male animals will adopt behavior, courtship rituals, and mating strategies that parallel those seen by female animals. Roughgarden suggests that it does not make sense to conceptualize such universal behavior as a disorder and that scientists should focus more on the adaptive consequences of gender-role diversity.

According to the DSM-IV-TR, GID can be diagnosed among children. GID in a child can be labeled in children as young as 2 to 4 years old (Green & Blanchard, 1995). GID is diagnosed on the basis of cross-gender behaviors, such as dressing in opposite-sex clothes, preferring opposite-sex playmates, and engaging in play that would usually be considered more typical of the opposite sex (e.g., a boy's playing with Barbie dolls), along with a persistently stated desire to be a member of the opposite sex.

The diagnosis of GID is more prevalent in children than in adults (Zucker & Bradley, 1995), perhaps because parents are often upset by their children adopting different gender roles. Based on clinic referral rates, it appears to be about six times more frequent in boys than girls (Zucker, Bradley, & Sanikhani, 1997). Most children with GID grow up to be comfortable with their biological sex in adulthood without professional intervention (Drummond et al., 2008; Zucker & Bradley, 1995). The vast majority of little boys engage in some traditional feminine play, and little girls in some traditional masculine play, with no identity conflicts whatsoever (Green, 1976). Aside from brief periods of play, about 1 percent of 4- or 5-year-old boys report wishing they were a girl at times, and about 5 percent of 4- or 5-year-old girls report wishing they were a boy (Bradley & Zucker, 1997). Cross-gender behaviors are so common that it should not be surprising that the vast majority of children with these behaviors do not grow up to be adults with GID. Because cross-gender behavior during childhood is common and because childhood GID diagnoses do not predict adulthood diagnoses, some argue that GID in childhood should be dropped from the DSM.

Etiology of Gender Identity Disorder

Genetic, neurobiological, and psychosocial causes of GID have been proposed. In part because this condition is so rare, there are few studies of the causes.

Genetic Factors   Some data suggest that gender identity may be at least partially genetic. Several twin studies suggest that some symptoms of gender identity during childhood are at least moderately heritable (Bailey, Dunne, & Martin, 2000; van Beijsterveldt, Hudziak, & Boomsma, 2006). These studies have looked at people with cross-gender behaviors, though, rather than those who met full diagnostic criteria for GID.

Neurobiological Factors   Levels of sex hormones in adulthood and during the pregnancy have both been hypothesized as causal factors in GID. People with and without GID do not consistently differ in hormone levels during adulthood (Bosinski et al., 1997). Rather, most current research focuses on the role of hormones during gestation. Research with humans and primates shows that offspring of mothers who have taken sex hormones during pregnancy often behave like members of the opposite sex and have anatomical abnormalities. For example, a series of studies suggest that girls with high levels of androgen exposure in utero tend to display more masculine-typed behaviors and attitudes than girls without high levels of androgen exposure (Berenbaum, 1999). Young boys whose mothers ingested female hormones when pregnant were found to be less athletic and to engage less in rough-and-tumble play than their male peers (Yalom, Green, & Fisk, 1973). Despite the evidence that in utero hormone exposure can shape cross-gender behaviors, these children do not declare themselves to be of the opposite gender (Berenbaum, 1999). Hence, prenatal sex hormones only seem to explain some aspects of gender identity, rather than providing a full explanation.

The case of Joan/John and others like it demonstrate a strong biological underpinning for gender identity; despite not having a penis and being treated as a girl throughout childhood, John never developed a female gender identity (Colapinto, 1997). One study suggests similar conclusions. Reiner and Gearhart (2004) followed up 14 genetic males who for medical reasons had been surgically changed to females as young infants and then raised as girls. Of the 14, 8 had fully adopted a male identity by age 16, and all showed interests and activities that were typical of males. Even with the attempts to raise these children as girls, biology seemed to have influenced identity to a strong extent.

Social and Psychological Factors   Masculinity and femininity are culturally shaped and defined, and heavily laden with value judgments and stereotyping. Our society is still sadly intolerant of boys who engage in activities more typical of girls. Girls can play games and dress in

Clinical Case: Joan/John

As there is so little research on the prospective predictors of GID, many people have looked to other literature to understand how gender identity develops. In 1965, Linda Thiessen gave birth to twin boys. During a surgery to correct a problem with the foreskin, the penis of John, one of the twins, was destroyed. With advice from John Money, a well-known sex researcher at Johns Hopkins University, the Thiessens decided to castrate John, construct female genitals, and raise him as a girl named Joan.

Several years later, Money began to discuss the case with other health professionals, describing it as a total success and using it to buttress his theory that gender identity is determined by the environment. But the facts suggest instead that there is a strong biological influence on gender identity.

Despite having been instructed to encourage feminine behavior in Joan, her parents reported that Joan behaved in a very boyish way. At age 2, she ripped off her first dress; during her preschool years, her play activities were clearly masculine. At age 11, Joan steadfastly held out against surgery to construct a more feminine vagina than the rudimentary one that had been created during the original surgery. By age 14, Joan had decided to stop living as a girl. Given Joan's behavior and distress, Joan's physicians finally recommended that she be told the whole story. She immediately decided to reverse the earlier treatments and changed her name back to John. She took male hormones, had her breasts removed, and had an artificial penis constructed. At age 21 John had another operation to improve his artificial penis, and at age 25 he married a woman.

Although dressing up is common in childhood, most people with GID trace their gender identity distress to childhood and report dressing in cross-gender clothes. (Francene Keery/Stock, Boston.)

Harisu was born a male, but after sex reassignment surgery at age 23 she became an extremely successful model and pop star in South Korea. (Sean Gallup/GettyImages, Inc.)

a manner more typical of boys and still conform to acceptable standards of behavior for girls (Williams, Goodman, & Green, 1985).

If gender-role behavior is environmentally shaped, some have suggested that GID could be shaped by environmental contingencies as well. One model of GID focuses on reinforcement of cross-gender behavior (Green, 1987). Most children engage in cross-gender behaviors at some point in time. Some parents and relatives may reinforce such behavior. Parents of children who show signs of GID often reveal that they did not discourage cross-dressing behavior in their children. This holds true especially for feminine boys—family members may have seen the behavior as cute. According to the reinforcement theory, such reactions on the part of the family to a child could contribute to the acquired gender identity (Zucker et al., 1993). As pointed out by Bailey (2003), though, family members and peers are often mercilessly cruel about cross-gender behavior—if environmental contingencies were powerful, one might expect these interpersonal punishments to dispel cross-gender behavior.

Treatments of Gender Identity Disorder

The most common treatment for GID is to change the body to suit the person's gender identity. A few case studies are available of behavioral treatment designed to change the psychology to match the person's body.

Changing the Body   People seeking hormones to change their sexual features are generally required to first undergo months of living as the desired gender or take part in psychotherapy to address feelings about gender roles (Harry Benjamin International Gender Dysphoria Association, 2001). A range of physical procedures are used to change the person's body. For example, a man may have electrolysis to remove facial hair, surgery to reduce the size of the chin and Adam's apple, and training to raise the pitch of the voice. Female hormones promote breast growth and soften the skin of men (Schaefer, Wheeler, & Futterweit, 1997). Some men also have plastic surgery to attain a more feminine facial appearance, larger breasts, or more curvaceous hips. Some take the additional step of having sex-reassignment surgery. It is typically recommended that cosmetic and hormonal changes be in place and that the person live as a member of the opposite sex for at least one year before surgery is performed.

In **sex-reassignment surgery**, the existing genitalia are altered to be more similar to those of the opposite sex. The first sex-reassignment operation took place in Europe in 1930, but the surgery that attracted worldwide attention was performed on an ex-soldier, Christine (originally George) Jorgensen, in Copenhagen, Denmark, in 1952.

For male-to-female reassignment surgery, most of the penis is removed, but some of the tissue and nerves are used to form an artificial vagina, labia, and clitoris. Heterosexual intercourse is possible after reassignment surgery for men, with sensitivity of nerves to stimulation preserved.

The female-to-male reassignment process is more difficult in some ways and less difficult in others. On the one hand, the surgically constructed penis is small and not capable of normal erection; artificial supports are therefore needed for sexual intercourse. An operation extends the urethra into the newly constructed penis to allow the person the social comfort of being able to use public urinals. On the other hand, less cosmetic follow-up is needed than for male-to-female reassignment because the male hormones prescribed to women seeking sexual reassignment drastically alter fat distribution and stimulate the growth of facial and body hair. The relatively greater ease of the cosmetic female-to-male change may be due in part to society's lesser focus on the physical attributes of men. A small, soft-spoken man with a relatively high-pitched voice may be more acceptable to society than a 6-foot-tall deep-voiced woman. Nevertheless, sex-reassignment surgery is chosen by many more men than women.

How beneficial is sex-reassignment surgery? Over the years, controversy has existed over its benefits, and the quality of the research is low (Carroll, 2000). A review by Green and Fleming (1990) of reasonably controlled outcome studies published between 1979 and 1989 with at least a one-year follow-up drew favorable conclusions. Of 130 female-to-male surgeries, about 97 percent could be judged satisfactory; of 220 male-to-female surgeries, 87 percent were satisfactory. Preoperative factors that seemed to predict favorable postsurgery adjustment were (1) reason-

Author and historian James Morris (in a 1960 picture), after sex-reassignment surgery, became Jan Morris (in a 1974 photograph). (Left: Corbis Images; right: Robin Laurence/New York Times Picture.)

able emotional stability, (2) successful adaptation in the new role for at least one year before the surgery, (3) adequate understanding of the actual limitations and consequences of the surgery, and (4) psychotherapy in the context of an established gender identity program. The authors caution, however, that satisfactory ratings meant only that the patients reported that they did not regret having had the surgery. One report from the University of Pennsylvania indicated that sexual responsiveness and sexual satisfaction increase dramatically after both male-to-female and female-to-male reassignments, with overall high satisfaction with the results of the surgery (Lief & Hubschman, 1993). In one follow-up study of people who had undergone sex-reassignment surgery, just over half reported satisfaction with their partnerships, as compared to one-third who were satisfied before the surgery (De Cuypere et al., 2005). Finally, one long-term study found that young men who had undergone sex reassignment were no longer gender-dysphoric, had no regrets about the procedures, and were otherwise functioning better than men who had been denied the hormonal treatment and surgery (Smith, van Goozen, & Cohen-Kettenis, 2001).

Behavioral Treatment to Alter Gender Identity   A few case reports exist of behavioral treatment designed to alter sex-role behaviors. These treatments have included helping men to shape specific behaviors, such as mannerisms and interpersonal behavior, to be more masculine (Barlow, Reynolds, & Agras, 1973). In three cases, these treatments were successful in helping patients change sex-role behavior, and changes were sustained (Barlow, Abel, & Blanchard, 1979). This work demonstrates that some sex-role behaviors may be amenable to change. But as the researchers pointed out, even the limited success of this program might not be generalizable. Their clients might have been different from others with GID because they wanted treatment to change their gender identity. Most people with GID are not interested in such treatment. For them, physically altering their bodies is the goal.

Check Your Knowledge 13.2

True or false?
1. A person who experiences a brief problem with sexual arousal, orgasm, or desire is likely to meet criteria for a sexual dysfunction.
2. The best treatment for premature ejaculation is Viagra.
3. Sex therapists may recommend that a woman with lack of orgasms practice masturbation without her partner present.

4. People with one sexual dysfunction tend to have other comorbid sexual dysfunctions.
5. Diagnostic criteria for GID include distress over sexual attraction to people of the same sex.

Quick Summary

GID is diagnosed when a person experiences long-term and intense discomfort with his or her gender identity. People with this disorder feel like they are trapped in the wrong body. Prevalence rates are low: about one in 30,000 men and one in 100,000 women meet formal diagnostic criteria. There is major debate about whether diagnosing this experience pathologizes naturally occurring diversity. There is also debate about the appropriateness of using this diagnosis during childhood. Because GID is so rare, researchers do not know much about the etiology. There is evidence that some cross-gender behavior is moderately heritable, but genetic studies do not focus on diagnosable levels of gender identity symptoms.

Some evidence suggests a role for exposure to atypically high levels of hormones in utero. Behavioral theory focuses on possible reinforcement of cross-gender roles, but this theory does a poor job of taking into account the extreme punishment often provoked by cross-gender behavior.

Treatments for GID involve surgical and hormonal procedures that change the person's sexual anatomy to match the internal identity. Behavioral treatment has been used for a small number of cases to change cross-gender behavior, but even when individuals change the way they act, they may retain an internal sense of identity as the other gender.

The Paraphilias

In DSM-IV-TR the **paraphilias** are a group of disorders defined by sexual attraction to unusual objects or sexual activities. In other words, there is a deviation (*para*) in what the person is attracted to (*philia*). The fantasies, urges, or behaviors last at least 6 months. Attractions to parts of the body, such as feet, are not diagnosed. Indeed, surveys have shown that many people occasionally fantasize about some of the activities we will be describing. For example, 50 percent of men report voyeuristic fantasies of peeping at unsuspecting naked women (Hanson & Harris, 1997). In a large group of people who volunteered for a study of sexuality and health, 7.7 percent of people reported that they had been aroused by spying on others having sex, and 3.1 percent of people reported that they had exposed their genitalia to a stranger at least once during their lifetime (Långström & Seto, 2006). Diagnoses of paraphilias, though, are meant to capture sexual urges that are more problematic and long-lasting than the occasional fantasy or sexual experimentation. Paraphilias are not diagnosed unless the fantasies or behaviors are recurrent and cause marked distress or impairment.

Accurate prevalence statistics are not available for the paraphilias. When responding to a community survey, many people with paraphilias may not reveal their proclivities. As some persons with paraphilias seek nonconsenting partners or otherwise violate people's rights in offensive ways (as we will see in exhibitionism and pedophilia), these disorders can have legal consequences. But statistics on arrests are likely to be underestimates because many crimes go unreported and some paraphilias (e.g., voyeurism) involve an unsuspecting victim. The data do indicate, though, that most people with paraphilias are male and heterosexual; even with masochism and pedophilia, which occur in noticeable numbers of women, men vastly outnumber women.

Clinical Case: William

William is a twenty-eight-year-old computer programmer who sought treatment after being arrested for voyeurism. William grew up as the second of four children in a conservative, religious family living in a rural area. He began to masturbate at age fifteen, and he did so while watching his sister urinate in their outhouse. Despite feeling very guilty, he continued to masturbate several times a week while having voyeuristic fantasies. A couple of times, he had masturbated while watching strangers undress.

As an adult, William was a timid, shy, and lonely man. He lived alone, and six months before the arrest, he had been rejected in a long-term relationship. In response, he withdrew from other social relationships and began drinking more alcohol. As his self-esteem deteriorated, his voyeuristic fantasies became more and more urgent.

One summer night, William had been feeling lonely and depressed, and he had been drinking heavily at a lounge with a topless dancer. After leaving the bar, he had been driving through a suburban neighborhood when he noticed someone in an upstairs window. Without thinking much, he had parked, erected a ladder he found near the house, and climbed up to the window to peep. The residents called the police when they heard him, and William was arrested. He was very shocked at the arrest, but knew that his behavior was destructive and he was motivated to change. [Rosen & Rosen (1981), pp. 452–453, Reprinted by permission of McGraw-Hill Book Company].

Table 13.4 Paraphilias Included in DSM-IV-TR

Paraphilia	Object of Sexual Attraction
Fetishism	An inanimate object
Transvestic fetishism	Cross-dressing
Pedophilia	Children
Voyeurism	Watching unsuspecting others undress or have sex
Exhibitionism	Exposing one's genitals to an unwilling stranger
Frotteurism	Sexual touching of an unsuspecting person
Sexual sadism	Inflicting pain
Sexual masochism	Receiving pain

DSM-IV-TR differentiates the paraphilias based on the source of arousal, for example, providing one diagnostic category for people whose sexual attractions are focused on inanimate objects and another diagnostic category for people whose attractions are focused on children (see Table 13.4). Here, we provide a clinical description of the paraphilias included in DSM-IV-TR. As we describe the symptoms, we describe the epidemiology of these disorders. Many people with paraphilias meet criteria for other paraphilias and for other DSM-IV-TR diagnoses, and we will discuss the most frequent comorbid conditions as we review epidemiology. Then we will discuss models of the etiology and treatment of these disorders.

Fetishism

Fetishism involves a reliance on an inanimate object for sexual arousal. The person with fetishism, almost always a man, has recurrent and intense sexual urges toward nonliving objects, called fetishes (e.g., women's shoes), and the presence of the fetish is strongly preferred or even necessary for sexual arousal.

Clothing (especially underwear), rubber products (like raincoats), and articles related to feet (stockings, women's shoes) are common fetishes. Some carry on their fetishism by themselves in secret by fondling, kissing, smelling, sucking, placing in their rectum, or merely gazing at the adored object as they masturbate. Others need their partner to don the fetish as a stimulant for intercourse. Some become interested in acquiring a collection of the desired objects, and they may even commit burglary week after week to add to their hoard.

The person with fetishism feels a compulsive attraction toward the object; the attraction is experienced as involuntary and irresistible. It is the degree of the erotic focus—the exclusive and very special status the object occupies as a sexual stimulant—that distinguishes fetishisms from the ordinary attraction that, for example, high heels may hold for heterosexual men in Western cultures. The person with a boot fetish must see or touch a boot to become aroused, and the arousal is overwhelmingly strong when a boot is present.

The disorder usually begins by adolescence, although the fetish may have acquired special significance even earlier, during childhood. People with fetishism often have other paraphilias, such as pedophilia, sadism, and masochism (Mason, 1997).

Transvestic Fetishism

Transvestic fetishism, or *transvestism*, refers to recurrent and intense sexual arousal from cross-dressing. The extent of transvestism varies from wearing women's underwear under conventional clothing to full cross-dressing. Some female impersonators in nightclubs cater to the delight that many people take in observing skilled cross-dressing. Unless the cross-dressing associated with sexual arousal, however, these impersonators do not meet criteria for transvestic fetishism. Transvestism also should not be confused with the cross-dressing associated with gender identity disorder. People with transvestic fetishism cross-dress for sexual arousal, unlike those with gender identity disorder.

DSM-IV-TR Criteria for Fetishism

- For at least 6 months, recurrent and intense sexually arousing fantasies, urges, or behaviors involving the use of nonliving objects
- Causes marked distress or impairment in functioning
- The sexually arousing objects are not limited to articles of female clothing used in cross-dressing or to devices designed to provide tactile genital stimulation, such as a vibrator

Many people experiment with fetishes. Fetishism is not diagnosed unless the attraction to fetishes causes marked distress or impairment. (Cindy Charles/PhotoEdit.)

FOCUS ON DISCOVERY 13.3

The Effects of Pedophilia: Outcomes After Childhood Sexual Abuse

In one major community survey, 13.5 percent of women and 2.5 percent of men reported experiencing some form of **childhood sexual abuse (CSA)** (Molnar et al., 2001). How does this all-too-common experience affect mental health during childhood and beyond? What can be done to protect children and to help children heal from CSA?

Effects on the Child

About half of children who are exposed to CSA will develop symptoms, such as depression, low self-esteem, conduct disorder, and anxiety disorders like posttraumatic stress disorder (PTSD). On the other hand, almost half of children who are exposed to CSA do not appear to experience immediate symptoms (Kuehnle, 1998). We have seen in previous chapters that a history of CSA is found among adults experiencing many different mental disorders—notably, dissociative identity disorder, eating disorders, borderline personality disorder, major depressive disorder, sexual dysfunctions, and substance abuse (Litrownik & Castillo-Cañez, 2000).

What factors contribute to how CSA affects a child? The odds that CSA will produce negative reactions will be increased when a perpetrator threatens a child, the child blames him- or herself, or the family is unsupportive (Kuehnle, 1998). Negative outcomes are more pronounced when the CSA involves sexual intercourse (Nelson et al., 2002). Levels of adulthood depression and anxiety symptoms also appear to be higher when the CSA started at an earlier age (Kaplow & Widom, 2007).

The research linking CSA to mental disorders has been mired in methodological issues. For example, sampling biases appear important, in that studies of college students with a history of CSA typically find small effects of CSA (Rind, Tromovitch, & Bauserman, 1998), but studies of clients in treatment may overestimate the role of abuse. Understanding the effects of CSA require studies of community samples that do not have these sampling biases.

A broader issue, though, is that families in which abuse happens are often experiencing a broad array of problems, such as substance dependence in one or both parents, which may be entangled with other genetic and environmental risks for psychopathology. Because of this, it is hard to isolate whether CSA is genuinely the factor that heightens the risk for a clinical disorder. Twin studies provide a way to disentangle these effects, particularly when one twin but not the other has been abused, because the twin who was not abused shares genetic, and at least some environmental, risk factors. In one study of almost 2,000 twin pairs, people with a history of CSA had substantially increased risk of depression, suicide, conduct disorder, alcohol dependence, social anxiety, rape during adulthood, and divorce compared to nonabused twins (Nelson et al., 2002).

The Issue of Betrayal

A child abuser is usually not a stranger. He may be a father, an uncle, a brother, a teacher, a coach, a neighbor, or even a cleric. The abuser is often an adult whom the child knows and trusts. When the abuser is someone close to the child, the child is likely to be torn by allegiance to the abuser on the one hand and, on the other hand, by fear, revulsion, and the knowledge that what is happening is wrong. The betrayal of this trust makes the crime more abhorrent than it would be if no prior relationship existed between abuser and child. Betrayal is also experienced by adults and children who are sexually abused by clergy or other people related to religious organizations.

During 2002–2003, more than 1,000 people filed claims accusing Catholic clergy of molesting them as children many years earlier (Sheler, 2003). As with childhood incest, molestation or sexual harassment by a religious authority figure violates trust and respect. The victim, whatever his or her age, cannot give meaningful consent. The power differential is just too great. Self-blame is likely to be strong in the victim because the

---

Clinical Case: Ruben

Ruben is a single, 32-year-old male photographer who sought treatment for his "abnormal sex drive." He reported that he was particularly concerned that he was more attracted to women's underwear than to the women themselves. Ruben reported that he remembered being excited by pictures of women in their underwear at age 7. He first reached orgasm at age 13 by masturbating while imagining women in their "panties." He began to steal underwear from his sister to use while masturbating. As he grew older, he would take opportunities to sneak into other women's rooms and steal their underwear. He began to have intercourse at age 18, and his preferred partner was a prostitute that he asked to wear underwear with the crotch removed while they had sex. He found that he preferred masturbating into stolen underwear more than sexual intercourse. He avoided dating "nice women," as he feared they would not understand his sexual behavior, and he also avoided friends who might encourage him to date such women. He had begun to experience significant depression over the ways in which his sexual behavior was limiting his social life. [Adapted from Spitzer et al. (1994).]

Transvestic fetishism usually begins with partial cross-dressing in childhood or adolescence. Always men, most cross-dress episodically rather than regularly. They tend to be otherwise masculine in appearance and demeanor. Many are married and lead otherwise conventional lives. Cross-dressing usually takes place in secret. Married men who engage in this behavior may feel guilt or shame about their behavior, and they sometimes hide their urges from their wives for years. The urge to cross-dress may become more frequent over time. Transvestism is often comorbid with other paraphilias, notably masochism (Zucker & Blanchard, 1997).

offender is part of the person's religion. If the priest or minister or rabbi is doing this, how can it be wrong?

Prevention

CSA prevention efforts have focused on elementary schools. Common elements include teaching children to recognize inappropriate adult behavior, resist inducements, leave the situation quickly, and report the incident to an appropriate adult (Wolfe, 1990). Children are taught to say no in a firm, assertive way when an adult talks to or touches them in a manner that makes them feel uncomfortable. Instructors may use comic books, films, and descriptions of risky situations to teach about sexual abuse and how children can protect themselves.

Evaluations of school programs suggest that they do increase awareness of sexual abuse. Researchers do not know whether children are able to translate what they have learned into overt behavior that reduces the problem (Wolfe, 1990).

Dealing with the Problem

When they suspect that something is awry, parents must raise the issue with their children; unfortunately, many adults are uncomfortable doing so. Physicians also need to be sensitized to signs of sexual abuse. Both sexual and nonsexual abuse are reportable offenses; professionals who suspect abuse are required by law to report their suspicions to the police or child protective agencies. When states first passed legislation requiring health care professionals and teachers to report suspected child abuse, confirmed cases skyrocketed. For a child, reporting sexual abuse can be extremely difficult. We tend to forget how helpless and dependent the child feels, and it is difficult to imagine how frightening it would be to tell one's parents that one had been fondled by a brother or grandfather.

Most cases of sexual abuse do not leave any physical evidence, such as torn vaginal tissue. Furthermore, there is no behavioral pattern, such as anxiety, depression, or increased sexual activity that unequivocally indicates that abuse has occurred (Kuehnle, 1998). Therefore, the child's own report is the primary source of information about whether CSA has occurred. The problem is that leading questions can produce some false reports. Great skill is required in questioning a child about possible sexual abuse to avoid biasing the youngster one way or the other. Some jurisdictions use innovative procedures to reduce the stress on the child while protecting the rights of the accused adult, for example, videotaped testimony, closed-courtroom trials, closed-circuit televised testimony, and special coaching sessions to explain what to expect in the courtroom (Wolfe, 1990). Having the child play with anatomically correct dolls can be useful in getting at the truth, but it should be only one part of an assessment, because many nonabused children portray such dolls having sexual intercourse (Jampole & Weber, 1987).

Parents go through their own crisis when they become aware that someone has been molesting their child. Shame, guilt, fear, and anger abound. In the case of incest, the victim's mother may be in a particularly difficult situation, sometimes torn between her partner and her child, sometimes facing financial uncertainty should the partner leave the home or be arrested. Sadly, a parent who is unable to face such threats may allow incest to continue. It is impossible to know what percentage of incest cases are not reported to the police, but it is safe to say that most are unreported, particularly if the offender is a family member (Finkelhor, 1983).

Many children need treatment (Litrownik & Castillo-Cañez, 2000). As with adult survivors of rape, posttraumatic stress disorder (PTSD) can be a consequence. Many interventions are similar to those used for PTSD in adults; the emphasis is on exposure to memories of the trauma through discussion in a safe and supportive therapeutic atmosphere (Johnson, 1987). It is also important for children to learn that healthy human sexuality is not about power and fear (McCarthy, 1986). Inhibitions about bodily contact can be addressed in group therapy settings via structured, nonsexual hand-holding and back rubs (Wolfe, 1990). As with rape, it is important to change the person's attribution of responsibility from "I was bad" to "He/she was bad." Intervention varies with the person's age—a 14-year-old does not need dolls to recount what was done, and a 3-year-old is not an appropriate candidate for group therapy. As yet there has been no controlled research on these various interventions, but uncontrolled studies are encouraging (E. M. Arnold et al., 2003).

Pedophilia and Incest

According to the DSM, **pedophilia** (*pedos*, Greek for "child") is diagnosed when adults derive sexual gratification through sexual contact with prepubertal children. DSM-IV-TR requires that the offender be at least 16 years old and at least 5 years older than the child. Despite these diagnostic criteria, some people with pedophilia also victimize adolescents (Marshall, 1997).

As in most paraphilias, a strong subjective attraction impels the behavior. Sometimes a man with pedophilia is content to stroke the child's hair, but he may also manipulate the child's genitalia, encourage the child to manipulate his, and, less often, attempt penile insertion. The molestations may be repeated over a period of weeks, months, or years if they are not discovered by other adults or if the child does not protest. Some people with pedophilia intentionally frighten the child by, for example, killing a pet and threatening further harm if the youngster tells his or her parents.

People with pedophilia generally molest children that they know, such as neighbors or friends of the family (Gebhard et al., 1965). Sadly, incidents abound involving scoutmasters, camp counselors, and clergy. People with pedophilia have increasingly used the Internet to acquire child pornography and to contact potential victims (Durkin, 1997). Most pedophilia does not involve violence other than the sexual act, although when it does, it is often a focus of lurid stories in the media. A minority of people with pedophilia, who might also meet diagnostic criteria for sexual sadism, inflict serious bodily harm on the object of their passion. Because overt physical force is seldom used in pedophilia, the child molester often denies that he is actually forcing himself on his victim. Despite their distorted beliefs, it must be acknowledged that child sexual abuse

> **DSM-IV-TR Criteria for Transvestic Fetishism**
>
> - For at least 6 months, recurrent and intense sexually arousing fantasies, urges, or behaviors involving cross-dressing in a heterosexual male
> - Causes marked distress or impairment in functioning
> - Can be associated with some discomfort with gender identity

inherently involves a betrayal of trust and other serious negative consequences (see Focus on Discovery 13.3 for a discussion of these consequences).

In one meta-analysis of 61 follow-up studies of 28,972 sexual offenders, sexual arousal in response to pictures of young children as measured by penile plethysmograph was one of the strongest predictors of repeated sexual offenses (Hanson & Bussiere, 1998). A study of 11 men with pedophilia found that they were attracted to pictures of children that were not designed to be provocative. These men became aroused viewing widely available materials, such as television ads and clothing catalogs picturing young children in underwear. In other words, men with pedophilia were sexually stimulated from sources that most did not find stimulating (Howitt, 1995).

Nonetheless, arousal in response to pictures of children is not a perfect predictor of pedophilia. Many men who are conventional in their sexual interests and behavior can be sexually aroused by erotic pictures of children. In a study using both self-report and penile plethysmographic measures, one-quarter of men drawn from a community sample showed or reported arousal when viewing sexually provocative pictures of children (Hall, Hicschman, & Oliver, 1995). Although this finding might seem disturbing, it highlights the importance of the distinction made by the DSM and by health professionals between fantasy and behavior. Pedophilia is diagnosed when adults either act on sexual urges toward children or are distressed by the urges.

Incest is listed in DSM-IV-TR as a subtype of pedophilia. Incest refers to sexual relations between close relatives for whom marriage is forbidden. It is most common between brother and sister. The next most common form, which is considered more pathological, is between father and daughter.

The taboo against incest is virtually universal in human societies (Ford & Beach, 951), with a notable exception of Egyptian pharaohs, who could marry their sisters or other females of their immediate families. In Egypt it was believed that the royal blood should not be contaminated by that of outsiders. The incest taboo makes sense according to present-day scientific knowledge. The offspring from a father–daughter or a brother–sister union have a greater probability of inheriting a pair of recessive genes, one from each parent. For the most part, recessive genes have negative biological effects, such as serious birth defects. The incest taboo, then, has adaptive evolutionary significance.

There is evidence that families in which incest occurs are unusually patriarchal, especially with respect to the subservient position of women relative to men (Alexander & Lupfer, 1987). Parents in these families also tend to be more neglectful and emotionally distant from their children (Madonna, Van Scoyk, & Jones, 1991).

Typically, men who commit incest abuse their postpubertal daughters, whereas men with nonincestual pedophilia are usually interested in prepubertal children. Consistent with this difference in the age of victims, men who molest children within their families show greater penile arousal (as measured by penile plethysmography) to adult heterosexual cues than do men who molest children who are unrelated to them (Marshall, Barbaree, & Christophe, 1986).

What are the demographic characteristics of people who engage in pedophilia and incest? People with pedophilia can be straight or gay, though most are heterosexual. Up to half of all child molestations, including those that take place within the family, are committed by adolescent males (Morenz & Becker, 1995). Consistent with this statistic, about half of adult offenders began their illegal behavior in their early teens. Academic problems are common, as are other criminal behaviors (Becker & Hunter, 1997). Most older heterosexual men with pedophilia are or have been married.

Psychologically, men with pedophilia demonstrate elevated impulsivity and psychopathy compared to the general population (Ridenour et al., 1997). These men often meet criteria for comorbid conduct disorder and substance abuse, and molestations are more likely to occur when the person with pedophilia is intoxicated. Somewhat more surprisingly, depression and anxiety disorders are also common (Galli et al., 1999). Evidence also suggests that men with pedophilia have sexual fantasies about children when their mood is negative, perhaps as a way to cope with their dysphoria; however,

DSM-IV-TR Criteria for Pedophilia

- For at least 6 months, recurrent and intense, sexually arousing fantasies, urges, or behaviors involving sexual contact with a prepubescent child
- Person has acted on these urges, or the urges and fantasies cause marked distress or interpersonal problems
- Person is at least 16 years old and 5 years older than the child

having the pedophilic fantasy appears to increase negative affect. Perhaps this downward spiral leads at some point to the person's acting on the impulse to molest a child (Looman, 1995).

Voyeurism

Now and then a man may happen to see a nude woman by chance without her knowledge. If his sex life is primarily conventional, he would not generally meet criteria for voyeurism. Similarly, voyeuristic fantasies are quite common in men but do not by themselves warrant a diagnosis (Hanson & Harris, 1997). **Voyeurism** involves an intense and recurrent desire to obtain sexual gratification by watching unsuspecting others in a state of undress or having sexual relations. For some men, voyeurism is their only sexual activity; for others, it is preferred but not absolutely essential for sexual arousal (Kaplan & Kreuger, 1997). As in the case of William earlier in this chapter, the looking, often called peeping, helps the person become sexually aroused and is sometimes essential for arousal. People with voyeurism achieve orgasm by masturbation, either while watching or later while remembering the peeping. Sometimes the person with voyeurism fantasizes about having sexual contact with the observed person, but it remains a fantasy; he or she seldom contacts the observed.

A true voyeur, almost always a man, does not find it particularly exciting to watch a woman who is undressing for his special benefit. The element of risk seems important, for the voyeur is excited by the anticipation of how the woman would react if she knew he was watching. As with all categories of illegal behavior, prevalence is difficult to assess since most illegal activities are not reported to the police. Indeed, people with voyeurism are most often charged with loitering rather than with peeping itself (Kaplan & Kreuger, 1997).

Voyeurism typically begins in adolescence. People who meet diagnostic criteria for voyeurism often have other paraphilias, but they do not tend to have elevated rates of other mental disorders.

Exhibitionism

Exhibitionism is a recurrent, intense desire to obtain sexual gratification by exposing one's genitals to an unwilling stranger, sometimes a child. It typically begins in adolescence. As with voyeurism, there is seldom an attempt to have actual contact with the stranger. Some exhibitionists, however, do get arrested for other crimes involving contact with a victim (Sugarman et al., 1994). Many exhibitionists masturbate during the exposure. In most cases there is a desire to shock or embarrass the observer.

The urge to expose seems overwhelming and virtually uncontrollable to the exhibitionist and is apparently triggered by anxiety and restlessness as well as by sexual arousal. One exhibitionist persisted in his practices even after suffering a spinal cord injury that left him without sensation or movement from the waist down (DeFazio & Cunningham, 1987). Because of the compulsive nature of the urge, the exposures may be repeated often and even in the same place and at the same time of day. At the time of the act, the social and legal consequences are far from their mind (Stevenson & Jones, 1972). In the desperation and tension of the moment, they may experience headaches and palpitations and have a sense of unreality (also called derealization). After exposing themselves, exhibitionists tend to flee and feel remorseful. Other paraphilias are very common in exhibitionists, notably voyeurism and frotteurism (see next section) (Freund, 1990).

Frotteurism

Frotteurism involves the sexually oriented touching of an unsuspecting person. The frotteur may rub his penis against a woman's thighs or buttocks or fondle her breasts or genitals. These attacks typically occur in places, such as a crowded bus or sidewalk, that provide

---

DSM-IV-TR Criteria for Voyeurism

- For at least 6 months, recurrent and intense sexually arousing fantasies, urges, or behaviors involving the observation of unsuspecting others who are naked or engaged in sexual activity
- Person has acted on these urges, or the urges and fantasies cause marked distress or interpersonal problems

---

DSM-IV-TR Criteria for Exhibitionism

- For at least 6 months, recurrent, intense, and sexually arousing fantasies, urges, or behaviors involving showing one's genitals to an unsuspecting stranger
- Person has acted on these urges, or the urges and fantasies cause marked distress or interpersonal problems

an easy means of escape. Frotteurism has not been studied very extensively. It appears to begin in adolescence and typically occurs along with other paraphilias (Kreuger & Kaplan, 2000).

Sexual Sadism and Sexual Masochism

Sexual sadism is defined by an intense and recurrent desire to obtain or increase sexual gratification by inflicting pain or psychological suffering (such as humiliation) on another. **Sexual masochism** is defined by an intense and recurrent desire to obtain or increase sexual gratification through being subjected to pain or humiliation. Some sadists achieve orgasm by inflicting pain, and some masochists achieve orgasm by being subjected to pain. For others, though, the sadistic and masochistic practices, such as spanking, are just one aspect of sexual activity.

Sadistic and masochistic behavior have become more accepted over time: 5 to 10 percent of the population has tried some form of sadomasochistic activity, such as blindfolding one's partner (Baumeister & Butler, 1997). Some clubs now cater to members seeking sadomasochistic partnerships. Most people who engage in sadomasochistic behaviors are relatively comfortable with their sexual practices (Spengler, 1977). Sadism and masochism are only diagnosed if the urges or behaviors cause distress or impairment. Most sadists establish relationships with masochists to derive mutual sexual gratification. Although many people are able to take both dominant and submissive roles, masochists outnumber sadists.

The manifestations of sexual masochism are varied. Examples include restraint (physical bondage), blindfolding, spanking, whipping, electric shocks, cutting, humiliation (e.g., being urinated or defecated on, being forced to wear a collar and bark like a dog, or being put on display naked), and taking the role of slave and submitting to orders and commands. The term *infantilism* refers to a desire to be treated like a helpless infant and clothed in diapers. One particularly dangerous form of masochism, called hypoxyphilia, can result in death or brain damage; it involves sexual arousal by oxygen deprivation, which can be achieved using a noose, a plastic bag, chest compression, or a chemical that produces a temporary decrease in brain oxygenation by peripheral vasodilation (American Psychiatric Association, 1994).

Sadism and masochism seem to begin by early adulthood. Both these disorders are found in straight and gay relationships. Surveys have found that 20 to 30 percent of the members of sadomasochistic clubs are female (Moser & Levitt, 1987), and it has been assumed that a similar gender ratio might be true of diagnosable sadism and masochism. Most sadists and masochists lead otherwise conventional lives, and there is some evidence that they are above average in income and educational status (Moser & Levitt, 1987). Alcohol abuse is common among sadists (Allnut et al., 1996).

Etiology of the Paraphilias

Of the many theories about the etiology of the paraphilias, the principal ones come from biological, psychodynamic, and behavioral perspectives. Because many people do not want to talk about their paraphilias, researchers have few opportunities to understand the causes of paraphilias.

Neurobiological Factors
Because the overwhelming majority of people with paraphilias are men, there has been speculation that androgens, or male hormones, play a role. Androgens regulate sexual desire, and sexual desire appears to be atypically high among people with paraphilias (Kafka, 1997). Findings of hormonal correlates of paraphilias are inconclusive, however. As to differences in the brain, a dysfunction in the temporal lobe may be relevant to a minority of cases of sadism and exhibitionism (Mason, 1997). If biology turns out to be important, it most likely will be but one factor in a complex network of causes that includes experience as a major player (Meyer, 1995).

DSM-IV-TR Criteria for Frotteurism
- For at least 6 months, recurrent and intense and sexually arousing fantasies, urges, or behaviors involving touching and rubbing up against a nonconsenting person
- Person has acted on these urges, or the urges and fantasies cause marked distress or interpersonal problems

DSM-IV-TR Criteria for Sexual Sadism
- For at least 6 months, recurrent intense and sexually arousing fantasies, urges, or behaviors involving acts in which the partner is humiliated or suffers physically
- Causes marked distress or impairment in functioning or the person has acted on these urges with a nonconsenting other

DSM-IV-TR Criteria for Sexual Masochism
- For at least 6 months, recurrent, intense, and sexually arousing fantasies, urges, or behaviors involving the act of being humiliated or beaten
- Causes marked distress or impairment in functioning

Check Your Knowledge 13.3

Choose the diagnostic category that best fits each vignette. If not diagnosable, state so.

1. Joe is only able to obtain sexual arousal by rubbing his body against strangers. He has worked out a set of rituals to engage in this behavior; he knows which bus routes and times will be most crowded, chooses a bus that tends to have many women, and times his attacks so that he can leave the bus at a stop along with many other people.

2. Sam and Terry enjoy a good sexual relationship. They have mutually satisfying sex at least weekly. Occasionally, Terry likes to be tied down before sex, but she is able to enjoy sex without bondage as well. Most of their sex life involves no hint of pain or bondage.

3. Victor secretly enjoys wearing his wife's underwear. When she is away, he dresses up, watches himself in the mirror, and masturbates. He finds this activity to be the most exciting sexual activity he has ever engaged in, and despite an incredible sense of embarrassment and shame, he feels he has no control over these urges. He fears that his wife would divorce him if she knew about his cross-dressing.

4. Matt only feels aroused when he is able to cause pain to someone before engaging in sex. Most of the time, he indulges in these activities at a sadomasochism club. He has not been able to sustain a relationship with any of the women he has met in clubs. He is deeply distressed by his inability to enjoy other forms of sexuality.

5. Ever since he was a small child, Dennis has felt like he was a girl. As a child, he would sneak into his mother's closet and dress up in her clothes. As he grew older, his belief that he was trapped in a boy's body became stronger. At age 20, he began taking female hormones, shaving his legs, dressing as a woman, and calling himself Deanna. He is very distressed about his gender identity as a woman.

6. Barry is a 40-year-old single man who has never had a sustained dating relationship or sexual partner. Several times a week, Barry parks his car at the beach, masturbates, and then finds a way to lure a woman to his car, usually by asking for directions. He is unable to have an orgasm unless the woman notices his erection. He has been arrested three times for this behavior.

Psychodynamic Perspectives   Psychodynamic theorists view paraphilias as a defense, guarding the ego from dealing with repressed fears and memories. The person with a paraphilia is seen as someone who is fearful of conventional heterosexual relationships, even when the relationships do not involve sex, because they are fixated at a pregenital stage of psychosexual development. Development is inadequate for social and sexual adult relationships (Lanyon, 1986). For example, fetishes, voyeurism, and pedophilia are seen as manifestations of intense castration anxiety that makes heterosexual sex with adult women too threatening. Castration anxiety leads the exhibitionist to reassure himself of his masculinity by showing his manhood (his genitals) to others (usually girls and women); it results in the sadist dominating others. Although many of the psychodynamic ideas have been influential, and some of these ideas have been picked up and reformulated by cognitive theorists, there is little research available regarding the psychodynamic theory of paraphilias.

Psychological Factors   Most psychological theories of the paraphilias involve a set of risk factors, including conditioning experiences, relationship histories, and cognition. Some behavioral theorists view the cause of paraphilias as classical conditioning that by chance has linked sexual arousal with unusual or inappropriate stimuli (Kinsey et al., 1948). For example, a young man may masturbate to images of women dressed in black leather boots. According to this theory, repetitions of these experiences make boots sexually arousing. Similar proposals have been made for transvestism, pedophilia, voyeurism, and exhibitionism. Although there is some minor support (e.g., Rachman, 1966), research has not supported most components of the orgasm conditioning hypothesis (O'Donohue & Plaud, 1994). As described later, however, some innovative therapeutic strategies have been developed based on these ideas.

From an operant conditioning perspective, many paraphilias are considered an outcome of inadequate social skills or reinforcement of unconventionality by parents or relatives. Evidence does indicate that men with pedophilia often have poor social skills (Dreznick, 2003). Paraphilias such as exhibitionism may thus be activities that substitute for more conventional relationships and sexual activity. On the other hand, the fact that many pedophiles and exhibitionists have conventional social- and sexual relationships indicates that the issue is more complex than a simple absence of nondeviant sexual outlets (Maletsky, 2000).

The childhood histories of people with paraphilias reveal that often they were exposed to physical abuse, sexual abuse, and poor parent–child relationships (Mason, 1997). These early experiences may contribute to the poor social skills and lack of intimate relationships often seen among those with paraphilias (Marshall, Serran, & Cortoni, 2000). But the widely accepted belief that sexual abuse in childhood predisposes people to paraphilic behavior (Worling, 1995) needs to be qualified by research showing that fewer than a third of adult sex offenders were sexually abused when they were below the age of 18 (Maletzky, 1993). It is also important to note that only a small percentage of sexually abused children develop pedophilia as adults. Distorted parent–child relationships may also create hostility, negative attitudes, and lack of empathy toward women, which may increase the chances of victimizing a woman.

Alcohol and negative affect often are the immediate triggers of incidents of pedophilia, voyeurism, and exhibitionism. This is consistent with evidence that alcohol decreases inhibition. Deviant sexual activity, like alcohol use, may be a means of escaping from negative affect (Baumeister & Butler, 1997).

Cognitive distortions also play a role in the paraphilias. For example, a voyeur may believe that a woman who left her blinds up while undressing wanted someone to look at her (Kaplan & Kreuger, 1997). A person with pedophilia may believe that children want to have sex with adults (Marshall, 1997). Table 13.5 contains examples of the kinds of unwarranted beliefs that may be associated with pedophilia and exhibitionism. Rape, a topic dealt with later in this chapter, is also included in the table.

Treatments for the Paraphilias

Because many of the behaviors involved in paraphilias are illegal, many people diagnosed with them are imprisoned and court-ordered into treatment. Outcomes for incarcerated juvenile and adult sex offenders are highly variable (Becker & Hunter, 1997; Maletzky, 2002). Data on treatment are hard to interpret for several reasons. First, most researchers avoid using control groups who receive no treatment—many researchers consider it unethical to withhold treatment when the consequences of sexual offenses are so severe. Second, it is difficult to compare findings because studies vary greatly. Some programs select the most problematic prisoners for treatment,

Table 13.5 Examples of Cognitive Distortions and Justifications in Sexual Paraphilias

Category	Pedophilia	Exhibitionism	Rape
Misattributing blame	"She started it by being too cuddly."	"She kept looking at me like she was expecting it."	"She was saying no, but her body said yes."
		"The way she was dressed, she was asking for it."	"I was always drinking when I did it."
Denying sexual intent	"I was just teaching her about sex . . . better from her father than from someone else."	"I was just looking for a place to pee."	"I was just trying to teach her a lesson; she deserved it."
		"My pants just slipped down."	
Debasing the victim	"She'd had sex before with her boyfriend."	"She was just a slut anyway."	"The way she came on to me at the party, she deserved it."
Minimizing consequences	"She has always been friendly to me, even afterward."	"I never touched her, so I couldn't have hurt her."	"She'd had sex with hundreds of guys before. It was no big deal."
	"She was messed up even before it happened."		
Deflecting censure	"This happened years ago. Why can't everyone forget about it?"	"It's not like I raped anyone."	"I only did it once."
Justifying the cause	"If I wasn't molested as a kid, I'd never have done this."	"If I knew how to get dates, I wouldn't have to expose."	"If my girlfriend gave me what I want, I wouldn't be forced to rape."

Source: Maletzky (2002).

whereas others treat those with the most promising prognoses, for example, first offenders. Some treatments have follow-up sessions after release, whereas others do not. Third, many studies do not evaluate whether treatment successes are sustained over time, even though recidivism increases as the years go by, especially when two years have passed since termination of treatment (Maletzky, 2002).

Sex offenders often lack motivation to change their illegal behavior. They may deny their problem, minimize the seriousness of their problem, believe that their victims will not be credible witnesses, and feel confident that they can control their behavior without professional assistance. Some blame the victim—even a child—for being overly seductive. For these reasons, such people are often judged to be inappropriate for treatment programs (Dougher, 1988); when they do become involved, they often drop out (Knopp, 1984). To enhance motivation for treatment, a therapist can do the following (Miller & Rollnick, 1991):

1. Empathize with the offender's reluctance to admit that he is an offender and to seek treatment, thereby reducing defensiveness and hostility

2. Point out that treatment might help him control his behavior better

3. Emphasize the negative consequences of refusing treatment (e.g., transfer to a less attractive incarceration setting if the person is already in custody) and of offending again (e.g., stiffer legal penalties)

4. Explain that there will be a psychophysiological assessment of the patient's sexual arousal, implying that this can reveal the patient's sexual proclivities without his admitting to them (Garland & Dougher, 1991)

With the foregoing as background, we now describe cognitive behavioral and biological treatments for the paraphilias. Then we consider legal efforts to protect the public from sex offenders.

Cognitive Behavioral Treatment   In the earliest years of behavioral treatment, paraphilias were narrowly viewed as attractions to inappropriate objects and activities. Looking to behavioral psychology for ways to reduce these attractions, researchers fixed on aversion therapy. Thus, a person with boot fetishism would be given a shock (on the hands or feet) or an emetic (a drug that produces nausea) when looking at a boot, a person with transvestism when cross-dressing, a person with pedophilia when gazing at a photograph of a nude child, and so on. A variation of aversion therapy based on imagery is covert sensitization, whereby the person imagines situations he finds inappropriately arousing and also imagines feeling sick or ashamed for feeling and acting this way. Versions of covert sensitization have been developed that pair the aversive imagery with a foul odor (Maletzky, 2000). Studies of covert sensitization have shown that it reduces deviant arousal, but little evidence is available that these techniques alone actually change the behavior (Maletzky, 2000).

Another aversion therapy technique is satiation, in which the man masturbates for a long time, typically after ejaculating, while fantasizing out loud about his deviant activity. The idea is that masturbation will continue for so long as to become aversive. Although aversion therapy may not completely eliminate the attraction, in some cases it provides the patient with a greater measure of control over the overt behavior (McConaghy, 1994).

Another technique entails imagining a typical deviant activity but changing its ending, as described in the following vignette.

> As you drive home one night you notice an attractive woman driver on your right in a van. She can see right into your car. You slow down and drive parallel with her as you begin to get aroused. You want to rub your penis and take it out to show her. However, the urge this time is weaker and you drive past her quickly without exposing. You feel good about yourself for being able to exert control. (Maletzky, 1997, p. 57)

Cognitive procedures are often used to counter the distorted thinking of people with paraphilias. Table 13.5 contains examples of cognitive distortions that would be targets for modification. For example, an exhibitionist might claim that the girls he exposes himself to are too young to be harmed by it. The therapist would counter this distortion by pointing out that the younger the victim, the worse the harm will be (Maletzky, 1997).

In general, cognitive and behavioral approaches have become more sophisticated and broader in scope since the 1960s, when the paraphilias were addressed almost exclusively through aversive conditioning and cognitive interventions. Current approaches combine these traditional approaches with techniques such as social skills training and sexual impulse control training (Maletzky, 2002). Training in empathy toward others is another increasingly common cognitive technique; teaching the sex offender to consider how his or her behavior would affect someone else may lessen the tendency to engage in such activities. Relapse prevention, modeled after the work on substance abuse described in Chapter 10, is also an important component of many broader treatment programs. A therapist who uses relapse prevention techniques would help a person identify situations and emotions that might trigger symptomatic behavior.

Comprehensive programs that include aversion therapy combined with other types of psychological interventions, such as social skills training, have some beneficial effects on pedophilia, transvestism, exhibitionism, and fetishism (Maletzky, 2002). Overall, both institution-based and outpatient programs that follow a cognitive behavioral model with sex offenders reduce recidivism more than what would be expected were no treatment at all attempted (Maletzky, 2002). These outcomes are much better for people with pedophilia than for rapists. Although sex offenders evoke disgust and fear from many people, efforts to treat such people, even if only minimally effective, are not only cost-effective but stand the chance of protecting others after the person is released from prison (Prentky & Burgess, 1990).

Biological Treatment   A variety of biological interventions have been tried on sex offenders. Castration, or removal of the testes, was used a great deal in western Europe two generations ago, with some apparent effectiveness in reducing the incidence of paraphilic behavior (e.g., Langeluddeke, 1963). Surgical castration is not a common treatment today due to major ethical concerns.

On the other hand, several medications have been used to treat paraphilias, particularly among sex offenders. Typically, these medications are used as a supplement to psychological treatment. Among men, sexual drive and functioning are regulated by androgens (testosterone and dihydrotestoterone). Hence, hormonal agents that reduce androgens have been used to treat paraphilias, including medroxyprogesterone acetate (MPA, trade name Depo-Provera), cyproterone acetate (CPA, Cyprostat), and luteinizing hormone–releasing hormone agents (LHRH). Beyond drugs that influence hormones, SSRI antidepressants have been shown to reduce sexual arousal, as well as orgasmic and ejaculatory capacity. Across treatment trials, researchers tend to measure sexual fantasies to deviant objects, sexual behaviors, and legal offenses. In some studies, sexual arousal to deviant objects is measured using the plethysmograph. A range of clinical trials have found that SSRIs, MPA, and CPA are effective in reducing arousal (Hill et al., 2003). SSRIs have also been found to be helpful as an addition to psychological treatment (Hill et al., 2003).

Despite the promising findings, many ethical issues are raised about the indefinite use of hormonal agents. Long-term use of hormonal agents is associated with a number of negative side effects, including infertility, liver problems, osteoporosis, and diabetes (Gunn, 1993). Informed consent concerning these risks must be obtained, and many patients will not agree to use these drugs long-term (Hill et al., 2003).

Efforts to Protect the Public: Megan's Law   The rates of recidivism after prison release have led to public pressure to forbid sexual offenders from returning to the locales where they were arrested. A further trend is exemplified in laws that allow police to publicize the whereabouts of registered sex offenders if they are considered to be a potential danger. These laws also permit citizens to use a national network of computerized police records to determine whether sex offenders are living in their neighborhoods (Ingram, 1996; Kempster, 1996).

Referred to by some as Megan's law, this statute and others like it across the United States arose from public outrage at the brutal murder of a second grader in New Jersey who was kidnapped while walking home from school. The person convicted of this crime was a twice-convicted child molester. Sadly, some neighborhoods have responded with vigilantism when residents become aware of sex offenders in their neighborhoods (Younglove & Vitello, 2003). It should come as no surprise that civil liberties groups are challenging these laws.

Check Your Knowledge 13.4

Answer the questions.
1. Which of the following has not been related to paraphilias?
   a. childhood abuse
   b. cognitive distortions
   c. permissive parenting
   d. negative affect

2. Currently the most commonly used biological treatments to reduce sexual desire and paraphilic behaviors are
   a. surgical castration
   b. hormonal agents and antidepressants
   c. antianxiety medications
   d. none of the above

Quick Summary

Paraphilias are defined by a sexual attraction to an unusual sexual object or activity that lasts at least 6 months and causes significant distress or impairment. The DSM-IV-TR diagnostic criteria for paraphilias are distinguished based on the object of sexual attraction, as shown in Table 13.4.

Researchers do not know the prevalence of these disorders, nor is much research available on the causes of paraphilias. Neurobiological factors that might be involved include excess levels of male hormones or, for some, dysfunction in the temporal lobes. Psychodynamic theory emphasizes conflicts between urges for sexual gratification and castration anxiety. Psychological theories focus on conditioning to inappropriate sexual objects, histories of physical and sexual abuse, poor parenting, social skill deficits hostility toward women, and cognitive distortions.

Treatment approaches must begin with a focus on engaging the client, which is often difficult to do. Cognitive behavioral approaches include various versions of aversion therapy, including covert sensitization and satiation. Cognitive techniques are used to challenge distorted beliefs about the consequences of sexual behaviors. Cognitive behavioral therapists also use techniques to improve social skills, to help people control impulses, to increase empathy for potential victims, and to identify potential high-risk situations for the return of symptoms. The most common medication treatments involve antidepressants or medications that reduce male hormone levels such as Depo-Provera. Laws have been passed that allow the public to access information about where sexual offenders live, but civil liberties groups are opposed to some aspects of these laws.

Rape

In legal terms, rape falls into two categories—forced and statutory. **Forced rape** is sexual intercourse with an unwilling partner. **Statutory rape** refers to sexual intercourse with a minor, someone under the age of consent (typically age 18). Because it is assumed that a person younger than the age of consent should not be held responsible for sexual activity with an older person, a charge of statutory rape can be made even if the minor reports consenting to sex willingly. Thus statutory rape need not involve force, only sex with a minor. We focus on forced rape in this section.

Twenty to 25 percent of American women will be raped during their lifetimes (Crowell & Burgess, 1996). Most women who are raped will experience symptoms of anxiety in the weeks after an attack (Rothbaum & Foa, 1993), and at least a third will develop PTSD (Breslau et al., 1999). More detail on PTSD and its treatment is provided in Chapter 5.

Rape is an important issue on college campuses. Table 13.6 shows findings from one study that asked college-age men and women the extent to which they had perpetrated or experienced physical coercion after a refusal of sexual contact. As shown, a discouraging 30 percent of female college students report that they have experienced the use of physical force, threats, or harm after they refused sexual contact with a person, with 8.7 percent reporting that they had experienced actual physical harm. In one survey of a representative sample of 4,446 women enrolled in college (Fisher, Cullen, & Turner, 2000), researchers provided carefully worded

Table 13.6 Behaviors That College Students Report after a Partner Refuses Sexual Contact

Tactic	Men Experiencing the Tactic, N=275 (%)	Women Experiencing the Tactic, N=381 (%)	Men Perpetrating the Tactic, N=275 (%)	Women Perpetrating the Tactic, N=381 (%)
Emotional manipulation and deception				
Repeatedly asking	36.9	65.8	29.2	13.9
Telling lies	21.5	42.4	16.2	3.1
Using authority of older age	8.7	13.4	0.7	0.3
Questioning target's sexuality	7.6	9.2	2.6	1.6
Threatening to break up	4.4	9.5	2.6	0.3
Using authority of position	3.3	5.3	1.1	0.5
Threatening self-harm	5.5	3.7	1.5	0.5
Threatening blackmail	3.6	2.4	1.5	0.8
One or more of the above	43.6	71.4	32.4	15.2
Exploitation of intoxication				
Taking advantage of a drunken target	29.5	42.1	12.9	5.0
Purposefully getting a target drunk	10.9	25.0	5.9	1.1
One or more of the above	30.5	43.8	13.1	5.2
Physical force or threats				
Blocking target's retreat	19.3	21.1	2.9	1.1
Using physical restraint	9.1	22.4	4.0	2.1
Using physical harm	6.2	8.7	1.1	0.5
Threatening physical harm	1.1	6.3	0.7	0.5
Tying up a target	3.6	0.8	1.1	1.1
Threatening with a weapon	1.1	1.8	0.7	0.3
One or more of the above	24.7	30.4	5.1	2.6

Note: Some percentages are based on less than the total N because of missing data.

Source: From Struckman-Johnson (1988).

questions about rape. The authors coded forcible vaginal, oral, or anal insertion of the penis, fingers, tongue, or objects as rape. About 3 percent of women reported that they had experienced an attempted or completed rape in the 7 months before the study. Rape occurs far too often.

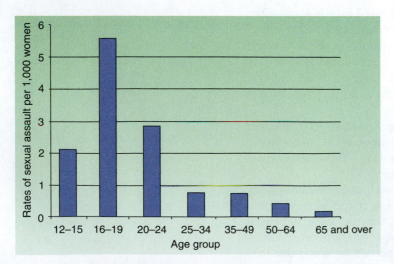

Figure 13.7 Annual rates of sexual assault victimization among women by age group. From National Center for Justice (2003).

The Crime

The specifics of rape cases vary widely. Up to 70 percent of rapes are associated with intoxication (Crowell & Burgess, 1996). In a very small percentage of cases, rapists murder their victims. Although men can be victims of sexual assault, our discussion focuses on women, because more than 90 percent of rapes are committed by men against women (Crowell & Burgess, 1996). Younger women and girls are much more likely to be victims of rape than are older women (see Figure 13.7).

About 70 percent of rapes are committed by someone known to the woman (National Center for Justice, 2003). Many believe rape should not be classified as a sexual crime, lest this terminology mask the violent nature of the act and create an atmosphere in which the sexual motives of the victim are questioned. In considering links between violence and rape, it is important to consider rape during wartime. The Crusaders raped their way across Europe on their holy pilgrimages in the eleventh through the thirteenth centuries; the

Germans raped as they rampaged through Belgium in World War I; U.S. forces raped women and girls as they searched and destroyed during the Vietnam War; Iraqi soldiers raped and brutalized women as they occupied Kuwait; U.S. soldiers humiliated Iraqi prisoners through various torture tactics, including rape. In 2008, the United Nations Security Council classified rape as a war crime. Hopefully, this ruling will make it less likely that rape will be tacitly condoned during war.

The Rapist: Understanding the Etiology of Rape

Is the rapist primarily someone who seeks the thrill of dominating and humiliating a woman through intimidation and often brutal assault? Is he an ordinarily unassertive man with a fragile ego who, feeling inadequate after disappointment and rejection in work or love, takes out his frustrations on an unwilling stranger? What types of characteristics distinguish rapists?

There is no DSM diagnosis to capture a tendency to rape, but there are several traits that appear elevated among rapists. Many rapists have unusually high hostility toward women (Malamuth, 1998). Other studies have found that rapists tend to respond with more sexual arousal than nonsexual offenders to images of coercive sexual activity (Lalumiere & Quinsey, 1994). Sexually aggressive men tend to show antisocial and impulsive personality traits (Crowell & Burgess, 1996).

Beyond violent tendencies, rapists may have specific sexual difficulties. In one major community survey, men who had assaulted women sexually were 3.5 times more likely to report erectile dysfunction than those who had not (Laumann et al., 1999). Rapists also appear to have a high sex drive; across a range of samples, sex drive (as measured by frequency of sexual outlets) was correlated with sexual coercion (Kafka, 1997). Some rapists seem to have problems distinguishing friendliness from seductiveness and in accurately reading cues from a woman indicating that she wants intimacies to cease (Malamuth & Brown, 1994).

Although there has been a long history of belief that rapists have poor social skills, a meta-analysis of studies on this topic suggests that any social skills deficits are minor and that they tend to be documented only among convicted rapists, not among those who escape legal charges (Dreznick, 2003). A more specific interpersonal skill, though, may be deficient.

From a sociological perspective, the more a society accepts interpersonal violence as a way to handle conflict and solve problems, the higher the frequency of rape (Sanday, 1981). It seems worth noting that in a controlled experiment, male college students who stated that they regarded rape as unacceptable were aroused by video portrayals of rape if the woman was depicted as having an orgasm during the assault (Malamuth & Check, 1983). Since the time this study was conducted, eight experiments have been conducted in which men are asked to watch videos that contain either sexual activities with violence or sexual activities without violence. A meta-analysis of these studies suggested that after watching videos that contained violence, men were significantly more likely to report that violence toward women was acceptable (Allen, D' Alessio, & Brezgel,1995). This research suggests that rape may be encouraged by pornography that depicts women enjoying violent sexual relations.

Psychological Treatment for Rapists

Treatment programs for incarcerated rapists are typically multidimensional. These programs often include cognitive techniques aimed at rapists' distorted beliefs and inappropriate attitudes toward women (such as the belief that women want to be raped—see Table 13.5), along with attempts to increase empathy with their victims, to promote anger management, to improve self-esteem, and to reduce substance abuse. These methods are often implemented in confrontational group therapy sessions that attempt to goad the rapist into taking

This famous scene from *Gone with the Wind* illustrates one of the myths about rape—that despite initial resistance, women like to be "taken." (Everett Collection, Inc.)

Rape victims of the war in Bosnia. Rape often occurs during war, but only recently has sexual assault been considered a war crime. (Andrew Kaiser-G.A.F.F./Sipa Press.)

responsibility for his aggressive behavior. As with the paraphilias, this therapy is sometimes supplemented with the use of biological treatments, like Depo-Provera, which reduce sex drive by lowering levels of male sex hormones.

Treatment studies are limited in that they often measure legal charges rather than the rate of deviant sexual behavior, thus underestimating relapse rates. Another issue is that studies have not typically included adequate control groups. Despite these problems, meta-analyses have led to the conclusion that cognitive therapy and biological interventions may lower recidivism somewhat (Hanson & Bussiere, 1998). One study is notable for the inclusion of a control group in comparison to cognitive behavioral treatment (Marques et al., 1994). That study found that among 59 rapists, 9 percent of men in the treatment group committed an offense during the 5-year follow-up period, compared to 28 percent in the no-treatment group.

Reforming the Legal System

Estimates are that less than half of rapes are reported (National Center for Victims of Violent Crime, 2004). Interviews with half a million women indicated three reasons for reluctance to report rape:

1. Considering the rape a private matter
2. Fearing reprisals from the rapist or his family or friends
3. Believing that police would be ineffective or insensitive (Wright, 1991).

Several legal reforms have been enacted to address these types of concerns. For example, all states now allow for prosecution of rapes that occur within marriages; the laws in most states consider the likely absence of witnesses for such a private act; the definition of rape typically includes forced oral and anal entry as well as vaginal penetration; and perhaps most importantly, information about the victim's previous sexual behavior and history is no longer admissible in court. Despite these changes, trials remain very stressful. Only a very small percentage of rapists are ultimately convicted of their crimes. Any familiarity of the victim with her assailant makes conviction of the man more difficult to achieve. Even though many rapists rape hundreds of times, they are only occasionally imprisoned for an offense.

Summary

Sexual Norms

• Sexual behavior and attitudes are heavily influenced by culture, and so any discussion of disorders in sexuality must be sensitive to the idea that norms are likely to change over time and place. Currently, a great deal of research is focused on gender differences in sexuality.

Sexual Dysfunctions

• The DSM categorizes four kinds of sexual dysfunctions: sexual desire disorders, sexual arousal disorders, orgasmic disorders, and sexual pain disorders. Many people experience brief sexual symptoms, but these are not diagnosable unless they are recurrent, cause either distress or impairment, and are not explained by medical conditions.

• Research on the etiology of sexual dysfunctions is difficult to conduct, as surveys may be inaccurate and laboratory measures may be difficult to gather. Researchers have identified many different variables that can contribute to sexual dysfunctions, including biological variables, previous sexual experiences, relationship issues, psychopathology, negative affect and low arousal, and negative cognitions.

• Many effective interventions for sexual dysfunctions are available, most of them cognitive behavioral. Sex therapy, aimed at reversing old habits and teaching new skills, was propelled into public consciousness by the Masters and Johnson work. Their method hinges on gradual, nonthreatening exposure to increasingly intimate sexual encounters and the sanctioning of sexuality by credible therapists. Sex therapists also aim to educate patients in sexual anatomy and physiology; reduce anxiety; teach communication skills;

and improve attitudes and thoughts about sexuality. Couples therapy is sometimes appropriate as well. Biological treatments such as Viagra may be used for the treatment of erectile dysfunction.

Gender Identity Disorder

- Gender identity disorder (GID) involves the deep and persistent conviction of the person that his or her anatomic sexual makeup and psychological sense of self as male or female are discrepant. Thus, a man with GID is physically male but considers himself a woman.
- Neurobiological models of GID emphasize genes and prenatal hormone exposure. Most research on neurobiology, though, has focused on sex-typed behavior and attitudes, rather than full-blown diagnoses, and even then, neurobiological variables account for only a certain amount of the variance. Another theory proposes that parents may have reinforced cross-gender behavior. This theory has been criticized, though, as peers are so harsh toward children who show cross-gender behaviors.
- The most common treatment for GID is sex-reassignment surgery to bring bodily features into line with gender identity. There are case reports that behavioral treatment can help a person minimize cross-gender behavior, but most persons with GID do not see this as a goal.

Paraphilias

- In the paraphilias, unusual imagery and acts are persistent and necessary for sexual gratification. The principal paraphilias are fetishism, transvestic fetishism, pedophilia, voyeurism, exhibitionism, frotteurism, sexual sadism, and sexual masochism.
- Efforts have also been made to detect hormonal anomalies in people with paraphilias, but the findings are inconclusive.
- According to the psychodynamic view, the person with a paraphilia is fearful of conventional heterosexual relationships; there is no empirical support for this idea. One behavioral view is that a fetishistic attraction to objects arises from accidental classical conditioning of sexual arousal, but this view has not received much empirical support. Another behavioral hypothesis posits deficiencies in social skills that make it difficult for the person to inter-

act normally with other adults, but again, there is limited support for this idea. Exposure to childhood sexual abuse may be a risk factor. Alcohol use may increase the odds of acting on sexual urges. Cognitive distortions appear to be involved.

- The most promising treatments for the paraphilias are cognitive behavioral. One conditioning procedure is to pair the inappropriate sexual object with painful or aversive events. Cognitive methods focus on the cognitive distortions of the person with a paraphilia. Social skills and empathy training are also common. Studies suggest that psychological treatments do reduce rates of legal offenses. SSRIs and drugs that reduce testosterone levels have both been found to reduce sex drive and deviant sexual behaviors, but because of the side effects, there are ethical issues involved in the long-term use of hormonal drugs.

Rape

- Rape, although it is not separately diagnosed in DSM-IV-TR, results in considerable psychological trauma for the victim and is far too prevalent. Some estimates suggest that 20 to 25 percent of women will be raped during their lifetime. The nature of rapes varies a great deal; some people rape strangers, but most rapes are committed by someone known to the woman. The inclusion of rape in a discussion of human sexuality is a matter of some controversy, as many theorists regard rape as an act of aggressive violence rather than of sex.
- Although there is no single profile that fits all rapists, variables that appear to distinguish rapists include hostility toward women, antisocial and impulsive personality traits, and high rates of sexual dysfunction. Social skills do not seem to be poor, except in convicted rapists. Many have emphasized that rape is likely to be more prevalent in cultural contexts that condone interpersonal violence.
- Psychological treatment programs focus on increasing empathy for victims, anger management, self-esteem, and substance abuse. Biological treatments, like those used for paraphilias, are used to decrease sex drive by lowering male hormone levels. Treatment has been shown to reduce the rate of recidivism. A major concern is that most rapes do not get reported to police, and so few rapists are convicted.

Answers to Check Your Knowledge Questions

13.1 1. d; 2. b; 3. a

13.2 1. F (explanation: unless the problem is recurrent and leads to distress or impairment, it cannot be diagnosed); 2. F; 3. T; 4. T; 5. F

13.3 1. frotterurism; 2. not a diagnosable disorder; 3. transvestic fetishism; 4. sexual sadism; 5. gender identity disorder; 6. exhibitionism

13.4 1. c; 2. b

Key Terms

childhood sexual abuse (CSA)	frotteurism	paraphilias	sexual masochism
desire phase	gender identity	pedophilia	sexual orientation
dyspareunia	gender identity disorder	penile plethysmograph	sexual response cycle
excitement phase	hypoactive sexual desire	premature ejaculation	sexual sadism
exhibitionism	disorder	resolution phase	spectator role
female orgasmic disorder	incest	sensate focus	statutory rape
female sexual arousal disorder	male erectile disorder	sex-reassignment surgery	transvestic fetishism
fetishism	male orgasmic disorder	sexual aversion disorder	vaginismus
forced rape	orgasm phase	sexual dysfunctions	voyeurism

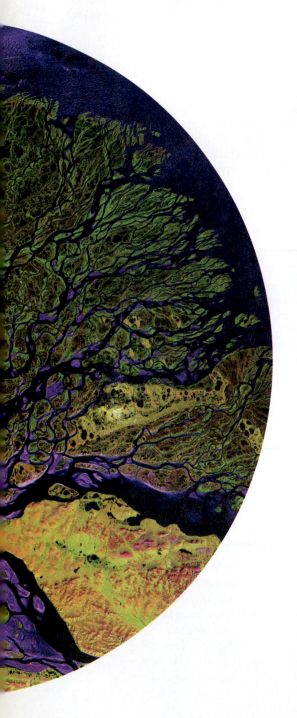

14 Disorders of Childhood

LEARNING GOALS

1. Be able to describe the issues in the classification of psychopathology in children.
2. Be able to discuss the description, etiology, and treatments for externalizing problems, including ADHD and conduct disorder, and for internalizing problems, including depression and anxiety disorders.
3. Be able to distinguish between the different learning disabilities as well as our current understanding of the causes and treatments for dyslexia.
4. Be able to describe the different systems for classifying mental retardation and the current research on causes and treatments.
5. Be able to describe the symptoms, causes, and treatments for autism and Asperger's disorder.

Clinical Case: Eric

"Eric. Eric? Eric!!" His teacher's voice and the laughter of his classmates roused the boy from his reverie. Glancing at the book of the girl sitting next to him, he noticed that the class was pages ahead of him. He was supposed to be answering a question about the Declaration of Independence, but he had been lost in thought, wondering about what seats he and his father would have for the baseball game they'd be attending that evening. A tall, lanky 12-year-old, Eric had just begun seventh grade. His history teacher had already warned him about being late to class and not paying attention, but Eric just couldn't seem to get from one class to the next without stopping for drinks of water or to investigate an altercation between classmates. In class, he was rarely prepared to answer when the teacher called on him, and he usually forgot to write down the homework assignment. He already had a reputation among his peers as an "airhead."

Eric's relief at the sound of the bell was quickly replaced by anxiety as he reached the playground for physical education. Despite his speed and physical strength, Eric was always picked last for baseball teams. His team was up to bat first, and Eric sat down to wait his turn. Absorbed in studying a pile of pebbles at his feet, he failed to notice his team's third out and missed the change of innings. The other team had already come in from the outfield before Eric noticed that his team was out in the field—too late to avoid the irate yells of his P.E. teacher to take his place at third base. Resolved to watch for his chance to field the ball, Eric nonetheless found himself without his glove on when a sharply hit ball rocketed his way; he had taken it off to toss it in the air in the middle of the pitch.

At home, Eric's father told him he had to finish his homework before they could go to the Dodgers game. He had only one page of math problems and was determined to finish them quickly. Thirty minutes later, his father emerged from the shower to find Eric building an elaborate Lego structure on the floor of his room; the math homework was half done. In exasperation, Eric's father left for the game without him.

At bedtime, frustrated and discouraged, Eric was unable to sleep. He often lay awake for what seemed like hours, reviewing the disappointments of the day and berating himself for his failures. On this night, he ruminated about his lack of friends, the frustration of his teachers, and his parents' exhortations to pay attention and "get it together." Feeling hopeless about doing better, despite his daily resolve, Eric often found his thoughts turning to suicide. Tonight he reviewed his fantasy of wandering out into the street in front of a passing car. Although Eric had never acted on his suicidal thoughts, he frequently replayed in his mind his parents' sorrow and remorse, his classmates' irritation with him, and the concern of his teachers.

T HE DISORDERS FOUND IN the DSM-IV-TR section entitled "Disorders Usually First Diagnosed in Infancy, Childhood, or Adolescence" cover a wide range of difficulties, from the attentional problems characteristic of attention-deficit/hyperactivity disorder, as in the case of Eric, to the sometimes serious intellectual deficits found in mental retardation, the sometimes callous disregard for the rights of others found in conduct disorder, the disturbances in mood found in anxiety and depression, the learning problems characteristic of learning disorders, and the language impairment and social and emotional difficulties of autistic disorder. Children typically have access to fewer social, financial, and psychological resources than do adults in dealing with such problems. Thus, whether children receive professional attention at all usually depends on the adults in their lives—parents, teachers, and school counselors. Although many childhood disorders can be treated in an outpatient setting with medication or psychotherapy, some disorders require stays in the hospital. As with adults, unfortunately, the availability of inpatient settings for children has also declined in recent years. For example, between 1990 and 2000, the average length of stay in a U.S. hospital for children declined from just over 12 days to 4.5 days (Case, et al., 2007).

Most psychological theories of childhood disorders, whether psychodynamic, behavioral, cognitive, or neurobiological, consider childhood experience and development critically important to adult mental health. Most theories also regard children as better able to change than adults and thus as particularly suitable for treatment. The number of children diagnosed with and treated for different psychological disorders has dramatically increased in recent years, but not without controversy (see Focus on Discovery 14.3). Also controversial is the tremendous increase in the number of medication prescriptions given to children. For example, antipsychotic medications for children increased fivefold between 1993 and 2002, with over one million such prescriptions given to children in 2002 (Olfson, Blanco, et al., 2006).

In this chapter we discuss several of the disorders that are most likely to arise in childhood and adolescence. We first consider disorders involving attention and socially unacceptable behavior, followed by depression and anxiety disorders. Finally, we discuss disorders in which the acquisition of cognitive, language, motor, or social skills is disturbed. These include learning disabilities as well as the most severe of developmental disorders, mental retardation and autistic disorder, which are usually chronic and often persist into adulthood.

Classification and Diagnosis of Childhood Disorders

Table 14.1 Chapters Where Disorders Are Discussed That Occur in Both Children and Adults

Substance-related disorders: Chapter 10

Schizophrenia: Chapter 11

Aftermath of child sexual abuse: Chapter 13

Somatoform disorders: Chapter 6

Dissociative disorders: Chapter 6

Eating disorders: Chapter 9

Parasomnias: Abnormal behavioral or physiological events occurring in association with sleep—for example, nightmare disorder, sleep terror disorder, and sleepwalking disorder (not covered in this text).

Before making a diagnosis of a particular disorder in children, clinicians must first consider what is typical for a particular age. The diagnosis of children who lie on the floor kicking and screaming when they don't get their way would be assessed differently at age two than at seven. The field of **developmental psychopathology** studies disorders of childhood within the context of life-span development, enabling us to identify behaviors that are considered appropriate at one stage but are disturbed at another.

Most childhood disorders, such as school phobia, are unique to children. Others, such as attention-deficit/hyperactivity disorder, have been conceptualized primarily as childhood disorders but may continue into adulthood. Still others, such as depression, may begin in childhood but are common in adulthood as well. The DSM descriptions of the disorders we cover in this chapter are provided in the DSM tables in the margins. Table 14.1 lists the chapters where we discuss other disorders that may occur in childhood but are primarily considered disorders of adulthood and so are not discussed here. Although eating disorders typically begin in adolescence, they are presented separately in Chapter 9.

The more prevalent childhood disorders are often categorized in two broad domains, externalizing disorders and internalizing disorders. **Externalizing disorders** are characterized by more outward-directed behaviors, such as aggressiveness, noncompliance, overactivity, and impulsiveness; the category includes attention-deficit/ hyperactivity disorder, conduct disorder, and oppositional defiant disorder. **Internalizing disorders** are characterized by more inward-focused experiences and behaviors such as depression, social withdrawal, and anxiety; the category includes childhood anxiety and mood disorders. Children and adolescents may exhibit symptoms from both domains, as described in the case of Eric.

The behaviors that comprise externalizing and internalizing disorders are prevalent across many countries, including Switzerland (Steinhausen & Metzke, 1998), Australia (Achenbach, Hensley, et al., 1990), Puerto Rico (Achenbach, Hensley, et al., 1990), Kenya (Weisz et al., 1993), and Greece (MacDonnald et al., 1995). Externalizing behaviors are consistently found more often among boys and internalizing behaviors more often among girls, at least in adolescence, across cultures (Weisz et al., 1987). Focus on Discovery 14.1 discusses the possible role of culture in the prevalence of these problem behaviors in children.

Attention-Deficit/Hyperactivity Disorder

The term *hyperactive* is familiar to most people, especially parents and teachers. The child who is constantly in motion—tapping fingers, jiggling legs, poking others for no apparent reason, talking out of turn, and fidgeting—is often called hyperactive. Often, these children also have difficulty concentrating on the task at hand for an appropriate period of time. When such problems are severe and persistent enough, these children may meet the criteria for diagnosis of **attention-deficit/hyperactivity disorder (ADHD)**. Recognizing the impact of ADHD on children and families, the U.S. Congress created a National ADHD Awareness Day, with the first such day being on September 7, 2004.

Clinical Descriptions, Prevalence, and Prognosis of ADHD

What distinguishes the typical range of hyperactive behaviors from a diagnosable disorder? When these behaviors are extreme for a particular developmental period, persistent across different situations, and linked to significant impairments in functioning, the diagnosis of ADHD may be appropriate (NIH Consensus Statement, 1998). The ADHD diagnosis does not properly apply to children who are rambunctious, active, or slightly distractible, for in the early school years children are often so (Whalen, 1983). Using the label simply because a child is more lively and more difficult to control than a parent or teacher would like is a serious mistake. The diagnosis of ADHD should be reserved for truly severe and persistent cases.

FOCUS ON DISCOVERY 14.1

The Role of Culture in Internalizing and Externalizing Behavior Problems

The values and mores of a culture may play a role in whether a certain pattern of child behavior develops or is considered a problem. One study found that in Thailand, children with internalizing behavior problems, such as fearfulness, were the ones most likely to be seen in clinics, whereas in the United States, those with externalizing behavior problems, such as aggressiveness and hyperactivity, were more commonly seen (Weisz et al., 1987). The researchers attributed these differences to the fact that Buddhism, which disapproves of and discourages aggression, is widely practiced in Thailand. They also cautioned that their results were based on assessment measures that were normed on U.S. samples and that additional work needed to be done to ensure that the assessment measures were valid for Thai children (see Chapter 3 for more on the issue of culture and assessment).

Findings from a follow-up study suggest that the behavior problems described in the same terms may not really be exactly the same across Thai and U.S. cultures (Weisz et al., 2003). The researchers compared specific behavior problems (e.g., somatic complaints, aggressive behavior) and broad domains (internalizing, externalizing) using U.S. and Thai assessment measures. The broad domains of internalizing and externalizing behaviors were found to be the same in Thai and U.S. children, but more specific categories within those domains were not. Among boys, somatic complaints were seen consistently across cultures, but shyness was seen less consistently. Among girls, shyness was seen consistently across cultures but verbal aggressive behavior was not.

These studies point to the importance of studying psychopathology across cultures. It is dangerous to assume that the measures we develop to assess psychopathology in the United States will work equally well across cultures. As the investigators cited above point out, our theories about the causes of psychopathology need to be able to account for cultural variation in such factors as parenting practices, beliefs and values, and the ways in which parents report on their child's behavior problems. This remains an urgent and important challenge for our field.

Thai teenagers serving as novices in a Buddhist temple. Buddhist culture may contribute to the relatively low prevalence of externalizing disorders in Thailand. (Paul Chesley/Stone/Getty Images.)

Children with ADHD seem to have particular difficulty controlling their activity in situations that call for sitting still, such as in the classroom or at mealtimes. When told to be quiet, they appear unable to stop moving or talking. Their activities and movements seem haphazard. They may quickly wear out their shoes and clothing, smash their toys, and exhaust their families and teachers.

Many children with ADHD have inordinate difficulty getting along with peers and establishing friendships (Blachman & Hinshaw, 2002; Hinshaw & Melnick, 1995), perhaps because their behavior is often aggressive and intrusive. Although these children are usually friendly and talkative, they often miss subtle social cues, such as noticing when other children are tiring of their constant jiggling. They also frequently misinterpret the wishes and intentions of their peers and make inadvertent social mistakes, such as reacting aggressively because they assume that a neutral action by a peer was meant to be aggressive. (Such cognitive misattributions are also found in some children with conduct disorder.)

A study involving observation of children playing tabletop football demonstrated that children with ADHD, particularly those who are also aggressive, have different social goals than other children. Children with ADHD who were also aggressive approached the game with sensation-seeking goals, such as making trouble, achieving domination, and showing off, whereas the other children were more likely to have the goal of playing fair (Melnick & Hinshaw, 1996). In another study, children were asked to instant-message (IM) other children in what appeared to be an online chat room (Mikami et al., 2007). Actually, children were interacting with four simulated peers on the computer, and thus all children got the same IMs from the simulated peers. The researchers coded the messages and the participants' reported experiences of the chat elicited in subsequent interviews. Children with ADHD were more likely to IM

DSM-IV-TR Criteria for Attention-Deficit/ Hyperactivity Disorder

- Either A or B:
  A. Six or more manifestations of inattention present for at least 6 months to a maladaptive degree and greater than what would be expected, given a person's developmental level, for example, careless mistakes, not listening well, not following instructions, easily distracted, forgetful in daily activities.
  B. Six or more manifestations of hyperactivity-impulsivity present for at least 6 months to a maladaptive degree and greater than what would be expected, given a person's developmental level, e.g., squirming in seat, running about inappropriately (in adults, restlessness), acting as if "driven by a motor," incessant talking.
- Some of the above present before age 7
- Present in two or more settings, e.g., at home, school or work
- Significant impairment in social, academic, or occupational functioning
- Not part of other disorders such as schizophrenia, an anxiety disorder, or a mood disorder

statements that were hostile and off the topic than were children without ADHD, and children's chat room experiences were related to other measures of social skills difficulties, suggesting that this common way of "interacting" with peers, even though not face-to-face, is also impaired among children with ADHD.

Children with ADHD can know what the socially correct action is in hypothetical situations but be unable to translate this knowledge into appropriate behavior in real-life social interactions (Whalen & Henker, 1985, 1991). Children with ADHD are often singled out very quickly and rejected or neglected by their peers. For example, in a study of previously unacquainted boys at a summer camp, boys with ADHD who exhibited a number of externalizing behaviors, such as overt aggression and noncompliance, were regarded quite negatively by their peers during the first day of camp, and these impressions remained unchanged throughout the 6-week camp period (Erhardt & Hinshaw, 1994; Hinshaw et al., 1997).

Because the symptoms of ADHD are varied, DSM-IV-TR includes three subcategories:

1. Predominantly inattentive type: Children whose problems are primarily those of poor attention.
2. Predominantly hyperactive-impulsive type: Children whose difficulties result primarily from hyperactive/impulsive behavior.
3. Combined type: Children who have both sets of problems.

Eric, the boy described at the beginning of the chapter, most likely would meet criteria for the predominantly inattentive type. The combined type comprises the majority of children with ADHD. These children are more likely than those with other subtypes to develop conduct problems and oppositional behavior, to be placed in special classes for children with behavior problems, and to have difficulties interacting with their peers (Faraone et al., 1998). Children with attentional problems but with otherwise developmentally appropriate activity levels appear to have more difficulties with focused attention or speed of information processing (Barkley, Grodzinsky, & DuPaul, 1992), perhaps associated with problems involving the neurotransmitter dopamine and certain areas of the brain, including the prefrontal cortex (Krause et al., 2003), topics to which we turn to below.

A difficult differential diagnosis is between ADHD and conduct disorder, which involves gross violation of social norms. An overlap of 30 to 90 percent between the two categories (Hinshaw, 1987) has caused some researchers to assert that these two types of externalizing disorders are actually one and the same. There are some differences, however. ADHD is associated more with off-task behavior in school, cognitive and achievement deficits, and a better long-term prognosis. Children with ADHD act out less in school and elsewhere and are less likely to be aggressive and to have antisocial parents. Their home life is also usually marked by less family hostility, and they are at less risk for delinquency and substance abuse in adolescence compared to children with conduct disorder (Faraone et al., 1997; Hinshaw, 1987; Jensen, Martin, & Cantwell, 1997).

When these two disorders occur in the same child, the worst features of each are manifest. Such children exhibit the most serious antisocial behavior, are most likely to be rejected by their peers, have the worst academic achievement, and have the poorest prognosis (Hinshaw & Lee, 2003). Girls with both ADHD and conduct disorder exhibit more antisocial behavior, other psychopathology, and risky sexual behavior than girls with only ADHD (Monuteaux et al., 2007).

Internalizing disorders, such as anxiety and depression, also frequently co-occur with ADHD. Recent estimates suggest that as many as 30 percent of children with ADHD may have comorbid internalizing disorders (e.g., Jensen et al., 1997; MTA Cooperative Group, 1999b). In addition, about 15 to 30 percent of children with ADHD have a learning disability in math, reading, or spelling (Barkley, DuPaul, & McMurray, 1990; Casey, Rourke, & Del Dotto, 1996), and many children with ADHD are placed in special educational programs because of their difficulty in adjusting to a typical classroom environment (Barkley et al., 1990).

Although having both ADHD and conduct disorder is associated with substance use and abuse, a prospective study found that that the hyperactive symptoms of ADHD predicted subsequent substance (nicotine, alcohol, illicit drugs) use at age 14 and abuse or dependence at age 18 even after controlling for symptoms of conduct disorder, and this was equally true for boys and girls (Elkins, McGue, & Iacono, 2007).

The consensus on prevalence estimates of ADHD is that about 3 to 7 percent of school-age children worldwide currently have ADHD (APA, 2000). When similar criteria for ADHD are used across countries as diverse as the United States, Kenya, China, and Thailand, the prevalence rates are similar (Anderson, 1996); however, using the same criteria may not adequately capture cultural differences in ADHD (see Focus on Discovery 14.1).

Much evidence indicates that ADHD is more common in boys than in girls, but exact figures depend on whether the sample is taken from clinic referrals or from the general population. Boys are more likely to be referred to clinics because of a higher likelihood of aggressive and antisocial behavior. Until recently, very few carefully controlled studies of girls with ADHD were conducted. Because so little research has been done with female samples, it is important to document the characteristics, correlates, comorbid disorders, and other social and cognitive deficits in a carefully selected sample of girls with ADHD. Two groups of researchers have conducted such studies (Biederman & Faraone, 2004; Hinshaw, 2002). One research group examined a large and ethnically diverse sample of girls with and without ADHD and reported a number of key findings at the initial assessment and then again five years later (Hinshaw et al., 2002, 2006):

Stephen Hinshaw, a renowned developmental psychopathology researcher and expert on mental illness stigma, is conducting one of the largest ongoing studies of girls with ADHD. (Courtesy Stephen Hinshaw, Ph.D.)

- Similar to findings with male samples, girls with the combined type had more disruptive behavior symptoms than girls with the inattentive type.

- Girls with the combined type were more likely to have a comorbid diagnosis of conduct disorder or oppositional defiant disorder than girls without ADHD, and this difference remained five years after initial diagnosis.

- Girls with the combined type were viewed more negatively by peers than girls with the inattentive type and girls without ADHD; girls with the inattentive type were also viewed more negatively than girls without ADHD.

- Girls with ADHD were likely to be more anxious and depressed than were girls without ADHD, and this remained true five years after initial diagnosis.

- Girls with ADHD exhibited a number of neuropsychological deficits, particularly in executive functioning (e.g., planning, solving problems), compared with girls without ADHD, replicating other findings (Castellanos et al., 2000).

- By adolescence, girls with ADHD were more likely to have symptoms of an eating disorder and substance abuse than girls without ADHD.

At one time it was thought that ADHD simply went away by adolescence. However, this belief has been challenged by numerous longitudinal studies (Barkley et al., 2002; Biederman et al., 1996; Hinshaw et al., 2006; Lee et al., 2008; Weiss & Hechtman, 1993). Although some children show reduced severity of symptoms in adolescence, 65 to 80 percent of children with ADHD still meet criteria for the disorder in adolescence (Biederman et al., 2006; Hart et al., 1995; Hinshaw et al., 2006). Table 14.2 provides a catalogue of behaviors that are found more often among adolescents with ADHD than among adolescents without it. Many children with ADHD do not appear to take a "hit" with respect to academic achievement, however—many studies indicate that achievement is within the average range for both adolescent boys (Lee et al., 2008) and girls (Hinshaw et al., 2006).

In adulthood, most people with ADHD are employed and financially independent, but some studies have found adults with ADHD are generally at a lower socioeconomic level and change jobs more frequently than is typical (Mannuzza et al., 1991; Weiss & Hechtman, 1993). The rates of ADHD in adulthood vary depending on the method of assessment (Barkley et al., 2002). Specifically, when ADHD in adulthood is assessed by self-reports of adults who had ADHD as children, only about 10 percent meet criteria for ADHD. In contrast, when ADHD is assessed by the parents of these same adults who had had ADHD as children, more than half meet criteria for ADHD. Whose assessments are correct? This question is impossible to answer. It may be the case that the adults with ADHD are less aware of their symptoms, or it could be that the parents' reports are influenced by their memories of their children. Findings from a review of the studies that have assessed ADHD longitudinally into adulthood indicate that up to 15 percent of people continue to meet full DSM-IV-TR criteria as 25-year-old adults. Even more people—close to 60 percent—continued to meet the

Aggression is not uncommon among boys with ADHD, and it contributes to their being rejected by peers. (Alamy Images.)

Table 14.2 Behaviors in Adolescents with and without ADHD

Behavior	Percentage of Adolescents Who Show this Behavior	
	With ADHD	**Without ADHD**
Blurts out answers	65.0	10.6
Distracted easily	82.1	15.2
Doesn't complete tasks before moving to another	77.2	16.7
Doesn't sustain attention	79.7	16.7
Doesn't follow instructions	83.7	12.1
Doesn't listen to others well	80.5	15.2
Engages in physically dangerous activities	37.4	3.0
Fidgets	73.2	10.6
Finds it hard to play quietly	39.8	7.6
Gets out of seat often	60.2	3.0
Interrupts others	65.9	10.6
Loses things needed for tasks	62.6	12.1
Talks a lot	43.9	6.1

Source: Adapted from Barkley et al. (1990).

DSM-IV-TR criteria for ADHD in partial remission as adults (Faraone, Biederman, & Mick, 2005). Thus, ADHD symptoms appear to decline with age, but they do not entirely go away for many people with ADHD.

Etiology of ADHD

Genetic Factors   Substantial evidence indicates that a genetic predisposition toward ADHD plays a role (Thapar et al., 2007). Adoption studies (e.g., Sprich et al., 2000) and numerous large-scale twin studies (e.g., Levy et al., 1997; Sherman, Iacono, & McGue, 1997) indicate a genetic component to ADHD, with heritability estimates as high as 70 to 80 percent (Tannock, 1998). Molecular genetics studies that seek to identify genes linked to ADHD are underway. Some of the more promising findings involve genes associated with the neurotransmitter dopamine. Specifically, two different dopamine genes have been implicated in ADHD: a dopamine receptor gene called DRD4 (e.g., Faraone et al., 2001) and a dopamine transporter gene called DAT1 (Krause et al., 2003; Waldman et al., 1998). The evidence in support of DRD4's association with ADHD is stronger at this point, as several different studies have consistently found a relationship between this gene and ADHD. Findings for DAT1 are more mixed, with some studies finding a link and others not finding a link with ADHD (Thapar et al., 2007). Even with these promising findings, most investigators agree that a single gene will not ultimately account for ADHD. Rather, several genes interacting with environmental factors will provide the most complete picture of the cause of ADHD. For example, recent studies have found that the DRD4 or DAT1 genes are associated with increased risk of ADHD only among those who also had particular environmental factors—namely, prenatal maternal nicotine or alcohol use (Brookes et al., 2006; Neuman et al., 2007). Additional gene–environment interaction studies are underway, and if these findings are replicated, we will have a clearer picture of how genes and environments interact in ADHD.

Neurobiological Factors   Studies suggest that brain structure and function differ in children with and without ADHD, particularly in areas of the brain linked to the neurotransmitter dopamine. For example, studies of brain structure have found that dopaminergic areas of the brain, such as the caudate nucleus, globus pallidus, and frontal lobes, are smaller in children with ADHD than children without ADHD (Castellanos et al., 2002; Swanson et al., 2007). Studies of brain function have found that children with ADHD exhibit less activation in frontal areas of

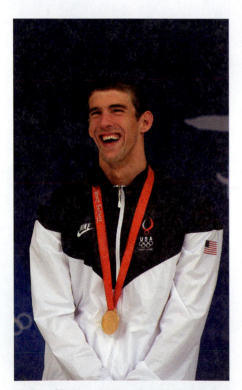

Michael Phelps who won 8 gold medals in swimming at the 2008 Olympics also struggled with ADHD as a child. (Heinz Kluetmeier/Sports Illustrated/Getty Images, Inc.)

the brain while performing different cognitive tasks (Casey & Durston, 2006; Nigg & Casey, 2005; Rubia et al., 1999). Moreover, children with ADHD perform poorly on neuropsychological tests that rely on the frontal lobes (such as inhibiting behavioral responses), providing further support for the theory that a basic deficit in this part of the brain may be related to the disorder (Barkley, 1997; Nigg, 2001; Nigg & Casey, 2005; Tannock, 1998).

Perinatal and Prenatal Factors   Other neurobiological risk factors for ADHD include a number of perinatal and prenatal complications. Low birth weight, for example, is a quite specific predictor of the development of ADHD (e.g., Bhutta et al., 2002; Breslau et al., 1996; Whitaker et al., 1997). However, the impact of low birth weight on later symptoms of ADHD can be mitigated by greater maternal warmth (Tully et al., 2004). Other complications associated with childbirth, as well as mothers' use of substances such as tobacco (discussed below) and alcohol, are also predictive of ADHD symptoms (Tannock, 1998).

Environmental Toxins   Early theories of ADHD that were quite popular in the 1970s involved the role of environmental toxins in the development of hyperactivity. One theory of hyperactivity enjoyed much attention in the popular press for many years (Feingold, 1973). Feingold proposed that additives and artificial colors in foods upset the central nervous systems of children who were hyperactive, and he prescribed a diet free of them. However, well-controlled studies of the so-called Feingold diet have found that very few children with ADHD respond positively to it (Goyette & Conners, 1977). Even though these early findings did not support Feingold's theory, researchers continue to examine how different elements of the diet, particularly additives, may influence hyperactive behavior. These later studies use more sophisticated research designs, such as placebo-controlled, double-blind studies, but the results remain modest. For example, a meta-analysis of 15 studies found a small effect size for artificial food coloring on hyperactive behavior among children with ADHD (Schnab & Trinh, 2004). A recent study found a similarly small effect of food additives and artificial food coloring on hyperactive behavior among children in the community (McCann et al. 2007). Thus, there is limited evidence that food additives impact hyperactive behavior. The popular view that refined sugar can cause ADHD has not been supported by careful research (Wolraich, Wilson, & White, 1995).

Although some evidence suggests that lead poisoning may be associated to a small degree with symptoms of hyperactivity and attentional problems (Braun et al., 2006; Thompson et al., 1989), most children with lead poisoning do not develop ADHD, and most children with ADHD do not show elevated levels of lead in the blood. However, given the unfortunate frequency with which children are exposed to low levels of lead, investigators continue to examine whether lead exposure might play a role, however small, in the etiology of ADHD (Nigg, 2006).

Nicotine—specifically, maternal smoking—is an environmental toxin that may play a role in the development of ADHD. One study found that 22 percent of mothers of children with ADHD reported smoking a pack of cigarettes per day during pregnancy, compared with 8 percent of mothers whose children did not develop ADHD (Milberger et al., 1996). This effect remained even after controlling for maternal depression and alcohol use (Chabrol et al., 1997). A twin study found that maternal smoking predicted ADHD symptoms even after controlling for genetic influences and other environmental risk factors (Thapar et al., 2003). Finally, a review of 24 studies examining the association between maternal smoking and ADHD found that exposure to tobacco in utero was associated with ADHD symptoms (Linnet et al., 2003). Several animal studies conducted since the 1980s indicate that chronic exposure to nicotine increases dopamine release in the brain and causes hyperactivity (e.g., Fung & Lau, 1989; Vaglenova et al., 2004). Furthermore, withdrawal from nicotine is associated with decreases in dopamine release in the brain and causes irritability. On the basis of these data, researchers hypothesize that maternal smoking can affect the dopaminergic system of the developing fetus, resulting in behavioral disinhibition and ADHD.

Psychological Factors in ADHD   Although research results support neurological and genetic factors more than psychological factors in the etiology of ADHD, the parent–child relationship interacts with these neurobiological factors in a complex way to contribute to ADHD

Children born to mothers who smoked cigarettes during pregnancy have an increased risk for ADHD. (Richard Phelps/Photo Researchers.)

symptom expression (Hinshaw et al., 1997). Just as parents of children with ADHD may give them more commands and have negative interactions with them (Anderson, Hinshaw, & Simmel, 1994; Heller et al., 1996), so these children have been found to be less compliant and more negative in interactions with their parents (Barkley, Karlsson, & Pollard, 1985; Tallmadge & Barkley, 1983). Certainly, it must be difficult to parent a child who is impulsive, aggressive, noncompliant, and unable to follow instructions. As we will discuss shortly, stimulant medication has been shown to reduce hyperactivity and increase compliance in some children with ADHD. Significantly, when such medication is used, either alone or in combination with behavioral treatment, the parents' commands, negative behavior, and ineffective parenting also decrease (Barkeley, 1990; Wells et al., 2000), suggesting that the child's behavior has at least some negative effect on the parents' behavior.

It is also important to consider a parent's own history of ADHD. As noted above, there appears to be a substantial genetic component to ADHD. Thus, it is not surprising that many parents of children with ADHD have ADHD themselves. In one study that examined couples' parenting practices with their ADHD children, fathers who had a diagnosis of ADHD were less effective parents, suggesting that parental psychopathology may make parenting all the more difficult (Arnold, O'Leary, & Edwards, 1997). Family characteristics thus may well contribute to maintaining or exacerbating the symptoms and consequences of ADHD; however, there is little evidence to suggest that families actually cause ADHD (Johnston & Marsh, 2001).

Treatment of ADHD

We now turn to treatments for ADHD. ADHD is typically treated with medication and with behavioral therapies based on operant conditioning.

Stimulant Medications   Stimulant medications, such as methylphenidate, or Ritalin, have been prescribed for ADHD since the early 1960s. Other medications approved by the FDA to treat ADHD include Adderall, Concerta, and Strattera. In 2006, an estimated 2.5 million children in the United States were taking stimulant medication (National Survey on Children's Health, 2003), including almost 10 percent of all 10-year-old boys. The prescription of these medications has sometimes continued into adolescence and adulthood in light of the accumulating evidence that the symptoms of ADHD do not usually disappear with the passage of time.

The drugs used to treat ADHD reduce disruptive behavior and improve ability to concentrate. Numerous controlled studies comparing stimulants with placebos in double-blind designs have shown short-term improvements in concentration, goal-directed activity, classroom behavior, and social interactions with parents, teachers, and peers, as well as reductions in aggressiveness and impulsivity in about 75 percent of children with ADHD (Spencer et al., 1996; Swanson et al., 1995).

The best-designed randomized controlled trial of treatments for ADHD was the Multimodal Treatment of Children with ADHD (MTA) study. Conducted at six different sites for 14 months with nearly 600 children with ADHD, the study compared standard community-based care and three other treatments: (1) medication alone, (2) medication plus intensive behavioral treatment, involving both parents and teachers, and (3) intensive behavioral treatment alone. Across the 14-month period, children receiving medication alone had fewer ADHD symptoms than children receiving intensive behavioral treatment alone. The combined treatment was slightly superior to the medication alone and had the advantage of not requiring as high a dosage of Ritalin to reduce ADHD symptoms. In addition, the combined treatment yielded improved functioning in areas such as social skills more than did the medication alone. The medication alone and the combined treatment were superior to community-based care, though the behavioral treatment alone was not (MTA Cooperative Group, 1999a,1999b).

In secondary analyses undertaken to clarify the key findings from the MTA study, researchers reported that the behavioral treatment alone was superior to community-based care at three of the six sites, but not at the other three (Swanson et al., 2001). In addition, further comparisons of the combined treatment with treatment by medication alone suggested that 20 percent more children who received the combined treatment achieved an excellent treatment response. The combined treatment was also associated with fewer behavioral problems at school, and

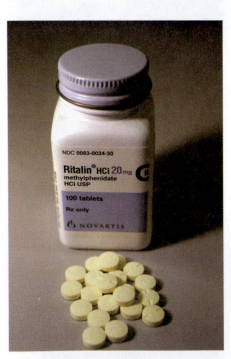

Ritalin is a commonly prescribed and effective drug treatment for ADHD. (Allan Tannenbaum/The Image Works.)

additional analyses suggest that this effect may be linked to a decrease in negative and ineffective parenting (Hinshaw et al., 2000). Finally, analyses that examined treatment effects by ethnicity indicated that white, African American, and Latino children benefited equally from treatment, particularly from the combined treatment (L.E. Arnold et al., 2003).

Despite the promising findings on the efficacy of stimulant medications for ADHD, other research indicates that these drugs may not improve academic achievement over the long haul (Weiss & Hechtman, 1993; Whalen & Henker, 1991). Although children in the MTA study who received stimulant medication (either alone or in the combined treatment group) still had a reduction in ADHD symptoms, the effect was substantially smaller than it was during the original study (MTA Cooperative Group, 2004). At the three-year follow-up of the MTA study, there were no longer any significant differences between the original treatment groups in terms of their ADHD symptoms (Jensen et al., 2007). In other words, the relatively superior effects of medication that were observed in the combined treatment and medication alone groups did not persist three years later, at least for some of the children (Swanson, Hinshaw et al., 2007).

Does this mean that stimulant medication is not all that effective for children with ADHD? No. The MTA study demonstrates that carefully prescribed and managed stimulant medication is effective for children with ADHD. However, the follow-up findings suggest that stimulant medication might be more effective for some children more than others.

These findings are important in light of the side effects that stimulant medication can have, such as transient loss of appetite, weight loss, stomach pain, and sleep problems. In May 2006, the Food and Drug Administration recommended but did not mandate that a "black box" warning, the strongest possible safety warning the FDA can issue for medications, about cardiovascular risks (e.g., heart attack) be added to stimulant medications. In February 2007, the FDA mandated that drug makers develop patient medication guides to describe these risks to consumers.

Psychological Treatment   Other promising treatments for ADHD involve parent training and changes in classroom management (Chronis, Jones, & Raggi, 2006). These programs have demonstrated at least short-term success in improving both social and academic behavior. In these treatments, children's behavior is monitored at home and in school, and they are reinforced for behaving appropriately—for example, for remaining in their seats and working on assignments. Point systems and daily report cards (DRCs) are typical components of these programs. Children earn points or stars for behaving in certain ways; the children can then spend their earnings for rewards. The DRC also allows parents to see how their child is doing in school. The focus of these programs is on improving academic work, completing household tasks, or learning specific social skills, rather than on reducing signs of hyperactivity, such as running around and jiggling. Accumulating evidence supports the efficacy of parent-training programs, although it is unclear whether they improve children's behavior beyond the effects of treatment with medication (Abikoff & Hechtman, 1996; Anastopoulos et al., 1993; MTA Cooperative Group, 1999a, 1999b).

School interventions for children with ADHD include training teachers to understand the unique needs of these children and to apply operant techniques in the classroom (Welsh et al., 1997), providing peer tutoring in academic skills (DuPaul & Henningson, 1993), and having teachers provide daily reports to parents about in-school behavior, which are followed up with rewards at home (Kelley, 1990). Research has demonstrated that certain classroom structures can help children with ADHD. Ideally, teachers vary the presentation format and materials used for tasks, keep assignments brief and provide immediate feedback on whether they have been done correctly, have an enthusiastic and task-focused style, provide breaks for physical exercise, use computer-assisted drill programs, and schedule academic work during the morning hours. Such environmental changes are designed to accommodate the limitations imposed by this disorder rather than to change the disorder itself.

Point systems and star charts, which are common in classrooms, are particularly useful in the treatment of ADHD. (Lew Merrim/Photo Researchers.)

Finally, findings from the just-mentioned MTA study indicate that intensive behavioral therapies can be very helpful to children with ADHD. In that study, some of the children participated in an intensive eight-week summer program that included a number of validated behavioral treatments. At the end of the summer program, children receiving the combined treatment had very few significant improvements over children receiving the intensive behavioral treatment alone (L. E. Arnold et al., 2003; Pelham et al., 2000). This finding suggests that intensive behavioral therapy may be as effective as Ritalin combined with a less intensive behavioral therapy.

Check Your Knowledge 14.1 (Answers are at the end of the chapter.)

True or false?
1. The two broad domains of childhood psychopathology are internalizing disorders and externalizing disorders.
2. Girls with the combined type of ADHD have more severe problems than girls with the predominantly inattentive type, similar to findings with boys.

3. Dopamine has been investigated in ADHD, particularly genes for the DRD4 receptors.
4. The most effective treatment for ADHD is behavioral treatment without medication.

Conduct Disorder

Conduct disorder is another externalizing disorder. The DSM-IV-TR criteria for conduct disorder focus on behaviors that violate the basic rights of others and that violate major societal norms. Nearly all such behavior is also illegal. The symptoms of conduct disorder must be frequent and severe enough to go beyond the mischief and pranks common among children and adolescents. These behaviors include aggression and cruelty toward people or animals, damaging property, lying, and stealing. Often the behavior is marked by callousness, viciousness, and lack of remorse, making conduct disorder during childhood one of the criteria for adult antisocial personality disorder (see p. 368).

A related but less well understood externalizing disorder in the DSM-IV-TR is **oppositional defiant disorder** (ODD). There is some debate as to whether ODD is distinct from conduct disorder, a precursor to it, or an earlier and milder manifestation of it (Hinshaw & Lee, 2003; Lahey, McBurnett, & Loeber, 2000). ODD is diagnosed if a child does not meet the criteria for conduct disorder—most especially, extreme physical aggressiveness—but exhibits such behaviors as losing his or her temper, arguing with adults, repeatedly refusing to comply with requests from adults, deliberately doing things to annoy others, and being angry, spiteful, touchy, or vindictive.

Commonly comorbid with ODD are ADHD, learning disorders, and communication disorders, but ODD is different from ADHD in that the defiant behavior is not thought to arise from attentional deficits or sheer impulsiveness. One manifestation of difference is that children with ODD are more deliberate in their unruly behavior than children with ADHD. Although conduct disorder is three to four times more common among boys than among girls, research suggests that boys are only slightly more likely to have ODD, and some studies find no difference in prevalence rates for ODD between boys and girls (Loeber et al., 2000). Because of ODD's somewhat uncertain status, we will focus here on the more serious diagnosis of conduct disorder.

Conduct disorder is diagnosed among those who are aggressive, steal, lie, and vandalize property. (Ken Lax/Photo Researchers.)

Clinical Description, Prevalence, and Prognosis of Conduct Disorder

Perhaps more than any other childhood disorder, conduct disorder is defined by the impact of the child's behavior on people and surroundings. Schools, parents, peers, and the criminal justice system usually determine which externalizing behaviors constitute unacceptable conduct.

Many children with conduct disorder display other problems, such as substance abuse and internalizing disorders. The Pittsburgh Youth Study, a longitudinal investigation of conduct disorder in boys, found a strong association between substance use and delinquent acts (van Kammen, Loeber, & Stouthamer-Loeber, 1991). For example, among seventh graders who reported having tried marijuana, more than 30 percent had attacked someone with a weapon and 43 percent admitted breaking and entering; fewer than 5 percent of children who reported no substance use had committed these acts. Some research suggests that conduct disorder precedes substance use problems (Nock et al., 2006), but other findings suggest that conduct disorder and substance use occur concomitantly, with the two conditions exacerbating each other (Loeber et al., 2000). Further, some evidence indicates that comorbid conduct disorder and substance use portend a more severe outcome for boys than for girls (Whitmore et al., 1997).

Anxiety and depression are common among children with conduct disorder, with comorbidity estimates varying from 15 to 45 percent (Loeber & Keenan, 1994; Loeber et al., 2000). Evidence suggests that conduct disorder precedes depression and most anxiety disorders, with the exceptions of specific and social phobias, which appear to precede conduct disorder (Nock et al., 2006). Girls with conduct disorder may be at higher risk for developing comorbid disorders, including anxiety, depression, substance abuse, and ADHD, than are boys with conduct disorder (Loeber & Keenan, 1994).

Recent estimates suggest that conduct disorder is fairly common, with a prevalence rate of 9.5 percent (Nock et al., 2006). A review of epidemiological studies suggests the prevalence rates range from 4 to 16 percent for boys and 1.2 to 9 percent for girls (Loeber et al., 2000). As shown in Figure 14.1, both the incidence and the prevalence of serious lawbreaking peak sharply at around age 17 and drop precipitously in young adulthood (Moffitt, 1993). Not all the criminal acts represented in Figure 14.1 are marked by the viciousness and callousness that are often a part of conduct disorder, but the figure illustrates the problem of antisocial behavior in children and adolescents.

Moffitt (1993) has theorized that two different courses of conduct problems should be distinguished. Some people seem to show a life-course-persistent pattern of antisocial behavior, beginning to show conduct problems by age three and continuing to commit serious transgressions into adulthood. Others are adolescence-limited—they have typical childhoods, engage in high levels of antisocial behavior during adolescence, and have typical, nonproblematic adulthoods. Moffitt proposed that the adolescence-limited form of antisocial behavior is the result of a maturity gap between the adolescent's physical maturation and his or her opportunity to assume adult responsibilities and obtain the rewards usually accorded such behavior. The life-course-persistent type is 10 to 15 times more common among boys than girls, suggesting it is almost exclusively a type affecting boys (Moffitt, 2006).

Cumulative evidence supports this distinction (Moffitt, 2007). For example, children with the life-course-persistent form of conduct disorder do indeed show an early onset of antisocial behavior that persists through adolescence, and these children have a number of other problems, such as academic underachievement, neuropsychological deficits, and comorbid ADHD (Moffitt & Caspi, 2001). Other evidence supports the notion that children with the life-course-persistent type have more severe neuropsychological deficits and family psychopathology, and these findings have been replicated across cultures (Hinshaw & Lee, 2003).

The original sample from which Moffitt and colleagues made the life-course-persistent and adolescent-limited distinction has now been followed into early adulthood (age 26). Those who were classified as life-course-persistent continue to have the most severe problems, including psychopathology, lower levels of education, partner and child abuse, and violent behavior. However, those classified as adolescent-limited, who were expected to "grow out" of their aggressive and antisocial behavior, have apparently not done so. The participants, now in their

DSM-IV-TR Criteria for Conduct Disorder

- Repetitive and persistent behavior pattern that violates the basic rights of others or conventional social norms as manifested by the presence of three or more of the following in the previous 12 months and at least one of them in the previous six months:

  A. Aggression to people and animals, e.g., bullying, initiating physical fights, physically cruel to people or animals, forcing someone into sexual activity

  B. Destruction of property, e.g., fire-setting, vandalism

  C. Deceitfulness or theft, e.g., breaking into another's house or car, conning, shoplifting

  D. Serious violation of rules, e.g., staying out at night before age 13 in defiance of parental rules, truancy before age 13

- Significant impairment in social, academic, or occupational functioning

- If person older than 18, criteria not met for antisocial personality disorder

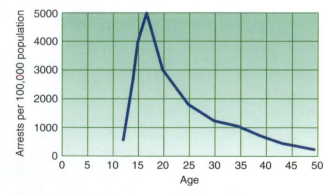

Figure 14.1 Arrest rates across ages for the crimes of homicide, forcible rape, robbery, aggravated assault, and auto theft. From "Criminal Career Research: Its Value for Criminology," by A. Blumstein, J. Cohen, and D. P. Farrington, 1988. *Criminology, 26,* p. 11. Copyright © 1988 by the American Society of Criminology. Adapted by permission.

Chapter 14 Disorders of Childhood

Children with the life-course-persistent type of conduct disorder continue to have trouble with the law into their mid-twenties. (The Image Works.)

mid-twenties, continue to have troubles with substance abuse and dependence, impulsivity, crime, and overall mental health (Moffitt et al., 2002). Additional follow-ups of this sample will help us learn whether or not these maladaptive patterns get better toward the later twenties or early thirties.

The prognosis for children diagnosed as having conduct disorder is mixed. Conduct disorder in childhood does not inevitably lead to antisocial behavior in adulthood, though it certainly is a predisposing factor. For example, a longitudinal study indicated that although about half of boys with conduct disorder did not fully meet the criteria for the diagnosis at a later assessment (1 to 4 years later), almost all of them continued to demonstrate some conduct problems (Lahey et al., 1995).

Etiology of Conduct Disorder

It seems clear that multiple factors are involved in the etiology of conduct disorder, including genetic, neurobiological, psychological, and social factors that interact in a complex manner (Figure 14.2). A review concluded that the evidence favors an etiology that includes heritable temperamental characteristics that interact with other neurobiological difficulties (e.g., neuropsychological deficits) as well as with a whole host of environmental factors (e.g., parenting, school performance, peer influences) (Hinshaw & Lee, 2003).

Genetic Factors The evidence for genetic influences in conduct disorder is mixed, although heritability likely plays a part. For example, a study of over 3,000 twin pairs indicated only modest genetic influence on childhood antisocial behavior; family–environment influences were more significant (Lyons et al., 1995). However, a study of over 2,600 twin pairs in Australia found a substantial genetic influence and almost no family–environment influence for childhood symptoms of conduct disorder (Slutske et al., 1997). The authors of the latter study point out that differences in the samples may have accounted for the different findings.

Three large-scale adoption studies, in Sweden, Denmark, and the United States, have been conducted, but two of them focused on the heritability of criminal behavior rather than conduct disorder (Simonoff, 2001). As with most traits, these studies indicate that criminal and antisocial behavior is accounted for by both genetic and environmental factors. Interestingly, despite different prevalence rates for boys and girls, the evidence favoring genetic and environmental contributions to conduct disorder and antisocial behavior does not differ between boys and girls. A meta-analysis of twin and adoption studies of antisocial behavior indicated that 40 to 50 percent of antisocial behavior was heritable (Rhee & Waldman, 2002).

Distinguishing types of conduct problems may help to clarify findings on the heritability of conduct disorder. Evidence from twin studies indicates that aggressive behavior (e.g., cruelty to animals, fighting, destroying property) is clearly heritable, whereas other delinquent behavior (e.g., stealing, running away, truancy) may not be (Edelbrock et al., 1995; Rhee & Waldman, 2002). Other evidence suggests that the time when antisocial and aggressive behavior problems begin is related to heritability. For example, aggressive and antisocial behaviors that begin in childhood, as in the case of Moffitt's life-course-persistent type, are more heritable than similar behaviors that begin in adolescence (Taylor, Iacono, & McGue, 2000).

One elegant study examined the interaction between genetic and environmental factors in predicting later adult antisocial behavior (Caspi et al., 2002). It examined the MAOA gene, which is located on the X chromosome and releases an MAO enzyme,

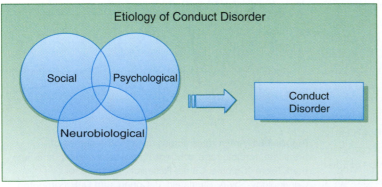

Figure 14.2 Neurobiological, psychological, and social factors all play a role in conduct disorder.

which metabolizes a number of neurotransmitters, including dopamine, serotonin, and norepinephrine. This gene varies in its activity, with some people having high MAOA activity and others having low MAOA activity. Using a large sample of over 1,000 children from Dunedin, New Zealand (the same sample that was the basis for Moffitt's characterization of the life-course-persistent and adolescent-limited types of conduct disorder), the researchers measured MAOA activity and assessed the extent to which the children had been maltreated. Being maltreated as a child was not enough to predict later conduct disorder, nor was the presence of low MAOA activity. Rather, those children who were both maltreated and had low MAOA activity were more likely to develop conduct disorder than either children who were maltreated but had high MAOA activity or children who were not maltreated but had low MAOA activity. Thus, both environment and genes mattered. A meta-analysis of several such studies confirms these findings: being maltreated was linked to later antisocial behavior only via genetics (Taylor & Kim-Cohen, 2007).

Neuropsychological Factors and the Autonomic Nervous System   Neuropsychological deficits have been implicated in the childhood profiles of children with conduct disorder (Lynam & Henry, 2001; Moffitt, Lynam, & Sylva, 1994). These deficits include poor verbal skills, difficulty with executive functioning (the ability to anticipate, plan, use self-control, and solve problems), and problems with memory. In addition, children who develop conduct disorder at an earlier age (i.e., life-course-persistent type) have an IQ score of one standard deviation below age-matched peers without conduct disorder, and this IQ deficit is apparently not attributable to lower socioeconomic status or school failure (Lynam, Moffitt, & Stouthamer-Loeber, 1993; Moffitt & Silva, 1988).

Other studies indicate that autonomic nervous system abnormalities are associated with antisocial behavior in adolescents. Specifically, lower levels of resting skin conductance and heart rate are found among adolescents with conduct disorder, suggesting that they have lower arousal levels than adolescents without conduct disorder (Raine, Venables, & Williams, 1990; Ortiz & Raine, 2004). Why does low arousal matter? Similar to findings on adult antisocial personality disorder (Chapter 12), these studies suggest that adolescents who exhibit antisocial behavior may not fear punishment as much as adolescents who don't exhibit such behavior. Thus, these children may be more likely to behave in antisocial ways without the fear that they will get caught. The fear of getting caught keeps most children from breaking the law.

Psychological Factors   An important part of typical child development is the growth of moral awareness—the acquisition of a sense of what is right and wrong and the ability, even desire, to abide by rules and norms. Most people refrain from hurting others not only because it is illegal but also because it would make them feel guilty to do otherwise. Children with conduct disorder seem to be deficient in this moral awareness, lacking remorse for their wrongdoing (Cimbora & McIntosh, 2003).

Behavioral theories that look to both modeling and operant conditioning provide useful explanations of the development and maintenance of conduct problems. For example, children who are physically abused by parents are likely to be aggressive when they grow up (Coie & Dodge, 1998). Children may also imitate aggressive acts seen elsewhere, such as on television (Huesmann & Miller, 1994). Since aggression is often an effective, albeit unpleasant, means of achieving a goal, it is likely to be reinforced. Thus, aggressive behavior is likely to be maintained. Modeling may help explain the onset of delinquent behavior among adolescents who had not previously shown conduct problems. Perhaps these adolescents imitate the behavior of persistently antisocial peers who are seen as enjoying high-status possessions and sexual opportunities (Moffitt, 1993).

In addition, parenting characteristics such as harsh and inconsistent discipline and lack of monitoring are consistently associated with antisocial behavior in children. Perhaps children who do not experience negative consequences for early misbehavior later develop more serious conduct problems (Coie & Dodge, 1998).

A social-cognitive perspective on aggressive behavior (and, by extension, conduct disorder) comes from the work of Kenneth Dodge and associates. Dodge has constructed a social information processing theory of child behavior that focuses on how children process information about their world and how these cognitions markedly affect their behavior (Crick & Dodge, 1994).In one of his early studies (Dodge & Frame, 1982), Dodge found that the cognitive processes of aggressive children had a particular bias; these children interpreted ambiguous acts,

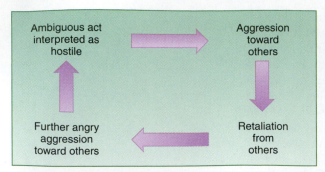

Figure 14.3 Dodge's cognitive theory of aggression. The interpretation of ambiguous acts as hostile is part of a vicious cycle that includes aggression toward and from others.

such as being bumped in line, as evidence of hostile intent. Such perceptions may lead these children to retaliate aggressively for actions that may not have been intended as provocative. This can create a vicious cycle: their peers, remembering these aggressive behaviors, may tend to be aggressive more often against them, further angering the already aggressive children (see Figure 14.3). Deficits in social information processing also predict antisocial behavior among adolescents (Crozier et al., 2008). More recently, Dodge and colleagues have linked deficits in social information processing to heart rate among adolescents who exhibit antisocial behavior. Specifically, low heart rate predicted antisocial behavior among male adolescents independent from social information processing deficits, a finding consistent with studies reviewed earlier on low arousal and conduct problems. However, the link between high heart rate and antisocial behavior was accounted for by social information processing deficits for both male and female adolescents (Crozier et al., 2008).

Peer Influences   Investigations of how peers influence aggressive and antisocial behavior in children have focused on two broad areas: (1) acceptance or rejection by peers and (2) affiliation with deviant peers. Studies have shown that being rejected by peers is causally related to aggressive behavior, particularly in combination with ADHD (Hinshaw & Melnick, 1995). Other studies have shown that being rejected by peers can predict later aggressive behavior, even after controlling for prior levels of aggressive behavior (Coie & Dodge, 1998). Associating with other deviant peers also increases the likelihood of delinquent behavior (Capaldi & Patterson, 1994). One question that remains to be answered is whether children with conduct disorder choose to associate with like-minded peers, thus continuing on their path of antisocial behavior, or if simply being around deviant peers can help initiate antisocial behavior.

Sociocultural Factors   Poverty and urban living are associated with higher levels of delinquency. Unemployment, poor educational facilities, disrupted family life, and a subculture that deems delinquency acceptable are all contributing factors (Lahey et al., 1999; Loeber & Farrington, 1998). The combination of early antisocial behavior in the child and socioeconomic disadvantage in the family predicts early criminal arrests (Patterson, Crosby, & Vuchinich, 1992).

A study of African American and white youths drawn from the Pittsburgh Youth Study indicates that the commonly found greater severity of delinquent acts among African Americans appears to be linked to their living in poorer neighborhoods, not to their race (Peeples & Loeber, 1994). The researchers designated neighborhoods as "underclass" or "non-underclass" based on factors such as family poverty, families with no one employed, and male joblessness. In the total sample—ignoring differences in socioeconomic status—African American youths were more likely than white youths to have committed serious delinquent acts (e.g., car theft, breaking and entering, aggravated assault). But African American youths who were not living in underclass neighborhoods did not differ from white youths in serious delinquent behavior. Social factors matter. The strongest correlates of delinquency other than neighborhood were hyperactivity and lack of parental supervision; once these factors were controlled, residence in underclass neighborhoods was significantly related to delinquent behavior, whereas ethnicity was not.

Treatment of Conduct Disorder

The treatment of conduct disorder appears to be most effective when addressing the multiple systems involved in the life of a child (family, peers, school, neighborhood).

Family Interventions   Some of the most promising approaches to treating conduct disorder involve intervening with the parents and families of the child. In addition, evidence suggests intervening early, if even just briefly, can make an impact. In a recent randomized controlled trial (D.S. Shaw et al., 2006), researchers compared what is called the "family check up (FCU)" treatment to no treatment. FCU involves three meetings to get to know, assess, and provide feedback to parents regarding their children and parenting practices. In this study, FCU was offered to families with toddlers who were at high risk of developing conduct problems (based on the presence of conduct or substance abuse problems in parents or early signs of conduct behavior in the children). This brief, three-session intervention was associated with less disruptive behavior compared to no treatment, even two years after the intervention.

Gerald Patterson and colleagues have worked for over four decades developing and testing a behavioral program called **parent management training (PMT)**, in which parents are taught to modify their responses to their children so that prosocial rather than antisocial behavior is consistently rewarded. Parents are taught to use techniques such as positive reinforcement when the child exhibits positive behaviors and time-out and loss of privileges for aggressive or antisocial behaviors.

This treatment has been modified by others, but, in general, it is the most efficacious intervention for children with conduct disorder and oppositional defiant disorder. Both parents' and teachers' reports of children's behavior and direct observation of behavior at home and at school support the program's effectiveness (Kazdin, 2005; Patterson, 1982). PMT has been shown to alter parent–child interactions, which in turn is associated with a decrease in antisocial and aggressive behavior (Dishion & Andrews, 1995; Dishion, Patterson, & Kavanagh, 1992). PMT has also been shown to improve the behavior of siblings and reduce depression in mothers involved in the program (Kazdin, 1985). PMT has been adapted for Latino families and has been shown to be effective in modifying parent and child behaviors (Martinez & Eddy, 2005).

Parent management training can be effective in treating conduct disorder. (David Young-Wolff/PhotoEdit.)

Longer-term follow-ups suggest that the beneficial effects of PMT persist for one to three years (Brestan & Eyberg, 1998; Long et al., 1994). Parent and teacher training approaches have been incorporated into larger community-based programs such as Head Start and have been shown to reduce childhood conduct problems and increase positive parenting behaviors (Webster-Stratton, 1998; Webster-Stratton, Reid & Hammond, 2001). (See Focus on Discovery 14.2 for more on Head Start.)

FOCUS ON DISCOVERY 14.2

Head Start: A Successful Community-Based Prevention Program

Head Start is a federally funded program whose goal is to prepare children from low-income families to succeed in the regular school setting. The impetus for the program came during the 1960s, when national attention in the United States was directed to the problems of hunger and civil rights.

The core of the Head Start program is community-based preschool education, focusing on the early development of cognitive and social skills. Head Start contracts with professionals in the community to provide children with health and dental services, including vaccinations, hearing and vision testing, medical treatment, parent training, and nutrition information (Office of Head Start: *http://www.acf.hhs.gov/programs/ohs*). Mental health services are another important component of the Head Start program. Psychologists may identify children with psychological problems and consult with teachers and staff to help make the preschool environment sensitive to psychological issues; for example, they may share knowledge of child development, consult on an individual case, or help staff address parents' concerns. Head Start programs are designed to be sensitive to cultural and ethnic factors affecting children and their families. Social workers can serve as advocates for a child's family, linking families with needed social services and encouraging parents to get involved with their children's education.

A comparison of Head Start children with other disadvantaged children who attended either a different preschool or no preschool showed that Head Start children improved significantly more than both groups on social-cognitive ability and motor impulsivity; the relative improvement was strongest for African American children, particularly those whose initial ability was below average. Although the Head Start program succeeded in enhancing the functioning of the neediest children, they were still behind their peers in terms of absolute cognitive levels after one year in the program (Lee, Brooks-Gunn, & Schnur, 1988). Other reports confirm the value of Head Start in helping poor children improve their intellectual functioning (e.g., Cronan et al., 1996; Perkins, 1995; Schleifer, 1995). The National Head Start Impact study, mandated by Congress in 1998, is a randomized, controlled clinical trial of Head Start that is studying close to 5,000 children in Head Start programs across the country. Data collection for the study began in 2002, and the study seeks to address how Head Start impacts school readiness and what types of children benefit the most from Head Start. Preliminary results, released in 2005, showed that 3- and 4-year-olds demonstrated gains in pre-reading skills and vocabulary, but not in math or oral comprehension after one year in the program (U.S. Department of Health and Human Services, Administration for Children and Families, 2005). These children also showed a decline in behavior problems, and parents of children in Head Start read to their children more often. Plans are to follow the children at the end of kindergarten, first grade, and third grade. More detailed analyses will allow for the examination of what particular types of interventions work best in particular locations and with particular types of children.

Multisystemic Treatment   A promising treatment for serious juvenile offenders is multisystemic treatment (MST) (Borduin et al., 1995). MST involves delivering intensive and comprehensive therapy services in the community, targeting the adolescent, the family, the school, and, in some cases, the peer group (Figure 14.4). The treatment is based on the view that conduct problems are influenced by multiple factors within the family as well as between the family and other social systems.

The strategies used by MST therapists are varied, incorporating behavioral, cognitive, family-systems, and case-management techniques. The therapy's uniqueness lies in emphasizing individual and family strengths, identifying the social context for the conduct problems, using present-focused and action-oriented interventions, and using interventions that require daily or weekly efforts by family members. Treatment is provided in "ecologically valid" settings, such as the home, school, or local recreational center, to maximize the chances that improvement will carry through into the regular daily lives of children and their families. MST has been shown to be effective in a number of studies (Henggeler et al., 1998; Henggeler & Sheidow, in press; Ogden & Halliday-Boykins, 2004).

In comparison with adolescents who received an equivalent number of sessions (about 25) of traditional individual therapy in an office setting, adolescents who received MST showed fewer behavior problems and far fewer arrests over the following four years. For example, whereas more than 70 percent of the adolescents receiving traditional therapy were arrested in the four years after treatment, only 22 percent of those completing MST were arrested. In addition, assessment of other family members indicated that parents involved in MST had fewer psychiatric symptoms, and families were more supportive and showed less conflict and hostility in videotaped interactions. In contrast, the quality of interactions in the families of the adolescents receiving traditional individual therapy deteriorated after treatment. Even the adolescents receiving MST who dropped out of treatment within four sessions were arrested significantly less than adolescents who completed the full course of traditional individual therapy.

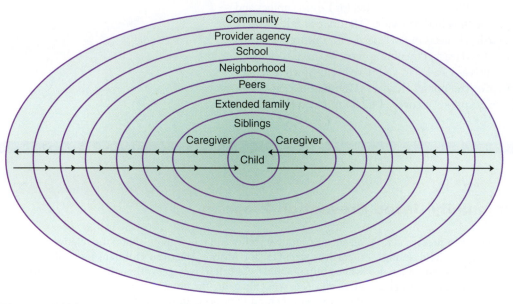

Figure 14.4 Multisystemic treatment (MST) includes consideration of many different factors when developing a child's treatment, including family, school, community, and peers.

Quick Summary

ADHD and conduct disorder are referred to as externalizing disorders. They appear across cultures, although there are also differences in the manifestation of externalizing symptoms in different cultures. Both disorders are more common in boys than girls, though research has begun to examine externalizing problems in girls. A number of factors work together to cause ADHD and conduct disorder. Genetic factors play a particularly important role in ADHD but are also implicated in conduct disorder. Neurobiological research has implicated areas of the brain and neurotransmitters such as dopamine in ADHD; neuropsychological deficits are seen in both disorders. Other risk factors for ADHD include low birth weight and maternal smoking. Family and peer variables are also important factors to consider, especially in how they interact with genetic vulnerabilities. The most effective treatment for ADHD is a combination of medication, such as Ritalin, and behavioral therapy. For conduct disorder, family-based treatments, such as PMT, are effective, as are treatments that include multiple points for intervention, as in MST.

Check Your Knowledge 14.2

Fill in the blanks.

1. Moffitt and colleagues have provided a good deal of evidence for two types of conduct disorder. The _____ type is associated with an early age of onset and continued problems into adolescence and adulthood. The _____ type begins in the teenage years and is hypothesized to remit by adulthood, though a recent follow-up study has not supported the idea that this type remits.

2. Comorbidity is common in conduct disorder. Other problems that co-occur with conduct disorder include: _____, _____, _____, and _____.

3. A successful treatment for conduct disorder that involves the family is called _____. Another successful community-focused treatment that works with the child, parents, peers, and schools is _____.

Depression and Anxiety in Children and Adolescents

So far, we have discussed disorders that are specific to children. The internalizing disorders, which include depression and anxiety disorders, first begin in childhood but are quite common in adults as well. Much richer descriptions of these disorders are presented in Chapter 5 (anxiety disorders) and Chapter 8 (mood disorders). Here, we describe the ways in which the symptoms, etiology, and treatment of these disorders differ in children as compared to adults.

Depression and anxiety disorders commonly co-occur with ADHD and conduct disorder, as we have already noted. Furthermore, depression and anxiety disorders commonly co-occur with each other among children, as they do among adults. Although early research indicated that depression and anxiety can be distinguished in children and adolescents in much the same way as among adults—that is, children with depression show low levels of positive affect and high levels of negative affect, and children with anxiety show high levels of negative affect but do not show low levels of positive affect (Lonigan, Phillips, & Hooe, 2003)—more recent research calls this into question (Anderson & Hope, 2008). Next, we consider in more detail some of the etiological factors and treatment considerations for childhood depression and anxiety.

Depression

Clinical Descriptions and Prevalence of Depression in Childhood and Adolescence
There are both similarities and differences in the symptomatology of children and adults with major depressive disorder (Garber & Flynn, 2001). Children and adolescents ages 7 to 17 and adults both tend to show the following symptoms: depressed mood, inability to experience pleasure, fatigue, concentration problems, and suicidal ideation. Children and adolescents differ from adults in showing more guilt and lower rates of early-morning wakefulness, early-morning depression, loss of appetite, and weight loss. As in adults, depression in children is recurrent. Longitudinal studies have demonstrated that both children and adolescents with major depression are likely to continue to exhibit significant depressive symptoms when assessed even four to eight years later (Garber, Kelly, & Martin, 2002; Lewinsohn et al., 2000).

In general, depression occurs in less than 1 percent of preschoolers (Kashani & Carlson, 1987; Kashani, Holcomb, & Orvaschel, 1986) and in 2 to 3 percent of school-age children (Cohen et al., 1993; Costello et al., 1988). By adolescence, rates of depression are comparable to those of adults (Angold & Rutter, 1992; Kashani et al., 1987).

The prevalence among adolescent girls (7 to 13 percent) is almost twice that among adolescent boys, just as we have seen with adult depression (see Focus on Discovery 8.1). Although adolescent girls experience depression more often than adolescent boys, there are no differences in the types of symptoms they experience (Lewinsohn et al., 2003). Interestingly, the gender difference does not occur before age 12; the full gender difference does not emerge until adolescence (Hankin et al., 1998).

Etiology of Depression in Childhood and Adolescence   What causes a young person to become depressed? As with adults, evidence suggests that genetic factors play a role (Klein et al., 2001). Indeed, the results of genetic studies with adults (see Chapter 8) apply to children and adolescents also, since genetic influences are present from birth, though they may not be expressed right away.

Studies of depression in children have also focused on family and other relationships as sources of stress that might interact with a genetic diathesis. As with adults, early adversity and negative life events also play a role (Garber, 2006). One recent study found that early adversity (e.g., financial hardship, maternal depression, chronic illness as a child) predicted depression between ages 15 and 20, particularly among those adolescents who had experienced a number of negative life events by age 15 (Hazel et al., 2008).

Having a mother or father who is depressed increases the chances of being depressed as a child or adolescent; less is known about the reasons for these linkages (Garber et al., 2002; Kane & Garber, 2004; Lewinsohn et al., 2000). We know that depression in either or both spouses is often associated with marital conflict; we should expect, therefore, that depression will have negative effects on their children, and it does (Hammen, 1997). Rejection by parents is modestly associated with depression in childhood, as confirmed by a recent meta-analysis of 45 studies (McLeod, Weisz, & Wood, 2007). The effect size for parental rejection was considered small across the studies, suggesting that factors other than parental rejection play a larger role in causing depression in childhood.

Once depression begins, it clearly leads to negativity in relationships. Children with depression and their parents have been shown to interact with each other in negative ways; for example, they show less warmth and more hostility toward each other than is the case with children without depression and their parents (Chiariello & Orvaschel, 1995). Children and adolescents experiencing major depression also have poor social skills and impaired relationships with siblings and friends (Lewinsohn et al., 1994). Children with depression have fewer and less satisfying contacts with their peers, who often reject them because they are not enjoyable to be around (Kennedy, Spence, & Hensley, 1989). These negative interactions in turn may aggravate the negative self-image and sense of worth that the depressed child already has (Coyne, 1976). That is, interpersonal problems are probably not just a consequence of depression, but also probably intensify and maintain the depression.

Consistent with both Beck's theory and the hopelessness theory of depression (see Chapter 8), cognitive distortions and negative attributional styles are associated with depression in children and adolescents in ways similar to what has been found with adults (Garber et al., 2002; Lewinsohn et al., 2000). For example, cognitive research with children with depression indicates that their outlooks are more negative than are those of children without depression and resemble those of adults with depression (Prieto, Cole, & Tageson, 1992). Negative thoughts and hopelessness also predict a slower time to recovery from depression among adolescents (Rhode et al., 2006). As with interpersonal functioning, it is important to remember that depression can make children think more negatively (Cole et al., 1998). Hence, it is important to consider longitudinal research.

A key question in the study of children with depression is: when do children actually develop stable attributional styles? That is, can young children have a stable way of thinking about themselves in the midst of such profound cognitive development? Recall from Chapter 8 that attributions can vary in whether they are stable (things will always be bad), internal (it is my fault that things are bad), and global (all aspects of life are bad) negative thoughts. A recent longitudinal study examined the development of attributional style in children (Cole et al., 2008). Specifically, the researchers prospectively studied three groups of children for four years each. At year one of the study, the three groups were (1) children in second grade, (2) children in fourth grade, and (3) children in sixth grade. These three groups were followed yearly until the children were in grades 5, 7, and 9, respectively. Participants completed child and adolescent versions of an attributional style questionnaire along with measures of depression. The results of the study revealed a number of key findings. First, all children could complete the attributional style measure and do so in a manner that was reliable and consistent. However, children's attributional style changed over the course of development. Specifically, attributions became more stable rather than internal or global as children got older. In addition, attributional style didn't appear to be a stable style until children were early adolescents. Finally and importantly, attributional style did not interact with negative life events to predict depression (i.e., it was not a cognitive diathesis) for young children. It wasn't until the children were in eighth or ninth grade that support for attributional style as a cognitive diathesis emerged. Thus, results of this study suggest that attributional style becomes style-like by early adolescence, and by the middle school years, it serves as a cognitive diathesis for depression.

Treatment of Childhood and Adolescent Depression   Research on the safety and efficacy of medications for childhood and adolescent depression has lagged behind research with adults (Emslie & Mayes, 2001). The side effects experienced by some children taking antidepressants include diarrhea, nausea, sleep problems, and agitation (Barber, 2008). In general, evidence suggests that selective serotonin reuptake inhibitors (SSRIs) are superior to tricyclic antidepressants (Emslie, Mayes, & Hughes, 2000; Lynch, Glod, & Fitzgerald, 2001; Wagner & Ambrosini, 2001). Some studies have shown that antidepressant drugs are no better than placebos in children and adolescents (Geller et al., 1992; Keller et al., 2001); however, a recent major trial provided some support for the efficacy of antidepressants. That is, a randomized controlled trial comparing Prozac, cognitive behavioral therapy (CBT), and both combined for adolescents with depression called the Treatment for Adolescents with Depression Study (TADS) found that the combined treatment was the most effective through 12 weeks and that there were modest advantages of Prozac compared to cognitive behavior therapy (March et al., 2004). This pattern of results remained true after 36 weeks (TADS team, 2007). A recent meta–analysis of 27 randomized controlled trials of antidepressant medication treatment for depression and anxiety disorders in children found that the medications were most effective for anxiety disorders other than obsessive compulsive disorder (OCD) and less effective for OCD and depression (Bridge et al., 2007).

Several concerns have been raised about antidepressants, though. A first concern is the potential for side effects. More importantly, concerns with respect to suicidality have prompted a series of recent hearings about antidepressants in the United States and Britain. For example, in the study cited above (March et al., 2004), 7 out of 439 adolescents attempted suicide, of whom 6 were in the Prozac group and 1 was in the CBT group. (See Focus on Discovery 14.3 for more on this complex issue). Evidence is controversial, though, and suicide effects likely occur early in treatment. In the major meta-analysis described above, researchers looked at suicidality rates in the studies of depression (Bridge et al., 2007). The risk of suicidal ideation was 3 percent for those children taking antidepressants and 2 percent for those taking placebo. It is important to note that this analysis shows that children taking medication were at risk for suicidal ideation, not that medication caused the suicide thoughts or attempts. There were no completed suicides in any of the 27 studies reviewed.

Most psychosocial interventions are modeled after treatments developed for adults. Several innovations have been made to adapt these treatments, though. For example, interpersonal therapy has been modified for use with depressed adolescents by focusing on issues of concern to adolescents, such as peer pressure, the stress inherent in the transition from childhood to adulthood, and the conflict between dependency on parents (and parental figures, like teachers) and the drive to be independent (Moreau et al., 1992). Cognitive behavioral treatments in school settings appear to be effective and are associated with more rapid reduction of symptoms than family or supportive therapy (Curry, 2001). About 63 percent of adolescents with depression treated with CBT show significant improvement at the end of treatment (Lewinsohn & Clarke, 1999). However, another study indicated that this favorable outcome does not hold up after treatment is over (Birmaher et al., 2000). A study designed to identify what types of adolescents might benefit the most from CBT found that CBT was most beneficial for Caucasian adolescents, those adolescents with good coping skills at pretreatment, and adolescents with recurrent depression (Rhode et al., 2006). The clinical case of Sharon illustrates CBT techniques with an adolescent. If these findings hold up, it suggests that other types of interventions may be effective for ethnic minority adolescents and for those who are experiencing their first episode of depression.

Clinical Case: Sharon

When initially seen, Sharon was extremely dysphoric, experienced recurrent suicidal ideation, and displayed a number of vegetative signs of depression. . . . [After being] placed on antidepressant medication . . . she was introduced to a cognitive behavioral approach to depression. . . . She was able to understand how her mood was affected by her thoughts and behavior and was able to engage in behavioral planning to increase the occurrence of pleasurable and mastery-oriented events. Sharon manifested extremely high standards for evaluating her performance in a number of areas, and it became clear that her parents also ascribed to these standards, so that family therapy sessions were held to encourage Sharon and her parents to reevaluate their standards.

Sharon had difficulty with the notion of changing her standards and noted that when she was not depressed she actually valued her perfectionism. At that point she resisted the therapy because she perceived it as trying to change something she valued in herself. With this in mind, we began to explore and identify those situations or domains in which her perfectionism worked for her and when and how it might work against her. She became increasingly comfortable with this perspective and decided she wanted to continue to set high standards regarding her performance in mathematical course work (which was a clear area of strength), but she did not need to be so demanding of herself regarding art or physical education. [Adapted from Braswell & Kendall (1988, p. 194).]

A meta-analysis of 35 studies of psychotherapy for depression in children and adolescents found that therapy had a modest effect (Weisz, McCarty, & Valeri, 2006) and that cognitive therapy was no better than noncognitive therapy. Though therapy was effective in the short term, the long-term effects were not as robust. Thus, although psychotherapy is effective, we need to devise more effective treatments.

A good deal of work has focused on how to prevent the onset of depression in adolescents and children. A recent meta-analysis examined two types of preventive interventions for depression: selective and universal (Horowitz & Garber, 2006). Selective prevention programs target particular youth based on family risk factors (e.g., parents with depression), environmental factors (e.g., poverty), or personal factors (e.g., hopelessness). Universal programs are targeted toward large groups, typically in schools, and seek to provide education and information about depression. Results of the meta-analysis indicated that selective prevention programs were more effective than universal programs in preventing depression symptoms among adolescents.

Anxiety

Just about every child experiences fears and worries as part of the normal course of development. Common fears, most of which are outgrown, include fear of the dark and of imaginary creatures (in children under 5) and fear of being separated from parents (in children under 10). In general, as with adults, fears are reported more often for girls than for boys (Lichtenstein & Annas, 2000), though this sex difference may be due at least in part to social pressures on boys that make them reluctant to admit that they are afraid of things.

The seriousness of some childhood anxiety problems should not be underestimated. Not only do children suffer, as do adults, from the aversiveness of being anxious—simply put, anxiety doesn't feel good—but their anxiety may also work against their acquisition of skills appropriate to various stages of their development. For example, a child who is painfully shy and finds interacting with peers virtually intolerable is unlikely to learn important social skills. This deficit may persist as the child grows into adolescence and will form the foundation of still further social difficulties. Then, whether in the workplace or at college, the adolescent's worst fear—"people will dislike and reject me"—is likely to be realized as his or her awkward, even off-putting behavior toward others produces rejecting and avoiding responses.

Clinical Descriptions and Prevalence of Anxiety in Childhood and Adolescence

For fears and worries to be classified as disorders according to DSM-IV-TR criteria, children's functioning must be impaired; unlike adults, however, children need not regard their fear as excessive or unreasonable, because children sometimes are unable to make such judgments.

Based on these criteria, about 12 to 20 percent of children and adolescents would be diagnosed as having an anxiety disorder, making these among the most common disorders of childhood (Achenbach et al., 1995; Shaffer et al., 1996). Although most unrealistic childhood fears dissipate over time, it is also the case that most anxious adults can trace their anxiety back to childhood.

One childhood fear, **school phobia**, sometimes called *school refusal*, has serious academic and social consequences for the child and can be extremely disabling. Two types of school phobia have been identified. The more common type is associated with *separation anxiety*—children worry constantly that some harm will befall their parents or themselves when they are away from their parents. When at home, such children shadow one or both of their parents. Since the beginning of school is often the first circumstance that requires lengthy and frequent separations of children from their parents, separation anxiety is often a principal cause of school phobia.

A second type of school phobia is associated with a true fear of school—either a fear specifically related to school or a more general fear (social phobia). Children with this type of school phobia generally begin refusing to go to school later in life and have more severe and pervasive avoidance of school. Their fear is more likely to be related to specific aspects of the school environment, such as worries about academic failure or discomfort with peers.

Another common anxiety disorder among children and adolescents is social phobia. Most classrooms include at least one or two children who are extremely quiet and shy. Often these children will play only with family members or familiar peers, avoiding strangers both young and old. Their shyness may prevent them from acquiring skills and participating in a variety of activities enjoyed by most of their peers, for they avoid playgrounds and stay out of games played by other children. Extremely shy children may refuse to speak at all in unfamiliar social circumstances, a condition called *selective mutism*. In crowded rooms, they cling and whisper to their parents, hide behind the furniture, cower in corners, and may even have tantrums. At home, they ask their parents endless questions about situations that worry them. Withdrawn children usually have warm and satisfying relationships with family members and family friends, and they show a desire for affection and acceptance.

The point at which this kind of behavior becomes a problem severe enough to be diagnosed as social phobia varies; few reliable statistics have been compiled on the frequency of this disorder. One estimate is that 1 percent of children and adolescents have social phobia (Kashani & Orvaschel, 1990); it is more of a problem with adolescents, who have a more acute concern about the opinions of others than younger children do.

Some children exhibit intense anxiety in specific social situations. For example, when such children were asked to keep daily diaries of anxiety-producing events, they reported experiencing anxiety three times more frequently than did other children, with concerns about such activities as reading aloud before a group, writing on the board, and performing in front of others. They reported crying, avoidance, and somatic complaints such as shakiness and nausea when faced with these tasks (Beidel, 1991).

Children who are exposed to traumas such as chronic abuse, community violence, and natural disasters may experience symptoms of posttraumatic stress disorder (PSTD) similar to those experienced by traumatized adults. As with adults, these symptoms fall into three broad categories: (1) reexperiencing the traumatic event, as in nightmares, flashbacks, or intrusive thoughts; (2) avoiding trauma-related situations or information and experiencing a general numbing of responses, as in feelings of detachment or anhedonia; and (3) hyperarousal, which can include irritability, sleep problems, and hypervigilance (Davis & Siegal, 2000). Some symptoms in children differ from those in adults; for example, children may exhibit signs of agitation instead of extreme fear or hopelessness.

Obsessive compulsive disorder (OCD) is also found among children and adolescents, with prevalence estimates ranging from 1 to 4 percent (Flament et al., 1988; Heyman et al., 2003). The symptoms in childhood are similar to symptoms in adulthood: both obsessions and compulsions are involved. The most common obsessions in childhood involve dirt or contamination as well as aggression; recurrent thoughts about sex or religion become more common in adolescence (Turner, 2006). OCD in children is more common in boys than girls, but this sex difference does not remain in adolescence or adulthood.

School phobia is most commonly associated with separation anxiety disorder, an intense fear of being away from parents or other attachment figures. (David Young-Wolff/PhotoEdit.)

FOCUS ON DISCOVERY 14.3

Controversies in the Diagnosis and Treatment of Children with Psychopathology

In recent years, the number of children diagnosed with psychological disorders has risen, as has the number of children taking psychoactive medications. These increases raise several questions:

Has there truly been an increase in the number of children with psychological disorders?

Have our diagnostic system and assessment measures improved enough to identify children once overlooked?

Are children being misdiagnosed and then treated for problems they do not have?

Are medications safe for children?

Will medication use lead to later drug use or abuse among children?

Here we briefly discuss some of the recent controversies and current evidence in some of these areas.

Bipolar Disorder in Children

For years, professionals thought bipolar disorders were very rare or even nonexistent among children. Today, however, diagnoses of bipolar disorders in children have increased 50-fold. One of the difficult diagnostic issues facing mental health professionals is distinguishing bipolar disorders from ADHD. Agitated behavior can be a sign of both, and only through careful and thorough assessments can the distinction be made. An additional controversy is whether the diagnostic criteria for bipolar disorders in children are the same as the criteria for bipolar disorders in adults. Some argue that the criteria for children should include explosive but brief outbursts of emotion and behavioral dysregulation (e.g., Biederman et al., 2000), but these are fundamentally different from the current DSM-IV-TR criteria for bipolar I disorder (see Chapter 8). And emotion dysregulation is also present in ADHD (Carlson & Meyer, 2006; Dickstein & Liebenluft, 2006). Yet the current DSM criteria apply mainly to adults and may not do a good job of characterizing bipolar disorders, particularly bipolar I disorder, among children. Nevertheless, the American Academy of Child and Adolescent Psychiatry recommends using the adult DSM-IV criteria for diagnosing bipolar disorder in children and adolescents (McClellan et al., 2007). These guidelines also recommend that impairment be identified in two different settings (e.g., home, school), a requirement not found in the DSM-IV-TR. Studies are just now emerging to differentiate bipolar disorder in children from other forms of severe emotion dysregulation with respect to behavior and brain function (Harvey, Mullin, & Hinshaw, 2006; Leibenluft & Rich, 2008). Additional research on bipolar disorders in children, particularly longitudinal research, is clearly needed to sort through these issues.

Antidepressant Medications

In 2002, physicians wrote close to 11 million prescriptions for antidepressant medications for children and adolescents (*New York Times*, September 15, 2004). In the fall of 2004, the Federal Drug Administration (FDA) held a series of hearings on the safety of treating children and adolescents with antidepressant medications. These hearings were prompted by research reports, one of which was kept quiet within the FDA, suggesting that children and adolescents with depression who were taking antidepressant medication were more likely to become suicidal than children who were not taking these medications. Earlier in 2004, Great Britain had prohibited the use of all antidepressants for the treatment of adolescent depression. This decision was based on a review of the research suggesting that the risk of suicide was greater for adolescents taking these medications than adolescents not taking them.

Concerns over the safety of the medications were joined by concerns that these medications were not all that effective in treating depression among children and adolescents. Findings from the TADS (Treatment of Adolescent Depression Study) study, perhaps the largest randomized controlled clinical trial of antidepressant treatment for adolescents, were reported in August 2004 (March et al., 2004). In this study, the most effective treatment was a combination of Prozac and cognitive behavioral therapy (CBT). Prozac alone was slightly better than CBT alone. However, the authors also reported that six adolescents taking Prozac attempted suicide, whereas only one receiving CBT attempted suicide. These seven were from a sample of over 400 and thus represented around 1.5 percent of the sample. The participants in the study were randomly assigned to treatment conditions, so it is less likely that the adolescents taking Prozac were more seriously ill or suicidal than the ones receiving CBT.

Antidepressants can take as long as 3–4 weeks to start working (see Chapter 8), and one analysis of adolescent suicide attempts and antidepressant use found that the risk for suicide was highest in the first 3–4 weeks of treatment. Thus, it could be the case that the medications did not have sufficient time to begin working in the adolescents who attempted suicide. It may also be true that the combined treatment in the TADS study was most effective because CBT began working earlier in the course of treatment. These sorts of issues will need to be sorted out in future studies.

At the end of the FDA hearings, the panel mandated a "black box warning" to accompany information sent to physicians on their use with adolescents. This is the strongest safety warning the FDA can issue with medications. Since then, the numbers of prescriptions for antidepressants have declined. Although suicides among youths have decreased at the same time, there are too many other variables that have changed during this time to know whether the reduction in antidepressant use explains the dropoff in suicide rates.

Stimulant Medications

Over the past two decades, the number of children taking stimulant medications such as Ritalin has risen dramatically (e.g., Angold et al., 2000). Does the use of stimulant medications lead to increases in illicit drug use among children? Two recent prospective, longitudinal studies suggest that the answer to this question is no. In one study, two groups of children with ADHD were studied for 13 years (Barkley et al., 2003). One group of children had been treated with stimulant medication for $3\frac{1}{2}$ years on average and the other group had never received stimulant medication. Consistent with a number of other studies, at follow-up in young adulthood, those who had taken stimulant medication were not more likely to have used illicit drugs than those who had not been treated with stimulant medication, with one exception—those who had taken stimulant medication were at great risk for having tried cocaine. However, after controlling for the severity of conduct disorder symptoms, the relationship between stimulant medication use and trying cocaine disappeared. This suggests that having severe conduct disorder symptoms accounts for the link between stimulant medication and trying cocaine, not the use of stimulant medication per se.

The second study followed into adulthood a group of children with reading disorders who had been treated with stimulant medications for 12 to 18 weeks and compared them to a group of children with reading disorders who had not received stimulant medication. Sixteen years after the medication treatment, the two groups did not differ in their use of illicit drugs (Mannuzza, Klein, & Moulton, 2003).

Autism: Diagnosis and Causes

The number of cases of autism has increased dramatically over the past 10 years. For example, a 14-state study conducted by the Centers for Disease Control and Prevention (CDC) reported the prevalence rate of autism-spectrum disorders (autism, Asperger's disorder) to be 1 in 150 children, up from earlier reports of about 1 in 500 (CDC, 2007). Why has there been such an increase? Are there that many more children with autism, or have mental health professionals gotten better at making a diagnosis? Autism wasn't formally recognized in the DSM until 1980. With the availability of formalized diagnostic criteria, mental health professionals are likely doing a better job now of identifying autism. In addition, the diagnostic criteria have broadened quite a bit between the publication of DSM-III in 1980 and the release of DSM-IV in 1994. More children meet the criteria for a diagnosis of autism today under the broader criteria of DSM-IV than they did under the more narrow criteria of DSM-III (Gernsbacher, Dawson, & Goldsmith, 2005). Additionally, there is greater public awareness of autism, and this may spur families to seek out mental health professionals for a formal psychological assessment. Some children with autism may have been diagnosed with mental retardation in years past; it is likely that more children are now being correctly diagnosed. Also, the delay in or lack of language acquisition has become a widely recognized warning sign among parents and mental health professionals that autism may be a consideration. In addition, public schools are mandated by law to provide services for children with autism, and this may have helped families seek a formal diagnosis. Indeed, the number of children classified as having an autism-spectrum disorder and thus qualifying for special education services increased between 1994 and 2006 by nearly 200,000.

With the increase in autism has come an increase in parents and families advocating for their children. Parents have been particularly worried that autism may be caused by vaccines routinely given to toddlers. The MMR vaccine (for measles, mumps, and rubella) is given to children right around the age when autism signs and symptoms begin to appear. A related concern is that the product used to preserve these vaccines, a substance called thimerosal that contains mercury, may be responsible for autism.

However, there is not much evidence to link autism with either the MMR vaccine or thimerosal. Vaccines have not been stored in thimerosal for the last several years, and even those vaccines that were stored in thimerosal contained very small amounts of mercury (CDC: *www.cdc.gov/ncbddd/autism/vaccines.htm*). One study examined the number of autism diagnoses reported to the California Department of Developmental Services between 1995 and 2007 (Schecter & Grether, 2008). By 2001, all but the smallest trace of thimerosal had been removed from childhood vaccines. If thimerosal was causing autism, the decline in its use in vaccines might correspond to a decrease in the number of new cases of autism. However, the study found no such association. In fact, the number of new cases of autism increased. In May 2004, the Institute of Medicine published the results of its comprehensive review of its available evidence on the link between MMR and autism. This report concluded that the MMR vaccines are not responsible for autism (Institute of Medicine, 2004).

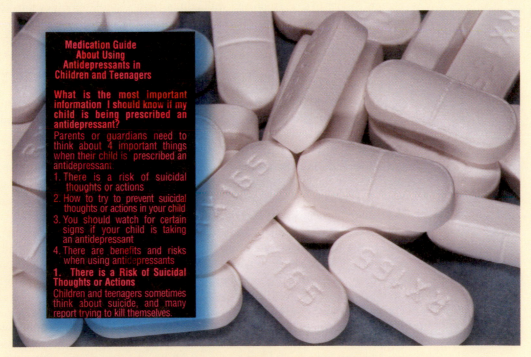

The FDA required black box warnings be put on antidepressants for use with adolescents. (Scott Camazine/Phototake.)

Etiology of Anxiety Disorders in Childhood and Adolescence As with adults, genetics plays a role in anxiety among children, with heritability estimates ranging from 29 to 50 percent in one recent study (Lau et al., 2007). However, genes appear to do their work via the environment, with genetics playing a stronger role in separation anxiety in the context of more negative life events experience by a child (Lau et al., 2007).

Parenting practices play a small role in childhood anxiety. Specifically, parental control, more than parental rejection, is associated with childhood anxiety. However, parental control accounted for only 4 percent of the variance in childhood anxiety according to a recent meta-analysis of 47 studies (McLeod, Weisz, & Wood, 2007). Thus, 96 percent of the variance is accounted for by other factors. Other psychological factors that predict anxiety symptoms among children and adolescents include emotion-regulation problems and insecure attachment in infancy (Bosquet & Egeland, 2006).

Theories of the etiology of social phobia in children are generally similar to theories of social phobia in adults. For example, research has shown that children with anxiety disorders overestimate the danger in many situations and underestimate their ability to cope with them (Boegels & Zigterman, 2000). The anxiety created by these cognitions then interferes with social interaction, causing the child to avoid social situations and thus not to get much practice at social skills. In adolescence, peer relationships are important. Specifically, a longitudinal study found that adolescents who perceived that they were not accepted by their peers were more likely to be socially anxious (Teachman & Allen, 2007).

Theories about the causes of PTSD in children are similar to the theories for adults. There must be exposure to a trauma, either experienced or witnessed. Like adults, children who have a propensity to experience anxiety may be at more risk for developing PTSD after exposure to trauma. Specific risk factors for children may include level of family stress, coping styles of the family, and past experiences with trauma (Martini et al., 1990). Some theorists suggest that parental reactions to trauma can help to lessen children's distress; specifically, if parents appear in control and calm in the face of stress, a child's reaction may be less severe (Davis & Siegal, 2000).

Treatment of Anxiety in Childhood and Adolescence How are childhood fears overcome? Many simply dissipate with time and maturation. For the most part, treatment of such fears is similar to that employed with adults, with suitable modifications to accommodate the different abilities and circumstances of childhood. The major focus of these treatments is on exposure to the feared object. Millions of parents help children overcome fears by exposing them gradually to feared objects, often while acting simultaneously to inhibit their anxiety. If a little girl fears school, a parent takes her by the hand and walks her slowly toward the building. Offering rewards for moving closer to a feared object or situation can also be encouraging to a child who is afraid. Compared to exposure treatments for adults, treatments may be modified for children by including more modeling (seeing an adult approach the feared object) and more reinforcement.

One treatment approach that has empirical support for the treatment of anxiety in children and adolescents is cognitive behavioral therapy (Compton et al., 2004). Evidence indicates that such therapy can be helpful to many children with anxiety disorders (Kendall et al., 2004). This type of treatment typically involves working with both children and parents. Beyond exposure, the treatment includes psychoeducation, cognitive restructuring, modeling, skills training, and relapse prevention (Kendall, Aschenbrand, & Hudson, 2003; Velting, Setzer, & Albano, 2004). One of the more widely used treatments is called the Coping Cat (Kendall et al., 2003). This treatment is used with children between the ages of 7 and 13; it focuses on confronting fears, developing new ways to think about fears, exposure to feared situations, practice, and relapse prevention. Parents are also included in a couple of sessions. At least two randomized controlled clinical trials have shown this treatment to be effective (Kendall, 1994; Kendall et al., 1997). A follow-up study of children who received this treatment found that after 7 years, most children were still anxiety-free. Furthermore, the children who remained anxiety-free after 7 years were less likely to have used drugs such as alcohol or marijuana than children for whom the treatment was less effective (Kendall et al., 2004).

More recently, Kendall and colleagues conducted a randomized controlled trial comparing individual CBT, family CBT, and family psychoeducation for the treatment of childhood anxiety. Both individual and family CBT included the Coping Cat workbook, both were more effective than family psychoeducation at reducing anxiety (Kendall et al. 2008), and the effects lasted one year after treatment. The family CBT was more effective than individual CBT when both parents had an anxiety disorder. This study points to the importance of considering not only the child's anxiety but also levels of parental anxiety when deciding on a treatment for childhood anxiety.

Only a few studies have examined the efficacy of cognitive behavior therapy for OCD in children and adolescents, with only four randomized controlled clinical trials published thus far. Two recent reviews suggest that CBT is an effective treatment for children and adolescents (Freeman et al., 2007). CBT appears to be equally as effective as medication, and CBT plus medication is more effective than medication alone, but not than CBT alone (O'Kearney et al., 2008). CBT does not appear to be as effective for very young children (e.g., ages 3 or 4).

Very few studies have evaluated the efficacy of treatment of PTSD among children and adolescents. The limited available research suggests that cognitive behavioral treatments, along with family involvement, are beneficial (Yule & Canterbury, 1996).

Quick Summary

Anxiety disorders and depression in children are referred to as internalizing disorders. Depression in childhood and adolescence looks similar to depression in adulthood, although there are notable differences. In childhood, depression affects boys and girls equally, but in adolescence girls are affected twice as often as boys. Genetics and stressful life events play a role in depression in childhood. Research on cognitive factors in childhood depression supports the notion that attributional style also plays a role; however, this work must consider the developmental stage of the child. Treatment for depression among children is facing a good deal of controversy, at least where medication is concerned. A randomized controlled trial found that

a combination of medication and CBT was the most effective treatment. Concerns about the effect of medications on suicide risk need to be addressed.

Anxiety and fear are typical in childhood. When fears interfere with functioning, such as keeping a child from school, intervention is warranted. Theories about the causes of anxiety disorders in children are similar to theories about their causes in adulthood, though less research has been done with children on, for example, cognitive factors. Cognitive behavioral therapy is an effective intervention for a number of different anxiety disorders in childhood. Other problems, such as PTSD in childhood, require additional study.

Learning Disabilities

Clinical Case: Tim

Several years ago, Tim was a student in one of our undergraduate courses who showed an unusual pattern of strengths and weaknesses. His comments in class were exemplary, but his handwriting was sometimes indecipherable and his spelling was very poor. After the instructor had noted these problems on his midterm examination, Tim came to see him and explained that he was dyslexic and that it

took him a long time to complete the weekly reading assignments and to write papers and exams. The instructor decided to give Tim extra time for written work because he was obviously of superior intelligence and highly motivated to excel. Given this chance, he earned an A in the course and when he graduated, he was admitted to a leading law school.

A **learning disability** is a condition in which a person shows a problem in a specific area of academic, language, speech, or motor skills that is not due to mental retardation or deficient educational opportunities. Children with a learning disability are usually of average or above-average intelligence but have difficulty learning some specific skill in the affected area (e.g., arithmetic or reading), and thus their progress in school is impeded.

Clinical Descriptions

The term *learning disabilities* is not used by DSM-IV-TR but is used by most mental health professionals to group together three categories of disorders that do appear in DSM-IV-TR: learning disorders, communication disorders, and motor skills disorder. These disorders are described briefly in Table 14.3. Any of these disorders may apply to a child who fails to develop to the degree appropriate to his or her intellectual level in a specific academic, language, or motor skill area. Learning disabilities are often identified and treated within the school system rather than through mental health clinics. An older study suggested that the disorders are only slightly more common in boys (Shaywitz et al., 1990), but a recent study of four large epidemiological samples indicates that reading disorders, at least, are far more common in boys than in girls (Rutter et al., 2004).

Etiology of Learning Disabilities

Most research on learning disabilities concerns dyslexia, perhaps because it is the most prevalent of this group of disorders: it affects 5 to 10 percent of school-age children. Although studies on mathematics disorder are beginning to emerge, research has advanced more slowly in this area.

Etiology of Dyslexia Family and twin studies confirm that there is a heritable component to dyslexia (Pennington, 1995; Raskind, 2001). Furthermore, the genes that are associated with dyslexia are the same genes associated with typical reading abilities (Plomin & Kovas, 2005). These so-called "generalist genes" are thus important for understanding normal as well as abnormal reading abilities.

There is fairly good consensus among investigators that the core deficits in dyslexia include problems in language processing. Evidence from psychological, neuropsychological, and neuroimaging studies supports this contention. Research points to one or more problems in language processing that might underlie dyslexia, including perception of speech and analysis of the sounds of spoken language and their relation to printed words (Mann & Brady, 1988), difficulty recognizing rhyme and alliteration (Bradley & Bryant, 1985), problems with rapidly naming familiar objects (Scarborough, 1990; Wolf, Bally, & Morris, 1986), and delays in learning syntactic rules

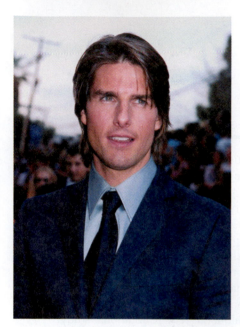

Tom Cruise, a highly successful actor, suffers from dyslexia. (AP/Wide World Photos.)

Table 14.3 Learning Disorders in DSM-IV-TR

Learning Disorders include three categories:

- **Reading disorder**, better known as **dyslexia**, involves significant difficulty with word recognition, reading comprehension, and typically written spelling as well.
- **Disorder of written expression** involves an impairment in the ability to write (including spelling errors, errors in grammar and punctuation, and very poor handwriting).
- **Mathematics disorder** involves difficulty in rapidly and accurately recalling arithmetic facts, counting objects correctly and quickly, and aligning numbers in columns.

Communication Disorders include three categories:

- **Expressive language disorder** involves difficulty expressing oneself in speech, including difficulties in word finding, speaking in phrases only by age 4, below-age-level use of grammar.
- **Phonological disorder** involves correct comprehension and sufficient vocabularly use, but unclear speech and improper articulation. For example, *blue* comes out *bu*, and *rabbit* sounds like *wabbit*. With speech therapy, complete recovery occurs in almost all cases, and milder cases may recover spontaneously by age 8.
- **Stuttering** is a disturbance in verbal fluency that is characterized by one or more of the following speech patterns: frequent repetitions or prolongations of sounds, long pauses between words, substituting easy words for those that are difficult to articulate (e.g., words beginning with certain consonants), and repeating whole words (e.g., saying "go-go-go-go" instead of just a single "go"). DSM-IV-TR estimates that up to 80 percent of people with stuttering recover, most of them without professional intervention, before the age of 16.

Motor skills disorder, also referred to as *developmental coordination disorder*, involves marked impairment in the development of motor coordination that is not explainable by mental retardation or a disorder such as cerebral palsy.

(Scarborough, 1990). Many of these processes fall under what is called *phonological awareness*, which is believed to be critical to the development of reading skills (Anthony & Lonigan, 2004).

Studies using various brain-imaging techniques support the idea that children with dyslexia have a problem in phonological awareness. These studies show that areas in the left temporal, parietal, and occipital regions of the brain are important for phonological awareness, and these same regions are centrally involved in dyslexia.

For example, a study using fMRI found that, compared with children without dyslexia, children with dyslexia failed to activate the temporoparietal area during a phonological processing task (Temple et al., 2001). A larger study using fMRI found that compared to children without dyslexia, children with dyslexia showed less activation in the left temporoparietal and occipitotemporal areas while doing a number of reading relevant tasks, such as identifying letters and sounding out words (Shaywitz et al., 2002). A treatment study showed that after a year of intensive treatment for reading problems, children with dyslexia were better readers and also showed greater activation in the left temporoparietal and occipitotemporal areas while completing a reading task, compared to a group of children who received a less intensive treatment (Shaywitz et al., 2004).

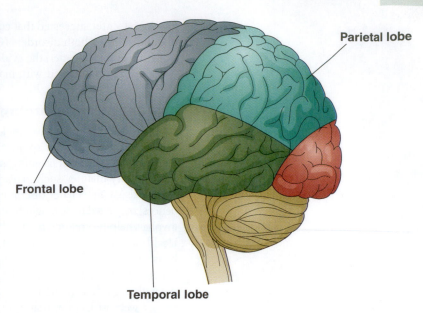

Figure 14.5 Areas of the brain implicated in dyslexia include parts of the frontal, parietal, and temporal lobes, at least in Western cultures.

Similar findings using fMRI have been found among adults with dyslexia (Horwitz, Ramsey, & Donahue, 1998; Klingberg et al., 2000). An fMRI study with adults examined three different types of readers (Shaywitz et al., 2003). The first group was called persistently poor readers (PPR)—they had trouble reading early in school (second grade) and later in school (ninth or tenth grade). The second group was called accuracy improved (AI)—they had trouble reading early in school but not later in school. The third group was called nonimpaired readers (NI)—they had no trouble with reading either early or late in school. On behavioral reading tasks completed outside the scanner, the PPR group performed more poorly than the AI and NI groups. On many tests, the AI group performed as well as the NI group, suggesting they had compensated for their early reading problems. However, the brain-imaging results told a different story. Specifically, the NI group activated the traditional areas of the brain linked to reading: the left temporal-parietal-occipital regions. However, the AI group did not show as much activation in these areas but did show activation in areas on the right side of the brain, suggesting that their compensation for early reading problems relied on areas of the brain not traditionally involved in reading. Paradoxically, the PPR group also activated the left side of the brain linked with reading. However, this group of poor readers also activated other areas of the brain associated with memory, suggesting that they were trying to rely on memorization of words to read rather than on language areas more efficiently used in reading.

It should be noted that the fMRI studies discussed above were done with children and adults in the United States who spoke English. A study examining Chinese children with dyslexia failed to find a problem with the temporoparietal area of the brain during reading tasks; instead, the left middle frontal gyrus showed less activation (Siok et al., 2004). The investigators speculate that the differences between the English and Chinese languages of may account for the different brain regions involved. Reading English requires putting together letters that represent sounds. Reading Chinese, in contrast, requires putting together symbols that represent meanings. Indeed, reading Chinese requires mastery of nearly 6,000 different symbols. Thus, Chinese relies more on visual processing, while English relies more on sound processing.

Etiology of Mathematics Disorder   Only one twin study has been conducted on the heritability of mathematics disorder, finding a heritability estimate of 0.38 (Alacorn et al., 1997). There is also evidence of some genetic influence on individual variations in math skills. In particular, the type of math disability that involves poor semantic memory is most likely to be heritable. A study of over 250 twin pairs conducted through the Colorado Learning Disabilities

Recent interventions for dyslexia have improved children's reading. (Scholastic Studio 10/Index Stock.)

Research Center suggested that common genetic factors underlie both reading and math deficits in children with both disorders (Gillis & DeFries, 1991; Plomin & Kovas, 2005). Furthermore, as with reading disorder, the evidence suggests that any genes associated with mathematics disorder are also associated with mathematics ability (Plomin & Kovas, 2005).

Treatment of Learning Disabilities

Several strategies are used to treat learning disabilities, both in school programs and in private tutoring. Traditional linguistic approaches, used primarily in cases of reading and writing difficulties, focus on instruction in listening, speaking, reading, and writing skills in a logical, sequential, and multisensory manner, such as reading out loud under close supervision. In young children, readiness skills, such as letter discrimination, phonetic analysis, and learning letter–sound correspondences, may need to be taught before explicit instruction in reading is attempted. Phonics instruction involves helping children master the task of converting sounds to words (National Institute of Child Health and Human Development, 2000). Findings from the National Reading Panel, a comprehensive review of the research on teaching children to read, indicate that phonics instruction is beneficial for children with reading difficulties. Like the clinical case of Tim described earlier, people with dyslexia can often succeed in college with the aid of instructional supports, such as podcast or webcast lectures that can be re-reviewed, tutors, and untimed tests. Colleges are required by law to provide special services to help such students, and public schools are now required to provide transitional vocational and career planning for older adolescents with learning disabilities.

One promising development in treating communication disorders (Merzenich et al., 1996; Tallal et al., 1996) is based on previous findings that children with such disorders have difficulty discriminating certain sounds. Researchers developed special computer games and audiotapes that slow speech sounds. After intensive training with these modified speech stimuli for 1 month, children with severe language disorders were able to improve their language skills to the point at which they were functioning as typically developing children do. Similar training using unmodified speech stimuli resulted in very little progress.

Based on their promising initial findings, these investigators expanded the treatment, now called Fast ForWord, and conducted a larger study including 500 children from the United States and Canada. Children received daily training for 6 to 8 weeks, and results again indicated that the intervention was effective. Children improved in speech, language, and auditory processing skills by about $1\frac{1}{2}$ years of ability (Tallal et al., 1998). The researchers speculate that this training method may even help prevent dyslexia, since many reading-disordered children had difficulties understanding language as young children.

Most children with learning disabilities have probably experienced a great deal of frustration and failure, eroding their motivation and confidence. Whatever their design, treatment programs should provide opportunities for children to experience feelings of mastery and self-confidence. Rewarding small steps can be useful in increasing the child's motivation, helping the child focus attention on the learning task, and reducing behavioral problems caused by frustration.

Mental Retardation

In this section, we first examine the DSM-IV-TR perspective on **mental retardation** and then discuss the approach of the American Association on Intellectual and Developmental Disabilities, the principal professional organization devoted to research, education, and application in the field of mental retardation.

Diagnosis and Assessment of Mental Retardation

Mental Retardation in DSM-IV-TR   The DSM-IV-TR diagnostic criteria for mental retardation, an Axis II disorder, include (1) significantly below average intellectual functioning, (2) deficits in adaptive behavior, and (3) an onset prior to age 18.

Intelligence Test Scores   About two-thirds of the population achieves IQ (intelligent quotient) test scores between 85 and 115. Those with a score below 70 to 75, two standard deviations below the mean of the population, meet the criterion of "significant subaverage general intellectual functioning." About 3 percent of the population falls into this category.

Adaptive Functioning Adaptive functioning refers to mastering childhood skills such as toileting and dressing; understanding the concepts of time and money; being able to use tools, to shop, and to travel by public transportation; and becoming socially responsive. An adolescent, for example, is expected to be able to apply academic skills, reasoning, and judgment to daily living and to participate in group activities. An adult is expected to be self-supporting and to assume social responsibilities. Several tests have been constructed to assess adaptive behavior. Best known are the Adaptive Behavior Scale, or ABS (Nihira et al., 1975), and the Vineland Adaptive Behavior Scales (Sparrow, Ballo, & Cicchetti, 1984; see Table 14.4).

Table 14.4 Sample Items from the Vineland Adaptive Behavior Scales

Age (Years)	Adaptive Ability
2	Says at least 50 recognizable words. Removes front-opening coat, sweater, or shirt without assistance.
5	Tells popular story, fairy tale, lengthy joke, or plot of television program. Ties shoelaces into a bow without assistance.
8	Keeps secrets or confidences for more than 1 day. Orders own meal in a restaurant.
11	Uses the telephone for all kinds of calls without assistance. Watches television or listens to radio for information about a particular area of interest.
16	Looks after own health. Responds to hints or indirect cues in conversation.

Source: From Sparrow et al, (1984).

Age of Onset The third DSM-IV-TR criterion is that mental retardation must be manifested before age 18, to rule out classifying as mental retardation any deficits in intelligence and adaptive behavior that result from injury or illnesses occurring later in life.

Levels of Mental Retardation Table 14.5 shows the four levels of mental retardation recognized in DSM-IV-TR, each corresponding to a specific range of IQ scores. However, because IQ is not the sole basis of diagnosis, persons with a low IQ score but no deficits in adaptive behavior would not be considered to have mental retardation. In practice, the IQ criterion is usually applied only after deficits in adaptive behavior have been identified.

The Approach of the American Association on Intellectual and Developmental Disabilities The American Association on Intellectual and Developmental Disabilities (AAIDD) is an organization whose mission is to "promote progressive policies, sound research, effective practices, and universal human rights for people with intellectual disabilities" (AAIDD: www.aaidd.org). The group changed its name in 2006 (it was formerly know as the American Association of Mental Retardation) in large part to acknowledge that intellectual disability is now

Table 14.5 DSM-IV-TR Categories of Mental Retardation

Mild mental retardation (50–55 to 70 IQ). About 85 percent of all those with IQs of less than 70 are classified as having mild mental retardation.

Moderate mental retardation (35–40 to 50–55 IQ). About 10 percent of those with IQs of less than 55 are classified as having moderate mental retardation.

Severe mental retardation (20–25 to 35–40 IQ). About 3 to 4 percent of those with IQs less than 40 are classified as having severe mental retardation.

Profound mental retardation (below 20–25 IQ). About 1 to 2 percent of people with IQs less than 25 are classified as having profound mental retardation.

Source: DSM-IV-TR (APA 2000).

DSM-IV-TR Criteria for Mental Retardation

- Significantly below average intellectual functioning, IQ less than 70
- Deficits in adaptive social functioning in at least two of the following areas: communication, self-care, home living, interpersonal skills, use of community resources, ability to make own decisions, functional academic skills, leisure, work, health, and safety
- Onset before age 18

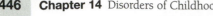

Table 14.6 The AAIDD Definition of Intellectual Disability (Mental Retardation)

Mental retardation is a disability characterized by significant limitations both in intellectual functioning and in adaptive behavior as expressed in conceptual, social, and practical adaptive skills.

This disability originates before age 18.

Five Assumptions Essential to the Application of the Definition

1. Limitations in present functioning must be considered within the context of community environments typical of the individual's age, peers, and culture.

2. Valid assessment considers cultural and linguistic diversity as well as differences in communication, sensory, motor, and behavioral factors.

3. Within an individual, limitations often coexist with strengths.

4. An important purpose of describing limitations is to develop a profile of needed supports.

5. With appropriate personalized supports over a sustained a period, the life functioning of the person with mental retardation generally will improve.

Source: © 2002 American Association on Mental Retardation. Reproduced with permission of the American Association on Mental Retardation in the format Textbook via Copyright Clearance Center.

the preferred term over mental retardation (Schalock et al., 2007). AAIDD has been in existence since 1876 and has routinely published guidelines for classifying and defining mental retardation that are less focused on identifying severity of disability and more on determining what steps are necessary to facilitate higher functioning. The 10th edition of the AAIDD guidelines for defining intellectual disability was published in 2002; the guidelines are presented in Table 14.6. These guidelines are followed by professionals more than are the DSM-IV-TR criteria.

Professionals are encouraged to identify an individual's strengths and weaknesses on psychological, physical, and environmental dimensions with a view toward determining the kinds and degrees of support needed to enhance the person's functioning in different domains. The approach focuses more on what people can do than on what they cannot do and directs professional attention to how best to make positive changes in the people's lives.

The AAIDD approach encourages a more individualized assessment of a person's skills and needs than does the DSM-IV-TR. As an example of the AAIDD approach to classification,

When assessing adaptive behavior, the environment must be considered. A person living in a rural community may not need the same skills as those needed by someone living in New York City, and vice versa. (Left: Gene Peach/Liaison Agency, Inc./Getty Images; right: Joseph Rodriguez/Black Star.)

consider Roger, a 24-year-old man with an IQ of 45 who has attended a special program for people with mental retardation since he was 6. According to DSM-IV-TR, he would be considered moderately mentally retarded. Based on this diagnosis, he would not be expected to be able to live independently, get around on his own, or progress beyond second grade. The AAIDD classification system, however, would emphasize what is needed to maximize Roger's functioning. Thus, a clinician might discover that Roger can use the bus system if he takes a route familiar to him, and thus he might be able to go to a movie by himself from time to time. And although he cannot prepare complicated meals, he might be able to learn to prepare frozen entrées in a microwave oven. The assumption is that by building on what he can do, Roger will make more progress.

In the schools, an individualized educational placement (IEP) is based on the person's strengths and weaknesses and on the amount of instruction needed. Students are identified by the classroom environment they are judged to need. This approach can lessen the stigmatizing effects of having mental retardation and may also encourage a focus on what can be done to improve the student's learning.

Etiology of Mental Retardation

At this time, the primary cause of mental retardation can be identified in only 25 percent of the people affected. The causes that can be identified are typically neurobiological.

Genetic or Chromosomal Abnormalities   Chromosomal abnormalities occur in just under 5 percent of all recognized pregnancies. Most of these pregnancies end in miscarriage. In all, about one-half of one percent of newborns have a chromosomal abnormality (Smith, Bierman, & Robinson, 1978). A significant proportion of these infants die soon after birth. Of the babies who survive, the majority have **Down syndrome**, or *trisomy 21*. Down syndrome is found in about 1 in 800 to 1,200 live births.

Down syndrome is named after the British physician Langdon Down, who first described its clinical signs in 1866. In 1959 the French geneticist Jerome Lejeune and colleagues identified its genetic basis. Human beings normally possess 46 chromosomes, inheriting 23 from each parent. People with Down syndrome almost always have 47 chromosomes instead of 46. During maturation of the egg, the two chromosomes of pair 21, the smallest ones, fail to separate. If the egg unites with a sperm, there will be three of chromosome 21—thus the technical term *trisomy 21*.

People with Down syndrome have mental retardation as well as some distinctive physical signs, such as short and stocky stature; oval, upward-slanting eyes; a prolongation of the fold of the upper eyelid over the inner corner of the eye; sparse, fine, straight hair; a wide and flat nasal bridge; square-shaped ears; a large, furrowed tongue, which may protrude because the mouth is small and its roof low; and short, broad hands.

About 40 percent of children with Down syndrome have heart problems; a small minority may have blockages of the upper intestinal tract; and about one in six dies during the first year. Mortality after age 40 is high.

Another chromosomal abnormality that can cause mental retardation is **fragile X syndrome**, which involves a mutation in the fMR1 gene on the X chromosome (National Fragile X Foundation: www.fragilex.org). Physical symptoms associated with fragile X include facial features such as large, underdeveloped ears and a long, thin face. Many people with fragile X syndrome have mental retardation. Others have average IQ but show problems such as learning disabilities, difficulties on neuropsychological tests, and mood lability. About a third of children with fragile X syndrome also exhibit autism-spectrum behaviors, suggesting that the fMR1 gene may be one of the many genes that contribute to autism (Hagerman, 2006).

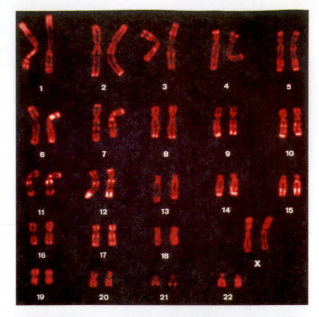

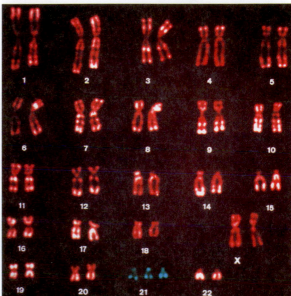

(Top) The normal complement of chromosomes is 23 pairs. (Bottom) In Down syndrome, there are three copies (a trisomy) of chromosome 21. (Kunkel/Phototake.)

Child with Down syndrome. (Terry McKoy/Index Stock.)

Recessive-Gene Diseases   Several hundred recessive-gene diseases have been identified, and many of them cause mental retardation. Here we discuss one recessive-gene disease, phenylketonuria.

In **phenylketonuria (PKU),** the infant, born without obvious signs of difficulty, soon begins to suffer from a deficiency of a liver enzyme, phenylalanine hydroxylase. This enzyme is needed to convert phenylalanine, an amino acid contained in protein, to tyrosine, an amino acid that is essential for the production of certain hormones, such as epinephrine. Because of this enzyme deficiency, phenylalanine and its derivative, phenylpyruvic acid, are not broken down and instead build up in the body's fluids. This buildup eventually damages the brain because the unmetabolized amino acid interferes with the process of myelination, the sheathing of neuron axons, which is essential for neuronal function. Myelination supports the rapid transmittal of neuronal impulses. The neurons of the frontal lobes, the site of many important cognitive functions, such as decision making, are particularly affected, and mental retardation can be profound.

Although PKU is rare, with an incidence of about 1 in 14,000 live births, it is estimated that 1 person in 70 is a carrier of the recessive gene. A blood test is available for prospective parents who have reason to suspect that they might be carriers. Pregnant women who carry the recessive gene must monitor their diet closely so that the fetus will not be exposed to toxic levels of phenylalanine (Baumeister & Baumeister, 1995). State laws require testing newborns for PKU. After the newborn with PKU has consumed milk for several days, an excess amount of unconverted phenylalanine can be detected in the blood. If the test is positive, the parents are taught to provide the infant a diet low in phenylalanine.

Parents are encouraged to introduce the special diet as early as possible and to maintain it indefinitely. Studies have indicated that children whose dietary restrictions stop at age 5–7 begin to show subtle declines in functioning, particularly in IQ, reading, and spelling (Fishler et al., 1987; Legido et al., 1993). Even among children with PKU who maintain the diet, however, deficits in perceptual, memory, and attentional abilities have been observed (Banich et al., 2000; Huijbregts et al., 2002).

Infectious Diseases   While in utero the fetus is at increased risk of mental retardation resulting from maternal infectious diseases such as rubella (German measles). The consequences of these diseases are most serious during the first trimester of pregnancy, when the fetus has no detectable immunological response, that is, its immune system is not developed enough to ward off infection. Cytomegalovirus, toxoplasmosis, rubella, herpes simplex, HIV, and syphilis are all maternal infections that can cause both physical deformities and mental retardation in the fetus. The mother may experience slight or no symptoms from the infection, but the effects on the developing fetus can be devastating.

Infectious diseases can also affect a child's developing brain after birth. Encephalitis and meningococcal meningitis may cause brain damage and even death if contracted in infancy or early childhood. In adulthood, these infections are usually far less serious. There are several forms of childhood meningitis, a disease in which the protective membranes of the brain are acutely inflamed and fever is very high.

Accidents   In the United States, accidents are the leading cause of severe disability and death in children over one year of age. Falls near-drownings, and automobile accidents are among the most common mishaps in early childhood and may cause head injuries leading to varying degrees of mental retardation. Laws mandating that children sit in safety seats and wear seat belts in automobiles and that they wear protective helmets when bicycling play a major role in reducing the incidence of mental retardation in children.

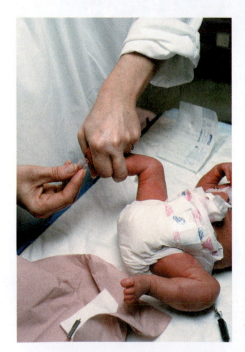

States require that newborns be tested for PKU. If excess phenylalanine is found in the blood, a special diet is recommended for the baby. (Garo/Photo Researchers, Inc.)

Environmental Hazards   Several environmental pollutants are implicated in mental retardation. One such pollutant is mercury, which may be ingested by eating affected fish. Another is lead, which is found in lead-based paints, smog, and the exhaust from automobiles that burn leaded gasoline. Lead poisoning can cause kidney and brain damage as well as anemia, mental retardation, seizures, and death. Lead-based paint is now prohibited in the United States, but it is still found in older homes, where children may eat pieces that flake off.

Treatment of Mental Retardation

Residential Treatment   Since the 1960s, there have been serious and systematic attempts to educate children with mental retardation as fully as possible. Most people with mental retardation can acquire the competence needed to function effectively in the community. The trend has been to provide these people with educational and community services rather than institutionalizing them in hospitals, where they receive mainly custodial care.

Since 1975, people with mental retardation have had a legal right to appropriate treatment in the least restrictive setting. Ideally, adults with mental retardation live in small to medium-sized residences that are integrated into the community. Medical care is provided, and trained, live-in supervisors and aides help with residents' special needs around the clock. Residents are encouraged to participate in household routines to the best of their abilities. Many adults with mental retardation have jobs and are able to live independently in their own apartments. Others live semi-independently in apartments housing three to four adults; generally, a counselor provides aid in the evening.

Behavioral Treatments   Early-intervention programs using behavioral techniques have been developed to improve the level of functioning of people with mental retardation. Specific behavioral objectives are defined, and children are taught skills in small, sequential steps (Reid, Wilson, & Faw, 1991).

Children with severe mental retardation usually need intensive instruction to be able to feed, toilet, and groom themselves. To teach a child a particular routine, the therapist usually begins by dividing the targeted behavior, such as eating, into smaller components: pick up spoon, scoop food from plate onto spoon, bring spoon to mouth, remove food with lips, chew, and swallow food. Operant conditioning principles are then applied to teach the child these components of eating. For example, the child may be reinforced for successive approximations to picking up the spoon until he or she is able to do so. This operant approach, sometimes called *applied behavior analysis*, is also used to reduce inappropriate and self-injurious behavior. These behaviors can often be reduced by reinforcing substitute behaviors.

Studies of these programs indicate consistent improvements in fine motor skills, acceptance by others, and self-help skills. However, the programs appear to have little effect on gross motor skills and linguistic abilities, and no long-term improvements in IQ or school performance have been demonstrated.

Cognitive Treatments   Many children with mental retardation fail to use strategies in solving problems, and when they do use strategies, they often do not use them effectively. Self-instructional training teaches these children to guide their problem-solving efforts through speech.

For example, one group of researchers taught high school students with IQs below 40 to make their own buttered toast and clean up after themselves (Hughes, Hugo, & Blatt, 1996). A teacher would demonstrate and verbalize the steps involved in solving a problem, such as the toaster's being upside down or unplugged. The young people learned to talk themselves through the steps using simple verbal or signed instructions. For example, when the toaster was presented upside down, the person would be taught to first state the problem ("Won't go in"), then to state the response ("Turn it"), self-evaluate ("Fixed it"), and self-reinforce ("Good"). They were rewarded with praise and high-fives when they verbalized and solved the problem correctly. Several studies have demonstrated that even people with severe mental retardation can learn self-instructional approaches to problem solving and then generalize the strategy to new tasks, including taking lunch orders at a cafeteria and performing janitorial duties (Hughes & Agran, 1993).

Computer-Assisted Instruction   Computer-assisted instruction is increasingly found in educational and treatment settings of all kinds; it may be especially well suited to the education of people with mental retardation.

Although lead-based paint is now illegal, it can still be found in older homes. Eating these paint chips can cause lead poisoning, which can cause mental retardation. (James Keyser/Time Inc. Picture Collection.)

Computer-assisted instruction is well suited for applications in the treatment of mental retardation. (Robin Nelson/PhotoEdit.)

The visual and auditory components of computers maintain the attention of distractible students; the level of the material can be geared to the individual, ensuring successful experiences; and the computer can meet the need for numerous repetitions of material without becoming bored or impatient, as a human teacher might. For example, computers have been used to help people with mental retardation learn to use an ATM (Davies, Stock, & Wehmeyer, 2003). PDAs or smart phones can be enormously helpful by serving as aids for reminders, directions, instructions, and daily tasks.

Quick Summary

Learning disorders, communication disorders, and motor skills disorders are all referred to by mental health professionals as learning disabilities. Most research has been conducted on learning disorders, particularly dyslexia. Children with dyslexia have significant difficulty with word recognition, reading comprehension, and typically written spelling as well. Research has uncovered how the brain is involved in dyslexia, particularly areas of the brain that support language, including the temporoparietal and occipitotemporal areas. However, important cultural differences have been noted, suggesting that there may not be one universal mechanism to account for dyslexia. The ways in which different languages are supported by the brain will be an important part of future research. Interventions for dyslexia involve inten-

sive work on reading and language skills. Not only are these interventions successful, but they may also promote changes in the brain that could contribute to the longer-term success of the treatment.

The DSM-IV-TR continues to include categories of mental retardation based on IQ scores (mild, moderate, severe, profound). However, most professionals agree that this approach is not particularly helpful for treatment. The approach of the AAIDD stresses the importance of identifying an individual's strengths and weaknesses. There are a number of known causes of mental retardation, including chromosomal abnormalities, brain injury, infections, and toxins. Environmental influences such as poverty and nutrition are believed to play a part in milder forms of mental retardation.

Check Your Knowledge 14.3

Answer the questions.
1. Which of the following is not considered a learning disability?
   a. mathematics disorder
   b. dyslexia
   c. mental retardation
   d. expressive language disorder
2. A recent study examining children with dyslexia who spoke either Chinese or English found:
   a. The left middle frontal gyrus showed less activation during reading among Chinese-speaking children with dyslexia.
   b. The left temporoparietal cortex showed less activation during reading among Chinese-speaking children with dyslexia.

   c. The left middle frontal gyrus showed less activation during reading among English-speaking children with dyslexia.
   d. The left temporoparietal cortex showed more activation during reading among English-speaking children with dyslexia.
3. Which of the following has not been established as a cause for mental retardation?
   a. chromosomal abnormalities such as trisomy 21
   b. PKU
   c. lead poisoning
   d. All the above have been found to cause mental retardation.

Autistic Disorder

Imagine that you are in a special education classroom for children. You are taking a course on child disabilities, and one of the requirements is to volunteer some time in this class. One of the children in the room is standing in front of a fish tank. You notice his graceful, deft movements, his dreamy smile, and the remote look in his eyes. You start talking to him about the fish, but instead of acknowledging your comment, or even your presence, he begins rocking back and forth while continuing to smile, as if enjoying a private joke. Later, you ask the teacher about the boy, and she tells you that he has autistic disorder.

Clinical Descriptions

Autistic disorder was identified in 1943 by a psychiatrist at Johns Hopkins, Leo Kanner, who, in the course of his clinical work, noted 11 disturbed children who behaved in ways that were not common in children with mental retardation or schizophrenia. He named the syndrome *early infantile autism* because he observed that "there is from the start an extreme autistic aloneness that, whenever possible, disregards, ignores, shuts out anything that comes to the child from the outside" (Kanner, 1943).

Kanner considered autistic aloneness the most fundamental symptom. He also learned that these 11 children had been unable from the beginning of life to relate to people in the ordinary way. They were severely limited in language and had a strong, obsessive desire for everything about them to remain unchanged. Despite its early description by Kanner and others (Rimland, 1964), the disorder was not accepted into official diagnostic nomenclature until the publication of DSM-III in 1980.

Autistic disorder begins in early childhood and can be evident in the first months of life. It affects about one of every 150 children. Studies show that about four times more boys than girls have autism (Volkmar, Szatmari, & Sparrow, 1993). There has been a large increase in the number of autism diagnoses over the past 25 years—close to a 300 percent increase in California, for example (Maugh, 2002) (see Focus on Discovery 14.3 for more on this). Autism is found in all socioeconomic, ethnic, and racial groups. The diagnosis of autism is remarkably stable. In one recent study, only 1 out of 84 children diagnosed with autism at age 2 no longer met the diagnostic criteria at age 9 (Lord et al., 2006).

Asperger's disorder is often regarded as a mild form of autism. The disorder is named after Hans Asperger, who in 1944 described the syndrome as being less severe and with fewer communication deficits than autism. Social relationships are poor and stereotyped behavior is intense and rigid, but language and intelligence are intact. It is not clear if Asperger's disorder differs qualitatively from autistic disorder or if it differs only in severity. More research has been conducted in the last 10 years on Asperger's disorder, perhaps due to the recognition of this condition among adults who for years wondered why they were different from others. Adults with Asperger's disorder are now more frequently recognized and treated by mental health professionals (Gaus, 2007).

Autism and Asperger's disorder are considered two types of **pervasive developmental disorders** (PDDs), a term first introduced in DSM-III. Two other PDDs are described in Table 14.7. When applied to autism, the term *pervasive developmental disorder* implies that autism involves a serious abnormality in the developmental process itself and thus differs from the mental disorders that originate in adulthood. Because there is not as much research on the other pervasive developmental disorders, we focus here on autism.

Autism and Mental Retardation   Many children with autism score below 70 on standardized intelligence tests, which sometimes makes it difficult to distinguish between autistic disorder and mental retardation. There are important differences, however. Children with mental retardation usually score poorly on all parts of an intelligence test, but children with autism may score

---

Table 14.7 Additional Pervasive Developmental Disorders in DSM-IV-TR

Rett's disorder is very rare and is found only in girls. Development is entirely normal until the first or second year of life, when the growth of the child's head decelerates. She loses the ability to use her hands for purposeful movements, instead engaging in stereotyped movements such as hand wringing or hand washing; walks in an uncoordinated manner; learns only poorly to speak and to understand others; and is profoundly retarded. The child does not relate well to others, though this may improve later in life.

Childhood disintegrative disorder occurs in children who have had normal development in the first 2 years of life followed by significant loss of social, play, language, and motor skills. Abnormalities in social interaction and communication and the presence of stereotyped behavior are very similar to those in autism. There has been considerable debate concerning the validity of childhood disintegrative disorder and whether it is distinct from autistic disorder (Hendry, 2000).

DSM-IV-TR Criteria for Autistic Disorder

- A total of six or more items from A, B, and C below, with at least two from A and one each from B and C:

  A. Impairment in social interactions as manifested by at least two of the following:

  Marked impairment in use of nonverbal behaviors such as eye contact, facial expression, body language

  Deficit in development of peer relationships appropriate to developmental level

  Lack of spontaneous sharing of things or activities with others

  Lack of social or emotional reciprocity

  B. Impairment in communication as manifested by at least one of the following:

  Delay in or total lack of spoken language without attempts to compensate by nonverbal gestures

  In those who have some speech, marked impairment in ability to initiate or sustain a conversation with another

  Repetitious or idiosyncratic language

  Lack of developmentally appropriate play

  C. Repetitive or stereotyped behaviors or interests, manifested by at least one of the following:

  Abnormal preoccupation with objects or activities

  Rigid adherence to certain rituals

  Stereotyped mannerisms

  Abnormal preoccupation with parts of objects

- Delays or abnormal functioning in at least one of the following areas, beginning before age 3: social interactions, language for communication with others, or imaginative play

- Disturbance not better described as Rett's disorder or childhood disintegrative disorder

poorly on those subtests related to language, such as tasks requiring abstract thought, symbolism, or sequential logic (Carpentieri & Morgan, 1994). They usually obtain better scores on items requiring visual-spatial skills, such as matching designs in block-design tests and putting together disassembled objects (Rutter, 1983). Sensorimotor development is the area of greatest relative strength among children with autism. These children, who may show severe and profound deficits in cognitive abilities, can be quite graceful and adept at swinging, climbing, or balancing, whereas children with mental retardation are much more delayed in areas of gross motor development, such as learning to walk. Sometimes they may have isolated skills that reflect great talent, such as the ability to multiply two four-digit numbers rapidly in their heads. They may also have exceptional long-term memory, being able to recall the exact words of a song heard years earlier.

People with autism who have an IQ score greater than 70 or 80 are sometimes referred to as high-functioning. The term *high-functioning* can be misleading, though (Gaus, 2007). Studies comparing these high-functioning people with a control group matched on age, IQ, and education still find differences between the groups. For example, one study found that high-functioning people with autism performed faster but less accurately on a sentence-comprehension test compared to a control group without autism but with equivalent IQ scores (Just et al., 2004). As part of this study, fMRI revealed that the patterns of brain activation also differed between the two groups. Specifically, compared to the control group, the high-functioning group showed greater activation in the areas of the brain linked to language comprehension and less activation in the areas linked to language production. In addition, the connectivity of the different areas of the brain linked with language was significantly lower among the high-functioning autism group than among the control group, suggesting that there is less coordination among the areas of the brain that support language processing among people with autism.

Social and Emotional Disturbances   Children with autism can have profound problems with the social world (Dawson et al., 2004). They rarely approach others and may look through or past people or turn their backs on them. For example, one study found that children with autism rarely offered a spontaneous greeting or farewell (either verbally or through smiling, making eye contact, or gesturing) when meeting or departing from an adult (Hobson & Lee, 1998). Another study found that one-year-old children with autism attended to other people's faces far

less often at their birthday parties than did children without autism (Osterling & Dawson, 1994). Few children with autism initiate play with other children, and they are usually unresponsive to any who may approach them. Children with autism do sometimes make eye contact, but their gaze has an unusual quality. Typically, children gaze to gain someone's attention or to direct the other person's attention to an object; children with autism generally do not (Dawson et al., 2004). This is often referred to as a problem in **joint attention**. That is, interactions that require two people to pay attention to each other, whether speaking or communicating emotion nonverbally, are impaired in children with autism.

A study with adults found that people with autism pay attention to different parts of faces than do people without autism (Spezio et al., 2007). In order to figure out what type of emotion a face is displaying, perceivers typically need to look at the upper and lower face. Some emotions carry a lot of information in the eyes (e.g., anger, happiness). In the study, adults with autism focused their gaze mostly on the mouth region and almost entirely neglected the eye region. This relative neglect likely contributes to their difficulties in perceiving emotion in other people.

Heather Kuzmich, a finalist on the television show *America's Next Top Model*, also has Asperger's disorder. (© Circe Hamilton/CameraPress/Retna.)

Consistent with the findings showing that children with autism do not pay attention to other people's faces or capture their gaze, fMRI studies have found that people with autism do not show activation in the fusiform gyrus, the area of the brain most often associated with identifying faces, when completing face perception or identity tasks (Pierce et al., 2001, 2004). Instead, other areas of the brain show activation during these tasks, suggesting perhaps a less efficient system for identifying faces. A different fMRI study examined blood flow changes in the brain during processing of emotional facial expressions. In people with autism, the areas of the brain associated with the processing of faces (temporal lobe region) and emotion (amygdala) were not activated during this task (Critchley et al., 2001).

When someone else initiates play, children with autism may be compliant and engage in the activity for a period of time. Physical play, such as tickling and wrestling, may not be enjoyable to children with autism. Observations of their spontaneous play in an unstructured setting reveal that children with autism spend much less of their time engaged in symbolic play, such as making a doll drive to the store or pretending that a block is a car, than do either children with mental retardation or typically developing children of comparable mental age (Sigman et al., 1987).

Children with autism do not often play or socially interact with other children. (Ellen B. Senisi.)

Some children with autism appear not to recognize or distinguish one person from another, but some of these children can become preoccupied with and form strong attachments to simple inanimate objects (e.g., keys, rocks, a wire-mesh basket, light switches, a large blanket) and to more complex mechanical objects (e.g., refrigerators and vacuum cleaners). If the object is something they can carry, they may walk around with it in their hands, and this may prevent them from learning to do more useful things.

Some researchers have proposed that children with autism have a deficient "theory of mind" and that this is their core deficit, leading to the kinds of social dysfunctions we have described here (Gopnik, Capps, & Meltzoff, 2000; Sigman, 1994). *Theory of mind* refers to a person's understanding that other people have desires, beliefs, intentions, and emotions that may be different from one's own. This ability is crucial for understanding and successfully engaging in social interactions. Theory of mind typically develops over the period between $2\frac{1}{2}$ and 5 years of age. Children with autism seem not to undergo this developmental milestone and thus seem unable to understand others' perspectives and emotional reactions. Research has also shown that people with autism (and those with Asperger's disorder) have disturbances in areas of the brain linked to abilities needed for a theory of mind (Castelli et al., 2002).

Although high-functioning children with autism can learn to understand emotional experiences, they "answer questions about . . . emotional experiences like normal children answer difficult arithmetic questions" (Sigman, 1994, p. 151), with concentrated effort. Laboratory studies of children with high-functioning autism have found that they may recognize others' emotions without really understanding them (Capps, Yirmiya, & Sigman, 1992; Capps et al., 1999). For example, when asked to explain why someone was angry, a child with autism responded "because he was yelling" (Capps, Losh, & Thurber, 2000).

Communication Deficits   Even before they acquire language, some children with autism show deficits in communication. Babbling, a term describing the utterances of infants before they begin to use words is less frequent in infants with autism and conveys less information than it does in other infants (Ricks, 1972). By 2 years of age, most typically developing children use words to represent objects in their surroundings and construct one- and two-word sentences to express more complex thoughts, such as "Mommy go" or "Me juice." In contrast, children with autism lag well behind in these abilities and often show other language disturbances.

One such feature associated with autism is **echolalia**, in which the child echoes, usually with remarkable fidelity, what he or she has heard another person say. The teacher may ask a child with autism, "Do you want a cookie?" The child's response may be, "Do you want a cookie?" This is immediate echolalia. In delayed echolalia, the child may be in a room with the television on and appear to be completely uninterested. Several hours later or even the next day, the child may echo a word or phrase from the television program.

Another language abnormality common in the speech of children with autism is **pronoun reversal**, in which children refer to themselves as "he," "she," or "you" (or even by their own name). For example:

Parent: What are you doing, Johnny?
Child: He's here.
Parent: Are you having a good time?
Child: He knows it.

Pronoun reversal is closely linked to echolalia—when children with autism use echolalic speech, they refer to themselves as they have heard others speak of them and misapply pronouns. Children with autism are very literal in their use of words. If a father provided positive reinforcement by putting his daughter on his shoulders when she learned to say the word *yes*, then the child might say *yes* to mean she wants to be lifted onto her father's shoulders. Or a child may say "do not drop the cat" to mean "no," because a parent had used these emphatic words when the child was about to drop the family feline.

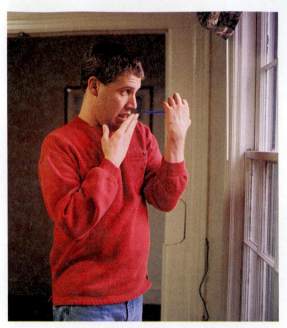

People with autism frequently engage in stereotyped behavior, such as ritualistic hand movements. (Nancy Pierce/Photo Researchers.)

Repetitive and Ritualistic Acts   Children with autism can become extremely upset over changes in their daily routines and surroundings. An offer of milk in a different drinking cup or a rearrangement of furniture may make them cry or precipitate a temper tantrum.

An obsessional quality may pervade the behavior of children with autism. In their play, they may continually line up toys or construct intricate patterns with household objects. As they grow older, they may become preoccupied with train schedules, subway routes, and number sequences. Children with autism are also likely to perform a more limited number of behaviors than children without autism and are less likely to explore new surroundings.

Children with autism may also display stereotypical behavior, peculiar ritualistic hand movements, and other rhythmic movements, such as endless body rocking, hand flapping, and walking on tiptoe. They may spin and twirl string, crayons, sticks, and plates, twiddle their fingers in front of their eyes, and stare at fans and other spinning things. Researchers often describe these as self-stimulatory activities. The children may become preoccupied with manipulating an object and may become very upset when interrupted.

Prognosis for Autistic Disorder   What happens to children with autism when they reach adulthood? Kanner (1973) reported on the adult status of nine of the eleven children described in his original paper on autism. Two had developed epileptic seizures; one of these had died, and the other was in a state hospital. Four others had spent most of their lives in hospitals. Of the remaining three, one was still mute but was working on a farm and as an orderly in a nursing home. The other two had made satisfactory recoveries; although both still lived with their parents and had little social life, they were gainfully employed and had developed some recreational interests.

Similar outcomes have been found in more recent population-based, follow-up studies (Gillberg, 1991; Nordin & Gillberg, 1998; Von Knorring & Hagglof, 1993). Generally, children with higher IQs who learn to speak before age six have the best outcomes, and a few of these function fairly well in adulthood. For example, a recent longitudinal study of children with autism from preschool to early adulthood found that IQs over 70 predicted more strengths and fewer weaknesses on the Vineland scales (see Table 14.4) as they grew older (McGovern & Sigman, 2005), and outcomes were better for those who had interacted and engaged more with their peers. Follow-up studies focusing on high-functioning people with autism have indicated that most do not require residential care and some are able to attend college and support themselves through employment (Yirmiya & Sigman, 1991). Still, many independently functioning adults with autism continue to show impairment in social relationships (Howlin,

Mawhood, & Rutter, 2000; Howlin, Goode, Hutton, & Rutter, 2004). Focus on Discovery 14.4 describes a woman with autism whose adult life is remarkable for its professional distinction blended with autistic social and emotional deficits.

Etiology of Autistic Disorder

The earliest theorizing about the etiology of autism was that psychological factors were responsible for its development. This narrow and faulty perspective has been replaced in recent years by theories based on evidence that genetic and neurological factors are important in the etiology of this puzzling syndrome. Despite the lack of empirical support for these psychological theories, they gained enough recognition to place a tremendous emotional burden on parents who were told that they were at fault for their child's autism.

Genetic Factors   Evidence strongly suggests a genetic component for autistic disorder. For example, the risk of autism among siblings of people with the disorder is about 75 times greater than it is among siblings of people who do not have autistic disorder (McBride, Anderson, & Shapiro, 1996). Even stronger evidence for genetic transmission of autism comes from twin studies, which have found 60 to 91 percent concordance for autism between identical twins, compared with concordance rates of 0 to 20 percent between fraternal twins (Bailey et al., 1995; Le Couteur et al., 1996).

A series of studies following twins and families with a member with autism suggests that autism is linked genetically to a broader spectrum of deficits in communication and social interaction (Bailey et al., 1995; Bolton et al., 1994; Folstein & Rutter, 1977a, 1977b). For example, most of the identical twins without autism evidenced communication deficits, such as delayed development of language abilities or reading impairments, as well as severe social deficits, including no social contacts outside the family, lack of responsiveness to social cues or conventions, and little or no spontaneous affection shown toward caregivers. In contrast, fraternal twins of children with autism are almost always normal in their social and language development and live independently in adulthood (Le Couteur et al., 1996). Taken together, the evidence from family and twin studies strongly supports a genetic basis for autistic disorder.

Molecular genetics studies are beginning to pinpoint areas of the genome that may confer risk for autism. For example, a study in 2008 found that a deletion on chromosome 16 was associated with autism in three different samples (Weiss et al., 2008). The deletion represents a genetic flaw—it was not supposed to be deleted—and the researchers suggest that although it is not clear why the flaw occurs, it is nonetheless associated with an increased risk of developing autism.

Neurological Factors   More and more research is linking the language, social, and emotional deficits in autism to the brain. A number of studies examining the brain in autism have been well replicated, allowing for a clearer picture of what may go wrong in the brain among people with autism. What remains to be figured out is why the brain goes awry early in development.

Studies using magnetic resonance imaging (MRI) found that, overall, the brains of adults and children with autism are larger than the brains of adults and children without autism (Courchesne, Carnes, & Davis, 2001; Piven et al., 1995, 1996). This same finding has been supported by studies using the measurement of head circumference as an indicator of brain size (Courchesne, Carper, & Akshoomoff, 2003). What makes these findings more interesting and puzzling is that most children with autism are born with brains of a relatively normal size; however, between the ages of 2 and 4, the brains of children with autism become significantly larger (Courchesne, 2004). Having a larger-than-normal brain is not necessarily a good thing, as it might indicate that neurons are not being pruned correctly. The pruning of neurons is an important part of brain maturation; older children have fewer connections between neurons than do babies. Adding further to this puzzle, brain growth in autism appears to slow abnormally in later childhood. It will be important for investigators to figure out how this pattern of brain growth is linked to the signs and symptoms of autism. It is worth noting that the areas of the brain that are "overgrown" in autism include the frontal, temporal, and cerebellar, which have been linked with language, social, and emotional functions.

FOCUS ON DISCOVERY 14.4

The Story of a Woman with High-Functioning Autism

Temple Grandin is a woman with autism. She also has a Ph.D. in animal science, runs her own business designing machinery for use with farm animals, and is on the faculty at Colorado State University. Two autobiographical books (Grandin, 1986, 1995) and a profile by neurologist Oliver Sacks (1995) provide a moving and revealing portrait of the mysteries of autism. (Because of her high level of intellectual functioning, the diagnosis of Asperger's disorder might be applicable. Controversy exists, however, as to whether this should be a separate diagnostic entity or viewed as a less severe form of autism.)

Lacking understanding of the complexities and subtleties of human social discourse, deficient in the ability to empathize with others, Grandin sums up her relationship to the nonautistic world saying, "Much of the time I feel like an anthropologist on Mars" (Sacks, 1995, p. 259).

Grandin recalls from her childhood sudden impulsive behavior and violent rages as well as hyperfocused attention, "a selectivity so intense that it could create a world of its own, a place of calm and order in the chaos and tumult" (Sacks, 1995, p. 254). She describes "sensations heightened, sometimes to an excruciating degree [and] she speaks of her ears, at the age of 2 or 3, as helpless microphones, transmitting everything, irrespective of relevance, at full, overwhelming volume" (Sacks, 1995, p. 254).

Grandin was diagnosed with autism in 1950 at age three. She had no speech at all, and doctors predicted that institutionalization would be her fate. However, with the help of a therapeutic nursery school and speech therapy and with the support of her family, she learned to speak by age six and began to make more contact with others. Still, as an adolescent observing other children interact, Grandin "sometimes wondered if they were all telepathic" (Sacks, 1995, p. 272), so mysterious did she find the ability of normal children to understand each other's needs and wishes, to empathize, to communicate.

Visiting her one day at her university, Sacks made several observations that convey the autistic flavor of this uncommon person:

She sat me down [in her office] with little ceremony, no preliminaries, no social niceties, no small talk about my trip or how I liked Colorado. She plunged straight into talking of her work, speaking of her early interests in psychology and animal behavior, how they were connected with self-observation and a sense of her own needs as an autistic person, and how this had joined with the [highly developed] visualizing and engineering part of her mind to point her towards the special field she had made her own: the design of farms, feedlots, corrals, slaughterhouses—systems of many sorts for animal management.

She spoke well and clearly, but with a certain unstoppable impetus and fixity. A sentence, a paragraph, once started, had to be completed; nothing left implicit, hanging in the air. (Sacks, 1995, pp. 256–257)

In her own writings, Grandin points out that many people with autism are great fans of *Star Trek*, and especially the characters of Spock and Data, the former a member of the Vulcan race, purely intellectual, logical beings who eschew any consideration of the emotional side of life, and the latter an android, a highly sophisticated computer housed in a human body and, like Spock, lacking in emotion. (One of the dramatic themes involving both characters was, of course, their flirtation with the experience of human emotion, portrayed with particular poignancy by Data. This is a theme in Grandin's life as well.) As Grandin (1995) wrote at age 47:

All my life I have been an observer, and I have always felt like someone who watches from the outside. I could not participate in the social interactions of high school life.

Even today, personal relationships are something I don't really understand. I've remained celibate because doing so helps me avoid the many complicated situations that are too difficult for me to handle. [M]en who want to date often don't understand how to relate to a woman. They [and I myself] remind me of Data, the android on Star Trek. In one episode, Data's attempts at dating were a disaster. When he tried to be romantic [by effecting a change in a subroutine of his computer program], he complimented his date by using scientific terminology. Even very able adults with autism have such problems. (pp. 132–133)

Other areas of the brain are implicated in autism as well. Sixteen MRI and autopsy studies from nine independent research groups all found abnormalities in the cerebellum of children with autism (Haas et al., 1996), and more recent studies have confirmed this finding (e.g., Hardan et al., 2001). Another study found that the commonly observed tendency of children with autism to explore their surroundings less than other children do is correlated with a larger-than-normal cerebellum (Pierce & Courchesne, 2001). Neurological abnormalities in people with autism suggest that in the course of development, their brain cells fail to align properly and do not form the network of connections found in normal brains.

A pair of recent studies examined the size of the amygdalae among children and adults with autism. Given that autism is associated with social and emotional difficulties, and that the amygdalae are associated with social and emotional behavior, it stands to reason that the amygdalae might be involved in autism. One study found that the amygdalae were larger among children with autism (Munson et al., 2006), and larger amygdalae at ages 3 or 4 predicted more difficulties in social behavior and communication at age 6. This finding is consistent with studies showing overgrowth of other brain areas. However, the other study found that *small* amygdalae size in autism was correlated with difficulties in emotional face perception and less gaze in the eye region of faces during the perception task (Nacewicz et al., 2006). How can we make sense

Some of the deficiencies of people with autism make them charmingly honest and trustworthy. "Lying," wrote Grandin, "is very anxiety-provoking because it requires rapid interpretations of subtle social cues [of which I am incapable] to determine whether the other person is really being deceived" (Grandin, 1995, p. 135).

Grandin's professional career is impressive. She uses her remarkable powers of visualization and her empathy for farm animals to design machines such as a chute leading cows to slaughter that takes them on a circular route, protecting them from awareness of their fate until the moment of death. She has also designed and built a "squeeze machine," a device that provides comforting hugs without the need for human contact. It has "two heavy, slanting wooden sides, perhaps four by three feet each, pleasantly upholstered with a thick, soft padding. They [are] joined by hinges to a long, narrow bottom board to create a V-shaped, body-sized trough. There [is] a complex control box at one end, with heavy-duty tubes leading off to another device, in a closet. [An] industrial compressor exerts a firm but comfortable pressure on the body, from the shoulders to the knees" (Sacks, 1995, pp. 262–263). Her explanation of the rationale behind this contraption is that as a little girl she longed to be hugged but was also very fearful of physical contact with another person. When a favorite, large-bodied aunt hugged her, she felt both overwhelmed and comforted. Terror commingled with pleasure.

She started to have daydreams—she was just five at the time—of a magic machine that could squeeze her powerfully but gently, in a huglike way, and in a way entirely commanded and controlled by her. Years later, as an adolescent, she had seen a picture of a squeeze chute designed to hold or restrain calves and realized that that was it: a little modification to make it suitable for human use, and it could be her magic machine. (Sacks, 1995, p. 263)

After watching her demonstrate the machine and trying it himself, Sacks observed:

It is not just pleasure or relaxation that Temple gets from the machine but, she maintains, a feeling for others. As she lies in her machine, she says, her thoughts often turn to her mother, her favorite aunt, her teachers. She feels their love for her, and hers for them. She feels that the machine opens a door into an otherwise closed emotional world and allows her, almost teaches her, to feel empathy for others. (Sacks, 1995, p. 264)

Sacks has great admiration for Grandin's professional success and for the interesting and productive life she has made for herself, but when it comes to human interactions, it is clear that she does not get it. "I was struck by the enormous difference, the gulf, between Temple's immediate, intuitive recognition of animal moods and signs and her extraordinary difficulties understanding human beings, their codes and signals, the way they conduct themselves" (Sacks, 1995, p. 269).

Accounts such as those of Grandin and Sacks can provide insight into how people adapt to their own idiosyncrasies, using the sometimes peculiar gifts they have been given and working around the deficiencies with which they have been saddled. "Autism, while it may be pathologized as a syndrome, must also be seen as a whole mode of being, a deeply different mode or identity, one that needs to be conscious (and proud) of itself," wrote Sacks (1995, p. 277). "At a recent lecture, Temple ended by saying, 'If I could snap my fingers and be nonautistic, I would not—because then I wouldn't be me. Autism is part of who I am'" (Sacks, 1995, p. 291).

Temple Grandin, Ph.D., was diagnosed with autism in early childhood, but has had a successful academic career. (Rosalie Winard Photography.)

of the seemingly different findings? Participants in the study by Nacewicz and colleagues were older, suggesting that the brain changes continue throughout in development may be differentially related to social and emotional impairments.

Treatment of Autistic Disorder

The most promising efforts at treatment of autistic disorder are psychological. Various treatments that combine psychological treatment and drugs have been studied as well, but with few positive results. Treatments for children with autism are usually aimed at reducing their unusual behavior and improving their communication and social skills. In most cases, the earlier the intervention begins, the better the outcome. Identifying autism early is a key priority for the field. In a promising longitudinal study, children at high risk for developing autism (parent or sibling with an autism-spectrum disorder) were studied beginning at age 14 months. Even though these children did not yet have language, the researchers were able to identify deficits in joint attention and communication that allowed for an early provisional diagnosis of autism (Landa, Holman, & Garrett-Mayer, 2007).

It is important to note that even though genetic and neurological factors in the etiology of autism have much more empirical support than psychological factors, it is the psychological

Ivar Lovaas, a behavior therapist, is noted for his operant-conditioning treatment of children with autism. (Courtesy of Susan Oliver Young.)

treatments that currently show the most promise, not medications. The lesson is that a neurological defect may well be treatable psychologically.

Behavioral Treatment   Ivar Lovaas, a leading clinical researcher at the University of California at Los Angeles, conducted an intensive operant conditioning based program of behavioral treatment with young (under four years old) children with autism (Lovaas, 1987). Therapy encompassed all aspects of the children's lives for more than 40 hours a week over more than two years. Parents were trained extensively so that treatment could continue during almost all the children's waking hours. Nineteen children receiving this intensive treatment were compared with 40 children who received a similar treatment for less than 10 hours per week. Both groups of children were rewarded for being less aggressive, more compliant, and more socially appropriate—for example, talking and playing with other children. The goal of the program was to mainstream the children, the assumption being that children with autism, as they improve, benefit more from being with typically developing peers than from remaining by themselves or with other seriously disturbed children.

The results of this landmark study were dramatic and encouraging. The IQs for the intensive-therapy group averaged 83 in first grade (after about two years in the intensive therapy) compared with about 55 for the other group; 12 of the 19 reached the normal range, compared with only 2 (of 40) of the others. Furthermore, 9 of the 19 in the intensive-therapy group were promoted to second grade in a regular public school, whereas only 1 of the much larger group achieved this level of functioning. A follow-up of these children four years later indicated that the intensive-treatment group maintained their gains in IQ, adaptive behavior, and grade promotions in school (McEachin, Smith, & Lovaas, 1993). Although critics have pointed out weaknesses in the study's methodology and outcome measures (Schopler, Short, & Mesibov, 1989), this ambitious program confirms the benefits of intensive therapy with the heavy involvement of both professionals and parents in dealing with the challenges of autistic disorder.

One of the weaknesses of the study was that it was not a randomized, controlled clinical trial. There has only been one randomized controlled clinical trial to examine the efficacy of intensive behavioral treatment on a broader scale. This study compared an intensive behavioral treatment (about 25 hours a week, instead of 40) to a treatment that consisted of parent training only (Smith, Groen, & Wynn, 2000). Although the behavioral treatment was more effective than parent training alone, the children in this study did not show the same gains as in the study discussed above (Lovaas, 1987), perhaps due to the fact that the treatment was implemented for fewer hours.

Other research suggests that education provided by parents is more beneficial to the child than is clinic- or hospital-based treatment. Parents are present in many different situations and thus can help children generalize the gains they make. For example, one group of researchers demonstrated that 25 to 30 hours of parent training was as effective as 200 hours of direct clinic treatment in improving the behavior of children with autism (Koegel et al., 1982). This research group has also focused on comparing different strategies for behavioral parent training, with interesting discoveries. They found that parents could be more effective when taught to focus on increasing their children's general motivation and responsiveness rather than being taught to focus on changing individually targeted problem behaviors in a sequential manner (Koegel, Bimbela, & Schreibman, 1996). For example, allowing the child to choose the teaching materials, providing natural reinforcers (e.g., play and social praise) rather than edible reinforcers, and reinforcing attempts to respond as well as correct responses all led to improved family interactions and more positive communication between parents and their children with autism. This more focused approach to treatment is called *pivotal response treatment* (PRT), a term based on the notion that intervening in a key, or pivotal, area may lead to changes in other areas. At least 10 studies have found PRT to be effective (reviewed in Koegel, Koegel, & Brookman, 2003).

Other interventions seek to improve children's problems in joint attention and communication. In a recent randomized controlled clinical trial, children ages 3 and 4 with autism were randomly assigned to a joint attention (JA) intervention, a symbolic play (SP) intervention, or a control group (Kasari, Freeman, & Paparella, 2006). All children were already part of an early-intervention program; the JA and SP interventions were additional interventions provided to the children in 30-minute daily blocks for 6 weeks. Children in the JA and SP treatments showed more improvement than children in the control group, and at 6 and 12 months after the treatment, children in the JA and SP groups had greater expressive language skills than children in the control group (Kasari et al., 2008).

Drug Treatment   The most commonly used medication for treating problem behaviors in children with autism is haloperidol (trade name Haldol), an antipsychotic medication used in the treatment of schizophrenia. Some controlled studies have shown that this drug reduces social withdrawal, stereotyped motor behavior, and such maladaptive behaviors as self-mutilation and aggression (Anderson et al., 1989; McBride et al., 1996; Perry et al., 1989). Many children do not respond positively to the drug, however, and it has not shown any positive effects on other aspects of autistic disorder, such as social functioning and language impairments (Holm & Varley, 1989). Haloperidol also has serious side effects (Posey & McDougle, 2000). In a longitudinal study, over 30 percent of children with autism developed drug-related dyskinesias, or jerky muscle disturbances, although most went away after the drug was withdrawn (Campbell et al., 1997).

Evidence that children with autism may have elevated blood levels of serotonin (Anderson & Hoshino, 1987) encouraged research on medications that reduce the action of serotonin. There was an initial flurry of enthusiastic claims that the drug fenfluramine, a drug known to lower serotonin levels in rats and monkeys, was associated with dramatic improvement in the behavior and thought processes of children with autism (Ritvo et al., 1983), but later studies delivered much more modest findings (Leventhal et al., 1993; Rapin, 1997). Although fenfluramine may work with some children with autism to slightly improve their social adjustment, attention span, activity level, and stereotyped behavior, no consistent effect has been shown on cognitive measures such as IQ or language functioning.

Researchers have also studied naltrexone, an opioid receptor antagonist, and found that this drug reduces hyperactivity in children with autism and produces a moderate improvement in the initiation of social interactions (Aman & Langworthy, 2000; P. A. Williams et al., 2001; Willemsen-Swinkels, Buitelaar, & van Engeland, 1996). One controlled study suggested mild improvements in the initiation of communication as well (Kolmen et al., 1995), but others found no changes in communication or social behavior (Feldman, Kolmen, & Gonzaga, 1999; Willemsen-Swinkels et al., 1995, 1996). The drug does not appear to affect the core symptoms of autism, and some evidence suggests that at some doses it may increase self-injurious behavior (Anderson et al., 1997).

In sum, pharmacological treatment of autism is, at this point, less effective than behavioral treatments.

Check Your Knowledge 14.4

True or false?
1. All children with autism also have mental retardation.
2. Children with autism have difficulty recognizing emotions in others.

3. Medication is an effective treatment for autistic disorder.

Summary

Clinical Descriptions

- Childhood disorders are often organized into two domains: externalizing disorders and internalizing disorders. Externalizing disorders are characterized by such behaviors as aggressiveness, noncompliance, overactivity, and impulsiveness; they include attention-deficit/hyperactivity disorder, conduct disorder, and oppositional defiant disorder. Internalizing disorders are characterized by such behaviors as depression, social withdrawal, and anxiety, they include childhood anxiety and mood disorders.
- Attention-deficit/hyperactivity disorder (ADHD) is a persistent pattern of inattention and/or hyperactivity and impulsivity that is more frequent and more severe than what is typically observed in children of a given age. Conduct disorder is sometimes a precursor to antisocial personality disor-

der in adulthood, though many children carrying the diagnosis do not progress to that extreme. It is characterized by high and widespread levels of aggression, lying, theft, vandalism, cruelty to other people and to animals, and other acts that violate laws and social norms.

- Mood and anxiety disorders in children share similarities with the adult forms of these disorders. However, differences that reflect different stages of development are also important.

- Learning disorders are diagnosed when a child fails to develop to the degree expected for his or her intellectual level in a specific academic, language, or motor skill area. These disorders are often identified and treated within the school system rather than through mental health clinics.

• The DSM-IV-TR diagnostic criteria for mental retardation are subaverage intellectual functioning and deficits in adaptive behavior, with onset before the age of 18. Most professionals, however, focus more on the strengths of people with mental retardation than on their assignment to a particular level of severity. This shift in emphasis is associated with increased efforts to design psychological and educational interventions that make the most of individuals' abilities.

• Autistic disorder begins early in life, and the number of diagnoses has risen dramatically in recent years. The major symptoms are a failure to relate to other people; communication problems, consisting of either a failure to learn any language or speech irregularities, such as echolalia and pronoun reversal; and theory of mind problems.

Etiology

• There is strong evidence for genetic and neurobiological factors in the etiology of ADHD. Low birth weight and maternal smoking are also risk factors. Family factors interact with these genetic vulnerabilities.

• Among the apparent etiological and risk factors for conduct disorder are a genetic predisposition, inadequate learning of moral awareness, modeling and direct reinforcement of antisocial behavior, negative peer influences, and living in impoverished and crime-ridden areas.

• Etiological factors for mood and anxiety disorders in children are believed to be largely the same as in adulthood, though additional research is needed.

• There is mounting evidence that the most widely studied of the learning disorders, dyslexia, has genetic and other neurobiological components.

• The more severe forms of mental retardation have a neurological basis, such as the chromosomal trisomy that causes Down syndrome. Certain infectious diseases in the pregnant mother, such as HIV, rubella, and syphilis, as well as illnesses that affect the child directly, such as encephalitis, can stunt cognitive and social development, as can malnutrition, severe falls, and automobile accidents that injure the brain. Environmental factors are considered the principal causes of milder mental retardation.

• Family and twin studies give compelling evidence of a genetic predisposition in autism. Abnormalities have been found in the brains of children with autism, including an overgrowth of the brain by age 2 and abnormalities in the cerebellum.

Treatment

• A combined treatment including stimulant drugs, such as Ritalin, and reinforcement for staying on task has shown effectiveness in reducing the symptoms of ADHD.

• The most promising approach to treating young people with conduct disorder involves intensive intervention in multiple systems, including the family, school, and peer systems.

• The most effective intervention for mood and anxiety disorders is cognitive behavioral therapy. Medication is effective for depression among adolescents, though its use is not without controversy.

• The most widespread interventions for dyslexia are educational.

• Many children with mental retardation who would formerly have been institutionalized are now being educated in the public schools. In addition, using applied behavioral analysis, self-instructional training, and modeling, behavior therapists have been able to successfully treat many of the behavioral problems of people with mental retardation and to improve their intellectual functioning.

• The most promising treatments for autism are psychological, involving intensive behavioral interventions and work with parents. Various drug treatments have been used but have proved less effective than behavioral interventions.

Answers to Check Your Knowledge Questions

14.1 1. T; 2. T; 3. T; 4. F

14.2 1. life-course-persistent, adolescent-limited; 2. ADHD, substance abuse, depression, anxiety; 3. parent management training, multisystemic treatment.

14.3 1. c; 2. a; 3. d

14.4 1. F; 2. T; 3. F

Key Terms

Asperger's disorder
attention-deficit/hyperactivity disorder (ADHD)
autistic disorder
childhood disintegrative disorder
communication disorders
conduct disorder
developmental psychopathology

disorder of written expression
Down syndrome (trisomy 21)
echolalia
expressive language disorder
externalizing disorders
fragile X syndrome
internalizing disorders
joint attention
learning disabilities
learning disorders

mathematics disorder
mental retardation
motor skills disorder
multisystemic treatment (MST)
oppositional defiant disorder
parent management training (PMT)
pervasive developmental disorders
phenylketonuria (PKU)

phonological disorder
pronoun reversal
reading disorder (dyslexia)
Rett's disorder
school phobia
stuttering

15 Late Life and Psychological Disorders

LEARNING GOALS

1. Be able to describe common misconceptions about age-related changes and to understand genuine age-related changes.
2. Be able to discuss issues involved in conducting research on aging.
3. Be able to explain the symptoms of dementia and delirium, and understand current approaches to etiology and treatment.
4. Be able to describe the prevalence, etiology, and treatment of psychological disorders in the elderly.
5. Be able to explain the issues involved with community living, assisted living, and nursing homes.

Clinical Case: Henry

Henry was a 56-year-old businessman who was hospitalized for cervical disk surgery. Because he was busy as well as anxious about the surgery, he had canceled two previous admissions. Although Henry drank heavily, his drinking had never interfered with his business performance. There were no immediate complications of the surgery. He seemed to be making a normal recovery initially. During the third postoperative night, though, Henry became quite restless and could not sleep. The next day he appeared severely fatigued. The next night his restlessness worsened, and he became fearful. Later in the night, he thought that he saw people hiding in his room, and shortly before dawn he told the nurse that he saw strange little animals running over his bed and up the curtains. By morning rounds, the patient was very frightened, lethargic, and distractible. He was incoherent when he tried to talk about the night before. "He knew who he was and where he was but did not know the date or when he had had his surgery. During that day his mental status fluctuated, but by nightfall he had become grossly disoriented and agitated. At this point, psychiatric consultation was obtained."

The consultant diagnosed Henry with delirium, probably due to several factors: withdrawal from alcohol, use of strong analgesics, and stress of the operation. The treatment consisted of a reduction in pain medications, partial illumination of the room at night, a family member present at all times, along with 50 mg of chlorpromazine (Thorazine) three times daily and 500 mg of chloral hydrate at bedtime. Treatment reversed his confusion within 2 days, and he was able to return home in a week with no symptoms (Strub & Black, 1981, pp. 89–90).

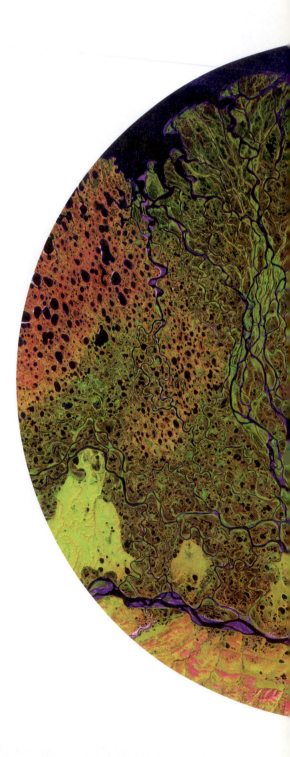

AS WE AGE, PHYSIOLOGICAL changes are inevitable, and there may be many emotional and mental changes as well. This chapter examines how issues like these influence mental health in late life. We begin by reviewing some general topics critical to the study of late life. We look next at dementia and delirium, two cognitive disorders. Then we examine a set of questions about mental illness in late life. Are older people at lower risk for mental disorders than young people? Do emotional problems develop in people who did not have them when younger? Are late-life manifestations of mental illness caused by the same factors that trigger early onsets? Which treatments successfully address mental health problems among the elderly? Finally, we discuss issues of living situations for older adults.

Aging: Issues and Methods

In contrast to the esteem in which they are held in most Asian countries, older adults are generally not treated well in the United States. The process of growing old is feared by many, even abhorred. Perhaps our lack of regard for older adults stems from our own deep-seated fear of growing old. The old person with serious infirmities is an unwelcome reminder that we all may one day walk with an unsteady gait, see less clearly, taste food less keenly, and experience more physical illness.

The social problems of aging may be especially severe for women. Even with the consciousness-raising of the past three decades, our society does not readily accept women with wrinkles and sagging bodies. Although men with gray hair at the temples and even baldness are often seen as distinguished, signs of aging in women are not valued in the United States and many other countries. The cosmetics and plastic-surgery industries make billions of dollars each year exploiting the fear inculcated in women about looking their age.[1] According to some experts, however, being female confers certain mental health benefits as people age, perhaps best evidenced by the lower rates of suicide in women compared to men (a topic we will discuss later in the chapter).

The old are usually defined as those over the age of 65, an arbitrary point set largely by social policies rather than any physiological process. To have some rough demarcation points, gerontologists usually divide people over age 65 into three groups: the young-old, those aged 65 to 74; the old-old, those aged 75 to 84; and the oldest-old, those over age 85.

People spend billions of dollars per year on cosmetics and plastic surgery to reduce signs of aging. (Courtesy of BooneOakley.)

---

[1]We should point out, though, that increasing numbers of men are undergoing plastic surgery in an effort to look younger than their years.

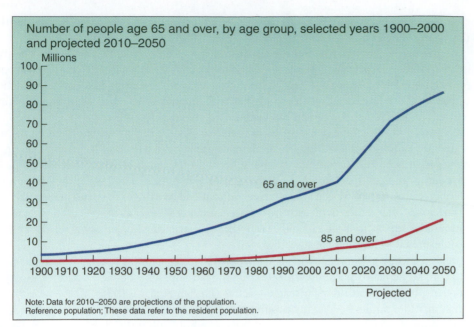

Figure 15.1 shows:
Number of people age 65 and over, by age group, selected years 1900–2000 and projected 2010–2050

Note: Data for 2010–2050 are projections of the population.
Reference population; These data refer to the resident population.

Figure 15.1 The number of old and old-old U.S. citizens is on the rise. From U.S. Census Bureau, Decennial Census and Projections.

Edna Parker died in 2008 at the age of 115. The number of centenarians (people who live to be more than 100 years old) in the United States is expected to grow 10-fold by the year 2050. (©AP/Wide World Photos.)

At the time of the last census, people 65 and older comprised 12.4 percent (35 million) of the U.S. population. Figure 15.1 shows the dramatic increase in the number of older Americans over time. As of 1999, there were 70,000 Americans at least 100 years old; by 2050, that number is expected to grow more than 10-fold to over 800,000 (U.S. Bureau of the Census, 1999).

Given these statistics, it is not surprising that 69 percent of practicing psychologists conduct clinical work with older adults (Qualls et al., 2002). A major concern, though, is that fewer than 30 percent of psychologists report receiving any formal training about late-life issues (Qualls et al., 2002). APA ethical principles state that it is important for psychologists working with the elderly to examine their stereotypes about late life (APA, 2004).

Myths about Late Life

Most people in the United States have certain assumptions about old age. Common myths include the idea that we will become doddering and befuddled. We worry that we will be unhappy, cope poorly with troubles, and become focused on our poor health. We worry that we will become lonely and that our sex lives will become unsatisfying.

Each of these myths has been debunked. As we will see, severe cognitive problems do not occur for most people in late life, though a mild decline in cognitive functioning is common (Langa et al., 2008). Elderly people (age 60 and older) actually experience less negative emotion than do young people (age 18–30 years) (Lawton et al., 1992). Although some might suspect that these findings are artifacts of a reluctance of older individuals to describe negative feelings to researchers, laboratory studies indicate that the elderly are actually more skilled at regulating their emotions. For example, when older people are asked to think or talk about emotionally charged topics, they display less physiological reactivity than do younger people (Kisley, Wood, & Burroughs, 2007; Levenson, Carstensen, & Gottman, 1994). When viewing positive images, they show more robust brain activation in key emotion regions than do younger people (Mather et al., 2004). Older people are actually likely to underreport somatic symptoms, perhaps because of beliefs that aches and pains are an inevitable part of late life.

Ageism refers to discrimination against someone because of his or her age. In one form of ageism, countermyth, we especially applaud achievements of the elderly, as in former President Bush's parachute jump. (AP/Wide World Photos.)

Contrary to stereotypes, many older people maintain an active interest in sex. Studies indicate that the frequency of sexual activity among healthy couples in their seventies remains high. (FPG International/Getty Images.)

The quality of sleep diminishes as people age. (Corbis Digital Stock.)

As illustrated by John Glenn's space flight, advancing age need not lead to a curtailment of activities. (NASA/CNP/Archive Photos.)

People in late life are no more likely to meet criteria for somatization or hypochondriasis than are the young (Regier et al., 1988; Siegler & Costa, 1985).

Another myth, that older people are lonely, has received considerable attention. The truth is that the number of social activities is unrelated to psychological well-being among older people (Carstensen, 1996). As we age, our interests shift away from seeking new social interactions to cultivating those few social relationships that really matter to us, such as those with family and close friends. This phenomenon has been called **social selectivity.**

When we have less time ahead of us, we tend to place a higher value on emotional intimacy than on exploring the world. This preference applies not just to older people but also to younger people who see themselves as having limited time, such as when they are preparing to move far away from their home (Frederickson & Carstensen, 1990) or if they have a life-threatening illness. When we can't see a future without end, we prefer to spend our limited time with our closest ties rather than with casual acquaintances, such as strangers in a recreation center for older adults. To those unfamiliar with these age-related changes, social selectivity could be misinterpreted as harmful social withdrawal.

Finally, contrary to popular belief, older people have considerable sexual interest and capacity (Deacon, Minichiello, & Plummer, 1995). Among participants who have a partner, most who are in good physical health remain sexually active (Lindau et al., 2007).

In sum, older adults have many positive life experiences, many coping mechanisms, and much wisdom on which to draw. Many stereotypes we hold about the elderly are false. Beyond questioning assumptions, it is important to recognize the diversity of older people. Not only are older people different from one another, but they are more different from one another than are people in any other age group. People tend to become less alike as they grow older. That all old people are alike is a prejudice held by many people. A moment's honest reflection may reveal that certain traits come to mind when we hear that a person is age, say, 67. But to know that a person is 67 years old is actually to know very little about him or her. Each older person brings to late life a developmental history that makes his or her reactions to common problems unique.

The Problems Experienced in Late Life

We know that mental health is tied to the physical and social problems in a person's life. As a group, no other people have more of these problems than the elderly. They have them all— physical decline and disabilities, sensory and neurological deficits, loss of loved ones, the cumulative effects of a lifetime of many unfortunate experiences, and social stresses such as ageism. (Ageism can be defined as discrimination against any person, young or old, based on chronological age, such as when a professor in his or her late sixties is considered too old to continue teaching at a university, or when it is assumed that a person older than 75 has nothing to contribute to the conversation.) As many as 80 percent of elderly people have at least one major medical condition (National Academy on an Aging Society, 1999).

One particular facet of aging deserves particular attention. As people age, the quality and depth of sleep declines, so that by age 65, 25 percent of people report insomnia (Mellinger, Balter, & Uhlenhuth, 1985). Rates of sleep apnea, a disorder in which a person stops breathing for seconds to minutes during the night, also increase with age (Prechter & Shepard, 1990). Insomnia is often caused by medication side effects (Rodin, McAvay, & Timko, 1988) or by pain from medical problems (Prinz & Raskin, 1978). Untreated and chronic sleep deficits can worsen both physical and psychological health problems and can even increase risk of mortality (Ancoli et al., 1996).

Several problems are evident in the medical treatment available during late life. One of the main difficulties is that the chronic health problems of older people seldom diminish; physicians focused on identifying cures can become frustrated when none are available (Zarit, 1980). Other problems result from the time pressure of the health care system. All too often, doctors do not check to see if the person is taking other medications or seeing other doctors. *Polypharmacy,* the prescribing of multiple drugs to a person, can result; this increases the risk of adverse drug reactions that may cause numerous side effects, toxicity, and allergic reactions. Often, physicians then prescribe more medications to combat the side effects, thus continuing the vicious circle.

Further complicating the picture is the fact that most psychoactive drugs are tested on younger people; gauging the appropriate dose for the less efficient metabolism of the kidneys and liver of the older person represents a challenge for the medical practitioner—side effects and toxicity are much more common (Gallo & Lebowitz, 1999). The increased sensitivity to medication side effects is a particular problem with psychiatric medications—we will discuss some major problems in using antipsychotic medications, antidepressants, and benzodiazapines later in the chapter. One review of medical charts of more than 750,000 elderly patients found that more than one-fifth had filled a prescription for a medication deemed inappropriate for people over the age of 65 due to serious side effects (Curtis et al., 2004). Therefore, it is important that the primary care physician of elderly people keep track of all prescribed medications taken, discontinue nonessential drugs, and prescribe only the minimum dosages needed.

Research Methods in the Study of Aging

Research on aging requires an understanding of several special issues. Chronological age is not as simple a variable in psychological research as it might seem. Because other factors associated with age may be at work, we must be cautious when we attribute differences in age groups solely to the effects of aging. In the field of aging, as in studies of childhood development, a distinction is made among three kinds of effects (see Table 15.1):

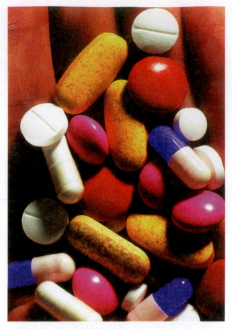

Polypharmacy is all too common in late life. (Tony Why/Phototake.)

- **Age effects** are the consequences of being a certain chronological age.
- **Cohort effects** are the consequences of growing up during a particular time period with its unique challenges and opportunities. For example, experiences like the Great Depression, a world war, or 9/11 each shape experiences and attitudes. Similarly, the expectations for marriage have changed drastically in the past century, at least in Western societies, from a focus on stability to a focus on happiness and personal fulfillment.
- **Time-of-measurement effects** are confounds that arise because events at a particular point in time can have a specific effect on a variable that is being studied (Schaie & Hertzog, 1982). For example, people tested right after Hurricane Katrina in New Orleans might demonstrate elevated levels of anxiety.

Two major research designs are used to assess developmental change: cross-sectional and longitudinal (see pp. 105–106 for more detail on these designs). In cross-sectional studies, the investigator compares different age groups at the same moment in time on the variable of interest. Suppose that in 1995 we took a poll in the United States and found that many interviewees over age 80 spoke with a European accent, whereas those in their forties and fifties did not. Could we conclude that as people grow older, they develop European accents? Hardly! Cross-sectional studies do not examine the same people over time; consequently, they do not provide clear information about how people change as they age.

In longitudinal studies, the researcher periodically retests one group of people using the same measure over a number of years or decades. For example, the Baltimore Longitudinal Study of Aging is one of the longest-running studies of aging. Beginning in the 1950s, researchers have been following 1,400 men and women to see how their lifestyles, medical conditions, and psychological health change over time. In this study, a great deal has been

Table 15.1 Age, Cohort, and Time-of-Measurement Effects		
Age Effects	**Cohort Effects**	**Time-of-Measurement Effects**
The effects of being a certain age; e.g., being old enough to receive Social Security	The effects of having grown up during a particular time period; e.g., frugality may be increased among those who lived through the Great Depression of the 1930s	The effects of testing people at a particular time in history; e.g., people became more frank during the 1990s to surveys about their sexual behavior, as media discussion of sexuality increased

learned about mental health and aging. For example, researchers were able to combat myths that people become unhappier over time. Rather, people who were happy at age 30 tended to be happy as they moved into late life (Costa, Metter, & McCrae, 1994). In general, longitudinal designs allow us to trace individual patterns of consistency or change over time. Although longitudinal studies offer fundamental advantages, results can be biased by attrition, in which participants drop out of the study due to death, immobility, or lack of interest. When people are no longer available for follow-up because of death, this is called **selective mortality**. The tendency for less healthy individuals to die more quickly can lead to biased samples in long-term follow-up studies. Selective mortality results in a particular form of bias, in that results obtained with the remaining sample are more relevant to drawing conclusions about relatively healthy people and less relevant to drawing conclusions about unhealthy people. Beyond attrition due to death, people with the most problems are likely to drop out from a study, whereas the people who remain are usually healthier than the general population. Attrition is an important issue in studies of aging and mental health, as psychological disorders have been shown to predict disease and death (Kiecolt-Glaser & Glaser, 2002).

Cohort effects refer to the fact that people of the same chronological age may differ considerably depending on when they were born. (Top: Liaison/Getty Images, Inc.; bottom: Marc Romanelli/Getty Images.)

Quick Summary

As the number of older people in the United States burgeons, more and more mental health professionals are working with this population. Unfortunately, even mental health professionals tend to hold certain stereotypes about late life. It is important to recognize that, as they age, most people tend to become more effective at regulating emotions, to remain invested in sexuality, to downplay medical symptoms, and to focus on core relationships over superficial social acquaintances and activities. The challenges of late life do include insomnia and declining health for many people. As increasing numbers of chronic health problems emerge, polypharmacy becomes an issue for many. Compounding the hazards of polypharmacy, people become more sensitive to medication side effects and toxicity as they age.

In research on aging, it is difficult to disentangle age effects, cohort effects, and time-of-measurement effects. Cross-sectional studies do not help distinguish age and cohort effects. Longitudinal studies provide more clarity about age and cohort effects, but the validity of findings can be challenged by attrition. One form of attrition, selective mortality, is particularly important to consider in studies of aging.

Check Your Knowledge 15.1 (Answers are at the end of the chapter.)

True or false?
1. Most people develop major memory problems in late life.
2. Sexual interest typically declines as people age.

3. Side effects of medications are of less concern as people age, because most people adjust to them over time.
4. Most people become unhappier as they age.

Cognitive Disorders in Late Life

Most elderly people do not have cognitive disorders. Indeed, the prevalence of cognitive impairment has declined among people over the age of 70 in the United States in the last 15 years, perhaps because of improvements in diet, medical care, and education levels over time (Langa et al., 2008). Nonetheless, cognitive disorders account for more hospital admissions and inpatient days than any other geriatric condition (Zarit & Zarit, 1998). Cognitive impairment is not a separate DSM category but is a characteristic of more than one disorder (e.g., depression, dementia, delirium). We will examine two principal types of cognitive disorders: dementia, a deterioration of cognitive abilities, and delirium, a state of mental confusion. For each, we will consider the clinical description and types as well as causal factors and treatment.

Dementia

Dementia is a general descriptive term for the deterioration of cognitive abilities to the point that social and occupational functions are impaired. Most dementias develop very slowly over a period of years; subtle cognitive and behavioral deficits can be detected well before the person shows any noticeable impairment (Small et al., 2000). Not all people with mild cognitive symptoms develop dementia, though. Among adults with mild cognitive impairment, about 10 percent per year will develop dementia; among adults without mild cognitive impairment, about 1 percent per year will develop dementia (Bischkopf, Busse, & Angermeyer, 2002).

Difficulty remembering things, especially recent events, is the most prominent symptom of dementia. People may leave tasks unfinished because they forget to return to them after an interruption. The person who had started to fill a teapot at the sink leaves the water running. As the dementia progresses, a parent is unable to remember the name of a daughter or son and later may not even recall that he or she has children or recognize them when they come to visit. Hygiene may become poor because the person forgets to bathe or dress adequately. People with dementia also get lost, even in familiar surroundings. Judgment may become faulty, and the person may have difficulty comprehending situations and making plans or decisions. People with dementia lose control of their impulses; they may use coarse language, tell inappropriate jokes, shoplift, and make sexual advances to strangers. The ability to deal with abstract ideas deteriorates, and disturbances in emotions are common, including symptoms of depression, flatness of affect, and sporadic emotional outbursts. Delusions and hallucinations can occur (APA, 2000). People with dementia are likely to show language disturbances as well, such as vague patterns of speech. Despite intact sensory functioning, they may also have trouble recognizing familiar surroundings or naming common objects. Episodes of delirium, a state of great mental confusion (discussed in detail later), may also occur.

The course of dementia may be progressive, static, or remitting, depending on the cause. Many people with progressive dementia eventually become withdrawn and apathetic. In the terminal phase of the illness, the person's personality loses its sparkle and integrity. Relatives and

Clinical Case: Ellen

"I am so glad you came," Ellen says when I greet her. She is sitting at the dining room table sipping juice, a slender, almost frail woman. But Ellen has presence. She has the posture of a dancer: shoulders back, neck elongated, head up, and the gaunt face of a once beautiful woman, with large milky hazel eyes and high patrician cheekbones. She smiles and reaches for my hand. "It is so nice of you to visit," she says.

Ellen is gracious and polite, but the truth is, she doesn't remember me. She doesn't remember that we've visited a half dozen times before, that a few days ago we had tea together, that just yesterday I sat on her bed for a half hour massaging her hands with rosemary mint lotion. Ellen, like the 43 others living at this residential care facility, has Alzheimer's disease. Her short-term memory is shot, and her long-term memory is quirky and dreamlike, with images that are sometimes bright and lucid, and other times so out of focus that she can hardly make them out. Her life is like a puzzle someone took apart when she wasn't looking. She can see some of the pieces, but she can no longer see how they fit together (quoted in Kessler, 2004, p. 1).

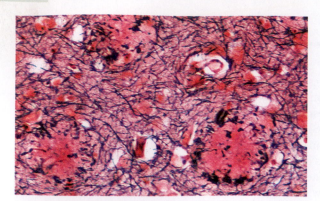

In this photograph of brain tissue from a person with Alzheimer's disease, the waxy amyloid shows up as areas of dark pink. (Martin Rotker/Phototake.)

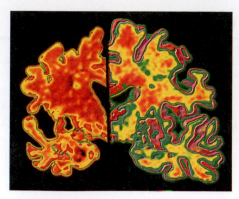

Computer-generated images of a brain of a person with Alzheimer's disease and a healthy brain. Note that the person's brain (left) has shrunk considerably owing to the loss of nerve cells. (Alfred Pasieka/Photo Researchers, Inc.)

friends say that the person is just not himself or herself anymore. Social involvement with others keeps narrowing. Finally, the person is oblivious to his or her surroundings.

Worldwide prevalence estimates of dementia in 2000 were over 25 million, which represents about 0.4 percent of the world population (Wimo et al., 2003). The prevalence of dementia increases with advancing age. Across international studies, the prevalence of dementia is 1 to 2 percent in people aged 60 to 69, 3 to 6 percent in those aged 70 to 79, more than 10 percent in those aged 80 to 84, and more than 20 percent in those 85 or older (Ferri et al., 2005).

There are many different types of dementia. Here we discuss four: Alzheimer's disease, the most well-researched form; frontotemporal dementia, defined by the areas of the brain that are most affected; vascular dementia, caused by cerebrovascular disease; and dementia with Lewy bodies, defined by the presence of Lewy bodies (abnormal deposits on neurons in the brain). After discussing these four, we briefly describe other causes of dementia. By far, the most common form of dementia is Alzheimer's disease. That is, as many as 80 percent of dementias are diagnosed as Alzheimer's disease (Terry, 2006).

Alzheimer's Disease   In **Alzheimer's disease**, initially described by the German neurologist Alois Alzheimer in 1906, the brain tissue irreversibly deteriorates, and death usually occurs within 12 years after the onset of symptoms. Over 50,000 Americans die each year from this disease, and in 2000, it was the seventh leading cause of death among men and women over the age of 65 (NCHS, 2004). The illness may begin with absentmindedness, irritability, and difficulties in concentration and in memory for new material. These shortcomings may be overlooked for several years but eventually interfere with daily living. As the disease develops, problems with language skills and word finding intensify. Visual-spatial abilities decline, which can be expressed in **disorientation** (confusion with respect to time, place, or identity) and trouble copying figures. People with the disorder are typically unaware of their cognitive problems initially, and they may blame others for lost objects, even to the point of developing delusions of being persecuted. Memory continues to deteriorate, and the person becomes increasingly disoriented and agitated. Depression is common, occurring in up to 30 percent of people with Alzheimer's disease (Strauss & Ogrocki, 1996).

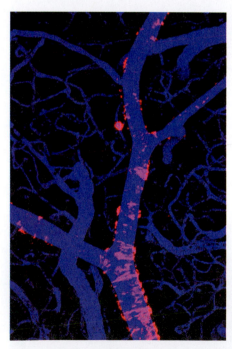

Plaques as shown using Pittsburgh Compound-B PET imaging. (Courtesy Dr. Claudia Prada/Dr. Brian Bacskai/Massachusettes General Hospital/Prada et al., J. Neurosci. 27(8):1973-80, 2007.)

People with Alzheimer's disease have more **plaques** (small, round beta-amyloid protein deposits that are outside the neurons) and **neurofibrillary tangles** (twisted protein filaments composed largely of the protein, tau, in the cell bodies of neurons) than would be expected for the person's age. The plaques are most densely present in the frontal cortex of people with Alzheimer's disease (Klunk et al., 2004). Tangles are most densely present in the hippocampus, an area that is important for memory. Over time, as the disease progresses, plaques and tangles spread through more of the brain.

There have been terrific developments in brain-imaging techniques for measuring plaques and tangles in recent years. Plaques can be measured using a specialized type of PET scan, using Pittsburgh Compound-B (PIB) (Klunk et al., 2004). Plaques and tangles can be measured using [F-18]FDDNP PET scans (Small et al., 2006).

These plaques and tangles appear related to a host of brain changes. At early stages, there seems to be a loss of synapses for acetylcholinergic (Ach) and glutamatergic neurons (Selkoe, 2002). Over time, neurons also begin to die. As neurons die, the cerebral cortex, the entorhinal cortex, and the hippocampus shrink, and later the frontal, temporal, and parietal lobes shrink. As this happens, the ventricles become enlarged. The cerebellum, spinal cord, and motor and sensory areas of the cortex are less affected, which is why people with Alzheimer's do not appear to have anything physically wrong with them until late in the disease process. For some time people with Alzheimer's are able to walk around normally, and their overlearned habits, such as making small talk, remain intact, so that in short encounters strangers may not notice anything amiss. About 25 percent of people with Alzheimer's disease eventually develop brain deterioration that leads to motor deficits.

In the largest twin study of Alzheimer's disease, a heritability estimate of 79 percent was reported. That is, about 79 percent of the variance in onset of Alzheimer's disease appears related to genes, and about 21 percent of the variance appears related to environmental factors (Gatz et al., 2006).

Among early-onset (before age 60) cases, which account for fewer than 5 percent of all cases of Alzheimer's disease, the pattern of inheritance suggests the operation of a single, dominant gene. Because people with Down's syndrome often develop Alzheimer's disease if they survive until middle age, interest focused initially on chromosome 21, which is aberrant in Down syndrome (see p. 447). A gene controlling the formation of beta-amyloid protein (which forms plaques) was identified on the long arm of chromosome 21, and studies have demonstrated that this gene causes the development of about 5 percent of cases of early-onset Alzheimer's disease. Dominant genes causing a small percentage of early-onset cases of Alzheimer's disease have also been found on chromosomes 1 and 14.

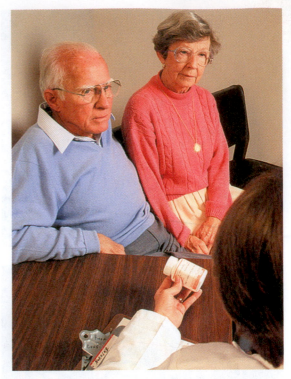

The frequency of Alzheimer's disease increases with advanced age. (Will & Deni McIntyre/Science Source/Photo Researchers, Inc.)

Most late-onset cases of Alzheimer's disease exhibit a particular form of a gene on chromosome 19, called the apolipoprotein E 4 or APOE-4 allele. Having one E 4 allele increases the risk of Alzheimer's disease to 30 percent, and having two alleles brings the risk to above 90 percent (Cummings & Cole, 2002). People with two of the E 4 alleles show abnormal glucose metabolism in the cortex even before the onset of any symptoms, but this has not been shown among people of color (Reiman et al., 1996). The gene appears related to the production of beta-amyloid proteins. Variants of several other genes also increase risk for Alzheimer's disease, including mutations of APP, PSEN1, PSEN2, and a polymorphism in UBQLN1.

Beyond genes, as mentioned before, twin studies suggest that the environment is likely to play a role in Alzheimer's. Engagement in intellectual activities has received a great deal of attention, with some proposing a "use it or lose it" model of Alzheimer's.

Strong cognitive ability before disease onset may offer some protection from Alzheimer's. This possibility was demonstrated in a study of nuns. In the weeks before the nuns took their religious vows, they had written autobiographies. Years later, after the nuns died, researchers were able to code these autobiographies for their linguistic ability, general knowledge, vocabulary skills, and other cognitive abilities. Excerpts from two of these autobiographies illustrate the range of linguistic ability among the nuns:

- *Low linguistic ability: I was born in Eau Claire, Wis. on May 24, 1913 and was baptized in St. James church.*
- *High linguistic ability: The happiest day of my life so far was my First Communion Day which was in June nineteen hundred and twenty when I was but eight years of age, and four years later I was confirmed by Bishop D. D. (Snowden et al., 1996, p. 530).*

Low linguistic ability was found in 90 percent of those who developed Alzheimer's disease many years later and in only 13 percent of those who didn't (Snowden et al., 1996).

Increasingly, researchers have focused on whether engagement in a broader range of cognitive activities can be protective. For example, regular reading of the newspaper is related to lower risk (Wilson et al., 2002). One meta-analysis of 29,000 persons drawn from 22 representative community samples suggested that frequent cognitive activity (for example, reading and puzzle solving) is related to a 46 percent decrease in risk of Alzheimer's disease compared to infrequent

DSM-IV-TR Criteria for Dementia

Of the Alzheimers type:

- Multiple cognitive deficits manifested by both A and B:
  A. Memory impairment
  B. One or more of the following: aphasia (language disturbance), apraxia (impairment in doing something even though motor components intact), agnosia (failure to identify objects despite sensory perception), and disturbance in executive functioning (i.e., planning, organizing, sequencing, and abstracting)
- Significant impairment and decline in social or occupational functioning
- Gradual onset and continuing cognitive decline
- Above cognitive deficits not due to substance use, other psychological disorders, delirium, or other medical conditions that cause progressive decline or dementia.

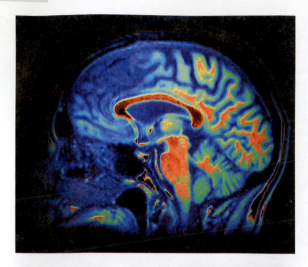

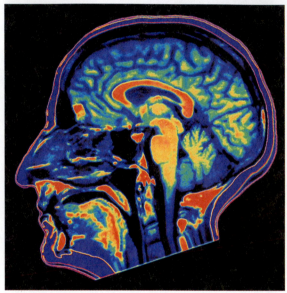

The image on the top is an MRI scan of a person with frontal temporal dementia (FTD). The image on the bottom is an MRI scan of a healthy person. The scan of the person on the top shows the atropy, or loss of brain volume, in the frontal region. FTD is also characterized by atrophy in the temporal regions. (Top: Zephyr/Photo Researchers, Inc.; bottom: Scott Camazine/Photo Researchers, Inc.)

cognitive activity (Valenzuela & Sachdev, 2006). Among people with similar levels of plaques and tangles in their brain, those with higher levels of cognitive activity show fewer cognitive symptoms. That is, cognitive activity seems to protect against the expression of underlying neurobiological disease (Wilson et al., 2007).

Researchers are focused on early identification of people at high risk for Alzheimer's, spurred by the hope that early intervention might prevent the development of the disease. Recent research focuses on differentiating people who do and do not progress from mild cognitive impairment to Alzheimer's disease. Promising results have been obtained using neuropsychological tests; assays of tau, amyloid, and other proteins in the blood (Ray et al., 2007); and brain imaging (den Heijer et al., 2006; Sunderland et al., 2006). To date, however, it remains difficult to know who will develop Alzheimer's disorder in the context of these early signs of cognitive decline.

Frontotemporal Dementia   As suggested by the name, **frontotemporal dementia (FTD)** is defined by a loss of neurons in frontal and temporal regions of the bran. FTD typically begins in the mid to late fifties, although many investigators believe that subtle changes in behavior, personality, and emotion can begin much earlier (e.g., Geschwind et al., 2001). The social and emotional changes in FTD are major and take a heavy toll on the loved ones of the affected person. Unlike Alzheimer's disease, memory is not severely impaired in FTD. Instead, executive functions, which include things such as planning, problem solving, and goal-directed behavior, are more impaired in FTD compared to Alzheimer's (Kramer et al., 2003). For example, the successful and savvy businessman may begin to make terrible investments (Levenson & Miller, 2007). Ability to recognize and regulate emotion is also impaired in FTD (Levenson & Miller, 2007). FTD often progresses rapidly. In one study, the average time from diagnosis to death was less than 5 years (Levenson & Miller, 2007).

The neuronal deterioration of FTD occurs predominantly in the amygdala, anterior temporal lobes, prefrontal cortex, and other regions involving serotonergic neurons (Miller et al., 1997). Pick's disease, one cause of frontotemporal dementia, is characterized by the presence of Pick bodies, spherical inclusions within neurons. FTD has a strong genetic component, although there may be multiple genetic pathways involved (Cruts et al., 2006).

Vascular Dementia   Vascular dementia is diagnosed when the cognitive symptoms of dementia are a consequence of cerebrovascular disease. Most commonly, the person had a series of strokes in which a clot formed, impairing circulation and causing cell death. Genetic factors appear to be of no importance (Bergem, Engedal, & Kringlen, 1997). Rather risk for vascular dementia involves the same risk factors described for cardiovascular disease in general—for example, a high level of "bad" (LDL) cholesterol, cigarette smoking, and elevated blood pressure (Moroney et al., 1999). Because strokes and cardiovascular disease can strike different regions of the brain, the symptoms of vascular dementias can vary a good deal. Vascular dementias are more common among African Americans than Caucasians (e.g., Froehlich, Bogardus, & Inouye, 2001). The onset of symptoms can be more rapid in vascular dementia than in other forms of dementia. Vascular dementia can co-occur with Alzheimer's disorder.

Dementia with Lewy Bodies   Dementia with Lewy bodies (DLB) can be divided into two subtypes, depending on whether it occurs in the context of Parkinson's disease or not. About 80 percent of people with Parkinson's disease will develop DLB, but some people without Parkinson's will develop DLB as well.

The symptoms associated with this type of dementia are often hard to distinguish from the symptoms of Parkinson's (such as the shuffling gait) and Alzheimer's disease (such as loss of memory). DLB is more likely than Alzheimer's disease to include prominent visual hallucinations and fluctuating cognitive symptoms (APA, 2004). People with DLB are often extremely sensitive to the physical side effects of antipsychotic medications. Another distinct symptom of DLB is that people often experience intense dreams accompanied by levels of movement and vocalizing that may make them seem as though they are "acting out their dreams" (McKeith et al., 2005). Imaging research suggests unusual patterns of dopamine activity in the basal ganglia, a region of the brain that is involved in Parkinson's disease, among people with DLB (McKeith et al., 2005).

Dementias Caused by Disease and Injury   A number of other medical concerns can produce dementia. Encephalitis, a generic term for any inflammation of brain tissue, is caused by viruses that enter the brain. Meningitis, an inflammation of the membranes covering the outer brain, is usually caused by a bacterial infection. Both encephalitis and meningitis can cause dementia. The organism that produces the venereal disease syphilis (*Treponema pallidum*) can invade the brain and cause dementia. HIV, head traumas, brain tumors, nutritional deficiencies (especially of B-complex vitamins), kidney or liver failure, and endocrine gland problems such as hyperthyroidism can result in dementia. Exposure to toxins (such as lead or mercury) and chronic substance use are both additional causes.

Treatment of Dementia   Despite numerous investigations, no treatment has been found that can reverse dementia. Some drugs, as described below, may provide modest protection against decline in cognitive functions. For treatment providers and family members, the desire for cures is intense, and sadly, the literature is replete with examples of failed efforts. For example, attempts to help people with Alzheimer's reminisce about key memories or treatments designed to provide additional sensory stimulation have shown effects that are miniscule at best (APA, 2007; Kasl-Godley & Gatz, 2000). Similarly, early-heralded gains with Vitamin E, statins, and nonsteroidal anti-inflammatory drugs have failed to find support in more careful research (Shumaker, Legault, & Coker, 2006).

Medications   Because Alzheimer's disease involves the death of brain cells that secrete acetylcholine, various medications are used to increase the levels of this neurotransmitter. Acetylcholinesterase inhibitors (drugs that interfere with the breakdown of acetylcholine), such as donepezil (Aricept) and rivastigmine (Exelon), are the standard treatment for Alzheimer's disease (Cummings, 2000). Meta-analyses of dozens of controlled trials indicate that this class of drugs is associated with slightly less decline in memory than is observed on placebo (Birks, 2006). In addition to acetylcholinesterase inhibitors, namenda (Memantine), a drug that affects glutamate receptors believed to be involved in memory, has shown small effects in placebo-controlled trials (Winblad & Portis, 1999).

A major effort is underway to find medications to prevent the onset of Alzheimer's disease. Recall that beta-amyloid plaques appear tied to the development of Alzheimer's disease. Based on this, one line of this research is focusing on processes involved in the creation of amyloid from its precursor protein (Rosenberg, 2005).

Beyond the memory loss, Alzheimer's disease can produce many other psychological symptoms. For example, as many as 30 percent of people with Alzheimer's disease will evidence depression, and so antidepressants are often used to address these symptoms (Lyketsos et al., 2000). Agitation, aggression, and paranoid symptoms are common concerns as the disease progresses. In a study of 421 people with Alzheimer's, atypical antipsychotic medications were found to provide small gains compared to placebo in relieving paranoia, aggression, and anger (Sultzer et al., 2008). Unfortunately, antipsychotic medications increase the risk of death among elderly people with dementia (FDA, 2005; Gill et al., 2007). Despite this, antipsychotic medications are all too commonly prescribed for people with dementia when behavioral interventions could be effective without the same risks.

Compared to Alzheimer's disease, much less is known about treatments for the other forms of dementia. No medications have been shown to have robust effects on the symptoms of FTD, although SSRIs have been prescribed with modest success (Pasquier et al., 2003). Namenda (Memantine) and some cholinesterase inhibitors have been shown to lead to a slightly slower cognitive decline in vascular dementia (Malouf & Birks, 2004). Cholinesterase inhibitors also have been shown to slow declines in dementia with Lewy bodies (Maidment, Fox, & Boustani,

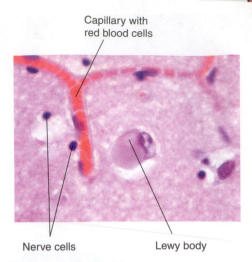

Capillary with red blood cells

Nerve cells   Lewy body

Dementia with Lewy bodies is defined by the presence of abnormal deposits called Lewy bodies. In this form of dementia, the Lewy bodies are found throughout the brain. (Courtesy of James Lowe, University of Nottingham, Nottingham, United Kingdom)

Former president Ronald Reagan died from Alzheimer's disease. His daughter wrote the following about his disease: " . . . the past is like the rudder of a ship. It keeps you moving through the present, steers you into the future. Without it, without memory, you are unmoored, a wind-tossed boat with no anchor. You learn this by watching someone you love drift away" (Davis, 2002). (Reuter/Steve Grayson/Archive Photos.)

Providing memory aids is one way of combating memory loss.
(RubberBall/SuperStock, Inc.)

2006). Unfortunately, many people discontinue these drugs due to aversive side effects such as nausea (Maidment et al., 2006).

Psychological Treatments Supportive psychotherapy can help families and patients deal with the effects of the disease. Generally, the therapist allows opportunities for the person with dementia and the family to discuss the illness. The therapist also provides accurate information about the illness, helps family members care for the person in the home, and encourages a realistic rather than a catastrophic attitude in dealing with the many specific challenges that this cognitive disorder presents (Knight, 1996). In contrast to what we have seen in dealing with virtually all other psychological problems, it may not be desirable to get people with Alzheimer's to admit to their problems, for their denial may be the most effective coping mechanism available (Zarit, 1980). See Focus on Discovery 15.1 for more detail on treatments offered to support caregivers.

Naturalistic (nontreatment) and treatment studies suggest that exercise may ward off memory problems. For example, in one study of people over the age of 65, exercising three times per week was related to less risk of developing Alzheimer's disease over a 6-year period (Larson et al., 2006). Intervention researchers are building on these findings. In a meta-analysis of 12 studies including 423 people assigned to exercise and 397 control participants, exercise programs have shown cognitive benefits for those with mild to moderate cognitive deficits (Heyn, Abreu, & Ottenbacher, 2004). Exercise programs have also been shown to improve cognitive functioning among those already diagnosed with Alzheimer's disease (Cott et al., 2002).

Behavioral approaches have been used to reduce disruptive behavior and depression in people with Alzheimer's. For example, self-care skills can be improved, verbal outbursts diminished, and depressed mood lifted with the application of appropriate reinforcement contingencies (Kasl-Godley & Gatz, 2000). Music may help reduce agitation and disruptive behavior while it is being played (Livingston et al., 2005). Given how sensitive older people can be to medications, these behavioral interventions can be quite important.

Check Your Knowledge 15.2

Answer the questions.
1. A plaque is:
    a. a small round beta-amyloid protein deposit
    b. a protein filament composed of the protein tau
    c. a buildup of the myelin sheath surrounding neurons in the hippocampus
    d. a small white spot on a brain scan
2. A neurofibrillary tangle is:
    a. a small, round beta-amyloid protein deposit
    b. a protein filament composed of the protein tau
    c. a buildup of the myelin sheath surrounding neurons in the hippocampus
    d. a small white spot on a brain scan
3. Which neurotransmitter is most involved in Alzheimer's disease?
    a. dopamine
    b. serotonin
    c. GABA
    d. acetylcholine
4. Which genes are most involved in Alzheimer's disease?
    a. the E 4 allele
    b. the C 5 allele
    c. the E 6 allele
    d. all of the above
5. FTD involves profound changes in:
    a. memory
    b. social and emotional behavior
    c. language
    d. attention

FOCUS ON DISCOVERY 15.1

Support for Caregivers

For every person with a severely disabling dementia living in an institution, there are at least two living in the community, usually supported by a family (especially wives and daughters). Caregiving for dementia requires much more time than caregiving for most other disorders (Ory et al., 1999) and has been shown to be extremely stressful across a number of cultures (Torti et al., 2004). Caregivers are at risk for clinical depression and anxiety (Dura, Stukenberg, & Kiecolt-Glaser, 1991), physical illness (Vitaliano, Zhang, & Scanlan, 2003), and decreased immune functioning (Kiecolt-Glaser et al., 1991) compared to noncaregivers. Further, for some caregivers, depression and loneliness persist long after their ill spouse has died (Robinson-Whelan et al., 2001).

Despite the obvious toll of caretaking, some caregivers seem to adjust to these stresses without developing symptoms. A key question, then, is what predicts resiliency? Caregivers are less likely to develop depression and anxiety when the patient's problem behaviors are less severe, when social support is available, and when financial resources are adequate to handle medical expenses. African American caregivers typically report less stress and depression in their roles as caregivers than Caucasian Americans do (Connell & Gibson, 1997). Certain cognitive attitudes might be protective as well (e.g., Gatz, Bengtson, & Blam, 1990). For example, it may be less stressful for a caregiver to adopt an accepting attitude toward the patient's behavior—"There's nothing I can do to change the situation, so let me just resign myself to it and make the necessary adjustments"—rather than take a more active approach—"How can I get mom to remember to put her coat on before leaving the house?" In a study by Knight, Lutzky, and Olshevski (1992), efforts to help distressed caregivers solve problems and accept responsibility actually increased their stress as measured by cardiovascular reactivity. Knight and colleagues speculate that problem-solving training may reinforce the view that the caregiver is responsible for the patient's problem behaviors.

Families can be helped, however, to cope better with the daily stress of having a family member with Alzheimer's. For example, because people with Alzheimer's have great difficulty placing new information into memory, they can engage in a reasonable conversation but forget a few minutes later what has been discussed. A caregiver may become impatient unless he or she understands that this impairment is to be expected because of the brain damage. Family members can learn communication strategies to adapt to the memory loss. For example, families can ask questions that embed the answer. For example, it is much easier to respond to "Was the

person you just spoke to on the phone Harry or Tom?" than to "Who just called?"

It is also useful for caregivers to understand that patients do not always recognize their limitations and may try to engage in activities beyond their abilities, sometimes dangerously so. Caregivers must set limits regarding dangerous activities. For example, caregivers often need to tell a relative with Alzheimer's disease that driving is off-limits (and then remove car keys, as they can assume that the relative will forget the new rule).

Caregivers need opportunities to vent their feelings of guilt and resentment. Many of their frustrations cannot and should not be shared with the person with dementia, and so having sources of support outside the home can be a big help. Some caregivers may need permission and support to take time off (Olshevski, Katz, & Knight, 1999). Because the family caregivers are so powerfully affected, it is recommended that they be given respites from their task. The person may be hospitalized for a week, a health care worker may take over to give the family an opportunity for a holiday, or the person may be enrolled at an adult day-care center.

Programs that teach coping strategies for the caregivers (e.g., increasing pleasant activities, exercise or social support) as well as individual behavioral therapy have been shown to relieve caregiver burden (Selwood et al., 2007). Programs lasting at least six weeks (Selwood et al., 2007) or offering multiple components (e.g., psychoeducation about dementia, case-management services, and cognitive behavioral strategies) more consistently reduce caregiver's distress (Acton & Kang, 2001). A study of 1,222 caregivers found that multicomponent programs were particularly helpful for female caregivers and for those with less education (Gitlin et al., 2003). Caregiver support programs have been found to be effective in improving the immune function of caregivers (Garand et al., 2002), decreasing medical costs of the person with dementia, and slowing the timing of institutionalization (Teri et al., 2003).

Caring for a relative with Alzheimer's disease is a source of severe stress. (David Young-Wolff/PhotoEdit.)

New research is examining the best ways to integrate caregiver programs into the medical system. Researchers have shown that these programs can be offered effectively in HMO settings, improving the ease of access (Toseland et al., 2004). One study found that providing social work consultation to caregivers improved the quality of medical treatment provided to people with Alzheimer's disease (Vickrey et al., 2006). Unfortunately, these caregiver support programs remain inaccessible for many people; only half of physicians provide caregivers with such programs (Rosen et al., 2002).

Delirium

The term **delirium** is derived from the Latin words *de*, meaning "out of," and *lira*, meaning "track." The term implies being off track or deviating from the usual state (Wells & Duncan, 1980). As illustrated in the clinical case of Henry at the beginning of this chapter, delirium is typically described as a clouded state of consciousness. The two most common symptoms are extreme trouble focusing attention and profound disturbances in the sleep/wake cycle (Meagher, 2007). Patients, sometimes rather suddenly, have so much trouble focusing attention that they cannot maintain a coherent stream of thought. The sleep/wake cycle becomes disturbed, making patients drowsy during the day yet awake and agitated at night. Vivid dreams and nightmares are common. People with delirium may be impossible to engage in conversation because of their wandering attention and fragmented thinking. In severe delirium, speech is rambling and incoherent. Bewildered and confused, some people with delirium may become so disoriented that they are unclear about what day it is, where they are, and even who they are. Memory impairment, especially for recent events, is common.

In the course of a 24-hour period, people with delirium have lucid intervals and become alert and coherent. They are usually worse during sleepless nights and in the dark. These daily fluctuations help distinguish delirium from other syndromes, especially Alzheimer's disease.

Perceptual disturbances are frequent in delirium. People mistake the unfamiliar for the familiar; for example, they may state that they are at home instead of in a hospital. Although visual hallucinations are common, they are not always present. Delusions—beliefs contrary to reality—have been noted in about 25 percent of older adults with delirium (Camus et al., 2000). These delusions tend to be poorly worked out, fleeting, and changeable.

Swings in activity and mood accompany these disordered thoughts and perceptions. People with delirium can be erratic, ripping their clothes one moment and sitting lethargically the next. People with delirium may also shift rapidly from one emotion to another—depression, anxiety, fright, anger, euphoria, and irritability. Fever, flushed face, dilated pupils, tremors, rapid heartbeat, elevated blood pressure, and incontinence of urine and feces are common. If delirium worsens, the person may become stuporous and lethargic (Webster & Holroyd, 2000).

As noted in the diagnostic criteria, delirium is caused by medical conditions. Several causes of delirium in older adults have been identified: drug intoxications and drug-withdrawal reactions, metabolic and nutritional imbalances (as in uncontrolled diabetes, thyroid dysfunction, kidney or liver failure, congestive heart failure, or malnutrition), infections or fevers (like pneumonia or urinary tract infections), neurological disorders (like head trauma or seizures), and the stress of major surgery, most commonly hip surgery (Knight, 1996; Zarit & Zarit, 1998). As in the case of Henry at the start of this chapter, however, delirium usually has more than one cause.

People of any age are subject to delirium, but it is more common among children and older adults. Among older adults, it is particularly common in nursing homes and hospitals. For example, one study found that 6 to 12 percent of nursing home residents developed delirium in the course of one year (Katz, Parmelee, & Brubaker, 1991), and rates much higher than this have been found in elderly hospital patients (Meagher, 2001). For example, in one study, 46 percent of patients with hip fractures experienced delirium (Marcantonio et al., 2001).

Why are older adults so vulnerable to delirium? Many explanations have been offered: the physical declines of late life, the increased susceptibility to chronic diseases, the many medications prescribed for older people, and the greater sensitivity to drugs. One other factor, brain damage, increases the risk of delirium. Older people with dementia appear to be the most susceptible to delirium. A retrospective review of 100 hospital admissions of people of all ages who had a diagnosis of delirium revealed that 44 percent of them had delirium superimposed on another brain condition (Purdie, Honigman, & Rosen, 1981).

Unfortunately, delirium is often misdiagnosed (Knight, 1996). For example, among 77 hospitalized older adults who had clear symptoms of delirium, about 60 percent had no notation of delirium in the hospital chart (Lauril et al., 2004). Physicians are particularly unlikely to detect delirium when lethargy is present (Cole, 2004).

Delirium is often misdiagnosed when a person has dementia. Table 15.2 compares the features of dementia and delirium. Knight (1996) offers a useful suggestion for distinguishing delirium from dementia:

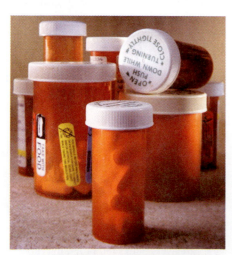

Medication misuse, whether deliberate or inadvertent, can be a serious problem among older people and can cause delirium. (Eric Kamp/Phototake.)

The clinical "feel" of talking with a person with delirium is rather like talking to someone who is acutely intoxicated or in an acute psychotic episode. Whereas the demented patient may not remember the name of the place where she or he is, the delirious patient may believe it is a different sort of place altogether, perhaps mistaking a psychiatric ward for a used car lot. (pp. 96–97)

Detecting and treating delirium is of fundamental importance. Untreated, the mortality rate for delirium is high; more than one-third of people with the condition die within a year, either from exhaustion or from the medical condition causing the delirium (McCusker, Cole, & Abrahamowicz, 2002). Beyond the risk of death, elderly adults who develop delirium in the hospital are at an increased risk for further cognitive decline (Jackson et al., 2004).

Table 15.2 Comparative Features of Dementia and Delirium

Dementia	Delirium
Gradual deterioration of abilities	Rapid onset
Deficits in memory for recent events	Trouble concentrating and staying with a train of thought
Not explained by another medical condition	Secondary to another medical condition
Usually progressive and nonreversible	Fluctuations over the course of a day
Treatment offers only minimal benefit	Usually reversible by treating underlying condition, but potentially fatal if cause—e.g., malnutrition—not treated
Prevalence increases with age	Prevalence is high in the very young as well as the old

Treatment of Delirium   Complete recovery from delirium is possible if the underlying cause is treated promptly and effectively. The older adult who has a cognitive impairment must be examined thoroughly for all possible reversible causes of the disorder, such as drug intoxication, infections, fever, and malnutrition, and then treated accordingly. Beyond treating the underlying medical conditions, the most common treatment is atypical antipsychotic medications (Lonergen, Britton, & Luxenberg, 2007). It usually takes one to four weeks for the condition to clear; it takes longer in older people than in younger people.

Because of the high rates of delirium in hospitalized older adults, one study examined the efficacy of primary prevention strategies—in other words, the aim was to prevent delirium from starting. The researchers randomly assigned 852 hospitalized patients who were 70 years of age or older to receive either standard medical care only or standard medical care along with an intervention designed to prevent delirium. This intervention addressed risk factors for delirium such as sleep deprivation, immobility, dehydration, visual and hearing impairment, and cognitive impairment. The patients who received the intervention were significantly less likely to develop delirium, and for those who did develop delirium, the symptoms cleared more quickly (Inouye et al., 1999).

The high risk of delirium among people with dementia raises another set of prevention issues. The family of a person with dementia should learn the symptoms of delirium and know about its reversible nature, so that they do not interpret the onset of delirium as a new stage of a progressive dementia. With proper diagnosis and treatment, the person can usually return to the earlier state.

Quick Summary

Dementia is a broad term to capture cognitive decline, most commonly a decline in memory for recent events. As cognitive deficits become more widespread and profound, social and occupational functioning becomes more and more disturbed. Dementia affects approximately 1 to 2 percent of people in their sixties but more than 20 percent of people over the age of 80. There are many types of dementia, including Alzheimer's, frontotemporal, vascular, dementia with Lewy bodies, and dementia from other medical causes.

Alzheimer's disease is characterized by plaques and tangles in the brain. It has been related to the APOE-4 allele. The expression of genetic vulnerability, though, is influenced by environmental and psychological events, such as depression, and baseline cognitive ability and activity. The FDA has approved acetylcholinesterase inhibitors and Memantine for the treatment of Alzheimer's disease, but these medications offer modest effects. Psychoeducation may be helpful for some people during the early stages of Alzheimer's but is not helpful as the dementia symptoms become more profound. Exercise appears to improve cognitive functioning for people with mild cognitive impairment as well as those with Alzheimer's disease. Caregivers of people with Alzheimer's are at high risk for depression and anxiety. Multimodal interventions that address a range of caregiver issues, including even periods of respite from caretaking, offer some protection against psychological symptoms.

Frontotemporal dementia (FTD) is characterized by neuronal deterioration in the amygdala, frontal, and temporal lobes. Pick's disease is one form of FTD. The primary symptoms of FTD include marked changes in social and emotional behavior.

Vascular dementia affects subcortical areas of the brain and often occurs after a stroke. Genetic factors do not play a direct role in vascular dementia.

Dementia with Lewy bodies is characterized by visual hallucinations, fluctuations in cognitive functioning, supersensitivity to side effects of antipsychotic medications, and intense dreams during which the person moves and talks. It is believed that DLB is related to dysfunction in basal ganglia neurons.

Delirium is a cognitive disorder characterized by clouded consciousness, disorientation, and inability to follow conversation. Mood and symptoms tend to vary throughout the day. Delirium is most likely to affect children and older adults; among the elderly, it is particularly common in hospitals and nursing homes. By definition, delirium is secondary to an underlying medical condition. If the underlying medical condition is treated, full recovery from delirium can be expected. Delirium is often not detected, though, and the risk of further cognitive decline and even death is quite high when symptoms are not addressed.

Check Your Knowledge 15.3

Answer the questions.

1. Dementia is commonly characterized by:
   a. anxiety
   b. memory loss
   c. frank disorganization
   d. sad mood

2. Delirium is characterized by:
   a. anxiety
   b. memory loss
   c. frank disorganization
   d. sad mood

3. Mary, a 70-year-old woman, was hospitalized for hip surgery. Although there were no immediate complications of the surgery, her son became concerned when he visited her that night because she was not making any sense. She thanked him for checking her into the Ritz Carlton and laughed giddily when he told her that she was in the hospital. Half an hour later, she began sobbing. Although she seemed fine the next morning, symptoms of acute confusion reemerged by lunchtime. Which diagnosis is most likely for Mary?
   a. Alzheimer's disease
   b. frontotemporal dementia
   c. mania
   d. delirium

Psychological Disorders in Late Life

Above, we described the cognitive disorders, which become more common as people age. Here, though, we turn to issues in understanding how aging relates to the other psychological disorders, such as depressive disorders, anxiety disorders, and substance abuse. We first look at the prevalence of mental disorders in late life. Then we consider questions about whether there are unique aspects of etiology and treatment when these disorders occur among older adults compared to younger adults.

The DSM criteria for older adults are the same as those for younger adults. This is because the symptoms of mental disorders are assumed to be the same in adulthood and late life, even though little research tests this assumption (Gatz, Kasl-Godley, & Karel, 1996).

Prevalence: How Common Are Psychological Disorders in Late Life?

How likely are older people to have mental disorders? Current estimates indicate that persons over age 65 have the lowest overall prevalence of mental disorders of all age groups (see Table 15.3). Note that the rates of schizophrenia and bipolar disorder in late life are particularly low. [These rates are so low that we will not focus on schizophrenia and bipolar disorder in this chap-

Table 15.3 One-Year Prevalence Rates of Mental Illness in Older and Younger Generations as Estimated in the Epidemiological Catchment Area Data

	One-Year Prevalence Rate (%)	
Disorder	Age 18–54	Age 55+
Any anxiety disorder	13.1	11.4
Simple phobia	8.3	7.3
Social phobia	2.0	1.0
Agoraphobia	4.9	4.1
Panic disorder	1.6	0.5
Obsessive-compulsive disorder	2.4	1.5
Any mood disorder	7.1	4.4
Major depressive disorder	5.3	3.7
Dysthymia	1.6	1.6
Bipolar I	1.1	0.2
Bipolar II	0.6	0.1
Schizophrenia	1.3	0.6
Antisocial personality disorder	2.1	0.0
Anorexia nervosa	0.1	0.0

Source: U.S. Department of Health and Human Services (1999).

ter, other than to note that treatments for older and younger people appear comparable (Jeste et al., 2003).] Prevalence rates for alcohol abuse or dependence are less than 2 percent in late life (Helzer, Burnam, & McEvoy, 1991). In one major NIMH survey (Regier et al., 1988), none of those aged 65 and older met criteria for a drug abuse or dependency disorder. These rates of substance abuse and dependence are much lower than the rates that have been determined for the general adult population (p. 279). Even rates of depression and anxiety appear lower than in younger populations. In sum, most people 65 years of age and older are free from serious psychopathology. Nonetheless, 10 to 20 percent do have psychological problems severe enough to warrant professional attention (Gatz et al., 1996).

Why are rates of psychopathology so low in late life? There are several completely different answers to these questions. Some have advised caution in interpreting such data, as a set of methodological issues must be considered. It also appears that there may be some processes related to aging that promote better mental health.

Methodologically, older adults may be more uncomfortable acknowledging and discussing mental health problems compared to younger people. Similarly, older people might feel embarrassed about describing drug use.

In addition to reporting bias, there are potential cohort effects. That is, the next generation of people to become old may manifest more depression, anxiety, and substance abuse than people who are already older (Zarit & Zarit, 1998).

Beyond these explanations, people with mental illness are at risk for dying earlier—before age 65—for several different reasons. Among heavy drinkers, the peak years for death from cirrhosis are between 55 and 64 years of age, and cardiovascular disease is also common (Shaper, 1990). Cardiovascular disease is also more common among people with a history of anxiety disorders, depressive disorders, and bipolar disorder (Kubzanski et al., 2007). Even milder psychological disorders compromise immune function, and as people age, they become particularly sensitive to these immune effects (Kiecolt-Glaser & Glaser, 2001). This may lead to worse outcomes for many medical conditions that are more common as people age. Psychological disorders are associated with increased mortality (Angst et al., 2002; Enger et al., 2004; King, 2005). For example, Frojdh and colleagues (2003) conducted surveys with over 1,200 elderly people living in Sweden. Compared to those with low scores, those who obtained high scores on a self-report measure of depression were 2.5 times as likely to die within the next six years. Because people with mental illness may die earlier, research studies on aging may suffer from the issue of selective mortality.

These three methodological issues—response biases, cohort effects, and selective mortality—could help explain the low prevalence of psychological disorders in late life. Most researchers, though, believe that aging is also genuinely related to better mental health. Above, we described findings that emotional coping improves as people age. This should translate into a decrease in psychological disorders. Some longitudinal studies suggest that many people who experience psychopathology early in life seem to grow out of those symptoms. For example, longitudinal studies indicate that heavy drinkers tend to drink less as they enter late life (Fillmore, 1987). Findings like these suggest that enhanced coping abilities developed across the life course may help protect people from mental illness during late life.

In sum, studies suggest lower rates of mental illness among the elderly. Although some methodological issues (low levels of disclosure, cohort effects, and selective mortality) might explain part of this effect, it is also possible that some people become more psychologically healthy as they age.

Beyond examining the prevalence rates of disorder, it is important to consider the incidence rates, or how many people are experiencing the onset of a new disorder. Most people who have an episode of a psychological disorder late in life are experiencing a recurrence of a disorder that started earlier in life, rather than an initial onset. For example, 97 percent of older adults with generalized anxiety disorder reported that their anxiety symptoms began before the age of 65 (Alwahhabi, 2003), and 94 percent of older adults with major depressive disorder had experienced depressive episodes earlier in life (Norton et al., 2006). Late onset is also extremely rare for schizophrenia (Karon & VandenBos, 1998). In contrast, late-onset alcohol dependence is more common among older adults with drinking problems (Liberto, Oslin, & Ruskin, 1996).

Medical Issues in Diagnosing Psychological Disorders

DSM criteria specify that a psychological disorder should not be diagnosed if the symptoms can be accounted for by a medical condition or medication side effects. Because medical conditions are more common in the elderly, it is particularly important to rule out such explanations. Medical problems such as thyroid problems, Addison's disease, Cushing's disease, Parkinson's disease, Alzheimer's disease, hypoglycemia, anemia, and vitamin deficiencies can produce symptoms that mimic schizophrenia, depression, or anxiety (Marengo & Westermeyer, 1996). Angina, congestive heart failure, and excessive caffeine consumption may all cause a faster heart rate, which can be mistaken as a symptom of anxiety (Fisher & Noll, 1996). Age-related deterioration in the vestibular system (inner-ear control of one's sense of balance) can account for panic symptoms such as severe dizziness (Raj, Corvea, & Dagon, 1993). Antihypertensive medication, hormones, corticosteroids, and antiparkinsonism medications may contribute to depression or anxiety (Spar & LaRue, 1990).

Major Depressive Disorder

The epidemiology of depression in late life shares many parallels with patterns observed earlier in life. For example, during late life, depression is more likely to occur in women than men, and depressive episodes tend to co-occur with anxiety and alcohol abuse (Gallo & Lebowitz, 1999). Researchers initially believed that symptoms of depression differed in late life, but researchers have identified only one consistent difference—cognitive symptoms (such as memory deficits and confusion) appear more pronounced when depression emerges in late life compared to earlier adulthood, as discussed next.

Depression versus Dementia Depression is likely to produce more cognitive impairment in the elderly than it does in younger people (Lockwood et al., 2000). The frequent presence of cognitive symptoms in late-life depression can make it hard to differentiate whether memory problems are due to dementia or to depression. Indeed, depression in older adults is often misdiagnosed as dementia because of the severe cognitive impairment. No single neuropsychological test can clearly differentiate people with depression from those with dementia, although researchers are working hard to develop a battery of specific memory tests that would help make this distinction (Swainson et al., 2001). When depressive symptoms are present, a good course of action is to treat them and hope that cognitive symptoms are improved in the process. Although treating depression is likely to bring some relief from cognitive symptoms, many elderly people who show cog-

Although depression is less common among older adults than younger ones, it accounts for a very large proportion of the psychiatric hospital admissions among the aged. (David Young-Wolff/PhotoEdit.)

nitive deficits during their depressive episodes will continue to experience at least mild cognitive problems after they recover from the depressive symptoms (Bhalla et al., 2006).

Of course, people can have both dementia and depression. Cognitive difficulties in late life do predict increases in depression over time (Vinkers et al., 2004). And the opposite direction of effects seems to occur as well: a lifetime history of depression predicts more decline in cognitive functioning (Ganguli et al., 2006); a twofold increase in risk for Alzheimer's disease (Ownby et al., 2006); and, among those who develop Alzheimer's disease, a faster progression of the illness (Rapp et al., 2006).

Etiology of Depression in Older Adults   Many of the causes of depression in older adults parallel those seen among younger adults. On the other hand, some new problems emerge during late life that can trigger depression.

A body of evidence has emerged about people who develop a first episode of depression after age 65. These late-onset first episodes seem particularly tied to vascular disease. For example, more than 20 percent of people develop a depressive episode in the 18 months after a myocardial infarction (Frasure-Smith, Lesperance, & Talajic, 1995). Moreover, a meta-analysis of 98 studies indicates that when the brains of people with late-onset depression are imaged, small white spots, called white matter hyperintensities (WMH), are often present (Herrmann, Le Masurier, & Ebmeier, 2008). WMH are more common as people age and are associated with cardiovascular risk factors, but they appear to be about twice as common among people with late-onset depression as they are in age-matched persons who do not experience depression. Taken together, these findings suggest that strokes and other vascular disease could explain the development of some late-onset depressions. The opposite direction of effects also has been shown. That is, increasing evidence suggests that depression can also contribute to cardiovascular disease, a topic we cover in Focus on Discovery 15.2.

FOCUS ON DISCOVERY 15.2

Depression and Cardiovascular Disease

It is now well established that depression predicts a worse outcome for people with cardiovascular disease. Indeed, in one meta-analysis, authors were able to compile the findings of 22 prospective studies that controlled for baseline medical and cardiovascular factors. Across those studies, depression was found to be related to a 90 percent increase in the risk of onset of cardiovascular disease and a 60 percent increase in the severity of cardiovascular disease over time (Nicholson, Kuper, & Hemingway, 2006). A separate meta-analysis shows that depression is also related to increased risk of death from cardiovascular disease, even after controlling for baseline cardiovascular health (Barth, Schumacher, & Herrmann-Lingen, 2004).

Given these disturbing findings, a high priority has been placed on whether these depressions are relieved by standard treatments. Several major studies have been conducted to examine this question. For example, in one study, more than 2,400 people who had just experienced a myocardial infarction (MI) and had at least mild symptoms of depression were randomly assigned to receive cognitive behavior therapy (CBT) or standard medical care. If people receiving CBT continued to show high levels of depression after five sessions, Sertraline was prescribed as well. Active intervention did lead to significant reductions in depression compared to placebo treatment (Berkman et al., 2003). In contrast to these promising results for CBT, interpersonal psychotherapy does not appear to significantly reduce depression in this population (Lesperance et al., 2007).

Researchers have also examined how well antidepressants work within this population. Tricyclic antidepressants are not recommended, because they have been found to be associated with twice the risk of subsequent

MI as compared to placebos in this population (Cohen, Gibson & Alderman, 2000). Better evidence has emerged for selective serotonin reuptake inhibitors (SSRIs), such as fluoxetine (Prozac), among people who are depressed after an MI. For example, in one study, 369 people were randomly assigned to receive Sertraline (an SSRI) or a placebo for 24 weeks. Sertraline was effective—and particularly effective for the people with severe and recurrent depression (Glassman et al., 2002).

While it is clear that depression can be treated among people who have had an MI, treatment has not been found to reduce the risk of death from cardiovascular disease. More specifically, many of the treatment studies have documented slightly lower rates of death in the treatment group than in the control group, but the number of deaths is small enough that such findings do not achieve statistical significance (Glassman, 2005). Carney and his colleagues reasoned that it isn't whether or not a person receives treatment that should matter, but rather, whether or not treatment worked. In a more careful analysis of people prescribed antidepressants after an MI, actual improvement in depression predicted greater likelihood of survival (Carney et al., 2004). This would suggest that it may be important to offer aggressive treatment, to ensure full relief from depression.

A major goal, then, is to help medical teams to routinely screen for depression and provide treatment. Many physicians are likely to dismiss symptoms of depression in a patient who has just had a heart attack, assuming that people might be understandably distressed by their recent change in health. However, depression relief may be an important component of medical recovery.

Beyond the specific ties to cardiovascular disease, poor physical health is a major risk factor for depression among older adults. Medical illness and physical disabilities (such as trouble walking) are major predictors of the onset of depressive symptoms in late life (Schoevers et al., 2006). As we grow older, we are more likely to experience a number of life events that would be expected to cause depression, such as the death of a spouse, social isolation, and retirement. Rates of depression do increase markedly in the year after people become widowed (Bruce, 2002). On the other hand, the number of people in a person's network (social isolation) is not as strongly linked to depression in late life as it is in middle age (Bruce et al., 2002), perhaps because older people place less emphasis on casual social contacts than younger people do (see the earlier discussion of social selectivity in older adults). Furthermore, most people do not become depressed after retirement. Any ill effects of retirement may have more to do with the poor health and low incomes of some retirees and less with retirement per se (Pahkala, 1990). Successful adjustment to retirement is tied to positive marital relationships, high education, high job prestige before retirement, and high self-efficacy and self-esteem (Kim & Moen, 2001). For many older adults, retirement ushers in a satisfying period of life (Wolfe, Morrow, & Frederickson, 1996). We would do well to assume that adaptation rather than depression is the common reaction to loss and stress in late life.

Treatment of Depression   Many primary care physicians do not diagnose, and therefore do not treat, depression (Wolfe et al., 1996). In one study of 599 people who were at least 85 years of age, only 25 percent of people who met criteria for major depressive disorder were diagnosed with such by their primary care doctor, and very few received appropriate treatment (Stek et al., 2004).

At least 20 high-quality studies have been conducted to examine psychotherapy for late-life depression (Scogin et al., 2005). As with younger adults, research supports the use of cognitive and behavioral approaches (Scogin et al., 2005). Several of the psychotherapy findings, though, contrast with those observed in younger adults. Interpersonal psychotherapy does not appear to be more effective than a placebo in preventing relapse among older adults with depression (Reynolds et al., 2006). Other treatments that have received little attention for depression occurring earlier in life appear helpful for late-life depression. These include short-term psychodynamic therapy (Gallagher & Thompson, 1983) as well as reminiscence therapy, in which people review significant positive and negative events in their life histories to gain perspective (Scogin et al., 2005).

At least 17 studies now indicate that antidepressant medications, such as selective serotonin reuptake inhibitors (SSRIs), are more effective than placebos are for treatment of late-life depression (Roose & Schatzberg, 2005). About 60 percent of elderly people with depression respond to antidepressant treatments as compared to about 40 percent of patients who respond to placebo (Delano-Wood & Abeles, 2005). Cognitive behavioral therapy provides additional relief when added to antidepressant medication (Unutzer et al., 2002).

Despite the encouraging findings for antidepressant medications, either alone or in combination with psychological treatment, some caution is merited. Older adults are likely to be highly sensitive to the side effects of antidepressant drugs, such as postural hypotension (a fall in blood pressure when standing up), which causes some people to become dizzy when they stand up and then to fall. (Falls in older adults are far more serious than they are for younger people. Broken bones take much longer to heal, and certain head injuries can be fatal.) Moreover, older people are at high risk for toxic reactions to medications of all kinds. Side effects of antidepressants may also be problematic among older adults (Menting et al., 1996). In one clinical trial, 76 percent of elderly people taking SSRIs experienced at least some side effects, and 25 percent discontinued medications because of side effects. Side effects and drug discontinuation rates are worse for tricyclic antidepressants than for SSRIs among the elderly (Mottram, Wilson, & Strobl, 2006). Although not all studies have found such high side effect rates, the lower tolerability of antidepressants among the elderly suggests that nonpharmacological approaches are particularly important (Scoggin & McElerath, 1994). Indeed, Landreville and colleagues (2001) found that elderly people with depression reported that they would rather receive cognitive therapy than antidepressant medications.

Some psychiatrists recommend electroconvulsive therapy (p. 241), particularly for elderly people who had an earlier favorable response to it (Sackeim, 2004). ECT does involve significant side effects, though, including cardiovascular risks that may be of particular concern among the elderly (Delano-Wood & Abeles, 2005). Cognitive side effects also appear more severe among elderly compared to younger patients (Sackeim et al., 2007).

One innovative program addressed depression among elderly people with chronic medical illnesses. Although chronic medical illnesses increase risk for depression, problems with mobility can interfere with attending therapy sessions. Ciechanowski and colleagues (2004), then, looked at how therapy would work if it were offered in the home. The treatment they offered had a great deal in common with psychological treatments covered in Chapter 8; it included problem solving for improving life situations, increasing behavioral activation, and other standard techniques. If warranted, recommendations were made to primary care providers for antidepressant medications. In this way, the study was not designed to look at psychological treatment so much as to provide some form of depression treatment for this highly vulnerable population. People were randomly assigned to receive either depression treatment or treatment as usual (standard medical care). Findings of this study offer good news and bad news. On the good side, depression treatment was significantly more likely to produce remission (33 percent) than treatment as usual (12 percent). On the downside, even with depression treatment, two-thirds of people continued to experience depressive symptoms, and treatment also did not improve quality of life. The findings suggest that depression treatment helps but also that it is hard to restore all aspects of life when older people face such severe medical conditions.

Suicide   The risk factors for suicide in the elderly are parallel with those in younger people (see Chapter 8). For example, in older and younger people, depression is the major risk factor. Beyond depression, it is worth noting that physical illness, loss of loved ones, and dire financial circumstances, problems that are widespread among older adults, are important risk factors for suicide.

Regardless of the reasons, the elevated suicide rates for people over age 65 are a concern: older adults are three times more likely to kill themselves than younger adults are (McIntosh, 1995). The suicide rate for men increases in a linear fashion with age from adolescence onward, whereas the rate for women peaks in their fifties and then slowly declines across the rest of the life span (McIntosh, 1995). Older Caucasian men are more likely to commit suicide than are members of any other group; the peak ages for committing suicide in this group are from 80 to 84 (Conwell, 2001). Although African American men are less likely to die from suicide than Caucasian men are, the rate of suicide increases with age among African American men (Alston, Rankin, & Harris, 1995).

Older persons are less likely to communicate their intentions to commit suicide and more likely to use lethal methods than are younger people (Conwell, 2001). Once people are past age 65, their attempts rarely fail (Butler, Lewis, & Sunderland, 1998). Furthermore, the statistics are probably underestimates; older adults have many opportunities to neglect their diet or medications, thus killing themselves in a more passive fashion.

One treatment program to reduce depression and suicidality among the elderly draws on the finding that elderly people are more likely to visit primary care doctors than to see specialty mental health providers. Bruce and colleagues (2004) screened for depression among people over the age of 60 who were seeking medical care. People with symptoms were offered an antidepressant medication, and if they did not want medication, they were offered a chance to receive psychological treatment. Interestingly, although the people had not been seeking depression treatment, about 90 percent of them accepted either medication or psychological treatment when they were offered. Compared to people who received typical medical care, those who received either medication or psychological treatment obtained faster relief from their depression and from suicidal ideation, differences that were still observable at a one year follow-up.

Anxiety Disorders

In general, symptoms of anxiety disorders do not differ as people enter late life (Gretarsdortir et al., 2004). GAD is the most common anxiety disorder among the elderly (Alwahhabi, 2003). Posttraumatic stress disorder (PTSD) is seen among some older war veterans (Cook, 2001) and has been observed among older people after traumatic health crises (Scogin, 1998). One study found that even 50 years after the event, many veterans are still affected by their war experiences (Hunt & Robbins, 2001).

Beyond ruling out medical explanations, causes of anxiety disorders are often related to the circumstances of getting older (Fisher & Noll, 1996)—threats of social isolation, poverty,

As with younger adults, anxiety disorders are more prevalent than depression. Worries about illnesses and becoming incapacitated may be a focus of concerns. (Zac Macaulay/The Image Bank/Getty Images.)

and medical difficulties become more prominent as people age. In addition to aging-relevant causes, anxiety in late life appears related to some of the same risk factors that are known to increase risk of anxiety disorders earlier in life, such as neuroticism (Schuurmans et al., 2005).

Anxiety problems in older adults seem to respond to the same types of psychological treatments found useful with younger adults (see Chapter 5), but less controlled research is available. For example, cognitive behavioral treatment has been found to be fairly helpful in reducing symptoms of anxiety (Ayers et al., 2007).

Short-acting benzodiazepines are the most widely used treatment for anxiety disorders in the elderly (Alwahhabi, 2003). Unfortunately, older adults are particularly sensitive to side effects from this class of medications—longitudinal research has shown that benzodiazepine use in older adults is predictive of increased morbidity, cognitive decline, and urinary incontinence (Alwahhabi, 2003). Indeed, given the concerns about how dangerous these medications can be for older adults, the federal government has now instituted guidelines that long-term care facilities should limit the use of short-acting benzodiazepines to less than 10 continuous days and the use of longer-acting benzodiazepines to less than four months. Despite these guidelines, more than 20 percent of nursing home residents are prescribed benzodiazepines, and eight percent use them for more than four months (Svarstad & Mount, 2001). A central goal, then, is to identify medications with fewer side effects. Busiperone (BusPar), which has fewer side effects, has been shown to be effective in one study of GAD. Surprisingly, researchers know little about anti-depressant medications for treatment of anxiety in older adults, despite their efficacy in younger populations.

Delusional (Paranoid) Disorders

Symptoms of paranoia, such as Jeanine's fears in the upcoming clinical case that her husband and her neighbors were trying to hurt her, are found in many older people with psychiatric disorders. For example, in a study of people age 85 and older, psychiatric interviews with family members and key informants suggested that 6.9 percent of people had experienced at least mild paranoid symptoms in the past year (Ostling & Skoog, 2002). In evaluating whether such symptoms merit diagnosis, though, clinicians must be sensitive to the fact that older people are often mistreated. Others may talk about them behind their backs or even to their faces, and people may take advantage of older adults in many ways. That is, complaints from an older person concerning persecution may be justified.

Although paranoia in older people may be the continuation of a disorder that began earlier in life, the most common causes of paranoia in late life are delirium and dementia (Livingston et al., 2001). Paranoid ideation also has been linked to loss of hearing or sight (Ostling & Skoog, 2002). An older person who is having trouble hearing may believe that other people are whispering about him or her. Beyond cognitive and sensory declines, increases in social isolation can trigger paranoid symptoms (Gurland, 1991). This isolation limits the person's opportunities to check his or her suspicions about the world, making it easier for delusions to take hold. A good evaluation, then, will incorporate medical, cognitive, sensory, and social assessments.

If paranoid symptoms are secondary to delirium or sensory impairment, treatment should address these issues. Otherwise, the treatment of paranoia is much the same for older adults as for younger adults. Although controlled data on the treatment of paranoia in older adults are lacking, supportive approaches to establish rapport, complemented by cognitive therapy, are recommended. Studies indicate that delusions in older people can be treated with some success with antipsychotic medications (Schneider, 1996), although people who are experiencing paranoia are generally suspicious of the motives of those who give them drugs. Toxicity from medications must also be considered, given the particular sensitivity of older people to drugs.

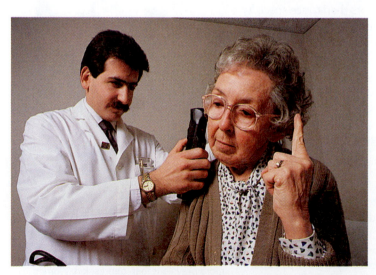
Loss of hearing is common in the elderly and can create the sense that others are whispering behind their back. (J. Griffin/The Image Works.)

Clinical Case: Jeanine

Jeanine was a 66-year-old married woman who reluctantly agreed to a clinical evaluation. She [had] a six-week history of bizarre delusions and hallucinations of her husband spraying the house with a fluid that smelled like "burned food." She complained that he sprayed the substance everywhere around the house, including draperies and furniture, although she had never seen him do it. She could smell the substance almost constantly, and she said that it affected her head, chest, and rectum. She also complained that someone in the neighborhood had been throwing bricks and rocks at her house. In addition, she suspected her husband of having affairs with other women, whose footprints she claimed to have seen near home.

During the interview, Jeanine was sullen toward the interviewer. She looked very sad at times and would occasionally wipe away a tear, but her predominant affect was extreme hostility about her husband's alleged behavior (Varner & Gaitz, 1982, p. 108).

Substance Abuse and Dependence

Although few people meet diagnostic criteria for alcohol or substance abuse, a fair number of people drink heavily during late life (Molgaard et al., 1990). It is important, then, to consider that the physiological consequences of alcohol become more intense as people age. For example, tolerance for alcohol diminishes with age, in part because the ratio of body water to body mass decreases with time, resulting in higher blood alcohol concentration per unit of alcohol imbibed (Morse, 1988). In addition, older people metabolize alcohol more slowly. Thus, the drug may cause greater changes in brain chemistry and may more readily bring on toxic effects, such as delirium and memory problems, in older people (Brandt et al., 1983).

Because older adults tend not to go to work regularly and may not even be seen in public for days or weeks at a time, consequences of drugs may continue for a long time without being noticed. Compounding these issues, clinicians may be less likely to look for substance abuse in older people than in younger people and instead may attribute symptoms such as poor motor coordination and impaired memory to a medical problem or to late-life depression. Indeed, substance problems are often comorbid with major depression (Liberto et al., 1996). If substance abuse goes unrecognized, treatment will be severely compromised.

The misuse of prescription and over-the-counter medicines is a much greater problem than abuse of alcohol or illegal drugs in the elderly (LaRue, Dessonville, Jarvik et al., 1985). Elderly people have a higher rate of legal drug intake than any other group; although they constitute only 13 percent of the population, they consume about one-third of all prescribed medications (Weber, 1996). Older people also use more antianxiety medications than any other age group: rates of benzodiazepine use in older adults have been estimated at 14 to 37 percent (Wetherell, 1998). The use of benzodiazapines and sleep aids can create physical as well as psychological dependency. Many people may have trouble recognizing that the medications that were prescribed for them by a respected and trusted doctor may be addictive and problematic.

Check Your Knowledge 15.4

True or false?
1. Mental illnesses occur more often as people age.
2. Most mental illnesses among older adults are continuations of illnesses that they had earlier in life.
3. Elderly men are more likely to kill themselves than are younger men.

Adjusting Treatment with Older Adults

Several barriers may prevent older people from receiving adequate mental health care. First, older people may hold more negative beliefs about mental illness and treatment. Second, older people are less likely than younger adults to be assessed and referred for mental health care (Knight, 1996).

Even when an elderly person can access treatment, clinicians tend to expect less success in treating older people than in treating younger people (Knight, 1996). Yet, as described above, research shows that psychological treatments can be successful for older people. Indeed, with increasing years come increasing reflectiveness and a tendency to be philosophical about life (Neugarten, 1977), traits that bode well for psychotherapeutic interventions.

Although psychological treatment tends to be successful with the elderly, it may be important to adjust the process in several ways. Many of the emotional concerns of older adults may be realistic reactions to problems in aging, and pragmatic supports may be a better approach in those circumstances than attempts to help a person see the problem differently. For example, some clinicians focus on here-and-now practical problems in a more active and directive manner; they provide information, take the initiative in seeking out agencies for necessary services, and help clients through the maze of federal and local laws and offices that are in place to help them. Some treatments focus on helping the older person create a sense of meaning as he or she approaches the end of life.

It is also important to consider how cognitive characteristics of aging influence psychological treatment (Knight, 1996). For example, certain kinds of thinking simply take longer for many older people. Older people also tend to experience some diminution in the number of things that they can keep in mind at any one time. Explanations may have to be paced carefully. Researchers have developed accommodations, such as the use of more in-session summaries, to help compensate for the memory loss that some older clients experience.

Therapists, usually many years younger than these patients, can find that their interactions with patients touch on sensitive personal areas of their own, such as worries about their own aging process and mortality. As Knight, Kelly, and Gatz (1992) noted, working with older adults "will challenge therapists intellectually and emotionally to reach a maturity beyond their years" (p. 546).

Being able to use a computer and access the Internet is one way older adults can increase their social connectedness. (Digital Vision/Getty Images.)

Quick Summary

The prevalence of psychological disorders is lower among older adults than it is for any other age group. The psychological disorders that are present during late life usually represent a recurrence or continuation of symptoms that first emerged earlier in life. Some have argued that the low rates of mental illness could be an artifact of less disclosure among older people, could be a cohort effect, or could reflect selective mortality. Most researchers, though, believe that increased coping abilities might help explain the lower rates of disorder as people age. When psychological symptoms are present in the elderly, it is important to screen for medical causes.

Certain issues should be considered in thinking about specific psychological disorders in late life. For example, cognitive symptoms may be a prominent symptom of depression during late life, so that differential diagnosis with dementia is important. Late-life depression may also be related to cardiovascular conditions. Aggressive depression treatment is particularly important among people with a history of myocardial infarction. Although the base rates of depression are low, suicide rates are high among older men, in part because suicide attempts made by older people are likely to be lethal. Aside from cognitive disorders, anxiety disorders are the most common mental health problem faced in late life and may often be tied to the stresses involved in aging. Unfortunately, benzodiazepines are widely prescribed for the elderly despite clear evidence for dangerous side effects. Symptoms of paranoia become more common as people age and may be triggered by sensory loss, dementia, or social isolation. Alcohol and substance abuse are rare, but inappropriate use of prescription or over-the-counter medications is a concern. Treatment for most conditions parallels the treatment used with younger adults, but some innovations have been made, such as providing more in-session summaries and offering treatment in the home or through primary care. Contrary to stereotypes, older people tend to benefit a great deal from psychological treatments.

Living Situations: Community Living, Nursing Homes, and Other Alternatives

At any given time, 95 percent of older persons reside in the community. Many of these people are frail and have an urgent need for help with daily living arrangements (Meeks & Murrell, 1997). Some communities and for-profit agencies are organized to provide services such as the following:

- Daily phone calls to older persons living alone to check that they are all right
- Home services that deliver hot meals
- Volunteers who cook meals, do household chores, and do minor repairs
- Home visits by health professionals
- Adult day services that provide health and social services in a group setting
- Senior centers, which serve hot lunches, help with state and federal forms, and also provide opportunities for socializing.

Available services can be matched with the needs of the older person (Evashwick, 2001).

Because mental health and physical health problems are so interwoven, interdisciplinary collaboration is critical with older clients. Focus on Discovery 15.3 describes the kind of interdisciplinary team effort that can serve the needs of older adults. A set of studies now clearly show that such community services as described above, coupled with careful coordination of services among health care providers, can enhance the quality of life as well as reduce hospitalization and institutionalization rates for older people (Johri, Beland, & Bergman, 2003).

FOCUS ON DISCOVERY 15.3

Interdisciplinary Teamwork in Health Care for the Elderly

The health problems of older adults—including psychological problems—are often more complex and chronic than are those of younger adults and of children (Birren & Schaie, 2001). Thus, the guiding principle that organizes the work of gerontological practitioners is interdisciplinary cooperation (Zeiss & Steffen, 1996). Professionals from several disciplines must work collaboratively to help older adults deal with psychological difficulties (Zeiss & Steffen, 1996). Figure 15.2 portrays how different professionals can work separately (the nonoverlapping areas) and collaboratively (the overlapping areas) to provide assessment and intervention. For example, although the medical doctor serves as the primary care physician, the cognitive screening (how well the person remembers and thinks about things) can be done by the psychologist.

Not all geriatric problems require interdisciplinary coordination, but as Zeiss and Steffen (1996) argue, even a seemingly straightforward health problem in an older adult can benefit from an interdisciplinary approach. They give an example of an 80-year-old woman with bronchitis. Can she be adequately treated by a physician alone? Maybe not. It may be essential to know that she is a caregiver for a husband with dementia, what other medications she is taking, what her immune status is, and other issues pertinent to her physical and emotional well-being. Social workers, psychologists, or other team members may be essential in planning not only acute treatment for her bronchitis but also backup care for her husband.

Coordination of care helps to prevent premature institutionalization among the elderly. Sadly, health care practices in the United States are behind those of other countries in developing "single point of entry" insurance systems, designed to facilitate coordinating health care needs across multiple agencies and providers (Johri et al., 2003).

Social work: Facilitate use of community resources; hold family meetings

Family counseling

Coordinate placement for discharge planning

Psychology: Personality and behavioral assessment, psychotherapy, behavioral medicine intervention

Planning and counseling during chronic or terminal illness

Occupational therapy: Assess and increase activities of daily living; energy conservation; assess home hazards

Decide on equipment needs

Nursing: Screen for psychosocial and functional problems, refer to case management

Cognitive assessment

Physical assessment and treatment planning; coordinate with other providers

Medication education

Monitor medication regimen

Medicine: Serves as primary care M.D.; monitor diagnosis and treatment

Pharmacy: Medication review; facilitate pharmacy dispensing

Figure 15.2 Geriatric interdisciplinary-team role map. Note both the separate and the overlapping areas of expertise. From Zeiss & Steffen (1996).

Mere availability of services is not enough. Services must be coordinated, and in most localities they are not. All too often an older person and his or her family are shuffled from one agency to another, getting lost in Kafkaesque bureaucracies. Even professionals who have experience with the system often have difficulty working through it to get needed services for their clients. Frustrating rules abound. In some states, for example, Medicare does not always pay for rehabilitation services, such as physical therapy, after a broken hip has healed. As a consequence, many older people do not regain as much function as they might; thus, they may experience additional physical and emotional deterioration, exacerbations that require more expensive services.

A growing number of older persons live with family members who help manage tasks of daily living. As changes in physical health or cognitive abilities become too daunting for community living, some people move to nursing homes, assisted living facilities, or retirement communities to receive more support. At any point in time, about 5 percent of elderly people live in long-term care facilities, but at least 40 percent of the elderly will spend some time in one of these facilities (Seperson et al., 2002).

Nursing Homes

The common myth about nursing homes is that families dump their older relatives into these institutions at the first sign of frailty. Rather, most families explore all their alternatives and exhaust their resources before they institutionalize an older relative. Thus, the decision to institutionalize comes as a last resort. For many families, the additional support and the relief from the difficulties of daily caretaking can actually improve the quality of relationships (Smith & Bengtson, 1979).

Nonetheless, nursing homes may have unintended negative consequences on some residents. Consider a classic study by Blenker (1967). Older adults who went to a family service center were randomly assigned to one of three treatments: intensive, intermediate, and minimal. Intensive treatment involved the services of a nurse and a social worker; intermediate treatment involved somewhat less professional attention; minimal treatment consisted of information and referral to community-based services. One might expect intensive treatment to have been the most effective, but after 6 months the death rate of members of the intensive-care group was four times that of people in the minimal-care group! The intermediate-care group was also better off than the intensive-care group; the death rate of its members was "only" twice that of the minimal-care group.

What happened? It turned out that the major factor was being placed in an institution such as a nursing home. A person was much more likely to be institutionalized if a nurse and social worker were intensively involved in planning his or her care, and the excessive death rates were found in people who were institutionalized. Since people had been assigned randomly to the three treatments, it is unlikely that the death rates were related to any pretreatment differences.

What is it about some nursing homes that could contribute to decline? First, the stress of relocating to a new setting is believed to play a role in increased mortality (Schultz & Brenner, 1977). Beyond this, in many nursing homes, the nature of care discourages maintenance of whatever self-care skills and autonomous activities the resident may be capable of. Residents of nursing homes, even if they are able to do so, are often not permitted to cook, do their laundry, buy groceries, or tend the yard. Even more limiting, some facilities feed residents to speed mealtime, even when a resident is able to feed himself or herself. As residents lose their autonomy in these daily tasks, a sense of control is eroded.

In a nursing home, small ways of giving residents a sense of control may mean a lot. In one study, Rodin and Langer (1977) gave one group of residents a variety of decisions to make themselves, instead of the staff's making decisions for them; they were also given plants to take care of. A control group was told how eager the staff was to take care of them; the plants they were given were looked after by the staff. Members of the group given enhanced

Among community-based services are day-care centers, where older people participate in various activities, such as exercise classes. (Corbis Images/SuperStock, Inc.)

responsibility—and presumably a sense of greater control—tested higher on measures of alertness, happiness, and well-being three weeks later and even 18 months later. More importantly, 18 months later only half as many members of the experimental group had died—7 of 47, compared with 13 of 44 for the control group. More recently, programs that give nursing home residents responsibility for plants and pets have been found to significantly diminish helplessness and boredom of the residents (Bergman-Evans, 2004).

During the late 1980s a series of investigations into lax practices in nursing homes led to governmental reforms. Despite resulting improvements in most nursing homes, serious problems remain with many of them (Senate Special Committee on Aging, March 2002). For example, nursing assistants are often inadequately trained, overworked, and underpaid—and it is the nursing assistants, not the professional nursing staff or physicians, who have by far the most contact with nursing home residents. In one study, nursing assistants were found to have committed a set of harmful, even fatal, errors, such as failure to wash hands, to note dehydration, and to attend to bedsores (Pyle, 1999). There is little doubt that nursing homes still need reform.

National policy now mandates that people with primary mental illnesses should not be admitted to nursing homes. Despite that ruling, some people develop mental illnesses after admission, some people with mental illnesses were already living in nursing homes before the ruling, and others were admitted because diagnoses were not caught at admission. It has been estimated that 80 percent of people living in nursing homes have mental illness or dementia (Reichman et al., 1998), and 44 percent report significant symptoms of depression (Teresi et al., 2001).

Clearly, then, there is a need for mental health services in these settings. Beyond evidence that psychological disorders can be effectively treated, interventions such as behavior therapy have been found to be quite effective in reducing unwanted behaviors and improving overall functioning in nursing home residents with dementia. In fact, medication can often be significantly reduced once behavior therapy has been implemented (Mansdorf et al., 1999).

Many nursing homes do provide mental health care. Indeed, one-third of mental health and substance-abuse treatment costs for the elderly are provided to nursing homes (Harwood et al., 2003). Nonetheless, nursing homes vary substantially in their access to quality mental health care. Almost half of nursing home administrators report that they do not have access to adequate mental health consultation (Reichman et al., 1998). Many of the staff working in nursing homes are untrained in managing behaviorally disruptive residents. Instead, nursing homes often rely on an off-site mental health provider who meets with a client and provides written recommendations for staff members to follow. One study of 523 nursing homes found that less than a third of written recommendations for mental health care were implemented by staff (Snowden & Roy-Byrne, 1998). These gaps in service are particularly sad, given that mental health interventions are shown to be helpful in late life.

In an attempt to improve the quality of care, the federal government now mandates that the care provided to each client in a nursing home be evaluated using quality control indices at admission and annually. Many of these indices are designed to assess whether procedures are in place to address depression, memory problems, and other psychological conditions. Average indices for each facility are included in a national database in order to allow researchers, reviewers, and policy makers to make data-guided decisions (*http://www.cms.hhs.gov/NursingHomeQualityInits*).

Alternative Living Settings

Assisted living has become a popular alternative to nursing homes for many older adults who require some assistance with daily activities (AARP, 1999). In contrast to nursing homes, assisted-living facilities resemble hotels with separate suites for the residents as well as dining rooms and on-site amenities such as beauty and barber shops. The philosophy of assisted living stresses autonomy, dignity, and privacy (AARP, 1999). Assisted living may sometimes go by other names, such as group homes or board-and-care. Many such residences are quite luxurious, with attentive staff, nursing and medical assistance readily available, daily activities such

Nursing homes play a major role in the institutional care of the aged. They have often been criticized for the poor care they provide as well as the lack of stimulation in the environment. (Jose Luis Pelaez/Corbis Stock Market.)

CCRCs often provide extensive opportunities for social contact. (Keith Brofsky/ PhotoDisc, Inc./Getty Images.)

as games and movies, and other services all designed to provide help for older adults too infirm to live on their own but not so infirm as to require a nursing home. Although assisted-living facilities can be costly, they are often more affordable than nursing homes.

In addition to assisted-living facilities and nursing homes, continuing care retirement communities (CCRCs) offer a continuum of care that enables residents to move from one housing option to another depending on their needs. These facilities combine independent living, assisted living, and nursing homes together on the same grounds. Residents may begin living in independent housing and move to other housing options as they require more assistance with their activities of daily living. The cost of living in these communities is quite high. Depending on the specific CCRC, residents may own or rent their apartment. Most CCRCs require their potential residents to pass a medical examination and demonstrate that they can still live relatively independently before they can join the community.

Check Your Knowledge 15.5

Answer the questions.
1. The most common living situation for people in late life is:
   a. in the community
   b. in a continuing care retirement community
   c. in a nursing home
   d. in a group home
2. National legislation focused on improving the quality of care in nursing homes has:
   a. ignored mental health issues
   b. broadly described the need for mental health care

   c. provided specific guidelines about certain forms of mental health treatment
   d. is nonexistent
3. National legislation concerning older people with current psychological disorders:
   a. mandates that they should only be placed in nursing homes with good psychiatric coverage
   b. mandates that they should not be placed in nursing homes
   c. does not address proper placement of this population

Summary

Aging: Issues and Methods

- As life expectancy continues to improve, it will become even more important to learn about the disorders suffered by some older people and the most effective means of treating them.
- Several stereotypes about aging are false. Generally, people in late life report low levels of negative emotion, are not inappropriately concerned with their health, and are not lonely. Elderly couples report active sex lives as long as health problems do not interfere. On the other hand, poverty, stigma, and physical disease are common challenges for people as they age.
- In research studies, differences between a younger and an older group could reflect either cohort effects or effects of chronological age. Longitudinal studies are more helpful for making this distinction than cross-sectional studies are.

Cognitive Disorders in Late Life

- Serious cognitive disorders affect a small minority of older people. Two principal disorders have been distinguished: dementia and delirium.
- In dementia, the person's intellectual functioning declines and memory, abstract thinking, and judgment deteriorate. As the dementia progresses, the person comes to seem like another person altogether and, in the end, may become oblivious to his or her surroundings. A variety of diseases can cause this deterioration. The most common is Alzheimer's disease. Genes play a major role in the etiology of Alzheimer's disease. A history of depression is a risk factor, and exercise and cognitive activity appear to be protective.
- Other forms of dementia include frontotemporal dementia, vascular dementia, dementia with Lewy bodies, and dementia due to other medical conditions.

- Dementia usually responds only minimally to medication treatment, but the person and the family affected by the disease can be counseled on how to make the remaining time manageable and even rewarding. Exercise programs for people with dementia may help improve cognitive functioning.
- In delirium, there is a sudden clouding of consciousness and other problems in thinking, feeling, and behaving: fragmented and undirected thought, incoherent speech, inability to sustain attention, hallucinations, illusions, disorientation, lethargy or hyperactivity, and mood swings. The condition is reversible, provided that the underlying cause is adequately treated. Causes include overmedication, infection of brain tissue, high fevers, malnutrition, dehydration, endocrine disorders, head trauma, cerebrovascular problems, and surgery.

Psychological Disorders in Late Life

- Data indicate that persons over age 65 have the lowest overall rates of psychiatric disorders of all age groups. When older people experience psychological disorders, the symptoms are often a recurrence of a disorder that first emerged earlier in life.
- In older adults, depression tends to be accompanied by more cognitive impairment. When the onset of a first episode of depression occurs after age 65, cardiovascular disease is often a cause. Depression is also predictive of worse outcomes of cardiovascular diseases.
- Suicide attempts of older people are more likely to result in death than those of younger people, and the group with the highest rate of suicide is elderly Caucasian men.
- Anxiety disorders are more prevalent than depression among older adults.

- Delusional (paranoid) disorder may also be seen in older people. Sometimes onset occurs in the context of brain disorders, sensory losses, or increasing social isolation.
- Medication treatments for psychological disorders are similar in effectiveness during adulthood and late life, but they must be used with caution because the elderly are more sensitive to side effects and toxicity.

Adjusting Treatment with Older Adults

- Many of the treatments shown to help most psychological disorders in adulthood appear to be helpful for late-life disorders. For example, cognitive behavioral psychotherapy is effective for depression and for anxiety.
- Psychological treatments may need to be tailored to the needs of older people. Clinicians should sometimes be active and directive, providing information and seeking out the agencies that give the social services needed by their clients.

Living Situations: Community Living, Nursing Homes, and Other Alternatives

- Most older persons reside in the community.
- Nursing homes sometimes do little to encourage residents to maintain whatever capacities they have. Both physical and mental deterioration may occur. Serious neglect can be found in some nursing homes, and access to mental health care is limited. Several efforts have been made to correct these deficiencies.
- An increasingly popular alternative is assisted-living facilities.

Answers to Check Your Knowledge Questions

15.1 1. F; 2. F; 3. F; 4. F
15.2 1. a; 2. b; 3. d; 4. a; 5. b
15.3 1. b; 2. c; 3. d

15.4 1. F; 2. T; 3. T
15.5 1. a; 2. c; 3. b

Key Terms

age effects	dementia	frontotemporal dementia (FTD)	social selectivity
Alzheimer's disease	dementia with Lewy bodies	neurofibrillary tangles	time-of-measurement effects
cohort effects	(DLB)	plaques	
delirium	disorientation	selective mortality	

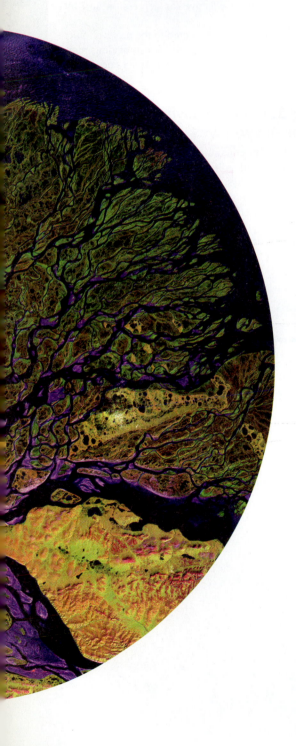

16 Psychological Treatment

LEARNING GOALS

1. Be able to describe the major forms of psychological treatments.
2. Be able to explain standards and issues for psychotherapy outcome research and the major research findings.
3. Be able to discuss different approaches for adapting psychotherapies for people from diverse ethnic and cultural backgrounds.
4. Be able to understand the basic goals of psychotherapy process research and some of the factors that predict better treatment outcome within different forms of therapy.
5. Be able to discuss the goals of community psychology and political trends in that field.

IN CHAPTERS 1 AND 2 we described the major approaches to psychological therapeutic intervention, and in Chapters 5 through 15 we reviewed how these approaches work for specific disorders. We now discuss some broader issues in psychological treatment. First, we review some of the major forms of therapy. Although cognitive behavioral therapies have received a lot of attention in previous chapters, here we also cover psychodynamic therapies, experiential therapies, couples therapies, and family therapies. Our goal is to provide a richer description of the philosophy behind these treatments as well as specific intervention strategies. To illustrate some of the treatments, we will include brief case studies. After describing the different forms of therapy, we provide an overview of treatment outcome research, which strives to address whether a given treatment works. We describe standards to evaluate treatment outcome studies as well as issues in applying those standards. With the standards in mind, we discuss the findings for the different types of therapy. A major concern is that most treatment outcome research has not addressed whether these treatments work well for diverse populations. We describe the small literature regarding ethnicity and treatment outcome. Then we discuss different approaches to enhancing the validity of therapy for people from different ethnic and cultural backgrounds. After providing an overview of the treatment outcome research, we consider psychotherapy process research, which attempts to understand the mechanisms involved in effective treatment. We close with a discussion of community psychology, a field that focuses on making interventions available on a broad social scale rather than with one person at a time.

Specific Treatment Approaches

We begin with an overview of several specific therapeutic approaches. For each therapy, we consider some issues in how to apply techniques and to refine the treatments.

Psychodynamic Treatment

As we noted in Chapter 1, psychoanalysis was originally developed by Freud and his colleagues. They proposed that symptoms were caused by unconscious conflicts and so developed a set of strategies to help clients gain insight into these underlying conflicts. The approach evolved over time, and today most people use psychodynamic therapies that tend to be briefer and more active. Psychoanalytic and psychodynamic treatments, though, both emphasize the importance of early parental relations and unconscious motivations in the genesis of symptoms. Both treatments, then, involve helping the client develop insight.

In psychoanalytic and psychodynamic treatments, the goal of the therapist is to understand the person's early-childhood experiences, the nature of their key relationships, and the patterns in their current relationships. The therapist is listening for core emotional and relationship themes that surface again and again. One way for the therapist to understand core themes is to watch the way that the client begins to relate to the therapist. Some clients express helpless bewilderment, perhaps a clue to underlying conflicts between helplessness and autonomy. Others develop fears that the therapist is secretly annoyed at them, perhaps providing a clue that the client has internalized an idea of relationships as overly punitive. To help the client gain insight, a core aspect of these interventions is interpretation, in which the therapist points out patterns in relationships and emotions that a client may not have realized. Insight is conceptualized as a process in which the client develops a new understanding and, with this understanding, experiences a cathartic release of emotions.

It has been assumed that psychoanalytic therapists would be more passive than psychodynamic therapists. The classic image of a psychoanalytic therapist is of a person who sits behind the client, providing a tabula rasa, or blank slate, as the client free-associates. In a report of a large psychoanalytic psychotherapy project, Wallerstein (1989) reported that in actual practice psychodynamic and psychoanalytic therapists appeared pretty similar; both were fairly active and engaged.

As we discuss treatment outcome research later, it is worth noting that the core goal of psychodynamic treatment is to improve insight and self-understanding. Symptom reduction is expected to happen as a consequence of this improved awareness, but it is not the central concern. Because of this, treatment outcome studies have been accused of focusing on the wrong goal due to their almost exclusive focus on symptom reduction as the measure of success.

Experiential Therapies

Experiential therapies were first developed in the mid-twentieth century and have continued to evolve since that time. Experiential approaches all share a belief that humans are innately good. In this way, experiential therapies differ from the psychodynamic focus on the unconscious as a caldron of powerfully negative impulses and motivations that must be managed. Experiential therapists emphasize the creative and expressive aspects of people, rather than the problematic and symptomatic features on which psychoanalysts often seem to concentrate. In experiential therapies, the therapist aims to promote growth by helping clients to understand and value their internal emotions and needs. The goal of the therapist is to provide a safe relationship so that clients can explore their emotions (Elliot, Greenberg & Lietaer, 2004). To do so, the therapist uses **empathy**, the accurate awareness of the client's emotions. Because we have not reviewed these in much detail elsewhere in the book, we describe three of these approaches here: client-centered therapy, Gestalt therapy, and emotion-focused therapy.

Carl Rogers, who developed client-centered therapy, proposed that the key ingredient in therapy is the attitude and style of the therapist rather than specific techniques. (Roger Ressmeyer/Corbis Images.)

Client-Centered Therapy   The American psychologist Carl Rogers (1902–1987) developed **client-centered therapy** based on a humanistic perspective. Humanism holds that if unfettered by groundless fears and societal restrictions, human beings will develop normally, even exceptionally, much as a healthy plant will naturally develop from a seed if given enough light, air, and water without harmful or limiting conditions. Rogers (1951, 1961) developed a therapy that included the following assumptions:

1. People can be understood only from the vantage point of their own perceptions and feelings.
2. Humans are innately good, effective, and self-directed. Humans share an innate tendency for **self-actualization,** or the potential to fulfill one's potential.
3. People's innate goodness and effectiveness is thwarted by too many internalized demands and preferences from others and from society.

In the empty-chair technique, the client projects a person, object, or situation onto an empty chair and then talks to it. (Copyright John Wiley & Sons, Inc.)

The therapeutic goals include helping people listen to their own internal feelings and needs rather than responding to externally imposed demands. The therapist's job is to create a therapeutic relationship that fosters a return to the client's basic nature. The therapist promotes growth by totally accepting the person for who he or she is and by providing what Rogers called **unconditional positive regard**. Other people set what Rogers called "conditions of worth"— "I will love you if." In contrast, the client-centered therapist values clients as they are—with unconditional positive regard—even if the therapist does not approve of their behavior. The therapist must deeply care for and respect a client for the simple reason that he or she is another human being struggling to live and grow.

Gestalt Therapy   A central goal of **Gestalt therapy**, derived from the work of Freidrich (Fritz) S. Perls (1893–1970), is to help clients to be aware of how they block themselves from experiencing their emotions and satisfying their needs. Gestalt therapists focus on what a client is doing here and now in the session, without delving into the past. The therapist attempts to help clients become more aware of and more expressive of their feelings and needs.

Compared to client-centered therapies, Gestalt therapy is noted for its emphasis on techniques. Here is a small sample of Gestalt techniques.

- *Language.* To help clients take responsibility for their lives, the therapist instructs them to change "it" language into "I" language.

  Therapist: What do you hear in your voice?
  Patient: My voice sounds like it is crying.
  Therapist: Can you take responsibility for that by saying, I am crying?
  (Levitsky & Perls, 1970, p. 142)

  This simple change in language reduces the client's sense of being alienated from aspects of his or her being.

- *The empty chair.* In the empty-chair technique, a client projects a feeling, person, object, or situation and then talks to the projection. For example, if a client is crying about childhood abuse, the Gestalt therapist might ask the client to pretend that the abuser is in an empty chair opposite the client and to speak to the abuser. This tactic increases the client's awareness of his or her feelings. A variation of the empty chair is the two-chair technique— the client moves to the chair that he or she has been talking to and responds as if he or she were the projected person or feeling.

- *Attention to nonverbal and paralinguistic cues.* Therapists are trained to pay attention to nonverbal and paralinguistic cues given by the client, including body movements, facial expressions, gestures, and tone of voice. Often without realizing it, people use nonverbal or paralinguistic cues to negate their words with their hands or their eyes. Perls placed emphasis on observing these cues to determine what clients might really be feeling. "What we say is mostly lies or bullshit. But the voice is there, the gesture, the posture, the facial expression" (Perls, 1969, p. 54).

Gestalt therapy forcefully conveys the message that a person can make the existential choice to be different at any time and that the therapist will not tolerate stagnation. Undoubtedly this optimistic view helps many people change.

Freidrich (Fritz) Perls, the colorful founder of Gestalt therapy. (Courtesy Harriet F. Schenker, Gestalt Institute of Cleveland.)

Emotion-Focused Therapy   Greenberg (2002) developed *emotion-focused therapy,* which incorporates elements of client-centered therapy and Gestalt techniques. Within this approach, the therapist focuses on the idea that some emotions are adaptive, in that they are accurate responses to a given situation, whereas others are maladaptive—responses that are biased by previous experiences. Maladaptive emotions are based on an underlying loneliness, abandonment, worthlessness, anger, or inadequacy. When these feelings surface repetitively, they damage a person's relationships and lifestyle. The goal, then, is for a client to become more aware of these maladaptive emotions, to understand the source of these feelings, and to learn skills to regulate emotions.

Clinical Case: An Example of Emotion-Focused Therapy

In emotion-focused therapy, the therapist will use a number of strategies to help clients develop a better understanding of their adaptive and maladaptive emotions. These include focusing on the present experience, as reflected nonverbally. By helping clients put their emotions into words, the therapist can begin to distinguish between healthy and unhealthy emotions as well as the needs that are driving those feelings.

In the session described below, the client began by describing the loneliness he had experienced in his previous marriage. He was harshly self-critical about the distance in the marriage (an unhealthy emotional pattern), and the therapist was helping him see this pattern. He began to talk about his amazement that his current girlfriend wanted closeness.

As my client talked about his girlfriend's active pursuit of him, he held his arms and hands straight out, gesturing that his response to her pursuit was to protectively hold her at bay. Paying attention to his hand movements, I asked him what it was like when he was approached by her. He said that he initially feels anxious when she

approaches and that he internally pulls back. On further exploration of this feeling, I encouraged him first to own this possibly unhealthy fear rather than avoid or ignore it. He talked first about how unworthy he felt and then about how he was afraid to let anyone close for fear of being known and rejected again. This led back to his feelings of having been dropped by his ex-wife, not for another man but for her art. I shared with him that I could imagine how unimportant that must have left him feeling. His experience of feeling rejected was further evoked and intensified when I asked him to pretend his ex-wife was sitting in the chair across from him. I asked him to imagine telling her how unlovable this had made him feel. This helped him access his feeling of having been poorly treated by her. A feeling of anger emerged. He felt more empowered, because he was able to feel angry at the offense rather than rejected and sad. The session concluded with the client clearly describing his need to feel loved and to be self-affirming and his intention to continue to seek the closeness he wanted with his girlfriend. (Greenberg, 2002, p. 104)

Behavioral Therapies

Exposure (see p. 45) is one of the best-established behavioral approaches. Beyond exposure, operant techniques, which involve manipulating rewards and punishment, have been found to be successful with a wide range of behavioral problems in both adults and children. Inroads in treating substance abuse have been made by reinforcing behavior that is incompatible with the use of a drug to deal with the stresses of everyday life (Higgins, Budney, & Sigmon, 2001). Linehan's dialectical behavior therapy (p. 377) also contains important operant elements for the management of suicidality. Another successful example of operant conditioning is **behavioral activation (BA) therapy** of depression (Jacobson, Martell, & Dimidjian, 2001, p. 239), which involves helping a person engage in tasks that provide an opportunity for positive reinforcement. See Focus on Discovery 16.1 for a discussion of self-control and operant contingencies.

Operant techniques such as systematically rewarding desirable behavior and extinguishing undesirable behavior have been particularly successful in the treatment of many childhood problems (Kazdin & Weisz, 1998). Consider how much of children's behavior is subject to the control of others-children tend to be supervised fairly continually by teachers at school and by parents at home. The behavior therapist can work with parents and teachers to change rewards and punishments for a child. A broad range of childhood problems are treated with through operant conditioning, including bed-wetting, thumb-sucking, nail-biting, aggression, tantrums, disruptive classroom behavior, poor school performance, extreme social withdrawal, mental retardation, and autistic disorder (Kazdin & Weisz, 1998).

Once contingencies shape a behavior, a key goal is to maintain the effects of treatment. If a therapist or a teacher has been providing reinforcement, one might not expect this person to keep providing reinforcement forever. This issue has been addressed in several ways. Because laboratory findings indicate that intermittent reinforcement—rewarding a response only a portion of the times it appears—makes new behavior more enduring, many operant programs move away from continuous schedules of reinforcement once desired behavior is occurring regularly.

Exposure treatment is one of the most well-supported approaches for anxiety disorders. (Michael Newman/PhotoEdit.)

FOCUS ON DISCOVERY 16.1

Self-Control—Outside a Behavioral Paradigm?

How do people change the way they think or behave? How do dieters resist a piece of chocolate cake, or alcoholics resist a drink, or angry people resist the urge to hurl a criticism at another person? Each of these impulses require people to control themselves, despite the conflicting possibility of reinforcement from taking another path. Self-control, then, involves consciously deciding to engage in a certain type of thought or behavior that requires some effort and is not explained by the immediate external contingencies. Most of us have decided to engage in some form of self-control.

Impulse control disorders, such as pathological gambling, may be related to poor self-control. (Doublas Kirkland/Corbis Images.)

Operant theory seems to assume that people passively respond to reinforcement and punishments in the environment. How can these models account for a person's ability to resist reinforcement in the hopes of improving life longer term?

Psychoanalytic writers posit that the ego controls the id's desire to indulge in immediate gratification. Behaviorists, especially Skinner (1953), objected to this explanation, as there is no way to observe the ego. Skinner argued that people engage in self-control by arranging the environment so that only certain controlling stimuli are present. A person wishing to lose weight rids the house of fattening foods and avoids standing by the food table at a party. Behavior remains a function of the surroundings, but the surroundings are controlled by the person. One way to control the environment is to promise oneself reinforcement after a goal is met (Bandura & Perloff, 1967). For example, one author of this book uses the strategy of promising herself a wonderful meal once she finishes a chapter. By setting up rewards for accomplishing a goal, self-control is promoted. Note that to account for self-control, behavior theorists incorporate cognition.

Muraven and Baumeister (2000) have described a model of self-control as an internal resource. They argue that we all have a certain amount of self-control and that some people tend to have more than others. Like a muscle, self-control can be strengthened but can also be exhausted. An interesting aspect of this model is the idea that there is a limit to how many self-regulatory goals a person can pursue at one time. For example, people trying to control their emotions after a major breakup (self-control over emotional expression) may find it harder to stick with their diet (self-control over their eating patterns). This model suggests that therapists should be careful not to assign their clients too many goals for self-improvement at once.

For example, if a teacher has succeeded in helping a disruptive child spend more time sitting by praising the child generously for each math problem finished while seated, the teacher will gradually reward the child for every other success, and ultimately only infrequently. Another strategy is to move from artificial reinforcers to those that occur naturally in the social environment. A token program might be maintained only long enough to encourage certain desired behavior, after which the person is weaned to naturally occurring reinforcers, such as praise from peers. If reinforcers are not likely to be available consistently in the natural environment, therapists sometimes manipulate surroundings to support behavioral changes. For example, in the treatment of children with autism, parents are taught how to provide reinforcement for good behavior (McEachin, Smith, & Lovaas, 1993). Hence, parent training often becomes an integral part of behavior therapy for children. Similarly, treatment for many anxiety disorders now includes partners and family members so that they can provide new reinforcement contingencies.

Cognitive Treatment

All cognitive approaches have one thing in common. They emphasize that how people construe themselves and the world is a major determinant of psychological disorders. By changing cognition, therapists hope that people can change their feelings, behaviors, and symptoms. In cognitive therapy, the therapist typically begins by helping clients become more aware of their maladaptive thoughts. People with depression may not realize how often they think

Clinical Case: An Example of Beck's Cognitive Therapy

The examples here illustrate ways of beginning to challenge a patient's negative cognitions.

> *Therapist: You said that you feel like a failure since Bill left you. How would you define "failure"?*
> *Patient: Well, the marriage didn't work out.*
> *Therapist: So, you believe that the marriage didn't work out because you, as a person, are a failure?*
> *Patient: If I had been successful, then he would still be with me.*
> *Therapist: So, would we conclude that we can say, "People whose marriages don't work out are failures"?*
> *Patient: No, I guess I wouldn't go that far.*
> *Therapist: Why not? Should we have one definition of failure for you and another for everyone else?*

People who define "failure" as less than "extraordinarily successful" can see that their definitions are polarized in all-or-nothing terms—that is, "complete success" vs. "complete failure." A variation on this technique is to ask the patient how others would define "success" or "failure."

> *Therapist: You can see that your definition of failure is quite different from the way other people might see it. Few people would say that a person who is divorced is a failure. Let's focus on the positive end right now. How would most people define "success" in a person?*
> *Patient: Well, they might say that someone has success when they accomplish some of their goals.*
> *Therapist: OK. So, would we say that if someone accomplishes some goals they have success?*
> *Patient: Right.*
> *Therapist: Would we also say that people can have different degrees of success? Some people accomplish more goals than others?*
> *Patient: That sounds right.*
> *Therapist: So, if we applied this to you, would we say that you have accomplished some of your goals in life?*
> *Patient: Yes, I did graduate from college and I have been working for the past six years. I've been busy raising Ted—he had some medical problems a couple of years ago, but I got the right doctors for him.*
> *Therapist: So, would we call these some successful behaviors on your part?*
> *Patient: Right. I've had some successes.*
> *Therapist: Is there a contradiction, then, in your thinking—calling yourself a "failure" but saying that you have had several successes?*
> *Patient: Yes, that doesn't make sense, does it?* (quoted in Leahy, 2003, pp. 38–39).

self-critically, and those with anxiety disorders may not realize that they tend to be overly sensitive to possible threats in the world. The therapist begins by tracking the daily thoughts a person experiences but then moves to understanding more about core cognitive biases and schemata that might shape those daily negative thoughts. Although many would imagine that cognitive therapy might be dry and unemotional, some cognitions are affect-laden, sometimes referred to as "hot cognitions." Beck argued that "emotions are the royal road to cognition." That is, during highly distressed states, clients may have access to their most negative thoughts.

The roots of cognitive therapy included Beck's cognitive therapy and Ellis's **rational-emotive behavior therapy (REBT)**. There have also been many recent innovations in cognitive behavior therapy (CBT). These treatments include dialectical behavior therapy (see Chapter 12), mindfulness-based cognitive therapy (see Chapter 8), and acceptance and commitment therapy. The newer treatments differ from traditional CBT by incorporating a focus on spirituality, values, emotion, and acceptance (Hayes et al., 2004). One theme that emerges across these manuals is acceptance (see Focus on Discovery 16.2). Another theme involves strategies to minimize emotional avoidance. For example, in acceptance and commitment therapy (Hayes, 2005), a person might be taught that much of the destructive power of emotions lies in the way we respond to them cognitively and behaviorally. An overarching goal of these therapies is to help a person learn to be more aware of emotions but to avoid immediate, impulsive reactions to that emotion. In the case of mindfulness-based cognitive therapy, this is facilitated through the use of meditation (Segal, Williams, & Teasdale, 2003). Overall a rich array of cognitive behavioral approaches have been developed.

Couples Therapy

Conflict is inevitable in any long-term partner relationship, whether the two people are married or not, or of the opposite sex or not. About 50 percent of marriages in the United States end in divorce, and most of these divorces happen within the first seven years of marriage (Snyder,

FOCUS ON DISCOVERY 16.2

Acceptance in Couples Therapy

The notion of acceptance in therapy dates back at least to Sigmund Freud. As Christensen and Jacobson (2000) indicate, the use of interpretation in psychoanalytic couples therapy (e.g., Scharff, 1995) can help partners understand that displeasing behaviors stem from childhood wounds, thereby fostering greater acceptance. But the concept assumes greater primacy in the work of Carl Rogers, whose client-centered therapy rested on the belief that "conditions of worth" should not be set for others. Rather, we should try to accept clients as worthy people deserving of respect regardless of their behavior at any point in time. Albert Ellis's rational-emotive behavioral therapy also emphasized acceptance by encouraging people to renounce many of the demands they impose on themselves and on others. As described on p. 378, Linehan's dialectical behavior therapy (1993) emphasizes the importance of the therapist providing genuine caring and acceptance for the client with borderline personality disorder.

Drawing on earlier work, Neil Jacobson and Andrew Christensen (1996) developed integrative behavioral couples therapy (IBCT). The goal of this therapy is to uncover the major variables driving the couple's distress rather than to create superficial behavioral changes. For example, whereas traditional behavior therapists might focus on discrete observable behavior, such as lack of sex or frequent arguments, integrative therapists might focus on a partner's feeling that he or she is not loved by the other partner. Jacobson and Christensen argue that traditional behavioral couples therapists have overlooked the importance of accepting a partner while at the same time hoping for and encouraging change. To address this, IBCT supplements traditional behavior therapy techniques with a focus on acceptance. This shift in therapeutic attention provides one example of recent versions of cognitive behavioral therapies being enriched by attention to broader goals.

IBCT includes a set of techniques to promote acceptance. One technique, known as "unified detachment," is used to help partners gain a degree of emotional distance from their problems (Cordova, Jacobson, & Christensen, 1998). Usually, couples in conflict are stuck blaming and criticizing each other. In unified detachment, couples are taught to focus on describing what happens in their interaction as objectively as possible, without trying to evaluate who is at fault or who caused a fight. They are taught to understand processes that can intensify conflicts, such as escalation (increasing tension as couples expand the focus of a conflict), polarization (increasing stalemate as people try to defend their positions), and alienation (increasing loneliness as conflict continues). Responses differ once an argument becomes heated—some people tend to accuse, others avoid conflict, and some do both. Couples are taught to take a step back, carefully observe their interactions, and label the processes that influence their conflict.

Beyond gaining perspective on conflicts, couples are even encouraged to embrace the differences that have become a source of conflict (Jacobson, 1992). "What one partner sees as the other partner's 'uptightness' might be the 'stability' that first attracted him/her. Or alternatively, what one partner sees as the other's 'flakiness' or 'irresponsibility' might be the 'free-spiritedness' or 'rebelliousness' that so attracted him or her in the beginning of their relationship. The therapist must help the partners notice the positive aspects of what they have come to see as purely negative behavior. And often this behavior is in some way related to a quality one partner once found attractive about the other" (Wheeler, Christensen, & Jacobson, 2001, p. 617). In every relationship, there are differences that are impossible to change; rather than futile attempts to remake a person, the idea is to appreciate differences.

Is acceptance tantamount to resignation, to accepting a status quo that keeps one or both partners in a destructive relationship, one that perhaps demeans one partner to satisfy the selfish demands of the other? Jacobson and Christensen argue that acceptance is actually affirmative. By truly understanding and appreciating differences, it is hoped that couples achieve a more fundamental closeness. And some behavioral changes that were formerly unreachable in behavioral couples therapy with direct attempts at change might actually be facilitated by embedding such efforts within a context of acceptance.

Castellani, & Whisman, 2006). People in a distressed marriage are two to three times as likely to experience a psychological disorder (Whisman & Uebelacker, 2006). In some couples, distress may be a consequence of the psychological disorder, but it is also clear that distress can trigger many psychological disorders. Couples therapy is often used in the treatment of psychological disorders, particularly when they occur in the context of major relationship distress. We describe a few of the predictors of relationship distress and then discuss several forms of couples therapy.

Understanding relationships is complex, but several patterns have been shown to predict distress over time. Some couples adopt the strategy of avoiding disagreements and conflicts. For couples who believe in the fairy-tale ending, "And they lived happily ever after," signs of conflict are threatening and must be ignored. Such patterns may keep the peace for a short time, but dissatisfaction takes a toll over time. Because the partners do not quarrel, they may appear to be a perfect couple to observers, but the lack of open communication produces emotional distance. Whereas disagreement among couples may be related to unhappiness in the short term, expression of differences predicts more satisfaction over time (Gottman & Krokoff, 1989).

One particularly destructive interaction pattern is known as the *demand–withdraw cycle*. In this pattern, one partner attempts to discuss a problem and the other withdraws from such efforts. This withdrawal generates more demands from the first spouse, who tries harder and harder to engage the other, only to be met with more avoidance. And so the cycle escalates. Christensen and Heavey (1990) suggest that there are sex differences in this pattern; women tend to assume the demanding role, whereas men usually withdraw. This process can reverse when the husband initiates discussion of his concerns (which men tend to do less often)—then, sometimes, the wife withdraws (Klinetob & Smith, 1996). In a subtler version of withdrawal, called "stonewalling," one person becomes very quiet. Although it can look like the person is uncaring, psychophysiological studies suggest that people who are stonewalling show incredibly high arousal (Gottman, 1994). Beyond the cycle of cricitism and withdrawal just described, couples who are defensive with each other or express contempt toward each other are at high risk for marital dissatisfaction and divorce (Gottman, 1994).

In couples therapies, the therapist works with both partners together to reduce relationship distress. Most couples treatments focus on improving communication, problem solving, satisfaction, trust, and positive feelings. To enhance communication, each partner is trained to listen empathically to the other and to state clearly to the partner what he or she understands is being said and what feelings underlie those remarks.

Despite the common ground, there are also major differences across forms of couples therapy. Therapists choose techniques to match their theoretical orientation. A psychoanalytically oriented couples therapist will attend to possible unconscious factors in each person's behavior toward the other, whereas a behavioral couples therapist will focus on maladaptive behavioral patterns that are being unwittingly reinforced in the relationship. Behavioral couples therapists often assign homework, such as asking couples to practice active listening skills for half an hour after dinner or to schedule a romantic activity. Table 16.1 outlines the major goals in different forms of couples therapies. See Focus on Discovery 16.2, for one example of a way that behavioral couples therapy has been expanded to include new ideas and procedures.

When a problem involves a couple, treatment is most effective if the couple is seen together. (Gary Corner/Alamy.)

Family Therapy

Family therapy is based on the idea that the problems of the family influence each member and that the problems of each member influence the family. As such, family therapy is used to address specific symptoms of a given family member, particularly for the treatment of child-hood problems.

Over time, family therapy approaches have evolved to include a broader array of strategies (Sexton, Alexander, & Mease, 2004), often carefully integrated into the school and community (Liddle, 1999). Some family therapists focus on roles within the family, asking questions about whether parents assume an appropriate level of responsibility. Sometimes family therapists attend

Table 16.1 Goals in Different Forms of Couples Therapy

Type of Couples Therapy	Chief Goal
Psychodynamic insight-oriented couples therapy	To help clients understand the interpersonal dynamics and needs that each partner brings to the relationship and how these influence their emotional reactions (Snyder, Wills, & Grady-Fletcher, 1991).
Behavioral couples therapy	To increase the rate of pleasant interactions and decrease the rate of unpleasant interactions (Wood & Jacobson, 1985).
Cognitive behavioral couples therapy	To supplement the behavioral approach with procedures designed make less negative interpretations of each others' actions (Wheeler, Christenson, & Jacobson, 2001).
Integrative behavioral couples therapy	To supplement the behavioral approach with procedures designed to foster acceptance of the partner (Christensen, Jacobson, & Babcock, 1995).
Emotionally focused therapy	To improve emotional engagement and responsiveness to each other's needs; to address "innate adaptive needs for protection, security, and connectedness with significant others" (Johnson & Greenberg, 1995, p. 124).

Clinical Case: Clare

Clare, a 17-year-old female who lived with her parents and her 15-year-old brother, was referred for family-focused treatment (FFT) of bipolar disorder as an adjunct to medication treatment. She had received a diagnosis of bipolar I disorder in early adolescence and was treated with lithium carbonate and quetiapine but had never fully responded to medications.

During an individual assessment session, Clare explained that she thought about suicide almost daily and had made two prior attempts, both by overdosing on her parents' medications. Clare had kept both attempts secret from her parents. Ethically, clinicians need to take steps to keep a client safe, and in this case, one measure would be to let Clare's parents know about her suicidality. The clinician explained this to Clare.

The first goal in family-focused treatment is to provide psychoeducation about bipolar disorder. As the symptoms of bipolar disorder were being reviewed, the clinician asked Clare to discuss her suicide attempts with her parents. When Clare did so, her parents were surprised. Her father, who had experienced his own father's suicide, was particularly concerned.

After psychoeducation, a goal in FFT is to choose one problem for the family to address and to help them learn new problem-solving skills in the process. In this family, the focus of problem solving was how to keep Clare safe from her suicidal impulses. To begin problem solving, the therapist works with the family to define the problem and its context. The therapist asked the family to discuss situations that seemed to place Clare at most risk for suicide. The family was able to pinpoint that both previous attempts had followed interpersonal losses.

The next phase of problem solving is to generate potential solutions. To help with this process, the clinician framed questions in the problem-solving process for the family, including whether Clare could share her suicidal thoughts with her parents, how to establish whether she was safe, what responses would be helpful from them, and what other protective actions should be taken. Using this structure, the family was able to agree on the plan that Clare would phone or page her parents when she was feeling self-destructive. Clare and her parents generated a plan in which her parents would help Clare engage in positive and calming activities

until her suicidal thoughts were less intrusive. Clare and her parents reported feeling closer and more optimistic.

The therapist then began to conduct the next phase of therapy, which focused directly on symptom management. This phase consisted of training Clare to monitor her moods, to identify triggers for mood changes, and to help her cope with those triggers.

As is typical in FFT, the clinician introduced the communication enhancement module during session eight. A goal of this module is to role-play new communication skills. Family members practice skills such as "active listening" by paraphrasing and labeling the others' statements and by asking clarifying questions. At first, Clare and her brother protested against the role-play exercises.

Clare experienced another loss during this period, in that her one and only close long-term friend announced that she was going to be moving out of state. Clare took an overdose of Tylenol as a suicide attempt. Afterward, she became afraid, induced vomiting, and later told her parents about the attempt.

The next session focused on the suicide attempt. Her parents, particularly her father, were hurt and angry. Clare reacted angrily and defensively. The therapist asked the family to practice active listening skills regarding Clare's suicidality. Clare explained that she had acted without even thinking about the family agreement because she had been so distressed about the idea of losing her friend. Clare's parents were able to validate her feelings using active listening skills. The therapist reminded the parents that suicidal actions are common in bipolar disorder and noted that Clare's ability to be honest about her suicide attempt was an indicator of better family connectedness. The therapist also recommended that Clare see her psychiatrist, who increased her dosage of lithium.

By the end of treatment after nine months, Clare had not made any more suicide attempts, had become more willing to take her medications, and felt closer to her parents. Like many people with bipolar disorder, though, she remained mildly depressed. Clare and her family continued to see the therapist once every three months for ongoing support. [Adapted from Miklowitz and Taylor (2005) with permission of the author.]

to whether a given person in the family has been "scapegoated," or unfairly blamed for a broader issue in the family. Many family therapists teach strategies to help families communicate and problem-solve more effectively.

Family therapy is often tailored to the specific disorder. In family approaches for conduct disorder, the therapist may focus on improving parental monitoring and discipline. For adolescents with other externalizing problems, the goal of family therapy may be to improve communication, to change roles, or to address a range of family problems. With disorders like schizophrenia and bipolar disorder, family therapy often includes psychoeducation as a supplement for the medication treatment provided to the individual. Psychoeducation focuses on improving understanding of the disorder, reducing expressed family criticism and hostility, and helping families learn skills for managing symptom (Miklowitz et al., 2003; see the clinical case of Clare). For people with substance-abuse problems, family therapy has been used to help clients recognize the need for treatment. In sum, the goals and strategies of family therapy will be adjusted to meet the needs of different clients.

Quick Summary

Psychoanalytic and psychodynamic treatments focus on how early childhood relationships shape interpersonal and emotional concerns in current life. Therapists uses transference, or the client's ways of responding to the therapist, as a way of understanding the themes in a client's relationships. They use interpretation to increase the client's insight into unconscious conflicts.

Experiential therapies emphasize the goodness of humans. Humanistic therapy focuses on providing the client with unconditional positive regard as a way to promote growth. Gestalt therapy provides a number of techniques to enhance emotional awareness. Emotion-focused therapy aims to help clients become more aware of their feelings and to differentiate adaptive emotions (based on the current context) from maladaptive emotions (held over from previous life experiences).

The most-researched form of behavioral therapy is exposure treatment, used in the treatment of anxiety disorders. Operant conditioning is used to treat many other disorders. In operant approaches, attention must be given to how to sustain the effects of treatment once therapy ends.

There are several forms of cognitive therapy. Beck's cognitive therapy of depression focuses on overly negative cognitions about the self and the world. Several new cognitive behavioral treatments have been developed in the past few years that focus on fostering acceptance, diminishing emotional avoidance, and other broader goals in managing thoughts and emotions.

Behavioral couples therapy focuses on communication and problem solving. Integrative behavioral couples therapy supplements this approach with techniques to bolster acceptance of differences. Emotionally focused couples therapy places an emphasis on developing strategies for enhancing closeness. Insight-oriented couples therapy helps each partner consider the childhood experiences that might drive behavior in their relationship. Family therapy can include psychoeducation about symptoms, communication training, and problem solving.

Check Your Knowledge 16.1 (Answers are at the end of the chapter.)

Choose the answer that best fits the statement.
1. All forms of psychoanalytic therapy are long.
2. The form of therapy that is most associated with the idea that humans naturally develop toward being positive and good is:

a. Psychodynamic therapy
b. Humanistic therapy
c. Behavioral therapy
d. Individualistic therapy

Treatment Outcome Research

Researchers have been studying treatment outcomes, or how well different therapies work, for decades. **Outcome research** is designed to address a simple question: does therapy work? The clear answer is yes. Hundreds of studies have examined whether people who receive psychotherapy fare better than those who do not. In meta-analyses of more than 300 studies, researchers have found that there is a moderately positive effect of treatment. About 75 percent of people who enter treatment achieve at least some improvement (Lambert & Ogles, 2004). As shown in Figure 16.1, these effects appear to be more powerful than the passage of time or support from friends and family. Eysenck (1952) had earlier questioned the effectiveness of most kinds of insight-oriented psychotherapy, finding that treated clients' rates of improvement were no better than the spontaneous remission rate. Eysenck's criticisms were compellingly rebutted by a number of scholars (e.g., Bergin, 1971) and continue to be rebutted by the accumulation of studies showing that therapy does work. On the other hand, it is also clear that therapy does not always work. About 30 percent of people do not improve in therapy (see Figure 16.1).

Because there are hundreds and hundreds of studies on psychotherapy, there is a need for people to systematically cull through the articles and identify the treatments that have strong support. In 1995, a

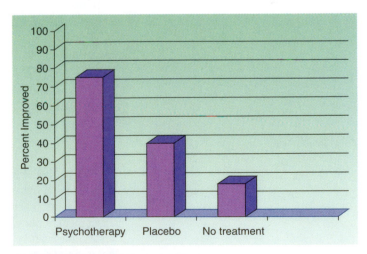

Figure 16.1 Summary of percent of people who achieve improvement across outcome for psychotherapy, placebo, and no treatment across studies. [Drawn from Lambert (2004). Psychotherapeutically-speaking—updates from the Division of Psychotherapy (29). With permission of the author and of APA.]

Table 16.2 Examples of Empirically Supported Treatments for Adult Disorders

Depression	*PTSD*
Cognitive therapy	Exposure
Behavior therapy	Eye movement desensitization and
Interpersonal psychotherapy	reprocessing (although see p. 150)
Generalized anxiety disorder	*Schizophrenia*
Cognitive therapy	Social skills training
Applied relaxation	Behavioral family therapy
	Supported employment programs
Social phobia	
Exposure	*Alcohol abuse and dependence*
Cognitive behavioral group therapy	Community reinforcement approach
Systematic desensitization	*Relationship distress*
Simple phobia	Behavioral couples therapy
Exposure	Emotion-focused therapy
Guided mastery	Insight-oriented couples therapy
Systematic desensitization	*Sexual dysfunctions*
Obsessive-compulsive disorder	Partner assisted sexual skills training
Exposure and response prevention	*Bulimia*
Cognitive therapy	Cognitive behavior therapy
Agoraphobia	Interpersonal psychotherapy
Exposure	*Borderline personality disorder*
Cognitive behavior therapy	Dialectical behavior therapy
Panic	
Cognitive therapy	
Exposure	
Applied relaxation	

Drawn from Chambless et al. (1998) and the Dissemination Subcommittee of the Committee on Science and Practice (2008) Available at *http://www.apa.org/divisions/div12/journals.html#Anchor-EMPIRICALLY-49575*.

task force for the American Psychological Association defined standards for research on psychotherapy and then published a report on the therapies that had received empirical support (Task Force on Promotion and Dissemination of Psychological Treatments, 1995). The report was updated in 2008 (see Table 16.2). The goal was to help clinicians draw more easily on this rapidly growing literature about **empirically supported treatments (ESTs)** to provide consumers with the best available treatments. These summaries also might help defend the role of psychotherapy with managed care agencies and insurance companies, who have increasingly demanded research evidence before they are willing to pay for treatments.

What are the standards for treatment **outcome research** to be seen as valid? Several different working groups have come up with slightly different answers to this question. At a minimum, most researchers agree that a treatment study should include the following criteria:

- A clear definition of the sample being studied, such as a description of diagnoses
- A clear description of the treatment being offered, as in a treatment manual (described below)
- Reliable and valid outcome measures
- Inclusion of a control or comparison treatment condition
- Random assignment of clients to treatment or comparison conditions
- A large enough sample for statistical tests

Studies in which clients are randomly assigned to receive active treatment or a comparison (either no treatment, a placebo, or another treatment) are called **randomized controlled trials (RCTs)**. These studies can be considered an experiment, in which the independent variable is the treatment and the dependent variable is the clients' outcome.

Many different types of control groups can be included in psychotherapy research. Although some people argue that the inclusion of a control group may be unethical (Wolitzky, 1995), it is difficult to make a compelling case for any treatment when treatment outcome studies do not include a control group of some form. A no-treatment control group allows researchers to test whether the mere passage of time helps as much as treatment does. A stricter test compares the treatment group to an attention-control group in which clients see a therapist regularly for support and encouragement (the "attention" component), but they do not receive what is considered to be the "active ingredient" in the kind of therapy being tested (e.g., exposure to a feared situation in a behavioral treatment of a phobia). The strictest type of design includes an active-treatment control group, in which researchers compare the new treatment against a well-tested treatment. This type of design allows researchers to make comparative statements about two treatments.

Issues in Treatment Outcome Research

As shown by the complexities in choosing a control group, designing treatment trials is difficult. Some aspects of the APA task force recommendations have been hotly debated. For example, failure for a treatment to appear on the APA task force list of empirically supported treatments (Table 16.2) could simply reflect a lack of careful studies. As you can see, most of the treatments listed are cognitive behavioral. Although we will discuss research supporting many other treatments in this chapter, cognitive behavioral treatments are featured in the APA list because the studies for these treatments have met the strict APA criteria. We turn toward four other issues that are a subject of debate: the need to track which treatments are harmful, the use of treatment manuals, the nature of samples within treatment studies, and the generalizability of findings to the real world.

Can Therapy be Harmful?   The APA guidelines have been criticized because they do not consider whether treatments have been harmful. Despite the substantial evidence that therapies, on average, tend to be helpful, this does not mean that they help everyone. Indeed, a small number of people may be in worse shape after therapy. Estimating how often therapy is harmful is not easy. Up to 10 percent of people are more symptomatic after therapy than they were before therapy began (Lilienfeld, 2007). Does this mean that therapy harmed them? Maybe not. Without a careful control group, it is hard to know whether symptoms would have worsened even without therapy. Unfortunately, few researchers report the percentage of people who worsened in the different branches of RCTs.

Nonetheless, it is important to be aware that several treatments have been found to be harmful to some people. That is, evidence that these treatments can be harmful for some people has emerged from multiple studies or from case reports of sudden deteriorations as treatment was implemented. See Table 16.3 for a summary of

Troubled people may talk about their problems with friends or seek professional therapy. Treatment is typically sought by those for whom the advice and support of family or friends have not provided relief. (Top: Rhoda Sidney/PhotoEdit; bottom: Esbin-Anderson/The Image Works.)

Table 16.3 Treatments Found to be Harmful in Multiple Studies or Case Reports

Treatment	Negative Effects
Critical incident stress debriefing	Heightened risk for posttraumatic symptoms
Scared Straight	Exacerbation of conduct problems
Facilitated communication	False accusations of child abuse against family members
Attachment therapies (e.g., rebirthing)	Death and serious injury to children
Recovered-memory techniques	Production of false memories of trauma
Dissociative identity disorder-oriented therapy	Induction of "alter" personalities
Grief counseling for people with normal bereavement reactions	Increases in depressive symptoms
Expressive-experiential therapies	Exacerbation of painful emotions
Boot-camp interventions for conduct disorder	Exacerbation of conduct problems
DARE programs	Increased intake of alcohol and cigarettes

Drawn from Lilienfeld (2007).

TREATMENT MANUALS FOR PRACTITIONERS

Treating *the* Trauma of Rape

Cognitive-Behavioral Therapy for PTSD

Edna B. Foa
Barbara Olasov Rothbaum

A treatment manual provides specific procedures for a therapist to use in working with a client. Although they are increasingly standard in research trials, many therapists still say they don't use them. From Edna B. Foa and Barbara Olasov Rothbaum, *Treating the Trauma of Rape: Cognitive-Behavioral Therapy for PTSD*. Represented with permission of Guilford Publications.

treatments that have been found to be harmful. Just as there is debate about the APA task force recommendations, there is debate about the list provided in Table 16.3. For example, although some studies found that group interventions for conduct disorder were associated with negative outcomes (presumably because peers teach each other bad behaviors), one review found little evidence to support the harmful effects of such interventions (Weiss et al., 2005). We should note that harmful effects of treatment are not exclusive to therapy; the FDA has issued warnings that antidepressants and antiseizure medications can increase the risk of suicidality and that antipsychotic medications can increase the risk of death among the elderly.

The Use of Treatment Manuals   Treatment manuals are detailed books on how to conduct a particular psychological treatment—they provide specific procedures for the therapist to follow at each stage of treatment. The use of manuals has been a major advance in psychotherapy research (e.g., Nathan & Gorman, 2002) and is required to receive grant funding for treatment outcome research. Without a manual, it is hard to know what therapists actually do, because a therapist's descriptions of a session or allegiance to an orientation might not capture what really happens (London, 1964). With manuals, someone reading a psychotherapy study can have an idea of what happened in therapy sessions.

The purpose of using treatment manuals is to help therapists to be more similar in what they do. That is, the goal is to minimize differences across therapists. However, therapists vary even in RCTs. For example, in the well-known NIMH Treatment of Depression Collaborative Research Program, therapists differed in how well they implemented the manuals. Some therapists were more successful than others using the same manual (Blatt et al., 1996). Research suggests that sometimes these differences between therapists can be greater than the differences between treatments (Beutler, 1997). Maintaining precision in delivering therapy is a challenge—almost no other experiments in science attempt to control the independent variable (in this case, the intervention condition) for months (Westen, Novotny, & Thompson-Brenner, 2004).

Although manuals help us to know what the therapists in a study actually did, some have argued that manuals might be too limiting for a good therapist (Beutler, 1999; Goldfried & Davison, 1994). Outside of RCTs, therapists tend to tailor treatment to the client (Haaga & Stiles, 2000) so that they are more responsive to a client's needs. In contrast, the very essence of treatment manuals is to minimize the tailoring of intervention to individual clients. The problem is that if a therapist adheres too rigidly to a treatment manual, the client can feel that his or her particular concerns are not being addressed (Henry et al., 1993).

Some of this debate about manuals could be resolved by research to compare results when therapists either do or do not use manuals. Some studies have suggested that manuals do not make a major difference in outcomes (Beutler et al., 2004). But the clear guidelines provided by manuals seem to help novice therapists more than experienced therapists (Multon, Kivlighan, & Gold, 1996). Further, in one meta-analysis of brief psychodynamic treatment studies, those that involved treatment manuals achieved greater gains than those with no treatment manuals (Anderson & Lambert, 1995). The challenge, then, might be to provide manuals that give therapists a clear road map but do not constrain experienced therapists to the point where their flexibility is diminished. One way to do this is to provide manuals that give therapists lots of freedom—for example, promoting the goal of exposure treatment for anxiety disorders but also giving a menu of options of how to conduct exposure (Kendall & Beidas, 2007).

Defining a Sample   Randomized controlled trials (RCTs) typically focus on treating people who have a certain DSM diagnosis. For example, many major studies have recruited people who met DSM criteria for major depressive disorder. But depressions are not all caused by the same factors (e.g., negative cognitive styles). Some have argued that we should be designing studies focused on people with similar psychological profiles (Persons, 1991). For example, clients with negative cognitive styles can be assigned to cognitive therapy, whereas those with significant family distress can be assigned to family therapy (Beevers & Miller, 2005). Beutler and colleagues (2003) have conducted research to demonstrate the effectiveness of matching clients to treatment based on their coping styles. Hence, some have argued that it would be better to choose a treatment based on a person's profile of risk factors for psychopathology rather than on their diagnosis.

Beyond concerns about the best basis for defining a sample, there are concerns about the number of people who are excluded in treatment research. In a typical RCT, researchers might include people who meet diagnostic criteria for a given disorder but exclude those who have more than one disorder, acute suicidality (for ethical reasons), or other characteristics. Some participants might not be willing to take part in a study in which they might be assigned to an ineffective treatment (the control condition). As it turns out, researchers exclude almost as many people as they recruit into these studies (Westen et al., 2004). This situation creates problems with generalizing from controlled studies to the actual practice of psychotherapy in the real world, a topic we consider next.

Treating Disorders in the Real World   Controlled RCTs, typically conducted in academic research settings, are designed to determine the **efficacy** of a treatment, that is, whether a treatment works under the purest of conditions. Because of the kinds of concerns just raised, academic research might not inform us about how these treatments work with broader samples in the hands of nonacademic therapists. We need to determine not just the efficacy of a treatment but also its **effectiveness**, that is, how well the treatment works in the real world. Studies of effectiveness might do the following:

- Include people with a broader range of problems (such as comorbid conditions)
- Provide less intensive supervision of therapists
- Examine a broader range of outcomes, such as whether clients believe they were helped and feel satisfied with their lives at the end of treatment
- Rely on briefer assessments

As you might expect, when clients have more serious diagnostic complications and providers have less support, even medications tend to look less powerful than they do in careful efficacy studies (Rush et al., 2006). Effectiveness research can focus on how to foster better treatment in the community. For example, one study examined whether medication treatment of depression in the community was improved by providing psychiatrists with easily navigated hand-held computers programmed to provide quick feedback and assistance regarding treatment decisions (Trivedi et al., 2004). If it is hard to foster good medication treatment, one can imagine that interventions as complicated as a 16-session course of psychotherapy will be challenged by real-world hurdles, too. Even though such studies may incorporate less experimental control, they are fundamentally important in evaluating how well these treatment approaches will work in the real world. Beyond some important surveys of how people see the therapy they have received (see *Consumer Reports*, 1995), effectiveness studies do provide support for cognitive behavioral treatments of anxiety (e.g., Wade, Treat, & Stuart, 1998) and depression (e.g., Persons, Bostrom, & Bertagnolli, 1999). Effectiveness studies also provide support for offering psychotherapy as a supplement to medication for bipolar disorder (Miklowitz et al., 2007).

Even with increasing evidence that these treatments work in the real world, there is a big gap between what happens in research centers and the real world (see Focus on Discovery 16.3 for a discussion of how economic issues shape treatment in the real world). Even though more than 145 treatment manuals have been recognized as empirically supported (Chambless & Ollendick, 2001), therapists in the community seem relatively unaware of these manuals. For example, Addis and Krasnow (2000) reported that 23 percent of therapists surveyed said they had not heard of treatment manuals, and another 38 percent reported that they had heard of them but did not know what they were. Hopefully, more clinicians have heard about these treatment manuals since the survey was done, but clearly this demonstrates a need to work harder on getting research findings into the hands of therapists and consumers! One way to do this has been to recommend that graduate students in psychology be taught empirically supported treatments (Crits-Christoph et al., 1995).

FOCUS ON DISCOVERY 16.3

Stepped Care: An Economic Approach to Treatment Decisions

Partly in response to managed care, a strategy from medicine called **stepped care** is becoming more widely used in psychology and psychiatry (Haaga, 2000). Stepped care refers to the practice of beginning treatment efforts with the least expensive intervention possible and moving on to more expensive interventions only if necessary (see Figure 16.2). For example, a client with mild depression might be offered a self-help book that has been shown to be helpful in reducing symptoms (McKendree-Smith, Floyd, & Scogin, 2003). After a month, people who do not gain symptom relief would be offered psychotherapy or antidepressant medication.

There is growing evidence that pretty minimal levels of intervention can be helpful for many people, and some people may actually prefer to receive help in the privacy of their home. Computerized cognitive behavioral interventions have been developed for anxiety and depression. One meta-analysis of 12 randomized controlled trials showed an interesting pattern of findings (Spek et al., 2007). First, these programs have yielded only small effects on depression. Second, Internet programs have been moderately helpful for the relief of anxiety symptoms. Third, effects are much more substantial when the Internet program is supplemented with some form of therapist contact. Beyond the growing literature on computer-based intervention materials, brief written materials appear to be extremely helpful for many people who want to gain better control over drinking habits (Apodaca & Miller, 2003).

There are risks associated with low-intensity treatments. If the initial intervention does not help, the client may lose heart and drop out of treatment altogether. Consider one example of stepped care. In a study of weight loss, researchers initially assigned 26 clients to receive basic education about how to lose weight. Only 4 of the 26 clients, though, were able to reach their desired weight (Black & Threlfall, 1986). Bibliotherapy was added, and the remaining 22 clients reached their desired weight. In this type of circumstance, it would make sense to start with the more powerful intervention to avoid the demoralization that can arise when initial treatment efforts fail (Wilson, Vitousek, & Loeb, 2000). Effective stepped care programs will depend on using minimal treatments that have strong research backing (Rosen, 2004). Planning stepped care interventions requires a delicate juggling act to consider economics, illness severity, and the relative efficacy of different approaches.

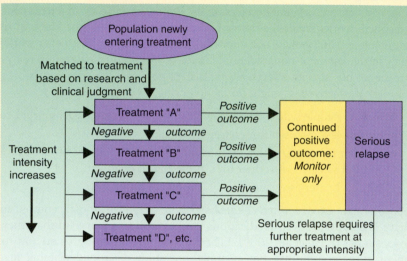

Figure 16.2 Stepped care involves starting with the least expensive intervention and moving on to more expensive interventions only if needed. From Sobell, M. B., & Sobell, L. C. (2000). Stepped Care as a Heuristic Approach to the Treatment of Alcohol Problems. *Journal of Consulting and Clinical Psychology, 68,* 573–579. Adapted with permission from *Addictive Behaviors across the Lifespan: Prevention, Treatment, and Policy Issues* (p. 150), by J. S. Baier, G. A. Marlatt, & R. J. McMahon (Eds.), 1993, Beverly Hills, CA: Sage.

Check Your Knowledge 16.2

Circle all that apply for the following questions.

1. Which of the following are the elements of an RCT by definition?
   a. randomization
   b. a comparison condition
   c. medications
   d. double-blind procedures
2. Which of these are common problems in treatment outcome studies?
   a. nonrepresentative samples
   b. no way to measure improvement
   c. variability across therapists
   d. treatment manuals constrain therapists
   e. lack of generalizability to the real world
   f. lack of clarity about treatment goals
3. The goal of effectiveness studies is to determine whether a treatment works
   a. under the best possible conditions
   b. under real-world conditions

The Evidence from Randomized Controlled Trials

We've described a set of issues in conducting and evaluating treatment outcome studies. But hundreds and hundreds of studies have been conducted to test different forms of psychotherapy, and at this point, a large literature has been amassed to support the helpfulness of therapy. We turn now to a discussion of the findings in regard to the different therapies we have described above.

Traditional Psychoanalytic Treatment   There are only four outcome studies of long-term psychoanalytic treatment (Bachrach et al., 1991). Major reviews of research on classical psychoanalysis suggest the following conclusions (Henry et al., 1994; Luborsky & Spence, 1978):

- Clients with severe psychopathology (e.g., schizophrenia) do not do as well as those with anxiety disorders. This is understandable in view of Freud's emphasis on less severe disorders.
- People with more education tend to do better in psychoanalysis than those with less education.
- Poor outcomes are more likely when a therapist makes frequent interpretations of transference reactions—for example, indicating to a male client that his behavior toward the therapist seems to reflect unresolved conflicts with his mother.

Each of the available studies of long-term psychoanalysis, though, has methodological problems, the most limiting of which is the lack of a control group. Because of this, we do not know whether psychoanalysis achieves more than the passage of time or the support of close others. This is not to say that psychoanalysis does no good, only that clear evidence is lacking as to its specific efficacy.

Perhaps the most ambitious attempt to evaluate the efficacy of psychoanalysis was the Menninger Foundation Psychotherapy Research Project, which began in the mid-1960s. In this study, 42 clients—mostly Caucasian clients with anxiety, depression, or both—were seen in either psychoanalysis or short-term psychodynamic psychotherapy. In both groups about 60 percent of the clients improved. There were no significant differences between the two groups either immediately after treatment or at follow-up 2 to 3 years later (Wallerstein, 1986, 1989).

Brief Psychodynamic Treatments   The picture emerging from outcome studies on brief psychodynamic treatment is inconsistent but generally positive. A meta-analysis of more than 25 studies suggested that brief psychodynamic therapy achieved moderately positive outcomes compared to no treatment (Anderson & Lambert, 1995). As reviewed by Goldfried, Greenberg, and Marmar (1990), brief psychodynamic therapy has been found to be helpful in treating bereavement (Marmar & Horowitz, 1988), job-related distress and anxiety disorders (Koss & Shiang, 1994), posttraumatic stress disorder (Horowitz, 1988) and psychopathy (Salekin, 2002).

Although psychodynamic treatment has received support, there are three important caveats:

- Psychodynamic treatment offers an advantage compared to control conditions only when treatment lasts more than 20 sessions; effects of briefer psychodynamic treatment (less than 20 sessions) appear comparable to control conditions (Abbass et al., 2008).
- Psychodynamic treatments have not been found to be more helpful than general treatment as offered in the community (Abbass et al., 2008).
- Brief psychodynamic therapies are likely to fare best when therapists use a manual and receive specific training in these approaches (Anderson & Lambert, 1995).

Taken together, these findings suggest that psychodynamic treatments can be helpful but also that there is more research needed.

Experiential Therapies   More than 100 treatment outcome studies have been conducted on experiential approaches (Elliot et al., 2004). Compared to wait-list and no-treatment controls, these treatments tend to have a positive effect. It does appear that experiential therapies, like most psychotherapies, are more likely to relieve symptoms of less severe problems, like anxiety and depression, than more severe problems, like schizophrenia. Of the different experiential treatments, emotion-focused therapy, developed by Greenberg and colleagues (2002), appears to have the strongest results. Of concern, two studies have suggested that Gestalt therapy and related approaches that emphasize expressing feelings (without much help in understanding those feelings and dealing with them constructively) lead to deterioration in about 15 percent of people (Beutler et al., 1984; Mohr et al., 1990).

Cognitive Behavior Therapy   Treatment outcome research supports the use of exposure to treat a wide variety of anxiety disorders, including simple phobias, posttraumatic stress disorder, obsessive-compulsive disorder, panic disorder, and agoraphobia (Chambless & Ollendick, 2001). Although most of the research has been done with adults, children also benefit from exposure treatment (Kazdin & Weisz, 1998). Exposure consistently performs better than other treatment approaches for anxiety disorders (Emmelkamp, 2004).

Beck's cognitive therapy (CBT) has received more intensive study than other forms of CBT (Hollon, Haman, & Brown, 2002). Beck's therapy achieves greater short-term improvement than wait-list controls, noncognitive behavioral treatments, and a heterogeneous group of other psychotherapies (Dobson, 1989). Beck's CBT also has proven efficacy in treating depression in children (Stark et al., 1998) as well as adolescents (Brent et al., 1997).

Other forms of CBT have received empirical support as well. A range of studies have shown positive effects of rational emotive behavior therapy for both adults and children (Chambless & Ollendick, 2001; Kendall et al., 1995). Marlatt's relapse prevention treatment has been shown to work better than attention-control or no-treatment conditions in a series of randomized controlled trials for substance abuse and appears to have particular promise when researchers study clients over longer follow-up periods (Witkiewitz & Marlatt, 2004). In a review of 16 meta-analyses, CBT was noted to be a well-supported intervention for schizophrenia, anxiety disorders, bulimia nervosa, and pain disorders, and to show small effects for sexual offenders (Butler et al., 2006).

There are relatively few treatment outcome studies available regarding the new approaches to CBT that focus on acceptance and emotional avoidance. The available studies have been criticized methodologically (Öt, 2008), but the early evidence is also promising. Preliminary evidence suggests that these types of approaches are helpful for problems that are quite difficult to address, such as borderline personality disorder, recurrent major depression, severe couples distress, and opiate addiction (Hayes et al., 2004). It is also worth noting that these approaches have become extremely popular with therapists—so popular that some have cautioned that we need to hold back against adopting them until more data can be accrued (Corrigan, 2001). Indeed, Teasdale (2004), one of the developers of mindfulness-based cognitive therapy, has argued for the need to proceed cautiously, with a strong sense of theory and a good knowledge of which conditions these treatments have been shown to help.

One of the positive aspects of cognitive therapy is that people may learn skills that help them even after they stop seeing a therapist. For example, CBT appears to help prevent future episodes of depression (Bockting et al., 2005). Given that as many as 50 percent of people with a first episode of depression will experience a second episode (APA, 2000), this is an important issue and suggests that CT has an important advantage compared to medication treatment (Vittengl et al., 2007). In one study of CBT for drug abuse, researchers found that clients who received CBT actually improved further after treatment stopped (Carroll, Rounsaville, Nich, et al., 1994). The investigators speculated that CBT had taught clients coping skills that they were able to implement after therapy ended.

One final issue is worth noting about cognitive therapy. Somewhat surprisingly, therapist experience doesn't seem to matter much in predicting outcomes of many treatments. Cognitive therapy, though, may be harder to implement than other types of therapy are. Research shows that therapist experience is related to better outcomes in cognitive therapy of major depressive disorder (DeRubeis et al., 2005) and panic disorder (Huppert et al., 2001).

Couples Therapy   A meta-analysis of more than 163 studies suggests that couples therapies work. About 80 percent of couples who receive couples therapy report being more satisfied than those who received no treatment (Shadish & Baldwin, 2003). Couples therapy is also more successful than individual therapy is for reducing couples' distress (Baucom et al., 1998; Sexton et al., 2004). When individual therapy is used to treat couples problems, about 10 percent get worse. Brief premarital training in communication skills can improve future relationship satisfaction and divorce rates compared with no intervention (Markman et al., 1989).

By far, behavioral couples therapy has received more attention than other forms of therapy. At least 30 RCTs of behavioral couples therapy have been conducted, and only 4 RCTs of emotion-focused couples therapy have been conducted. Behavioral couples therapy clearly reduces relationship distress compared to no-treatment and placebo-controlled treatments, and many of the gains last a year after therapy ends (Baucom et al., 1998; Sexton et al., 2004). Adding a cognitive component to behavioral couples therapy does not appear to add to the positive outcomes (Montag & Wilson, 1992).

Even though behavioral couples therapy has achieved support across a range of studies, the outcomes of behavioral couples therapy research are not as good as one might hope (Jacobson et al., 1984). Across all studies, no more than half the treated couples are happily married at the end of treatment (even if they had improved some during treatment). Interestingly, three therapies that include an emotionally relevant component have achieved positive results compared to behavioral couples therapy, including emotionally focused therapy (Johnson & Greenberg, 1995), psychodynamic insight-oriented therapy (Snyder, Wills, & Grady-Fletcher, 1991), and integrative couples behavior therapy (Christensen et al., 2006). Insight-oriented therapy was even found to be superior to behavioral couples therapy over a four-year follow-up in terms of divorce rates and marital satisfaction (Snyder et al., 1991).

Some research has focused on couples therapy as a way to address symptoms in one of the partners. For example, couples therapy has been found to be helpful in the treatment of sexual disorders, alcohol abuse (Sexton et al., 2004), and depression (O'Leary & Beach, 1990). Hence, psychological disorders that occur in the context of relationship problems may respond well to couples therapy.

Family Therapy   Family therapy has been found to have efficacy in reducing symptoms of a broad range of disorders, including agoraphobia, substance abuse, schizophrenia, and bipolar disorder (Lebow & Gurman, 1995). Family interventions for schizophrenia lead to substantially lower relapse rates, even two years after treatment (McFarlane et al., 2003).

Choosing between Therapies   The evidence above suggests that many different forms of therapy are helpful. Is there enough evidence to help consumers know whether one treatment is better than another? There is more debate about this issue of how different treatments compare than we can cover well here.

In one review, the authors concluded that brief psychodynamic treatment achieved comparable results to other kinds of therapies (Anderson & Lambert, 1995). Similarly, one study found that brief psychodynamic therapy was as helpful as cognitive therapy for certain personality disorders (Svartberg, Stiles, & Seltzer, 2004). There is a fair amount of controversy about these comparisons between treatments, though (see Lamberg & Ogles, 2004, for a discussion of how different reviewers find different patterns). Some of this debate may concern which studies and treatments should be included in a review. For example interpersonal psychotherapy, a well-validated treatment for depression (see p. 237), builds on the psychodynamic emphasis on relationships, but it does not focus on the therapeutic relationship or a person's history. Should this be included in reviews of psychodynamic therapy? Reviewers differ on decisions such as this. As a result, some reviews find a small advantage for cognitive behavioral therapies, whereas others do not.

Researchers have also compared experiential therapies, particularly emotion-focused therapy, with cognitive behavioral treatment. One comprehensive review suggests that if there is an advantage to CBT, it is probably fairly small (Elliot et al., 2004).

CBT does appear to fare better than other psychological treatments for anxiety disorders. Overall, however, the dominance of CBT approaches in Table 16.2 reflects that there are more carefully controlled trials available of CBT than of experiential therapies.

For the treatment of depression, eight studies have compared couples treatment and individual treatment. It turns out that both have similar effects in relieving depression, and couples therapy is more helpful in relieving relationship problems (Barbato & D'Avanzo, 2008). Similarly, family therapy has been found to be as helpful as interpersonal or cognitive therapy offered as a supplement to medications in bipolar disorder (Miklowitz et al., 2007).

Finally, a good deal of research has examined whether cognitive therapy offers an advantage compared to more strict behavioral interventions. Much of this work has been focused on anxiety disorders. In many forms of anxiety disorders, cognitive therapy does not yield better outcomes than exposure treatment alone (see Chapter 5 for more detail). Similarly, two major studies suggest that the behavioral activation component of depression treatment may be as helpful as a more complex therapy that combines behavioral activation with cognitive components (Dimidjian et al., 2006; Jacobson et al., 1996).

The Importance of Culture and Ethnicity in Psychological Treatment

Above, we described concerns about who is recruited into treatment studies. As it turns out, one of the major gaps in treatment outcome studies has been the exclusion of people from diverse cultural and ethnic backgrounds. Most studies enroll predominantly white, non-Latino clients, so samples are often not diverse enough to examine how treatment effects vary for differing groups of people. But there are many reasons to suspect that these treatments may not meet the needs of minority group members. For example, people from minority groups are much less likely to receive treatment for mental health conditions [U.S. Department of Health and Human Services (USDHHS), 2002]. As shown in Table 16.4, there are also dramatic differences in rates of treatment seeking by country among people with psychological disorders (Wang, Simon et al., 2007).

We believe it is important to consider some of the issues that may limit how well therapies work for people from different backgrounds. We do want to raise one caveat. Our discussion of ethnic and cultural factors in intervention runs the risk of stereotyping because we are going to review generalizations about the way a group of people react to psychological assistance. People from minority groups can differ as much from each other as their racial or ethnic group differs from another racial or ethnic group. It is important to consider the degree to which the person is *assimilated* into the majority culture and holds the same values as the majority culture (Sue & Sue, 2008). Nonetheless, a consideration of group characteristics is important and is part of a specialty called ethnic-minority mental health.

It is usually assumed that clients do better with therapists who are similar to them in cultural and ethnic background. Indeed, many minority clients report that they would prefer to

Table 16.4 Percent of People Diagnosed with a Psychological Disorder (*N*=5,630) Who Sought Treatment by Severity of the Disorder and Country

	Severe	Moderate	Mild
Nigeria	21.3	13.8	10.0
China	11.0	23.5	1.7
Colombia	27.8	10.3	7.8
South Africa	26.2	26.6	23.1
Ukraine	25.7	21.2	7.6
Lebanon	20.1	11.6	4.0
Mexico	25.8	17.9	11.9
Belgium	60.9	36.5	13.9
France	48.0	29.4	21.1
Israel	53.1	32.3	14.4
Germany	40.0	23.9	20.3
Italy	51.0	25.9	17.3
Japan	24.2	24.2	12.8
Netherlands	50.4	31.3	16.1
New Zeeland	56.6	39.8	22.2
Spain	58.7	37.4	17.3
United States	59.7	39.9	26.2

Drawn from a World Health Organization study reported by Wang, Aguilar-Gaxiola et al. (2007).

see someone from a similar background (Lopez, Lopez, & Fong, 1991). Such preferences may be particularly strong when individuals maintain a strong identification with their ethnic group (Ponce & Atkinson, 1989). Many clients believe that therapists of similar background, perhaps even of the same gender, will understand their life circumstances more quickly. Despite this assumption, it has *not* been demonstrated that better outcomes are achieved when client and therapist are similar in race or ethnicity (Beutler, Machado, & Neufeldt, 1994), nor that clients are more likely to continue treatment when there is a match (Maramba & Nagayama-Hall, 2002). **Cultural competence** may matter more than ethnic matching. A therapist who is not a member of the same racial or ethnic group as the client might still understand the client and create a good therapeutic relationship if he or she is familiar with the client's culture (USDHHS, 2002). We provide a brief glimpse of the kinds of knowledge related to cultural competence in Focus on Discovery 16.4.

Although many minority clients report that they would like to see a minority therapist, cultural sensitivity appears to be more important to outcome than a match of ethnicity between the client and therapist. (Lew Merrim/Photo Researchers, Inc.)

Here, we highlight work by a few researchers who have begun to provide data on whether currently available treatments work well when offered to people from different backgrounds. Then we turn to new treatments that have been developed to draw on the strengths of people from different backgrounds.

Overall, there are far too few studies on whether treatments are valid for any specific minority group (Chambless & Ollendick, 2001). Nonetheless, several studies have tested whether standard empirically validated treatments work well for culturally diverse populations. For example a group version of interpersonal psychotherapy for depression was found to be efficacious for people living in Ugandan villages (Bolton et al., 2003). Several studies support the efficacy of CBT for anxiety disorders among African American clients (Miranda et al., 2005). Two studies have found comparable efficacy for CBT of childhood anxiety disorders across ethnicities, and findings of several studies indicate that the effects of treatments for childhood disruptive disorders, including CBT and family therapy, do not differ by ethnicity (Miranda et al., 2005).

Even though there is a small amount of evidence that established treatments are helpful for minority populations, many theorists argue that treatments should be adapted to be more culturally sensitive. As outlined by Duran and colleagues (2004), established treatments may need to be modified to change the role of the therapist, the types of intervention strategies used, the content of the intervention, and how to present certain content. For example, in refining an established treatment manual for stress management in an HIV-positive population, changes were made to the ways that assertiveness training was covered, new content was introduced on coping strategies and spirituality, and an array of other changes were made based on feedback from therapists and clients. Early results suggest that these efforts were a good idea; in a small group of HIV-positive Latino men, culturally sensitive treatment was found to produce significantly larger changes in depression, functioning, denial, and even HIV symptoms compared to a no-treatment control.

One approach to developing culturally sensitive interventions is to draw on strengths that might be promoted by a given culture. For example, Latino culture emphasizes family values and spirituality. Weisman (2005) modified traditional family therapy for schizophrenia to build on these values, with a more explicit focus on spirituality and family coping. Another team modified cognitive behavioral therapy and interpersonal psychotherapy for depression to incorporate family values. Puerto Rican adolescents who received culturally sensitive CBT demonstrated significantly more decrease in depressive symptoms than did those who received IPT or a control condition (Rosello, Bernal, & Rivera-Medina, 1998). Hence, early data suggests that tailoring interventions to culturally relevant strengths can bolster applicability.

Amy Weisman's research focuses on how to modify family treatment for schizophrenia to draw on strengths of Latino families. (Courtesy of Amy Weisman, University of Miami.)

Another example of innovative approaches is illustrated by the work of Ricardo Muñoz and colleagues, who have conducted research for years to examine how to treat depression among low-income, predominantly minority women in San Francisco. Their team first tailored cognitive behavioral therapy for depression so that it could be offered in a primary care group setting, such that it would be more widely accessible for people who might not seek out formal psychotherapy. Results of this intervention were successful (Muñoz et al., 1995). More recently, they modified the

FOCUS ON DISCOVERY 16.4

Cultural Competence

A good therapist takes the perspective of his or her client. This process can be more challenging when a therapist and a client are from different backgrounds. It is important for therapists to be aware of differences across ethnic groups in social experiences that may have shaped a client's life experiences, community values, implicit ideas about how to express emotions, and expectancies about therapy. Here, we give examples of how just a few of these issues may shape the therapeutic process.

African Americans

Racial stereotypes on the part of white therapists may be one barrier to African American clients receiving treatment. One experiment revealed that white therapists rated case study information about African American clients as reflecting more pathology than did African American therapists and also considered photographs of the clients less attractive (Atkinson et al., 1996).

Therapists need to accept that virtually all African Americans have encountered prejudice and racism, and many must wrestle with their rage at a majority culture that is sometimes insensitive to and unappreciative of the emotional consequences of growing up as a member of a feared, resented, and sometimes hated minority (USDHHS, 2002). And, like members of all the minority groups discussed in this section, many African Americans have been subjected to hate crimes. One survey of African American clients suggested that many felt that their therapists were insensitive to these issues (Thompson et al., 2004).

In evaluating differences in outcomes for African Americans, as with many ethnic minorities, it is important to consider that some effects are driven by poverty. For example, in a major study of treatment for attention-deficit/hyperactivity disorder, outcomes were worse for African American children than they were for white children; on the other hand,

these differences were entirely explained by ethnic differences in poverty (MTA Cooperative Group, 1999b).

Latinos

The life experiences of Latino Americans vary a great deal depending on the region they originally came from—Mexico, Cuba, Puerto Rico, Central America, or South America. As is the case with other minority groups, generalizations are to be made with caution.

Therapy with most Latinos should appreciate that the culture may prohibit men from expressing weakness and fear. In addition, religion plays a very strong role in most Latin cultures and therefore needs to be considered in therapy with Latinos (USDHHS, 2002). Cognitive behavior therapy may be more acceptable than insight-oriented psychotherapy to some Latinos because it provides education, clear advice, and problem solving. This didactic and educational style of cognitive behavior therapy may demystify the process, thus reducing possible stigmatizing effects (Organista & Munoz, 1996). As with African Americans, though, many of the patterns described here apply more to lower-income people than higher-income people, regardless of race or ethnicity. This means that socioeconomic class has to be considered. There is no reason to assume that higher-income Latinos will find therapy less suitable than do Anglos.

Asian Americans and Pacific Islanders

Asian Americans and Pacific Islanders comprise more than three dozen distinct subgroups (e.g., Filipino, Chinese, Japanese, Vietnamese, Hawaiian, Samoan). They differ on dimensions such as how well they speak English, whether they came as refugees from war or terrorism in their homeland, and how much they identify with their native land (Sue & Sue, 2008). In

content of this intervention to be more specific to the concerns of African American women, including bolstering material to combat social isolation, to be sensitive to the high rates of trauma experienced in this population, to challenge myths of the superhuman African American woman, and to address family issues. African American women stated that they would rather receive the tailored intervention, and it produced a significantly larger reduction in depressive symptoms than a traditional CBT intervention (Kohn et al., 2002; Miranda et al., 2006).

Quick Summary

Treatment outcome research focuses on whether a given treatment works well. A number of groups have attempted to provide clear standards for psychotherapy research and to summarize the current state of knowledge about the validity of psychotherapy. With some minor variations in criteria, these groups have tended to emphasize the importance of clearly defining the sample and treatment regimen, random assignment to either the active treatment or a control comparison, and reliable and valid measures of outcome. These standards have provoked major debate. Treatment researchers and clinicians have raised concerns that evaluations of treatments should pay attention to the number of people who are harmed by treatments, that

control groups may not always be ethical, that treatment manuals can be constraining, that diagnosis might not be the best way to choose a treatment, and that the samples in some treatment studies are not representative. One type of research focuses on the effectiveness of treatment, or the utility of a given treatment in the real world.

A large number of RCTs now support the efficacy of psychotherapy compared to wait-list controls or no treatment. More specifically, researchers have amassed evidence to support brief psychodynamic, experiential, cognitive behavioral, couples, and family therapies. Cognitive behavioral treatments have received more extensive study than any other form of psychotherapy. Generally differences between

general, these groups show a greater tendency than whites to be ashamed of emotional suffering and to be reluctant to seek out professional help.

The stereotype of Asian Americans as invariably being highly educated, earning good salaries, and being emotionally well adjusted is belied by the facts. The discrimination suffered in the United States and in many other countries is as severe as that endured by other minority groups (Sue & Sue, 2008). In the United States, for example, over 120,000 Japanese Americans—70,000 of them born in the United States (USDHHS, 2002)—were imprisoned in concentration camps and prisons for several years during World War II. More subtle discrimination remains in more recent times. Sue and Sue (2008) advise therapists to be sensitive to the personal losses that many Asian refugees have suffered. Given the importance of family ties, it is also important to be sensitive to the losses that family members may have endured.

Asian Americans in the United States are often caught between two cultures. One form of resolution is to identify vigorously with majority values and denigrate anything Asian, a kind of racial self-hate. Others, torn by conflicting loyalties, experience poorly expressed rage at a discriminatory Western culture. Acculturation, then, is important to consider.

Many cultural differences in values, particularly concerning relationships and emotional expression, have implications for how to conduct psychotherapy with Asian Americans and Pacific Islanders. Therapists should be aware that Asian Americans may initially describe stress in physical terms, such as headaches and fatigue, even though they are aware of emotional symptoms and will endorse those when asked directly (Chang et al., 2008). Generally, Asians respect structure and formality in interpersonal relationships more than Westerners, who can often favor informality. People from the Pacific Islands, however, may prefer friendliness and informality. For Asians, respect for authority may interfere with discussing differences openly. It may be more comfortable to agree with a therapist, even if that means that differences of opinion are so extreme as to keep the person from continuing in treatment. Asian Americans may also consider some areas off-limits for discussion with a therapist, for example, the nature of the marital relationship, especially sex. Finally, many Asian Americans prefer a structured approach to therapy over a reflective one (Iwamasa, 1993).

American Indians and Alaskan Natives

Like other minorities, American Indians and Alaskan Natives (sometimes referred to collectively as Native Americans or First Americans) are a highly heterogeneous group, with more than 500 tribes residing in the United States and many in Canada as well, speaking more than 200 languages, some of them as dissimilar to each other as English is to Chinese (Fleming, 1992).

American Indians and to a lesser but still significant extent Alaskan Natives have experienced severe institutional discrimination for over 300 years. They have been forbidden to speak their own language, driven from the land that their tribes had inhabited for hundreds of years, forbidden to engage in traditional native spiritual practices (in the case of American Indians), forced onto reservations in undesirable locations without regard for the special sanctity that land has for them, and subjected to other indignities. In recent years, however, their social and economic conditions have been improving, and tribes are achieving more control over their lives (USDHHS, 2002).

Because it is common for different family members to provide care for Native American children, the pattern of a child moving among different households is not necessarily a sign of trouble. A youngster's avoidance of eye contact is a traditional sign of respect but may be misconstrued by someone unfamiliar with the culture (Everett, Proctor, & Cartmell, 1989). As with members of other minority groups, conflicts about identification can be severe—young people can be torn between traditional values and those of the decidedly more privileged majority culture, which may underlie the high rates of truancy, substance abuse, and suicide among Native American young people (Red Horse, 1982). Drug abuse, especially alcoholism, is a widespread problem in some tribes and can lead to child abuse, particularly when there is family conflict. A value placed on cooperativeness rather than competitiveness can be misinterpreted by a culturally unaware therapist as lack of motivation. The importance of family may make it advisable to conduct treatment in the home and to engage family members in the process (Sue & Sue, 2008).

---

cognitive behavioral treatments and other forms of treatment are quite small, but cognitive behavior therapy for anxiety disorders appears to be more effective than other treatments.

Minority groups are less likely to receive psychotherapy for psychological concerns. Matching therapist and client ethnicity is not helpful for therapy outcomes; rather, enhancing the cultural competence of therapists is the goal. The few researchers who have tested treatment manuals developed for majority populations generally find such psychotherapies work with minority groups, although sometimes they observe less positive effect than seen in initial trials. Some researchers are working on ways to tailor treatment approaches to fit with culturally relevant values.

Check Your Knowledge 16.3

Answer the questions.

1. Which treatment has **not** been shown to have efficacy compared to treatment as provided in the community?
   a. traditional psychoanalysis
   b. short-term psychodynamic therapy
   c. experiential therapy
   d. behavior therapy
   e. cognitive therapy

2. In the few available studies, cognitive behavioral treatments appear to offer more relief than experiential treatments for which disorders?

   a. schizophrenia
   b. depression
   c. anxiety disorders
   d. all psychological disorders

3. A couple comes for treatment of incessant conflicts. They are likely to show the strongest marital improvements if you offer them:
   a. individual cognitive behavioral treatment for both partners
   b. couples therapy

Psychotherapy Process Research

Treatment works for most people. But nonetheless, a careful review of the data suggests there is room for improvement—some people with serious mental illness don't seek treatment, others leave treatment early, still others don't find treatment helps them change, and for a very few, problems actually worsen during treatment. A growing number of theorists have suggested that one way to address these issues would be to draw from the best ideas in different treatment approaches (Castonguay et al., 2003). Treatments can be refined by studying what predicts good (or bad) outcomes. This is the goal of psychotherapy process research. Broadly, there are two types of **process research:**

- In the **common factors** approach, researchers try to understand the common ingredients that help all forms of therapy succeed (Goldfried, 2004).

- In research on *mechanisms of change*, researchers try to understand the unique processes involved when specific forms of therapy succeed. For example, does cognition have to change for cognitive therapy to work?

We cover these two different approaches next.

Common Factors Research

Well-documented common factors include a strong rationale for how treatment will work (which might bolster hope), therapist expectations for change, and a strong therapeutic relationship (Wampold, 2001). Bandura (1977) suggests that all therapeutic procedures work by giving the person a sense of mastery or *self-efficacy*. Here, we focus on a topic that has been studied in more than 1,000 studies using many different methods: the therapeutic relationship (Orlinsky, Ronnestad, & Willutzki, 2004).

Regardless of theoretical orientation, a good relationship between client and therapist is important. People are not likely to reveal deeply personal information if they do not trust their therapists. The heart of psychotherapy involves cooperation between a therapist and a client on making changes.

The term **therapeutic alliance** (also called the **working alliance**) describes the collaborative relationship between therapist and client, in which they share an affective bond and an ability to agree on treatment goals. In a meta-analysis of 79 studies, Martin, Garske, and Davis (2000) found that therapeutic alliance predicted a small but consistent amount of the variance in outcome across a broad range of psychological disorders, treatment approaches, and outcome measures. Overall, therapeutic alliance (measured with self-report scales given to the therapists or the client) accounted for at least 5 percent of the variability in outcome. This may seem like a really small piece of the pie! A few issues help put this in context. First, most therapists do establish good relationships with their clients—there may not be many terrible relationships being studied. Second, it is possible that other types of measures, like behaviorally based codes of actual interactions, would yield stronger effects. For example, across dozens of studies, clients' reports of empathy account for about 10 percent of the variance in outcome after treatment (Greenberg et al., 2001). Other variables that seem to be predictive include therapist friendliness and interpersonal flexibility (Beutler et al., 2004). Third, some data suggest that the quality of the therapeutic relationship influences variables that are not usually measured in these studies, such as whether a person leaves treatment (Horvath, 2001). Nonetheless, while it is clear that the therapeutic relationship is important, the research does not justify the assertion that the relationship alone produces change.

There are different views on how a good therapeutic alliance works (Henry et al., 1994). In client-centered therapy, a good relationship is assumed to be one of the critical ingredients for change (Elliott et al., 2004). In psychoanalysis, it might make interpretations more effective, thus having an indirect effect. Although the therapeutic relationship might not have received much direct attention in early cognitive manuals, it is central in some of the newer manuals, such as the manual for Linehan's dialectical behavior therapy. No matter how the alliance works, research suggests that a good relationship is important for any therapeutic approach (Martin et al., 2000).

Many researchers have focused on what fosters a strong therapeutic relationship. In most studies, the therapeutic alliance is measured after a couple sessions of treatment. Several studies sug-

A strong relationship between therapist and client is widely regarded as essential for implementing treatment procedures. A great deal of research has focused on the therapeutic alliance. (Esbin-Andersonage/ Age Fotostock America, Inc.)

gest that the therapeutic alliance is predicted by the degree of relief that patients are already getting from their symptoms (Crits-Cristoph, Gibbons, & Hearon, 2006). Nonetheless, even if you control for the early symptom relief, therapeutic alliance still predicts outcome (Klein et al., 2003).

Because therapeutic alliance matters, studies focus on how a therapist can promote a good relationship. Not surprisingly, these studies find that therapists who convey empathy and positive regard, who show their engagement in nonverbal behaviors (e.g., nodding their head, smiling, or leaning forward), and who are flexible but set consistent goals for treatment are able to promote stronger relationships (Ackerman & Hilsenroth, 2003). Beyond the therapists' behaviors, therapeutic relationships are also undoubtedly influenced by characteristics of the client as well as of the therapy.

Mechanisms of Change Research

Beyond the therapeutic relationship, researchers have focused on whether treatments actually change the mechanisms that each therapy is designed to target. For example, traditional behavioral couples therapy (BCT) focuses on communication training and integrative couples behavioral therapy (ICBT) focuses on acceptance. As one might expect, then, BCT produces more change in communication, and ICBT produces more change in acceptance (Doss et al., 2005).

A large body of research focuses on whether cognitive therapy works by changing negative cognitions. Many studies have found that clients who receive cognitive therapy become substantially less negative in their thinking (Jarrett et al., 2007). You might expect that this would answer the question of whether treatments actually change underlying mechanisms. But that is only part of the story. Some researchers have examined cognitive changes that occur during other forms of treatment. In one study, Jacobson and colleagues (1996) offered either traditional cognitive therapy or just one of the components of cognitive therapy—*behavioral activation*, which involves helping a person engage in more pleasant activities in the hopes that they will gain more positive reinforcement. During behavioral activation, the therapist does not talk about cognition. As it turns out, behavioral activation achieved similar results to cognitive therapy in terms of changes in cognitive variables among clients with depression. These results suggest that you can change cognition without offering cognitive therapy. Indeed, adding cognitive therapy to medication treatment does not influence the degree of change in negative cognitions; patients who receive medication treatment demonstrate just as much improvement in their negative cognitions as do those who receive cognitive therapy as well as medication treatment (Jarrett et al., 2007). The simplest way to understand this is that symptom relief (from many different treatments) helps people see the world and themselves less negatively. Indeed, careful analyses suggest that symptoms are driving the negative cognitions rather than that cognitions are driving symptoms (Jarrett et al., 2007).

These studies of cognitive therapy pose quite a challenge. As you can imagine, this is a major topic of research. Some researchers have suggested that maybe we need to be much more specific in how we think about what aspects of cognition need to change.

One example of this type of approach comes from work by David Clark (1994). Clark sees the driving force of panic disorder as cognitive misinterpretation of bodily sensations, such that a person believes that a small change in heart rate portends catastrophe. His treatment manual is designed to address this cognitive process, which is much more specific than general negative thoughts. In support of his proposed mechanism, clients who took part in treatment and yet retained cognitive misinterpretations of bodily sensations at the end of treatment were likely to relapse within a year.

One study has looked at very focused aspects of cognition in the context of therapy for depression. These authors reasoned that the key ingredient might not be whether a client's thoughts were negative at the end of therapy—most clients are pretty positive by the time depression is relieved. Rather, the authors argued that it might matter whether clients had the skills to ward off negative thoughts when they did occur. They had clients rate what they would do if they heard negative news about themselves (e.g., you aren't picked for a job), and they had observers rate how savvy clients seemed to be about using cognitive strategies during their therapy sessions. These two measures of the ability to challenge negative thinking predicted outcomes. That is, the ability to learn very specific skills to ward off negative thinking was associated with less risk of depression relapse (Strunk et al., 2007). These findings illustrate how sophisticated researchers will need to be to understand the mechanisms involved in therapeutic change.

It is hoped that by building our knowledge about the processes guiding therapeutic improvement, we can design better treatments. For example, Persons (2005) recommends conceptualizing the mechanisms that will be most important for a given person to obtain relief from symptoms and gathering data on whether treatment is working to change those processes. Similarly, Rosen and Davison (2003) have argued that we should be defining empirically supported principles of change rather than empirically supported treatments. That is, we should focus on the mechanisms that can successfully be changed in therapy and study when it would be most helpful to address those mechanisms. Many researchers have argued that we should be more focused on testing our ability to change these specific mechanisms than on comparing entire treatment packages.

Quick Summary

Process research focuses on understanding how therapy works. Common factors research attempts to find the predictors of good outcomes that work across different forms of therapy, including a strong therapeutic alliance. Other research is focused on mechanisms of change that might operate within specific forms of therapy. Some feel that process research may help us avoid a proliferation of treatment manuals, by encouraging us to go back to the basic elements of which strategies work for whom, at what time.

Check Your Knowledge 16.4

Fill in the blanks.
1. Treatment outcome studies test _____.
2. Process research focuses on _____.

True or False?
3. True or False? Cognitive therapy is the only treatment that changes negative cognitive styles.

Community Psychology and Prevention Science

Community psychology aims to change large systems to help groups of people rather than individuals. Community psychologists are invested in reaching out to large populations to prevent the onset or recurrence of physical or mental disorders. Community psychology gained popularity in the 1960s, during a period of tremendous social activism. Cities and college campuses erupted in riots, and many ethnic-minority groups demonstrated against racism and political repression. This social upheaval encouraged looking at social institutions for causes of individual suffering. Against this backdrop, mental health professionals began to shift from a focus on individual-level risk factors to a focus on large-scale social problems, such as poverty, overcrowding, violence, racism, poor education, segregation, and the alienation felt in large cities. Community psychology's emphasis on prevention became especially important in the United States, where a large gap had developed between the need for mental health care and the availability of services (Weissberg, Caplan, & Sivo, 1989).

These large-scale issues in understanding mental health have not gone away. We have described the prevalence of rape, child abuse, and homelessness in other chapters—ongoing problems of this magnitude call for interventions at a system level. Beyond evidence for social pressures on mental health, the high prevalence rates of depression, anxiety, and substance-abuse disorders demand approaches to identification and prevention that will reach a lot of people.

Researchers working from the perspective of community psychology have developed a number of techniques to evaluate the prevalence of risk factors using epidemiological studies, to reduce environmental risk factors, and to strengthen protective factors. Researchers may gather data using epidemiological research and then use that data to develop interventions, such as mass media campaigns, instructional programs in schools, or other techniques to reach a large number of people. These strategies have been called prevention science (Heller, Wyman, & Allen, 2000).

Many prevention science projects have worked well (Heller et al., 2000). Massive studies have been conducted to understand the epidemiology of risk factors in the general U.S. population (Kessler, Berglund, et al., 2005). Large-scale programs, such as National Depression Awareness Day, are implemented across the United States to enhance the detection of depression and other disorders. Jose Szapocznik has earned awards for his work on how community and school systems influence family and child mental health (APA, 2002), and the former president of the APA, Martin Seligman (1998), has conducted studies of how to prevent depression by teaching positive thinking skills to school children. Large-scale studies have considered how well medications and therapy can be implemented in community clinics, and a set of researchers are trying to develop therapies that can be efficiently offered over the web. We have previously described many other successful community psychology programs, including interventions to address depression when people seek primary care (p. 245) or through workplace interventions (p. 237), and suicide prevention centers with telephone hotlines (p. 251).

The success of these programs, coupled with the vast numbers of people affected by mental health problems, indicate that there is an ongoing need for this type of science. That is, there is a need for people who specialize in understanding how broad social systems influence mental health, how to develop effective prevention programs, how to develop national policies that will diminish stigma, and how to increase the accessibility and sensitivity of services for the needs of a diverse population.

Summary

Specific Treatment Approaches:

- Psychodynamic treatments focus on unconscious conflicts and childhood experiences that shape emotions and relationships in a person's current life.
- Experiential psychotherapies emphasize freedom to choose, personal growth, personal responsibility, and emotional awareness. Variants of these approaches include Rogers's client-centered therapy, Gestalt therapy, and emotion-focused therapy.
- Behavioral treatments include exposure treatment and treatments based on operant principles. Cognitive therapies vary in the targets of their work, but a core goal is often to challenge underlying negative schemata. Cognitive behavioral treatments have evolved over the past 10 years to incorporate themes like acceptance, emotional avoidance, spirituality and meaning.
- Couples therapy helps distressed couples resolve the inevitable conflicts in any ongoing relationship of two adults living together. Many different forms of couples therapy have been developed, including behavioral couples therapy, integrative behavioral couples therapy, emotionally focused couples therapy, and insight-oriented couples therapy.
- Family therapy includes many different techniques to address different family and individual concerns.

Challenges in Evaluating Treatment Outcomes

- Research on the effectiveness of various forms of psychological treatments has been conducted for many decades. Overall, this research suggests that about 75 percent of people gain some improvement from therapy. Therapy also seems to be more helpful than a placebo or the passage of time.
- Efforts have been made to define standards for research on psychotherapy trials and to summarize current knowledge on which psychological treatments work. These standards typically include the need to randomly assign participants to treatment or a control, to use a treatment manual, to define the treated sample carefully, and to use reliable and valid outcome measures. It is hoped that these efforts will help disseminate the best available therapeutic practices to clinicians and their clients as well as provide insurance companies with the data to support the use of psychotherapy.
- Controversy exists about research standards: most standards do not consider the proportion of patients who are harmed by a treatment, a large proportion of clients are excluded or will not take part in clinical trials, cultural diversity is lacking in most trials, many treatment approaches remain untested, and treatment manuals could constrain a talented therapist. A broader concern is that a huge gap exists between what happens in the research world and the real world. Efficacy research focuses on how well therapies work in carefully controlled experiments, whereas effectiveness research focuses on how well therapies work in the real world.

Specific Treatment Approaches: Treatment Outcome Research

- Treatment outcome research supports the efficacy of psychodynamic, experiential, cognitive behavioral, couples, and family therapy approaches compared to no treatment. Differences in how well these active forms of psychotherapy perform are quite small, but behavioral approaches offer a clear advantage for the treatment of anxiety disorders.
- Couples therapy offers an advantage compared to individual therapy in reducing couples' distress. Promising evidence exists for integrative behavioral couples therapy, emotion-focused couples therapy, and insight-oriented couples therapy as compared to standard behavioral couples therapy.

- Family therapy has been shown to be successful in the treatment of externalizing disorders among children and adolescents, in helping people with substance abuse accept the need for treatment, and in reducing relapse among adults with schizophrenia and bipolar disorder.

The Importance of Culture and Ethnicity in Psychological Treatment

- Clinicians offering treatment to minority clients must be sensitive to the cultural values and events that shape the way people may approach relationships, therapy, and emotional expression. Little empirical research is available on how psychotherapies work for people from diverse backgrounds, but minority status is associated with less use of therapy. Researchers have developed modifications of some treatments to be more culturally sensitive.

Psychotherapy Process Research

- Common factors research identifies variables that predict outcomes across a broad range of therapies, such as the quality of the therapeutic alliance.
- Process researchers also examine mechanisms of change. For example, researchers conduct studies on whether it is necessary to change cognition in order for cognitive therapy to work.

Community Psychology and Prevention Science

- Community psychology aims to understand and prevent disorder on a large scale.

Answers to Check Your Knowledge Questions

16.1. 1. f; 2. b
16.2. 1. a, b; 2. a, c, d, e; 3. b

16.3. 1. a; 2. c; 3. b
16.4. 1. Whether a given treatment works; 2. How a treatment works; 3. F

Key Terms

behavioral activation (BA)
   therapy
client-centered therapy
common factors
cultural competence
effectiveness

efficacy
emotion-focused therapy
empathy
empirically supported
   treatments (ESTs)
Gestalt therapy

outcome research
process research
randomized controlled trials
   (RCTs)
self-actualization
stepped care

therapeutic (working) alliance
unconditional positive regard

17 Legal and Ethical Issues

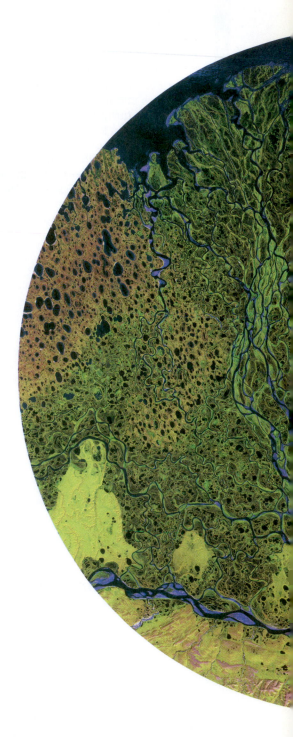

LEARNING GOALS

1. Be able to differentiate the legal concepts of insanity and the various standards for the insanity defense.
2. Be able to describe the issues surrounding competency to stand trial.
3. Be able to delineate the conditions under which a person can be committed to a hospital under civil law.
4. Be able to discuss the difficulties associated with predicting dangerousness and the issues surrounding the rights to receive and refuse treatment.
5. Be able to describe the ethics surrounding psychological research and therapy.

Amendment I   *Congress shall make no law respecting an establishment of religion, or prohibiting the free exercise thereof; or abridging the freedom of speech, or of the press; or the right of the people peaceably to assemble, and to petition the Government for a redress of grievances.*

Amendment IV   *The right of the people to be secure in their persons, houses, papers, and effects, against unreasonable searches and seizures, shall not be violated. . . .*

Amendment V   *No person . . . shall be compelled in any criminal case to be a witness against himself, nor be deprived of life, liberty, or property, without due process of law. . . .*

Amendment VI   *In all criminal prosecutions, the accused shall enjoy the right to a speedy and public trial . . . to be confronted with the witnesses against him; to have compulsory process for obtaining witnesses in his favor, and to have the Assistance of Counsel for his defense.*

Amendment VIII   *Excessive bail shall not be required, nor excessive fines imposed, nor cruel and unusual punishment inflicted.*

Amendment XIII   *. . . Neither slavery nor involuntary servitude, except as a punishment for crime whereof the party shall have been duly convicted, shall exist within the United States, or any place subject to their jurisdiction. . . .*

Amendment XIV   *. . . No State shall . . . deprive any person of life, liberty, or property, without due process of law; nor deny to any person within its jurisdiction the equal protection of the laws.*

Amendment XV   *. . . The right of citizens of the United States to vote shall not be denied or abridged by the United States or by any State on account of race, color, or previous condition of servitude.*

THESE ELOQUENT STATEMENTS DESCRIBE and protect some of the rights of U.S. citizens and others residing in the United States. Against what are these rights being protected? Be mindful of the circumstances under which most of these statements were issued. After the Constitutional Convention had delineated the powers of government in 1787, the first Congress saw fit in 1789 to amend what had been framed and to set specific limits on the federal

Clinical Case: David

David had been hearing voices for several days. Unable to drown them out with music or talking, he became more and more troubled. The voices were telling him that he was the one chosen by God to rid the world of evil. David went to the emergency room of the local hospital seeking relief. Instead of being admitted, David was given a prescription for Haldol and sent on his way. Two days later, David took a loaded gun into the busy train station and began shooting. He killed two people and injured four others. When he was arrested, David told the police he was answering to God. His speaking was disorganized and hard to follow, and he expressed a number of paranoid beliefs.

David was found competent to stand trial because he understood that he was charged with murder and he was able to help his attorney with his defense. At trial, David entered a plea of "not guilty by reason of insanity" (NGRI). His defense lawyer arranged for David to be evaluated by a psychologist. The psychologist concluded that David had schizophrenia, paranoid type, and that at the time of the crime he was unable to discern right from wrong (he thought his behavior was the right thing to do since God was directing him) and unable to conform his behavior to the requirements of the law. The prosecution did not dispute these findings, and the case was set-

tled before going to trial. David was committed to the local forensic hospital for an indeterminate period of time. He was to remain there until he was no longer dangerous and mentally ill. Periodic evaluations would be conducted to see if David could be transferred to a less secure hospital.

After seven years in the hospital, David had done very well. He took his prescribed medication (Zyprexa), was never in a physical altercation with other patients, participated in individual and group therapy, worked in the hospital machine shop, and served as a team leader for the unit he was living in. David felt horribly remorseful for the crimes he had committed, and he recognized that he had schizophrenia that would require treatment for the rest of his life. The treatment team on the unit all agreed that David was no longer dangerous and that his schizophrenia was under control with the medication. They recommended that he be transferred to a less secure psychiatric hospital. David's attorney presented the case before a judge in the courtroom that was part of the hospital. The attorneys for the state objected to David's release, arguing that David could stop taking his medications and become violent again. The judge agreed that release was premature at this time and ordered that David remain in the forensic hospital for another year before being evaluated again.

government. This was accomplished with what came to be called the Bill of Rights, which are the first 10 amendments to the Constitution. Amendments beyond the original 10 have been added since that time. The philosophical ideal of the U.S. government is to allow citizens the maximum degree of liberty consistent with preserving order in the community at large.

We open our final chapter in this way because the legal and mental health systems collaborate continually, although often subtly, to deny a substantial proportion of the U.S. population their basic civil rights. With the best of intentions, judges, governing boards of hospitals, legal associations, and professional mental health groups have worked over the years to protect society at large from the actions of people regarded as mentally ill and considered dangerous to themselves or to others. But in so doing they have denied many thousands of people their basic civil rights.

People with mental illness who have broken the law or who are alleged to have done so are subject to **criminal commitment**, a procedure that confines a person in a mental hospital either for determination of competency to stand trial or after acquittal by reason of insanity. **Civil commitment** is a set of procedures by which a person who is deemed mentally ill and dangerous but who has not broken a law can be deprived of liberty and placed in a psychiatric hospital. In this chapter we look at these legal procedures in depth. Then we turn to an examination of some important ethical issues as they relate to therapy and research.

Criminal Commitment

We examine first the role of psychiatry and psychology in the criminal justice system. Almost as early as the concept of mens rea, or "guilty mind," and the rule "No crime without an evil intent" had begun to be accepted in English common law, the concept of *insanity* was taken into consideration. Broadly speaking, insanity refers to a disordered mind, and a disordered mind may be regarded as unable to formulate and carry out a criminal purpose (Morse, 1992). In other words, a disordered mind cannot be a guilty mind, and only a guilty mind can engender culpable actions.

It is important to note that insanity is a legal concept, not a psychological one. As such, its definition comes from court proceedings. In today's courts, judges and lawyers call on psychiatrists and clinical psychologists for assistance in dealing with criminal acts thought to result from the accused person's disordered mental state. Although the insanity defense was developed to protect people's rights, in practice, the insanity defense often results in a greater denial of liberties than they would otherwise experience.

The Insanity Defense

The **insanity defense** is the legal argument that a defendant should not be held responsible for an illegal act if it is attributable to mental illness or mental retardation that interferes with rationality or that results from some other excusing circumstance, such as not knowing right from wrong. A staggering amount of material has been written on the insanity defense, even though it is pleaded in less than 1 percent of all cases that reach trial and even when pleaded, it is rarely successful (Morse, 1982b; Steadman, 1979; Steadman et al., 1993).

Because an insanity defense is based on the accused's mental condition at the time the crime was committed, retrospective, often speculative, judgment on the part of attorneys, judges, jurors, and mental health professionals is required. And disagreement between defense and prosecution psychiatrists and psychologists is the rule.

Mental illness and crime do not go hand in hand. A person can be diagnosed as mentally ill and be held responsible for a crime. However, the most heinous or bizarre crime can be committed by someone who has no mental illness at all, despite our tendency to think someone must have been "crazy" to commit such a crime. Indeed, decades of social psychological research tell us that otherwise normal people can do horrendous, criminal acts under the right circumstances or contexts (Aronson, 2004).

The insanity pleas available in state and federal courts in the United States have been crafted from a series of legal definitions and precedents that we review below. Broadly, there are two different kinds of insanity pleas today. With the **not guilty by reason of insanity (NGRI)** plea, there is no dispute over whether the person actually committed the crime—both sides agree that the person did the crime. However, due to the person's insanity at the time of the crime, the defense attorney argues that the person should not be held responsible for the crime and should thus be acquitted of the crime. The successful NGRI plea indicates the person is not held responsible for the crime due to his or her mental illness. People acquitted with the NGRI plea are committed indefinitely to a forensic hospital. That is, they are only released from forensic hospitals if they are deemed no longer dangerous and no longer mentally ill (we discuss the difficulties in making these determinations below).

A forensic hospital looks very much like a regular hospital except that the perimeter of the grounds is secured with gates, barbed wires, or electric fences. Inside the hospital, doors to the different units may be locked, and bars may be placed on windows on the lower floors. Patients do not stay in jail cells, however. They stay in either individual or shared rooms. Security professionals are on hand to keep patients safe. They typically do not carry weapons of any sort, and they may be dressed in regular clothing rather than uniforms.

The second insanity plea is **guilty but mentally ill (GBMI)**. Initially adopted by Michigan in 1975, this plea allows an accused person to be found legally guilty of a crime—thus maximizing the chances of incarceration—but allows for psychiatric judgment on how to deal with the convicted person if he or she is considered to have been mentally ill when the act was committed. Thus, even a seriously ill person can be held morally and legally responsible for a crime but can then, in theory, be committed to a prison hospital or other suitable facility for psychiatric treatment rather than to a regular prison for punishment. In reality, however, people judged GBMI are usually put in the general prison population, where they may or may not receive treatment. As of 2004, at least ten states had adopted some or all of the GBMI provisions; four states have both NGRI and GBMI available. Table 17.1 compares these two insanity pleas. Three states—Idaho, Montana, and Utah—do not allow for any insanity defense.

We now turn to how these two pleas were developed by reviewing the legal precedents throughout history that set the stage for our current definitions of insanity.

Table 17.1 Comparing NGRI and GBMI

	NGRI	GBMI
Responsibility for crime	Not responsible	Responsible
Where committed	Forensic hospital	Prison
Given sentence?	No	Yes
When released	When no longer dangerous and mentally ill	End of sentence, but could then be committed civilly if dangerous and mentally ill
Treatment given?	Yes	Possibly

Landmark Cases and Laws   Several court rulings and established principles bear on the problems of legal responsibility and mental illness. Table 17.2 summarizes these rulings and principles.

Irresistible Impulse   The **irresistible impulse** concept was formulated in 1834 in a case in Ohio. According to this concept, if a pathological impulse or uncontrollable drive compelled the person to commit the criminal act, an insanity defense is legitimate. The irresistible-impulse test was confirmed in two subsequent court cases, *Parsons v. State* and *Davis v. United States*.[1]

The M'Naghten Rule   The **M'Naghten rule** was formulated in the aftermath of a murder trial in England in 1843. The defendant, Daniel M'Naghten, had set out to kill the British prime minister, Sir Robert Peel, but had mistaken Peel's secretary for Peel. M'Naghten claimed that he had been instructed to kill Lord Peel by the "voice of God." The judges ruled that

> to establish a defense of insanity, it must be clearly proved that, at the time of the committing of the act, the party accused was labouring under such a defect of reason, from disease of the mind, as not to know the nature and quality of the act he was doing; or if he did know it, that he did not know he was doing what was wrong.

As of 2004, this right–wrong test was the sole test in 20 states and in 4 others was applied in conjunction with irresistible impulse.

Table 17.2 Landmark Cases and Laws Regarding the Insanity Defense

Irresistible impulse (1834) M'Naghten rule (1843)	A pathological impulse or drive that the person could not control compelled that person to commit a criminal act. The person did not know the nature and quality of the criminal act in which he or she engaged, or, if the person did know it, the person did not know what he or she was doing was wrong.
American Law Institute guidelines (1962)	1. The person's criminal act is a result of "mental disease or defect" that results in the person's not appreciating the wrongfulness of the act or in the person's inability to behave according to the law (combination of M'Naghten rule and irresistible impulse).
	2. "[T]he terms 'mental disease or defect' do not include an abnormality manifested only by repeated criminal or otherwise antisocial conduct" (American Law Institute, 1962).
Insanity Defense Reform Act (1984)	1. The person's criminal act is a result of severe mental illness or defect that prevents the person from understanding the nature of his or her crime.
	2. The burden of proof is shifted from the prosecution to the defense. The defense has to prove that the person is insane.
	3. If the person is judged to have recovered from mental illness, then instead of being released from the prison hospital, the person remains incarcerated for at least as long as he or she would have been imprisoned if convicted.
Guilty but mentally ill (1975)	The person can be found legally guilty of a crime—thus maximizing the chances of incarceration—and the person's mental illness plays a role in how he or she is dealt with. Thus, even a seriously ill person can be held morally and legally responsible but can then be committed to a prison hospital or other suitable facility for psychiatric treatment rather than to a regular prison for punishment.

---

[1]*Parsons v. State*, 2 So. 854, 866-67 (Ala. 1887); *Davis v. United States*, 165 U.S. 373, 378 (1897).

American Law Institute Guidelines   In 1962 the American Law Institute (ALI) proposed its own guidelines, which were intended to be more specific and informative to lay jurors than were other tests. The **American Law Institute guidelines** state the following:

1. A person is not responsible for criminal conduct if at the time of such conduct as a result of mental disease or defect he lacks substantial capacity either to appreciate the criminality (wrongfulness) of his conduct or to conform his conduct to the requirements of law.

2. As used in the article, the terms "mental disease or defect" do not include an abnormality manifested only by repeated criminal or otherwise antisocial conduct (American Law Institute, 1962, p. 66).

The first ALI guideline combines the M'Naghten rule and the concept of irresistible impulse. The phrase "substantial capacity" in the first guideline is designed to limit an insanity defense to those with the most serious mental disorders. The second guideline concerns those who are repeatedly in trouble with the law; repetitive criminal behavior and psychopathy are not evidence for insanity.

As of 2004, the ALI test was in use in 20 states. Until 1984, it was in use in all federal courts. In the 1980s a major effort began in the United States to clarify the legal defense of insanity at the federal level.

Insanity Defense Reform Act   In a highly publicized trial in March 1981, John Hinckley Jr. received an NGRI verdict for his assassination attempt against President Ronald Reagan. After the NGRI verdict, the court received a flood of mal from citizens outraged that a would-be assassin of a U.S. president had not been held criminally responsible and had only been committed to an indefinite stay in a mental hospital until deemed mentally healthy enough for release. Their outrage reflects the public misperceptions about the insanity defense. The public often believes that a person is "getting away" with a crime when found NGRI and that he or she will be released from the hospital in short order. In reality, many people who are committed to a forensic hospital stay there longer than they would have stayed in prison had they been given a sentence (as vividly illustrated in the clinical case below of Michael Jones). With respect to John Hinckley, he has been committed to St. Elizabeth's Hospital, a public mental hospital in Washington, D.C., for over 25 years. Although he can be released whenever his mental health is deemed adequate, this has not yet happened. He has slowly won more freedoms: In 2003, a judge ruled that Hinckley could have six day-long unsupervised visits with his parents outside St. Elizabeth's hospital but only in the Washington, D.C., area. In 2005, a judge allowed Hinckley to have seven overnight visits with his parents at their home in Virginia. As of 2007, doctors need give four days advance notice to the Secret Service, instead of two weeks, when Hinckley visits his parents.

Because of the publicity surrounding the trial and the public outrage at the NGRI verdict, the insanity defense became a target of vigorous criticism from many quarters. As Judge Parker, who presided at the trial, put it: "For many, the [Hinckley] defense was a clear manifestation of the failure of our criminal justice system to punish people who have clearly violated the law" (quoted in Simon & Aaronson, 1988, p. vii).

As a consequence of political pressures to "get tough" on criminals, Congress enacted the Insanity Defense Reform Act in October 1984, addressing the insanity defense for the first time at the federal level. This new law, which has been adopted in all federal courts, contains several provisions designed to make it more difficult to plead NGRI.

- It eliminates the irresistible-impulse component of the ALI rules. This volitional and behavioral aspect of the ALI guidelines had been strongly criticized because one could regard any criminal act as arising from an inability to stay within the limits of the law.

- It changes the ALI's "lacks substantial capacity . . . to appreciate" to "unable to appreciate." This alteration in the cognitive component of the law is intended to tighten the grounds for an insanity defense by making more stringent the criterion for impaired judgment.

- The act also stipulates that the mental disease or defect must be "severe," the intent being to exclude insanity defenses on the basis of disorders such as antisocial personality disorder. Also abolished by the act were defenses relying on "diminished capacity" or "diminished

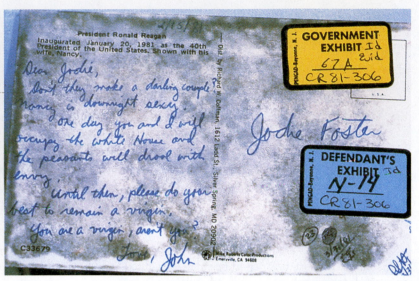

John Hinckley, President Reagan's assailant, wrote this letter to actress Jodie Foster expressing his dream of marrying her and becoming president. (R. Mims/Corbis Sygma.)

responsibility," based on such mitigating circumstances as extreme passion or "temporary insanity." Again, the purpose was to make it harder to mount an insanity defense.

- It shifts the burden of proof from the prosecution to the defense. Instead of the prosecution's having to prove that the person was sane beyond a reasonable doubt at the time of the crime (the most stringent criterion, consistent with the constitutional requirement that people are considered innocent until proved guilty), the defense must prove that the defendant was not sane and must do so with "clear and convincing evidence" (a less stringent but still demanding standard of proof). Table 17.3 shows the different standards of proof used in U.S. courts. The heavier burden now placed on the defense is, like the other provisions, designed to make it more difficult to relieve a defendant of moral and legal responsibility.[2]

- Finally, the new act responds to what many felt was the most troublesome feature of the existing laws—that the person could be released from commitment after a shorter period of time than would be allowed under an ordinary sentence. According to this act, if the person is judged to have recovered from mental illness, then instead of being released from the prison hospital, he or she can be incarcerated up to the maximum time allowable for the crime.

Table 17.3 Standards of Proof

Standard	Certainty Needed to Convict (%)
Beyond a reasonable doubt	95
Clear and convincing evidence	75
Beyond a preponderance of the evidence	51

Guilty but Mentally Ill Some states have created what seems to be a compromise verdict—guilty but mentally ill (GBMI). A GBMI verdict, as mentioned, allows the usual sentence to be imposed but also allows for the person to be treated for mental illness during incarceration, though treatment is not guaranteed. If the person is still considered to be dangerous or mentally ill after serving the imposed prison sentence, he or she may be committed to a mental hospital under civil law proceedings.

Critics of the GBMI verdict argue that it does not benefit criminal defendants with mental illness and does not result in appropriate treatment for those convicted (Woodmansee, 1996). A 1997 South Carolina Supreme Court case[3] found that South Carolina's GBMI statute did

---

[2]According to Simon and Aaronson (1988), this provision arose in large measure from the inability of the prosecution to prove John Hinckley's sanity when he shot Reagan and three others. Several members of the jury testified after the trial to a subcommittee of the Senate Judiciary Committee that the judge's instructions on the burden of proof played a role in their verdict of NGRI. Even before the act, almost half the states required that the defendant must prove insanity, but only one, Arizona, had the "clear and convincing" standard. A majority of the states now place the burden of proof on the defense, albeit with the least exacting of legal standards of proof, "by a preponderance of the evidence."

[3]*South Carolina v. Hornsby*, 484 S.E.2d 869 (S.C. Sup. Ct. 1997).

provide some benefit because it mandated that convicted people with mental illness receive mental health evaluations before being placed in the general prison population. Unfortunately, these assessments have not been shown to lead to better treatment. Other critics of the GBMI verdict note that the verdict is confusing and even deceiving to jurors. Jurors believe that GBMI is not as "tough" as a guilty verdict, but in reality people receving a GBMI verdict often receive harsher punishment (i.e., longer time incarcerated) than if they had been found guilty (Melville & Naimark, 2002).

One of the more famous cases involving the GBMI verdict was the 1992 conviction of Jeffrey Dahmer in Milwaukee, Wisconsin. He had been accused of and had admitted to butchering, cannibalizing, and having sex with the corpses of 15 boys and young men. Dahmer entered the insanity plea allowed in Wisconsin—guilty but mentally ill—and his sanity was the sole focus of an unusual trial that had jurors listening to conflicting testimony from mental health experts about the defendant's state of mind during the serial killings to which he had confessed. They had to decide whether he had had a mental disease that prevented him from knowing right from wrong or from being able to control his actions. Even though there was no disagreement that he was mentally ill, diagnosable as having some sort of paraphilia, Dahmer was deemed sane and therefore legally responsible for the grisly murders. The judge sentenced him to 15 consecutive life terms. Later, another inmate in prison killed him.

In the case of Michael Jones, the court considered whether someone who was found NGRI could be kept in a hospital longer than the person might have spent in prison had he or she been found guilty of the crime. Jones argued that he should be released; the Supreme Court disagreed. According to the court ruling, Jones could not be punished for the crime because his insanity left him legally blameless—this is the logic of the insanity defense. Jones would have been released from prison sooner had he pleaded guilty.

Jeffrey Dahmer, who admitted to butchering, cannibalizing, and having sex with the corpses of 15 boys and young men, was found guilty but mentally ill. (Reuters/Corbis Images.)

Clinical Case: Michael Jones

To illustrate the predicament that a person can get into by raising insanity as a condition for a criminal act, we consider a celebrated—some would call it infamous—Supreme Court case.[4]

Michael Jones was arrested, unarmed, on September 19, 1975, for attempting to steal a jacket from a department store in Washington, D.C. He was charged the next day with attempted petty larceny, a misdemeanor punishable by a maximum prison sentence of 1 year. The court ordered that he be committed to St. Elizabeth's Hospital for a determination of his competency to stand trial.

On March 2, 1976, almost six months after the alleged crime, a hospital psychologist reported to the court that Jones was competent to stand trial, although he had "schizophrenia, paranoid type." The psychologist also reported that the alleged crime resulted from Jones's condition, his paranoid schizophrenia. This comment is noteworthy because the psychologist was not asked to offer an opinion on Jones's state of mind during the crime, only on whether Jones was competent to stand trial. Jones then pleaded not guilty by reason of insanity. Ten days later, on March 12, the court found him NGRI and formally committed him to St. Elizabeth's Hospital for treatment of his mental disorder.

On May 25, 1976, a customary 50-day hearing was held to determine whether Jones should remain in the hospital any longer. A psychologist from the hospital testified that Jones still suffered from paranoid schizophrenia and was a danger to himself and to others. A second hearing was held on February 22, 1977, 17 months after Jones's commitment to St. Elizabeth's, for determination of competency. The defendant demanded release since he had already been hospitalized longer than the 1-year maximum sentence he would have served had he been found guilty of the theft of the jacket. The court denied the request and returned him to St. Elizabeth's.

In response to an appeal, the District of Columbia Court of Appeals agreed with the original court. Ultimately, in November 1982, more than seven years after his hospitalization, Jones's appeal to the Supreme Court was heard. On June 29, 1983, by a five-to-four decision, the Court affirmed the earlier decision: Jones was to remain at St. Elizabeth's. Jones was fully released from St. Elizabeth's in August 2004, 28 years after the crime!

The Court was also concerned about Jones's dangerousness. Jones argued in his petition to the Supreme Court that his theft of the jacket was not dangerous because it was not a violent crime. The Court stated, however, that for there to be violence in a criminal act, the act itself need not be dangerous. It cited a previous decision that a nonviolent theft of an article such as

[4]*Jones v. United States*, 463 U.S. 354 (1983).

a watch may frequently result in violence through the efforts of the criminal to escape, or of the victim to protect his or her property, or of the police to apprehend the fleeing thief.[5]

The dissenting justices of the Court commented that the longer someone such as Jones had to remain in the hospital, the harder it would be for him to demonstrate that he was no longer a dangerous person or mentally ill. Extended institutionalization would likely make it more difficult for him to afford medical experts other than those associated with the hospital and to behave like someone who was not mentally ill. Given that Jones remained in the hospital for 28 years, it would seem that the dissenting justices were correct.

Quick Summary

Insanity is a legal term, not a mental health term. Meeting the legal definition is not necessarily the same thing as having a diagnosable mental illness and vice versa. The insanity defense is the legal argument that a defendant should not be held responsible for an illegal act if it is attributable to mental illness that interferes with rationality or that results from some other excusing circumstance, such as not knowing right from wrong; the not guilty by reason of insanity (NGRI) plea signifies that an accused person should not be held responsible for the crime due to his or her mental illness. The guilty but mentally ill (GBMI) plea signifies that an accused person is legally guilty of a crime but can then, in theory, be committed to a prison hospital or other suitable facility for psychiatric treatment rather than to a regular prison for punishment.

The irresistible-impulse standard suggested that an impulse or drive that the person could not control compelled that person to commit the criminal act. The M'Naghten rule specified that a person could not distinguish right from wrong at the time of the crime because of the person's mental illness. The first part of the American Law Institute guidelines combines the M'Naghten rule and the concept of irresistible impulse. The second concerns those who are repeatedly in trouble with the law; they are not to be deemed mentally ill only because they keep committing crimes. The Insanity Defense Reform Act shifted the burden of proof from the prosecution to the defense, removed the irresistible impulse component, changed wording of substantial capacity, and specified that mental illness must be severe. The Jones case illustrates a number of the complexities associated with the insanity defense.

Check Your Knowledge 17.1 (Answers are at the end of the chapter.)

Match the statement with the correct insanity standard.
1. can't control behavior
2. found guilty
3. doesn't know right from wrong
4. affirmative defense

a. GBMI
b. NGRI
c. irrestible impulse
d. M'Naghten rule

Competency to Stand Trial

The insanity defense concerns the accused person's mental state at the time of the crime. An important consideration before deciding what kind of defense to adopt is whether the accused person is competent to stand trial at all. In the U.S. criminal justice system, **competency to stand trial** must be decided before it can be determined whether a persoon is responsible for the crime of which he or she is accused. It is possible for a person to be judged competent to stand trial and then be judged not guilty by reason of insanity.

The legal standard for being competent to stand trial has not changed since it was articulated by a 1960 U.S. Supreme Court decision:[6] "The test [is] whether [the defendant] has sufficient present ability to consult with his lawyer with a reasonable degree of rational understanding, and whether he has a rational as well as a factual understanding of the proceedings against him."

With the 1966 Supreme Court case *Pate v. Robinson*[7] as precedent, the defense attorney, prosecutor, or judge may raise the question of mental illness whenever there is reason to believe that

---

[5]*Overholser v. O'Beirne*, 302 F.2d 85, 861 (D.C. Cir. 1961).
[6]*Dusky v. United States*, 362 U.S. 402 (1960).
[7]*Pate v. Robinson*, 383 U.S. 375 (1966).

the accused person's mental condition might interfere with his or her upcoming trial. Another way to look at competency is that the courts do not want a person to be brought to trial **in absentia** ("not present"), which is a centuries-old principle of English common law that refers here to the person's mental state, not his or her physical presence. If, after examination, the person is deemed too mentally ill to participate meaningfully in a trial, the trial is delayed, and the accused person is placed in a hospital with the hope that means of restoring adequate mental functioning can be found.

If a court fails to order a hearing when there is evidence that raises a reasonable doubt about competency to stand trial, or if it convicts a legally incompetent defendant, there is a violation of due process.[8] Once competency is questioned, there must be a preponderance of evidence (see Table 17.3) showing that the defendant is competent to stand trial.[9] As just indicated, the test to be applied is whether the defendant is able to consult adequately with his or her lawyer and whether he or she can understand the proceedings.[10] The court has to consider evidence such as irrational behavior as well as any medical or psychological data that might bear on the defendant's competency.[11] However, analogous to the insanity defense, being deemed mentally ill does not necessarily mean that the person is incompetent to stand trial; a person with schizophrenia, for example, may still understand legal proceedings and be able to assist in his or her defense (Winick, 1997). In Focus on Discovery 17.1, we consider the case of Andrea Yates, who was found competent to stand trial despite clear agreement that she was mentally ill.

Being judged incompetent to stand trial can have severe consequences for the individual. Bail is automatically denied, even if it would be routinely granted had the question of incompetency not been raised. The person is usually kept in a hospital for the pretrial examination. During this period the accused person is supposed to receive treatment to render him or her competent to stand trial.[12] In the meantime, he or she may lose employment and undergo the trauma of being separated from family and friends and from familiar surroundings for months

Clinical Case: Yolanda

Yolanda, a 51-year-old African American woman, was arrested after taking a box of doughnuts from the local QuickMart. At the time of her arrest, she claimed she needed the doughnuts to feed the seven babies growing inside her. She said that Malcolm X was the father of her soon-to-be-born children and that she would soon assume the position of Queen of the New Cities. When asked what the New Cities were, she responded this was a new world order that would be in place following the alignment of the clouds with the planets Jupiter, Saturn, and Venus. Yolanda's public defender immediately realized that Yolanda was not ready for trial; she asked for a competency hearing and arranged for a psychologist to conduct an evaluation. Yolanda was diagnosed with schizophrenia, disorganized type, and her thought disturbance was found to be so profound that she was not able to understand that she had been charged with a crime. Furthermore, she was unable to help her attorney prepare a defense. Instead, Yolanda viewed her attorney as a threat to her unborn babies (she was not pregnant) and feared the attorney would keep her from assuming her rightful position as queen. At her competency hearing, the judge declared that Yolanda was not competent to stand trial and that she be committed to the local forensic hospital for a period of three months, after which another competency evaluation would be held.

At the hospital, Yolanda was prescribed Olanzapine, and her thinking became more coherent and organized after two months. One of the unit's psychologists worked with Yolanda, teaching her about the criminal justice system. She worked to help Yolanda understand what the charge of theft meant and what a defense attorney, prosecuting attorney, judge, and jury were. At the end of three months, a different psychologist evaluated Yolanda and recommended that she now be considered competent to stand trial. Yolanda's public defender came to the hospital and met with her to discuss the case. Yolanda was able to help her attorney by telling her about her past hospitalizations and treatment history for schizophrenia. Yolanda realized she was not pregnant but still held onto beliefs about the New Cities. Still, Yolanda understood that she had stolen the doughnuts and this was why she had to go to court. At her next competency hearing, Yolanda was deemed competent to stand trial. Two months later, she went to court again. This time, she entered a plea of NGRI. After a short trial, the judge accepted her NGRI plea and she returned to the forensic hospital. The treatment goals were now focused on helping Yolanda recover from schizophrenia, not on restoring her competency to stand trial.

---

[8]*United States v. White*, 887 F.2d 705 (6th Cir. 1989); *Wright v. Lockhart*, 914 F.2d 1093, cert. denied, 111 S.Ct. 1089 (1991).
[9]*United States v. Frank*, 956 F.2d 872, cert. denied, 113 S.Ct. 363 (1992); *United States v. Blohm*, 579 F.Supp. 495 (1983).
[10]*Frank*, 956 F.2d at 872; *Wright v. Lockhart*, 914 F.2d 1093 (8th Cir. 1990).
[11]*United States v. Hemsi*, 901 F.2d 293 (2d Cir. 1990); *Balfour v. Haws*, 892 F.2d 556 (7th Cir. 1989).
[12]*United States v. Sherman*, 912 F.2d 907 (7th Cir. 1990).

FOCUS ON DISCOVERY 17.1

Another Look at Insanity versus Mental Illness

On June 20, 2001, believing that her five children, ranging in age from six months to seven years, were condemned to eternal damnation, 37-year-old Andrea Yates, who lived with her husband and children in Houston, Texas, systematically drowned each child in a bathtub. As recounted on the CNN website:

> . . . when the police reached [the] modest brick home on Beachcomber Lane in suburban Houston, they found Andrea drenched with bathwater, her flowery blouse and brown leather sandals soaking wet. She had turned on the bathroom faucet to fill the porcelain tub and moved aside the shaggy mat to give herself traction for kneeling on the floor. It took a bit of work for her to chase down the last of the children; toward the end, she had a scuffle in the family room, sliding around on wet tile. . . . She dripped watery footprints from the tub to her bedroom, where she straightened the blankets around the kids in their pajamas once she was done with them. She called 911 and then her husband. "It's time. I finally did it," she said before telling him to come home and hanging up.

The nation was horrified by her actions, and in the months following the murders, information became known about Yates' frequent bouts of depression, especially after giving birth, as well as her several suicide attempts and hospitalizations for severe depression.

Eight months later her trial was held. The defense argued that she was mentally ill at the time of the murders—and for many periods of time preceding the events—and that also she have been unable to distinguish right from wrong when she put her children to death. The prosecution argued that she had known right from wrong and therefore should be found guilty. On two things the defense and the prosecution agreed: (1) she had murdered her children, and (2) she was mentally ill at the time of the murder. Where they disagreed was on the crucial question as to whether her mental illness entailed not being able to distinguish right or wrong, the familiar M'Naghten principle of criminal responsibility.

This trial shows the difficulty of making a successful insanity defense and is a vivid example of the critical difference between mental illness and insanity. No one disagreed that she was severely depressed,

Andrea Yates, who drowned her five children, pled NGRI. Although she was suffering from mental illness, her initial plea was unsuccessful because she was judged capable of knowing right from wrong. After the initial verdict was thrown out, her NGRI plea was successful in the second trial. (©AP/Wide World Photos.)

probably psychotic, when she killed her five small children. But, as we have seen, mental illness is not the same as legal insanity. Employing the right–wrong principle, the jury deliberated for only 3 hours and 40 minutes on March 12, 2002, and delivered a verdict of guilty. They had rejected the defense's contention that Ms. Yates could not distinguish right from wrong at the time of the crime. On March 15, the jury decided to spare her life and recommended to the presiding judge that she get life in prison, not being eligible for parole for 40 years.

The trial and the guilty verdict occasioned impassioned discussion in the media and among thousands of people. How could the jury not have considered her insane? If such a person is not insane, who could be judged to be so? Should the right–wrong M'Naghten principle be dropped from the laws of half the states in the United States? Didn't her phoning 911 to report what she had done prove that she knew she had done something very wrong? Didn't the careful and systematic way she killed her children reflect a mind that, despite her deep depression and delusional thinking, could formulate a complex plan and execute it successfully? Had she received proper treatment from psychiatrists, especially from the one who had recently taken her off the antidepressant medication that had been helping her and had sent her home without adequate follow-up?

As it turns out, these questions were addressed in the Yates case after all. In January 2005, an appeals court overturned Yates's murder conviction because the jury had heard false testimony from one of the expert witnesses that may have unduly influenced their decision. The prosecution witness testified that Yates's behavior may have been influenced by an episode of the television show *Law and Order* that showed a woman with depression drowning her children, suggesting she knew right from wrong. However, there was no such episode on this television show, so Yates could not have been thus influenced. A new trial was conducted, and on July 26, 2006, after 3 days of deliberations, the new jury found Yates not guilty by reason of insanity. She was placed in a forensic hospital in Texas, and she will remain there until she is no longer considered dangerous.

or even years, perhaps making his or her emotional condition even worse and thus making it all the more difficult to show competency to stand trial. Until the 1970s, some people languished in prison hospitals for many years waiting to be found competent to stand trial.

A 1972 Supreme Court case, *Jackson v. Indiana*,[13] forced the states to a speedier determination of incompetency. The case concerned a deaf and mute man with mental retardation who

---

[13]*Jackson v. Indiana*, 406 U.S. 715 (1972).

was deemed not only incompetent to stand trial but unlikely ever to become competent. The Court ruled that the length of pretrial confinement must be limited to the time it takes to determine whether treatment during this detainment is likely to render the defendant competent to stand trial. If the defendant is unlikely ever to become competent, the state must, after this period, either institute civil commitment proceedings or release the defendant. Laws in most states define more precisely the minimal requirements for competency to stand trial, ending the latitude that has deprived thousands of people of their rights to due process (Fourteenth Amendment) and a speedy trial (Sixth Amendment). Defendants today cannot be committed for determination of competency for a period longer than the maximum possible sentence they face.[14]

Medication has had an impact on the competency issue. The concept of "synthetic sanity" (Schwitzgebel & Schwitzgebel, 1980) has been used to argue that if a drug, such as Thorazine, temporarily produces a bit of rationality in an otherwise incompetent defendant, the trial may proceed. The likelihood that the defendant will again become incompetent to stand trial if the drug is withdrawn does not disqualify the person from going to court.[15] However, the individual rights of the defendant are to be protected against forced medication, because there is no guarantee that such treatment would render the person competent to stand trial, and there is a chance that it might cause harm. A subsequent Supreme Court ruling[16] held that a criminal defendant generally cannot be forced to take medication in an effort to render him or her competent to stand trial. In general, the courts have responded to the existence of powerful psychoactive medications by requiring safeguards against their involuntary use to ensure that the defendant's civil rights are protected, even when a drug might restore legal competency to stand trial.[17]

In 2003, the Supreme Court ruled that forced medication to restore competency could be used only in very limited circumstances.[18] In this case, St. Louis dentist Charles Sell had been charged in 1997 with two different counts of fraud and with conspiring to kill a former employee and an FBI agent who arrested him. Sell was later diagnosed with delusional disorder and was found incompetent to stand trial. This was in essence a nonviolent crime, and the Supreme Court did not see that forced medication was justified in this case. The court ruled that forced medication could be used only if alternative treatments had failed; medication is likely to be effective; medication won't interfere with a person's right to defend him- or herself at trial, and there is an important government interest in trying the defendant for a serious crime.

If the defendant wishes, the effects of the medication must be explained to the jury, lest—if the defendant is pleading NGRI—the jury conclude from the defendant's relatively rational drug-produced demeanor that he or she could not have been insane at the time of the crime.[19] This requirement acknowledges that juries form their judgments of legal responsibility or insanity at least in part based on how the defendant appears during the trial. If the defendant appears healthy, the jury may be less likely to believe that the crime was an act of a disturbed mental state rather than of free will—even though an insanity defense has to do with the defendant's state of mind during the crime, not his or her psychological state during the trial.

Even if a person with a mental disorder is found competent to stand trial, that person may not be able to serve as his or her own defense attorney. A 2008 U.S. Supreme Court decision (*Indiana v. Edwards*) held that a judge may deny the right of self-represnentation if it is clear that the defendant would not receive a fair trial. Focus on Discovery 17.2 discusses the unusual challenge posed by dissociative identity disorder in criminal commitments.

Insanity, Mental Retardation, and Capital Punishment

As we have just seen, an accused person's mental state can be taken into consideration to determine whether he or she is competent to stand trial and/or should be held legally responsible for a criminal act. On very rare occasions, the sanity or mental capacity of a person also becomes

---

[14]*United States v. DeBellis*, 649 F.2d 1 (1st Cir. 1981); *State v. Moore*, 467 N.W. 2d 201 (Wis. Ct. App. 1991).
[15]*State v. Hampton*, 218 So.2d 311 (La. 1969); *State v. Stacy*, no. 446 (Crim. App., Knoxville, Tenn., August 4, 1977); *United States v. Hayes*, 589 F.2d 811 (1979).
[16]*Riggins v. Nevada*, 504 U.S. 127 (1992).
[17]*United States v. Waddell*, 687 F. Supp. 208 (1988).
[18]*Sell v. United States*, 539 U.S. 02-5664 (2003).
[19]*State v. Jojola*, 553 F.2d 1296 (N.M. Ct. App. 1976).

FOCUS ON DISCOVERY 17.2

Dissociative Identity Disorder and the Insanity Defense

Imagine that as you are having a cup of coffee one morning, you hear pounding at the front door. You hurry to answer and find two police officers staring grimly at you. One of them asks, "Are you Jane Smith?" "Yes," you reply. "Well, ma'am, you are under arrest for grand theft and for the murder of John Doe." The officer then reads you your Miranda rights against self-incrimination, handcuffs you, and takes you to the police station, where you are allowed to call your lawyer.

This would be a scary situation for anybody. What is particularly frightening and puzzling to you and your lawyer is that you have absolutely no recollection of having committed the crime that a detective later describes to you. You are horrified that you cannot account for the time period when the murder was committed—in fact, your memory is startlingly blank for that entire time. And, as if this were not bizarre enough, the detective then shows you a videotape in which you are clearly firing a gun at a bank teller during a holdup. "Is that you in the videotape?" asks the detective. You confer with your lawyer, saying that it certainly looks like you, including the clothes, but you are advised not to admit anything one way or the other.

Let's move forward in time now to your trial some months later. Witnesses have come forward and identified you beyond a reasonable doubt. There is no one you know who can testify that you were somewhere other than at the bank on the afternoon of the robbery and the murder. But did you murder the teller in the bank? You are able to assert honestly to yourself and to the jury that you did not. And yet even you have been persuaded that the person in the videotape is you—and that that person committed the robbery and the murder.

Because of the strange nature of the case, your lawyer arranged prior to the trial to have you interviewed by a psychiatrist and a clinical psychologist, both of them well-known experts in forensics. Through extensive questioning they have decided that you have dissociative identity disorder (DID, formerly called multiple personality disorder) and that the crimes were committed not by you, Jane Smith, but by your rather violent alter, Laura. Indeed, during one of the interviews, Laura emerged and boasted about the crime, even chuckling over the fact that you, Jane, would be imprisoned for it.

Can DID be an excusing condition for a criminal act? Should Jane Smith be held responsible for a crime committed by her alter, Laura?

In reviews of the DID literature and of its forensic implications, Elyn Saks (1997) of the University of Southern California Law Center argued that DID should be regarded as a special case in mental health law and that a new legal principle should be established. Her argument takes issue with legal practice that would hold a person with DID responsible for a crime as long as the personality acting at the time of the crime intended to commit it.

What is intriguing about Saks's argument is that she devotes a major portion of it to defining personhood. What is a person? Is a person the body we inhabit? Well, most of the time our sense of who we are as persons does not conflict with the bodies we have come to know as our own or rather, as us. But in DID there is a discrepancy. The body that committed the crimes at the bank was Jane Smith. But it was her alter, Laura, who committed the crimes. Saks argues that, peculiar as it may sound, the law should be interested in the body only as a container for the person. It is the person who may or may not be blameworthy, not the body. Nearly all the time they are one and the same, but in the case of DID they are not. In a sense, Laura committed the murder by using Jane's body.

Then is Jane blameworthy? The person Jane did not commit the crime; she did not even know about it. For the judge to sentence Jane—or, more specifically, the body in the courtroom who usually goes by that name—would be unjust, argues Saks, for Jane is descriptively innocent. To be sure, sending Jane to prison would punish Laura, for whenever Laura would emerge, she would find herself imprisoned. But what of Jane? Saks concludes that it is unjust to imprison Jane because she is not blameworthy. Rather, we must find her not guilty by reason of dissociative identity disorder and remand her for treatment of the disorder.

Dissociative identity disorder would not, however, be a justification for a verdict of NGRI if the alter that did not commit the crime was aware of the other alter's criminal intent and did not do anything to prevent the criminal act. Under these circumstances, argues Saks, the first alter would be complicit in the crime and would therefore be somewhat blameworthy. A comparison Saks draws is to Robert Louis Stevenson's fictional character of Dr. Jekyll and Mr. Hyde. Jekyll made the potion that caused the emergence of Mr. Hyde, his alter, with the foreknowledge that Hyde would do evil. So even though Jekyll was not present when Hyde was in charge, he would nonetheless be blameworthy because of his prior knowledge of what Hyde would do—not to mention that he, Jekyll, had concocted the potion that created his alter, Hyde.

Saks is optimistic about the effectiveness of therapy for DID and believes that people like Jane/Laura can be integrated into one personality and then released to rejoin society. Saks goes so far as to argue that people with DID who are judged dangerous but who have not committed a crime should be subject to civil commitment, even though this would be tantamount to preventive detention. In this way, she suggests, future crimes might be avoided.

Poster for the classic film about Jekyll and Hyde. (Jerry Ohlinger's Movie Material Store)

an issue after a conviction. The question is, should a person who is sentenced to be put to death (i.e., capital punishment) by the state have to be legally sane at the time of the execution? Furthermore, what if the person is deemed so mentally retarded as to not understand what is about to happen to him or her?

The question of insanity and capital punishment arose in April 1998 in California in the case of Horace Kelly, a 39-year-old man who had been found guilty of the rapes and murders of two women and the slaying of an 11-year-old boy in 1984. Although Kelly's mental state had not been an issue at the time of his trial, his lawyers argued—12 years later and just days before his scheduled execution by lethal injection—that his mental health had deteriorated during his imprisonment on death row to such an extent that one of his defense attorneys referred to him as a "walking vegetable." They made reference to a 1986 Supreme Court ruling[20] stating that it is a violation of the Eighth Amendment (which prohibits cruel and unusual punishment) for an insane individual to be executed.

Evidence of mental illness during Kelly's imprisonment included psychiatrists' reports of delusions, hallucinations, and inappropriate affect. He was also described by fellow inmates and by guards as hoarding his feces and smearing them on the walls of his prison cell. By 1995, after 10 years on death row, one court-appointed psychiatrist had concluded that Kelly was legally insane. On the other hand, another psychiatrist reported that when asked what being executed would mean for him, Kelly had given the rational reply that he would not be able to have a family; he was also able to name two of his victims and beat the psychiatrist had in several games of tic-tac-toe. A federal judge decided in June 1998 and the U.S. Supreme Court concurred in April 1999 to stay (delay) Kelly's execution and allow his lawyers to argue, among other things, that he should not be put to death because he was insane. After these arguments, Kelly's execution was permanently stayed.

In 2007, the U.S. Supreme Court overturned another death sentence in the case of Scott Panetti[21]. Panetti shot and killed his estranged wife's parents in 1992. He had been diagnosed with schiozophrenia and had been hospitalized numerous times prior to the murders. At his trial, Panetti served as his own attorney, dressed up as a cowboy (he had narrowly been deemed competent to stand trial). The court transcripts are filled with incoherent ramblings from him. For example, he tried to subpoena Jesus Christ. In his closing arguments, he said:

> The ability to reason correctly. Common sense, the common sense, the horse sense. This is Texas and we're not talking loopholes and if we're talking—well, let's talk a lariat. Let's talk a catch rope . . .

He was sentenced to death by a Texas court, and this sentence was upheld by an appeals court. The U.S. Supreme Court ruled, however, that Panetti could not understand why he was to be put to death given his mental state and returned the case for further evaluation of insanity by a lower court.

Eighteen of the 38 states that allow capital punishment already prohibit the execution of the people with mental retardation on Eighth Amendment grounds against cruel and unusual punishment. In 2002, the United States Supreme Court ruled in a six-to-three decision in the case of *Atkins v. Virginia* that capital punishment of those with mental retardation constitutes cruel and unusual punishment, which is prohibited by the Eighth Amendment. The Supreme Court left open the question of what constitutes mental retardation, however, leaving it up to the states to decide how to remain within the requirements of the Eighth Amendment. As illustrated in the case of Daryl Akins, the definitions of mental retardation can vary quite a bit from state to state.

If a person should not be executed due to insanity, what are the ethics of providing medications to improve a person's mental state? Increasing attention is being paid to this issue. In February 2002, for example, the Georgia Board of Pardons and Paroles threw out the death sentence of a convicted rapist and murderer on the grounds that he was delusional (note that he had not been found NGRI and that he had been on death row for nearly 16 years). What makes this case significant is that the person had been forced to take psychoactive medication that improved his mental condition enough to meet the federal standard that only a person who is legally sane can be executed (Weinstein, 2002).

---

[20]*Ford v. Wainright*, 477 U.S. 399 (1986).
[21]*Panetti v. Quarterman*, 551 U. S. (2007)

Clinical Case: Daryl Atkins

Daryl Atkins was sentenced to death in Virginia for a kidnapping and murder he was convicted of in 1996. His IQ was rated at 59, which placed him in the range of the moderately retarded. His defense attorney argued that his intellectual limitations rendered capital punishment unconstitutional because he lacked understanding of the consequences of his actions and was therefore not as morally culpable for his acts as a person of normal intelligence.

Following the 2002 Supreme Court ruling (*Atkins v. Virginia*), the state of Virginia subsequently defined mental retardation as consisting of an IQ score of 70 or less along with difficulties in self-care and social interaction. In Virginia, a defendant must convince the jury of mental retardation using the standard "beyond a preponderance of the evidence" (see Table 17.3). Since 1998, Atkins had been given

an IQ test at least four times. He scored below 70 on two testing occasions (scores of 59 and 67) and above 70 on two other testing occasions (scores of 74 and 76). In August 2005, a Virginia jury decided that Daryl Atkins did not meet Virginia's definition of mental retardation. Thus, even though the *Atkins* case effectively abolished the practice of executing people with mental retardation, Daryl Atkins could have been put to death in Virginia because the state jury's decision paved the way for the original death sentence to be carried out. However, in January 2008 a Virginia judge changed Atkins's death sentence to life imprisonment. The reason for this change was not due to any rethinking of Atkins's mental capacity. Rather, it was due to prosecutorial misconduct (improper witness coaching) that was revealed by one of the attorneys.

Check Your Knowledge 17.2

True or false?

1. The *Jackson* case established that people who will not be restored to competency should be found NGRI.
2. To be competent to stand trial, a person must be able to understand the charges and assist his or her attorney.
3. The Supreme Court ruled that executing prisoners with mental illness constitutes cruel and unusual punishment.

Civil Commitment

Historically, governments have had a duty to protect their citizens from harm. We take for granted the right and duty of government to set limits on our freedom for the sake of protecting us. Few drivers, for example, question the legitimacy of the state's imposing limits on them by providing traffic signals that often make them stop when they would rather go. Government has a long-established right as well as an obligation to protect us both from ourselves—the *parens patriae*, "power of the state"—and from others—the police power of the state. Civil commitment is one further exercise of these powers.

In virtually all states, a person can be committed to a psychiatric hospital against his or her will if a judgment is made that he or she is (1) mentally ill and (2) a danger to self—that is, the person is suicidal or unable to provide for the basic physical needs of food, clothing, and shelter—or to others (Perlin, 1994). At present, dangerousness to others is more often the principal criterion in court rulings that point to imminent dangerousness as (e.g., the person is right on the verge of committing a violent act).[22] In some states, a finding of imminent dangerousness must be evidenced by a recent overt act, attempt, or threat; however, there are some states that do not require an overt act [*In Re: Albright*, 836 P.2d 1 (Kan. App. 1992)]. Such commitment is supposed to last for only as long as the person remains dangerous.[23]

---

[22]*Suzuki v. Yuen*, 617 F.2d 173 (9th Cir. 1980).
[23]*United States v. DeBellis*, 649 F.2d 1 (1st Cir. 1981).

Specific commitment procedures generally fit into one of two categories, formal and informal. Formal (or judicial) commitment is by order of a court. It can be requested by any responsible citizen—usually the police, a relative, or a friend—seeks the commitment. If a judge believes that there is a good reason to pursue the matter, he or she will order a mental health examination. The person has the right to object to these attempts to "certify" him or her, and a court hearing can be scheduled to allow the person to present evidence against commitment.

Informal, emergency commitment of people with mental illness can be accomplished without initially involving the courts. For example, if a hospital administrative board believes that a voluntary patient requesting discharge is too mentally ill and dangerous to be released, it is able to detain the patient with a temporary, informal commitment order.

Any person acting in an out-of-control, dangerous fashion may be taken immediately to a psychiatric hospital by the police. Perhaps the most common informal commitment procedure is the 2PC, or two physicians' certificate. In most states, two physicians, not necessarily psychiatrists, can sign a certificate that allows a person to be incarcerated for some period of time, ranging from 24 hours to as long as 20 days. Detainment beyond this period requires formal judicial commitment.

Civil commitment affects far more people than criminal commitment. It is beyond the scope of this book to examine in detail the variety of state civil commitment laws and regulations; each state has its own, and they are in almost constant flux. Our aim is to present an overview that will provide a basic understanding of the issues and of current directions of change.

Preventive Detention and Problems in the Prediction of Dangerousness

The perception is widespread that people with mental illness account for a significant proportion of the violence that besets contemporary society, but this is not the case (Bonta, Law, & Hanson, 1998; Monahan, 1992). Only about 3 percent of the violence in the United States is clearly linked to mental illness (Swanson et al., 1990). Moreover, about 90 percent of people diagnosed with psychotic disorders (primarily schizophrenia) are not violent (Swanson et al., 1990). People with mental illness—even allowing for their relatively small numbers—do not account for a large proportion of violent offenses, especially when compared with people who abuse drugs or alcohol and people who are in their teens and twenties, are male, and are poor (Corrigan & Watson, 2005; Mulvey, 1994). The MacArthur Violence Risk Assessment Study, a large prospective study of violent behavior among persons recently discharged from psychiatric hospitals, found that people with mental illness who were not substance abusers were no more likely to engage in violence than are people without mental illness who were not substance abusers (Steadman et al., 1998). Also, when people with mental illness do act aggressively, it is usually against family members or friends, and the incidents tend to occur at home (Steadman et al., 1998). Additional findings from the MacArthur study indicated that people with delusions were not more violent than people without delusions, regardless of whether they had comorbid substance abuse (Appelbaum, Robbins, & Monahan, 2000). However, men with threat delusions were more likely to be violent than men without threat delusions or women with any type of delusion (Teasdale, Silver, & Monahan, 2006). Another analysis from the study found that people with mental illness reported more violent thoughts while in the

People with mental illness are not necessarily more likely to be violent than people without mental illness, contrary to the way movies often portray people with mental illness. (The Kobal Collection, Ltd.)

hospital compared to people not in the hospital (Grisso et al, 2000). However, these people were not necessarily more likely to actually be violent once they left the hospital. Actual violent behavior was found only among a subsample of people with mental illness (e.g., those with a diagnosis of substance abuse or those who had severe symptoms and persistent violent thoughts). By and large, then, the general public is seldom affected by violence from people with mental illness, even though certain people with mental illness can and will be violent.

The Prediction of Dangerousness   Civil commitment is necessarily a form of preventive detention; the prediction is made that a person judged mentally ill may in the future behave in a dangerous manner and should therefore be detained. But the entire U.S. legal and constitutional system is organized to protect people from preventive detention. Thus, unless mental illness comes into the picture, a person can generally be imprisoned only after having been found guilty of committing a crime (or, if accused and not yet convicted, denied bail if the crime was especially heinous and if the person poses a risk of leaving the jurisdiction to avoid trial). Furthermore, ordinary prisoners are routinely released from prison even though statistics show that many will commit additional crimes.

But what if a person openly threatens to inflict harm on others, such as an individual who for an hour each day stands in the street and shouts threats to people in a nearby apartment house? Does the state have to wait until the person acts on the threats? Usually not. In such a case the civil commitment process can be brought into play if the person is deemed not only an imminent danger to others but also mentally ill (Perlin, 1994).

The likelihood of committing a dangerous act is central to civil commitment, but is dangerousness easily predicted? Early studies examining the accuracy of predictions that a person would commit a dangerous act found that mental health professionals were poor at making this judgment (e.g., Kozol, Boucher, & Garofalo, 1972; Monahan, 1973, 1976), but these studies had several methodological problems (Monahan, 1978).

Newer research suggests that greater accuracy can be achieved than previously assumed in predicting dangerousness in the longer term (Campbell, Stefan, & Loder, 1994; Monahan, 1984; Monahan & Steadman, 1994; Steadman et al., 1998). Violence prediction is most accurate under the following conditions:

- If a person has been repeatedly violent in the recent past, it is reasonable to predict that he or she will be violent in the near future unless there have been major changes in the person's attitudes or environment.

- If violence is in the person's distant past, and if it was a single but very serious act, and if that person has been incarcerated for a period of time, then violence can be expected on release if there is reason to believe that the person's predetention personality and physical abilities have not changed and if the person is going to return to the same environment in which he or she was previously violent.

- Even with no history of violence, violence can be predicted if the person is judged to be on the brink of a violent act, for example, if the person is pointing a loaded gun at an occupied building.

As noted earlier, the presence of substance abuse significantly raises the rate of violence, and this is true for people with and without other mental disorders (Gendreau, Little, & Goggin, 1996; Steadman et al., 1998).

Violence among people with mental illness is often associated with medication noncompliance (Monahan, 1992; Steadman et al., 1998). **Outpatient commitment** is one way of increasing medication compliance. It is an arrangement whereby a patient is allowed to leave the hospital but must live in a halfway house or other supervised setting and report to a mental health agency frequently. To the extent that outpatient commitment increases compliance with medication regimens and other mental health treatment—and evidence indicates that it does (Munetz et al., 1996)—we can expect violence to be reduced. Indeed, support services, such as halfway houses, can markedly reduce the chances that a person who might otherwise be prone to committing a violent act will actually commit one (Dvoskin &

Steadman, 1994). For a discussion of therapists' responsibilities to predict dangerousness, see Focus on Discovery 17.3.

Toward Greater Protection of Patients' Rights

The U.S. Constitution is a remarkable document. It lays down the basic duties of elected federal officials and guarantees a set of civil rights. But there is often some distance between the abstract delineation of a civil right and its day-to-day implementation. Moreover, judges must interpret the Constitution as it bears on specific contemporary problems. Since nowhere in this cornerstone of U.S. democracy is there specific mention of people with mental illness, lawyers and judges interpret various sections of the document to justify what they consider necessary in society's treatment of people whose mental health is in question.

Beginning in the 1970s, a number of court decisions were rendered to protect people from being involuntarily hospitalized unless absolutely necessary. For example, a 1976 federal court decision in Wisconsin, *Lessard v. Schmidt*,[24] gives a person threatened with civil commitment the right to timely written notice of the proceeding, opportunity for a hearing with counsel, the right to have the hearing decided by a jury, Fifth Amendment protection against self-incrimination, and other similar procedural safeguards already accorded defendants in criminal actions, including being present at any hearing to decide the need for commitment.[25] Such protections are to be provided even under emergency commitment conditions.[26] A 1979 Supreme Court decision, *Addington v. Texas*,[27] further provides that the state must produce clear and convincing evidence that a person is mentally ill and dangerous before he or she can be involuntarily committed to a psychiatric hospital. In 1980, the Ninth Circuit Court of Appeals ruled that this danger must be imminent.[28] Clearly, the intent is to restrict the state's power to curtail individual freedoms because of mental illness. Although protection of the rights of people with mental illness adds to the burden of both civil courts and state and county mental hospital staffs, it is a price a free society must pay. Being hospitalized against one's wishes is less likely today, in large part due to changes in health care that emphasize outpatient care over inpatient care. In fact, it is increasingly difficult to hospitalize a patient today who is in real need of at least a short hospital stay. However, many rights of people with mental illness are still curtailed. An analysis of mental health–related bills introduced in state legislatures in 2002 (Corrigan et al., 2005) found that 75 percent of these contracted liberties of people with mental illness (e.g., allowing involuntary medication) and 33 percent contracted privacy rights (e.g., sharing mental health records in the interest of public safety) (see also Focus on Discovery 1.1 in Chapter 1).

We turn now to a discussion of several issues and trends that revolve around the protections provided to those with mental disorders: the principle of the least restrictive alternative; the right to treatment; the right to refuse treatment; and, finally, the way in which these several themes conflict in efforts to provide humane mental health treatment while respecting individual rights. We will see that competing interests operate to create a complex and continually changing picture.

Least Restrictive Alternative   As noted earlier, civil commitment rests on presumed dangerousness, a condition that may vary depending on the circumstances. A person may be deemed dangerous if living in an apartment by himself or herself, but not dangerous if living in a residential treatment home and taking prescribed medications every day under medical supervision. The **least restrictive alternative** to freedom is to be provided when treating people with mental disorders and protecting them from harming themselves and others. A number of court rulings require that only those people who cannot be adequately looked after in less restrictive settings be placed in hospitals.[29] In general terms, mental health professionals have to provide the treatment that restricts the patient's liberty to the least possible degree while remaining workable.[30] It is unconstitutional to

---

[24]*Lessard v. Schmidt*, 349 F.Supp. 1078 (E.D. Wisc. 1972), vacated and remanded on other grounds, 94 S.Ct. 713 (1974), reinstated in 413 F.Supp. 1318 (E.D. Wisc. 1976).

[25]*In Re: Lawaetz* 728 F.2d 225 (3d Cir. 1984).

[26]*Doremus v. Farrell*, 407 F.Supp. 509 (1975).

[27]*Addington v. Texas*, 441 U.S. 418 (1979).

[28]*Suzuki v. Yuen*, 617 F.2d at 173.

[29]*Lake v. Cameron*, 267 F. Supp 155 (D.C. Cir. 1967); *Lessard*, 349 F. Supp. at 1078.

[30]*In Re: Tarpley*, 556 N.E.2d, superseded by 581 N.E.2d 1251 (1991).

FOCUS ON DISCOVERY 17.3

The *Tarasoff* Case—The Duty to Warn and to Protect

The client's right to privileged communication—the legal right of a client to require that what goes on in therapy remain confidential—is an important protection, but it is not absolute. Society has long stipulated certain conditions in which confidentiality in a relationship should not be maintained because of the harm that can befall others. A famous California court ruling in 1974[a] described circumstances in which a therapist not only may but *must* breach the sanctity of a client's communication. First, we describe the facts of the case.

Clinical Case

In the fall of 1968, Prosenjit Poddar, a graduate student from India studying at the University of California at Berkeley, met Tatiana (Tanya) Tarasoff at a folk dancing class. They saw each other weekly during the fall, and on New Year's Eve she kissed him. Poddar interpreted this act as a sign of formal engagement (as it might have been in India, where he was a member of the Harijan, or "untouchable," caste). But Tanya told him that she was involved with other men and indicated that she did not wish to have an intimate relationship with him.

Poddar was depressed as a result of the rebuff, but he saw Tanya a few times during the spring (occasionally tape-recording their conversations in an effort to understand why she did not love him). Tanya left for Brazil in the summer, and Poddar, at the urging of a friend, went to the student health facility, where a psychiatrist referred him to a psychologist for psychotherapy. When Tanya returned in October 1969, Poddar discontinued therapy. Based in part on Poddar's stated intention to purchase a gun, the psychologist notified the campus police, both orally and in writing, that Poddar was dangerous and should be taken to a community mental health center for psychiatric commitment.

The campus police interviewed Poddar, who seemed rational and promised to stay away from Tanya. They released him and notified the health service. No further efforts at commitment were made because the supervising psychiatrist apparently decided that there was no need and, as a matter of confidentiality, requested that the letter to the police as well as certain therapy records be destroyed.

On October 27, Poddar went to Tanya's home armed with a pellet gun and a kitchen knife. She refused to speak to him. He shot her with the pellet gun. She ran from the house; he pursued, caught, and repeatedly and fatally stabbed her. Poddar was found guilty of voluntary manslaughter rather than first- or second-degree murder. The defense established with the aid of the expert testimony of three psychiatrists that Poddar's diminished mental capacity, paranoid schizophrenia, precluded the malice necessary for first- or second-degree murder. After his prison term, he returned to India, where, according to his own report, he is happily married (Schwitzgebel & Schwitzgebel, 1980, p. 205).

Under the privileged communication statute of California, the counseling center psychologist properly breached the confidentiality of the professional relationship and took steps to have Poddar civilly committed, for he judged Poddar to be an imminent danger. Poddar had stated that he intended to purchase a gun, and by his other words and actions he had convinced the therapist that he was desperate enough to harm Tarasoff. What the psychologist did not do, and what the court decided he should have done, was to warn the likely victim, Tanya Tarasoff, that her former friend had bought a gun and might use it against her. As stated by the California Supreme Court in *Tarasoff*: "Once a therapist does in fact determine, or under applicable professional standards reasonably should have determined, that a patient poses a serious danger of violence to others, he bears a duty to exercise reasonable care to protect the foreseeable victims of that danger." The *Tarasoff* ruling requires clinicians, in deciding when to violate confidentiality, to use the very imperfect skill of predicting dangerousness. Since the original ruling, it has been extended in several ways.

Extending Protection to Foreseeable Victims

A subsequent California court ruling[b] held by a bare majority that foreseeable victims include those in close relationship to the identifiable victim. In this instance, a mother was hurt by a shotgun fired by the dangerous patient, and her 7-year-old son was present when the shooting took place. The boy later sued the psychologists for damages brought on by emotional trauma. Since a young child is likely to be in the company of his or her mother, the court concluded in *Hedlund* that the *Tarasoff* ruling extended to the boy.

Extending Protection Further to Potential Victims

A 1983 decision of a federal circuit court in California[c] ruled that Veterans Administration psychiatrists should earlier have warned the murdered lover of an outpatient, Phillip Jablonski, that she was a foreseeable victim, even

---

[a] *Tarasoff v. Regents of the University of California,* 529 P.2d 553 (Cal. 1974), vacated, reheard in bank, and affirmed, 131 Cal. Rptr. 14, 551 P.2d 334 (1976). The 1976 California Supreme Court ruling was by a four-to-three majority.
[b] *Hedlund v. Superior Court,* 34 Cal.3d 695 (1983).
[c] *Jablonski by Pahls v. United States,* 712 F.2d 391 (1983).

---

confine a person with mental illness who is nondangerous and who is capable of living on his or her own or with the help of willing and responsible family or friends.[31] Of course, this principle has meaning only if society provides suitable residences and treatments, which rarely happens.

Right to Treatment   Another aspect of civil commitment that has come to the attention of the courts is the so-called right to treatment. If a person is deprived of liberty because he or she is mentally ill and is a danger to self or others, is the state not required to provide treatment to alleviate these problems? This important question has been the subject of several court cases.

[31]*Project Release v. Prevost,* 722 F.2d 960 (2d Cir. 1983).

though the patient had never made an explicit threat against her to the therapists. The reasoning was that Jablonski, having previously raped and otherwise harmed his wife, would likely direct his continuing "violence . . . against women very close to him" (p. 392).

The court also found the hospital psychiatrists negligent in not obtaining Jablonski's earlier medical records. These records showed a history of harmful violent behavior, which, together with the threats his lover was complaining about, should have moved the hospital to institute emergency civil commitment. The court ruled that the failure to warn was a proximate or immediate cause of the woman's murder. Proper consideration of the medical records, said the judge, would have convinced the psychiatrists that Jablonski was a real danger to others and should be committed.

This broadening of the duty to warn and protect has placed mental health professionals in California in an even more difficult predicament, for the potentially violent patient need not even mention the specific person he or she may harm. It is up to the therapist to deduce who are possible victims, based on what he or she can learn of the patient's past and present circumstances.

Extending Protection to Potential Victims as Yet Unknown

Many courts have augmented the duty to warn and protect to foreseeable victims of child abuse and even to possible victims as yet unknown. In one such case,[d] a medical student underwent his own psychoanalysis as one of the requirements to become a psychoanalyst. During the therapy, he admitted that he was a pedophile. Later in his training, he saw a male child as a patient as part of his psychiatric residency and sexually assaulted the boy. The court decided that the training analyst, who was not only the student's therapist but also an instructor in the school, had reason to know that his patient-student "posed a specific threat to a specific group of persons, namely future minor patients, with whom [the student] would necessarily interact as part of his training" (p. 8). Even though the student did not have child patients at the time he revealed his pedophilia (and thus there were

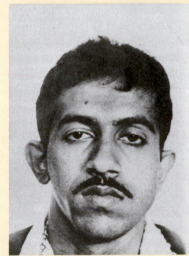

Prosenjit Poddar was convicted of manslaughter in the death of Tatiana Tarasoff. The court ruled that his therapist, who had become convinced Poddar might harm Tarasoff, should have warned her of the impending danger. (©AP/Wide World Photos.)

no specific people whom the instructor could warn and take steps to protect), the supervisor—as his instructor, not just his therapist—was judged to have sufficient control over the student's professional training and activities (specifically, the power to keep the student from pursuing his interests in working with children) for the *Tarasoff* ruling to be relevant.

Extending Protection Based on Families' Reports

In 2004, a California appeals court ruled that therapists have a duty to warn a possible victim if the threat is reported by a member of the patient's family.[e] In this case, a therapist learned about a threat not from his patient but from a family member of his patient. His patient revealed to his parents that he had thoughts of killing his ex-girlfriend's new boyfriend. The parents contacted the therapist about this threat. The therapist did not contact the new boyfriend, who was later killed by his patient. The parents of the boyfriend sued for wrongful death, saying the therapist should have warned their son. The court agreed and ruled that a close family member is in essence a part of the patient, and thus a therapist does have a duty to warn potential victims if notified by a close family member of a patient.

Extending Protection to Property

Tarasoff was further extended by a Vermont State Supreme Court ruling, *Peck v. Counseling Service of Addison County,*[f] which held that a mental health practitioner has a duty to warn a third party if there is a danger of damage to property. The case involved a 29-year-old male patient who, after a heated argument with his father, told his therapist that he wanted to get back at his father and indicated that he might do so by burning down his father's barn. He proceeded to do just that. No people or animals were harmed in the fire; the barn housed no animals and was located 130 feet away from the parents' home. The court's conclusion that the therapist had a duty to warn was based on reasoning that arson is a violent act and therefore a lethal threat to people who may be in the vicinity of the fire.

---

[d] *Almonte v. New York Medical College,* 851 F. Supp. 34, 40 (D. Conn. 1994) (denying motion for summary judgment).

[e] *Ewing v. Goldstein,* Cal. App. 4th B163112.2d. (2004).

[f] *Peck v. Counseling Service of Addison County,* 499 A.2d 422 (Vt. 1985).

The right to treatment was extended to all civilly committed patients in a landmark 1972 case, *Wyatt v. Stickney.*[32] In that case, an Alabama federal court ruled that treatment is the only justification for the civil commitment of people with mental illness to a state mental hospital. As stated by Judge Frank Johnson, "to deprive any citizen of his or her liberty upon the altruistic theory that the confinement is for humane and therapeutic reasons and then fail to provide adequate treatment violates the very fundamentals of due process." People with mental illness who are hospitalized "have a constitutional right to receive such individual treatment as

---

[32]*Wyatt v. Stickney,* 325 F.Supp. 781 (M.D. Ala. 1971), enforced in 334 F.Supp. 1341 (M.D. Ala. 1971), 344 F.Supp. 373, 379 (M.D. Ala. 1972), *aff'd sub nom Wyatt v. Anderholt,* 503 F.2d 1305 (5th Cir. 1974).

Civil commitment supposedly requires that the person be dangerous. But in actual practice, the decision to commit can be based on a judgment of severe disability, as in the case of some people who are homeless. (Corbis Images.)

will give each of them a realistic opportunity to be cured or to improve his or her mental condition." This ruling, upheld on appeal, is frequently cited as ensuring protection of people confined by civil commitment, at least to the extent that the state cannot simply put them away without meeting minimal standards of care. In fact, when people with mental retardation (as opposed to those judged to be mentally ill) are released from an institution, health officials are not relieved of their constitutional duty to provide reasonable care and safety as well as appropriate training.[33]

The *Wyatt* ruling was significant, because previously the courts had asserted that it was beyond their competence to pass judgment on the care given to people with mental illness, and they had assumed that mental health professionals possessed special and exclusive knowledge about psychopathology and its treatment. Repeated reports of abuses, however, gradually prodded the judicial system to rule on what went on within the walls of psychiatric hospitals. The *Wyatt* decision set forth very specific requirements for psychiatric hospitals—for example, dayrooms of at least 40 square feet, curtains or screens for privacy in multipatient bedrooms, and no physical restraints except in emergency situations. The ruling also specified how many mental health professionals ought to be in the hospital. When the *Wyatt* action was taken, Alabama state mental facilities averaged one physician per 2,000 patients, an extreme situation.[34] After *Wyatt*, there were to be at least two psychiatrists for every 250 patients. Similar protections have been extended to people with mental retardation.[35]

The *Wyatt* ruling appeared to have been weakened by a later Supreme Court decision, *Youngberg v. Romeo*,[36] regarding the treatment of a boy with mental retardation, Nicholas Romeo, who had been placed in physical restraints on occasion to keep him from hurting himself and others. While maintaining that people with mental illness have a right to reasonable care and safety, this 1982 decision deferred to the professional judgment of the mental health professionals responsible for the boy. However, the 1990 *Thomas S. v. Flaherty* decision held that professional judgment is not the final word when it comes to constitutional protections of people with mental retardation in public hospitals, a ruling more in line with *Wyatt*.

In a celebrated case, *O'Connor v. Donaldson*,[37] that eventually went to the Supreme Court in 1975, a civilly committed patient sued two state hospital doctors for his release and for monetary damages on the grounds that he had been kept against his will for 14 years without being treated and without being dangerous to himself or to others. In January 1957, at the age of 49, Kenneth Donaldson was committed to the Florida state hospital at Chattahoochee on petition of his father, who felt that his son was delusional. At a brief court hearing, a county judge found that Donaldson had paranoid schizophrenia and committed him for "care, maintenance, and treatment."

In 1971, Donaldson sued Dr. O'Connor, the hospital superintendent, and Dr. Gumanis, a hospital psychiatrist, for release. Evidence presented at the trial in a U.S. District Court in Florida indicated that the hospital staff could have released Donaldson at any time after they determined that he was not a dangerous person. Testimony made it clear that at no time during his hospitalization had Donaldson's conduct posed any real danger to others or to himself. Furthermore, just before his commitment in 1957 he had been earning a living and taking adequate care of himself (and immediately on discharge he secured a job in hotel administration). Nonetheless, O'Connor had repeatedly refused the patient's requests for release, feeling it was his duty to determine whether a committed patient could adapt successfully outside the hospital. His judgment was that Donaldson could not. In deciding the question of dangerousness on the basis of how well the patient could live outside the institution, O'Connor was applying a more restrictive standard than that required by most state laws.

[33]*Thomas S. v. Flaherty*, 902 F.2d 250, cert. denied, 111 S.Ct. 373 (1990).

[34]The underlying assumption is that patients civilly committed to public mental hospitals will receive adequate care, but the evidence for this level of care is weak. Even though the extremely negligent conditions that the *Wyatt* decision remedied in Alabama are seldom found today, it is questionable, argued Morse (1982c), whether forced hospitalization benefits patients. At the very least, however, public mental hospitals can provide shelter, food, protection, and custodial care, which many deinstitutionalized patients lack.

[35]*Feagley v. Waddill*, 868 F.2d 1437 (5th Cir. 1989).

[36]*Youngberg v. Romeo*, 102 S.Ct. 2452 (1982).

[37]*O'Connor v. Donaldson*, 95 S.Ct. 2486 (1975).

The evidence indicated that Donaldson received only custodial care during his hospitalization. No treatment that could conceivably alleviate his assumed mental illness was undertaken. The therapy that O'Connor claimed Donaldson was undergoing consisted of being kept in a large room with 60 other patients. Donaldson had been denied privileges to stroll around the hospital grounds or even to discuss his case with Dr. O'Connor. O'Connor also regarded as delusional Donaldson's expressed desire to write a book about his hospital experiences (which Donaldson did after his release; the book sold well).

The Supreme Court ruled on June 26, 1975, that "a State cannot constitutionally confine . . . a nondangerous individual who is capable of surviving safely in freedom by himself or with the help of willing and responsible family members or friends." In 1977, Donaldson settled for $20,000 from Dr. Gumanis and from the estate of Dr. O'Connor, who had died during the appeals process.

Because of this decision, a committed patient's status must be periodically reviewed, for the grounds on which a patient was committed cannot be assumed to continue in effect forever. This position seems straightforward enough, yet it may still be overlooked. For example, a 1986 court decision involved a woman with mental retardation who had spent her entire adult life in a state institution after having been committed at age 15; during her 20 years of confinement, she was never given a hearing to reconsider the grounds for the original commitment.[38]

Kenneth Donaldson, displaying a copy of the Supreme Court opinion stating that nondangerous people with mental illness cannot be confined against their will under civil commitment. (©AP/Wide World Photos.)

Right to Refuse Treatment   Does a committed patient have the right to refuse treatment or a particular kind of treatment? The answer is yes, but with qualifications.

The right of committed patients to refuse medication is hotly debated. Psychiatrist E. Fuller Torrey (1996) asserts that because many people with mental illness have no insight into their condition, they believe they do not need any treatment and thus subject themselves and their loved ones to sometimes desperate and frightening situations by refusing medication or other modes of therapy, most of which involve hospitalization. Torrey's arguments plead for consideration of the costs of untreated mental illness.

On the other hand, there are many arguments against forcing a person to take medications. The side effects of most antipsychotic drugs are often aversive to the patient and are sometimes harmful and irreversible in the long run. As many as one-third of people with mental illness who take medications may not benefit from them.

Some court decisions illustrate the difficult issues that arise when the right to refuse treatment is debated. In a 1979 decision on some cases in which "unjustified polypharmacy" and "force or intimidation" had allegedly been applied without due consideration for the serious negative side effects of medications, the judge in a New Jersey federal district court concluded that medications can actually inhibit recovery and that, therefore, except in emergencies, even an involuntarily committed patient can refuse to take them, based on the rights of privacy (First Amendment) and due process (Fourteenth Amendment).[39] The judge ordered that advocates be available in each public hospital to help patients exercise the right to refuse treatment and that a listing of all the side effects of the medications that might be given to the patients be posted in each hospital. In a reconsideration of this case, however, the judge stated that the opinion of the health professional must take precedence over the right to refuse treatment when patients are a danger to themselves or to others, in other words, in emergency situations.[40]

The question of the right to refuse medication continues to be the subject of lawsuits. Although there is inconsistency across jurisdictions and the forensic picture is always changing, there is a trend toward granting even involuntarily committed patients certain rights to refuse medication, based on the constitutional protections of freedom from physical invasion, freedom of thought, and the right to privacy.[41] In an extension of the least-restrictive-treatment principle, the court in *United States v. Charters* ruled that the government cannot force

---

[38]*Clark v. Cohen*, 794 F.2d 79, cert. denied, 479 U.S. 962 (1986).

[39]*Rennie v. Klein*, Civil Action No. 77-2624, Federal District Court of New Jersey, 14 September 1979.

[40]*Rennie v. Klein*, 720 F.2d 266 (3d Cir. 1983).

[41]*United States v. Charters*, 829 F.2d 479 (1987); *United States v. Watson*, 893 F.2d 970 (1990).

antipsychotic drugs on a person only on the supposition that at some future time he or she might become dangerous. The threat to the public safety has to be clear and imminent to justify the risks and restrictions that such medications pose, and it must be shown that less intrusive intervention will not likely reduce impending danger to others. In other words, forcible medication necessarily restricts liberty in addition to whatever physical risks it could bring; there has to be a very good reason to deprive a person of liberty and privacy via such intrusive measures. For example, a ruling in favor of forcible medication was made in a case of a person who had been threatening to assassinate the president of the United States. He posed a threat to his own safety, and he could be shown by clear and convincing evidence to be seriously mentally impaired.[42] Decisions of health professionals are nevertheless subject to judicial review.[43]

When someone already hospitalized is believed to be too psychotic to give informed consent about a treatment, mental health law sometimes invokes the doctrine of substituted judgment, the decision that the patient would have made if he or she had been able or competent to make a decision.[44] This principle creates as many problems as it solves. Deciding when a patient is competent to refuse treatment is one of the most controversial topics in the mental health law literature (e.g., Appelbaum & Grisso, 1995; Grisso & Appelbaum, 1991; Winick, 1997).

To complicate matters even further, research findings indicate that many hospitalized patients, although showing impairment in their ability to think and make decisions, nonetheless demonstrate enough legally relevant abilities to be considered competent to participate in treatment decisions. Specifically, they have the ability to state a choice, to understand relevant information, to understand the nature of the situation they are in, and to think reasonably about the information pertaining to their treatment. For example, people diagnosed with schizophrenia that initially show major cognitive impairments that can interfere with their capacity to make treatment decisions for themselves usually improve enough after a few weeks of medication to be able to participate in decisions about their future therapy (Appelbaum & Grisso, 1995; Applebaum et al., 1999).

Rights to Treatment, to Refuse Treatment, and to Be Treated in the Least Restrictive Setting—Can They Be Reconciled?

We have reviewed several legal principles that guide the courts and mental health professionals in meeting their constitutional obligations to civilly committed patients. Actions taken to implement one principle may conflict with another, however. The basic question is whether the right to be treated in the least restrictive fashion can be reconciled with both the right to treatment and the right to refuse treatment.

One approach to the conflict between right to treatment and right to refuse treatment is the so-called **advanced directive**, a legal document modeled after living wills. An advanced directive is composed by people who are legally competent and able to make decisions and specify how they want to be treated in the event that, sometime in the future, they need psychological or medical therapy but are mentally unfit to make decisions bearing on their therapy. The document may state what procedures the person consents to or refuses. Or the document may name another person to make such decisions. Many states now have laws that make such documents legally binding.

The use of advanced directives may enable people who are psychologically troubled but still competent to have more power over their future health care. But can such people really know what they will want or need if and when they become legally incompetent in the future? We can expect the debates on this issue of patient autonomy to continue.

Deinstitutionalization, Civil Liberties, and Mental Health

Court rulings such as *Wyatt v. Stickney* and *O'Connor v. Donaldson* put mental health professionals on notice to be careful about keeping people in psychiatric hospitals against their will and to attend more to the specific treatment needs of people with mental illness. Pressure was placed

---

[42]*Dautremont v. Broadlawns Hospital*, 827 F.2d 291 (8th Cir. 1987).
[43]*United States v. Charters*, 863 F.2d 302, cert. denied, 494 U.S. 1016 (1990).
[44]*Guardianship of Weedon*, 565 N.E. 2d 432, 409 Mass. 196 (1991).

on state governments to upgrade the quality of care in hospitals. In view of the abuses that have been documented in hospital care, these are surely encouraging changes. But the picture is not all that rosy. For judges to declare that patient care must meet certain minimal standards does not automatically translate into realization of that praiseworthy goal. Money is not in unlimited supply, and the care of people with mental illness has not been one of government's high priorities.

Beginning in the 1960s, many states embarked on a policy referred to as *deinstitutionalization*, discharging as many patients as possible from mental hospitals and discouraging admissions. Indeed, civil commitment is more difficult to achieve now than it was in the 1950s and 1960s, despite the fact that some people with mental illness need short stays in a hospital.

The population of state mental hospitals peaked in the 1950s at more than half a million patients. By 2000, these numbers had dropped to around 50,000. The number of hospitals continues to decline: there were 273 state mental hospitals in 1992 but only 195 in 2000 (Geller, 2006). The maxim is now "Treat them in the community," the assumption being that virtually anything is preferable to institutionalization.

Unfortunately, there are woefully inadequate resources for such treatment in the community. Some effective programs were described in Chapter 11, but these are very much the exception, not the rule. The state of affairs in cities is an unrelenting crisis for the hundreds of thousands of people with mental illness who have been released since the 1960s without adequate community services to help them. Many patients discharged from hospitals are eligible for benefits from the Veterans Administration and for Social Security Disability Insurance, but a large number are not receiving this assistance. Rates of homelessness have soard among the mentally ill, and homeless persons do not have fixed addresses and need help in establishing eligibility and residency for the purpose of receiving benefits. The state of homelessness undoubtedly exacerbates the emotional suffering of people with mental illness. People with mental illness are an especially defenseless segment of the homeless population.

Deinstitutionalization may be a misnomer. *Transinstitutionalization* may be more apt, for declines in the census of psychiatric hospitals have occasioned increases in the presence of people with mental illness in nursing homes, the mental health departments of nonpsychiatric hospitals, and prisons (Cloud, 1999; Kiesler, 1991), and these settings are by and large not equipped to handle the particular needs of people with mental illness.

Indeed, jails and prisons have become the new "hospitals" for the people with mental illness in the twenty-first century. A study by the Justice Department found that 16.2 percent of the population in prison or jails is seriously mentally ill (BJS, 1999). The Los Angeles County Jail may now be the country's largest mental "hospital" facility, with 1,500 inmates believed to have a serious mental illness (CAPT, 2000). Have we come that far from the days of the abysmal institutions that we discussed in Chapter 1? Clearly, we need to do more.

> It is deplorable and outrageous that this state's prisons appear to have become a repository for a great number of its mentally ill citizens. Persons who, with psychiatric care, could fit well into society, are instead locked away, to become wards of the state's penal system. Then, in a tragically ironic twist, they may be confined in conditions that nurture, rather than abate, their psychoses. Judge William Wayne Justice, Ruiz v. Johnson, 37 F. Supp.2d 855 (S.D. Texas, 1999).

Police officers are now called on to do the work of mental health professionals. They are often the first to come in contact with a person with mental illness and can make decisions as to whether a person should be taken to a hospital or jail. In several cities, mental health professionals have teamed up with police officers to form mobile crisis units (Lamb, Weinberger, & DeCuir, 2002). These units consist of trained mental health professionals who work in conjunction with local police to find the best option for a person with mental illness in the community. Because police officers are increasingly called on to work with people with mental illness, communities are recognizing the need for the police to receive proper training. New laws passed in the past decade including America's Law Enforcement and Mental Health Project Act (2000) and the later extension of this, called the Mentally Ill Offender Treatment and Crime Reduction Act (2004), provide funding for such training. These laws also provide funds to set up what are referred to as mental health courts in local communities. The idea is that people with mental illness who commit a crime may be better served by courts that can monitor treatment availability and adherence.

The approach of building partnerships between mental health professionals and law enforcement led to the creation of the Consensus Project (www.consensusproject.org). The Council of State Governments coordinated collaboration between criminal justice, mental health, and local and national lawmakers. A report entitled *Criminal Justice/Mental Health Consensus Project* was released in 2002, and it has been influential in increasing awareness of the large numbers of people with mental illness who are now housed in jails rather than in treatment facilities. The report outlines a number of policy ideas, all aimed at increasing cooperation between mental health and criminal justice and ultimately benefiting those with mental illness who are in the criminal justice system or who are at risk of becoming involved (e.g., sent to jail rather than treatment following a public outburst that reflects an exacerbation of illness).

Quick Summary

The legal standard for competency to stand trial requires that the accused understand the charges against him or her and be able to assist his or her attorney in the defense. Someone who is judged incompetent to stand trial receives treatment to restore competence and then returns to face the charges. The *Jackson* case specified that the pretrial period can be no longer than it takes to determine whether a person will ever become competent to stand trial. The use of medication to restore competency to stand trial can be used in limited circumstances.

The U.S. Supreme Court has ruled that it is unconstitutional (a violation of the Eighth Amendment, which prohibits cruel and unusual punishment) to execute people who are deemed legally insane or mentally retarded. Individual states can determine what constitutes mental retardation and insanity.

A person can be civilly committed to a hospital against his or her wishes if the person is mentally ill and a danger to self or others. Formal commitment requires a court order; informal commitment does not. People with mental illness who are not substance abusers are not necessarily more likely to engage in violence than are non–mentally ill people who are not substance abusers.

Early studies on the prediction of dangerousness had a number of flaws. Later research has shown that repeated acts of violence, a single serious violent act, being on the brink of violence, and medication noncompliance can maximize accuracy in predictions.

Court cases have tried to balance a person's rights with the rights of society to be protected. The least restrictive alternative to freedom is to be provided when treating people with mental disorders and protecting them from harming themselves and others. A series of court cases have generally supported the notion that those people committed to a hospital have the right to receive treatment. People with mental illness have the right to refuse treatment as well, except when doing so poses a danger to self or others.

The advanced directive is a legal document composed by people who are legally competent and able to make decisions and specify how they want to be treated in the event that, sometime in the future, they need psychological or medical therapy but are mentally unfit to make decisions bearing on their therapy.

Beginning in the 1960s, large numbers of patients were released from hospitals in what has been called deinstitutionalization. Unfortunately, there are not enough treatment options available in the community. Jails and prisons are now the new "hospitals" for people with mental illness. Police officers are called on to do the work once reserved for mental health professionals. Partnerships between police, courts, and community mental health providers are promising for helping people with mental illness.

Check Your Knowledge 17.3

True or false?

1. People with schizophrenia who have delusions are more likely to be violent than those without delusions.
2. Past violence is a predictor of future violence.
3. Court decisions have determined that hospitalized patients do not have a right to treatment unless they are dangerous.
4. People with mental illness can refuse treatment if they are found incompetent to stand trial after being charged with a nonviolent offense.

Ethical Dilemmas in Therapy and Research

The legal trends reviewed thus far in this chapter place limits on the activities of mental health professionals. These legal constraints are important, for laws are one of society's strongest means of encouraging all of us to behave in certain ways. Mental health professionals also have ethical constraints. Ethics statements are designed to provide an ideal, to review moral issues of right and wrong that may or may not be reflected in the law. All professional groups promulgate "should." These ethics guidelines describe what therapists and researchers should do with their patients, clients, and research participants. Courts have also ruled on some of these questions. Most of the time what we believe is unethical is also illegal, but sometimes existing laws are in conflict with our moral sense of right and wrong. The American Psychological Association publishes a *Code of Ethics* that includes the ethical standards that constrain research and practice in psychology (APA, 2002; http://www.apa.org/ethics). We examine now the ethics of making psychological inquiries and interventions into the lives of other human beings.

Ethical Restraints on Research

The training of scientists equips them to pose interesting questions, sometimes even important ones, and to design research that is as free as possible of confounds. They have no special qualifications, however, for deciding whether a particular line of research with people should be followed. Society needs knowledge, and a scientist has a right in a democracy to seek that knowledge. However, the ordinary citizens who participate in experiments must be protected from unnecessary harm, risk, humiliation, and invasion of privacy.

Perhaps the most reprehensible ethical insensitivity was evidenced in the brutal experiments conducted by German physicians on concentration camp prisoners during World War II. One experiment, for example, investigated how long people lived when their heads were bashed repeatedly with a heavy stick. Clearly, such actions violate our sense of decency and morality. The Nuremberg Trials, conducted by the Allies following the war, brought these and other barbarisms to light and meted out severe punishment (including the death penalty) to some of the soldiers, physicians, and Nazi officials who had engaged in or contributed to such actions, even when they claimed that they had merely been following orders.

It would be reassuring to be able to say that such gross violations of human decency take place only during incredible and cruel epochs such as the Third Reich, but unfortunately this is not the case. Spurred on by a blind enthusiasm for their work, researchers in the United States and other countries have sometimes dealt with human participants in reproachable ways.

For example, one experiment conducted after World War II compared penicillin with a placebo as a treatment to prevent rheumatic fever. Even though penicillin had already been acknowledged as the drug of choice for people with a streptococcal respiratory infection in order to protect them from later contracting rheumatic fever, placebos were administered to 109 service personnel without their knowledge or permission. More participants received penicillin than received the placebo, but three members of the control group contracted serious illnesses—two had rheumatic fever and one acute nephritis, a kidney disease. None of those who had received penicillin contracted such illnesses (Beecher, 1966).

Half a century later, in January 1994, spurred on by Eileen Welsome, a journalist who won a Pulitzer Prize for her investigative reporting on the issue, the United States Energy Department began to publicize numerous experiments conducted in the 1950s through the 1970s that had exposed hundreds of people—usually without their informed consent or prior knowledge—to harmful doses of radiation. Particular concern was expressed because the overwhelming majority were people of low socioeconomic status, members of ethnic minorities, people with mental retardation, nursing

Defendants at the Nuremberg trials. (Corbis-Bettmann.)

home patients, or prisoners. The scientists, for the most part supported in their research with federal funds, understood that the risks were great even though relatively little was known about the harmful effects of radiation at the time. Some of these experiments involved giving women in the third trimester of pregnancy a radioactive tonic to determine safe levels of exposure and irradiating the testicles of prisoners to find out the degree of radiation that service personnel could endure without negative effects on sperm production.

Responding to the many instances of harm inflicted on research participants, several international codes of ethics for the conduct of scientific research have been developed—the Nuremberg Code formulated in 1947 in the aftermath of the Nazi war-crime trials, the 1964 Declaration of Helsinki, and statements from the British Medical Research Council. In 1974, the U.S. Department of Health, Education, and Welfare began to issue guidelines and regulations governing scientific research that employs human and animal participants. In addition, a blue-ribbon panel, the National Commission for the Protection of Human Subjects of Biomedical and Behavioral Research, issued a report in 1978 that arose from hearings and inquiries into restrictions that the U.S. government might impose on research performed with patients in psychiatric hospitals, prisoners, and children. These various codes and principles are continually being reevaluated and revised as new challenges are posed to the research community.

For the past 40 years, the proposals of behavioral researchers, many of whom conduct experiments related to psychopathology and therapy, have been reviewed for safety and general ethical propriety by institutional review boards in hospitals, universities, and research institutes. Such committees—and this is significant—comprise not only behavioral scientists but also citizens from the community. They are able to block any research proposal or require questionable aspects to be modified if in their collective judgment the research would put participants at too great a risk. Such committees now also pass judgment on the scientific merits of proposals, the rationale being that it is not ethical to recruit participants for studies that will not yield valid data (Capron, 1999). In 2000, universities and other research institutions were required to begin certifying researchers on the basis of special coursework and examinations concerning research ethics. Researchers who receive funds from federal agencies, such as the National Institute of Mental Health, are also required to receive specialized training in research ethics.

Informed Consent

A core component of ethical research is **informed consent**. The investigator must provide enough information to enable people to decide whether they want to be in a study. Researchers must describe the study clearly, including any risks involved. Researchers should disclose even minor risks that could occur from a study, including emotional distress from answering personal questions or side effects from drugs. There must be no coercion in obtaining informed consent. Participants must understand that they have every right not to take part in the study or to withdraw from the study at any point, without any fear of penalty. For example, a psychologist might want to determine whether imagery helps students to associate one word with another. One group of students might be asked to associate pairs of words in their minds by generating a wacky image connecting the two, such as a cat riding on a bicycle. Current procedure allows prospective participants to decide that the experiment is likely to be boring and to decline to participate.

A central issue is that potential participants must be able to understand the study and associated risks. What if the prospective participant is a child with mental retardation, unable to understand fully what is being asked? In clinical settings, researchers must ascertain that patients are not having trouble understanding the study.

Irwin and colleagues (1985) found that although most people with mental illness said they understood the benefits and side effects of their drugs, only a quarter of them could actually demonstrate such understanding when queried specifically. The authors concluded that simply reading information to hospitalized patients—especially the more severely ill ones—is no guarantee that they fully comprehend; therefore, informed consent cannot be said to have been obtained. The report of the National Bioethics Advisory Commission pointed to many published experiments involving people with mental illness in which no effort was made to determine whether the research participants had the decision-making capacity to give informed consent

(Capron, 1999). Instead of simply allowing a guardian or family member to make the decision for the patient, the commission proposed that a health professional who has nothing to do with the particular study make a judgment on whether a given patient can give informed consent. The commission also recommended that if a guardian is allowed to give consent on behalf of a patient judged incompetent to do so, the guardian's own ability to give consent also be evaluated (Capron, 1999).

Still, as with the right to refuse treatment, there is recognition that being judged mentally ill does not necessarily mean being incapable of giving informed consent (Appelbaum & Gutheil, 1991). For example, although people with schizophrenia may do more poorly than people without schizophrenia on tests designed to assess decision-making skills, people with schizophrenia can give informed consent if a more detailed procedure describing a study is included—for example, one that describes what they will be asked to do and what they will see and explains that their participation is voluntary and that it in no way will impact their treatment (Carpenter et al., 2000; Wirshing et al., 1998).

The issue of informed consent is also of concern to researchers and clinicians who work with people with Alzheimer's disease. As with schizophrenia, having an Alzheimer's diagnosis does not necessarily mean a person cannot provide informed consent (Marson, Huthwaite, & Hupert, 2004). Measures have been developed to assess capacity for consent in this population, and this will continue to be an area of active research as the number of people over age 65 continues to increase (Marson, 2001).

These results point to the importance of examining each person individually for ability to give informed consent, rather than assuming that a person is unable to do so by virtue of being hospitalized for schizophrenia or Alzheimer's disease. Thus, having a mental disorder does not necessarily mean that a person cannot give informed consent.

Confidentiality and Privileged Communication

When people consult a psychiatrist or clinical psychologist, they are assured by professional ethics codes that what goes on in the session will remain confidential. **Confidentiality** means that nothing will be revealed to a third party except for other professionals and those intimately involved in the treatment, such as a nurse or medical secretary.

A **privileged communication** goes even further. It is communication between parties in a confidential relationship that is protected by law. The recipient of such a communication cannot legally be compelled to disclose it as a witness. The right of privileged communication is a major exception to the access courts have to evidence in judicial proceedings. Society believes that in the long term the interests of people are best served if communications to a spouse and to certain professionals remain off limits to the prying eyes and ears of the police, judges, and prosecutors. The privilege applies to such relationships as those between husband and wife, physician and patient, pastor and penitent, attorney and client, and psychologist and patient. The legal expression is that the patient or client "holds the privilege," which means that only he or she may release the other person to disclose confidential information in a legal proceeding.

There are important limits to a client's right of privileged communication, however. For example, this right is eliminated for any of the following reasons in some states:

- The client has accused the therapist of malpractice. In such a case, the therapist can divulge information about the therapy in order to defend himself or herself in any legal action initiated by the client.
- The client is less than 16 years old and the therapist has reason to believe that the child has been a victim of a crime such as child abuse. In fact, the psychologist is required to report to the police or to a child welfare agency within 36 hours any suspicion he or she has that the child client has been physically abused, including any suspicion of sexual molestation.
- The client initiated therapy in hopes of evading the law for having committed a crime or for planning to do so.
- The therapist judges that the client is a danger to self or others and disclosure of information is necessary to ward off such danger (recall Focus on Discovery 17.3 on *Tarasoff*).

Who Is the Client or Patient?

Is it always clear to the clinician who the client is? In private therapy, when an adult pays a clinician a fee for help with a personal problem that has nothing to do with the legal system, the consulting individual is clearly the client. But an individual may be seen by a clinician for an evaluation of his or her competency to stand trial, or the clinician may be hired by an individual's family to assist in civil commitment proceedings. Perhaps the clinician is employed by a state mental hospital as a regular staff member and sees a particular patient about problems in controlling aggressive impulses.

It should be clear, although it sometimes is not, that in these instances the clinician is serving more than one client. In addition to the patient, he or she serves the family or the state, and it is incumbent on the mental health professional to inform the patient that this is so. This dual allegiance does not necessarily indicate that the patient's own interests will be sacrificed, but it does mean that discussions will not inevitably remain secret and that the clinician may in the future act in a way that displeases or even seriously compromises the interests of the patient.

Quick Summary

Ethical restraints on research are necessary to avoid the abuses that have occurred in the past. Since the Nuremberg Codes of 1947, a number of ethical codes regarding psychological research have been developed. Research must be approved for safety and ethics by an institutional review board. Universities and other research institutions, as well as federal grant-funding agencies, require that researchers receive specialized training and certification in research ethics, on the basis of special coursework and examinations, to make it less likely that research participants will be put at risk.

Special precautions must be taken to ensure that research participants with mental illness fully understand the risks and benefits of any research they are asked to participate in and that particular care be taken to make certain that they can decline or withdraw from research without feeling coerced. Informed consent procedures must include enough information about the research so that participants know about the risks and feel free to withdraw without penalty.

In therapy sessions, patients have the right to have what is discussed kept confidential (can't be disclosed to a third party), and this discussion is considered a privileged communication (information in confidential relationship protected by law). However, confidentiality and the privileged communication can be broken if an individual is a danger to self or others, is suing a therapist for malpractice, is a child under 16 who has been the victim of a crime or abuse, or is trying to evade the law for a crime committed or planned.

Summary

- Some civil liberties are rather routinely set aside when mental health professionals and the courts judge that mental illness has played a decisive role in determining an individual's behavior. This may occur through criminal or civil commitment.

- Criminal commitment sends a person to a hospital either before a trial for an alleged crime, because the person is deemed incompetent to stand trial, or after an acquittal by reason of insanity.

- A person who is considered mentally ill and dangerous to self and to others, although he or she has not broken a law, can be civilly committed to hospital or be allowed to live outside of a hospital but only under supervision and with restrictions placed on his or her activities.

- Several landmark cases and principles in law address the conditions under which a person who has committed a crime might be excused from legal responsibility for it—that is, not guilty by reason of insanity. These involve the presence of an irresistible impulse and the notion that some people may not be able to distinguish between right and wrong (the M'Naghten rule). The Insanity Defense Reform Act of 1984 made it harder for accused criminals to argue insanity as defense.

- Today, the defense of guilty but mentally ill is in use in a number of states.

- There is an important difference between mental illness and insanity. The latter is a legal concept. A person can be diagnosed as mentally ill and yet be deemed sane enough both to stand trial and to be found guilty of a crime.

- Court rulings have provided greater protection to all committed people with mental illness, particularly those under civil commitment. They have the right to written notification, to counsel, to a jury decision concerning their commitment, and to Fifth Amendment protection against self-incrimination; the right to the least restrictive treatment setting; the right to be treated; and, in most circumstances, the right to refuse treatment, particularly any procedure that entails considerable risk.

- Ethical issues concerning research include restraints on what kinds of research are allowable and the duty of scientists to obtain informed consent from prospective human participants.

- In the area of therapy, ethical issues concern the right of clients to confidentiality and the question of who is the client (e.g., an individual or the hospital that is paying the clinician).

Answers to Check Your Knowledge Questions

17.1 1. c; 2. a; 3. d; 4. b

17.2 1. F; 2. T; 3. T

17.3 1. F; 2. T; 3. F; 4. T

Key Terms

advanced directive

American Law institute
    guidelines

civil commitment

competency to stand trial

confidentiality

criminal commitment

guilty but mentally ill (GBMI)

in absentia

informed consent

insanity defense

irresistible impulse

least restrictive alternative

M'Naghten rule

not guilty by reason of insanity
    (NGRI)

outpatient commitment

privileged communication

Glossary

acute stress disorder. A short-lived anxiety reaction to a traumatic event; if it lasts more than a month, it is diagnosed as posttraumatic stress disorder.

addiction. See *substance dependence*.

adoptees method. Research method that studies children who were adopted and reared completely apart from their parents, thereby eliminating the influence of being raised by disordered parents.

advanced directive. Legal document in which an individual—before becoming incapable of making such decisions—prescribes and proscribes certain courses of action to be taken to preserve his or her health or terminate life support.

age effects. The consequences of being a given chronological age. Compare *cohort effects*.

agonist. A drug that stimulates receptors normally specific to a particular neurotransmitter.

agoraphobia. Literally, fear of the marketplace. Fear of being in crowded or open places. Anxiety about situations in which it would be embarrassing or difficult to escape if panic symptoms occurred; most commonly diagnosed in some individuals with panic disorder.

AIDS (acquired immunodeficiency syndrome). A fatal disease transmitted by transfer of the human immunodeficiency virus, usually during sexual relations or by using needles previously infected by an HIV-positive person; it compromises the immune system to such a degree that the person ultimately dies from one of any number of infections.

allele. Any of the various forms in which a particular gene is found.

allostatic load. The physiological burden of high levels of stress hormones such as cortisol; may lead to disease susceptibility because of altered immune system functioning.

alogia. A negative symptom in schizophrenia, marked by poverty of speech.

alternate-form reliability. See *reliability*.

altruistic suicide. As defined by Durkheim, self-annihilation that the person feels will serve a social purpose, such as the self-immolations practiced by Buddhist monks during the Vietnam War.

Alzheimer's disease. A dementia involving a progressive atrophy of cortical tissue and marked by memory impairment, intellectual deterioration, and, in more extreme cases, involuntary movements of limbs, occasional convulsions, and psychotic behavior. See also *plaques* and *neurofibrillary tangles*.

American Law Institute guidelines. Rules proposing that insanity is a legitimate defense plea if, during criminal conduct, an individual could not judge right from wrong or control his or her behavior as required by law. Repetitive criminal acts are disavowed as a sole criterion. Compare *M'Naghten rule* and *irresistible impulse*.

amphetamines. A group of stimulating drugs that produce heightened levels of energy and, in large doses, nervousness, sleeplessness, and paranoid delusions.

amygdala. A subcortical structure of the temporal lobe involved in attention to emotionally salient stimuli and memory of emotionally relevant events.

anal stage. In psychoanalytic theory, the second psychosexual stage, which occurs during the second year of life when the anus is considered the principal erogenous zone.

analogue experiment. An experimental study of a phenomenon different from but related to the actual interests of the investigator; for example, animal research used to study human disorders, or research on mild symptoms used as a bridge to clinical disorders.

analytical psychology. A variation of Freud's psychoanalysis introduced by Carl Jung, focusing less on biological drives and more on factors such as self-fulfillment, the collective unconscious, and religious symbolism.

anesthesia. An impairment or loss of sensation, usually of touch but sometimes of the other senses, that is often part of conversion disorder.

anger-in theory. The view that psychophysiological disorders, such as essential hypertension, arise from a person's not expressing anger or resentment.

angina pectoris. See *coronary heart disease*.

anhedonia. A negative symptom in schizophrenia or a symptom in depression in which the individual experiences a loss of interest and pleasure. See *anticipatory pleasure* and *consummatory pleasure*.

anomic suicide. As defined by Durkheim, self-annihilation triggered by a person's inability to cope with sudden and unfavorable change in a social situation.

anorexia nervosa. A disorder in which a person refuses to maintain normal weight, has an intense fear of becoming obese, and feels fat even when emaciated.

Antabuse. A drug that makes the drinking of alcohol produce nausea and other unpleasant effects; trade name for disulfiram.

antagonist. A drug that dampens the effect of a neurotransmitter on its receptors; for example, many dopamine antagonists block dopamine receptors.

anterior cingulate. In the subcortical region of the brain, the anterior portion of the cingulate gyrus, stretching about the corpus callosum.

anticipatory pleasure. Expected or anticipated pleasure for events, people, or activities in the future. See *consummatory pleasure*.

antidepressant. Any drug that alleviates depression; also widely used to treat anxiety disorders.

antipsychotic drugs. Psychoactive drugs, such as Thorazine, that reduce psychotic symptoms but have long-term side effects resembling symptoms of neurological diseases.

antisocial personality disorder. Personality disorder defined by the absence of concern for others' feelings or social norms, a pervasive pattern of rule breaking, and the presence of conduct disorder by age 15.

anxiety. An unpleasant feeling of fear and apprehension accompanied by increased physiological arousal; in learning theory, considered a drive that mediates between a threatening situation and avoidance behavior. Anxiety can be assessed by self-report, by measuring physiological arousal, and by observing overt behavior.

anxiety disorders. Disorders in which fear or tension is overriding and the primary disturbance; include phobic disorders, panic disorder, generalized anxiety disorder, obsessive-compulsive disorder, acute stress disorder, and posttraumatic stress disorder. These disorders form a major category in DSM-IV-TR.

Anxiety Sensitivity Index (ASI). A test that measures the extent to which people respond fearfully to their bodily sensations; predicts the degree to which unexplained physiological arousal leads to panic attacks.

anxiolytics. Minor tranquilizers or benzodiazepines used to treat anxiety disorders.

asociality. A negative symptom of schizophrenia marked by an inability to form close relationships and to feel intimacy.

Asperger's disorder. Pervasive developmental disorder believed to be a mild form of autism in which social relationships are poor and stereotyped behavior is intense and rigid, but language and intelligence are intact.

asthma. A disorder characterized by narrowing of the airways and increased secretion of mucus, often causing extremely labored and wheezy breathing.

asylums. Refuges established in western Europe in the fifteenth century to confine and provide for the mentally ill; forerunners of the mental hospital.

attachment theory. The type or style of an infant's attachment to his or her caregivers can set the stage for psychological health or problems later in development

attention-deficit/hyperactivity disorder (ADHD). A disorder in children marked by difficulties in focusing adaptively on the task at hand, inappropriate fidgeting and antisocial behavior, and excessive non-goal-directed behavior.

attribution. The explanation a person has for why an event or behavior has occurred.

attributional style. A person's relatively consistent approach to attribution; for example, the consistent attribution of negative life events to internal, stable, and global causes is thought to dispose to depression.

autistic disorder. Pervasive developmental disorder in which the child's world is one of profound aloneness: speech is often absent, and the child has an obsessive need for everything to remain the same.

autonomic nervous system (ANS). The division of the nervous system that regulates involuntary functions; innervates endocrine glands, smooth muscle, and heart muscle; and initiates the physiological changes that are part of the expression of emotion. See *sympathetic* and *parasympathetic nervous systems*; compare *somatic nervous system*.

aversive conditioning. Process believed to underlie the effectiveness of aversion therapy.

avoidant personality disorder. Personality disorder defined by aloofness and extreme sensitivity to potential rejection, despite an intense desire for affiliation and affection.

avolition. A negative symptom in schizophrenia in which the individual lacks interest and drive.

barbiturates. A class of addictive synthetic sedatives; in large doses, can cause death by almost completely relaxing the diaphragm.

behavior genetics. The study of individual differences in behavior that are attributable to differences in genetic makeup.

behavior therapy. A branch of psychotherapy conceived narrowly as the application of classical and operant conditioning to the alteration of clinical problems, but more broadly as applied experimental psychology in a clinical context.

behavioral activation (BA) therapy. Clinical approach to depression that seeks to increase participation in positively reinforcing activities.

behavioral assessment. A sampling of ongoing cognitions, feelings, and overt behavior in their situational context. Compare *projective test* and *personality inventory*.

behavioral inhibition. The tendency to exhibit anxiety or to freeze when facing threat. In infants, it manifests as a tendency to become agitated and cry when faced with novel stimuli and may be a heritable predisposition for the development of anxiety disorders.

behavioral couples therapy. Clinical approach to depression in which a couple works to improve communication and satisfaction; more likely to relieve relationship distress than individual cognitive therapy.

behavioral medicine. An interdisciplinary field concerned with integrating knowledge from medicine and behavioral science to understand health and illness and to prevent as well as treat psychophysiological disorders and other illnesses in which a person's psyche plays a role. See also *health psychology*.

behaviorism. The school of psychology originally associated with John B. Watson, who proposed that observable behavior, not consciousness, is the proper subject matter of psychology. Contemporary behaviorists do use mediational concepts, provided they are firmly anchored to observables.

benzodiazepines. Any of several drugs commonly used to treat anxiety, such as Valium and Xanax.

beta blockers. Any of numerous beta-adrenergic antagonists, competitive inhibitors of a class of receptors for the hormone adrenaline; are approved as cardiovascular drugs but often used to treat social phobia, despite a lack of demonstrated efficacy.

binge eating disorder. Categorized in DSM-IV-TR as a diagnosis in need of further study; includes recurrent episodes of unrestrained eating.

bipolar I disorder. A diagnosis defined on the basis of at least one lifetime episode of mania. Most people with this disorder also experience episodes of major depression.

bipolar II disorder. A form of bipolar disorder, diagnosed in those who have experienced at least one major depressive episode and at least one episode of hypomania.

blindsight. Conversion disorder wherein patients have suffered lesions in the visual cortex and report themselves blind but can perform well on some specific visual tests.

body dysmorphic disorder. A somatoform disorder marked by preoccupation with an imagined or exaggerated defect in appearance—for example, facial wrinkles or excess facial or body hair.

body mass index (BMI). Measure of body fat calculated by dividing weight in kilograms by height in meters squared; considered a more valid estimate of body fat than many others.

BOLD (blood oxygenation level dependent). The signal detected by functional MRI studies of the brain; measures blood flow and thus neural activity in particular regions.

borderline personality disorder. Personality disorder defined by impulsiveness and unpredictability, an uncertain self-image, intense and unstable social relationships, and extreme swings of mood.

brain stem. The part of the brain connecting the spinal cord with the cerebrum; contains the pons and medulla oblongata and functions as a neural relay station.

brief psychotic disorder. A disorder in which a person has a sudden onset of psychotic symptoms—incoherence, loose associations, delusions, hallucinations—immediately after a severely disturbing event; the symptoms last more than I day but no more than I month. Compare *schizophreniform disorder*.

brief therapy. Time-limited psychotherapy, usually ego-analytic in orientation and lasting no more than 25 sessions.

bulimia nervosa. A disorder characterized by episodic, uncontrollable eating binges followed by purging either by vomiting or by taking laxatives.

caffeine. Perhaps the world's most popular drug; a generalized stimulant of body systems, including the sympathetic nervous system. Though seldom viewed as a drug, caffeine is addictive, produces tolerance, and subjects habitual users to withdrawal.

cardiovascular disorders. Medical problems involving the heart and the blood circulation system, such as hypertension or coronary heart disease.

case study. The collection of historical or biographical information on a single individual, often including experiences in therapy.

catatonia. Constellation of schizophrenic symptoms including repetitive, peculiar, complex gestures, and, in some cases, an almost manic increase in overall activity level.

catatonic features. Immobility or excessive and peculiar physical movements characterizing a subtype of episodes of major depressive disorder or mania.

catatonic immobility. A fixity of posture, sometimes grotesque, maintained for long periods, with accompanying muscular rigidity, trancelike state of consciousness, and waxy flexibility.

catatonic schizophrenia. A subtype of schizophrenia whose primary symptoms alternate between stuporous immobility and excited agitation.

categorical classification. An approach to assessment in which a person is or is not a member of a discrete grouping. Compare *dimensional classification*.

cathartic method. A therapeutic procedure to relieve emotional suffering introduced by Breuer and developed further by Freud in the late nineteenth century, whereby a patient recalls and relives an earlier emotional catastrophe and reexperiences the tension and unhappiness.

central nervous system. The part of the nervous system that in vertebrates consists of the brain and spinal cord, to which all sensory impulses are transmitted and from which motor impulses pass out; supervises and coordinates the activities of the entire nervous system.

cerebellum. An area of the hindbrain concerned with balance, posture, and motor coordination.

cerebral cortex. The thin outer covering of each of the cerebral hemispheres; highly convoluted and composed of nerve cell bodies that constitute the gray matter of the brain.

cerebrum. The two-lobed structure extending from the brain stem and constituting the anterior (frontal) part of the brain; the largest and most recently developed portion of the brain, responsible for coordinating sensory and motor activities and performing higher cognitive processes.

childhood disintegrative disorder. Pervasive developmental disorder characterized by significant loss of social, play, language, and motor skills after the second year of life, with abnormalities in social interaction and communication similar to autism.

childhood sexual abuse (CSA). Sexual contact with a minor.

chromosomes. The threadlike bodies within the nucleus of the cell, composed primarily of DNA and bearing the genetic information of the organism.

civil commitment. A procedure whereby a person can be legally certified as mentally ill and hospitalized, even against his or her will. Compare *criminal commitment* and *outpatient commitment*.

classical conditioning. A basic form of learning, sometimes referred to as Pavlovian conditioning, in which a neutral stimulus is repeatedly paired with another stimulus (called the unconditioned stimulus, UCS) that naturally elicits a certain desired response (called the unconditioned response, UCR). After repeated trials, the neutral stimulus becomes a conditioned stimulus (CS) and evokes the same or a similar response, now called the conditioned response (CR). Compare *operant conditioning*.

client-centered therapy. A humanistic-existential insight therapy, developed by Carl Rogers, that emphasizes the importance of the therapist understanding the client's subjective experiences and assisting the client to gain more awareness of current motivations for behavior: the goal is not only to reduce anxieties but also to foster actualization of the client's potential.

clinical interview. General term for conversation between a clinician and a patient that is aimed at determining diagnosis, history, causes for problems, and possible treatment options.

clinical psychologist. An individual who has earned a Ph.D. degree in psychology or a Psy. D. and whose training has included an internship in a mental hospital or clinic.

clinical significance. The degree to which effect size is large enough to be meaningful in predicting or treating a clinical disorder. Compare *statistical significance*.

cocaine. A pain-reducing, stimulating, and addictive alkaloid obtained from coca leaves that increases mental powers, produces euphoria, heightens sexual desire, and in large doses causes paranoia and hallucinations.

cognition. The process of knowing; the thinking, judging, reasoning, and planning activities of the human mind. Behavior is now often explained as depending on these processes.

cognitive behavior therapy (CBT). Behavior therapy that incorporates theory and research on cognitive processes such as thoughts, perceptions, judgments, self-statements, and tacit assumptions; a blend of both the cognitive and behavioral paradigms.

cognitive behavioral paradigm. General view that people can best be understood by studying how they perceive and structure their experiences and how this influences behavior.

cognitive biases. Tendencies to perceive events in a negative manner, for example, by attending to or remembering negative information more than positive information; hypothesized to be driven by underlying negative schemata.

cognitive enhancement therapy (CET). Also known as cognitive training, treatment that seeks to improve basic cognitive functions such as verbal learning ability in people with schizophrenia, meanwhile reducing symptoms as well.

cognitive restructuring. Any behavior therapy procedure that attempts to alter the manner in which a client thinks about life so that he or she changes overt behavior and emotions.

cognitive therapy. See *cognitive restructuring.* See also *cognitive behavior therapy.*

cohort effects. The consequences of having been born in a given year and having grown up during a particular time period with its own unique pressures, problems, challenges, and opportunities. Compare *age effects.*

collective unconscious. Jung's concept that every human being carries within the wisdom, ideas, and strivings of those who have come before.

common factors. An approach to psychotherapeutic integration that aims to understand the common ingredients that work across different forms of therapy, such as rationale for how treatment will take place, therapist expectations for change, and a strong therapeutic relationship.

communication disorders. Learning disabilities in a child who fails to develop to the degree expected by his or her intellectual level in a specific language skill area; include expressive language disorder, phonological disorder, and stuttering.

comorbidity. The co-occurrence of two disorders, as when a person has depression and social phobia.

competency to stand trial. A legal decision as to whether a person can participate meaningfully in his or her own defense.

compulsion. The irresistible impulse to repeat an irrational act or thought over and over again. Compare *obsession.*

concordance. As applied in behavior genetics, the similarity in psychiatric diagnosis or in other traits within a pair of twins.

concurrent validity. See *validity.*

conditioned response (CR). See *classical conditioning.*

conditioned stimulus (CS). See *classical conditioning.*

conduct disorder. Pattern of extreme disobedience in youngsters, including theft, vandalism, lying, and early drug use; may be precursor of antisocial personality disorder.

confidentiality. A principle observed by lawyers, doctors, pastors, psychologists, and psychiatrists which dictates that the contents of a professional and private relationship are not divulged to anyone else. See also *privileged communication.*

construct validity. The extent to which scores or ratings on an assessment instrument relate to other variables or behaviors according to some theory or hypothesis.

consummatory pleasure. Pleasure experienced in-the-moment or in the presence of a pleasurable stimulus. See *anticipatory pleasure.*

content validity. See *validity.*

control group. Those for whom the active condition of the independent variable is not administered, thus forming a baseline against which the effects of the active condition of the independent variable can be evaluated.

controlled drinking. A pattern of alcohol consumption that is moderate, avoiding the extremes of total abstinence and of inebriation.

conversion disorder. A somatoform disorder in which sensory or motor function is impaired, even though there is no detectable neurological explanation for the deficits.

coping. How people try to deal with problems, in particular the typically negative emotions elicited by stress; generally includes problem-focused, emotion-focused, and avoidance actions and efforts.

coronary heart disease (CHD). Angina pectoris, chest pains caused by insufficient supply of blood and thus oxygen to the heart; and myocardial infarction, or heart attack, in which the blood and oxygen supply is reduced so much that heart muscles are damaged.

corpus callosum. The large band of nerve fibers connecting the two cerebral hemispheres.

correlation. The tendency for two variables, such as height and weight, to covary.

correlation coefficient. A statistic ranging in value from –1.00 to +1.00 that measures the degree to which two variables are related. The sign indicates whether the relationship is positive or negative, and the magnitude indicates the strength of the relationship.

correlational method. The research strategy used to establish whether two or more variables are related without manipulating the independent variable. Relationships may be positive—as values for one variable increase, those for the other do also—or negative—as values for one variable increase, those for the other decrease. Compare *experiment.*

cortisol. A "stress hormone" secreted by the adrenal cortices; helps the body prepare to face threats.

counseling psychologist. A doctoral-level mental health professional whose training is similar to that of a clinical psychologist, though usually with less emphasis on research and serious psychopathology.

crack. A rock-crystal form of cocaine that is heated, melted, and smoked; more often used in poorer urban areas than conventional cocaine.

criminal commitment. A procedure whereby a person is confined in a mental hospital either for determination of competency to stand trial or after acquittal by reason of insanity. Compare *civil commitment.*

criterion validity. See *validity.*

cross-dependent. Acting on the same receptors, as methadone does with heroin.

cross-fostering. Research method that studies offspring who were adopted and reared completely apart from their biological parents, where the adoptive parent has a particular disorder but the biological parent does not, thereby introducing the influence of being raised by disordered parents.

cross-sectional design. Studies in which different age groups are compared at the same time. Compare *longitudinal design.*

CT or **CAT scan.** Refers to computerized axial tomography, a method of diagnosis in which X-rays are taken from different angles and then analyzed by computer to produce a representation of the part of the body in cross section.

cultural competence. The capacity of a therapist to understand the patient's cultural framework and its implications for therapeutic work.

Cushing's syndrome. An endocrine disorder usually affecting young women, produced by oversecretion of cortisone and marked by mood swings, irritability, agitation, and physical disfigurement.

cyclothymic disorder. A form of bipolar disorder characterized by swings between elation and depression over at least a 2-year period, but with moods not so severe as manic or major depressive episodes.

cytokines. Immune system molecules, released by activated macrophages, which help initiate such bodily responses to infection as fatigue, fever, and activation of the HPA axis.

defense mechanisms. In psychoanalytic theory, reality-distorting strategies unconsciously adopted to protect the ego from anxiety.

delirium. A state of great mental confusion in which consciousness is clouded, attention cannot be sustained, and the stream of thought and speech is incoherent. The person is probably disoriented, emotionally erratic, restless or lethargic, and often has illusions, delusions, and hallucinations.

delirium tremens (DTs). One of the withdrawal symptoms that sometimes occurs when a period of heavy alcohol consumption is terminated; marked by fever, sweating, trembling, cognitive impairment, and hallucinations.

delusional disorder. A disorder in which the individual has persistent delusions and is very often contentious but has no disorganized thinking or hallucinations.

delusions. Beliefs contrary to reality, firmly held in spite of evidence to the contrary and common in paranoid disorders: of control, belief that one is being manipulated by some external force such as radar, television, or a creature from outer space; of grandeur, belief that one is an especially important or powerful person; of persecution, belief that one is being plotted against or oppressed by others.

dementia. Deterioration of mental faculties—memory, judgment, abstract thought, control of impulses, intellectual ability—that impairs social and occupational functioning and eventually changes the personality. See *Alzheimer's disease.*

dementia praecox. An older term for schizophrenia, believed then to be an incurable and progressive deterioration of mental functioning beginning in adolescence.

dementia with Lewy bodies (DLB). Form of dementia recently categorized as distinct from Parkinson's disease; characterized by shuffling gait, memory loss, and hallucinations and delusions.

demonology. The doctrine that a person's abnormal behavior is caused by an autonomous evil spirit.

dependent personality disorder. A disorder in which people are overly concerned about maintaining relationships. People with this disorder often allow others to make decisions for them and are reticent to make demands that could challenge relationships.

dependent variable. In a psychological experiment, the behavior that is measured and is expected to change with manipulation of the independent variable.

depersonalization. An alteration in perception of the self in which the individual loses a sense of reality and feels estranged from the self and perhaps separated from the body; may be a temporary reaction to stress and fatigue or part of panic disorder, depersonalization disorder, or schizophrenia.

depersonalization disorder. A dissociative disorder in which the individual feels unreal and estranged from the self and surroundings enough to disrupt functioning. People with this disorder may feel that their extremities have changed in size or that they are watching themselves from a distance.

derealization. Loss of the sense that the surroundings are real; present in several psychological disorders, such as panic disorder, depersonalization disorder, and schizophrenia.

desire phase. The first stage of the sexual response cycle, characterized by sexual interest or desire, often associated with sexually arousing fantasies.

detoxification. The initial stage in weaning an addicted person from a drug; involves medical supervision of the sometimes painful withdrawal.

developmental psychopathology. The field that studies disorders of childhood within the context of normal life-span development.

diagnosis. The determination that the set of symptoms or problems of a patient indicates a particular disorder.

Diagnostic and Statistical Manual of Mental Disorders. See *DSM-IV-TR.*

dialectical behavior therapy. A therapeutic approach to borderline personality disorder that combines client-centered empathy and acceptance with behavioral problem solving, social skills training, and limit setting.

diathesis. Predisposition toward a disease or abnormality.

diathesis–stress. As applied in psychopathology, a view that assumes that individuals predisposed toward a particular mental disorder will be particularly affected by stress and will then manifest abnormal behavior.

dimensional classification. An approach to assessment in which a person is placed on a continuum. Compare *categorical classification.*

directionality problem. A difficulty that arises in the correlational method of research when it is known that two variables are related but it is unclear which is causing the other.

disorder of written expression. Difficulties writing without errors in spelling, grammar, or punctuation.

disorganized behavior. Symptom of schizophrenia that is marked by odd behaviors that do not appear organized, such as bouts of agitation, unusual dress, or childlike, silly behavior.

disorganized schizophrenia. In this subtype of schizophrenia (formerly called hebephrenia), the person has diffuse and regressive symptoms; is given to silliness, facial grimaces, and inconsequential rituals; and has constantly changeable moods and poor hygiene.

disorganized speech. Speech found in schizophrenia patients that is marked by poorly organized ideas and speech that is difficult for others to understand; also known as formal thought disorder.

disorganized symptoms. Broad category of symptoms in schizophrenia that includes disorganized speech, disorganized thinking, and disorganized behavior.

disorientation. A state of mental confusion with respect to time, place, identity of self, other persons, and objects.

dissociation. A process whereby a group of mental processes is split off from the main stream of consciousness, or behavior loses its relationship with the rest of the personality.

dissociative amnesia. A dissociative disorder in which the person suddenly becomes unable to recall important personal information to an extent that cannot be explained by ordinary forgetfulness.

dissociative disorders. Disorders in which the normal integration of consciousness, memory, or identity is suddenly and temporarily altered; include dissociative amnesia, dissociative fugue, dissociative identity disorder (multiple personality), and depersonalization disorder.

dissociative fugue. Disorder in which the person experiences total amnesia, moves, and establishes a new identity.

dissociative identity disorder (DID). A rare dissociative disorder (formerly called multiple personality disorder, or MPD) in which two or more fairly distinct and separate personalities are present within the same individual, each with his or her own memories, relationships, and behavior patterns, with only one of them dominant at any given time.

dizygotic (DZ) twins. Birth partners who developed from separate fertilized eggs and who are only 50 percent alike genetically, just as siblings born from different pregnancies involving the same father; also called fraternal twins. Compare *monozygotic twins.*

dopamine. Central nervous system neurotransmitter, a catecholamine that is also a precursor of norepinephrine and apparently figures in schizophrenia and Parkinson's disease.

dopamine theory. The view that schizophrenia is linked to an increase in the number of dopamine receptors.

double-blind procedure. A method for reducing the biasing effects of the expectations of research participant and experimenter; neither is allowed to know whether the independent variable of the experiment is being applied to the participant.

Down syndrome (trisomy 21). A form of mental retardation caused by a third copy of a particular chromosome; involves an IQ usually less than 50 as well as distinctive physical characteristics.

DSM-IV-TR. The current *Diagnostic and Statistical Manual of Mental Disorders* of the American Psychiatric Association.

dyslexia (reading disorder). A learning disorder involving significant difficulty with word recognition, reading comprehension, and (typically) spelling.

dyspareunia. Persistent or recurrent pain during sexual intercourse not attributable to a medical problem.

dysthymic disorder. Depressive symptoms that last for at least 2 years but do not meet criteria for the diagnosis of major depressive disorder.

echolalia. The immediate or delayed repetition of the words of others, often found in autistic children.

ecological momentary assessment (EMA). Form of self-observation involving collection of data in real time (e.g., diaries) regarding thoughts, moods, and stressors.

Ecstasy. A relatively new hallucinogen, chemically similar to mescaline and the amphetamines.

effectiveness. How well a therapeutic treatment works in the real world, in the hands of broader samples of nonacademic, less supervised therapists. Compare *efficacy.*

efficacy. How well a therapeutic treatment works under rarified, academic research conditions. Compare *effectiveness.*

ego. In psychoanalytic theory, the predominantly conscious part of the personality, responsible for decision making and for dealing with reality.

ego analysis. An important set of modifications of classical psychoanalysis, based on a conception of the human being as having a stronger, more autonomous ego with gratifications independent of id satisfactions. Sometimes called ego psychology.

egoistic suicide. As defined by Durkheim, self-annihilation committed because the individual feels extreme alienation from others and from society.

electrocardiogram (EKG). A recording of the electrical activity of the heart, made with an electrocardiograph.

electroconvulsive therapy (ECT). A treatment that produces a convulsion by passing electric current through the brain; despite public concerns about this treatment, it can be useful in alleviating profound depression.

electrodermal responding. A recording of the minute electrical activity of the sweat glands on the skin, allowing inference of an emotional state.

electroencephalogram (EEG). A graphic recording of electrical activity of the brain, usually of the cerebral cortex, but sometimes of lower areas.

emotion. The expression, experience, and physiology that guide responses to problems and challenges in the environment.

emotion-focused therapy. An experiential therapeutic approach developed by Greanberg that focuses on helping clients differentiate maladaptive from adaptive emotions, as well as promoting better acceptance, understanding, and regulation of emotions.

empathy. Awareness and understanding of another's feelings and thoughts.

empirically supported treatments (ESTs). Approaches whose efficacy has been demonstrated and documented through research that meets the APA's standards for research on psychotherapy.

endorphins. Opiates produced within the body; may have an important role in the processes by which the body builds up tolerance to drugs and is distressed by their withdrawal.

enzyme. A complex protein that acts as a catalyst in regulating metabolic activities.

epidemiology. The study of the frequency and distribution of illness in a population.

episodic disorder. A condition, such as major depressive disorder, whose symptoms dissipate but that tends to recur.

essential hypertension. A disorder characterized by high blood pressure that cannot be traced to an organic cause; over time causes degeneration of small arteries, enlargement of the heart, and kidney damage.

etiology. All the factors that contribute to the development of an illness or disorder.

excitement phase. As applied by Masters and Johnson, the second stage of the sexual response cycle, characterized by pleasure associated with increased blood flow to the genitalia.

executive functioning. The cognitive capacity to plan how to do a task, how to devise strategies, and how to monitor one's performance.

exhibitionism. Marked preference for obtaining sexual gratification by exposing one's genitals to an unwilling observer.

exorcism. The casting out of evil spirits by ritualistic chanting or torture.

experiment. The most powerful research technique for determining causal relationships; involves the manipulation of an independent variable, the measurement of a dependent variable, and the random assignment of participants to the several different conditions being investigated. Compare *correlational method.*

experimental effect. A statistically significant difference between two groups experiencing different manipulations of the independent variable.

explicit memory. Memory involving the conscious recall of experiences; the area of deficits typically seen in dissociative amnesia. Compare *implicit memory.*

exposure. Real-life (in vivo) or imaginal confrontation of a feared object or situation, especially as a component of systematic desensitization. See also *imaginal exposure.*

exposure and response prevention (ERP). The most widely used and accepted treatment of obsessive-compulsive disorder, in which the sufferer is prevented from engaging in compulsive ritual activity and instead faces the anxiety provoked by the stimulus, leading eventually to extinction of the conditioned response (anxiety).

expressed emotion (EE). Hostility, criticism, and emotional overinvolvement directed from other people toward the patient, usually within a family.

expressive language disorder. Communication disorder of childhood involving difficulties expressing thoughts and emotions in speech.

external validity. The extent to which the results of a study can be considered generalizable.

externalizing disorders. Domain of childhood disorders characterized by outward-directed behaviors, such as aggressiveness, noncompliance, overactivity, and impulsiveness; the category includes attention-deficit/hyperactivity disorder, conduct disorder, and oppositional defiant disorder. Compare *internalizing disorders*.

extinction. The elimination of a classically conditioned response by the omission of the unconditioned stimulus. In operant conditioning, the elimination of the conditioned response by the omission of reinforcement.

extraversion. Personality trait associated with frequent experiences of positive affect and social engagement.

factitious disorder. Disorder in which the individual's physical or psychological symptoms appear under voluntary control and are adopted merely to assume the role of a sick person; called factitious disorder by proxy or Munchausen syndrome when a parent produces a physical illness in a child.

falsifiability. The extent to which a scientific assertion is amenable to systematic probes, any one of which could negate the scientist's expectations.

family method. A research strategy in behavior genetics in which the frequency of a trait or of abnormal behavior is determined in relatives who have varying percentages of shared genetic background.

family-focused treatment (FFT). With the goal of reducing the likelihood of relapse of bipolar disorder or schizophrenia, treatment that aims to educate the person's family about illness, enhance communication, and develop problem-solving skills.

fear. A reaction to real or perceived immediate danger in the present; can involve arousal, or sympathetic nervous system activity.

fear circuit. Set of brain structures, including the amygdala, that tend to be activated when the individual is feeling anxious or fearful; especially active among people with anxiety disorders.

fear-of-fear hypothesis. A cognitive model for the etiology of agoraphobia; suggests the condition is driven by negative thoughts about the consequences of having a panic attack in public.

female orgasmic disorder. A recurrent and persistent delay or absence of orgasm in a woman during sexual activity adequate in focus, intensity, and duration; in many instances the woman may experience considerable sexual excitement.

female sexual arousal disorder. Formerly called frigidity, the inability of a female to reach or maintain the lubrication–swelling stage of sexual excitement or to enjoy a subjective sense of pleasure or excitement during sexual activity.

fetal alcohol syndrome (FAS). Retarded growth of the developing fetus and infant involving cranial, facial, and limb anomalies as well as mental retardation; caused by heavy consumption of alcohol by the mother during pregnancy.

fetishism. Reliance on an inanimate object for sexual arousal.

five-factor model. A personality theory that isolates five major dimensions of personality: neuroticism, extraversion, openness to experience, agreeableness, and conscientiousness.

fixation. In psychoanalytic theory, the arrest of psychosexual development at a particular stage through too much or too little gratification at that stage.

flashback. An unpredictable recurrence of experiences from an earlier drug high.

flat affect. A negative symptom of schizophrenia that involves a lack of outward expression of emotion.

flight of ideas. A symptom of mania that involves a rapid shift in conversation from one subject to another with only superficial associative connections.

forced rape. The legal term for rape, forced sexual intercourse, or other (especially) penetrative sexual activity with another person. Compare *statutory rape*.

fragile X syndrome. Malformation (or even breakage) of the X chromosome, associated with moderate mental retardation; symptoms include large, underdeveloped ears; a long, thin face; a broad nasal root; enlarged testicles in males; and, in many cases, attention deficits and hyperactivity.

free association. A key psychoanalytic procedure in which the analysand is encouraged to give free rein to his or her thoughts and feelings, verbalizing whatever comes into the mind without monitoring its content. The assumption is that over time, repressed material will come forth for examination by both analysand and psychoanalyst.

frontal lobe. The anterior portion of each cerebral hemisphere, in front of the central sulcus; active in reasoning and other higher mental processes.

frontal-subcortical dementias. Dementias that involve impairment of both cognitive and motor functions; include Huntington's chorea, Parkinson's disease, normal pressure hydrocephalus, and vascular dementia.

frontotemporal dementia (FTD). Dementia that begins typically in the mid to late fifties, characterized by deficits in executive functions such as planning, problem solving, and goal-directed behavior as well as recognition and comprehension of emotions in others. Compare *Alzheimer's disease*.

frotteurism. The sexually oriented touching of an unsuspecting person, typically in public places that provide an easy means of escape.

functional magnetic resonance imaging (fMRI). Modification of magnetic resonance imaging (MRI) that allows researchers to take pictures of the brain so quickly that metabolic changes can be measured, resulting in a picture of the brain at work rather than of its structure alone.

functional social support. The quality of a person's relationships, for example, a good versus a distressed marriage. Compare *structural social support*.

G-proteins. Guanine nucleotide-binding proteins that serve to modulate activity within the postsynaptic cell, are implicated in mania and depression, and are possibly the intracellular target of lithium.

gamma-aminobutyric acid (GABA). Inhibitory neurotransmitter that may be involved in the anxiety disorders.

gender identity. The ingrained sense a person has of being either a man or a woman.

gender identity disorder. Adult disorder in which there is an incongruence between anatomic sex and self-identified gender that causes distress for the person.

gene. The smallest portion of DNA within a chromosome that functions as a piece of functional hereditary information.

gene expression. The switching on and off of the reading (transcription and translation) of genes into their products (usually proteins) and thus their associated phenotypes.

gene–environment interaction. The influence of genetics on an individual's sensitivity or reaction to an environmental event. Compare *reciprocal gene–environment interaction*.

general adaptation syndrome (GAS). Hans Selye's model to describe the biological reaction of an organism to sustained and unrelenting stress; the several stages culminate in death, in extreme circumstances.

general paresis. Infection of the central nervous system by the spirochete *Treponema pallidum*, which destroys brain tissue; marked by eye disturbances, tremors, and disordered speech as well as severe intellectual deterioration and psychotic symptoms.

generalized anxiety disorder (GAD). Disorder characterized by anxiety so chronic, persistent, and pervasive that it seems free-floating. The individual is jittery and strained, distractible, and worried that something bad is about to happen. A pounding heart, fast pulse and breathing, sweating, flushing, muscle aches, a lump in the throat, and an upset gastrointestinal tract are some of the bodily indications.

genetic marker. A DNA polymorphism linked to a gene critical to the inheritance of a particular form of psychopathology. See *linkage analysis*.

genetic paradigm. Since the early twentieth century, the approach to human behavior that focuses on both heritability of traits and complex interactions between genes and environment.

genital stage. In psychoanalytic theory, the final psychosexual stage, reached in adulthood, in which heterosexual interests predominate.

genotype. An individual's unobservable, genetic constitution, that is, the totality of genes present in the cells of an individual; often applied to the genes contributing to a single trait. Compare *phenotype*.

Gestalt therapy. A humanistic therapy, developed by Fritz Perls, that encourages clients to satisfy emerging needs so that their innate goodness can be expressed, to increase their awareness of unacknowledged feelings, and to reclaim parts of their personality that have been denied or disowned.

grandiose delusions. Found in paranoid schizophrenia, delusional disorder, and mania, an exaggerated sense of one's importance, power, knowledge, or identity. See also *delusions*.

gray matter. The neural tissue—made up largely of nerve cell bodies—that constitutes the cortex covering the cerebral hemisphere, the nuclei in lower brain areas, columns of the spinal cord, and the ganglia of the autonomic nervous system. Compare *white matter*.

guilty but mentally ill (GBMI). Insanity plea in which a mentally ill person can be held morally and legally responsible for a crime but can then, in theory, be sent to a prison hospital or other suitable facility for psychiatric treatment rather than to a regular prison for punishment. In reality, however, people judged GBMI are usually put in the general prison population, where they may or may not receive treatment. Compare *not guilty by reason of insanity*.

hallucinations. Perceptions in any sensory modality without relevant and adequate external stimuli.

hallucinogen. A drug or chemical, such as LSD, psilocybin, or mescaline, whose effects include hallucinations; often called a psychedelic.

harmful dysfunction. Proposed definition of mental disorder that contains both a value judgment (harmful) and a putatively objective scientific component (dysfunction).

hashish. The dried resin of the cannabis plant, stronger in its effects than the dried leaves and stems that constitute marijuana.

health psychology. A branch of psychology dealing with the role of psychological factors in health and illness. See also *behavioral medicine*.

heritability. The extent to which variability in a particular behavior/disorder within a population can be attributed to genetic factors.

heroin. An extremely addictive narcotic drug derived from morphine.

high-risk method. A research technique involving the intensive examination of people, such as the offspring of people with schizophrenia, who have a high probability of later developing a disorder.

hippocampus. In the subcortical region of the brain, the long, tubelike structure that stretches from the septal area into the temporal lobe.

histrionic personality disorder. Personality disorder defined by overly dramatic behavior, emotional excess, and sexually provocative behavior.

hopelessness theory. Cognitive theory of depression that began with learned helplessness theory, was modified to incorporate attributions, and has been modified again to emphasize hopelessness—an expectation that desirable outcomes will not occur and that no available responses can change the situation.

HPA axis. The neuroendocrine connections among hypothalamus, pituitary gland, and adrenal cortex, central to the body's response to stress.

humanistic therapy. An insight therapy that emphasizes freedom of choice, growth of human potential, the joys of being a human being, and the importance of the patient's phenomenology; sometimes called an experiential therapy.

hydrocodone. An opiate combined with other drugs such as acetaminophen to produce prescription pain medications, including the commonly abused drug Vicodin. See also *oxycodone*.

hypnosis. A trancelike state or behavior resembling sleep, induced by suggestion, characterized primarily by increased suggestibility.

hypoactive sexual desire disorder. Absence of or deficiency in sexual fantasies and urges. Compare *sexual aversion disorder*.

hypochondriasis. A somatoform disorder in which the person, misinterpreting rather ordinary physical sensations, is preoccupied with fears of having a serious disease.

hypomania. An extremely happy or irritable mood accompanied by symptoms like increased energy and decreased need for sleep, but without the significant functional impairment associated with mania.

hypothalamus. In the subcortical region of the brain, the structure that regulates many visceral processes, including metabolism, temperature, perspiration, blood pressure, sleeping, and appetite.

hypothesis. Specific expectation or prediction about what should occur or be found if a theory is true or valid.

id. In psychoanalytic theory, that part of the personality present at birth, comprising all the energy of the psyche and expressed as biological urges that strive continually for gratification.

ideas of reference. Delusional thinking that reads personal significance into seemingly trivial remarks or activities of others and completely unrelated events.

imaginal exposure. Treatment for anxiety disorders that involves visualizing feared scenes for extended periods of time. Frequently used in the treatment of posttraumatic stress disorder when in vivo exposure to the initial trauma cannot be conducted.

implicit memory. Memory that underlies behavior but is based on experiences that cannot be consciously recalled; typically not compromised in cases of dissociative amnesia. Compare *explicit memory*.

in absentia. Literally, "in one's absence." Courts are concerned that a person be able to participate personally and meaningfully in his or her own trial and not be tried in absentia because of a distracting mental disorder.

in vivo. As applied in psychology, taking place in a real-life situation.

inappropriate affect. Emotional responses that are out of context, such as laughter when hearing sad news.

incest. Sexual relations between close relatives, most often between daughter and father or between brother and sister.

incidence. In epidemiological studies of a particular disorder, the rate at which new cases occur in a given place at a given time. Compare *prevalence*.

independent variable. In a psychological experiment, the factor, experience, or treatment that is under the control of the experimenter and that is expected to have an effect on participants as assessed by changes in the dependent variable.

index case (proband). The person who in a genetic investigation bears the diagnosis or trait in which the investigator is interested.

individual psychology. A variation of Freud's psychoanalysis introduced by Alfred Adler, focusing less on biological drives and more on such factors as people's conscious beliefs and goals for self-betterment.

informed consent. The agreement of a person to serve as a research participant or to enter therapy after being told the possible outcomes, both benefits and risks.

insanity defense. The legal argument that a defendant should not be held responsible for an illegal act if the conduct is attributable to mental illness. See *not guilty by reason of insanity* and *guilty but mentally ill*.

intelligence quotient (IQ). A standardized measure indicating how far an individual's raw score on an intelligence test is from the average raw score of his or her chronological age group.

intelligence test. A standardized means of assessing a person's current mental ability, for example, the Stanford–Binet test or the Wechsler Adult Intelligence Scale.

interleukin-6 (IL-6). A proinflammatory cytokine; elevated levels can result from stress as well as infection and have been linked to numerous diseases in older adults.

internal consistency reliability. See *reliability*.

internal validity. See *validity*.

internalizing disorders. Domain of childhood disorders characterized by inward-focused experiences and behaviors, such as depression, social withdrawal, and anxiety; the category includes childhood anxiety and mood disorders. Compare *externalizing disorders*.

interoceptive conditioning. Classical conditioning of panic attacks in response to internal bodily sensations of arousal (as opposed to the external situations that trigger anxiety).

interpersonal psychotherapy (IPT). A short-term, here-and-now focused psychological treatment initially developed for depression and influenced by the psychodynamic emphasis on relationships.

interpretation. In psychoanalysis, a key procedure in which the psychoanalyst points out to the analysand where resistance exists and what certain dreams and verbalizations reveal about impulses repressed in the unconscious; more generally, any statement by a therapist that construes the client's problem in a new way.

interrater reliability. See *reliability*.

irresistible impulse. The term used in an 1834 Ohio court ruling on criminal responsibility which determined that an insanity defense can be established by proving that the accused had an uncontrollable urge to perform the act.

joint attention. Interactions between two people require paying attention to each other, whether speaking or communicating emotion nonverbally. This is impaired in children with autism.

la belle indifférence. The blasé attitude people with conversion disorder have toward their symptoms.

latency period. In psychoanalytic theory, the years between ages 6 and 12, during which id impulses play a minor role in motivation.

law of effect. A principle of learning that holds that behavior is acquired by virtue of its consequences.

learned helplessness theory. The theory of depression etiology that individuals, through unpleasant experiences and traumas against which their efforts were ineffective, acquire passivity and a sense of being unable to act and to control their lives.

learning disabilities. General term for learning disorders, communication disorders, and motor skills disorder.

learning disorders. A set of developmental disorders encompassing dyslexia, mathematics disorder, and disorder of written expression; characterized by failure to develop in a specific academic area to the degree expected by the child's intellectual level.

least restrictive alternative. The legal principle according to which a hospitalized patient must be treated in a setting that imposes as few restrictions as possible on his or her freedom.

libido. Freudian term for the life-integrating instinct or force of the id; sometimes equated with sexual drive.

linkage analysis. A molecular genetic technique wherein occurrence of a disorder in a family is evaluated in parallel with inheritance of a known genetic (DNA) marker.

lithium. A drug useful in treating both mania and depression in bipolar disorder.

locus ceruleus. The brain region in the fear circuit that is especially important in panic disorder; the major source in the brain of norepinephrine, which helps trigger sympathetic nervous system activity.

longitudinal design. Investigation that collects information on the same individuals repeatedly over time, perhaps over many years, in an effort to determine how phenomena change. Compare *cross-sectional design*.

loose associations (derailment). In schizophrenia, an aspect of disorganized thinking wherein the patient has difficulty sticking to one topic and drifts off on a train of associations evoked by an idea from the past.

LSD. *d*-lysergic acid diethylamide, a drug synthesized in 1938 and discovered by accident to be a hallucinogen in 1943.

magnetic resonance imaging (MRI). A technique for measuring the structure (or, in the case of functional magnetic resonance imaging, the activity) of the living brain. The person is placed inside a large circular magnet that causes hydrogen atoms to move; the return of the atoms to their original positions when the current to the magnet is turned off is translated by a computer into pictures of brain tissue.

major depressive disorder (MDD). A disorder of individuals who have experienced episodes of depression but not of mania. Depression episodes are marked by sadness or loss of pleasure, accompanied by symptoms such as feelings of worthlessness and guilt, withdrawal from others, loss of sleep, appetite, sexual desire, and either lethargy or agitation.

male erectile disorder. A recurrent and persistent inability to attain or maintain an erection until completion of sexual activity.

male orgasmic disorder. A recurrent and persistent delay or absence of ejaculation after an adequate phase of sexual excitement.

malingering. Faking a physical or psychological incapacity in order to avoid a responsibility or gain an end, where the goal is readily recognized from the individual's circumstances distinct from conversion disorder, in which the incapacity is assumed to be beyond voluntary control.

mania. Intense elation or irritability, accompanied by symptoms such as excessive talkativeness, rapid thoughts, distractibility, grandiose plans, heightened activity, and insensitivity to the negative consequences of actions.

marriage and family therapist. A mental health professional who specializes in treating couples and families and how these relationships impact mental health. Training can be at the masters or Ph.D. level, and some M.S.W. programs offer training in marriage and family therapy.

marijuana. A drug derived from the dried and ground leaves and stems of the female hemp plant *Cannabis sativa*.

mathematics disorder. Learning disorder characterized by difficulty recalling arithmetic facts, counting objects, and aligning numbers in columns.

MDA. Methylenedioxyamphetamine, a chemical component of Ecstasy; first synthesized in 1910 but not broadly known as a psychedelic until the 1960s.

MDMA. Methylenedioxymethamphetamine, a chemical component of Ecstasy; initially used as an appetite suppressant for World War 1 soldiers and derived from precursors found in nutmeg, dill, saffron, and sassafras.

melancholic. Subtype of major depressive disorder in which the individual is unable to feel better even momentarily when something good happens, regularly feels worse in the morning and awakens early, and suffers a deepening of other symptoms of depression.

mental disorder. The DSM-IV-TR defines mental disorder as a clinically significant behavioral or psychological syndrome or patterns. The definition includes a number of key features, including distress, disability or impaired functioning, violation of social norms, and dysfunction.

mental retardation. Subnormal intellectual functioning associated with impairment in adaptive behavior and identified at an early age.

mescaline. A hallucinogen and alkaloid that is the active ingredient of peyote.

mesmerize. The first term for *hypnotize*, after Franz Anton Mesmer, an Austrian physician who in the late eighteenth century treated and cured hysterical or conversion disorders with what he considered the animal magnetism emanating from his body and permeating the universe.

meta-analysis. A quantitative method of analyzing the results of a set of studies on a topic, by standardizing the results.

metabolic syndrome (of CHD). Combination of particular risk factors—abdominal obesity, insulin resistance, high blood pressure, low HDL cholesterol, and heightened inflammation—disposing to onset of coronary heart disease.

metabolite. A chemical breakdown product of an endogenous molecule, such as a neurotransmitter, or of an exogenous drug; used to gauge current or recent level of its precursor.

metacognition. The knowledge people have about the way they know and learn about their world, for example, recognizing the usefulness of a map in finding their way in a new city.

methadone. A synthetic addictive heroin substitute for treating those addicted to heroin that eliminates its effects and the cravings.

methamphetamine. An amphetamine derivative whose abuse skyrocketed in the 1990s.

mindfulness-based cognitive therapy (MBCT). Recent adaptation of cognitive therapy/restructuring that focuses on relapse prevention after successful treatment for recurrent episodes of major depression; aims to "decenter" the person's perspective in order to break the cycle between sadness and thinking patterns.

Minnesota Multiphasic Personality Inventory (MMPI). A lengthy personality inventory that identifies individuals with states such as anxiety, depression, masculinity–femininity, and paranoia, through their true–false replies to groups of statements.

mixed episodes. Bipolar episodes characterized by severe symptoms of both mania and depression within the same week.

M'Naghten rule. An 1843 British court decision stating that an insanity defense can be established by proving that the defendant did not know what he or she was doing or did not realize that it was wrong.

modeling. Learning by observing and imitating the behavior of others, or teaching by demonstrating and providing opportunities for imitation.

molecular genetics. Studies that seek to determine the components of a trait that are heritable by identifying relevant genes and their functions.

monoamine oxidase (MAO) inhibitors. A group of antidepressant drugs that prevent the enzyme monoamine oxidase from deactivating catecholamines and indolamines.

monozygotic (MZ) twins. Genetically identical twins who have developed from a single fertilized egg. Compare *dizygotic twins*.

mood disorders. Disorders, such as depressive disorders or mania, in which there are disabling disturbances in emotion.

moral treatment. A therapeutic regimen, introduced by Philippe Pinel during the French Revolution, whereby mentally ill patients were released from their restraints and were treated with compassion and dignity rather than with contempt and denigration.

morphine. An addictive narcotic alkaloid extracted from opium, used primarily as an analgesic and as a sedative.

motor skills disorder. A learning disability characterized by marked impairment in the development of motor coordination that is not accounted for by a physical disorder such as cerebral palsy.

Mowrer's two-factor model. Mowrer's theory of avoidance learning according to which (1) fear is attached to a neutral stimulus by pairing it with a noxious unconditioned stimulus, and (2) a person learns to escape the fear elicited by the conditioned stimulus, thereby avoiding the unconditioned stimulus.

multiaxial classification system. Classification having several dimensions, all of which are employed in categorizing; DSM-IV-TR is an example.

multisystemic treatment (MST). Treatment for serious juvenile offenders that involves delivering intensive and comprehensive therapy services in the community, targeting the adolescent, the family, the school, and, in some cases, the peer group, in ecologically valid settings and using varied techniques.

myocardial infarction. Heart attack. See *coronary heart disease*.

narcissistic personality disorder. Personality disorder defined by extreme selfishness and self-centeredness; a grandiose view of one's uniqueness, achievements, and talents; an insatiable craving for admiration and approval from others; willingness to exploit others to achieve goals; and expectation of much more from others than one is willing to give in return.

negative affect. Constellation of negative emotions that is elevated in both anxiety and depression.

negative reinforcement. The strengthening of a tendency to exhibit desired behavior by rewarding responses in that situation with the removal of an aversive stimulus.

negative symptoms. Behavioral deficits in schizophrenia, which include flat affect, anhedonia, asociality, alogia, and avolition. Compare *positive symptoms*.

negative triad. In Beck's theory of depression, a person's negative views of the self, the world, and the future, in a reciprocal causal relationship with pessimistic assumptions (schemata) and cognitive biases such as selective abstraction.

nerve impulse. A wave of depolarization that propagates along the neuron and causes the release of neurotransmitter; action potential.

neurofibrillary tangles. Abnormal protein filaments present in the cell bodies of brain cells in patients with Alzheimer's disease.

neurologist. A physician who specializes in medical diseases that affect the nervous system, such as muscular dystrophy, cerebral palsy, or Alzheimer's disease.

neuron. A single nerve cell.

neuropsychological tests. Psychological tests, such as the Luria–Nebraska, that can detect impairment in different parts of the brain.

neuropsychologist. A psychologist who studies how brain dysfunction affects cognition, emotion, and behavior.

neuroscience paradigm. A broad theoretical view that holds that mental disorders are caused in part by some aberrant process directed by the brain.

neuroses. Old term for a large group of nonpsychotic disorders characterized by unrealistic anxiety, depression, and other associated problems. See *anxiety disorders*.

neuroticism. The tendency to react to events with greater-than-average negative affect; a strong predictor of onset of anxiety disorders and depression.

neurotransmitters. Chemical substances important in transferring a nerve impulse from one neuron to another; for example, serotonin and norepinephrine.

nicotine. The principal alkaloid of tobacco (an addicting agent).

nitrous oxide. A gas that, when inhaled, produces euphoria and sometimes giddiness.

nonshared environment. Factors distinct among family members, such as relationships with friends or specific experiences unique to a person. Compare *shared environment*.

nonverbal memories. Memories based on connections between sensory stimuli and external events.

norepinephrine. A catecholamine neurotransmitter of the central nervous system, disturbances in the tracts of which apparently figure in depression and mania. It is also a sympathetic nervous system neurotransmitter, a hormone released in addition to epinephrine and similar in action, and a strong vasoconstrictor.

not guilty by reason of insanity (NGRI). Insanity plea that specifies an individual is not to be held legally responsible for the crime because the person had a mental illness at the time of the crime. Different states and federal law have different standards for defining mental illness and what must be demonstrated by the defense.

In most cases, the defense must show that because of the mental illness, the accused person could not conform his or her behavior to the law and did not know right from wrong when the crime was committed. Compare *guilty but mentally ill.*

obese. Currently defined as exhibiting a body mass index (BMI) of greater than 30.

Object relations theory. Variant of psychoanalytic theory that focuses on the way children internalize (*introject*) images of the people who are important to them (e.g., their parents), such that these internalized images (*object representations*) become part of the ego and influence how the person reacts to the world.

obsession. An intrusive and recurring thought that seems irrational and uncontrollable to the person experiencing it. Compare *compulsion.*

obsessive-compulsive disorder (OCD). An anxiety disorder in which the mind is flooded with persistent and uncontrollable thoughts or the individual is compelled to repeat certain acts again and again, causing significant distress and interference with everyday functioning.

obsessive-compulsive personality disorder. Personality disorder defined by inordinate difficulty making decisions, hyperconcern with details and efficiency, and poor relations with others due to demands that things be done just so, as well as the person's unduly conventional, serious, formal, and stingy emotions.

occipital lobe. The posterior portion of each cerebral hemisphere, situated behind the parietal lobe and above the temporal lobes; responsible for reception and analysis of visual information and for some visual memory.

operant conditioning. The acquisition or elimination of a response as a function of the environmental contingencies of reinforcement and punishment. Compare *classical conditioning.*

opiates. A group of addictive sedatives that in moderate doses relieve pain and induce sleep.

opium. One of the opiates, the dried, milky juice obtained from the immature fruit of the opium poppy; an addictive narcotic that produces euphoria and drowsiness while reducing pain.

oppositional defiant disorder. An externalizing disorder of children marked by high levels of disobedience to authority but lacking the extremes of conduct disorder.

oral stage. In psychoanalytic theory, the first psychosexual stage, which extends into the second year; during it the mouth is the principal erogenous zone.

orbitofrontal cortex. The portion of the frontal lobe located just above the eyes; one of three closely related brain regions that are unusually active in individuals with obsessive-compulsive disorder.

orgasm phase. The third stage of the sexual response cycle, characterized by a peak of sexual pleasure, generally including ejaculation in men and contraction of the outer vaginal walls in women.

outcome research. Research on the efficacy of psychotherapy. Compare *process research.*

outpatient commitment. A form of civil commitment consistent with the principle of least restrictive alternative, whereby the person is not hospitalized but rather is allowed to remain free in the community under legal/medical constraints that ensure, for example, that prescribed medication is taken and other measures are observed.

oxycodone. An opiate combined with other drugs to produce prescription pain medications, including the commonly abused drug OxyContin. See also *hydrocodone.*

pain disorder. A somatoform disorder in which the person complains of severe and prolonged pain that is not fully explainable by organic pathology and is thus assumed to be caused or intensified by psychological factors.

panic attack. A sudden attack of intense apprehension, terror, and impending doom, accompanied by symptoms such as labored breathing, nausea, chest pain, feelings of choking and smothering, heart palpitations, dizziness, sweating, and trembling.

panic control therapy (PCT). A cognitive behavior treatment, based on the tendency of individuals with panic disorder to overreact to bodily stimuli, in which sensations are induced physically and coped with under safe conditions.

panic disorder. An anxiety disorder in which the individual has sudden, inexplicable, and frequent panic attacks; in DSM-IV-TR, diagnosed as with or without agoraphobia. See *panic attack.*

paradigm. A set of basic assumptions that outlines the universe of scientific inquiry, specifying both the concepts regarded as legitimate and the methods to be used in collecting and interpreting data.

paranoia. The general term for delusions of persecution, of grandiosity, or both; found in several pathological conditions, delusional disorders, paranoid schizophrenia, and paranoid personality disorder but can also be produced by large doses of certain drugs, such as cocaine or alcohol.

paranoid personality disorder. Personality disorder defined by expectation of mistreatment at the hands of others, suspicion, secretiveness, jealousy, argumentativeness, unwillingness to accept blame, and cold and unemotional affect.

paranoid schizophrenia. A type of schizophrenia in which the patient has numerous systematized delusions as well as hallucinations and ideas of reference. He or she may also be agitated, angry, and argumentative.

paraphilias. Sexual attraction to unusual objects and sexual activities unusual in nature.

parasympathetic nervous system. The division of the autonomic nervous system that is involved with maintenance; controls many of the internal organs and is active primarily when the organism is not aroused. Compare *sympathetic nervous system.*

parent management training (PMT). Behavioral program in which parents are taught to modify their responses to their children so that prosocial rather than antisocial behavior is consistently rewarded.

parietal lobe. The middle division of each cerebral hemisphere, situated behind the central sulcus and above the lateral sulcus; the receiving center for sensations of the skin and of bodily positions.

PCP. Phencyclidine, also known by street names such as angel dust, PeaCE Pill, and zombie; this very powerful and hazardous drug causes profound disorientation, agitated and often violent behavior, and even seizures, coma, and death.

pedophilia. A paraphilia defined by a marked preference for obtaining sexual gratification through contact with people defined legally as underage.

penile plethysmograph. A device for detecting blood flow and thus for recording changes in the size of the penis.

personality disorders. A group of disorders, listed separately on Axis II of the DSM-IV-TR, involving longstanding, inflexible, and maladaptive personality traits that impair social and occupational functioning.

personality inventory. A self-report questionnaire comprised of statements assessing habitual behavioral and affective tendencies.

pervasive developmental disorders. Severe childhood conditions, encompassing autistic disorder, Rett's disorder, childhood disintegrative disorder, and Asperger's disorder, marked by profound disturbances in social relations and oddities in behavior.

PET scan. Computer-generated picture of the living brain, created by analysis of emissions from radioactive isotopes injected into the bloodstream.

phallic stage. In psychoanalytic theory, the third psychosexual stage, extending from ages 3 to 5 or 6, during which maximal gratification is obtained from genital stimulation.

phenotype. The totality of physical characteristics and behavioral traits of an individual, or a particular trait exhibited by an individual; the product of interactions between genetics and the environment over the course of development. Compare *genotype.*

phenylketonuria (PKU). A genetic deficiency in a liver enzyme, phenylalanine hydroxylase, that causes severe mental retardation unless phenylalanine can be largely restricted from the diet.

phobia. An anxiety disorder in which there is intense fear and avoidance of specific objects and situations, recognized as irrational by the individual.

phonological disorder. Communication disorder in childhood in which some words sound like baby talk because the person is not able to make certain speech sounds.

placebo. Any inactive therapy or chemical agent, or any attribute or component of such a therapy or chemical, that affects a person's behavior for reasons related to his or her expectation of change.

placebo effect. The action of a drug or psychological treatment that is not attributable to any specific operations of the agent. For example, a tranquilizer can reduce anxiety both because of its special biochemical action and because the recipient expects relief. See *placebo.*

plaques. Small, round areas composed of remnants of lost neurons and beta-amyloid, a waxy protein deposit; present in the brains of patients with Alzheimer's disease.

pleasure principle. In psychoanalytic theory, the demanding manner by which the id operates, seeking immediate gratification of its needs.

polydrug abuse. The misuse of more than one drug at a time, such as drinking heavily and taking cocaine.

polygenic. As applied to psychopathology or any other trait, caused by multiple genes contributing their effects, typically during multiple stages of development.

polymorphism. Any specific difference in DNA sequence that exists within a population.

positive affect. A constellation of particular positive emotions, such as excitement, that also reflect a general engagement with the environment; dampened in depression but not in anxiety.

positive reinforcement. The strengthening of a tendency to exhibit desired behavior by rewarding responses in that situation with a desired reward.

positive symptoms. Behavioral excesses in schizophrenia, such as hallucinations and delusions. Compare *negative symptoms.*

postpartum onset. Onset within 4 weeks postpartum, characterizing a subtype of episodes of major depressive disorder or mania.

posttraumatic model (of DID). Etiological model of dissociative identity disorder that assumes the condition begins in childhood as a result of severe physical or sexual abuse. Compare *sociocognitive model*.

posttraumatic stress disorder (PTSD). An anxiety disorder in which a particularly stressful event, such as military combat, rape, or a natural disaster, brings in its aftermath intrusive reexperiencing of the trauma, a numbing of responsiveness to the outside world, estrangement from others, and a tendency to be easily startled, as well as nightmares, recurrent dreams, and otherwise disturbed sleep.

predictive validity. See *validity*.

predisposition. An inclination or diathesis to respond in a certain way, either inborn or acquired; in abnormal psychology, a factor that lowers the ability to withstand stress and inclines the individual toward pathology.

prefrontal cortex. The region of the frontal lobe of the brain that helps maintain an image of threats and rewards faced, as well as maintain focus and plan relevant to those threats and rewards.

premature ejaculation. Inability of the male to inhibit his orgasm long enough for mutually satisfying sexual relations.

prepared learning. In classical conditioning theory, a biological predisposition to associate particular stimuli readily with the unconditioned stimulus.

prevalence. In epidemiological studies of a disorder, the percentage of a population that has the disorder at a given time. Compare *incidence*.

privileged communication. The communication between parties in a confidential relationship that is protected by statute, which a spouse, doctor, lawyer, pastor, psychologist, or psychiatrist thus cannot be forced to disclose, except under unusual circumstances.

process research. Research on the mechanisms by which a therapy may bring improvement. Compare *outcome research*.

prognosis. A prediction of the likely course and outcome of an illness. Compare *diagnosis*.

projective hypothesis. The notion that standard but highly unstructured stimuli, as found in the Rorschach assessment's series of inkblots, are necessary to bypass defenses in order to reveal unconscious motives and conflicts.

projective test. A psychological assessment device, such as the Rorschach series of inkblots, employing a set of standard but vague stimuli, on the assumption that unstructured material will allow unconscious motivations and fears to be uncovered.

pronoun reversal. A speech problem in which the child refers to himself or herself as "he," "she," or "you" and uses "I" or "me" in referring to others; often found in the speech of children with autistic disorder.

pruning. In neural development, the selective loss of synaptic connections, especially in the fine-tuning of brain regions devoted to sensory processing.

psilocybin. A psychedelic drug extracted from the mushroom *Psilocybe mexicana*.

psyche. In psychoanalytic theory, the totality of the id, ego, and superego, including both conscious and unconscious components.

psychiatric nurse. A nurse, typically with a bachelor's degree, who receives specialized training in mental illness. A nurse practitioner may prescribe psychiatric medications.

psychiatrist. A physician (M.D.) who has taken specialized postdoctoral training, called a residency, in the diagnosis, treatment, and prevention of mental disorders.

psychoactive medications. Prescribed chemical compounds—for example, Prozac—having a psychological effect that alters mood or thought process.

psychoanalysis. Primarily the therapy procedures pioneered by Freud, entailing free association, dream analysis, and working through the transference neurosis. More recently the term has come to encompass the numerous variations on basic Freudian therapy.

psychodynamic paradigm. General view based on psychodynamic and psychoanalytic theory.

psychoanalytic theory. Theory originating with Freud that psychopathology results from unconscious conflicts in the individual.

psychoeducational approaches. Especially with bipolar disorder and schizophrenia, the component of treatment that helps people learn about symptoms, expected time course, triggers for symptoms, and treatment strategies.

psychological factors affecting medical condition. A diagnosis in DSM-IV-TR that a physical illness is caused in part or exacerbated by psychological stress.

psychological tests. Standardized procedures designed to measure performance on a particular task or to assess personality.

psychoneuroimmunology. Field that studies how psychological factors (especially stressors) impact the immune system (adversely).

psychopathology. The field concerned with the nature and development of mental disorders.

psychopathy. A personality syndrome related to antisocial personality disorder but defined by an absence of emotion, impulsivity, manipulativeness, and irresponsibility.

psychophysiology. The discipline concerned with the bodily changes that accompany psychological events.

psychotherapy. A primarily verbal means of helping troubled individuals change their thoughts, feelings, and behavior to reduce distress and to achieve greater life satisfaction.

psychotic features. Delusions or hallucinations characterizing a subtype of episodes of major depressive disorder or mania. Also used to refer to positive symptoms of schizophrenia.

random assignment. A method of assigning people to groups by chance (e.g., using a flip of a coin). The procedure helps to ensure that groups are comparable before the experimental manipulation begins.

randomized controlled trials (RCTs). Studies in which clients are randomly assigned to receive either active treatment or a comparison (a placebo condition involving no treatment, or else an active-treatment control group that receives another treatment); experimental treatment studies, where the independent variable is the treatment type and the dependent variable is client outcome.

rapid cycling. Term applied to bipolar disorders if the person has experienced at least four episodes within the past year.

rational-emotive behavior therapy (REBT). A cognitive-restructuring behavior therapy introduced by Albert Ellis and based on the assumption that much disordered behavior is rooted in absolutistic, unrealistic demands and goals, such as, "I must be universally loved."

reactivity. The phenomenon wherein behavior changes because it is being observed.

reading disorder. See *dyslexia*.

reality principle. In psychoanalytic theory, the manner in which the ego delays gratification and otherwise deals with the environment in a planned, rational fashion.

receptor. A protein embedded in a neural cell membrane that interacts with one or more neurotransmitters. Nonneural receptor proteins include hormone receptors.

reciprocal gene–environment interaction. The genetic predisposition for an individual to seek out certain environments that increase the risk of developing a particular disorder. Compare *gene–environment interaction*.

reliability. The extent to which a test, measurement, or classification system produces the same scientific observation each time it is applied. Reliability types include test–retest, the relationship between the scores that a person achieves when he or she takes the same test twice; interrater, the relationship between the judgments that at least two raters make independently about a phenomenon; split-half, the relationship between two halves of an assessment instrument that have been determined to be equivalent; alternate-form, the relationship between scores achieved by people when they complete two versions of a test that are judged to be equivalent; and internal consistency, the degree to which different items of an assessment are related to one another.

repression. A defense mechanism whereby impulses and thoughts unacceptable to the ego are pushed into the unconscious.

residual schizophrenia. Diagnosis given to patients who have had an episode of schizophrenia but who presently show no psychotic symptoms, though signs of the disorder do exist.

resolution phase. The fourth and final stage of the sexual response cycle, characterized by an abatement of muscle tension, relaxation, and a sense of well-being.

Rett's disorder. A very rare pervasive developmental disorder found only in girls, with onset in the first or second year of life; symptoms include decelerated head growth, lost ability to use hands purposefully, uncoordinated walking, poor speech production and comprehension, and poor interpersonal relations. The child may improve later in life but usually will remain severely or profoundly mentally retarded.

reuptake. Cellular process by which released neurotransmitters are taken back into the presynaptic cell, terminating their present postsynaptic effect but making them available for subsequent modulation of nerve impulse transmission.

reversal (ABAB) design. An experimental design in which behavior is measured during a baseline period (A), during a period when a treatment is introduced (B), during the reinstatement of the conditions that prevailed in the baseline period (A), and finally during a reintroduction of the treatment (B); commonly used in operant research to isolate cause–effect relationships.

reward system. System of brain structures involved in the motivation to pursue rewards. Believed to be involved in depression, mania, schizophrenia, and substance dependence.

risk factor. A condition or variable that increases the likelihood of developing a disorder.

Rorschach Inkblot Test. A projective test in which the examinee is instructed to interpret a series of 10 inkblots reproduced on cards.

safety behaviors. Behaviors used to avoid experiencing anxiety in feared situations, such as the tendency of people with social phobia to avoid looking at other people (so as to avoid perceiving negative feedback) or the tendency of people with panic disorder to avoid exercise (so as to avoid somatic arousal that could trigger a panic attack).

schema. A mental structure for organizing information about the world. Pl.: *schemata*.

schizoaffective disorder. Diagnosis applied when a patient has symptoms of both mood disorder and either schizophreniform disorder or schizophrenia.

schizoid personality disorder. Personality disorder defined by emotional aloofness; indifference to the praise, criticism, and feelings of others; maintenance of few, if any, close friendships; and solitary interests.

schizophrenia. A group of psychotic disorders characterized by major disturbances in thought, emotion, and behavior; disordered thinking in which ideas are not logically related; faulty perception and attention; bizarre disturbances in motor activity; flat or inappropriate emotions; reduced tolerance for stress in interpersonal relations and withdrawal from people and reality, often into a fantasy life of delusions and hallucinations. See *schizoaffective disorder*, *schizophreniform disorder*, and *brief psychotic disorder*.

schizophreniform disorder. Diagnosis given to people who have all the symptoms of schizophrenia for more than 2 weeks but less than 6 months. See *brief psychotic disorder*.

schizotypal personality disorder. Personality disorder defined by eccentricity, oddities of thought and perception (magical thinking, illusions, depersonalization, derealization), digressive speech involving overelaborations, and social isolation; under stress, behavior may appear psychotic.

school phobia. An acute, irrational dread of attending school, usually accompanied by somatic complaints; the most common phobia of childhood.

second-generation antipsychotic drugs. Any of several drugs, such as clozapine, used to treat schizophrenia that produce fewer motor side effects than traditional antipsychotics while reducing positive and disorganized symptoms at least as effectively; may, however, be associated with increased and serious side effects of other varieties.

second messengers. Intracellular molecules whose levels are increased by sustained activity of neurotransmitter, for example, receptors, and which affect the resting states of ion channels or regulate gene expression of receptor molecules, thus modulating the cell's sensitivity to neurotransmitter.

secondhand smoke. Also referred to as environmental tobacco smoke (ETS), the smoke from the burning end of a cigarette; contains higher concentrations of ammonia, carbon monoxide, nicotine, and tar than the smoke inhaled by the smoker.

sedatives. Drugs that slow bodily activities, especially those of the central nervous system; used to reduce pain and tension and to induce relaxation and sleep.

selective mortality. The tendency for less healthy individuals to die more quickly, which leads to biased samples in long-term follow-up studies.

selective serotonin reuptake inhibitors (SSRIs). Any of various drugs that inhibit the presynaptic reuptake of the neurotransmitter serotonin, thereby prolonging its effects on postsynaptic neurons.

self-actualization. Fulfilling one's potential as an always growing human being; believed by client-centered therapists to be the core motive of all humans.

self-monitoring. In behavioral assessment, a procedure whereby the individual observes and reports certain aspects of his or her own behavior, thoughts, or emotions.

sensate focus. A term applied to exercises prescribed at the beginning of the Masters and Johnson sex therapy program, in which partners are instructed to fondle each other to give pleasure but to refrain from intercourse, thus reducing anxiety about sexual performance.

separation anxiety disorder. A disorder in which the child feels intense fear and distress when away from someone on whom he or she is very dependent; said to be a significant cause of school phobia.

septal area. In the subcortical region of the brain, the area anterior to the thalamus.

serotonin. A neurotransmitter of the central nervous system whose disturbances apparently figure in depression.

serotonin transporter gene. A particular gene critical to the gene–environment interactions that apparently contribute to the development of depression.

sex-reassignment surgery. An operation removing existing genitalia and constructing a substitute for the genitals of the opposite sex.

sexual aversion disorder. Avoidance of nearly all genital contact with other people. Compare *hypoactive sexual desire disorder*.

sexual dysfunctions. Dysfunctions in which the appetitive or psychophysiological changes of the normal sexual response cycle are inhibited. Compare *hypoactive sexual desire disorder*.

sexual masochism. A marked preference for obtaining or increasing sexual gratification through subjection to pain or humiliation.

sexual orientation. An individual's emotional, romantic, or sexual attraction toward other people that is stable and enduring.

sexual response cycle. The general pattern of sexual physical processes and feelings, made up of four phases: appetitive interest, excitement, orgasm, and resolution.

sexual sadism. A marked preference for obtaining or increasing sexual gratification by inflicting pain or humiliation on another person.

shaping. In operant conditioning, reinforcing responses that are successively closer approximations to the desired behavior.

shared environment. Factors that family members have in common, such as income level, child-rearing practices, and parental marital status and quality. Compare *nonshared environment*.

single-subject experimental design. A design for an experiment conducted with a single subject. Typically, behavior is measured within a baseline condition, then during an experimental or treatment condition, and finally within the baseline condition again.

social phobia. A collection of fears linked to the presence of other people.

social selection theory. An attempt to explain the correlation between social class and schizophrenia by arguing that people with schizophrenia tend to move downward in socioeconomic status. Compare *sociogenic hypothesis*.

social selectivity. The late-life shift in interest away from seeking new social interactions and toward cultivating those few social relationships that matter most, such as with family and close friends.

social worker. A mental health professional who holds a master of social work (M.S.W.) degree.

social skills training. Behavior therapy procedures, such as modeling and behavior rehearsal, for teaching individuals how to meet others, talk to them and maintain eye contact, give and receive criticism, offer and accept compliments, make requests and express feelings, and otherwise improve their relations with other people.

sociocognitive model (of DID). Etiological model of dissociative identity disorder that considers the condition to be the result of learning to enact social roles, though not through conscious deception, but in response to suggestion. Compare *posttraumatic model (of DID)*.

sociogenic hypothesis. An idea that seeks causes in social conditions, for example, that being in a low social class can cause one to become schizophrenic. Compare *social selection theory*.

somatic arousal. Sweaty palms, fast heart rate, and so on; expected to increase in anxiety but not in depression.

somatic nervous system. The division of the nervous system that controls muscles under voluntary control. Compare *autonomic nervous system*.

somatization disorder. A somatoform disorder, once called Briquet's syndrome, in which the person continually seeks medical help for recurrent and multiple physical symptoms that have no discoverable physical cause, despite a complicated medical history that is dramatically presented. Compare *hypochondriasis*.

somatoform disorders. Disorders in which symptoms suggest a physical problem but have no known physiological cause; believed to be linked to psychological conflicts and needs but not voluntarily assumed. See *somatization disorder (Briquet's syndrome)*, *conversion disorder*, *pain disorder*, and *hypochondriasis*.

specific phobia. An unwarranted fear and avoidance of a specific object or circumstance, for example, fear of nonpoisonous snakes or fear of heights.

spectator role. As applied by Masters and Johnson, a pattern of behavior in which the individual's focus on and concern with sexual performance causes him or her to be an observer rather than a participant and thus impedes natural sexual responses.

standardization. The process of constructing a normed assessment procedure that meets the various psychometric criteria for reliability and validity.

statistical significance. A result that has a low probability of having occurred by chance alone and is by convention regarded as important. Compare *clinical significance*.

statutory rape. Sexual intercourse between an adult and someone who is under the age of consent, as fixed by local statute. Compare *forced rape*.

stepped care. The practice of beginning treatment with the least intrusive intervention possible and moving on to more intensive efforts only if necessary.

stigma. The pernicious beliefs and attitudes held by a society, ascribed to groups considered deviant in some manner, such as people with mental illness.

stimulant. A drug, such as cocaine, that increases alertness and motor activity and at the same time reduces fatigue, allowing an individual to remain awake for an extended period of time.

stress. State of an organism subjected to a stressor; can take the form of increased autonomic activity and in the long term can cause breakdown of an organ or development of a mental disorder.

stress management. A range of psychological procedures that help people control and reduce their stress or anxiety.

structural social support. A person's network of social relationships, for example, number of friends. Compare *functional social support*.

structured interview. An interview in which the questions are set out in a prescribed fashion for the interviewer; assists professionals in making diagnostic decisions based on standardized criteria.

stuttering. Communication disorder of childhood marked by frequent and pronounced verbal dysfluencies, such as repetitions of certain sounds.

substance abuse. The use of a drug to such an extent that the person is often intoxicated throughout the day and fails in important obligations and in attempts to abstain, but there is no physiological dependence.

substance dependence. The abuse of a drug sometimes accompanied by a physiological dependence on it, made evident by tolerance and withdrawal symptoms; also called addiction.

substance-related disorders. Disorders in which drugs such as alcohol and cocaine are abused to such an extent that behavior becomes maladaptive; social and occupational functioning are impaired, and control or abstinence becomes impossible. Reliance on the drug may be either psychological, as in substance abuse, or physiological, as in substance dependence (addiction).

subthreshold symptoms. Symptoms of a disorder that are clinically significant but do not meet full diagnostic criteria.

suicide. The intentional taking of one's own life.

suicide prevention centers. Staffed primarily by paraprofessionals who are trained to be empathic and to encourage suicidal callers—assumed to be ambivalent—to consider nondestructive ways of dealing with what is bothering them.

superego. In psychoanalytic theory, the part of the personality that acts as the conscience and reflects society's moral standards as learned from parents and teachers.

sympathetic nervous system. The division of the autonomic nervous system that acts on bodily systems—for example, contracting the blood vessels, reducing activity of the intestines, and increasing the heartbeat—to prepare the organism for exertion, emotional stress, or extreme cold. Compare *parasympathetic nervous system*.

symptom. An observable physiological or psychological manifestation of a disease.

synapse. Small gap between two neurons where the nerve signal passes electrically or chemically from the axon of the first to the dendrites, cell body, or axon of the second.

systematic desensitization. A major behavior therapy procedure that has a fearful person, while deeply relaxed, imagine a series of progressively more fearsome situations, such that fear is dispelled as a response incompatible with relaxation; useful for treating psychological problems in which anxiety is the principal difficulty.

tardive dyskinesia. A muscular disturbance of patients who have taken phenothiazines for a very long time, marked by involuntary motor movements such as lip smacking and chin wagging.

temporal lobe. A large region of each cerebral hemisphere situated below the lateral sulcus and in front of the occipital lobe; contains primary auditory and general association areas.

test–retest reliability. See *reliability*.

thalamus. A major brain relay station consisting of two egg-shaped lobes; receives impulses from all sensory areas except the olfactory and transmits them to the cerebrum for higher processing.

Thematic Apperception Test (TAT). A projective test consisting of black-and-white pictures, each depicting a potentially emotion-laden situation, about each of which the examinee is instructed to make up a story. See also *projective hypothesis*.

theory. A formally stated and coherent set of propositions that explain and logically order a range of phenomena, generating testable predictions or hypotheses.

therapeutic (working) alliance. The collaborative relationship between therapist and patient, in which they share an affective bond and an ability to agree on treatment goals.

third-variable problem. The difficulty in the correlational method of research whereby the relationship between two variables may be attributable to a third factor.

thought suppression. Key feature of obsessive-compulsive disorder; has the paradoxical effect of inducing preoccupation with the object of thought.

time-of-measurement effects. A possible confound in longitudinal studies whereby conditions at a particular point in time can have a specific effect on a variable that is being studied over time.

time-out. An operant-conditioning procedure in which, after bad behavior, the person is temporarily removed from a setting where reinforcers can be obtained and placed in a less desirable setting, for example, in a boring room.

token economy. A behavior therapy procedure, based on operant-conditioning principles, in which hospitalized patients are given scrip rewards, such as poker chips, for socially constructive behavior. The tokens can be exchanged for desirable items and activities such as cigarettes and extra time away from the ward.

tolerance. A physiological process in which greater and greater amounts of an addictive drug are required to produce the same effect. See also *substance dependence*.

transference. The venting of the analysand's emotions, either positive or negative, by treating the psychoanalyst as the symbolic representative of someone important in the past.

transvestic fetishism. The practice of dressing in the clothing of the opposite sex, for the purpose of sexual arousal.

tricyclic antidepressants. A group of antidepressants with molecular structures characterized by three fused rings; interfere with the reuptake of norepinephrine and serotonin.

tryptophan. Amino acid that is the major precursor of serotonin; experimental depletion has found that a lowered serotonin level causes temporary depressive symptoms in people with a personal or family history of depression.

twin method. Research strategy in behavior genetics in which concordance rates of monozygotic and dizygotic twins are compared.

Type A behavior pattern. One of two contrasting psychological patterns revealed through studies seeking the cause of coronary heart disease. Type A people are competitive, rushed, hostile, and overcommitted to their work, and are believed to be at heightened risk for heart disease; Type B people are more relaxed and relatively free of pressure.

unconditional positive regard. According to Rogers, a crucial attitude for the client-centered therapist to adopt toward the client, who needs to feel complete acceptance as a person in order to evaluate the extent to which current behavior contributes to self-actualization.

unconditioned response (UCR). See *classical conditioning*.

unconditioned stimulus (UCS). See *classical conditioning*.

unconscious. A state of unawareness without sensation or thought; in psychoanalytic theory, the part of the personality, in particular the id impulses or energy, of which the ego is unaware.

undifferentiated schizophrenia. Diagnosis for patients whose symptoms either do not fit any listed category of schizophrenia or meet the criteria for more than one subtype.

vaginismus. Painful, spasmodic contractions of the outer third of the vagina, making penetration impossible or extremely difficult.

validity. In research, includes internal, the extent to which results can be confidently attributed to the manipulation of the independent variable, and external, the extent to which results can be generalized to other populations and settings. Validity as applied to psychiatric diagnoses includes concurrent, the extent to which previously undiscovered features are found among patients with the same diagnosis, and predictive, the extent to which predictions can be made about the future behavior of patients with the same diagnosis. Validity as applied to psychological and psychiatric measures includes content validity, the extent to which a measure adequately samples the domain of interest, and criterion, the extent to which a measure is associated in an expected way with some other measure (the criterion). See also *construct validity*.

ventricles. Cavities deep within the brain, filled with cerebrospinal fluid, that connect to the spinal cord.

voyeurism. Marked preference for obtaining sexual gratification by watching others in a state of undress or having sexual relations.

white matter. Neural tissue, particularly of the brain and spinal cord, consisting of tracts or bundles of myelinated (sheathed) nerve fibers. Compare *gray matter*.

withdrawal. Negative physiological and psychological reactions evidenced when a person suddenly stops taking an addictive drug; cramps, restlessness, and even death are examples. See *substance dependence*.

References

Abbass, A. A., Hancock, J. T., Henderson, J., & Kisely, S. (2008). Short-term psychodynamic psychotherapies for common mental disorders. *Cochrane Database of Systematic Reviews*, Issue 4. Art. No.: CD004687. DOI: 10.1002/14651858.CD004687.pub3.

Abbey, S. E., & Stewart, D. E. (2000). Gender and psychosomatic aspects of ischemic disease. *Journal of Psychosomatic Research*, 48, 417–423.

Abikoff, H. B., & Hechtman, L. (1996). Multimodal therapy and stimulants in the treatment of children with attention-deficit hyperactivity disorder. In E. D. Hibbs & P.S. Jensen (Eds.), *Psychosocial treatments for child and adolescent disorders: Empirically based strategies for clinical practice* (pp. 341–369). Washington, DC: American Psychological Association.

Abou-Saleh, M. T., Younis, Y., & Karim, L. (1998). Anorexia nervosa in an Arab culture. *International Journal of Eating Disorders*, 23, 207–212.

Abramson, L. Y., Metalsky, G. I., & Alloy, L. B. (1989). Hopelessness depression: A theory-based subtype of depression. *Psychological Review*, 96, 358–372.

Abramson, L. Y., Seligman, M. E. P., & Teasdale, J. D. (1978). Learned helplessness in humans: Critique and reformulation. *Journal of Abnormal Psychology*, 87, 49–74.

Achenbach, T. M., Bird, H. R., Canino, G., Phares, V., Gould, M. S., & Rubio-Stipec, M. (1990). Epidemiological comparisons of Puerto Rican and U.S. mainland children: Parent, teacher and self-reports. *Journal of the American Academy of Child and Adolescent Psychiatry*, 29, 84–93.

Achenbach, T. M., Hensley, V. R., Phares, V., & Grayson, D. (1990). Problems and competencies reported by parents of Australian and American children. *Journal of Child Psychology and Psychiatry*, 31, 265–286.

Achenbach, T. M., Howell, C. T., McConaughy, S. H., & Stanger, C. (1995). Six-year predictors of problems in a national sample of children and youth: I. Cross-informant syndromes. *Journal of the American Academy of Child and Adolescent Psychiatry*, 34, 336–347.

Ackerman, S. J., & Hilsenroth, M. J. (2003). A review of therapist characteristics and techniques positively impacting the therapeutic alliance. *Clinical Psychology Review*, 23, 1–33.

Acocella, J. (1999). *Creating hysteria: Women and multiple personality disorder*. San Francisco: Jossey-Bass.

Acton, G. J., & Kang, J. (2001). Interventions to reduce the burden of caregiving for an adult with dementia: A meta-analysis. *Research in Nursing and Health*, 24, 349–360.

Addis, M. E., & Krasnow, A. D. (2000). A national survey of practicing psychologists' attitudes toward psychotherapy treatment manuals. *Journal of Consulting and Clinical Psychology*, 68, 331–339.

Adler, A. (1930). *Guiding the child on the principles of individual psychology*. New York: Greenberg.

Adler, P. S., & Ditto, B. (1998). Psychophysiological effects of interviews about emotional events on offspring of hypertensives and normotensives. *International Journal of Psychophysiology*, 28, 263–271.

Adler, R. H., Zamboni, P., Hofer, T., & Hemmeler, W. (1997). How not to miss a somatic needle in a haystack of chronic pain. *Journal of Psychosomatic Research*, 42, 499–505.

Afflek, G., Apter, A., Tennen, H., Reisine, S., Barrows, E., Willard, A., et al. (2000). Mood states associated with transitory changes in asthma symptoms and peak expiratory flow. *Psychosomatic Medicine*, 62, 61–68.

Agras, W. S., Crow, S. J., Halmi, K. A., Mitchell, J. E., Wilson, G. T., & Kraemer, H. C. (2000). Outcome predictors for the cognitive-behavioral treatment of bulimia nervosa: Data from a multisite study. *American Journal of Psychiatry*, 157, 1302–1308.

Agras, W. S., Rossiter, E. M., Arnow, B., et al. (1994). One-year follow-up of psychosocial and pharmacologic treatments for bulimia nervosa. *Journal of Clinical Psychiatry*, 55, 179–183.

Agras, W. S., Rossiter, E. M., Arnow, B., Schneider, J. A., Telch, C. F., Raeburn, S. D., Bruce, B., Perl, M., & Koran, L. M. (1992). Pharmacologic and cognitive-behavioral treatment for bulimia nervosa: A controlled comparison. *American Journal of Psychiatry*, 149, 82–87.

Ainsworth, M. S., Blehar, M. C., Waters, E., & Wall, S. (1978). *Patterns of attachment: A psychological study of the strange situation*. Oxford, UK: Erlbaum.

Akyuez, G., Dogan, O., Sar, V., Yargic, L. I., & Tutkun, H. (1999). Frequency of dissociative disorder in the general population in Turkey. *Comprehensive Psychiatry*, 40, 151–159.

Albarracon, D., Gillette, J., Earl, A., Glasman, L. R., Durantini, M. R., & Ho., M. H. (2005). A test of major assumptions about behavior change: A comprehensive look at HIV prevention interventions since the beginning of the epidemic. *Psychological Bulletin*, 131, 856–897.

Albee, G. W., Lane, E. A., & Reuter, J. M. (1964). Childhood intelligence of future schizophrenics and neighborhood peers. *Journal of Psychology*, 58, 141–144.

Albertini, R. S., & Phillips, K. A. (1999). Thirty-three cases of body dysmorphic disorder in children and adolescents. *Journal of the American Academy of Child and Adolescent Psychiatry*, 38, 453–459.

Alden, L. E. (1989). Short-term structured treatment for avoidant personality disorder. *Journal of Consulting and Clinical Psychology*, 57, 756–764.

Alden, L. E., Laposa, J. M., Taylor, C. T., & Ryder, A. G. (2002). Avoidant personality disorder: Current status and future directions. *Journal of Personality Disorders*, 16, 1–29.

Alegria, M., Canino, G., Shrout, P. E., Woo, M., Duan, N., & Vila, D. (2008). Prevalence of mental illness in immigrant and non-immigrant U.S. Latino groups. *American Journal of Psychiatry*, 165, 359–369.

Alegria, M., Woo, M., Cao, Z., Torres, M., Meng, X-L., & Striegel-Moore, R. (2007). Prevalence and correlates of eating disorders among Latinos in the United States. *International Journal of Eating Disorders*, 40, s15-s21.

Alexander, F. (1950). *Psychosomatic medicine*. New York: Norton.

Alexander, P. C., & Lupfer, S. L. (1987). Family characteristics and long-term consequences associated with sexual abuse. *Archives of Sexual Behavior*, 16, 235–245.

Alferi, S. M., Carver, C. S., Antoni, M. H., Weiss, S., & Duran, R. E. (2001). An exploratory study of social support, distress, and life disruption among low-income Hispanic women under treatment for early stage breast cancer. *Health Psychology*, 20, 41–46.

Allan, C., Smith, I., & Mellin, M. (2000). Detoxification from alcohol: A comparison of home detoxification and hospital-based day patient care. *Alcohol & Alcoholism*, 35, 66–69.

Alldridge, P. (1979). Hospitals, mad houses, and asylums: Cycles in the care of the insane. *British Journal of Psychiatry*, 134, 321–324.

Allen, P. D., Johns, L. C., Fu, C. H. Y., Broome, M. R., Vythelingum, G. N., & McGuire, P. K. (2004). Misattribution of external speech in patients with hallucinations and delusions. *Schizophrenia Research*, 69, 277–287.

Allen, M., D'Alessio, D., & Brezgel, K. (1995). A meta-analysis summarizing the effects of pornography: II. Aggression after exposure. *Human Communication Research*, 22, 258–283.

Allnutt, S. H., Bradford, J. M., Greenberg, D. M., & Curry, S. (1996). Co-morbidity of alcoholism and the paraphilias. *Journal of Forensic Science*, 41, 234–239.

Alloy, L. B., Abramson, L. Y., Hogan, M. E., Whitehouse, W. G., Rose, D. T., Robinson, M. S., Kim, R. S., & Lapkin, J. B. (2000). The Temple-Wisconsin Cognitive Vulnerability to Depression Project: Lifetime history of Axis I psychopathology in individuals at high and low cognitive risk for depression. *Journal of Abnormal Psychology*, 109, 403–418.

Alloy, L. B., Abramson, L. Y., Whitehouse, W. G., Hogan, M. E., Panzarella, C., & Rose, D. T. (2006). Prospective incidence of first onsets and recurrences of depression in individuals at high and low cognitive risk for depression. *Journal of Abnormal Psychology*, 115, 145–156.

Almada, S. J. (1991). Neuroticism and cynicism and risk of death in middle aged men: The Western Electric study. *Psychosomatic Medicine*, 53, 165–175.

Alston, M. H., Rankin, S. H., & Harris, C. A. (1995). Suicide in African American elderly. *Journal of Black Studies*, 26, 31–35.

Alwahhabi, F. (2003). Anxiety symptoms and generalized anxiety disorder in the elderly: A review. *Harvard Review of Psychiatry*, 11, 180–193.

Amador, X. F., Flaum, M., Andreasen, N. C., Strauss, D. H., Yale, S. A., et al. (1994). Awareness of illness in schizophrenia and schizoaffective and mood disorder. *Archives of General Psychiatry*, 51, 826–836.

Aman, M. G., & Langworthy, K. (2000). Pharmacotherapy for hyperactivity in children with autism and other pervasive developmental disorders. *Journal of Autism and Developmental Disorders*, 30, 451–459.

American Association of Retired Persons. (1999). *Assisted living in the United States*. AARP Publication FS62R. Retrieved from www.aarp.org

American Heart Association. (2004). *Heart disease and stroke statistics–2004 update.* Dallas, TX: Author.

American Law Institute. (1962). *Model penal code: Proposed official draft.* Philadelphia: Author.

American Psychiatric Association. (1993). Practice guidelines for major depressive disorder in adults. *American Journal of Psychiatry, 150,* entire issue.

American Psychiatric Association. (1994). *Diagnostic and statistical manual of mental disorders. (DSM-IV). (4th ed.).* Washington, DC: Author.

American Psychiatric Association (2004). Practice guidelines for the treatment of patients with schizophrenia (2nd ed.). Retrieved from http://www.psych.org

American Psychiatric Association. (2007). Treatment of patients with Alzheimer's disease and other dementias (2nd ed.). *APA Practice Guidelines.* Washington, DC: Author.

American Psychiatric Association. *Diagnostic and statistical manual of mental disorders. (DSM-IV-TR).* First edition, 1952; second edition, 1968; third edition, 1980; revised, 1987; fourth edition, 1994; revised 2000. Washington, DC: Author.

American Psychological Association. (2002). Ethical principles of psychologists and code of conduct. *American Psychologist, 57,* 1060–1073. Available from the APA Web site: http://www.apa.org/ethics/code2002.html

American Psychological Association. (2004). Guidelines for psychological practice with older adults. *American Psychologist, 59,* 236–260.

Amir, N., Beard, C., Burns, M., & Bomyea, J. (2008, in press). Attention modification program in individuals with generalized anxiety disorder. *Journal of Abnormal Psychology.*

Amir, N., Foa, E. B., & Coles, M. E. (1998). Negative interpretation bias in social phobia. *Behaviour Research and Therapy, 36,* 945–957.

Anand A. et al. (2000). Brain SPECT imaging of amphetamine-induced dopamine release in euthymic BPD patients. *American Journal of Psychiatry, 157,* 1109–1114.

Anastopoulos, A. D., Shelton, T., DuPaul, G. J., & Guevremont, D. C. (1993). Parent training for attention deficit hyperactivity disorder: Its impact on parent functioning. *Journal of Abnormal Child Psychology, 20,* 503–520.

Ancoli, I. S., Kripke, D. F., Klauber, M. R., Fell, R., Stepnowsky, C., Estline, E., et al. (1996). Morbidity, mortality and sleep-disordered breathing in community dwelling elderly. *Sleep: Journal of Sleep Research and Sleep Medicine, 19,* 277–282.

Andersen, B. L., Cyranowski, J. M., & Aarestad, S. (2000). Beyond artificial, sex-linked distinctions to conceptualize female sexuality: Comment on Baumeister (2000).

Andersen, B. L. Cyranowski, J. M., & Espindle, D. (1999). Men's sexual self-schema. *Journal of Personality and Social Psychology, 76,* 645–661.

Andersen, S. M. & Chen, S. (2002). The relational self: An interpersonal social-cognitive theory. *Psychological Review, 109,* 619–645.

Andersen, S. M., Reznik, I., & Manzella, L. M. (1996). Eliciting transient affect, motivation, and expectancies in transference: Significant-other representations and the self in social relations. *Journal of Personality and Social Psychology, 71,* 1108–1129.

Andersen, B. L., Kiecolt-Glaser, J. K., & Glaser, R. (1994). A biobehavioral model of cancer stress and disease course. *American Psychologist, 49,* 389–404.

Anderson, C. A., Hinshaw, S. P., & Simmel, C. (1994). Mother-child interactions in ADHD and comparison boys: Relationships to overt and covert externalizing behavior. *Journal of Abnormal Child Psychology, 22,* 247–265.

Anderson, E. M., & Lambert, M. J. (1995). Short-term dynamically oriented psychotherapy: A review and metaanalysis. *Clinical Psychology Review, 15,* 503–514.

Anderson, E. R., & Hope, D. A. (2008). A review of the tripartite model for understanding the link between anxiety and depression in youth. *Clinical Psychology Review, 28,* 275–287.

Anderson, G. M., & Hoshino, Y. (1987). Neurochemical studies of autism. In D. J. Cohen, A. M. Donnellan, & R. Paul (Eds.), *Handbook of autism and pervasive developmental disorders* (pp. 166–191). New York: Wiley.

Anderson, J. C. (1996). Is childhood hyperactivity the product of Western culture? *Lancet, 348,* 73–74.

Anderson, L. T., Campbell, M., Adams, P., Small, A. M., Perry, R., & Shell, J. (1989). The effects of haloperidol on discrimination learning and behavioral symptoms in autistic children. *Journal of Autism and Developmental Disorders, 19,* 227–239.

Anderson, M. C., & Green, C. (2001). Suppressing unwanted memories by executive control. *Nature, 410,* 366–369.

Anderson, S., Hanson, R., Malecha, M., Oftelie, A., Erickson, C., & Clark, J. M. (1997). The effectiveness of naltrexone in treating task attending, aggression, self-injury, and stereotypic mannerisms of six young males with autism or pervasive developmental disorders. *Journal of Developmental and Physical Disabilities, 9,* 211–221.

Andreano, J. M., & Cahill, L. (2006). Glucocorticoid release and memory consolidation in men and women. *Psychological Science, 17,* 466–470.

Andreasen, N. C., Olsen, S. A., Dennert, J. W., & Smith, M. R. (1982). Ventricular enlargement in schizophrenia: Relationship to positive and negative symptoms. *American Journal of Psychiatry, 139,* 297–302.

Anglin, M. D., Burke, C., Perrochet, B., Stamper, E., & Dawud-Noursi, S. (2000). History of the methamphetamine problem. *Journal of Psychoactive Drugs, 32,* 137–141.

Angold, A., Erkanli, A., Egger, H. L., & Costello, E. J. (2000). Stimulant treatment for children: A community perspective. *Journal of the American Academy of Child and Adolescent Psychiatry, 39,* 975–984.

Angold, A., & Rutter, M. (1992). Effects of age and pubertal status on depression in a large clinical sample. *Development and Psychopathology, 4,* 5–28.

Angrist, B., Lee, H. K., & Gershon, S. (1974). The antagonism of amphetamine-induced symptomatology by a neuroleptic. *American Journal of Psychiatry, 131,* 817–819.

Angst, F., Stassen, H. H., Clayton, P. J., & Angst, J. (2002). Mortality of patients with mood disorders: Follow-up over 34–38 years. *Journal of Affective Disorders, 68,* 167–181.

Angst, J. (1998). Sexual problems in healthy and depressed persons. *International Clinical Psychopharmacology, 13* (Suppl. 6), S1–S4.

Anthony, J. L., & Lonigan, C. L. (2004). The nature of phonological awareness: Converging evidence from four studies of preschool and early grade school children. *Journal of Educational Psychology, 96,* 43–55.

Antoni, M. H., Cruess, D. G., Cruess, S., et al. (2000). Cognitive-behavioral stress management intervention effects on anxiety, 24-hr urinary norepinephrine output, and T-cytotoxic/suppressor cells over time among symptomatic HIV-infected gay men. *Journal of Consulting and Clinical Psychology, 68,* 31–45.

Antony, M. M., & Barlow, D. H. (2004). Specific phobias. In D. H. Barlow (Ed.), *Anxiety and its disorders: The nature and treatment of anxiety and panic* (pp. 380–417). New York: Guilford.

Apodaca, T. R., & Miller, W. R. (2003). A meta-analysis of the effectiveness of bibliotherapy for alcohol problems. *Journal of Clinical Psychology, 59,* 289–304.

Appel, L. J., Moore, T. J., Obarzanek, E., Vollmer, W. M., Svetkey, L. P., Sacks, F. M., Bray, G. A., Vogt, T. M., Cutler, J. A., Windhauser, M. M., Lin, P.-H., & Karanja, N., for the DASH Collaborative Research Group. (1997). A clinical trial of the effects of dietary patterns on blood pressure. *New England Journal of Medicine, 336,* 1117–1124.

Appelbaum, P. S. (2006). Law and psychiatry "depressed? get out!": Dealing with suicidal students on college campuses. *Psychiatric Services, 57,* 914–916.

Appelbaum, P. S., & Grisso, T. (1995). The MacArthur Treatment Competence Study: 1. Mental illness and competence to consent to treatment. *Law and Human Behavior, 19,* 105–126.

Appelbaum, P. S., Grisso, T., Frank, E., O'Donnel, S., & Kupfer, D. (1999). Capacities of depressed patients to consent to research. *American Journal of Psychiatry, 156,* 1380–1384.

Appelbaum, P. S., & Gutheil, T. (1991). *Clinical handbook of psychiatry and the law.* Baltimore: Williams & Wilkins.

Appelbaum, P. S., Robbins, P. C., & Monahan, J. (2000). Violence and delusions: Data from the MacArthur Violence Risk Assessment Study. *American Journal of Psychiatry, 157,* 566–557.

Appignannesi, L. (2008). *Mad, bad, and sad: Women and the mind doctors.* New York: W. W. Norton.

Apt, C., & Hurlbert, D. H. (1994). The sexual attitudes, behavior, and relationships of women with histrionic personality disorder. *Journal of Sex and Marital Therapy, 20,* 125–133.

Apter, A. J., Affleck, G., Reisine, S. T., Tennen, H. A., Barrows, E., Wells, M., et al. (1997). Perception of airway obstruction in asthma: Sequential daily analyses of symptoms, peak expiratory flow rate, and mood. *Journal of Allergy and Clinical Immunology, 99,* 605–612.

Araujo, A.B., Durante, R., Feldman, H.A., Goldstein, I., & McKinley, J.B. (1998). The relationship between depressive symptoms and male erectile dysfunction: Cross-sectional results from the Massachusetts Male Aging Study. *Psychosomatic Medicine, 60,* 458–465.

Arbisi, P. A., Ben-Porath, Y. S., & McNulty, J. (2002). A comparison of MMPI-2 validity in African American and Caucasian psychiatric patients. *Psychological Assessment, 14,* 3–15.

Arentewicz, G., & Schmidt, G. (1983). *The treatment of sexual disorders: Concepts and techniques of couple therapy.* New York: Basic Books.

Arias, E., Anderson, R. N., Kung, H. C., Murphy, S. L., & Kochanek, K. D. (2003). *Deaths: Final reports, 52.* DHHS Publication No. 2003–1120. Hyattsville, MD: National Center for Health Statistics.

Arndt, I. O., Dorozynsky, L., Woody, G. E., McLellan, A. T., & O'Brien, C. P. (1992). Desipramine treatment of cocaine dependence in methadone-maintained patients. *Archives of General Psychiatry, 49,* 888–893.

Arnold, E. H., O'Leary, S. G., & Edwards, G. H. (1997). Father involvement and self-reported parenting of children with attention deficit hyperactivity disorder. *Journal of Consulting and Clinical Psychology, 65,* 337–342.

Arnold, E. M., Kirk, R. S., Roberts, A. C., Griffith, D. P., Meadows, K., Julian, J., et al. (2003). Treatment of incarcerated, sexually-abused adolescent females: An outcome study. *Journal of Child Sexual Abuse, 12*(1), 123–139.

Arnold, L. E., Elliott, M., Sachs, L., et al. (2003). Effects of ethnicity on treatment attendance, stimulant response/dose, and 14-month outcome in ADHD. *Journal of Consulting and Clinical Psychology, 71,* 713–727.

Arnold, L. M., Keck, P. E., Jr., Collins, J., Wilson, R., Fleck, D. E., Corey, K. B., Amicone, J., Adebimpe, V. R., & Strakowski, S. M. (2004). Ethnicity and first-rank symptoms in patients with psychosis. *Schizophrenia Research, 67,* 207–212.

Arnow, B., Kenardy, J., & Agras, W. S. (1992). Binge eating among the obese. *Journal of Behavioral Medicine, 15,* 155–170.

Aronson, E. (2004). *The social animal* (9th ed.). New York: Worth.

Artiles, A. J., & Trent, S. C. (1994). Overrepresentation of minority students in special education: A continuing debate. *Journal of Special Education, 27,* 410–437.

Ashbaugh, A. R., Antony, M. M., McCabe, R. E., Schmidt, L. A., & Swinson, R. P. (2005). Self-evaluative biases in social anxiety. *Cognitive Therapy and Research, 29,* 387–398.

Ashton, H., & Young, A. H. (2003). GABA-ergic drugs: Exit stage left, enter stage right. *Journal of Psychopharmacology, 17,* 174–178.

Asmundson, G. J., Larsen, D. K., & Stein, M. B. (1998). Panic disorder and vestibular disturbance: An overview of empirical findings and clinical implications. *Journal of Psychosomatic Research, 44,* 107–120.

Atkinson, D. R., Brown, M. T., Parham, T. A., & Matthews, L. G. (1996). African American client skin tone and clinical judgments of African American and European American psychologists. *Professional Psychology: Research and Practice, 27,* 500–505.

Attia, E., Haiman, C., Walsh, B. T., & Flater, S. R. (1998). Does fluoxetine augment the inpatient treatment of anorexia nervosa? *American Journal of Psychiatry, 155,* 548–551.

Aubry, J., Gervasoni, N., Osiek, C., Perret, G., Rossier, M. F., Bertschy, G., et al. (2007). The DEX/CRH neuroendocrine test and the prediction of depressive relapse in remitted depressed outpatients. *Journal of Psychiatric Research, 41,* 290–294.

Avissar, S., Nechamkin, Y., Barki-Harrington, L., Roitman, G., & Schreiber, G. (1997). Differential G protein measures in mononuclear leukocytes of patients with bipolar mood disorder are state dependent. *Journal of Affective Disorders, 43,* 85–93.

Avissar, S., Schreiber, G., Nechamkin, Y., Nehaus, I., Lam, G., et al. (1999). The effects of seasons and light therapy on G protein levels in mononuclear leukocytes in patients with seasonal affective disorder. *Archives of General Psychiatry, 56,* 178–184.

Ayanian, J. Z., & Cleary, P. D. (1999). Perceived risks of heart disease and cancer among cigarete smokers. *JAMA, 281,* 1019–1021.

Ayers, C. R., Sorrell, J. T., Thorp, S. R., & Wetherell, J. L. (2007). Evidence-based psychological treatments for late-life anxiety. *Psychology and Aging, 22,* 8–17.

Bach, A. K., Wincze, J. P., & Barlow, D. H. (2001). Sexual dysfunction. In D. H. Barlow (Ed.), *Clinical handbook of psychological disorders* (pp. 562–608). New York: Guilford.

Bach, G. R. (1966). The marathon group: Intensive practice of intimate interactions. *Psychological Reports, 181,* 995–1002.

Bach, P. B., Cramer, L. D., Warren, J. L., & Begg, C. B. (1999). Racial differences in the treatment of early-stage lung cancer. *New England Journal of Medicine, 341,* 1198–1205.

Bachrach, H., Galatzer-Levy, R., Skolnikoff, A., & Waldron, S. (1991). On the efficacy of psychoanalysis. *Journal of the American Psychoanalytic Association, 39,* 871–916.

Baer, J. S., & Lichtenstein, E. (1988). Cognitive assessment. In D. M. Donovan & G. A. Marlatt (Eds.), *Assessment of addictive behaviors* (pp. 189–213). New York: Guilford.

Baer, L., & Jenike, M. A. (1992). Personality disorders in obsessive-compulsive disorder. *Psychiatric Clinics of North America, 15,* 803–812.

Baer, R. A., & Sekirnjak, G. (1997). Detection of underreporting on the MMPI-II in a clinical population. Effects of information about validity scales. *Journal of Personality Assessment, 69,* 555–567.

Bagby, M. R., Nicholson, R. A., Bacchionchi, J. R., et al. (2002). The predictive capacity of the MMPI-2 and PAI validity scales and indexes to detect coached and uncoached feigning. *Journal of Personality Assessment, 78,* 69–86.

Bailey, A., LeCouteur, A., Gottesman, I., Bolton, P., Simonoff, E., Yuzda, E., & Rutter, M. (1995). Autism as a strongly genetic disorder: Evidence from a British twin study. *Psychological Medicine, 25,* 63–77.

Bailey, J. M. (2003). *The man who would be queen.* Washington, DC: Joseph Henry Press.

Bailey, J. M., Dunne, M. P., & Martin, N. G. (2000). Genetic and environmental influences on sexual orientation and its correlates in an Australian twin sample. *Journal of Personality and Social Psychology, 78,* 524–536.

Baker, B., Paquette, M., Szalai, J., Driver, H., Perger, T., Helmers, K., et al. (2000). The influence of marital adjustment on 3-year left ventricular mass and ambulatory blood pressure in mild hypertension. *Archives of Internal Medicine, 160,* 3453–3458.

Baker, L. A., Jacobson, K. C., Raine, A., Lozano, D. I., & Bezdjian, S. (2007). Genetic and environmental bases of childhood antisocial behavior: A multi-informant twin study. *Journal of Abnormal Psychology, 116,* 219–235.

Ball, J., & Lehder Roberts, D. (2004). *Oxycodone, hydrocodone, and polydrug use 2002. The DAWN Report.* Office of Applied Statistics, Substance Abuse and Mental Health Services Administration, U.S. Department of Health and Human Services. Bethesda, MD.

Ball, J. C., & Ross, A. (1991). *The effectiveness of methadone maintenance treatment.* New York: Springer-Verlag.

Bancroft, J., Loftus, J., & Long, J. S. (2003). Distress about sex: A national survey of women in heterosexual relationships. *Archives of Sexual Behavior, 32,* 193–208.

Bandura, A. (1977). Self-efficacy: Toward a unifying theory of behavioral change. *Psychological Review, 84,* 191–215.

Bandura, A., Blanchard, E. B., & Ritter, B. (1969). Relative efficacy of desensitization and modeling approaches for inducing behavioral, affective, and attitudinal changes. *Journal of Personality and Social Psychology, 13,* 173–199.

Bandura, A., & Menlove, F. L. (1968). Factors determining vicarious extinction of avoidance behavior through symbolic modeling. *Journal of Personality and Social Psychology, 8,* 99–108.

Bandura, A., & Perloff, B. (1967). Relative efficacy of self-monitored and externally imposed reinforcement systems. *Journal of Personality and Social Psychology, 7,* 111–116.

Banich, M. T., Passarotti, A. M., White, D. A., Nortz, M. J., & Steiner, R. D. (2000). Interhemispheric interaction during childhood: II. Children with early-treated phenylketonuria. *Developmental Neuropsychology, 18,* 53–71.

Bankier, B., Aigner, M., & Bach, M. (2001). Alexithymia in DSM-IV disorder: Comparative evaluation of somatoform disorder, panic disorder, obsessive-compulsive disorder, and depression. *Psychosomatics: Journal of Consultation Liaison Psychiatry, 42,* 235–240.

Banks, S. M., Salovey, P., Greener, S., Rothman, A. J., et al. (1995). The effects of message framing on mammography utilization. *Health Psychology, 14,* 178–184.

Barbato, A., & D'Avanzo, B. (2008). Efficacy of couple therapy as a treatment for depression: A meta-analysis. *Psychiatric Quarterly, 79,* 121–132.

Barber, C. (2008). *Comfortably numb.* New York: Pantheon.

Barbini, B., Benedetti, F., Colombo, C., Dotoli, D., Bernasconi, A., Cigala-Fulgosi, M, et al. (2005). Dark therapy for mania: A pilot study. *Bipolar Disorders, 7,* 98–101.

Barch, D. M., Carter, C. S., Braver, T. S., et al. (2001). Selective deficits in prefrontal cortex function in medication naïve patients with schizophrenia. *Archives of General Psychiatry, 58,* 280–288.

Barch, D. M., Carter, C. S., MacDonald, A. W., Braver, T. S., & Cohen, J. D. (2003). Context processing deficits in schizophrenia: Diagnostic specificity, four-week course, and relationship to clinical symptoms. *Journal of Abnormal Psychology, 112,* 132–143.

Barch, D. M., Csernansky, J. G., Conturo, T., & Snyder, A. Z. (2002). Working and long-term memory deficits in schizophrenia: Is there a common prefrontal mechanism? *Journal of Abnormal Psychology, 111,* 478–494.

Bardone-Cone, A. M., Wonderlich, S. A., Frost, R. O., Bulik, C. M., Mitchell, J., et al. (2007). Perfectionism and eating disorders: Current status and future directions. *Clinical Psychology Review, 27,* 384–405.

Barefoot, J. C., Dahlstrom, G., & Williams, R. B. (1983). Hostility, CHD incidence, and total mortality: A 25-year follow-up study of 255 physicians. *Psychosomatic Medicine, 45,* 59–63.

Bar-Haim, Y., Lamy, D., Lee, P., Bakermans-Kranenburg, M. J., & van Ijzendoorn, M. H. (2007). Threat-related attentional bias in anxious and nonanxious individuals: A meta-analytic study. *Psychological Bulletin, 133,* 1–24.

Barkley, R. A. (1990). *Attention-deficit hyperactivity disorder: A handbook for diagnosis and treatment.* New York: Guilford.

Barkley, R. A. (1997). Behavioral inhibition, sustained attention, and executive function: Constructing a unifying theory of ADHD. *Psychological Bulletin, 121,* 65–94.

Barkley, R. A., DuPaul, G. J., & McMurray, M. B. (1990). A comprehensive evaluation of attention deficit disorder with and without hyperactivity defined by research criteria. *Journal of Consulting and Clinical Psychology, 58,* 775–789.

Barkley, R. A., Fischer, M., Edelbrock, C. S., & Smallish, L. (1990). The adolescent outcome of hyperactive children diagnosed by research criteria: 1. An 8 year prospective follow-up study. *Journal of the American Academy of Child and Adolescent Psychiatry, 29,* 546–557.

Barkley, R. A., Fischer, M., Smallish, L., & Fletcher, K. (2002). The persistence of attention-deficit hyperactivity disorder into young adulthood as a function of reporting source and definition of disorder. *Journal of Abnormal Psychology, 111,* 279–289.

Barkley, R. A., Fischer, M., Smallish, L., & Fletcher, K. (2003). Does the treatment of attention-deficit/hyperactivity disorder with stimulants contribute to drug use/abuse? A 13 year prospective study. *Pediatrics, 111,* 97–109.

Barkley, R. A., Grodzinsky, G., & DuPaul, G. J. (1992). Frontal lobe functions in attention deficit disorder with and without hyperactivity: A review and research report. *Journal of Abnormal Child Psychology, 20,* 163–188.

Barkley, R. A., Karlsson, J., & Pollard, S. (1985). Effects of age on the mother-child interactions of hyperactive children. *Journal of Abnormal Child Psychology, 13,* 631–638.

Barlow, D. H. (2004). *Anxiety and its disorders: The nature and treatment of anxiety and panic.* New York: Guilford.

Barlow, D. H., Abel, G. G., & Blanchard, E. B. (1979). Gender identity change in transsexuals. *Archives of General Psychiatry, 36,* 1001–1007.

Barlow, D. H., Blanchard, E. B., Vermilyea, J. A., Vermilyea, B. B., & DiNardo, P. A. (1986). Generalized anxiety and generalized anxiety disorder: Description and reconceptualization. *American Journal of Psychiatry, 143,* 40–44.

Barlow, D. H., Gorman, J. M., Shear, M. K., & Woods, S. W. (2000). Cognitive-behavioral therapy, imipramine, or their combination for panic disorder: A randomized controlled trial. *Journal of the American Medical Association, 283,* 2529–2536.

Barlow, D. H., Raffa, S. D., & Cohen, E. M. (2002). Psychosocial treatments for panic disorders, phobias, and generalized anxiety disorder. In J. M. Gorman & P. E. Nathan (Eds.), *A guide to treatments that work* (2nd ed., pp. 301–335). London: Oxford University Press.

Barlow, D. H., Reynolds, E. J., & Agras, W. S. (1973). Gender identity change in a transsexual. *Archives of General Psychiatry, 29,* 569–576.

Barlow, D. H., Vermilyea, J., Blanchard, E., Vermilyea, B., DiNardo, P., & Cerny, J. (1985). The phenomenon of panic. *Journal of Abnormal Psychology, 94,* 320–328.

Barnett, P. A., & Gotlib, I. H. (1988). Psychosocial functioning and depression: Distinguishing among antecedents, concomitants, and consequences. *Psychological Bulletin, 104,* 97–126.

Barsky, A. (2006). "Doctor, are you sure my heart is okay?" Cognitive-behavioral treatment of hypochondriasis. In R. L. Spitzer, M. B. W. First, J. B. Williams, & M. Gibbon (Eds.), *DSM-IV-TR® casebook: Volume 2. Experts tell how they treated their own patients* (pp. 251–261). Washington, DC: American Psychiatric Association.

Barsky, A. J., & Ahern, D. K. (2004). Cognitive behavior therapy for hypochondriasis: A randomized controlled trial. *Journal of the American Medical Association, 291,* 1464–1470.

Barsky, A. J., Brener, J., Coeytaux, R. R., & Cleary, P. D. (1995). Accurate awareness of heartbeat in hypochondriacal and non-hypochondriacal patients. *Journal of Psychosomatic Research, 39,* 489–497.

Barsky, A. J., Fama, J. M., Bailey, E. D., & Ahern, D. K. (1998). A prospective 4- to 5-year study of DSM-III-R hypochondriasis. *Archives of General Psychiatry, 55,* 737–744.

Barsky, A. J., Orav, E. J., & Bates, D. W. (2005). Somatization increases medical utilization and costs independent of psychiatric and medical comorbidity. *Archives of General Psychiatry, 62,* 903–910.

Barth, J., Schumacher, M., & Herrmann-Lingen, C. (2004). Depression as a risk factor for mortality in patients with coronary heart disease: A meta-analysis. *Psychosomatic Medicine, 66,* 802–813.

Bartlik, B., & Goldberg, J. (2000). Female sexual arousal disorder. In S. R. Lieblum & R. C. Rosen (Eds.), *Principles and practice of sex therapy* (3rd ed., pp. 85–117). New York: Guilford.

Bass, E., & Davis, L. (1994). *The courage to heal: A guide for women survivors of child sexual abuse.* New York: Harper Collins.

Basson, R., Brotto, L. A., Laan, E., Redmond, G., & Utian, W. H. (2005). Assessment and management of women's sexual dysfunctions: Problematic desire and arousal. *Journal Sexual Medicine, 2,* 291–300.

Bateman, A. W., & Fonagy, P. (2004). Mentalization-based treatment of BPD. *Journal of Personality Disorders, 18,* 36–51.

Baucom, D. H., Shoham, V., Mueser, K. T., Daiuto, A. D., & Stickle, T. R. (1998). Empirically supported couple and family interventions for marital distress and adult mental health problems. *Journal of Consulting and Clinical Psychology, 66,* 53–88.

Baumeister, A. A., & Baumeister, A. A. (1995). Mental retardation. In M. Hersen & R. T. Ammerman (Eds.), *Advanced abnormal child psychology* (pp. 283–303). Hillsdale, NJ: Erlbaum.

Baumeister, R. F. (2000). Gender differences in erotic plasticity: The female sex drive as socially flexible and responsive. *Psychological Bulletin, 126*(3), 347–374.

Baumeister, R. F., & Butler, J. L. (1997). Sexual masochism: Deviance without pathology. In D. R. Laws & W. O'Donohue (Eds.), *Sexual deviance* (pp. 225–239). New York: Guilford.

Baumeister, R. F., Catanese, K. R., & Vohs, K. (2001). Is there a gender difference in strength of sex drive? Theoretical views, conceptual distinctions, and a review of relevant evidence. *Personality and Social Psychology Review, 5*(3), 242–273.

Baxter, L. R., Ackermann, R. F., Swerdlow, N. R., Brody, A., Saxena, S., Schwartz, J. M., Gregoritch, J. M., Stoessel, P., & Phelps, M. E. (2000). Specific brain system mediation of obsessive-compulsive disorder responsive to either medication or behavior therapy. In W. K. Goodman, M. V. Rudorfer, & J. D. Maser (Eds.), *Obsessive-compulsive disorder: Contemporary issues in treatment* (pp. 573–610). Mahwah, NJ: Erlbaum.

Bazanis, E., Rogers, R. D., Dowson, J. H., Taylor, P., Meux, C., Staley, C., et al. (2002). Neurocognitive deficits in decision-making and planning of patients with DSM-IIIR borderline personality disorder. *Psychological Medicine, 32,* 1395–1405.

Beck, A. T. (1967). *Depression: Clinical, experimental and theoretical aspects.* New York: Harper & Row.

Beck, A. T. (1976). *Cognitive therapy and the emotional disorders.* New York: International Universities Press.

Beck, A. T., & Emery, R. (1985). *Anxiety disorders and phobias: A cognitive perspective.* New York: Basic Books.

Beck, A. T., & Freeman, A. (1990). *Cognitive therapy for personality disorders.* New York: Guilford.

Beck, A. T., Kovacs, M., & Weissman, A. (1975). Hopelessness and suicidal behavior: An overview. *Journal of the American Medical Association, 234,* 1146–1149.

Beck, A. T., & Rector, N. A. (2000). Cognitive therapy of schizophrenia: A new therapy for the new millennium. *American Journal of Psychotherapy, 54,* 291–300.

Beck, A. T., Rector, N., & Stolar, N. (2004, October). *The negative symptoms of schizophrenia: A cognitive perspective.* Paper presented at the annual meeting of the Society for Research in Psychopathology, St. Louis, MO.

Beck, J. G. (1995). Hypoactive sexual desire disorder: An overview. *Journal of Consulting and Clinical Psychology, 63,* 919–927.

Beck, J. G., & Bozman, A. (1995). Gender differences in sexual desire: The effects of anger and anxiety. *Archives of Sexual Behavior, 24,* 595–612.

Becker, J. V., & Hunter, J. A. (1997). Understanding and treating child and adolescent sexual offenders. In T. H. Ollendick & R. J. Prinz (Eds.), *Advances in clinical child psychology* (pp. 177–196). New York: Plenum.

Beecher, H. K. (1966). Ethics and clinical research. *New England Journal of Medicine, 274,* 1354–1360.

Beevers, C. G., & Miller, I. W. (2005). Unlinking negative cognition and symptoms of depression: Evidence of a specific treatment effect for cognitive therapy. *Journal of Consulting and Clinical Psychology, 73,* 68–77.

Beidel, D. C. (1991). Social phobia and overanxious disorder in school-age children. *Journal of the American Academy of Child and Adolescent Psychiatry, 30,* 545–552.

Bellack, A. S., & Hersen, M. (1998). *Behavioral assessment: A practical handbook* (4th ed.). Boston: Allyn & Bacon.

Benkelfat, C., Ellenbogen, M. A., Dean, P., Palmour, R. M., & Young, S. N. (1994). Mood-lowering effect of tryptophan depletion: Enhanced susceptibility in young men at genetic risk for major affective disorders. *Archives of General Psychiatry, 51,* 687–700.

Benowitz, N. L., & Peng, M. W. (2000). Non-nicotine pharmacotherapy for smoking cessation. *CNS Drugs, 13,* 265–285.

Benowitz, N., Pérez-Stable, E., Herrera, B., & Jacob, P. (2002). Slower metabolism and reduced intake of nicotine from cigarette smoking in Chinese-Americans. *Journal of the National Cancer Institute, 94,* 108–115.

Ben-Porath, Y. S., & Butcher, J. N. (1989). The comparability of MMP-I and MMPI-2 scales and profiles. *Psychological Assessment, 1,* 345–347.

Berenbaum, H., & Oltmanns, T. F. (1992). Emotional experience and expression in schizophrenia and depression. *Journal of Abnormal Psychology, 101,* 37–44.

Berenbaum, S. A. (1999). Effects of early androgens on sex-typed activities and interests in adolescents with congenital adrenal hyperplasia. *Hormones and Behavior, 35,* 102–110.

Bergem, A. L., Engedal, K., & Kringlen, E. (1997). The role of heredity in late-onset Alzheimer's disease and vascular dementia: A twin study. *Archives of General Psychiatry, 54,* 264–270.

Bergin, A. E. (1971). The evaluation of therapeutic outcomes. In A. E. Bergin & S. L. Garfield (Eds.), *Handbook of psychotherapy and behavior change: An empirical analysis,* 217–270 New York: Wiley.

Bergman-Evans, B. (2004). Beyond the basics: Effects of the eden alternative model on quality of life issues. *Journal of Gerontological Nursing, 30,* 27–34.

Berkman, L. F., Blumenthal, J., Burg, M., Carney, R. M., et al. (2003). Effects of treating depression and low perceived social support on clinical events after myocardial infarction: The Enhancing Recovery in Coronary Heart Disease Patients (ENRICHD) Randomized Trial. *Journal of the American Medical Association, 289,* 3106–3116.

Berman, L., Berman, J., Miles, M., Pollets, D., & Powell, J. A. (2003). Genital self-image as a component of sexual health: Relationship between genital self-image, female sexual function, and quality of life measures. *Journal of Sex and Marital Therapy, 29* (Suppl. 1), 11–21.

Bernstein, D. P., Kasapis, C., Bergman, A., Weld, E., Mitropoulou, V., et al. (1997). Assessing Axis II disorders by informant interview. *Journal of Personality Disorders, 11,* 158–167.

Berry, J. C. (1967). *Antecedents of schizophrenia, impulsive character and alcoholism in males.* Paper presented at the 75th annual convention of the American Psychological Association, Washington, DC.

Bettocchi, C., Verze, P., Palumbo, F., Arcaniolo, D., & Mirone, V. (2008) Ejaculatory disorders: Pathophysiology and management. *Nature Clinical Practice Urology, 5,* 93–103.

Beutler, L. E. (1997). The psychotherapist as a neglected variable in psychotherapy: An illustration by reference to the role of therapist experience and training. *Clinical Psychology: Science and Practice, 4,* 44–52.

Beutler, L. E. (1999). Manualizing flexibility: The training of eclectic therapists. *Journal of Clinical Psychology, 55,* 399–404.

Beutler, L. E., Frank, M., Schieber, S. C., Calvert, S., & Gaines, J. (1984). Comparative effects of group psychotherapies in a short-term inpatient setting: An experience with deterioration effects. *Psychiatry, 47,* 66–76.

Beutler, L. E., Machado, P. P. P., & Neufeldt, S. A. (1994). Therapist variables. In S. L. Garfield, & A. E. Bergin (Eds.), *Handbook of psychotherapy and behavior change* (pp. 229–269). Oxford, UK: John Wiley & Sons.

Beutler, L. E., Malik, M., Alimohamed, S., Harwood, T. M., Talebi, H., Noble, S., & Wong, E. (2004). Therapist variables. In M. J. Lambert (Ed.), *Bergin and Garfield's handbook of psychotherapy and behavior change* (5th ed., pp. 227–306). New York: Wiley.

Beutler, L. E., Moleiro, C., Malik, M., Harwood, T. M., Romanelli, R., Gallagher-Thompson, D., & Thompson, L. (2003). A comparison of the dodo, EST, and ATI factors among comorbid stimulant-dependent, depressed patients. *Clinical Psychology and Psychotherapy, 10,* 69–85.

Bhalla, R., Butters, M. A., Mulsant, B. H., Begley, A. E., Zmuda, M. D., Schoderbek, B., et al. (2006). Persistence of neuropsychologic deficits in the remitted state of late-life depression. *American Journal of Geriatric Psychiatry, 14,* 419–427.

Bhutta, A. T., Cleves, M. A., Casey, P. H., Cradock, M. M., & Anand, K. J. (2002). Cognitive and behavioral outcomes of school-aged children who were born preterm: A meta-analysis. *Journal of the American Medical Association, 288,* 728–737.

Biederman, J., & Faraone, S. (2004). The Massachusetts General Hospital studies of gender influences on attention-deficit/hyperactivity disorder in youth and relatives. *Psychiatric Clinics of North America, 27,* 215–224.

Biederman, J., Faraone, S., Milberger, S., Curtis, S., Chen, L., Marrs, A., Ouellette, C., Moore, P., & Spencer, T. (1996). Predictors of persistence and remission of ADHD into adolescence: Results from a four-year prospective follow-up study. *Journal of the American Academy of Child and Adolescent Psychiatry, 35,* 343–351.

Biederman, J., Mick, E., Faraone, S. V., et al. (2000). Pediatric mania: A developmental subtype of bipolar disorder? *Biological Psychiatry, 48,* 458–466.

Biederman, J., Monuteasu, M. C., Mick, E., Spencer, T., Wilens, T. E., Silva, J. M., Snyder, L. E., & Faraone, S. V. (2006). Young adult outcome of attention deficit hyperactivity disorder: A controlled 10-year follow-up study. *Psychological Medicine, 36,* 167–179.

Biederman, J., Rosenbaum, J. F., Hirshfeld, D. R., & Faraone, S. V. (1990). Psychiatric correlates of behavioral inhibition in young children of parents with and without psychiatric disorders. *Archives of General Psychiatry, 47,* 21–26.

Bierut, L. J., Dinwiddie, S. H., Begleiter, H., Crowe, R. R., Hesselbrock, V., et al. (1998). Familial transmission of substance dependence: Alcohol, marijuana, cocaine, and habitual smoking: A report from the Collaborative Study on the Genetics of Alcoholism. *Archives of General Psychiatry, 55,* 982–994.

Biglan, A., Hops, H., & Sherman, L. (1988). Coercive family processes and maternal depression. In R. J. McMahon & R. DeV. Peter (Eds.), *Marriages and families: Behavioral treatments and processes* (pp. 72–103). New York: Brunner/Mazel.

Binzer, M., & Kullgren, G. (1996). Conversion symptoms: What can we learn from previous studies? *Nordic Journal of Psychiatry, 50,* 143–152.

Birbaumer, N., Veit, R., Lotze, M., Erb, M., Hermann, C., Grodd, W., & Flor. H. (2005). Deficient fear conditioning in psychopathy: A functional magnetic resonance imaging study. *Archives of General Psychiatry, 62,* 799–805.

Birks, J. (2006). Cholinesterase inhibitors for Alzheimer's disease. *Cochrane Database of Systematic Reviews,* (1) doi:10.1002/14651858.

Birmaher, B., Brent, D. A., Kolko, D., Baugher, M., Bridge, J., Holder, D., Iyengar, S., & Ulloa, R. E. (2000). Clinical outcome after short-term psychotherapy for adolescents with major depressive disorder. *Archives of General Psychiatry, 57,* 29–36.

Birnbaum, G. E., Reis, H. T., Mikulincer, M., Gillath, O., & Orpaz, A. (2006). When sex is more than just sex: Attachment orientations, sexual experience, and relationship quality. *Journal of Personality and Social Psychology, 91,* 929–943.

Birren, J. E., & Schaie, K. W. (Eds.). (2001). *Handbook of the psychology of aging* (5th ed.). San Diego: Academic Press.

Bischkopf, J., Busse, A., & Angermeyer, M. C. (2002). Mild cognitive impairment: A review of prevalence, incidence and outcome according to current approaches. *Acta Psychiatrica Scandinavia, 106,* 403–414.

BJS. (1999). *Mental health and treatment of inmates and probationers.* Bureau of Justice Statistics Special Report. Department of Justice. NJDC174463.

Blachman, D. R., & Hinshaw, S. P. (2002). Patterns of friendship among girls with and without attention-deficit/hyperactivity disorder. *Journal of Abnormal Child Psychology, 30,* 625–640.

Black, D. R., & Threlfall, W. E. (1986). A stepped approach to weight control: A minimal intervention and a bibliotherapy problem-solving program. *Behavior Therapy, 17,* 144–157.

Black, D. W., Baumgard, C. H., & Bell, S. E. (1995). A 16- to 45-year follow-up of 71 men with antisocial personality disorder. *Comprehensive Psychiatry, 36,* 130–140.

Blair, R. J. D., Jones, L., Clark, F., & Smith, M. (1997). The psychopathic individual: A lack of responsiveness to distress cues? *Psychophysiology, 34,* 192–198.

Blanchard, J. J., & Brown, S. B. (1998). Structured diagnostic interviews. In C. R. Reynolds (Ed.), *Comprehensive clinical psychology: Vol. 3. Assessment* (pp. 97–130). New York: Elsevier.

Blanchard, J. J., Squires, D., Henry, T., Horan, W. P., Bogenschutz, M., et al. (1999). Examining an affect regulation model of substance abuse in schizophrenia: The role of traits and coping. *Journal of Nervous and Mental Disease, 187,* 72–79.

Blatt, S. J., Sanislow, C. A., III, Zuroff, D. C., & Pilkonis, P. A. (1996). Characteristics of effective therapists: Further analyses of data from the national institute of mental health treatment of depression collaborative research program. *Journal of Consulting and Clinical Psychology, 64,* 1276–1284.

Blenker, M. (1967). Environmental change and the aging individual. *Gerontologist, 7,* 101–105.

Blumberg, H. P., Stern, E., Ricketts, S., Martinez, D., de Asis, J., White, T., et al. (1999). Rostral and orbital prefrontal cortex dysfunction in the manic state of bipolar disorder. *American Journal of Psychiatry, 156,* 1986–1988.

Blumenthal, J. A., Sherwood, A., Gullette, E. C. D., et al. (2002). Biobehavioral approaches to the treatment of essential hypertension. *Journal of Consulting and Clinical Psychology, 70,* 569–589.

Bockhoven, J. (1963). *Moral treatment in American psychiatry.* New York: Springer-Verlag.

Bockting, C. L. H., Schene, A. H., Spinhoven, P., Koeter, M. W. J., Wouters, L. F., Huyser, J., et al. (2005). Preventing relapse/recurrence in recurrent deprssion with cognitive therapy: A randomized controlled trial. *Journal of Consulting and Clinical Psychology, 73,* 647–657.

Boegels, S. M., & Zigterman, D. (2000). Dysfunctional cognitions in children with social phobia, separation anxiety disorder, and generalized anxiety disorder. *Journal of Abnormal Child Psychology, 28,* 205–211.

Bogenschutz, M. P., & Nurnberg, G. (2004). Olanzapine versus placebo in the treatment of borderline personality disorder. *Journal of Clinical Psychiatry, 65,* 104–109.

Bohne, A., Keuthen, N. J., Wilhelm, S., Deckersback, T., & Jenike, M. A. (2002). Prevalence of symptoms of body dysmorphic disorder and its correlates: A cross-cultural comparison. *Psychosomatics, 43,* 486–490.

Bolton, P., Bass, J., Neugebauer, R., Verdeli, H., Clougherty, K. F., Wickramaratne, P., Speelman, L., Ndogoni, L., & Weissman, M. (2003). Group interpersonal psychotherapy for depression in rural Uganda: A randomized controlled trial. *Journal of the American Medical Association, 289,* 3117–3124.

Bolton, P., MacDonald, H., Pickles, A., Rios, P., Goode, S., Crowson, M., Bailey, A., & Rutter, M. (1994). A case control family history study of autism. *Journal of Child Psychology and Psychiatry, 35,* 877–900.

Bonanno, G. A. (2004). Loss, trauma, and human resilience: Have we underestimated the human capacity to thrive after extremely aversive events? *American Psychologist, 59,* 20–28.

Bonanno, G. A., Wortman, C. B., Lehman, D. R., Tweed, R. G., Haring, M., Sonnega, J., et al. (2002). Resilience to loss and chronic grief: A prospective study from preloss to 18-months postloss. *Journal of Personality and Social Psychology, 83,* 1150–1164.

Bonta, J., Law, M., & Hanson, K. (1998). The prediction of criminal and violent recidivism among mentally disordered offenders. *Psychological Bulletin, 123,* 123–142.

Boon, S., & Draijer, N. (1993a). *Multiple personality disorder in the Netherlands.* Amsterdam: Swets & Zeitlinger.

Boon, S., & Draijer, N. (1993b). Multiple personality disorder in the Netherlands: A clinical investigation of 71 cases. *American Journal of Psychiatry, 150,* 489–494.

Boos, H. B., Aleman, A., Cahn, W., Hulshoff, H., & Kahn, R. S.(2007). Brain volumes in relatives of patients with schizophrenia: A meta-analysis. *Archives of General Psychiatry, 64,* 297–304.

Borch-Jacobsen, M. (1997, April 24). Sybil: The making of a disease? An interview with Dr. Herbert Spiegel. *New York Review of Books,* p. 60.

Borduin, C. M., Mann, B. J., Cone, L. T., Henggeler, S. W., Fucci, B. R., Blaske, D. M., & Williams, R. A. (1995). Multisystemic treatment of serious juvenile offenders: Long-term prevention of criminality and violence. *Journal of Consulting and Clinical Psychology, 63,* 569–578.

Borkovec, T. D., & Newman, M. G. (1998). Worry and generalized anxiety disorder. In P. Salkovskis (Ed.), *Comprehensive clinical psychology,* 157–178 Oxford: Elsevier.

Bornstein, R. F. (1997). Dependent personality disorder in the DSM-IV and beyond. *Clinical Psychology: Science and Practice, 4,* 175–187.

Bornstein, R. F. (2003). Behaviorally referenced experimentation and symptom validation: A paradigm for 21st-century personality disorder research. *Journal of Personality Disorders, 17,* 1–18.

Bosinski, H. A., Peter, M., Bonatz, G., Arndt, R., Heidenreich, M., et al. (1997). A higher rate of hyper-adrenergic disorders in female-to-male transsexuals. *Psychoneuroendocrinology, 22,* 361–380.

Bosquet, M. & Egeland, B. (2006). The development and maintenance of anxiety symptoms from infancy through adolescence in a longitudinal sample. *Development and Psychopathology, 18,* 517–550.

Bostwick, J. M., & Pankratz, V. S. (2000). Affective disorders and suicide risk: A reexamination. *American Journal of Psychiatry, 157,* 1925–1932.

Bouton, M. E., Mineka, S., & Barlow, D. H. (2001). A modern learning theory perspective on the etiology of panic disorder. *Psychological Review, 108,* 4–32.

Bouton, M. E., & Waddell, J. (2007). Some biobehavioral insights into persistent effects of emotional trauma. In L. J. Kirmayer, R. Lemelson, & M. Barad (Eds.), *Understanding trauma: Integrating biological, clinical, and cultural perspectives* (pp. 41–59). New York: Cambridge University Press.

Bowden, C. L., Lecrubier, Y., Bauer, M., Goodwin, G., Greil, W., Sachs, G., & von Knorring, L. (2000). Maintenance therapies for classic and other forms of bipolar disorder. *Journal of Affective Disorders, 59,* S57–S67.

Bowers, M. B., Jr. (1974). Central dopamine turnover in schizophrenic syndromes. *Archives of General Psychiatry, 31,* 50–54.

Bowers, W. A., & Ansher, L.S. (2008). The effectiveness of cognitive behavioral therapy on changing eating disorder symptoms and psychopathy of 32 anorexia nervosa patients at hospital discharge and one year follow-up. *Annals of Clinical Psychiatry, 20,* 79–86.

Boyle, M. (1991). *Schizophrenia: A scientific delusion?* New York: Routledge.

Bradley, L., & Bryant, P. E. (1985). *Rhyme and reason in reading and spelling.* Ann Arbor: University of Michigan Press.

Bradley, R., Greene, J., Russ, E., Dutra, L., & Westen, D. (2005). A multidimensional meta-analysis of psychotherapy for PTSD. *American Journal of Psychiatry, 162,* 214–227.

Bradley, S. J., & Zucker, K. J. (1997). Gender identity disorder: A review of the past 10 years. *Journal of the American Academy of Child and Adolescent Psychiatry, 36,* 872–880.

Brandon, T. H., Collins, B. N., Juliano, L. M., & Lazev, A. B. (2000). Preventing relapse among former smokers: A comparison of minimal interventions through telephone and mail. *Journal of Consulting and Clinical Psychology, 68,* 103–113.

Brandon, T. H, Vidrine, J. I., & Litvin, E. B. (2007). Relapse and relapse prevention. *Annual Review of Clinical Psychology, 3,* 257–284.

Brandon, Y. H., Zelman, D. C., & Baker, T. B. (1987). Effects of maintenance sessions on smoking relapse: Delaying the inevitable? *Journal of Consulting and Clinical Psychology, 55,* 780–782.

Brandt, J., Buffers, N., Ryan, C., & Bayog, R. (1983). Cognitive loss and recovery in chronic alcohol abusers. *Archives of General Psychiatry, 40,* 435–442.

Bransford, J. D., & Johnson, M. K. (1973). Considerations of some problems of comprehension. In W. G. Chase (Ed.), *Visual information processing.* New York: Academic Press.

Braswell, L., & Kendall, P. C. (1988). Cognitive-behavioral methods with children. In K. S. Dobson (Ed.), *Handbook of cognitive-behavioral therapies.* New York: Guilford.

Braun, J. M., Kahn, R. S., Froehlich, T., Auinger, P., & Lanphear, B. (2006). Exposures to environmental toxicants and attention deficit hyperactivity disorder in U.S. children. *Environmental Health Perspectives, 114,* 1904–1909.

Brecher, E. M., & the Editors of *Consumer Reports.* (1972). *Licit and illicit drugs.* Mount Vernon, NY: Consumers Union.

Bremner, J. D., Vythilingam, M., Vermetten, E., Southwick, S. M., McGlashan, T., Nazeer, A., et al. (2003). MRI and PET study of deficits in hippocampal structure and function in women with childhood sexual abuse and post-traumatic stress disorder. *American Journal of Psychiatry, 160,* 924–932.

Brems, C. (1995). Women and depression: A comprehensive analysis. In E. E. Beckham & W. Leber (Eds.), *Handbook of depression* (2nd ed., pp. 539–566). New York: Guilford.

Brennan, P. L., Schutte, K. K., & Moos, R. H. (1999). Reciprocal relations between stressors and drinking behavior: A three-wave panel study of late middle-aged and older women and men. *Addiction, 94,* 737–749.

Brent, D. A., Holder, D., Kolko, D., Birmaher, B., Baugher, M., et al. (1997). A clinical psychotherapy trial for adolescent depression comparing cognitive, family, and supportive therapy. *Archives of General Psychiatry, 54,* 877–885.

Breslau, J., Aguilar-Gaxiola, A., Kendler, K. S., Su, M., Williams, D., & Kessler, R. (2006). Specifying race-ethnic differences in risk for psychiatric disorder in a USA national sample. *Psychological Medicine, 36,* 57–68.

Breslau, N., Brown, G. G., Del Dotto, J. E., Kumar, S., Ezhuthachan, S., Andreski, P., & Hufnagle, K. G. (1996). Psychiatric sequalae of low birth weight at 6 years of age. *Journal of Abnormal Child Psychology, 24,* 385–400.

Breslau, N., Chilcoat, H. D., Kessler, R. C., & Davis, G. C. (1999). Previous exposure to trauma and PTSD effects of subsequent trauma: Results from the Detroit Area Survey of Trauma. *American Journal of Psychiatry, 156,* 902–907.

Breslau, N., Davis, G. C., & Andreski, P. (1995). Risk factors for PTSD-related traumatic events: A prospective analysis. *American Journal of Psychiatry, 152,* 529–535.

Breslau, N., Lucia, V., & Alvarado, G. F. (2006). Intelligence and other predisposing factors in exposure to trauma and posttramatic stress disorder: A follow-up study at age 17 years. *Archives of General Psychiatry, 63,* 1238–1245.

Brestan, E. V., & Eyberg, S. M. (1998). Effective psychosocial treatment of conduct disordered children and adolescents: 29 years, 82 studies, and 5275 kids. *Journal of Clinical Child Psychology, 27,* 180–189.

Breuer, J., & Freud, S. (1982). *Studies in hysteria.* (J. Strachey, Trans. and Ed., with the collaboration of A. Freud). New York: Basic Books. (Original work published 1895)

Brewerton, T. D., Lydiard, B. R., Laraia, M. T., Shook, J. E., & Ballenger, J. C. (1992). CSF beta-endorphin and dynorphin in bulimia nervosa. *American Journal of Psychiatry, 149,* 1086–1090.

Brewin, C. R., Andrews, B., & Valentine, J. D. (2000). Meta-analysis of risk factors for posttraumatic stress disorder in trauma-exposed adults. *Journal of Consulting and Clinical Psychology, 68,* 748–766.

Brewin, C. R., & Holmes, E. A. (2003). Psychological theories of posttraumatic stress disorder. *Clinical Psychology Review, 23,* 339–376.

Brewin, C. R., Kleiner, J. S., Vasterling, J. J., & Field, A. P. (2007). Memory for emotionally neutral information in posttraumatic stress disorder: A meta-analytic investigation. *Journal of Abnormal Psychology, 116,* 448–463.

Brezo, J., Paris, J., & Turecki, G. (2006). Personality traits as correlates of suicidal ideation, suicide attempts, and suicide completions: A systematic review. *Acta Psychiatrica Scandinavica, 113,* 180–206.

Brickman, A. S., McManus, M., Grapentine, W. L., & Alessi, N. (1984). Neuropsychological assessment of seriously delinquent adolescents. *Journal of the American Academy of Child Psychiatry, 23,* 453–457.

Bridge, J. A., Iyengar, S., Salary, C. B., et al. (2007). Clinical response and risk for reported suicidal ideation and suicide attempts in pediatric antidepressant treatment: A meta-analysis of randomized controlled trials. *Journal of the American Medical Association, 297,* 1683–1696.

Briere, J., Scott, C., & Weathers, F. (2005). Peritraumatic and persistent dissociation in the presumed etiology of PTSD. *American Journal of Psychiatry, 162,* 2295–2301.

Brisson, C., Laflamme, N., Moisan, J., Miloît, A., Mâsse, B., & Vézina, M. (1999). Effect of family responsibilities and job strain on ambulatory blood pressure among white collar women. *Psychosomatic Medicine, 61,* 205–213.

Brody, A. L., Saxena, S., Stoessel, P., Gillies, L. A., Fairbanks, L. A., Alborzian, S., Phelps, M. E., Huang, S. C., Wu, H. M., Ho, M. L., Ho, M. K., Au, S. C., Maidment, K., & Baxter, L. R., Jr. (2001). Regional brain metabolic changes in patients with major depression treated with either paroxetine or interpersonal therapy: Preliminary findings. *Archives of General Psychiatry, 58,* 631–640.

Brookes, K., Mill, J., Guindalini, C., Curran, S., Xu, X., Knight, J., Chen, C. K., Huang, Y. S., Sentha, V., Taylor, E., Chen, W., Breen, G., & Asherson, P. (2006). A common haplotype of the dopamine transporter gene associated with attention-deficit/hyperactivity disorder and interacting with maternal use of alcohol during pregnancy. *Archives of General Psychiatry, 63,* 74–81.

Brown, A. S. (2006). Prenatal infection as a risk factor for schizophrenia. *Schizophrenia Bulletin, 32,* 200–202.

Brown, A. S., Begg, M. D., Gravenstein, S., Schaefer, C. A., Wyatt, R. J., Bresnahan, M., Babulas, V. P., & Susser, E. S. (2004). Serologic evidence of prenatal influenza in the etiology of schizophrenia. *Archives of General Psychiatry, 61,* 774–780.

Brown, A. S., Bottiglieri, T., Schaefer, C. A., Quesenberry, C.P., Jr, Liu, L., Bresnahan, M., & Susser, E.S. (2007). Elevated prenatal homocysteine levels as a risk factor for schizophrenia. *Archives of General Psychiatry, 64,* 31–39.

Brown, A.S., Schaefer, C.A., Quesenberry, C.P., Jr, Liu, L., Babulas, V.P., & Susser, E.S. (2005). Maternal exposure to toxoplasmosis and risk of schizophrenia in adult offspring. *American Journal of Psychiatry, 162,* 767–773.

Brown, D., Scheflin, A. W., & Whitfield, C. L. (1999). Recovered memories: The current weight of the evidence in science and in the courts. *The Journal of Psychiatry and Law, 27,* 5–156.

Brown, G. K., Beck, A. T., Steer, R. A., & Grisham, J. R. (2000). Risk factors for suicide in psychiatric outpatients: A 20-year prospective study. *Journal of Consulting and Clinical Psychology, 68,* 371–377.

Brown, G. K., Henriques, G. R., Ratto, C., & Beck, A. T. (2002). *Cognitive therapy treatment manual for suicide attempters.* Philadelphia: University of Pennsylvania.

Brown, G. K., Ten Have, T., Henriques, G. R., Xie, S. X., Hollander, J. E., & Beck, A. T. (2005). Cognitive therapy for the prevention of suicide attempts. *Journal of the American Medical Association, 294,* 563–570.

Brown, G. W., & Andrews, B. (1986). Social support and depression. In R. Trumbull & M. H. Appley (Eds.), *Dynamics of stress: Physiological, psychological, and social perspectives* (pp. 257–282). New York: Plenum.

Brown, G. W., Bone, M., Dalison, B., & Wing, J. K. (1966). *Schizophrenia and social care.* London: Oxford University Press.

Brown, G. W., & Harris, T. O. (1978). *The Bedford College lifeevents and difficulty schedule: Directory of contextual threat of events.* London: Bedford College, University of London.

Brown, S. A., Vik, P. W., McQuaid, J. R., Patterson, T. L., Irwin, M. R., et al. (1990). Severity of psychosocial stress and outcome of alcoholism treatment. *Journal of Abnormal Psychology, 99,* 344–348.

Brown, T. A., Campbell, L. A., Lehman, C. L., et al. (2001). Current and lifetime comorbidity of the DSM-IV anxiety and mood disorders in a large clinical sample. *Journal of Abnormal Psychology, 110,* 585–599.

Brownell, K. D., & Horgen, K. B. (2003). *Food fight: The inside story of the food industry, America's obesity crisis, and what we can do about it.* Chicago: Contemporary Books.

Bruce, M. L. (2002). Psychosocial risk factors for depressive disorders in late life. *Biological Psychiatry, 175,* 175–184.

Bruce, M. L., Ten Have, T. R., Reynolds, C. F. III, Katz, I. I., et al. (2004). Reducing suicidal ideation and depressive symptoms in depressed older primary care patients. *Journal of the American Medical Association, 291,* 1081–1091.

Bruch, H. (1980). Preconditions for the development of anorexia nervosa. *American Journal of Psychoanalysis, 40,* 169–172.

Bryant, R. A., & Guthrie, R. M. (2007). Maladaptive self-appraisals before trauma exposure predict posttraumatic stress disorder. *Journal of Consulting and Clinical Psychology, 75,* 812–815.

Bryant, R. A., Mastrodomenico, J., Felmingham, K. L., Hopwood, S., Kenny, L., Kandris, E., et al. (2008). Treatment of acute stress disorder: A randomized controlled trial. *Archives of General Psychiatry, 65,* 659–667.

Bryant, R. A., & McConkey, K. M. (1989). Visual conversion disorder: A case analysis of the influence of visual information. *Journal of Abnormal Psychology, 98,* 326–329.

Bryant, R. A., Sackville, T., Dang, S. T., Moulds, M., & Guthrie, R. (1999). Treating acute stress disorder: An evaluation of cognitive behavior therapy and supporting counseling techniques. *American Journal of Psychiatry, 156,* 1780–1786.

Buchanan, R. W., Vladar, K., Barta, P. E., & Pearlson, G. D. (1998). Structural evaluation of the prefrontal cortex in schizophrenia. *American Journal of Psychiatry, 155,* 1049–1055.

Bucher, J. A., Houts, P. S., Nezu, C. M., & Nezu, A. M. (1999). Improving problem-solving skills of family caregivers through group education. *Journal of Psychosocial Oncology, 16,* 73–84.

Buchsbaum, M. S., Kessler, R., King, A., Johnson, J., & Cappelletti, J. (1984). Simultaneous cerebral glucography with positron emission tomography and topographic electroencephalography. In G. Pfurtscheller, E. J. Jonkman, & F. H. Lopes da Silva (Eds.), *Brain ischemia: Quantitative EEG and imaging techniques* 263–269. Amsterdam: Elsevier.

Budney, A. J., Moore, B. A., Rocha, H. L., & Higgens, S. T. (2006). Clinical trial of abstinence-based vouchers and cognitive behavior therapy for cannabis dependence. *Journal of Consulting and Clinical Psychology, 74,* 307–316.

Bulik, C. M., Sullivan, P. F., Wade, T. D., & Kendler, K. S. (2000). Twin studies of eating disorders: A review. *International Journal of Eating Disorders, 27,* 1–20.

Bulik, C. M., Wade, T. D., & Kendler, K. S. (2000). Characteristics of monozygotic twins discordant for bulimia nervosa. *International Journal of Eating Disorders, 29,* 1–10.

Bullers, S., Cooper, M. L., & Russell, M. (2001). Social network drinking and adult alcohol involvement: A longitudinal exploration of the direction of influence. *Addictive Behaviors, 26,* 181–199.

Burke, B. L., Arkowitz, H., & Menchola, M. (2003). The efficacy of motivational interviewing: A meta-analysis of controlled clinical trials. *Journal of Consulting and Clinical Psychology, 71,* 843–861.

Burne, S. M., & McLean, N. J. (2002). The cognitive behavioral model of bulimia nervosa: A direct evaluation. *International Journal of Eating Disorders, 31,* 17–31.

Burris, K. D., Molski, T. F., Xu, C., Ryan, E., Tottori, K., Kikuchi, T., Yocca F. D., & Molinoff, P. B. (2002). Aripiprazole, a novel antipsychotic, is a high-affinity partial agonist at human dopamine D2 receptors. *Journal of Pharmacology and Experimental Therapies, 302,* 381–389.

Bushman, B. J., & Cooper, H. M. (1990). Effects of alcohol on human aggression: An integrative research review. *Psychological Bulletin, 107,* 341–354.

Bustillo, J. R., Lauriello, J., Horan, W. P., & Keith, S. J. (2001). The psychosocial treatment of schizophrenia: An update. *American Journal of Psychiatry, 158,* 163–175.

Butcher, J. N., Dahlstrom, W. G., Graham, J. R., Tellegen, A., & Kraemer, B. (1989). *Minnesota Multiphasic Personality Inventory–2: Manual for administration and scoring.* Minneapolis: University of Minnesota Press.

Butler, A. C., Chapman, J. E., Forman, E. M., & Beck, A. T. (2006). The empirical status of cognitive-behavioral therapy: A review of meta-analyses. *Clinical Psychology Review, 26,* 17–31.

Butler, L. D., Duran, R. E. F., Jasiukaitis, P., Koopman, C., & Spiegel, D. (1996). Hypnotizability and traumatic experience: A diathesis-stress model of dissociative symptomatology. *American Journal of Psychiatry, 153,* 42–63.

Butler, R. N., Lewis, M. I., & Sunderland, T. (1998). *Aging and mental health: Positive psychosocial and biomedical approaches* (5th ed.). Boston: Allyn & Bacon.

Butzlaff, R. L., & Hooley, J. M. (1998). Expressed emotion and psychiatric relapse: A meta-analysis. *Archives of General Psychiatry, 55,* 547–553.

Byne, W., Buchsbaum, M. S., Mattiace, L. A., et al. (2002). Postmortem assessment of thalamic nuclear volume in subjects with schizophrenia. *American Journal of Psychiatry, 159,* 59–65.

Caccioppo, J. T., Klein, D. J., Bernston, G. G., & Hatfield, E. (1998). The psychophysiology of emotion. In M. Lewis & E. Haviland (Eds.), *Handbook of emotions* (pp. 119–142). New York: Guilford.

Cadenhead, K. S., Light, G. A., Geyer, M. A., McDowell, J. E., & Braff, D. L. (2002). Neurobiological measures of schizotypal personality disorder: Defining an inhibitory endophenotype? *American Journal of Psychiatry, 159,* 869–871.

Cadoret, R. J., Yates, W. R., Troughton, E., Woodworth, G., & Stewart, M. A. (1995). Adoption study demonstrating two genetic pathways to drug abuse. *Archives of General Psychiatry, 52,* 42–52.

Cahill, K., Stead, L., & Lancaster, T. (2007). Nicotine receptor partial agonists for smoking cessation. *Cochrane Database Systematic Reviews.* CD006103.

Calabrese, J. R., Bowden, C. L., Sachs, G. S., Ascher, J. A., Monaghan, E., & Rudd, G. D. (1999). A double-blind placebo-controlled study of lamotrigine monotherapy in outpatients with bipolar I depression. *Journal of Clinical Psychiatry, 60,* 79–84.

Calabrese, J. R., Bowden, C. L., Sachs, G., Yatham, L. N., Behnke, K., Mehtonen, O. P., et al. (2003). A placebo-controlled 18-month trial of lamotrigine and lithium maintenance treatment in recently depressed patients with bipolar I disorder. *Journal of Clinical Psychiatry, 64,* 1013–1024.

Caldwell, M. B., Brownell, K. D., & Wilfley, D. (1997). Relationship of weight, body dissatisfaction, and self-esteem in African American and white female dieters. *International Journal of Eating Disorders, 22,* 127–130.

Calhoun, V. D., Pekar, J. J., & Pearlson, G. D. (2004). Alcohol intoxication effects on simulated driving: Exploring alcohol-dose effects on brain activation using functional MRI. *Neuropsychopharmacology, 29,* 2197–2107.

Caligiuri, M. P., Brown, G. G., Meloy, M. J., Eberson, S. C., Kindermann, S. S., Frank, L. R., et al. (2003). An fMRI study of affective state and medication on cortical and subcortical brain regions during motor performance in bipolar disorder. *Psychiatry Research, 123,* 171–182.

Camí, J., & Farré, M. (2003). Drug addiction. *New England Journal of Medicine, 349,* 975–986.

Campbell, J., Stefan, S., & Loder, A. (1994). Putting violence in context. *Hospital and Community Psychiatry, 45,* 633.

Campbell, M., Armenteros, J. L., Malone, R. P., Adams, P. B., Eisenberg, Z. W., & Overall, J. E. (1997). Neuroleptic-related dyskinesias in autistic children: A prospective, longitudinal study. *Journal of the American Academy of Child and Adolescent Psychiatry, 36,* 835–843.

Campbell, W. K., Bosson, J. K., Goheen, T. W., Lakey, C. E., & Kernis, M. H. (2007). Do narcissists dislike themselves "deep down inside"? *Psychological Science, 18,* 227–229.

Camus, V., Burtin, B., Simeone, I., et al. (2000). Factor analysis supports the evidence of existing hyperactive and hypoactive subtypes of delirium. *International Journal of Geriatric Psychiatry, 15,* 313–316.

Canivez, G. L., & Watkins, M. W. (1998). Long-term stability of the Wechsler Intelligence Scale for Children (3rd ed.). *Psychological Assessment, 10,* 285–291.

Cannon, T. D., Cadenhead, K., Cornblatt, B., Woods, S.W, Addington, J., Walker, E., Seidman, L.J., Perkins, D., Tsuang, M., McGlashan, T., & Heinssen, R. (2008). Prediction of psychosis in youth at high clinical risk: A multisite longitudinal study in North America. *Archives of General Psychiatry, 65,* 28–37.

Cannon, T. D., Kaprio, J., Lonnqvist, J., Huttunen, M., & Koskenvuo, M. (1998). The genetic epidemiology of schizophrenia in a Finnish twin cohort: A population-based modeling study. *Archives of General Psychiatry, 55,* 67–74.

Cannon, T. D., & Mednick, S. A. (1993). The schizophrenia high-risk project in Copenhagen: Three decades of progress. *Acta Psychiatrica Scandanavica, 87,* 33–47.

Cannon, T. D., Mednick, S. A., & Parnas, J. (1990). Antecedents of predominantly negative and predominantly positive-symptom schizophrenia in a high-risk population. *Archives of General Psychiatry, 47,* 622–632.

Cannon, T. D., van Erp, T. G., Rosso, I. M., et al. (2002). Fetal hypoxia and structural brain abnormalities in schizophrenic patients, their siblings, and controls. *Archives of General Psychiatry, 59,* 35–42.

Capaldi, D. M., & Patterson, G. R. (1994). Interrelated influences of contextual factors on antisocial behavior in childhood and adolescence for males. In D. C. Fowles, P. Sutker, & S. H. Goodman (Eds.), *Progress in experimental personality and psychopathology research* (pp. 165–198). New York: Springer-Verlag.

Capps, L., Losh, M., & Thurber, C. (2000). "The frog ate the bug and made his mouth sad": Narrative competence in children with autism. *Journal of Abnormal Child Psychology, 28,* 193–204.

Capps, L., Rasco, L., Losh, M., & Heerey, E. (1999, April). *Understanding of self-conscious emotions in high-functioning children with autism*. Paper presented at the biennial meeting of the Society for Research in Child Development, Albuquerque, NM.

Capps, L., Yirmiya, N., & Sigman, M. (1992). Understanding of simple and complex emotion in high-functioning children with autism. *Journal of Child Psychology and Psychiatry, 33,* 1169–1182.

Capron, A. M. (1999). Ethical and human rights issues in research on mental disorders that may affect decision-making capacity. *The New England Journal of Medicine, 340,* 1430–1434.

CAPT. (2000). Prisons: The nation's new mental institutions. *Outreach.* Retrieved from http://www.psych-health. com/mental8. htm

Cardno, A. G., Marshall, E. J., Coid, B., Macdonald, A. M., Ribchester, T. R., et al. (1999). Heritability estimates for psychotic disorders: The Maudsley Twin Psychosis Series. *Archives of General Psychiatry, 56,* 162–170.

Carey, K. B., Carey, M. P., Maisto, S. A., & Henson, J. M. (2006). Brief motivational interventions for heavy college drinkers: A randomized controlled trial. *Journal of Consulting and Clinical Psychology, 74,* 943–954.

Carlbring, P., Bohman, S., Brunt, S., Buhrman, M., Westling, B. E., Ekselius, L., et al. (2006). Remote treatment of panic disorder: A randomized trial of Internet-based cognitive behavior therapy supplemented with telephone calls. *American Journal of Psychiatry, 163,* 2119–2125.

Carlson, G. A., & Meyer, S. E. (2006). Phenomenology and diagnosis of bipolar disorder in children, adolescents, and adults: Complexities and developmental issues. *Development and Psychopathology, 18,* 939–969.

Carlsson, A., Hanson, L. O., Waters, N., & Carlsson, M. L. (1999). A glutamatergic deficiency model of schizophrenia. *British Journal of Psychiatry, 174,* 2–6.

Carney, R. M., Blumenthal, J. A., Freedland, K. E., Youngblood, M., Veith, R. C., Burg, M. M., et al. (2004). Depression and late mortality after myocardial infarction in the enhancing recovery in coronary heart disease (ENRICHD) study. *Psychological Medicine, 66,* 466–474.

Carpenter, W. T., Gold, J. M., Lahti, A. C., Queern, C. A., Conley, R. R., Bartko, J. J., Kovnick, J., & Appelbaum, P. S. (2000). Decisional capacity for informed consent in schizophrenia research. *Archives of General Psychiatry, 57,* 533–538.

Carpenter, W. T., Heinrichs, D. W., & Wagman, A. M. I. (1988). Deficit and nondeficit forms of schizophrenia: The concept. *American Journal of Psychiatry, 145,* 578–583.

Carpentieri, S. C., & Morgan, S. B. (1994). Brief report: A comparison of patterns of cognitive functioning of autistic and nonautistic retarded children on the Stanford-Binet (4th ed.). *Journal of Autism and Developmental Disorders, 24,* 215–223.

Carr, A. T. (1971). Compulsive neurosis: Two psychophysiological studies. *Bulletin of the British Psychological Society, 24,* 256–257.

Carr, E. G., Levin, L., McConnachie, G., Carlson, J. I., Kemp, D. C., & Smith, C. E. (1994). *Communication based intervention for problem behavior.* Baltimore: Paul H. Brookes.

Carr, R. E. (1998). Panic disorder and asthma: Causes, effects, and research implications. *Journal of Psychosomatic Research, 44,* 43–52.

Carr, R. E. (1999). Panic disorder and asthma. *Journal of Asthma, 36,* 143–152.

Carrasco, J. L., Dyaz-Marsa, M., Hollander, E., Cesar, J., & Saiz-Ruiz, J. (2000). Decreased monoamine oxidase activity in female bulimia. *European Neuropsychopharmacology, 10,* 113–117.

Carroll, K. M., Ball, S. A., Nich, C., et al. (2001). Targeting behavioral therapies to enhance naltrexone treatment of opioid dependence: Efficacy of contingency management and significant other involvement. *Archives of General Psychiatry, 58,* 755–761.

Carroll, K. M., Easton, C. J., Nich, C., Hunkele, K. A., Neavins, T. M., et al. (2006). The use of contingency management and motivational/skills-building therapy to treat young adults with marijuana dependence. *Journal of Consulting and Clinical Psychology, 74,* 955–966.

Carroll, K. M., Rounsaville, B. J., Gordon, L. T., Nich, C., Jatlow, P., Bisighini, R. M., & Gawin, F. H. (1994). Psychotherapy and pharmacotherapy for ambulatory cocaine abusers. *Archives of General Psychiatry, 51,* 177–187.

Carroll, K. M., Rounsaville, B. J., Nich, C., Gordon, L. T., & Gawin, F. (1995). Integrating psychotherapy and pharmacotherapy for cocaine dependence: Results from a randomized clinical trial. In L. S. Onken, J. D. Blaine, & J. J. Boren (Eds.), *Integrating behavioral therapies with medications in the treatment of drug dependence* (pp. 19–36). Rockville, MD: National Institute on Drug Abuse.

Carroll, K. M., Rounsaville, B. J., Nich, C., Gordon, L. T., Wirtz, P. W., & Gawin, F. (1994). One-year follow-up of psychotherapy and pharmacotherapy for cocaine dependence. *Archives of General Psychiatry, 51,* 989–997.

Carroll, R. A. (2000). Assessment and treatment of gender dysphoria. In S. R. Lieblum & R. C. Rosen (Eds.), *Principles and practice of sex therapy* (pp. 368–397). New York: Guilford.

Carstensen, L. L. (1996). Evidence for a life-span theory of socioemotional selectivity. *Current Directions in Psychological Science, 4,* 151–156.

Carter, F. A., McIntosh, V. V. W., Joyce, P. R., Sullivan, P. F., & Bulik, C. M. (2003). Role of exposure with response prevention in cognitive-behavioral therapy for bulimia nervosa: Three-year follow-up results. *International Journal of Eating Disorders, 33,* 127–135.

Carver, C. S., Pozo, C., Harris, S. D., Noriega, V., Scheier, M., Robinson, D., Ketcham, A., Moffat, F. L., & Clark, K. (1993). How coping mediates the effect of optimism on distress: A study of women with early stage breast cancer. *Journal of Personality and Social Psychology, 65,* 375–390.

Carver, C. S., & Scheier, M. F. (1999). Stress, coping, and self-regulatory processes. In L. A. Pervin & O. P. John (Eds.), *Handbook of personality* (2nd ed., pp. 553–575). New York: Guilford.

Case, B. G., Olfson, M., Marcus, S. C., & Siegel, C. (2007). Trends in the inpatient mental health treatment of children and adolescents in US community hospitals between 1990 and 2000. *Archives of General Psychiatry, 64,* 89–96.

Casey, B. J., & Durston, S. (2006). From behavior to cognition to the brain and back: What have we learned from functional imaging studies of attention deficit hyperactivity disorder? *American Journal of Psychiatry, 163,* 957–960.

Casey, J. E., Rourke, B. P., & Del Dotto, J. E. (1996). Learning disabilities in children with attention deficit disorder with and without hyperactivity. *Child Neuropsychology, 2,* 83–98.

Casper, M. L., Barnett, E., Halverson, J. A., Elmes, G. A., Braham, V. E., Majeed, Z. A., Boom, A. S., & Stanley, S. (2000). *Women and heart disease: An atlas of racial and ethnic disparities in mortality* (2nd ed.). Office for Social and Environmental Health Research, West Virginia University, and the National Center for Chronic Disease Prevention and Health Promotion, Centers for Disease Control and Prevention, Atlanta, GA.

Caspi, A., McClay, J., Moffitt, T. E., Mill, J., Martin, J., Craig, I. W., Taylor, A., & Poulton, R. (2002). Role of genotype in the cycle of violence in maltreated children. *Science, 297,* 851–854.

Caspi, A. & Moffitt, T. E. (2006). Gene–environment interactions in psychiatry: Joining forces with neuroscience. *Nature Reviews Neuroscience, 7,* 583–590.

Caspi, A., Sugden, K., Moffitt, T. E., Taylor, A., Craig, I. W., Harrington, H., et al. (2003). Influence of life stress on depression: Moderation by a polymorphism in the 5-HTT gene. *Science, 301,* 386–389.

Castellanos, F. X., Lee, P. P., Sharp, W., Jeffries, N. O., Greenstein, D. K., et al. (2002). Developmental trajectories of brain volume abnormalities in children and adolescents with attention-deficit/hyperactivity disorder. *Journal of the American Medical Association, 288,* 1740–1748.

Castellanos, F. X., Marvasti, F. F., Ducharme, J. L., Walter, J. M., Israel, M. E., Krain, A., Pavlovsky, C., & Hommer, D. W. (2000). Executive function oculomotor tasks in girls with ADHD. *Journal of the American Academy of Child and Adolescent Psychiatry, 39,* 644–650.

Castelli, F., Frith, C., Happe, F., & Frith, U. (2002). Autism, Asperger syndrome and brain mechanisms for the attribution of mental states to animated shapes. *Brain, 125,* 1839–1849.

Castells, X., Casas, M., Vidal, X., Bosch, R., Roncero, C., Ramos-Quiroga, J. A., et al. (2007). Efficacy of CNS stimulant treatment for cocaine dependence. A systematic review and meta-analysis of randomized controlled clinical trials. *Addiction, 102,* 1871–1887.

Castle, D. J., & Murray, R. M. (1993). The epidemiology of late-onset schizophrenia. *Schizophrenia Bulletin, 19,* 691–700.

Castonguay, L. G., Reid, J. J., Jr., Halperin, G. S., & Goldfried, M. R. (2003). Psychotherapy integration. In T. A. Widiger & G. Stricker (Eds.), *Handbook of psychology: Clinical psychology* (Vol. 8, pp. 327–366). New York: Wiley.

Celebucki, C. C., Wayne, G. F., Connolly, G. N., Pankow, J. F., & Chang, E. I. (2005). Characterization of measured menthol in 48 U.S. cigarette sub-brands. *Nicotine & Tobacco Research, 7,* 523–531.

Centers for Disease Control and Prevention (CDC). (2006). Homicides and suicides—National violent death reporting system, United States, 2003–2004. *American Journal of Medicine, 296,* 506–510.

Centers for Disease Control and Prevention (CDC). (2007). Prevalence of autism spectrum disorders — Autism and developmental disabilities monitoring network, 14 sites, United States, 2002. *MMWR, 56,* 12–28.

Cerny, J. A., Barlow, D. H., Craske, M. G., & Himadi, W. G. (1987). Couples treatment of agoraphobia: A two year follow-up. *Behavior Therapy, 18,* 401–415.

Chabrol, H., Peresson, G., Milberger, S., Biederman, J., & Faraone, S. V. (1997). ADHD and maternal smoking during pregnancy. *American Journal of Psychiatry, 154,* 1177–1178.

Chambers, K. C., & Bernstein, I. L. (1995). Conditioned flavor aversions. In R. L. Doty (Ed.), *Handbook of olfaction and gustation* (pp. 745–773). New York: Marcel Dekker.

Chambers, R. A., Taylor, J. R., & Potenza, M. N. (2003). Developmental neurocircuitry of motivation in adolescence: A critical period of addiction vulnerability. *American Journal of Psychiatry, 160,* 1041–1052.

Chambless, D. L., & Ollendick, T. H. (2001). Empirically supported psychological interventions: Controversies and evidence. *Annual Review of Psychology, 52,* 685–716.

Chambless, D. L., Sanderson, W. C., Shoham, V., Johnson, S. B., Pope, K. S., Crits-Christoph, P., Baker, M., Johnson, B., Woody, S. R., Sue, S., Beutler, L. E., Williams, D. A., & McCurry, S. (1998). An update on empirically validated therapies. *The Clinical Psychologist, 49,* 5–18.

Chang, L., Cloak, C. C., & Ernst, T. (2003). Magnetic resonance spectroscopy studies of GABA in neuropsychiatric disorders. *Journal of Clinical Psychiatry, 64* (Suppl. 3), 7–14.

Chang, S. M., Hahm, B., Lee, J., Shin, M. S., Jeon, H. J., Hong, J., et al. (2008). Cross-national difference in the prevalence of depression caused by the diagnostic threshold. *Journal of Affective Disorders, 106,* 159–167.

Chard, K. M. (2005). An evaluation of cognitive processing therapy for the treatment of posttraumatic stress disorder related to childhood sexual abuse. *Journal of Consulting and Clinical Psychology, 73,* 965–971.

Charney, D. S., Nemeroff, C. B., Lewis, L., et al. (2002). National Depressive and Manic Depressive Association Consensus statement on the use of placebo in clinical trials of mood disorders. *Archives of General Psychiatry, 59,* 262–270.

Charuvastra, A., & Cloitre, M. (2008). Social bonds and posttraumatic stress disorder. *Annual Review of Psychology, 59,* 301–328.

Chase, A. (1980). *The legacy of Malthus.* Urbana: University of Illinois Press.

Chassin, L., Curran, P. J., Hussong, A. M., & Colder, C. R. (1996). The relation of parent alcoholism to adolescent substance abuse: A longitudinal follow-up. *Journal of Abnormal Psychology, 105,* 70–80.

Chassin, L., Pitts, S. C., DeLucia, C., & Todd, M. (1999). A longitudinal study of children of alcoholics: Predicting young adult substance use disorders, anxiety, and depression. *Journal of Abnormal Psychology, 108,* 106–119.

Chavira, D. A., Stein, M. B., & Malcarne, V. L. (2002). Scrutinizing the relationship between shyness and social phobia. *Journal of Anxiety Disorders, 16,* 585–598.

Chen, E., Bloomberg, G. R., Fisher, E. B., & Strunk, R. C. (2003). Predictors of repeat hospitalizations in children with asthma: The role of psychosocial and socioenvironmental factors. *Health Psychology, 22,* 12–18.

Chen, S., Boucher, H. C., & Parker Tapias, M. (2006). The relational self revealed: Integrative conceptualization and implications for interpersonal life. *Psychological Bulletin, 132,* 151–179.

Chen, Y., Levy, D. L., Nakayama, K., Matthysse, S., et al. (1999). Dependence of impaired eye tracking on velocity discrimination in schizophrenia. *Archives of General Psychiatry, 56,* 155–161.

Chernoff, R. A. (1998). *The short and long-term behavioral outcomes of HIV prevention interventions: A critical evaluation.* Unpublished manuscript.

Chesney, M. A., Barrett, D. C., & Stall, R. (1998). Histories of substance use and risk behavior: Precursors to HIV seroconversion in homosexual men. *American Journal of Public Health, 88,* 113–116.

Chi, J. S., Poole, W. K., Kandefer, S. C., & Kloner, R. A. (2003). Cardiovascular mortality in New York City after September 11, 2001. *American Journal of Cardiology, 92,* 857–861.

Chiariello, M. A., & Orvaschel, H. (1995). Patterns of parent–child communication: Relationship to depression. *Clinical Psychology Review, 15,* 395–407.

Chorpita, B. F., Brown, T. A., & Barlow, D. H. (1998). Perceived control as a mediator of family environment in etiological models of childhood anxiety. *Behavior Therapy, 29,* 457–476.

Chorpita, B. F., Vitali, A. E., & Barlow, D. H. (1997). Behavioral treatment of choking phobia in an adolescent: An experimental analysis. *Journal of Behavior Therapy and Experimental Psychiatry, 28,* 307–315.

Choy, Y., Fyer, A. J., & Lipsitz, J. D. (2007). Treatment of specific phobia in adults. *Clinical Psychology Review, 27,* 266–286.

Christakis, N., & Fowler, J. (2008). The collective dynamics of smoking in a large social network. *New England Journal of Medicine, 358,* 2249–2258.

Christensen, A., Atkins, D. S., Yi, J., Baucom, D. H., & George, W. H. (2006). Couple and individual adjustment for 2 years following a randomized clinical trial comparing traditional versus integrative behavioral couple therapy. *Journal of Consulting and Clinical Psychology, 74,* 1180–1191.

Christensen, A., & Heavey, C. L. (1990). Gender and social structure in the demand/withdraw pattern of marital conflict. *Journal of Personality and Social Psychology, 59,* 73–81.

Christensen, A., & Jacobson, N. S. (2000). *Reconcilable differences.* New York: Guilford.

Chronis, A. M., Jones, H. A., & Raggi, V. L. (2006). Evidence-based psychosocial treatments for children and adolescents with attention-deficit/hyperactivity disorder. *Clinical Psychology Review, 26,* 486–502.

Chu, J. A., Frey, L. M., Ganzel, B. L., & Matthews, J. A. (1999). Memories of childhood abuse: Dissociation, amnesia, and corroboration. *American Journal of Psychiatry, 156,* 749–755.

Chua, S. T., & McKenna, P. T. (1995). Schizophrenia—a brain disease? *British Journal of Psychiatry, 166,* 563–582.

Ciechanowski, P., Wagner, E., Schmaling, K., Schwartz, S., Williams, B., Diehr, P., et al. (2004). Community integrated home-based depression treatment in older adults: A randomized controlled trial. *Journal of the American Medical Association, 291,* 1569–1577.

Cimbora, D. M., & McIntosh, D. N. (2003). Emotional responses to antisocial acts in adolescent males with conduct disorder: A link to affective morality. *Journal of Clinical Child and Adolescent Psychology, 32,* 296–301.

Cinciripini, P. M., Lapitsky, L. G., Wallfisch, A., Mace, R., Nezami, E., & Van Vunakis, H. (1994). An evaluation of a multicomponent treatment program involving scheduled smoking and relapse prevention procedures: Initial findings. *Addictive Behaviors, 19,* 13–22.

Cipriani, A., Pretty, H., Hawton, K., & Geddes, J. R. (2005). Lithium in the prevention of suicidal behavior and all-cause mortality in patients with mood disorders: A systematic review of randomized trials. *American Journal of Psychiatry, 162,* 1805–1819.

Clark, D. A. (1997). Twenty years of cognitive assessment: Current status and future directions. *Journal of Consulting and Clinical Psychology, 65,* 996–1000.

Clark, D. M. (1994). Cognitive therapy for panic disorder. In J. D. Maser & B. E. Wolfe (Eds.), *Treatment of panic disorder: A consensus development conference* (pp. 121–132). Washington, DC: American Psychiatric Association.

Clark, D. M. (1996). Panic disorder: From theory to therapy. In P. M. Salkovskis (Ed.), *Frontiers of cognitive therapy* (pp. 318–344). New York: Guilford.

Clark, D. M., Ehlers, A., Hackmann, A., McManus, F., Fennell, M., Grey, N., et al. (2006). Cognitive therapy versus exposure and applied relaxation in social phobia: A randomized controlled trial. *Journal of Consulting and Clinical Psychology, 74,* 568–578.

Clark, D. M., Ehlers, A., McManus, F., Hackmann, A., Fennell, M., Campbell, H., Flower, T., Davenport, C., & Louis, B. (2003). Cognitive therapy versus fluoxetine in generalized social phobia: A randomized control trial. *Journal of Consulting and Clinical Psychology, 71,* 1058–1067.

Clark, D. M., Salkovskis, P. M., Hackmann, A., Wells, A., Ludgate, J., & Gelder, M. (1999). Brief cognitive therapy for panic disorder: A randomized controlled trial. *Journal of Consulting and Clinical Psychology, 67,* 583–589.

Clark, D. M., & Wells, A. (1995). A cognitive model of social phobia. In R. Heimberg, M. R. Liebowitz, D. A. Hope, & F. R. Schneier (Eds.), *Social phobia: Diagnosis, assessment and treatment* (pp. 69–93). New York: Guilford.

Clark, L. A. (2007). Assessment and diagnosis of personality disorder: Perennial issues and an emerging reconceptualization. *Annual Review of Psychology, 58,* 227–257.

Clark, L. A., & Livesley, W. J. (2002). Two approaches to identifying the dimensions of personality disorder: Convergence on the five-factor model. In T. A. Widiger & P. T. J. Costa (Eds.), *Personality disorders and the five-factor model of personality* (pp. 161–176). Washington, DC: American Psychological Association.

Clark, L. A., Watson, D., & Mineka, S. (1994). Temperament, personality, and the mood and anxiety disorders. *Journal of Abnormal Psychology, 103,* 103–116.

Clarkin, J. F., Levy, K. N., Lenzenweger, M. F., & Kernberg, O. F. (2007). Evaluating three treatments for borderline personality disorder: A multiwave study. *American Journal of Psychiatry, 164,* 922–928.

Classen, C., Koopman, C., Hales, R., & Spiegel, D. (1998). Acute stress disorder as a predictor of posttraumatic stress disorder. *American Journal of Psychiatry, 155,* 620–624.

Clayton, R. R., Catterello, A., & Walden, K. P. (1991). Sensation seeking as a potential mediating variable for school-based prevention intervention: A two-year follow-up of DARE. *Health Communication, 3,* 229–239.

Cleckley, H. (1976). *The mask of sanity* (5th ed.). St. Louis: Mosby.

Cloninger, R. C., Martin, R. L., Guze, S. B., & Clayton, P. L. (1986). A prospective follow-up and family study of somatization in men and women. *American Journal of Psychiatry, 143,* 713–714.

Cloud, J. (1999, June 7). Mental health reform: What it would really take. *Time,* pp. 54–56.

Coe, C. L., Kramer, M., Kirschbaum, C., Netter, P., & Fuchs, E. (2002). Prenatal stress diminishes cytokine production after an endotoxin challenge and induces glucocorticoid resistance in juvenile rhesus monkeys. *Journal of Clinical Endocrinology and Metabolism, 87,* 675–681.

Coe, C. L., & Lubach, G. R. (2005). Prenatal origins of individual variation in behavior and immunity. *Neuroscience and Biobehavioral Reviews, 25,* 39–49.

Coe, C. L., Lubach, G. R., & Schneider, M.L. (1999). Neuromotor and socioemotional behavior in the young monkey is presaged by prenatal conditions. In M. Lewis & D. Ramsay (Eds.), *Soothing and stress* (pp. 19–38). Mahwah, NJ: Erlbaum.

Cohen, D., Taieb, O., Flament, M., Benoit, N., Chevret, S., Corcos, M., Fossati, P., Jeammet, P., Allilaire, J. F., & Basquin, M. (2000). Absence of cognitive impairment at long-term follow-up in adolescents treated with ECT for severe mood disorder. *American Journal of Psychiatry, 157,* 460–462.

Cohen, P. (2008, February 2). Midlife suicide rises, puzzling researchers. *New York Times,* pp. 1–4.

Cohen, P., Cohen, J., Kasen, S., et al. (1993). An epidemiological study of disorders in late childhood and adolescence: I. Age and gender-specific prevalence. *Journal of Child Psychology & Psychiatry, 34,* 851–867.

Cohen, R. M., Nordahl, T. E., Semple, W. E., Andreason, P., et al. (1997). The brain metabolic patterns of clozapine and fluphenazine-treated patients with schizophrenia during a continuous performance task. *Archives of General Psychiatry, 54,* 481–486.

Cohen, S., Doyle, W. J., Skoner, D. P., Rabin, B. S., & Gwaltney, J. M. (1997). Social ties and susceptibility to the common cold. *Journal of the American Medical Association, 277,* 1940–1945.

Cohen, S., Frank, E., Doyle, W. J., Rabin, B. S., et al. (1998). Types of stressors that increase susceptibility to the common cold in healthy adults. *Health Psychology, 17,* 214–223.

Cohen, S., Tyrell, D. A. J., & Smith, A. P. (1991). Psychological stress and susceptibility to the common cold. *New England Journal of Medicine, 325,* 606–612.

Cohen, S., & Wills, T. A. (1985). Stress, social support, and the buffering process. *Psychological Bulletin, 98,* 310–357.

Coie, J. D., & Dodge, K. A. (1998). Aggression and antisocial behavior. In W. Damon (Series Ed.) & N. Eisenberg (Vol. Ed.), *Handbook of child psychology: Vol. 3: Social, emotional and personality development* (pp. 779–862). New York: Wiley.

Colapinto, J. (1997). The true story of Joan/John. *Rolling Stone,* pp. 55ff.

Cole, D. A., Ciesla, J. A., Dallaire, D. H., et al. (2008). Emergence of attributional style and its relations to depressive symptoms. *Journal of Abnormal Psychology, 117,* 16–31.

Cole, D. A., Martin, J. M., Peeke, L. G., Seroczynski, A. D., & Hoffman, K. (1998). Are cognitive errors of underestimation predictive or reflective of depressive symptoms in children?: A longitudinal study. *Journal of Abnormal Psychology, 107,* 481–496.

Cole, D. A., Martin, J. M., Powers, B., & Truglio, R. (1990). Modeling causal relations between academic and social competence and depression: A multitrait-multimethod longitudinal study of children. *Journal of Abnormal Psychology, 105,* 258–270.

Cole, M. G. (2004). Delirium in elderly patients. *American Journal of Geriatric Psychiatry, 12,* 7–21.

Colfax, G., Vittinghoff, E., Husnik, M. J., et al. (2004). Substance use and sexual risk: A participant and episode-level analysis among a cohort of men who have sex with men. *American Journal of Epidemiology, 159,* 1002–1012.

Colom, F., Vieta, E., Martinez-Aran, A., Reinares, M., Goikolea, J. M., Benabarre, A., Torrent, C., Comes, M., Corbella, B., Parramon, G., & Corominas, J. (2003). A randomized trial on the efficacy of group psychoeducation in the prophylaxis of recurrences in bipolar patients whose disease is in remission. *Archives of General Psychiatry, 60,* 402–407.

Colombo, C., Benedetti, F., Barbini, B., Campori, E., & Smeraldi E. (1999). Rate of switch from depression into mania after therapeutic sleep deprivation in bipolar depression. *Psychiatry Research, 86,* 267–270.

Comer, S. D., Hart, C. L., Ward, A. S., Haney, M., Foltin, R. W., & Fischman, M. W. (2001). Effects of repeated oral methamphetamine administration in humans. *Psychopharmacology, 155,* 397–404.

Community Epidemiology Work Group. (2003). *Epidemiologic trends in drug abuse.* National Institute of Drug Abuse. Bethesda MD.

Compas, B. E., Haaga, D. A. F., Keefe, F. J., Leitenberg, H., & Williams, D. A. (1998). Sampling of empirically supported psychological treatments from health psychology: Smoking, chronic pain, cancer, and bulimia nervosa. *Journal of Consulting and Clinical Psychology, 66,* 89–112.

Compton, D. R., Dewey, W. L., & Martin, B. R. (1990). Cannabis dependence and tolerance production. *Advances in Alcohol and Substance Abuse, 9,* 129–147.

Compton, S. N., March, J. M., Brent, D., Albano, A. M., Weersing, R., & Curry, J. (2004). Cognitive-behavioral psychotherapy for anxiety and depressive disorders in children and adolescents: An evidence-based medicine review. *Journal of the American Academy of Child and Adolescent Psychiatry, 43,* 930–959.

Conceicao do Rosario-Campos, M., Leckman, J. F., Mercadante, M. T., et al. (2001). Adults with early-onset obsessive-compulsive disorder. *American Journal of Psychiatry, 158,* 1899–1903.

Conley, R. R., Love, R. C., Kelly, D. L., & Bartko, J. J. (1999). Rehospitalization rates of patients recently discharged on a regimen of risperidone or clozapine. *American Journal of Psychiatry, 156,* 863–868.

Conley, R. R., & Mahmoud, R. (2001). A randomized double-blind study of risperidone and olanzapine in the treatment of schizophrenia or schizoaffective disorder. *American Journal of Psychiatry, 158,* 765–774.

Connell, C. M., & Gibson, G. D. (1997). Racial, ethnic, and cultural differences in dementia caregiving: Review and analysis. *Gerontologist, 37,* 355–364.

Consumer Reports. (1995, November). Mental health: Does therapy help? *Consumer Reports,* pp. 734–739.

Conwell, Y. (2001). Suicide in later life: A review and recommendations for prevention. *Suicide and Life-Threatening Behavior, 31,* 32–47.

Cook, J. M. (2001). Post-traumatic stress disorder in older adults. *PTSD Research Quarterly, 12*(3), 1–3.

Cook, M., & Mineka, S. (1989). Observational conditioning of fear to fear-relevant versus fear-irrelevant stimuli in rhesus monkeys. *Journal of Abnormal Psychology, 98,* 448–459.

Cooke, D. J., & Michie, C. (1999). Psychopathy across cultures: North America and Scotland compared. *Journal of Abnormal Psychology, 108,* 58–68.

Cookson, W. O. C. M., & Moffatt, M. F. (1997). Asthma: An epidemic in the absence of infection? *Science, 275,* 41–42.

Cookson, W. O. C. M., & Moffatt, M. F. (2000). Genetics of asthma and allergic disease. *Human Molecular Genetics, 9,* 2359–2364.

Coolidge, F. L., & Segal, D. L. (1998). Evolution of personality disorder diagnosis in the Diagnostic and Statistical Manual of Mental Disorders. *Clinical Psychology Review, 18,* 585–589.

Coons, P. M., & Bowman, E. S. (2001). Ten-year follow-up study of patients with dissociative identity disorder. *Journal of Trauma and Dissociation, 2,* 73–89.

Cooper, M. L., Frone, M. R., Russell, M., & Mudar, P. (1995). Drinking to regulate positive and negative emotion: A motivational model of alcoholism. *Journal of Personality and Social Psychology, 69,* 961–974.

Copolov, D. L., Mackinnon, A., & Trauer, T. (2004). Correlates of the affective impact of auditory hallucinations in psychotic disorders. *Schizophrenia Bulletin, 30,* 163–171.

Corder, R., Douthwaite, J. A., Lees, D. M., Khan, N. Q., Viseu dos Santos, A. C., Wood, E. G., & Carrier, M. J. (2001). Endothelin-1 synthesis is reduced by red wine. *Nature, 414,* 863–864.

Cordova, J. V., Jacobson, N. S., & Christensen, A. (1998). Acceptance vs. change in behavioral couples therapy: Impact on client communication processes in the therapy session. *Journal of Marital and Family Therapy, 24,* 437–455.

Cornblatt, B., & Erlenmeyer-Kimling, L. E. (1985). Global attentional deviance in children at risk for schizophrenia: Specificity and predictive validity. *Journal of Abnormal Psychology, 94,* 470–486.

Corrigan, P. W. (2001). Getting ahead of the data: A threat to some behavior therapies. *The Behavior Therapist, 24,* 189–193.

Corrigan, P. W., & Watson, A. C. (2005). Findings from the National Comorbidity Survey on the frequency of violent behavior in individuals with psychiatric disorders. *Psychiatry Research, 136,* 153–162.

Corrigan, P. W., Watson, A. C., Heyrman, J. D., Warpinski, A., Gracia, G., Slopen, N., & Hall, L. L., (2005). Structural stigma in state legislatures. *Psychiatric Services, 56,* 557–563.

Coryell, W., & Schlesser, M. (2001). The dexamethasone suppression test and suicide prevention. *Archives of General Psychiatry, 158,* 748–753.

Costa, P. T., Metter, E. J., & McCrae, R. R. (1994). Personality stability and its contribution to successful aging. *Journal of Geriatric Psychiatry, 27,* 41–59.

Costa, P. T., Metter, E. J., & McCrae, R. R. (1994). Personality stability and its contribution to successful aging. *Journal of Geriatric Psychiatry, 27,* 41–59.

Costello, E. J., Costello, A. J., Edelbrock, C., Burns, B. J., Dulcan, M. K., Brent, D., & Janiszewski, S. (1988). Psychiatric disorders in pediatric primary care. *Archives of General Psychiatry, 45,* 1107–1116.

Cott, C. A., Dawson, P., Sidani, S., & Wells, D. (2002). The effects of a walking/talking program on communication, ambulation and functional status in residents with Alzheimer disease. *Alzheimer Disease and Associated Disorders, 16,* 81–87.

Courchesne, E. (2004). Brain development in autism: Early overgrowth followed by premature arrests of growth. *Mental Retardation and Developmental Disabilities Research Reviews, 10,* 106–111.

Courchesne, E., Carnes, B. S., & Davis, H. R. (2001). Unusual brain growth patterns in early life in patients with autistic disorder: An MRI study. *Neurology, 57,* 245–254.

Courchesne, E., Carper, R., & Akshoomoff, N. (2003). Evidence of brain overgrowth in the first year of life in autism. *Journal of the American Medical Association, 290,* 337–344.

Cox, B. J., Clara, I. P., & Enns, M. W. (2002). Posttraumatic stress disorder and the structure of common mental disorders. *Depression and Anxiety, 15,* 168–171.

Coyne, J. C. (1976). Depression and the response of others. *Journal of Abnormal Psychology, 85,* 186–193.

Coyne, J. C. (1994). Self-reported distress: Analog or ersatz depression? *Psychological Bulletin, 116,* 29–45.

Craske, M. G., & Barlow, D. H. (2001). Panic disorder and agoraphobia. In D. H. Barlow (Ed.), *Clinical handbook of psychological disorders* (pp. 1–59). New York: Guilford.

Craske, M. G., Maidenberg, E., & Bystritsky, A. (1995). Brief cognitive-behavioral versus nondirective therapy for panic disorder. *Journal of Behavior Therapy & Experimental Psychiatry, 26,* 113–120.

Craske, M., & Mystkowski, J. (2006). Exposure therapy and extinction: Clinical studies. In M. G. Craske, D. Hermans, & D. Vansteenwegen (Eds.), *Fear and learning from basic processes to clinical implications* (pp. 217–233). Washington, DC: American Psychological Association.

Crawford, T. N., Cohen, P., Johnson, J. G., Kasen, S., First, M. B., Gordon, K., & Brook, J. S. (2005). Self-reported personality disorder in the children in the community sample: Convergent and prospective validity in late adolescence and adulthood. *Journal of Personality Disorders, 19*, 30–52.

Creamer, M., Burgess, P., & McFarlane, A. C. (2001). Posttraumatic stress disorder: Findings from the Australian national survey of mental health and well-being. *Psychological Medicine, 31*, 1237–1247.

Creer, T. L. (1982). Asthma. *Journal of Consulting and Clinical Psychology, 50*, 912–921.

Crick, N. R., & Dodge, K. A. (1994). A review and reformulation of social information-processing mechanisms in children's social adjustment. *Psychological Bulletin, 115*, 74–101.

Critchley, H. D., Daly, E. M., Bullmore, E. T., Williams, S. C. R., Van Amelsvoort, T., Robertson, D. M., Rowe, A., Phillips, M., McAlonan, G., Howlin, P., & Murphy, D. G. M. (2001). The functional neuroanatomy of social behaviour: Changes in cerebral blood flow when people with autistic disorder process facial expressions. *Brain, 123*, 2203–2212.

Crits-Christoph, P., & Barber, J. P. (2002). Psychological treatments for personality disorders. In P. E. Nathan & J. M. Gorman (Eds.), *A guide to treatments that work.* New York: Oxford University Press 641–658.

Crits-Christoph, P., Chambless, D. L., Frank, E., Brody, C., et al. (1995). Training in empirically validated treatments: What are clinical psychology students learning? *Professional Psychology: Research and Practice, 26*, 514–522.

Crits-Cristoph, P., Gibbons, M. B. C., & Hearon, B. (2006). Does the alliance cause good outcome? Recommendations for future research on the alliance. *Theory, Research, Practice, Training, 43*, 280–285.

Critser, G. (2003). *Fatland: How Americans became the fattest people in the world.* Boston: Houghton Mifflin.

Cronan, T. A., Cruz, S. G., Arriaga, R. I., & Sarkin, A. J. (1996). The effects of a community-based literacy program on young children's language and conceptual development. *American Journal of Community Psychology, 24*, 251–272.

Cronbach, L. J., & Meehl, P. E. (1955). Construct validity in psychological tests. *Psychological Bulletin, 52*, 281–302.

Crow, T. J. (1980). Molecular pathology of schizophrenia: More than one disease process? *British Medical Journal, 280*, 784–788.

Crowell, N. A., & Burgess, A. W. (1996). *Understanding violence against women.* Washington, DC: National Academy Press.

Crozier, J. C., Dodge, K. A., Griffith, R., et al. (2008). Social information processing and cardiac predictors of adolescent antisocial behavior. *Journal of Abnormal Psychology, 117*, 253–267.

Cruts, M., Gijselinck, I., van der Zee, J., Engelborghs, S., Wils, H., Pirici, D., et al. (2006). Null mutations in progranulin cause ubiquitin-positive frontotemporal dementia linked to chromosome 17q21. *Nature, 442*, 920–924.

Csernansky, J. G., Mahmoud, R., & Brenner, R. (2002). A comparison of risperidone and haloperidol for the prevention of relapse in patients with schizophrenia. *The New England Journal of Medicine, 356*, 16–22.

Cummings, J. L. (2000). Cholinesterase inhibitors: A new class of psychotropic compounds. *American Journal of Psychiatry, 157*, 4–15.

Cummings, J. L., & Cole, G. (2002). Alzheimer disease. *Journal of the American Medical Association, 287*, 2335–2338.

Cummings, J. L., & Cunningham, K. (1992). Obsessive-compulsive disorder in Huntington's disease. *Biological Psychiatry, 31*, 263–270.

Curry, J. F. (2001). Specific psychotherapies for childhood and adolescent depression. *Biological Psychiatry, 49*, 1091–1100.

Curtin, J. J., Lang, A. R., Patrick, C. J., & Strizke, W. G. K. (1998). Alcohol and fear-potentiated startle: The role of competing cognitive demands in the stress-reducing effects of intoxication. *Journal of Abnormal Psychology, 107*, 547–557.

Curtis, L. H., Ostbye, T., Sendersky, V., Hutchison, S., Dans, P. E., Wright, A., Woolsey, R. L., & Schulman, K. A. (2004). Inappropriate prescribing for elderly Americans in a large outpatient population. *Archives of Internal Medicine, 164*, 1621–1625.

D'Silva, K., Duggan, C., & McCarthy, L. (2004). Does treatment really make psychopaths worse? A review of the evidence. *Journal of Personality Disorders, 18*, 163–177.

Dallery, J., Silverman, K., Chutuape, M. A., Bigelow, G. E., & Stitzer, M. (2001). Voucher-based reinforcement of opiate plus cocaine abstinence in treatment-resistant methadone patients: Effects of reinforcer magnitude. *Experimental & Clinical Psychopharmacology, 9*, 317–325.

Dallman, M. F., Pecoraro, N., Akana, S. F., La Fleur, S. E., Gomez, F., Houshyar, H., Bell, M. E., Bhatnagar, S., Laugero, K. D., & Manalo, S. (2003). Chronic stress and obesity: A new view of comfort food. *Proceedings of the National Academy of Sciences, 100*, 11696–11701.

Dare, C., LeGrange, D., Eisler, I., & Rutherford, J. (1994). Redefining the psychosomatic family: Family process of 26 eating disordered families. *International Journal of Eating Disorders, 16*, 211–226.

Davidson, R. J., Pizzagalli, D., & Nitschke, J. B. (2002). The representation and regulation of emotion in depression: Perspectives from affective neuroscience. In C. L. Hammen & I. H. Gotlib (Eds.), *Handbook of depression* (pp. 219–244). New York: Guilford.

Davidson, R. J., Pizzagalli, D., Nitschke, J. B., & Putnam, K. (2002). Depression: Perspectives from affective neuroscience. *Annual Review of Psychology, 53*, 545–574.

Davies, D. K., Stock, S. E., & Wehmeyer, M. (2003). Application of computer simulation to teach ATM access to individuals with intellectual disabilities. *Education & Training in Developmental Disabilities, 38*, 451–456.

Davila, J., Hammen, C. L., Burge, D., Paley, B., & Daley, S. E. (1995). Poor interpersonal problem solving as a mechanism of stress generation in depression among adolescent women. *Journal of Abnormal Psychology, 104*, 592–600.

Davis, C. (1996). The interdependence of obsessive-compulsiveness, physical activity, and starvation: A model for anorexia nervosa. In W. F. Epling & W. D. Pierce (Eds.), *Activity nervosa: Theory, research, and treatment* (pp. 209–218). Mahwah, NJ: Erlbaum.

Davis, J. M. (1978). Dopamine theory of schizophrenia: A two-factor theory. In L. C. Wynne, R. L. Cromwell, & S. Matthysse (Eds.), *The nature of schizophrenia.* New York: Wiley.

Davis, K. L., Kahn, R. S., Ko, G., & Davidson, M. (1991). Dopamine and schizophrenia: A review and reconceptualization. *American Journal of Psychiatry, 148*, 1474–1486.

Davis, L., & Siegel, L. J. (2000). Posttraumatic stress disorder in children and adolescents: A review and analysis. *Clinical Child and Family Psychology Review, 3*, 135–153.

Davis, M. C., Matthews, K. A., & Twamley, E. W. (1999). Is life more difficult on Mars or Venus? A meta-analytic review of sex differences in major and minor life events. *Annals of Behavioral Medicine, 21*, 83–97.

Davison, G. C., & Thompson, R. F. (1988). Stress management. In D. Druckman & J. A. Swets (Eds.), *Enhancing human performance: Issues, theories, and techniques.* Washington, DC: National Academy Press.

Davison, G. C., Haaga, D. A., Rosenbaum, J., Dolezal, S. L., & Weinstein, K. A. (1991). Assessment of self-efficacy in articulated thoughts: "States of mind" analysis and association with speech anxious behavior. *Journal of Cognitive Psychotherapy: An International Quarterly, 5*, 83–92.

Davison, G. C., Navarre, S. G., & Vogel, R. S. (1995). The articulated thoughts in simulated situations paradigm: A think-aloud approach to cognitive assessment. *Current Directions in Psychological Science, 4*, 29–33.

Davison, G. C., Robins, C., & Johnson, M. K. (1983). Articulated thoughts during simulated situations: A paradigm for studying cognition in emotion and behavior. *Cognitive Therapy and Research, 7*, 17–40.

Davison, G. C., & Zighelboim, V. (1987). Irrational beliefs in the articulated thoughts of college students with social anxiety. *Journal of Rational-Emotive Therapy, 5*, 238–254.

Dawson, G., Toth, K., Abbott, R., Osterling, J., Munson, J., Estes, A., & Liaw, J. (2004). Early social attention impairments in autism: Social orienting, joint attention, and attention to distress. *Developmental Psychology, 40*, 271–283.

Dawson, M. E., Schell, A. M., & Banis, H. T. (1986). Greater resistance to extinction of electrodermal responses conditioned to potentially phobic CSs: A noncognitive process? *Psychophysiology, 23*, 552–561.

Day, N. L., Leech, S. L., Richardson, G. A., Cornelius, M. D., Robles, N., & Larkby, C. (2004). Prenatal alcohol exposure predicts continued deficits in offspring size at 14 years of age. *Alcoholism: Clinical and Experimental Research, 26*, 1584–1591.

Day, N. L., & Richardson, G. A. (2004). An analysis of the effects of prenatal alcohol exposure on growth: A teratologic model. *American Journal of Medical Genetics Part C (Seminar in Medical Genetics), 127C*, 28–34.

De Cuypere, G., TSjoen, G., Beerten, R., Selvaggi, G., De Sutter, P., Hoebeke, P., et al. (2005). Sexual and physical health after sex reassignment surgery. *Archives of Sexual Behavior, 34*, 679–690.

de Graaf, R., Bijl, R. V., Ravelli, A., Smit, F., & Vollenbergh, W. A. M. (2002). Predictors of first incidence of DSM-III-R psychiatric disorders in the general population: Findings from the Netherlands mental health survey and incidence study. *Acta Psychiatrica Scandinavica, 106*, 303–313.

De Souza, E. B., Battaglia, G., & Insel, T. L. (1990). Neurotoxic effect of MDMA on brain serotonin neurons: Evidence from neurochemical and radioligand binding studies. *Annual Proceedings of the New York Academy of Science, 600*, 682–697.

de Wit, H., & Zacny, J. (2000). Abuse potential of nicotine replacement therapies. In K. J. Palmer (Ed), *Smoking cessation* (pp. 79–92). Kwai Chung, Hong Kong: Adis International Publications.

Deacon, S., Minicchiello, V., & Plummer, D. (1995). Sexuality and older people: Revisiting the assumptions. *Educational Gerontology, 21*, 497–513.

Deary, V., Chalder, T., & Sharpe, M. (2007). The cognitive behavioural model of medically unexplained symptoms: A theoretical and empirical review. *Clinical Psychology Review, 27*, 781–797.

Deep, A. L., Lilenfeld, L. R., Plotnicov, K. H., Pollice, C., & Kaye, W. H. (1999). Sexual abuse in eating disorder subtypes and control women: The role of cormorbid substance dependence in bulimia nervosa. *International Journal of Eating Disorders, 25*, 1–10.

DeFazio, A., & Cunningham, K. A. (1987). A paraphilia in a spinal-cord-injured patient: A case report. *Sexuality and Disability, 8,* 247–254.

DeJong, W., & Kleck, R. E. (1986). The social psychological effects of overweight. In C. P. Herman, M. P. Zanna, & E. T. Higgins (Eds.), *Physical appearance, stigma, and social behavior*. Hillside, NJ: Erlbaum.

Delano-Wood, L., & Abeles, N. (2005). Late-life depression: Detection, risk reduction, and somatic intervention. *Clinical Psychology Science and Practice, 12,* 207–217.

deLint, J. (1978). Alcohol consumption and alcohol problems from an epidemiological perspective. *British Journal of Alcohol and Alcoholism, 17,* 109–116.

DeLisi, L. E., Shaw, S. H., Crow, T. J., et al. (2002). A genome-wide scan for linkage to chromosomal regions in 382 sibling pairs with schizophrenia or schizoaffective disorder. *American Journal of Psychiatry, 159,* 803–812.

den Heijer, T., Vermeer, S. E., Clarke, R., Oudkerk, M., Koudstaal, P. J., Hofman, A., & Breteler, M. M. B. (2002). Homocysteine and brain atrophy on MRI of non-demented elderly. *Brain, 126*(1), 170–175.

Depression Guidelines Panel. (1993). *Depression in primary care: Vol. 2. Treatment of major depression. Clinical practice guideline No. 5.* (AHCPR publication No. 93–0551). Rockville, MD: U.S. Department of Health and Human Services, Public Health Service, Agency for Health Care Policy and Research.

Depue, R. A., Collins, P. F., & Luciano, M. (1996). A model of neurobiology: Environment interaction in developmental psychopathology. In M. F. Lenzenweger & J. J. Haugaard (Eds.), *Frontiers of developmental psychopathology* (pp. 44–76). New York: Oxford University Press.

Depue, R. A., & Iacono, W. G. (1989). Neurobehavioral aspects of affective disorders. In L. W. Porter & M. R. Rosenzweig (Eds.), *Annual review of psychology* (pp. 457–492). Palo Alto, CA: Annual Reviews, Inc.

DeRubeis, R. J., & Crits-Christoph, P. (1998). Empirically supported individual and group psychological treatments for adult mental disorders. *Journal of Consulting and Clinical Psychology, 66,* 37–52.

DeRubeis, R. J., Gelfand, L. A., Tang, T. Z., & Simons, A. D. (1999). Medications versus cognitive behavior therapy for severely depressed outpatients: Mega-analysis of four randomized comparisons. *American Journal of Psychiatry, 156,* 1007–1013.

DeRubeis, R. J., Hollon, S. D., Amsterdam, J. D., Shelton, R. C., Young, P. R., Salomon, R. M., et al. (2005). Cognitive therapy vs medications in the treatment of moderate to severe depression. *Archives of General Psychiatry, 62,* 409–416.

Detweiler, J. B., Bedell, B. T., Salovey, P., Pronin, E., & Rothman, A. J. (1999). Message framing and sunscreen use: Gain-framed messages motivate beach-goers. *Health Psychology, 18,* 9–196.

Dew, M. A., Bromet, E. J., Brent, D., & Greenhouse, J. B. (1987). A quantitative literature review of the effectiveness of suicide prevention centers. *Journal of Consulting and Clinical Psychology, 55,* 239–244.

Dickerson, S. S., & Kemeny, M. E. (2004). Acute stressors and cortisol responses: A theoretical integration and synthesis of laboratory research. *Psychological Bulletin, 130,* 355–391.

Dickey, C. C., McCarley, R. W., & Shenton, M. E. (2002). The brain in schizotypal personality disorder: A review of structural MRI and CT findings. *Harvard Review of Psychiatry, 10,* 1–15.

Dickstein, D. P. & Leibenluft, E. (2006). Emotion regulation in children and adolescents: Boundaries between normalcy and bipolar disorder. *Development and Psychopathology, 18,* 1105–1131.

Dieserud, G., Roysamb, E., Braverman, M. T., Dalgard, O. S., & Ekeberg, O. (2003). Predicting repetition of suicide attempt: A prospective study of 50 suicide attempters. *Archives of Suicide Research, 7,* 1–15.

DiFranza, J. R., Richards, J. W., Paulman, P. M., Wolf-Gillespie, N., Fletcher, C., et al. (1991). RJR Nabisco's cartoon camel promotes Camel cigarettes to children. *Journal of the American Medical Association, 266,* 3149–3153.

Dimidjian, S., Hollon, S. D., Dobson, K. S., Schmaling, K. B., Kohlenberg, R. J., Addis, M. E., et al. (2006). Randomized trial of behavioral activation, cognitive therapy, and antidepressant medication in the acute treatment of adults with major depression. *Journal of Consulting and Clinical Psychology, 74,* 658–670.

DiNardo, P. A., O'Brien, G. T., Barlow, D. H., Waddell, M. T., & Blanchard, E. B. (1993). Reliability of the DSM-III-R anxiety disorders categories using the Anxiety Disorders Interview Schedule-Revised (ADIS-R). *Archives of General Psychiatry, 50,* 251–256.

Dishion, T. J., & Andrews, D. W. (1995). Preventing escalation in problem behaviors with high-risk young adolescents: Immediate and 1-year outcomes. *Journal of Consulting and Clinical Psychology, 63,* 538–548.

Dishion, T. J., Patterson, G. R., & Kavanagh, K. A. (1992). An experimental test of the coercion model: Linking theory, measurement, and intervention. In J. McCord & R. E. Tremblay (Eds.), *Preventing antisocial behavior* (pp. 253–282). New York: Guilford.

Dixon, L., Scott, J., Lyles, A., Fahey, A., Skinner, A., & Shore, A. (1997). Adherence to schizophrenia PORT family treatment recommendations. *Schizophrenia Research, 24,* 221.

Dobson, K. S. (1989). A meta-analysis of the efficacy of cognitive therapy for depression. *Journal of Consulting and Clinical Psychology, 57,* 414–419.

Dodge, K. A., & Frame, C. L. (1982). Social cognitive biases and deficits in aggressive boys. *Child Development, 53,* 620–635.

Doerr, P., Fichter, M., Pirke, K. M., & Lund, R. (1980). Relationship between weight gain and hypothalamic-pituitary-adrenal function in patients with anorexia nervosa. *Journal of Steroid Biochemistry, 13,* 529–537.

Dohrenwend, B. P., Levav, P. E., Schwartz, S., Naveh, G., Link, B. G., Skodol, A. E., & Stueve, A. (1992). Socioeconomic status and psychiatric disorders: The causation-selection issue. *Science, 255,* 946–952.

Dolan, B. (1991). Cross-cultural aspects of anorexia and bulimia: A review. *International Journal of Eating Disorders, 10,* 67–78.

Dolder, C. R., Lacro, J. P., Dunn, L. B., & Jeste, D. V. (2002). Antipsychotic medication adherence: Is there a difference between typical and atypical agents? *American Journal of Psychiatry, 159,* 103–108.

Doll, H. A., & Fairburn, C. G. (1998). Heightened accuracy of self-reported weight in bulimia nervosa: A useful cognitive "distortion." *International Journal of Eating Disorders, 24,* 267–273.

Dombrovsky, A. Y., Lenze, E. J., Dew, M. A., Mulsant, B. H., Pollock, B. G., Houck, P. R., & Reynolds, C. F., III. (2007). Maintenance treatment for old-age depression preserves health-related quality of life: A randomized, controlled trial of paroxetine and interpersonal psychotherapy. *Journal of the American Geriatrics Society, 55,* 1325–1332.

Doss, B. D., Thum, Y. M., Sevier, M., Atkins, D. C., & Christensen, A. (2005). Improving relationships: Mechanisms of change in couple therapy. *Journal of Consulting and Clinical Psychology, 73,* 624–633.

Dougher, M. J. (1988). Clinical assessment of sex offenders. In B. K. Schwartz (Ed.), *A practitioner's guide to treating the incarcerated male sex offender* (pp. 77–84). Washington, DC: U.S. Department of Justice.

Draguns, J. G. (1989). Normal and abnormal behavior in cross-cultural perspective: Specifying the nature of their relationships. In J. J. Berman (Ed.), *Nebraska symposium on motivation*. Lincoln: University of Nebraska Press.

Drevets, W. C., Price, J. L., Simpson, J. R. J., Todd, R. D., Reich, T., Vannier, M., et al. (1997). Subgenual prefrontal cortex abnormalities in mood disorders. *Nature, 386,* 824–827.

Dreznick, M. T. (2003). Heterosocial competence of rapists and child molesters: A meta-analysis. *Journal of Sex Research, 40,* 170–178.

Drug Enforcement Administration. (2001). *Working to prevent the diversion and abuse of Oxycontin*. Drug Enforcement Administration, Office of Diversion Control. Washington, DC.

Drummond, K. D., Bradley, S., Peterson-Badali, M., & Zucker, K. J. (2008). A follow-up study of girls with gender identity disorder. *Developmental Psychology, 44,* 34–45.

Drury, V., Birchwood, M., Cochrane, R., & Macmillan, R. (1996). Cognitive therapy and recovery from acute psychosis: A controlled trial. *British Journal of Psychiatry, 169,* 593–601.

Duffy, F. F., West, J. C., Wilk, J., Narrow, W. E., Hales, D., Thompson, J., et al. (2004). Mental health practitioners and trainees. In R. W. Manderscheid, & M. J. Henderson (Eds.), *Mental health, United States, 2002.* [DHHS Publication No. (SMA) 3938] Rockville, MD: Substance Abuse and Mental Health Services Administration.

Dugas, M. J., Marchand, A., & Ladouceur, R. (2005). Further validation of a cognitive-behavioral model of generalized anxiety disorder: Diagnostic and symptom specificity. *Journal of Anxiety Disorders, 19,* 329–343.

Duke, M. P. (1994). Chaos theory and psychology: Seven propositions. *Genetic, Social, & General Psychology Monographs, 120,* 267–286.

Duman, R. S., Nakagawa, S. & Malberg, J. (2001). Regulation of adult neurogenesis by psychotropic drugs and stress. *Journal of Pharmacology and Experimental Therapeutics, 299,* 401–407.

Duman, R. S., Heninger, G. R., & Nestler, E. J. (1997). A molecular and cellular theory of depression. *Archives of General Psychiatry, 54,* 597–606.

DuPaul, G. J., & Henningson, P. N. (1993). Peer tutoring effects on the classroom performance of children with attention deficit hyperactivity disorder. *School Psychology Review, 22,* 134–143.

Dura, J. R., Stukenberg, K. W., & Kiecolt-Glaser, J. K. (1991). Anxiety and depressive disorders in adult children caring for demented parents. *Psychology and Aging, 6,* 467–473.

Duran, R. E. F., Bedoya, A., Stoelb, B., Antoni, M., & Schneiderman, N. (August, 2004). *Adapting a manualized group intervention for Spanish-speaking, HIV-positive men and women living with HIV: El Proyecto ARMESE.* Paper presented at the annual conference of the American Psychological Association. Honolulu, Hawaii.

Durantini, M. R., AlbarracPn, D., Mitchell, A., L., Earl, A., Glasman, L. R., & Gillette, J., (2006). Conceptualizing the influence of social agents of behavior change: A meta-analysis of the effectiveness of HIV-prevention interventionists for different groups. *Psychological Bulletin, 132,* 212–248.

Durkheim, E. (1951). *Suicide.* (J. A. Spaulding & G. Simpson, Trans.). New York: Free Press. (Original work published 1897.)

Durkin, K. L. (1997). Misuse of the Internet by pedophiles: Implications for law enforcement and probation practice. *Federal Probation, 61,* 14–18.

Dusseldorp, E., van Elderen, T., Maes, S., Meulman, J., & Kraaij, V. (1999). A meta-analysis of psychoeducation programs for coronary heart disease patients. *Health Psychology, 18,* 506–519.

Dvoskin, J. A., & Steadman, H. J. (1994). Using intensive case management to reduce violence by mentally ill persons in the community. *Hospital and Community Psychiatry, 45,* 679–684.

Dworkin, R. H., & Lenzenweger, M. F. (1984). Symptoms and the genetics of schizophrenia: Implications for diagnosis. *American Journal of Psychiatry, 141,* 1541–1546.

Dworkin, R. H., Lenzenweger, M. F., & Moldin, S. O. (1987). Genetics and the phenomenology of schizophrenia. In P. D. Harvey & E. F. Walker (Eds.), *Positive and negative symptoms of psychosis.* Hillsdale, NJ: Erlbaum.

Eaker, E. D., Pinsky, J., & Castelli, W. P. (1992). Myocardial infarction and coronary death among women: Psychosocial predictors from a 20 year follow-up of women in the Framingham study. *American Journal of Epidemiology, 135,* 854–864.

Eddy, K. T., Keel, P. K., Dorer, D. J., Delinsky, S. S., Franko, D. L., & Herzog, D. B. (2002). Longitudinal comparison of anorexia nervosa subtypes. *International Journal of Eating Disorders, 31,* 191–201.

Edelbrock, C., Rende, R., Plomin, T., & Thompson, L. A. (1995). A twin study of competence and problem behavior in childhood and early adolescence. *Journal of Child Psychology and Psychiatry and Allied Disciplines, 36,* 775–789.

Eder, W., Ege, M. J., & von Mutius, E. (2006). The asthma epidemic. *New England Journal of Medicine, 355,* 2226–2235.

Edvardsen, J., Torgersen, S., Røysamb, E., Lygren, S., Skre, I., Onstad, S., et al. (2008). Heritability of bipolar spectrum disorders: Unity or heterogeneity? *Journal of Affective Disorders, 106,* 229–240.

Egan, T. (1990). As memory and music faded, Alzheimer patient met death. *The New York Times, June,* A1, A16.

Ehlers, A., Mayou, R. A., & Bryant, B. (1998). Psychological predictors of chronic posttraumatic stress disorder after motor vehicle accidents. *Journal of Abnormal Psychology, 107,* 508–519.

Eich, E., Macaulay, D., Loewenstein, R. J., & Dihle, P. H. (1997). Memory, amnesia, and dissociative identity disorder. *Psychological Science, 8,* 417–422.

Eley, T. C., Lichtenstein, P., & Moffitt, T. E. (2003). A longitudinal behavioral genetic analysis of the etiology of aggressive and nonaggressive antisocial behavior. *Development and Psychopathology, 15,* 383–402.

Elkin, I., Gibbons, R. D., Shea, M. T., & Shaw, B. F. (1996). Science is not a trial (but it can sometimes be a tribulation). *Journal of Consulting and Clinical Psychology, 64,* 92–103.

Elkin, I., Shea, M. T., Watkins, J. T., Imber, S. D., Sotsky, S. M., Collins, J. F., Glass, D. R., Pilkonis, P. A., Leber, W. R., Docherty, J. P., Fiester, S. J., & Parloff, M. B. (1989). NIMH Treatment of Depression Collaborative Research Program: 1. General effectiveness of treatments. *Archives of General Psychiatry, 46,* 971–983.

Elkins, I., King, S. M., McGue, M., & Iacono, W. (2006). Personality traits and the development of alcohol, nicotine, and illicit drug disorders: Prospective links from adolescence to young adulthood. *Journal of Abnormal Psychology, 115,* 26–39.

Elkins, I., McGue, M., & Iacono, W. (2007). Prospective effects of attention-deficit/hyperactivity disorder, conduct disorder, and sex on adolescent substance use and abuse. *Archives of General Psychiatry, 64,* 1145–1152.

Elkis, H., Friedman, L., Wise, A., & Meltzer, H. T. (1995). Meta-analysis of studies of ventricular enlargement and cortical sulcal prominence in mood disorders. *Archives of General Psychiatry, 52,* 735–746.

Ellenberger, H. F. (1972). The story of "Anna O": A critical review with new data. *Journal of the History of the Behavioral Sciences, 8,* 267–279.

Elliott, R., Greenberg, L. S., & Lietaer, G. (2004). Research on experiential psychotherapies. In M. J. Lambert (Ed.), *Bergin and Garfield's handbook of psychotherapy and behavior change* (5th ed., pp. 493–539). New York: Wiley.

Ellis, A. (1991). The revised ABC's of rational-emotive therapy (RET). *Journal of Rational-Emotive and Cognitive Behavior Therapy, 9,* 139–172.

Ellis, A. (1993). Changing rational-emotive therapy (RET) to rational emotive behavior therapy (REBT). *The Behavior Therapist, 16,* 257–258.

Ellis, A. (1995). Changing rational-emotive therapy (RET) to rational emotive behavior therapy (REBT). *Journal of Rational-Emotive and Cognitive Behavior Therapy, 13,* 85–89.

Elzinga, B. M., Phaf, R. H., Ardon, A. M., & van Dyck, R. (2003). Directed forgetting between, but not within, dissociative personality status. *Journal of Abnormal Psychology, 112,* 237–243.

Emmelkamp, P. M. G. (2004). Behavior therapy with adults. In M. J. Lambert (Ed.), *Bergin and Garfield's handbook of psychotherapy and behavior change* (5th ed., pp. 393–446). New York: Wiley.

Emslie, G., & Mayes, T. N. (2001). Mood disorders in children and adolescents: Psychopharmacological treatment. *Biological Psychiatry, 49,* 1082–1090.

Emslie, G. J., Mayes, T. L., & Hughes, C. W. (2000). Updates in the pharmacologic treatment of childhood depression. *Psychiatric Clinics of North America, 23,* 813–835.

Engdahl, B., Dikel, T. N., Eberly, R., & Blank, A. (1997). Posttraumatic stress disorder in a community group of former prisoners of war: A normative response to severe trauma. *American Journal of Psychiatry, 154,* 1576–1581.

Engelhard, I. M., Huijding, J., van den Hout, Marcel, A., & de Jong, Peter J. (2007). Vulnerability associations and symptoms of post-traumatic stress disorder in soldiers deployed to Iraq. *Behaviour Research and Therapy, 45,* 2317–2325.

Enger, C., Weatherby, L., Reynolds, R. F., Glasser, D. B., & Walker, A. M. (2004). Serious cardiovascular events and mortality among patients with schizophrenia. *Journal of Nervous and Mental Disease, 192,* 19–27.

Enserink, M. (1999). Drug therapies for depression: From MAO inhibitors to substance. *Science, 284,* 239.

Epel, E. S., McEwen, B. S., & Ickovics, J. R. (1998). Embodying psychological thriving: Physical thriving in response to stress. *Journal of Social Issues, 54,* 301–322.

Epling, W. F., & Pierce, W. D. (1992). *Solving the anorexia puzzle.* Toronto: Hogrefe & Huber.

Epping-Jordan, J. E., Compas, B. E., & Howell, D. C. (1994). Predictors of cancer progression in young adult men and women: Avoidance, intrusive thoughts, and psychological symptoms. *Health Psychology, 13,* 539–547.

Epstein, H. (2007). *The invisible cure: Why we are losing the fight against AIDS in Africa.* New York: Picador.

Epstein, J. A., Botvin, G. J., & Diaz, T. (2001). Linguistic acculturation associated with higher marijuana and polydrug use among Hispanic adolescents. *Substance Use & Misuse, 36,* 477–499.

Erdberg, P., & Exner, J. E., Jr. (1984). Rorschach assessment. In G. Goldstein & M. Hersen (Eds.), *Handbook of psychological assessment.* New York: Pergamon.

Erhardt, D., & Hinshaw, S. P. (1994). Initial sociometric impressions of attention-deficit hyperactivity disorder and comparison boys: Predictions from social behaviors and nonverbal behaviors. *Journal of Consulting and Clinical Psychology, 62,* 833–842.

Erikson, E. (1950). *Childhood and society.* New York: Norton.

Erlenmeyer-Kimling, L. E., & Cornblatt, B. (1987). The New York high-risk project: A follow-up report. *Schizophrenia Bulletin, 13,* 451–461.

Escobar, J. I., Burnam, M. A., Karno, M., Forsythe, A., Golding, J. M., et al. (1987). Somatization in the community. *Archives of General Psychiatry, 44,* 713–720.

Evans, P. D., & Edgerton, N. (1990). Life events as predictors of the common cold. *British Journal of Medical Psychology, 64,* 35–44.

Evans, R. J. (2001). Social influences in etiology and prevention of smoking and other health threatening behaviors in children and adolescents. In A. Baum, T. A. Revenson, & J. E. Singer (Eds.), *Handbook of health psychology* (pp. 459–468). Mahwah, NJ: Erlbaum.

Evashwick, C. J. (2001). Definition of the continuum of care. In C. J. Evashwick (Ed.), *The continuum of long-term care* (pp. 3–13). Albany, NY: Delmar.

Everett, F., Proctor, N., & Cartmell, B. (1989). Providing psychological services to American Indian children and families. In D. R. Atkinson, G. Morten, & D. W. Sue (Eds.), *Counseling American Minorities* (3rd ed.). Dubuque, IA: W.C. Brown.

Everill, J. T., & Waller, G. (1995). Reported sexual abuse and eating psychopathology: A review of the evidence for a causal link. *International Journal of Eating Disorders, 18,* 1–11.

Everson, S. A., Kaplan, G. A., Goldberg, D. A., & Salonen, J. T. (1996). Anticipatory blood pressure response to exercise predicts future high blood pressure in middle-aged men. *Hypertension, 27,* 1059–1064.

Everson, S. A., Kauhanen, J., Kaplan, G. A., Goldberg, D. E., Julkunen, J., et al. (1997). Hostility and increased risk of mortality and acute myocardial infarction: The mediating role of behavioral risk factors. *American Journal of Epidemiology, 146,* 142–152.

Exner, J. E. (1978). *The Rorschach: A comprehensive system: Vol. 2. Current research and advanced interpretation.* New York: Wiley.

Exner, J. E., Jr. (1986). *The Rorschach: A comprehensive system: Vol. 1. Basic foundations* (2nd ed.). New York: Wiley.

EXPLORE Study Team. (2004). Effects of a behavioural intervention to reduce acquisition of HIV infection among men who have sex with men: The EXPLORE randomised controlled study. *Lancet, 364,* 41–50.

Eysenck, H. J. (1952). The effects of psychotherapy: An evaluation. *Journal of Consulting Psychology, 16,* 319–324.

Faber, S. D., & Burns, J. W. (1996). Anger management style, degree of expressed anger, and gender influence cardiovascular recovery from interpersonal harassment. *Journal of Behavioral Medicine, 19,* 31–53.

Fabrega, H., Jr. (2002). Evolutionary theory, culture and psychiatric diagnosis. In M. Maj & W. Gaebel (Eds.), *Psychiatric diagnosis and classification* (pp. 107–135). New York: Wiley.

Fairburn, C. G. (1985). Cognitive-behavioral treatment for bulimia. In D. M. Garner & P. E. Garfinkel (Eds.), *Handbook of psychotherapy for anorexia nervosa and bulimia* (pp. 160–192). New York: Guilford.

Fairburn, C. G. (1997). Eating disorders. In D. M. Clark & C.G. Fairburn (Eds.), *Science and practice of cognitive behavior therapy* (pp. 209–243). New York: Oxford University Press.

Fairburn, C. G., Agras, W. S., & Wilson, G. T. (1992). The research on the treatment of bulimia nervosa: Practical and theoretical implications. In G. H. Anderson & S. H. Kennedy (Eds.), *The biology of feast and famine: Relevance to eating disorders.* New York: Academic Press.

Fairburn, C. G., Cooper, Z., Doll, H. A., & Welch, S. L. (1999). Risk factors for anorexia nervosa: Three integrated case-control comparisons. *Archives of General Psychiatry, 56,* 468–478.

Fairburn, C. G., Jones, R., Peveler, R., Carr, S. J., Solomon, R. A., O'Connor, M. E., Burton, J., & Hope, R. A. (1991). Three psychological treatments for bulimia nervosa. *Archives of General Psychiatry, 48,* 463–469.

Fairburn, C. G., Jones, R., Peveler, R. C., Hope, R. A., & O'Connor, M. E. (1993). Psychotherapy and bulimia nervosa: The longer-term effects of interpersonal psychotherapy, behavior therapy, and cognitive therapy. *Archives of General Psychiatry, 50,* 419–428.

Fairburn, C. G., Marcus, M. D., & Wilson, G. T. (1993). Cognitive behaviour therapy for binge eating and bulimia nervosa: A comprehensive treatment manual. In C. G. Fairburn & G. T. Wilson (Eds.), *Binge eating: Nature, assessment, and treatment.* New York: Guilford.

Fairburn, C. G., Norman, P. A., Welch, S. L., O'Connor, M. E., Doll, H. A., & Peveler, R. C. (1995). A prospective study of outcome in bulimia nervosa and the long-term effects of three psychological treatments. *Archives of General Psychiatry, 52,* 304–312.

Fairburn, C. G., Shafran, R., & Cooper, Z. (1999). A cognitive behavioural theory of anorexia nervosa. *Behaviour Research and Therapy, 37,* 1–13.

Fairburn, C. G., Stice, E., Cooper, Z., Doll, H. A., Norman, P. A., & O'Connor, M. E. (2003). Understanding persistence in bulimia nervosa: A 5-year naturalistic study. *Journal of Consulting and Clinical Psychology, 71,* 103–109.

Fairburn, C. G., Welch, S. L., Doll, H. A., Davies, B. A., & O'Connor, M. E. (1997). Risk factors for bulimia nervosa: A community-based case-control study. *Archives of General Psychiatry, 54,* 509–517.

Fairburn, C. G., Welch, S. L., & Hay, P. J. (1993). The classification of recurrent overeating: The "binge eating disorder" proposal. *International Journal of Eating Disorders, 13,* 155–159.

Falloon, I. R. H., Boyd, J. L., McGill, C. W., Razani, J., Moss, H. B., & Gilderman, A. N. (1982). Family management in the prevention of exacerbation of schizophrenia: A controlled study. *New England Journal of Medicine, 306,* 1437–1440.

Falloon, I. R. H., Boyd, J. L., McGill, C. W., Williamson, M., Razani, J., Moss, H. B., Gilderman, A. M., & Simpson, G. M. (1985). Family management in the prevention of morbidity of schizophrenia. *Archives of General Psychiatry, 42,* 887–896.

Fanous, A. H., Prescott, C. A., & Kendler, K. S. (2004). The prediction of thoughts of death or self-harm in a population-based sample of female twins. *Psychological Medicine, 34,* 301–312.

Faraone, S. V., Biederman, J., Jetton, J. G., & Tsuang, M. T. (1997). Attention deficit disorder and conduct disorder: Longitudinal evidence for a family subtype. *Psychological Medicine, 27,* 291–300.

Faraone, S. V., Biederman, J., & Mick, E. (2005). The age-dependent decline of attention deficit hyperactivity disorder: A meta-analysis of follow-up studies. *Psychological Medicine, 36,* 159–165.

Faraone, S. V., Biederman, J., Weber, W., & Russell, R. L. (1998). Psychiatric, neuropsychological, and psychosocial features of DSM-IV subtypes of attention-deficit/hyperactivity disorder: Results from a clinically referred sample. *Journal of the American Academy of Child and Adolescent Psychiatry, 37,* 185–193.

Faraone, S. V., Doyle, A. E., Mick, E., & Biederman, J. (2001). Meta-analysis of the association between the 7repeat allele of the dopamine d(4) receptor gene and attention deficit hyperactivity disorder. *American Journal of Psychiatry, 158,* 1052–1057.

Faraone, S. V., Taylor, L., & Tsuang, M. (2002). The molecular genetics of schizophrenia: An emerging consensus. *Expert reviews in molecular medicine, 23.* Retrieved from http://www.expertreviews.org/02004751h.htm

Faravelli, C., Salvatori, S., Galassi, F., & Aiazzi, L. (1997). Epidemiology of somatoform disorders: A community survey in Florence. *Social Psychiatry and Psychiatric Epidemiology, 32,* 24–29.

Farina, A. (1976). *Abnormal psychology.* Englewood Cliffs, NJ: Prentice-Hall.

Faustman, W. O., Bardgett, M., Faull, K. F., Pfefferman, A., & Cseransky, J. G. (1999). Cerebrospinal fluid glutamate inversely correlates with positive symptom severity in unmedicated male schizophrenic/schizoaffective patients. *Biological Psychiatry, 45,* 68–75.

Favaro, A., & Santonastaso, P. (1997). Suicidality in eating disorders: Clinical and psychological correlates. *Acta Psychiatrica Scandanavica, 95,* 508–514.

Febbraro, G. A. R., & Clum, G. A. (1998). Meta-analytic investigation of the effectiveness of self-regulatory components in the treatment of adult behavior problems. *Clinical Psychology Review, 18,* 143–161.

Feingold, B. F. (1973). *Introduction to clinical allergy.* Springfield, IL: Charles C. Thomas.

Feldman, H. A., Goldstein, I., Hatzichristou, G., Krane, R. J., & McKinlay, J. B. (1994). Impotence and its medical and psychosocial correlates: Results of the Massachusetts male aging study. *Journal of Urology, 151,* 54–61.

Feldman, H. M., Kolmen, B. K., & Gonzaga, A. M. (1999). Naltrexone and communication skills in young children with autism. *Journal of the American Academy of Child & Adolescent Psychiatry, 38,* 587–593.

Feldman Barrett, L. (2003). So you want to be a social neuroscientist? *APS Observer, 16,* 5–7.

Ferguson, C. P., La Via, M. C., Crossan, P. J., & Kaye, W. H. (1999). Are SSRIs effective in underweight anorexia nervosa? *International Journal of Eating Disorders, 25,* 11–17.

Ferguson, S. B., Shiffman, S., & Gwaltney, C. J. (2006). Does reducing withdrawal severity mediate nicotine patch efficacy? A randomized clinical trial. *Journal of Consulting and Clinical Psychology, 74,* 1153–1161.

Fergusson, D. M., & Horwood, L. J. (2000). Does cannabis use encourage other forms of illicit drug use? *Addiction, 95,* 505–520.

Ferri, C. P., Prince, M., Brayne, C., Brodaty, H., & Lyketsos, C. G. (2005). Global prevalence of dementia: A delphi consensus study. *Lancet, 366,* 2112–2117.

Ferri, M., Amato, L., & Davoli, M. (2008). Alcoholics anonymous and other 12 step programmes for alcohol dependence (review). *Cochrane Database of Systematic Reviews,* Issue 3. Art. No.: CD005032. DOI: 10.1002/14651858. CD005032.pub2.

Fertuck, E. A., Lenzenweger, M. F., Clarkin, J. F., Hoermann, S., & Stanley, B. (2006). Executive neurocognition, memory systems, and borderline personality disorder. *Clinical Psychology Review, 26,* 346–375.

Fiellin, D. A., O'Connor, P. G., Chawarski, M., Pakes, J. P., Pantalon, M. V., & Schottenfeld, R. S. (2001). Methadone maintenance in primary care: A randomized controlled trial. *Journal of the American Medical Association, 286,* 1724–1731.

Fillmore, K. M. (1987). Prevalence, incidence and chronicity of drinking patterns and problems among men as a function of age: A longitudinal and cohort analysis. *British Journal of Addiction, 82,* 77–83.

Fillmore, K. M., & Caetano, R. (1980, May 22). *Epidemiology of occupational alcoholism.* Paper presented at the National Institute on Alcohol Abuse and Alcoholism's Workshop on Alcoholism in the Workplace, Reston, VA.

Finkelhor, D. (1983). Removing the child—Prosecuting the offender in cases of sexual abuse: Evidence from the national reporting system for child abuse and neglect. *Child Abuse and Neglect, 7,* 195–205.

Finlay-Jones, R. (1989). Anxiety. In G. W. Brown & T. O. Harris (Eds.), *Life events and illness* (pp. 95–112). New York: Guilford.

Finney, J. W., & Moos, R. H. (1998). Psychosocial treatments for alcohol use disorders. In P. E. Nathan & J. M. Gorman (Eds.), *A guide to treatments that work* (pp. 156–166). New York: Oxford University Press.

Fiorentine, R., & Hillhouse, M. P. (2000). Exploring the additive effects of drug misuse treatment and twelve step involvement: Does twelve-step ideology matter? *Substance Use & Misuse, 35,* 367–397.

Fischer, M. (1971). Psychoses in the offspring of schizophrenic monozygotic twins and their normal cotwins. *British Journal of Psychiatry, 118,* 43–52.

Fishbain, D. A., Cutler, R., Rosomoff, H. L., & Rosomoff, R. S. (2000). Evidence-based data from animal and human experimental studies on pain relief with antidepressants: A structured review. *Pain Medicine, 1,* 310–316.

Fisher, B. S., Cullen, F. T., & Turner, M. G. (2000). *The sexual victimization of college women.* Retrieved from http://www.ojp.usdoj.gov

Fisher, J. E., & Noll, J. P. (1996). Anxiety disorders. In L. L. Carstensen, B. A. Edelstein, & L. Dornbrand (Eds.), *The practical handbook of clinical gerontology* (pp. 304–323). Thousand Oaks, CA: Sage.

Fishler, K., Azen, C. G., Henderson, R., Friedman, E. G., & Koch, R. (1987). Psychoeducational findings among children treated for phenylketonuria. *American Journal of Mental Deficiency, 92,* 65–73.

Fitzgibbons, M. L., Spring, B., Avellone, M. E., Blackman, L. R., Pingitore, R., & Stolley, M. R. (1998). Correlates of binge eating in Hispanic, black, and white women. *International Journal of Eating Disorders, 24,* 43–52.

Flament, M. F., Whitaker, A., Rapoport, J. L., Davies, M., Berg, C. Z., Kalikow, K., et al. (1988). Obsessive compulsive disorder in adolescence: An epidemiological study. *Journal of the American Academy of Child and Adolescent Psychiatry, 27,* 764–771.

Flaum, M., Amador, X., Gorman, J., Bracha, H. S., Edell, W., McGlashan, T., Pandurangi, A., Knedler, K. S., Robinson, D., Lieberman, J., Ontiveros, A., Tohen, M., McGorry, P., Tyrrell, G., Arndt, S., & Andreasen, N. C. (1998). DSM-IV field trial for schizophrenia and other psychotic disorders. *DSM-IV sourcebook* (pp. 687–713). Washington, DC: American Psychological Association.

Fleming, C. M. (1992). American Indians and Alaska Natives: Changing societies past and present. In M. A. Orlandi, R. Weston, & L. G. Epstein (Eds.), *Cultural competence for evaluators: A guide for alcohol and other drug abuse prevention practitioners working with ethnic/racial communities* (OSAP cultural competence series 1, pp. 147–171). Rockville, MD: U.S. Department of Health & Human Services.

Foa, E. B., & Franklin, M. E. (2001). Obsessive-compulsive disorder. In D. H. Barlow (Ed.), *Clinical handbook of psychological disorders* (pp. 209–263). New York: Guilford.

Foa, E. B., Libowitz, M. R., Kozak, M. J., Davies, S., Campeas, R., Franklin, M. E., et al. (2005). Randomized, placebo-controlled trail of exposure and ritual prevention, clomipramine, and their combination in the treatment of obsessive-compulsive disorder. *American Journal of Psychiatry, 162,* 151–161.

Foa, E. B., & Meadows, E. A. (1997). Psychosocial treatments for posttraumatic stress disorder: A critical review. *Annual Review of Psychology, 48,* 449–480.

Foa, E. B., Riggs, D. S., Marsie, E. D., & Yarczower, M. (1995). The impact of fear activation and anger on the efficacy of exposure treatment for posttraumatic stress disorder. *Behavior Therapy, 26,* 487–499.

Folkman, S., & Moskowitz, J. T. (2000). Positive affect and the other side of coping. *American Psychologist, 55,* 647–654.

Folstein, S., & Rutter, M. (1977a). Genetic influences and infantile autism. *Nature, 265,* 726–728.

Folstein, S., & Rutter, M. (1977b). Infantile autism: A genetic study of 21 twin pairs. *Journal of Child Psychology and Psychiatry, 18,* 291–321.

Food and Drug Administration (FDA). (April 11, 2005). *Deaths with antipsychotics in elderly patients with behavioral disturbances* (Public Health Advisory). Retrieved from http://www.fda.gov/cder/drug/advisory/antipsychotics.htm

Food and Drug Administration (FDA). (2008). *Serious health risks with antiepileptic drugs* (Public Health Advisory). Retrieved from www.fda.gov/consumer/updates/antiepileptic020508.html.

Ford, C. S., & Beach, F. A. (1951). *Patterns of sexual behavior.* New York: Harper.

Ford, C. V. (1995). Dimensions of somatization and hypochondriasis. Special Issue: Malingering and conversion reactions. *Neurological Clinics, 13,* 241–253.

Ford, C. V., & Folks, D. G. (1985). Conversion disorders: An overview. *Psychosomatics, 26,* 371–383.

Ford, J. M., Mathalon, D. H., Whitfield, S., Faustman, W. O., & Roth, W. T. (2002). Reduced communication between frontal and temporal lobes during talking in schizophrenia. *Biological Psychiatry, 51,* 485–492.

Forster, H. P., Emanuel, E., & Grady, C. (2001). The 2000 revision of the Declaration of Helsinki: A step forward or more confusion. *Lancet, 358,* 1449–1453.

Fowler, I. L., Carr, V. J., Carter, N. T., & Lewin, T. J. (1998). Patterns of current and lifetime substance use in schizophrenia. *Schizophrenia Bulletin, 24,* 443–455.

Frackeiwicz, E. J., Sramek, J. J., Herrera, J. M., Kurtz, N. M., & Cutler, N. R. (1997). Ethnicity and antipsychotic response. *Annals of Pharmacotherapy, 31,* 1360–1369.

Fraley, R. C., & Shaver, P. R. (2000). Adult romantic attachment: Theoretical developments, emerging controversies, and unanswered questions. *Review of General Psychology, 4,* 132–154.

Francis, D., Diorio, J., Liu, D., & Meaney, M. J. (1999). Nongenomic transmission across generations of maternal behavior and stress responses in the rat. *Science, 286,* 1155–1158.

Frank, E., Kupfer, D. J., Perel, J. M., Cornes, C., Jarrett, D. B., et al. (1990). Three-year outcomes for maintenance therapies in recurrent depression. *Archives of General Psychiatry, 47,* 1093–1099.

Frank, E., Kupfer, D. J., Thase, M. E., Mallinger, A. G., Swartz, H. A., Fagiolini, A. M., et al. (2005). Two-year outcomes for interpersonal and social rhythm therapy in individuals with bipolar I disorder. *Archives of General Psychiatry, 62,* 996–1004.

Frank, J. D. (1978). *Effective ingredients of successful psychotherapy.* Oxford, UK: Brunner/Mazel.

Franklin, M. E., & Foa, E. B. (1998). Cognitive-behavioral treatments for obsessive-compulsive disorder. In P. E. Nathan & J. M. Gorman (Eds.), *A guide to treatments that work* (pp. 339–357). New York: Oxford University Press.

Franko, D. L., & Keel, P. K. (2006). Suicidality in eating disorders: Occurrence, correlates, and clinical implications. *Clinical Psychology Review 26,* 769–782.

Frasure-Smith, N., & Lesperance, F. (2008). Depression and anxiety as predictors of 2-year cardiac events in patients with stable coronary artery disease. *Archives of General Psychiatry, 65,* 62–71.

Frederickson, B. L., & Carstensen, L. L. (1990). Choosing social partners: How old age and anticipated endings make people more selective. *Psychology and Aging, 5,* 335–347.

Fredrickson, B. L., & Kahneman, D. (1993). Duration neglect in retrospective evaluations of affective episodes. *Journal of Personality and Social Psychology, 65,* 20–28.

Fredrickson, B. L., & Levenson, R. W. (1998). Positive emotions speed recovery from the cardiovascular sequelae of negative emotions. *Cognition and Emotion, 12,* 191–200.

Fredrickson, B. L., Maynard, K. E., Helms, M. J., Haney, T. L., Siegler, I. C., & Barefoot, J. C. (2000). Hostility predicts magnitude and duration of blood pressure response to anger. *Journal of Behavioral Medicine, 23,* 229–243.

Fredrickson, B. L., & Roberts, T. A. (1997). Objectification theory: Toward understanding women's lived experience and mental health risks. *Psychology of Women Quarterly, 21,* 173–206.

Fredrickson, B. L., Roberts, T. A., Noll, S. M., Quinn, D. M., & Twenge, J. M. (1998). That swimsuit becomes you: Sex differences in self-objectification, restrained eating, and math performance. *Journal of Personality and Social Psychology, 78,* 269–284.

Fredrikson, M., Annas, P., & Wik, G. (1997). Parental history, aversive exposure and the development of snake and spider phobia in women. *Behaviour Research and Therapy, 35,* 23–28.

Freeman, J. B., Choate-Summers, M. L., Moore, P. S., Garcia, A. M., Sapyta, J. J., Leonard, H. L., & Franklin, M. E. (2007). Cognitive behavioral treatment for young children with obsessive-compulsive disorder. *Biological Psychiatry, 61,* 337–343.

Freeston, M. H., Dugas, M. J., & Ladoceur, R. (1996). Thoughts, images, worry, and anxiety. *Cognitive Therapy and Research, 20,* 265–273.

Fremouw, W. J., De Perczel, M., & Ellis, T. E. (1990). *Suicide risk: Assessment and response guidelines.* New York: Pergamon.

French, S. A., Story, M., Neumark-Sztainer, D., Downes, B., Resnick, M., et al. (1997). Ethnic differences in psychosocial and health behavior correlates of dieting, purging, and binge eating in a population-based sample of adolescent females. *International Journal of Eating Disorders, 22,* 315–322.

Freud, A. (1966). *The ego and mechanisms of defense.* New York: International Universities Press. (Original work published 1946)

Freud, S. (1950). Mourning and melancholia. In *Collected papers* (Vol. 4). London: Hogarth and the Institute of Psychoanalysis (Original work published 1917)

Freund, K. (1990). Courtship disorders. In W. L. Marshall, D. R. Laws, & H. E. Barbaree (Eds.), *Handbook of sexual assault: Issues, theories, and treatment* (pp. 195–207). New York: Plenum.

Fried, P., Watkinson, B., James, D., & Gray, R. (2002). Current and former marijuana use: Preliminary findings of a longitudinal study of effects on IQ in young adults. *CMAJ, 166,* 887–891.

Friedman, M. (1969). *Pathogenesis of coronary artery disease.* New York: McGraw-Hill.

Friedman, M. S., Powell, K. E., Hutwagner, L., Graham, L. M., & Teague, W. G. (2001). Impact of changes in transportation and commuting behaviors during the 1996 summer Olympic games in Atlanta on air quality and childhood asthma. *Journal of the American Medical Association, 285,* 897–905.

Friedman, M., Thoresen, C. E., Gill, J. J., Ulmer, D., Thompson, L., Powell, L., Price, A., Elek, S. R., Rabin, D. D., Breall, W. S., Piaget, G., Dixon, T., Bourg, E., Levy, R., & Tasto, D. I. (1982). Feasibility of altering type A behavior pattern after myocardial infarction. *Circulation, 66,* 83–92.

Friedmann, P. D., Lemon, S. C., & Stein, M. D. (2001). Transportation and retention in outpatient drug abuse treatment programs. *Journal of Substance Abuse Treatment, 21,* 97–103.

Friedrich, M. J. (2002). Epidemic of obesity expands its spread to developing countries. *Journal of the American Medical Association, 287,* 1382–1386.

Froehlich, T. E., Bogardus, S. T., & Inouye, S. K. (2001). Dementia and race: Are there differences between African Americans and Caucasians? *Journal of the American Gerontological Society, 49,* 477–484.

Frojdh, K., Hakansson, A., Karlsson, I., Molarius, A., Frojdh, K., Hakansson, A., et al. (2003). Deceased, disabled or depressed—a population-based 6-year followup study of elderly people with depression. *Social Psychiatry and Psychiatric Epidemiology, 38,* 557–562.

Fromm-Reichmann, F. (1948). Notes on the development of treatment of schizophrenics by psychoanalytic psychotherapy. *Psychiatry, 11,* 263–273.

Frost, D. O., & Cadet, J.-L. (2000). Effects of methamphetamine-induced toxicity on the development of neural circuitry: A hypothesis. *Brain Research Reviews, 34,* 103–118.

Fuller, R. K. (1988). Disulfiram treatment of alcoholism. In R. M. Rose & J. E. Barrett (Eds.), *Alcoholism: Treatment and outcome.* New York: Raven.

Fumeron, F., Betoulle, D., Nicaud, V., Evans, A., Kee, F., Ruidavets, J. B., Arveiler, D., Luc, G., & Cambien, F. (2002). Serotonin transporter gene polymorphism and myocardial infarction: Étude Cas-T Âmoins de l'Infarctus du Myocarde (ECTIM). *Circulation, 105,* 2943–2945.

Fung, Y. K., & Lau, Y-S. (1989). Effects of prenatal nicotine exposure on rat striatal dopaminergic and nicotinic systems. *Pharmacology, Biochemistry & Behavior, 33,* 1–6.

Furnham, A., & Baguma, P. (1994). Cross-cultural differences in the evaluation of male and female body shapes. *International Journal of Eating Disorders, 15,* 81–89.

Galea, S., Ahern, J., Resnick, H., Kilpatrick, D., Bucuvalas, M., Gold, J., & Vlahov, D. (2002). Psychological sequelae of the September 11 terrorist attacks in New York City. *New England Journal of Medicine, 346,* 982–987.

Gallagher, D., & Thompson, L. W. (1983). Cognitive therapy for depression in the elderly. A promising model for treatment and research. In L. D. Breslau & M. R. Haug

(Eds.), *Depression and aging: Causes, care and consequences*. New York: Springer-Verlag.

Galli, V., McElroy, S. L., Soutullo, C. A., Kizer, D., Raute, N., et al. (1999). The psychiatric diagnoses of twenty-two adolescents who have sexually molested children. *Comprehensive Psychiatry, 40*, 85–88.

Gallo, C. L., & Pfeffer, C. R. (2003). Children and adolescents bereaved by a suicidal death: Implications for psychosocial outcomes and interventions. In A. Apter & R. A. King (Eds.), *Suicide in children and adolescents* (pp. 294–312). New York: Cambridge University Press.

Gallo, J. J., & Lebowitz, B. D. (1999). The epidemiology of common late-life mental disorders in the community: Themes for the new century. *Psychiatric Services, 50*, 1158–1166.

Ganellan, R. J. (1996). Comparing the diagnostic efficiency of the MMPI, MCMI-II, and Rorschach: A review. *Journal of Personality Assessment, 67*, 219–243.

Ganguli, M., Du, Y., Dodge, H. H., Ratcliff, G. G., & Chang, C.-C. H. (2006). Depressive symptoms and cognitive decline in late life: A prospective epidemiological study. *Archives of General Psychiatry, 63*, 153–160.

Garand, L., Buckwalter, K. C., Lubaroff, D., Tripp-Reimer, T., Frantz, R. A., & Ansley, T. N. (2002). A pilot study of immune and mood outcomes of a community-based intervention for dementia caregivers: The PLST intervention. *Archives of Psychiatric Nursing, 16*, 156–167.

Garb, I. I. N. (1997). Race bias, social class bias, and gender bias in clinical judgment. *Clinical Psychology: Science and Practice, 4*, 99–120.

Garber, J. (2006). Depression in children and adolescents: Linking risk research and prevention. *American Journal of Preventative Medicine, 31*, 5104–5125.

Garber, J., & Flynn, C. (2001). Vulnerability to depression in childhood and adolescence. In R. M. Ingram & J. M. Price (Eds.), *Vulnerability to psychopathology: Risk across the lifespan* (pp. 175–225). New York: Guilford.

Garber, J., Kelly, M. K., & Martin, N. C. (2002). Developmental trajectories of adolescents' depressive symptoms: Predictors of change. *Journal of Consulting and Clinical Psychology, 70*, 79–95.

Garbutt, J. C., Mayo, J. P., Little, K. Y., Gillette, G. M., Mason, G. A., et al. (1994). Dose-response studies with protirelin. *Archives of General Psychiatry, 51*, 875–883.

Gard, D. E., Kring, A. M., Germans Gard, M., Horan, W. P., & Green, M. F. (2007). Anhedonia in schizophrenia: Distinctions between anticipatory and consummatory pleasure. *Schizophrenia Research, 93*, 253–260.

Garety, P. A., Fowler, D., & Kuipers, E. (2000). Cognitive behavioral therapy for medication-resistant symptoms. *Schizophrenia Bulletin, 26*, 73–86.

Garfinkel, P. E., Goering, E. L., Goldbloom, S. D., Kennedy, S., Kaplan, A. S., & Woodside, D. B. (1996). Should amenorrhea be necessary for the diagnosis of anorexia nervosa? *British Journal of Psychiatry, 168*, 500–506.

Garfinkel, P. E., Kennedy, S. H., & Kaplan, A. S. (1995). Views on classification and diagnosis of eating disorders. *Canadian Journal of Psychiatry, 40*, 445–456.

Garland, R. J., & Dougher, M. J. (1991). Motivational interviewing in the treatment of sex offenders. In W. R. Miller & S. Rollnick (Eds.), *Motivating interviewing: Preparing people to change addictive behavior* (pp. 303–313). New York: Guilford.

Garner, D. M. (1997). Psychoeducational principles. In D. M. Garner & P. E. Garfinkel (Eds.), *Handbook of treatment for eating disorders* (pp. 145–177). New York: Guilford.

Garner, D. M., Garfinkel, P. E., Schwartz, D., & Thompson, M. (1980). Cultural expectation of thinness in women. *Psychological Reports, 47*, 483–491.

Garner, D. M., Olmsted, M. P., & Polivy, J. (1983). Development and validation of a multidimensional eating disorder inventory for anorexia nervosa and bulimia. *International Journal of Eating Disorders, 2*, 15–34.

Garner, D. M., Vitousek, K. M., & Pike, K. M. (1997). Cognitive-behavioral therapy for anorexia nervosa. In D. M. Garner & P. E. Garfinkel (Eds.), *Handbook of treatment for eating disorders* (pp. 94–144). New York: Guilford.

Gatchel, R. J., Peng, Y. B., Peters, M. L., Fuchs, P. N., & Turk, D. C. (2007). The biopsychosocial approach to chronic pain: Scientific advances and future directions. *Psychological Bulletin, 133*, 581–624.

Gatz, M., Bengtson, V. L., & Blum, M. J. (1990). Caregiving families. In J. E. Birren & K. W. Schaie (Eds.), *Handbook of the psychology of aging* (3rd ed., pp. 404–426). New York: Academic Press.

Gatz, M., Kasl-Godley, J. E., & Karel, M. J. (1996). Aging and mental disorders. In J. E. Birren & K. W. Schaie (Eds.), *Handbook of the psychology of aging 367–382*. San Diego, CA: Academic Press.

Gatz, M., Reynolds, C. A., Fratiglioni, L., Johansson, B., Mortimer, J. A., Berg, S., et al. (2006). Roles of genes and environments for explaining Alzheimer disease. *Archives of General Psychiatry, 63*, 168–174.

Gaus, V. L. (2007). *Cognitive behavior therapy for adults with Asperger's syndrome*. New York: Guilford.

Gaw, A. C. (2001). *Concise guide to cross-cultural psychiatry*. Washington, DC: American Psychiatric Association.

Ge, X., Conger, R. D., Cadoret, R. J., Neiderhiser, J. M., Yates, W., et al. (1996). The developmental interface between nature and nurture: A mutual influence model of child antisocial behavior and parent behaviors. *Developmental Psychology, 32*, 574–589.

Gebhard, P. H., Gagnon, J. H., Pomeroy, W. B., & Christenson, C. V. (1965). *Sex offenders*. New York: Harper & Row.

Geddes, J. R., Carney, S. M., Davies, C., Furukawa, T. A., Frank, E., Kupfer, D. J., & Goodwin, G. (2003). Relapse prevention with antidepressant drug treatment in depressive disorders: A systematic review. *Lancet, 361*, 653–661.

Geller, B., Cooper, T. B., Graham, D., Fetner, H., Marstellar, F., & Wells, J. (1992). Pharmacokinetically designed double-blind placebo-controlled study of nortriptyline in 6- to 12-year-olds with major depressive disorder. *Journal of the American Academy of Child and Adolescent Psychiatry, 31*, 34–44.

Geller, J. L. (2006). A history of private psychiatric hospitals in the USA: From start to almost finished. *Psychiatric Quarterly, 77*, 1–41.

Gendall, K. A., Bulik, C. M., Joyce, P. R., McIntosh, V. V., & Carter, F. A. (2000). Menstrual cycle irregularity in bulimia nervosa: Associated factors and changes with treatment. *Journal of Psychosomatic Research, 49*, 409–415.

Gendreau, P., Little, T., & Goggin, C. (1996). A meta-analysis of the predictors of adult offender recidivism: What works! *Criminology, 34*, 575–607.

General Register Office. (1968). *A glossary of mental disorders*. London.

Geracioti, T. D., Baker, D. G., Ekhator, N. N., et al. (2001). CSF norepinephrine concentrations in posttraumatic stress disorder. *American Journal of Psychiatry, 158*, 1227–1230.

Geraerts, E., Schooler, J. W., Merckelbach, H., Jelicic, M., Hauer, B. J. A., & Ambadar, Z. (2007). The reality of recovered memories: Corroborating continuous and discontinuous memories of childhood sexual abuse. *Psychological Science, 18*, 564–568.

Gerlach, A. L., Wilhelm, F. H., Gruber, K., & Roth, W. T. (2001). Blushing and physiological arousability in social phobia. *Journal of Abnormal Psychology, 110*, 247–258.

Gernsbacher, M. A., Dawson, M., & Goldsmith, H. H. (2005). Three reasons not to believe in an autism epidemic. *Current Directions in Psychological Science, 14*, 55–58.

Gerra, G., Zaimovic, A., Ferri, M., Zambelli, U., Timpano, M., Neri, E., Marzocchi, G. F., Delsignore, R., & Brambilla, F. (2000). Long-lasting effects of (6)3, 4-methylenedioxymethamphetamine (Ecstasy) on serotonin system function in humans. *Biological Psychiatry, 47*, 127–136.

Geschwind, D. H., Robidoux, J., Alarcon, M., et al. (2001). Dementia and neurodevelopmental predisposition: Cognitive dysfunction in presymptomatic subjects precedes dementia by decades in frontotemporal dementia. *Annals of Neurology, 50*, 741–746.

Ghaemi, S. N., Boiman, E. E., & Goodwin, F. K. (2000). Diagnosing bipolar disorder and the effect of antidepressants: A naturalistic study. *Journal of Clinical Psychiatry, 61*, 804–808.

Ghaemi, S. N., & Goodwin, F. K. (2003). Introduction to special issue on antidepressant use in bipolar disorder. *Bipolar Disorders, 5*, 385–387.

Giancola, P., & Corman, M. (2007). Alcohol and aggression: A test of the attention-allocation model. *Psychological Science, 18*, 649–655.

Gibson, D. R. (2001). Effectiveness of syringe exchange programs in reducing HIV risk behavior and seroconversion among injecting drug users. *AIDS, 15*, 1329–1341.

Gidron, Y., Davidson, K., & Bata, I. (1999). The short-term effects of a hostility reduction intervention in CHD patients. *Health Psychology, 18*, 416–420.

Giesen-Bloo, J., van Dyck, R., Spinhoven, P., van Tilburg, W., Dirksen, C., van Asselt, T., et al. (2006). Outpatient psychotherapy for borderline personality disorder: Randomized trial of schema-focused therapy vs. transference-focused psychotherapy. *Archives of General Psychiatry, 63*, 649–658.

Gilbert, A. R., Rosenberg, D. R., Harenski, K., et al. (2001). Thalamic volumes in patients with first episode schizophrenia. *American Journal of Psychiatry, 158*, 618–624.

Gilbertson, M. W., Shenton, M. E., Ciszewski, A., Kasai, K., Lasko, N. B., Orr, S. P., et al. (2002). Smaller hippocampal volume predicts pathologic vulnerability to psychological trauma. *Nature Neuroscience, 5*, 1242–1247.

Gilbody, S., Whitty, P., Grimshaw, J., & Thomas, R. (2003). Educational and organizational interventions to improve the management of depression in primary care: A systematic review. *Journal of the American Medical Association, 289*, 3145–3151.

Gill, S., Bronskill, S. E., Normand, S. T., Anderson, G. M., Sykora, K., Lam, K., et al. (2007). Antipsychotic drug use and mortality in older adults with dementia. *Annuals of Internal Medicine, 146*, 775–786.

Gillberg, C. (1991). Outcome in autism and autistic-like conditions. *Journal of the American Academy of Child and Adolescent Psychiatry, 30*, 375–382.

Gillespie, K., Duffy, M., Hackmann, A., & Clark, D. M. (2002). Community based cognitive therapy in the treatment of post-traumatic stress disorder following the Omaha bomb. *Behaviour Research and Therapy, 40*, 345–357.

Gillis, J. J., & DeFries, J. C. (1991). Confirmatory factor analysis of reading and mathematics performance measures in the Colorado Reading Project. *Behavior Genetics, 21*, 572–573.

Gitlin, L. N., Belle, S. H., Burgio, L. D., Czaja, S. J., Mahoney, D., Gallagher-Thompson, D., et al. (2003). Effect of multicomponent interventions on caregiver burden and depression: The REACH Multisite Initiative at 6-month follow-up. *Psychology and Aging, 18*, 361–374.

Glass, C. R., & Arnkoff, D. B. (1997). Questionnaire methods of cognitive self-statement assessment. *Journal of Consulting and Clinical Psychology, 65*, 911–927.

Glassman, A. H. (2005). Does treating post-myocardial infarction depression reduce medical mortality? *Archives of General Psychiatry, 62*, 711–712.

Glassman, A. H., O'Connor, C. M., Califf, R. M., Swedberg, K., Schwartz, P., Bigger, J. T., et al. (2002). Sertraline treatment of major depression in patients with acute MI or unstable angina. *Journal of American Medical Association, 288*, 701–709.

Glassman, A. H., & Shapiro, P. A. (1998). Depression and the course of cardiovascular disease. *American Journal of Psychiatry, 155*, 4–11.

Glatt, S. J., Faraone, S. V., & Tsuang, M. (2003). Meta-analysis identifies an association between the dopamine D2 receptor gene and schizophrenia. *Molecular Psychiatry, 8*, 911–915.

Gleaves, D. H. (1996). The sociocognitive model of dissociative identity disorder: A reexamination of the evidence. *Psychological Bulletin, 120*, 42–59.

Gleick, J. (1987). *Chaos: Making a new science.* New York: Penguin.

Glenn, A. L., Raine, A., Venables, P. H., & Mednick, S. A. (2007). Early temperamental and psychophysiological precursors of adult psychopathic personality. *Journal of Abnormal Psychology, 116,* 508–518.

Godart, N. T., Flament, M. F., Lecrubier, Y., & Jeammet, P. (2000). Anxiety disorders in anorexia nervosa and bulimia nervosa: Co morbidity and chronology of appearance. *European Psychiatry, 15*, 38–45.

Goenjian, A. K., Walling, D., Steinberg, A. M., Karayan, I., Najarian, L. M., & Pynoos, R. (2005). A prospective study of posttraumatic stress and depressive reactions among treated and untreated adolescents 5 years after a catastrophic disaster. *American Journal of Psychiatry, 162*, 2302–2308.

Goldapple, K., Segal, Z., Garson, C., Lau, M., Bieling, P., Kennedy, S., & Mayberg, H. (2004). Modulation of cortical-limbic pathways in major depression. *Archives of General Psychiatry, 61*, 34–41.

Goldberg, T. E., & Weinberger, D. R. (2004). Genes and the parsing of cognitive processes. *Trends in Cognitive Sciences, 8*, 325–335.

Golden, C. J. (1981a). The Luria-Nebraska Children's Battery: Theory and formulation. In G. W. Hynd & J. E. Obrzut (Eds.), *Neuropsychological assessment and the school-age child: Issues and procedures.* New York: Grune & Stratton.

Golden, C. J. (1981b). A standardized version of Luria's neuropsychological tests: A quantitative and qualitative approach to neuropsychological evaluation. In S. B. Filskov & T. J. Boil (Eds.), *Handbook of clinical neuropsychology.* New York: Wiley.

Golden, C. J., Hammeke, T., & Purisch, A. (1978). Diagnostic validity of a standardized neuropsychological battery derived from Luria's neuropsychological tests. *Journal of Consulting and Clinical Psychology, 46*, 1258–1265.

Golden, R. N., Gaynes, B. N., Ekstrom, R. D., Hamer, R. M., Jacobsen, F. M., Suppes, T., et al. (2005). The efficacy of light therapy in the treatment of mood disorders: A review and meta-analysis of the evidence. *American Journal of Psychiatry, 162*, 656–662.

Goldfried, M. R. (2004). Integrating integratively oriented brief psychotherapy. *Journal of Psychotherapy Integration, 14,* 93–105.

Goldfried, M. R., & Davison, G. C. (1994). *Clinical behavior therapy* (expanded ed.). New York: Wiley.

Goldfried, M. R., Greenberg, L. S., & Marmar, C. (1990). Individual psychotherapy: Process and outcome. *Annual Review of Psychology, 41*, 659–688.

Golding, J. M., Smith, G. R., & Kashner, T. M. (1991). Does somatization disorder occur in men? Clinical characteristics of women and men with unexplained somatic symptoms. *Archives of General Psychiatry, 48*, 231–235.

Goldman-Rakic, P. S., & Selemon, L. D. (1997). Functional and anatomical aspects of prefrontal pathology in schizophrenia. *Schizophrenia Bulletin, 23*, 437–458.

Goldstein, A. J., & Chambless, D. L. (1978). A reanalysis of agoraphobic behavior. *Behavior Therapy, 9*, 47–59.

Goldstein, Alan J., de Beurs, E., Chambless, D L., & Wilson, K. A. (2000). EMDR for panic disorder with agoraphobia: Comparison with waiting list and credible attention–placebo control conditions. *Journal of Consulting and Clinical Psychology, 68*, 947–956.

Golier, J., & Yehuda, R. (1998). Neuroendocrine activity and memory-related impairments in posttraumatic stress disorder. *Development and Psychopathology, 10*, 857–869.

Gomez, F. C., Piedmont, R. L., & Fleming, M. Z. (1992). Factor analysis of the Spanish version of the WAIS: The Escala de Inteligencia Wechsler para Adultos (EIWA). *Psychological Assessment, 4*, 317–321.

Goodenow, C., Reisine, S. T., & Grady, K. E. (1990). Quality of social support and associated social and psychological functions in women with rheumatoid arthritis. *Health Psychology, 9*, 266–284.

Goodkin, K., Baldewicz, T. T., Blaney, N. T., et al. (2001). Physiological effects of bereavement and bereavement support group interventions. In M. Stroebe, R. O. Hansson, et al. (Eds.), *Handbook of bereavement research: Consequences, coping, and care* (pp. 671–703). Washington, DC: American Psychological Association.

Goodman, G. S., Ghetti, S., Quas, J. A., Edelstein, R. S., Alexander, K. W., Redlich, A. D., et al. (2003). A prospective study of memory for child sexual abuse: New findings relevant to the repressed-memory controversy. *Psychological Science, 14*, 113–118.

Goodsitt, A. (1997). Eating disorders: A self-psychological perspective. In D. M. Garner & P. E. Garfinkel (Eds.), *Handbook of treatment for eating disorders* (pp. 205–228). New York: Guilford.

Goodwin, D. K. (2003, February 17). The man in our memory. *New York Times,* Op-Ed section.

Goodwin, F., & Jamison, K. (1990). *Manic-depressive illness.* New York: Oxford University Press.

Gopnik, A., Capps, L., & Meltzoff, A. N. (2000). Early theories of mind: What the theory can tell us about autism. In S. Baren-Cohen, H. Tager-Flusberg, & D. Cohen (Eds.), *Understanding other minds* (2nd ed., pp. 50–72). Oxford, UK: Oxford University Press.

Gordon, K. H., Perez, M., & Joiner, T. E. (2002). The impact of racial stereotypes on eating disorder recognition. *International Journal of Eating Disorders, 32*, 219–224.

Gorenstein, E. E., & Newman, J. P. (1980). Disinhibitory psychopathology: A new perspective and a model for research. *Psychological Review, 87*, 301–315.

Gorman, J. M., Kent, J., Martinez, J., Browne, S., Coplan, F., & Papp, L. A. (2001). Physiological changes during carbon dioxide inhalation in patients with panic disorder, major depression, and premenstrual dysphoric disorder. *Archives of General Psychiatry, 58*, 125–131.

Gortner, E. T., Gollan, J. K., Dobson, K. S., & Jacobson, N. S. (1998). Cognitive-behavioral treatment for depression: Relapse prevention. *Journal of Consulting and Clinical Psychology, 66*, 377–384.

Gotlib, I. H., & Krasnoperova, E. (1998). Biased information processing as a vulnerability factor for depression. *Behavior Therapy, 29*, 603–617.

Gotlib, I. H., Lewinsohn, P. R., & Seeley, J. R. (1995). Symptoms versus a diagnosis of depression: Differences in psychosocial functioning. *Journal of Consulting and Clinical Psychology, 63*, 90–100.

Gotlib, I. H., & Robinson, L. A. (1982). Responses to depressed individuals: Discrepancies between self-report and observer-rated behavior. *Journal of Abnormal Psychology, 91*, 231–240.

Gottesman, I. I., & Goldsmith, H. H. (1994). Developmental psychopathology of antisocial behavior: Inserting genes into its ontogenesis and epigenesis. In C. A. Nelson (Ed.), *Threats to optimal development 69–104.* Hillsdale, NJ: Erlbaum.

Gottesman, I. I., McGuffin, P., & Farmer, A. E. (1987). Clinical genetics as clues to the "real" genetics of schizophrenia. *Schizophrenia Bulletin 69–104, 13*, 23–47.

Gottesman, I., & Shields, J. (1972). *Schizophrenia and genetics: A twin study vantage point.* New York: Academic Press.

Gottman, J. M. (1994). *What predicts divorce? The relationship between marital processes and marital outcome.* Hillsdale, NJ: Erlbaum.

Gottman, J. M., & Krokoff, L. J. (1989). Marital interaction and satisfaction: A longitudinal view. *Journal of Consulting and Clinical Psychology, 57*, 47–52.

Gould, E., Otto, M. W., & Pollack, M. H. (1995). A meta-analysis of treatment outcome for panic disorder. *Clinical Psychology Review, 15*, 819–844.

Gould, R. A., Safren, S. A., Washington, D. O., & Otto, M. W. (2004). A meta-analytic review of cognitive-behavioral treatments. In R. G. Heimberg, C. L. Turk, & D. S. Mennin (Eds.), *Generalized anxiety disorder* (pp. 248–264). New York: Guilford.

Goyette, C. H., & Conners, C. K. (1977). *Food additives and hyperkinesis.* Paper presented at the 85th annual convention of the American Psychological Association. San Francisco, CA.

Grabe, S., & Hyde, J. S. (2006). Ethnicity and body dissatisfaction among women in the United States: A meta-analyis. *Psychological Bulletin, 132*, 622–640.

Graham, J. R. (1988). *Establishing validity of the revised form of the MMPI.* Symposium presentation at the 96th annual convention of the American Psychological Association, Atlanta.

Graham, J. R. (1990). *MMPI-2: Assessing personality and psychopathology.* New York: Oxford University Press.

Grandin, T. (1986). *Emergence: Labeled autistic.* Novato, CA: Arena Press.

Grandin, T. (1995). *Thinking in pictures.* New York: Doubleday.

Grant, B. F., & Dawson, D. A. (1997). Age of onset at alcohol use and its association with DSM-IV alcohol abuse and dependence: Results from the national longitudinal epidemiologic survey. *Journal of Substance Abuse, 9*, 103–110.

Green, M. F. (1996). What are the functional consequences of neurocognitive deficits in schizophrenia? *American Journal of Psychiatry, 153*, 321–330.

Green, M. F., Kern, R. S., Braff, D. L., & Mintz, J. (2000). Neurocognitive deficits and functional outcome in schizophrenia: Are we measuring the "right stuff"? *Schizophrenia Bulletin, 26*, 119–136.

Green, M. F., Marshall, B. D., Wirshing, W. C., Ames, D., Marder, S. R., McGurk, S., Kern, R. S., & Mintz, J. (1997). Does risperidone improve verbal working memory in treatment-resistant schizophrenia? *American Journal of Psychiatry, 154*, 799–804.

Green, M. F., Nuechterlein, K. H., Gold, J. M., et al. (2004). Approaching a consensus cognitive battery for clinical trials in schizophrenia: The NIMH-MATRICS conference to select cognitive domains and test criteria. *Biological Psychiatry, 56*, 301–307.

Green, M. J., Cahill, C. M., & Malhi, G. S. (2007). The cognitive and neurophysiological basis of emotion dysregulation in bipolar disorder. *Journal of Affective Disorders, 103*, 29–42.

Green, R. (1976). One hundred ten feminine and masculine boys: Behavioral contrasts and demographic similarities. *Archives of Sexual Behavior, 5*, 425–446.

Green, R. (1987). Gender identity in childhood and later sexual orientation: Follow-up of 78 males. In A. Thomas & S. Chess (Eds.), *Annual progress in child psychiatry and child development, 1986* (pp. 214–220). Philadelphia: Brunner/Mazel.

Green, R., & Blanchard, R. (1995). Gender identity disorders. In H. I. Kaplan & B. J. Sadock (Eds.), *Comprehensive textbook of psychiatry* (pp. 1347–1360). Baltimore: Williams & Wilkins.

Green, R., & Fleming, D. T. (1990). Transsexual surgery follow-up: Status in the 1990s. In J. Bancroft, C. Davis, & D. Weinstein (Eds.), *Annual review of sex research* (pp. 163–174). Society for the Scientific Study of Sexuality, Allentown. Vol. 1.

Greenberg, L. (2002). *Emotion-focused therapy: Coaching clients to work through their feelings*. Washington, DC: American Psychological Association.

Greenberg, L. S., Watson, J. C., Elliot, R., & Bohart, A. C. (2001). Empathy. *Psychotherapy: Theory, Research, Practice, Training, 38*, 380–384.

Greenblatt, J. C., Gfroerer, J. C., & Melnick, D. (1995). Increasing morbidity and mortality associated with abuse of methamphetamines—United States, 1991–1994. *Morbidity and Mortality Weekly Report, 44*, 882–886.

Greenwood, T. A., Braff, D. L., Light, G. A., Cadenhead, K. S., Calkins, M. E., et al. (2007). Initial heritability analyses of endophenotypic measures for schizophrenia: The consortium on the genetics of schizophrenia. *Archives of General Psychiatry, 64*, 1242–1250.

Greeven, A., van Balkom, A. J. L. M., Visser, S., Merkelbach, J. W., van Rood, Y. R., van Dyck, R., et al. (2007). Cognitive behavior therapy and paroxetine in the treatment of hypochondriasis: A randomized controlled trial. *American Journal of Psychiatry, 164*, 91–99.

Gretarsdottir, E., Woodruff Borden, J., Meeks, S., Depp, C. A., Gretarsdottir, E., Woodruff Borden, J., et al. (2004). Social anxiety in older adults: Phenomenology, prevalence, and measurement. *Behaviour Research and Therapy, 42*, 459–475.

Grice, D. E., Halmi, K. A., Fichter, M. M., Strober, M., Woodside, D. B., Treasure, J. T., Kaplan, A. S., Magistretti, P. J., Goldman, D., Bulik, C. M., Kaye, W. H., & Berrettini, W. H. (2002). Evidence for a susceptibility gene for anorexia nervosa on chromosome 1. *American Journal of Human Genetics, 70*, 787–792.

Grillon, C. (2002). Startle reactivity and anxiety disorders: Aversive conditioning, context, and neurobiology. *Biological Psychiatry, 52*, 958–975.

Grilo, C.M. (2007). Treatment of binge eating disorder. In S. Wonderlich, J. E. Mitchell, M. de Zwaan, & H. Steiger (Eds.), *Annual review of eating disorders* (pp. 23–34). Oxford, UK: Radcliffe.

Grilo, C. M., Shea, M. T., Sanislow, C. A., Skodol, A. E., Gunderson, J. G., Stout, R. L., et al. (2004). Two-year stability and change of schizotypal, borderline, avoidant, and obsessive-compulsive personality disorders. *Journal of Consulting and Clinical Psychology, 72*, 767–775.

Grilo, C. M., Shiffman, S., & Carter-Campbell, J. T. (1994). Binge eating antecedents in normal weight nonpurging females: Is there consistency? *International Journal of Eating Disorders, 16*, 239–249.

Grinker, R. R., & Spiegel, J. P. (1944). *Management of neuropsychiatric casualties in the zone of combat: Manual of military neuropsychiatry*. Philadelphia: W. B. Saunders.

Grinspoon, L., & Bakalar, J. B. (1995). Marijuana as medicine: A plea for reconsideration. *Journal of the American Medical Association, 273*, 1875–1876.

Grisso, T., & Appelbaum, P. S. (1995). Mentally ill and non-mentally ill patients' abilities to understand informed consent disclosures for medication: Preliminary data. *Law and Human Behavior, 15*, 377–388.

Grisso, T., Davis, J., Vesselinov, R., Appelbaum, P. S., & Monahan, J. (2000). Violent thoughts and violent behavior following hospitalization for mental disorder. *Journal of Consulting and Clinical Psychology, 68*, 388–398.

Groesz, L. M., Levine, M. P., & Murnen, S. K. (2002). The effect of experimental presentation of thin media images on body dissatisfaction: A meta-analytic review. *International Journal of Eating Disorders, 31*, 1–16.

Gross, C., Zhuang, X., Stark, K., Ramboz, S., Oosting, R., Kirby, L., Santarelli, L., Beck, S., & Hen, R. (2002). Serotonin 1A receptor acts during development to establish normal anxiety-like behaviour in the adult. *Nature, 416*, 396–400.

Grossman, D. (1995). *On killing: The psychological cost of learning to kill in war and society*. Boston: Little, Brown.

Gruber, K., Chutuape, M. A., & Stitzer, M. L. (2000). Reinforcement-based intensive outpatient treatment for inner city opiate abusers: A short-term evaluation. *Drug & Alcohol Dependence, 57*, 211–223.

Grundy, S. M., Brewer, B., Jr., Cleeman, J. I., et al. (2004). Definition of metabolic syndrome: Report of the National Heart, Lung and Blood Institute/American Heart Association Conference on scientific issues related to definition. *Circulation, 109*, 433–438.

Guastella, A. J., Richardson, R., Lovibond, P. F., Rapee, R. M., Gaston, J. E., Mitchell, P., et al. (2008). A randomized controlled trial of D-cycloserine enhancement of exposure therapy for social anxiety disorder. *Biological Psychiatry, 63*, 544–549.

Gump, B. S., Matthews, K. A., & Räikkönen, K. (1999). Modeling relationships among socioeconomic status, hostility, cardiovascular reactivity, and left ventricular mass in African American and white children. *Health Psychology, 18*, 140–150.

Gunn, J. (1993). Castration is not the answer. *British Medical Journal, 307*, 790–791.

Gur, R. E., & Pearlson, G. D. (1993). Neuroimaging in schizophrenia research. *Schizophrenia Bulletin, 19*, 337–353.

Gur, R. E., Turetsky, B. I., Cowell, P. E., et al. (2000). Temporolimbic volume reductions in schizophrenia. *Archives of General Psychiatry, 57*, 769–776.

Gurland, B. (1991). Epidemiology of psychiatric disorders. In J. Sadavoy, L. W. Lazarus, & L. F. Jarvik (Eds.), *Comprehensive review of geriatric psychiatry* (pp. 25–40). Washington, DC: American Psychiatric Press.

Gustad, J., & Phillips, K. A. (2003). Axis I comorbidity in body dysmorphic disorder. *Comprehensive Psychiatry, 44*, 270–276.

Guthrie, R. M., & Bryant, R. A. (2005). Auditory startle response in firefighters before and after trauma exposure. *American Journal of Psychiatry, 162*, 283–290.

Gutman, D. A., & Nemeroff, C. B. (2003). Persistent central nervous system effects of an adverse early environment: Clinical and preclinical studies. *Physiology and Behavior, 79*, 471–478.

Guyll, M., & Contrada, R. J. (1998). Trait hostility and ambulatory cardiovascular activity: Responses to social interaction. *Health Psychology, 17*, 30–39.

Guyll, M., Matthews, K. A., & Bromberger, J. T. (2001). Discrimination and unfair treatment: Relationship to cardiovascular reactivity among African American and European American women. *Health Psychology, 20*, 315–325.

Gwynn, R. C. (2004). Risk factors for asthma in US adults: Results from the 2000 Behavioral Risk Factor Surveillance System. *Journal of Asthma, 41*, 91–98.

Haaga, D. A. F. (1989). Articulated thoughts and endorsement procedures for cognitive assessment in the prediction of smoking relapse. *Psychological Assessment: A Journal of Consulting and Clinical Psychology, 1*, 112–117.

Haaga, D. A. F. (1990). Issues in relating self-efficacy to smoking relapse: Importance of an "Achilles' Heel" situation and of prior quitting experience. *Journal of Substance Abuse, 2*, 191–200.

Haaga, D. A. F. (2000). Introduction to the special section on stepped care models in psychotherapy. *Journal of Consulting and Clinical Psychology, 68*, 547–548.

Haaga, D. A. F., Dyck, M. J., & Ernst, D. (1991). Empirical status of cognitive theory of depression. *Psychological Bulletin, 110*, 215–236.

Haaga, D. A. F., & Stiles, W. B. (2000). Randomized clinical trials in psychotherapy research: Methodology, design, and evaluation. In R. E. Ingram & C. Snyder (Eds.), *Handbook of psychological change: Psychotherapy processes & practices for the 21st century* (pp. 14–39). New York: Wiley.

Haas, R. H., Townsend, J., Courchesne, E., Lincoln, A. J., Schreibman, L., & Yeung-Courchesne, R. (1996). Neurologic abnormalities in infantile autism. *Journal of Child Neurology, 11*, 84–92.

Hacking, I. (1998). *Mad travelers: Reflections on the reality of transient mental illness*. Charlottesville: University Press of Virginia.

Haddock, G., Tarrier, N., Spaulding, W., Yusupoff, L. K., & McCarthy, E. (1998). Individual cognitive-behavior therapy in the treatment of hallucinations and delusions: A review. *Clinical Psychology Review, 18*, 821–838.

Hagerman, R. (2006). Lessons from fragile X regarding neurobiology, autism, and neurodegeneration. *Developmental and Behavioral Pediatrics, 27*, 63–74.

Halbreich, U., Alarcon, R. D., Calil, H., Douki, S., Gaszner, P., Jadresic, E., et al. (2007). Special research report: Culturally-sensitive complaints of depressions and anxieties in women. *Journal of Abnormal Psychology, 102*, 159–176.

Halkitis, P. N., Parsons, J. T., & Stirratt, M. J. (2001). A double epidemic: Crystal methamphetamine drug use in relation to HIV transmission among gay men. *Journal of Homosexuality, 41*, 17–35.

Hall, G. C. (2001). Psychotherapy research with ethnic minorities: Empirical, ethical, and conceptual issues. *Journal of Consulting and Clinical Psychology, 69*(3), 502–510.

Hall, G. C., Hirschman, R., & Oliver, L. L. (1995). Sexual arousal and arousability to pedophilic stimuli in a community sample of normal men. *Behavior Therapy, 26*, 681–694.

Halmi, K. A., Sunday, S. R., Strober, M., Kaplan, A., Woodside, D. B., Fichter, N., Treasure, J., Berrettini, W. H., & Kaye, W. (2000). Perfectionism in anorexia nervosa: Variation by clinical subtype, obsessionality, and pathological eating behavior. *American Journal of Psychiatry, 157,* 1799–1805.

Hammen, C. (1997). Children of depressed parents: The stress context. In S. A. Wolchik & I. N. Sandler (Eds.), *Handbook of children's coping: Linking theory and intervention. Issues in clinical child psychology* (pp. 131–157). New York: Plenum Press.

Hankin, B. J., Abramson, L. Y., Moffitt, T. E., Silva, P. A., McGee, R., et al. (1998). Development of depression from preadolescence to young adulthood: Emerging gender differences in a 10-year longitudinal study. *Journal of Abnormal Psychology, 107,* 128–140.

Hankin, B. L., & Abramson, L. Y. (2001). Development of gender differences in depression: An elaborated cognitive vulnerability-transactional stress theory. *Psychological Bulletin, 127,* 773–796.

Hankin, B. L., Mermelstein, R., & Roesch, L. (2007). Sex differences in adolescent depression: Stress exposure and reactivity models. *Child Development, 78,* 279–295.

Hansen, W. B. (1992). School-based substance abuse prevention: A review of the state of the art in curriculum, 1980–1990. *Health Education Research: Theory and Practice, 7,* 403–430.

Hansen, W. B. (1993). School-based alcohol prevention programs. *Alcohol Health and Research World, 18,* 62–66.

Hansen, W. B., & Graham, J. W. (1991). Preventing alcohol, marijuana, and cigarette use among adolescents: Peer pressure resistance training versus establishing conservative norms. *Preventive Medicine, 20,* 414–430.

Hanson, R. K., & Bussiere, M. T. (1998). Predicting relapse: A meta-analysis of sexual offender recidivism studies. *Journal of Consulting and Clinical Psychology, 66,* 348–362.

Hanson, R. K., & Harris, A. J. R. (1997). Voyeurism: Assessment and treatment. In D. R. Laws & W. O'Donohue (Eds.), *Sexual deviance* (pp. 311–331). New York: Guilford.

Hanson, R. K., Hunsley, J., & Parker, K. C. H. (1988). The relationship between WAIS subtest reliability, "g" loadings, and meta-analytically derived validity estimates. *Journal of Clinical Psychology, 44,* 557–563.

Hardan, A. Y., Minshew, N. J., Harenski, K., & Keshavan, M. S. (2001). Posterior fossa magnetic resonance imaging in autism. *Journal of the American Academy of Child and Adolescent Psychiatry, 40,* 666–672.

Hare, E. (1969). *Triennial statistical report of the Royal Maudsley and Bethlem Hospitals.* London: Bethlem and Maudsley Hospitals.

Hare, R. D. (2003). *The Hare psychopathy checklist* (rev. ed.). Toronto: Multi-Health System.

Hare, R. D., Hart, S. D., & Harpur, T. J. (1991). Psychopathy and the DSM-IV criteria for antisocial personality disorder. *Journal of Abnormal Psychology, 100,* 391–398.

Hare, R. D., & Neumann, C. N. (2007). The PCL-R assessment of psychopathy: Development, structural properties, and new directions. In C. Patrick (Ed.), *Handbook of psychopathy* (pp. 58–88). New York: Guilford.

Hariri, A. R., Drabant, E. M., Munoz, K. E., Kolachana, B. S., Mattay, V. S., Egan, M. F., & Weinberger, D. R. (2005). A susceptibility gene for affective disorders and the response of the human amygdala. *Archives of General Psychiatry, 62,* 146–152.

Harkin, A., Connor, T. J., Mulrooney, J., Kelly, J. P., & Leonard, B. E. (2001). Prior exposure to methylenedioxyamphetamine (MDA) induces serotonergic loss and changes in spontaneous exploratory and amphetamine-induced behaviors in rats. *Life Sciences, 68,* 1367–1382.

Harrington, A. (2008). *The cure within: A history of mind-body medicine.* New York, NY: Norton.

Harrison, P. J. (2002). The neuropathology of primary mood disorder. *Brain, 125,* 1428–1449.

Harrison, P. J., & Weinberger, D. R. (2004). Schizophrenia genes, gene expression, and neuropathology: On the matter of their convergence. *Molecular Psychiatry, 10,* 1–29.

Harrow, M., Goldberg, J. F., Grossman, L. S., & Meltzer, H. Y. (1990). Outcome in manic disorders: A naturalistic follow-up study. *Archives of General Psychiatry, 47,* 665–671.

Harry Benjamin International Gender Dysphoria Association. (2001). *The standards of care of gender identity disorders* (6th version). Dusseldorf: Symposion.

Hart, E. L., Lahey, B. B., Loeber, R., Applegate, B., & Frick, P. J. (1995). Developmental changes in attention-deficit hyperactivity disorder in boys: A four-year longitudinal study. *Journal of Abnormal Child Psychology, 23,* 729–750.

Hartmann, H. (1958). *Ego psychology and the problem of adaptation.* New York: International Universities Press.

Hartung, C. M., & Widiger, T. A. (1998). Gender differences in the diagnosis of mental disorders: Conclusions and controversies of the DSM-IV. *Psychological-Bulletin, 123,* 260–278.

Hartz, D. T., Fredrick-Osborne, S. L., & Galloway, G. P. (2001). Craving predicts use during treatment for methamphetamine dependence: A prospective repeated measures, within-subjects analysis. *Drug and Alcohol Dependence, 63,* 269–276.

Harvard Mental Health Letter. (1995, July). *Schizophrenia update–Part II, 12,* 1–5.

Harvey, A. G., & Bryant, R. A. (2002). Acute stress disorder: A synthesis and critique. *Psychological Bulletin, 128,* 886–902.

Harvey, A. G., Mullin, B. C., & Hinshaw, S. P. (2006). Sleep and circadian rhythms in children and adolescents with bipolar disorder. *Development and Psychopathology, 18,* 1147–1168.

Harvey, A. G., Watkins, E., Mansell, W., & Shafran, R. (2004). *Cognitive behavioural processes across psychological disorders: A transdiagnostic approach to research and treatment.* Oxford, UK: Oxford University Press.

Harvey, P. D., Green, M. F., Keefe, R. S. I., & Velligan, D. (2004). Changes in cognitive functioning with risperidone and olanzapine treatment: A large-scale, double-blind, randomized study. *Journal of Clinical Psychiatry, 65,* 361–372.

Harvey, P. D., Green, M. F., McGurk, S., & Meltzer, H. Y. (2003). Changes in cognitive functioning with risperidone and olanzapine treatment: A large-scale, doubleblind, randomized study. *Psychopharmacology, 169,* 404–411.

Harwood, H. J., Mark, T. L., McKusick, D. R., Coffey, R. M., King, E. C., & Genuardi, J. S. (2003). National spending on mental health and substance abuse treatment by age of clients, 1997. *Journal of Behavioral Health Services and Research, 30,* 433–443.

Hasin, D. S., Stinson, F. S., Ogburn, E., & Grant, B. F. (2007). Prevalence, correlates, disability, and comorbidity of DSM-IV alcohol abuse and dependence in the United States: Results from the National Epidemiologic Survey on Alcohol and Related Conditions. *Archives of General Psychiatry, 64,* 830–842.

Haslam, C., Brown, S., Atkinson, S., & Haslam, R. (2004). Patients' experiences of medication for anxiety and depression: Effects on working life. *Family Practice, 21,* 204–212.

Haslam, N., & Kim, H. C. (2002). Categories and continua: A review of taxometric research. *Genetic, Social, and General Psychology Monographs, 128,* 271–320.

Hathaway, S. R., & McKinley, J. C. (1943). *MMPI manual.* New York: Psychological Corporation.

Hawkins, J. D., Graham, J. W., Maguin, E., Abbott, R., et al. (1997). Exploring the effects of age of alcohol use initiation and psychosocial risk factors on subsequent alcohol misuse. *Journal of Studies on Alcohol, 58,* 280–290.

Hawton, K., Catalan, J., Martin, P., & Fagg, J. (1986). Long-term outcome of sex therapy. *Behaviour Research and Therapy, 24,* 665–675.

Hay, P., & Fairburn, C. G. (1998). The validity of the DSM-IV scheme for classifying eating disorders. *International Journal of Eating Disorders, 23,* 7–15.

Hayes, S. C. (2005). *Get out of your mind and into your life: The new acceptance and commitment therapy.* Okland, CA: New Harbinger Publications.

Hayes, S. C., Masuda, A., Bissett, R., Luoma, J., & Guerrero, L.F.(2004). DBT, FAR and ACT: How empirically oriented are the new behavior therapy technologies? *Behavior Therapy, 35,* 35–54.

Haynes, S. N., & Horn, W. F. (1982). Reactivity in behavioral observation: A review. *Behavioral Assessment, 4,* 369–385.

Hazel, N. A., Hamman, C., Brennan, P. A., & Najman, J. (2008). Early childhood adversity and adolescent depression: The mediating role of continued stress. *Psychological Medicine, 38,* 581–589.

Heatherton, T. F., & Baumeister, R. F. (1991). Binge eating as escape from self-awareness. *Psychological Bulletin, 110,* 86–108.

Heatherton, T. F., Herman, C. P., & Polivy, J. (1991). Effects of physical threat and ego threat on eating behavior. *Journal of Personality and Social Psychology, 60,* 138–143.

Hecker, M. H. L., Chesney, M., Black, G. W., & Frautsch, N. (1988). Coronary-prone behavior in the Western Collaborative Group Study. *Psychosomatic Medicine, 50,* 153–164.

Heim, E., Valach, L., & Schaffner, L. (1997). Coping and psychosocial adaptation: Longitudinal effects over time and stages in breast cancer. *Psychosomatic Medicine, 59,* 408–418.

Heimberg, R. G., Dodge, C. S., Hope, D. A., Kennedy, C. R., Zollo, L. J., & Becker, R. E. (1990). Cognitive behavioral treatment for social phobia: Comparison with a credible placebo control. *Cognitive Therapy and Research, 14,* 1–23.

Heinrichs, R. W., & Zakzanis, K. K. (1998). Neurocognitive deficits in schizophrenia: A quantitative review of the evidence. *Neuropsychology, 12,* 426–445.

Heinssen, R. K., Liberman, R. P., & Kopelowicz, A. (2000). Psychosocial skills training for schizophrenia: Lessons from the laboratory. *Schizophrenia Bulletin, 26,* 21–46.

Heiss, G., Wallace, R., Anderson, G. L., Aragaki, A., Beresford, S. A. A., et al. (2008). Health risks and benefits 3 years after stopping randomized treatment with estrogen and progestin. *Journal of the American Medical Association, 299,*1036–1045.

Heller, K., Wyman, M. F., & Allen, S. M. (2000). Future directions for prevention science: From research to adoption. In C. R. Snyder & R. E. Ingram (Eds.), *Handbook of psychological change: Psychotherapy processes & practices for the 21st century* (pp. 660–680). New York: Wiley.

Heller, T. L., Baker, B. L., Henker, B., & Hinshaw, S. P. (1996). Externalizing behavior and cognitive functioning from preschool to first grade: Stability and predictors. *Journal of Clinical Child Psychology, 25,* 376–387.

Helmuth, L. (2003). In sickness or in health? *Science, 302*(5646), 808–810.

Helzer, J. E., Burnam, A., & McEvoy, L. T. (1991). Alcohol abuse and dependence. In L. Robins & D. Reiger (Eds.), *Psychiatric disorders in America: The Epidemiologic Catchment Area Study* (pp. 9–38). New York: Free Press.

Hendry, C. N. (2000). Childhood disintegrative disorder: Should it be considered a distinct diagnosis? *Clinical Psychology Review, 20,* 77–90.

Henggeler, S. W., Schoenwald, S. D., Borduin, C. M., Rowland, M. D., & Cunningham, P. B. (1998). *Multisystemic treatment of antisocial behavior in children and adolescents.* New York: Guilford.

Henggeler, S. W., & Sheidow, A. J. (in press). Multisystemic therapy with substance abusing adolescents: A synthesis of the research. In N. Jainchill (Ed.), *Understanding and treating substance use disorders.* Kingston, NJ: Civic Research Institute.

Henningfield, J. E., Michaelides, T., & Sussman, S. (2000). Developing treatment for tobacco addicted youth—issues and challenges. *Journal of Child & Adolescent Substance Abuse, 9,* 5–26.

Henriques, G., Wenzel, A., Brown, G. K., & Beck, A. T. (2005). Suicide attempters' reaction to survival as a risk factor for eventual suicide. *American Journal of Psychiatry, 162,* 2180–2182.

Henriques, J. B., & Davidson, R. J. (2000). Decreased responsiveness to reward in depression. *Cognition and Emotion, 14,* 711–724.

Henry, W. P., Schacht, T. E., Strupp, H. H., Butler, S. F., & Binder, J. L. (1993). Effects of training in time-limited dynamic psychotherapy: Mediators of therapists' responses to training. *Journal of Consulting and Clinical Psychology, 61,* 441–447.

Henry, W. P., Strupp, H. H., Schacht, T. E., & Gaston, L. (1994). Psychodynamic approaches. In S. L. Garfield & A. E. Bergin (Eds.), *Handbook of psychotherapy and behavior change* (pp. 467–508). Oxford, UK: Wiley.

Herbert, J. D. (1995). An overview of the current status of social phobia. *Applied and Preventive Psychology, 4,* 39–51.

Herbert, M. A, Gerry, N. P., McQueen, I. M., Heid, A. P., , Illig, T., et al. (2006). Common genetic variant is associated with adult and childhood obesity. *Science, 312,* 279–312.

Herman, C. P., Polivy, J., Lank, C., & Heatherton, T. F. (1987). Anxiety, hunger, and eating. *Journal of Abnormal Psychology, 96,* 264–269.

Herman, J. L., Perry, J. C., & van der Kolk, B. A. (1989). Childhood trauma in borderline personality disorder. *American Journal of Psychiatry, 146,* 490–495.

Herpetz, S. C., Dietrich, T. M., Wenning, B., et al. (2001). Evidence of abnormal amygdala functioning in borderline personality disorder: A functional MRI study. *Biological Psychiatry, 50,* 292–298.

Herrmann, L. L., Le Masurier, M., & Ebmeier, K. P. (2008). White matter hyperintensities in late life depression: A systematic review. *Journal of Neurology, Neurosurgery, and Psychiatry, 79,* 619–624.

Hersen, M., & Barlow, D. H. (1976). *Single case experimental designs: Strategies for studying behavior change.* New York: Pergamon.

Herz, M. I., Lamberti, J. S., Mintz, J., et al. (2000). A program for relapse prevention in schizophrenia: A controlled study. *Archives of General Psychiatry, 57,* 277–284.

Herzog, D. B., Greenwood, D. N., Dorer, D. J., Flores, A. T., Ekeblad, E. R., Richards, A., Blais, M. A., & Keller, M. B. (2000). Mortality in eating disorders: A descriptive study. *International Journal of Eating Disorders, 28,* 20–26.

Heston, L. L. (1966). Psychiatric disorders in foster home reared children of schizophrenic mothers. *British Journal of Psychiatry, 112,* 819–825.

Hettema, J. M., Neale, M. C., & Kendler, K. S. (2001). A review and meta-analysis of the genetic epidemiology of the anxiety disorders. *American Journal of Psychiatry, 158,* 1568–1578.

Hettema, J. M., Prescott, C. A., Myers, J. M., Neale, M. C., & Kendler, K. S. (2005). The structure of genetic and environmental risk factors for anxiety disorders in men and women. *Archives of General Psychiatry, 62,* 182–189.

Heuser, I., Yassouridis, A., & Holsboer, F. (1994). The combined dexamethasone CRH test: A refined laboratory test for psychiatric disorders. *Journal of Psychiatric Research, 28,* 341–346.

Heyman, I., Fombonne, E., Simmons, H., Ford, T., Meltzer, H., & Goodman, R. (2003). Prevalence of obsessive–compulsive disorder in the British nationwide survey of child mental health. *International Review of Psychiatry, 15,* 178–184.

Heyn, P., Abreu, B. C., & Ottenbacher, K. J. (2004). Meta-analysis: The effects of exercise training on elderly persons with cognitive impairment and dementia: A meta-analysis. *Archives of Physical Medicine and Rehabilitation, 85,* 1694–1704.

Hibbeln, J. R., Nieminen, L. R. G., Blasbalg, T. L., Riggs, J. A., & Lands, W. E. M. (2006). Healthy intakes of n-3 and n-6 fatty acids: Estimations considering worldwide diversity. *Journal of Clinical Nutrition, 83,* 1483S–1493S.

Hietala, J., Syvalahti, E., Vuorio, K., Nagren, K., Lehikoinen, P., et al. (1994). Striatal D2 dopamine receptor characteristics in drug-naive schizophrenic patients studied with positron emission tomography. *Archives of General Psychiatry, 51,* 116–123.

Higgins, S. T., Budney, A. J., & Sigmon, S. C. (2001). Cocaine dependence. In D. H. Barlow (Ed.), *Clinical handbook of psychological disorders: A step-by-step treatment manual* (pp. 434–469). New York: Guilford.

Hill, A., Briken, P., Kraus, C., Strohm, K., & Berner, W. (2003). Differential pharmacological treatment of paraphilias and sex offenders. *International Journal of Offender Therapy and Comparative Criminology, 47*(4), 407–421.

Hinshaw, S. P. (1987). On the distinction between attentional deficits/hyperactivity and conduct problems/aggression in child psychopathology. *Psychological Bulletin, 101,* 443–463.

Hinshaw, S. P. (2007). Preadolescent girls with attention-deficit/hyperactivity disorder: I. Background characteristics, comorbidity, cognitive and social functioning, and parenting practices. *Journal of Consulting and Clinical Psychology, 70,* 1086–1098.

Hinshaw, S. P. (2007). *The mark of shame: The stigma of mental illness and an agenda for change.* New York: Oxford University Press.

Hinshaw, S. P., Carte, E. T., Sami, N., Treuting, J. J., & Zupan, B. A. (2002). Preadolescent girls with attention-deficit/hyperactivity disorder: II. Neuropsychological performance in relation to subtypes and individual classification. *Journal of Consulting and Clinical Psychology, 70,* 1099–1111.

Hinshaw, S. P., & Lee, S. S. (2003). Oppositional defiant and conduct disorders. In E. J. Mash & R. A. Barkley (Eds.), *Child psychopathology* (2nd ed., pp. 144–198). New York: Guilford.

Hinshaw, S. P., & Melnick, S. M. (1995). Peer relationships in boys with attention-deficit hyperactivity disorder with and without comorbid aggression. *Development and Psychopathology, 7,* 627–647.

Hinshaw, S. P., Owens, E. B., Sami, N., & Fargeon, S. (2006). Prospective follow-up of girls with attention-deficit/hyperactivity disorder into adolescence: Evidence for continuing cross-domain impairment. *Journal of Consulting and Clinical Psychology, 74,* 489–499.

Hinshaw, S. P., Owens, E. B., Wells, K. C., et al. (2000). Family processes and treatment outcome in the MTA: Negative/ineffective parenting practices in relation to multimodal treatment. *Journal of Abnormal Child Psychology, 28,* 555–568.

Hinshaw, S. P., Zupan, B. A., Simmel, C., Nigg, J. T., & Melnick, S. (1997). Peer status in boys with and without attention-deficit hyperactivity disorder: Predictions from overt and covert antisocial behavior, social isolation, and authoritative parenting beliefs. *Child Development, 68,* 880–896.

Hinton, D., Ba, P., Peou, S., & Um, K. (2000). Panic disorder among Cambodian refugees attending a psychiatric clinic. *General Hospital Psychiatry, 22,* 437–444.

Hinton, E., Um, K., & Ba, P. (2001). *Kyol goeu* ('wind overload'). Part II: Prevalence, characteristics, and mechanisms of *kyol goeu* and near *kyol goeu* episodes of Khmer patients attending a psychiatric clinic. *Transcultural Psychiatry, 38,* 433–460.

Hirsch, C. R., & Clark, D. M. (2004). Mental imagery and social phobia. In J. Yiend (Ed.), *Cognition, emotion and psychopathology: Theoretical, empirical and clinical directions* (pp. 232–250). Cambridge, UK: Cambridge University Press.

Ho, B.C., Milev, P., O'Leary, D. S., Librant, A., Flaum, M., Andreasen, N. C., & Wassink, T. (2006). Cognitive and magnetic resonance imaging brain morphometric correlates of brain-derived neurotrophic factor Val66Met gene polymorphism in patients with schizophrenia and healthy volunteers. *Archives of General Psychiatry, 63,* 731–740.

Ho, B.C., Nopoulos, P., Flaum, M., Arndt, S., & Andreasen, N. C. (1998). Two-year outcome in first-episode schizophrenia: Predictive value of symptoms for quality of life. *American Journal of Psychiatry, 155,* 1196–1201.

Hobfoll, S. E., Spielberger, C. D., Breznitz, S., Figley, C., Folkman, S., Lepper-Green, B., Meichenbaum, D., Milgram, N. A., Sandler, I., Sarason, I., & van der Kolk, B. (1991). War-related stress: Addressing the stress of war and other traumatic events. *American Psychologist, 46,* 848–855.

Hobson, R. P., & Lee, A. (1998). Hello and goodbye: A study of social engagement in autism. *Journal of Autism and Developmental Disorders, 28,* 117–127.

Hodges, E. L., Cochrane, C. E., & Brewerton, T. D. (1998). Family characteristics of binge-eating disorder patients. *International Journal of Eating Disorders, 23,* 145–151.

Hoebel, B. G., & Teitelbaum, P. (1966). Weight regulation in normal and hypothalamic hyperphagic rats. *Journal of Comparative and Physiological Psychology, 61,* 189–193.

Hoek, H. W., & van Hoeken, D. (2003). Review of the prevalence and incidence of eating disorders. *International Journal of Eating Disorders, 34,* 383–396.

Hofmann, S. G., & Barlow, D. H. (2004). Social phobia (social anxiety disorder). In D. H. Barlow (Ed.), *Anxiety and its disorders: The nature and treatment of anxiety and panic* (pp. 454–476). New York: Guilford.

Hofmann, S. G., Levitt, J. T., Hoffman, E. C., Greene, K., Litz, B. T., & Barlow, D. H. (2001). Potentially traumatizing events in panic disorder and other anxiety disorders. *Depression and Anxiety, 13,* 101–102.

Hofmann, S. G., Meuret, A. E., Smits, J. A. J., Simon, N. M., Pollack, M. H., Eisenmenger, K., Shiekh, M., & Otto, M. W. (2006). Augmentation of exposure therapy with D-cycloserine for social anxiety disorder. *Archives of General Psychiatry, 63,* 298–304.

Hogarty, G. E., Anderson, C. M., Reiss, D. J., Kornblith, S. J., Greenwald, D. P., et al. (1986). Family psychoeducation, social skills training, and maintenance chemotherapy in the aftercare treatment of schizophrenia: 1. One-year effects of a controlled study on relapse and expressed emotion. *Archives of General Psychiatry, 43*, 633–642.

Hogarty, G. E., Anderson, C. M., Reiss, D. J., Kornblith, S. J., Greenwald, D. P., Ulrich, R. F., Carter, M., & The Environmental-Personal Indicators in the Course of Schizophrenia (EPICS) Research Group. (1991). Family psychoeducation, social skills training, and maintenance chemotherapy in the aftercare treatment of schizophrenia. *Archives of General Psychiatry, 48*, 340–347.

Hogarty, G. E., Flesher, S., Ulrich, R., et al. (2004). Cognitive enhancement therapy for schizophrenia: Effects of a 2-year randomized trial on cognition and behavior. *Archives of General Psychiatry, 61*, 866–876.

Holder, H. D., Longabaugh, R., Miller, W. R., & Rubonis, A. V. (1991). The cost effectiveness of treatment for alcoholism: A first approximation. *Journal of Studies on Alcohol, 52*, 517–540.

Hollander, E., Allen, A., Lopez, R. P., Bienstock, C. A., Grossman, R., Siever L. J., et al. (2001). A preliminary double-blind, placebo-controlled trial of divalproex sodium in borderline personality disorder. *Journal of Clinical Psychiatry, 62*, 199–203.

Hollingshead, A. B., & Redlich, F. C. (1958). *Social class and mental illness: A community study.* New York: Wiley.

Hollon, S., & DeRubeis, R. (2003). *Cognitive therapy for depression.* Paper presented at the annual conference of the American Psychiatric Association, Philadelphia, PA.

Hollon, S. D., DeRubeis, R. J., Shelton, R. C., Amsterdam, J. D., Salomon, R. M., O'Reardon, J. P., et al. (2005). Prevention of relapse following cognitive therapy vs medications in moderate to severe depression. *Archives of General Psychiatry, 62*, 417–422.

Hollon, S. D., Haman, K. L., & Brown, L. L. (2002). Cognitive-behavioral treatment of depression. In C. L. Hammen & I. H. Gotlib (Eds), *Handbook of depression* (pp. 383–403). New York: Guilford.

Hollon, S. D., Thase, M. E., & Markowitz, J. C. (2002). Treatment and prevention of depression. *Psychological Science in the Public Interest, 3*, 39–77.

Holm, V. A., & Varley, C. K. (1989). Pharmacological treatment of autistic children. In G. Dawson (Ed.), *Autism: Nature, diagnosis, and treatment* (pp. 386–404). New York: Guilford.

Holmes, T. H., & Rahe, R. H. (1967). The social readjustment rating scale. *Journal of Psychosomatic Research, 11*, 213–218.

Holzman, P. S. (1985). Eye movement dysfunctions and psychosis. *Review of Neurobiology, 27*, 179–205.

Hong, J. P., Samuels, J., Bienvenu, O. J., Hsu, F. C., Eaton, W. W., Costa, P. T., Jr., et al. (2005). The longitudinal relationship between personality disorder dimensions and global functioning in a community-residing population. *Psychological Medicine, 35*, 891–895.

Hope, D. A., Heimberg, R. G., & Bruch, M. A. (1995). Dismantling cognitive-behavioral group therapy for social phobia. *Behaviour Research and Therapy, 33*, 637–650.

Horan, W. P., Kring, A. M., & Blanchard, J. J. (2006). Anhedonia in schizophrenia: A review of assessment strategies. *Schizophrenia Bulletin, 32*, 259–273.

Horney, K. (1942). *Self-analysis.* New York: Norton.

Horowitz, J. L., & Garber, J. (2006). The prevention of depressive symptoms in children and adolescents: A meta-analytic review. *Journal of Consulting and Clinical Psychology, 74*, 401–415.

Horowitz, M. J. (1988). *Introduction to psychodynamics: A new synthesis.* New York: Basic Books.

Horton, A. M. Jr. (2008). The Halstead-Reitan Neuropsychological Test Battery: Past, present, and future. In A. M. Horton & D. Wedding (Eds)., *The neuropsychology handbook* (3rd Ed., pp. 251–278). New York: Springer.

Horvath, A. O. (2001). The alliance. *Psychotherapy: Theory, Research, Practice Training, 38*, 365–372.

Horwitz, B., Rumsey, J. M., & Donahue, B. C. (1998). Functional connectivity of the angular gyrus in normal reading and dyslexia. *Proceedings of the National Academy of Science, 95*, 8939–8944.

Houts, A. C. (2001). Harmful dysfunction and the search for value neutrality in the definition of mental disorder: Response to Wakefield, Part 2. *Behaviour Research and Therapy, 39*, 1099–1132.

Howitt, D. (1995). Pornography and the paedophile: Is it criminogenic? *British Journal of Medical Psychology, 68*, 15–27.

Howlin, P., Goode, S., Hutton, J., & Rutter, M. (2004). Adult outcome for children with autism. *Journal of Child Psychology and Psychiatry, 45*, 212–229.

Howlin, P., Mawhood, L., & Rutter, M. (2000). Autism and developmental receptive language disorder—A follow-up comparison in early adult life. II. Social, behavioral, and psychiatric outcomes. *Journal of Child Psychiatry and Psychology, 41*, 561–578.

Hser, Y., Anglin, M. D., & Powers, K. (1993). A 24-year follow-up of California narcotics addicts. *Archives of General Psychiatry, 50*, 577–584.

Hsu, L. K. G. (1990). *Eating disorders.* New York: Guilford.

Hudson, J. I., Hiripi, E., Pope, H.G. Jr., & Kessler, R.C. (2007). The prevalence and correlates of eating disorders in the National Comorbidity Survey Replication. *Biological Psychology, 61*, 348–58.

Hudson, J. I., Lalonde, J. K., Berry, J. M., Pindyck, L. J., Bulick, C. et al. (2006). Binge-eating disorder as a distinct familial phenotype in obese. *Archives of General Psychology, 63*, 3138–319.

Huesmann, L. R., & Miller, L. S. (1994). Long-term effects of repeated exposure to media violence in childhood. In L. R. Huesmann (Ed.), *Aggressive behavior: Current perspectives* (pp. 153–186). New York: Plenum.

Huether, G., Zhou, D., & Ruther, E. (1997). Causes and consequences of the loss of serotonergic presynapses elicited by the consumption of 3-4 methylenedioxymethamphetamine (MDMA, "ecstasy") and its congeners. *Journal of Neural Transmission, 104*, 771–794.

Hughes, C., & Agran, M. (1993). Teaching persons with severe disabilities to use self-instruction in community settings: An analysis of applications. *The Journal of the Association for Persons with Severe Handicaps, 18*, 261–274.

Hughes, C., Hugo, K., & Blatt, J. (1996). Self-instructional intervention for teaching generalized problem-solving within a functional task sequence. *American Journal on Mental Retardation, 100*, 565–579.

Hughes, J., Stead, L., & Lancaster, T. (2004). Antidepressants for smoking cessation. *Cochrane Database Systematic Review;* CD000031.

Hughes, J. R., Higgins, S. T., Bickel, W. K., Hunt, W. K., & Fenwick, J. W. (1991). Caffeine self-administration, withdrawal, and adverse effects among coffee drinkers. *Archives of General Psychiatry, 48*, 611–617.

Hughes, J. R., Higgins, S. T., & Hatsukami, D. K. (1990). Effects of abstinence from tobacco: A critical review. In L. T. Kozlowski, H. Annis, H. D. Cappell, F. Glaser, M. Goodstadt, Y. Israel, H. Kalant, E. M. Sellers, & J. Vingilis (Eds.), *Research advances in alcohol and drug problems.* New York: Plenum.

Hughes, S. L., Ulasevich, A., Weaver, F. M., et al. (1997). Impact of home care on hospital days: A meta-analysis. *Health Services Research, 32*, 415–432.

Huijbregts, S. C. J., de Sonneville, L. M. J., Licht, R., van Spronsen, F. J., Verkerk, P. H., & Sergeant, J. A. (2002). Sustained attention and inhibition of cognitive interference in treated phenylketonuria: Associations with concurrent and lifetime phenylalanine concentrations. *Neuropsychologia. 40*, 7–15.

Hulley, S. Grady, D., Bush, T., Furberg, C., Herrington, D., Riggs, B., & Vittinghoff, E. (1998). Randomized trial of estrogen plus progestin for secondary prevention of coronary heart disease in postmenopausal women. Heart and Estrogen/progestin Replacement Study (HERS) Research Group. *Journal of the American Medical Association, 280*, 605–613.

Hunsley, J., & Bailey, J. M. (1999). The clinical utility of the Rorschach: Unfulfilled promises and an uncertain future. *Psychological Assessment, 11*, 266–277.

Hunt, N., & Robbins, I. (2001). The long-term consequences of war: The experience of world war II. *Aging & Mental Health, 5*, 183–190.

Hunter, R. & Macalpine, I. (1963). *Three hundred years of psychiatry 1535–1860.* Oxford, England: Oxford University Press.

Huntjen, R. J. C., Postma, A., Peters, M. L., Woertman, L., & van der Hart, O. (2003). Interidentity amnesia for neutral, episodic information in dissociative identity disorder. *Journal of Abnormal Psychology, 112*, 290–297.

Huppert, J. D., Bufka, L. F., Barlow, D. H., Gorman, J. M., Shear, M. K., & Woods, S. W. (2001). Therapists, therapist variables, and cognitive-behavioral therapy outcome in a multicenter trial for panic disorder. *Journal of Consulting and Clinical Psychology, 69*, 747–755.

Hurlburt, R. T. (1979). Random sampling of cognitions and behavior. *Journal of Research on Personality, 13*, 103–111.

Hurlburt, R. T. (1997). Randomly sampling thinking in the natural environment. *Journal of Consulting and Clinical Psychology, 65*, 941–949.

Hussong, A. M., Hicks, R. E., Levy, S. A., & Curran, P. J. (2001). Specifying the relations between affect and heavy alcohol use among young adults. *Journal of Abnormal Psychology, 110*, 449–461.

Hyland, M. E. (1990). The mood-peak flow relationship in adult asthmatics: A pilot study of individual differences and direction of causality. *British Journal of Medical Psychology, 63*, 379–384.

Hyman, S. E. (2002). Neuroscience, genetics, and the future of psychiatric diagnosis. *Psychopathology, 35*, 139–144.

Hypericum Depression Trial Study Group. (2002). Effect of *Hypericum perforatum* (St. John's wort) in major depressive disorder: A randomized controlled trial. *Journal of the American Medical Association, 287*, 1807–1814.

Iacono, W. G., Morean, M., Beiser, M., Fleming, J. A., et al. (1992). Smooth pursuit eye-tracking in first episode psychotic patients and their relatives. *Journal of Abnormal Psychology, 101*, 104–116.

IBM, "Financial Authority for Education," IBM Case Study, 2002, www-306.ibm.com/software/success/cssdb.nsf/CS/KHAL-62GL7N? OpenDocument&Site=gicss67educ (accessed Septemer 2008).

IMS Health (2008). IMS national prescription audit PlusTM.(2006). Retrieved from http://www.imshealth.com/portal/site/imshealth.

Ingram, C. (1996, September 26). Bill signed to let police tell of sex offenders' whereabouts. *Los Angeles Times*, pp. A3, A19.

Inouye, S. K., Bogardus, S. T., Jr., Charpentier, P. A., Leo-Summers, L., Acampora, D., Holford, T. R., & Cooney, L. M., Jr. (1999). A multicomponent intervention to prevent delirium in hospitalized older patients. *New England Journal of Medicine, 340,* 669–676.

Insel, T. R., Scanlan, J., Champoux, M., & Suomi, S. J. (1988). Rearing paradigm in a nonhuman primate affects response to B-CCE challenge. *Psychopharmacology, 96,* 81–86.

Institute of Medicine. (1990). *Treating drug problems.* Washington, DC: National Academy Press.

Institute of Medicine. (1999). *Marijuana and medicine: Assessing the science base.* Washington, DC: National Academy Press.

Institute of Medicine. (2004). *Immunization safety review: Vaccines and autism.* Washington, DC: National Academies Press.

Iribarren, C., Sidney, S., Bild, D. E., Liu, K., Markovitz, J. H., Roseman, J. M., & Matthews, K. A. (2000). Association of hostility with coronary artery calcification in young adults. *Journal of the American Medical Association, 283,* 2546–2551.

Irvin, J. E., Bowers, C.A., Dunn, M. E., & Wang, M. C. (1999). Efficacy of relapse prevention: A meta-analytic review. *Journal of Consulting and. Clinical Psychology, 67,* 563–570.

Irwin, M., Lovitz, A., Marder, S. R., Mintz, J., Winslade, W. J., van Putten, T., & Mills, M. J. (1985). Psychotic patients' understanding of informed consent. *American Journal of Psychiatry, 142,* 1351–1354.

Ishikawa, S. S., Raine, A., Lencz, T., Bihrle, S., & Lacasse, L. (2001). Autonomic stress reactivity and executive functions in successful and unsuccessful criminal psychopaths from the community. *Journal of Abnormal Psychology, 110,* 423–432.

Ito, T., Miller, N., & Pollack, V. E. (1996). Alcohol and aggression: A meta-analysis on the moderating effects of inhibitory cues, triggering events, and self-focused attention. *Psychological Bulletin, 120,* 60–82.

Ivanoff, A., Jang, S. J., Smyth, N. J., & Linehan, M. M. (1994). Fewer reasons for staying alive when you are thinking of killing yourself: The Brief Reasons for Living Inventory. *Journal of Psychopathology and Behavioral Assessment, 16,* 1–13.

Ivarsson, T., Råstam, M., Weitz, E., Gilberg, I. C., & Gilberg, G. (2000). Depressive disorders in teen-age-onset anorexia nervosa: A controlled longitudinal, partly community-based study. *Comprehensive Psychiatry, 41,* 398–403.

Iwamasa, G. Y. (1993). Asian Americans and cognitive behavioral therapy. *The Behavior Therapist, 16,* 233–235.

Jablonsky, A., Sartorius, N., Cooper, J. E., Anker, A., Korten, A., & Bertelson, A. (1994). Culture and schizophrenia. *British Journal of Psychiatry, 165,* 434–436.

Jackson, C. (1997). Testing a multi-stage model for the adoption of alcohol and tobacco behaviors by children. *Addictive Behaviors, 22,* 1–14.

Jackson, J. C., Gordon, S. M., Hart, R. P., Hopkins, R. O., & Ely, E. W. (2004). The association between delirium and cognitive decline: A review of the empirical literature. *Neuropsychology Review, 14,* 87–98.

Jackson, K. M., Sher, K. J., & Wood, P. K. (2000). Trajectories of concurrent substance use disorders: A developmental, typological approach to comorbidity. *Alcoholism: Clinical & Experimental Research, 24,* 902–913.

Jackson, R. W., Treiber, F. A., Turner, J. R., Davis, H., & Strong, W. B. (1999). Effects of race, sex, and socioeconomic status upon cardiovascular stress responsivity and recovery in youth. *International Journal of Psychophysiology, 31,* 111–119.

Jacob, R. G., Thayer, J. F., Manuck, S. B., Muldoon, M. F., Tamres, L. K., et al. (1999). Ambulatory blood pressure responses and the circumplex model of mood: A 4-day study. *Psychosomatic Medicine, 61,* 319–333.

Jacobi, E. A. (2004). Prevalence, co-morbidity and correlates of mental disorders in the general population: Results from the German health interview and examination survey. *Psychological Medicine, 34,* 597–611.

Jacobsen, L. K., Southwick, S. M., & Kosten, T. R. (2001). Substance use disorders in patients with posttraumatic stress disorder: A review of the literature. *American Journal of Psychiatry, 158,* 1184–1190.

Jacobson, N. S., Follette, W. C., Revenstort, D., Bowcon, D. H., Halweg, K., Nargolin, G. (1984). Variability in outcome and clinical significance of behavioral marital therapy: A reanalysis of outcome data. *Journal of Consulting and Clinical Psychology, 52,* 497–504.

Jacobson, N. S. (1992). Behavioral couple therapy: A new beginning. *Behavior Therapy, 23,* 493–506.

Jacobson, N. S., & Christensen, A. (1996). *Integrative couple therapy: Promoting acceptance and change.* New York: Norton.

Jacobson, N. S., Dobson, K. S., Fruzzetti, A. E., & Schmaling, K. B. (1991). Marital therapy as a treatment for depression. *Journal of Consulting and Clinical Psychology, 59,* 547–557.

Jacobson, N. S., Dobson, K. S., Truax, P. A., Addis, M. E., Koerner, K., Gollan, J. K., Gortner, E., & Prince, S. E. (1996). A component analysis of cognitive-behavioral treatment for depression. *Journal of Consulting and Clinical Psychology, 64,* 295–304.

Jacobson, N. S., & Gortner, E. T. (2000). Can depression be de-medicalized in the 21st century?: Scientific revolutions, counter-revolutions and the magnetic field of normal science. *Behaviour Research & Therapy, 38,* 103–117.

Jacobson, N. S., Martell, C. R., & Dimidjian, S. (2001). Behavioral activation treatment for depression: Returning to contextual roots. *Clinical Psychology: Science and Practice, 8,* 255–270.

Jacobson, N. S., Roberts, L. J., Berns, S. B., & McGlinchey, J. B. (1999). Methods for defining and determining the clinical significance of treatment effects: Description, application, and alternatives. *Journal of Consulting and Clinical Psychology, 67(3),* 300–307.

Jaffe, J. H. (1985). Drug addiction and drug abuse. *In Goodman and Gilman's pharmacological basis of therapeutic behavior.* New York: Macmillan.

Jaffee, S. R., Moffitt, T. E., Caspi, A., Taylor, A., & Arseneault, L. (2002). Influence of adult domestic violence on children's internalizing and externalizing problems: An environmentally informative twin study. *Journal of the American Academy of Child and Adolescent Psychiatry, 41,* 1095–1103.

Jamison, K. R. (1992). *Touched with fire: Manic-depressive illness and the artistic temperament.* New York: Free Press.

Jampole, L., & Weber, M. K. (1987). An assessment of the behavior of sexually abused and nonsexually abused children with anatomically correct dolls. *Child Abuse and Neglect, 11,* 187–192.

Jang, K. L., Livesley, W. J., Angleitner, A., Riemann, R., & Vernon, P. A. (2002). Genetic and environmental influences on the covariance of facets defining the domains of the five-factor model of personality. *Personality and Individual Differences, 33,* 83–101.

Janicak, P. G., Davis, J. M., Preskorn, S. H., & Ayd, F. J. (1993). *Principles and practice of psychopharmacological therapy.* Baltimore, MD: Williams & Wilkins.

Jansen, M. A., Glynn, T., & Howard, J. (1996). Prevention of alcohol, tobacco and other drug abuse. *American Behavioral Scientist, 39,* 790–807.

Jarrell, M. P., Johnson, W. G., & Williamson, D. A. (1986). *Insulin and glucose response in the binge purge episode of bulimic women.* Paper presented at the annual convention of the Association for Advancement of Behavior Therapy, Chicago.

Jarrett, R. B., Vittengl, J. R., Doyle, K., & Clark, L. A. (2007). Changes in cognitive content during and following cognitive therapy for recurrent depression: Substantial and enduring, but not predictive of change in depressive symptoms. *Journal of Consulting and Clinical Psychology, 75,* 432–446.

Jasnoski, M. L., & Kugler, J. (1987). Relaxation, imagery, and neuroimmunomodulation. *Annals of the New York Academy of Sciences, 496,* 722–730.

Jeans, R. F. I. (1976). An independently validated case of multiple personality. *Journal of Abnormal Psychology, 85,* 249–255.

Jelicic, M., Geraerts, E., Merckelbach, H., & Guerrieri, R. (2004). Acute stress enhances memory for emotional words, but impairs memory for neutral words. *International Journal of Neuroscience, 114,* 1343–1351.

Jeng, J. C., Wang, L. R., Chou, C-S., Shen, J., & Tzeng, C. R. (2006). Management and outcome of primary vaginismus. *Journal of Sex & Marital Therapy, 32* (supplement 5), 379–387.

Jenike, M. A., Baer, L., & Minichiello, W. E. (1986). *Obsessive-compulsive disorders: Theory and management.* Littleton, MA: PSG.

Jenike, M. A., & Rauch, S. L. (1994). Managing the patient with treatment-resistant obsessive-compulsive disorder: Current strategies. *Journal of Clinical Psychiatry, 55,* 11–17.

Jensen, P. S., Arnold, L. E., Swanson, J., Vitiello, B., Abikoff, H. B., Greenhill, L. L., et al. (2007). Follow-up of the NIMH MTA study at 36 months after randomization. *Journal of the American Academy of Child and Adolescent Psychiatry, 46,* 988–1001.

Jensen, P. S., Martin, D., & Cantwell, D. P. (1997). Comorbidity in ADHD: Implications for research, practice, and DSM-V. *Journal of the American Academy of Child and Adolescent Psychiatry, 36,* 1065–1079.

Jernigan, D. H., Ostroff, J., Ross, C., & O'Hara, J. A., III. (2004). Sex differences in adolescent exposure to alcohol advertising in magazines. *Archives of Pediatric and Adolescent Medicine, 158,* 702–704.

Jeste, D. V., Barak, Y., Madhusoodanan, S., Grossman, F., & Gharabawi, G. (2003). International multisite doubleblind trial of the atypical antipsychotics risperidone and olanzapine in 175 elderly patients with chronic schizophrenia. *American Journal of Geriatric Psychiatry, 11,* 638–647.

Jimerson, D. C., Lesem, M. D., Kate, W. H., & Brewerton, T. D. (1992). Low serotonin and dopamine metabolite concentrations in cerebrospinal fluid from bulimic patients with frequent binge episodes. *Archives of General Psychiatry, 49,* 132–138.

Jimerson, D. C., Wolfe, B. E., Metzger, E. D., Finkelstein, D. M., Cooper, T. B., et al. (1997). Decreased serotonin function in bulimia nervosa. *Archives of General Psychiatry, 54,* 529–536.

Johnson, D. R. (1987). The role of the creative arts therapist in the diagnosis and treatment of psychological trauma. *The Arts in Psychotherapy, 14,* 7–13.

Johnson, N. J., Backlund, E., Sorlie, P. D., & Loveless, C. A. (2000). Martial status and mortality: The National Longitudinal Mortality Study. *Annals of Epidemiology, 10,* 224–238.

Johnson, J., Weissman, M. M., & Klerman G. L. (1992). Service utilization and social morbidity associated with depressive symptoms in the community. *Journal of the American Medical Association, 267,* 1478–1483.

Johnson, S. L. (2005). Mania and dysregulation in goal pursuit: A review. *Clinical Psychology Review, 25,* 241–262.

Johnson, S. L., Cueller, A. K., Ruggero, C., Winett-Perlman, C., Goodnick, P., White, R., et al. (2008). Life events as predictors of mania and depression in bipolar I disorder. *Journal of Abnormal Psychology, 117,* 268–277.

Johnson, S. L., & Kizer, A. (2002). Bipolar and unipolar depression: A comparison of clinical phenomenology and psychosocial predictors. In C. L. Hammen & I. H. Gotlib (Eds.), *Handbook of depression* (pp. 141–165). New York: Guilford.

Johnson, S. L., & Leahy, R. (Eds.). (2002). *Psychosocial approaches to bipolar disorder.* New York: Guilford.

Johnson, S. L., Sandrow, D., Meyer, B., Winters, R., Miller, I., Solomon, D., & Keitner, G. (2000). Increases in manic symptoms after life events involving goal attainment. *Journal of Abnormal Psychology, 109,* 721–727.

Johnson, S. M., & Greenberg, L. S. (1995). The emotionally focused approach to problems in adult attachment. In A. S. Gurman & N. S. Jacobson (Eds.), *Clinical handbook of couple therapy* (pp. 121–141). New York: Guilford.

Johnson, W. G., Tsoh, J. Y., & Varnado, P. J. (1996). Eating disorders: Efficacy of pharmacological and psychological interventions. *Clinical Psychology Review, 16,* 457–478.

Johnston, C., & Marsh, E. J. (2001). Families of children with attention-deficit/hyperactivity disorder: Review and recommendations for future research. *Clinical Child and Family Psychology Review, 4,* 183–207.

Johnston, L. D., O'Malley, P. M., & Bachman, J. G. (2001). *Monitoring the future national results on adolescent drug use, 1975–2000: Vol. II. College students and adults ages 19–40* (NIH Publication No. 01–4925). Bethesda, MD: National Institute on Drug Abuse.

Johri, M., Beland, F., & Bergman, H. (2003). International experiments in integrated care for the eldery: A synthesis of the evidence. *International Journal of Geriatric Psychiatry, 18,* 222–235.

Joiner, T. E. J. (1995). The price of soliciting and receiving negative feedback: Self-verification theory as a vulnerability to depression theory. *Journal of Abnormal Psychology, 104,* 364–372.

Joiner, T. E., Alfano, M. S., & Metalsky, G. I. (1992). When depression breeds contempt: Reassurance seeking, self-esteem, and rejection of depressed college students by their roommates. *Journal of Abnormal Psychology, 101,* 165–173.

Joiner, T. E. J., Brown, J. S., & Wingate, L. R. (2005). The psychology and neurobiology of suicidal behavior. *Annual Review of Psychology, 56,* 287–314.

Joiner, T. E. J., Voelz, Z. R., & Rudd, M. D. (2001). For suicidal young adults with comorbid depressive and anxiety disorders, problem-solving treatment may be better than treatment as usual. *Professional Psychology: Research and Practice, 32,* 278–282.

Joiner, T. E., Vohs, K. D., & Heatherton, T. F. (2000). Three studies on the factorial distinctiveness of binge eating and bulimic symptoms among non-clinical men and women. *International Journal of Eating Disorders, 27,* 198–205.

Jones, P. B., Barnes, T. R. E., Davies, L., Dunn, G., Lloyd, H., et al. (2006). Randomized controlled trial of the effect on quality of life of second- vs first-generation antipsychotic drugs in schizophrenia: Cost Utility of the Latest Antipsychotic Drugs in Schizophrenia Study (CUtLASS 1). *Archives of General Psychiatry, 63,* 1079–1087.

Jorenby, D. E., Leischow, S. J., Nides, M. A., Rennard, S. I., Johnston, J. A., et al. (1999). A controlled trial of sustained-release buproprion, a nicotine patch, or both for smoking cessation. *New England Journal of Medicine, 340,* 685–691.

Jorm, A. F., Christensen, H., Henderson, A. S., Jacomb, P. A., Korten, A. E., & Rodgers, B. (2000). Predicting anxiety and depression from personality: Is there a synergistic effect of neuroticism and extraversion? *Journal of Abnormal Psychology, 109,* 145–149.

Judd, L. L. (1997). The clinical course of unipolar depressive disorders. *Archives of General Psychiatry, 54,* 989–992.

Judd, L. L., Akiskal, H. S., Maser, J. D., Zeller, P. J., Endicott, J., et al. (1998). A prospective 12-year study of subsyndromal and syndromal depressive symptoms in unipolar major depressive disorders. *Archives of General Psychiatry, 55,* 694–701.

Judd, L. L., Schettler, P. J., Solomon, D. A., Maser, J. D., Coryell, W., Endicott, J., et al. (2008). Psychosocial disability and work role function compared across the long-term course of bipolar I, bipolar II and unipolar major depressive disorders. *Journal of Affective Disorders, 108,* 49–58.

Junkert-Tress, B., Schnierda, U., Hartkamp, N., Schmitz, N., & Tress, W. (2001). Effects of short-term dynamic psychotherapy for neurotic, somatoform, and personality disorders: A prospective 1-year follow-up study. *Psychotherapy Research, 11,* 187–200.

Just, M. A., Cherkassky, V. L., Keller, T. A., & Minshew, N. J. (2004). Cortical activation and synchronization during sentence comprehension in high-functioning autism: Evidence of underconnectivity. *Brain, 127,* 1811–1821.

Kable, J. A., & Coles, C. D. (2004). The impact of prenatal alcohol exposure on neurophysiological encoding of environmental events at six months. *Alcoholism: Clinical and Experimental Research, 28,* 489–496.

Kafka, M. P. (1997). Hypersexual desire in males: An operational definition and clinical implications for males with paraphilias and paraphilia-related disorders. *Archives of Sexual Behavior, 26(5),* 505–526.

Kagan, J., & Snidman, N. (1999). Early childhood predictors of adult anxiety disorders. *Biological Psychiatry, 46,* 1536–1541.

Kalichman, S. C. (1995). *Understanding AIDS: A guide for mental health professionals.* Washington, DC: American Psychological Association.

Kalichman, S. C. (1996). *Answering your questions about AIDS.* Washington, DC: American Psychological Association.

Kamarck, T. W., Annunziato, B., & Amateau, L. M. (1995). Affiliations moderate the effects of social threat on stress-related cardiovascular responses: Boundary conditions for a laboratory model of social support. *Psychosomatic Medicine, 57,* 183–194.

Kamarck, T. W., Everson, S. A., Kaplan, G. A., Manuck, S. B., Jennings, J. R., et al. (1997). Exaggerated blood pressure responses during mental stress are associated with enhanced carotid atherosclerosis in middle-aged Finnish men. *Circulation, 96,* 3842–3848.

Kamarck, T. M., Shiffman, S. M., Smithline, L., Goodie, J. L., Paty, J. A., et al. (1998). Effects of task strain, social conflict, and emotional activation on ambulatory cardiovascular activity: Daily life consequences of recurring stress in a multiethnic adult sample. *Health Psychology, 17,* 17–29.

Kandel, D. B. (2002). *Stages and pathways of drug involvement: Examining the gateway hypothesis.* New York: Cambridge University Press.

Kane, J. M., Marder, S. R., Schooler, N. R., et al. (2001). Clozapine and haloperidol in moderately refractory schizophrenia: A 6-month randomized and doubleblind comparison. *Archives of General Psychiatry, 58,* 965–972.

Kane, J., Honigfeld, G., Singer, J., Meltzer, H., and the Clozapine Collaborative Study Group. (1988). Clozapine for treatment resistant schizophrenics. *Archives of General Psychiatry, 45,* 789–796.

Kane, P., & Garber, J. (2004). The relations among depression in fathers, children's psychopathology, and father–child conflict: A meta-analysis. *Clinical Psychology Review, 24,* 339–360.

Kanner, L. (1943). Autistic disturbances of affective contact. *Nervous Child, 2,* 217–250.

Kanner, L. (1973). *Childhood psychosis: Initial studies and new insights.* Washington, DC: V. H. Winston and Sons.

Kapczinski, F., Lima, M. S., Souza, J. S., Cunha, A., & Schmitt, R. (2002). Antidepressants for generalized anxiety disorder. *Cochrane Database of Systematic Reviews, 2003,* Issue 2. Art. No.: CD003592. DOI: 10.1002/14651858. CD003592.

Kaplan, H. S. (1974). *The new sex therapy.* New York: Brunner/Mazel.

Kaplan, H. S. (1997). Sexual desire disorders (hypoactive sexual desire and sexual aversion). In G. O. Gabbard & S. D. Atkinson (Eds.), *Synopsis of treatments of psychiatric disorders* (2nd ed., pp. 771–780). Washington, DC: American Psychiatric Press.

Kaplan, J. R., Manuck, S. B., Williams, J. K., & Strawn, W. (1994). Psychosocial influences on atherosclerosis: Evidence for efforts and mechanisms in nonhuman primates. In J. Blascovich & E. S. Katkin (Eds.), *Cardiovascular reactivity* (pp. 3–26). Washington, DC: American Psychological Association.

Kaplan, M. (1983). A woman's view of DSM-III. *American Psychologist, 39,* 786–792.

Kaplan, M. S., & Kreuger, R. B. (1997). Voyeurism: Psychopathology and theory. In D. R. Laws & W. O'Donohue (Eds.), *Sexual deviance* (pp. 297–310). New York: Guilford.

Kaplow, J. B., & Widom, C. S. (2007). Age of onset of child maltreatment predicts long-term mental health outcomes. *Journal of Abnormal Psychology, 116,* 176–187.

Kaptchuk, T. J., Kelley, J. M., Conboy, L. A., Davis, R. B., Kerr, C. E., Jacobson, E. E., et al. (2008). Components of placebo effect: Randomised controlled trial in patients with irritable bowel syndrome. *British Medical Journal (Clinical Research Ed.), 336,* 999–1003.

Karasek, R. A. (1979). Job demands, job decision latitude, and mental strain: Implications for job redesign. *Administrative Science, 24,* 285–308.

Karkowski, L. M., Prescott, C. A., & Kendler, K. S. (2000). Multivariate assessment of factors influencing illicit substance use in twins from female-female pairs. *Amercian Journal of Medical Genetics and Neuropsychiatric Genetics, 96,* 665–670.

Karon, B. P., & VandenBos, G. R. (1998). Schizophrenia and psychosis in elderly populations. In I. H. Nordhus, G. R. VandenBos, S. Berg, & P. Fromholt (Eds.), *Clinical geropsychology* (pp. 219–227). Washington, DC: American Psychological Association.

Kasari, C., Freeman, S., & Paparella, T. (2006). Joint attention and symbolic play in young children with autism: A randomized controlled intervention study. *Journal of Child Psychology and Psychiatry, 47,* 611–620.

Kasari, C., Paparella, T., Freeman, S., & Jahromi, L. B. (2008). Language outcome in autism: Randomized comparison of joint attention and play interventions. *Journal of Consulting and Clinical Psychology, 76,* 125–137.

Kashani, J. H., Beck, N. C., Hoeper, E. W., Fallahi, C., Corcoran, C. M., McAllister, J. A., Rosenberg, T. K., & Reid, J. C. (1987). Psychiatric disorders in a community sample of adolescents. *American Journal of Psychiatry, 144,* 584–589.

Kashani, J. H., & Carlson, G. A. (1987). Seriously depressed preschoolers. *American Journal of Psychiatry, 144,* 348–350.

Kashani, J. H., Holcomb, W. R., & Orvaschel, H. (1986). Depression and depressive symptoms in preschool children from the general population. *American Journal of Psychiatry, 143,* 1138–1143.

Kashani, J. H., & Orvaschel, H. (1990). A community study of anxiety in children and adolescents. *American Journal of Psychiatry, 147,* 313–318.

Kashden, J., & Franzen, M. D. (1996). An interrater reliability study of the Luria-Nebraska Neuropsychological Battery Form-II quantitative scoring system. *Archives of Clinical Neuropsychology, 11,* 155–163.

Kasl-Godley, J., & Gatz, M. (2000). Psychosocial intervention for individuals with dementia: An integration of theory, therapy, and a clinical understanding of dementia. *Clinical Psychology, 20*(6), 755–782.

Kassel, J. D., & Shiffman, S. (1997). Attentional mediation of cigarette smoking's effect on anxiety. *Health Psychology, 16,* 359–368.

Kassel, J. D., Stroud, L. R., & Paronis, C. A. (2003). Smoking, stress, and negative affect: Correlation, causation, and context across stages of smoking. *Psychological Bulletin, 129,* 270–304.

Kassel, J. D., & Unrod, M. (2000). Smoking, anxiety, and attention: Support for the role of nicotine in attentionally mediated anxiolysis. *Journal of Abnormal Psychology, 109,* 161–166.

Kassett, J. A., Gershon, E. S., Maxwell, M. E., et al. (1989). Psychiatric disorders in the first-degree relatives of probands with bulimia nervosa. *American Journal of Psychiatry, 146,* 1468–1471.

Kaszniak, A. W., Nussbaum, P. D., Berren, M. R., & Santiago, J. (1988). Amnesia as a consequence of male rape: A case report. *Journal of Abnormal Psychology, 97,* 100–104.

Kato, T. (2007). Molecular genetics of bipolar disorder and depression. *Psychiatry and Clinical Neurosciences, 61,* 3–19.

Katz, E. C., Gruber, K., Chutuape, M. A., & Stitzer, M. L. (2001). Reinforcement-based outpatient treatment for opiate and cocaine abusers. *Journal of Substance Abuse Treatment, 20,* 93–98.

Katz, H. M., & Gunderson, J. G. (1990). Individual psychodynamically oriented psychotherapy for schizophrenic patients. In M. I. Herz, S. J. Keith, & J. P. Docherty (Eds.), *Handbook of schizophrenia: Psychosocial treatment of schizophrenia* (pp. 69–90). Amsterdam: Elsevier.

Katz, I. R., Parmelee, P., & Brubaker, K. (1991). Toxic and metabolic encephalopathies in long-term care patients. *International Psychogeriatrics, 3,* 337–347.

Kawachi, I., Colditz, G. A., Ascherio, A., Rimm, E. B., Giovannucci, E., et al. (1994). Prospective study of phobic anxiety and risk of coronary heart disease in men. *Circulation, 89,* 1992–1997.

Kawachi, I., Sparrow, D., Spiro, A., Vokonas, P., & Weiss, S. T. (1996). A prospective study of anger and coronary heart disease: The normative aging study. *Circulation, 94,* 2090–2094.

Kawakami, N., Shimizu, H., Haratani, T., Iwata, N., & Kitamura, T. (2004). Lifetime and 6-month prevalence of DSM-III-R psychiatric disorders in an urban community in Japan. *Psychiatry Research, 121,* 293–301.

Kaye, W. H., Ebert, M. H., Raleigh, M., & Lake, R. (1984). Abnormalities in CNS monoamine metabolism in anorexia nervosa. *Archives of General Psychiatry, 41,* 350–355.

Kaye, W. H., Greeno, C. G., Moss, H., Fernstrom, J., Lilenfeld, L. R., Wahlund, B., Weltzin, T. E., & Mann, J. J. L. (1998). Alterations in serotonin activity and platelet monoamine oxidase and psychiatric symptoms after recovery from bulimia nervosa. *Archives of General Psychiatry, 55,* 927–935.

Kazdin, A. E. (1985). *Treatment of antisocial behavior in children and adolescents.* Homewood, IL: Dorsey.

Kazdin, A. E. (2005). *Parent management training: Treatment for oppositional, aggressive, and antisocial behavior in children and adolescents.* New York: Oxford University Press.

Kazdin, A. E., & Weisz, J. R. (1998). Identifying and developing empirically supported child and adolescent treatments. *Journal of Consulting and Clinical Psychology, 66,* 19–36.

Keane, T. M., & Barlow, D. H. (2004). Posttraumatic stress disorder. In D. H. Barlow (Ed.), *Anxiety and its disorders: The nature and treatment of anxiety and panic* (pp. 418–454). New York: Guilford.

Keane, T. M., Fairbank, J. A., Caddell, J. M., & Zimering, R. T. (1989). Implosive (flooding) therapy reduces symptoms of PTSD in Vietnam combat veterans. *Behavior Therapy, 20,* 245–260.

Keane, T. M., Gerardi, R. J., Quinn, S. J., & Litz, B. T. (1992). Behavioral treatment of posttraumatic stress disorder. In S. M. Turner, K. S. Calhoun, & H. E. Adams (Eds.), *Handbook of clinical behavior therapy* (2nd ed., pp. 87–97). New York: Wiley.

Keane, T. M., Marshall, A. D., & Taft, C. T. (2006). Posttraumatic stress disorder: Etiology, epidemiology, and treatment outcome. *Annual Review of Clinical Psychology, 2,* 161–197.

Keane, T. M., Zimering, R. T., & Caddell, J. (1985). A behavioral formulation of posttraumatic stress disorder in Vietnam veterans. *The Behavior Therapist, 8,* 9–12.

Kearney, P. M., Whelton, M., Reynolds, K., Whelton, P. K., & He, J. (2004). Worldwide prevalence of hypertension: A systematic review. *Journal of Hypertension, 22,* 11–19.

Keefe, R. S. E., Bilder, R. M., Davis, S. M., Harvey, P. D., Palmer, B. W., et al. (2007). Neurocognitive effects of antipsychotic medications in patients with chronic schizophrenia in the CATIE trial. *Archives of General Psychiatry, 64,* 633–647.

Keel, P. K., Baxter, M. G., Heatherton, T. F., & Joiner, T. E. (2007). A 20-year longitudinal study of body weight, dieting, and eating disorder symptoms. *Journal of Abnormal Psychology, 116,* 422–432.

Keel, P. K., & Klump, K. L. (2003). Are eating disorders culture-bound syndromes? Implications for conceptualizing their etiology. *Psychological Bulletin, 129,* 747–769.

Keel, P. K., & Mitchell, J. E. (1997). Outcome in bulimia nervosa. *American Journal of Psychiatry, 154,* 313–321.

Keel, P. K., Mitchell, J. E., Davis, T. L., & Crow, S. J. (2002). Long-term impact of treatment in women diagnosed with bulimia nervosa. *International Journal of Eating Disorders, 31,* 151–158.

Keel, P. K., Mitchell, J. E., Miller, K. B., Davis, T. L., & Crowe, S. J. (1999). Long-term outcome of bulimia nervosa. *Archives of General Psychiatry, 56,* 63–69.

Keilp, J. G., Sackeim, H. A., Brodsky, B. S., Oquendo, M. A., Malone, K. M., & Mann, J. J. (2001). Neuropsychological dysfunction in depressed suicide attempters. *Archives of General Psychiatry, 158,* 735–741.

Keller, M. B., Lavori, P. W., Kane, J. M., & Gelenberg, A. J. (1992). Subsyndromal symptoms in bipolar disorder: A comparison of standard and low serum levels of lithium. *Archives of General Psychiatry, 49,* 371–376.

Keller, M. B., Ryan, N. D., Strober, M., Klein, R. G., Kutcher, S. P., Birmaher, B., et al. (2001). Efficacy of paroxetine in the treatment of adolescent major depression: A randomized, controlled trial. *Journal of the American Academy of Child & Adolescent Psychiatry, 40,* 762–772.

Keller, M. B., Yonkers, K. A., Warshaw, M. G., Pratt, L. A., Golan, J., Mathews, A. O., et al. (1994). Remission and relapse in subjects with panic disorder and agoraphobia: A prospective short interval naturalistic follow-up. *Journal of Nervous and Mental Disorders, 182,* 290–296.

Kellerman, J. (1989). *Silent partner.* New York: Bantam Books.

Kelley, M. L. (1990). *School-home notes: Promoting children's classroom success.* New York: Guilford.

Kellner, C. H., Fink, M., Knapp, R., Petrides, G., Husain, M., Rummans, T., et al. (2005). Relief of expressed suicidal intent by ECT: A consortium for research in ECT study. *American Journal of Psychiatry, 162,* 977–982.

Kelly, J. A. (1995). *Changing HIV risk behavior: Practical strategies.* New York: Guilford.

Keltner, D., & Bonanno, G. A. (1997). A study of laughter and dissociation: Distinct correlates of laughter and smiling during bereavement. *Journal of Personality & Social Psychology, 73,* 687–702.

Keltner, D., & Kring, A. M. (1998). Emotion, social function, and psychopathology. *Review of General Psychology, 2,* 320–342.

Kemeny, M. E. (2003). The psychobiology of stress. *Current Directions in Psychological Science, 12,* 124–129.

Kempster, N. (1996, August 25). Clinton orders tracking of sex offenders. *Los Angeles Times,* p. A20.

Kenardy, J., & Taylor, C. B. (1999). Expected versus unexpected panic attacks: A naturalistic prospective study. *Journal of Anxiety Disorders, 13,* 435–445.

Kendall, P. C. (1994). Treating anxiety disorders in youth: Results of a randomized clinical trial. *Journal of Consulting and Clinical Psychology, 62,* 100–110.

Kendall, P. C., Aschenbrand, S. G., & Hudson, J. L. (2003). Child-focused treatment of anxiety. In A. E. Kazdin & J. R. Weisz (Eds.), *Evidence-based psychotherapies for children and adolescents* (pp. 81–100). New York: Guilford.

Kendall, P. C., & Beidas, R. S. (2007). Trail for dissemination of evidence-based practices for youth: Flexibility within fidelity. *Professional Psychology: Research and Practice, 38,* 13–20.

Kendall, P. C., Flannery-Schroeder, E. C., Panichelli-Mindel, S., Southam-Gerow, M., Henin, A., & Warman, M. (1997). Therapy for youths with anxiety disorders: A second randomized clinical trial. *Journal of Consulting and Clinical Psychology, 65,* 366–380.

Kendall, P. C., Haaga, D. A. F., Ellis, A., Bernard, M., DiGiuseppe, R., & Kassinove, H. (1995). Rational-emotive therapy in the 1990s and beyond: Current status, recent revisions, and research questions. *Clinical Psychology Review, 15,* 169–185.

Kendall, P. C., Hudson, J. L., Gosch, E., Flannery-Schroeder, E., & Suveg, C. (2008). Cognitive-behavioral therapy for anxiety disordered youth: A randomized clinical trial evaluating child and family modalities. *Journal of Consulting and Clinical Psychology, 76,* 282–297.

Kendall, P. C., & Ingram, R. E. (1989). Cognitive-behavioral perspectives: Theory and research on depression and anxiety. In D. Watson & P. C. Kendall (Eds.), *Personality, psychopathology, and psychotherapy* (pp. 27–53). San Diego, CA: Academic Press.

Kendall, P. C., Safford, S., Flannery-Schroeder, E., & Webb, A. (2004). Child anxiety treatment: Outcomes in adolescence and impact on substance use and depression at 7.4-year follow-up. *Journal of Consulting and Clinical Psychology, 72,* 276–287.

Kendler, K. S. (1993). Twin studies of psychiatric illness: Current status and future directions. *Archives of General Psychiatry, 50,* 905–914.

Kendler, K. S. (1997). The diagnostic validity of melancholic major depression in a population-based sample of female twins. *Archives of General Psychiatry, 54,* 299–304.

Kendler, K. S., & Baker, J. (2007). Genetic influences on measures of the environment: A systematic review. *Psychological Medicine, 37,* 615–626.

Kendler, K. S., & Gardner, C. O. (1998). Boundaries of major depression: An evaluation of DSM-IV criteria. *American Journal of Psychiatry, 155,* 172–177.

Kendler, K. S., Gatz, M., Gardner, C. O., & Pedersen, N. L. (2006a). Personality and major depression: A Swedish longitudinal, population-based twin study. *Archives of General Psychiatry, 63,* 1113–1120.

Kendler, K. S., Hettema, J. M., Butera, F., Gardner, C. O., & Prescott, C. A. (2003). Life event dimensions of loss, humiliation, entrapment, and danger in the prediction of onsets of major depression and generalized anxiety. *Archives of General Psychiatry, 60,* 789–796.

Kendler, K. S., Jacobson, K. C., Prescott, C. A., & Neale, M. C. (2003). Specificity of genetic and environmental risk factors for use and abuse/dependence of cannabis, cocaine, hallucinogens, sedatives, stimulants, and opiates in male twins. *American Journal of Psychiatry, 160,* 687–695.

Kendler, K. S., Karkowski, L. M., & Prescott, C. A. (1999). Causal relationship between stressful life events and the onset of major depression. *American Journal of Psychiatry, 156,* 837–841.

Kendler, K. S., Karkowski-Shuman, L., & Walsh, D. (1996). Age of onset in schizophrenia and risk of illness in relatives. *British Journal of Psychiatry, 169,* 213–218.

Kendler, K. S., Kuhn, J. W., Vittum, J., Prescott, C. A., & Riley, B. (2005). The interaction of stressful life events and a serotonin transporter polymorphism in the prediction of episodes of major depression: A replication. *Archives of General Psychiatry, 62,* 529–535.

Kendler, K. S., Myers, J., & Prescott, C. A. (2002). The etiology of phobias: An evaluation of the stress-diathesis model. *Archives of General Psychiatry, 59,* 242–249.

Kendler, K. S., Myers, J., Prescott, C. A., & Neale, M. C. (2001). The genetic epidemiology of irrational fears and phobias in men. *Archives of General Psychiatry, 58,* 257–267.

Kendler, K. S., Myers, J., Torgersen, S., Neale, M. C., & Reichborn-Kjennerud, T. (2007). The heritablity of cluster A personality disorders assessed by both personal interview and questionnaire. *Psychological Medicine, 37,* 655–665.

Kendler, K. S., Neale, M. C., & Walsh, D. (1995). Evaluating the spectrum concept of schizophrenia in the Roscommon Family Study. *American Journal of Psychiatry, 152,* 749–754.

Kendler, K. S., & Prescott, C. A. (1998). Cannabis use, abuse, and dependence in a population-based sample of female twins. *American Journal of Psychiatry, 155,* 1016–1022.

Kendler, K. S., Prescott, C. A., Myers, J., & Neale, M. C. (2003). The structure of genetic and environmental risk factors for common psychiatric and substance use disorders in men and women. *Archives of General Psychiatry, 60,* 929–937.

Kennedy, E., Spence, S. H., & Hensley, R. (1989). An examination of the relationship between childhood depression and social competence amongst primary school children. *Journal of Child Psychology and Psychiatry, 30,* 561–573.

Kernberg, O. F. (1985). *Borderline conditions and pathological narcissism.* Northvale, NJ: Jason Aronson.

Kerns, J. G., & Berenbaum, H. (2002). Cognitive impairments associated with formal thought disorder in people with schizophrenia. *Journal of Abnormal Psychology, 111,* 211–224.

Kerns, J. G., & Berenbaum, H. (2003). The relationship between formal thought disorder and executive functioning component processes. *Journal of Abnormal Psychology, 112,* 339–352.

Keshavan, M. S., Rosenberg, D., Sweeney, J. A., & Pettegrew, J. W. (1998). Decreased caudate volume in neuroleptic-naive psychotic patients. *American Journal of Psychiatry, 155,* 774–778.

Kessel, N., & Grossman, G. (1961). Suicide in alcoholics. *British Medical Journal, 2,* 1671–1672.

Kessler, L. (2004, August 22). Dancing with Rose: A strangely beautiful encounter with Alzheimer's patients provides insights that challenge the way we view the disease. *LA Times Magazine, 1–10.*

Kessler, R. C., Berglund, P., Demler, O., Jin, R., Merikangas, K. R., & Walters, E. E. (2005). Lifetime prevalence and age-of-onset distributions of DSM-IV disorders in the national comorbidity survey replication. *Archives of General Psychiatry, 62,* 593–602.

Kessler, R. C., Chiu, W. T., Demler, O., & Walters, E. E. (2005). Prevalence, severity, and comorbidity of 12-month DSM-IV disorders in the National Comorbidity Survey Replication. *Archives of General Psychiatry, 62,* 617–627.

Kessler, R. C., Chiu, W. T., Jin, R., Ruscio, A. M., Shear, K., & Walters, E. E. (2006). The epidemiology of panic attacks, panic disorder, and agoraphobia in the National Comorbidity Survey Replication. *Archives of General Psychiatry, 63,* 415–424.

Kessler, R. C., Crum, R. M., Warner, L. A., Nelson, C. B., et al. (1997). Lifetime co-occurrence of DSM-IIIR alcohol dependence with other psychiatric disorders in the National Comorbidity Study. *Archives of General Psychiatry, 54,* 313–321.

Kessler, R. C., Heeringa, S., Lakoma, M. D., et al. (2008). Individual and society effects of mental disorders on earnings in the United States: Results from the National Comorbidity Survey Replication. *American Journal of Psychiatry, 165,* 703–711.

Kessler, R. C., McGonagle, K. A., Zhao, S., Nelson, C. B., et al. (1994). Lifetime and 12-month prevalence of DSM-III-R psychiatric disorders in the United States: Results from the National Comorbidity Study. *Archives of General Psychiatry, 51,* 8–19.

Kessler, R. C., & McLeod, J. D. (1985). Social support and mental health in community samples. In S. Cohen & L. Syme (Eds.), *Social support and health* (pp. 219–240). Orlando, FL: Academic Press.

Kety, S. S., Rosenthal, D., Wender, P. H., & Schulsinger, F. (1976). Mental illness in the adoptive and biological families of adopted individuals who have become schizophrenic. In R. R. Fieve, D. Rosenthal, & H. Brill (Eds.), *Genetic research in psychiatry.* Baltimore, MD: Johns Hopkins University Press.

Kety, S. S., Wender, P. H., Jacobsen, B., Ingraham, L. T., Jansson, L., et al. (1994). Mental illness in the biological and adoptive relatives of schizophrenic adoptees: Replication of the Copenhagen study in the rest of Denmark. *Archives of General Psychiatry, 51,* 442–468.

Keys, A., Brozek, J., Hsu, L. K. G., McConoha, C. E., & Bolton, B. (1950). *The biology of human starvation.* Minneapolis: University of Minnesota Press.

Kiecolt-Glaser, J. K., Bane, C., Glaser, R., & Malarkey, W. B. (2003). Love, marriage, and divorce: Newlyweds' stress hormones foreshadow relationship changes. *Journal of Consulting and Clinical Psychology, 71,* 176–188.

Kiecolt-Glaser, J., Dura, J. R., Speicher, C. E., & Trask, O. (1991). Spousal caregivers of dementia victims: Longitudinal changes in immunity and health. *Psychosomatic Medicine, 54,* 345–362.

Kiecolt-Glaser, J. K., Garner, W., Speicher, C. E., Penn, G. M., Holliday, J., & Glaser, R. (1984). Psychosocial modifiers of immunocompetence in medical students. *Psychosomatic Medicine, 46,* 7–14.

Kiecolt-Glaser, J. K., & Glaser, R. (2001). Stress and immunity: Age enhances the risks. *Current Directions in Psychological Science, 10,* 18–21.

Kiecolt-Glaser, J. K., & Glaser, R. (2002). Depression and immune function: Central pathways to morbidity and mortality. *Journal of Psychosomatic Research, 53,* 873–876.

Kiecolt-Glaser, J. K., Glaser, R., Williger, D., Stout, J., Messick, G., Sheppard, S., Ricker, D., Romischer, S. C., Briner, W., Bonnell, G., & Donnerberg, R. (1985). Psychosocial enhancement of immunocompetence in a geriatric population. *Health Psychology, 4,* 25–41.

Kiecolt-Glaser, J. K., McGuire, L., Robles, T. F., & Glaser, R. (2002). Psychoneuroimmunology and psychosomatic medicine: Back to the future. *Psychosomatic Medicine, 64,* 15–28.

Kieseppa, T., Partonen, T., Haukka, J., Kaprio, J., & Lonnqvist, J. (2004). High concordance of bipolar I disorder in a nationwide sample of twins. *American Journal of Psychiatry, 161,* 1814–1821.

Kiesler, C. A. (1991). Changes in general hospital psychiatric care. *American Psychologist, 46,* 416–421.

Kihlstrom, J. F. (1994). Dissociative and conversion disorders. In D. J. Stein & J. E. Young (Eds.), *Cognitive science and clinical disorders* 247–270. San Diego, CA: Academic Press.

Kihlstrom, J. F., Tataryn, D. J., & Holt, I. P. (1993). Dissociative disorders. In P. B. Sutker & H. E. Adams (Eds.), *Comprehensive handbook of psychopathology* (pp. 203–234). New York: Plenum.

Killen, J. D., Fortmann, S. P., Murphy, G. M., Jr., Hayward, C., Arredondo, C., et al. (2006). Extended treatment with bupropion SR for cigarette smoking cessation. *Journal of Consulting and Clinical Psychology, 74,* 286–294.

Killen, J. D., Robinson, T. N., Haydel, K. F., Hayward, C., et al. (1997). Prospective study of risk factors for the initiation of cigarette smoking. *Journal of Consulting and Clinical Psychology, 65,* 1011–1016.

Killen, J. D., Taylor, C. B., Hayward, C., Haydel, K. F., Wilson, D. M., Hammer, L., Kraemer, H., Blair-Greiner, A., & Strachowski, D. (1996). Weight concerns influence the development of eating disorders: A 4-year prospective study. *Journal of Consulting and Clinical Psychology, 64,* 936–940.

Killen, J. D., Taylor, C. B., Hayward, C., Wilson, D. M., Haydel, K. F., et al. (1994). Pursuit of thinness and onset of eating disorders in a community sample of adolescent girls. *International Journal of Eating Disorders, 16,* 227–238.

Kim, E. (2005). The effect of the decreased safety behaviors on anxiety and negative thoughts in social phobics. *Journal of Anxiety Disorders, 19,* 69–86.

Kim, E. D., & Lipshultz, L. I. (1997). Advances in the evaluation and treatment of the infertile man. *World Journal of Urology, 15,* 378–393.

Kim, J. E., & Moen, P. (2001). Is retirement good or bad for subjective well-being? *Current Directions in Psychological Science* (Special Issue), *10*(3), 83–86.

King, D. A. (2005). Introduction to the special issue. *Clinical Psychology Science and Practice, 12,* 203–206.

Kinsey, A. C., Pomeroy, W. B., & Martin, C. E. (1948). *Sexual behavior in the human male.* Philadelphia: Saunders.

Kinzl, J. F., Traweger, C., Trefalt, E., Mangweth, B., & Biebl, W. (1999). Binge eating disorder in females: A population based investigation. *International Journal of Eating Disorders, 25,* 287–292.

Kirkbride, J. B., Fearon, P., Morgan, C., Dazzon, P., Morgan, K., et al. (2006). Heterogeneity in the incidence of schizophrenia and other psychotic illnesses: Results from the 3-center Aesop study. *Archives of General Psychiatry, 63,* 250–258.

Kirkpatrick, B., Fenton, W., Carpenter, W.T., & Marder, S.R. (2006). The NIMH-MATRICS consensus statement on negative symptoms. *Schizophrenia Bulletin, 32,* 296–303.

Kirmayer, L. J. (2001). Cultural variations in the clinical presentation of depression and anxiety: Implications for diagnosis and treatment. *Journal of Clinical Psychiatry, 62* (Suppl. 13), 22–28.

Kirmayer, L. J., Robbins, J. M., & Paris, J. (1994). Somatoform disorders: Personality and social matrix of somatic distress. *Journal of Abnormal Psychology, 103,* 125–136.

Kirmayer, L. J., & Young, A. (1998). Culture and somatization: Clinical, epidemiological, and ethnographic perspectives. *Psychosomatic Medicine, 60,* 420–430.

Kirsch, I. (2000). Are drug and placebo effects in depression additive? *Biological Psychiatry, 47,* 733–735.

Kirschbaum, C., Prussner, J. C., & Stone, A. A. (1995). Persistent high cortisol responses to repeated psychological stress in a subpopulation of healthy men. *Psychosomatic Medicine, 57,* 468–474.

Kisiel, C. L., & Lyons, J. S. (2001). Dissociation as a mediator of psychopathology among sexually abused children and adolescents. *American Journal of Psychiatry, 158,* 1034–1039.

Kisley, M. A., Wood, S., & Burrows, C. L. (2007). Looking at the sunny side of life: Age-related change in an event-related potential measure of the negativity bias. *Psychological Science, 18,* 838.

Klein, D. N., Durbin, C. E., Shankman, S. A., & Santiago, N. J. (2002). Depression and personality. In C. L. Hammen & I. H. Gotlib (Eds.), *Handbook of depression* (pp. 115–140). New York: Guilford.

Klein, D. N., Lewinsohn, P. M., Seeley, J. R., & Rohde, P. A. (2001). A family study of major depressive disorder in a community sample of adolescents. *Archives of General Psychiatry, 58,* 13–20.

Klein, D. N., Schwartz, J. E., Rose, S., & Leader, J. B. (2000). Five-year course and outcome of dysthymic disorder: A prospective, naturalistic follow-up study. *American Journal of Psychiatry, 157,* 931–939.

Klein, D. N., Schwartz, J. E., Santiago, N. J., Vivian, D., Vocisano, C., Castonguay, L. G., et al. (2003). Therapeutic alliance in depression treatment: Controlling for prior change and patient characteristics. *Journal of Consulting and Clinical Psychology, 71,* 997–1006.

Klein, D. N., Shankman, S. A. M. A., & Rose, S. M. A. (2006). Ten-year prospective follow-up study of the naturalistic course of dysthymic disorder and double depression. *American Journal of Psychiatry, 163,* 872–880.

Kleinman, A. (1986). *Social origins of distress and disease: Depression, neurasthenia, and pain in modern China.* New Haven, CT: Yale University Press.

Klerman, G. L. (1988). Depression and related disorders of mood (affective disorders). In A. M. Nicholi, Jr. (Ed.), *The new Harvard guide to psychiatry.* Cambridge, MA: Harvard University Press.

Klerman, G. L., Weissman, M. M., Rounsaville, B. J., & Chevron, E. S. (1984). *Interpersonal psychotherapy of depression.* New York: Basic Books.

Klinetob, N. A., & Smith, D. A. (1996). Demand-withdraw communication in marital interaction: Tests of interspousal contingency and gender role hypotheses. *Journal of Marriage and the Family, 58,* 945–957.

Klingberg, T., Hedehus, M., Temple, E., Salz, T., Gabrieli, J. D., Moseley, M. E., & Poldrack, R. A. (2000). Microstructure of temporo-parietal white matter as a basis for reading ability: Evidence from diffusion tensor magnetic resonance imaging. *Neuron, 25,* 493–500.

Klinnert, M. D., Mrazek, P. J., & Mrazek, D. A. (1994). Early asthma onset: The interaction between family stressors and adaptive parenting. *Psychiatry, 57,* 51–61.

Klintsova, A. Y., Scamra, C., Hoffman, M., Napper, R. M. A., Goodlett, C. R., & Greenough, W. T. (2002). Therapeutic effects of complex motor training on motor performance deficits induced by neonatal binge-like alcohol exposure in rats: II. A quantitative stereological study of synaptic plasticity in female rat cerebellum. *Brain Research, 937,* 83–93.

Klonsky, E. D., Oltmanns, T. F., & Turkheimer, E. (2002). Informant-reports of personality disorder: Relations to self-reports and future research directions. *Clinical Psychology: Science and Practice, 9,* 300–311.

Kluft, R. P. (1994). Treatment trajectories in multiple personality disorder. *Dissociation, 7,* 63–75.

Klump, K. L., McGue, M., & Iacono, W. G. (2000). Age differences in genetic and environmental influences on eating attitudes and behaviors in preadolescent and adolescent female twins. *Journal of Abnormal Psychology, 109,* 239–251.

Klump, K. L., McGue, M., & Iacono, W. G. (2002). Genetic relationships between personality and eating attitudes and behaviors. *Journal of Abnormal Psychology, 111,* 380–389.

Klunk, W. E., Engler, H., Nordberg, A., Wang, Y., Blomqvist, G., & Holt, D. P. (2004). Imaging brain amyloid in Alzheimer's disease with Pittsburgh compound-b. *Annuals of Neurology, 55,* 306–319.

Knight, B. G. (1996). *Psychotherapy with older adults* (2nd ed.). Thousand Oaks, CA: Sage.

Knight, B. G., Kelly, M., & Gatz, M. (1992). Psychotherapy and the older adult. In H. J. Freudenberger & D. K. Freedheim (Eds.), *History of psychotherapy: A century of change* (pp. 528–551). Washington, DC: American Psychological Association.

Knight, B. G., Lutzky, S. M., & Olshevski, J. L. (1992). *A randomized comparison of stress reduction training to problem solving training for dementia caregivers: Processes and outcomes.* Unpublished manuscript, University of Southern California, Los Angeles.

Knopp, E. H. (1984). *Retraining adult sex offenders.* New York: Safer Society Press.

Kochanek, K. D., Murphy, S. L., Anderson, R. N., & Scott, C. (2004). Deaths: Final data for 2002. *National vital statistics reports, 53*(5). Hyattsville, MD: National Center for Health Statistics.

Koegel, R. L., Bimbela, A., & Schreibman, L. (1996). Collateral effects of parent training on family interactions. *Journal of Autism and Developmental Disorders, 26,* 347–359.

Koegel, R. L., Koegel, L. K., & Brookman, L. I. (2003). Empirically supported pivotal response interventions with children with autism. In A. E. Kazdin & J. R. Weisz (Eds.), *Evidence-based psychotherapies for children and adolescents* (pp. 341–357). New York: Guilford.

Koegel, R. L., Schreibman, L., Britten, K. R., Burkey, J. C., & O'Neill, R. E. (1982). A comparison of parent training to direct child treatment. In R. L. Koegel, A. Rincover, & A.L. Egel (Eds.), *Educating and understanding autistic children.* San Diego, CA: College-Hill.

Koenigsberg, H. W., Reynolds, D., Goodman, M., New, A. S., Mitropoulou, V., Trestman, R. L., et al. (2003). Risperidone in the treatment of schizotypal personality disorder. *Journal of Clinical Psychiatry, 64,* 628–634.

Koenigsberg, H. W., Woo-Ming, A. M., & Siever, L. J. (2002). Pharmacological treatments for personality disorders. In P. E. Nathan & J. M. Gorman (Eds.), *A guide to treatments that work* 625–641. New York: Oxford University Press.

Kohn, L. P., Oden, T., Munoz, R. F., Robinson, A., & Leavitt, D. (2002). Adapted cognitive behavioral group therapy for depressed low-income African American women. *Community Mental Health Journal, 38*(6), 497–504.

Kohn, M. L. (1968). Social class and schizophrenia: A critical review. In D. Rosenthal & S. S. Kety (Eds.), *The transmission of schizophrenia.* Elmsford, NY: Pergamon.

Kohut, H. (1971). *The analysis of the self.* New York: International Universities Press.

Kohut, H. (1977). *The restoration of the self.* New York: International Universities Press.

Koivuma-Honkanen, H., Honkanen, R., Viinamäki, H., Heikkilä, K., Kaprio, J., & Koskenvuo, M. (2001). Life satisfaction and suicide: A 20-year follow-up study. *American Journal of Psychiatry, 158,* 433–439.

Koller, E. A., Cross, J. T., Doraiswamy, P. M., & Malozowski, S. N. (2003). Pancreatitis associated with atypical antipsychotics: From the Food and Drug Administration's MedWatch surveillance system and published reports. *Pharmacotherapy, 23,* 1123–1130.

Kolmen, B. K., Feldman, H. E., Handen, B. L., & Janosky, J. E. (1995). Naltrexone in young autistic children: A double-blind, placebo-controlled crossover study. *Journal of the American Academy of Child and Adolescent Psychiatry, 34,* 223–231.

Koob, G. F. (2008). A role for brain systems in addiction. *Neuron, 59,* 11–34.

Koob, G. F., Caine, B., Hyytia, P., Markou, A., Parsons, L. H., Roberts, A. J., Schulteis, G., & Weiss, F. (1999). Neurobiology of drug addiction. In M. D. Glantz & C. R. Hartel (Eds.), *Drug abuse: Origins and interventions* (pp. 161–190). Washington, DC: American Psychological Association.

Koob, G. F., & Le Moal (2008). Addiction and the brain anti-reward system. *Annual Review of Psychology, 59,* 29–53.

Koons, C. R., Robins, C. J., Tweed, J. L., Lynch, T. R., Gonzalez, A. M., Morse, J. Q., et al. (2001). Efficacy of dialectical behavior therapy in women veterans with borderline personality disorder. *Behavior Therapy, 32,* 371–390.

Kopelowicz, A., & Liberman, R. P. (1998). Psychosocial treatments for schizophrenia. In P. E. Nathan & J. M. Gorman (Eds.), *A guide to treatments that work* (pp. 190–211). New York: Oxford University Press.

Kopelowicz, A., Liberman, R. P., & Zarate, R. (2002). Psychosocial treatments for schizophrenia. In P. E. Nathan & J. M. Gorman (Eds.), *A guide to treatments that work* (pp. 201–229). New York: Oxford University Press.

Koss, M. P., & Shiang, J. (1994). Research on brief psychotherapy. In A. E. Bergin & S. L. Garfield (Eds.), *Handbook of psychotherapy and behavior change* (4th ed., pp. 664–700). New York: Wiley.

Kosten, T. R., Morgan, C. M., Falcione, J., & Schottenfeld, R. S. (1992). Pharmacotherapy for cocaine-abusing methadone-maintained patients using amantadine or desipramine. *Archives of General Psychiatry, 49*, 894–898.

Kosten, T. R., & Ziedonis, D. M.(1997). Substance abuse and schizophrenia: Editors' introduction. *Schizophrenia Bulletin, 23*, 181–186.

Kozak, M. J., Liebowitz, M., & Foa, E. B. (2000). Cognitive behavior therapy and pharmacotherapy for OCD: The NIMH-sponsored collaborative study. In W. K. Goodman, M. V. Rudorfer, & J. D. Maser (Eds.), *Obsessive-compulsive disorder: Contemporary issues in treatment* (pp. 501–503). Mahwah, NJ: Erlbaum.

Kozel, N. J., & Adams, E. H. (1986). Epidemiology of drug abuse: An overview. *Science, 234*, 970–974.

Kozol, H., Boucher, R., & Garofalo, R. (1972). The diagnosis and treatment of dangerousness. *Crime and Delinquency, 18*, 37–92.

Kramer, J. H., Jurik, J., Sha, S. J., Rankin, K. P., Rosen, H. J., Johnson, J. K., & Miller, B. L. (2003). Distinctive neuropsychological patterns in frontotemporal dementia, semantic dementia, and Alzheimer disease. *Cognitive and Behavioral Neurology, 16*, 211–218.

Kranzler, H. R., & Van Kirk, J. (2001). Efficacy of naltrexone and acamprosate for alcoholism treatment: A meta-analysis. *Alcoholism: Clinical & Experimental Research, 25*, 1335–1341.

Krause, K.-H., Dresel, S. H., Krause, J., La Fougere, C., & Ackenheil, M. (2003). The dopamine transporter and neuroimaging in attention deficit hyperactivity disorder. *Neuroscience and Biobehavioral Reviews, 27*, 605–613.

Kreslake, J. M., Wayne, G. F., Alpert, H. R., Koh, H. K., & Connolly, G. N. (2008). Tobacco industry control of menthol in cigarettes and targeting of adolescents and young adults. *American Journal of Public Health, 98*, 1685–1692.

Kreuger, R. B., & Kaplan, M. S. (2000). Evaluation and treatment of sexual disorders: Frottage. In L. Vandecreek & T. L. Jackson (Eds), *Innovations in clinical practice: A source book* (Vol. 18, pp. 185–197). Sarasota, FL: Professional Resource Press/Professional Resource Exchange.

Kreyenbuhl, J., Zito, J. M., Buchanan, R. W., Soeken, K. L., & Lehman, A. F. (2003). Racial disparity in the pharmacological management of schizophrenia. *Schizophrenia Bulletin, 29*, 183–193.

Kring, A. M. (1999). Emotion in schizophrenia: Old mystery, new understanding. *Current Directions in Psychological Science, 8*, 160–163.

Kring, A. M. (2000). Gender and anger. In A. H. Fischer (Ed.), *Gender and emotion* (pp. 211–231). Cambridge: Cambridge University Press.

Kring, A. M., & Moran, E. K. (2008). Emotional response deficits in schizophrenia: Insights from affective science. *Schizophrenia Bulletin, 34*, 819–834.

Kring, A. M., & Neale, J. M. (1996). Do schizophrenics show a disjunctive relationship among expressive, experiential and physiological components of emotion? *Journal of Abnormal Psychology, 105*, 249–257.

Krinsley, K. E., Gallagher, J. G., Weathers, F. W., Kutter, C. J., & Kaloupek, D. G. (2003). Consistency of retrospective reporting about exposure to traumatic events. *Journal of Traumatic Stress, 16*, 399–409.

Kroenke, K. (2007). Efficacy of treatment for somatoform disorders: A review of randomized controlled trials. *Psychosomatic Medicine, 69*, 881–888.

Krueger, R. F. (1999). Personality traits in late adolescence predict mental disorders in early adulthood: A prospective-epidemiological study. *Journal of Personality, 67*, 39–65.

Krueger, R. F., Markon, K. E., Patrick, C. J., & Iacono, W. G. (2005). Externalizing psychopathology in adulthood: A dimensional-spectrum conceptualization and its implications for DSM-V. *Journal of Abnormal Psychology, 114*, 537–550.

Kruger, S., Seminowicz, D., Goldapple, K., Kennedy, S. H., & Mayberg, H. S. (2003). State and trait influences on mood regulation in bipolar disorder: Blood flow differences with an acute mood challenge. *Biological Psychiatry, 54*, 1274–1283.

Krystal, J. H., Cramer, J. A., Krol, W. F., et al. (2001). Naltrexone in the treatment of alcohol dependence. *The New England Journal of Medicine, 345*, 1734–1739.

Kubansky, L. D., & Kawachi, I. (2000). Going to the heart of the matter: Do negative emotions cause coronary heart disease? *Journal of Psychosomatic Research, 48*, 323–337.

Kuehnle, K. (1998). Child sexual abuse evaluations: The scientist-practitioner model. *Behavioral Sciences & the Law, 16*, 5–20.

Kuhn, T. S. (1970). *The structure of scientific revolutions.* Chicago: University of Chicago Press. (Original work published 1962)

Kunkel, D., Wilcox, B. L., Cantor, J., Palmer, E., Linn, S., & Dowrick, P. (2004). *Report of the APA Task Force on Advertising and Children.* Washington, DC: American Psychological Association. Retrieved July 14, 2008, from http://www.apa.org/releases/childrenads.pdf

Kunst-Wilson, W. R., & Zajonc, R. B. (1980). Affective discrimination of stimuli that cannot be recognized. *Science, 207*, 557–558.

Kupfer, D. J. (2005). The increasing medical burden in bipolar disorder. *Journal of the American Medical Association, 293*, 2528–2530.

Kupfer, D. J., First, M. B., & Regier, D. A. (2002). *A research agenda for DSM-V.* Arlington, VA: APPI.

Ladoceur, R., Dugas, M. J., Freeston, M. H., Leger, E., Gagnon, F., & Thibodeau, N. (2000). Efficacy of a new cognitive-behavioral treatment for generalized anxiety disorder: Evaluation in a controlled clinical trial. *Journal of Consulting and Clinical Psychology, 68*, 957–996.

Lahey, B. B., Loeber, R., Burke, J. D., & Applegate, B. (2005). Predicting future antisocial personality disorder in males from a clinical assessment in childhood. *Journal of Consulting and Clinical Psychology, 73*, 389–399.

Lahey, B. B., McBurnett, K., & Loeber, R. (2000). Are attention-deficit/hyperactivity disorder and oppositional defiant disorder developmental precursors to conduct disorder? In A. J. Sameroff, M. Lewis, et al. (Eds.), *Handbook of developmental psychopathology* (2nd ed., pp. 431–446). New York: Kluwer Academic/Plenum.

Lahey, B. B., Miller, T. L., Gordon, R. A., & Riley, A. W. (1999). Developmental epidemiology of the disruptive behavior disorders. In H. C. Quay & A. Hogan (Eds.), *Handbook of disruptive behavior disorders* (pp. 23–48). New York: Plenum.

Lam, D. H., Bright, J., Jones, S., Hayward, P., Schuck, N., Chisholm, D., et al. (2000). Cognitive therapy for bipolar illness—a pilot study of relapse prevention. *Cognitive Therapy and Research, 24*, 503–520.

Lam, R. W., Levitt, A. J., Levitan, R. D., Enns, M. W., Morehouse, R., Michalak, E. E., & Tam, E. M. (2006). The Can-SAD study: A randomized controlled trial of the effectiveness of light therapy and fluoxetine in patients with winter seasonal affective disorder. *American Journal of Psychiatry, 163*, 805–812.

Lamb, H. R., Weinberger, L. E., & DeCuir, W. J. (2002). The police and mental health. *Psychiatry Services, 53*, 1266–1271.

Lambert, M. J. (2004). Psychotherapeutically speaking-updates from the Division of Psychotherapy (29). Retrieved from http://www.divisionofpsychotherapy.org/updates.php

Lambert, M. J., & Ogles, B. M. (2004). The efficacy and effectiveness of psychotherapy. In M. J. Lambert (Ed.), *Bergin and Garfield's handbook of psychotherapy and behavior change* (5th ed., pp. 139–193). Hoboken, NJ: Wiley.

Landa, R. J., Holman, K. C., & Garrett-Mayer, E. (2007). Social and communication development in toddlers with early and later diagnosis of autism spectrum disorders. *Archives of General Psychiatry, 64*, 853–864.

Landreville, P., Landry, J., Baillargeon, L., Guerette, A., & Matteau, E. (2001). Older adults' acceptance of psychological and pharmacological treatments for depression. *Journal of Gerontology: Psychological Sciences, 56B*(5), P285–P291.

Lane, E. A., & Albee, G. W. (1965). Childhood intellectual differences between schizophrenic adults and their siblings. *American Journal of Orthopsychiatry, 35*, 747–753.

Lang, A. R., Goeckner, D. J., Adessor, V. J., & Marlatt, G. A. (1975). Effects of alcohol on aggression in male social drinkers. *Journal of Abnormal Psychology, 84*, 508–518.

Langa, K. M., Larson, E. B., Karlawish, J. H., Cutler, D. M., Kabeto, M. U., Kim, S. Y., et al. (2008). Trends in the prevalence and mortality of cognitive impairment in the United States: Is there evidence of a compression of cognitive morbidity? *Alzheimer's & Dementia: The Journal of the Alzheimer's Association, 4*, 134–144.

Langeluddeke, A. (1963). *Castration of sexual criminals.* Berlin: de Gruyter.

Langenbucher, J., Martin, C. S., Labouvie, E., Sanjuan, P. M., Bavly, L., & Pollock, N. K. (2000). Toward the DSM-V: The withdrawal-gate model versus the DSM-IV in the diagnosis of alcohol abuse and dependence. *Journal of Consulting & Clinical Psychology, 68*, 799–809.

Långström, N., & Seto, M. C. (2006). Exhibitionistic and voyeuristic behavior in a Swedish national population survey. *Archives of Sexual Behavior, 35*, 427–435.

Lantz, P. M., House, J. S., Lepkowski, J. M., Williams, D. R., et al. (1998). Socioeconomic factors, health behaviors, and mortality. *Journal of the American Medical Association, 279*, 1703–1708.

Lanyon, R. I. (1986). Theory and treatment in child molestation. *Journal of Consulting and Clinical Psychology, 54*, 176–182.

Larson, E. B., Wang, L., Bowen, J. D., McCormick, W. C., Teri, L., Crane, P., et al. (2006). Exercise is associated with reduced risk for incident dementia among persons 65 years of age and older. *Annuals of Internal Medicine, 144*, 73–81.

Larsson, H., Andershed, H., & Lichtenstein, P. (2006). A genetic factor explains most of the variance in psychopathic personality. *Journal of Abnormal Psychology, 115*, 221–230.

Larsson, H., Tuvblad, C., Rijsdijk, F. V., Andershed, H., Grann, M., & Lichtenstein, P. (2007). A common genetic factor explains the association between psychopathic personality and antisocial behavior. *Psychological Medicine, 37*, 15–26.

LaRue, A., Dessonville, C., & Jarvik, L. F. (1985). Aging and mental disorders. In J. E. Birren & K. W. Schaie (Eds.), *Handbook of psychology of aging* (2nd ed.). New York: Van Nostrand-Reinhold.

Lau, J. Y. F., Gregory, A. M., Goldwin, M. A., Pine, D. S., & Eley, T. C. (2007). Assessing gene–environment interactions on anxiety symptom subtypes across childhood and adolescence. *Development and Psychopathology, 19*, 1129–1146.

Laumann, E. O., Gagnon, J. H., Michael, R. T., & Michaels, S. (1994). *The social organization of sexuality.* Chicago: University of Chicago Press.

Laumann, E. O., Nicolosi, A., Glasser, D. B., Paik, A., Gingell, C., Moreira, E., et al. (2005). Sexual problems among women and men aged 40–80 y: Prevalence and correlates identified in the global study of sexual attitudes and behaviors. *International Journal of Impotence Research, 17,* 39–57.

Laumann, E. O., Paik, A., & Rosen, R. C. (1999). Sexual dysfunction in the United States: Prevalence and predictors. *Journal of the American Medical Association, 281*(6), 537–544.

Lauril, J. V., Pitkala, K. H., Strandberg, T. E., & Tilvis, R. S. (2004). Detection and documentation of dementia and delirium in acute geriatric wards. *General Hospital Psychiatry, 26,* 31–35.

Lavoie, K. L., Miller, S. B., Conway, M., & Fleet, R. P. (2001). Anger, negative emotions, and cardiovascular reactivity during interpersonal conflict in women. *Journal of Psychosomatic Research, 15,* 503–512.

Law, M., & Tang, J. L. (1995). An analysis of the effectiveness of interventions intended to help people stop smoking. *Archives of Internal Medicine, 155,* 1933–1941.

Lawton, M., Kleban, M. H., Dean, J., & Rajagopal, D. (1992). The factorial generality of brief positive and negative affect measures. *Journals of Gerontology, 47,* P228–P237.

Lazarus, R. S., & Folkman, S. (1984). *Stress, appraisal, and coping.* New York: Springer-Verlag.

Le Couteur, A., Bailey, A., Goode, S., Pickles, A., Robertson, S., Gottesman, I., & Rutter, M. (1996). A broader phenotype of autism: The clinical spectrum in twins. *Journal of Child Psychology and Psychiatry and Allied Disciplines, 37,* 785–801.

le Grange, D., Crosby, R. D., Rathouz, P. J. & Leventhal, B. L. (2007). A randomized controlled comparison of family-based treatment and supportive psychotherapy for adolescent bulimia nervosa. *Archives of General Psychiatry, 64,* 1049–1056.

le Grange, D., & Lock, J. A. (2005). The dearth of psychological treatment studies for anorexia nervosa. *International Journal of Eating Disorders, 37,* 79–91.

Leahy, R. L. (2003). *Cognitive therapy techniques: A practitioner's guide.* New York: Guilford Press.

Lebow, J. L., & Gurman, A. S. (1995). Research assessing couple and family therapy. *Annual Review of Psychology, 46,* 27–57.

Lecci, L., & Cohen, D. (2007). Altered processing of health threat words as a function of hypochondriacal tendencies and experimentally manipulated beliefs. *Cognition and Emotion, 21,* 211–224.

Lechner, S. C., Antoni, M. H., Lydston, D., Laperrier, A., Ishii, M., Devieux, J., Stanley, H., Ironson, G., Schneiderman, N., Brondolo, E., Tobin, J., & Weiss, S. (2003). Cognitive-behavioral interventions improve quality of life in women with AIDS. *Journal of Psychosomatic Research, 54,* 253–261.

Lee, S. S., Lahey, B., Owens, E. B., & Hinshaw, S. P. (2008). Few preschool boys and girls with ADHD are well-adjusted during adolescence. *Journal of Abnormal Child Psychology, 36,* 373–383.

Lee, S., Lee, A. M., Ngai, E., Lee, D. T. S., & Wing, Y. K. (2001). Rationale for food refusal in Chinese patients with anorexia nervosa. *International Journal of Eating Disorders, 29,* 224–229.

Lee, V. E., Brooks-Gunn, J., & Schnur, E. (1988). Does Head Start work? A 1-year follow-up comparison of disadvantaged children attending Head Start, no preschool, and other preschool programs. *Developmental Psychology, 24,* 210–222.

Leenaars, A. A., & Lester, D. (1995). Impact of suicide prevention centers on suicide in Canada. *Crisis, 16,* 39.

Legido, A., Tonyes, L., Carter, D., Schoemaker, A., DiGeorge, A., & Grover, W. D. (1993). Treatment variables and intellectual outcome in children with classic phenylketonuria: A single-center-based study. *Clinical Pediatrics, 32,* 417–425.

Lehman, A. F., Kreyenbuhl, J., Buchanan, R. W., et al. (2004). The Schizophrenia Patient Outcomes Research Team (PORT): Updated treatment recommendations 2003. *Schizophrenia Bulletin, 30,* 193–217.

Lehman, A. F., Steinwachs, D. M., & the survey coinvestigators from the Schizophrenia Patient Outcomes Research Team (PORT) client survey. (1998). Patterns of usual care for schizophrenia: Initial results from the Schizophrenia Patient Outcomes Research Team (PORT) client survey. *Schizophrenia Bulletin, 24,* 11–20.

Lehrer, P. M., & Woolfolk, R. L. (1993). *Principles and practice of stress management* (2nd ed.). New York: Guilford.

Leibenluft, E. (1996). Women with bipolar illness: Clinical and research issues. *American Journal of Psychiatry, 153,* 163–173.

Leibenluft, E., & Rich, B. A. (2008). Pediatric bipolar disorder. *Annual Review of Clinical Psychology, 4,* 163–187.

Leiblum, S. R. (1997). Sexual pain disorders. In G. O. Gabbard & S. D. Atkinson (Eds.), *Synopsis of treatments of psychiatric disorders* (2nd ed., pp. 805–810). Washington, DC: American Psychiatric Press.

Leischow, S. J., Ranger-Moore, J., & Lawrence, D. (2000). Addressing social and cultural disparities in tobacco use. *Addictive Behaviors, 25,* 821–831.

Leit, R. A., Gray, J. J., & Pope, H. G. (2002). The media's presentation of the ideal male body: A cause for muscle dysmorphia? *International Journal of Eating Disorders, 31,* 334–338.

Leit, R. A., Pope, H. G., & Gray, J. J. (2001). Cultural expectations of muscularity in men: The evolution of Playgirl centerfolds. *International Journal of Eating Disorders, 29,* 90–93.

Leitenberg, H., Gross, H., Peterson, H., & Rosen, J. C. (1984). Analysis of an anxiety model in the process of change during exposure plus response prevention treatment of bulimia nervosa. *Behavior Therapy, 15,* 3–20.

Lenzenweger, M. F. (2001). Reaction time slowing during high-load, sustained-attention task performance in relation to psychometrically identified schizotypy. *Journal of Abnormal Psychology, 110,* 290–296.

Lenzenweger, M. F., Dworkin, R. H., & Wethington, E. (1991). Examining the underlying structure of schizophrenic phenomenology: Evidence for a 3-process model. *Schizophrenia Bulletin, 17,* 515–524.

Lenzenweger, M. F., Lane, M. C., Loranger, A. W., & Kessler, R. C. (2007) DSM-IV personality disorders in the national comorbidity survey replication. *Biological Psychiatry, 62,* 553–564.

Leon, A. C., Portera, L., & Weissman, M. M. (1995). The social costs of anxiety disorders. *British Journal of Psychiatry, 166* (Suppl. 27), 19–22.

Leon, G. R., Fulkerson, J. A., Perry, C. L., & Early-Zald, M. B. (1995). Prospective analysis of personality and behavioral vulnerabilities and gender influences in the later development of disordered eating. *Journal of Abnormal Psychology, 104,* 140–149.

Leon, G. R., Fulkerson, J. A., Perry, C. L., Peel, P. K., & Klump, K. L. (1999). Three to four year prospective evaluation of personality and behavioral risk factors for later disordered eating in adolescent girls and boys. *Journal of Youth and Adolescence, 28,* 181–196.

Lerman, C., Caporaso, N. E., Audrain, J., Main, D., Bowman, E. D., et al. (1999). Evidence suggesting the role of specific genetic factors in cigarette smoking. *Health Psychology, 18,* 14–20.

Leslie, D. L., & Rosenheck, R. A. (2004). Incidence of newly diagnosed diabetes attributable to atypical antipsychotic medications. *American Journal of Psychiatry, 161,* 1709–1711.

Lesperance, F, Frasure-Smith, N., Koszycki, D., Laliberte, M., van Zyl, L. T., Baker, B., et al. (2007). Effects of citalopram and interpersonal psychotherapy on depression in patients with coronary artery disease: The Canadian Cardiac Randomized Evaluation of Antidepressant and Psychotherapy Efficacy (CREATE) trial. *Journal of the American Medical Association, 297,* 367–379.

Lester, D. (1991). Do suicide prevention centers prevent suicide? *Homeostasis in Health and Disease, 33,* 190–194.

Lester, D. (1995). Which nations establish suicide prevention centers? *Psychological Reports, 77,* 1298.

Leucht, S., Barnes, T. R. E., Kissling, W., Engel, R. R., Correll, C., & Kane, J. M. (2003). Relapse prevention in schizophrenia with new-generation antipsychotics: A systematic review and exploratory meta-analysis of randomized, controlled trials. *American Journal of Psychiatry, 160,* 1209–1222.

Levav, I., Kohn, R., Golding, J. M., & Weissman, M. M. (1997). Vulnerability of Jews to major depression. *American Journal of Psychiatry, 154,* 941–947.

Levenson, R. W., Carstensen, L. L., & Gottman, J. M. (1994). Influence of age and gender on affect, physiology, and their interrelations: A study of long-term marriages. *Journal of Personality and Social Psychology, 67,* 56–68.

Levenson, R. W., & Miller, B. L. (2007). Loss of cells—Loss of self: Frontotemporal lobar degeneration and human emotion. *Current Directions in Psychological Science, 16,* 289–294.

Levenston, G. K., Patrick, C. J., Bradley, M. M., & Lang, P. J. (2000). The psychopath as observer: Emotion and attention in picture processing. *Journal of Abnormal Psychology, 109,* 373–385.

Leventhal, B. L., Cook, E. H., Morford, M., Ravitz, A. J., Heller, W., & Freedman, D. X. (1993). Clinical and neurochemical effects of fenfluramine in children with autism. *The Journal of Neuropsychiatry and Clinical Neurosciences, 5,* 307–315.

Leverich, G. S., Altshuler, L. L., Frye, M. A., Suppes, T., McElroy, S. L., Keck, P. E., et al. (2006). Risk of switch in mood polarity to hypomania or mania in patients with bipolar depression during acute and continuation trials of venlafaxine, sertraline, and bupropion as adjuncts to mood stabilizers. *American Journal of Psychiatry, 163,* 232–239.

Levine, R., "Risk Management Systems: Understanding the Needs," Information *Strategy—The Executive Journal*, Summer 2004.

Levitan, R. D., Kaplan, A. S., Joffe, R. T., Levitt, A. J., & Brown, G. M. (1997). Hormonal and subjective responses to intravenous meta-chlorophenylpiperazine in bulimia nervosa. *Archives of General Psychiatry, 54,* 521–528.

Levitsky, A., & Perls, F. S. (1970). The rules and games of Gestalt therapy. In J. Fagan & I. L. Shepherd (Eds.), *Gestalt therapy now: Theory, techniques, applications.* Palo Alto, CA: Science & Behavior Books.

Levy, F., Hay, D. A., McStephen, M., Wood, C., & Waldman, I. (1997). Attention-deficit hyperactivity disorder: A category or a continuum? Genetic analysis of a large-scale twin study. *Journal of the American Academy of Child and Adolescent Psychiatry, 36,* 737–744.

Lewinsohn, P. M., & Clarke, G. N. (1999). Psychosocial treatments for adolescent depression. *Clinical Psychology Review, 19*, 329–342.

Lewinsohn, P. M., Joiner, T. E., & Rohde, P. (2001). Evaluation of cognitive diathesis-stress models in predicting major depressive disorder. *Journal of Abnormal Psychology, 110*, 203–215.

Lewinsohn, P. M., Petit, J. W., Joiner, T. E., & Seeley, J. R. (2003). The symptomatic expression of major depressive disorder in adolescents and young adults. *Journal of Abnormal Psychology, 112*, 244–252.

Lewinsohn, P. M., Roberts, R. E., Seeley, J. R., Rohde, P., Gotlib, I. H., & Hops, H. (1994). Adolescent psychopathology: 2. Psychosocial risk factors for depression. *Journal of Abnormal Psychology, 103*, 302–315.

Lewinsohn, P. M., Rohde, P., Seeley, J. R., Klein, D. N., & Gotlib, I. H. (2000). Natural course of adolescent major depressive disorder in a community sample: Predictors of recurrence in young adults. *American Journal of Psychiatry, 157*, 1584–1591.

Lewis, C.M., Levinson, D.F., Wise, L.H., DeLisi, L.E., Straub, R.E., Hovatta, I., et al. (2003). Genome scan meta-analysis of schizophrenia and bipolar disorder: II. Schizophrenia. *American Journal of Human Genetics, 73*, 34–48.

Lewis, D. O., Yeager, C. A., Swica, Y., Pincus, J. H., & Lewis, M. (1997). Objective documentation of child abuse and dissociation on 12 murderers with dissociative identity disorder. *American Journal of Psychiatry, 154*, 1703–1710.

Lewis, S.W., Barnes, T. R. E., Davies, L., Murray, R. M., Dunn, G., et al. (2006). Randomized controlled trial of effect of quality of life of prescription of clozapine vs other second generation antipsychotic drugs in resistant schizophrenia. *Schizophrenia Bulletin, 32*, 715–723.

Li, F., Duncan, T. E., & Hops, H. (2001). Examining developmental trajectories in adolescent alcohol use using piecewise growth mixture modeling analysis. *Journal of Studies on Alcohol, 62*, 199–210.

Liberman, R. P., Eckman, T. A., Kopelowicz, A., & Stolar, D. (2000). *Friendship and intimacy module.* Camarillo, CA: Psychiatric Rehabilitation Consultants, PO Box 2867, Camarillo, CA 93011.

Liberman, R. P., Wallace, C. J., Blackwell, G., Kopelowicz, J. V., et al. (1998). Skills training versus psychosocial occupational therapy for persons with persistent schizophrenia. *American Journal of Psychiatry, 155*, 1087–1091.

Liberto, J. G., Oslin, D. W., & Ruskin, P. E. (1996). Alcoholism in the older population. In L. L. Carstensen, B. A. Edelstein, & L. Dornbrand (Eds.), *The practical handbook of clinical gerontology* (pp. 324–348). Thousand Oaks, CA: Sage.

Lichenstein, P., & Annas, P. (2000). Heritability and prevalence of specific fears and phobias in childhood. *Journal of Child Psychology & Psychiatry & Allied Disciplines, 41*, 927–937.

Liddle, H. A. (1999). Theory development in a family-based therapy for adolescent drug abuse. *Journal of Clinical Child Psychology, 28*, 521–532.

Lieb, R., Meinlschmidt, G., & Araya, R. (2007). Epidemiology of the association between somatoform disorders and anxiety and depressive disorders: An update. *Psychosomatic Medicine, 69*, 860–863.

Lieberman, J. A. (2006). Comparing effectiveness of antipsychotic drugs. *Archives of General Psychiatry, 63*, 1069–1072.

Lieberman, J. A., Stroup, T. S., et al. (2005). Effectiveness of antipsychotic drugs in patients with chronic schizophrenia. *New England Journal of Medicine, 353*, 1209–1223.

Liebowitz, M. R., Heimberg, R. G., Fresco, D. M., Travers, J., & Stein, M. B. (2000). Social phobia or social anxiety disorder: What's in a name? *Archives of General Psychiatry, 57*, 191–192.

Liechti, M. E., Baumann, C., Gamma, A., & Vollenweider, F. X. (2000). Acute psychological effects of 3, 4-methylenedioxymethamphetamine (MDMA, 'Ecstasy') are attenuated by the serotonin uptake inhibitor citalopram. *Neuropsychopharmacology, 22*, 513–521.

Lief, H. I., & Hubschman, L. (1993). Orgasm in the post-operative transsexual. *Archives of Sexual Behavior, 22*, 145–155.

Light, K. C., Dolan, C. A., Davis, M. R., & Sherwood, A. (1992). Cardiovascular responses to an active coping challenge as predictors of blood pressure patterns 10 to 15 years later. *Psychosomatic Medicine, 54*, 217–230.

Lilenfeld, L. R., Kaye, W. H., Greeno, C. G., Merikangas, K. R., Plotnicov, K., et al. (1998). A controlled family study of anorexia nervosa and bulimia nervosa: Psychiatric disorders in first-degree relatives and effects of proband comorbidity. *Archives of General Psychiatry, 55*, 603–610.

Lilenfeld, L. R., Kaye, W. H., Greeno, C. G., Merikangas, K. R., Plotnicov, K., et al. (1999). Psychiatric disorders in women with bulimia nervosa and their first-degree relatives: Effects of comorbid substance dependence. *International Journal of Eating Disorders, 22*, 253–264.

Lilienfeld, S. O. (2007). Psychological treatments that cause harm. *Perspectives on Psychoogical Science, 2*, 53–70.

Lilienfeld, S. O., Lynn, S. J., Kirsch, I., Chaves, J. F., et al. (1999). Dissociative identity disorder and the sociogenic model: Recalling lessons from the past. *Psychological Bulletin, 125*, 507–523.

Lilienfeld, S. O., & Marino, L. (1999). Essentialism revisited: Evolutionary theory and the concept of mental disorder. *Journal of Abnormal Psychology, 108*, 400–411.

Lilienfeld, S. O., Wood, J. M., & Garb, H. N. (2000). The scientific status of projective techniques. *Psychological Science in the Public Interest, 1*, 27–66.

Lilly, R., Quirk, A., Rhodes, T., & Stimson, G. V. (2000). Sociality in methadone treatment: Understanding methadone treatment and service delivery as a social process. *Drugs: Education, Prevention & Policy, 7*, 163–178.

Lim, K. O., Adalsteinssom, E., Spielman, D., Sullivan, E. V., Rosenbloom, M. J., & Pfefferman, A. (1998). Proton magnetic resonance spectroscopic imaging of cortical gray and white matter in schizophrenia. *Archives of General Psychiatry, 55*, 346–353.

Lim, S., & Kim, J. (2005). Cognitive processing of emotional information in depression, panic, and somatoform disorder. *Journal of Abnormal Psychology, 114*, 50–61.

Lindau, S. T., Schumm, L. P., Laumann, E. O., Levinson, W., O'Muircheartaigh, C. A., & Waite, L. J. (2007). A study of sexuality and health among older adults in the United States. *The New England Journal of Medicine, 357*, 762–774.

Lindemann, E., & Finesinger, I. E. (1938). The effect of adrenalin and mecholyl in states of anxiety in psychoneurotic patients. *American Journal of Psychiatry, 95*, 353–370.

Linehan, M. M. (1987). Dialectical behavior therapy for borderline personality disorder. *Bulletin of the Menninger Clinic, 51*, 261–276.

Linehan, M. M. (1993). *Cognitive-behavioral treatment of borderline personality disorder.* New York: Guilford.

Linehan, M. M. (1997). Behavioral treatments of suicidal behaviors: Definitional obfuscation and treatment outcomes. In D. M. Stoff & J. J. Mann (Eds.), *Neurobiology of suicide* (pp. 302–327). New York: Annals of the New York Academy of Sciences.

Linehan, M. M., Armstrong, H. E., Suarez, A., Allmon, D., & Heard, H. L. (1991). Cognitive-behavioral treatment of chronically parasuicidal borderline patients. *Archives of General Psychiatry, 48*, 1060–1064.

Linehan, M. M., Goodstein, J. L., Nielsen, S. L., & Chiles, J. A. (1983). Reasons for staying alive when you are thinking of killing yourself. *Journal of Consulting and Clinical Psychology, 51*, 276–286.

Linehan, M. M., & Heard, H. L. (1999). Borderline personality disorder: Costs, course, and treatment outcomes. In N. E. Miller & K. M. Magruder (Eds.), *Cost-effectiveness of psychotherapy: A guide for practitioners, researchers, and policymakers* (pp. 291–305). London: Oxford University Press.

Linehan, M. M., Heard, H. L., & Armstrong, H. E. (1993). Naturalistic follow-up of a behavioral treatment for chronically parasuicidal borderline patients. *Archives of General Psychiatry, 50*, 971–974.

Linehan, M. M., Schmidt, H., Dimeff, L. A., Craft, J. C., Kanter, J., & Comtois, K. A. (1999). Dialectical behavior therapy for patients with borderline personality disorder and drug-dependence. *American Journal on Addictions, 8*, 279–292.

Linehan, M. M., & Shearin, E. N. (1988). Lethal stress: A social-behavioral model of suicidal behavior. In S. Fisher & J. Reason (Eds.), *Handbook of life stress, cognition, and health.* New York: Wiley.

Link, B., Cullen, F., Frank, J., & Wozniak, J. (1987). The social rejection of former mental patients: Understanding why labels matter. *American Journal of Sociology, 92*, 1401–1500.

Links, P., Steiner, M., Boiago, I., & Irwin, D. (1990). Lithium therapy for borderline patients: Preliminary findings. *Journal of Personality Disorders, 4*, 173–181.

Linnet, K. M., Dalsgaard, S., Obel, C., et al. (2003). Maternal lifestyle factors in pregnancy risk of attention deficit hyperactivity disorder and associated behaviors: Review of the current evidence. *American Journal of Psychiatry, 160*, 1028–1040.

Linney, J. A. (1989). Optimizing research strategies in the schools. In L. A. Bond & B. E. Compas (Eds.), *Primary prevention and promotion in the schools* (pp. 50–76). Newbury Park, CA: Sage.

Liotti, M., Mayberg, H. S., McGinnis, S., Brannan, S. L., & Jerabek, P. (2002). Unmasking disease-specific cerebral blood flow abnormalities: Mood challenge in patients with remitted unipolar depression. *American Journal of Psychiatry, 159*, 1830–1840.

Lipsitz, J. D., Mannuzza, S., Klein, D. F., Ross, D. C., & Fyer, A. J. (1999). Specific phobia 10–16 years after treatment. *Depression and Anxiety, 10*, 105–111.

Litrownik, A. F., & Castillo-Cañez, I. (2000). Childhood maltreatment: Treatment of abuse and incest survivors. In C. R. Snyder & R. E. Ingram (Eds.), *Handbook of psychological change* (pp. 520–545). New York: Wiley.

Litz, B. T., Gray, M. J., Bryant, R. A., & Adler, A. B. (2002). Early intervention for trauma: Current status and future directions. *Clinical Psychology: Science and Practice, 9*, 112–134.

Livesley, W. J., Schroeder, M. L., & Jackson, D. N. (1990). Dependent personality disorder and attachment problems. *Journal of Personality Disorders, 4*, 131–140.

Livingston, G., Johnston, K., Katona, C., Paton, J., & Lyketsos, C. G. (2005). Systematic review of psychological approaches to the management of neuropsychiatric symptoms of dementia. *American Journal of Psychiatry, 162,* 1996–2021.

Livingston, G., Kitchen, G., Manela, M., Katona, C., & Copeland, J. (2001). Persecutory symptoms and perceptual disturbance in a community sample of older people: The Islington study. *International Journal of Geriatric Psychiatry, 16,* 462–468.

Lock, J., & le Grange, D. (2001). Can family-based treatment of anorexia nervosa be manualized? *Journal of Psychotherapy Practice and Research, 10,* 253–261.

Lock, J., le Grange, D., Agras, W. S., & Dare, C. (2001). *Treatment manual for anorexia nervosa: A family-based approach.* New York: Guilford.

Lockwood, K. A., Alexopoulos, G. S., Kakuma, T., & van Gorp, W. G. (2000). Subtypes of cognitive impairment in depressed older adults. *American Journal of Geriatric Psychiatry, 8,* 201–208.

Loeber, R., Burke, J. D., Lahey, B. B., Winters, A., & Zera, M. (2000). Oppositional defiant and conduct disorder: A review of the past 10 years, Part I. *Journal of the American Academy of Child & Adolescent Psychiatry, 39,* 1468–1484.

Loeber, R., & Farrington, D. P. (1998). *Serious and violent juvenile offenders: Risk factors and successful interventions.* Thousand Oaks, CA: Sage.

Loeber, R., & Hay, D. (1997). Key issues in the development of aggression and violence from childhood to early adulthood. *Annual Review of Psychology, 48,* 371–410.

Loeber, R., & Keenan, K. (1994). Interaction between conduct disorder and its comorbid conditions: Effects of age and gender. *Clinical Psychology Review, 14,* 497–523.

Loewenstein, R. J. (1991). Psychogenic amnesia and psychogenic fugue: A comprehensive review. In A. Tasman & S. M. Goldfinger (Eds.), *American Psychiatric Press review of psychiatry* (pp. 189–222). Washington, DC: American Psychiatric Press.

Loftus, E. F. (1993). The reality of repressed memories. *American Psychologist, 48,* 518–537.

Loftus, E. F. (1997). Memory for a past that never was. *Current Directions in Psychological Science, 6,* 60–62.

Logan, T. K., Cole, J., & Leukefeld, C. (2002). Women, sex, and HIV: Social and contextual factors, meta-analysis of published interventions, and implications for practice and research. *Psychological Bulletin, 128,* 851–885.

Lohmueller, K. E., Pearce, C. L., Pike, M., Lander, E. S., & Hirschhorn, J. N. (2003). Meta-analysis of genetic association studies supports a contribution of common variants to susceptibility to common disease. *Nature Genetics, 33,* 177–182.

London, P. (1964). *The modes and morals of psychotherapy.* New York: Holt, Rinehart & Winston.

Lonergan, E., Britton, A. M., & Luxenberg, J. (2007). Antipsychotics for delirium. *Cochrane Database of Systematic Reviews,* (2) doi:10.1002/14651858.

Long, P., Forehand, R., Wierson, M., & Morgan, A. (1994). Does parent training with young noncompliant children have long-term effects? *Behaviour Research and Therapy, 32,* 101–107.

Longshores, D., Urada, D., Evans E., Hser, Y. J., Prendergast, M., Hawken, A. Buch, T., & Ettner, S. (2003). *Evaluation of the Substance Abuse and Crime Prevention Act, 2003 report.* Retrieved from http://www.uclaisap.org/prop36/html/reports.html.

Lonigan, C. J., Phillips, B. M., & Hooe, E. S. (2003). Relations of positive and negative affectivity to anxiety and depression in children: Evidence from a latent variable longitudinal study. *Journal of Consulting and Clinical Psychology, 71,* 465–481.

Looman, J. (1995). Sexual fantasies of child molesters. *Canadian Journal of Behavioural Science, 27,* 321–332.

Looney, S. W., & el-Mallakh, R. S. (1997). Meta-analysis of erythrocyte NA, K-ATPase activity in bipolar illness. *Depression and Anxiety, 5,* 53–65.

Looper, K. J., & Kirmayer, L. J. (2002). Behavioral medicine approaches to somatoform disorders. *Journal of Consulting and Clinical Psychology, 70,* 810–827.

Lopez, S. (2008). *The soloist: A lost dream, an unlikely friendship, and the redemptive power of music.* New York: Putnam.

Lopez, S. R. (1989). Patient variable biases in clinical judgment: Conceptual overview and methodological considerations. *Psychological Bulletin, 106,* 184–203.

Lopez, S. R. (1994). Latinos and the expression of psychopathology: A call for direct assessment of cultural influences. In C. Telles & M. Karno (Eds.), *Latino mental health: Current research and policy perspectives 109–127.* Los Angeles: UCLA.

Lopez, S. R. (1996). Testing ethnic minority children. In B. B. Wolman (Ed.), *The encyclopedia of psychology, psychiatry, and psychoanalysis.* New York: Holt.

Lopez, S. R. (2002). Teaching culturally informed psychological assessment: Conceptual issues and demonstrations. *Journal of Personality Assessment, 79,* 226–234.

Lopez, S. R., Lopez, A. A., & Fong, K. T. (1991). Mexican Americans' initial preferences for counselors: The role of ethnic factors. *Journal of Counseling Psychology, 38,* 487–496.

Lopez, S. R., Nelson, K. A., Snyder, K. S., & Mintz, J. (1999). Attributions and affective reactions of family members and course of schizophrenia. *Journal of Abnormal Psychology, 108,* 307–314.

Lopez-Ibor, J. J., Jr. (2003). Cultural adaptations of current psychiatric classifications: Are they the solution? *Psychopathology, 36,* 114–119.

Lopez Leon, S., Croes, E. A., Sayed-Tabatabaei, F. A., Claes, S., Van Broekhoven, C., & van Duijn, C. M. (2005). The dopamine D4 receptor gene 48-base-pair repeat polymorphism and mood disorders: A meta-analysis. *Biological Psychiatry, 57,* 999–1003.

LoPiccolo, J. (1992). Post-modern sex therapy for erectile failure. In R. C. Rosen & S. R. Leiblum (Eds.), *Erectile failure: Assessment and treatment 171–197.* New York: Guilford.

LoPiccolo, J., & Hogan, D. R. (1979). Multidimensional treatment of sexual dysfunction. In O. F. Pomerleau & J. P. Brady (Eds.), *Behavioral medicine: Theory and practice 174–204.* Baltimore, MD: Williams & Wilkins.

LoPiccolo, J., & Lobitz, W. C. (1972). The role of masturbation in the treatment of orgasmic dysfunction. *Archives of Sexual Behavior, 2,* 163–171.

Lorber, M. F. (2004). Psychophysiology of aggression, psychopathy, and conduct problems: A meta-analysis. *Psychological Bulletin, 130,* 531–552.

Lord, C., Risi, S., DiLavore, P. S., Shulman, C., Thurm, A., & Pickles, A. (2006). Autism from 2 to 9 years of age. *Archives of General Psychiatry, 63,* 694–701.

Lovaas, O. I. (1987). Behavioral treatment and normal educational and intellectual functioning in young autistic children. *Journal of Consulting and Clinical Psychology, 55,* 3–9.

Lovallo, W. R., & Al'Absi, M. (1998). Hemodynamics during rest and behavioral stress in normotensive men at high risk for hypertension. *Psychophysiology, 35,* 47–53.

Luborsky, L., & Spence, D. P. (1978). Quantitative research on psychoanalytic therapy. In S. L. Garfield & A. E. Bergin (Eds.), *Handbook of psychotherapy and behavior change: An empirical analysis* (2nd ed.). New York: Wiley.

Lutgendorf, S., Antoni, M. H., Ironson, G., Klimas, N., Kumar, M., Starr, K., McCabe, P., Cleven, K., Fletcher, M. A., & Schneiderman, N. (1997). Cognitive-behavioral stress management decreases dysphoric mood and herpes simplex virus-type 2 antibody titers in symptomatic HIV-seropositive gay men. *Journal of Consulting and Clinical Psychology, 65,* 31–43.

Lyketsos, C. G., Sheppard, J. M. E., Steele, C. D., Kopunek, S., Steinberg, M., Baker, A. S., et al. (2000). Randomized, placebo-controlled, double-blind clinical trial of sertraline in the treatment of depression complicating Alzheimer's disease: Initial results from the depression in Alzheimer's disease study. *American Journal of Psychiatry, 157,* 1686–1689.

Lykken, D. T. (1957). A study of anxiety in the sociopathic personality. *Journal of Abnormal and Social Psychology, 55,* 6–10.

Lynam, D., & Henry, B. (2001). The role of neuropsychological deficits in conduct disorders. In J. Hill & B. Maughan (Eds.), *Conduct disorders in childhood and adolescence* (pp. 235–263). New York: Cambridge University Press.

Lynam, D., Moffitt, T. E., & Stouthamer-Loeber, M. (1993). Explaining the relation between IQ and delinquency: Race, class, test motivation, school failure, or self-control. *Journal of Abnormal Psychology, 102,* 187–196.

Lynam, D. R., & Widiger, T. A. (2001). Using the five-factor model to represent DSM-IV personality disorders: An expert consensus approach. *Journal of Abnormal Psychology, 110,* 401–412.

Lynch, A., Glod, C. A., & Fitzgerald, F. (2001). Psychopharmacologic treatment of adolescent depression. *Archives of Psychiatric Nursing, 15,* 41–47.

Lynch, J. W., Kaplan, G. A., Cohen, R. D., Tuomilehto, J., & Salonen, J. T. (1996). Do cardiovascular risk factors explain the relation between socioeconomic status, risk of all-cause mortality, cardiovascular mortality, and acute myocardial infarction? *American Journal of Epidemiology, 144,* 934–942.

Lynch, J., Kaplan, G. A., Salonen, R., & Salonen, J. T. (1997). Workplace demands, economic reward, and the progression of atherosclerosis. *Circulation, 96,* 302–307.

Lynch, J., Krause, N., Kaplan, G. A., Tuomilehto, J., & Salonen, J. T. (1997). Workplace conditions, socioeconomic status, and the risk of mortality and acute myocardial infarction. *American Journal of Public Health, 87,* 617–622.

Lynch, T. R., Rosenthal, M. Z., Kosson, D. S., Cheavens, J. S., Lejuez, C. W., & Blair, R. J. R. (2006). Heightened sensitivity to facial expressions of emotion in borderline personality disorder. *Emotion, 6,* 647–655.

Lynn, S. J., Lock, T., Loftus, E. F., Krackow, E., & Lilienfeld, S. O. (2003). The remembrance of things past: Problematic memory recovery techniques in psychotherapy. In S. J. Lynn & S. O. Lilienfeld (Eds.), *Science and pseudoscience in clinical psychology* (pp. 205–239). New York: Guilford.

Lyons, M. J., True, W. R., Eisen, S. A., et al. (1995). Differential heritability of adult and juvenile antisocial traits. *Archives of General Psychiatry, 52,* 906–915.

Ma, S. H., & Teasdale, J. D. (2004). Mindfulness-based cognitive therapy for depression: Replication and exploration of differential relapse prevention effects. *Journal of Consulting and Clinical Psychology, 72,* 31–40.

MacDonald, A. W., III, & Carter, C. S. (2003). Event-related fMRI study of context processing in dorsolateral prefrontal cortex of patients with schizophrenia. *Journal of Abnormal Psychology, 112,* 689–697.

MacDonald, A. W., III, & Chafee, D. (2006). Translational and developmental perspective on *N*-methyl-D-aspartate synaptic deficits in schizophrenia. *Development and Psychopathology, 18,* 853–876.

MacDonald, V. M., Tsiantis, J., Achenbach, T. M., Motti-Stefanidi, F., & Richardson, C. (1995). Competencies and problems reported by parents of Greek and American children, ages 6–11. *European Child and Adolescent Psychiatry, 4,* 1–13.

MacGregor, M. W. (1996). Multiple personality disorder: Etiology, treatment, and techniques from a psychodynamic perspective. *Psychoanalytic Psychology, 13,* 389–402.

Madonna, P. G., Van Scoyk, S., & Jones, D. B. (1991). Family interactions within incest and nonincest families. *American Journal of Psychiatry, 148,* 46–49.

Maffei, C., Fossati, A., Agostini, I., Barraco, A., et al. (1997). Interrater reliability and internal consistency of the Structured Clinical Interview for Axis II Personality Disorders (SCID-II), Version 2.0. *Journal of Personality Disorders, 11,* 279–284.

Mahoney, L. J. (1977). Early diagnosis of breast cancer: The breast self-examination problem. *Progress in Clinical and Biological Research, 12,* 203–206.

Maidment, I., Fox, C., & Boustani, M. (2006). Cholinesterase inhibitors for Parkinson's disease dementia. *Cochrane Database of Systematic Reviews, (1)* Retrieved from http://www.cochrane.org/reviews/en/ab004747.html

Maier, S. F., & Watkins, L. R. (1998). Cytokines for psychologists: Implications of bidirectional immune-to-brain communication for understanding behavior, mood, and cognition. *Psychological Review, 105,* 83–107.

Main, M., Kaplan, K., & Cassidy, J. (1985). Security in infancy, childhood, and adulthood: A move to the level of representation. *Monographs of the Society for Research in Child Development, 50* (1–2, Serial No. 209).

Maj, M., Pirozzi, R., Magliono, L., & Bartoli, L. (1998). Long-term outcome of lithium prophylaxis in bipolar disorder: A 5-year prospective study of 402 patients at a lithium clinic. *American Journal of Psychiatry, 155,* 30–35.

Malamuth, N. M. (1998). An evolutionary-based model integrating research on the characteristics of sexually coercive men. In J. G. Adair & D. Belanger (Eds.), *Advances in psychological science: Vol. 1: Social, personal, and cultural aspects.* (pp. 151–184). Hove, UK: Psychology Press/Erlbaum.

Malamuth, N. M., & Brown, L. M. (1994). Sexually aggressive men's perceptions of women's communications: Testing three explanations. *Journal of Personality and Social Psychology, 67,* 699–712.

Malamuth, N. M., & Check, J. V. P. (1983). Sexual arousal to rape depictions: Individual differences. *Journal of Abnormal Psychology, 92,* 55–67.

Malaspina, D., Goetz, R. R., Yale, S., et al. (2000). Relation of familial schizophrenia to negative symptoms but not to the deficit syndrome. *American Journal of Psychiatry, 157,* 994–1003.

Malcolm, R., Herron, J. E., Anton, R. F., Roberts, J., & Moore, J. (2000). Recurrent detoxification may elevate alcohol craving as measured by the Obsessive Compulsive Drinking scale. *Alcohol, 20,* 181–185.

Maldonado, J. R., Butler, L. D., & Spiegel, D. (1998). Treatments for dissociative disorders. In P. E. Nathan & J. M. Gorman (Eds.), *A guide to treatments that work* (pp. 423–446). New York: Oxford University Press.

Maletzky, B. M. (1993). Factors associated with success and failure in the behavioral and cognitive treatment of sex offenders. *Annals of Sex Research, 6,* 241–258.

Maletzky, B. M. (1997). Exhibitionism: Assessment and treatment. In D. R. Laws & W. O'Donohue (Eds.), *Sexual deviance* (pp. 40–74). New York: Guilford.

Maletzky, B. M. (2000). Exhibitionism. In M. Hersen & M. Biaggio (Eds.), *Effective brief therapy: A clinician's guide* (pp. 235–257). New York: Plenum.

Maletzky, B. M. (2002). The paraphilias: Research and treatment. In P. E. Nathan & J. M. Gorman (Eds.), *A guide to treatments that work* (pp. 525–558). New York: Oxford University Press.

Malik, S., Wong, N. D., Franklin, S. S., Kamath, T. V., L'Italien, G. J., Pio, J. R., & Williams, G. R. (2004). Impact of the metabolic syndrome on mortality from coronary heart disease, cardiovascular disease, and all causes in United States adults. *Circulation, 110,* 1245–1250.

Malizia, A. L. (2003). Brain imaging and anxiety disorders. In D. Nutt & J. Ballenger (Eds.), *Anxiety disorders* (pp. 201–228). Malden, MA: Blackwell.

Malone, K. M., Oquendo, M. A., Haas, G. L., Ellis, S. P., Li, S., & Mann, J. J. (2000). Protective factors against suicidal acts in major depression: Reasons for living. *American Journal of Psychiatry, 157,* 1084–1088.

Malouf, R., & Birks, J. (2004). Donepezil for vascular cognitive impairment. *Cochrane Database of Systematic Reviews, (1)* doi:10.1002/14651858

Mangweth, B., Hausmann, A., Walch, T., Hotter, A., Rupp, C. I., Biebl, W. et al., (2004). Body-fat perception in men with eating disorders. *International Journal of Eating Disorders, 35,* 102–108.

Manji, H. K., Chen, G., Shimon, H., Hsiao, J. K., Potter, W. Z., & Belmaker, R. H. (1995). Guanine nucleotide-binding proteins in bipolar affective disorder: Effects of long-term lithium treatment. *Archives of General Psychiatry, 52,* 135–144.

Mann, J. J., Huang, Y. Y., Underwood, M. D., Kassir, S. A., Oppenheim, S., Kelly, T. M., et al. (2000). A serotonin transporter gene promoter polymorphism (5-HTTLPR) and prefrontal cortical binding in major depression and suicide. *Archives of General Psychiatry, 57,* 729–738.

Mann, V. A., & Brady, S. (1988). Reading disability: The role of language deficiencies. *Journal of Consulting and Clinical Psychology, 56,* 811–816.

Mannuzza, S., Klein, R. G., Bonagura, N., Malloy, P., Giampino, T. L., & Addalli, K. A. (1991). Hyperactive boys almost grown up: 5. Replication of psychiatric status. *Archives of General Psychiatry, 48,* 77–83.

Mannuzza, S., Klein, R. G., & Moulton, J. L. (2003). Does stimulant medication place children at risk for adult substance abuse? A controlled, prospective follow-up study. *Journal of Child and Adolescent Psychopharmacology, 13,* 273–282.

Mansdorf, I. J., Calapai, P., Caselli, L., & Burstein, Y. (1999). Reducing psychotropic medication usage in nursing home residents: The effects of behaviorally oriented psychotherapy. *The Behavior Therapist, 22,* 21–39.

Manuck, S. B., Kaplan, J. R., & Clarkson, T. B. (1983). Behaviorally induced heart rate reactivity and atherosclerosis in cynomolgus monkeys. *Psychosomatic Medicine, 49,* 95–108.

Maramba, G. G., & Nagayama-Hall, G. C. (2002). Meta-analyses of ethnic match as a predictor of dropout, utilization, and level of functioning. *Cultural Diversity and Ethnic Minority Psychology, 8,* 290–297.

Marcantonio, E. R., Flacker, J. M., Wright, R. J., & Resnick, N. M. (2001). Reducing delirium after hip fracture: A randomized trial. *Journal of the American Geriatrics Society, 49,* 516–522.

March, J., Silva, S., Petrycki, S., et al. (2004). Fluoxetine, cognitive-behavioral therapy, and their combination for adolescents with depression: Treatment for adolescents with depression study (TADS) randomized controlled trial. *Journal of the American Medical Association, 292,* 807–820.

Marcus, D. K., Gurley, J. R., Marchi, M. M., & Bauer, C. (2007). Cognitive and perceptual variables in hypochondriasis and health anxiety: A systematic review. *Clinical Psychology Review, 27,* 127–139.

Marcus, J., Hans, S. L., Nagier, S., Auerbach, J. G., Mirsky, A. F., & Aubrey, A. (1987). Review of the NIMH Israeli kibbutz-city and the Jerusalem infant development study. *Schizophrenia Bulletin, 13,* 425–438.

Marder, S. R., Wirshing, W. C., Glynn, S. M., Wirshing, D. A., Mintz, J., & Liberman, R. P. (1999). Risperidone and haloperidol in maintenance treatment: Interactions with psychosocial treatments. *Schizophrenia Research, 36,* 288.

Marengo, J., & Westermeyer, J. F. (1996). Schizophrenia and delusional disorder. In L. L. Carstensen, B. A. Edelstein, & L. Dornbrand (Eds.), *The practical handbook of clinical gerontology* (pp. 255–273). Thousand Oaks, CA: Sage.

Margraf, J., Ehlers, A., & Roth, W. T. (1986). Sodium lactate infusions and panic attacks: A review and critique. *Psychosomatic Medicine, 48,* 23–51.

Markman, H. J., Floyd, F. J., Stanley, S. M., & Storaasli, R. D. (1988). Prevention of marital distress: A longitudinal investigation. *Journal of Consulting and Clinical Psychology, 56,* 210–217.

Markowitz, J. C. (1994). Psychotherapy of dysthymia. *American Journal of Psychiatry, 151,* 1114–1121.

Marks, I. M. (1995). Advances in behavioral-cognitive therapy of social phobia. *Journal of Clinical Psychiatry, 56,* 25–31.

Marks, I., Lovell, K., Noshirvani, H., Livanou, M., & Thrasher, S. (1998). Treatment of posttraumatic stress disorder by exposure and/or cognitive restructuring: A controlled study. *Archives of General Psychiatry, 55,* 317.

Markus, M.L. *Systems in Organizations.* Pitman, Marshfield. Mass., 1984.

Marlatt, G. A. (1983). The controlled drinking controversy: A commentary. *American Psychologist, 38,* 1097–1110.

Marlatt, G. A., & Gordon, J. R. (Eds.). (1985). *Relapse prevention: Maintenance strategies in the treatment of addictive behaviors.* New York: Guilford.

Marlowe, D. H. (2001). *Psychological and psychosocial consequences of combat and deployment: With special emphasis on the Gulf War.* Santa Monica, CA: RAND.

Marmar, C., & Horowitz, M. J. (1988). Diagnosis and phase-oriented treatment of post-traumatic stress disorders. In J. Wilson (Ed.), *Human adaptation to extreme stress: From the Holocaust to Vietnam.* New York: Brunner/Mazel.

Marmot, M. G., Bosma, H., Hemingway, H., Brunner, E., & Stansfeld, S. (1997). Contribution of job control and other risk factors to social variations in coronary heart disease incidence. *Lancet, 350,* 235–239.

Marques, J. K., Day, D. M., Nelson, C., & West, M. A. (1994). Effects of cognitive-behavioral treatment on sex offender recidivism: Preliminary results of a longitudinal study. *Criminal Justice and Behavior, 21*(1), 28–54.

Marrazzi, M. A., & Luby, E. D. (1986). An auto-addiction model of chronic anorexia nervosa. *International Journal of Eating Disorders, 5,* 191–208.

Marsh, A. A., & Blair, R. J. R. (2008). Deficits in facial affect recognition among antisocial populations: A meta-analysis. *Neuroscience and Biobehavioral Reviews, 32,* 454–465.

Marshall, L. A., & Cooke, D. J. (1999). The childhood experiences of psychopaths: A retrospective study of familial and societal factors. *Journal of Personality Disorders, 13,* 211–225.

Marshall, W. L. (1997). Pedophilia: Psychopathology and theory. In D. R. Laws & W. O'Donohue (Eds.), *Sexual deviance* (pp. 152–174). New York: Guilford.

Marshall, W. L., Barbaree, H. E., & Christophe, D. (1986). Sexual offenders against female children: Sexual preferences for age of victims and type of behaviour. *Canadian Journal of Behavioural Science, 18,* 424–439.

Marshall, W. L., Serran, G. A., & Cortoni, F. A. (2000). Childhood attachments, sexual abuse, and their relationship to adult coping in child molesters. *Sexual Abuse: A Journal of Research and Treatment, 12,* 17–26.

Marson, D. C. (2001). Loss of competency in Alzheimer's disease: Conceptual and psychometric approaches. *International Journal of Law and Psychiatry, 24,* 267–283.

Marson, D. C., Huthwaite, J. S., & Hebert, K. (2004). Testamentary capacity and undue influence in the elderly: A jurisprudent therapy perspective. *Law and Psychology Review, 28,* 71–96.

Martell, C. R., Addis, M. E., & Jacobson, N. S. (Eds.). (2001). *Ending depression one step at a time: The new behavioral activation approach to getting your life back.* New York: Oxford University Press.

Martin, D. J., Garske, J. P., & Davis, M. K. (2000). Relation of the therapeutic alliance with outcome and other variables: A meta-analytic review. *Journal of Consulting and Clinical Psychology, 68,* 438–450.

Martinez, C., & Eddy, M. (2005). Effects of culturally adapted parent management training on Latino youth behavioral health outcomes. *Journal of Consulting and Clinical Psychology, 73,* 841–851.

Martini, D. R., Ryan, C., Nakayama, D., & Ramenofsky, M. (1990). Psychiatric sequelae after traumatic injury: The Pittsburgh regatta accident. *Journal of the American Academy of Child and Adolescent Psychiatry, 29,* 70–75.

Mason, B. J. (2001). Treatment of alcohol-dependent outpatients with acamprosate: A clinical review. *Journal of Clinical Psychiatry, 62,* 42–48.

Mason, F. L. (1997). Fetishism: Psychopathology and theory. In D. R. Laws & W. O'Donohue (Eds.), *Sexual deviance* (pp. 75–91). New York: Guilford.

Masters, W. H., & Johnson, V. E. (1966). *Human sexual response.* Boston: Little, Brown.

Masters, W. H., & Johnson, V. E. (1970). *Human sexual inadequacy.* Boston: Little, Brown.

Mather, M., Canli, T., English, T., Whitfield, S., Wais, P., Ochsner, K., Gabrieli, J. D. E., & Carstensen, L. L. (2004). Amygdala responses to emotionally valenced stimuli in older and younger adults. *Psychological Science, 15,* 259–263.

Mathews, A., & MacLeod, C. (2002). Induced processing biases have causal effects on anxiety. *Cognition and Emotion, 16,* 331–354.

Matsuda, L. A., Lolait, S. J., Brownstein, M. J., Young, A. C., & Bonner, T. I. (1990). Structure of a cannabinoid receptor and functional expression of the cloned cDNA. *Nature, 346,* 561–564.

Matt, G. E., Vazquez, C., & Campbell, W. K. (1992). Mood-congruent recall of affectively toned stimuli: A metaanalytic review. *Clinical Psychology Review, 12,* 227–255.

Matthews, K. A., Owens, J. F., Kuller, L. H., Sutton-Tyrrell, K., & Jansen-McWilliams, L. (1998). Are hostility and anxiety associated with carotid atherosclerosis in health postmenopausal women? *Psychosomatic Medicine, 60,* 633–638.

Maugh, T. H., II. (2002, October 18). "Sobering" state report calls autism an epidemic. *Los Angeles Times,* pp. A1, A25.

Mayer, E. A., Berman, S., Suyenobu, B., Labus, J., Mandelkern, M. A., Naliboff, B. D., et al. (2005). Differences in brain responses to visceral pain between patients with irritable bowel syndrome and ulcerative colitis. *Pain, 115,* 398–409.

Mays, V., Cochran, S., & Barnes, N. W. (2007). Race, race-based discrimination, and health outcomes among African Americans. *Annual Review of Psychology, 58,* 201–225.

Mayne, T. J. (2001). Emotions and health. In T. J. Mayne & G. A. Bonanno (Eds.), *Emotions: Current issues and future directions* (pp. 361–397). New York: Guilford.

Mayou, R., Kirmayer, L. J., Simon, G., Kroenke, K., & Sharpe, M. (2005). Somatoform disorders: Time for a new approach in DSM-V. *American Journal of Psychiatry, 162,* 847–855.

McBride, P. A., Anderson, G. M., & Shapiro, T. (1996). Autism research: Bringing together approaches to pull apart the disorder. *Archives of General Psychiatry, 53,* 980–983.

McCabe, R. E., McFarlane, T., Polivy, J., & Olmsted, M. (2001). Eating disorders, dieting, and the accuracy of self-reported weight. *International Journal of Eating Disorders, 29,* 59–64.

McCann, D., Barrett, A., Cooper, A., et al. (2007). Food additives and hyperactive behaviour in 3-year-old and 8/9-year-old children in the community: A randomised, double-blinded, placebo-controlled trial. *Lancet, 370,* 1560–1567.

McCarthy, B. W. (1986). A cognitive-behavioral approach to understanding and treating sexual trauma. *Journal of Sex and Marital Therapy, 12,* 322–329.

McCarty, D., Caspi, Y., Panas, L., Krakow, M., & Mulligan, D. H. (2000). Detoxification centers: Who's in the revolving door? *Journal of Behavioral Health Services & Research, 27,* 245–256.

McCarthy, D. E., Piasecki, T. M., Fiore, M. C., & Baker, T. (2006). Life before and after quitting smoking: An electronic diary study. *Journal of Abnormal Psychology, 115,* 454–466.

McClellan, J., Kowatch, R., & Findling, R. L. (2007). Practice parameter for the assessment and treatment of children and adolescents with bipolar disorder. *Journal of the American Academy of Child and Adolescent Psychiatry, 46,* 107–125.

McConaghy, N. (1993). *Sexual behavior: Problems and management.* New York: Plenum.

McConaghy, N. (1994). Paraphilias and gender identity disorders. In M. Hersen & R. T. Ammerman (Eds.), *Handbook of prescriptive treatments for adults* (pp. 317–346). New York: Plenum.

McCormick, N. B. (1999). When pleasure causes pain: Living with interstitial cystitis. *Sexuality and Disability, 17,* 7–18.

McCrady, B. S., & Epstein, E. E. (1995). Directions for research on alcoholic relationships: Marital and individual-based models of heterogeneity. *Psychology of Addictive Behaviors, 9,* 157–166.

McCrae, R. R., & Costa, P. T., Jr. (1990). *Personality in adulthood.* New York: Guilford.

McCusker, J., Cole, M., & Abrahamowicz, M. (2002). Delirium predicts 12-month mortality. *Archives of Internal Medicine, 162,* 457–463.

McDonough, M., & Kennedy, N. (2002). Pharmacological management of obsessive-compulsive disorder: A review for clinicians. *Harvard Review of Psychiatry, 10,* 127–137.

McEachin, J. J., Smith, T., & Lovaas, O. I. (1993). Long-term outcome for children with autism who received early intensive behavioral treatment. *American Journal on Mental Retardation, 97,* 359–372.

McEvoy, J. P., Johnson, J., Perkins, D., Lieberman, J. A., Hamer, R. M., Keefe, R. S. E., et al. (2006). Insight in first episode psychosis. *Psychological Medicine, 36,* 1385–1393.

McEwen, B. S., & Seeman, T. (1999). Protective and damaging effects of the mediators of stress: Elaborating the concepts of allostasis and allostatic load. In N. E. Adler, M. Marmot, B. E. McEwen, & J. Stewart (Eds.), *Socioeconomic status and health in industrial nations: Social, psychological, and biological pathways* (pp. 30–47). New York: New York Academy of Sciences.

McFall, R. M., & Hammen, C. L. (1971). Motivation, structure, and self-monitoring: Role of nonspecific factors in smoking reduction. *Journal of Consulting and Clinical Psychology, 37,* 80–86.

McFarlane, T., Polivy, J., & Herman, C. P. (1998). Effects of false weight feedback on mood, self-evaluation, and food intake in restrained and unrestrained eaters. *Journal of Abnormal Psychology, 107,* 312–318.

McFarlane, W. R., Dixon, L., Lukens, E., & Lucksted, A. (2003). Family psychoeducation and schizophrenia: A review of the literature. *Journal of Marital and Family Therapy, 29,* 223–245.

McFarlane, W. R., Lukens, E., Link, B., Dushay, R., Deakins, S., Newmark, M., Dunne, E. J., Horen, B., & Toran, J. (1995). Multiple-family groups and psychoeducation in the treatment of schizophrenia. *Archives of General Psychiatry, 52,* 679–687.

McGhie, A., & Chapman, I. S. (1961). Disorders of attention and perception in early schizophrenia. *British Journal of Medical Psychology, 34,* 103–116.

McGlashan, T. H., Grilo, C. M., Skodol, A. E., Gunderson, J. G., Shea, M. T., Morey, L. C., et al. (2000). The collaborative longitudinal personality disorders study: Baseline Axis I/II and II/II diagnostic co-occurrence. *Acta Psychiatrica Scandinavica, 102,* 256–264.

McGlashan, T. H., & Hoffman, R. E. (2000). Schizophrenia as a disorder of developmentally reduced synaptic connectivity. *Archives of General Psychiatry, 57,* 637–648.

McGovern, C.W., & Sigman, M. (2005). Continuity and change from early childhood to adolescence in autism. *Journal of Child Psychology and Psychiatry, 46,* 401–408.

McGue, M., Pickens, R. W., & Svikis, D. S. (1992). Sex and age effects on the inheritance of alcohol problems: A twin study. *Journal of Abnormal Psychology, 101,* 3–17.

McGuire, P. K., Bench, C. J., Frith, C. D., & Marks, I. M. (1994). Functional anatomy of obsessive-compulsive phenomena. *British Journal of Psychiatry, 164,* 459–468.

McGuire, P. K., Shah, G. M. S., & Murray, R. M. (1993). Increased blood flow in Broca's area during auditory hallucinations in schizophrenia. *Lancet, 346,* 596–600.

McGuire, P. K., Silbersweig, D. A., & Frith, C. D. (1996). Functional neuroanatomy of verbal self-monitoring. *Brain, 119,* 907–917.

McIntosh, J. L. (1995). Suicide prevention in the elderly (age 65–99). *Suicide and Life Threatening Behavior, 25,* 180–192.

McIntyre-Kingsolver, K., Lichtenstein, E., & Mermelstein, R. J. (1986). Spouse training in a multicomponent smoking-cessation program. *Behavior Therapy, 17,* 67–74.

McKeith, I. G., Dickson, D. W., Lowe, J., Emre, M., O'Brien, J. T., Feldman, H., et al. (2005). Diagnosis and management of dementia with Lewy bodies; third report of the DLB consortium. *Neurology, 65,* 1863–1872.

McKeller, J., Stewart, E., & Humphreys, K. (2003). Alcoholics Anonymous involvement and positive alcohol-related outcomes: Cause, consequence, or just a correlate? A prospective 2-year study of 2,319 alcohol dependent men. *Journal of Consulting and Clinical Psychology, 71,* 302–308.

McKendree-Smith, N. L., Floyd, M., & Scogin, F. R. (2003). Self-administered treatments for depression: A review. *Journal of Clinical Psychology, 59,* 275–288.

McKim, W. A. (1991). *Drugs and behavior: An introduction to behavioral pharmacology.* Englewood Cliffs, NJ: Prentice-Hall.

McKinley, N. M., & Hyde, J. S. (1996). The objectified body consciousness scale: Development and validation. *Psychology of Women Quarterly, 20,* 181–216.

McKown, C., & Weinstein, R. S. (2003). The development and consequences of stereotype consciousness in middle childhood. *Child Development, 74,* 498–515.

McMullen, S., & Rosen, R. C. (1979). Self-administered masturbation training in the treatment of primary orgasmic dysfunction. *Journal of Consulting and Clinical Psychology, 47,* 912–918.

McNally, R. J. (1987). Preparedness and phobias: A review. *Psychological Bulletin, 101,* 283–303.

McNally, R. J. (1997). Atypical phobias. In G. C. L. Davey (Ed.), *Phobias: A handbook of theory, research and treatment* (pp. 183–199). Chichester, UK: Wiley.

McNally, R. J. (2003). *Remembering trauma.* Cambridge, MA: Belknap Press of Harvard University Press.

McNally, R. J., Caspi, S. P., Riemann, B. C., & Zeitlin, S. B. (1990). Selective processing of threat cues in posttraumatic stress disorder. *Journal of Abnormal Psychology, 99,* 398–406.

McNally, R. J., Clancy, S. A., Barrett, H. M., & Parker, H. A. (2004). Inhibiting retrieval of trauma cues in adults reporting histories of childhood sexual abuse. *Cognition and Emotion, 18,* 479–493.

McNally, R. J., Caspi, S. P., Riemann, B. C., & Zeitlin, S. B. (1990). Selective processing of threat cues in posttraumatic stress disorder. *Journal of Abnormal Psychology, 99,* 398–402.

McNally, R. J., Lasko, N. B., Clancy, S. A., Macklin, M. L., Pitman, R. K., & Orr, S. P. (2004). Psychophysiological responding during script-driven imagery in people reporting abduction by space aliens. *Psychological Science, 15,* 493–497.

McNally, R. J., Ristuccia, C. S., & Perlman, C. A. (2005). Forgetting trauma cues in adults reporting continuous or recovered memories of childhood sexual abuse. *Psychological Science, 16,* 336–340.

McNeil, T. F., Cantor-Graae, E., & Weinberger, D. R. (2000). Relationship of obstetric complications and differences in size of brain structures in monozygotic twin pairs discordant for schizophrenia. *American Journal of Psychiatry, 157,* 203–212.

Meagher, D. J. (2001). Delirium: Optimizing management. *British Medical Journal, 322,* 144–149.

Meagher, D. J., Moran, M., Raju, B., Gibbons, D., & Donnelly, S. (2007). Phenomenology of delirium: Assessment of 100 adult cases using standardised measures. *British Journal of Psychiatry, 190,* 135–141.

Meana, M., Binik, I., Khalife, S., & Cohen, D. (1997). Dyspareunia: Sexual dysfunction or pain syndrome? *Journal of Nervous and Mental Disease, 185,* 561–569.

Meana, M., Binik, I., Khalife, S., & Cohen, D. (1998). Affect and marital adjustment in women's ratings of dyspareunic pain. *Canadian Journal of Psychiatry, 43,* 381–385.

Meaney, M. J., Brake, W., & Gratton, A. (2002). Environmental regulation of the development of mesolimbic dopamine systems: A neurobiological mechanism for vulnerability to drug abuse? *Psychoneuroendocrinology, 27,* 127–148.

Mednick, S. A., Huttonen, M. O., & Machon, R. A. (1994). Prenatal influenza infections and adult schizophrenia. *Schizophrenia Bulletin, 20,* 263–268.

Mednick, S. A., Machon, R., Hottunen, M. O., & Bonett, D. (1988). Fetal viral infection and adult schizophrenia. *Archives of General Psychiatry, 45,* 189–192.

Mednick, S. A., & Schulsinger, F. (1968). Some premorbid characteristics related to breakdown in children with schizophrenic mothers. In D. Rosenthal & S. S. Kety (Eds.), *The transmission of schizophrenia.* Elmsford, NY: Pergamon.

Medvedev, Z. (1972). *A question of madness.* New York: Knopf.

Meeks, S., & Murrell, S. A. (1997). Mental illness in late life: Socioeconomic conditions, psychiatric symptoms, and adjustment of long term sufferers. *Psychology and Aging, 12,* 296–308.

Meier, B. (2003). *Pain killer: A "wonder" drug's trail of addiction and death.* Emmaus, PA: Rodale Books.

Meier, D. E., Emmons, C. A., Wallenstein, S., Quill, T., Morrison, R. S., & Cassel, C. K. (1998). A national survey of physician-assisted suicide and euthanasia in the United States. *New England Journal of Medicine, 338,* 1193–1201.

Melamed, B. G., & Siegel, L. J. (1975). Reduction of anxiety in children facing hospitalization and surgery by use of filmed modeling. *Journal of Consulting and Clinical Psychology, 43,* 511–521.

Mellinger, G. D., Balter, M. B., & Uhlenhuth, E. H. (1985). Insomnia and its treatment. *Archives of General Psychiatry, 42,* 225–232.

Melnick, S. M., & Hinshaw, S. P. (1996). What they want and what they get: The social goals of boys with ADHD and comparison boys. *Journal of Abnormal Child Psychology, 24,* 169–185.

Meltzer, H. Y. (2003). Suicide in schizophrenia. *Journal of Clinical Psychiatry, 64,* 1122–1125.

Meltzer, H. Y., Cola, P., & Way, L. E. (1993). Cost effectiveness of clozapine in neuroleptic-resistant schizophrenia. *American Journal of Psychiatry, 150,* 1630–1638.

Melville, J. D., & Naimark, D. (2002). Punishing the insane: The verdict of guilty but mentally ill. *Journal of the American Academy of Psychiatry and the Law, 30,* 553–555.

Menezes, N. M., Arenovich, T., & Zipursky, R. B. (2006). A systematic review of longitudinal outcome studies of first-episode psychosis. *Psychological Medicine, 36,* 1349–1362.

Mennin, D. S., Heimberg, R. G., & Turk, C. L. (2004). Clinical presentation and diagnostic features. In R. G. Heimberg, C. L. Turk, & D. S. Mennin (Eds.), *Generalized anxiety disorder* (pp. 3–28). New York: Guilford.

Mennin, D. S., Heimberg, R. G., Turk, C. L., & Fresco, D. M. (2002). Applying an emotion regulation framework to integrative approaches to generalized anxiety disorder. *Clinical Psychology: Science and Practice, 9,* 135–141.

Menting, J., Honig, A., Verhey, F., & Hartmans, M. (1996). Selective serotonin reuptake inhibitors (SSRIs) in the treatment of elderly depressed patients: A qualitative analysis of the literature on their efficacy and side-effects. *International Clinical Psychopharmacology, 11,* 165–175.

Menzies, R. G., & Clarke, J. C. (1995). The etiology of phobias: A nonassociative account. *Clinical Psychology Review, 15,* 23–48.

Merckelbach, H., Dekkers, T., Wessel, I., & Roefs, A. (2003). Dissociative symptoms and amnesia in Dutch concentration camp survivors. *Comprehensive Psychiatry, 44,* 65–69.

Merikangas, K. R., Stolar, M., Stevens, D. E., Goulet, J., Preisig, M. A., et al. (1998). Familial transmission of substance use disorders. *Archives of General Psychiatry, 55,* 973–981.

Merzenich, M. M., Jenkins, W. M., Johnson, P., Schreiner, C., Miller, S. L., & Tallal, P. (1996). Temporal processing deficits of language-learning impaired children ameliorated by training. *Science, 271,* 77–81.

Meston, C. M., & Gorzalka, B. B. (1996). The effects of sympathetic activation on physiological and subjective sexual arousal in women. *Behaviour Research and Therapy, 33,* 651–664.

Metz, M. E., Pryor, J. L., Nesvacil, L. J., Abuzzahab, F., et al. (1997). Premature ejaculation: A psychophysiological review. *Journal of Sex and Marital Therapy, 23,* 3–23.

Meyer, G. J., & Archer, R. P. (2001). The hard science of Rorschach research: What do we know and where do we go? *Psychological Assessment, 13,* 486–502.

Meyer, J. K. (1995). Paraphilias. In H. I. Kaplan & B. J. Sadock (Eds.), *Comprehensive textbook of psychiatry* (pp. 1334–1347). Baltimore, MD: Williams & Wilkins.

Meyer, V. (1966). Modification of expectations in cases with obsessional rituals. *Behaviour Research and Therapy, 4,* 273–280.

Meyer, V., & Chesser, E. S. (1970). *Behavior therapy in clinical psychiatry.* Baltimore, MD: Penguin.

Meyer, W., Bockting, W., Cohen-Kettenis, P., Coleman, E., Di Ceglie, D., Devor, H., et al. (2001). The standards of care for gender identity disorders—[Sixth Version]. *The International Journal of Transgenderism, 5.* Retrieved from http://www.symposion.com/ijt/soc_2001/index.htm.

Meyerhoefer, C. D. & Zuvekas, S. H. (2008). The Shape of Demand: What Does It Tell Us about Direct-to-Consumer Marketing of Antidepressants? The B.E. Journal of Economic Analysis & Policy Advances, 8, Article 4.).

Meyerowitz, B. E., & Chaiken, S. (1987). The effect of message framing on breast self-examination attitudes, intentions, and behavior. *Journal of Personality and Social Psychology, 52,* 500–510.

Meyerowitz, B. E., Richardson, J., Hudson, S., & Leedham, B. (1998). Ethnicity and cancer outcomes: Behavioral and psychosocial considerations. *Psychological Bulletin, 123,* 47–70.

Micallef, J., & Blin, O. (2001). Neurobiology and clinical pharmacology of obsessive-compulsive disorder. *Clinical Neuropharmacology, 24,* 191–207.

Micheal, T., Blechert, J., Vriends, N., Margraf, J., & Wilhelm, F. H. (2007). Fear conditioning in panic disorder: Enhanced resistance to extinction. *Journal of Abnormal Psychology, 116,* 612–617.

Mikami, A. Y., Huang-Pollack, C. L., Pfiffner, L. J., McBurnett, K., & Hangai, D. (2007). Social skills differences among attention-deficit/hyperactivity disorder types in a chat room assessment task. *Journal of Abnormal Child Psychology, 35,* 509–521.

Miklowitz, D. J. (1985). *Family interaction and illness outcome in bipolar and schizophrenic patients.* Unpublished doctoral dissertation, University of California at Los Angeles.

Miklowitz, D. J., George, E. L., Richards, J. A., Simoneau, T. L., & Suddath, R. L. (2003). A randomized study of family-focused psychoeducation and pharmacotherapy in the outpatient management of bipolar disorder. *Archives of General Psychiatry, 60,* 904–912.

Miklowitz, D. J., & Goldstein, M. J. (1997). *Bipolar disorder: A family-focused treatment approach.* New York: Guilford.

Miklowitz, D. J., Otto, M. W., Frank, E., Reilly-Harrington, N. A., Wisniewski, S. R., Kogan, J. N., et al. (2007). Psychosocial treatments for bipolar depression: A 1-year randomized trial from the systematic treatment enhancement program. *Archives of General Psychiatry, 64,* 419–427.

Miklowitz, D. J., Simoneau, T. L., Sachs-Ericsson, N., Warner, R., & Suddath, R. (1996). Family risk indicators in the course of bipolar affective disorder. In E. Mundt et al. (Eds.), *Interpersonal factors in the origin and course of affective disorders* (pp. 204–217). London: Gaskell.

Miklowitz, D. J., & Taylor, D. O. (2005). Family-focused treatment of the suicidal bipolar patient. Unpublished manuscript.

Milberger, S., Biederman, J., Faraone, S. V., & Chen, L. (1996). Is maternal smoking during pregnancy a risk factor for attention deficit hyperactivity disorder in children? *American Journal of Psychiatry, 153,* 1138–1142.

Miller, B. D., & Wood, B. L. (1994). Psychophysiologic reactivity in asthmatic children: A cholinergically mediated confluence of pathways. *Journal of the American Academy of Adolescent Psychiatry, 33,* 1236–1245.

Miller, B. L., Ikonte, C., Ponton, M., & Levy, M. (1997). A study of the Lund Manchester research criteria for frontotemporal dementia: Clinical and single-photon emission CT correlations. *Neurology, 48,* 937–942.

Miller, G. E., Chen, E., & Zhou, E. S. (2007). If it goes up, must it come down? Chronic stress and the hypothalamic-pituitary-adrenocortical axis in humans. *Psychological Bulletin, 133,* 25–45.

Miller, M. A., & Rahe, R. H. (1997). Life changes scaling for the 1990s. *Journal of Psychosomatic Research, 13,* 279–292.

Miller, T. Q., & Volk, R. J. (1996). Weekly marijuana use as a risk factor for initial cocaine use: Results from a six wave national survey. *Journal of Child and Adolescent Substance Abuse, 5,* 55–78.

Miller, W. R., & Rollnick, S. (Eds.). (1991). *Motivational interviewing: Preparing people to change addictive behavior.* New York: Guilford.

Millon, T. (1996). *Disorders of personality: DSM-IV and beyond* (2nd ed.). New York: Wiley.

Milrod, B., Leon, A. C., Busch, F., Rudden, M., Schwalberg, M., Clarkin, J., et al. (2007). A randomized controlled clinical trial of psychoanalytic psychotherapy for panic disorder. *American Journal of Psychiatry, 164,* 265–272.

Mineka, S., & Öhman, A. (2002). Born to fear: Nonassociative vs. associative factors in the etiology of phobias. *Behaviour Research and Therapy, 40,* 173–184.

Mineka, S., & Sutton, J. (2006). Contemporary learning theory perspectives on the etiology of fear and phobias. In M. G. Craske, D. Hermans, & D. Vansteenwegen (Eds.), *Fear and learning: From basic processes to clinical implications* (pp. 75–97). Washington, DC: American Psychological Association.

Mineka, S., Watson, D., & Clark, L. A. (1998). Comorbidity of anxiety and unipolar mood disorders. *Annual Review of Psychology, 49,* 377–412.

Mineka, S., & Zinbarg, R. (1998). Experimental approaches to the anxiety and mood disorders. In J. G. Adair, D. Belanger, & K. L. Dion (Eds.), *Advances in psychological science: Vol. 1. Social, personal, and cultural aspects* (429–454). Hove, UK: Psychology Press/Erlbaum, Taylor & Francis.

Mineka, S., & Zinbarg, R. (2006). A contemporaty learning theory perspective on the etiology of anxiety disorders: It's not what you thought it was. *American Psychologist, 61,* 10–26.

Miranda, J., Bernal, G., Lau, A., Kohn, L., Hwang, W., & LaFromboise, T. (2005). State of the science on psychosocial interventions for ethnic minorities. *Annual Review of Psychology, 1,* 113–142.

Miranda, J., Green, B. L., Krupnick, J. L., Chung, J., Siddique, J., Belin, T., et al. (2006). One-year outcomes of a randomized clinical trial treating depression in low-income minority women. *Journal of Consulting and Clinical Psychology, 74,* 99–111.

Mishkind, M. E., Rodin, J., Silberstein, L. R., & Striegel-Moore, R. H. (1986). The embodiment of masculinity: Cultural, psychological, and behavioral dimensions. *American Behavioral Scientist, 29,* 545–562.

Mitchell, J. E. (1992). Subtyping of bulimia nervosa. *International Journal of Eating Disorders, 11,* 327–332.

Mitchell, J. T., & Everly, G. S., Jr. (2000). Critical incident stress management and critical incident stress debriefings: Evolutions, effects and outcomes. In J. P. Wilson & B. Raphael (Eds.), *Psychological debriefing: Theory, practice and evidence* (pp. 71–90). New York: Cambridge University Press.

Mitte, K. (2005). Meta-analysis of cognitive-behavioral treatments for generalized anxiety disorder: A comparison with pharmacotherapy. *Psychological Bulletin, 131,* 785–795.

Mittleman, M. A., Maclure, M., Sherwood, J. B., Murly, R. P., Tofler, G. A., et al. (1997). Triggering of acute myocardial infarction onset by episodes of anger. *Circulation, 92,* 1720–1725.

Modestin, J. (1992). Multiple personality disorder in Switzerland. *American Journal of Psychiatry, 149,* 88–92.

Moene, F. C., Landberg, E. H., Hoogduin, K. A., et al. (2000). Organic syndromes diagnosed as conversion disorder: Identification and frequency in a study of 85 patients. *Journal of Psychosomatic Research, 49,* 7–12.

Moffitt, T. E. (1993). Adolescence-limited and life-course-persistent antisocial behavior: A developmental taxonomy. *Psychological Review, 100,* 674–701.

Moffitt, T. E. (2005). The new look of behavioral genetics in developmental psychopathology: Gene–environment interplay in antisocial behaviors. *Psychological Bulletin, 131,* 533–554.

Moffitt, T. E. (2006). Life-course-persistent versus adolescent-limited antisocial behavior. In D. Cicchetti & D. Cohen (Eds.), *Developmental psychopathology* (2nd ed., pp. 570–598). New York: Wiley.

Moffitt, T. E. (2007). A review of research on the taxonomy of life-course persistent versus adolescence-limited antisocial behavior. In D. J. Flannery, A. T. Vazsonyi, & I. D. Waldman (Eds.), *The Cambridge handbook of violent behavior and aggression* (pp. 49–74). New York: Cambridge University Press.

Moffitt, T. E., & Caspi, A. (2001). Childhood predictors differentiate life-course persistent and adolescence-limited antisocial pathways among males and females. *Development and Psychopathology, 13,* 355–375.

Moffitt, T. E., Caspi, A., Harrington, H., & Milne, B. J. (2002). Males on the life-course persistent and adolescence-limited antisocial pathways: Follow-up at age 26. *Development and Psychopathology 14,* 179–207.

Moffitt, T. E., Lynam, D., & Silva, P. A. (1994). Neuropsychological tests predict persistent male delinquency. *Criminology, 32,* 101–124.

Moffitt, T. E., & Silva, P. A. (1988). IQ and delinquency: A direct test of the differential detection hypothesis. *Journal of Abnormal Psychology, 97,* 330–333.

Mohr, D. C., Beutler, L. E., Engle, D., Shoham-Salomon, V., Bergan, J., Kaszniak, A. W., et al. (1990). Identification of patients at risk for nonresponse and negative outcome in psychotherapy. *Journal of Consulting and Clinical Psychology, 58,* 622–628.

Molgaard, C. A., Nakamura, C. M., Stanford, E. P., Peddecord, K. M., & Morton, D. J. (1990). Prevalence of alcohol consumption among older persons. *Journal of Community Health, 15,* 239–251.

Molnar, B. E., Buka, S. L., & Kessler, R. C. (2001). Child sexual abuse and subsequent psychopathology: Results from the National Comorbidity Survey. *American Journal of Public Health, 91*(5), 753–760.

Monahan, J. (1973). The psychiatrization of criminal behavior. *Hospital and Community Psychiatry, 24,* 105–107.

Monahan, J. (1976). The prevention of violence. In J. Monahan (Ed.), *Community mental health and the criminal justice system.* Elmsford, NY: Pergamon.

Monahan, J. (1978). Prediction research and the emergency commitment of dangerous mentally ill persons: A reconsideration. *American Journal of Psychiatry, 135,* 198–201.

Monahan, J. (1984). The prediction of violent behavior: Toward a second generation of theory and policy. *American Journal of Psychiatry, 141,* 10–15.

Monahan, J. (1992). Mental disorder and violent behavior: Perceptions and evidence. *American Psychologist, 47,* 511–521.

Monahan, J., & Shah, S. (1989). Dangerousness and commitment of the mentally disordered in the United States. *Schizophrenia Bulletin, 15,* 541–553.

Monahan, J., & Steadman, H. (1994). Toward a rejuvenation of risk assessment research. In J. Monahan & H. Steadman (Eds.), *Violence and mental disorder: Developments in risk assessment.* Chicago: University of Chicago Press.

Moniz, E. (1936). *Tentatives operatoires dans le traitement de ceretaines psychoses.* Paris: Mason.

Monroe, S. M., & Harkness, K. L. (2005). Life stress, the "kindling" hypothesis, and the recurrence of depression: Considerations from a life stress perspective. *Psychological Review, 112,* 417–445.

Monsen, K., & Monsen, J. T. (2000). Chronic pain and psychodynamic body therapy: A controlled outcome study. *Psychotherapy: Theory, Research, Practice, Training, 37,* 257–269.

Monson, R., & Smith, C. R. (1983). Current concepts in psychiatry: Somatization disorder in primary care. *New England Journal of Medicine, 308,* 1464–1465.

Montag, K. R., & Wilson, G. L. (1992). An empirical evaluation of behavioral and cognitive-behavioral group marital treatments with discordant couples. *Journal of Sex and Marital Therapy, 18,* 255–272.

Monuteaux, M., Faraone, S. V., Gross, L., & Biederman, J. (2007). Predictors, clinical characteristics, and outcome of conduct disorder in girls with attention-deficit/hyperactivity disorder: A longitudinal study. *Psychological Medicine, 37,* 1731–1741.

Moos, R. H., & Humphreys, K. (2004). Long-term influence of duration and frequency of participation in Alcoholics Anonymous on individuals with alcohol use disorders. *Journal of Consulting and Clinical Psychology, 72,* 81–90.

Mora, S., Redberg, R. F., Cui, Y., Whiteman, M. K., Flaws, J. A., Sharrett, A. R., & Blumenthal, R. S. (2003). Ability of exercise testing to predict cardiovascular and all-cause death in asymptomatic women: A 20-year follow-up of the lipid research clinics prevalence study. *Journal of the American Medical Association, 290,* 1600–1607.

Moran, M. (1991). Psychological factors affecting pulmonary and rheumatological diseases: A review. *Psychosomatics, 32,* 14–23.

Moreau, D., Mufson, L., Weissman, M. M., & Klerman, G. L. (1992). Interpersonal psychotherapy for adolescent depression: Description of modification and preliminary application. *Journal of the Academy of Child and Adolescent Psychiatry, 30,* 642–651.

Moreland, K., Wing, S., Diez Roux, A., & Poole, C. (2002). Neighborhood characteristics associated with the location of food stores and food services places. *American Journal of Preventive Medicine, 22,* 23–29.

Morenz, B., & Becker, J. V. (1995). The treatment of youthful sexual offenders. *Applied and Preventive Psychology, 4,* 247–256.

Morey, L. C. (1988). Personality disorders in DSM-III and DSM-III-R: Convergence, coverage, and internal consistency. *American Journal of Psychiatry, 145,* 573–577.

Morey, L. C., Gunderson, J., Quigley, B. D., & Lyons, M. (2000). Dimensions and categories: The "big five" factors and the DSM personality disorders. *Assessment, 7,* 203–216.

Morf, C. C., & Rhodewalt, F. (2001). Unraveling the paradoxes of narcissism: A dynamic self-regulatory processing model. *Psychological Inquiry, 12,* 177–196.

Morgan, C. A., III, Hazlett, G., Wang, S., Richardson, E. G., Jr., Schnurr, P., & Southwick, S. M. (2001). Symptoms of dissociation in humans experiencing acute, uncontrollable stress: A prospective investigation. *American Journal of Psychiatry, 158,* 1239–1247.

Morgan, M. J. (2000). Ecstasy (MDMA): A review of its possible persistent psychological effects. *Psychopharmacology, 152,* 230–248.

Morgenstern, J., Blanchard, K. A., Morgan, T. J., Labouvie, E., & Hayaki, J. (2001). Testing the effectiveness of cognitive-behavioral treatment for substance abuse in a community setting: Within treatment and posttreatment findings. *Journal of Consulting and Clinical Psychology, 69,* 1007–1017.

Morgenstern, J., Langenbucher, J., Labouvie, E., & Miller, K. J. (1997). The comorbidity of alcoholism and personality disorders in a clinical population: Prevalence rates and relation to alcohol typology variables. *Journal of Abnormal Psychology, 106,* 74–84.

Morin, C. M., Colecchi, C., Stone, J., Sood, R., & Brink, D. (1999). Behavioral and pharmacological therapies for late-life insomnia: A randomized controlled trial. *Journal of the American Medical Association, 281,* 991–999.

Morley, S. (1997). Pain management. In A. Baum, S. Newman, J. Weinman, R. West, & C. McManus (Eds.), *Cambridge handbook of psychology, health and medicine* (pp. 234–237). Cambridge, UK: Cambridge University Press.

Morokoff, P. J., & Gilliland, R. (1993). Stress, sexual functioning, and marital satisfaction. *Journal of Sex Research, 30,* 43–53.

Moroney, J. T., Tang, M.-X., Berglund, L., Small, S., Merchant, C., et al. (1999). Low-density lipoprotein cholesterol and the risk of dementia with stroke. *Journal of the American Medical Association, 282,* 254–260.

Morriss, R. K., Faizal, M. A., Jones, A. P., Williamson, P. R., Bolton, C., & McCarthy, J. P. (2007). Interventions for helping people recognise early signs of recurrence in bipolar disorder. *Cochrane Database of Systematic Reviews,* CD004854.

Morse, R. M. (1988). Substance abuse among the elderly. *Bulletin of the Menninger Clinic, 52,* 259–268.

Morse, S. J. (1982a). Failed explanation and criminal responsibility: Experts and the unconscious. *Virginia Law Review, 678,* 971–1084.

Morse, S. J. (1982b). A preference for liberty: The case against involuntary commitment of the mentally disordered. *California Law Review, 70,* 54–106.

Morse, S. J. (1992). The "guilty mind": Mens rea. In D. K. Kagehiro & W. S. Laufer (Eds.), *Handbook of psychology and law* (pp. 207–229). New York: Springer-Verlag.

Moscicki, E. K. (1995). Epidemiology of suicidal behavior. In M. M. Silverman & R. W. Maris (Eds.), *Suicide prevention: Toward the year 2000* (pp. 22–35). New York: Guilford.

Moser, C., & Levitt, E. E. (1987). An exploratory descriptive study of a sadomasochistically oriented sample. *The Journal of Sex Research, 23,* 322–337.

Moses, J. A., & Purisch, A. D. (1997). The evolution of the Luria-Nebraska Battery. In G. Goldstein & T. Incagnoli (Eds.), *Contemporary approaches to neuropsychological assessment* (pp. 131–170). New York: Plenum.

Moses, J. A., Schefft, B. A., Wong, J. L., & Berg, R. A. (1992). Interrater reliability analyses of the Luria-Nebraska neuropsychological battery, form II. *Archives of Clinical Neurology, 7,* 251–269.

Moskowitz, J. T. (2003). Positive affect predicts lower risk of AIDS mortality. *Psychosomatic Medicine, 65,* 620–626.

Mottram, P., Wilson, K., & Strobl, J. (2006). Antidepressants for depressed elderly. *Cochrane Database of Systematic Reviews,* (1) doi:DOI: 10.1002/14651858.

Mowrer, O. H. (1947). On the dual nature of learning: A reinterpretation of "conditioning" and "problem-solving." *Harvard Educational Review, 17,* 102–148.

MTA Cooperative Group. (1999a). A 14-month randomized clinical trial of treatment strategies for attention-deficit/hyperactivity disorder. *Archives of General Psychiatry, 56,* 1073–1086.

MTA Cooperative Group. (1999b). Moderators and mediators of treatment response for children with attention-deficit/hyperactivity disorder. *Archives of General Psychiatry, 56,* 1088–1096.

MTA Cooperative Group. (2004). National Institute of Mental Health multimodal treatment study of ADHD follow-up: Changes in effectiveness and growth after the end of treatment. *Pediatrics, 113,* 762–769.

Mueser, K. T., Bellack, A. S., & Blanchard, J. J. (1992). Comorbidity of schizophrenia and substance abuse: Implications for treatment. *Journal of Consulting and Clinical Psychology, 60,* 845–856.

Mueser, K. T., & Berenbaum, H. (1990). Psychodynamic treatment for schizophrenia: Is there a future? *Psychological Medicine, 20,* 253–262.

Mueser, K. T., Bond, G. R., Drake, R. E., & Resnick, S. G. (1998). Models of community care for severe mental illness: A review of research on case management. *Schizophrenia Bulletin, 24,* 37–74.

Mufson, L., Weissman, M. M., Moreau, D., & Garfinkel, R. (1999). Efficacy of interpersonal psychotherapy for depressed adolescents. *Archives of General Psychiatry, 56,* 573–579.

Multon, K. D., Kivlighan, D. M., & Gold, P. B. (1996). Changes in counselor adherence over the course of training. *Journal of Counseling Psychology, 43,* 356–363.

Mulvey, E. P. (1994). Assessing the evidence of a link between mental illness and violence. *Hospital and Community Psychiatry, 45,* 663–668.

Mundle, G., Bruegel, R., Urbaniak, H., Laengle, G., Buchkremer, G., & Mann, K. (2001). Kurzund mittelfristige Erfolgsraten ambulanter Entwoehnungsbehandlungen fuer alkoholabhaengige Patienten. Eine 6-, 18, und 36-Monats-Katamnese. Short and medium-term outcome of outpatient treatment for alcohol dependent patients in Germany—A 6-, 18-, and 36-month follow-up. *Fortschritte der Neurologie Psychiatrie, 69,* 374–378.

Mundo, E., Maina, G., & Uslenghi, C. (2000). Multicentre, double-blind comparison of fluvoxamine and clomipramine in the treatment of obsessive-compulsive disorder. *International Clinical Psychopharmacology, 15,* 69–76.

Munetz, M. R., Grande, T., Kleist, J., & Peterson, G. A. (1996). The effectiveness of outpatient civil commitment. *Psychiatric Services, 47,* 1251–1253.

Muñoz, R. F., Ying, Y. W., Bernal, G., Perez-Stable, E. J., et al. (1995). Prevention of depression with primary care patients: A randomized controlled trial. *American Journal of Community Psychology, 23,* 199–222.

Munro, S., Thomas, K. L., & Abu-Shaar, M. et al. (1993). Molecular characterization of a peripheral receptor for cannabinoids. *Nature, 365,* 61–65.

Munson, J., Dawson, G., Abbott, R., et al. (2006). Amygdalar volume and behavioral development in autism. *Archives of General Psychiatry, 63,* 686–693.

Muntner, P., He, J., Cutler, J. A., Wildman, R. P., & Whelton, P. K. (2004). Trends in blood pressure among adolescents and children. *Journal of the American Medical Association, 291,* 2107–2113.

Muraven, M., & Baumeister, R. F. (2000). Self-regulation and depletion of limited resources: Does self-control resemble a muscle? *Psychological Bulletin, 126,* 247–259.

Murphy, J. (1976). Psychiatric labeling in cross-cultural perspective. *Science, 191,* 1019–1028.

Murphy, J. K., Stoney, C. M., Alpert, B. S., & Walker, S. S. (1995). Gender and ethnicity in children's cardiovascular reactivity: 7 years of study. *Health Psychology, 14,* 48–55.

Murray, C. J. L., & Lopez, A. D. (1996). *The global burden of disease: A comprehensive assessment of disease, injuries, and risk factors in 1990 and projected to 2020.* Cambridge, MA: Harvard University Press.

Musselman, D. L., Evans, D. L., & Nemeroff, C. B. (1998). The relationship of depression to cardiovascular disease: Epidemiology, biology, and treatment. *Archives of General Psychiatry, 55,* 580–592.

Mustonen, T. K., Spencer, S. M., Hoskinson, R. A., Sachs, D. P. L., & Garvey, A. J. (2005). The influence of gender, race, and menthol content on tobacco exposure measures. *Nicotine & Tobacco Research, 7,* 581–590.

Myin-Germeys, I., van Os, J., Schwartz, J. E., et al. (2001). Emotional reactivity to daily life stress in schizophrenia. *Archives of General Psychiatry, 58,* 1137–1144.

Nacewicz, B. M., Dalton, K. M., Johnstone, T., et al. (2006). Amygdala volume and nonverbal social impairment in adolescent and adult males with autism. *Archives of General Psychiatry, 63,* 1417–1448.

Naranjo, C. A., Tremblay, L. K., & Busto, U. E. (2001). The role of the brain reward system in depression. *Progress in Neuro-Psychopharmacology & Biological Psychiatry, 25,* 781–823.

Nasser, M. (1988). Eating disorders: The cultural dimension. *Social Psychiatry and Psychiatric Epidemiology, 23,* 184–187.

Nasser, M. (1997). *Culture and weight consciousness.* London: Routledge.

Nathan, P. E., & Gorman, J. M. (Eds.). (2002). *A guide to treatments that work* (2nd ed.). London: Oxford University Press.

National Academy on an Aging Society. (1999). *Challenges for the 21st century: Chronic and disabling conditions.* Retrieved from http://www.agingsociety.org/agingsociety/ publications/chronic/index.html

National Center for Health Statistics. (2004). *Healthy People, 2004.* Retrieved from http://www.cdc.gov/nchs/hus.htm

National Center for Justice. (2003). *National crime victimization survey*. Unpublished document (National Center for Justice, Document NCJ 206348).

National Center for Victims of Violent Crime. (2004). *Sexual violence*. Unpublished document number 32291. Retrieved from http://www.ncvc.org/ncvc/ main.aspx? dbID=DBStatistics584

National Center on Addiction and Substance Abuse at Columbia University (2005). Under the counter: The diversion and abuse of controlled prescription drugs in the U.S.

National Heart, Lung and Blood Institute. (1998a). *Behavioral research in cardiovascular, lung, and blood health and disease*. Washington, DC: U.S. Department of Health and Human Services.

National Heart, Lung, and Blood Institute. (1998b, June). *Clinical guidelines of the identification, evaluation, and treatment of overweight and obese adults*. Retrieved July 25, 2001, from www.nhlbi.nih.gov/guidelines/obesity/obhome.htm

National Highway Transportation & Safety Administration. (2003). *Traffic safety facts 2003: Alcohol* (DOT Publication No. HS 809 761). Washington, DC: National Center for Statistics and Analysis, U.S. Department of Transportation.

National Highway Transportation Safety Administration. (2005). 2004 traffic safety annual assessment—Early results (DOT Publication No. HS 809 897). National Center for Statistics and Analysis, U.S. Department of Transportation.

National Institute of Child Health and Human Development. (2000). *Report of the National Reading Panel. Teaching children to read: An evidence-based assessment of the scientific research literature on reading and its implications for reading instruction*. Retrieved from http://www. nichd.nih.gov/publications/nrp/smallbook. htm

National Institutes of Health. (1998, November 16–18). *Diagnosis and treatment of attention deficit hyperactivity disorder*. Retrieved from http://consensus.nih.gov/1998/ 1998AttentionDeficitHyperactivityDisorder110htmlhtm

National Institute of Mental Health (NIMH) Multisite HIV Prevention Trial Group. (1998). The NIMH multisite HIV prevention trial: Reducing HIV sexual risk behavior. *Science, 280*, 1889–1894.

National Institute on Alcohol Abuse and Alcoholism. (2001). *Alcohol Alert No. 51: Economic perspectives in alcoholism research*. Rockville, MD. (http://www.niaaa.nih. gov/publications/aa51-text.htm)

National Institute on Alcohol Abuse and Alcoholism. (1997). Youth drinking: Risk factors and consequences. *Alcohol Alert*, 1–7.

National Institute on Alcohol Abuse and Alcoholism. (2002). *A call to action: Changing the culture of drinking at U.S. colleges*. (NIH Publication No. 02–5010). Task Force of the National Advisory Council on Alcohol Abuse and Alcoholism. National Institutes of Health, U.S. Department of Health and Human Service. (www.collegedrinkingprevention.gov).

National Institute on Drug Abuse (NIDA). (2004a). *NIDA InfoFacts: Crack and cocaine*. Washington, DC: National Institute on Drug Abuse, National Institute of Health, U.S. Department of Health and Human Services. (http://www.drugabuse.gov)

National Institute on Drug Abuse (NIDA). (2004c). *NIDA InfoFacts: Nationwide trends*. Washington, DC. National Institute on Drug Abuse, National Institute of Health, U.S. Department of Health and Human Services. (http://www.drugabuse.gov)

National Survey on Children's Health (2003). Retrieved from *http://www.nschdata.org/Content/Default.aspx*

NCHS. (2004). *NCHS data on Alzheimer's Disease*. Washington, DC. National Center for Health Statistics, Centers for Disease Control. (http://www.cdc.gov/nchs/ data/factsheets /Alzheimers.pdf)

Neale, J. M., & Liebert, R. M. (1986). Science and behavior: An introduction to methods of research (3rd ed.). Englewood Cliffs, NJ: Prentice-Hall.

Neale, J. M., & Oltmanns, T. (1980). *Schizophrenia*. New York: Wiley.

Neisser, U. (1976). *Cognition and reality*. San Francisco: Freeman.

Neisser, U., & Harsch, N. (1991). Phantom flashbulbs: False recognitions of hearing the news about *Challenger*. In E. Winograd & U. Neisser (Eds.), *Affect and accuracy of recall: Studies of "flashbulb" memories* (9–31). New York: Cambridge University Press.

Nelson, E. C., Heath, A. C., Madden, P. A. F., Cooper, L., Dinwiddie, S. H., Bucholz, K. K., et al,. (2002). Association between self-reported childhood sexual abuse and adverse psychosocial outcomes: A twin study. *Archives of General Psychiatry, 59*, 139–145.

Nelson, J. C., & Davis, J. M. (1997). DST studies in psychotic depression: A meta-analysis. *American Journal of Psychiatry, 154*, 1497–1503.

Nelson, M. D., Saykin, A. J., Flashman, L. A., & Riordin, H. J. (1998). Hippocampal volume reduction in schizophrenia as assessed by magnetic resonance imaging: A meta analytic study. *Archives of General Psychiatry, 55*, 433–440.

Nelson, R. O., Lipinski, D. P., & Black, J. L. (1976). The reactivity of adult retardates' self-monitoring: A comparison among behaviors of different valences, and a comparison with token reinforcement. *Psychological Record, 26*, 189–201.

Nelson, T. L., Palmer, R. F., & Pederson, N. L. (2004). The metabolic syndrome mediates the relationship between cynical hostility and cardiovascular disease. *Experimental Aging Research, 30*, 163–177.

Nemeroff, C. B., & Schatzberg, A. F. (1998). Pharmacological treatment of unipolar depression. In P. E. Nathan & J. M. Gorman (Eds.), *A guide to treatments that work* (pp. 212–225). New York: Oxford University Press.

Nestadt, G., Romanoski, A., Chahal, R., Merchant, A., et al. (1990). An epidemiological study of histrionic personality disorder. *Psychological Medicine, 20*, 413–422.

Nestle, M. (2002). *Food politics: How the food industry influences nutrition and health*. Berkeley: University of California Press.

Neugarten, B. L. (1977). Personality and aging. In J. E. Birren & K. W. Schaie (Eds.), *Handbook of the psychology of aging* (pp. 626–649). New York: Van Nostrand.

Neugebauer, R. (1979). Mediaeval and early modern theories of mental illness. *Archives of General Psychiatry, 36*, 477–484.

Neuman, R. J., Lobos, E., Reich, W., Henderson, C. A., Sun, L. W., & Todd, R. D. (2007). Prenatal smoking exposure and dopaminergic genotypes interact to cause a severe ADHD subtype. *Biological Psychiatry, 61*, 1320–1328.

Neumeister, A., Konstantinidis, A., Praschak Rieder, N., Willeit, M., Hilger, E., Stastny, J., et al. (2001). Monoaminergic function in the pathogenesis of seasonal affective disorder. *International Journal of Neuropsychopharmacology, 4*, 409–420.

Neumeister, A., Konstantinidis, A., Stastny, J., Schwarz, M. J., Vitouch, O., Willeit, M., et al. (2002). Association between the serotonin transporter gene promoter polymorphism (5-HTTLPR) and behavioral responses to tryptophan depletion in healthy women with and with-

out family history of depression. *Archives of General Psychiatry, 59*, 613–620.

Neuner, F., Schauer, M., Klaschik, C., Karunakara, U., & Ebert, T. (2004). A comparison of narrative exposure therapy, supportive counseling, and psychoeducation for treating posttraumatic stress disorder in an african refugee settlement. *Journal of Consulting and Clinical Psychology, 72*, 579–587.

Newman, D. L., Moffitt, T. E., Caspi, A., & Silva, P. A. (1998). Comorbid mental disorders: Implications for treatment and sample selection. *Journal of Abnormal Psychology, 107*, 305–311.

Newman, J. P., Patterson, C. M., & Kosson, D. S. (1987). Response perseveration in psychopaths. *Journal of Abnormal Psychology, 96*, 145–149.

Newman, J. P., Schmitt, W. A., & Voss, W. D. (1997). The impact of motivationally neutral cues on psychopathic individuals: Assessing the generality of the response modulation hypothesis. *Journal of Abnormal Psychology, 196*, 563–575.

Nezu, A. A., Nezu, C. M., Friedman, S. H., Houts, P. S., & Faddis, S. (1997). The Project Genesis: Application of problem-solving therapy to individuals with cancer. *The Behavior Therapist, 20*, 155–158.

Nicholson, A., Kuper, H., & Hemingway, H. (2006). Depression as an aetiologic and prognostic factor in coronary heart disease: A meta-analysis of 6362 events among 146538 participants in 54 observational studies. *European Heart Journal, 27*, 2763–2774.

Niederdeppe, J., Farrelly, M. C., & Haviland, M. L. (2004). Confirming "truth": More evidence of a successful tobacco countermarketing campaign in Florida. *American Journal of Public Health, 94*, 255–257.

Niedhammer, I., Goldberg, M., Leclerc, A., David, S., et al. (1998). Psychosocial work environment and cardiovascular risk factors in an occupational cohort in France. *Journal of Epidemiology and Community Health, 52*, 93–100.

Nietzel, M. T., & Harris, M. J. (1990). Relationship of dependency and achievement/autonomy to depression. *Clinical Psychology Review, 10*, 279–297.

Nigg, J. T. (2001). Is ADHD a disinhibitory disorder? *Psychological Bulletin, 127*, 571–598.

Nigg, J. T. (2006). *What causes ADHD? Toward a multi-path model for understanding what goes wrong and why*. New York: Guilford.

Nigg, J. T., & Casey, B. J. (2005). An integrative theory of attention-deficit/ hyperactivity disorder based on the cognitive and affective neurosciences. *Development and Psychopathology, 17*, 785–806.

Nigg, J. T., & Goldsmith, H. H. (1994). Genetics of personality disorders: Perspectives from personality and psychopathology research. *Psychological Bulletin, 115*, 346–380.

Nihira, K., Foster, R., Shenhaas, M., & Leland, H. (1975). *AAMD–Adaptive Behavior Scale*. Washington, DC: American Association on Mental Deficiency.

Noble, E. P. (2003). D2 dopamine receptor gene in psychiatric and neurologic disorders and its phenotypes. *American Journal of Medical Genetics, 116B*, 103–125.

Nobler, M. S., Oquendo, M. A., Kegeles, L. S., Malone, K. M., Campbell, C., Sackheim, H. A., et al. (2001). Decreased regional brain metabolism after ECT. *American Journal of Psychiatry, 158*, 305–308.

Nock, M. K., Kazdin, A. E., Hiripi, E., & Kessler, R. C. (2006). Prevalence, subtypes, and correlates of DSM-IV conduct disorder in the National Comorbidity Survey Replication. *Psychological Medicine, 36*, 699–710.

Nolen-Hoeksema, S. (2001). Gender differences in depression. *Current Directions in Psychological Science, 10*, 173–176.

Nolen-Hoeksema, S., Girgus, J. S., & Seligman, M. E. (1986). Learned helplessness in children: A longitudinal study of depression, achievement, and explanatory style. *Journal of Personality and Social Psychology, 51,* 435–442.

Nolen-Hoeksema, S., Morrow, J., & Fredrickson, B. (1993). Response styles and the duration of episodes of depressed mood. *Journal of Abnormal Psychology, 102,* 20–28.

Noll, S. M., & Fredrickson, B. L. (1998). A mediational model linking self-objectification, body shame, and disordered eating. *Psychology of Women Quarterly, 22,* 623–636.

Nopoulos, P., Flaum, M., & Andreasen, N. C. (1997). Sex differences in brain morphology in schizophrenia. *American Journal of Psychiatry, 154,* 1648–1654.

Nordin, V., & Gillberg, C. (1998). The long-term course of autistic disorders: Update on follow-up studies. *Acta Psychiatrica Scandinavica, 97,* 99–108.

Norman, R. M., Malla, A. K., McLean, R. S., McIntosh, E. M., Neufeld, R. W., et al. (2002). An evaluation of a stress management program for individuals with schizophrenia. *Schizophrenia Research, 58,* 292–303.

Norton, G. R., Cox, B. J., & Malan, J. (1992). Non-clinical panickers: A critical review. *Clinical Psychology Review, 12,* 121–139.

Norton, J. P. (1982). *Expressed emotion, affective style, voice tone and communication deviance as predictors of offspring schizophrenia spectrum disorders.* Unpublished doctoral dissertation, University of California, Los Angeles.

Norton, M. C., Skoog, I., Toone, L., Corcoran, C., Tschanz, J. T., Lisota, R. D., et al. for the Cache County Investigators. (2006). Three-year incidence of first-onset depressive syndrome in a population sample of older adults: The Cache County Study. *American Journal of Geriatric Psychiatry, 14,* 237–245.

Noshirvani, H. F., Kasvikis, Y., Marks, I. M., Tsakiris, F., & Monteiro, W. O. (1991). Gender-divergent aetiological factors in obsessive compulsive disorder. *The British Journal of Psychiatry, 158,* 260–263.

Nourkova, V., Bernstein, D. M., & Loftus, E. F. (2004). Biography becomes autobiography: Distorting the subjective past. *American Journal of Psychology, 117,* 65–80.

Noyes, R. (1999). The relationship of hypochondriasis to anxiety disorders. *General Hospital Psychiatry, 21,* 8–17.

O'Brien, W. H., & Haynes, S. N. (1995). Behavioral assessment. In L. A. Heiden & M. Hersen (Eds.), *Introduction to clinical psychology* (pp. 103–139). New York: Plenum.

O'Connor, L. E., Berry, J. W., Weiss, J., Schweitzer, D., & Sevier, M. (2000). Survivor guilt, submissive behaviour and evolutionary theory: The down-side of winning in social comparison. *British Journal of Medical Psychology, 73,* 519–530.

O'Donnell, P., & Grace, A. A. (1998). Dysfunctions in multiple interrelated systems as the neurobiological bases of schizophrenic symptom clusters. *Schizophrenia Bulletin, 24,* 267–283.

O'Donohue, W. (1993). The spell of Kuhn on psychology: An exegetical elixir. *Philosophical Psychology, 6,* 267–287.

O'Donohue, W., Dopke, C. A., & Swingen, D. N. (1997). Psychotherapy for female sexual dysfunction: A review. *Clinical Psychology Review, 17,* 537–566.

O'Donohue, W., & Plaud, J. J. (1994). The conditioning of human sexual arousal. *Archives of Sexual Behavior, 23,* 321–344.

O'Farrell, T. J., & Fals-Stewart, W. (2000). Behavioral couples therapy for alcoholism and drug abuse. *Journal of Substance Abuse Treatment, 18,* 51–54.

O'Kearney, R.T., Anstey K.J., & von Sanden C. (2006). Behavioural and cognitive behavioural therapy for obsessive compulsive disorder in children and adolescents. *Cochrane Database of Systematic Reviews 2006,* Issue 4.

O'Leary, D. S., Block, R. I., Flaum, M., Schultz, S. K., Ponto, L. L., Boles, Watkins, G. L., Hurtig, R. R., Andreasen, N. C., & Hichwa, R. D. (2000). Acute marijuana effects on rCBF and cognition: A PET study. *Neuroreport: For Rapid Communication of Neuroscience Research, 11,* 3835–3841.

O'Leary, K. D., & Beach, S. R. (1990). Marital therapy: A viable treatment for depression and marital discord. *American Journal of Psychiatry, 147,* 183–186.

O'Leary, K. D., & Wilson, G. T. (1987). *Behavior therapy: Application and outcome.* Englewood Cliffs, NJ: Prentice-Hall.

O'Loughlin, J. O., Paradis, G., Kim, W., DiFranza, J., Meshefedjian, G., McMillan-Davey, E., Wong, S., Hanley, J., & Tyndale, R. F. (2005). Genetically decreased CYP2A6 and the risk of tobacco dependence: A prospective study of novice smokers. *Tobacco Control, 13,* 422–428.

O'Neal, J. M. (1984). First person account: Finding myself and loving it. *Schizophrenia Bulletin, 10,* 109–110.

Ockene, J. K., Mermelstein, R. J., Bonollo, D. S., Emmons, K. M., Perkins, K. A., Voorhees, C. C., & Hollis, J. F. (2000). Relapse and maintenance issues for smoking cessation. *Health Psychology, 19,* 17–31.

Oei, T. P. S., & Dingle, G. (2008). The effectiveness of group cognitive behaviour therapy for unipolar depressive disorders. *Journal of Affective Disorders, 107,* 5–21.

Oetting, E. R., Deffenbacher, J. L., Taylor, M. J., Luther, N., Beauvais, F., & Edwards, R. W. (2000). Methamphetamine use by high school students: Recent trends, gender and ethnicity differences, and use of other drugs. *Journal of Child & Adolescent Substance Abuse, 10,* 33–50.

Office of Applied Studies. (2002). *Results from the 2001 National Household Survey on Drug Abuse: Vol. I. Summary of national findings* (DHHS Publication No. SMA 02–3758, NHSDA Series H-17). Rockville, MD: Substance Abuse and Mental Health Services Administration.

Ogden, C. L., Carroll, M.D., & Flegal, K. M. (2008). High body mass index for age among US children and adolescents, 2003–2006. *Journal of the American Medical Association, 299,* 2401–2405.

Ogden, C.L., Carroll, M.D., McDowell, M.A., & Flegal, K.M. (2007). Obesity among adults in the United States—No change since 2003–2004 (NCHS Data Brief No 1). Hyattsville, MD: National Center for Health Statistics.

Ogden, T., & Halliday-Boykins, C. A. (2004). Multisystemic treatment of antisocial adolescents in Norway: Replication of clinical outcomes outside the US. *Child and Adolescent Mental Health, 9,* 77–83.

Ogrodniczuk, J. S., & Piper, W. E. (2001). Day treatment for personality disorders: A review of research findings. *Harvard Review of Psychiatry, 9,* 105–117.

Öhman, A., Flykt, A., & Esteves, F. (2001). Emotion drives attention: Detecting the snake in the grass. *Journal of Experimental Psychology: General, 137,* 466–478.

Öhman, A., & Mineka, A. (2003). The malicious serpent: Snakes as a prototypical stimulus for an evolved module of fear. *Current Directions in Psychological Science, 12,* 5–9.

Öhman, A., & Soares, J. J. F. (1994). "Unconscious anxiety": Phobic responses to masked stimuli. *Journal of Abnormal Psychology, 103,* 231–240.

Olatunji, B. O., Cisler, J. M., & Tolin, D. F. (2007). Quality of life in the anxiety disorders: A meta-analytic review. *Clinical Psychology Review, 27,* 572–581.

Olff, M., Langeland, W. L., Draijer, N., & Gersons, B. P. R. (2007). Gender differences in posttraumatic stress disorder. *Psychological Bulletin, 133,* 183–204.

Olfson, M., Blanco, C., Liu, L., Moreno, C., & Laje, G. (2006). National trends in the outpatient treatment of children and adolescents with antipsychotic drugs. *Archives of General Psychiatry, 63,* 679–687.

Olfson, M., Marcus, S. C., Tedeschi, M., & Wan, G. J. (2006). Continuity of antidepressant treatment for adults with depression in the United States. *Archives of General Psychiatry, 163,* 101–108.

Olivardia, R., Pope, H. G., Mangweth, B., & Hudson, J. I. (1995). Eating disorders in college men. *American Journal of Psychiatry, 152,* 1279–1284.

Olshevski, J. L., Katz, A. D., & Knight, B. (1999). *Stress reduction for caregivers.* Philadelphia, PA: Brunner/Mazel.

Olsson, A., Nearing, K. I., & Phelps, E. A. (2007). Learning fears by observing others: The neural systems of social fear transmission. *Social Cognitive and Affective Neuroscience Advance Assess, 2,* 3–11.

Ono, Y., Yoshimura, K., Sueoka, R., Yaumachi, K., et al. (1996). Avoidant personality disorder and *taijin kyoufu:* Sociocultural implications of the WHO/ADAMHA International Study of Personality Disorders in Japan. *Acta Psychiatrica Scandinavica, 93,* 172–176.

Organista, K. C., & Munoz, R. F. (1996). Cognitive behavioral therapy with Latinos. *Cognitive and Behavioral Practice, 3,* 255–270.

Orlinsky, D. E., Ronnestad, M. H., & Willutzki, U. (2004). Fifty years of psychotherapy process-outcome research: Continuity and change. In M. J. Lambert (Ed.), *Bergin and Garfield's handbook of psychotherapy and behavior change* (5th ed., pp. 307–389). Hoboken, NJ: Wiley.

Orr, S. P., Metzger, L. J., Lasko, N. B., Macklin, M. L., Hu, F. B., Shalev, A. Y., et al. (2003). Physiologic responses to sudden, loud tones in monozygotic twins discordant for combat exposure: Association with posttraumatic stress disorder. *Archives of General Psychiatry, 60,* 283–288.

Orth-Gomer, K., & Unden, A. L. (1990). Type A behavior, social support, and coronary risk: Interaction and significance for mortality in cardiac patients. *Psychosomatic Medicine, 52,* 59–72.

Ortiz, J., & Raine, A. (2004). Heart rate level and antisocial behavior in children and adolescents: A meta-analysis. *Journal of the American Academy of Child and Adolescent Psychiatry, 43,* 154–162.

Ory, M., Hoffman, R. R., Yee, J. L., Tennstedt, S., & Schulz, R. (1999). Prevalence and impact of caregiving: A detailed comparison between dementia and nondementia caregivers. *The Gerontologist, 39,* 177–185.

Osby, U., Brandt, L., Correia, N., Ekbom, A., & Sparen, P. (2001). Excess mortality in bipolar and unipolar disorder in Sweden. *Archives of General Psychiatry, 58,* 844–850.

Öst, L. G. (2008). Efficacy of the third wave of behavioral therapies: A systematic review and meta-analysis. *Behaviour Research and Therapy, 46,* 296–321.

Öst, L. G., Ferebee, I., & Furmark, T. (1997). One-session group therapy of spider phobia: Direct versus indirect treatments. *Behaviour Research and Therapy, 35,* 21–72

Osterling, J., & Dawson, G. (1994). Early recognition of children with autism: A study of first birthday home videotapes. *Journal of Autism and Developmental Disorders, 24,* 247–257.

Ostling, S., & Skoog, I. (2002). Psychotic symptoms and paranoid ideation in a nondemented population-based sample of the very old. *Archives of General Psychiatry, 59*, 53–59.

Otto, M. W., Wilhelm, S., Cohen, L. S., and Harlow, B. L. (2001). Prevalence of body dysmorphic disorder in a community sample of women. *American Journal of Psychiatry, 158*, 2061-2063.

Otto, M. W., Teachman, B. A., Cohen, L. S., Soares, C. N., Vitonis, A. F., & Harlow, B. L. (2007). Dysfunctional attitudes and episodes of major depression: Predictive validity and temporal stability in never-depressed, depressed, and recovered women. *Journal of Abnormal Psychology, 116*, 475–483.

Otway, L. J., & Vignoles, V. L. (2006). Narcissism and childhood recollections: A quantitative test of psychoanalytic predictions. *Personality and Social Psychology Bulletin, 32*, 104–116.

Ouimette, P. C., Finney, J. W., & Moos, R. H. (1997). Twelve-step and cognitive-behavioral treatment for substance abuse: A comparison of treatment effectiveness. *Journal of Consulting and Clinical Psychology, 65*, 230–240.

Owen, M. J., Williams, N. M., & O'Donovan, M. C. (2004). The molecular genetics of schizophrenia: New findings promise new insights. *Molecular Psychiatry, 9*, 14–27.

Owen, P. P., & Laurel-Seller, E. (2000). Weight and shape ideals: Thin is dangerously in. *Journal of Applied Social Psychology, 54*, 682–687.

Ownby, R. L., Crocco, E., Acevedo, A., John, V., & Loewenstein, D. (2006). Depression and risk for Alzheimer disease: Systematic review, meta-analysis, and meta-regression analysis. *Archives of General Psychiatry, 63*, 530–538.

Pahkala, K. (1990). Social and environmental factors and depression in old age. *International Journal of Geriatric Psychiatry, 5*, 99–113.

Pantelis, C., Velakoulis, D., McGorry, P. D., et al. (2003). Neuroanatomical abnormalities before and after onset of psychosis: A cross-sectional and longitudinal MRI comparison. *Lancet, 361*, 281–288.

Paris, J. (2002). Implications of long-term outcome research for the management of patients with borderline personality disorder. *Harvard Review of Psychiatry, 10*, 315–323.

Pasquier, F., Fukui, T., Sarazin, M., Pijnenburg, Y., Diehl, J., Grundman, M., & Miller, B. L. (2003). Laboratory investigations and treatment in frontotemporal dementia. *Annals of Neurology, 54*(Suppl 5), S32–S35.

Patel, S. T., Zhang, L., Martenyi, F., Lowe, S. L., Jackson, K. A., et al. (2007). Activation of mGlu2/3 receptors as a new approach to treat schizophrenia: A randomized phase 2 clinical trial. *Nature Medicine, 13*, 1102–1107.

Patterson, C. M., & Newman, J. P. (1993). Reflectivity and learning from aversive events: Toward a psychological mechanism for the syndromes of disinhibition. *Psychological Review, 100*, 716–736.

Patterson, G. R. (1982). *Coercive family process.* Eugene, OR: Castilia.

Patterson, G. R., Crosby, L., & Vuchinich, S. (1992). Predicting risk for early police arrest. *Journal of Quantitative Criminology, 8*, 335–355.

Paulhus, D. L. (1998). Interpersonal and intrapsychic adaptiveness of trait self-enhancement: A mixed blessing? *Journal of Personality and Social Psychology, 74*, 1197–1208.

Paulus, M. P., Tapert, S. F., & Schuckit, M. A. (2005). Neural activation patterns of methamphetamine-dependent subjects during decision making predict relapse. *Archives of General Psychiatry, 62*, 761–768.

Paxton, S. J., Schutz, H. K., Wertheim, E. H., & Muir, S. L. (1999). Friendship clique and peer influences on body image concerns, dietary restraint, extreme weight-loss behaviors, and binge eating in adolescent girls. *Journal of Abnormal Psychology, 108*, 255–264.

Payne, A., & Blanchard, E. B. (1995). A controlled comparison of cognitive therapy and self-help support groups in the treatment of irritable bowel syndrome. *Journal of Consulting and Clinical Psychology, 63*, 779–786.

Peeples, F., & Loeber, R. (1994). Do individual factors and neighborhood context explain ethnic differences in juvenile delinquency? *Journal of Quantitative Criminology, 10*, 141–157.

Pelham, W. E., Gnagy, E. M., Greiner, A. R., Hoza, B., Hinshaw, S. P., Swanson, J. M., Simpson, S., Shapiro, C., Bukstein, O., Baron-Myak, C., & McBurnett, K. (2000). Behavioral versus behavioral plus pharmacological treatment for ADHD children attending a summer treatment program. *Journal of Abnormal Child Psychology, 28*, 507–525.

Penn, D. L., Chamberlin, C., & Mueser, K. T. (2003). The effects of a documentary film about schizophrenia on psychiatric stigma. *Schizophrenia Bulletin, 29*, 383–391.

Penn, D. L., & Mueser, K. T. (1996). Research update on the psychosocial treatment of schizophrenia. *American Journal of Psychiatry, 153*, 607–617.

Pennebaker, J. W., Kiecolt-Glaser, J. K., & Glaser, R. (1988). Disclosure of traumas and immune function: Health implications for psychotherapy. *Journal of Consulting and Clinical Psychology, 56*, 239–245.

Pennington, B. F. (1995). Genetics of learning disabilities. *Journal of Child Neurology, 10*, S69–S77.

Peplau, L. A. (2003). Human sexuality: How do men and women differ? *Current Directions in Psychological Science, 12*, 37–40.

Perez, M., & Joiner, T. E. (2003). Body image dissatisfaction and disordered eating in black and white women. *International Journal of Eating Disorders, 33*, 342–350.

Perez, M., Voelz, Z. R., Pettit, J. W., & Joiner, T. E. (2002). The role of acculturative stress and body dissatisfaction in predicting bulimic symptomatology across ethnic groups. *International Journal of Eating Disorders, 31*, 442–454.

Perkins, D. D. (1995). Speaking truth to power: Empowerment ideology as social intervention and policy. *American Journal of Community Psychology, 23*, 765–794.

Perkins, K. A., Ciccocioppo, M., Conklin, C. A., Milanek, M. E., Grottenthaler, A., & Sayette, M. A. (2008). Mood influences on acute smoking responses are independent of nicotine intake and dose expectancy. *Journal of Abnormal Psychology, 117*, 79–93.

Perkonigg, A., Pfister, H., Stein, M. B., Hofler, M., Lieb, R., Maercker, A., et al. (2005). Longitudinal course of posttraumatic stress disorder and posttraumatic stress. *American Journal of Psychiatry, 162*, 1320–1327.

Perlin, M. L. (1994). *Law and mental disability.* Charlottesville, VA: Michie Company.

Perls, F. S. (1969). *Gestalt therapy verbatim.* Moab, UT: Real People Press.

Perry, J. C., Banon, E., & Ianni, F. (1999). Effectiveness of psychotherapy for personality disorders. *American Journal of Psychiatry, 156*, 1312–1321.

Perry, R., Campbell, M., Adams, P., Lynch, N., Spencer, E. K., Curren, E. L., & Overall, J. E. (1989). Long-term efficacy of haloperidol in autistic children: Continuous versus discontinuous administration. *Journal of the American Academy of Child and Adolescent Psychiatry, 28*, 87–92.

Persing, J. S., Stuart, S. P., Noyes, R., & Happel, R. L. (2000). Hypochondriasis: The patient's perspective. *International Journal of Psychiatry in Medicine, 30*, 329–342.

Persons, J. B. (1991). Psychotherapy outcome studies do not accurately represent current models of psychotherapy: A proposed remedy. *American Psychologist, 46*, 99–106.

Persons, J. B. (2005). Empiricism, mechanism, and the practice of cognitive-behavior therapy. *Behavior Therapy, 36*, 107–118.

Persons, J. B., Bostrom, A., & Bertagnolli, A. (1999). Results of randomized controlled trials of cognitive therapy for depression generalize to private practice. *Cognitive Therapy Research, 23*, 535–548.

Perugi, G., Akiskal, H. S., Giannotti, D., Frare, F., et al. (1997). Gender-related differences in body dysmorphic disorder. *Journal of Nervous and Mental Disease, 185*, 578–582.

Peterson, C., Maier, S. F., & Seligman, M. E. P. (1993). *Learned helplessness: A theory for the age of personal control.* London: Oxford University Press.

Petry, N. M., Alessi, S. M., & Hanson, T. (2007). Contingency management improves abstinence and quality of life in cocaine abusers. *Journal of Consulting and Clinical Psychology, 75*, 307–315.

Petry, N. M., Alessi, S. M., Marx, J., Austin, M., & Tardif, M. (2005). Vouchers versus prizes: Contingency management treatment of substance abusers in community settings. *Journal of Consulting and Clinical Psychology, 73*, 1005–1014.

Petry, N. M., Martin, B., Cooney, J. L., & Kranzler, H. R. (2000). Give them prizes and they will come: Contingency management for treatment of alcohol dependence. *Journal of Consulting and Clinical Psychology, 68*, 250–257.

Phillips, D. P. (1974). The influence of suggestion on suicide: Substantive and theoretical implications of the Werther effect. *American Sociological Review, 39*, 340–354.

Phillips, D. P. (1985). The found experiment: A new technique for assessing impact of mass media violence on real-world aggressive behavior. In G. Comstock (Ed.), *Public communication and behavior* (Vol. 1). New York: Academic Press.

Phillips, K. A. (2006). "I look like a monster": Pharmacotherapy and cognitive-behavioral therapy for body dysmorphic disorder. In R. L. Spitzer, M. B. First, J. B. W. Williams, & M. Gibbon (Eds.), *DSM-IV-TR case book: Vol. 2. Experts tell how they treated their own patients* (pp. 263–276). Washington, DC: American Psychiatric Publishing.

Phillips, K. A., McElroy, S. L., Dwight, M. M., et al. (2001). Delusionality and response to open-label fluvoxamine in body dysmorphic disorder. *Journal of Clinical Psychiatry, 62*, 87–91.

Phillips, K. A., Pagano, M. E., Menard, W., & Stout, R. L. (2006). A 12-month follow-up study of the course of body dysmorphic disorder. *American Journal of Psychiatry, 163*, 907–912.

Phillips, L. J., Francey, S. M., Edwards, J., & McMurray, N. (2007). Stress and psychosis: Towards the development of new models of investigation. *Clinical Psychology Review, 27*, 307–317.

Phillips, M. L., Drevets, W. C., Rauch, S. L., & Lane, R. (2003). Neurobiology of emotion perception II: Implications for major psychiatric disorders. *Biological Psychiatry, 54*, 515–528.

Phillips, M. R., Li, X., & Zhang, Y. (2002). Suicide rates in China, 1995–99. *Lancet, 359*, 835–840.

Piasecki, T. M. (2006). Relapse to smoking. *Clinical Psychology Review, 26*, 196–225.

Pierce, J. P., Choi, W. S., Gilpin, E. A., Farkas, A. J., & Berry, C. C. (1998). Tobacco ads, promotional items linked with teen smoking. *Journal of the American Medical Association, 279,* 511–515.

Pierce, J. M., Petry, N. M., Stitzer, M. L., Blaine, J., Kellog, S., et al. (2006). Effects of lower-cost incentives on stimulant abstinence in methadone maintenance treatment. *Archives of General Psychiatry, 63,* 201–208.

Pierce, K., & Courchesne, E. (2001). Evidence for a cerebellar role in reduced exploration and stereotyped behavior in autism. *Biological Psychiatry, 49,* 655–664.

Pierce, K., Haist, F., Sedaghadt, F., & Corchesne, E. (2004). The brain response to personally familiar faces in autism: Findings of fusiform activity and beyond. *Brain, 127,* 1–14.

Pierce, K., Muller, R. A., Ambrose, J., Allen, G., & Courchesne, E. (2001). Face processing occurs outside the fusiform 'face area' in autism: Evidence from functional MRI. *Brain, 124,* 2059–2073.

Pietromonaco, P. R., & Barrett, L. F. (1997). Working models of attachment and daily social interactions. *Journal of Personality and Social Psychology, 73,* 1409–1423.

Pike, K. M., Dohm, F., Striegel-Moore, R. H., Wilfley, D. E., & Fairburn, C. M. (2001). A comparison of black and white women with binge eating disorder. *American Journal of Psychiatry, 158,* 1455–1460.

Pilling, S., Bebbington, P., Kuipers, E., Garety, P., Geddes, L., Martindale, B., Orbach, G., & Morgan, C. (2002). Psychological treatments in schizophrenia: II. Meta-analyses of randomized controlled trials of social skills training and cognitive remediation. *Psychological Medicine, 32,* 783–791.

Pineles, S. L., & Mineka, S. (2005). Attentional biases to internal and external sources of potential threat in social anxiety. *Journal of Abnormal Psychology, 114,* 314–318.

Piper, A., Jr., Pope, H. G., Jr., & Borowiecki J. J., III. (2000). Custer's last stand: Brown, Scheffn, and Whitfiled's latest attempt to salvage "dissociative amnesia." *Journal of Psychiatry and the Law, 28,* 149–213.

Pitman, R. K., Orr, S. P., Altman, B., & Longpre, R. E. (1996). Emotional processing during eye movement desensitization and reprocessing therapy of Vietnam veterans with chronic posttraumatic stress disorder. *Comprehensive Psychiatry, 37,* 419–429.

Piven, J., Arndt, S., Bailey, J., & Andreasen, N. (1996). Regional brain enlargement in autism: A magnetic resonance imaging study. *Journal of the American Academy of Child and Adolescent Psychiatry, 35,* 530–536.

Piven, J., Arndt, S., Bailey, J., Havercamp, S., Andreasen, N. C., & Palmer, P. (1995). An MRI study of brain size in autism. *American Journal of Psychiatry, 152,* 1145–1149.

Placidi, G. P., Oquendo, M. A., Malone, K. M., Huang, Y. Y., Ellis, S. P., & Mann, J. J. (2001). Aggressivity, suicide attempts, and depression: Relationship to cerebrospinal fluid monoamine metabolite levels. *Biological Psychiatry, 50,* 783–791.

Plomin, R. (1999). Genetics and general cognitive ability. *Nature, 402,* C25–C29.

Plomin, R., DeFries, J. C., Craig, I. W., & McGuffin, P. (2003). *Behavioral genetics in the postgenomic era.* Washington, DC: APA Books.

Plomin, R., & Kovas, Y. (2005). Generalist genes and learning disabilities. *Psychological Bulletin, 131,* 592–617.

Plomin, R., & McGuffin, P. (2003). Psychopathology in the postgenomic era. *Annual Review of Psychology, 54,* 205–228.

Plummer, D. C., and D. W. McCoy, "Achieving Agility: The View through a Conceptual Framework," Gartner Research, ID Number:

Pole, N., Gone, J. P., & Kulkarni, M. (2008). Posttraumatic stress disorder among ethnoracial minorities in the United States. *Clinical Psychology Science and Practice, 15,* 35–61.

Polich, J. M., Armor, D. J., & Braiker, H. B. (1980). Patterns of alcoholism over four years. *Journal of Studies on Alcohol, 41,* 397–415.

Polivy, J. (1976). Perception of calories and regulation of intake in restrained and unrestrained eaters. *Addictive Behaviors, 1,* 237–244.

Polivy, J., Heatherton, T. F., & Herman, C. P. (1988). Self-esteem, restraint and eating behavior. *Journal of Abnormal Psychology, 97,* 354–356.

Polivy, J., & Herman, C. P. (1985). Dieting and binging: A causal analysis. *American Psychologist, 40,* 193–201.

Polivy, J., Herman, C. P., & Howard, K. (1980). The Restraint Scale. In A. Stunkard (Ed.), *Obesity.* Philadelphia: Saunders.

Polivy, J., Herman, C. P., & McFarlane, T. (1994). Effects of anxiety on eating: Does palatability moderate distress-induced overeating in dieters? *Journal of Abnormal Psychology, 103,* 505–510.

Pollack, M. H., Zainelli, R., Goddard, A., et al. (2001). Paroxetine in the treatment of generalized anxiety disorder: Results of a placebo-controlled, flexible dosage trial. *Journal of Clinical Psychiatry, 62,* 350–357.

Polonsky, D. C. (2000). Premature ejaculation. In R. C. Rosen & S. R. Leiblum (Eds.), *Principles and practice of sex therapy* (3rd ed., pp. 305–332). New York: Guilford.

Pomerleau, O. F., Collins, A. C., Shiffman, S., & Pomerleau, C. S. (1993). Why some people smoke and others do not: New perspectives. *Journal of Consulting and Clinical Psychology, 61,* 723–731.

Ponce, F., & Atkinson, D. (1989). Mexican-Americans and acculturation, counselor ethnicity, counseling style, and perceived counselor credibility. *Journal of Counseling Psychology, 36,* 203–208.

Poole, D. A., Lindsay, D. S., Memon, A., & Bull, R. (1995). Psychotherapy and the recovery of memories of childhood sexual abuse: U.S. and British practitioners' opinions, practices and experiences. *Journal of Consulting and Clinical Psychology, 63,* 426–437.

Pope, H. G. J., Poliakoff, M. B., Parker, M. P., Boynes, M., & Hudson, J. J. (2006). Is dissociative amnesia a culture-bound syndrome? Findings from a survey of historical literature. *Psychological Medicine, 37,* 1067–1068.

Pope, K. S. (1998). Pseudoscience, cross-examination, and scientific evidence in the recovered memory controversy. *Psychology, Public Policy, and Law, 4,* 1160–1181.

Porter, S., Yuille, J. C., & Lehman, D. R. (1999). The nature of real, implanted, and fabricated memories for emotional childhood events: Implications for the recovered memory debate. *Law and Human Behavior, 23,* 415–537.

Posey, M. J., & McDougle, C. M. (2000). The pharmacotherapy of target symptoms associated with autistic disorder and other pervasive developmental disorders. *Harvard Review of Psychiatry, 8,* 45–63.

Potkin, S. G., Alva, G., Fleming, K., et al. (2002). A PET study of the pathophysiology of negative symptoms in schizophrenia. *American Journal of Psychiatry, 159,* 227–237.

Powell, R. A., & Gee, T. L. (2000). "The effects of hypnosis on dissociative identity disorder: A reexamination of the evidence": Reply. *Canadian Journal of Psychiatry, 45,* 848–849.

Prechter, G. C., & Shepard, J. W. J. (1990). Sleep and sleep disorders in the elderly. In R. J. Martin (Ed.), *Cardiorespiratory disorders during sleep* (pp. 365–386). Armonk, NY: Futura Publishing.

Prentky, R., & Burgess, A. W. (1990). Rehabilitation of child molesters: A cost-benefit analysis. *American Journal of Orthopsychiatry, 60*(1), 108–117.

Pressman, S. D., & Cohen, S. (2005). Does positive affect influence health? *Psychological Bulletin, 131,* 925–971.

Price, R. A., Cadoret, R. J., Stunkard, A. J., & Troughton, E. (1987). Genetic contributions to human fatness: An adoption study. *American Journal of Psychiatry, 144,* 1003–1008.

Prien, R. F., & Potter, W. Z. (1993). Maintenance treatment for mood disorders. In D. L. Dunner (Ed.), *Current psychiatric therapy* (pp. 255–260). Philadelphia: Saunders.

Prieto, S. L., Cole, D. A., & Tageson, C. W. (1992). Depressive self-schemas in clinic and nonclinic children. *Cognitive Therapy and Research, 16,* 521–534.

Primack, B. A., Bost, J. E., Land, S. R., & Fine, M. J. (2007). Volume of tobacco advertising in African American markets: Systematic review and meta-analysis. *Public Health Reports, 122,* 607–615.

Prinz, P., & Raskind, M. (1978). Aging and sleep disorders. In R. Williams & R. Karacan (Eds.), *Sleep disorders: Diagnosis and treatment* (pp. 303–322). New York: Wiley.

Pryor, T., Wiederman, M. W., & McGilley, B. (1996). Clinical correlates of anorexia subtypes. *International Journal of Eating Disorders, 19,* 371–379.

Przeworski, A., & Newman, M. G. (2006). Efficacy and utility of computer-assisted cognitive behavioural therapy for anxiety disorders. *Clinical Psychologist, 10,* 43–53.

Pu, T., Mohamed, E., Imam, K., & El-Roey, A. M. (1986). One hundred cases of hysteria in eastern Libya. *British Journal of Psychiatry, 148,* 606–609.

Purdie, F. R., Honigman, T. B., & Rosen, P. (1981). Acute organic brain syndrome: A view of 100 cases. *Annals of Emergency Medicine, 10,* 455–461.

Putnam, F. W. (1993). Dissociative disorders in children: Behavioral profiles and problems. *Child Abuse and Neglect, 17,* 39–45.

Putnam, F. W. (1996). A brief history of multiple personality disorder. *Child and Adolescent Psychiatric Clinics of North America, 5,* 263–271.

Putnam, F. W., Guroff, J. J., Silberman, E. K., Barban, L., & Post, R. M. (1986). The clinical phenomenology of multiple personality disorder: Review of 100 recent cases. *Journal of Clinical Psychiatry, 47,* 285–293.

Pyle, A. (1999, May 28). Seeking a remedy for nursing homes' ills. *Los Angeles Times,* pp. A1–A30.

Qualls, S. H., Segal, D. L., Norman, S., Niederehe, G., & Gallagher-Thompson, D. (2002). Psychologists in practice with older adults: Current patterns, sources of training, and need for continuing education. *Professional Psychology: Research and Practice, 33,* 435–442.

Rachman, S. (1977). The conditioning theory of fear acquisition: A critical examination. *Behaviour Research and Therapy, 15,* 375–387.

Rachman, S. (1997). A cognitive theory of obsessions. *Behaviour Research and Therapy, 35,* 793–802.

Rachman, S., & de'Silva, P. (1978). Abnormal and normal obsessions. *Behaviour Research and Therapy, 16,* 233–248.

Rachman, S. J. (1966). Sexual fetishism: An experimental analogue. *Psychological Record, 16,* 293–296.

Rachman, S. J., & Wilson, G. T. (1980). *The effects of psychological therapy* (2nd ed.). Elmsford, NY: Pergamon.

Räikkönen, K., Matthews, K. A., Flory, J. D., & Owens, J. F. (1999). Effects of hostility on ambulatory blood pressure and mood during daily living. *Health Psychology, 18,* 44–53.

Räikkönen, K., Matthews, K. A., & Salomen, K. (2003). Hostility predicts metabolic syndrome risk factors in children and adolescents. *Health Psychology, 22,* 279–286.

Raine, A., Venables, P. H., & Williams, M. (1990). Relationships between central and autonomic measures of arousal at age 15 years and criminality at age 24 years. *Archives of General Psychiatry, 47,* 1003–1007.

Raine, A., & Yang, Y. (2007). The neuroanatomical bases of psychopathy: A review of brain imaging findings. In C. J. Patrick (Ed.), *Handbook of psychopathy* (pp. 278–295). New York: Guilford.

Raj, B. A., Corvea, M. H., & Dagon, E. M. (1993). The clinical characteristics of panic disorder in the elderly: A retrospective study. *Journal of Clinical Psychiatry, 54,* 150–155.

Rajkowska, G., Halaris, A., & Selemon, L. D. (2001). Reductions in neuronal and glial density characterize the dorsolateral prefrontal cortex in bipolar disorder. *Biological Psychiatry, 49,* 741–752.

Rao, Y., Hoffmann, E., Zia, M., et al. (2000). Duplications and defects in the CYP2A6 gene: Identification, genotyping, and in vivo effects on smoking. *Molecular Pharmacology, 58,* 747–755.

Rapaport, D. (1951). *The organization and pathology of thought.* New York: Columbia University Press.

Rapee, R., Mattick, R., & Murrell, E. (1986). Cognitive mediation in the affective component of spontaneous panic attacks. *Journal of Behavior Therapy and Experimental Psychiatry, 17,* 245–253.

Rapin, I. (1997). Autism. *New England Journal of Medicine, 337,* 97–104.

Rapoport, J. L., Swedo, S. E., & Leonard, H. L. (1992). Childhood obsessive compulsive disorder. *Journal of Clinical Psychiatry, 53*(4, Suppl.), 11–16.

Rapp, M. A., Schnaider-Beeri, M., Grossman, H. T., Sano, M., Perl, D. P., Purohit, D. P., et al. (2006). Increased hippocampal plaques and tangles in patients with Alzheimer disease with a lifetime history of major depression. *Archives of General Psychiatry, 63,* 161–167.

Raskind, W. H. (2001). Current understanding of the genetic basis of reading and spelling disability. *Learning Disability Quarterly, 24,* 141–157.

Rassin, E., Merckelbach, H., Muris, P., & Schmidt, H. (2001). The thought-action fusion scale: Further evidence for its reliability and validity. *Behaviour Research and Therapy, 39,* 537–544.

Rassin, E., Muris, P., Schmidt, H., & Merckelbach, H. (2000). Relationships between thought-action fusion, thought suppression and obsessive-compulsive symptoms: A structural equation modeling approach. *Behaviour Research and Therapy, 38,* 889–897.

Rather, B. C., Goldman, M. S., Roehrich, L., & Brannick, M. (1992). Empirical modeling of an alcohol expectancy memory network using multidimensional scaling. *Journal of Abnormal Psychology, 101,* 174–183.

Rauch, S. L., & Jenike, M. A. (1998). Pharmacological treatment of obsessive compulsive disorder. In Jack M. Gorman & Peter E. Nathan (Eds.), *A guide to treatments that work* (pp. 358–376). London: Oxford University Press.

Rauch, S. L., Phillips, K. A., Segal, E., Makris, N., Shin, L. M., Whalen, P. J., et al. (2003). A preliminary morphometric magnetic resonance imaging study of regional brain volumes in body dysmorphic disorder. *Psychiatry Research: Neuroimaging, 122,* 13–19.

Rauch, S. L., Whalen, P. J., Shin, L. M., McInerney, S. C., Macklin, M. L., Lasko, N. B., Orr, S. P., & Pitman, R. K. (2000). Exaggerated amygdala response to masked facial stimuli in posttraumatic stress disorder: A functional MRI study. *Biological Psychiatry, 47,* 769–776.

Rawson, R. A., Martinelli-Casey, P., Anglin, M. D., et al. (2004). A multi-site comparison of psychosocial approaches for the treatment of methamphetamine dependence. *Addiction, 99,* 708–717.

Ray, S., Britschgi, M., Herbert, C., Takeda-Uchimura, Y., Boxer, A., Blennow, K., et al. (2007). Classification and prediction of clinical Alzheimer's diagnosis based on plasma signaling proteins. *Nature Medicine, 13,* 1359–1362.

Reas, D. L., Williamson, D. A., Martin, C. K., & Zucker, N. L. (2000). Duration of illness predicts outcome for bulimia nervosa: A long-term follow-up study. *International Journal of Eating Disorders, 27,* 428–434.

Rechlin, T., Loew, T. H., & Joraschky, P. (1997). Pseudoseizure "status." *Journal of Psychosomatic Research, 42,* 495–498.

Rector, N. A., Beck, A. T., & Stolar, N. (2005). The negative symptoms of schizophrenia: A cognitive perspetive. *Canadian Journal of Psychiatry, 50,* 247–257.

Red Horse, Y. (1982). A cultural network model: Perspectives for adolescent services and paraprofessional training. In S. Manson (Ed.), *New directions in prevention among American Indians and Alaskan Native communities.* Portland: Oregon Health Sciences University.

Redmond, D. E. (1977). Alterations in the function of the nucleus locus coeruleus. In I. Hanin & E. Usdin (Eds.), *Animal models in psychiatry and neurology.* New York: Pergamon.

Regeer, E. J., ten Have, M., Rosso, M. L., van Roijen, L. H., Vollebergh, W., & Nolen, W. A. (2004). Prevalence of bipolar disorder in the general population: A reappraisal study of the Netherlands mental health survey and incidence study. *Acta Psychiatrica Scandinavica, 110,* 374–382.

Regier, D. A., Boyd, J. H., Burke, J. D., & Rae, D. S. (1988). One-month prevalence of mental disorders in the United States: Based on five epidemiologic catchment area sites. *Archives of General Psychiatry, 45,* 977–986.

Regier, D. A., Narrow, W. E., Rae, D. S., & Manderscheid, R. W. (1993). The de facto US mental and addictive disorders service system: Epidemiologic catchment area prospective 1-year prevalence rates of disorders and services. *Archives of General Psychiatry, 50,* 85–94.

Regland, B., Johansson, B.V., Grenfeldt, B., Hjelmgren, L.T., & Medhus, M. (1995). Homocysteinemia is a common feature of schizophrenia. *Journal of Neural Transmission: General Section, 100,* 165–169.

Reich, D., & Zanarini, M. C. (2001). Developmental aspects of borderline personality disorder. *Harvard Review of Psychiatry, 9,* 294–301.

Reichborn-Kjennerud, T., Czajkowski, N., Neale, M. C., Ørstavik, R. E., Torgersen, S., Tambs, K., et al. (2007). Genetic and environmental influences on dimensional representations of DSM-IV cluster C personality disorders: A population-based multivariate twin study. *Psychological Medicine, 37,* 645–653.

Reichborn-Kjennerud, T., Czajkowski, N., Torgersen, S., Neale, M. C., Orstavik, R. E., Tambs, K., et al. (2007). The relationship between avoidant personality disorder and social phobia: A population-base twin study. *American Journal of Psychiatry, 164,* 1722–1728.

Reichman, W. E., Coyne, A. C., Borson, S., et al. (1998). Psychiatric consultation in the nursing home: A survey of six states. *American Journal of Geriatric Psychiatry, 6,* 320–327.

Reid, D. H., Wilson, P. G., & Faw, G. D. (1991). Teaching self-help skills. In J. L. Matson & J. A. Mulick (Eds.), *Handbook of mental retardation.* New York: Pergamon Press.

Reilly-Harrington, N. A., Alloy, L. B., Fresco, D. M., & Whitehouse, W. G. (1999). Cognitive styles and life events interact to predict bipolar and unipolar symptomatology. *Journal of Abnormal Psychology, 108,* 567–578.

Reiman, E. M., Caselli, R. J., Yun, L., Chen, K., Bandy, D., et al. (1996). Preclinical evidence of Alzheimer's disease in persons homozygous for the E4 allele for apolipoprotein E. *New England Journal of Medicine, 334,* 752–756.

Reimherr, F. W., Strong, R. E., Marchant, B. K., Hedges, D. W., & Wender, P. H. (2001). Factors affecting return of symptoms 1 year after treatment in a 62-week controlled study of fluoxetine in major depression. *Journal of Clinical Psychiatry, 62,* 16–23.

Reiner, W. G., & Gearhart, J. P. (2004). Discordant sexual identity in some genetic males with cloacal exstrophy assigned to female sex at birth. *New England Journal of Medicine, 350,* 333–341.

Reiser, M. F., Brust, A. A., Shapiro, A. P., Baker, H. M., Ranschoff, W., & Ferris, E. B. (1950). Life situations, emotions and the course of patients with arterial hypertension. *Research Publications of the Association for Research in Nervous & Mental Disease, 29,* 870–880.

Reiss, D., Heatherington, E. M., Plomin, R., Howe, G. W., Simmens, S. J., et al. (1995). Genetic questions for environmental studies: Differential parenting and psychopathology in adolescence. *Archives of General Psychiatry, 52,* 925–936.

Reissing, E. D., Binik, Y. M., & Khalife, S. (1999). Does vaginismus exist? A critical review of the literature. *Journal of Nervous and Mental Disease, 187,* 261–274.

Renneberg, B., Goldstein, A. J., Phillips, D., & Chambless, D. L. (1990). Intensive behavioral group treatment of avoidant personality disorder. *Behavior Therapy, 21,* 363–377.

Renshaw, D. C. (2001). Women coping with a partner's sexual avoidance. *Family Journal—Counseling & Therapy for Couples & Families, 9,* 11–16.

Resick, P. A., Nishith, P., & Griffin, M. G. (2003). How well does cognitive-behavioral therapy treat symptoms of complex PTSD? An examination of child sexual abuse survivors within a clinical trial. *CNS Spectrums, 8,* 351–355.

Resick, P. A., Nishith, P., Weaver, T. L., Astin, M. C., & Feuer, C. A. (2002). A comparison of cognitive-processing therapy with prolonged exposure and a waiting condition for the treatment of chronic posttraumatic stress disorder in female rape victims. *Journal of Consulting and Clinical Psychology, 70,* 867–879.

Ressler, K. J., & Nemeroff, C. B. (1999). Role of norepinephrine in the pathophysiology and treatment of mood disorders. *Biological Psychiatry, 46,* 1219–1233.

Ressler, K. J., Rothbaum, B. O., Tannenbaum, L., Anderson, P., Graap, K., Zimand, E., et al. (2004). Cognitive enhancers as adjuncts to psychotherapy: Use of D-cycloserine in phobic individuals to facilitate extinction of fear. *Archives of General Psychiatry, 61,* 1136–1144.

Rey, J. M., Martin, A., & Krabman, P. (2004). Is the party over? Cannabis and juvenile psychiatric disorder: The past 10 years. *Journal of the American Academy of Child and Adolescent Psychiatry, 43,* 1194–1205.

Reynolds, C. R., Chastain, R. L., Kaufman, A. S., & McLean, J. E. (1997). Demographic characteristics and IQ among adults: Analysis of the WAIS-R standardization sample as a function of the stratification variables. *Journal of School Psychology, 25,* 323–342.

Rhee, S. H. & Waldman, I. D. (2002). Genetic and environmental influences on antisocial behavior. A meta-analysis of twin and adoption studies. *Psychological Bulletin, 128,* 490–529.

Rhode, P., Seeley, J. R., Kaufman, N. K, Clarke, G. N., & Stice, E. (2006). Predicting time to recovery among depressed adolescents treated in two psychosocial group interventions. *Journal of Consulting and Clinical Psychology, 74,* 80–88.

Richards, P. S., Baldwin, B. M., Frost, H. A., Clark-Sly, J. B., Berrett, M. E., & Hardman, R. K. (2000). What works for treating eating disorders? Conclusions of 28 outcome reviews. *Eating Disorders, 8,* 189–206.

Richards, R. L., Kinney, D. K., Lunde, I., Benet, M., & Merzel, A. (1988). Creativity in manic-depressives, cyclothymes, their normal relatives, and control subjects. *Journal of Abnormal Psychology, 97,* 281–288.

Ricks, D. M. (1972). *The beginning of vocal communication in infants and autistic children.* Unpublished doctoral dissertation, University of London.

Ridenour, T. A., Miller, A. R., Joy, K. L., & Dean, R. S. (1997). "Profile" analysis of the personality characteristics of child molesters using the MMPI-2. *Journal of Clinical Psychology, 53,* 575–586.

Ridker, P. M., Cook, N. R., Lee, I.-M., Gordon, D., Gaziano, J. M., Manson, J. E., Hennekens, C. H., & Buring, J. E. (2005). A randomized trial of low-dose aspirin in the primary prevention of cardiovascular disease in women. *Journal of the American Medical Association, 352,* 1293–1304.

Ridley, M. (2003). *Nature via nurture: Genes, experience, and what makes us human.* UK: London Harper Collins.

Rieder, R. O., Mann, L. S., Weinberger, D. R., van Kammen, D. P., & Post, R. M. (1983). Computer tomographic scans in patients with schizophrenia, schizoaffective, and bipolar affective disorder. *Archives of General Psychiatry, 40,* 735–739.

Rief, W., & Auer, C. (2001). Is somatization a habituation disorder? Physiological reactivity in somatization syndrome. *Psychiatry Research, 101,* 63–74.

Rief, W., Buhlmann, U., Wilhelm, S., Borkenhagen, A., & Brähler, E. (2006). The prevalence of body dysmorphic disorder: A population-based survey. *Psychological Medicine, 36,* 877–885.

Riley, A. J., & Riley, E. J. (1978). A controlled study to evaluate directed masturbation in the management of primary orgasmic failure in women. *British Journal of Psychiatry, 133,* 404–409.

Rimland, B. (1964). *Infantile autism.* New York: Appleton-Century-Crofts.

Rind, B., Tromovitch, P., & Bauserman, R. (1998). A meta-analytic examination of assumed properties of child sexual abuse using college students. *Psychological Bulletin, 124,* 22–53.

Ringwalt, C., Ennett, S. T., & Holt, K. D. (1991). An outcome evaluation of Project DARE (Drug Abuse Resistance Education). *Health Education Research, 6,* 327–337.

Rinne, T., van den Brink, W., Wouters, L., & van Dyck, R. (2002). SSRI treatment of borderline personality disorder: A randomized, placebo-controlled clinical trial for female patients with borderline personality disorder. *American Journal of Psychiatry, 159,* 2048–2054.

Ritsher, J. B., Struening, E. L., Hellman, F., & Guardino, M. (2002). Internal validity of an anxiety disorder screening instrument across five ethnic groups. *Psychiatry Research, 111,* 199–213.

Ritvo, E. R., Freeman, B. J., Geller, E., & Yuwiler, A. (1983). Effects of fenfluramine on 14 outpatients with the syndrome of autism. *Journal of the American Academy of Child Psychiatry, 22,* 549–558.

Ritz, T., & Roth, W. T. (2003). Behavioral interventions in asthma: Breathing training. *Behavior Modification, 27,* 710–730.

Roan, S. (1992, October 15). Giving up coffee tied to withdrawal symptoms. *Los Angeles Times,* p. A26.

Robbins, S. J., Ehrman, R. N., Childress, A. R., Cornish, J. W., & O'Brien, C. P. (2000). Mood state and recent cocaine use are not associated with levels of cocaine cue reactivity. *Drug and Alcohol Dependence, 59,* 33–42.

Roberts, B. W., Kuncel, N. R., Shiner, R., Caspi, A., & Goldberg, L. R. (2007). The power of personality: The comparative validity of personality traits, socioeconomic status, and cognitive ability for predicting important life outcomes. *Perspectives on Psychological Science, 2,* 313–345.

Robiner, W. N. (2006). The mental health professions: Workforce supply and demand, issues, and challenges. *Clinical Psychology Review, 26,* 600–625.

Robinson, L. A., Klesges, R. C., Zbikowski, S. M., & Glaser, R. (1997). Predictors of risk for different stages of adolescent smoking in a biracial sample. *Journal of Consulting and Clinical Psychology, 65,* 653–662.

Robinson, N. S., Garber, J., & Hillsman, R. (1995). Cognitions and stress: Direct and moderating effects on depression versus externalizing symptoms during the junior high school transition. *Journal of Abnormal Psychology, 104,* 453–463.

Robinson, T. E., & Berridge, K. C. (1993). The neural basis of drug craving: An incentive sensitization theory of addiction. *Brain Research Reviews, 18,* 247–191.

Robinson, T. E., & Berridge, K. C. (2003). Addiction. *Annual Review of Psychology, 54,* 25–53.

Robinson-Whelan, S., Tada, Y., McCallum, R. C., McGuire, L., & Kiecolt-Glaser, J. K. (2001). Long-term caregiving: What happens when it ends? *Journal of Abnormal Psychology, 110,* 573–584.

Robles, T. F., & Kiecolt-Glaser, J. K. (2004). The physiology of marriage: Pathways to health. *Physiology and Behavior, 79,* 409–416.

Rodin, J., & Langer, E. J. (1977). Long-term effects of a control-relevant intervention with the institutionalized aged. *Journal of Personality and Social Psychology, 35,* 897–902.

Rodin, J., McAvay, G., & Timko, C. (1988). A longitudinal study of depressed mood and sleep disturbances in elderly adults. *Journal of Gerontology: Psychological Sciences, 43,* 45–53.

Roemer, L., Molina, S., & Borkovec, T. D. (1997). An investigation of worry content among generally anxious individuals. *Journal of Nervous and Mental Disease, 185,* 314–319.

Roemer, L., Orsillo, S. M., & Barlow, D. H. (2004). Generalized anxiety disorder. In D. H. Barlow (Ed.), *Anxiety and its disorders: The nature and treatment of anxiety and panic* (pp. 477–515). New York: Guilford.

Roesch, S. C., & Weiner, B. (2001). A meta-analytic review of coping with illness: Do causal attributions matter? *Journal of Psychosomatic Research, 50,* 205–219.

Rogers, C. R. (1951). *Client-centered therapy.* Boston: Houghton Mifflin.

Rogers, C. R. (1961). *On becoming a person: A therapist's view of psychotherapy.* Boston: Houghton Mifflin.

Rogler, L. H., & Hollingshead, A. B. (1985). *Trapped: Families and schizophrenia* (3rd ed.). Maplewood, NJ: Waterfront Press.

Rohan, K. J., Roecklein, K. A., Lindsey, K. T., Johnson, L. G., Lippy, R. D., Lacy, T. J., et al. (2007). A randomized controlled trial of cognitive-behavioral therapy, light therapy, and their combination for seasonal affective disorder. *Journal of Consulting and Clinical Psychology, 75,* 489–500.

Romans, S. E., Gendall, K. A., Martin, J. L., & Mullen, P. E. (2001). Child sexual abuse and later disordered eating: A New Zealand epidemiological study. *International Journal of Eating Disorders, 29,* 380–392.

Roose, S. P., & Schatzberg, A. F. (2005). The efficacy of antidepressants in the treatment of late-life depression. *Journal of Clinical Psychopharmacology, 25,* S1–S7.

Rose, J. E., Brauer, L. H., Behm, F. M., Cramblett, M., Calkins, K., & Lawhon, D. (2004). Psychopharmacological interactions between nicotine and ethanol. *Nicotine and Tobacco Research, 6,* 133–144.

Rosen, C. S., Chow, H. C., Greenbaum, M. A., Finney, J. F., Moos, R. H., Sheikh, J. I., et al. (2002). How well are clinicians following dementia practice guidelines? *Alzheimer Disease and Associated Disorders, 16,* 15–23.

Rosen, G. M. (2004). Remembering the 1978 and 1990 task forces on self-help therapies. *Journal of Clinical Psychology, 60,* 111–113.

Rosen, G. M., & Davison, G. C. (2003). Psychology should list empirically supported principles of change (ESPs) and not credential trade-marked therapies or other treatment packages. *Behavior Modification, 27,* 300–312.

Rosen, L. N., Targum, S. D., Terman, M., Bryant, M. J., Hoffman, H., Kasper, S. F., et al. (1990). Prevalence of seasonal affective disorder at four latitudes. *Psychiatry Research, 31,* 131–144.

Rosen, R. C. (2000). Medical and psychological interventions for erectile dysfunction: Toward a combined treatment approach. In S. R. Lieblum & R. C. Rosen (Eds.), *Principles and practice of sex therapy* (pp. 276–304). New York: Guilford.

Rosen, R. C., & Leiblum, S. R. (1995). Treatment of sexual disorders in the 1990s: An integrated approach. *Journal of Consulting and Clinical Psychology, 63,* 877–890.

Rosen, R. C., Leiblum, S. R., & Spector, I. (1994). Psychologically based treatment for male erectile disorder: A cognitive-interpersonal model. *Journal of Sex and Marital Therapy, 20,* 67–85.

Rosen, R. C., & Rosen, L. (1981). *Human sexuality.* New York: Knopf.

Rosenberg, R. N. (2005). Translational research on the way to effective therapy for Alzheimer disease. *Archives of General Psychiatry, 62,* 1186–1192.

Rosenfarb, I. S., Goldstein, M. J., Mintz, J., & Neuchterlein, K. H. (1994). Expressed emotion and subclinical psychopathology observable within transactions between schizophrenics and their family members. *Journal of Abnormal Psychology, 104,* 259–267.

Rosengren, A., Hawken, S., Ounpuu, S., Sliwa, K., Zubaid, M., et al. (2004). Association of psychosocial risk factors with risk of acute myocardial infarction in 11,119 cases and 13,648 controls from 52 countries (the INTERHEART study): Case-control study. *Lancet 364,* 953–962.

Rosenheck, R., Cramer, J., Allan, E., Erdos, J., Frisman, J., et al. (1999). Cost-effectivness of clozapine in patients with high and low levels of hospital use. *Archives of General Psychiatry, 56,* 565–572.

Rosenkranz, M. A., Jackson, D. C., Dalton, K. M., Dolski, I., Ryff, C. D., Singer, B. H., Muller, D., Kalin, N. H., & Davidson, R. J. (2003). Affective style and *in vivo* immune response: Neurobehavioral mechanisms. *PNAS, 100,* 11148–11152.

Rosenman, R. H., Brand, R. J., Jenkins, C. D., Friedman, M., Straus, R., & Wurm, M. (1975). Coronary heart disease in the Western Collaborative Group Study: Final follow-up experience of 8 years. *Journal of the American Medical Association, 233,* 872–877.

Rosman, B. L., Minuchin, S., & Liebman, R. (1975). Family lunch session: An introduction to family therapy in anorexia nervosa. *American Journal of Orthopsychiatry, 45,* 846–852.

Rosman, B. L., Minuchin, S., & Liebman, R. (1976). Input and outcome of family therapy of anorexia nervosa. In J. L. Claghorn (Ed.), *Successful psychotherapy.* New York: Brunner/Mazel.

Ross, C. A. (1989). *Multiple personality disorder: Diagnosis, clinical features, and treatment.* New York: Wiley.

Ross, C. A. (1991). Epidemiology of multiple personality disorder and dissociation. *Psychiatric Clinics of North America, 14,* 503–517.

Ross, G. J., Waller, G., Tyson, M., & Elliott, P. (1998). Reported sexual abuse and subsequent psychopathology among women attending psychology clinics: The mediating role of dissociation. *British Journal of Clinical Psychology, 37,* 313–326.

Rossiter, E. M., & Agras, W. S. (1990). An empirical test of the DSM-III-R definition of binge. *International Journal of Eating Disorders, 9,* 513–518.

Rost, K., Kashner, T. M., & Smith, G. R. (1994). Effectiveness of psychiatic intervention with somatization disorder patients: Improved outcomes at reduced costs. *General Hospital Psychiatry, 16,* 381–387.

Rothbaum, B. O., & Foa, E. B. (1993). Subtypes of post-traumatic stress disorder and duration of symptoms. In J. R. T. Davidson & E. B. Foa (Eds.), *Post-traumatic stress disorder: DSM-IV and beyond* (pp. 23–35). Washington, DC: American Psychiatric Press.

Rothbaum, B. O., Foa, E. B., Murdock, T., Riggs, D. S., & Walsh, W. (1992). A prospective examination of post-traumatic stress disorder in rape victims. *Journal of Traumatic Stress, 5,* 455–475.

Rothbaum, B. O., Hodges, L., Alarcon, R., Ready, D., Shahar, F., Graap, K., Pair, J., Hebert, P., Gotz, D., Will, B., & Baltzell, D. (1999). Virtual reality exposure therapy for PTSD Vietnam veterans: A case study. *Journal of Traumatic Stress, 12*(2), 263–271.

Rothman, A. J., & Salovey, P. (1997). Shaping perceptions to motivate healthy behavior: The role of message framing. *Psychological Bulletin, 121,* 3–19.

Roughgarden, J. (2004). *Evolution's rainbow: Diversity, gender, and sexuality in nature and people.* Berkeley, CA: University of California Press.

Roughten, E. C., Schneider, M. L., Bromley, L. J., & Coe, C. L. (1998). Maternal activation during pregnancy alters neurobehavioral state in primate infants. *American Journal of Occupational Therapy, 52,* 90–98.

Rowland, D. L., Cooper, S. E., & Slob, A. K. (1996). Genital and psychoaffective responses to erotic stimulation in sexually functional and dysfunctional men. *Journal of Abnormal Psychology, 105,* 194–203.

Roy, A. (1982). Suicide in chronic schizophrenia. *British Journal of Psychiatry, 141,* 171–180.

Roy, A. (1994). Recent biologic studies on suicide. *Suicide and Life Threatening Behaviors, 24,* 10–24.

Roy, A. (1995). Suicide. In H. I. Kaplan & B. J. Sadock (Eds.), *Comprehensive textbook of psychiatry* (pp. 1739–1752). Baltimore, MD: Williams & Wilkins.

Roy-Byrne, P. P., & Cowley, D. S. (1998). Pharmacological treatment of panic, generalized anxiety, and phobic disorders. In P. E. Nathan & J. M. Gorman (Eds.), *A guide to treatments that work* (pp. 319–338). New York: Oxford University Press.

Roy-Byrne, P. P., Katon, W., Cowley, D. S., & Russo, J. (2001). A randomized effectiveness trial of collaborative care for patients with panic disorder in primary care. *Archives of General Psychiatry, 58,* 869–876.

Rubia, K., Overmeyer, S., Taylor, E., Brammer, M., Williams, S. C. R., et al. (1999). Hypofrontality in attention deficit hyperactivity disorder during higher-order motor control: A study with functional MRI. *American Journal of Psychiatry, 156,* 891–896.

Ruchsow, M., Walter, H., Buchheim, A., Martius, P., Spitzer, M., Kachele, H., et al. (2006). Electrophysiological correlates of error processing in borderline personality disorder. *Biological Psychology, 72,* 133–140.

Rude, S. S., Valdez, C. R., Odom, S., & Ebrahimi, A. (2003). Negative cognitive biases predict subsequent depression. *Cognitive Therapy and Research, 27,* 415–429.

Rumbak, M. J., Kelso, T. M., Arheart, K. L., & Self, T. H. (1993). Perception of anxiety as a contributing factor in asthma: Indigent versus non-indigent. *Journal of Asthma, 30,* 165–169.

Rush, A. J., Beck, A. T., Kovacs, M., & Hollon, S. D. (1977). Comparative efficacy of cognitive therapy and pharmacotherapy in the treatment of depressed outpatients. *Cognitive Therapy and Research, 1,* 17–39.

Rush, A. J., Trivedi, M., Wisniewski, S. R., Nierenberg, A. A., Stewart, J. W., Warden, D, et al. (2006). Acute and longer-term outcomes in depressed outpatients requiring one or several treatment steps: A STAR*D report. *American Journal of Psychiatry, 163,* 1905–1917.

Rutherford, M. J., Cacciola, J. S., & Alterman, A. I. (1999). Antisocial personality disorder and psychopathy in cocaine-dependent women. *American Journal of Psychiatry, 156,* 849–856.

Rutledge, T., Reis, S. E., Olson, M., Owens, J., Kelsey, S. F., Pepine, C. J., Reichek, N., Rogers, W. J., Merz, N. B., Sopko, G., Cornell, C. E., & Matthews, K. A. (2001). Psychosocial variables are associated with atherosclerosis risk factors among women with chest pain: The WISE study. *Psychosomatic Medicine, 63,* 282–288.

Rutter, M. (1983). Cognitive deficits in the pathogenesis of autism. *Journal of Child Psychology and Psychiatry, 2,* 513–531.

Rutter, M., Caspi, A., Fergusson, D., Horwood, L. J., Goodman, R., Maughan, B., Moffitt, T. E., Meltzer, H., & Carroll, J. (2004). Sex differences in developmental reading disability: New findings from 4 epidemiological studies. *Journal of the American Medical Association, 291,* 2007–2012.

Rutter, M., & Silberg, J. (2002). Gene-environment interplay in relation to emotional and behavioral disturbance. *Annual Review of Psychology, 53,* 463–490.

Sabol, S. Z., Nelson, M. L., Fisher, C., Gunzerath, L., Brody, C. L., et al. (1999). A genetic association for cigarette smoking behavior. *Health Psychology, 18,* 7–13.

Sacco, R. L., Elkind, M., Boden-Albala, B., Lin, I., Kargman, D. E., et al. (1999). The protective effect of moderate alcohol consumption on ischemic stroke. *Journal of the American Medical Association, 281,* 53–60.

Sachs, G. S., & Thase, M. E. (2000). Bipolar disorder therapeutics: Maintenance treatment. *Biological Psychiatry, 48,* 573–581.

Sackheim, H. A. (2004). Electroconvulsive therapy in late-life depression. In H. A. Sackeim & S. P. Roose (Eds.), *Late-life depression* (pp. 241–278). New York: Oxford University Press.

Sackeim, H. A., & Lisanby, S. H. (2001). Physical treatments in psychiatry: Advances in electroconvulsive therapy, transcranial magnetic stimulation, and vagus nerve stimulation. In M. M. Weissman (Ed.), *Treatment of depression: Bridging the 21st century* (pp. 151–174). Washington, DC: American Psychiatric Publishing.

Sackeim, H. A., Nordlie, J. W., & Gur, R. C. (1979). A model of hysterical and hypnotic blindness: Cognition, motivation and awareness. *Journal of Abnormal Psychology, 88,* 474–489.

Sackeim, H. A., Prudic, J., Fuller, R., Keilp, J., Lavori, P. W. & Olfson, M. (2007). The cognitive effects of electroconvulsive therapy in community settings. *Neuropsychopharmacology, 32,* 244–254.

Sacks, O. (1995). *An anthropologist on Mars.* New York: Knopf.

Saffer, H. (1991). Alcohol advertising bans and alcohol abuse: An international perspective. *Journal of Health Economics, 10,* 65–79.

Saha, S., Chant, D., & McGrath, J. (2007). A systematic review of mortality in schizophrenia: Is the differential mortality gap worsening over time? *Archives of General Psychiatry, 64,* 1123–1131.

Sakel, M. (1938). The pharmacological shock treatment of schizophrenia. *Nervous and Mental Disease Monograph, 62.*

Saks, E. R. (1997). *Jekyll on trial: Multiple personality disorder and criminal law.* New York: New York University Press.

Saks, E. R. (2007). *The center cannot hold: My journey through madness.* New York: Hyperion.

Salamone, J. D. (2000). A critique of recent studies on placebo effects of antidepressants: Importance of research on active placebos. *Psychopharmacology, 152,* 1–6.

Salan, S. E., Zinberg, N. E., & Frei, E. (1975). Antiemetic effect of delta-9-THC in patients receiving cancer chemotherapy. *New England Journal of Medicine, 293,* 795–797.

Salekin, R. T. (2002). Psychopathy and therapeutic pessimism: Clinical lore or clinical reality? *Clinical Psychology Review, 22,* 79–112.

Salem, J. E., & Kring, A. M. (1998). The role of gender differences in the reduction of etiologic heterogeneity in schizophrenia. *Clinical Psychology Review, 18,* 795–819.

Salkovskis, P. M. (1996). Cognitive-behavioral approaches to understanding obsessional problems. In R. M. Rapee (Ed.), *Current controversies in anxiety disorders 103–133.* New York: (pp. 103–113) Guilford.

Samuel, D. B., & Widiger, T. A. (2006). Clinicians' judgments of clinical utility: A comparison of the DSM-IV and five-factor models. *Journal of Abnormal Psychology, 115,* 298–308.

Samuels, J., Eaton, W. W., Bienvenu, O. J., III, Brown, C., Costa, P. T., Jr., & Nestadt, G. (2002). Prevalence and correlates of personality disorders in a community sample. *British Journal of Psychiatry, 180,* 536–542.

Sanchez. D. T., & Kiefer, A. K. (2007). Body concerns in and out of the bedroom: Implications for sexual pleasure and problems. *Archives of Sexual Behavior, 36,* 808–820.

Sanday, P. R. (1981). The socio-cultural context of rape: A cross-cultural study. *The Journal of Social Issues, 37,* 5–27.

Sandberg, S., Järvenpää, S., Paton, J. Y., & McCann, D. C. (2004). Asthma exacerbations in children immediately following stressful life events: A Cox's hierarchical regression. *Thorax, 49,* 1046–1051.

Sanderson, W. C., Rapee, R. M., & Barlow, D. H. (1989). The influence of an illusion of control on panic attacks induced via inhalation of 5.5% carbon dioxide-enriched air. *Archives of General Psychiatry, 46,* 157–162.

Santarelli, L., Saxe, M., Gross, C., Surget, A., Battaglia, F., Dulawa, S., Weisstaub, N., Lee, J., Duman, R., Arancio, O., Belzung, C., & Hen, R. (2003). Requirement of hippocampal neurogenesis for the behavioral effects of antidepressants. *Science, 301*, 805–809.

Sareen, J., Cox, B. J., Afifi, T. O., de Graaf, R., Asmundson, G. J. G., ten Have, M., et al. (2005). Anxiety disorders and risk for suicidal ideation and suicide attempts: A population-based longitudinal study of adults. *Archives of General Psychiatry, 62*, 1249–1257.

Sartorius, N., Jablensky, A., Korten, A., Ernberg, G., et al. (1986). Early manifestations and first-contact incidence of schizophrenia in different cultures: A preliminary report on the initial evaluation phase of the WHO Collaborative Study on Determinants of Outcome of Severe Mental Disorders. *Psychological Medicine, 16*, 909–928.

Sartorius, N., Shapiro, R., & Jablonsky, A. (1974). The international pilot study of schizophrenia. *Schizophrenia Bulletin, 2*, 21–35.

Saulsman, L. M., & Page, A. C. (2004). The five-factor model and personality disorder empirical literature: A meta-analytic review. *Clinical Psychology Review, 23*, 1055–1085.

Sbrocco, T., Weisberg, R. B., Barlow, D. H., & Carter, M. M. (1997). The conceptual relationship between panic disorder and male erectile dysfunction. *Journal of Sex and Marital Therapy, 23*, 212–220.

Scarborough, H. S. (1990). Very early language deficits in dyslexic children. *Child Development, 61*, 128–174.

Schaefer, L. C., Wheeler, C. C., & Futterweit, W. (1997). Gender identity disorders (transsexualism). In G. O. Gabbard & S. D. Atkinson (Eds.), *Synopsis of treatments of psychiatric disorders* (2nd ed., pp. 843–858). Washington, DC: American Psychiatric Press.

Schaie, K. W., & Hertzog, C. (1982). Longitudinal methods. In B. B. Wolman (Ed.), *Handbook of developmental psychology* (pp. 91–115). Englewood Cliffs, NJ: Prentice-Hall.

Scharff, J. S. (1995). Psychoanalytic marital therapy. In N. S. Jacobson & A. S. Gurman (Eds.), *Clinical handbook of couple therapy*. New York: Guilford.

Schecter, R., & Grether, J. K. (2008). Continuing increases in autism reported to California's Developmental Services System. *Archives of General Psychiatry, 65*, 19–24.

Scheier, M. F., & Carver, C. S. (1987). Dispositional optimism and physical well-being: The influence of generalized outcome expectancies on health. *Journal of Personality and Social Psychology, 55*, 169–210.

Scherk, H., Pajonk, F. G., & Leucht, S. (2007). Second-generation antipsychotic agents in the treatment of acute mania: A systematic review and meta-analysis of randomized controlled trials. *Archives of General Psychiatry, 64*, 442–455.

Schilder, P. (1953). *Medical psychology*. New York: International Universities Press.

Schleifer, M. (1995). Should we change our views about early childhood education? *Alberta Journal of Educational Research, 41*, 355–359.

Schlundt, D. G., & Johnson, W. G. (1990). *Eating disorders: Assessment and treatment.* Needham Heights, MA: Allyn & Bacon.

Schmidt, E., Carns, A., & Chandler, C. (2001). Assessing the efficacy of rational recovery in the treatment of alcohol/drug dependency. *Alcoholism Treatment Quarterly, 19*, 97–106.

Schmidt, N. B., Lerew, D. R., & Jackson, R. J. (1999). Prospective evaluation of anxiety sensitivity in the pathogenesis of panic: Prospective evaluation of spontaneous panic attacks during acute stress. *Journal of Abnormal Psychology, 106*, 355–364.

Schmidt, N. B., Woolaway-Bickel, K., & Bates, M. (2000). Suicide and panic disorder: Integration of the literature and new findings. In M. D. Rudd & T. E. Joiner (Eds.), *Suicide science: Expanding the boundaries* (pp. 117–136). New York: Kluwer Academic/Plenum.

Schmitt, D. P., et al. (2003). Universal sex differences in the desire for sexual variety: Tests from 52 nations, 6 continents and 13 islands. *Journal of Personality and Social Psychology, 85*, 85–104.

Schneider, J. (1996). Geriatric psychopharmacology. In L. L. Carstensen, B. A. Edelstein, & L. Dornbrand (Eds.), *The practical handbook of clinical gerontology* (pp. 481–542). Thousand Oaks, CA: Sage.

Schoeneman, T. J. (1977). The role of mental illness in the European witch-hunts of the sixteenth and seventeenth centuries: An assessment. *Journal of the History of the Behavioral Sciences, 13*, 337–351.

Schoevers, R. A., Smit, F., Deeg, D. J. H., Cuijpers, P., Dekker, J., van Tilburg, W., et al. (2006). Prevention of late-life depression in primary care: Do we know where to begin? *American Journal of Psychiatry, 163*, 1611–1621.

Schopler, E., Short, A., & Mesibov, G. (1989). Relation of behavioral treatment to "normal functioning": Comment on Lovaas. *Journal of Consulting and Clinical Psychology, 57*, 162–164.

Schreiber, F. L. (1973). *Sybil*. Chicago: Regnery.

Schuckit, M. A., Daeppen, J.-B., Danko, G. P., Tripp, M. L., Smith, T. L., et al. (1999). Clinical implications for four drugs of the DSM-IV distinction between substance with and without a physiological component. *American Journal of Psychiatry, 156*, 41–49.

Schuckit, M. A., Daeppen, J.-B., Tipp, J. E., Hesselbrock, M., & Bucholz, K. K. (1998). The clinical course of alcohol-related problems in alcohol dependent and nonalcohol dependent drinking women and men. *Journal of Studies on Alcohol, 59*, 581–590.

Schuckit, M. A., Smith, T. L., Danko, G. P., Bucholz, K. K., Reich, T., & Bierut, L. (2001). Five-year clinical course associated with DSM-IV alcohol abuse or dependence in a large group of men and women. *American Journal of Psychiatry, 158*, 1084–1090.

Schuepbach, W. M. M., Adler, R. H., & Sabbioni, M. E. E. (2002). Accuracy of clinical diagnosis of 'psychogenic disorders' in the presence of physical symptoms suggesting a general medical condition: A 5-year follow-up in 162 patients. *Psychotherapy and Psychosomatics, 71*, 11–17.

Schultz, R., & Brenner, G. (1977). Relocation of the aged: A review and theoretical analysis. *Journal of Gerontology, 32*, 323–333.

Schumacher, J. E., Milby, J. B., Wallace, D., Meehan, D-C., Kertesz, S., et al. (2007). Meta-analysis of day treatment and contingency-management dismantling research: Birmingham homeless cocaine studies (1990–2005). *Journal of Consulting and Clinical Psychology, 75*, 823–828.

Schuurmans, J., Comijs, H., Beekman, A., de Beurs, E., Deeg, D., Emmelkamp, P., et al. (2005). The outcome of anxiety disorders in older people at 6-year follow-up: Results from the longitudinal aging study Amsterdam. *Acta Psychiatrica Scandinavica, 111*, 420–428.

Schwartz, J. E., Warren, K., & Pickering, T. G. (1994). Mood, location and physical position as predictors of ambulatory blood pressure and heart rate: Application of a multilevel random effects model. *Annals of Behavioral Medicine, 16*, 210–220.

Schwartz, M. B., Chambliss, O. H., Brownell, K. D., Blair, S., & Billington, C. (2003). Weight bias among health professionals specializing in obesity. *Obesity Research, 11*, 1033–1039.

Schweizer, E., Rickels, K., Case, G., & Greenblatt, D. J. (1990). Long-term therapeutic use of benzodiazapines: Effects of gradual taper. *Archives of General Psychiatry, 47*, 908–915.

Schwitzgebel, R. L., & Schwitzgebel, R. K. (1980). *Law and psychological practice*. New York: Wiley.

Scogin, F. (1998). Anxiety in old age. In I. H. Nordhus, G. R. VandenBos, S. Berg, & P. Fromholt (Eds.), *Clinical geropsychology* (pp. 205–209). Washington, DC: American Psychological Association.

Scogin, F., & McElreath, L. (1994). Efficacy of psychosocial treatments for geriatric depression: A quantitative review. *Journal of Consulting and Clinical Psychology, 62*, 69–74.

Scogin, F., Welsh, D., Hanson, A., Stump, J., & Coates, A. (2005). Evidence-based psychotherapies for depression in older adults. *Clinical Psychology Science and Practice, 12*, 222–236.

Scroppo, J. C., Drob, S. L., Weinberger, J. L., & Eagle, P. (1998). Identifying dissociative identity disorder: A self-report and projective study. *Journal of Abnormal Psychology, 107*, 272–284.

Scully, J. A., Tosi, H., & Banning, K. (2000). Life event checklists: Revisiting the Social Readjustment Rating Scale after 30 years. *Educational and Psychological Measurement, 60*, 864–876.

Seedat, S., & Matsunaga, H. (2006). Cross-national and ethnic issues in OC spectrum disorders. Unpublished manuscript.

Seeman, T. E., Singer, B. H., Rowe, J. W., Horwitz, R. I., & McEwen, B. S. (1997). Price of adaption—Allostatic load and its health consequences: MacArthur studies of successful aging. *Archives of Internal Medicine, 157*, 2259–2268.

Seeman, T. E., & Syme, S. L. (1987). Social networks and coronary artery disease: A comparison of the structure and function of social relations as predictors of disease. *Psychosomatic Medicine, 49*, 381–406.

Segal, Z. V., Kennedy, S., Gemar, M., Hood, K., Pedersen, R., & Buis, T. (2006). Cognitive reactivity to sad mood provocation and the prediction of depressive relapse. *Archives of General Psychiatry, 63*, 749–755.

Segal, Z. V., Williams, J. M., & Teasdale, J. D. (2001). *Mindfulness-based cognitive therapy for depression*. New York: Guilford.

Segal, Z. V., Williams, J. M. G., & Teasdale, J. D. (2003). Mindfulness-based cognitive therapy for depression: A new approach to preventing relapse. *Psychotherapy Research, 13*, 123–125.

Segerstrom, S. C., & Miller, G. E. (2004). Psychological stress and the immune system: A meta-analytic study of 30 years of inquiry. *Psychological Bulletin, 130*, 601–630.

Segerstrom, S. C., Taylor, S. E., Kemeny, M. E., & Fahey, J. L. (1998). Optimism is associated with mood, coping, and immune change in response to stress. *Journal of Personality and Social Psychology, 74*, 1646–1655.

Segraves, K. B., & Segraves, R. T. (1991). Hypoactive sexual desire disorder: Prevalence and comorbidity in 906 subjects. *Journal of Sex and Marital Therapy, 17*, 55–58.

Segraves, R. T. (2003). Recognizing and reversing sexual side effects of medications. In S. B. Levine, C. B. Candace, et al. (Eds.), *Handbook of clinical sexuality for mental health professionals* (pp. 377–391). New York: Brunner-Routledge.

Segraves, R. T., & Althof, S. (1998). Psychotherapy and pharmacotherapy of sexual dysfunctions. In P. E. Nathan & J.M. Gorman (Eds.), *A guide to treatments that work.* (pp. 358–376) NY: Oxford.

Segurado, R., Detera-Wadleigh, S. D., Levinson, D. F., Lewis, C. M., Gill, M., Nurnberger, J. I., et al. (2003). Genome scan meta-analysis of schizophrenia and bipolar disorder, part III: Bipolar disorder. *The American Journal of Human Genetics, 73*, 49–62.

Seidler, G. H., & Wagner, F. E. (2006). Comparing the efficacy of EMDR and trauma-focused cognitive-behavioral therapy in the treatment of PTSD: A meta-analytic study. *Psychological Medicine, 36*, 1515–1522.

Seligman, M. E. P. (1971). Phobias and preparedness. *Behavior Therapy, 2*, 307–320.

Seligman, M. E. P. (1974). Depression and learned helplessness. In R. J. Friedman & M. M. Katz (Eds.), *The psychology of depression: Contemporary theory and research*. Washington, DC: Winston-Wiley.

Seligman, M. E. P. (1998). President's column: Positive social science. *APA Monitor, 29*, 2–5.

Seligman, M. E., Maier, S. F., & Geer, J. H. (1968). Alleviation of learned helplessness in the dog. *Journal of Abnormal Psychology, 73*, 256–262.

Selkoe, D. J. (2002). Alzheimer's disease is a synaptic failure. *Science, 298*, 789–791.

Selling, L. S. (1940). *Men against madness*. New York: Greenberg.

Selwood, A., Johnson, K., Katona, C., Lyketsos, C., & Livingson, G. (2007). Systematic review of the effect of psychological interventions on family caregivers of people with dementia. *Journal of Affective Disorders, 101*, 75–89.

Selye, H. (1950). *The physiology and pathology of exposure to stress*. Montreal: Acta.

Senate Special Committee on Aging.(2002). Retrieved from http://www.gpo.gov/congress/senate/senate22sh107.html

Sensky, T., Turkington, D., Kingdon, D., et al. (2000). A randomized controlled trial of cognitive-behavioural therapy for persistent symptoms in schizophrenia resistant to medication. *Archives of General Psychiatry, 57*, 165–172.

Seperson, S.B. (2002). Demographics about aging. In S. B. Seperson & C. R. Hegeman (Eds.), *Elder care and service learning: A handbook* (pp. 17–30). Westport, CT: Auburn House.

Serdula, M. K., Mokdad, A. H., Williamson, D. F., Galuska, D. A., et al. (1999). Prevalence of attempting weight loss and strategies for controlling weight. *Journal of the American Medical Association, 282*, 1353–1358.

Sexton, T. L., Alexander, J. F., & Mease, A. L. (2004). Levels of evidence for the models and mechanisms of therapeutic change in family and couple therapy. In M. J. Lambert (Ed.), *Bergin and Garfield's handbook of psychotherapy and behavior change* (5th ed., pp. 590–646). Hoboken, NJ: Wiley.

Shachnow, J., Clarkin, J., DiPalma, C.-S., Thurston, F., et al. (1997). Biparental psychopathology and borderline personality disorder. *Psychiatry—Interpersonal and Biological Processes, 60*, 171–181.

Shadish, W. R., & Baldwin, S. A. (2003). Meta-analysis of MFT interventions. *Journal of Marital and Family Therapy, 29*, 547–570.

Shaffer, D., Fisher, P., Dulcan, M., Davis, D., Piacentini, J., Schwab-Stone, M., et al. (1996). The NIMH Diagnostic Interview Schedule for Children, Version 2.3 (DISC 2.3): Description, acceptability, prevalence rates, and performance in the MECA study. *Journal of the American Academy of Child and Adolescent Psychiatry, 49*, 865–877.

Shaffer, D., Fisher, P., Lucas, C. P., et al. (2000). NIMH Diagnostic Interview for Children Version IV (NIMH DISC-IV): Description, differences from previous versions, and reliability of some common diagnoses. *Journal of the American Academy of Child & Adolescent Psychiatry, 39*, 28–38.

Shaper, A. G. (1990). Alcohol and mortality: A review of prospective studies. *British Journal of Addiction, 85*, 837–847.

Shapiro, D., Goldstein, I. B., & Jamner, L. D. (1995). Effects of anger and hostility, defensiveness, gender and family history of hypertension on cardiovascular reactivity. *Psychophysiology, 32*, 425–435.

Shapiro, D., Jamner, L. D., & Goldstein, I. B. (1993). Ambulatory stress psychophysiology: The study of "compensatory and defensive counterforces" and conflict in a natural setting. *Psychosomatic Medicine, 55*, 309–323.

Shapiro, F. (1999). Eye movement desensitization and reprocessing (EMDR) and the anxiety disorders: Clinical and research implications of an integrated psychotherapy treatment. *Journal of Anxiety Disorders, 13*, 35–67.

Sharkansky, E. J., King, D. W., King, L. A., et al. (2000). Coping with Gulf War combat stress: Mediating and moderating effects. *Journal of Abnormal Psychology, 109*, 188–197.

Shaw, D.S., Dishion, T. J., Supplee, L., Gardner, F., & Arnds, K. (2006). Randomized trial of a family-centered approach to the prevention of early conduct problems: 2-year effects of the family check-up in early childhood. *Journal of Consulting and Clinical Psychology, 74*, 1–9.

Shaw, L. J., Bairy Merz, C. N., Pepine, C. J., Reis, S. E., Bittner, V. E., et al. (2006). Insights from the NHLBI-sponsored Women's Ischemia Syndrome Evaluation (WISE) study. Part I: Gender differences in traditional and novel risk factors, symptom evaluation, and gender-optimized diagnostic strategies. *Journal of the American College of Cardiology, 47*, 4S-20S.

Shaywitz, B. A., Shaywitz, S. E., Blachman, B. A., et al. (2004). Development of left occipitotemporal systems for skilled reading in children after a phonologically-based intervention. *Biological Psychiatry, 55*, 926–933.

Shaywitz, S. E., Shaywitz, B. A., Fletcher, J. M., & Escobar, M. D. (1990). Prevalence of reading disability in boys and girls. *Journal of the American Medical Association, 264*, 998–1002.

Shaywitz, S. E., Shaywitz, B. A., Fulbright, R. K., et al. (2003). Neural systems for compensation and persistence: Young adult outcome of childhood reading disability. *Biological Psychiatry, 54*, 25–33.

Shaywitz, B. A., Shaywitz, S. E., Pugh, K. R., et al. (2002). Disruption of posterior brain systems for reading in children with developmental dyslexia. *Biological Psychiatry, 52*, 101–110.

Shea, M. T., Elkin, I., Imber, S. D., Sotsky, S. M., Watkins, J. T., Collins, J. F., Beckham, E., Glass, D. R., Dolan, R. T., & Parloff, M. B. (1992). Course of depressive symptoms over follow-up: Findings from the National Institute of Mental Health Treatment of Depression Collaborative Research Program. *Archives of General Psychiatry, 49*, 782–787.

Shea, M. T., Stout, R., Gunderson, J., Morey, L. C., Grilo, C. M., & McGlashan, T., et al. (2002). Short-term diagnostic stability of schizotypal, borderline, avoidant, and obsessive-compulsive personality disorders. *American Journal of Psychiatry, 159*, 2036–2041.

Sheler, J. L. (2003). A stubborn scandal: A year later, the church falls short on many reforms. U.S. *News & World Report*. Retrieved from www.usnews.com/usnews/culture/articles/30616/16catholic.htm

Sheline, Y. I. (2000). 3D MRI studies of neuroanatomic changes in unipolar major depression: The role of stress and medical comorbidity. *Biological Psychiatry, 48*, 791–800.

Sheline, Y. I. et al. (2003). Neuroimaging studies of mood disorder effects on the brain. *Biological Psychiatry, 54*, 338–352.

Sheline, Y., Barch, D., Donnelly, J. M., Ollinger, J. M., Snyder, A. Z., & Mintun, M. A. (2001). Increased amygdala response to masked emotional faces in depressed subjects resolves with antidepressant treatment: An fMRI study. *Biological Psychiatry, 50*, 651–658.

Shelton, J. D., Halperin, D. T., Nantulya, V., Potts, M., Gayle, H. D., & Holmes, K. K. (2004). Partner reduction is crucial for balanced "ABC" approach to HIV prevention. *BMJ, 328*, 891–893.

Shelton, R. C., Mainer, D. H., & Sulser, F. (1996). cAMP-dependent protein kinase activity in major depression. *American Journal of Psychiatry, 153*, 1037–1042.

Shen, G. H. C., Sylvia, L. G., Alloy, L. B., Barrett, F., Kohner, M., Iacoviello, B., et al. (2008). Lifestyle regularity and cyclothymic symptomatology. *Journal of Clinical Psychology, 64*, 482–500.

Sher, K. J., Walitzer, K. S., Wood, P. K., & Brent, E. F. (1991). Characteristics of children of alcoholics: Putative risk factors, substance use and abuse, and psychopathology. *Journal of Abnormal Psychology, 100*, 427–448.

Sher, K. J., Wood, M. D., Wood, P. K., & Raskin, G. (1996). Alcohol outcome expectancies and alcohol use: A latent variable cross-lagged panel study. *Journal of Abnormal Psychology, 105*, 561–574.

Shergill, S. S., Brammer, M. J., Williams, S. C., Murray, R. M., & McGuire, P. K. (2000). Mapping auditory hallucinations in schizophrenia using functional magnetic resonance imaging. *Archives of General Psychiatry, 57*, 1033–1038.

Sherman, D. K., Iacono, W. G., & McGue, M. K. (1997). Attention-deficit hyperactivity disorder dimensions: A twin study of inattention and impulsivity-hyperactivity. *Journal of the American Academy of Child and Adolescent Psychiatry, 36*, 745–753.

Shestyuk, A. Y., Deldin, P. J., Brand, J. E., & Deveney, C. M. (2005). Reduced sustained brain activity during processing of positive emotional stimuli in major depression. *Biological Psychiatry, 57*, 1089–1096.

Shiffman, S., Gwaltney, C. J., Balabanis, M. H., Liu, K. S., Paty, J. A., Kassel, J. D., Hickcox, M., & Gnys, M. (2002). Immediate antecedents of cigarette smoking: An analysis from ecological momentary assessment. *Journal of Abnormal Psychology, 111*, 531–545.

Shiffman, S., Paty, J. A., Gwaltney, C. J., & Dang, Q. (2004). Immediate antecedents of cigarette smoking: An analysis of unrestricted smoking patterns. *Journal of Abnormal Psychology, 113*, 166–171.

Shiffman, S., & Waters, A. J. (2004). Negative affect and smoking lapses: A prospective analysis. *Journal of Consulting and Clinical Psychology, 72*, 192–201.

Shin, L. M., Wright, C. I., Cannistraro, P. A., Wedig, M. M., McMullin, K., Martis, B., et al. (2005). A functional magnetic resonance imaging study of amygdala and medial prefrontal cortex responses to overtly presented fearful faces in posttraumatic stress disorder. *Archives of General Psychiatry, 62*, 273–281.

Shneidman, E. S. (1973). Suicide. In *Encyclopedia Britannica*. Chicago: Encyclopedia Britannica.

Shneidman, E. S. (1987). A psychological approach to suicide. In G. R. VandenBos & B. K. Bryant (Eds.), *Cataclysms, crises, and catastrophes: Psychology in action*. Washington, DC: American Psychological Association.

Shobe, K. K., & Kihlstrom, J. F. (1997). Is traumatic memory special? *Current Directions in Psychological Science, 6*, 70–74.

Shobe, K. K., & Schooler, J. W. (2001). Discovery fact and fiction: Case-based analyses of authentic and fabricated memories of abuse. In G. M. Davies & T. Dalgleish (Eds.), *Recovered memories: Seeking the middle ground* (pp. 95–151). Chichester, UK: Wiley.

Shumaker, S. A., Legault, C., & Coker, L. H. (2006). Behavior-based interventions to enhance cognitive functioning and independence in older adults. *Journal of the American Medical Association, 296,* 2852–2854.

Shumaker, S. A., Legault, C., Kuller, L., et al. (2004). Conjugated equine estrogens and incidence of probable dementia and mild cognitive impairment in postmenopausal women: Women's health initiative memory study. *Journal of the American Medical Association, 291,* 2947–2958.

Shumaker, S. A., Legault, C., Rapp, S. R., et al. (2003). Estrogen plus progestin and the incidence of dementia and mild cognitive impairment in postmenopausal women. *Journal of the American Medical Association, 289,* 2651–2662.

Siegler, I. C., & Costa, P. T., Jr. (1985). Health behavior relationships. In J. E. Birren & K. W. Schaie (Eds.), *Handbook of the psychology of aging* (2nd ed.). New York: Van Nostrand-Reinhold.

Siegman, A. W., Townsend, S. T., Civelek, A. C., & Blumenthal, R. S. (2000). Antagonistic behavior, dominance, hostility, and coronary heart disease. *Psychosomatic Medicine, 62,* 248–257.

Siever, L. J., Torgersen, S., Gunderson, J. G., Livesley, W. J., & Kendler, K. S. (2002). The borderline diagnosis. III: Identifying endophenotypes for genetic studies. *Biological Psychiatry, 51,* 964–968.

Sigman, M. (1994). What are the core deficits in autism? In S. H. Broman & J. Grafman (Eds.), *Atypical cognitive deficits in developmental disorders: Implications for brain function* (pp. 139–157). Hillsdale, NJ: Erlbaum.

Sigman, M., Ungerer, J. A., Mundy, P., & Sherman, T. (1987). Cognition in autistic children. In D. J. Cohen, A. M. Donnellan, & R. Paul (Eds.), *Handbook of autism and pervasive developmental disorders* (pp. 103–120). New York: Wiley.

Silberg, J., Pickles, A, Rutter, M., Hewitt, J., Simonoff, E., et al. (1999). The influence of genetic factors and life stress on depression among adolescent girls. *Archives of General Psychiatry, 56,* 225–32.

Silberg, J., Rutter, M., Meyer, J., Maes, H., Hewitt, J., Simonoff, E., Pickles, A., Loeber, R., & Eaves, L. (1996). Genetic and environmental influences on the covariation between hyperactivity and conduct disturbance in juvenile twins. *Journal of Child Psychology and Psychiatry, 37,* 803–816.

Silbersweig, D., Clarkin, J. F., Goldstein, M., Kernberg, O. F., Tuescher, O., Levy, K. N., et al. (2007). Failure of frontolimbic inhibitory function in the context of negative emotion in borderline personality disorder. *American Journal of Psychiatry, 164,* 1832–1841.

Silverman, K., Evans, S. M., Strain, E. C., & Griffiths, R. R. (1992). Withdrawal syndrome after the double-blind cessation of caffeine consumption. *New England Journal of Medicine, 327,* 1109–1114.

Silverman, K., Higgins, S. T., Brooner, R. K., Montoya, I. D., Cone, E. J., Schuster, C. R., & Preston, K. I. (1996). Sustained cocaine abstinence in methadone maintenance patients through voucher-based reinforcement therapy. *Archives of General Psychiatry, 53,* 409–413.

Simeon, D., Gross, S., Guralnik, O., Stein, D. J., Schmeidler, J., & Hollander, E. (1997). Feeling unreal: 30 cases of DSM-III-R depersonalization disorder. *American Journal of Psychiatry, 154,* 1107–1112.

Simon, G. E. (1998). Management of somatoform and factitious disorders. In P. E. Nathan & J. M. Gorman (Eds.), *A guide to treatments that work* (pp. 408–422). New York: Oxford University Press.

Simon, G. E., Goldberg, D. P., Von Korff, M., & Ustun, T. B. (2002). Understanding cross-national differences in depression prevalence. *Psychological Medicine, 32,* 585–594.

Simon, G. E., & Gureje, O. (1999). Stability of somatization disorder and somatization symptoms among primary care patients. *Archives of General Psychiatry, 56,* 90–95.

Simon, G. E., Ludman, E. J., Bauer, M. S., Unutzer, J., & Operskalski, B. (2006). Long-term effectiveness and cost of a systematic care program for bipolar disorder. *Archives of General Psychiatry, 63,* 500–508.

Simon, G., Ormel, J., VonKorff, M., & Barlow, W. (1995). Health care costs associated with depressive and anxiety disorders in primary care. *The American Journal of Psychiatry, 152,* 352–357.

Simon, G. E., Von Korff, M., Piccinelli, M., Fullerton, C., & Ormel, J. (1999). An international study of the relation between somatic symptoms and depression. *New England Journal of Medicine, 341,* 1329–1335.

Simon, G. E., Von Korff, M., Rutter, C. M., & Peterson, D. A. (2001). Treatment process and outcomes for managed care patients receiving new antidepressant prescriptions from psychiatrists and primary care physicians. *Archives of General Psychiatry, 58,* 395–401.

Simon, G. E., Gureje, O., Fullerton, C. (2001). Course of hypochondriasis in an international primary care study, *General Hospital Psychiatry, 23,* 51-55.

Simon, R. J., & Aaronson, D. E. (1988). *The insanity defense: A critical assessment of law and policy in the post-Hinckley era.* New York: Praeger.

Simonoff, E. (2001). Genetic influences on conduct disorder. In J. Hill & B. Maughan (Eds.), *Conduct disorders in childhood and adolescence* (pp. 202–234). Cambridge, UK: Cambridge University Press.

Singer, R., & Ryff, C. D. (1999). Hierarchies of life histories and associated health risks. In N. E. Alder, M. Marmot, B. E. McEwen, & J. Stewart (Eds.), *Socioeconomic status and health in industrial nations: Social, psychological, and biological pathways* (pp. 96–115). New York: New York Academy of Sciences.

Sinha, S. S., Mohlman, J., & Gorman, J. M. (2004). Neurobiology. In R. G. Heimberg, C. L. Turk, & D. S. Mennin (Eds.), *Generalized anxiety disorder* (pp. 187–218). New York: Guilford.

Siok, W. T., Perfetti, C. A., Lin, Z., & Tan, L. H. (2004). Biological abnormality of impaired reading is constrained by culture. *Nature, 431,* 71–76.

Skinner, B. F. (1953). *Science and human behavior.* New York: Macmillan.

Skinstad, A. H., & Swain, A. (2001). Comorbidity in a clinical sample of substance abusers. *American Journal of Drug and Alcohol Abuse, 27,* 45–64.

Skoog, G., & Skoog, I. (1999). A 40-year follow-up of patients with obsessive-compulsive disorder. *Archives of General Psychiatry, 56,* 121–130.

Slater, E. (1961). The thirty-fifth Maudsley lecture: Hysteria 311. *Journal of Mental Science, 107,* 358–381.

Slater, E., & Glithero, E. (1965). A follow-up of patients diagnosed as suffering from hysteria. *Journal of Psychosomatic Research, 9,* 9–13.

Sloan, D. M., Strauss, M. E., & Wisner, K. L. (2001). Diminished response to positive stimuli by depressed women. *Journal of Abnormal Psychology, 110,* 488–493.

Slutske, W. S., Heath, A. C., Dinwiddie, S. H., Madden, P. A. F., Bucholz, K. K., Dunne, M. P., Statham, D. J., &

Martin, N. G. (1997). Modeling genetic and environmental influences in the etiology of conduct disorder: A study of 2,682 adult twin pairs. *Journal of Abnormal Psychology, 106,* 266–279.

Small, B. J., Fratiglioni, L., Viitanen, M., et al. (2000). The course of cognitive impairment in preclinical Alzheimer disease. *Archives of Neurology, 57,* 839–844.

Small, G. W., Kepe, V., Ercoli, L. M., Siddarth, P., Bookheimer, S. Y., Miller, K. J., et al. (2006). PET of brain amyloid and tau in mild cognitive impairment. *The New England Journal of Medicine, 355,* 2652–2663.

Smart, R. G., & Ogborne, A. C. (2000). Drug use and drinking among students in 36 countries. *Addictive Behaviors, 25,* 455–460.

Smith, D. W., Bierman, E. L., & Robinson, N. M. (1978). *The biologic ages of man: From conception through old age.* Philadelphia: Saunders.

Smith, G. (1992). The epidemiology and treatment of depression when it coincides with somatoform disorders, somatization, or panic. *General Hospital Psychiatry, 14,* 265–272.

Smith, G. T., Goldman, M. S., Greenbaum, P. E., & Christiansen, B. A. (1995). Expectancy for social facilitation from drinking: The divergent paths of high expectancy and low expectancy adolescents. *Journal of Abnormal Psychology, 104,* 32–40.

Smith, J. E., Meyers, R. J., & Miller, W. R. (2001). The community reinforcement approach to the treatment of substance use disorders. *American Journal on Addictions, 10,* 51–59.

Smith, K. F., & Bengston, V. L. (1979). Positive consequences of institutionalization: Solidarity between elderly parents and their middle aged children. *The Gerontologist, 5,* 438–447.

Smith, M. L., Glass, G. V., & Miller, T. I. (1980). *The benefits of psychotherapy.* Baltimore, MD: Johns Hopkins University Press.

Smith, S. M., Stinson, F. S., Dawson, D. A., Goldstein, R., Huang, B., & Grant, B. F. (2006). Race/ethnic differences in the prevalence and co-occurrence of substance use disorders and independent mood and anxiety disorders: Results from the National Epidemiologic Survey on Alcohol and Related Conditions. *Psychological Medicine, 36,* 987–998.

Smith, S. S., Jorenby, D. E., Fiore, M. C., Anderson, J. E., Mielke, M. M., Beach, K. E., Piasecki, T. M., & Baker, T. B. (2001). Strike while the iron is hot: Can stepped-care treatments resurrect relapsing smokers? *Journal of Consulting & Clinical Psychology, 69,* 429–439.

Smith, T., Groen, A., & Wynn, J. W. (2000). Randomized trial of intensive early intervention for children with pervasive developmental disorder. *Research in Developmental Disabilities, 21,* 297–309.

Smith, Y. L. S., van Goozen, S. H. M., & Cohen-Kettenis, P. T. (2001). Adolescents with gender identity disorder who were accepted or rejected for sex reassignment surgery: A prospective follow-up study. *Journal of the American Academy of Child and Adolescent Psychiatry, 40,* 472–481.

Smoller, J. W., Pollack, M. H., Wassertheil-Smoller, S., Jackson, R. D., Oberman, A., Wong, N. D., et al. (2007). Panic attacks and risk of incident cardiovascular events among postmenopausal women in the women's health initiative observational study. *Archives of General Psychiatry, 64,* 1153–1160.

Smyth, J., Wonderlich, S. A., Heron, K. E., Sliwinski, M. J., Crosby, R. D., et al. (2007). Daily and momentary mood and stress are associated with binge eating and vomiting in bulimia nervosa patients in the natural environment. *Journal of Consulting and Clinical Psychology, 75,* 629–638.

Snowden, M., & Roy-Byrne, P. (1998). Mental illness and nursing home reform: OBRA-87 ten years later. *Psychiatric Services, 49,* 220–233.

Snowden, D. A., Kemper, S. J., Mortimer, J. A., Greiner, L. H., et al. (1996). Linguistic ability in early life and cognitive function and Alzheimer's disease in late life: Findings from the nun study. *Journal of the American Medical Association, 275,* 528–534.

Snyder, D. K., Castellani, A. M., & Whisman, M. A. (2006). Current status and future directions in couple therapy. *Annual Review of Psychology, 57,* 317–344.

Snyder, D. K., Wills, R. M., & Grady-Fletcher, A. (1991). Long-term effectiveness of behavioral versus insight-oriented marital therapy: A 4-year follow-up study. *Journal of Consulting and Clinical Psychology, 59,* 138–141.

Sobczak, S., Honig, A., Nicolson, N. A., & Riedel, W. J. (2002). Effects of acute tryptophan depletion on mood and cortisol release in first-degree relatives of type I and type II bipolar patients and healthy matched controls. *Neuropsychopharmacology, 27,* 834–842.

Sobczak, S., Honig, A., van Duinen, M. A., & Riedel, W. J. (2002 a, b). Serotonergic dysregulation in bipolar disorders: A literature review of serotonergic challenge studies. *Bipolar Disorders, 4,* 347–356.

Sobell, L. C., & Sobell, M. B. (1996). *Timeline Followback user's guide: A calendar method for assessing alcohol and drug use.* Toronto, Canada: Addiction Research Foundation.

Sobell, L. C., Toneatto, A., & Sobell, M. B. (1990). Behavior therapy. In A. S. Bellack & M. Hersen (Eds.), *Handbook of comparative treatments for adult disorders* (pp. 479–505). New York: Wiley.

Sobell, M. B., & Sobell, L. C. (1976). Second-year treatment outcome of alcoholics treated by individualized behavior therapy: Results. *Behaviour Research and Therapy, 14,* 195–215.

Sobell, M. B., & Sobell, L. C. (1993). *Problem drinkers: Guided self-change treatment.* New York: Guilford.

Sobell, M. B., & Sobell, L. C. (2000). Stepped care as a heuristic approach to the treatment of alcohol problems. *Journal of Consulting and Clinical Psychology, 68,* 573–579.

Soler, J., Pascual, J. C., Campins, J., Barrachina, J., Puigdemont, D., Alvarez, E., et al. (2005). Double-blind, placebo-controlled study of dialectical behavior therapy plus olanzapine for borderline personality disorder. *American Journal of Psychology, 162,* 1221–1224.

Soloff, P. H., Meltzer, C. C., Greer, P. J., et al. (2000). A fenfluramine-activated FDG-PET study of borderline personality disorder. *Biological Psychiatry, 47,* 540–547.

Solomon, D. A., Keller, M. B., Leon, A. C., Mueller, T. I., Lavori, P. W., Shea, M. T., Coryell, W., Warshaw, M., Turvey, C., Maser, J. D., & Endicott, J. (2000). Multiple recurrences of major depressive disorder. *American Journal of Psychiatry, 157,* 229–233.

Soomro, G. M., Altman, D., Rajagopal, S., & Oakley-Browne, M. Selective serotonin re-uptake inhibitors (SSRIs) versus placebo for obsessive compulsive disorder (OCD). (2008). *The Cochrane Database of Systematic Reviews,* Issue 1. Art. No.: CD001765. DOI: 10.1002/14651858.CD001765.pub3.

Soyka, M., Horak, M., Morhart, V., & Moeller, H. J. (2001). Modellprojekt "Qualifizierte ambulante Entgiftung" [Qualified outpatient detoxification]. *Nervenarzt, 72,* 565–569.

Spanos, N. P. (1994). Multiple identity enactments and multiple personality disorder: A sociocognitive perspective. *Psychological Bulletin, 116,* 143–165.

Spanos, N. P., Weekes, J. R., & Bertrand, L. D. (1985). Multiple personality: A social psychological perspective. *Journal of Abnormal Psychology, 94,* 362–376.

Spar, J. E., & LaRue, A. (1990). *Geriatric psychiatry.* Washington, DC: American Psychiatric Press.

Sparrow, S. S., Ballo, D. A., & Cicchetti, D. V. (1984). *Vineland Adaptive Behavior Scales.* Circle Pines, MI: American Guidance Service.

Spek, V., Cuijpers, P., Nyklicek, I., Riper, H., Keyzer, J., & Pop, V. (2007). Database of abstracts of reviews of effects (DARE)—short record display: Internet-based cognitive behaviour therapy for symptoms of depression and anxiety: A meta-analysis. *Psychological Medicine, 37,* 319–328.

Spencer, S. J., Steele, C. M., & Quinn, D. M. (1999). Stereotype threat and women's math performance. *Journal of Experimental Social Psychology, 35,* 4–28.

Spencer, T., Biederman, J., Wilens, T., Harding, M., O'Donnell, D., & Griffin, S. (1996). Pharmacotherapy of attention-deficit hyperactivity disorder across the life cycle. *Journal of the American Academy of Child and Adolescent Psychiatry, 35,* 409–432.

Spengler, A. (1977). Manifest sadomasochism of males: Results of an empirical study. *Archives of Sexual Behavior, 6,* 441–456.

Spezio, M. L., Adolphs, R., Hurley, R. S., & Piven, J. (2007). Abnormal use of facial information in high-functioning autism. *Journal of Autism and Developmental Disorders, 37,* 929–939.

Spiess, W. F. J., Geer, J. H., & O'Donohue, W. T. (1984). Premature ejaculation: Investigation of factors in ejaculatory latency. *Journal of Abnormal Psychology, 93,* 242–245.

Spitzer, M., & Petry, N. (2006). Contingency management for treatment of substance abuse. *Annual Review of Clinical Psychology, 2,* 411–434.

Spitzer, R. L., Gibbon, M., Skodol, A. E., Williams, J. B. W., & First, M. B. (Eds.). 1994. *DSM-IV casebook: A learning companion to the Diagnostic and Statistical Manual of Mental Disorders* (4th ed.). Washington, DC: American Psychiatric Press.

Spitzer, R. L., Gibbon, M., & Williams, J. B. W. (1996). *Structured clinical interview of DSM-IV Axis I disorders.* New York: New York State Psychiatric Institute, Biometrics Research Department.

Spitzer, R. M., Stunkard, A., Yanovski, S., Marcus, M. D., Wadden, T., et al. (1993). Binge eating disorders should be included in DSM-IV. *International Journal of Eating Disorders, 13,* 161–169.

Spoth, R. A., Guyll, M., & Day, S. X. (2002). Universal family-focused interventions in alcohol-use prevention: Cost-benefit analyses of two interventions. *Journal of Studies on Alcohol, 63,* 219–228.

Spoth, R. A., Redmond, C., Shin, C., & Azevedo, K. (2004). Brief family intervention effects on adolescent substance initiation: School-level growth curve analyses 6 years following baseline. *Journal of Consulting and Clinical Psychology, 72,* 535–542.

Sprich, S., Biederman, J., Crawford, M. H., Mundy, E., & Faraone, S. V. (2000). Adoptive and biological families of children and adolescents with ADHD. *Journal of the American Academy of Child and Adolescent Psychiatry, 39,* 1432–1437.

Stack, S. (2000). Media impacts on suicide: A quantitative review of 293 findings. *Social Science Quarterly, 81,* 957–971.

Stacy, A. W., Newcomb, M. D., & Bentler, P. M. (1991). Cognitive motivation and drug use: A 9-year longitudinal study. *Journal of Abnormal Psychology, 100,* 502–515.

Stahl, S. (2006). *Essential psychopharmacology: The prescriber's guide: Revised and updated edition* (Essential psychopharmacology series). Cambridge, UK: Cambridge University Press.

Stanford, J. L., & Greenberg, R. S. (1989). Breast cancer incidence in young women by estrogen receptor status and race. *American Journal of Public Health, 79,* 71–73.

Stanley, M. A., & Turner, S. M. (1995). Current status of pharmacological and behavioral treatment of obsessive-compulsive disorder. *Behavior Therapy, 26,* 163–186.

Stanton, A. H., Gunderson, J. G., Knapp, P. H., Frank, A. E., Vanicelli, M. L., Schnitzer, R., & Rosenthal, R. (1984). Effects of psychotherapy in schizophrenia. *Schizophrenia Bulletin, 10,* 520–563.

Stark, K. D., Schmidt, K., Joiner, T. E., & Lux, M. G. (1998). Cognitive triad: Relationship to depressive symptoms, parents' cognitive triad, and perceived parental messages. *Journal of Abnormal Child Psychology, 24,* 615–631.

Stark, K. D., Swearer, S., Sommer, D., Hickey, B. B., Napolitano, S., Kurowski, C., and Dempsey, M. (1998). School-based group treatment for depressive disorders in children. In K. C. Stoiber & T. R. Kratochwill (Eds.), *Handbook of group intervention for children and families* (pp. 68–99). Needham Heights, MA: Allyn & Bacon.

Stead, L. F., Perera, R., Bullen, C., Mant, D., & Lancaster, T. (2008). Nicotine replacement therapy for smoking cessation. *Cochrane Database of Systematic Reviews.* No.: CD000146. DOI: 10.1002/14651858.CD000146.pub3.

Steadman, H. J. (1979). *Beating a rap: Defendants found incompetent to stand trial.* Chicago: University of Chicago Press.

Steadman, H. J., McGreevy, M. A., Morrissey, J. P., Callahan, L. A., Robbins, P. C., & Cirincione, C. (1993). *Before and after Hinckley: Evaluating insanity defense reform.* New York: Guilford.

Steadman, H. J., Mulvey, E. P., Monahan, J., Robbins, P. C., Appelbaum, P. S., Grisso, T., Roth, L. H., & Silver, E. (1998). Violence by people discharged from acute psychiatric inpatient facilities and by others in the same neighborhoods. *Archives of General Psychiatry, 55,* 393–401.

Steele, C. M., & Josephs, R. A. (1988). Drinking your troubles away: 2. An attention-allocation model of alcohol's effects on psychological stress. *Journal of Abnormal Psychology, 97,* 196–205.

Steele, C. M., & Josephs, R. A. (1990). Alcohol myopia: Its prized and dangerous effects. *American Psychologist, 45,* 921–933.

Steen, R.G., Mull, C., McClure, R., Hamer, R.M.,& Lieberman, J.A. (2006). Brain volume in first-episode schizophrenia: Systematic review and meta-analysis of magnetic resonance imaging studies. *British Journal of Psychiatry, 188,* 510–518

Steiger, H., Gauvin, L., Jabalpurwala, S., & Séguin, J. R. 1999. Hypersensitivity to social interactions in bulimic syndromes: Relationship to binge eating. *Journal of Consulting and Clinical Psychology, 67,* 765–775.

Stein, D. J., Ipser, J. C., & van Balkom, A. J. (2004). Pharmacotherapy for social anxiety disorder. *Cochrane Database of Systematic Reviews,* Issue 4. Art. No.: CD001206. DOI: 10.1002/14651858.CD001206.pub2.

Stein, D. J., Ipser, J. C., & van Seedat, S. (2000). Pharmacotherapy for post traumatic stress disorder (PTSD). *Cochrane Database of Systematic Reviews,* Issue 4. Art. No.: CD002795. DOI: 10.1002/14651858. CD002795.pub2.

Stein, E. A., Pankiewicz, J., Harsch, H. H., Cho, J.-K., Fuller, S. A., et al. (1998). Nicotine-induced limbic cortical activation in the human brain: A functional MRI study. *American Journal of Psychiatry, 155,* 1009–1015.

Stein, L. I., & Test, M. A. (1980). Alternative to mental hospital treatment: I. Conceptual model, treatment program, and clinical evaluation. *Archives of General Psychiatry, 37,* 392–397.

Stein, M. B. (1998). Neurobiological perspectives on social phobia: From affiliation to zoology. *Biological Psychiatry, 44,* 1277–1285.

Stein, M. B., Liebowitz, M. R., Lydiard, R. B., Pitts, C. D., Bushnell, W., & Gergel, I. (1998). Paroxetine treatment of generalized social phobia (social anxiety disorder): A randomized clinical trial. *Journal of the American Medical Association, 280,* 708–713.

Steinberg, J. S., Arshad, A., Kowalski, M., et al. (2004). Increased incidence of life-threatening ventricular arrhythmias in implantable defibrillator patients after the World Trade Center attack. *Journal of the American College of Cardiology, 44,* 1261–1264.

Steinhausen, H. C., & Metzke, C. W. (1998). Youth self-report of behavioral and emotional problems in a Swiss epidemiological study. *Journal of Youth and Adolescence, 27,* 429–441.

Stek, M. L., Gussekloook, J., Beekman, A. T. F., van Tilburg, W., & Westendorp, R. G. J. (2004). Prevalence, correlates and recognition of depression in the oldest old: The Leiden 85-plus study. *Journal of Affective Disorders, 78,* 193–200.

Steketee, G., & Barlow, D. H. (2004). Obsessive-compulsive disorder. In D. H. Barlow (Ed.), *Anxiety and its disorders: The nature and treatment of anxiety and panic* (pp. 516–550). New York: Guilford.

Steketee, G., & Frost, R. O. (1998). Obsessive-compulsive disorder. In A. S. Bellack & M. Hersen (Eds.), *Comprehensive clinical psychology: Vol. 6. Adults: Clinical formulation and treatment.* Oxford: Pergamon.

Steketee, G., & Frost, R. (2003). Compulsive hoarding: Current status of the research. *Clinical Psychology Review, 23,* 905–927.

Stephens, J. H., & Kamp, M. (1962). On some aspects of hysteria: A clinical study. *Journal of Nervous and Mental Disease, 134,* 305–315.

Stephens, R. S., Roffman, R. A., & Simpson, E. E. (1993). Adult marijuana users seeking treatment. *Journal of Consulting and Clinical Psychology, 61,* 1100–1104.

Steptoe, A. (1997). Stress management. In A. Baum, S. Newman, J. Weinman, R. West, & C. McManus (Eds.), *Cambridge encyclopedia of psychology, health and medicine* (pp. 262–264). Cambridge, UK: Cambridge University Press.

Stern, G. S., & Berrenberg, J. L. (1979). Skill-set, success outcome, and mania as determinants of the illusion of control. *Journal of Research in Personality, 13,* 206–222.

Stern, R. S., & Cobb, J. P. (1978). Phenomenology of obsessive-compulsive neurosis. *British Journal of Psychiatry, 132,* 233–234.

Stevenson, J., & Jones, I. H. (1972). Behavior therapy technique for exhibitionism: A preliminary report. *Archives of General Psychiatry, 27,* 839–841.

Stewart, W. F., Ricci, J. A., Chee, E., Hahn, S. R., & Morganstein, D. (2003). Cost of lost productive work time among US workers with depression. *Journal of the American Medical Association, 289,* 3135–3144.

Stice, E. (2001). A prospective test of the dual-pathway model of bulimic pathology: Mediating effects of dieting and negative affect. *Journal of Abnormal Psychology, 110,* 124–135.

Stice, E., & Agras, W. S. (1999). Subtyping bulimics along dietary restraint and negative affect dimensions. *Journal of Consulting and Clinical Psychology, 67,* 460–469.

Stice, E., Barrera, M., & Chasin, L. (1998). Prospective differential prediction of adolescent alcohol use and problem use: Examining the mechanisms of effect. *Journal of Abnormal Psychology, 107,* 616–628.

Stice, E., Burton, E. M., & Shaw, H. (2004). Prospective relations between bulimic pathology, depression, and substance abuse: Unpacking comorbidity in adolescent girls. *Journal of Consulting and Clinical Psychology, 72,* 62–71.

Stice, E., & Fairburn, C. G. (2003). Dietary and dietary-depressive subtypes of bulimia nervosa show differential symptom presentation, social impairment, comorbidity, and course of illness. *Journal of Consulting and Clinical Psychology, 71,* 1090–1094.

Stice, E., Marti, C. N., Spoor, S., Presnell, K., & Shaw, H. (2008). Dissonance and healthy weight eating disorder prevention programs: Long-term effects from a randomized efficacy trial. *Journal of Consulting and Clinical Psychology, 76,* 329–240.

Stice, E., Shaw, H., & Marti, C. N. (2007). A meta-analytic review of eating disorder prevention programs: Encouraging findings. *Annual Review of Clinical Psychology, 3,* 207–231.

Stinson, F. S., Ruan, W. J., Pickering, R., & Grant, B. F. (2006). Cannabis use disorders in the U.S.A.: Prevalence, correlates, and comorbidity. *Psychological Medicine, 36,* 1447–1460.

Stone, A. A., Bovbjerg, D. H., Neale, J. M., Napoli, A., Valdimarsdottir, H., et al. (1992). Development of common cold symptoms following experimental rhinovirus infection is related to prior stressful life events. *Behavioral Medicine, 18,* 115–120.

Stone, A. A., & Neale, J. M. (1982). Development of a methodology for assessing daily experiences. In A. Baum & J. Singer (Eds.), *Environment and health.* Hillsdale, NJ: Erlbaum.

Stone, A. A., Reed, B. R., & Neale, J. M. (1987). Changes in daily event frequency precede episodes of physical symptoms. *Journal of Human Stress, 13,* 70–74.

Stone, A. A., Schwartz, J., Neale, J. M., Shiffman, S., Marco, C. A., et al. (1998). A comparison of coping assessed by ecological momentary assessment and retrospective recall. *Journal of Personality and Social Psychology, 74,* 1670–1680.

Stone, A. A., & Shiffman, S. (1994). Ecological momentary assessment (EMA) in behavioral medicine. *Annals of Behavioral Medicine, 16,* 199–202.

Stone, G. (1982). Health Psychology, a new journal for a new field. *Health Psychology, 1,* 1–6.

Stone, M. H. (1987). Psychotherapy of borderline patients in light of long-term follow-up. *Bulletin of the Menninger Clinic, 51,* 231–247.

Stone, M. H. (1993). *Abnormalities of personality. Within and beyond the realm of treatment.* New York: Norton.

Stopa, L., & Clark, D. M. (2000). Social phobia and interpretation of social events. *Behaviour Research and Therapy, 38,* 273–283.

Stormer, S. M., & Thompson, J. K. (1996). Explanations of body image disturbance: A test of maturational status, negative verbal commentary, and sociological hypotheses. *International Journal of Eating Disorders, 19,* 193–202.

Story, M., French, S. A., Resnick, M. D., & Blum, R. W. (1995). Ethnic/racial and socioeconomic differences in dieting behaviors and body image perceptions in adolescents. *International Journal of Eating Disorders, 18,* 173–179.

Stoving, R. K., Hangaard, J., Hansen-Nord, M., & Hagen, C. (1999). A review of endocrine changes in anorexia nervosa. *Journal of Psychiatric Research, 33,* 139–152.

Strain, E. C., Bigelow, G. E., Liebson, I. A., & Stitzer, M. L. (1999). Moderate- vs low-dose methadone in the treatment of opioid dependence. *Journal of the American Medical Association, 281,* 1000–1005.

Strakowski, S. M., Sax, K. W., Setters, M. J., Stanton, S. P., & Keck, P. E. (1997). Lack of enhanced behavioral response to repeated d-amphetamine challenge in first-episode psychosis: Implications for sensitization model of psychosis in humans. *Biological Psychiatry, 42,* 749–755.

Strassberg, D. S., Kelly, M. P., Carroll, C., & Kircher, J. C. (1987). The psychophysiological nature of premature ejaculation. *Archives of Sexual Behavior, 16*(4), 327–336.

Strauss, J. S., Carpenter, W. T., & Bartko, J. J. (1974). The diagnosis and understanding of schizophrenia: Part 3. Speculations on the processes that underlie schizophrenic signs and symptoms. *Schizophrenia Bulletin, 1,* 61–69.

Strauss, M. E., & Ogrocki, P. K. (1996). Confirmation of an association between family history of affective disorder and the depressive syndrome in Alzheimer's disease. *American Journal of Psychiatry, 153,* 1340–1342.

Streeton, C., & Whelan, G. (2001). Naltrexone, a relapse prevention maintenance treatment of alcohol dependence: A meta-analysis of randomized controlled trials. *Alcohol & Alcoholism, 36,* 544–552.

Streltzer, J., & Johansen, L. (2006). Prescription drug dependence and evolving beliefs about chronic pain management. *American Journal of Psychiatry, 163,* 594–598.

Striegel-Moore, R. H., Cachelin, F. M., Dohm, F.-A., Pike, K. M., Wilfely, D. E., & Fairburn, C. G. (2001). Comparison of binge eating disorder and bulimia nervosa in a community sample. *International Journal of Eating Disorders, 29,* 157–165.

Striegel-Moore, R. H., & Franco, D. L. (2003). Epidemiology of binge eating disorder. *International Journal of Eating Disorders, 34,* S19–S29.

Striegel-Moore, R. H., & Franco, D. L. (2008). Should binge eating disorder be included in the DSM-V? A critical review of the state of the evidence. *Annual Review of Clinical Psychology, 4,* 305–324.

Striegel-Moore, R. H., Garvin, V., Dohm, F.-A., & Rosenheck, R. (1999a). Eating disorders in a national sample of hospitalized male and female veterans: Prevalence and psychiatric comorbidity. *International Journal of Eating Disorders, 25,* 405–414.

Striegel-Moore, R. H., Garvin, V., Dohm, F. A., & Rosenheck, R. (1999b). Psychiatric comorbidity of eating disorders in men: A national study of hospitalized veterans. *International Journal of Eating Disorders, 25,* 399–404.

Striegel-Moore, R. H., Schreiber, G. B., Lo, A., Crawford, P., Obarzanek, E., & Rodin, J. (2000). Eating disorder symptoms in a cohort of 11 to 16-year-old black and white girls: The NHLBI growth and health study. *International Journal of Eating Disorders, 27,* 49–66.

Striegel-Moore, R. H., Wilson, G. T., Wilfley, D. E., Elder, K. A., & Brownell, K. D. (1998). Binge eating in an obese community sample. *International Journal of Eating Disorders, 23,* 27–36.

Stritzke, W. G. K., Patrick, C. J., & Lang, P. J. (1995). Alcohol and emotion: A multidimensional approach incorporating startle probe methodology. *Journal of Abnormal Psychology, 104,* 114–122.

Strober, M., Freeman, R., Lampert, C., Diamond, J., & Kaye, W. (2000). Controlled family study of anorexia nervosa and bulimia nervosa: Evidence of shared liability and transmission of partial syndromes. *American Journal of Psychiatry, 157,* 393–401.

Strober, M., Freeman, R., Lampert, C., Diamond, J., & Kaye, W. (2001). Males with anorexia nervosa: A controlled study of eating disorders in first-degree relatives. *International Journal of Eating Disorders, 29,* 264–269.

Strober, M., Freeman, R., & Morrell, W. (1997). The long-term course of severe anorexia nervosa in adolescents: Survival analysis of recovery, relapse, and outcome predictors over 10–15 years in a prospective study. *International Journal of Eating Disorders, 22,* 339–360.

Strober, M., Lampert, C., Morrell, W., Burroughs, J., & Jacobs, C. (1990). A controlled family study of anorexia nervosa: Evidence of family aggregation and lack of shared transmission with affective disorders. *International Journal of Eating Disorders, 9,* 239–253.

Stroebe, M., Stroebe, W., & Abakoumkin, G. (2005). The broken heart: Suicidal ideation in bereavement. *American Journal of Psychiatry, 162,* 2178–2180.

Strub, R. L., & Black, F. W. (1981). *Organic brain syndromes: An introduction to neurobehavioral disorders.* Philadelphia: F.A. Davis.

Struckman-Johnson, C. (1988). Forced sex on dates: It happens to men, too. *Journal of Sex Research, 24,* 234–241.

Strunk, D. R., DeRubeis, R. J., Chiu, A. W., & Alvarez, J. (2007). Patients' competence in and performance of cognitive therapy skills: Relation to the reduction of relapse risk following treatment for depression. *Journal of Consulting and Clinical Psychology, 75,* 523–530.

Styron, W. (1992). *Darkness visible: A memoir of madness.* New York: Vintage.

Substance Abuse and Mental Health Services Administration (SAMHSA). *Highlights–2006.* Office of Applied Studies. Treatment Episode Data Set (TEDS). National Admissions to Substance Abuse Treatment Services, DASIS Series: S-40, DHHS Publication No. (SMA) 08–4313, Rockville, MD.

Substance Abuse and Mental Health Services Administration (SAMHSA). (2004). *Overview of findings from the 2003 National Survey on Drug Use and Health* (Office of Applied Studies, NSDUH Series H-24, DHHS Publication No. SMA 04–3963). Rockville, MD.

Substance Abuse and Mental Health Services Administration (SAMHSA). (2007). *Results from the 2006 National Survey on Drug Use and Health: National findings* (Office of Applied Studies, NSDUH Series H-32, DHHS Publication No. SMA 07–4293). Rockville, MD.

Suddath, R. L., Christison, G. W., Torrey, E. F., Cassonova, M. F., Weinberger, D. R., et al. (1990). Anatomical abnormalities in the brains of monozygotic twins discordant for schizophrenia. *New England Journal of Medicine, 322,* 789–793.

Sugarman, P., Dumughn, C., Saad, K., Hinder, S., & Bluglass, S. (1994). Dangerousness in exhibitionists. *Journal of Forensic Psychiatry, 5,* 287–296.

Sullivan, J. M. (2000). Cellular and molecular mechanisms underlying learning and memory impairments produced by cannabinoids. *Learning and Memory, 7,* 132–139.

Sullivan, P. F. (1995). Mortality in anorexia nervosa. *American Journal of Psychiatry, 152,* 1073–1075.

Sullivan, P. F., Neale, M. C., & Kendler, K. S. (2000). Genetic epidemiology of major depression: Review and metaanalysis. *American Journal of Psychiatry, 157,* 1552–1562.

Suls, J., & Bunde, J. (2005). Anger, anxiety, and depression as risk factors for cardiovascular disease: The problems and implications of overlapping affective dispositions. *Psychological Bulletin, 131,* 260–300.

Sultzer, D. L., Davis, S. M., Tariot, P. N., Dagerman, K. S., Lebowitz, B. D., & Lyketsos, C. G. (2008). Clinical symptom responses to atypical antipsychotic medications in Alzheimer disease: Phase 1 outcomes from the CATIE-AD effectiveness trial. *American Journal of Psychiatry, 165,* 844–854.

Sunderland, T., Hampel, H., Takeda, M., Putnam, K. T., & Cohen, R. M. (2006). Biomarkers in the diagnosis of Alzheimer's disease: Are we ready? *Journal of Geriatric Psychiatry and Neurology, 19,* 172–179.

Surles, R. C., Blanch, A. K., Shern, D. L., & Donahue, S. A. (1992). Case management as a strategy for systems change. *Health Affairs, 11,* 151–163.

Susser, E., Neugebauer, R., Hoek, H. W., Brown, A. S., Lin, S., et al. (1996). Schizophrenia after prenatal famine: Further evidence. *Archives of General Psychiatry, 53,* 25–31.

Susser, E., & Wanderling, J. (1994). Epidemiology of non-affective acute remitting psychosis versus schizophrenia: Sex and sociocultural setting. *Archives of General Psychiatry, 51,* 294–301.

Sussman, S. (1996). Development of a school-based drug abuse prevention curriculum for high-risk youth. *Journal of Psychoactive Drugs, 28,* 169–182.

Sussman, S., Dent, C. W., McAdams, L., Stacy, A. W., Burton, D., & Flay, B. R. (1994). Group self-identification and adolescent cigarette smoking: A 1-year prospective study. *Journal of Abnormal Psychology, 103,* 576–580.

Sussman, S., Dent, C. W., Simon, T. R., Stacy, A. W., Galaif, E. R., Moss, M. A., Craig, S., & Johnson, C. A. (1995). Immediate impact of social influence-oriented substance abuse prevention curricula in traditional and continuation high schools. *Drugs and Society, 8,* 65–81.

Sussman, S., Stacy, A. W., Dent, C. W., Simon, T. R., & Johnson, C. A. (1996). Marijuana use: Current issues and new research directions. *The Journal of Drug Issues, 26,* 695–733.

Sussman, T., Dent, C. W., & Lichtman, K. L. (2001). Project EX: Outcomes of a teen smoking cessation program. *Addictive Behaviors, 26,* 425–438.

Sutcliffe, J. P., & Jones, J. (1962). Personal identity, multiple personality, and hypnosis. *International Journal of Clinical and Experimental Hypnosis, 10,* 231–269.

Sutker, P. B., & Adams, H. E. (2001). *Comprehensive handbook of psychopathology* (3rd ed.). New York: Kluwer Academic/Plenum.

Sutker, P. B., Uddo, M., Brailey, K., Vasterling, J. J., & Errera, P. (1994). Psychopathology in war-zone deployed and nondeployed Operation Desert Storm troops assigned grave registration duties. *Journal of Abnormal Psychology, 103,* 383–390.

Suzuki, K., Takei, N., Kawai, M., Minabe, Y., & Mori, N. (2003). Is *taijin kyofusho* a culture-bound syndrome? *American Journal of Psychiatry, 160,* 1358.

Svarstad, B. L., & Mount, J. K. (2001). Chronic benzodiazepine use in nursing homes: Effects of federal guidelines, resident mix, and nurse staffing. *Journal of the American Geriatrics Society, 49,* 1673–1678.

Svartberg, M., Stiles, T. C., & Seltzer, M. H. (2004). Randomized, controlled trial of the effectiveness of short-term dynamic psychotherapy and cognitive therapy for cluster C personality disorders. *American Journal of Psychiatry, 161,* 810–817.

Swain, J., Koszycki, D., Shlik, J., & Bradwein, J. (2003). In D. Nutt & J. Ballenger (Eds.), *Anxiety disorders* (pp. 269–295). Malden, MA: Blackwell.

Swainson, R., Hodges, J. R., Galton, C. J., Semple, J., Michael, A., Dunn, B. D., Iddon, J. L., Robbins, T. W., & Sahakian, B. J. (2001). Early detection and differential diagnosis of Alzheimer's disease and depression with neuropsychological tasks. *Dementia and Geriatric Cognition Disorders, 12,* 265–280.

Swanson, J. M. Hinshaw, S. P., Arnold, L. E., Gibbons, R., Marcus, S., Hur, K., et al. (2007). Secondary evaluations of MTA 36-month outcomes: Propensity score and growth mixture model analyses. *Journal of the American Academy of Child and Adolescent Psychiatry, 46*(8), 1002–1013.

Swanson, J., Kinsbourne, M., Nigg, J., et al. (2007). Etiologic subtypes of attention-deficit/hyperactivity disorder: Brain imaging, molecular genetic and environmental factors and the dopamine hypothesis. *Neuropsychology Review, 17,* 39–59.

Swanson, J. M., Kraemer, H. C., Hinshaw, S. P., et al. (2001). Clinical relevance of the primary findings of the MTA: Success rates based on severity of ADHD and ODD symptoms at the end of treatment. *Journal of the American Academy of Child and Adolescent Psychiatry, 40,* 168–179.

Swanson, J., McBurnett, K., Christian, D. L., & Wigal, T. (1995). Stimulant medications and the treatment of children with ADHD. In T. H. Ollendick & R. J. Prinz (Eds.), *Advances in clinical child psychology* (Vol. 17, pp. 265–322). New York: Plenum.

Swanson, J. W., Holzer, C. E., Ganju, V. K., & Jono, R. T. (1990). Violence and psychiatric disorder in the community: Evidence from the Epidemiological Catchment Area surveys. *Hospital and Community Psychiatry, 41,* 761–770.

Sweet, J. J., Carr, M. A., Rossini, E., & Kasper, C. (1986). Relationship between the Luria-Nebraska Neuropsychological Battery and the WISC-R: Further examination using Kaufman's factors. *International Journal of Clinical Neuropsychology, 8,* 177–180.

Sweet, R. A., Mulsant, B. H., Gupta, B., Rifai, A. H., Pasternak, R. E., et al. (1995). Duration of neuroleptic treatment and prevalence of tardive dyskinesia in late life. *Archives of General Psychiatry, 52,* 478–486.

Szasz, T. S. (1999). *Fatal freedom: The ethics and politics of suicide.* Westport, CT: Praeger.

Szczypka, M. S., Kwok, K., Brot, M. D., Marck, B. T., Matsumoto, A. M., Donahue, B. A., & Palmiter, R. D. (2001). Dopamine production in the caudate putamen restores feeding in dopamine-deficient mice. *Neuron, 30,* 819–828.

Szechtman, H., & Woody, E. (2004). Obsessive-compulsive disorder as a disturbance of security motivation. *Psychological Review, 111,* 111–127.

TADS team (2007). The treatment for adolescents with depression study (TADS): Long term effectiveness and safety outcomes. *Archives of General Psychiatry, 64,* 1132–1144.

Tallal, P., Merzenich, M., Miller, S., & Jenkins, W. (1998). Language learning impairment: Integrating research and remediation. *Scandinavian Journal of Psychology, 39,* 197–199.

Tallal, P., Miller, S. L., Bedi, G., Byma, G., Wang, X., Nagarajan, S. S., Schreiner, C., Jenkins, W. M., & Merzenich, M. M. (1996). Language comprehension in language-learning impaired children improved with acoustically modified speech. *Science, 271,* 81–84.

Tallmadge, J., & Barkley, R. A. (1983). The interactions of hyperactive and normal boys with their mothers and fathers. *Journal of Abnormal Child Psychology, 11,* 565–579.

Tannock, R. (1998). Attention deficit hyperactivity disorder: Advances in cognitive, neurobiological, and genetic research. *Journal of Child Psychology and Psychiatry, 39,* 65–100.

Task Force on Promotion and Dissemination of Psychological Procedures. (1995). Training in and dissemination of empirically-validated psychological treatments: Report and recommendations. *The Clinical Psychologist, 48*, 3–23.

Taylor, A., & Kim-Cohen, J. (2007). Meta-analysis of gene–environment interactions in developmental psychopathology. *Development and Psychopathology, 19*, 1029–1037.

Taylor, C. B., Hayward, C., King, R., et al. (1990). Cardiovascular and symptomatic reduction effects of alprazolam and imipramine in patients with panic disorder: Results of a double-blind, placebo-controlled trial. *Journal of Clinical Psychopharmacology, 10*, 112–118.

Taylor, J., Iacono, W. G., & McGue, M. (2000). Evidence for a genetic etiology of early-onset delinquency. *Journal of Abnormal Psychology, 109*, 634–643.

Taylor, J., Loney, B. R., Bobadilla, L., Iacono, W. G., & McGue, M. (2003). Genetic and environmental influences on psychopathy trait dimensions in a community sample of male twins. *Journal of Abnormal Child Psychology, 31*, 633–645.

Taylor, S. E., Kemeny, M. E., Aspinwall, L. G., Schneider, S. G., Rodriguez, R., & Herbert, M. (1992). Optimism, coping, psychological distress, and high-risk sexual behavior among men at risk for acquired immunodeficiency syndrome (AIDS). *Journal of Personality and Social Psychology, 63*, 460–473.

Teachman, B. A., & Allen, J. P. (2007). Development of social anxiety: Social interaction predictors of implicit and explicit fear of negative evaluation. *Journal of Abnormal Child Psychology, 35*, 63–78.

Teasdale, B., Silver, E., & Monahan, J. (2006). Gender, threat/control-override delusions and violence. *Law and Human Behavior, 30*, 649–658.

Teasdale, J. D. (1988). Cognitive vulnerability to persistent depression. *Cognition and Emotion, 2*, 247–274.

Teasdale, J. D. (2004, September). Mindfulness and the third wave of cognitive-behavioural therapies. Keynote Address at the 34th annual conference of the European Association for Behavioural and Cognitive Therapies, Manchester, England.

Teasdale, J. D., Segal, Z. V., Williams, J. M. G., Ridgeway, V. A., Soulsby, J. M., & Lau, M. A. (2000). Prevention of relapse/recurrence in major depression by mindfulness-based cognitive therapy. *Journal of Consulting & Clinical Psychology, 68*, 615–623.

Tedeschi, R. G., Park, C. L., & Calhoun, L. G. (1998). Posttraumatic growth: Conceptual issues. In R. G. Tedeschi, Park, C. L., & Calhoun, L. G. (Eds.), *Posttraumatic growth: Positive changes in the aftermath of trauma* (pp. 1–22). Thousand Oaks, CA: Sage.

Telch, M. J. & Harrington, P. J. (1992). *Anxiety sensitivity and unexpectedness of arousal in mediating affective response to 35% carbon dioxide inhalation.* Unpublished manuscript.

Telch, M. J., Lucas, J. A., Schmidt, N. B., & Hanna, H. H. (1993). Group cognitive-behavioral treatment of panic disorder. *Behaviour Research and Therapy, 31*, 279–287.

Telch, M. J., Shermis, M. D., & Lucas, J. A. (1989). Anxiety sensitivity: Unitary personality trait or domain-specific appraisals? *Journal of Anxiety Disorders, 3*, 25–32.

Temple, E., Poldrack, R. A., Salidas, J., Deutsch, G. K., Tallal, P., Merzenich, M. M., & Gabrieli, J. D. E. (2001). Disrupted neural responses to phonological and orthographic processing in dyslexic children: An fMRI study. *Neuroreport, 12*, 299–307.

Teresi, J., Abrams, R., Holmes, D., Ramirez, M., & Eimicke, J. (2001). Prevalence of depression and depression recognition in nursing homes. *Social Psychiatry and Psychiatric Epidemiology, 36*, 613–620.

Teri, L., Gibbons, L. E., McCurry, S. M., Logsdon, R. G., Buchner, D. M., Barlow, W. E., et al. (2003). Exercise plus behavioral management in patients with Alzheimer disease: A randomized controlled trial. *Journal of the American Medical Assocaition, 290*, 2015–2022.

Terman, M., & Terman, J. S. (2006). Controlled trial of naturalistic dawn simulation and negative air ionization for seasonal affective disorder. *Archives of General Psychiatry, 163*, 2126–2133.

Terman, M., Terman, J. S., & Ross, D. C. (1998). A controlled trial of timed bright light and negative air ionization for treatment of winter depression. *Archives of General Psychiatry, 55*, 875–882.

Terry, D. J., & Hynes, G. J. (1998). Adjustment to a low-control situation: Reexamining the role of coping responses. *Journal of Personality and Social Psychology, 74*, 1078–1092.

Terry, R. D. (2006). Alzheimer's disease and the aging brain. *Journal of Geriatric Psychiatry and Neurology, 19*, 125–128.

Thapar, A., Fowler, T., Rice, F., et al. (2003). Maternal smoking during pregnancy and attention deficit hyperactivity disorder symptoms in offspring. *American Journal of Psychiatry, 160*, 1985–1989.

Thapar, A., Langley, K., Owen, M. J., & O'Donovan, M. C. (2007). Advances in genetic findings on attention deficit hyperactivity disorder. *Psychological Medicine, 37*, 1681–1692.

Thase, M. E., Jindal, R., & Howland, R. H. (2002). Biological aspects of depression. In C. L. Hammen & I. H. Gotlib (Eds.), *Handbook of depression* (pp. 192–218). New York: Guilford.

Thase, M. E., & Rush, A. J. (1997). When at first you don't succeed: Sequential strategies for antidepressant nonresponders. *Journal of Clinical Psychiatry, 58*(Suppl. 13), 23–29.

The ESEMeD/MHEDEA 2000 Investigators. (2004). Prevalence of mental disorders in Europe: Results from the European Study of the Epidemiology of Mental Disorders (ESEMeD) project. *Acta Psychiatrica Scandinavica, 109* (Suppl. 420), 21–27.

Theobald, H., Bygren, L. O., Carstensen, J., & Engfeldt, P. A. (2000). Moderate intake of wine is associated with reduced total mortality and reduced mortality from cardiovascular disease. *Journal of Studies on Alcohol, 61*, 652–656.

Thiruvengadam, A. P., & Chandrasekaran, K. (2007). Evaluating the validity of blood-based membrane potential changes for the identification of bipolar disorder I. *Journal of Affective Disorders, 100*, 75–82.

Thoits, P. A. (1985). Self-labeling processes in mental illness: The role of emotional deviance. *American Journal of Sociology, 92*, 221–249.

Thomas, C., Turkheimer, E., & Oltmanns, T. F. (2003). Factorial structure of pathological personality as evaluated by peers. *Journal of Abnormal Psychology, 112*, 81–91.

Thomas, G., Reifman, A., Barnes, G. M., & Farrell, M. P. (2000). Delayed onset of drunkenness as a protective factor for adolescent alcohol misuse and sexual risk taking: A longitudinal study. *Deviant Behavior, 21*, 181–200.

Thomas, K. M., Drevets, W. C., Dahl, R. E., Ryan, N. D., Birmaher, B., & Eccard, C. H., et al. (2001). Amygdala response to fearful faces in anxious and depressed children. *Archives of General Psychiatry, 58*, 1057–1063.

Thomson, A. B., & Page, L. A. (2007). Psychotherapies for hypochondriasis. *Cochrane Database of Systematic Reviews*, Issue 4. Art. No.: CD006520. DOI: 10.1002/14651858.CD006520.pub2.

Thompson, G. O. B., Raab, G. M., Hepburn, W. S., Hunter, R., Fulton, M., & Laxen, D. P. H. (1989). Blood-lead levels and children's behaviour: Results from the Edinburgh lead study. *Journal of Child Psychology and Psychiatry, 30*, 515–528.

Thompson, P. M., Hayashi, H. M., Simon, S. L., et al. (2004). Structural abnormalities in the brains of human subjects who use methamphetamine. *Journal of Neuroscience, 24*, 6028–6036.

Tiefer, L. (2001). A new view of women's sexual problems: Why new? Why now? *Journal of Sex Research, 38*, 89–96.

Tiefer, L. (2003). Female sexual dysfunction (FSD): Witnessing social construction in action. *Sexualities, Evolution and Gender, 5*, 33–36.

Tiefer, L., Hall, M., and Tavris, C. (2002). Beyond dysfunction: A new view of women's sexual problems. *Journal of Sex & Marital Therapy, 28*, 225–232.

Tienari, P., Wynne, L. C., Laksy, K., Moring, J., Nieminen, P., Sorri, A., et al. (2003). Genetic boundaries of the schizophrenia spectrum: Evidence from the Finnish adoptive family study of schizophrenia. *American Journal of Psychiatry, 160*, 1587–1594.

Tienari, P., Wynne, L. C., Moring, J., et al. (1994). The Finnish adoptive family study of schizophrenia: Implications for family research. *British Journal of Psychiatry, 164*, 20–26.

Tienari, P., Wynne, L. C., Moring, J., et al. (2000). Finnish adoptive family study: Sample selection and adoptee DSM-III diagnoses. *Acta Psychiatrica Scandinavica, 101*, 433–443.

Tiihonen, J., Kuikka, J., Rasanen, P., Lepola, U., Kopenen, H., Liuska, A., Lehmusvaara, A., Vainio, P., Kononen, M., et al. (1997). Cerebral benzodiazepine receptor binding and distribution in generalized anxiety disorder: A fractal analysis. *Molecular Psychiatry, 2*, 463–471.

Timko, C., Moos, R. H., Finney, J. W., & Lesar, M. D. (2001). Long-term outcomes of alcohol use disorders: Comparing untreated individuals with those in Alcoholics Anonymous and formal treatment. *Journal of Studies on Alcohol, 61*, 529–540.

Tobin, D. L., Griffing, A., & Griffing, S. (1997). An examination of subtype criteria for bulimia nervosa. *International Journal of Eating Disorders, 22*, 179–186.

Tobler, N. S., Roona, M. A., Ochshorn, P., Marshall, D. G., Streke, A. V., & Stackpole, K. M. (2000). School-based adolescent drug prevention programs: 1998 metaanalysis. *Journal of Primary Prevention, 20*, 275–336.

Tolin, D. F., & Foa, E. B. (2006). Sex differences in trauma and posttraumatic stress disorder: A quantitative review of 25 years of research. *Psychological Bulletin, 132*, 959–992.

Tonigan, J. S., Miller, W. R., & Connors, G. J. (2000). Project MATCH client impressions about Alcoholics Anonymous: Measurement issues and relationship to treatment outcome. *Alcoholism Treatment Quarterly, 18*, 25–41.

Tonstad, S., Tonnesen, P., Hajek, P., Williams, K. E., Billing, C. B., & Reeves, K. R. (2006). Varenicline Phase 3 Study Group. Effect of maintenance therapy with varenicline on smoking cessation: a randomized controlled trial. *Journal of the American Medical Association, 296*, 64–71.

Torgersen, S. (1986). Genetics of somatoform disorder. *Archives of General Psychiatry, 43*, 502–505.

Torgersen, S., Lygren, S., Øien, P. A., Skre, I., Onstad, S., Edvardsen, J., et al. (2000). A twin study of personality disorders. *Comprehensive Psychiatry, 41*, 416–425.

Torrey, E. F. (1996). *Out of the shadows: Confronting America's mental health crisis.* New York: Wiley.

Torti, F. M., Gwyther, L. P., Reed, S. D., Friedman, J. Y., & Schulman, K. A. (2004). A multinational review of recent trends and reports in dementia caregiver burden. *Alzheimer's Disease and Associated Disorders, 18*, 99–109.

Toseland, R. W., McCallion, P., Smith, T., & Banks, S. (2004). Supporting caregivers of frail older adults in an HMO setting. *American Journal of Orthopsychiatry, 74*, 349–364.

Totterdell, P., & Kellett, S. (2008). Restructuring mood in cyclothymia using cognitive behavior therapy: An intensive time-sampling study. *Journal of Clinical Psychology, 64*, 501–518.

Tran, G. Q., Haaga, D. A. F., & Chambless, D. L. (1997). Expecting that alcohol will reduce social anxiety moderates the relation between social anxiety and alcohol consumption. *Cognitive Therapy and Research, 21*, 535–553.

Tremblay, L. K., Naranjo, C. A., Graham, S. J., Herrmann, N., Mayberg, H. S., Hevenor, S., et al. (2005). Functional neuroanatomical substrates of altered reward processing in major depressive disorder revealed by a dopaminergic probe. *Archives of General Psychiatry, 62*, 1228–1236.

Trierweiler, S. J., Neighbors, H. W., Munday, C., Thompson, E. E., Binion, V. J., & Gomez, J. P. (2000). Clinician attributions associated with the diagnosis of schizophrenia in African American and non-African American patients. *Journal of Consulting and Clinical Psychology, 68*, 171–175.

Trimpey, J., Velten, E., & Dain, R. (19993). Rational recovery from addictions. In W. Dryden & L. K. Hill (Eds). *Innovations in rational-emotive therapy* (pp. 253–271). Thousand Oaks, CA: Sage.

Trinder, H., & Salkovaskis, P. M. (1994). Personally relevant instrusions outside the laboratory: Long-term suppression increases intrusion. *Behaviour Research and Therapy, 32*, 833–842.

Trivedi, M. H., Rush, A. J., Crismon, M. L., Kashner, T. M., Toprac, M. G., Carmody, T. J., Key, T., et al. (2004). Clinical Results for Patients With Major Depressive Disorder in the Texas Medication Algorithm project. *Archives of General Psychiatry, 61*, 669–680.

Trivedi, M. H., Rush, A. J., Wisniewski, S. R., Nierenberg, A. A., Warden, D., Ritz, L., et al. (2006). Evaluation of outcomes with citalopram for depression using measurement-based care in STAR*D: Implications for clinical practice. *American Journal of Psychiatry, 163*, 28–40.

True, W. R., Rice, J., Eisen, S. A., Heath, A. C., Goldberg, J., Lyons, M. J., & Nowak, J. (1993). A twin study of genetic and environmental contributions to liability for posttraumatic stress symptoms. *Archives of General Psychiatry, 50*, 257–264.

True, W. R., Xiam, H., Scherrer, J. F., Madden, P., Bucholz, K. K., et al. (1999). Common genetic vulnerability for nicotine and alcohol dependence in men. *Archives of General Psychiatry, 56*, 655–662.

Trull, T. J, Stepp, S. D., & Durrett, C. A. (2003). Research on borderline personality disorder: An update. *Current Opinion in Psychiatry, 16*, 77–82.

Tsai, D. C., & Pike, P. L. (2000). Effects of acculturation on the MMPI-2 scores of Asian American students. *Journal of Personality Assessment, 74*, 216–230.

Tsai, G., Parssani, L. A., Slusher, B. S., Carter, R., Baer, L., et al. (1995). Abnormal excitatory neurotransmitter metabolism in schizophrenic brains. *Archives of General Psychiatry, 52*, 829–836.

Tsai, J. L. (2007). Ideal affect: Cultural causes and behavioral consequences. *Perspectives on Psychological Science, 2*, 242–259.

Tsai, J. L., et al. (2001). Culture, ethnicity, and psychopathology. In H. E. Adams & P. B. Sutker (Eds). *Comprehensive handbook of psychopathology* (3rd. ed., pp. 105–127). New York: Kluwer Academic/Plenum Publishers.

Tsai, J. L., Knutson, B. K., & Fung, H. H. (2006). Cultural variation in affect valuation. *Journal of Personality and Social Psychology, 90*, 288–307.

Tsai, J. L., Knutson, B., & Rothman, A. (2007). *The pursuit of ideal affect: Variation in mood-producing behavior.* Unpublished manuscript.

Tseng, W. S. (2001). *Handbook of cultural psychiatry.* San Diego, CA: Academic Press.

Tsuang, M. T., Lyons, M. J., Meyer, J. M., Doyle, T., Eisen, S. A., et al. (1998). Co-occurrence of abuse of different drugs in men: The role of drug-specific and shared vulnerabilities. *Archives of General Psychiatry, 55*, 967–972.

Tully, L. A., Arseneault, L., Caspi, A., Moffitt, T. E., & Morgan, J. (2004). Does maternal warmth moderate the effects of birth weight on twins' attention-deficit/hyperactivity disorder (ADHD) symptoms and low IQ? *Journal of Consulting and Clinical Psychology, 72*, 218–226.

Tune, L. E., Wong, D. F., Pearlson, G. D., Strauss, M. E., Young, T., et al. (1993). Dopamine D2 receptor density estimates in schizophrenia: A positron-emission tomography study with "C-methylspiperone." *Psychiatry Research, 49*, 219–237.

Tuomisto, M. T. (1997). Intra-arterial blood pressure and heart rate reactivity to behavioral stress in normotensive, borderline, and mild hypertensive men. *Health Psychology, 16*, 554–565.

Turk, C. L., Heimberg, R. G., & Hope, D. A. (2001). Social anxiety disorder. In D. H. Barlow (Ed.), *Clinical handbook of psychological disorders* (pp. 114–153). New York: Guilford.

Turk, D. C. (2001). Treatment of chronic pain: Clinical outcomes, cost-effectiveness, and cost benefits. *Drug Benefit Trends, 13*, 36–38.

Turk, D. C., Wack, J. T., & Kerns, R. D. (1985). An empirical examination of the "pain behavior" construct. *Journal of Behavioral Medicine, 8*, 119–130.

Turkheimer, E. (1998). Heritability and biological explanation. *Psychological Review, 105*, 782–791.

Turkheimer, E. (2000). Three laws of behavior genetics and what they mean. *Current Directions in Psychological Science, 9*, 160–164.

Turkheimer, E., Haley, A., Waldron, M., D'Onofrio, B., & Gottesman, I. I. (2003). Socioeconomic status modifies the heritability of IQ in young children. *Psychological Science, 6*, 623–628.

Turkington, D., Kingdom, D., & Turner, T. (2002). Effectiveness of a brief cognitive-behavioural intervention in the treatment of schizophrenia. *British Journal of Psychiatry, 180*, 523–527.

Turner, C. F., Ku, S. M., Rogers, L. D., Lindberg, J. H., & Pleck, F. L. (1998). Adolescent sexual behavior, drug use, and violence: Increased reporting with computer survey technology. *Science, 280*, 867–873.

Turner, C. M. (2006). Cognitive-behavioural theory and therapy for obsessive-compulsive disorder in children and adolescents: Current status and future directions. *Clinical Psychology Review, 26*, 912–948.

Turner, E. H., Matthews, A. M., Linardatos, E., Tell, R. A., & Rosenthal, R. (2008). Selective publication of antidepressant trials and its influence on apparent efficacy. *New England Journal of Medicine, 358*, 252–260.

Turner, S. M., Beidel, D. C., & Townsley, R. M. (1990). Social phobia: Relationship to shyness. *Behaviour Research and Therapy, 28*, 297–305.

Twamley, E. W., Jeste, D. V., & Bellack, A. S. (2003). A review of cognitive training in schizophrenia. *Schizophrenia Bulletin, 29*, 359–382.

Tyrer, P., Thompson, S., Schmidt, U., Jones, V., Knapp, M., Davidson, K., et al. (2003). Randomized controlled trial of brief cognitive behaviour therapy versus treatment as usual in recurrent deliberate self-harm: The POPMACT study. *Psychological Medicine, 33*, 969–976.

Tyrka, A. R., Waldron, I., Graber, J. A., & Brooks-Gunn, J. (2002). Prospective predictors of the onset of anorexic and bulimic syndromes. *International Journal of Eating Disorders, 32*, 282–290.

U.S. Bureau of the Census. (1999). *Current population reports, special studies.* Washington, DC: U.S. Government Printing Office.

U.S. Department of Health and Human Services (USDHHS). (1998b). *NHLBLI report of the Task Force on Behavioral Research in Cardiovascular, Lung, and Blood Health and Disease.* Washington, DC: U.S. Government Printing Office.

U.S. Department of Health and Human Services (USDHHS). (1999). *Mental health: A report of the Surgeon General—Executive summary.* Rockville, MD: U.S. Department of Health and Human Services, Substance Abuse and Mental Health Services Administration, Center for Mental Health Services, National Institutes of Health, National Institute of Mental Health.

U.S. Department of Health and Human Services (USDHHS). (2001a). *Mental health: Culture, race, and ethnicity—A supplement to mental health: A report of the Surgeon General.* Rockville, MD: U.S. Department of Health and Human Services, Substance Abuse and Mental Health Services Administration, Center for Mental Health Services.

U.S. Department of Health and Human Services (USDHHS). (2002). *Supplement to mental health: A report of the Surgeon General* (SMA-01–3613). Retrieved July 2, 2002, from http://www.mentalhealth.org/Publications/allpubs/SMA01–3613/sma-01–3613.pdf

U. S. Department of Health and Human Services (USDHHS). (2004b). HHS announces revised Medicare obesity coverage policy. News releases of the Centers for Medicare and Medicaid Services, Washington, D.C., July 15, 2004. Retrieved from http://hhs.gov/news/press/2004pres/20040715.html

U.S. Department of Health and Human Services (USDHHS). (2006). *The health consequences of involuntary exposure to tobacco smoke: A report of the Surgeon General.* Department of Health and Human Services, Centers for Disease Control and Prevention, Coordinating Center for Health Promotion.

U.S. Department of Health and Human Services (USDHHS), Administration for Children and Families. (2005). *Head Start impact study: First year findings.* Washington, DC.

Uchino, B. N., Cacioppo, J. T., & Kiecolt-Glaser, K. G. (1996). The relationship between social support and physiological processes: A review with emphasis on underlying mechanisms and implications for health. *Psychological Bulletin, 119*, 488–531.

Uchinuma, Y., & Sekine, Y. (2000). Dissociative identity disorder (DID) in Japan: A forensic case report and the recent increase in reports of DID. *International Journal of Psychiatry in Clinical Practice, 4*, 155–160.

Underhill, K., Montgomery, P., & Operario, D. (2007). Sexual abstinence only programmes to prevent HIV infection in high income countries: A systematic review. *BMJ, 335*, 248–252.

Unger, J. B., Boley Cruz, T., Schuster, D., Flora, J. A., & Anderson Johnson, C. (2001). Measuring exposure to pro- and anti-tobacco marketing among adolescents: Intercorrelations among measures and associations with smoking status. *Journal of Health Communication, 6*, 11–29.

Unutzer, J., Katon, W., Callahan, C. M., Williams, J. W., Hunkeler, E., Harpoole, L., et al. (2002). Collaborative care management of late-life depression in the primary care setting: A randomized controlled trial. *Journal of the American Medical Association, 288,* 2836–2845.

Vacha-Haase, T., Kogan, L. R., Tani, C. R., & Woodall, R. A. (2001). Reliability generalization: Exploring variation of reliability coefficients of MMPI clinical scale scores. *Educational and Psychological Measurement, 61,* 45–49.

Vaglenova, J., Birru, S., Pandiella, N. M., & Breese, C. R. (2004). An assessment of the long-term developmental and behavioral teratogenicity of prenatal nicotine exposure. *Behavioural Brain Research, 150,* 159–170.

Valencia, M., Racon, M. L., Juarez, F., & Murow, E. (2007). A psychosocial skills training approach in Mexican outpatients with schizophrenia. *Psychological Medicine, 37,* 1393–1402.

Valenti, A. M., Narendran, R., & Pristach, C. A. (2003). Who are patients on conventional antipsychotics? *Schizophrenia Bulletin, 29,* 195–200.

Valenzuela, M. J., & Sachdev, P. (2006). Brain reserve and dementia: A systematic review. *Psychological Medicine, 36,* 441–454.

Van Ameringen, M. A., Lane, R. M., Walker, J. R., et al. (2001). Sertraline treatment of generalized social phobia: A 20-week, double-blind, placebo-controlled study. *American Journal of Psychiatry, 158,* 275–281.

van Beijsterveldt, C. E. M., Hudziak, J. J., & Boomsma, D. (2006). Genetic and environmental influences on cross-gender behavior and relation to behavior problems: A study of Dutch twins at ages 7 and 10 years. *Archives of Sexual Behavior, 35,* 647–658.

van den Broucke, S., Vandereycken, W., & Vertommen, H. (1995). Marital communication in eating disorders: A controlled observational study. *International Journal of Eating Disorders, 17,* 1–23.

van der Sande, R., Buskens, E., Allart, E., van der Graaf, Y., & van Engeland, H. (1997). Psychosocial intervention following suicide attempt: A systematic review of treatment interventions. *Acta Psychiatrica Scandinavica, 96,* 43–50.

van der Veen, F. M., Evers, E. A., Deutz, N. E., & Schmitt, J. A. (2007). Effects of acute tryptophan depletion on mood and facial emotion perception related brain activation and performance in healthy women with and without a family history of depression. *Neuropsychopharmacology, 32,* 216–224.

van Elst, L. T. (2003). Frontolimbic brain abnormalities in patients with borderline personality disorder: A volumetric magnetic resonance imaging study. *Biological Psychiatry, 54,* 163–171.

van Elst, L. T., Thiel, T., Hesslinger, B., et al. (2001). Subtle prefrontal neuropathology in pilot magnetic resonance spectroscopy study in patients with borderline personality disorder. *Journal of Neuropsychiatry and Clinical Neuroscience, 13,* 511–514.

van Erp, T. G. M., Saleh, P. A., Huttunen, M., et al. (2004). Hippocampal volumes in schizophrenic twins. *Archives of General Psychiatry, 61,* 346–353.

van Kammen, W. B., Loeber, R., & Stouthamer-Loeber, M. (1991). Substance use and its relationship to conduct problems and delinquency in young boys. *Journal of Youth and Adolescence, 20,* 399–413.

Van Oppen, P., de Haan, E., Van Balkom, A. J. L. M., Spinhoven, P., et al. (1995). Cognitive therapy and exposure in vivo in the treatment of obsessive compulsive disorder. *Behaviour Research and Therapy, 33,* 379–390.

van Praag, H., Plutchik, R., & Apter, A. (Eds.), 1990. *Violence and suicidality.* New York: Brunner/Mazel.

Varner, R. V., & Gaitz, C. M. (1982). Schizophrenic and paranoid disorders in the aged. *Psychiatric Clinics of North America, 5,* 107–118.

Vasan, R., Larson, M. G., Liep, E. P., Evans, J. C., O'Donnell, C. J., et al. (2001). Impact of high-normal blood pressure on the risk of cardiovascular disease. *New England Journal of Medicine, 345,* 1291–1297.

Veale, D. (2000). Outcome of cosmetic surgery and "DIY" surgery in patients with body dysmorphic disorder. *Psychiatric Bulletin, 24,* 218–221.

Veale, D., Boocock, A., Gournay, K., et al. (1996). Body dysmorphic disorder: A cognitive-behavioral model and pilot randomized controlled trial. *Behaviour Research and Therapy, 34,* 717–729.

Vega, W. A., Kolody, B., Aguilar-Gaxiola, S., Adlerete, E., Catalana, R., & Caraveo-Anduaga, J. (1998). Lifetime prevalence of DSM-III-R psychiatric disorders among urban and rural Mexican Americans in California. *Archives of General Psychiatry, 55,* 771–778.

Velakoulis, D., Pantelis, C., McGorry, P. D., Dudgeon, P., Brewer, W., et al. (1999). Hippocampal volume in first episode psychoses and chronic schizophrenia: A high-resolution magnetic resonance imaging study. *Archives of General Psychiatry, 56,* 133–141.

Velting, O. N., Setzer, N. J., & Albano, A. M. (2004). Update on and advances in assessment and cognitive-behavioral treatment of anxiety disorders in children and adolescents. *Professional Psychology: Research and Practice, 35,* 42–54.

Ventura, J., Neuchterlein, K. H., Lukoff, D., & Hardesty, J. D. (1989). A prospective study of stressful life events and schizophrenic relapse. *Journal of Abnormal Psychology, 98,* 407–411.

Verheul, R. (2005). Clinical utility of dimensional models for personality pathology. *Journal of Personality Disorders, 19,* 283–302.

Vickrey, B. G., Mittman, B. S., Connor, K. I., Pearson, M., L., Della Penna, R. D., Ganiats, T. G., et al. (2006). The effect of a disease management intervention on quality and outcomes of demential care: A randomized, controlled trial. *Annuals of Internal Medicine, 145,* 713–726.

Vieta, E., Martinez-De-Osaba, M. J., Colom, F., Martinez-Aran, A., Benabarre, A., & Gasto, C. (1999). Enhanced corticotropin response to corticotropin-releasing hormone as a predictor of mania in euthymic bipolar patients. *Psychological Medicine, 29,* 971–978.

Vinkers, D. J., Gussekloo, J., Stek, M. L., Westendorp, Rudı G. J., & van der Mast, R. C. (2004). Temporal relation between depression and cognitive impairment in old age: Prospective population based study. *British Medical Journal, 329,* 881.

Vitaliano, P. P., Zhang, J., & Scanlan, J. M. (2003). Is caregiving hazardous to one's physical health? A meta-analysis. *Psychological Bulletin, 129,* 946–972.

Vitousek, K., & Manke, F. (1994). Personality variables and disorders in anorexia nervosa and bulimia nervosa. *Journal of Abnormal Psychology, 103,* 137–147.

Vittengl, J. R., Clark, L. A., Dunn, T. W., & Jarrett, R. B. (2007). Reducing relapse and recurrence in unipolar depression: A comparative meta-analysis of cognitive-behavior therapy's effects. *Journal of Consulting and Clinical Psychology, 75,* 475–488.

Vogel, V. G., Graves, D. S., Vernon, S. W., Lord, J. A., Winn, R. J., & Peters, G. N. (1990). Mammographic screening of women with increased risk of breast cancer. *Cancer, 66,* 1613–1620.

Volk, D. W., Austin, M. C., Pierri, J. N., et al. (2000). Decreased glutamic acid decarboxylase-67 messenger RNA expression in a subset of prefrontal cortical γ aminobutyric acid neurons in subjects with schizophrenia. *Archives of General Psychiatry, 57,* 237–248.

Volkmar, F. R., Szatmari, P., & Sparrow, S. S. (1993). Sex differences in pervasive developmental disorders. *Journal of Autism and Developmental Disorders, 23,* 579–591.

Volkow, N. D., Chang, L., Wang, G.-J., Fowler, J. S., Leonido-Lee, M., Franceschi, D., Sedler, M. J., Gatley, S. J., Hitzemann, R., & Ding, Y. S. (2001). Association of dopamine transporter reduction with psychomotor impairment in methamphetamine abusers. *American Journal of Psychiatry, 158,* 377–382.

Volkow, N. D., Wang, G. J., Fischman, M. W., & Foltin, R. W. (1997). Relationship between subjective effects of cocaine and dopamine transporter occupancy. *Nature, 386,* 827–830.

Volkow, N. D., Wang, G.-J., Fowler, J. S., Logan, J., Jayne, M., Franceschi, D., Wong, C., Gatley, S. J., Gifford, A. N., Ding, Y. S., & Pappas, N. (2002). "Nonhedonic" food motivation in humans involves dopamine in the dorsal striatum and methylphenidate amplifies this effect. *Synapse, 44,* 175–180.

Volpicelli, J. R., Rhines, K. C., Rhines, J. S., Volpicelli, L. A., et al. (1997). Naltrexone and alcohol dependence: Role of subject compliance. *Archives of General Psychiatry, 54,* 737–743.

Volpicelli, J. R., Watson, N. T., King, A. C., Shermen, C. E., & O'Brien, C. P. (1995). Effects of naltrexone on alcohol "high" in alcoholics. *American Journal of Psychiatry, 152,* 613–617.

von Krafft-Ebing, R. (1902). *Psychopathia sexualis.* Brooklyn, NY: Physicians and Surgeons Books.

Wade, T. D., Bulik, C. M., Neale, M., & Kendler, K. S. (2000). Anorexia nervosa and major depression: Shared genetic and environmental risk factors. *American Journal of Psychiatry, 157,* 469–471.

Wade, W. A., Treat, T. A., & Stuart, G. A. (1998). Transporting an empirically supported treatment for panic disorder to a service clinic setting: A benchmarking strategy. *Journal of Consulting and Clinical Psychology, 66,* 231–239.

Wagner, K. D., & Ambrosini, P. J. (2001). Childhood depression: Pharmacological therapy/treatment (pharmacotherapy of childhood depression). *Journal of Clinical Child Psychology, 30,* 88–97.

Wahl, O. F. (1999). Mental health consumers' experience of stigma. *Schizophrenia Bulletin, 25,* 467–478.

Wahlbeck, K., Cheine, M., Essali, A., & Adams, C. (1999). Evidence of clozapine's effectiveness in schizophrenia: A systemic review and meta-analysis of randomized trials. *American Journal of Psychiatry, 156,* 990–999.

Wakefield, J. (1992). Disorder as dysfunction: A conceptual critique of DSM-III-R's definition of mental disorder. *Psychological Review, 99,* 232–247.

Wakefield, J. C. (1999). Philosophy of science and the progressiveness of DSM's theory—neutral nosology: Response to Follette and Houts, Part 1. *Behaviour Research and Therapy, 37,* 963–969.

Wakefield, M., & Chaloupka, R. (2000). Effectiveness of comprehensive tobacco control programmes in reducing teenage smoking in the USA. *Tobacco Control, 9,* 177–186.

Waldenger, R. J., & Frank, A. E. (1989). Clinicians' experiences in combining medication and psychotherapy in the treatment of borderline patients. *Hospital and Community Psychiatry, 40,* 712–718.

Waldman, I. D., Rowe, D. C., Abramowitz, A., Kozel, S. T., Mohr, J. H., Sherman, S. L., Cleveland, H. H., Sanders, M. L., Gard, J. M., & Stever, C. (1998). Association and linkage of the dopamine transporter gene and attention-deficit hyperactivity disorder in children: Heterogeneity owing to diagnostic subtype and severity. *American Journal of Human Genetics, 63,* 1767–1776.

Waldron, I. (1976). Why do women live longer than men? *Journal of Human Stress, 2*, 1–13.

Walitzer, K. S., & Dearing. R. L. (2006). Gender differences in alcohol and substance use relapse. *Clinical Psychology Review, 26*, 128–148.

Walker, E. F., Davis, D. M., & Savoie, T. D. (1994). Neuromotor precursors of schizophrenia. *Schizophrenia Bulletin, 20*, 441–451.

Walker, E. F., Grimes, K. E., Davis, D. M., & Adina, J. (1993). Childhood precursors of schizophrenia: Facial expressions of emotion. *American Journal of Psychiatry, 150*, 1654–1660.

Walker, E., Kestler, L., Bollini, A., & Hochman, K. (2004). Schizophrenia: Etiology and course. *Annual Review of Psychology, 55*, 401–430.

Walker, E. F., Mittal, V., & Tessner, K. (2008). Stress and the hypothalamic pituitary adrenal axis in the developmental course of schizophrenia. *Annual Review of Clinical Psychology, 4*, 189–216.

Walker, E. F., & Tessner, K. (2008). Schizophrenia. *Perspectives on Psychological Science, 3*, 30–37.

Waller, D. A., Kiser, S., Hardy, B. W., Fuchs, I., & Feigenbaum, L. P. (1986). Eating behavior and plasma beta-endorphin in bulimia. *American Journal of Clinical Nutrition, 4*, 20–23.

Wallerstein, R. S. (1986). *Forty-two lives in treatment: A study of psychoanalysis and psychotherapy.* New York: Guilford.

Wallerstein, R. S. (1989). The Psychotherapy Research Project of the Menninger Foundation: An overview. *Journal of Consulting and Clinical Psychology, 57*, 195–205.

Walsh, B. T., Agras, S. W., Devlin, M. J., et al. (2000). Fluoxetine for bulimia nervosa following poor response to psychotherapy. *American Journal of Psychiatry, 157*, 1332–1334.

Walsh, B. T., Seidman, S. N., Sysko, R., & Gould, M. (2002). Placebo response in studies of major depression: Variable, substantial, and growing. *Journal of the American Medical Association, 287*, 1840–1847.

Walsh, B. T., Wilson, G. T., Loeb, K. L., Devin, M. J., et al. (1997). Medication and psychotherapy in the treatment of bulimia nervosa. *American Journal of Psychiatry, 154*, 523–531.

Walsh, T., McClellan, J. M., McCarthy, S. E., Addington, A. M., Pierce, S. B. et al. (2008). Rare structural variants disrupt genes in neurodevelopmental pathways in schizophrenia. *Science, 320*, 539–543.

Walters, G. L., & Clopton, J. R. (2000). Effect of symptom information and validity scale information on the malingering of depression on the MMPI-2. *Journal of Personality Assessment, 75*, 183–199.

Wampold, B. E. (2001). *The great psychotherapy debate: Models, methods, and findings.* Mahwah, NJ, Erlbaum.

Wang, M. Q., Fitzhugh, E. C., Eddy, J. M., Fu, Q., et al. (1997). Social influences on adolescents' smoking progress: A longitudinal analysis. *American Journal of Health Behavior, 21*, 111–117.

Wang, P. S., Aguilar-Gaxiola, S., Alonso, J., Angermeyer, M. C., Borges, G., Bromet, E. J., et al. (2007). Use of mental health services for anxiety, mood, and substance disorders in 17 courtries in the WHO world mental health surveys. *Lancet, 370*, 841–850.

Wang, P. S., Demler, O., & Kessler, R. C. (2002). Adequacy of treatment for serious mental illness in the United States. *American Journal of Public Health, 92*, 92–98.

Wang, P. S., Simon, G. E., Avorn, J., Azocar, F., Ludman, E. J., McCulloch, J., et al. (2007). Telephone screening, outreach and care management for depressed workers and impact on clinical and work productivity outcomes: A randomized trial. *Journal of the American Medical Association, 298*, 1401–1411.

Wannamethee, S. G., Shaper, A. G., & Walker, M. (1998). Changes in physical activity, mortality, and incidence of coronary heart disease in older men. *Lancet, 351*, 1603–1608.

Warwick, H. M. C., & Salkovskis, P. M. (2001). Cognitive-behavioral treatment of hypochondriasis. In D. R. Lipsitt & V. Starcevic (Eds.), *Hypochondriasis: Modern perspectives on an ancient malady* (pp. 314–328). London: Oxford University Press.

Waters, A., Hill, A., & Waller, G. (2001). Internal and external antecedents of binge eating episodes in a group of women with bulimia nervosa. *International Journal of Eating Disorders, 29*, 17–22.

Watkins, P. C. (2002). Implicit memory bias in depression. *Cognition and Emotion, 16*, 381–402.

Watson, D. (2005). Rethinking the mood and anxiety of disorders: A qualitative hierarchical model for DSM-V. *Journal of Abnormal Psychology, 114*, 522–536.

Watson, J. B., & Rayner, R. (1920). Conditioned emotional reactions. *Journal of Experimental Psychology, 3*, 1–14.

Watson, S., Thompson, J. M., Ritchie, J. C., Ferrier, I. N., & Young, A. H. (2006). Neuropsychological impairment in bipolar disorder: The relationship with glucocorticoid receptor function. *Bipolar Disorders, 8*, 85–90.

Watt, N. F. (1974). Childhood and adolescent roots of schizophrenia. In D. Ricks, A. Thomas, & M. Roll (Eds.), *Life history research in psychopathology* (Vol. 3). Minneapolis: University of Minnesota Press.

Watt, N. F., Stolorow, R. D., Lubensky, A. W., & McClelland, D. C. (1970). School adjustment and behavior of children hospitalized for schizophrenia as adults. *American Journal of Orthopsychiatry, 40*, 637–657.

Waxman, J. G., Cohen, E. N., Patchias, E., & Greenberger, M. D. (2004). *Making the grade: A national and state-by-state report card.* Retrieved from http://www.nwlc.org

Weaver, I. C. G., Cervoni, N., Champagne, F. A., D'Allesio, A. C., Shakti, S., Seck, J. R., Dymov, S., Szyf, M., & Meaney, J. J. (2004). Epigenetic programming by maternal behavior. *Nature Neuroscience, 7*, 847–854.

Weber, T. (1996, December 2). Tarnishing the golden years with addiction. *Los Angeles Times*, pp. A1, A37.

Webster, J. J., & Palmer, R. L. (2000). The childhood and family background of women with clinical eating disorders: A comparison with women with major depression and women without psychiatric disorder. *Psychological Medicine, 30*, 53–60.

Webster, R., & Holroyd, S. (2000). Prevalence of psychotic symptoms in delirium. *Psychosomatics, 41*, 519–522.

Webster-Stratton, C. (1998). Preventing conduct problems in Head Start children: Strengthening parenting competencies. *Journal of Consulting and Clinical Psychology, 66*, 715–730.

Webster-Stratton, C., Reid, M. J., & Hammond, M. (2001). Preventing conduct problems, promoting social competence: A parent and teacher training partnership in Head Start. *Journal of Clinical Child Psychology, 30*, 283–302.

Wechsler, D. (1968). *Escala de Inteligencia Wechsler para Adultos.* New York: Psychological Corporation.

Wegner, D. M., Schneider, D. J., Carter, S. R., & White, T. L. (1987). Paradoxical effects of thought suppression. *Journal of Personality and Social Psychology, 53*, 5–13.

Wehr, T. A., Duncan, W. C., Sher, L., Aeschbach, D., Schwartz, P. J., Turner, E. H., et al. (2001). A circadian signal of change of season in patients with seasonal affective disorder. *Archives of General Psychiatry, 58*, 1108–1114.

Wehr, T. A., Turner, E. H., Shimada, J. M., Lowe, C. H., Baker, C., & Leibenluft, E. (1998). Treatment of a rapidly cycling bipolar patient by using extended bed rest and darkness to stabilize the timing and duration of sleep. *Biological Psychiatry, 43*, 822–828.

Weickert, C. S., Straub, R. E., McClintock, B. W., et al. (2004). Human dysbindin (DTNBP1) gene expression in normal brain and in schizophrenic prefrontal cortex and mid brain. *Archives of General Psychiatry, 61*, 544–555.

Weidner, G., & Collins, R. L. (1993). Gender, coping, and health. In H. W. Krohne (Ed.), *Attention and avoidance.* New York: Springer-Verlag.

Weidner, G., Friend, R., Ficarroto, T. J., & Mendell, N. R. (1989). Hostility and cardiovascular reactivity to stress in women and men. *Psychosomatic Medicine, 51*, 36–45.

Weinberger, D. R. (1987). Implications of normal brain development for the pathogenesis of schizophrenia. *Archives of General Psychiatry, 44*, 660–669.

Weinberger, D. R., Berman, K. F., & Illowsky, B. P. (1988). Physiological dysfunction of dorsolateral prefrontal cortex in schizophrenia: 3. A new cohort and evidence for a monoaminergic mechanism. *Archives of General Psychiatry, 45*, 609–615.

Weinberger, D. R., Cannon-Spoor, H. E., Potkin, S. G., & Wyatt, R. J. (1980). Poor premorbid adjustment and CT scan abnormalities in chronic schizophrenia. *American Journal of Psychiatry, 137*, 1410–1413.

Weiner, B., Frieze, L., Kukla, A., Reed, L., Rest, S., & Rosenbaum, R. M. (1971). *Perceiving the causes of success and failure.* New York: General Learning Press.

Weiner, D. B. (1994). *Le geste de Pinel:* The history of psychiatric myth. In M. S. Micale & R. Porter (Eds.), *Discovering the history of psychiatry.* New York: Oxford.

Weinstein, H. (2002, February 19). Killer's sentence of death debated. *Los Angeles Times*, pp. A1, A14.

Weintraub, S., Prinz, R., & Neale, J. M. (1978). Peer evaluations of the competence of children vulnerable to psychopathology. *Journal of Abnormal Child Psychology, 6*, 461–473.

Weisberg, R. B., Brown, T. A., Wincze, J. P., & Barlow, D. H. (2001). Causal attributions and male sexual arousal: The impact of attributions for a bogus erectile difficulty on sexual arousal, cognitions, and affect. *Journal of Abnormal Psychology, 110*, 324–334.

Weisberg, R. W. (1994). Genius and madness? A quasiexperimental test of the hypothesis that manic-depression increases creativity. *Psychological Science, 5*, 361–367.

Weisman, A. (2005). Integrating culturally-based approaches with existing interventions for Hispanic/Latino families coping with schizophrenia. *Psychotherapy, 42*, 178–197.

Weisman, A. G., Nuechterlein, K. H., Goldstein, M. J., & Snyder, K. S. (1998). Expressed emotion, attributions, and schizophrenia symptom dimensions. *Journal of Abnormal Psychology, 107*, 355–359.

Weisman, C. S., & Teitelbaum, M. A. (1985). Physician gender and the physician–patient relationship: Recent evidence and relevant questions. *Social Science and Medicine, 20*, 1119–1127.

Weiss, B., Caron, A., Ball, S., Tapp, J., Johnson, M., & Weisz, J. R. (2005). Iatrogenic effects of group treatment for antisocial youth. *Journal of Consulting and Clinical Psychology, 73*, 1036–1044.

Weiss, G., & Hechtman, L. (1993). *Hyperactive children grown up* (2nd ed.). New York: Guilford.

Weiss, J., & Sampson, R. (1986). *The psychoanalytic process: Theory, clinical observations, and empirical research.* New York: Guilford.

Weiss, L. A., Shen, Y., Korn, J. M., et al. (2008). Association between microdeletion and microduplication at 16p11.2 and autism. *New England Journal of Medicine, 358,* 667–675.

Weissberg, R. P., Caplan, M. Z., & Sivo, P. J. (1989). A new conceptual framework for establishing school-based social competence promotion programs. In L. A. Bond & B. E. Compas (Eds.), *Primary prevention and promotion in the schools* (Vol. 12, pp. 255–296). Newbury Park, CA: Sage.

Weissman, A. N., & Beck, A. T. (1978). *Development and validation of the Dysfunctional Attitude Scale: A preliminary investigation.* Paper presented at the annual meeting of the American Educational Research Association, Toronto.

Weissman, M. M., Bland, R. C., Canino, G. J., Faravelli, C., Greenwald, S., et al. (1996). Cross-national epidemiology of major depression and bipolar disorder. *Journal of the American Medical Association, 276,* 293–299.

Weissman, M. M., Bland, R. C., Canino, G. J., Greenwald, S., Hwu, H. G., Joyce, P. R., et al. (1999). Prevalence of suicide ideation and suicide attempts in nine countries. *Psychological Medicine, 29,* 9–17.

Weisz, J. R., McCarty, C. A., & Valeri, S. M. (2006). Effects of psychotherapy for depression in children and adolescents: A meta-analysis. *Psychological Bulletin, 132,* 132–149.

Weisz, J. R., Sigman, M., Weiss, B., & Mosk, J. (1993). Parent reports of behavioral and emotional problems among children in Kenya, Thailand and the United States. *Child Development, 64,* 98–109.

Weisz, J. R., Suwanlert, S. C., Wanchai, W., & Bernadette, R. (1987). Over and undercontrolled referral problems among children and adolescents from Thailand and the United States: The wat and wai of cultural differences. *Journal of Consulting and Clinical Psychology, 55,* 719–726.

Weisz, J. R., Weiss, B., Suwanlert, S., & Wanchai, C. (2003). Syndromal structure of psychopathology in children of Thailand and the United States. *Journal of Consulting and Clinical Psychology, 71,* 375–385.

Wells, A. (1998). Cognitive therapy of social phobia. In N. Tarrier, A. Wells, & G. Haddock (Eds.), *Treating complex cases: The cognitive-behavioural approach* (pp. 1–26). Chichester, UK: Wiley.

Wells, C. E., & Duncan, G. W. (1980). *Neurology for psychiatrists.* Philadelphia: F. A. Davis.

Wells, K. C., Epstein, J. N., Hinshaw, S. P., et al. (2000). Parenting and family stress treatment outcomes in attention deficit hyperactivity disorder (ADHD): An empirical analysis in the MTA study. *Journal of Abnormal Child Psychology, 28,* 543–553.

Welsh, R., Burcham, B., DeMoss, K., Martin, C., & Milich, R. (1997). *Attention deficit hyperactivity disorder diagnosis and management: A training program for teachers.* Frankfort: Kentucky Department of Education.

Wender, P. H., Kety, S. S., Rosenthal, D., Schulsinger, F., Ortmann, J., & Lunde, I. (1986). Psychiatric disorders in the biological and adoptive families of adopted individuals with affective disorders. *Archives of General Psychiatry, 43,* 923–929.

Westen, D. (1998). The scientific legacy of Sigmund Freud: Toward a psychodynamically informed psychological science. *Psychological Bulletin, 124,* 333–371.

Westen, D., Novotny, C. M., & Thompson-Brenner, H. (2004). The empirical status of empirically supported psychotherapies: Assumptions, findings, and reporting in controlled clinical trials. *Psychological Bulletin, 130,* 631–663.

Westergaard, T., Mortensen, P. B., Pedersen, C. B., Wohlfahrt, J., & Melbye, M. (1999). Exposure to prenatal and childhood infections and the risk of schizophrenia: Suggestions from a study of sibship characteristics and influenza prevalence. *Archives of General Psychiatry, 56,* 993–998.

Wetherell, J. L. (1998). Treatment of anxiety in older adults. *Psychotherapy, 35,* 444–458.

Whalen, C. K. (1983). Hyperactivity, learning problems, and the attention deficit disorders. In T. H. Ollendick & M. Hersen (Eds.), *Handbook of child psychopathology.* New York: Plenum.

Whalen, C. K., & Henker, B. (1985). The social worlds of hyperactive (ADDH) children. *Clinical Psychology Review, 5,* 447–478.

Whalen, C. K., & Henker, B. (1991). Therapies for hyperactive children: Comparisons, combinations, and compromises. *Journal of Consulting and Clinical Psychology, 59,* 126–137.

Wheeler, J. G., Christensen, A., & Jacobson, N. S. (2001). Couple distress. In D. H. Barlow (Ed.), *Clinical handbook of psychological disorders: A step-by-step treatment manual* (pp. 609–630). New York: Guilford.

Whelton, P. K., Appel, L. J., Espeland, M. A., Applegate, W. B., Ettinger, W. H., Kostis, J. B., Kumanyika, S., Lacy, C. R., Johnson, K. C., Folmar, S., & Cutler, J. A. for the TONE Collaborative Research Group. (1998). Sodium reduction and weight loss in the treatment of hypertension in older persons: A randomized controlled trial of nonpharmacologic interventions in the elderly (TONE). *Journal of the American Medical Association, 279,* 839–846.

Whelton, P. K., He, J., Appel, L. J., et al. (2002). Primary prevention of hypertension. Clinical and public health advisory from the national high blood pressure education program. *Journal of the American Medical Association, 288,* 1882–1888.

Whisman, M. A. (2007) Marital distress and DSM-IV psychiatric disorders in a population-based national survey. *Journal of Abnormal Psychology, 116,* 638–643.

Whisman, M. A., & Bruce, M. L. (1999). Marital dissatisfaction and incidence of major depressive episode in a community sample. *Journal of Abnormal Psychology, 108,* 674–678.

Whisman, M. A., & Uebelacker, L. A. et al. (2006). Impairment and distress associated with relationship discord in a national sample of married or cohabiting adults. *Journal of Family Psychology, 20,* 369–377.

Whitaker, A. H., van Rossen, R., Feldman, J. F., Schonfeld, I. S., Pinto-Martin, J. A., Torre, C., Shaffer, D., & Paneth, N. (1997). Psychiatric outcomes in low birth weight children at age 6 years: Relation to neonatal cranial ultrasound abnormalities. *Archives of General Psychiatry, 54,* 847–856.

Whitaker, R. (2002). *Mad in America.* Cambridge, MA: Perseus.

White, K. S., & Barlow, D. H. (2004). Panic disorder and agoraphobia. In D. H. Barlow (Ed.), *Anxiety and its disorders: The nature and treatment of anxiety and panic* (pp. 328–379). New York: Guilford.

Whitmore, E. A., Mikulich, S. K., Thompson, L. L., Riggs, P. D., Aarons, G. A., & Crowley, T. J. (1997). Influences on adolescent substance dependence: Conduct disorder, depression, attention deficit hyperactivity disorder, and gender. *Drug and Alcohol Dependence 47,* 87–97.

Whittal, M. L., Agras, S. W., & Gould, R. A. (1999). Bulimia nervosa: A meta-analysis of psychosocial and pharmacological treatments. *Behavior Therapy, 30,* 117–135.

Wiborg, I. M., & Dahl, A. A. (1996). Does brief dynamic psychotherapy reduce the relapse rate of panic disorder? *Archives of General Psychiatry, 53,* 689–694.

Widiger, T. A., & Costa, P. T., Jr. (1994). Personality and personality disorders. *Journal of Abnormal Psychology, 95,* 43–51.

Widiger, T. A., Frances, A., & Trull, T. J. (1987). A psychometric analysis of the social-interpersonal and cognitive-perceptual items for schizotypal personality disorder. *Archives of General Psychiatry, 44,* 741–745.

Widiger, T. A., & Samuel, D. B. (2005). Diagnostic categories or dimensions? A question for the Diagnostic and Statistical Manual of Mental Disorders—Fifth Edition. *Journal of Abnormal Psychology, 114,* 494–504.

Wilcox, S., Evenson, K. R., Aragaki, A., Wassertheil-Smoller, S., Mouton, C. P., & Loevinger, B. L. (2003). The effects of widowhood on physical and mental health, health behaviors, and health outcomes: The Women's Health Initiative. *Health Psychology, 22,* 513–522.

Wildes, J. E., Emery, R. E., & Simons, A. D. 2001. The roles of ethnicity and culture in the development of eating disturbance and body dissatisfaction: A meta-analytic review. *Clinical Psychology Review, 21,* 521–551.

Wilfley, D. E., Welch, R. R, Stein, R. I., Spurrell, E. B., Cohen, L. R., et al. (2002). A randomized comparison of group cognitive-behavioral therapy and group interpersonal psychotherapy for the treatment of overweight individuals with binge eating disorder. *Archives of General Psychiatry, 59,* 713–721.

Willemsen-Swinkels, S. H. N., Buitelaar, J. K., & van Engeland, H. (1996). The effects of chronic naltrexone treatment in young autistic children: A double-blind placebo-controlled crossover study. *Biological Psychiatry, 39,* 1023–1031.

Willemsen-Swinkels, S. H. N., Buitelaar, J. K., Weijnen, F. G., & van Engeland, H. (1995). Placebo-controlled acute dosage naltrexone study in young autistic children. *Psychiatry Research, 58,* 203–215.

Willford, J. A., Richardson, G. A., Leech, S. L., & Day, N. L. (2004). Verbal and visuospatial learning and memory function in children with moderate prenatal alcohol exposure. *Alcoholism: Clinical and Experimental Research, 28,* 497–507.

Williams, C. J. (1999, May 27). In Kosovo, rape seen as awful as death. *Los Angeles Times,* pp. A1, A18.

Williams, J. (2003). Dementia and genetics. In R. Plomin, J. D. DeFries, et al. (Eds.), *Behavioral genetics in the postgenomic era* (pp. 503–527). Washington, DC: American Psychological Association.

Williams, J., McGuffin, P., Nothen, M., Owen, M. J., & Group, E. C. (1997). A meta-analysis of association between the 5-HT2a receptor T102C polymorphism and schizophrenia. *Lancet, 349,* 1221–1226.

Williams, J. B. W., Gibbon, M., First, M. B., Spitzer, R. L., Davies, M., et al. (1992). The Structured Clinical Interview for DSM-III-R (SCID): 2. Multisite test–retest reliability. *Archives of General Psychiatry, 49,* 630–636.

Williams, J. M. G., Watts, F. N., MacLeod, C., & Mathews, A. (1997). *Cognitive psychology and emotional disorders* (2nd ed.). New York: Wiley.

Williams, K., Goodman, M., & Green, R. (1985). Parent-child factors in gender role socialization in girls. *Journal of the American Academy of Child Psychiatry, 24,* 720–731.

Williams, P. A., Allard, A., Spears, L., Dalrymple, N., & Bloom, A. S. (2001). Brief report: Case reports on naltrexone use in children with autism: Controlled observations regarding benefits and practical issues in medication management. *Journal of Autism and Developmental Disorders, 31*, 103–108.

Williams, R. B., Marchuk, D. A., Gadde, K. M., Barefoot, J. C., Grichnik, K., Helms, M. J., Kuhn, C. M., Lewis, J. G., Schanberg, S. M., Stafford-Smith, M., Suarez, E. C., Clary, G. L., Svenson, I. K., & Siegler, I. C. (2001). Central nervous system serotonin function and cardiovascular responses to stress. *Psychosomatic Medicine, 63*, 300–305.

Williams, S. L., & Falbo, J. (1996). Cognitive and performance-based treatments for panic attacks in people with varying degrees of agoraphobic disability. *Behaviour Research and Therapy, 34*, 253–264.

Williamson, D. A., Goreczny, A. J., Davis, C. J., Ruggiero, L., & MacKenzie, S. L. (1988). Psychophysiological analysis of the anxiety model of bulimia nervosa. *Behavior Therapy, 19*, 1–9.

Wills, T. A., & Cleary, S. D. (1999). Peer and adolescent substance use among 6th–9th graders: Latent growth analysis of influence versus selection mechanisms. *Health Psychology, 18*, 453–463.

Wills, T. A., DuHamel, K., & Vaccaro, D. (1995). Activity and mood temperament as predictors of adolescent substance use: Test of a self-regulation model. *Journal of Personality and Social Psychology, 68*, 901–916.

Wills, T. A., Sandy, J. M., Shinar, O., & Yaeger, A. (1999). Contributions of positive and negative affect to adolescent substance use: Test of a bidimensional model in a longitudinal study. *Psychology of Addictive Behaviors, 13*, 327–338.

Wills, T. A, Sandy, J. M., & Yaeger, A. M. (2002). Stress and smoking in adolescence: A test of directional hypotheses. *Health Psychology, 21*, 122–130.

Wilsnack, R. W., Vogeltanz, N. D., Wilsnack, S. C., et al. (2000). Gender differences in alcohol consumption and adverse drinking consequences: Cross-cultural patterns. *Addiction, 95*, 251–265.

Wilson, G. T. (1995). Psychological treatment of binge eating and bulimia nervosa. *Journal of Mental Health (UK), 4*, 451–457.

Wilson, G. T., & Fairburn, C. G. (1998). Treatments for eating disorders. In P. Nathan & J. M. Gorman (Eds.), *A guide to treatments that work* (pp. 501–530). London: Oxford University Press.

Wilson, G. T., Loeb, K. L., Walsh, B. T., Labouvie, E., Petkova, E., Liu, X., & Waternaux, C. (1999). Psychological and pharmacological treatment of bulimia nervosa: Predictors and processes of change. *Journal of Consulting and Clinical Psychology, 67*, 451–459.

Wilson, G. T., & Pike, K. M. (1993). Eating disorders. In D. H. Barlow (Ed.), *Clinical handbook of psychological disorders* (pp. 278–317). New York: Guilford.

Wilson, G. T., & Pike, K. M. (2001). Eating disorders. In D. H. Barlow (Ed.), *Clinical handbook of psychological disorders.*(3rd ed., pp. 332–375). New York: Guilford.

Wilson, G. T., Vitousek, K. M., & Loeb, K. L. (2000). Stepped care treatment for eating disorders. *Journal of Consulting and Clinical Psychology, 68*, 564–572.

Wilson, R. S., Mendes de Leon, C., Barnes, L., et al. (2002). Participation in cognitively stimulation activities and risk of incident Alzheimer's disease. *Journal of the American Medical Association, 287*, 742–748.

Wilson, R. S., Scherr, P. A., Schneider, J. A., Tang, Y., & Bennett, D. A. (2007). Relation of cognitive activity to risk of developing Alzheimer disease. *Neurology, 69*, 1191–1920.

Wimo, A., Winblad, B., Aguero-Torres, A., & von Strauss, E. (2003). The magnitude of dementia occurrence in the world. *Alzheimer Disease and Associated Disorders, 17*, 63–67.

Winblad. B., & Portis, N. (1999). Memantine in severe dementia: Results of the 9M-Best Study (Benefit and efficacy in severely demented patients during treatment with memantine). *International Journal of Geriatric Psychiatry, 14*, 135–146.

Winchel, R. M., Stanley, B., & Stanley, M. (1990). Biochemical aspects of suicide. In S. J. Blumenthal & D. J. Kupfer (Eds.), *Suicide over the life cycle: Risk factors, assessment and treatment of suicidal patterns* (pp. 97–126). Washington, DC: American Psychiatric Press.

Winick, B. J. (1997). *The right to refuse mental health treatment.* Washington, DC: American Psychological Association.

Winkleby, M. A., Cubbin, C., Ahn, D. K., & Kraemer, H. C. (1999). Pathways by which SES and ethnicity influence cardiovascular risk factors. In N. E. Adler & M. Marmot (Eds.), *Socioeconomic status and health in industrialized nations: Social, psychological, and biological pathways* [*Annals of the New York Academy of Sciences* (Vol. 896)]. New York: New York Academy of Sciences.

Winkleby, M. A., Kraemer, H. C., Ahn, D. K., & Varady, A. N. (1998). Ethnic and socioeconomic differences in cardiovascular disease risk factors. *Journal of the American Medical Association,, 280*, 356–362.

Winston, A., Laikin, M., Pollack, J., Samstag, L. W., McCullough, L., & Muran, J. C. (1994). Short-term psychotherapy of personality disorders. *American Journal of Psychiatry, 151*, 190–194.

Wirshing, D. W., Wirshing, W. C., Marder, S. R., Liberman, R. P., & Mintz, J. (1998). Informed consent: Assessment of comprehension. *American Journal of Psychiatry, 155*, 1508–1511.

Wirz-Justice, A., Quinto, C., Cajochen, C., Werth, E., & Hock, C. (1999). A rapid-cycling bipolar patient treated with long nights, bedrest and light. *Biological Psychiatry, 45*, 1075–1077.

Witkiewitz, K., & Marlatt, G. A. (2004). Relapse prevention for alcohol and drug problems: That was zen, this is tao. *American Psychologist, 59*, 224–235.

Wittchen, H. U., & Jacobi, F. (2005). Size and burden of mental disorders in Europe—a critical review and appraisal of 27 studies. *European Neuropsychopharmacology, 15*, 357–376.

Wittchen, H.–U., Stein, M. B., & Kessler, R. C. (1999). Social fears and social phobia in a community sample of adolescents and young adults: Prevalence, risk factors and comorbidity. *Psychological Medicine, 29*, 309–323.

Wolf, M., Bally, H., & Morris, R. (1986). Automaticity, retrieval processes, and reading: A longitudinal study in average and impaired readers. *Child Development, 57*, 988–1000.

Wolfe, R., Morrow, J., & Frederickson, B. L. (1996). Mood disorders in older adults. In L. L. Carstensen, B. A. Edelstein, & L. Dornbrand (Eds.), *The practical handbook of clinical gerontology* (pp. 274–303). Thousand Oaks, CA: Sage.

Wolfe, V. V. (1990). Sexual abuse of children. In Bellack, A. S., Hersen, M., & Kazdin, A. E., (Eds.), *International handbook of behavior modification and therapy* (2nd ed., pp. 707–729). New York: Plenum.

Wolitzky, D. (1995). Traditional psychoanalytic psychotherapy. In A. S. Gurman & S. B. Messer (Eds.), *Essential psychotherapies: Theory and practice* (pp. 24–68). New York: Guilford.

Wolpe, J. (1958). *Psychotherapy by reciprocal inhibition.* Stanford, CA: Stanford University Press.

Wolraich, M. L., Wilson, D. B., & White, J. W. (1995). The effect of sugar on behavior or cognition in children: A meta-analysis. *Journal of the American Medical Association, 274*, 1617–1621.

Women's Health Initiative Screening Committee. (2004). Effects of conjugated equine estrogen in postmenopausal women with hysterectomy: The Women's Health Initiative randomized controlled trial. *Journal of the American Medical Association, 291*, 1701–1712.

Wonderlich, S. A., Crosby, R. D., Mitchell, J. E., Thompson, K. M., Redlin, J., Demuth, G., Smyth, J., & Haseltine, B. (2001). Eating disturbance and sexual trauma in childhood and adulthood. *International Journal of Eating Disorders, 30*, 401–412.

Wonderlich, S. A., Wilsnack, R. W., Wilsnack, S. C., & Harris, T. R. (1996). Childhood sexual abuse and bulimic behavior in a nationally representative sample. *American Journal of Public Health, 86*, 1082–1086.

Wong, D. F., Wagner, H. N., Tune, L. E., Dannals, R. F., Pearlson, G. D., Links, J. M., et al. (1986). Positron emission tomography reveals elevated D2 dopamine receptors in drug-naive schizophrenics. *Science, 234*, 1558–1562.

Woodmansee, M. A. (1996). The guilty but mentally ill verdict: Political expediency at the expense of moral principle. *Notre Dame Journal of Law, Ethics and Public Policy, 10*, 341–387.

Woodside, D. B., Bulik, C. M., Halmi, K. A., et al. (2002). Personality, perfectionism, and attitudes towards eating in parents of individuals with eating disorders. *International Journal of Eating Disorders, 13*, 290–299.

Woodside, D. B., Shekter-Wolfson, L. F., Garfinkel, P. E., & Olmsted, M. P. (1995). Family interactions in bulimia nervosa: Study design, comparisons to established population norms and changes over the course of an intensive day hospital treatment program. *International Journal of Eating Disorders, 17*, 105–115.

Woody, S. R., & Rodriguez, B. F. (2000). Self-focused attention and social anxiety in social phobics and normal controls. *Cognitive Therapy and Research, 24*, 473–488.

World Health Organization (WHO). (2001). *World health report: New understanding, new hope.* Geneva: Author.

World Health Organization (WHO). (2004). Prevalence, severity, and unmet need for treatment of mental disorders in the World Health Organization world mental health surveys. *Journal of the American Medical Association, 291*, 2581–2590.

Worling, J. R. (1995). Sexual abuse histories of adolescent male sex offenders: Differences on the basis of the age and gender of their victims. *Journal of Abnormal Psychology, 104*, 610–613.

Wouda, J. C., Hartman, P. M., Bakker, R. M., Bakker, J. O., et al. (1998). Vaginal plethysmography in women with dyspareunia. *Journal of Sex Research, 35*, 141–147.

Wright, M. J. (1991). Identifying child sexual abuse using the Personality Inventory for Children. *Dissertation Abstracts International, 52*, 1744.

Writing Committee for the ENRICHD Investigators. (2003). Effects of treating depression and low perceived social support on clinical events after myocardial infarction. *Journal of the American Medical Association, 289*, 3106–3116.

Writing Group for the Women's Health Initiative Investigators. (2002). Risks and benefits of estrogen plus estrogen plus progestin in healthy postmenopausal women. Principle results from the Women's Health Initiative randomized controlled trial. *Journal of the American Medical Association, 288*, 321–333.

Wu, L.T., Pilowsky, D. J., & Schlenger, W. E. (2004). Inhalant abuse and dependence among adolescents in the United State. *Journal of the American Academy of Child and Adolescent Psychiatry, 43*, 1206–1214.

Wurtele, S. K., & Miller-Perrin, C. L. (1987). An evaluation of side-effects associated with participation in a child sexual abuse prevention program. *Journal of School Health, 57*, 228–231.

Wykes, T., Steel, C., Everitt, T., & Tarrier, N. (2008). Cognitive behavior therapy for schizophrenia: Effect sizes, clinical models, and methodological rigor. *Schizophrenia Bulletin, 34*, 523–537.

Wylie, K. R. (1997). Treatment outcome of brief couple therapy in psychogenic male erectile disorder. *Archives of Sexual Behavior, 26*, 527–545.

Yalom, I. D., Green, R., & Fisk, N. (1973). Prenatal exposure to female hormones: Effect on psychosexual development in boys. *Archives of General Psychiatry, 28*, 554–561.

Yamagata, S., Suzuki, A., Ando, J., Ono, Y., Kijima, N., Yoshimura, K., et al. (2006). Is the genetic structure of human personality universal? A cross-cultural twin study from North America, Europe, and Asia. *Journal of Personality and Social Psychology, 90*, 987–998.

Yan, L. J., Hammen, C., Cohen, A. N., Daley, R. M., & Henry, R. M. (2004). Expressed emotion versus relationship quality variable in the prediction of recurrence in bipolar patients. *Journal of Affective Disorders, 83*, 199–206.

Yan, L. L., Liu, K., Matthews, K. A., Daviglus, M. L., Ferguson, T. F., & Kiefe, C. I. (2003). Psychosocial factors and risk of hypertension: The Coronary Artery Risk Development in Young Adults (CARDIA) Study. *Journal of the American Medical Association, 290*, 2138–2148.

Yanovski, S. Z. (2003). Binge eating disorder and obesity in 2003: Could treating an eating disorder have a positive effect on the obesity epidemic? *International Journal of Eating Disorders, 34*(Suppl), S117–S120.

Yerkes, R. M., & Dodson, J. D. (1908). The relation of strength of stimulus to rapidity of habit formation. *Journal of Comparative and Neurological Psychology, 18*, 459–482.

Yildiz, A., Guleryuz, S., Ankerst, D. P., Öngür, D., & Renshaw, P. F. (2008). Protein kinase C inhibition in the treatment of mania: A double-blind, placebo-controlled trial of tamoxifen. *Archives of General Psychiatry, 65*, 255–263.

Yoast, R., Williams, M. A., Deitchman, S. D., & Champion, H. C. (2001). Report of the Council on Scientific Affairs: Methadone maintenance and needle-exchange programs to reduce the medical and public health consequences of drug abuse. *Journal of Addictive Diseases, 20*, 15–40.

Yonkers, K. A., Dyck, I. R., Warshaw, M., & Keller, M. B. (2000). Factors predicting the clinical course of generalised anxiety disorder. *British Journal of Psychiatry, 176*, 544–549.

Young, A. S., Klap, R., Sherbourne, C. D., & Wells, K. B. (2001). The quality of care for depressive and anxiety disorders in the United States. *Archives of General Psychiatry, 58*, 55–61.

Younglove, J. A., & Vitello, C. J. (2003). Community notification provisions of "Megan's law" from a therapeutic jurisprudence perspective: A case study. *American Journal of Forensic Psychology, 21*, 25–38.

Yücel, M., Harrison, B. J., Wood, S. J., Fornito, A., Wellard, R. M., Pujol, J., et al. (2007). Functional and biochemical alterations of the medial frontal cortex in obsessive-compulsive disorder. *Archives of General Psychiatry, 64*, 946–955.

Yule, W., & Canterbury, R. (1996). The treatment of post-traumatic stress disorder in children and adolescents. *International Review of Psychiatry, 6*, 141–151.

Yung, A. R., McGorry, P. D., McFarlane, C. A., & Patton, G. (1995). The PACE Clinic: Development of a clinical service for young people at high risk of psychosis. *Australia Psychiatry, 3*, 345–349.

Yung, A. R., Phillips, L. J., Hok, P. Y., & McGorry, P. D. (2004). Risk factors for psychosis in an ultra high-risk group: Psychopathology and clinical features. *Schizophrenia Research, 67*, 131–142.

Yusuf, S., Hawken, S., Ounpuu, S., Dans, T., Avezum, A., et al. (2004) . Effect of potentially modifiable risk factors associated with myocardial infarction in 52 countries (the INTERHEART study): Case-control study. *Lancet, 364*, 937–952.

Zanarini, M. C., Frankenburg, F. R., Hennen, J., Reich, D. B., & Silk, K. R. (2004). Axis I comorbidity in patients with borderline personality disorder: 6-year follow-up and prediction of time to remission. *American Journal of Psychiatry, 161*, 2108–2114.

Zanarini, M. C., Frankenburg, F. R., Hennen, J., Reich, D. B., & Silk, K. R. (2006). Prediction of the 10-year course of borderline personality disorder. *American Journal of Psychiatry, 163*, 827–832.

Zanarini, M. C., Skodol, A. E., Bender, D., Dolan, R., Sanislow, C., Schaefer, E., et al. (2000). The Collaborative Longitudinal Personality Disorders Study: Reliability of Axis I and II diagnoses. *Journal of Personality Disorders, 14*, 291–299.

Zane, M. D. (1984). Psychoanalysis and contextual analysis of phobias. *Journal of the American Academy of Psychoanalysis, 12*, 553–568.

Zarit, S. H. (1980). *Aging and mental disorders: Psychological approaches to assessment and treatment.* New York: Free Press.

Zarit, S. H., & Zarit, J. M. (1998). *Mental disorders in older adults: Fundamentals of assessment and treatment.* New York: Guilford.

Zatzick, D. F., Marmer, C. R., Weiss, D. S., Browner, W. S., Metzler, T. J., et al. (1997). Posttraumatic stress disorder and functioning and quality of life in a nationally representative sample of male Vietnam veterans. *American Journal of Psychiatry, 154*, 1690–1695.

Zeiss, A. M., & Steffen, A. M. (1996). Interdisciplinary health care teams: The basic unit of geriatric care. In L. L. Carstensen, B. A. Edelstein, & L. Dornbrand (Eds.), *The practical handbook of clinical gerontology* (pp. 423–450). Thousand Oaks, CA: Sage.

Zellner, D. A., Harner, D. E., & Adler, R. L. (1989). Effects of eating abnormalities and gender on perceptions of desirable body shape. *Journal of Abnormal Psychology, 98*, 93–96.

Zheng, H., Sussman, S., Chen, X., Wang, Y., Xia, J., Gong, J., Liu, C., Shan, J., Unger, J., & Johnson, C. A. (2004). Project EX—A teen smoking cessation initial study in Wuhan, China. *Addictive Behaviors, 29*, 1725–1733.

Ziegler, F. J., Imboden, J. B., & Meyer, E. (1960). Contemporary conversion reactions: A clinical study. *American Journal of Psychiatry, 116*, 901–910.

Zilboorg, G., & Henry, G. W. (1941). *A history of medical psychology.* New York: Norton.

Zimmer, D. (1987). Does marital therapy enhance the effectiveness of treatment for sexual dysfunction? *Journal of Sex and Marital Therapy, 13*, 193–209.

Zimmer, L., & Morgan, J. P. (1995). *Exposing marijuana myths: A review of the scientific evidence.* New York: The Lindemith Center.

Zimmerman, M., & Mattia, J. I. (1999). Differences between clinical and research practices in diagnosing borderline personality disorder. *American Journal of Psychiatry, 156*, 1570–1574.

Zimmerman, M., Rothschild, L., & Chelminski, I. (2005). The prevalence of DSM-IV personality disorders in psychiatric outpatients. *American Journal of Psychiatry, 162*, 1911–1918.

Zinbarg, R. E., Brown, T. A., Barlow, D. H., & Rapee, R. M. (2001). Anxiety sensitivity, panic, and depressed mood: A reanalysis teasing apart the contributions of the two levels in the hierarchical structure of the Anxiety Sensitivity Index. *Journal of Abnormal Psychology, 110*, 372–377.

Zlotnick, C., Johnson, S. L., Miller, I. W., Pearlstein, T., & Howard, M. (2001). Postpartum depression in women receiving public assistance: Pilot study of an interpersonal therapy-oriented group intervention. *American Journal of Psychiatry, 158*, 638–640.

Zubin, J., & Spring, B. (1977). Vulnerability: A new view of schizophrenia. *Journal of Abnormal Psychology, 86*, 103–126.

Zucker, K. J., & Blanchard, R. (1997). Transvestic fetishism: Psychopathology and theory. In D. R. Laws & W. O'Donohue (Eds.), *Sexual deviance* (pp. 280–296). New York: Guilford.

Zucker, K. J., & Bradley, S. J. (1995). *Gender identity disorder and psychosexual problems in children and adolescents.* New York: Guilford.

Zucker, K. J., Bradley, S. J., & Sanikhani, M. (1997). Sex difference in referral rates of children with gender identity disorder: Some hypotheses. *Journal of Abnormal Child Psychology, 25*, 217–227.

Zucker, K. J., Wild, J., Bradley, S. J., & Stern, A. (1993). Physical attractiveness of boys with gender identity disorder. *Archives of Sexual Behavior, 22*, 23–36.

Quotation and Illustration Credits

Name Index

Subject Index

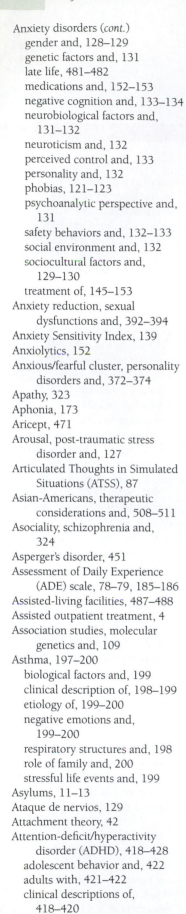

DSM-IV-TR Multiaxial Classification System

Axis I

Clinical syndromes:
Disorders Usually First Diagnosed in Infancy, Childhood, or Adolescence
Delirium, Dementia, Amnestic, and other Cognitive Disorders
Substance-related Disorders
Schizophrenia and Other Psychotic Disorders
Mood Disorders
Anxiety Disorders
Somatoform Disorders
Factitious Disorder
Dissociative Disorders
Sexual and Gender Identity Disorders
Eating Disorders
Sleep Disorders
Impulse Control Disorders Not Elsewhere Classified
Adjustment Disorders

Axis II

Mental Retardation
Personality Disorders

Axis III

General Medical Conditions

Axis IV
Psychosocial and Environmental Problems

Check:

_____ Problems with primary support group.
Specify:

_____ Problems related to the social environment.
Specify:

_____ Educational problem.
Specify:

_____ Occupational problem.
Specify:

_____ Housing problem.
Specify:

_____ Economic problem.
Specify:

_____ Problems with access to healthcare services.
Specify:

_____ Problems related to interaction with the legal system/crime.
Specify:

_____ Other psychosocial and environmental problems.
Specify: